8th Edition

Introduction to Comparative Politics

Political Challenges and Changing Agendas

Mark Kesselman
Columbia University

Joel Krieger
Wellesley College

William A. Joseph
Wellesley College

CENGAGE

Australia • Brazil • Mexico • Singapore • United Kingdom • United States

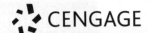

**Introduction to Comparative Politics:
Political Challenges and Changing
Agendas, 8th Edition**
Mark Kesselman, Joel Krieger,
William A. Joseph

Product Director: Paul Banks

Product Manager: Brad Potthoff

Project Manager: Julia Giannotti

Vendor Content Project Manager:
Kassi Radomski, Lumina Datamatics

Product Assistant: Danielle Gidley

Marketing Manager: Valerie Hartman

Content Project Manager: Corinna Dibble

Manufacturing Planner: Julio Esperas

IP Analyst: Alexandra Ricciardi

IP Project Manager: Reba Frederics

Production Service and Compositor:
MPS Limited

Art Director: Sarah Cole

Text and Cover Designer: Ke Design

Cover Image by Eli Asenova/Shutterstock.com

For product information and technology assistance, contact us at
Cengage Customer & Sales Support, 1-800-354-9706.

For permission to use material from this text or product, submit all
requests online at **www.cengage.com/permissions.**
Further permissions questions can be emailed to
permissionrequest@cengage.com.

Library of Congress Control Number: 2017946306

Student Edition:
ISBN: 978-1-337-56044-3

Loose-leaf Edition:
ISBN: 978-1-337-56049-8

Cengage
20 Channel Center Street
Boston, MA 02210
USA

Cengage is a leading provider of customized learning solutions with
employees residing in nearly 40 different countries and sales in more
than 125 countries around the world. Find your local representative at
www.cengage.com.

Cengage products are represented in Canada by Nelson Education, Ltd.

To learn more about Cengage platforms and services, visit
www.cengage.com.
Purchase any of our products at your local college store or at our
preferred online store **www.cengagebrain.com**.

Printed in the United States of America
Print Number: 01   Print Year: 2017

Brief Contents

PART I   **INTRODUCTION**

    CHAPTER 1: Introducing Comparative Politics   1

PART II   **CONSOLIDATED DEMOCRACIES**

    CHAPTER 2: Britain   38
    CHAPTER 3: France   84
    CHAPTER 4: Germany   133
    CHAPTER 5: European Union   183
    CHAPTER 6: Japan   228
    CHAPTER 7: India   276
    CHAPTER 8: The United States   324

PART III   **MIXED SYSTEMS**

    CHAPTER 9: Brazil   369
    CHAPTER 10: Mexico   415
    CHAPTER 11: South Africa   462
    CHAPTER 12: Nigeria   509
    CHAPTER 13: The Russian Federation   555

PART IV   **AUTHORITARIAN REGIMES**

    CHAPTER 14: Iran   607
    CHAPTER 15: China   653

Contents

Preface   xxiii

PART I   INTRODUCTION

Chapter 1   Introducing Comparative Politics   1
Mark Kesselman, Joel Krieger, and William A. Joseph

SECTION 1: Comparative Politics in a Volatile World   2
Making Sense of Turbulent Times   5

SECTION 2: What—and How—Comparative Politics Compares   6
Level of Analysis   9
Causal Theories   11

SECTION 3: Themes for Comparative Analysis   13
Theme 1: A Globalizing World of States   13
Theme 2: Governing the Economy   15
Theme 3: The Democratic Idea   17
Theme 4: The Politics of Collective Identities   20

SECTION 4: Classifying Political Systems   22

SECTION 5: Organization of the Text   26
The Making of the Modern State   26
Political Economy and Development   27
Governance and Policy-Making   27
Representation and Participation   28
Politics in Transition   28
Key Terms, Suggested Readings, and Suggested Websites   29

Contents

PART II   CONSOLIDATED DEMOCRACIES

Chapter 2   Britain   38

Joel Krieger

SECTION 1: The Making of the Modern British State   39

Politics in Action   39

Geographic Setting   39

Critical Junctures   41

*The Consolidation of the British State 41   The Seventeenth-Century Settlement 43
The Industrial Revolution and the British Empire 43   The British Empire 44
Industrial Change and the Struggle for Voting Rights 44   World Wars, Industrial Strife,
and the Depression (1914–1945) 44   Collectivist Consensus (1945–1979) 45
New Labour's Third Way 45   The Conservative–Liberal Coalition 46   Brexit 47*

The Four Themes and Britain   48

Britain in a Globalized World of States 48

Themes and Comparisons   50

SECTION 2: Political Economy and Development   50

State and Economy   50

*Economic Management 51   The Consensus Era 51   Thatcherite Policy Orientation 52
New Labour's Economic Policy Approach 52   The Coalition Government's Economic
Policy 52   New Labour Becomes Old Labour Once Again 52*

Social Policy   53

Society and Economy   53

Inequality and Ethnic Minorities 54   Inequality and Women 55

Environmental Issues   56

Britain in the Global Economy   56

SECTION 3: Governance and Policymaking   58

Organization of the State   58

The Executive   59

*Cabinet Government 59   Bureaucracy and Civil Service 61
Public and Semipublic Institutions 63*

Other State Institutions   64

The Military and the Police 64   The Judiciary 65   Subnational Government 65

The Policymaking Process   66

SECTION 4: Representation and Participation   67

The Legislature   67

*The House of Commons 67   The Legislative Process 67   The House of Lords 68
Reforms in Behavior 68   Structural Changes: Parliamentary Committees 69*

Contents

Political Parties and the Party System   69
The Labour Party 69   The Conservative Party 70   Liberal Democrats 71

Elections   72
The Electoral System and the 2010 Election 72   Gender, Ethnicity, and Representation 73   Trends in Electoral Behavior 74

Political Culture, Citizenship, and Identity   75
Social Class 75   National Identity 76

Interest Groups, Social Movements, and Protest   76

The Political Impact of Technology and the Media   77

SECTION 5: British Politics in Transition   78
Political Challenges and Changing Agendas   78
Constitutional Reform 78   Identities in Flux 79

Is Demography Destiny?   80

British Politics in Comparative Perspective   81

Chapter 3   France   **84**
Mark Kesselman

SECTION 1: The Making of the Modern French State   85
Politics in Action   85
Geographic Setting   86
Critical Junctures   88
Creating Modern France 88   The Ancien Régime 89   The Two Faces of the French Revolution (1789–1815) 90   Many Regimes, Slow Industrialization (1815–1940) 90 Vichy France (1940–1944) and the Fourth Republic (1946–1958) 91   The Fifth Republic (1958–present) 93   2002: The Le Pen Bombshells and Their Aftermath 94 The 2017 Presidential Elections: Reshuffling the Deck 95   France after September 11 95 The French "Non"—Now or Forever? 96

The Four Themes and France   96
France in a Globalized World of States 96   Governing the Economy 97 The Democratic Idea 97   Politics of Collective Identity 97

Themes and Comparisons   97

SECTION 2: Political Economy and Development   98
State and Economy   98
The New French Revolution 98   French-Style Economic Management 99   France's Economic Miracle 99   French Socialism in Practice—and Conservative Aftermath 99 France's Neoliberal Modernization Strategy 100   Assessing French Economic Performance 101

Society and Economy   101
Labor Relations 102   Inequality and Ethnic Minorities 102   Inequality and Women 102   The Generation Gap 103

Contents

Environmental Issues   103

France in the Global Economy   104

SECTION 3: Governance and Policy-Making   **105**

Organization of the State   105

The Executive   107

The President 107   The Prime Minister and Government 109   Bureaucracy and Civil Service 110   Public and Semipublic Agencies 111

Other State Institutions   111

The Judiciary 111   The Constitutional Council 112   State Council 112 Subnational Governments 112   The Military and Police 113

The Policy-Making Process   113

SECTION 4: Representation and Participation   **114**

The Legislature   114

How a Bill Becomes a Law 115   Electing the Legislature 116

Political Parties and the Party System   116

The Major Parties 116   Minor Parties 119

Elections   119

Political Culture, Citizenship, and Identity   121

Social Class 122   Ethnicity and Immigration 122   Citizenship and National Identity 123   Gender 124

Interest Groups, Social Movements, and Protest   125

French Trade Unions 125   Social Movements and Protest 126

The Political Impact of Technology and the Media   126

SECTION 5: French Politics in Transition   **127**

Political Challenges and Changing Agendas   128

Reshaping the French Social Model? 128   "Oui" to Roquefort Cheese, "Non" to Genetically Engineered Products 128   The Challenge of the FN 129 France Falling? 129   France's Relation to Terrorism 129

Is Demography Destiny?   130

French Politics in Comparative Perspective   130

Chapter 4   Germany   **133**

Wade Jacoby

SECTION 1: The Making of the Modern German State   **134**

Politics in Action   134

Geographic Setting   136

Critical Junctures   138

Contents

The Second Reich (1871–1918)   138   The Weimar Republic (1918–1933)   139
The Third Reich (1933–1945)   140   A Divided Germany (1945–1990)   141
The Challenge of German Unification (1990–2001)   142   Germany after
September 11, 2001   143

The Four Themes and Germany 144
Germany in a Globalized World of States   144

Comparisons 145

SECTION 2: Political Economy and Development **146**
State and Economy 146
The Social Market Economy   146   Semipublic Institutions   147   Current Strains on
the Social Market Economy   149

Society and Economy 150
Ethnicity and Economy   150   Gender and Economy   151

Environmental Issues 152
Germany in the Global Economy 152

SECTION 3: Governance and Policy-Making **154**
Organization of the State 154
Government Institutions   154

The Executive 155
The President   155   The Chancellor   155   The Cabinet   157   The Bureaucracy   158

Other State Institutions 158
The Military and Police   159   The Judiciary   160   Subnational Government   160

The Policy-Making Process 161

SECTION 4: Representation and Participation **162**
The Legislature 162
The Bundestag   163   The Bundesrat   165

Political Parties and the Party System 165
The Christian Democrats   166   The Social Democratic Party   166   The Greens   167
The Free Democratic Party   168   The Left Party   168   Alternative for Germany   169

Elections 169
Political Culture, Citizenship, and Identity 171
Refugees, Immigration, and Migrant Labor   171

Interest Groups, Social Movements, and Protest 172
The Political Impact of Technology and the Media 174

SECTION 5: German Politics in Transition **176**
Political Challenges and Changing Agendas 177
Is Demography Destiny? 178
German Politics in Comparative Perspective 179

Contents

Chapter 5 European Union   **183**

George Ross

SECTION 1: The Making of the European Union   **184**

Politics in Action   184

Geographic Setting   185

Critical Junctures   185

Four Themes and the European Union   187

Comparisons   188

SECTION 2: Political Economy and Development   **189**

Environmental Issues   194

SECTION 3: EU Governance and Policy-Making   **198**

Organizing a Nonstate: EU Institutions   198

The European Commission: Executive and Bureaucracy? 199   The Council of Ministers and the European Council 200

Other Institutions   201

The European Parliament: A European Legislature? 201   The European Union Court of Justice 203   The Eurogroup, Advisory Committees, Agencies 204

SECTION 4: The EU and Its Policies   **205**

Federal Policies   205

Building a European Market 205   Competition Policy 206

Agriculture   207

Regional Development   207

The EU Budget   208

EMU and the Euro   209

Shared Policies   209

Globalization and Competitiveness 209   Social Policy 210

Intergovernmental Europe?   211

Justice and Home Affairs 211   Foreign and Security Policy 212

SECTION 5: Representation and Participation in the EU   **215**

The European Parliament   217

Political Cultures, Citizenship, and Identities   217

Interest Groups, Social Movements, and Protest   218

Elections   221

The Political Impact of Technology and the Media   221

Contents

SECTION 6: Europolitics in Transition — 222
Political Challenges and Changing Agendas — 223
Is Demography Destiny? — 224
Politics in Comparative Perspective — 224
The EU: Summary and Prospects — 225

Chapter 6 Japan — 228

Shigeko Fukai and Haruhiro Fukui

SECTION 1: The Making of the Modern Japanese State — 229
Politics in Action — 229
Geographic Setting — 230
Critical Junctures — 231

*Premodern Japan 231   Meiji Restoration and Taisho Democracy (1868–1925) 235
Rise and Fall of Militarist Nationalism (1926–1945) 236   The Birth and Evolution of a
Pacifist Democracy (1945–Present) 237*

The Four Themes and Japan — 238

*Japan in a Globalized World of States 238   Governing the Economy 239
The Democratic Idea 239   Politics of Collective Identity 239*

Comparisons — 240

SECTION 2: Political Economy and Development — 241
State and Economy — 241
Society and Economy — 243
Environmental Issues — 245
Japan in the Global Economy — 246

SECTION 3: Governance and Policymaking — 248
Organization of the State — 248
The Executive — 250

Prime Minister and Cabinet 250   The National Bureaucracy 251

Other State Institutions — 253

*The Military 253   The Judiciary 253   The Police 255
Subnational Government 255*

The Policymaking Process — 256

SECTION 4: Representation and Participation — 257
The Legislature — 257
Political Parties and the Party System — 258
Elections — 261

Contents

Political Culture, Citizenship, and Identity   263

The Ainu and Okinawans 263   Outcast Groups 264   Koreans and Other Resident Foreigners 265

Interest Groups, Social Movements, and Protest   265

Women's Movement 267   Protest 268

The Political Impact of Technology and the Media   269

SECTION 5: Japanese Politics in Transition   **271**
Political Challenges and Changing Agendas   271
Is Demography Destiny?   272
Japanese Politics in Comparative Perspective   273

Chapter 7   India   **276**

Atul Kohli and Amrita Basu

SECTION 1: The Making of the Modern Indian State   **277**
Politics in Action   277
Geographic Setting   278
Critical Junctures   280

The Colonial Legacy (1757–1947) 281   The Nationalist Movement and Partition (1885–1947) 282   The Nehru Era (1947–1964) 283   The Indira Gandhi Era (1966–1984) 284   Coalition Governments (1989 to the Present) 286   September 11 and Its Aftermath 287

The Four Themes and India   288

India in a Globalized World of States 288   Governing the Economy 288 The Democratic Idea 288   The Politics of Collective Identity 288   Implications for Comparative Politics 288

SECTION 2: Political Economy and Development   **289**
State and Economy   290

The Economy after Independence 290   Economic Liberalization 291 Reforms in Agriculture 291

Society and Economy   292

Inequality and Social Welfare Policy 292

Environmental Issues   294
India in the Global Economy   295

SECTION 3: Governance and Policy-Making   **296**
Organization of the State   296
The Executive   298

The Prime Minister and Cabinet 298   The Prime Minister 298   The Cabinet 299 The Bureaucracy 299

Contents

Other State Institutions   300

The Military and the Police 300   The Judiciary 301   Subnational Government 302

The Policy-Making Process   303

SECTION 4: Representation and Participation   303

The Legislature   303

Political Parties and the Party System   305

*The Congress Party 307   The Janata Party and Janata Dal 307
The Bharatiya Janata Party (BJP) 308   The Communist Party of India (CPM) 309
The Aam Admi Party 309*

Elections   311

Political Culture, Citizenship, and Identity   311

Interest Groups, Social Movements, and Protest   312

The Political Impact of Technology and the Media   314

SECTION 5: Indian Politics in Transition   315

Political Challenges and Changing Agendas   315

*The Challenge of Ethnic Diversity 315   Political Violence 316   India-Pakistan
Tensions 316   Nuclear Weapons 316   Kashmir in a World of States 317
India's Regional Relations 317   Economic Performance 318   International Power
and Domestic Prosperity 319   Institutional Decay 319*

Is Demography Destiny?   320

Indian Politics in Comparative Perspective   321

Chapter 8   The United States   324

Louis DeSipio

SECTION 1: The Making of the Modern American State   325

Politics in Action   325

Geographic Setting   327

Critical Junctures   327

*The Revolutionary Era (1773–1789) 328   The Civil War and Reconstruction
(1861–1876) 330   The New Deal Era (1933–1940) 330   Divided Government,
Frequently Shifting Partisan Dominance, and Political Contestation of the Scope of
Government (1968 to the Present) 331   September 11, 2001, and Its Aftermath 332*

The Four Themes and the United States   332

*The United States in a Globalized World of States 332   Governing the Economy 333
The Democratic Idea 333   The Politics of Collective Identity 333*

Themes and Comparisons   334

SECTION 2: Political Economy and Development   334

State and Economy   334

Society and Economy   337

Contents

Environmental Issues   340

The United States in the Global Economy   341

SECTION 3: Governance and Policy-Making   **344**

Organization of the State   344

The Executive   346

The Presidency 346   The Cabinet and the Bureaucracy 347

Other State Institutions   348

The Judiciary 348   Subnational Government 349   The Military 350
National Security Agencies 350

The Policy-Making Process   350

SECTION 4: Representation and Participation   **352**

The Legislature   352

Political Parties and the Party System   354

Elections   356

Political Culture, Citizenship, and Identity   358

Interest Groups, Social Movements, and Protest   359

The Political Impact of Technology and the Media   361

SECTION 5: United States Politics in Transition   **362**

Political Challenges and Changing Agendas   362

Is Demography Destiny?   365

U.S. Politics in Comparative Perspective   365

PART III   MIXED SYSTEMS

Chapter 9   Brazil   **369**

Alfred P. Montero

SECTION 1: The Making of the Modern Brazilian State   370

Politics in Action   370

Geographic Setting   371

Critical Junctures   372

The Brazilian Empire (1822–1889) 372   The Old Republic (1889–1930) 373
The 1930 Revolution 374   The Populist Republic (1945–1964) 375   The Rise of
Bureaucratic Authoritarianism (1964–1985) 376   The Transition to Democracy and the
First Civilian Governments (1974–2001) 376   Brazil after September 11, 2001 378

The Four Themes and Brazil   380

Brazil in a Globalized World of States 380   Governing the Economy 380
The Democratic Idea 380   The Politics of Collective Identity 380

Themes and Comparisons   381

Contents

SECTION 2: Political Economy and Development 382

State and Economy 382

The Fiscal System 383 The Problem of Inflation 384

Society and Economy 385

The Welfare System 385 Agrarian Reform 387

Environmental Issues 387

Brazil in the Global Economy 388

SECTION 3: Governance and Policy-Making 390

Organization of the State 390

The Executive 391

The Bureaucracy: State and Semipublic Firms 393

Other State Institutions 394

The Judiciary 394 Subnational Government 395 The Military and the Police 395

The Policy-Making Process 396

SECTION 4: Representation and Participation 398

The Legislature 398

Political Parties and the Party System 399

Elections 402

Political Culture, Citizenship, and Identity 402

Interest Groups, Social Movements, and Protest 405

The Political Impact of Technology and the Media 406

SECTION 5: Brazilian Politics in Transition 407

Political Challenges and Changing Agendas 407

Is Demography Destiny? 410

Brazilian Politics in Comparative Perspective 410

Chapter 10 Mexico 415

Halbert Jones

SECTION 1: The Making of the Modern Mexican State 416

Politics in Action 416

Geographic Setting 419

Critical Junctures 420

Independence, Instability, and Dictatorship (1810–1910) 420 The Mexican Revolution and the Sonoran Dynasty (1910–1934) 422 Lázaro Cárdenas, Agrarian Reform, and the Workers (1934–1940) 423 The Politics of Rapid Development (1940–1982) 423 Crisis and Reform (1982–2000) 423 Since 2000: Mexico as a Multiparty Democracy 425

Contents

The Four Themes and Mexico 427

*Mexico in a Globalized World of States 427 Governing the Economy 427
The Democratic Idea 428 The Politics of Collective Identity 428*

Comparisons 429

SECTION 2: Political Economy and Development 430

State and Economy 430

*Import Substitution and Its Consequences 430 Sowing the Oil and Reaping a Crisis 432
New Strategies: Structural Reforms and NAFTA 433 The Mexican Economy Today 433*

Society and Economy 435

Environmental Issues 435

Mexico in the Global Economy 436

SECTION 3: Governance and Policy-Making 438

Organization of the State 438

The Executive 438

The President and the Cabinet 438 The Bureaucracy 440 The Parastatal Sector 441

Other State Institutions 441

The Military 441 The Judiciary 442 Subnational Government 443

The Policy-Making Process 444

SECTION 4: Representation and Participation 445

The Legislature 445

Political Parties and the Party System 446

The PRI 446 The PAN 448 The PRD and Morena 449 Other Parties 450

Elections 451

Political Culture, Citizenship, and Identity 451

Interest Groups, Social Movements, and Protest 452

The Political Impact of Technology and the Media 453

SECTION 5: Mexican Politics in Transition 455

Political Challenges and Changing Agendas 456

Is Demography Destiny? 458

Mexican Politics in Comparative Perspective 459

Chapter 11 South Africa **462**

Tom Lodge

SECTION 1: The Making of the Modern South African State 463

Politics in Action 463

Geographic Setting 465

Contents

Critical Junctures   465

Dynamics of the Frontier, 1779–1906   467   Imperialists Against Republicans, 1867–1910   468   The Origins of Modern Institutionalized Racism, 1910–1945   468 Apartheid and African Resistance, 1945–1960   469   The Sharpeville Massacre and Grand Apartheid, 1960–1976   469   Generational Revolt and Political Reform, 1976–1990   472   The South African Miracle, 1990–1999   472

The Four Themes and South Africa   474

South Africa in a Globalized World of States   474   Governing the Economy   474   The Democratic Idea   475   Collective Identity   475

Themes and Comparisons   475

SECTION 2: Political Economy and Development   476

State and Economy   476

Apartheid Economics   476   Liberalization and Deregulation   477

Society and Economy   478

Black Empowerment   479

Environmental Issues   480

South Africa in the Global Economy   481

SECTION 3: Governance and Policy-Making   483

Organization of the State   483

The Executive   484

Other State Institutions   487

The Judiciary and the Police   487   National Security Organizations   489 Subnational Government   489

The Policy-Making Process   491

SECTION 4: Representation and Participation   492

The Legislature   492

Political Parties and the Party System   493

The African National Congress   494   Smaller Parties   495

Elections   498

Political Culture, Citizenship, and Identity   500

Interest Groups, Social Movements, and Protest   500

The Political Impact of Technology and the Media   501

SECTION 5: South African Politics in Transition   502

Political Challenges and Changing Agendas   502

Economic Challenges   504

Is Demography Destiny?   505

South African Politics in Comparative Perspective   505

Contents

Chapter 12 Nigeria   **509**

Darren Kew and Peter M. Lewis

SECTION 1: The Making of the Modern Nigerian State   **512**

Politics in Action   512

Geographic Setting   513

Critical Junctures   515

The Precolonial Period (800–1900) *515*   *Colonial Rule and Its Impact (1860–1945)* *517*
Divisive Identities: Ethnic Politics Under Colonialism (1945–1960) *517*   *The First*
Republic (1960–1966) *518*   *Civil War and Military Rule (1966–1979)* *519*
The Second and Third Republics, and Predatory Military Rule (1979–1999) *520*
The Fourth Republic (1999–Present) *520*

The Four Themes and Nigeria   522

Nigeria in a Globalized World of States *522*   *Governing the Economy* *522*
The Democratic Idea *522*   *Collective Identities* *523*

Comparisons   523

SECTION 2: Political Economy and Development   **524**

State and Economy   524

Origins of Economic Decline *524*   *From 1985 to the Present: Deepening Economic Crisis*
and the Search for Solutions *524*

Society and Economy   527

Environmental Issues   529

Nigeria in the Global Economy   530

SECTION 3: Governance and Policy-Making   **532**

Organization of the State   532

The National Question and Constitutional Governance *532*   *Federalism and State*
Structure *532*

The Executive   534

The Bureaucracy *536*

Other State Institutions   536

The Military *536*   *The Judiciary* *537*   *Subnational Government* *538*

The Policy-Making Process   538

SECTION 4: Representation and Participation   **539**

The Legislature   539

Political Parties and the Party System   539

Elections   541

Political Culture, Citizenship, and Identity   542

Modernity Versus Traditionalism *542*   *Religion* *543*

Interest Groups, Social Movements, and Protest   544

The Political Impact of Technology and the Media   545

Contents

SECTION 5: Nigerian Politics in Transition   547

Political Challenges and Changing Agendas   547

Is Demography Destiny?   550

Nigerian Politics in Comparative Perspective   551

Chapter 13 The Russian Federation   555

Joan DeBardeleben

Section 1: The Making of the Modern Russian State   556

Politics in Action   556

Geographic Setting   558

Critical Junctures   559

*The Decline of the Russian Tsarist State and the Founding of the Soviet Union   559
The Bolshevik Revolution and the Establishment of Soviet Power (1917–1929)   559
The Stalin Revolution (1929–1953)   560   Attempts at De-Stalinization
(1953–1985)   561   Perestroika and Glasnost (1985–1991)   563   Collapse of the
USSR and the Emergence of the Russian Federation (1991 to the Present)   563*

The Four Themes and Russia   565

*Russia in a Globalized World of States   565   Governing the Economy   566
The Democratic Idea   566   The Politics of Collective Identity   566*

Comparisons   566

Section 2: Political Economy and Development   567

State and Economy   568

Society and Economy   570

Environmental Issues   572

Russia in the Global Economy   572

Section 3: Governance and Policy-Making   576

Organization of the State   576

The Executive   578

The National Bureaucracy   579   Public and Semipublic Institutions   580

Other State Institutions   581

The Judiciary   581   Subnational Governments   582   The Military and Security Organs   584

The Policy-Making Process   585

Section 4: Representation and Participation   586

The Legislature   586

Political Parties and the Party System   587

*The Dominant Party: United Russia   588   Other Parties Represented in the State
Duma   588   Western-Oriented Liberal Parties and Kremlin Critics: Marginalized   591*

Elections   592

Contents

Political Culture, Citizenship, and Identity..593

Interest Groups, Social Movements, and Protest..594

The Political Impact of Technology and the Media...596

SECTION 5: Russian Politics in Transition...**598**

Political Challenges and Changing Agendas..598

Is Demographic Destiny?...602

Russian Politics in Comparative Perspective...603

PART IV AUTHORITARIAN REGIMES

Chapter 14 Iran   607

Ervand Abrahamian

SECTION 1: The Making of the Modern Iranian State..**608**

Politics in Action..608

Geographic Setting...609

Critical Junctures...612

*The Safavids (1501–1722) 612   The Qajars (1794–1925) 613   The Pahlavis
(1925–1979) 613   The Islamic Revolution (1979) 615   The Islamic Republic
(1979–Present) 617   Iran after 9/11 618*

The Four Themes and Iran...619

*Iran in a Globalized World of States 619   Governing the Economy 620
The Democratic Idea 620   The Politics of Collective Identity 621*

Comparisons...621

SECTION 2: Political Economy and Development..**622**

State and Economy..622

Iran's Economy under the Islamic Republic 623

Society and Economy...624

Environmental Issues..626

Iran in the Global Economy..627

SECTION 3: Governance and Policy-Making...**629**

Organization of the State...629

The Executive...630

*The Leader and Major Organizations of Clerical Power 630   The Government
Executive 632   The Bureaucracy 633*

Other State Institutions...634

*The Judiciary 634   The Military 635   Subnational Government 636
Semipublic Institutions 636*

The Policy-Making Process...637

Contents

SECTION 4: Representation and Participation   **639**

The Legislature   640

Political Parties and the Party System   640

The Liberation Movement 640   The National Front 641   The Mojahedin 641
The Fedayin 641   The Tudeh (Party of the Masses) 641

Elections   641

Political Culture, Citizenship, and Identity   642

Interest Groups, Social Movements, and Protest   644

The Political Impact of Technology and the Media   645

SECTION 5: Iranian Politics in Transition   **646**

Political Challenges and Changing Agendas   647

Is Demography Destiny?   650

Iranian Politics in Comparative Perspective   650

Chapter 15 China   **653**

William A. Joseph

SECTION 1: The Making of the Modern Chinese State   **654**

Politics in Action   654

Geographic Setting   655

Critical Junctures   657

Warlords, Nationalists, and Communists (1912–1949) 658
Mao Zedong in Power (1949–1976) 659   Deng Xiaoping and the Transformation
of Chinese Communism (1977–1997) 661   From Revolutionaries to Technocrats
(1997–Present) 662

The Four Themes and China   663

China in a Globalized World of States 663   Governing the Economy 664   The
Democratic Idea 664   The Politics of Collective Identity 664

Comparisons   665

SECTION 2: Political Economy and Development   **666**

State and Economy   666

China Goes to Market 666   Remaking the Chinese Countryside 668

Society and Economy   669

Environmental Issues   671

China in the Global Economy   672

SECTION 3: Governance and Policy-Making   **674**

Organization of the State   674

The Executive   674

CCP Organization 674   PRC Organization 677

Contents

Other State Institutions   679

The Judiciary 679   Subnational Government 680   The Military, Police, and Internal Security 680

The Policy-Making Process   681

SECTION 4: Representation and Participation   **682**

The Legislature   682

Political Parties and the Party System   683

The CCP 683   China's Noncommunist "Democratic Parties" 684

Elections   685

Political Culture, Citizenship, and Identity   686

From Communism to Consumerism 686   China's Non-Chinese Citizens 687

Interest Groups, Social Movements, and Protest   689

Protest and the Party-State 689

The Political Impact of Technology and the Media   690

SECTION 5: Chinese Politics in Transition   **691**

Political Challenges and Changing Agendas   691

China and the Democratic Idea 693

Is Demography Destiny?   694

Chinese Politics in Comparative Perspective   695

China as a Communist Party-State 695   China as a Developing Country 696

Endnotes 701

Glossary 709

About the Editors and Contributors 721

Index 723

Preface

In the prefaces to several of the previous editions of *Introduction to Comparative Politics* (ICP), we brought up the title of Bob Dylan's 1964 song, "The Times, They Are a-Changin'" to describe how tumultuous politics around the world was when the book was published. Here is what we observed:

- "Politics throughout the world seems more troubled today than even a few years ago, when celebrations around the globe ushered in the new millennium."
  —*Introduction to Comparative Politics*, 3rd edition, © 2004.
- In recent years, the "world of politics was as turbulent as at any time in recent memory, with clear-cut trends more elusive than ever."
  —*Introduction to Comparative Politics*, 4th edition, © 2007.
- [We] have witnessed as much—or more—turmoil and uncertainty as the preceding years."
  —*Introduction to Comparative Politics*, 5th edition, © 2010.
- "The sixth edition of ICP . . . has been published soon after prodemocracy movements overthrew decades-old dictatorships in Tunisia and Egypt, and repressive regimes unleashed deadly force against similar movements in Algeria, Bahrain, Iran, Libya, Syria, and Yemen."
  —*Introduction to Comparative Politics*, 6th edition, © 2013
- "When it comes to the degree of uncertainty, and the range and depth of challenges faced by ordinary citizens who yearn for stability, less strife, and a widening circle of opportunities, the present edition is no different than its predecessors."
  —*Introduction to Comparative Politics*, 7th edition, © 2016

If there is a difference in the tone of the 8th edition of ICP, it may be that, although the times are certainly still a-changin', it now seems as if many of those political changes are for the worse. Where are equivalent developments fueling the optimism generated by the democratic promise of the fall of the Berlin Wall in 1989 or the Arab Spring in 2011?

The political climate in much of the world these days is cloudy indeed, and for all-too-good reasons. For a start, there have recently been heightened geopolitical tensions, which, in the case of North Korea's continuing development of nuclear weapons, threaten devastating military conflict. In addition, civil wars and ethnic violence have engulfed many regions of the world, unleashing great destruction of life and property and giving rise to waves of refugees—which in turn fuel a nativist backlash in countries that feel threatened by the influx of migrants seeking safe haven. Finally, the thickening storm clouds also include the increasingly palpable reality that climate change is accelerating, including rising sea levels, global warming, and more frequent extreme weather events. There is a scientific consensus that the change is largely due to human actions (i.e., a hyperindustrialized assault on nature). But, at least with regard to the latter, all is not bleak: there is increased recognition of the need for concerted action at the local, regional, national, and international levels.

Whatever the direction of change, our mission in this book has remained the same. It is not to promote optimism or pessimism, but, as we noted in the preface of prior editions of ICP, to provide a clear and comprehensive guide to unsettled political times through comparative analysis.

Country-by-Country Approach and Thematic Framework

We hope that the methods of comparative analysis will come alive as students examine similarities and differences among countries and within and between political systems. Our thematic approach facilitates disciplined analysis of political challenges and changing agendas within each country. Like previous editions of ICP, this edition employs a country-by-country approach structured around four core themes:

1. **A Globalizing World of States** focuses on the importance of state formation, the internal organization of the state, and the impact of the interstate system on political development. This theme emphasizes the interaction of globalization and state power.
2. **Governing the Economy** analyzes state strategies for promoting economic development and competitiveness, emphasizes the crucial role of economic performance in determining a state's political legitimacy, and stresses the interactive effects of economic globalization on domestic politics.
3. **The Democratic Idea** explores the challenges posed to the state by citizens' demands for greater participation and influence in democracies, mixed systems, and authoritarian regimes, and discusses the inevitable gap between the promise of democracy and its imperfect fulfillment.
4. **The Politics of Collective Identities** considers the political consequences of the complex interplay among class, race, ethnicity, gender, religion, and nationality.

Our approach to comparative politics stresses the analysis of each country's politics by applying these four themes within a context shaped by globalization. This approach strikes a balance between a fine-grained analysis of the richness of each country's distinctive pattern of political development and explicit cross-country comparative analysis. In so doing, our text teaches students that the study of comparative politics is defined by a method that investigates similarities and differences in cases and, at the same time, poses and attempts to answer searching questions that really matter in the lives of students as active citizens. These are questions embedded in the thematic scaffolding of ICP.

Chapter 1 begins this book by describing the comparative method, presenting in some detail our four-theme framework, discussing how we classify the political systems of the countries covered in this book, and providing an overview of the organization of the country chapters.

Consolidated Democracies, Hybrid States, and Authoritarian Regimes

We classify the thirteen countries in this edition of ICP in three categories:

- *Consolidated democracies* (Britain, France, Germany, Japan, India, and the United States)
- *Hybrid states* (Brazil, Mexico, South Africa, Nigeria, and Russia)
- *Authoritarian regimes* (Iran and China)

The book also includes a chapter on the European Union (EU), which, in addition to Britain, France, and Germany, is made up of twenty-five other member states that fall into the category of consolidated democracies. (Thanks to the outcome of the 2016 popular vote in the United Kingdom known as Brexit, Britain may no longer be a member of the EU during the life of this edition.)

In Chapter 1, we define the three regime types and explain the rationale for the typology. In particular, we warn against assuming that there is a linear movement from authoritarian regimes to hybrid states to consolidated democracies. Democratization is often a protracted process with ambiguous results or reversals, rather than a clearly delineated path toward completion. Thus, we stress that the countries that we classify as hybrid states are not riding a historical escalator mechanically leading to their transformation into stable or consolidated democracies. Indeed, we emphasize that in hybrid states, elements of democracy coexist with authoritarian practices, and that future political developments could lead any of these countries to move toward either more or less freedom for their citizens.

We also emphasize that the boundaries dividing the three groups are not airtight. Russia is a good example of a country on the cusp between a mixed system and an authoritarian regime. Furthermore, scholars disagree about the appropriate criteria for classifying regime types, as well as about how to classify particular cases. Indeed, instructors may find it fruitful to encourage class discussion of alternative conceptual schemes for classifying groups of countries and how to best characterize the political system of given countries.

NEW Eighth Edition Content

- A new subsection called "Is Demography Destiny?" examines the political importance of demographic changes such as the graying population, the youth bulge, and migration.
- The subsection on "The Political Impact of Technology" in the previous edition has been retitled "The Political Impact of Technology and the Media" and supplemented by additional material on the press, social media, and other means of communication in the Information Age.
- The thoroughly updated introduction and country chapters provide analyses of major recent political developments throughout the world, including discussion of the following:
  - The dramatic 2016 Brexit vote in Britain and its impact on British and EU politics, as well as the loss of its parliamentary majority by the governing Conservative Party a year later
  - The election in 2017 of political newcomer Emmanuel Macron as French president and the upending of France's party system
  - The surprising Electoral College victory of Donald J. Trump in the 2016 U.S. presidential election as the result of an unanticipated nationalist and populist upsurge
  - The impeachment and removal from office of Brazil's president, Dilma Rousseff, and corruption charges involving her successor, Michel Temer
  - The crisis in South African politics resulting from youth protest, the erosion of the domination of the African National Congress (ANC), and corruption charges against President Jacob Zuma
  - The 2016 election as president of Nigeria of retired general Muhammadu Buhari, who had previously served as the nation's head of state from 1983 to 1985 after taking power in a military coup d'état
  - The reelection in 2017 of the reform-minded Iranian president Hassan Rouhani
  - Russia's continuing drift toward authoritarianism under Vladimir Putin
  - The consolidation of personal power by the head of the Chinese Communist Party, Xi Jinping, to a degree unprecedented since the eras of Mao Zedong and Deng Xiaoping

Special Features That Teach

- **Country chapters** strike a balance between introducing comparative politics to students with little or no background in political science and maintaining coverage of the complexity of institutions, issues, processes, and events.
- **Consistent Country Chapter Organization.** At the beginning of each chapter, students will find a map, data on ethnicity, religion, and language specific to that country to aid in comparing countries, and some basic information about the country's political system. Each country chapter consists of five sections:
  - **The Making of the Modern State** begins with an opening vignette that illustrates an important feature of the country's contemporary politics. This is followed by a description of the country's geographic setting, a discussion of the critical junctures in the historical development of the state, and an overview of how the book's four central themes relate to the country. This section concludes by noting the significance of the country for the study of comparative politics.
  - **Political Economy and Development** analyzes the relationship between the state, the impact of economic development on society, current environmental issues, and the country's position in the global economy.

- **Governance and Policy-making** describes the general organization of the state, the executive branch, and other state institutions, including the judiciary, subnational levels of government, and the military, police, internal security, and other agencies of coercion. This section concludes with a description of the policy-making process.
- **Representation and Participation** covers the country's legislature, party system, elections, political culture, citizenship, national identity, interest groups, social movements, and protest. The final subsection is a newly expanded one on the political impact of technology and the media.
- **Politics in Transition** begins by highlighting a recent important development that is influencing the country's politics and then proceeds to an analysis of the major political challenges facing the country. This is followed by a new subsection on youth politics and the generational divide. The section ends with some concluding thoughts about the politics of the country in comparative perspective.
- **Focus questions** at the beginning of each major section in the country chapters provides students with some guidance about what is particularly important about that section.
- **Where Do You Stand?** questions at the end of each section in all chapters encourage students to develop and defend original arguments on controversial issues.
- An end-of-chapter **Summary** highlights the major themes and facts in the chapter.
- There are three **sidebar boxes** in each country chapter that highlight interesting and important aspects of politics:
    - The **Profile** box highlights biographies of important political leaders.
    - **The Global Connection** box provides links between domestic and international politics.
    - The **U.S. Connection** box compares an important feature of political institutions with its American counterpart or explores a crucial aspect of the country's relationship with the United States.
- **Making Connections** questions at the end of each sidebar box encourage students to link the topic of the box to the content of the chapter.
- **Maps, tables, charts, photographs, and political cartoons** enliven the text and present key information in clear and visually appealing ways. At the end of Chapter 1, various data are presented in a way that facilitates comparisons among the countries covered in this book.
- **Key terms** are set in boldface and defined in the margin of the page where the term is first introduced, as well as in a **glossary** at the end of the book. The glossary defines many key concepts that are used broadly in comparative politics.
- Each chapter concludes with a list of **suggested readings and websites**.

Not much is certain about what the political future will hold. But we believe that politics around the world will continue to be endlessly fascinating and that comparative analysis can be an important tool for trying to make sense of what happens and why. The times, indeed, are a-changin'! Welcome aboard!

MindTap

- **MindTap: Empower Your Students.** MindTap is a platform that propels students from memorization to mastery. It gives you complete control of your course so that you can provide engaging content, challenge every learner, and build student confidence. Customize interactive syllabi to emphasize priority topics, and then add your own material or notes to the eBook as desired. This outcomes-driven application gives you the tools needed to empower students and boost both understanding and performance.
- **Access Everything You Need in One Place.** Cut down on prep with the preloaded and organized MindTap course materials. Teach more efficiently with interactive multimedia, assignments, quizzes, and more. Give your students the power to read, listen, and study on their phones so that they can learn on their own terms.

- **Empower Students to Reach their Potential.** Twelve distinct metrics give you actionable insight into student engagement. Identify topics troubling your entire class and instantly communicate with those who are struggling. Students can track their scores to stay motivated to progress toward their goals.
- **Control Your Course—and Your Content.** Get the flexibility to reorder textbook chapters, add your own notes, and embed a variety of content, including Open Educational Resources (OER). Personalize course content to your students' needs. They can even read your notes, add their own, and highlight key text to aid their learning.
- **Get a Dedicated Team, Whenever You Need Them.** MindTap isn't just a tool—it's backed by a personalized team eager to support you. We can help set up your course and tailor it to your specific objectives, so you'll be ready to make an impact from day one. We'll be standing by to help you and your students until the final day of the term.

Supplemental Teaching and Learning Aids and Database Editions

Instructor Companion Website

The Instructor Companion Website is an all-in-one multimedia online resource for class preparation, presentation, and testing. Accessible through www.cengage.com/login with your faculty account, the site offers the following available for download:

- Book-specific Microsoft® PowerPoint® presentations
- A Test Bank compatible with multiple learning management systems
- An Instructor Manual
- PowerPoint image slides
- A JPEG Image Library

The Test Bank, offered in Blackboard, Moodle, Desire2Learn, Canvas, and Angel formats, contains Learning Objective–specific multiple-choice and essay questions for each chapter. Import the test bank into your LMS to edit and manage questions, and to create tests.

The Instructor's Manual contains chapter-specific learning objectives, an outline, key terms with definitions, and a chapter summary. In addition, it features a critical thinking question, lecture launching suggestion, and an in-class activity for each learning objective.

The PowerPoint presentations are ready-to-use, visual outlines of each chapter. These presentations can easily be customized for your lectures.

Cognero Test Bank

Cengage Learning Testing Powered by Cognero is a flexible online system that allows you to create, edit, and manage test bank content from multiple Cengage Learning solutions, create multiple test versions in an instant, and deliver tests from your LMS, your classroom, or wherever you want. The test bank for *Introduction to Comparative Politics*, 8th Edition, contains Learning Objective–specific multiple-choice and essay questions for each chapter.

Acknowledgments

We are grateful to several colleagues who have reviewed and critiqued past and current editions of ICP:

Neal Coates, *Abilene Christian University*
Joseph Ellis, *Wingate University*
Katharina Felts, *Loudoun Valley High School*

Elizabeth Heckman, *Westminster School*
Gunther Hega, *Western Michigan University*
Kira Hoilman, *Potomac Falls High School*
Debra Holzhauer, *Southeast Missouri State University*
Daniel Hoppe, *Stevens Point Area Senior High*
John Kunich, *UNC Charlotte*
Anika Leithner, *California Polytechnic State University*
Thomas Wood, *University of South Carolina, Aiken*

In addition, we thank the talented and professional staff who helped edit and publish the 8th edition of ICP: Brad Potthoff, Senior Product Manager; Kassi Radomski, Content Developer; Paul Banks, Product Director; and Danielle Gidley, Product Assistant.

M. K.
J. K.
W. A. J.

1

Introducing
Comparative Politics

Mark Kesselman, Joel Krieger, and William A. Joseph

COMPARATIVE POLITICS IN A VOLATILE WORLD

▽ Focus Questions

- How did the fall of the Berlin Wall in 1989 and the 9/11 terrorist attacks mark important turning points in world politics?

- Describe a discussion in which you used the comparative method to make a point.

Cold War

The hostile relations that prevailed between the United States and the Soviet Union from the late 1940s until the demise of the latter in 1991.

November 9, 1989, was a day that changed the world. The heavily guarded concrete wall that had divided communist-ruled East Berlin from democratic West Berlin for nearly three decades was opened, and thousands of East Berliners flooded across the border to freedom. Within weeks of the fall of the Berlin Wall, the entire Soviet empire in Eastern Europe had crumbled.

For the first decade or so after the Russian Revolution of 1917 that brought a communist regime to power, the Union of Soviet Socialist Republics (USSR, the formal name of the Soviet Union) was a weak and beleaguered country. But Soviet power and influence increased greatly as a result of the rapid industrialization achieved under Josef Stalin's brutal rule and Russia's crucial role in the Allied coalition that defeated the Axis powers (Nazi Germany, fascist Italy, and militarist Japan) in World War II. At the end of the war in 1945, the Soviet militarily occupied and installed pro-Soviet communist regimes in countries throughout Eastern Europe.

For nearly the entire following half-century, world politics was dominated by a conflict, known as the **Cold War**, that pitted the Soviet Union against the United States and their respective allies across the globe. By the mid-1980s, citizens of the USSR and the communist states of Eastern Europe had grown increasingly discontented due to the poor performance of their countries' centrally planned socialist economies and the harsh dictatorships under which they lived.

In 1985, a decisive change occurred when the reform-minded Mikhail Gorbachev became leader of the Communist Party of the Soviet Union (CPSU) and, as a result, ruler of the Soviet Union. Gorbachev introduced major political and economic reforms, with the goal of increasing support for the CPSU. He also ended repression of political opposition, relaxed controls on the media, and signaled that the Soviet Union would no longer interfere in the affairs of its Eastern European allies.

Gorbachev's reforms provide the context for understanding the significance of the Berlin Wall's fall on that fateful day in November 1989. In the preceding and subsequent months, every communist regime in Eastern Europe had crumbled in a series of largely peaceful revolutions. But Gorbachev's reform program failed to contain the winds of change, and in late December 1991, the USSR was dissolved and Russia was reborn. The Cold War was over.

The impact of the initial phase in this chain reaction of world-shaking political changes was analyzed in a widely noted 1989 article by political scientist Francis Fukuyama, entitled "The End of History?" (The article was later expanded into the similarly titled book *The End of History and the Last Man*.) Fukuyama argued that the end of the Cold War was not only immensely important in its own right but had even greater historical significance. It was, he said, "the end point of mankind's ideological evolution and the universalization of Western liberal democracy as the final form of human government."[1]

Several decades later, the idea that history ended with the collapse of communism in Eastern Europe and the Soviet Union and that Western democracy had vanquished all ideological challengers as a way to govern society seems extraordinarily quaint—and even rather naïve. In fairness, Fukuyama did not claim that important political challenges to **liberal democracy** would never recur. Rather, he claimed that the implosion of communism spelled an end to any globally influential ideological challenges to such a system of government and its underlying capitalist economy.

September 11, 2001, was another day that changed the world. The terrorist attacks on the World Trade Center and the Pentagon reflected the spread of an ideology, radical Islamism,* that challenges the very core values of liberal democracy. The persistence of Al-Qaeda, the organization that masterminded the 9/11 attacks, and the rise of the Islamic State are visible and violent reminders that Fukuyama's optimism may have been misguided.

Another source of recent monumental change in world politics was the Great Recession of 2008, which threw the global economy into a tailspin and undermined confidence in the liberal democracies where it started and where it hit hardest, particularly the United States. Partly in reaction to the impact of the recession, ultra-conservative, hypernationalist, xenophobic, and populist movements have arisen in Western Europe, all of which reject some of the basic tenets of liberal democracy and trends in globalized capitalism. Notable examples include the Brexit vote in June 2016, which started the process of Britain's withdrawal from the European Union, and the second-place finish in France's May 2017 presidential election of Marine Le Pen, the candidate of the far-right National Front. Many scholars and political analysts have argued that the victory of first-time politician and populist candidate Donald J. Trump in the U.S. presidential elections in November 2016 was also indicative of the diminished luster of liberal democracy for many American citizens.

At the same time, other political developments in the United States, Britain, and France suggest just how unpredictable the power of populism can be. The surprising strength of Bernie Sanders's ultimately unsuccessful challenge to the Democratic Party establishment's favored candidate, Hillary Clinton, in the primaries was propelled mostly by young voters who were angry about growing inequality in the United States and the economic and political power of Wall Street. In France, Le Pen was decisively defeated by political newcomer Emmanuel Macron, whose liberal party, En Marche ! (Forward !), was founded less than a year before he was elected president. And in Britain, pollsters and pundits (including political scientists) were confounded when Prime Minister Theresa May's pro-Brexit Conservative Party lost its parliamentary majority and the anti-Brexit Labour Party, with its new leader, Jeremy Corbyn, advocating a radical left program, gained a large number of seats in the June 2017 snap election. May has remained prime minister (at least for the moment), but she is greatly weakened politically.

The only thing that seems clear at the moment is that **populism**, which is defined more by an antiestablishment, "power to the people" message and anger against existing political norms and policies and elite concentrations of power than by any particular ideological orientation, is a political force to be reckoned with in many parts of the world today.

The People's Republic of China, one of the world's only remaining communist regimes, and by far the largest, has been the fastest-growing major economy in the world for three decades. Through its proactive role in forming multilateral organizations and its aid to and investment in developing countries, China has been increasingly successful in promoting its model of state-led development and strong,

liberal democracy

A democratic system of government that officially recognizes and legally protects individual rights and freedoms and in which the exercise of political power is constrained by the rule of law.

populism

A style of mobilization by a political party or movement that seeks to gain popular support by emphasizing antiestablishment rhetoric, decrying elite concentrations of power as the source of national decline, and promising to be responsive to the needs of ordinary people.

Islamism is the use of Islam as a political ideology. It is sometimes called *political Islam* and *Islamic fundamentalism*. All the world's other major religions also have taken political forms. For more on this topic, see Chapter 14, on Iran.

authoritarian government as an alternative to slow-growing, politically volatile, capitalist, and liberal democracies.

And under Vladimir Putin, Russia, which after the collapse of the Soviet Union was apparently embarking on a transition to liberal democracy, has instead drifted toward authoritarianism. More broadly, the think tank Freedom House concluded in its 2017 *Freedom in the World* report, "With populist and nationalist forces making significant gains in democratic states, 2016 marked the 11th consecutive year of decline in global freedom."[2]

The Russian military takeover and annexation of Crimea, which then was part of independent, democratic Ukraine, as well as Russian cyberinterference in the 2016 U.S. presidential election and 2017 French presidential election, have led to what some analysts have characterized as a new Cold War. Among the many developments that keep world politics unsettled and ever-changing are major violent conflicts in the Middle East (e.g., the ongoing civil war in Syria) and Africa (e.g., the activities of the terrorist group Boko Haram in Nigeria), a bellicose regime in North Korea that is rapidly improving its nuclear arsenal, and China's aggressive assertion of its power in the South China Sea.

Clearly, history hasn't ended. Therefore, if we want to understand how our world has gotten to this point and how history may unfold in the future, the study of **comparative politics**—the subfield of political science that focuses on the similarities and differences among different types of political systems—becomes particularly important. Our aim in *Introduction to Comparative Politics* (ICP) is to provide students with the tools to bring some order out of the apparent chaos of kaleidoscopic political change that has become the norm in the contemporary world.

comparative politics

The field within political science that focuses on domestic politics of countries and analyzes patterns of similarity and difference among countries.

The fall of the Berlin Wall on November 9, 1989, and the terrorist attack on the World Trade Center in New York and the Pentagon in Washington, DC, on September 11, 2001, mark two of the most transformational events in modern world politics.

AP Photo; Stacy Walsh Rosenstock/Alamy

This book describes and analyzes how thirteen countries and the European Union both shape and are shaped by the world order created by the watershed political events noted previously. Each of these events marks what we call a **critical juncture** in political history, not only in international relations, but also in that of the countries included here and of the European Union.

This chapter is designed to help students navigate the large volume of information provided in ICP by introducing a thematic framework that organizes the politics of each of the countries and is combined with a thorough analysis of the political institutions and processes of each country.

critical juncture

An important historical event when political actors make critical choices that shape institutions and future outcomes in both individual countries and the international system.

Making Sense of Turbulent Times

The flash of newspaper headlines, television sound bites, and endless tweets can make politics at home and abroad look overwhelming and chaotic. Political analysis involves more than blogging, talking heads, or Monday-morning quarterbacking. It requires a longer historical context, a thorough grasp of countries' institutional configurations (political systems), and a framework for understanding unfolding political developments.

This book describes and analyzes the political history, government institutions, policy-making processes, and other key aspects of politics in a range of countries that represent a variety of political systems around the world. ICP examines the political similarities and differences in politics in Britain, France, Germany, Japan, India, the United States, Brazil, Mexico, South Africa, Nigeria, Russia, Iran, and China. The European Union is also included in the book because it is the most important regional organization created to provide political and economic integration among a large group of countries that, despite all being democracies, have quite divergent national interests. Brexit has called into question the viability of this noble effort to overcome such differences in order to promote peace and prosperity among member-states. The European Union has profound implications for the field of comparative politics, which has been based on the assumption that the individual **nation-state** is the most important unit of analysis in understanding world politics.

By using a framework that facilitates comparing similarities and differences in a representative sample of countries, we can understand the longer-term causes of political changes and continuities within nations. Each chapter explores a country's political development by reference to four themes that are central for understanding politics in today's world:

nation-state

A distinct, politically defined territory in which the state and national identity (that is, a sense of solidarity and shared values based on being citizens of the same country) coincide.

- *The Globalizing World of States:* The historical formation, internal organization, and interaction of states within the international order
- *Governing the Economy:* The role of the state in economic management
- *The Democratic Idea:* The spread of democracy and the challenges of democratization
- *The Politics of Collective Identities:* The sources and political impact of diverse **collective identities**, including class, gender, ethnicity, nationality, and religion

These themes, discussed next, help us make political sense of both stable and tumultuous times in countries around the world.

While the contemporary period presents an extraordinary challenge to those who study comparative politics, the study of comparative politics also provides a unique opportunity for understanding this uncertain era. In order to appreciate

collective identities

The groups with which people identify, including gender, class, race, region, and religion, and which are the "building blocks" for social and political action.

the complexity of politics in countries around the world, we must look beyond any single national perspective. Today, business and trade, information technology, mass communications and culture, immigration and travel, and politics forge deep connections—as well as deep divisions—among people worldwide. We urgently need a global and comparative perspective as we explore the politics of different countries and their interaction and interdependence with one another.

There is an added benefit of studying comparative politics: by looking at political institutions, values, and processes in different countries, the student of comparative politics acquires analytical skills that can also be used to examine his or her own country. After you study comparative politics, you begin to think comparatively. As comparison becomes second nature, we hope that you will look at the politics of your own country differently, with a wider, deeper, and more analytical focus that will inspire new reflections, interpretations, and insights. The contemporary world provides a fascinating laboratory for the study of comparative politics. We hope that you share our sense of excitement in the challenging effort to understand the complex and ever-shifting terrain of contemporary politics throughout the world.

Where Do You Stand?

There are more than 200 countries in the world. Is it time for other countries to take on more of the burdens of global leadership that the United States has shouldered since the end of World War II?

In what ways do you think the study of comparative politics will change how you understand the United States—or whatever country you call home?

SECTION 2

WHAT—AND HOW—COMPARATIVE POLITICS COMPARES

⚑ Focus Questions

- What do we mean by globalization?

- How does increased cross-border contact among countries and peoples affect political, social, and cultural life within individual countries?

To "compare and contrast" is one of the most common human mental exercises, whether in the classroom study of literature, politics, or animal behavior, or in selecting dorm rooms or arguing with friends about your favorite movie. In the observation of politics, the use of comparisons is very old, dating in the Western world from the ancient Greek philosopher, Aristotle, who analyzed and compared the city-states of Greece in the fourth century BCE according to whether they were ruled by a single individual, a few people, or all citizens. The modern study of comparative politics refines and systematizes this age-old practice of evaluating some features of country X's politics by comparing it to the same features of country Y's politics.

Comparative politics is a subfield within the academic discipline of political science, as well as a method or approach to the study of politics.[3] The subject matter of comparative politics is the domestic, or internal, politics of countries.

The discipline of political science is usually defined as comprising four areas of specialization: comparative politics, American politics, international relations, and political theory.

Because it is widely believed that students living in the United States should study the politics of their own country in depth, American politics is usually treated as one of the four subfields of political science. It is also usual elsewhere to separate the study of politics at home and abroad, so students in Canada study Canadian politics as a distinct specialty, Japanese students learn about Japanese politics, and so on. However, there is no logical reason why the United States should not be included within the field of comparative politics—on the contrary, there is good reason to do so. Comparative study can make it easier to recognize what is distinctive about the United States and what features it shares with some other countries. For this reason, we have included a chapter on the United States in ICP.

Special mention should be made of the distinction between comparative politics and international relations. Comparative politics involves comparing domestic political institutions, processes, policies, conflicts, and attitudes *within* different countries; international relations involves studying the foreign policies of and interactions *among* countries, the role of international organizations such as the United Nations, and the growing influence of global actors, from multinational corporations to international human rights advocates to terrorist networks. In a globalized world, however, domestic and international politics routinely spill over into one another, so the distinction between the two fields is somewhat blurry. Courses in international relations nowadays often analyze how internal political processes affect states' behavior toward each other, while courses in comparative politics highlight the importance of transnational forces for understanding what goes on within a country's borders. One of the four themes that we use to analyze comparative politics, the "globalizing world of states," emphasizes the interaction of domestic and international forces in the politics of all nations.

It still makes sense to maintain the distinction between comparative politics and international relations. Much of the world's political activity continues to occur within national borders, and comparisons of domestic politics, institutions, and processes enable us to understand critical features that distinguish one country's politics from another's. Furthermore, we believe that despite increased international economic competition and integration (a key aspect of **globalization**), countries remain the fundamental building blocks in structuring most political activity. Therefore, ICP is built on in-depth case studies of a sample of important countries around the world.

The comparative approach principally analyzes similarities and differences among countries by focusing on selected political institutions and processes. As students of comparative politics (we call ourselves **comparativists**), we believe that we cannot make reliable statements about most political situations by looking at only one case. We often hear statements such as: "The United States has the best health care system in the world." Comparativists immediately wonder what kinds of health care systems exist in other countries, what they cost and how they are financed, how it is decided who can receive medical care, how effectively they deliver health care to their citizens, and so on. As we know from the ongoing political fight over the Affordable Care Act enacted during the Barack Obama administration (and the Republicans' proposed replacement, the American Health Care Act), there is little agreement about what "the best" means when it comes to health care systems, even within the United States. Is it the one that provides the widest access? The one that is the most technologically advanced? The one that is the most cost effective? The one that produces the healthiest population?

globalization

The intensification of worldwide interconnectedness associated with the increased speed and magnitude of cross-border flows of trade, investment and finance, and processes of migration, cultural diffusion, and communication.

comparativist

A political scientist who studies the similarities and differences in the domestic politics of various countries.

World Bank

An international financial institution (IFI) comprising over 180 member-states that provides low-interest loans, policy advice, and technical assistance to developing countries with the goal of reducing poverty.

Human Development Index (HDI)

A composite number used by the United Nations Development Programme (UNDP) to measure and compare levels of achievement in health, knowledge, and standard of living.

Global Gender Gap

A measure developed by the World Economic Forum of the extent to which women in 58 countries have achieved equality with men.

THE INTERNET AND THE STUDY OF COMPARATIVE POLITICS

The Internet can be a rich source of information about the politics of countries around the world. The following are some of the types of information you can find on the Web. We haven't included URLs since they change so often. But you should be able to find the websites easily through a key-word search on Google or another search engine.

- **Current events.** Most of the world's major news organizations have excellent websites. Among those, we recommend for students of comparative politics the sites of the British Broadcasting Corporation (BBC), Cable News Network (CNN), the *New York Times*, and the *Washington Post*.
- **Elections.** Results of recent (and often past) elections, data on voter turnout, and descriptions of different types of electoral systems can be found at the International Election Guide, Most Recent Elections by Country/Wikipedia, and the International Institute for Democracy and Electoral Assistance.
- **Statistics.** You can find data that are helpful both for understanding the political, economic, and social situations in individual countries and for comparing countries. Excellent sources of statistics are the Central Intelligence Agency (CIA) World FactBook, the United Nations Development Program (UNDP), and the **World Bank**.

   There are many websites that bring together data from other sources. These enable you not only to access the statistics, but also to chart or map them in a variety of ways. See, for example, Google Public Data, nationmaster.com, and gapminder.com.
- **Rankings and ratings.** Many organizations provide rankings or ratings of countries along a particular dimension, based on comparative statistical analysis. We provide the following examples of these in the data that appear at the end of this chapter: the UNDP **Human Development Index (HDI)**; the **Global Gender Gap**; the **Environmental Performance Index**; the **Corruption Perceptions Index**; and the **Economist Intelligence Unit Democracy**

Index. Others you might consult are the UNDP's Gender-Related Development Index (GDI) and Gender Empowerment Measure (GEM), the World Bank's Worldwide Governance Indicators, Freedom in the World ratings, the Index of Economic Freedom, and the Press Freedom Index. *A note of caution: Sites often have a political perspective that influences the way that they collect and analyze data. As with any Web source, be sure to check out who sponsors the site and what type of organization it is. And since Wikipedia is an open-source creation that can be edited by anyone, you should use it very carefully, and be sure to use other sources to verify any information that you find there.*
- **Official information and documents.** Most governments maintain websites in English. The first place to look is the website of the country's embassy in Washington, D.C.; Ottawa, or London. The United Nations delegations of many countries also have websites. Governments often have English-language versions of their official home pages, including governments with which the United States does not have official relations, such as Iran and North Korea.
- **The U.S. Department of State.** The State Department's website has background notes on most countries. American embassies around the world provide information on selected topics about the country in which they are based.
- **Maps.** The Perry-Castañeda Library Map Collection at the University of Texas is probably the best currently available online source of worldwide maps at an educational institution.
- **General resources on comparative politics.** See the list of suggested websites at the end of this chapter.

MAKING CONNECTIONS How has access to the Internet changed the way you do research? Is there a down side?

Environmental Performance Index

Developed by Yale University and Columbia University, a measure of how close countries come to meeting specific benchmarks for national pollution control and natural resource management.

None of us would declare the winner for Best Picture at the Academy Awards without seeing more than one—and preferably all—of the nominated movies! Shouldn't we be as critically minded and engaged when we are comparing and evaluating critical public policy issues?

Some comparativists focus on comparing government institutions, such as the legislature, executive, electoral systems, political parties, or the judiciaries of different countries.[4] Others compare specific political processes, such as voting or policies on a particular issue, such as education or the environment.[5] Some comparative political studies take a thematic approach, analyzing broad topics, such as the causes and consequences of nationalist movements or revolutions in different countries.[6] Comparative studies may also involve comparisons of an institution, policy, or process through time in one country or several countries. For example, some studies have analyzed a shift in the orientation of economic policy that occurred in many advanced capitalist countries in the 1980s from **Keynesianism**, an approach that gives priority to government regulation of the economy, to **neoliberalism**, which emphasizes the importance of market-friendly policies.[7] And many comparativists study politics within a single country, often using a framework that draws on similarities and differences with other countries.[8]

Level of Analysis

Comparisons can be useful for political analysis at several different levels of a country, such as cities, regions, provinces, or states. A good way to begin the study of comparative politics, however, is with countries. **Countries** are distinct, politically defined territories that encompass governments, composed of political institutions, as well as cultures, economies, and collective identities. Countries are often highly divided by internal conflicts, people within their borders may have close ties to those in other countries, and business firms based in one country may have operations in many others. Nevertheless, countries are still the major arena for organized political action in the modern world. Countries also have historically been among the most important sources of a people's collective political identity.

Within a given country, the **state** is almost always the most powerful cluster of institutions. But just what is the state? The way the term is used in comparative politics is probably unfamiliar to many students. In the United States, it usually refers to the states in the federal system—California, Illinois, New York, Texas, and so on. But in comparative politics, the term *state* refers to the key political institutions responsible for making, implementing, and adjudicating important policies in a country. Thus, we refer to the "German state" and the "Mexican state." The state is synonymous with what is often called the "government," as in the government of the United States. But the state also implies a durable entity that remains despite changes in ruling party or executive administration, and in which the institutions that comprise the state generally endure unless overthrown from within or conquered by other states in war.

The most important state institutions are the **executive**—usually, the president and/or prime minister and the **cabinet**. Other key state institutions include the military, police, and **bureaucracy**. In some countries, the executive includes the communist party leadership (such as in China), the head of a military government (as in Nigeria until 1999), or the supreme religious leader (as in the Islamic Republic of Iran). Alongside the executive, the **legislature** and the **judiciary** comprise the institutional apex of state power. The interrelationships and functions of these institutions vary from country to country and through time within countries.

States usually—but not necessarily successfully—claim the right to make rules (notably laws, administrative regulations, and court decisions) that are binding for people within the country. Even democratic states—in which top officials are chosen by procedures that allow all adult citizens to participate in politics—can survive only if they can keep order internally and protect their independence with regard to other states and external groups that may threaten them. Many countries have highly repressive states, whose political survival depends largely on the ability of the military

Corruption Perceptions Index

A measure developed by Transparency International that ranks countries in terms of the degree to which corruption is perceived to exist among public officials and politicians.

Economist Intelligence Unit Democracy Index

An index compiled by the Economist Intelligence Unit (EIU), based in the United Kingdom, that measures and rank the state of democracy in 167 countries. It classifies the world's states as Full Democracies, Flawed Democracies, Hybrid Regimes, and Authoritarian Regimes.

Keynesianism

Named after the British economist John Maynard Keynes, an approach to economic policy in which state fiscal policies are used to regulate the economy in an attempt to achieve stable economic growth.

neoliberalism

A term used to describe government policies aiming to promote free competition among business firms within the market, including reduced governmental regulation and social spending.

country

A territory defined by boundaries generally recognized in international law as constituting an independent nation.

state

The most powerful political institutions in a country, including the executive, legislative, and judicial branches of government, as well as the police and armed forces.

executive

The agencies of government that implement or execute policy. The chief executive, such as a prime minister or president, also plays a key policy-making role.

cabinet

The body of officials (e.g., ministers, secretaries) who direct executive departments presided over by the chief executive (e.g., prime minister or president).

bureaucracy

An organization structured hierarchically, in which lower-level officials are charged with administering regulations codified in rules that specify impersonal, objective guidelines for making decisions.

legislature

The political institutions in a country in which elected or appointed members are charged with responsibility for making laws and usually for authorizing the taxation and expenditure of the financial resources enabling the state to carry out its functions.

judiciary

The political institutions in a country responsible for the administration of justice, and in some countries, for determining the constitutionality of state decisions.

and police to suppress opposition. Even in such states, however, long-term stability requires that the ruling regime have some measure of political **legitimacy**—that is, the support of a significant segment of the citizenry (in particular, more influential citizens and groups) who believe that the state is entitled to demand compliance. Political legitimacy is greatly affected by the state's ability to "deliver the goods" to its people through satisfactory economic performance and at least a minimally satisfactory distribution of economic resources. Moreover, as upheavals in Libya, Tunisia, Yemen, Syria, and Egypt recently dramatized, legitimacy is much more secure when there is some measure of democracy. Thus, ICP looks closely at both the state's role in governing the economy and the extent of democracy within the state.

You will see from the country chapters in this book that the organization of state institutions varies widely, and that these differences have a powerful impact on political, economic, and social life. Therefore, we devote considerable attention to institutional variations, along with their political implications. Each country study begins with an analysis of how the state has evolved historically; that is, **state formation**.

One critical difference among states involves the extent to which citizens in a country share a common sense of nationhood; that is, a belief that the state's geographic borders coincide with the political identity of the people who live within those borders, which can be described as a sense of solidarity and shared values based on being citizens of the same country. When state boundaries and national identity coincide, the resulting formation is called a "nation-state." A major source of political instability can occur when they do not. In many countries around the world, nationalist movements within a state's borders challenge existing boundaries and seek to secede to form their own state, sometimes in alliance with movements from neighboring countries with whom they claim to share a common heritage. Such is the case with the Kurds, an ethnic group whose members live in Turkey, Syria, and Iraq. Many groups of Kurds have fought to establish an independent nation-state of

AP Photo/Muhammed Muheisen

Young people were at the forefront of the democracy movements that shook the Middle East and North Africa in 2011.

Kurdistan. When a nationalist movement has distinctive ethnic, religious, and/or linguistic ties opposed to those of other groups in the country, conflicts are likely to be especially intense. India and Nigeria, for example, have experienced particularly violent episodes of what has been termed "ethnonationalist" conflict. Tibet is an example of ethnic conflict within a country, China, the vast majority of whose population has a strong sense of Chinese national identity.

Causal Theories

Because countries are the basic building blocks in politics, and because states are the most significant political organizations within countries, these are two critical units for comparative analysis. The comparativist seeks to measure and explain similarities and differences among countries or states. One widely used approach in doing such comparative analysis involves developing a **causal theory**—a hypothesis that can be expressed formally in a causal mode: "If X happens, then Y will be the result." Such theories include a factor (the **independent variable**, symbolized by X) that is claimed to influence an outcome (the **dependent variable**, symbolized by Y) that the analyst wants to explain.

For example, it is commonly argued that if a country's economic pie shrinks, conflict among groups will intensify. This hypothesis claims what is called an "inverse correlation" between variables: as X varies in one direction (the economic pie shrinks), Y varies in the opposite direction (political and economic conflict over the economic pie increases). This relationship might be tested by statistical analysis of a large number (N) of cases (what is called "large N analysis") or by analyzing one or several country cases in depth to determine how relevant relationships have varied historically ("small N analysis"). Even when the explanation does not involve the explicit testing of hypotheses (and often it does not), comparativists try to identify significant patterns that help explain political similarities and differences among countries.

It is important to recognize the limits on just how "scientific" political science—and thus comparative politics—can be. Two important differences exist between the "hard" (or natural) sciences like physics and chemistry and the social sciences, which in addition to political science include anthropology, economics, psychology, and sociology. First, political scientists study people who exercise their political will and therefore may act in unpredictable ways, as the Arab Spring events of 2011 in the Middle East and North Africa and the U.S. presidential election of 2016 powerfully demonstrate. This does not mean that people choose in a totally arbitrary fashion. We choose within the context of material constraint, institutional dictates, and cultural preferences. But there will always be a gulf between the natural and social sciences because of their different objects of study.

In the natural sciences, experimental techniques can be applied to isolate the contribution of distinct factors to producing a particular outcome. It is possible to change the value or magnitude of a factor—for example, the force applied to an object or the amount of a chemical in a compound—and precisely measure how the outcome has consequently changed. There is a lively debate about whether the social sciences should seek scientific explanations comparable to what prevails in the natural sciences. An approach largely borrowed from economics, called **rational choice theory**, has become influential—and highly controversial—in political science, including comparative politics, in recent years.[9] Rational choice theory focuses on how individuals act strategically (that is, rationally) in an attempt to achieve goals

legitimacy

A belief by powerful groups and the broad citizenry that a state exercises rightful authority.

state formation

The historical development of a state, often marked by major stages, key events, or turning points (critical junctures) that influence the contemporary character of the state.

causal theory

An influential approach in comparative politics that involves trying to explain why "if X happens, then Y is the result."

independent variable

The variable symbolized by X in the statement that "If X happens, then Y will be the result;" in other words, the independent variable is a cause of Y (the dependent variable).

dependent variable

The variable symbolized by Y in the statement that "If X happens, then Y will be the result;" in other words, the dependent variable is the outcome of X (the independent variable).

rational choice theory

A largely quantitative approach to analyzing political decision making and behavior that assumes that individual actors rationally pursue their aims in an effort to achieve the most positive net result.

that maximize their interests. Such actions involve varied activities like voting for a particular candidate or rebelling against the government. Proponents of rational choice generally use quantitative methods to construct models of political behavior that they believe can be applied across all types of political systems and cultures. The appeal of rational choice theory lies in its capacity to provide theoretical and practical insights about comparative politics through formal models based on the assumption that individual actors pursue goals efficiently and strategically. But this approach has been criticized for claiming to explain large-scale and complex social phenomena by reference to individual choices while dismissing the importance of variations in historical experience, political culture, identities, institutions, and other key aspects of the political world.

The study of comparative politics offers many challenges, including the complexity of the subject matter, the fast pace of change in the contemporary world, and the impossibility of manipulating variables or replicating conditions in a truly scientific way. As a result, most comparativists probably agree on a middle course that avoids either focusing exclusively on one country or blending all countries indiscriminately into a grand theory. If we study only individual countries without any comparative framework, comparative politics would become merely the study of a series of isolated cases. It would therefore be impossible to recognize what is most significant in the collage of political characteristics that we find in the world's many countries. As a result, it would impossible to understand patterns of similarity and difference among countries, as well as what is and what is not unique about a country's political life.

If we go to the other extreme and try to make claims of universal applicability, we would tend to ignore significant national differences and patterns of variation. The political world is incredibly complex, shaped by an extraordinary array of factors and an almost endless interplay of variables. Indeed, following a brief period in the 1950s and 1960s when many comparativists tried—and failed—to develop a grand theory of political development that would apply to all countries, most comparativists now agree on the value of **middle-level theory**; that is, a theory focusing on specific features of the political world, such as institutions and policies, or classes of similar events, such as revolutions or elections.

Consider an example of middle-level theory that would help us understand a key political development in the contemporary world: theories about transitions from authoritarian to more democratic government. Comparativists have long analyzed the processes through which many countries with authoritarian governments, such as military **dictatorships** and one-party regimes, have developed more participatory and democratic regimes. In studying the process that they call **democratic transitions**, comparativists neither treat each national case as unique nor try to construct a universal pattern that ignores all differences.[10] Scholars of democratic transitions seek to identify the weak links in authoritarian regimes, such as declining economic performance, a decrease in the regime's repressive capacity, or a switch in loyalty by influential insiders, that result in the crumbling of the authoritarian regime.

We believe that students will be in a better position to understand the causes and consequences of such major developments after gaining a solid grasp of political similarities and differences in diverse countries around the world. It is this goal that we put front and center in ICP.

middle-level theory

A theory that seeks to explain phenomena in a limited range of cases, such as comparing presidential democracies (e.g. the United States) with parliamentary democracies (e.g. Britain).

dictatorship

A form of government in which power and political control are concentrated in one ruler or a few rulers who have concentrated and nearly absolute power.

democratic transition

The process of a state moving from an authoritarian to a democratic political system.

Where Do You Stand?

Is declining economic performance or political instability a greater threat to a regime?

THEMES FOR COMPARATIVE ANALYSIS

Our framework in *Introduction to Comparative Politics*, comprised of four core themes, provides a guide to understanding many features of contemporary comparative politics. But we urge students (and rely on instructors!) to challenge and amplify our interpretations. Further, we want to note that this textbook builds on existing theory but does not construct or test new hypotheses. That task is the goal of original scholarly studies.

Theme 1: A Globalizing World of States

Our first theme, *a globalizing world of states*, focuses on the central importance of states in the understanding of comparative politics. International organizations, such as the United Nations, private actors like transnational corporations, such as Apple and ExxonMobil, and nongovernmental organizations (NGOs), such as Amnesty International, play a crucial role in politics. But states are unique by (to a highly variable extent) providing security to their citizens, making and enforcing laws, and providing citizens with social protection to those in need.

Our "globalizing world of states" theme highlights that states are the basic building blocks in world politics. The theme also analyzes the importance of variations among the ways that states are organized—in other words, the mix of political institutions that distinguishes, for example, democratic from authoritarian regimes. Country chapters emphasize the importance of understanding similarities and differences in state formation and **institutional design.** We identify critical junctures of state formation: key events like colonial conquest, defeat in war, economic crises, or revolutions that affect and shape states. We also study variations in states' economic management strategies and capacities, diverse patterns of political institutions, such as the contrast between presidential and parliamentary forms in democratic states, the relationship of the state with social groups, and unresolved challenges that the state faces from within and outside its borders.

The "globalized world of states" theme also emphasizes the interaction between the national and the international levels in shaping the politics of all countries. Here, the theme points in two directions: One direction focuses on a state's influence in affecting other states and the international economic and political arena; the other focuses on the impact of international forces on the state's activities within the country's borders.

Regarding the first direction, states dwarf other influential actors, such as transnational corporations, in the exercise of power, whether with regard to war, peace, and national security or when it comes to providing educational opportunities, health care, and pensions (social security) to its citizens. The second direction of this theme underlines the multiple global forces that have significant impacts on the domestic politics of virtually all countries.[11] A wide array of international organizations and treaties, including the United Nations, the European Union, the **World Trade Organization (WTO)**, the World Bank, the **International Monetary Fund (IMF)**, and the **North American Free Trade Agreement (NAFTA)**, challenge the sovereign control of national governments within their own territories. Transnational

institutional design

The institutional arrangements that define the relationships between executive, legislative, and judicial branches of government and between the national government and subnational units, such as states in the United States.

World Trade Organization (WTO)

A global international organization that oversees the "rules of trade" among its member-states. The main functions of the WTO are to serve as a forum for its members to negotiate new agreements and resolve trade disputes. Its fundamental purpose is to lower or remove barriers to free trade.

International Monetary Fund (IMF)

The International Monetary Fund (IMF) is a global institution whose mandate is to "foster global monetary cooperation, secure financial stability, facilitate international trade, promote high employment and sustainable economic growth, and reduce poverty."

North American Free Trade Agreement (NAFTA)

A treaty among the United States, Mexico, and Canada implemented on January 1, 1994, that largely eliminates trade barriers among the three nations.

corporations, international banks, and currency traders in New York, London, Frankfurt, Hong Kong, and Tokyo affect countries and people throughout the world. A country's political borders do not protect its citizens from global warming, environmental pollution, terrorism, or infectious diseases that come from abroad.

Thanks to the global diffusion of radio, television, Twitter, and the Internet, as well as social media of all kinds, people nearly everywhere can become remarkably well informed about international developments. This knowledge may fuel popular demands that governments intervene to stop atrocities in, for example, faraway Kosovo, Rwanda, Libya, and Syria, or provide aid to the victims of natural disasters, as happened after devastating earthquakes in China in 2008 and Haiti in 2010, each of which killed many thousands of people. Further, heightened global awareness may encourage citizens to hold their own government to internationally recognized standards of human rights and democracy. Such awareness played a significant role in motivating people to join prodemocracy movements, such as those against authoritarian regimes in North Africa and the Middle East in the Arab Spring of 2011 and against China's refusal to allow freer elections in Hong Kong in 2014.

A puzzle: To what extent can even the most powerful states (including the United States) preserve their autonomy and impose their will on others in a globalized world? And in what ways are the poorer and less powerful countries particularly vulnerable to the pressures of globalization and disgruntled citizens?

Increasingly, the politics and policies of states are shaped by diverse international factors, often lumped together under the category of globalization. At the same time,

GLOBALIZATION

This cartoon portrays globalization flattening the world.

many states face increasingly restive constituencies within their country who challenge the power and legitimacy of central governments. In reading the country case studies in this book, try to assess how pressures from both above and below—outside and inside—influence a state's policies and its ability to retain citizen support.

Theme 2: Governing the Economy

The success of states in maintaining sovereign authority and control over their people is greatly affected by their ability to ensure that enough goods are produced and services delivered to satisfy the needs and demands of their populations. Citizen discontent with the inadequate economic performance of many countries ruled by a communist party was an important reason for the disintegration of the Soviet Union and its allies in Eastern Europe in 1989. In contrast, China's stunning success in promoting economic development has generated powerful support for the communist regime in that country.

The pursuit of effective economic performance is near the top of every state's political agenda, and "governing the economy"[12]—that is, how a state organizes production and the extent and nature of its intervention in the economy—is a key element in its overall pattern of governance. The strategies that states choose in an attempt to improve economic performance, deal with economic crises, and compete in international markets are at the core of governing the economy. A key contrast between various strategies is the relative balance of private market forces versus government direction of the economy.

The term **political economy** refers to the interaction between politics and economics (that is, to how government actions affect economic performance and how economic performance in turn affects a country's politics). We place great importance on political economy in ICP because we believe that politics in all countries is deeply influenced by the interaction between a country's government and the economy in both its domestic and international dimensions.

political economy

The study of the interaction between the state and the economy in a country; that is, how politics influences the economy and how the organization and performance of the economy influence the political process.

Is there a particular formula for governing the economy that produces maximum success in promoting national prosperity? In particular, is there an optimum balance between the extent of state direction of the economy and the extent of free markets—that is, the ability of private business firms to operate freely without government supervision and regulation? The answer is: probably not. On the one hand, some economic winners and some losers among the world's countries display a pattern of extensive state intervention in the economy. Similarly, other winners and losers engage in relatively little state intervention. Thus, it is not the *degree* of state intervention that distinguishes the economic success stories from those that have fared less well, but the *nature* of such intervention. For example, an influential study of the world's affluent capitalist economies identifies quite varying patterns of the state versus market balance associated with strong economic performance.[13] Studies that analyze the East Asian "miracle" economies show that in Japan and South Korea, the state played a critical role in promoting economic growth, whereas in China, the key was reducing the extensive role of the state in governing the economy.[14]

Comparative analysis of how well different states govern their economies becomes even more complex when one considers the appropriate yardstick to measure what constitutes economic success. Should economic performance be measured solely by how rapidly a country's economy grows? By how equitably it distributes the fruits of economic growth? By the quality of life of its citizenry, as measured by such criteria as life expectancy, level of education, and unemployment rate? What about the interrelationship between economic growth, environmental sustainability, and climate

communist party-state

A type of nation-state in which a communist party exercises a monopoly on political power and controls all important state institutions.

gross domestic product (GDP)

The total of all goods and services produced within a country that is used as a broad measure of the size of its economy.

change? These questions take us far outside the traditional realm of economics into the fields of political theory, economics, and ecology. We invite you to consider these questions as you study the political economies of the countries analyzed in this book.

A puzzle: What is the relationship between democracy and successful national economic performance? Students of political economy have long pondered this question—and have yet to produce fully satisfactory answers. Although all economies, even the most powerful, experience ups and downs, all durable democracies (with the partial exception of India) have been notable economic success stories. On the other hand, China, an authoritarian **communist party-state** that has enjoyed the highest growth rate among major economies in the world since the early 1990s, provides a vivid case of development without democracy. An influential study by political scientist Adam Przeworski and colleagues concludes, after an exhaustive comparison of the economic performance of democratic and authoritarian states, that there is no clear-cut answer to the question of which type of regime is better able to achieve superior economic performance.[15] Similarly, Nobel Prize–winning political economist Amartya Sen has argued, "There is no clear relation between economic growth and democracy in *either* direction."[16] As you read the country studies, try to identify why some states have been more successful than others in "governing the economy"; that is, fostering successful economic performance.

GLOBAL CONNECTION

How Is Development Measured?

As we have noted, we put particular importance on understanding the relationship between the political system and the economy in the study of the politics of any country and in our overall approach to comparative politics. Each of the country case studies describes and analyzes the role of the government in making economic policy. They also take special note of the impact of the global economy on national politics. This book makes frequent reference to two commonly used measures of the overall size or power of a country's economy:

- **Gross domestic product (GDP):** The value of the total goods and services produced by the country during a given year
- **Gross national product (GNP):** GDP plus income earned abroad by the country's residents

A country's GDP and GNP are different, but not hugely so. In this book, we usually use GDP. A country's GDP is a useful measure for understanding its overall power in the world economy. One way of calculating and comparing GDP is by converting countries' GDP into U.S. dollars (called GDP at official exchange rate, or nominal GDP). According this measure, here is the rank order of the world's ten largest economies: the United States, China, Japan, Germany, Britain, France, India, Italy, Brazil, and Canada.

Another increasingly popular way of calculating GDP is according to what is called **purchasing power parity (PPP)**. PPP is more sophisticated than the first method because it takes into account the real cost of living in a particular country by calculating how much it would take in the local currency to buy the same "basket of goods" in different countries. For example, how many dollars in the United States, pesos in Mexico, or rubles in Russia does it take to buy a certain amount of food or to pay for housing? According to PPP, China is the world's largest economy, followed by the United States, India, Japan, Russia, Brazil, Indonesia, Britain, and France.

However it is calculated, total GDP is an important way to compare the *overall size* of different economies. But in order to compare *standards of living* and *levels of economic development* around the world, the total GDP of a country needs to be divided by its population, which yields GDP *per capita* (per person). Because it takes into account the actual cost of living, the most revealing method is to use PPP in calculating GDP per capita. When using this procedure, for example, although China is the world's largest economy as measured by total GDP (PPP), it falls to 104th out of 230 economies in terms of its annual GDP (PPP) per capita ($15,400); India, the world's third-largest PPP economy, ranks 159th with a GDP/PPP per capita of $6,700.

(continued)

The charts and data at the end of this chapter provide total GDP (PPP and nominal) and GDP (PPP) per capita, as well as other economic, geographic, demographic, social, and political information for our country case studies. The Comparative Rankings (Table 1.1) at the end of this chapter provides several other ways of evaluating countries' economic, political, or public policy performance.

In 2014, an international team of scholars launched an important new comparative index that ranks countries according to what they called "social progress," which they defined as "the capacity of a society to meet the basic human needs of its citizens, establish the building blocks that allow citizens and communities to enhance and sustain the quality of their lives, and create the conditions for all individuals to reach their full potential." The **Social Progress Index (SPI)** is derived from more than fifty measures, such as access to shelter, health and wellness, ecosystem sustainability, personal freedom and choice, and tolerance and inclusion. Out of 133 countries, the three with the highest SPI in 2016 were Finland, Canada, and Denmark, while the three with the lowest were Chad, Afghanistan, and the Central African Republic. The countries covered in this book had the following SPI rankings: Brazil (46), Britain (9), China (84), France (18), Germany (15), India (98), Iran (93), Japan (14), Mexico (51), Nigeria (119), Russia (75), South Africa (59), and the United States (19).

MAKING CONNECTIONS As you look at the SPI rankings here, what in the country rankings makes you want to dig deeper because it seems surprising?

Theme 3: The Democratic Idea

One of the most important and astonishing political developments in recent years has been the rapid spread of **democracy** throughout much of the world. This provides powerful evidence of the strong appeal of democracy (that is, a regime in which citizens exercise substantial control over the choice of political leaders and the decisions made by their governments).

According to statistical analysis of numerous measures of political freedom and civil liberties, Freedom House has calculated that in 1973, there were 43 countries that could be considered "free" (or democratic), 38 that were "partly free," and 69 that should be classified as "not free."[17] In 2016, the count of free or democratic countries had increased to 87 free, with 59 partly free, and 49 not free. (See Figure 1.1.) In terms of population, 35 percent of the world's people lived in free countries in 1973, 18 percent in partly free, and 47 percent were citizens of countries ranked as not free. In 2016, the percentages were 39 percent free, 25 percent partly free, and 36 percent not free.

Political economist Amartya Sen has observed, "While democracy is not yet uniformly practiced, nor indeed uniformly accepted, in the general climate of world opinion, democratic governance has now achieved the status of being taken to be generally right."[18] As authoritarian rulers in countries from Albania to Zaire (now called the Democratic Republic of the Congo) have learned in recent decades, once persistent and widespread pressures for democratic participation develop, they are hard to resist. However, as brutal suppression of protesters in China (in 1989) and Libya and Bahrain (in 2011) demonstrated, dictators do not easily give up their power.

What determines the growth, stagnation, or decline of democracy in a country? Comparativists have devoted enormous energy to studying this question. One scholar notes, "For the past two decades, the main topic of research in comparative politics has been democratization."[19] Yet, for all the attention that it has received, there is no scholarly consensus on how and why democratization develops and becomes consolidated, remains incomplete, or is reversed. Just as there is no single route to economic prosperity, we have also learned that there is no one path to democracy,

gross national product (GNP)

GDP plus income earned by the country's residents; another broad measure of the size of an economy.

purchasing power parity (PPP)

A method of calculating the value of a country's currency based on the actual cost of buying goods and services in that country rather than how many U.S. dollars the currency is worth.

Social Progress Index (SPI)

A composite measurement of social progress in countries that takes into account basic needs, their food, shelter and security; access to health care, education, and a healthy environment; and the opportunity for people to improve their lives.

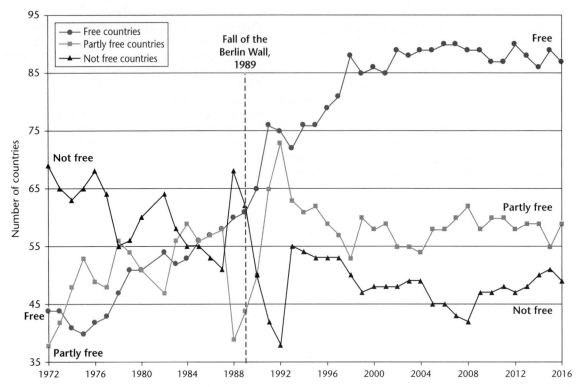

FIGURE 1.1 **Freedom in the World: The Spread of Democracy, 1972–2016.**

Source: Freedom House (www.freedomhouse.org).

democracy

From the Greek *demos* (the people) and *kratos* (rule), a political system featuring selection to major public offices through free and fair elections; the right of all adults to vote; political parties that are free to compete in elections; government that operates by equitable and relatively open procedures; protection of political rights and civil liberties; an independent judiciary (court system); and civilian control of the military.

and that democratic transitions can be slow, uncertain, and reversible. Many of the country studies in *Introduction to Comparative Politics* analyze the diverse causes and sources of support for and opposition to democracy; and some highlight the fragility of democratic transitions.

In certain historical settings, democracy may result from a standoff or compromise among political contenders for power in which no one group can gain sufficient strength to control outcomes by itself. The result is that they reluctantly settle for a democratic compromise in which power is shared. In some (but not all) cases, rival groups may conclude that democracy is preferable to civil war, or it may take a bloody civil war that produces stalemate to persuade competing groups to accept democracy as a second-best solution. Democracy may appeal to citizens in authoritarian nations because democratic regimes often rank among the world's most stable, affluent, and cohesive countries.

In other cases, a regional demonstration effect occurs in which a democratic transition in one country provokes democratic change in neighboring countries. This occurred in southern Europe in the 1970s, Latin America and parts of East Asia in the 1980s, Eastern and Central Europe in the 1990s, and, to a much more limited degree, in North Africa and the Middle East in 2011. Many scholars argue that another important pressure for democracy involves the universal human desire for dignity and equality. Even when dictatorial regimes appear to benefit their countries—for example, by promoting economic development or nationalist goals—citizens may demand democracy.

Is it possible to identify conditions that are necessary or sufficient for the democratic idea to take root and flourish? Comparativists have proposed, among such factors, secure national boundaries, a stable state, a certain level of economic development as measured by GDP per capita, the widespread acceptance of democratic values, and agreement on the rules of democratic politics among those contending for power. However, this laundry list of factors hardly resolves the matter since it leaves open which factors, if any, are essential, the balance among factors, the question of whether the sequence in which factors develop matters, and so on.

Institutional design also matters when it comes to producing stable democracies. Do certain kinds of political institutions facilitate compromise as opposed to polarization, and hence promote greater stability? The balance of scholarly opinion suggests, for example, that parliamentary systems that tie the fates of the legislators to that of the prime minister tend to produce more consensual outcomes than do presidential systems, where the legislature and executive are independent from each other and often compete in setting national political agendas. As you read the country studies, note the patterns of similarity and difference regarding the degree of conflict or polarization in presidential systems (such as the United States and Mexico) and compare those cases to parliamentary systems (such as Britain and Japan).

Although certain economic, cultural, and institutional features enhance the prospects of democratic transitions and consolidations, democracy has flourished in unlikely settings. India, for example, is a long-established democracy that ranks in the bottom quarter of the world's countries in terms of per capita income. Hundreds of millions of Indians live in dire poverty. Yet, despite some important instances of undemocratic practices, India has had a vibrantly functioning democratic system ever since it became independent in 1947. Democracy has also failed where it might be expected to flourish, most notably and tragically when the Nazi Party was elected into power in highly educated and relatively wealthy Germany in the 1930s.

Democracies vary widely in terms of how they have come into existence and in their concrete historical, institutional, economic, and cultural dimensions. As you read about the long-established democracies that are included in this book, think about and *compare* the varied ways in which they started on the path to democracy—for example, by revolutions early in their history (Britain, France, the United States), by peaceful transition from colonial rule (India), or by imposition by foreign powers after defeat (Germany and Japan).

Displacing authoritarian regimes and holding elections does not guarantee the survival or durability of a fledgling democracy. A wide gulf exists between what comparativists have termed a "*transition*" to democracy and the "*consolidation*" of democracy. A transition involves toppling an authoritarian regime and adopting the basic institutions and procedures of democracy; consolidation requires fuller adherence to democratic principles and making democratic government more sturdy and durable. Several country case studies in ICP—Brazil, Mexico, Nigeria, and South Africa—are transitional democracies. As you read those cases, think about the circumstances that led them to embark on that political path, how far along they are, and their prospects for becoming consolidated, durable democracies.

The theme of the democratic idea requires us to examine the incompleteness of democratic agendas, even in countries with the longest experiences of representative democracy. Citizens may invoke the democratic idea to demand that their governments be more responsive and accountable, as in the civil rights movement in the United States. **Social movements** in some democratic countries have targeted the state because of its actions or inactions in such varied spheres as environmental regulation, reproductive rights, and race or ethnic relations. Comparative studies confirm

social movement

Large-scale grassroots action that demands reforms of existing social practices and government policies.

that a large gap separates democratic ideals and the actual functioning of democratic political institutions in even the most democratic countries—and the gap may fuel social movements. Moreover, social movements often organize because citizens consider that political parties—presumably, the vehicle that typically represents citizen demands in democracies—are rigid and out of touch.

A puzzle: Is there a relationship between democracy and political stability? Comparativists have debated whether democratic institutions contribute to political stability or, on the contrary, may promote political disorder.[20] On the one hand, democracy by its very nature permits political opposition. One of its defining characteristics is competition among those who aspire to gain political office. Political life in democracies is often turbulent and unpredictable. On the other hand, and perhaps paradoxically, the very fact that political opposition and competition are legitimate in democracies can deepen support for the state. The democratic rules of the game may promote political stability by encouraging today's losers to reject the use of violence to press their claim to power. They may do so because they calculate that they have a good chance to win peacefully in future contests. Although deep flaws often mar democratic governance in countries that have recently toppled authoritarian regimes, one study finds that, once a country adopts a democratic regime, the odds are that it will endure.[21] As you learn about different countries, look for the stabilizing and destabilizing consequences of democratic transitions, the pressures (or lack of pressure) for democratization in authoritarian states, and the persistence of undemocratic elements even in established democracies.

Theme 4: The Politics of Collective Identities

How do individuals understand who they are in relation to the state and other citizens? How and why do they join in groups to advance shared political or other goals within a country? In other words, what are the sources of collective political identities? At one time, social scientists thought they knew. Scholars once argued that age-old loyalties of ethnicity, religious affiliation, race, and locality were in the process of being dissolved and displaced as a result of economic, political, and cultural modernization. Comparativists thought that **social class**—solidarities based on the shared experience of work or, more broadly, economic position in society—had become the most important (indeed, nearly the only) source of collective identity. They believed that in the future, the typical political situation would involve groups formed on the basis of economic interest pragmatically pursuing their objectives. We now know that the formation of group attachments and the interplay of politically relevant collective identities are far more complex and uncertain.

social class

A group whose members share common worldviews and aspirations determined largely by occupation, income, and wealth.

In many long-established democracies, the political importance of identities based on class membership has declined. Economically based sources of collective identity do remain significant in influencing citizens' party affiliation and preferences about economic policy, as well as their belief concerning how the economic pie should be divided and distributed. Especially in an era of austerity, and in particular among those struggling who cannot be assured of a decent existence, the struggle over who gets what—and who decides who gets what—can be fierce. Further, the days of class politics is clearly making a comeback, as suggested by the relatively successful campaigns recently of political candidates in many countries who advocate serving the needs of disadvantaged citizens. But contrary to earlier predictions, in many countries, nonclass identities have assumed growing, not diminishing, significance. Such identities are based on a sense of belonging to particular groups sharing a common language, region, religion, ethnicity, race, nationality, or gender. While these group identities may be correlated with economic status, they also may have a powerful appeal quite distinct from, and even at odds with, social class.

The politics of collective identity involves efforts to mobilize particular groups to influence political outcomes, ranging from the state's distribution of social welfare benefits, the basis for representation in the government, and even territorial claims. Identity-based conflicts occur in most societies. Politics in democratic regimes (and, often in a more concealed way, in authoritarian regimes as well) involves a tug of war among groups over relative power and influence, both symbolic and substantive. Issues of inclusion, political recognition, representation, resource allocation, and the capacity to shape public policies, such as immigration, education, and the status of minority languages, remain pivotal in many countries.

Questions of representation are especially hard to resolve: Which groups should be considered legitimate participants in the political game? Who speaks for the group or negotiates with a governmental authority on its behalf? Conflict about these issues can be intense because political leaders often seek to mobilize support by exploiting identity-based rivalries and by manipulating issues of identity and representation.

An especially important source of identity-based conflict involves ethnicity. And given the pace of migration and the tangled web of postcolonial histories that link colonizer to colonized, many countries are multi-ethnic. As political scientist Alfred Stepan points out, "[T]here are very few states in the entire world that are relatively homogeneous nation-states."[22] In Britain, France, Germany, and the United States, issues of nationality, citizenship, and immigration—often linked to ethnic or racial factors—have frequently been hot-button political issues. Ethnic conflicts have been particularly frequent and intense in postcolonial countries, such as in Nigeria, where colonial powers forced ethnic groups together when defining the country's boundaries and where borders were drawn with little regard to preexisting collective identities. In many postcolonial nations, the process of state formation has often sowed the seeds of future conflict.

Religion is another source of collective identity, as well as of severe political conflict, both within and among religious communities. For instance, violent conflict among religious groups has occurred recently in India, Sri Lanka, and Nigeria. Such conflicts may spill over national boundaries and involve an especially ugly form of globalization. For example, leaders of Al-Qaeda pointed to non-Muslim Western military forces stationed in what they regarded as the sacred soil of Saudi Arabia as a principal reason for the 9/11 attacks. At the same time, the political orientation of a particular religious community is not predetermined. The political posture associated with what it means to be a faithful Christian, Jew, Muslim, or Hindu cannot be determined from holy texts. Witness the intense conflict *within* most religious communities today that pits liberal, secular elements against those who defend what they claim is a more orthodox, traditional interpretation.

A puzzle: How do collective identities affect a country's **distributional politics**—that is, the process of deciding how resources are allocated (concretely, who gets what, when, and how?). Once identity demands are placed on the national agenda, can a government resolve them by distributing political, economic, and other resources in ways that redress the grievances of the minority or politically weaker identity groups?

Collective identities operate at the level of symbols, attitudes, values, and beliefs, as well as at the level of material resources. The contrast between material- and non-material-based identities and demands should not be exaggerated. In practice, most groups are animated both by feelings of attachment and solidarity and by the desire to obtain material benefits and political influence for their members. Nonetheless,

distributional politics

The use of power, particularly by the state, to allocate valued resources among competing groups.

the analytical distinction between material and nonmaterial demands remains useful because the relative balance between the two in fueling conflict varies widely in practice. Furthermore, nonmaterial aspects of collective identities may make political disputes over ethnicity or religion or language or nationality especially divisive and difficult to resolve because in such cases, it is harder to purchase peace through distributing material benefits.

These four themes provide our analytic scaffold. With an understanding of the method of comparative politics and the four themes in mind, we can now discuss the theoretical underpinnings for grouping the country studies in *Introduction to Comparative Politics,* as well as how the text is organized to help students master the basics of comparative analysis.

Where Do You Stand?

Do you agree with Nobel Prize–winner Amartya Sen (cited earlier) that "democratic governance has now achieved the status of being taken to be generally right" and is a "universal value" to which all nations should aspire? Why might some people think this is an ethnocentric point of view?

Are nonmaterial-based collective identities or economic interests more important to the understanding of comparative politics? Or, alternatively, to what extent and how does each shape the other?

SECTION 4

CLASSIFYING POLITICAL SYSTEMS

▼ Focus Questions

- What are the advantages of using a typology based on levels of adherence to democratic practices? What are the disadvantages?

- What other ways can you suggest of classifying the countries in *Introduction to Comparative Politics*?

typology

A method of classifying by using criteria that assign cases to categories whose members share common characteristics.

There are more than 200 states in the world today. Although each is unique, it is also the case that various groups of states share some important features. Therefore, it is useful to identify what distinguishes one category of states from other categories, as well as to study how a state moves from one category to another as circumstances evolve. When comparativists classify a large number of cases by assigning them to a smaller number of categories, or types, they introduce a typology—that is, an analytic construct that enables us to engage in comparisons yielding useful knowledge. In ICP, we employ a typology that distinguishes among consolidated democracies, hybrid states, and authoritarian regimes. We thus assign each country in ICP to one of these three categories.

Typologies can also be used as the basis for comparison within the same political category. For example, Britain and the United States are consolidated democracies. But Britain has a parliamentary form of government, and the United States has a presidential one. Since the two countries are members of the same basic regime type—consolidated democracy—we are better able to study the impact of their different institutional form of democracy (that is, parliamentary versus presidential forms). Analyzing how different mixes of democratic institutions work in practice is one of the important and intriguing questions that lies at the heart of comparative politics.

As with many important concepts in political science, the meaning of democracy is a contentious subject among political scientists and citizens. Should democracy be defined solely on the basis of the procedures used to select top governmental office-holders? For a political system to qualify as democratic, occupants of high office clearly must be selected on the basis of free and fair elections. However, are other elements also necessary for a system to qualify as democratic? For example, must there be respect for civil liberties, due process, the rule of law, freedom of expression and assembly, and the right to petition and criticize government without fear of reprisal? A narrow conception of democracy might not consider these elements as necessary. As a general matter, most comparativists, including the authors of ICP, support a richer conception of democracy, one that includes some or all of these additional core features.

Even more controversial is whether our definition of democracy should include substantial economic equality (or at least government policies ensuring limits on the permissible extent of economic inequality). That is, many comparativists argue that democracy requires some leveling of the economic playing field. What, then, does it say about the quality of present-day American democracy that the twenty richest people in the United States own more wealth than the entire bottom half of the population combined, and the richest 1 percent of Americans owns over one-third of all U.S. wealth?[23]

Another example: For a system to qualify as democratic, must government guarantee citizens at least a minimum level of social protection and security? Or is it not pertinent to consider this question in evaluating the existence or extent of democracy? The matter does not end there, for it is necessary to translate abstract values to actual political practice. Even in long-established democratic states, there remains a gap—often a substantial one—between the aspirations and ideals of democracy and the practice and results of the actual, existing democracy. For example, police abuse and unequal legal treatment of citizens who are poor or from a racial or ethnic minority are all too common in countries generally considered high in the democratic rankings, including the United States.

Consider another dilemma: we contend that democracy requires guaranteeing citizens the right of privacy. However, how should this right be defined and applied in an era of routine mass surveillance and intercepts of communications by `government? When does government surveillance, conducted in the name of preventing terrorism, infringe on citizens' right to privacy? Another example: We believe that democracy requires an independent judiciary. Yet how is judicial independence to be guaranteed when judges are elected, and therefore inclined to bow to public opinion, or appointed by elected representatives, and therefore inclined to defer to those who appoint them? Another puzzle: It is generally agreed that democracy requires freedom of religion—but how can we resolve the problem that the practice of religious freedom may infringe on the rights of other groups? Final example: While we contend that democracy requires substantial gender equality, this requirement may prove hard to define in theory—and even harder to achieve in practice!

We invite you to keep these issues in mind as you read the case studies of the **consolidated democracies**, which include Britain, France, Germany, Japan, India, and the United States. There is also a chapter on the European Union, which consists of consolidated democracies, including Britain (until Brexit is completed, if, in fact, that happens in the aftermath of the June 2017 elections in the United Kingdom), France, Germany, and the other countries of Western Europe, as well as democracies that were established more recently, including former communist states such as Hungary and Poland.

consolidated democracy

A democratic political system that has been solidly and stably established for an ample period of time and in which there is relatively consistent adherence to core democratic principles.

The Economist Intelligence Unit (EIU), a highly respected research and analysis organization, produces an annual Democracy Index that examines and ranks the state of democracy in countries around the world according to five variables: electoral process and pluralism, civil liberties, functioning of government, political participation, and political culture. In the 2016 Democracy Index, Germany and Britain were listed in the category of "Full Democracies." Japan, the United States, France, and India were included among "Flawed Democracies." (See the Comparative Rankings (Table 1.1) at the end of this chapter.) As you read the case studies, keep an eye out for ways in which some Consolidated Democracies might be considered Flawed Democracies.

The reason why we highlight the importance of adhering to democratic procedures and institutional arrangements becomes apparent when we turn to the second category of democracy that we use in this book. In **hybrid states**, the political system reflects a mix of both democratic and nondemocratic features, and a façade of democratic institutions often conceals numerous practices that violate some core features of democracy. As a general matter, although there is usually greater legal protection of citizen rights and liberties in hybrid states than in authoritarian regimes, there is considerably less than in consolidated democracies.

The hybrid states that are covered in ICP are Brazil, Mexico, Nigeria, Russia, and South Africa. Of these, Russia under Vladimir Putin is clearly the least democratic and has been described as an **illiberal democracy**. This is a type of political system where the government has been brought to power (and perhaps reelected) by at least partially free elections and may enjoy a high level of popular support. But once in power, the government takes steps to seriously limit political completion, undermine the rule of law, and deprive citizens of their basic rights.[24]

The contrast is with *liberal democracies*, which we call consolidated democracies. The word "liberal" in this context has nothing to do with liberal versus conservative as political ideologies; rather, it is meant to refer to political systems that conform to the core principles of democracy that we noted previously.

How do we define **authoritarian regimes**—the third kind of political system in our typology? The simplest way is to say that they lack most or all of the features of a democracy. Thus, authoritarian regimes lack effective procedures for selecting political leaders through competitive elections based on universal suffrage; they include few institutionalized procedures for holding those with political power accountable to the citizens of the country; dissent is severely restricted; people of different genders, racial groups, religions, and ethnicities do not enjoy equal rights; the legal system is highly politicized and the judiciary lacks the autonomy and power to check the administration or protect the rights of citizens; and the state routinely exercises extrajudicial coercion and violence.

Clearly, then, authoritarian states are not democracies. But it isn't good social science to define something only by what it is *not*. The term "authoritarianism" refers to political systems in which power (or authority) is highly concentrated in a single unaccountable individual, a small group of people, or one political party. Furthermore, those with power are not selected by truly competitive elections, they claim an exclusive right to govern, and they use arbitrary force, among other means, to impose their will and policies on those living under their authority.

As with states classified as democracies, there are an enormous variety of authoritarian regime types: communist party-states, in which the communist party directs the state (e.g., China and Cuba); theocracies, in which sovereign power is held by religious leaders and law is defined in religious terms (e.g., the Islamic Republic of Iran);

hybrid state

A country whose political systems exhibit some democratic and some authoritarian elements.

illiberal democracy

A state where the government has been brought to power (and perhaps reelected) by democratic election, but then takes steps to seriously limit political competition, undermine the rule of law, and deprive citizens of their basic rights.

authoritarian regime

A form of government in which power is highly concentrated at the top, political freedom is limited, and those with authority are not accountable to those they govern.

military governments (e.g., Thailand, after the army overthrew the parliamentary government in 2014; Brazil, 1964–1985; Nigeria, 1983–1999); absolute monarchies (e.g., Saudi Arabia); and personalistic dictatorships (e.g., Iran under the Shah, North Korea under Kim Jong-un).

Authoritarian regimes frequently claim that they embody a form of democracy, particularly in the contemporary era, when the democratic idea has become so persuasive and powerful. For example, according to the Chinese Communist Party, the political system of the People's Republic of China is based on "socialist democracy," which it claims is superior to the "bourgeois democracy" of capitalist countries that favors the interests of wealthier citizens. But most political scientists would conclude that there is little substance to these claims, and that in a state like China, dictatorship far outweighs democracy. As Chapter 15, on China, will describe, the Communist Party monopolizes most decision making, and its leaders are chosen in secret by the party elite rather than by popular election.

Nevertheless, even countries classified as authoritarian may include democratic values and practices. For example, in Iran, a theocratic authoritarian regime, there are vigorously contested multiparty elections, although the extent of contestation is limited by Islamic clergy, who ultimately exercise sovereign power. In China, a form of grassroots democracy has been implemented in the more than 600,000 rural villages where nearly half the population lives. Even though the Communist Party still oversees the process, China's rural dwellers now have real choice when they elect their local leaders. Such democratic elements in Iran and China are certainly significant in understanding politics in those countries; however, they do not fundamentally alter the authoritarian character of these states.

Our categories of consolidated democracies, hybrid states, and authoritarian regimes are not airtight, and some countries may straddle two categories. Consider Brazil, which we classify as a hybrid state. Ever since democracy was restored in 1984, following a period of harsh military rule, Brazil has compiled a solid record of democratic practice. For example, since the return of civilian rule, there have been several peaceful electoral alternations between dramatically different political coalitions. One might claim, therefore, that Brazil should be classified as a consolidated democracy. Our decision to designate Brazil as a hybrid state is based on the fact that there continues to be clear violations of democratic procedures, political corruption, lack of entrenched democratic values, and extensive inequality (which is heavily coded in racial terms).

Another example of the difficulty of classifying states: We consider India a consolidated democracy because it has generally respected most democratic procedures since it gained independence in 1947. There is intense political competition in India, elections are usually free and fair, and the Indian judiciary is quite independent. However, some might question our decision and claim that India should be considered a hybrid democracy. For example, India has repeatedly experienced scenes of horrific communal violence, in which large numbers of Muslim, Sikh, and Christian minorities have been brutally massacred, sometimes with the active complicity of state officials.

A further point about our typology is that the boundaries among categories are fluid. Some of the countries classified as mixed systems are experiencing such political turmoil that they could very well fall out of any category of democracy. Take Russia, for example, which we classify as a hybrid system, but whose trajectory in the last several years has been in the authoritarian direction. Since Putin's reelection as president in 2012, the Russian government has engaged in numerous undemocratic practices, including arbitrary detention and rigged trials of opponents, repeated violations of the constitution, and extensive political corruption. There are competitive (but not wholly fair) elections; multiple parties, but one dominant establishment party; a vocal and active opposition, but terrible violations of civil liberties across the board; not to mention dangerously bellicose foreign policy and blatant disregard for the sovereignty of Ukraine. We have kept Russia in the hybrid state camp for now, but we are fully aware of the ominous tendencies that may move Russia into the authoritarian slot in our typology in the next edition of this book.

As you read about the countries we now call hybrid states (Brazil, Mexico, Nigeria, Russia, and South Africa), think about whether they are moving in a more democratic or authoritarian direction—and the reasons for these political dynamics. It's a question like this that makes the study of comparative politics such a fascinating, constantly changing, often unpredictable, and, we think, important way of analyzing and understanding our contemporary world.

Where Do You Stand?

The EIU's Democracy Index classifies the United States as a "flawed democracy" rather than a full democracy. Do you agree? Why or why not?

Do you agree with our decision to classify Russia as a hybrid state that has important elements of both democracy and authoritarianism? (You probably will be in a better position to take a stand on this after you've read Chapter 13, on Russia.)

SECTION 5

ORGANIZATION OF THE TEXT

Focus Questions

- If you could choose one other country to study in a comparative politics course besides those included in this book, what would it be? Why? What would you like to know about politics in that country?

- We observe that a country's economy has an important impact on its politics, and vice versa. In what ways might this be the case?

We selected the countries for the case studies in this book on the basis of their significance in terms of our comparative themes and because they provide an extensive sample of types of political regimes, levels of economic development, and geographic regions. Although each of the country studies makes important comparative references, the studies primarily provide in-depth descriptions and analyses of the politics of individual countries. At the same time, the country studies have identical formats, with common section and subsection headings to help you make comparisons and explore similar themes across the various cases. And each chapter emphasizes the four themes that anchor analyses in *Introduction to Comparative Politics* and that enable you to engage in cross-country comparisons.

The following are brief summaries of the main sections and subsections of the country studies.

The Making of the Modern State

Section 1 in each chapter provides an overview of the forces that have shaped the state. We believe that understanding the contemporary politics of any country requires familiarity with the historical process of state formation. "Politics in Action" uses a specific event to illustrate an important political moment in the country's recent history and to highlight some of the critical political challenges that it faces. "Geographic Setting" locates the country in its regional context and discusses the political implications of this setting. "Critical Junctures" looks at some of the major stages and decisive turning points in the state's development. This should give you an overview of how the country assumed its current political shape. It is followed by a discussion of "The Four Themes and *Country X*," which applies the text's key themes to the making of the modern state. How has the country's political development been affected by its position in the globalized world of states—its relative ability to control external events and its regional and global status? What are the political implications of the state's approach to governing the economy? What has been the country's experience with the democratic idea? What are the important bases of collective identity in the country, and how do they influence the country's politics? Section 1 ends with a brief discussion ("Comparison") of how the country might usefully be compared to others, which you should keep in mind as you read the rest of the chapter.

Political Economy and Development

Section 2 analyzes the pattern of governing each country's economy, and it explores how economic development has affected political change. We locate this section toward the beginning of the country study because we believe that a country's economy has an important impact on its politics and vice versa. Within this section, there are several subsections. "State and Economy" discusses the basic organization of the country's economic system, focusing on the respective role of the state and markets in economic life. The subsection also examines the relationship between the government and other economic actors. "Society and Economy" examines the social implications of the country's economic situation. It describes the state's social welfare policies, such as health care, housing, and pension programs. It asks who benefits from the way that the economy functions, as well as how economic development creates or reinforces class, ethnic, gender, regional, or ideological themes in society. The next subsection, "Environmental Issues," analyzes the country's environmental politics and policies, since these are related to the process of economic development. Section 2 closes by examining the country's relationship to "The Global Economy." How have international economic issues affected the domestic political agenda? How have patterns of trade and foreign investment changed over time? What is the country's relationship to regional and international economic organizations? To what degree has the country been able to influence multilateral economic policies?

Governance and Policy-Making

In Section 3, we describe the state's major government institutions and policymaking procedures. "Organization of the State" lays out the fundamental principles on which the political system and the distribution of political power are based, the country's historical experience, constitution, and key state institutions. The chapter also outlines the basic structure of the state, including the relationships among different levels and branches of government. "The Executive" encompasses the key offices of the administrative branch (for example, presidents, prime ministers, communist party leaders) at the top of the political system, focusing on how they are selected and how they use their power to make policy. This subsection also analyzes the cabinet and the national bureaucracy, their relationship to the chief executive, and their role in policy-making. "Other State Institutions" examines the military, the judiciary and the legal system, semipublic agencies, and subnational government. "The Policy-Making Process" summarizes how public policy gets made and implemented in the country. It describes the roles of formal institutions and procedures, as well as informal aspects of policy-making, such as the influence of lobbyists and interest groups.

Representation and Participation

Section 4 focuses on the relationship between a country's state and society. How do different groups in society organize to further their political interests, how do they participate and get represented in the political system, and to what extent and how do they influence policy-making? Given the importance of the U.S. Congress in policy-making, American readers might expect to find the principal discussion of "The Legislature" in Section 3 ("Governance and Policy-Making") rather than Section 4. But the U.S. Congress is an exceptionally powerful legislature. In most other political systems, the executive dominates the policy process, even when it is ultimately responsible to the legislature (as is the case in parliamentary systems). In most countries other than the United States, the legislature functions primarily to represent and provide a forum for the political expression of various interests; it is only secondarily (and in some cases, such as China, only marginally) a policy-making body. Therefore, although this section does describe and assess the legislature's role in policy-making, its primary focus is on how the legislature represents or fails to represent different interests in society.

"Political Parties and the Party System" describes the overall organization of the party system and reviews the major parties. "Elections" discusses the election process and recent trends in electoral behavior. It also considers the significance of elections (or lack thereof) as a vehicle for citizen participation in politics and for possibly influencing changes in the government and government policy. "Political Culture, Citizenship, and Identity" examines how people perceive themselves as members of the political community, the nature and source of political values and attitudes, who is considered a citizen, and how different groups in society understand their relationship to the state. The topics covered may include political aspects of the educational system, religion, and ethnicity. We also ask how globalization affects collective identities and collective action. "Interest Groups, Social Movements, and Protest" discusses how groups in civil society pursue their political interests outside the party system. What is the relationship between the state and such organizations and movements? When and how do citizens engage in acts of protest? And how does the state respond when they do? The final subsection analyzes "The Political Impact of Technology and the Media" and assesses, for example, how the growth of the Internet and social media influences politics and how the state uses technology as an instrument of power.

Politics in Transition

In Section 5, we identify and analyze the major challenges confronting each country and revisit the book's four themes. "Political Challenges and Changing Agendas" lays out the major unresolved issues facing the country and how they may play out in the near future. Many of these challenges involve issues that have generated intense political tensions around the world in recent times—globalization, immigration, economic growth, inequality, human rights and civil liberties, and conflicts over collective identities. Others may be more unusual and specific to a particular country or group of countries, such as separatist movements. "Is Demography Destiny?" draws attention to the impact of important changes in the age distribution of the population—such as whether it is a graying population or a youth bulge—on the politics of the country, as well as how demographic composition and change may affect politics and policy-making. "Politics in Comparative Perspective" highlights the implications of the country case for the study of comparative politics. How does the history—and how will the future—of the country influence developments in a regional and global context? What does this case study tell us about politics in other countries that have similar political systems or that face similar kinds of political challenges?

Key Terms, Suggested Readings, and Suggested Websites

In the margin of the text, we briefly define key terms, highlighted in bold in the text, that we consider especially important for students of comparative politics to know. The key words in each chapter are also listed at the end of the chapter, and all key terms, with definitions, are included in the Glossary at the end of the book. Each chapter also has a list of books that reflect important current scholarship in the field, are interesting and accessible to undergraduates, or both. This introductory chapter ends with suggested readings that survey the scope and methods of comparative politics and illuminate important issues in the field. We also include a set of websites that will help you track developments and acquire timely information in the ever-changing world of comparative politics.

We realize that it is quite a challenge to begin a journey seeking to understand contemporary politics in countries around the globe. We hope that the timely information and thematic focus of ICP will prepare and encourage you to explore further the often troubling, sometimes inspiring, and endlessly fascinating world of comparative politics.

Where Do You Stand?

Are you optimistic or pessimistic about the spread of democracy around the world? Why?

Do you think that globalization will continue to erode the nation-state as the basic building block of politics in the world? Why or why not?

WHAT'S IN THE COMPARATIVE DATA CHARTS AND TABLES?

The following charts and tables present important factual and statistical information about each of the countries included in this book. We hope most of this information is self-explanatory, but a few points of clarification may be helpful.

The social and economic data mostly come from the CIA *World Factbook*, the World Bank *World Development Indicators*, and the United Nations *Human Development Report*, all of which are updated annually. These statistics are available at the following websites:

- https://www.cia.gov/library/publications/the-world -factbook/

- http://data.worldbank.org/
- http://hdr.undp.org/en/data

The data presented below are as up to date as possible. Several important terms used in the data, including gross domestic product (GDP), purchasing power parity (PPP), and Gini Index, are explained in the feature called "How Is Development Measured?" on pages 16–17, and are defined in the Glossary.

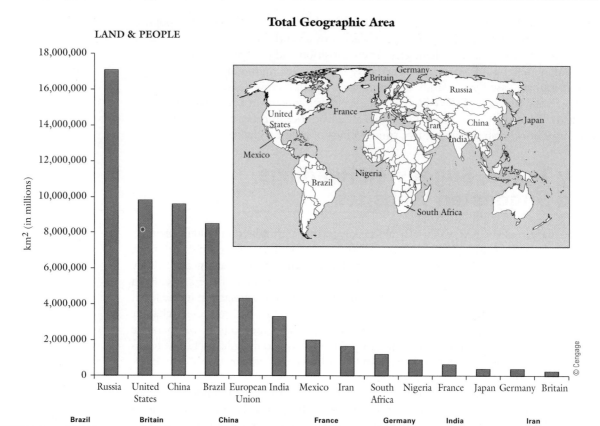

Total Geographic Area

LAND & PEOPLE

	Brazil	Britain	China	France	Germany	India	Iran
Official name	Federative Republic of Brazil	United Kingdom of Great Britain and Northern Ireland	People's Republic of China	French Republic	Federal Republic of Germany	Republic of India	Islamic Republic of Iran
Capital	Brasilia	London	Beijing	Paris	Berlin	New Delhi	Teheran
Comparative Size	Slightly smaller than the US	Slightly smaller than Oregon	Slightly smaller than the US	Slightly smaller than Texas	Slightly smaller than Montana	Slightly more than 1/3 the size of the US	Slightly smaller than Alaska
Annual Population growth	0.8%	0.5%	0.4%	0.4%	−0.2%	1.2%	1.2%
Major ethnic groups	White 47.7% ; Mulatto (mixed White and Black) 43.1%; Black 7.6%; Other (includes 0.5%; Asian) 1.6%	White 87.2%; Black 3.0%; Indian 2.3%; Pakistani 1.9%; Mixed 2.0%; Other 3.7%	Han Chinese 91.6%; Other nationalities 8.4%; (includes 55 ethnic minorities, such as Zhuang, Manchu, Hui, Miao, Uyghur, Yi, Mongol, Tibetan, and Korean)	*It is illegal in France to collect data about ethnicity.*	German 91.5%; Turkish 2.4%; Other 6.1%	*The government of India does not collect data on ethnicity.*	Persian 61%; Azeri 16%; Kurd 10%; Lur 6%; Baloch 2%; Arab 2%; Turkmen and Turkic 2%; Other 1%
Major religions	Roman Catholic 65.0%; Protestant 23.0%; Other Christian 0.9%; Other 4.0%; Folk Religions 2.8%; Unaffiliated 7.9%	Christian 59.5%; Muslim 4.4%; Hindu 1.3%; Other 2.0%; None 25.7%; Unspecified 7.2%	Buddhist 18.2%; Christian 5.1%; Muslim 1.8%; Folk Religions 21.9%; Unaffiliated 52.2%; Other 1.0% **Note:** Officially Atheist	Christians 63%; Unaffiliated 28%; Muslims 7.5%; Jews 0.5%; Other 1.0%;	None 36%; Roman Catholic 29%; Protestant 27 %; Muslim 4.4%; Other 3.6%	Hindu 79.8%; Muslim 14.2%; Christian 2.3%; Sikh 1.7%; Other 2.0%	Muslim 99.3%; (Shia 90-95%, Sunni 5-10%); Other 0.3%; (includes Zoroastrian, Jewish, Christian, and Baha'i); Unspecified 0.4%
Major languages	Portuguese	English The following are recognized regional languages: Scots, Scottish Gaelic Welsh, Irish, Cornish	Standard Chinese or Mandarin based on the Beijing dialect. Other major dialects include Cantonese and Shanghaiese. Also various minority languages; such as Tibetan and Mongolian	French	German	Hindi is the most widely spoken language and the primary tongue of 41% of the people There are 14 other official languages. English is the most important language for government and business.	Official language: Persian, spoken by 58% as a first language; 90%; can communicate in Persian. Other major languages: Azeri and Turkic; Kurdish Gilaki and Mazandarani; Luri Balochi; Arabic.

© Cengage

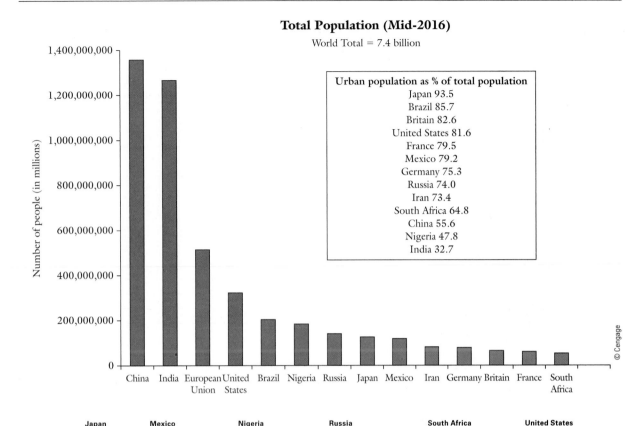

Total Population (Mid-2016)

World Total = 7.4 billion

Urban population as % of total population
Japan 93.5
Brazil 85.7
Britain 82.6
United States 81.6
France 79.5
Mexico 79.2
Germany 75.3
Russia 74.0
Iran 73.4
South Africa 64.8
China 55.6
Nigeria 47.8
India 32.7

© Cengage

	Japan	Mexico	Nigeria	Russia	South Africa	United States
Official name	Japan	United Mexican States	Federal Republic of Nigeria	Russian Federation	Republic of South Africa	United States of America
Capital	Tokyo	Mexico City	Abuja	Moscow	Pretoria	Washington, D.C.
Comparative size	Slightly smaller than California	Slightly less than three times the size of Texas	Slightly more than twice the size of California	Approximately 1.8 times the size of the US	Slightly less than twice the size of Texas	About half the size of Russia
Annual population growth	−0.2%	1.2%	2.4%	−0.1%	1.0%	0.8%
Major ethnic groups	Japanese 98.5%; Koreans 0.5%; Chinese 0.4%; Other 0.6%	Mestizo (Amerindian-Spanish) 62.0%; Predominantly Amerindian 21.0%; Amerindian 7.0%; Other (mostly European) 10.0%	More than 250 ethnic groups. The most populous and politically influential are: Hausa and Fulani 29.0%; Yoruba 21.0%; Igbo (Ibo) 18.0%; Ijaw 10.0%; Kanuri 4.0%; Ibibio 3.5%; Tiv 2.5%	Russian 77.7%; Tatar 3.7%; Ukrainian 1.4%; Bashkir 1.1%; Chuvash 1.0%; Chechen 1.0%; Other 10.2%; Unspecified 3.9% Nearly 200 national and/or ethnic groups are represented in Russia's 2010 census.	Black African 80.2%; White 8.4%; Colored (Mixed Race) 8.8%; Indian/Asian 2.5%	White 61.6%; Hispanic 17.6%; Black or African American 13.3%; Asian 5.6%; American Indian and Alaska Native 1.2%; Native Hawaiian and Other Pacific Islander 0.2%; Two or more races 2.9%
Major religions	Shinto 79.2%; Buddhist 66.8%; Christian 1.5%; Other 7.1% Note: Many Japanese practice both Shintoism and Buddhism	Catholic 82.7%; Pentecostal 1.6%; Jehovah's Witness 1.4%; Other Evangelical Churches 5.0%; Other 1.9%; None 4.7%; Unspecified 2.7%	Christian 49.3%; Muslim 48.8%; Other 1.9%	Russian Orthodox 70.6%; Other Christian 2.6%; Muslim 10%; Unaffiliated 16.2%; Other 1.6%	Protestant 73.2%; Catholic 7.4%; Muslim 1.7%; Hindu 1.1%; Unaffiliated 14.9%; Other 1.7%	Protestant 46.5%; Roman Catholic 20.8%; Jewish 1.9%; Mormon 1.6%; Other 6.4%; Unaffiliated 22.8%.
Major languages	Japanese	Spanish only 92.7%; Spanish and indigenous languages 5.7%; Indigenous only 0.8%; Unspecified 0.8%	English (official), Hausa, Yoruba, Igbo (Ibo), Fulani. Over 500 additional indigenous languages	Russian 85.7%; Tatar 3.2%; Chechen 1%; Other 10.1%	IsiZulu 22.7%; IsiXhosa 16.0%; Afrikaans 13.5%; English 9.6%; Sepedi 9.1%; Setswana 8%; Sesotho7.6%; Other 13.1%	Speak only English at home, 79.2%; Speak only Spanish at home, 12.9%; Speak only another language at home, 7.9%

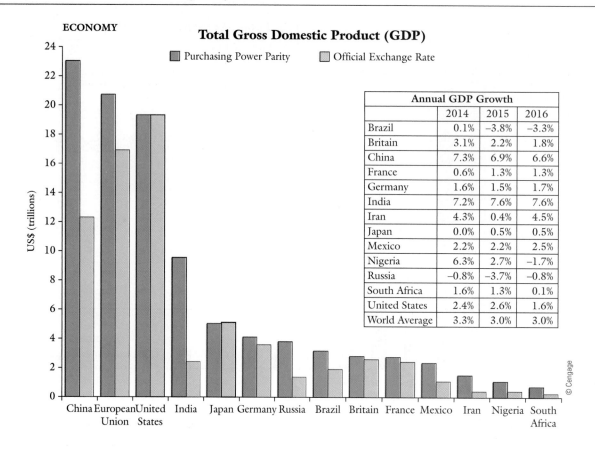

ECONOMY

Total Gross Domestic Product (GDP)

■ Purchasing Power Parity   □ Official Exchange Rate

US$ (trillions)

China European Union United States India Japan Germany Russia Brazil Britain France Mexico Iran Nigeria South Africa

© Cengage

Annual GDP Growth			
	2014	2015	2016
Brazil	0.1%	−3.8%	−3.3%
Britain	3.1%	2.2%	1.8%
China	7.3%	6.9%	6.6%
France	0.6%	1.3%	1.3%
Germany	1.6%	1.5%	1.7%
India	7.2%	7.6%	7.6%
Iran	4.3%	0.4%	4.5%
Japan	0.0%	0.5%	0.5%
Mexico	2.2%	2.2%	2.5%
Nigeria	6.3%	2.7%	−1.7%
Russia	−0.8%	−3.7%	−0.8%
South Africa	1.6%	1.3%	0.1%
United States	2.4%	2.6%	1.6%
World Average	3.3%	3.0%	3.0%

	Brazil	Britain	China	France	Germany	India	Iran
GDP average annual growth: 2006–2016	2.2%	1.3%	9.3%	0.9%	1.5%	7.4%	2.9%
GDP *per capita* average annual growth:							
2010–16	1.2%	1.2%	7.8%	0.6%	2.1%	6.0%	0.2%
2000–09	2.1%	1.2%	9.7%	0.7%	0.8%	5.1%	3.9%
1990–99	0.3%	1.8%	8.8%	1.6%	1.8%	3.7%	2.3%
1980–89	0.8%	2.5%	8.2%	1.8%	*Before German*	3.3%	−4.6%
1970–79	5.9%	2.8%	5.3%	3.4%	*Reunification*	0.6%	1.3%
GDP composition by economic sector							
Agriculture	6.3%	0.6%	8.6%	1.7%	0.6%	16.5%	9.3%
Industry	21.8%	19.2%	40.7%	19.4%	30.3%	29.7%	38.2%
Services	72.0%	80.2%	50.7%	78.8%	69.1%	53.2%	52.4%
Labor force by occupation							
Agriculture	15.7%	1.3%	33.6%	3.0%	1.2%	49.0%	16.3%
Industry	13.3%	15.2%	30.3%	21.3%	24.2%	20.0%	35.1%
Services	71.0%	83.5%	36.1%	75.7%	74.3.%	31.0%	48.6%
% of female population age 15+ in labor force	56.1%	60.0%	63.3%	50.5%	54.5%	26.9%	16.2%
Foreign trade as % of GDP							
Exports	13.0%	27.2%	27.3%	30.0%	46.8%	19.9%	24.2%
Imports	14.3%	29.3%	24.5%	31.4%	39.2%	22.5%	18.9%
Total	27.3%	56.5%	49.7%	61.4%	86.0%	43.4%	43.1%
Inequality							
Household income or consumption by % share							
Richest 10%	40.7%	24.7%	31.4%	26.8%	23.7%	29.8%	29.1%
Poorest 10%	1.2%	2.9%	2.1%	3.1%	3.4%	3.6%	2.9%
Gini Index *(0-100; higher = more unequal)*	51.9	32.4	46.9	30.1	27.0	33.6	44.5
Poverty							
Population in multidimensional poverty %	40.0%	—	43.3%	—	—	51.1%	—
Population below national poverty line %	8.9%	15.0%	6.1%	8.1%	15.5%	29.8%	18.7%

GDP Per Capita (US$ Purchasing Power Parity)

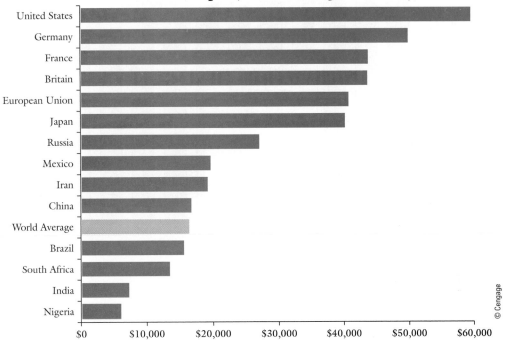

© Cengage

	Japan	Mexico	Nigeria	Russia	South Africa	United States
GDP average annual growth 2000–016	0.6%	2.4%	5.3%	2.2%	2.4%	1.5%
GDP *per capita* average annual growth						
2010–16	1.7%	1.8%	2.5%	1.3%	0.7%	1.4%
2000–09	0.4%	0.4%	6.1%	5.8%	2.0%	0.9%
1990–99	1.3%	1.7%	0.1%	−4.9%	−0.8%	2.0%
1980–89	3.7%	0.1%	−4.0%	*Before Collapse*	−0.3%	2.2%
1970–79	2.9%	3.3%	4.2%	*of Soviet Union*	1.0%	2.5%
GDP composition by economic sector						
Agriculture	1.1%	3.6%	20.9%	4.6%	2.4%	1.3%
Industry	26.2%	32.8%	20.4%	32.6%	28.9%	20.7%
Services	70.9%	63.6%	58.8%	62.8%	68.7%	78.0%
Labor force by occupation						
Agriculture	2.9%	13.4%	70.0%	9.4%	4.0%	0.7%
Industry	25.3%	24.1%	10.0%	27.6%	18.0%	23.3%
Services	69.7%	61.9%	20.0%	63.0%	66.0%	76.0%
% of female population age 15+ in labor force	49.0%	45.5%	48.5%	56.5%	46.3%	55.8%
Foreign trade as % of GDP						
Exports	17.6%	35.5%	10.7%	29.5%	30.7%	12.6%
Imports	18.0%	37.7%	10.8%	21.2%	31.7%	15.4%
Total	35.6%	72.8%	21.4%	50.7%	62.4%	28.0%
Inequality						
Household income or consumption by % share						
Richest 10%	24.8%	39.7%	32.7%	32.2%	51.3%	30.2 %
Poorest 10%	2.7%	1.9%	2.0%	2.3%	0.9%	1.7%
Gini Index *(0-100; higher = more unequal)*	37.9	48.3	43.7	42.0	62.5	45.0
Poverty						
Population in multidimensional poverty %	—	39.9%	54.8%	—	39.9%	—
Population below national poverty line %	16.1%	48.0%	60.5%	11.2%	35.9%	15.1%

Life Expectancy at Birth (Years)

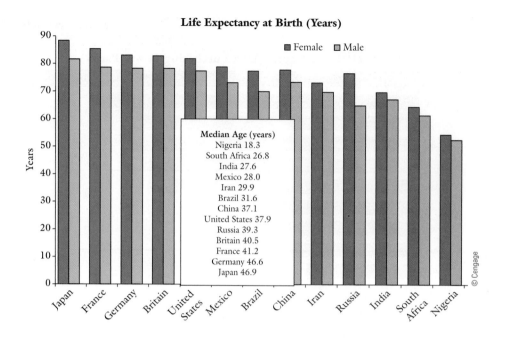

	Brazil	Britain	China	France	Germany	India	Iran
EDUCATION							
Adult literacy (% of population age 15+)	Female 92.9 Male 92.2	Female 99.0* Male 99.0*	Female 94.5 Male 98.2	Female 99.0* Male 99.0*	Female 99.0* Male 99.0*	Female 62.8 Male 80.9	Female 82.5 Male 91.2
School Completion Rate (% of age-eligible population}	Primary 93 Middle 60 Secondary 19 Tertiary 17	Primary 100 Middle 100 Secondary 90 Tertiary 46	Primary 91 Middle 77 Secondary 39 Tertiary 21	Primary 100 Middle 88 Secondary 88 Tertiary 45	Primary 100 Middle 85 Secondary 81 Tertiary 32	Primary 86 Middle 71 Secondary 30 Tertiary 15	Primary 97.5 Secondary 89.2 Tertiary n/a
Average (Mean) Years of School	9.9	12.7	9.7	11.3	14.1	8.8	7.8
HEALTH							
Physicians per 1000 population	1.9	2.8	1.4	3.2	3.9	0.7	0.9
Under 5 mortality rate/1000 live births	Female 14.9 Male 17.7	Female 3.8 Male 4.7	Female 10.0 Male 11.3	Female 3.9 Male 4.8	Female 3.4 Male 4.1	Female 49.2 Male 46.3	Female 14.9 Male 16.2
Adolescent fertility (births per 1000 women age 15–19)	67.7	13.9	7.3	8.8	6.4	23.3	26.3
Health spending per capita per year (US$ PPP)	$1318	$3377	$731	$4508	$5182	$267	$1082
Health spending as % of GDP	Public 4.5 Private 3.8	Public 8.3 Private 1.5	Public 2.5 Private 3.1	Public 9.0 Private 2.5	Public 8.7 Private 2.6	Public 1.3 Private 3.3	Public 2.8 Private 4.1
MILITARY SPENDING							
• as % of GDP	1.5	2.5	2.0	1.8	1.2	2.4	5.0
• per capita US$	$120	$854	$156	$792	$542	$40	$131
PHONES, COMPUTERS, TVS, & CARS							
• Fixed telephone lines (per 100 people)	21.4	52.6	16.5	59.9	54.9	2.0	38.3
• Cell phone subscriptions (per 100 people)	126.6	125.8	93.2	102.6	116.7	78.8	93.4
• People using the Internet (%)	59.1	92.0	50.3	84.7	87.6	26.0	44.1
• Households with computer (%)	53.5	89.9	49.6	89.3	91.0	14.1	53.4
• Households with television set (%)	98.0	99.0	n/a	99.0	99.0	47.0	98.0
• Motor vehicles (per 1000 people)	249.0	519.0	205.0	578.0	572.0	35.0	213.0
CRIME & INCARCERATION							
Homicides per 100,000 population	24.6	0.9	0.8	1.2	0.9	3.2	3.9
Prison inmates per 100,000 total population	316.0	146.0**	118.0	101.0	76.0	33.0	287.0
Crime Index (0-100, higher = more crime)	71.2	43.2	32.1	44.1	32.9	46.6	52.4
Safety Index (0-100, higher = safer)	28.8	56.9	67.9	55.9	67.1	53.4	47.6
POLITY							
Women members of national legislature (%)							
• Lower house or single house	10.7	30.0	25.2	25.8	37.0	11.8	5.9
• Upper house (if any)	14.8	25.7		27.3	39.1	11.1	
Governance Indicators (0-100, higher = better)							
• Voice and Accountability	60	92	5	86	96	61	5
• Political Stability & Absence of Violence	34	62	27	57	70	17	17
• Government Effectiveness	48	94	68	89	94	56	47
• Regulatory Quality	47	99	44	84	93	40	7
• Rule of Law	50	94	44	88	93	56	16
• Control of Corruption	41	94	50	88	93	44	32
Freedom on the Net rating • 0 = least free, 100 = most free	Partly Free 38	Free 23	Not Free 88	Free 25	Free 19	Partly Free 41	Not Free 87
Freedom House rating • 0 = least free, 100 = most free	Free 79	Free 95	Not Free 15	Free 90	Free 95	Free 77	Not Free 17

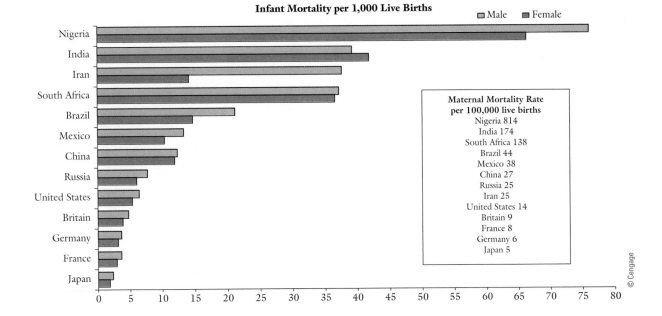

Infant Mortality per 1,000 Live Births — Male / Female

	Japan	Mexico	Nigeria	Russia	South Africa	United States
EDUCATION						
Adult literacy (% of population age 15+)	Female 99.0* Male 99.0*	Female 93.3 Male 95.6	Female 49.7 Male 69.2	Female 99.0* Male 99.0*	Female 93.1 Male 95.5	Female 99.0* Male 99.0*
School Completion Rate (% of age-eligible population)	Primary 100 Middle 100 Secondary 98 Tertiary 47	Primary 96 Middle 81 Secondary 50 Tertiary 28	Primary 68 Middle 52 Secondary 44 Tertiary 16	Primary 100 Middle 91 Secondary 89 Tertiary 55	Primary 93 Middle 75 Secondary 44 Tertiary 4	Primary 99 Middle 94 Secondary 91 Tertiary 40
Average (Mean) Years of School	11.5	10.8	7.7	11.5	10.3	13.5
HEALTH						
Physicians per 1000 population	2.3	2.1	0.4	4.3	0.8	2.5
Under 5 mortality rate/1000 live births	Female 2.5 Male 2.9	Female 11.9 Male 14.4	Female 102.3 Male 114.9	Female 8.4 Male 10.6	Female 37.3 Male 46.5	Female 5.9 Male 7.1
Adolescent fertility (births per 1000 women age 15–19)	4.0	62.2	109.3	22.7	44.4	21.2
Health spending per capita per year (US$ PPP)	$3727	$70	$217	$1838	$1148	$9403
Health spending as % of GDP	Public 8.6 Private 1.7	Public 3.3 Private 3.0	Public 0.9 Private 2.7	Public 3.7 Private 3.4	Public 4.2 Private 4.6	Public 8.3 Private 8.9
MILITARY SPENDING						
• as % of GDP	1.0	0.6	0.9	3.5	1.0	4.4
• per capita US$	$323	$64	$12	$454	$63	$ 1854
PHONES, COMPUTERS, TVS, AND CARS						
• Fixed telephone lines (per 100 people)	50.2	15.9	0.1	25.7	7.7	37.5
• Cell phone subscriptions (per 100 people)	125.5	85.3	82.2	160.0	159.3	117.6
• People using the Internet (%)	93.3	57.4	47.4	73.4	51.9	74.6
• Households with computer (%)	80.0	44.9	9.8	72.5	23.4	87.3
• Households with television set (%)	99.0	95.0	40.0	87.0	81.0	99.0
• Motor vehicles (per 1000 people)	591.0	275.0	31.0	293.0	165.0	797.0
CRIME & INCARCERATION						
Homicides per 100,000 population	0.3	15.7	10.3	9.5	33.0	3.9
Prison inmates per 100,000 total population	45.0	192.0	35.0	433.0	291.0	666.0
Crime Index (0-100, higher = more crime)	19.3	50.8	74.1	47.3	74.4	48.9
Safety Index (0-100, higher = safer)	80.7	49.2	25.9	52.7	21.6	51.1
POLITY						
Women members of national legislature (%)						
• Lower house or single house	9.3	42.6	5.6	15.8	42.1	19.3
• Upper house (if any))	20.7	36.7	6.5	17.1	35.2	21.0
Governance Indicators (0-100, higher = better)						
• Voice and Accountability	79	43	33	19	69	81
• Political Stability & Absence of Violence	82	18	6	13	39	70
• Government Effectiveness	96	62	17	48	65	90
• Regulatory Quality	85	66	22	32	64	88
• Rule of Law	89	38	13	26	59	90
• Control of Corruption	91	25	11	19	58	90
Freedom on the Net rating • 0 = least free, 100 = most free	Free 22	Partly Free 38	Partly Free 34	Not Free 65	Free 25	Free 18
Freedom House rating • 0 = least free, 100 = most free	Free 96	Partly Free 65	Partly Free 50	Not Free 20	Free 78	Free 89

* Developed countries have near universal adult *basic* literacy rates, but *functional* literacy—being literate enough to be able to function well in complex society—among the working age population is considerably lower. For the developed countries covered in this book, the percentage of adults considered to be at such a level of literacy are as follows Japan 92.1; Russia 86.9; Germany 82.5%; the United States 82.5%; and France 78.0%. (Based on OECD Skills Outlook 2013, Table A2.1, Percentage of adults scoring literacy proficiency Levels 3-5.)

** England and Wales. Northern Ireland = 75; Scotland 138

Table 1.1   Comparative Rankings

International organizations and research institutions have developed statistical methods to rate and rank different countries according to various categories of economic, social, political, and environmental performance. Such rankings can be controversial, but we think they provide an interesting approach to comparative analysis. Five examples of this approach are listed below. In addition to the countries included in this book (which are in bold), the top and bottom 5 countries in each of the rankings are also listed.

Human Development Index (HDI) is a measure used by the United Nations to compare the overall level of well-being in countries around the world. It takes into account life expectancy, education, and the standard of living.

2016 HDI Rankings:

Very High Human Development
1. Norway
2. Australia
3. Switzerland
4. **Germany**
5. Denmark
10. **United States**
16. **United Kingdom**
20. **Japan**
21. **France**
49. **Russia**

High Human Development
69. **Iran**
77. **Mexico**
79. **Brazil**
90. **China**

Medium Human Development
119. **South Africa**
130. **India**

Low Human Development
152. **Nigeria**
184. Burundi
185. Burkina Faso
186. Chad
187. Niger
188. Central African Republic

http://hdr.undp.org/en/composite/HDI/

Global Gender Gap measures the extent to which women have achieved equality with men in five critical areas: economic participation, economic opportunity, political empowerment, educational attainment, and health and well-being.

2016 Gender Gap Rankings:
1. Iceland
2. Finland
3. Norway
4. Sweden
5. Rwanda
13. **Germany**
15. **South Africa**
20. **Britain**
45. **United States**
66. **Mexico**
75. **Russia**
79. **Brazil**
99. **China**
85. **Brazil**
87. **India**
111. **Japan**
118. **Nigeria**
139. **Iran**
140. Chad
141. Saudi Arabia
142. Syria
143. Pakistan
144. Yemen

http://reports.weforum.org/global-gender-gap-report-2016/rankings/

Environmental Performance Index (EPI) measures how close countries come to meeting specific benchmarks for national pollution control and natural resource management.

2016 EPI Rankings:
1. Finland
2. Iceland
3. Sweden
4. Denmark
5. Slovenia
10. **France**
12. **Britain**
26. **United States**
30. **Germany**
32. **Russia**
39. **Japan**
46. **Brazil**
67. **Mexico**
81. **South Africa**
105. **Iran**
109. **China**
133. **Nigeria**
141. **India**
176. Afghanistan
177. Niger
178. Madagascar
179. Eretria
180. Somalia

http://epi.yale.edu/country-rankings

International Corruption Perceptions Index (CPI) defines corruption as the abuse of public office for private gain and measures the degree to which corruption is perceived to exist among a country's public officials and politicians.

2016 CPI Rankings:
1. Denmark
1. New Zealand
3. Finland
3. Sweden
5. Switzerland
10. **Britain**
10. **Germany**
18. **United States**
20. **Japan**
23. **France**
64. **South Africa**
79. **Brazil**
79. **China**
79. **India**
123. **Mexico**
131. Iran
131. **Russia**
136. **Nigeria**
170. Libya
170. Sudan
170. Yemen
173. Syria
174. North Korea
175. South Sudan
176. Somalia

http://www.transparency.org/news/feature/corruption_perceptions_index_2016

Identical numbers indicate a tie in the rankings

Economist Intelligence Unit Democracy Index categorizes four types of political systems based on five categories: electoral process and pluralism; civil liberties; the functioning of government; political participation; and political culture.

2016 Democracy Index:

Full Democracies
1. Norway
2. Iceland
3. Sweden
4. New Zealand
5. Denmark
13. **Germany**
16. **Britain**

Flawed Democracies
20. **Japan**
21. **United States**
24. **France**
32. **India**
39. **South Africa**
51. **Brazil**
67. **Mexico**
101. **Nigeria**

Authoritarian Regimes
134. **Russia**
136. **China**
154. **Iran**
163. Equatorial Guinea
164. Central African Republic
165. Chad
166. Syria
167. North Korea

https://en.wikipedia.org/wiki/Democracy_Index

Key Terms

authoritarian regime
bureaucracy
cabinet
causal theory
Cold War
collective identities
communist party-state
comparative politics
comparativist
consolidated democracy
Corruption Perceptions Index
country
critical juncture
democracy
democratic transition
dependent variable
dictatorship
distributional politics
Economist Intelligence Unit
   Democracy Index

Environmental Performance
   Index
executive
Global Gender Gap
globalization
gross domestic product (GDP)
gross national product (GNP)
Human Development Index
   (HDI)
hybrid state
illiberal democracy
independent variable
institutional design
International Monetary Fund
   (IMF)
judiciary
Keynesianism
legislature
legitimacy
liberal democracy

middle-level theory
nation-state
neoliberalism
North American Free Trade
   Agreement (NAFTA)
political economy
populism
purchasing power parity
   (PPP)
rational choice theory
social class
social movements
Social Progress Index (SPI)
state
state formation
sustainable development
typology
World Bank
World Trade Organization
   (WTO)

Suggested Readings

Acemoglu, Daron, and James A. Robinson. *Why Nations Fail: The Origins of Power, Prosperity, and Poverty.* New York: Crown Business, 2012.

Bueno de Mesquita, Bruce, and Alastair Smith. *The Dictator's Handbook: Why Bad Behavior Is Almost Always Good Politics.* New York: PublicAffairs, 2012.

Diamond, Larry, Marc F. Plattner, and Philip J. Costopoulos, eds. *Debates on Democratization.* Baltimore: Johns Hopkins University Press, 2010.

Diamond, Larry, and Marc F. Plattner, eds. *Democracy in Decline?* Baltimore: Johns Hopkins University Press, 2015.

Goldstone, Jack A. *Revolutions: A Very Short Introduction.* New York: Oxford University Press, 2014.

Grosby, Steven. *Nationalism: A Very Short Introduction.* New York: Oxford University Press, 2005.

Jansen, Jan C., and Jürgen Osterhammel. *Decolonization: A Short History.* Princeton, NJ: Princeton University Press, 2017.

Krieger, Joel, ed. *The Oxford Companion to Comparative Politics.* New York: Oxford University Press, 2013.

Steger, Manfred. *Globalization: A Very Short Introduction,* 4th ed. New York: Oxford University Press, 2017

Tepperman, Jonathan. *The Fix: How Nations Survive and Thrive in a World in Decline.* New York: Tim Duggan Books, 2016.

Suggested Websites

CIA World Factbook
https://www.cia.gov/library/publications/the-world-factbook

Election Guide (Consortium for Elections and Political Process Strengthening)
http://www.electionguide.org/

Freedom House
http://www.freedomhouse.org/

NationMaster
http://www.nationmaster.com/

PlanetRulers—Current Heads of State
https://planetrulers.com/

U.S. Bilateral Relations Fact Sheets
http://www.state.gov/r/pa/ei/bgn/

WorldStatesmen.org
http://www.worldstatesmen.org/

Britain

Joel Krieger

Official Name: United Kingdom of Great Britain and Northern Ireland

Location: Western Europe

Capital City: London

Population (2017): 64.2 million

Size: 244,820 sq. km.; slightly smaller than Oregon

THE MAKING OF THE MODERN BRITISH STATE

Politics in Action

Focus Questions ▽

Holding the English record for goals scored in World Cup matches, Gary Lineker, one of the finest strikers in English soccer history, is no stranger to the public eye.[1] In October 2016, when a group of child refugees from Calais landed in Britain, setting off a furious outcry by the country's right-wing tabloids, Lineker's single tweet, "The treatment by some towards these young refugees is hideously racist and utterly heartless. What's happening to our country?" transformed the athletic darling of the British public into an unlikely spokesman for the so-called Liberal Elite. Daring to go even further than the opposition Labour Party in defending a globalized Britain, Lineker set his sights on correcting many of the wrongs that he saw being created by the harsh anti-immigration and anti-European rhetoric that has become mainstream in recent British political discourse.

• How does the history of its empire still shape British politics today?

• What forces, both in the United Kingdom (UK) and abroad, conspired to lead Britain to exit the European Union (EU) in 2016?

Told repeatedly to "back off" and "stick to football," Lineker chose instead to use his celebrity to focus on something that he saw as an enormous problem: Brexit. Having spent numerous years playing in Barcelona, learning the language and cultures of other European nations, Lineker was sure that Brexit, the vote that his countrymen took on June 23, 2016, to split from the European Union, was a mistake. "As footballers, you just grow up with people from different backgrounds and different colors of skin," he said. "When you sit in a dressing room and you've got 15 teammates with you, you don't look around and think 'He's got black skin. He's Asian.' You think 'He's a great player. He's a good player. He needs to work.'" Lineker had urged Britain publicly to stay in the European Union before the referendum last June and condemned the vote afterward.

If soccer has showcased a growing racial and ethnic tolerance in British society, it has also mirrored the spectacular rise in income inequality that has developed in recent decades. If, as Lineker suggested, the popular sport thus stands as a kind of parable for all that has gone right and wrong in Britain in the past 30 years, it may also point to the political opportunities and challenges of the future. The competing demands of globalization and nationalist agendas will surely dominate the political agenda for the forseeable future, as Britain tries to negotiate a new place for its increasingly globalized citizens in a post-Brexit world.

Geographic Setting

Britain is the largest of the British Isles, a group of islands off the northwest coast of Europe that encompasses England, Scotland, and Wales. The second-largest island includes Northern Ireland and the independent Republic of Ireland. The term *Great Britain* includes England, Wales, and Scotland, but not Northern Ireland. We use the term *Britain* as shorthand for the United Kingdom of Great Britain and Northern Ireland.

1832
Reform Act expands voting rights.

1945–1979
Establishment of British welfare state; dismantling of British Empire

1914–1918
World War I

1650	1700	1750	1800	1900	1940	1950

1688
Glorious Revolution establishes power of Parliament.

1837–1901
Reign of Queen Victoria; height of British Empire

1939–1945
World War II

ca. 1750
Industrial Revolution begins in Britain.

1929–1939
Great Depression

Covering an area of approximately 94,000 square miles, Britain is roughly two-thirds the area of Japan, or approximately half the area of France. In 2017, the British population was approximately 64 million.

As an island off the shores of Europe, Britain was for centuries less subject to invasion and conquest than its continental counterparts. This gave the country a sense of security. The separation has also made many Britons feel that they are more apart from Europe than an intrinsic part of it—a sentiment that surely contributed to Britain's decision to break from the European Union. (See Figure 2.1 and Table 2.1.)

PATRICK HERTZOG/Getty Images

English forward Gary Lineker is tripped by Cameroon's goalkeeper Thomas N Kono (L) during the World Cup quarterfinal soccer match between England and Cameroon July 1990 in Naples.

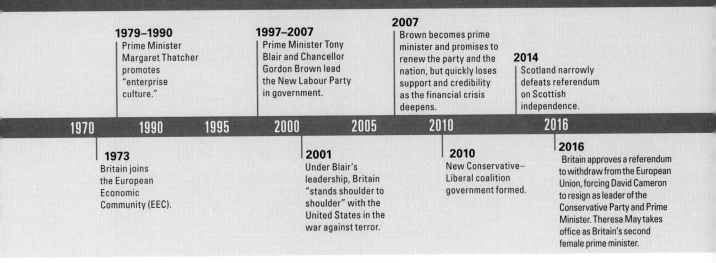

1979–1990
Prime Minister Margaret Thatcher promotes "enterprise culture."

1997–2007
Prime Minister Tony Blair and Chancellor Gordon Brown lead the New Labour Party in government.

2007
Brown becomes prime minister and promises to renew the party and the nation, but quickly loses support and credibility as the financial crisis deepens.

2014
Scotland narrowly defeats referendum on Scottish independence.

1970　1990　1995　2000　2005　2010　2016

1973
Britain joins the European Economic Community (EEC).

2001
Under Blair's leadership, Britain "stands shoulder to shoulder" with the United States in the war against terror.

2010
New Conservative–Liberal coalition government formed.

2016
Britain approves a referendum to withdraw from the European Union, forcing David Cameron to resign as leader of the Conservative Party and Prime Minister. Theresa May takes office as Britain's second female prime minister.

Critical Junctures

The Consolidation of the British State

The consolidation of the British state unified several kingdoms. After Duke William of Normandy defeated the English in the Battle of Hastings in 1066, the Norman monarchy eventually extended its authority throughout the British Isles, except for

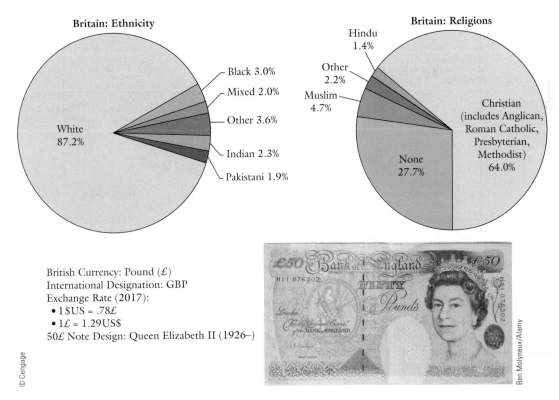

Britain: Ethnicity

White 87.2%
Black 3.0%
Mixed 2.0%
Other 3.6%
Indian 2.3%
Pakistani 1.9%

Britain: Religions

Hindu 1.4%
Other 2.2%
Muslim 4.7%
None 27.7%
Christian (includes Anglican, Roman Catholic, Presbyterian, Methodist) 64.0%

British Currency: Pound (£)
International Designation: GBP
Exchange Rate (2017):
- 1$US = .78£
- 1£ = 1.29US$

50£ Note Design: Queen Elizabeth II (1926–)

Ben Molyneux/Alamy

© Cengage

FIGURE 2.1 The British Nation at a Glance

Britain

0 — 100 Miles
0 — 100 Kilometers

Shetland Islands

Orkney Islands

Outer Hebrides

Inner Hebrides

SCOTLAND

North Sea

★Edinburgh
•Glasgow

NORTHERN IRELAND

Belfast★

Isle of Man

Irish Sea

REPUBLIC OF IRELAND

Dublin★

Isle of Anglesey

Manchester•
•Liverpool

WALES

ENGLAND

•Birmingham

Thames

Cardiff★
•Bristol
London

Chunnel

Southampton•

Isle of Wight

ATLANTIC OCEAN

•Plymouth

English Channel

FRANCE

© Cengage

Scotland. In the sixteenth century, legislation unified England and Wales legally, politically, and administratively. Scotland and England remained separate kingdoms until the Act of Union of 1707. After that, a common Parliament of Great Britain replaced the two separate parliaments of Scotland and of England and Wales.

Royal control increased after 1066, but the conduct of King John (1199–1216) fueled opposition from feudal barons. In 1215, they forced him to consent to a series of concessions that protected feudal landowners from abuses of royal power. These restrictions were embodied in the Magna Carta, a historic statement of the rights of a political community against the monarchical state. It has served as the inspiration for constitutions around the world that contain protections for citizens and groups from the arbitrary exercise of state power. In 1236, the term *Parliament* was first

Table 2.1	Political Organization
Political System	Parliamentary democracy, constitutional monarchy.
Regime History	Long constitutional history, origins subject to interpretation, usually dated from the seventeenth century or earlier.
Administrative Structure	Unitary state with fusion of powers. The UK Parliament has supreme legislative, executive, and judicial authority. Limited powers have been transferred to representative bodies in Scotland, Wales, and Northern Ireland.
Executive	Prime minister (PM), answerable to House of Commons, subject to collective responsibility of the cabinet; leader of the party that holds the majority in Parliament.
Legislature	Bicameral. House of Commons elected by single-member plurality system. Main legislative powers: to pass laws, provide for finance, scrutinize public administration and government policy. House of Lords, unelected upper house: limited powers to delay enactment of legislation and to recommend revisions. Since 2009, the judicial functions of Parliament were transferred to the UK Supreme Court. Recent reforms eliminated voting rights for most hereditary peers.
Judiciary	Independent, but with no power to judge the constitutionality of legislation or governmental conduct. UK Supreme Court, established in 2009, is the final court of appeal for all UK civil cases and criminal cases in England, Wales, and Northern Ireland.
Party System	Two-party dominant, with regional variations. Principal parties: Labour and Conservative; a center party (Liberal Democrat); national parties in Scotland, Wales, and Northern Ireland; and United Kingdom Independence Party (UKIP).

used officially for the gathering of feudal barons summoned by the king whenever he required their consent to special taxes. By the fifteenth century, Parliament had gained the right to make laws.

The Seventeenth-Century Settlement

By the sixteenth and seventeenth centuries, Britain was embroiled in a complex interplay of religious conflicts, national rivalries, and struggles between rulers and Parliament. These conflicts erupted in the civil wars of the 1640s, and later forced the removal of James II in 1688. This was the last successful revolution in British history.

This "Glorious Revolution" of 1688 also resolved long-standing religious conflict. The replacement of the Roman Catholic James II by the Protestant William and Mary ensured the dominance of the Church of England (or Anglican Church). To this day, the Church of England remains the established (official) church. By about 1700, a basic form of parliamentary democracy had emerged.

The Industrial Revolution and the British Empire

The Industrial Revolution, which took place from the mid-eighteenth century onward, involved rapid expansion of manufacturing production and technological innovation. It also led to vast social and economic changes and created pressures to make the country more democratic. Britain's competitive edge also dominated the international order. The Industrial Revolution transformed the British state and society.

Industrial Revolution

A period of rapid and destabilizing social, economic, and political changes caused by the introduction of large-scale factory production, originating in England in the middle of the eighteenth century.

Despite a gradually improving standard of living throughout the English population in general, industrialization disrupted lives and shattered old ways of life. Many field laborers lost their jobs, and many small landholders were squeezed off the land.

The British Empire

Britain relied on imported raw materials, and by 1800, it sold the vast majority of finished goods overseas. Growth depended on foreign markets, not domestic consumption. This export orientation made economic growth happen much faster than an exclusively domestic orientation would have allowed.

Because Britain needed overseas trade, its leaders worked aggressively to secure markets and expand the empire. Backed by the British navy, international trade made England the dominant military and economic world power. Britain led the alliance that toppled Napoleon in the early nineteenth century, enabling the country to maintain its dominant position in the world.

By 1870, British trade represented nearly one-quarter of the world total (see Figure 2.2), and by 1900, Queen Victoria (1837–1901) ruled an empire that included 25 percent of the world's population, exercising direct colonial rule over 50 countries, including India and Nigeria. Britain also dominated an extensive economic empire—a worldwide network of independent states, including China, Iran, and Brazil. Britain ruled as a **hegemonic power**, controlling alliances and shaping domestic political developments in countries throughout the world.

hegemonic power

A state that can control the pattern of alliances and terms of the international order and often shapes domestic political developments in countries throughout the world.

Industrial Change and the Struggle for Voting Rights

The Industrial Revolution shifted economic power from landowners to businessmen and industrialists. The first important step toward democratization began in the late 1820s, when the propertied classes and increasing popular agitation pressed Parliament to expand the right to vote. With Parliament under considerable pressure, the Reform Act of 1832 extended the vote to a section of the (male) middle class. (see Figure 2.3 on page 45).

The reform was narrow. Before 1832, less than 5 percent of the adult population could vote—but afterward, it grew to only about 7 percent. The reform showed that the strict property basis for political participation inflamed class-based tensions.

The Representation of the People Act of 1867 increased the electorate to 16 percent but left cities significantly underrepresented. The Franchise Act of 1884 nearly doubled the electorate. The Representation of the People Act of 1918 finally included nearly all adult men and women over age thirty. How slow a process was it? The struggle to extend the vote took place mostly without violence, but it lasted for centuries.

*As compared with the average rate of productivity in other members of the world economy.

FIGURE 2.2 World Trade and Relative Labor Productivity

Source: From Robert O. Keohane, *After Hegemony* (Princeton, NJ: Princeton University Press, 2005).

World Wars, Industrial Strife, and the Depression (1914–1945)

State involvement in the economy increased significantly during World War I (1914–1918). The state took control of numerous industries, including railways, mining, and shipping, and channeled resources into war production. After World War I, the state remained active in managing industry, but in a different way. Amid tremendous industrial disputes, the state fragmented the trade union movement and resisted demands for workers' control over production. This government manipulation of the economy openly contradicted the policy of laissez-faire (minimal government interference in the operation of economic markets) that generally characterizes Britain's approach to governing the economy.

Tensions between free-market principles and interventionist practices deepened with the Great Depression—occurring from 1929 throughout much of the 1930s—and World War II (1939–1945). Fear of economic depression and public yearnings for a better life after the war transformed the role of the state and led to a period of unusual political harmony.

laissez-faire

A term taken from the French, which means "to let do," it refers to the pattern in which state management is limited to such matters as enforcing contracts and protecting property rights, while private market forces are free to operate with only minimal state regulation.

Collectivist Consensus (1945–1979)

The term *collectivism* describes the consensus in politics after World War II, when most Britons and all the major political parties agreed that governments should work to narrow the gap between rich and poor and provide for basic necessities through public education, national health care, and other policies of the welfare state (a set of policies designed to provide health care, pensions, unemployment benefits, and assistance to the poor). They also accepted state responsibility for economic growth and full employment. British people came to expect that the state should be responsible for economic growth and full employment. In time, however, economic downturn and political stagnation unraveled the consensus.

welfare state

A set of public policies designed to provide for citizens' needs through direct or indirect provision of pensions, health care, unemployment insurance, and assistance to the poor.

New Labour's Third Way

Under the leadership of Tony Blair from 1997 to 2007, the Labour Party was determined to modernize itself. Although its official name did not change, the party was rebranded as "New Labour," promising what the British sociologist Anthony Giddens characterized as a "third-way" alternative to Thatcherism (the Conservative politics of the country under Prime Minister Margaret Thatcher) and the collectivism of traditional Labour. New Labour rejected interest-based politics, in which unions and working people tended to vote for Labour and businesspeople and the more prosperous voted for the Conservatives. Labour won in 1997 with support from across the socioeconomic spectrum.

Early in their careers, Tony Blair and Gordon Brown formed an alliance as rising stars in the Labour Party. Blair pushed the party to modernize and expand its political base well beyond its heritage as a labor party, while Brown became shadow chancellor under John Major (the opposition party's spokesman on the economy).

But after Labour took office, Blair and Brown became rivals rather than partners within the party. Prime Minister Blair won a third electoral victory in May 2005; however, due mainly to his support for the war in Iraq, his parliamentary majority was slashed by nearly 100 seats. In June 2007, Blair resigned and Gordon Brown became prime minister. A strong finance minister, Brown was not a nimble campaigner and was never able to get out from

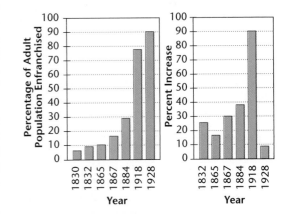

FIGURE 2.3 Expansion of Voting Rights
Expansion of the franchise in Britain was a gradual process. Despite reforms dating from the early nineteenth century, nearly universal adult suffrage was not achieved until 1928.

Source: Jorgen S. Rasumussen, *The British Political Process: Concentrated Power versus Accountability* (Belmont, CA: Wadsworth, 1993).

under the shadow cast by New Labour's role in the war in Iraq, a war that was extremely unpopular in the United Kingdom.

Brown's effectiveness as chancellor for 10 years and his highly praised efforts to stabilize the global economy during the "Great Recession" of 2008 were soon forgotten. Nor could Brown—or any prime minister—reduce the fear of sudden terrorist attacks that ordinary people in Britain have felt ever since bombs were set off in the London transport system on July 7, 2005 (referred to as "7/7" in the United Kingdom, much like the September 11, 2001, terrorist attacks are called "9/11").

The Conservative–Liberal Coalition

Ever since the Conservatives took power in 1990, many of the core principles of New Labour's approach have become widely shared across much of the political spectrum. When the Conservatives elected David Cameron as their leader in 2005, he took the party in a familiar mainstream direction, appealing directly to youth for political support and championing modernization and pragmatism. Young, smart, and telegenic, Cameron seemed to be stealing the thunder of New Labour and expanding the appeal of the Conservative Party by reaching out to youth and promoting agendas such as climate change, citizen activism, and promises to reduce both the global development gap and the gap between rich and poor in the United Kingdom—issues that had broad nonideological appeal. As a result, when the May 2010 election produced what the British call a "hung parliament"—an outcome after a general election when no party can control a majority of the seats in Parliament by itself —it was a stretch for the Conservatives and the Liberal Democrats to form a government, but it was not an unbridgeable gap.

The coalition government, like New Labour before it, characterized its governing objective as a blending of the Conservative belief in the dynamism of free markets with the Liberal Democrat commitment to decentralization. The result was captured in a new framework for governance, which the coalition partners called the "Big Society." The Big Society argued for wide-ranging initiatives to empower ordinary citizens to take control over their lives and shift the balance of power downward from the state to communities and individual citizens. Parents should be given the opportunity to start their own schools; citizens should be encouraged to take over the administration of post offices, to elect police commissioners, and to recall Members of Parliament (MPs) who violate the public trust. An innovative approach to governance in the United Kingdom, the Big Society was the "Big Idea"—the catchphrase and rebranding of politics apparently demanded of all new governments in the United Kingdom.

Despite his best efforts, Cameron's Big Society never caught on as a defining vision, nor was it able to successfully drive the agenda of the coalition government. To be fair, no government would have been able both to manage the consequences of the increasingly unpopular cuts demanded by the Great Recession of 2008 and to effectively galvanize the forces of globalization, which produced a set of international and domestic challenges that the Labour Party's policies were better suited to address.

But a coalition government turned out to be the least of the destabilizing and unexpected challenges defining British politics in the current period. First, in 2014, Britain narrowly fended off a Scottish referendum, which would have resulted in the breakup of Britain. Next, the United Kingdom Independence Party (UKIP) emerged on the scene under the leadership of Nigel Farage, a charismatic political figure who

led a movement to withdraw from the European Union. To this day the Labour Party has not been able to overcome the lingering aftereffects of Blair's disastrous decision to support the Anglo-American war in Iraq, nor has the uninspiring Jeremy Corbyn, who has led the party since 2015, been able to make any headway in challenging the growing dominance of the right-wing populist parties that now characterize European politics.

Brexit

A referendum vote was held on June 23, 2016, to determine whether the United Kingdom would remain in the European Union. The vote was 52 percent to 48 percent in favor of exiting, with a turnout of nearly 72 percent, meaning more than 30 million people voted. The result was a radical destabilization of British politics, as it became immediately clear that neither Britain's leaders nor the general public had any idea what their vote actually meant, or what it would accomplish. In the days following the vote confirming Britain's exit from the European Union, two of the top trending searches on Google were "What is Brexit?" and "What is the EU?" The decision to leave, led by Conservative MP Boris Johnson, led to the resignation of Prime Minister David Cameron, who, having argued that Britain should remain in the European Union, felt that he couldn't turn its exit into a success. Without so much as a general election, Conservative leader Theresa May took office as the second female prime minister in the country's history. It was, however, for the precise purpose of managing Britain's exit from the European Union effectively that May unexpectedly called for an early snap election, held in June 2017, hoping to increase her majority in Parliament. In light of her surprisingly poor showing in that election, the terms and timetable for leaving the European Union prove even more challenging, as both the United Kingdom and the European Union need time to negotiate the terms of the split, as well as to prepare for the impact of the decision, both economically and politically.

The Four Themes and Britain

Britain in a Globalized World of States

The first theme analyzes how a country's position in the globalizing world of states influences its ability to manage domestic and international challenges. A weaker international standing makes it difficult for a country to control international events or insulate itself from external pressure. Britain's ability to control the terms of trade and master political alliances during the nineteenth century confirms this maxim, but now times have changed.

Through gradual decolonization, Britain fell to second-tier status among the world's nations. Its formal empire shrank between the two world wars (1919–1939) as the so-called white dominions of Canada, Australia, and New Zealand gained independence. In Britain's Asian, Middle Eastern, and African colonies, pressure for political reforms that would lead to independence deepened during World War II and afterward. Beginning with the formal independence of India and Pakistan in 1947, an enormous empire dissolved in less than 20 years. Finally, in 1997, Britain returned the commercially vibrant crown colony of Hong Kong to China. The process of decolonization ended Britain's position as a dominant player in world politics.

 PROFILE

Theresa May

Theresa May is Britain's second female prime minister, following in the footsteps of the legendary Margaret Thatcher, a Conservative leader who has achieved the apex of political opportunity in a domain that is still very much dominated by men. May followed David Cameron after he resigned as prime minister within hours of the Brexit referendum. Within three weeks, on July 13, without either a general election or a full-blown Tory leadership contest, May assumed the position. She is an exceptionally experienced political figure, entering office after serving as Britain's home secretary for 6 years since the creation of the coalition government in 2010. (The Home Secretary is the British cabinet position in charge of domestic affairs, including security and terrorism.)

Like Thatcher and her immediate predecessor, Cameron, May stands for a formidable, no-nonsense, conservative leadership and a vision of Britain that recalls the days when the British Empire was the dominant global power. One of her top priorities has been making a success of Brexit and navigating the complex waters of British-European relationships that follow in its wake. Despite May's own misgivings about Brexit—she was a "Remain" supporter during the campaign—she has had no choice going forward but to manage the aftershocks of the decision as effectively as possible, both at home and abroad. Theresa May looked like a sure bet to remain as prime minister for the forseeable future and to ably lead Britain out of the EU. After she unexpectedly called for a snap election in April 2017, it was a

great surprise to all that thanks to lackluster campaigning on her part combined with issues raised by terror attacks in London and Manchester she lost rather than gained seats in June and was forced to scramble to stay in power. Minority governments, cobbled together by expediency rather than a coherent strategic vision, almost always fail in the end, and despite her long experience in government, Theresa May's political future remains clouded.

MAKING CONNECTIONS: Will Theresa May's extensive experience as Home Secretary ensure a smooth transition at 10 Downing Street in spite of the abrupt nature of her rise to power?

Now questions are emerging about how the Brexit decision will reorient Britain's place in the global order. Is Britain a world power, or just a middle-of-the-pack country in Europe? The answer is: Maybe both. Resulting from its role in World War II, Britain sits as a permanent member of the United Nations (UN) Security Council and is also a leading member of the world's select club of nuclear powers. What will happen to Britain's **special relationship** with the United States—one that has often helped stabilize a chaotic and increasingly uncertain global order—in an era characterized by the quixotic tendencies of the recently elected U.S. president Donald Trump and the historic rightward slide of politics through Europe?

special relationship

A unofficial term, first used by Winston Churchill, to describe the unusually close political, cultural, economic, and historical relations between the United States and the United Kingdom.

A second theme examines the strategies employed in governing the economy. Since the dawn of Britain's Industrial Revolution, prosperity at home has relied on superior competitiveness abroad. This is even truer with the intensified international competition and global production of today. Will Britain's "less-is-more," laissez-faire approach to economic governance, invigorated by partnerships between the state and key competitive businesses, sustain economic growth and competitiveness in a global context? Unlike other leading European powers like France, which remains committed to an approach to economic politic that is *dirigiste* (one in which the government takes direct responsibility for economic policy), in the United Kingdom, both governing and opposition leaders have been inclined to believe that government has a decreasing capacity to control the ebb and flow of economic developments. In the name of globalization, they have come to believe that Britain has fewer tools for sustaining economic competiveness over the long haul.

The Brexit vote will inevitably have a strong impact on Britain's economic future. Brexit supporters argue that as a result of the break, Britain will be able to forge closer trade links with countries outside the European Union and benefit from a reduction in the red tape generated in the EU capital of Brussels. Others disagree. In a 2017 report, the World Economic Forum noted that while the United Kingdom is currently one of the most competitive economies in the world, its future strength is uncertain: "Although the process and the conditions of Brexit are still unknown, it is likely to have a negative impact on the United Kingdom's competitiveness through goods and financial markets, as well as market size and, potentially, innovation."

Our third theme assesses the potent political influence of the democratic idea—the universal appeal of core values associated with parliamentary democracy as practiced first in the United Kingdom. Even in Britain, issues about democratic governance, citizen participation, and constitutional reform have been renewed with considerable force. The coalition government of 2010, the Scottish referendum of 2014 (with yet another on the horizon), and Brexit—this rapid succession of challenges to Britain's political institutions has unsettled the centuries-old British experience of the democratic idea, both from the perspective of government and within the lived experience of British citizens.

The fourth theme, the politics of collective identity, considers how individuals define themselves politically through group attachments, come together to pursue political goals, and face their status as political insiders or outsiders. Through the immigration of former colonial subjects to the United Kingdom, decolonization created a multiracial and multiethnic society. Issues of race, ethnicity, and cultural identity have challenged the long-standing British values of tolerance and consensus. The concept of "Britishness"—what the country stands for and who makes up the political community—continues to be fraught, especially in light of terrorist fears fueled by the Syrian refugee crisis, as well as the "America First" policy trumpeted by U.S. President Donald Trump.

Themes and Comparisons

Britain was the first nation to industrialize. For much of the nineteenth century, the British Empire was the world's dominant power, with a vast network of colonies. Britain was also the first nation to develop an effective parliamentary democracy.

British politics is often studied as a model of representative government. Named after the building that houses the British legislature in London, the **Westminster model** emphasizes that democracy rests on the supreme authority of a legislature—in Britain's case, the Parliament. Finally, Britain has long served as a model of gradual and peaceful evolution of democratic government in a world where transitions to democracy are often turbulent, interrupted, and uncertain. Given the recent challenges (UKIP, Brexit) to the stability of its parliamentary democracy, will Britain remain an effective example of this kind of government?

Westminster model

A form of democracy based on the supreme authority of Parliament and the accountability of its elected representatives; named for the Parliament building in London.

neoliberalism

A term used to describe government policies aiming to promote free competition among business firms within the market, including reduced governmental regulation and social spending.

Where Do You Stand?

What will be the effect of the Brexit vote on Britain's standing in the world?

The deck is stacked against the revival of the once powerful Labour Party. What will it take for this center-left party to return to its glory days when Tony Blair's New Labour was all the rage throughout Europe?

SECTION 2

POLITICAL ECONOMY AND DEVELOPMENT

▽ Focus Questions

- How will Britain manage its politics of austerity without succumbing to the right-wing populism that currently dominates European affairs?

- What are the key elements of the May government's approach to economic management in the post-Brexit environment?

The pressures of global competitiveness and the perceived advantages of a minimalist government have encouraged the adoption in many countries of neoliberal approaches to economic management. A legacy of Thatcher's Britain, **neoliberalism** was a key feature of Tony Blair's and Gordon Brown's New Labour governments. Its policies aimed to promote free competition, to interfere with entrepreneurs and managers as little as possible, and to create a business-friendly environment to attract foreign investment and spur innovation. Given that New Labour had long accepted the core principles of neoliberalism, the differences in economic policy between New Labour and the Conservative–Liberal coalition reflected changed circumstances—the economic crisis driven by the recession of 2008—more than fundamental ideological shifts.

State and Economy

In the 1980s, economic growth in Britain was low and unemployment high. Britain was routinely called the "sick man of Europe." But from the mid-1990s until the Great Recession of 2008, Britain avoided the high unemployment and recession that many EU nations suffered. The UK economy has run on a two-track pattern of growth, with a strong service sector (especially in financial services) offsetting a much weaker industrial sector. Until the global downturn of fall 2008, the British economy exhibited overall strength. With low unemployment, low interest rates, low inflation, and sustained growth, the UK performance was one of the best among the leading industrial economies. Weeks before the collapse of Lehman Brothers heralded the Great Recession, Brown warned at a meeting of Eurozone countries that the collapse of the U.S. housing market and the Great Recession to follow could be blamed on the United States, but he also insisted that these global problems required coordinated global solutions.

With the transition in 2010 from a New Labour to a Conservative–Liberal government, the policy orientation did not change at a stroke. Neoliberalism drove the economic policy of New Labour, and as a result, the economic performance of the UK economy was characterized by a patchwork neoliberal approach. Two central dimensions, economic management and social policy, captured the new role of the state and revealed its limitations. Although the UK economy has managed to create jobs since the recession, productivity growth has been low, a development reflected in low wage growth, with working households at risk of poverty. Both the coalition government and the Labour Party have been committed to balancing the budget, but with very different approaches. The coalition aimed to achieve fiscal responsibility through harsh spending cuts, but protecting the areas of health and education. The Labour Party, under Corbyn's leadership, has strongly criticized the government's austerity policies, proposing instead to deliver much-needed infrastructure that would expand economic activity and raise tax revenue.

Economic Management

Like all other states, the British state intervenes in economic life, sometimes with considerable force. However, the state has generally limited its role to broad policy instruments that influence the general economy (**macroeconomic policy**). How has the orientation of economic policy evolved during the postwar period?

macroeconomic policy

A policy intended to shape the overall economic system by concentrating on policy targets such as inflation and growth.

The Consensus Era

After World War II, the unity inspired by shared suffering during the war and the need to rebuild the country crystallized in the collectivist consensus. The state broadened and deepened its responsibilities for the economy.

The state assumed direct ownership of key industries. It also accepted the responsibility to secure low levels of unemployment (i.e., a policy of full employment), expand social services, maintain steady economic growth, keep prices stable, and achieve desirable balance-of-payments and exchange rates. The approach is called *Keynesian demand management,* or Keynesianism (named after the British economist John Maynard Keynes, 1883–1946).

Before Thatcher became leader of the Conservative Party in 1975, Conservative leaders generally accepted the collectivist consensus. By the 1970s, however, Britain was suffering economically, with no growth and growing political discontent. Investments declined, and trade union agitation increased. Industrial unrest in the winter of 1978–1979 dramatized Labour's inability to manage the trade unions. It seemed as if everyone was on strike. Strikes by truckers disrupted fuel supplies. Strikes by train drivers disrupted intercity commerce and visits to Granny. Some ambulance drivers refused to respond to emergency calls. Gravediggers refused to bury the dead.

Thatcher came to power a few months later, in May 1979. What was dubbed "the winter of discontent" destroyed Britain's collectivist consensus and discredited the Keynesian welfare state.

Thatcherite Policy Orientation

monetarism

An approach to economic policy that assumes a natural rate of unemployment, determined by the labor market, and rejects the instruments of government spending to run budgetary deficits for stimulating the economy and creating jobs.

The economic orientations of Thatcher and John Major, her successor, rejected Keynesianism. Monetarism emerged as the new economic doctrine. It assumed that there is a natural rate of unemployment that is determined by the labor market itself. State intervention to steer the economy should be limited to a few steps to foster appropriate rates of growth in the money supply and keep inflation low. Monetarism reflected a radical change from the postwar consensus regarding economic management. Not only was active government intervention considered unnecessary, it was seen as undesirable and destabilizing.

New Labour's Economic Policy Approach

As chancellor, and later as prime minister, Gordon Brown insisted on establishing a sound economy. He was determined to reassure international markets that the British economy was built on a platform of stability (i.e., low debt, low deficit, and low inflation) and that the Labour government could be counted on to run a tight financial ship. Only after he turned the public debt into a surplus did the "Iron Chancellor" reinvent himself as a more conventional Labour chancellor. Even then, Brown used economic growth to increase spending rather than cut taxes.

Brown claimed that since capital is international, mobile, and not subject to control, industrial policy and planning are futile if they focus on the domestic economy alone. Instead, government should improve the quality of labor through education and training, maintain labor market flexibility, and attract investment to Britain. Strict control of inflation and tough limits on public expenditure would promote both employment and investment opportunities. Economic policy should increase competitive strength through government–business partnerships and efforts to improve the skill of the workforce, and therefore the competitiveness of British industry.

The Coalition Government's Economic Policy

The centerpiece of the coalition government's approach to economic policy was its overarching commitment to deficit reduction as the necessary precondition for stabilizing the economy. Very soon after taking office, the coalition government engaged in a comprehensive spending review and a predictably harsh retrospective critique of the state of the economy that it inherited from New Labour. Given the still-fresh experience of the Great Recession caused by the global economic collapse of 2008, all eyes were turning to efforts to manage the politics of austerity in Britain.

New Labour Becomes Old Labour Once Again

By 2015, Ed Miliband, the leader of the Labour Party, was working hard (but not effectively) to establish his credibility on economic affairs even as the Conservatives were blaming Labour for the country's high debt and deficits, denying that Labour's plans would bring the deficits under control. After Miliband, things went from bad to worse as Corbyn, the new Labour leader, was unable to persuade anyone that he could orchestrate an alternative to the austerity measures that confounded British politics root and branch.

By all accounts, Theresa May has the fullest in-box of any newly installed prime minister in recent history. Alongside Brexit, managing the politics of austerity while securing sustainable economic growth are at the top of her agenda.

Social Policy

Historically, in the United Kingdom, welfare state provisions have interfered relatively little in the workings of the market, and policymakers do not see the reduction of group inequalities as the proper goal of the welfare state. In fact, through changes in government, there has been considerable continuity across the period of postwar consensus despite differences in perspectives on the welfare state. Thatcher assailed the principles of the welfare state enshrined by the collectivist era but accepted many of its policies. New Labour attempted to link social expenditures to improving skills, making everyone a stakeholder in society, and tried hard—with only limited success—to turn social policy into an instrument for improving education, skills, and competitiveness.

In 2016, in the first review of UK social policy since 2009, the UN Committee on Economic, Social, and Cultural Rights expressed "serious concerns" about growing inequality in the United Kingdom following 6 years of austerity policies under the Conservative government and the coalition that preceded it. The report's authors noted "the various changes in the entitlements to, and cuts in, social benefits," which it said disproportionately affected women, young people, ethnic minorities, and disabled people. The report was completed before the United Kingdom voted to leave the European Union, and since the vote, there has been a 57 percent spike in the number of reported hate crimes against migrants and ethnic minorities, according to the National Police Chiefs' Council.

Compared to the rest of Europe, the UK welfare state offers few comprehensive services, and the policies are not very generous. The lone exception is the National Health Service (NHS), which provides comprehensive and universal medical care and has long been championed as the jewel in the crown of the welfare state in Britain because it provides fine, low-cost medical care to all British citizens as a right. Despite periodic infusions of cash to temporarily stabilize it, the NHS is chronically underfunded, general practitioners are woefully underpaid, and it faces some of the same challenges as the United States in terms of managing health care costs, the excessive use of emergency rooms for medical care, and insufficient access to primary care physicians. According to a 2014 report of the European Commission, Britain has fewer doctors per capita than nearly all the other countries in the European Union.

Society and Economy

New Labour rejected both the cutbacks in social provisions of Conservative governments, which they characterized as mean-spirited, and the egalitarian traditions of Britain's collectivist era, which emphasized entitlements (or what in the United States is called "tax-and-spend liberalism"). Instead, New Labour focused its social policy on training and broader social investment as a more positive third-way alternative.

New Labour emphasized efficiencies and attempted to break welfare dependency. Its effort to identify comprehensive solutions to society's ills and reduce the tendency of government to let marginalized individuals fall by the wayside captures the third-way orientation of the New Labour project.

The economic upturn that began in 1992, combined with Major's moderating effects on the Thatcherite social policy agenda, narrowed inequality in the mid-1990s. Attention to social exclusion in its many forms and strong rates of growth were good omens for narrowing the gap between rich and poor. But even before the "Great Recession" of 2008, and despite New Labour's commitment to producing a more egalitarian society and reducing poverty, achieving success has proved very difficult.

UNICEF's report cards suggest that while the United Kingdom has made progress in addressing overall levels of child well-being since being ranked at the bottom of the chart in the early 2000s, its performance can be summed up as "could do better." The 2016 Report Card examines four domains of child well-being—income, education, health, and life satisfaction. Overall, the United Kingdom is ranked 14th out of 35 countries. It ranks in the middle of the pack in three of the four child well-being domains: 25th out of 37 on educational achievement gaps, 19th out of 35 on health gaps, and 20th out of 35 on life satisfaction gaps. In the plus column, however, the economic situations of the United Kingdom's poorest children did not dramatically fall following the recession.

Clear contrasts can be drawn here with many other countries hit hard by the economic crisis, particularly those in southern Europe. This reflects the comparatively strong role that social security benefits have played in protecting the incomes of many families with children in the United Kingdom. Indeed, across Europe, no other country's social security system does more to reduce the gap between the economic status of the poorest children and the average child. In a market-driven economy, however, it is extremely difficult for governments to effectively pursue goals such as eliminating childhood poverty, and social security protections for working-age people have been the major focal point of the United Kingdom's austerity agenda. Ongoing cuts to social security provisions are likely to affect the well-being of the poorest children in the United Kingdom in the future and to risk widening inequalities in child well-being still further.

Inequality and Ethnic Minorities

Ethnic minorities disproportionately suffer diminished opportunity in the United Kingdom. Despite the common and often disparaging references to ethnic minority individuals as "immigrants," members of ethnic minority groups in Britain are increasingly native-born. Today, fully one-third of the children born in England and Wales have at least one foreign-born parent—a figure that has risen by 21 percent since 2000—and in four London boroughs (Newham, Brent, Westminster, and Kensington and Chelsea), that number is 8 out of 10. Britain is positioned to become the most ethnically diverse Western nation by 2050. Unfortunately, this does not mean that it has resolved the challenges of social exclusion and marginalization of its ethnic minority members, and anti-immigrant sensibilities were a key factor in the Brexit vote.

Ethnic minorities, particularly young men, are subject to unequal treatment by the police and considerable physical harassment by citizens. They have experienced cultural isolation, as well as marginalization in the educational system, job training, housing, and labor markets. There is considerable concern about the apparent rise in racially motivated crime in major metropolitan areas with significant ethnic diversity.

Poor rates of economic success reinforce the sense of isolation and distinct collective identities, although in recent years the number of ethnic minority workers in the British workforce has soared to record levels. According to 2016 statistics from the Department for Work and Pensions (DWP), there are 670,000 more black and minority ethnic (BME) workers in employment in Great Britain than in 2010—an increase of around 24 percent. Of the ethnic minority population aged 16 to 24, 62 percent were in full-time education or work in 2015, compared to 43 percent of the entire population in that age bracket. The employment rate gap—the difference between the employment rates of the ethnic minority population and the overall population—has decreased by 0.5 percent since 2014. Women have played a role in this increase; statistics show that 109,000 more women from an ethnic minority have entered the workforce since 2014. The Pakistani and Bangladeshi populations have also seen a significant increase in employment rates, from around 42 percent in 2005 to a high of almost 55 percent in 2015.

DWP statistics show that people from ethnic minority groups are more likely to be employed in accommodation and food services, wholesale and retail trade, transportation and storage, and human health and social work. They are less likely to be employed in the manufacturing, construction, and education sectors. These same figures showed that there is slightly higher diversity among the male workforce than for females, with almost one in eight men of working age now from an ethnic minority background.

Inequality and Women

The United Kingdom's stubbornly wide gender pay gap is well known. Almost half a century after the Equal Pay Act of 1970, there is still an 18.1 percent difference in average pay between men and women. According to data from the Office of National Statistics (ONS) released in April 2016, while the gender pay gap for full-time employees has narrowed to 9.4 percent (the lowest it has been since the survey began in 1997), and the part-time gender pay gap has decreased from −6.8 percent in April 2015 to −6.0 percent in April 2016, there is evidence that the part-time gender pay gap has widened in the long term. While only 12 percent of men work part time, 41 percent of women do, leading to a major disparity. In addition, the gap is expected to widen as public sector cuts increase the number and percentage of women moving into the private sector—where the gender gap is greater than in the public sector. According to a 2016 study by Deloitte, the business advisory firm, unless action is taken to tackle it now, the hourly pay gap between men and women will not close until 2069.

Nor is the gender gap in the economy the only expression of gender bias in Britain. Despite the legal recognition of equality between women and men and the growing empowerment of women in nearly all spheres of social and political life in the United Kingdom—witness the recent election of Theresa May as Prime Minister—readily observable differences in the treatment and experiences of women and men persist. As every student reading this text knows instinctively, the terrain of gender in every society produces complicated evidence about the role of women in society. Where family dynamics and cultural habits intersect, however, gender divisions remain strong. Although women are far more likely to shoulder the additional burdens of childcare, eldercare, and housework, recent UK policy has favorably affected women's role. In 2013, the government implemented policies to provide early learning facilities for the 20 percent most disadvantaged 2-year-olds, and in 2014, it introduced early learning facilities for roughly 40 percent of all 2-year-olds. Clearly, these policies reduce the strain on women (and the increasing numbers of men) who juggle the responsibilities of work and family.

Environmental Issues

In Britain, as in much of the United States, recent extreme weather events have provoked intense debate about environmental issues. In 2013–2014, Britons suffered through the worst storms and tidal surges in 60 years on the North Sea coastline, with floods ruining Christmas and sparking intensified (and increasingly politicized and hostile) debate within the government and the scientific community about the role played by climate change in environmental disasters. In January 2017, London was put on "very high" pollution alert for the first time ever, after cold air and a stationary air pattern failed to clear the toxic air caused by diesel traffic and the high use of open fires. Some made comparisons to the Great Smog of December 1952, when fumes from factories and house chimneys were thought to have killed as many as 12,000 Londoners. The recent spike in air pollution has led London's mayor, Sadiq Khan, to announce a range of environmental policies for the capital, including expanding central London's low-emission zone, imposing a toxicity charge of $12/day for high-polluting vehicles, and introducing environmentally friendly cars and low-emission bus zones.

In general, the British public has expressed increasing concern about a variety of environmental issues, including acid rain, fracking, and the safety of the food supply. Environmental policy is hotly contested in the United Kingdom, perhaps most dramatically in 2009, when scientists at the University of East Anglia were accused of manipulating data to overstate the dangers of climate change, a controversy nicknamed "Climategate." In 2012, the UK government produced the first of what are intended to be 5-year climate risk assessment reports.

In general, environmental policy has reflected a cross-party consensus, although Labour has been accused by critics of an urban bias that neglects the needs of rural areas, a view exacerbated in 2013–2014 by the slow and ineffective response to extreme weather. Recently, Jeremy Corbyn pushed hard for a commitment to generate 65 percent of Britain's electricity from renewable resources by 2030, but it is not clear whether his specific proposals to make that target are in fact feasible.

Margaret Thatcher once led the world on environmental policy, particularly regarding the restoration of the ozone layer. Sadly the same cannot be said of Theresa May's approach to the current climate crisis. Her promise to ratify the Paris Agreement trailed the announcements of China and the United States, and she still hedges her bets on the all-important question of timing. In 2008, May was praised by the executive director of Friends of the Earth for her part in pushing the Climate Change Bill through Parliament. Since coming to power, however, her policies have failed to show much corresponding leadership on green issues. In fact, so far, the moves that her ministers have made seem to be taking their lead from business instead. In general, despite the professed cross-party commitment to effective environmental policy, tensions remain between a growing desire of many in Britain to "think Green" and the anti-regulatory, pro-business bias that makes effective environmental policy more difficult.

foreign direct investment (FDI)

Ownership of or investment in cross-border enterprises in which the investor plays a direct managerial role.

Britain in the Global Economy

Foreign direct investment (FDI) favors national systems, like those of Britain (and the United States), that rely mostly on private, contractual, and market-driven arrangements. Because of low costs, a business-friendly political climate, government-sponsored financial incentives, reduced trade union power, and a large pool of potential nonunionized recruits, the United Kingdom is a highly regarded location in Europe for FDI. Almost 1,600 new jobs a week were created by FDI between 2015 and 2016. Demonstrating Britain's attractiveness to an ever-widening pool of global investors, investments originated from a record 79 countries, and it became the top European destination for projects from emerging markets. Projects from Latin America rose by 240 percent, and those from Central and Eastern Europe surged by 131 percent.

The United Kingdom scores well in international comparisons of micro-economic competitiveness and growth competitiveness. It has also achieved significant competitive success in particular pockets of science-based, high-technology industries. Even before the Great Recession, however, the picture of UK global competitiveness was clouded by weak industrial performance. Gordon Brown's Britain preached a globalization-friendly model of flexible labor markets throughout the European Union, and its success in boosting Britain's economic performance in comparison with the rest of Europe won some reluctant admirers. However, under New Labour, Britain achieved an enviable record of growth, low inflation, and low unemployment, in part because of its sustained commitment to attract foreign investment and to assume an outward-looking competitive profile.

Of course, that international market-driven orientation of the British economy, combined with a hands-off antiregulatory approach, exposed Britons to enormous risk and a very severe downturn, with reverberating political consequences, when the global recession engulfed Britain in 2008. Until the Great Recession, the British economy exhibited an enviable growth model that was fueled by ready access to consumer credit and by the simultaneous "fool's paradise" of low interest rates, inflated housing values, low inflation, and highly questionable lending practices.[2]

Under the woeful conditions that the coalition government faced from its first days in office, its options for governing the economy were very limited. Rejecting the temptation to stimulate the economy through government spending, budgetary cuts were the first, second, and third priority, and effective economic management proved to be a daunting challenge that Cameron's coalition government was not able to meet. Britain's decision to exit the European Union raised the stakes even higher for the May government.

Left on its own to forge new trade agreements with Europe and the United States, Britain is in uncharted global economic waters. Will Theresa May be the next Margaret Thatcher and revitalize the special relationship between Britain and the United States to counteract the economic consequences of the strong break from Europe? Can she renegotiate Britain's trade relations with European countries on Britain's terms?

Where Do You Stand?

Will Theresa May be remembered for her canny ability to redefine the special relationship in the hothouse environment of the Trump administration?

How can Labour restore attention to issues of class and economic inequality to a credible economic policy in a global age?

GOVERNANCE AND POLICYMAKING

- What are the strengths and weaknesses of parliamentary democracy?

- How has the devolution of powers from the UK Parliament to Wales, Scotland, and Northern Ireland changed both the organizing principles of the state and politics in the United Kingdom?

The British constitution is notable for two features: its form and its age. Britain lacks a formal written constitution in the usual sense. There is no single unified and authoritative text (like the U.S. Constitution) that has special status above ordinary law and can be amended only by special procedures. Rather, the British constitution is a combination of statutory law (mainly acts of Parliament), common law, convention, and authoritative interpretations. Although it is often said that Britain has an unwritten constitution, this is not accurate. Authoritative legal treatises are written, of course, as are the much more significant acts of Parliament that define crucial elements of the political system. These acts define the powers of Parliament and its relationship with the monarchy, the rights governing the relationship between state and citizen, the relationship of constituent nations to the United Kingdom, the relationship of the United Kingdom to the European Union, and many other rights and legal arrangements. In fact, "What distinguishes the British constitution from others is not that it is unwritten, but rather that it is part written and uncodified."[3]

The conventions and acts of Parliament with constitutional implications began at least as early as the seventeenth century, notably with the Bill of Rights of 1689, which helped define the relationship between the monarchy and Parliament. "Britain's constitution presents a paradox," a British scholar of constitutional history has observed. "We live in a modern world but inhabit a pre-modern, indeed, ancient, constitution."[4]

Constitutional authorities have accepted the structure and principles of many areas of government for so long that the very appeal to convention itself has enormous cultural force. Thus, widely agreed-on rules of conduct, rather than law or U.S.-style checks and balances, set the limits of governmental power. Absolute principles of government are few, but those that exist are fundamental to the organization of the state and central to governance, policymaking, and patterns of representation. It will become clear in this discussion, however, that even the most time-encrusted principles of Britain's ancient constitutional traditions are subject to quick and potentially radical changes.

Organization of the State

The core of the British system is **parliamentary sovereignty**: to wit, Parliament can make or overturn any law; the executive, the judiciary, and the throne have no authority to restrict, veto, or otherwise overturn parliamentary action. In a classic **parliamentary democracy**, the prime minister is answerable to the House of Commons (the elected element of Parliament) and may be dismissed by it. That said, by joining the European Economic Community (EEC) in 1973 (now known as the *European Union*), Parliament accepted significant limitations on its power to act. It acknowledged that European law had force in the United Kingdom, without requiring parliamentary assent, and that European law overrode British law. It was in

parliamentary sovereignty

The doctrine that grants the legislature the power to make or overturn any law and permits no veto or judicial review.

parliamentary democracy

A system of government in which the chief executive is answerable to the legislature and may be dismissed by it.

no small measure the wish to escape the economic and legal encumbrances imposed by Britain's participation in the European Union that prompted the Brexit referendum.

Second, Britain has long been a **unitary state**. By contrast to the United States, where powers not delegated to the national government are reserved for the states, no powers are reserved constitutionally for subcentral units of government in the United Kingdom. However, the Labour government of Tony Blair introduced a far-reaching program of constitutional reform that created a quasi-federal system. Specified powers have been delegated (the British prefer to say *devolved*) to legislative bodies in Scotland and Wales, and to Northern Ireland as well, now that the long-standing conflict there seems settled. On September 18, 2014, the people of Scotland narrowly voted to remain as part of the United Kingdom, leaving the issues that prompted the referendum for Scottish independence unresolved. Eager to take charge of their own political destiny (and considerable financial resources) those who voted for Scottish independence expressed strong disagreements with both major parties in the United Kingdom on a range of economic and political issues.

Third, Britain has a system of **fusion of powers** at the national level: Parliament is the supreme legislative, executive, and judicial authority and includes the monarch, as well as the House of Commons and the House of Lords. The fusion of legislature and executive is also expressed in the function and personnel of the cabinet. U.S. presidents can direct or ignore their cabinets, which have no constitutionally mandated function, but the British cabinet bears enormous constitutional responsibility. Through collective decision-making, the cabinet—not an independent prime minister—shapes, directs, and takes responsibility for government. This core tenet, **cabinet government** may at critical junctures be observed more in principle than in practice, however. Particularly with strong prime ministers, such as Thatcher and Blair, who can rally—or bully—the cabinet, power gravitates to the prime minister.

Britain is a **constitutional monarchy**. The Crown passes by hereditary succession, but the government or state officials exercise nearly all powers of the Crown. Parliamentary sovereignty, parliamentary democracy, and cabinet government form the core of the British or Westminster model of government.

The Executive

The term *cabinet government* emphasizes the key functions that the cabinet exercises: responsibility for policymaking, supreme control of government, and coordination of all government departments. However, the term does not capture the full range of executive institutions, nor the scale and complexity of operations, nor the realities of a system in which power invariably flows upward to the prime minister. In addition, the executive reaches well beyond the cabinet. It extends from ministries (departments) and ministers to the civil service in one direction, and to Parliament (as we shall see in Section 4) in the other direction.

Cabinet Government

After a general election, the Crown invites the leader of the party that emerges from the election with control of a majority of seats in the House of Commons to form a government and serve as prime minister. The prime minister selects approximately two dozen ministers for the cabinet. Senior cabinet posts include the Foreign Office

unitary state

In contrast to a federal system, a system of government in which no powers are reserved for subnational units of government.

fusion of powers

A constitutional principle that merges the authority of branches of government, in contrast to the principle of separation of powers.

cabinet government

A system of government in which most executive power is held by the cabinet, headed by a prime minister.

constitutional monarchy

A system of government in which the head of state ascends by heredity but is limited in powers and constrained by the provisions of a constitution.

(equivalent to the U.S. secretary of state), the Home Office (ministry of justice or attorney general), and the chancellor of the exchequer (finance minister). Unlike the French Constitution, which prohibits a cabinet minister from serving in the legislature, British constitutional tradition requires overlapping membership between Parliament and cabinet. A member of the cabinet must be either a member of the House of Commons or, less often, a member of the House of Lords.

The cabinet room at 10 Downing Street (the prime minister's official residence) is a place of intrigue as well as deliberation. From the prime minister's viewpoint, the cabinet may appear as loyal followers or as ideological combatants, potential challengers for party leadership, and parochial advocates for pet programs that run counter to the overall objectives of the government. By contrast, the convention of collective responsibility normally unifies the cabinet. In principle, the prime minister must gain the support of a majority of the cabinet for a range of significant decisions, notably the budget and the legislative program.

The only other constitutionally mandated mechanism for checking the prime minister is the government's defeat on a vote of no confidence in the House of Commons (discussed further in Section 4). Since the defeat of a government by Parliament is rare and politically dangerous, the cabinet remains the only routine check on the prime minister.

Margaret Thatcher often attempted to galvanize loyalists in the cabinet and either marginalize or expel detractors. In the end, her treatment of the cabinet, which stretched British constitutional conventions, helped inspire the movement to unseat her as party leader. Her successor, John Major, returned to a more consultative approach.

Tony Blair, like Thatcher, narrowed the scope of collective responsibility. The prime minister, a few key cabinet members, and a handful of advisers made many important policy decisions in small, unofficial gatherings. The decision to go to war in Iraq, for example, underscored the cabinet's weakened capacity to exercise constitutional checks and balances. Skeptical about the effectiveness and centrality of the cabinet, as well as cabinet committees, Blair preferred to coordinate strategically important policy areas through highly politicized special units in the Cabinet Office. Under David Cameron, the role of the cabinet returned to its more traditional role of consultation and advice.

How does Theresa May run her cabinet? Due to her extensive experience in the Home Office, undoubtedly she has a clear understanding of the role of the prime minister, and unlike Cameron, she is not operating in a coalition government and has the united support of the Conservative Party. The cabinet operates within a broader cabinet system, or *core executive* (see Figure 2.4), and the prime minister controls many of the levers of power in the core executive. Because the prime minister is the head of the cabinet, his or her office helps develop policy, coordinates operations, and functions as a liaison with the media, the party, interest groups, and Parliament.

Cabinet committees (comprising ministers) and official committees (made up of civil servants) supplement the work of the cabinet. In addition, the treasury plays an important coordinating role through its budgetary control. The Cabinet Office supports day-to-day operations. Leaders in both the House of Commons and the House of Lords, the *whips*, smooth the passage of legislation sponsored by the government. Given that the government always has a working majority (except when the government declares a "free vote," which signals that a matter is either too controversial or too inconsequential to be introduced on behalf of the government), the outcome of a vote is seldom in doubt.

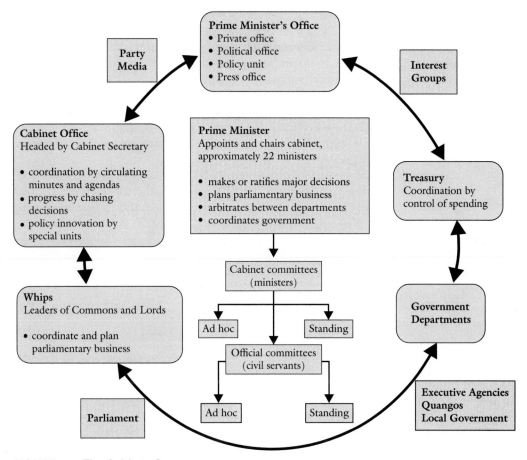

FIGURE 2.4 The Cabinet System
The cabinet is supported by a set of institutions that help formulate policy, coordinate operations, and facilitate support for government policy. Acting within a context set by the fusion of legislature and executive, the prime minister enjoys a great opportunity for decisive leadership that is lacking in a system of checks and balances and separation of powers among the branches of government.

Source: From Dennis Kavanagh, *British Politics: Continuities and Change*, 4th ed. (Oxford: Oxford University Press, 2000), p. 41. Data originally from HM Treasury Budget Bulletin.

Because the cabinet system and the core executive concentrate power at the top, London does not suffer from Washington-style gridlock. The risk in the United Kingdom is the opposite—excessive concentration of power by a prime minister who is prepared to manipulate cabinet and flout the conventions of collective responsibility.

Bureaucracy and Civil Service

Policymaking may appear to be increasingly concentrated in the prime minister's hands. When viewed from Whitehall (the London street where key UK units of government and administration are located), however, the executive may appear to be dominated by its vast administrative agencies. The range and complexity of state policymaking mean that the cabinet's authority must be shared with a vast set of unelected officials. Government departments are directed by members of the cabinet. Ministers are assisted by a very senior career civil servant, called a *permanent secretary*, who has chief administrative responsibility for running a department. Other senior civil servants, including deputy secretaries and undersecretaries, assist the permanent secretaries. In addition, the minister reaches into his or her department to appoint a principal private secretary, an up-and-coming civil servant who assists the minister as gatekeeper and liaison with senior civil servants.

Since nearly all legislation is introduced on behalf of the government and presented as the policy directive of a ministry, civil servants in Britain do much of the work of conceptualizing and refining legislation. (In the United States, committee staffers in Congress often perform this job.) Civil servants, more than ministers, assume operational duties.

As a result of the ongoing modernization of Whitehall, the civil service has been downsized and given a new corporate structure. Few at the top of these agencies (i.e., agency chief executives) are traditional career civil servants. There is growing

THE U.S. CONNECTION

Comparing the U.S. Presidential System to the British Parliamentary System

Political scientists—especially those engaged in comparative politics—often discuss how the design of political institutions affects political outcomes. Among the institutional differences that matter most is the distinction between presidential systems, such as that of the United States, and parliamentary systems, such as that of the United Kingdom.

In a presidential system, the legislature and executive are independent. Both the legislature and the chief executive have their own fixed schedules for election and their own political mandates. Legislators and presidents have been elected independent of each other. They have different constituencies and often have different political agendas. Each may even gain credibility and support by opposing the other. In presidential systems, the agenda and the authority of the president are often compromised when the president and the majority of legislators are from different parties—in fact, this is the rule rather than the exception in the United States and in many other presidential systems. Stalemates on key items of legislation are common. Between presidential elections, it is very difficult to remove a president, even one who has very little popular support or is suspected of acting unconstitutionally. It requires impeachment, which, in turn, requires a finding of extraordinary misconduct and a strong majority vote in the legislature.

Prime ministers, in contrast, must enjoy the support of the majority of the legislature to achieve office—and they must preserve that support to stay in office since prime ministers and their governments can fall if they lose a vote of no confidence in the legislature. Furthermore, in a parliamentary system, the timing of elections is typically not fixed (although the Cameron government has modified this rule to establish a 5-year, fixed-term Parliament). When riding high, the prime minister can call for a new election in an effort to win a new mandate and a deeper majority in Parliament. When in trouble, a prime minister can be sent packing in an instant through a vote of no confidence.

In a parliamentary system like Britain's, because the legislators and prime minister sink or swim together, they tend to cooperate and work through differences. In a presidential system like that of the United States, because the legislature and executive are mutually independent—one can swim, while the other sinks—the tendency for finger-pointing and stalemate is much greater.

But the distinctions should not be exaggerated. Powerful prime ministers such as Thatcher and Blair were routinely criticized for being too presidential. And in Britain, the threat that a prime minister faces of losing office through a vote of no confidence has all but disappeared—it has happened only once in more than 80 years. In fact, if recent history is a good predictor, an American president is more likely to face a bill of impeachment than a British prime minister is to face a serious vote of no confidence.

MAKING CONNECTIONS Is a parliamentary system more or less effective than a presidential system?

This analysis draws heavily from Alfred Stepan, with Cindy Skatch, "Constitutional Frameworks and Democratic Consolidation: Parliamentarism Versus Presidentialism," in Mark Kesselman and Joel Krieger, eds., *Readings in Comparative Politics: Political Challenges and Changing Agendas* (Boston: Houghton Mifflin, 2006), pp. 284–293.

Dan Kitwood/Getty Images

concern that the increasing importance of special advisers (who are both political policy advisers and civil servants) is eroding the impartiality of civil servants. Key special advisers played critical roles in making the case in the famous "dodgy dossier" of September 2002, alleging that the threat of weapons of mass destruction justified regime change in Iraq.

Public and Semipublic Institutions

Like other countries, Britain has institutionalized "semipublic" agencies, which are sanctioned by the state but lack direct democratic oversight. Examples include nationalized industries and nondepartmental public bodies.

Nationalized Industries The nationalization of basic industries—such as coal, iron and steel, and gas and electricity—was a central objective of the Labour government during the postwar collectivist era. By the end of the Thatcher era, the idea of public ownership had clearly run out of steam, and most of these giant state enterprises were privatized (i.e., sold to private, large-scale investors or sold in small units to ordinary citizens), as was the case with British Telecom (BT), the communications giant. More than 50 percent of the BT shares were sold to the public. When thinking of expanding state functions, we can look to a set of semipublic administrative organizations.

Nondepartmental Public Bodies Since the 1970s, an increasing number of administrative functions have been transferred to bodies that are typically part of the state in terms of funding, function, and appointment of staff, but operate at arm's length from ministers.

These nondepartmental public bodies (NDPBs) are better known as quasi-nongovernmental organizations, or **quangos**. They take responsibility for specific functions and can combine governmental and private-sector expertise. At the same time, they enable ministers to distance themselves from controversial areas of policy.

quango

The acronym for *quasi-nongovernmental organization*, the term used in Britain for a nonelected body that is outside traditional governmental departments or local authorities.

Alongside quangos, in recent years, the government has looked for ways to expand the investment of the private sector in capital projects such as hospitals and schools. Thus, New Labour continued the private finance initiative (PFI) that it inherited from the Conservatives as a key part of its signature modernization program and as a way to revitalize public services. The results have been controversial. Critics and supporters disagree about the quality of services provided and about whether taxpayers win or lose by the financial arrangements. In addition, the tendency of PFIs to blur the line between public and private raises important and controversial issues.[5] As of 2015, the United Kingdom owed more than 222 billion pounds ($275 billion)—a startling figure described by experts as a "financial disaster"—to banks and businesses as a result of these PFIs.

Other State Institutions

The Military and the Police

Those involved in security and law enforcement have enjoyed a rare measure of popular support in Britain. Constitutional tradition and professionalism distance the British police and military from politics.

In the case of the military, British policy since the Cold War remains focused on a gradually redefined set of North Atlantic Treaty Organization (NATO) commitments. Still ranked among the top five military powers in the world, Britain retains a global presence. In 1999, the United Kingdom strongly backed NATO's Kosovo campaign and pressed for ground troops. According to Blair, global interdependence rendered isolationism obsolete and inspired a commitment to a new ethical dimension in foreign policy. Throughout the war in Iraq and its bloody aftermath, Blair persistently sought to characterize Iraq as an extension of Kosovo—an effort to liberate Muslims from brutal dictatorships, whether Serbia's Slobodan Milosevic or Iraq's Saddam Hussein. Until Blair's decision to support the American plan to shift the main venue of the war on terror from Afghanistan to Iraq, the use of the military in international conflicts generated little opposition. It may be that the Iraq war was the exception that proved the rule that the United Kingdom could play an important role in the world of states, including the use of force, when justified, without losing public support. In 2011, the Cameron government played a leading role in the international effort, endorsed by the UN Security Council, to protect civilians and enhance the cause of rebels fighting the regime of Libyan dictator Muammar Gaddafi. Although Cameron enjoyed strong support for his decision to participate in the international coalition in the early stages, in August 2013, despite strong pressure from the United States and Cameron's best efforts, Parliament refused to authorize the use of force to quell the violence in Syria. More recently, however, Britain has joined the international coalition to defeat ISIS in Syria and to provide humanitarian aid to the region.

The police have traditionally operated as independent local forces throughout the country. Since the 1980s, the police have witnessed growth in government control, centralization, and level of political use. During the coal miners' strike of 1984–1985, the police operated to an unprecedented—and perhaps unlawful—degree as a national force coordinated through Scotland Yard (London police headquarters). Police menaced strikers and hindered miners from participating in strike support activities. This partisan use of the police in an industrial dispute flew in the face of constitutional traditions and offended some police officers and officials. During the 1990s, concerns about police conduct focused on police–community relations. These included race relations, corruption, and the interrogation and treatment of people held in custody.

The Judiciary

In Britain, the principle of parliamentary sovereignty has limited the role of the judiciary. Courts have no power to judge the constitutionality of legislative acts (**judicial review**). They can only determine whether policy directives or administrative acts violate common law or an act of Parliament. Hence, the British judiciary is generally less politicized and influential than its U.S. counterpart.

Jurists, however, have participated in the wider political debate outside court. They have headed royal commissions on the conduct of industrial relations, the struggle in riots over Northern Ireland in Britain's inner cities, and the suspicious death of a UN weapons inspector who challenged Blair's case for the war in Iraq. In recent years, Britain has witnessed dramatic institutional changes in law and the administration of justice, most notably the 2009 creation of the UK Supreme Court, which serves as the highest court of appeal, removing that authority from the House of Lords.

As a member of the European Union, Britain was bound to abide by the European Court of Justice (ECJ). For example, with the passage of the Human Rights Act in 1998, Britain was required to comply with the European Convention on Human Rights (ECHR). Also, the adoption of the ECHR forced Britain to curtail discrimination against gays in the military.

Subnational Government

The United Kingdom is a state comprising distinct nations (England, Scotland, Wales, and Northern Ireland). Because the British political framework has traditionally been unitary, not federal, for centuries, no formal powers devolved to either the nations within the United Kingdom or to subnational (really subcentral or sub-UK) units, as in the United States, Germany, or India. Historically, Parliament has asserted authority over all political units in the United Kingdom. No powers were reserved for any other unit of government: There are no states, and no powers were reserved for nations within the United Kingdom or for local government. Even so, nations were a significant aspect of collective identities in the United Kingdom, often exerting a powerful hold on their members. For many, to be Scottish or Welsh or English or Northern Irish was a core source of identity that created a sense of commonality and shared fates among members. Nations were not political units. But that is no longer true.

Recent constitutional reforms have introduced important modifications in the organizing principles of the United Kingdom. After referendums in Wales and Scotland in 1997, and in Northern Ireland and the Republic of Ireland (an independent country) in 1998, Blair's Labour government introduced a set of power-sharing arrangements (what the British call "devolution") to govern the arrangements among the UK Westminster Parliament, the Welsh Assembly, the Northern Ireland Assembly, and the Scottish Parliament. Finally, in 2014, Scottish voters narrowly defeated a referendum on Scottish independence.

In general, the UK government retains responsibility for all policy areas that have not been devolved and that are the traditional domain of nation-states. Westminster controls security and foreign policy, economic policy, trade, defense, and social

---

judicial review

The capacity of a high court to nullify actions by the executive and legislative branches of government that in its judgment violate the constitution.

security for the United Kingdom as a whole, except where it does not—that is, where specific powers have been ceded to Scotland, Northern Ireland, or Wales.

Of all the devolved nations and regions within the United Kingdom, Scotland and the Scottish government enjoy the most robust powers. Whereas Wales and Northern Ireland have relatively limited independent authority and have legislative arenas called *assemblies,* Scotland has a parliament and the Scottish government is responsible for crucial areas of policy, including education, health, and the administration of justice. Clearly, devolution involves both an element of federalism and a carefully crafted compromise. The UK Parliament is still the mother of all parliaments, but it has some potentially restive offspring!

It is important to note that every power devolved from the UK Parliament to the Scottish Parliament or the Welsh or Northern Ireland assembly chips away at the very core of parliamentary sovereignty that lies at the heart of the Westminster model. Devolution has also sparked a controversy about the asymmetry in voting rights that devolution produces.

What right should a Scottish MP have to vote on laws that might relate to England or Wales, while English and Welsh MPs cannot vote on some matters related to Scotland, in areas where policy had been devolved from the Westminster Parliament to the Scottish Parliament?

Devolution within England is also part of the reform process. Regional development agencies (RDAs) were introduced throughout England in 1999 to facilitate economic development at the regional level. Even though they are unelected bodies with no statutory authority, they have opened the door to popular mobilization in the long term for elected regional assemblies. In addition, the Blair government placed changes in the governance of London on the fast track. The introduction of a directly elected mayor of London in May 2000 marked an important reform, leading to the direct election of mayors in other major cities, such as Birmingham and putting into practice a process of decentralizing power.

The Policymaking Process

Parliamentary sovereignty is the core constitutional principle of the British political system. But for policymaking and policy implementation, the focus is not on Westminster, but rather on Whitehall.

The UK Parliament has little direct participation in policymaking. Policymaking emerges primarily from within the executive. There, decision-making is strongly influenced by policy communities—informal networks with extensive knowledge, access, and personal connections to those responsible for policy. In this private, hothouse environment, civil servants, ministers, and members of the policy communities work through informal ties. A cooperative style develops, as the ministry becomes an advocate for key players and civil servants may come to overidentify the public good with the advancement of policy within their area of responsibility.

Where Do You Stand?

Which is a more effective form of government: American checks and balances or British parliamentary democracy?

Does the strength of the cabinet and the power of the prime minister risk turning Britain into an elective dictatorship?

REPRESENTATION AND PARTICIPATION

As discussed in Section 3, parliamentary sovereignty is the core constitutional principle defining the role of the legislature and, in a sense, the whole system of British government. The executive or judiciary cannot set any act of Parliament aside, nor is any Parliament bound by the actions of any previous Parliament. Nevertheless, in practice, the control exerted by the House of Commons (or Commons)—the lower of the two houses of Parliament and by far the more powerful—is not unlimited. This section investigates the powers and role of Parliament, both the House of Commons and the House of Lords (or Lords). It also looks at the party system, elections, and contemporary currents in British political culture, citizenship, and identity. We close by offering an analysis of surprising new directions in political participation and social protest.

Focus Questions ⑦

• What are the political implications of Britain's departure from the European Union?

• How profoundly will Brexit transform Britain's historic model of parliamentary democracy?

The Legislature

Today, the Commons does not really legislate in a meaningful way. Its real function is to assent to government legislation since (with rare exceptions, such as the 2010 coalition government) a single governing party has a majority of the seats and can control the legislative agenda and pass legislation at will. In addition, the balance of effective oversight of policy has shifted from the legislature to executive agencies.

The House of Commons

The House of Commons, the lower house of Parliament, with 650 seats at the time of the 2017 election, exercises the main legislative power in Britain. Along with the two unelected elements of Parliament, the Crown and the House of Lords, the Commons has three main functions: (1) to pass laws, (2) to provide finances for the state by authorizing taxation, and (3) to review and scrutinize public administration and government policy.

In practical terms, the Commons has a limited legislative function. Nevertheless, it serves a very important democratic role. It provides a highly visible arena for policy debate and the partisan collision of political worldviews. The flash of rhetorical skills brings drama to Westminster. One crucial element of drama, however, is nearly always missing. The outcome is seldom in doubt. MPs from the governing party who consider rebelling against the leader of their respective parties or challenge the terms of the coalition agreement are understandably reluctant in a close and critical vote to force a general election. This would place their jobs in jeopardy. Only once since the defeat of Ramsay MacDonald's government in 1924 has a government been brought down by a defeat in the Commons (in 1979). Today, the balance of institutional power has shifted from Parliament to the governing party and the executive.

The Legislative Process

Bills must be introduced in the Commons and the Lords, although approval by the Lords is not required. Ideas for legislation come from political parties, pressure groups, think tanks, the prime minister's policy unit, or government departments. Proposed legislation, on behalf of the government, is then drafted by civil servants, circulated within Whitehall, approved by the cabinet, and then refined by the office of Parliamentary Counsel.

In the Commons, the bill usually comes to the floor three times. The bill is formally read upon introduction, printed, distributed, debated in general terms, and after an interval, given a second reading, followed by a vote. The bill then undergoes detailed review by a standing committee reflecting the overall party balance. It then goes through a report stage, during which new amendments may be introduced. In the third reading, the bill is considered in final form (and voted on) without debate.

A bill passed in the Commons follows a parallel path in the Lords. There, the bill is either accepted without change, amended, or rejected. The Lords passes bills concerning taxation or budgetary matters without alteration, but can add technical and editorial amendments to other bills (if approved by the Commons) to add clarity and precision. Finally, it receives royal assent (which is only a formality) and becomes an Act of Parliament.

The House of Lords

Traditionally, the House of Lords was a wholly unelected body comprised of hereditary peers (i.e., nobility of the rank of duke, marquis, earl, viscount, or baron), and life peers (appointed on the recommendation of the prime minister or the recently institutionalized House of Lords Appointment Commission). The Lords also includes the archbishops of Canterbury and York and some two dozen other bishops and archbishops of the Church of England. As part of a gradual reform agenda, in 1999, the right of all hereditary peers to sit and vote in the Lords was curtailed and that right limited to 92, pending further reform. In 2017 there were about 800 members eligible to take part in the work of the House of Lords.

The Lords serves mainly as a chamber of revision, providing expertise in redrafting legislation, with the power to suggest amendments to legislation in the Commons. The Lords can debate, refine, and delay—but not block—legislation. For example, in 2006, to protect the civil liberties of British Muslims, the Lords persuaded the Commons to water down a bill that prohibited incitement to violence on the grounds that the bill might be used to target Muslim clerics unfairly. It is interesting that when it comes to parliamentary reform, more attention has been paid in recent years to reform of the Lords—an issue that has repeatedly deadlocked, with multiple versions of reform in play, including the possibility of an elected upper chamber, which would bear some kinship to the U.S. Senate. Increasingly, the Lords engaged in unruly and inconclusive debate, challenging the coalition government on a variety of governance and substantive matters, for example, displaying firm resistance to reforms in the NHS and welfare benefits. It appears that in what might be the waning days of the House of Lords, members seem inclined to go out with a bang, not a whimper.

Reforms in Behavior

There have been a number of changes in the House of Commons, which, ironically, have been tamer than the potential changes afoot in the House of Lords. Since the 1970s, backbenchers (MPs of the governing party who have no governmental office and rank-and-file opposition members) have been markedly less deferential. A backbench rebellion against the Major government's EU policy in 1993, which was viewed by Thatcherites as dangerously pro-European, weakened the prime minister considerably and divided the party. In addition, one-third of Labour MPs defected on key votes authorizing the use of force in Iraq in 2003—a historic rebellion. Although more recently, in December 2016, the House of Commons held an emergency debate on international action to protect civilians in Aleppo and Syria, no clear plan of action emerged.

Structural Changes: Parliamentary Committees

In addition to the standing committees that routinely review bills, in 1979 the Commons extended the number and responsibilities of select committees, which help Parliament exert control over the executive by examining specific policies or aspects of administration.

The most controversial select committees monitor the major departments and ministries. Select committees hold hearings, take written and oral testimony, and question senior civil servants and ministers. Their reports have included strong policy recommendations at odds with government policy. These reforms have complicated the role of the civil service. Civil servants have been required to testify in a manner that may damage their ministers, revealing official culpability or flawed judgments. More significantly, in 2009, a tawdry scandal was uncovered that affected all the major parties. It concerned fraudulent claims by MPs (including ministers) for travel expenses and expenses for upkeep of extravagant homes away from London—in some cases, homes occupied by their lovers. The practice of fiddling expense accounts was widespread, and improprieties over expense accounts resulted in jail time in some cases.

Political Parties and the Party System

Britain is often referred to as a *two-party system,* but as the 2017 election made clear, that is a misnomer. It is true that from 1945 until the 2017 election, only leaders of the Labour or Conservative parties had served as prime ministers. And Conservative and Labour have been very closely matched. From 1945 through 2005, the Conservative and Labour parties each won eight general elections. In addition, throughout the postwar period, these two parties have routinely divided at least 85 percent of the seats in the Commons. But since the 1980s, the Liberal Democrats (Lib Dems) have become an important alternative. Britain also has several national parties: the Scottish National Party (SNP) in Scotland and the Plaid Cymru in Wales, as well as a roster of parties competing in Northern Ireland. The United Kingdom Independence Party (UKIP), founded in 1993 and initially dismissed as, in the words of David Cameron, "fruitcakes and loonies," has in recent years emerged as a powerful and disruptive force in British politics. The emergence of nationalist parties, combined with the increasing fragility of the two major parties, has increased the likelihood of coalition governments—as illustrated by the outcome of the 2017 elections.

The Labour Party

Fifty years ago, those not engaged in manual labor voted Conservative three times more commonly than they did Labour. More than two out of three manual workers, by contrast, voted Labour. Britain then conformed to one classic pattern of a Western European party system: a two-class/two-party system.

Since the mid-1970s, significant changes have developed in the party system, such as the decline in class-based voting and a growing disaffection with the moderate social democracy associated with the Keynesian welfare state. The Labour Party suffered from divisions between its trade unionist and parliamentary elements, constitutional wrangling over the power of trade unions to determine party policy at annual conferences, and disputes over how the leader would be selected. Divisions spilled over into foreign policy issues.

The 1980s and 1990s witnessed relative harmony within the party. Moderate trade union and parliamentary leadership agreed on major policy issues. Labour became a moderate, center-left party. Under the leadership of Tony Blair, Labour was rebranded as "New Labour," although its formal name stayed the same. After the party's defeat in the 2010 election, two close-knit brothers who had served in the cabinet, David Miliband, with close ties to Blair as foreign minister, and Ed Miliband, with close ties to Brown and former Secretary of State for Climate Change, were the top contenders to succeed Gordon Brown. In a dramatic contest for leadership of the Labour Party in September 2010, Ed Miliband, the younger brother, prevailed in a very close election, signaling a turn away from New Labour and an effort to turn the party in a more progressive direction. Miliband tried with only moderate success to rally the base, particularly among trade unionists and public-sector employees, who were feeling the pinch the hardest under the austerity policies of the Coalition government.

Jeremy Corbyn, elected leader of the Labour Party in 2015, has taken it into uncharted waters, moving it sharply to the left and inviting controversy over his support for the Palestinians. In the 2017 snap election, Corbyn surprised everyone with the fervor of his campaigning, and under his leadership, Labour managed to pick up 30 seats, effectively thwarting May's attempts to consolidate her conservative majority. It remains to be seen how Corbyn's Labour party can build on these recent electoral successes to develop a fitting alternative to the more centrist vision of "New Labour."

The Conservative Party

The Conservative Party dates back to the eighteenth century. Its pragmatism, flexibility, and organizational capabilities have made it one of the most successful and, at times, innovative center-right parties in Europe.

In 2003, the combative and experienced Michael Howard took over as party leader. For a time, the Conservatives seemed revitalized. But it was not easy for Howard to translate his assured performance from the front bench in Parliament into popular support, as effective opposition to New Labour proved elusive. Despite an energetic campaign in 2005, one likely to be remembered for the Conservatives' playing of the race and ethnicity card, electoral defeat led to his quick resignation. In December 2005, the Conservatives elected David Cameron as party leader in a landslide.

Cameron wasted little time in reorienting the party, modernizing its appeal, and reaching out beyond its traditional core values. He acknowledged that New Labour had been right in understanding the mood of Britain and right, also, to insist on achieving both social justice and economic success. Cameron also promised to reduce poverty both in Britain and globally, take on reducing climate change as a priority, and ensure security from terrorism. A testament to Blair's success, Cameron worked hard to reposition the Conservatives as a more centrist party that could compete effectively with post-Blair New Labour across the economic and social spectrum.

In a speech to the Conservative Party conference in October 2016, Theresa May outlined her vision of the Conservative Party. While praising Cameron's efforts at modernizing the party, she emphasized the need for it to change once again in light of the "quiet revolution" that voted to exit the European Union. The list of former British leaders with which she ended her speech (Benjamin Disraeli, Winston Churchill, Clement Attlee, and Margaret Thatcher) provides an interesting window into the influences that have formed her political identity and the agenda that she plans to pursue. Ideologically, May is difficult to place, with right-wing policies on immigration and education, a left-leaning attack on the excesses of the business community, and a populist concern for the growing inequality in society.

Liberal Democrats

Through the 1970s, the Liberal Party was the only centrist challenger to the Labour and Conservative parties. Since the 1980s, a changing roster of centrist parties posed an increasingly significant threat to the two-party dominance of Conservative and Labour. In 1981, the Social Democratic Party (SDP) formed out of a split within the Labour Party. After the Conservative victory in 1987, the Liberal Party and most of the SDP merged to form the Social and Liberal Democratic Party (now called the Liberal Democrats, or Lib Dems), which quickly emerged as a major political player.

In the 2001 general election, the party increased its vote tally by nearly one-fifth and won fifty-two seats, the most gained by a centrist third party since 1929. This success positioned the party as a potentially powerful center-left critic of New Labour. That said, at least until Blair's fortunes declined, Labour did not make it easy for them. As the Blair government began to spend massively to improve education and health care—an approach that would come to haunt them later—it narrowed the range of policy issues on which the Liberal Democrats could challenge New Labour. Party leader Charles Kennedy won the political gamble that he took in spring 2003 by opposing the war in Iraq, but it was not easy to take electoral advantage of Blair's political weakness. For a time, the fortunes of the Liberal Dems declined.

In December 2007, after two leadership turnovers, Nick Clegg, a 40-year-old ex-journalist and former member of the European Parliament, took over leadership of the Liberal Democrats. Clegg and his party faced an uphill battle to make the Lib Dems a serious contender in time for the 2010 election. But fueled by the country's fatigue with New Labour, combined with post-9/11 and 7/7 concerns about the erosion of civil liberties and Clegg's energetic and confident leadership, in fall 2008, Clegg launched a campaign to knock on 1 million doors to connect with ordinary citizens. The effort quickly catapulted the Liberal Democrats into serious contention.

In the wake of the Brexit vote, the Liberal Democrats have become increasingly focused on the needs of Britain's business community. On the day that the debate took place in Parliament to trigger Article 50 (which allows Britain to leave the European Union), Liberal Democrat MPs and Peers held a "Business and Brexit day," which specifically focused on meeting businesses and business leaders from across the country and addressing their concerns.

The unfamiliar terrain of the 2010 coalition government led many to be concerned that the two-party system in Britain was eroding. Some anticipated the emergence of a two-and-and-a-half party system, or even a more fluid multiparty system, with an enhanced role for less mainstream parties. This prospect provoked considerable handwringing, notably with reference to the far-right British National Party, which placed their first members in the European Parliament in 2009, and the UKIP, which, drawing on a deep reservoir of Britain's Euroskepticism, pushed Labour into third place.

Despite a broad but apparently shallow commitment to an environmentally responsible Britain, the Green Party performed badly in 2010, winning only one seat; meanwhile, the BNP and UKIP secured no seats. Even though radical right parties have not had the success in Britain that they have enjoyed in the rest of Europe, the UKIP's influence increased in recent years, especially thanks to its support for Brexit. However, its victory in promoting Brexit had the paradoxical effect of weakening its support once it had achieved its goal. It fared very poorly in the 2017 election and, in part due to the UK's "first past the post" voting system, failed to secure a single seat in Parliament

Elections

British general elections are exclusively for seats in the House of Commons. The prime minister is not directly elected as prime minister, but as an MP from a single constituency (electoral district). The queen invites the leader of the party that can control a majority in the Commons to become prime minister. Constituencies vary widely in size, but the average number of voters remains roughly comparable.

Traditionally, Parliament had a maximum life of 5 years, with no fixed term. The 2010 coalition agreement resulted in passage of the Fixed-Term Parliament Act of 2011, providing that parliamentary general elections must be held every 5 years, beginning in 2015. A vote of no confidence in the government, however, or a two-thirds majority vote in the House of Commons can still trigger a general election at any time. It was the latter that allowed Theresa May to call for a snap election in June 2017.

The Electoral System and the 2010 Election

Election for representatives in the Commons (MPs) is by a "first-past-the-post" principle in each constituency. In this single-member plurality system, the candidate who receives the most votes is elected. There is no requirement of a majority and no element of proportional representation (a system in which each party is given a percentage of seats in a representative assembly roughly comparable to its percentage of the popular vote).

This winner-take-all electoral system tends to exaggerate the size of the victory of the largest party and to reduce the influence of regionally dispersed lesser parties. This system is praised for increasing the chances that a party or coalition of parties will gain a majority of parliamentary seats and therefore form a stable government. Critics of the electoral system, however, charge that it does not give adequate representation to minority opinion.

hung parliament

A situation after an election when no single party comprises a majority in the Commons.

Contrary to the typical tendency of the winner-take-all electoral system, the 2010 election resulted in a **hung parliament** (a situation after an election when no single party comprises a majority in the Commons). Only after a quick set of negotiations could an arrangement be found to form a coalition government. Thus, 2010 was one for the record books. On the one hand, it was the exception that proves the rule. Ordinarily, Britain exhibits a stable, two-party-dominant system (Conservative and Labour), with support for a third party (Liberal Democrat) spread widely across the country, but too thinly for the party to win a substantial number of seats. The Liberal Democrats needed an exceptional stroke of luck to buck the trend—and they got it in 2010. The campaign by the Tories (Conservatives) peaked early, failed to inspire, and could not convince the electorate that they had the experience or were equipped to handle the enormous challenges of the economic downturn. Meanwhile, with Blair fatigue, an unpopular successor in Gordon Brown, and a failing economy, New Labour never really stood a chance to win the election outright.

The first televised debates ever in UK politics certainly enlivened the campaign. They also initially fueled a surge in popularity for the telegenic and media-savvy Liberal Democratic leader, Nick Clegg, who stole the show in the first debate by providing British viewers with a fresh and honest alternative to the status quo. In fact, for a time, "Cleggmania" produced polls showing the Lib Dems with an unprecedented one-third of the electorate behind them. For a brief moment, Britain enjoyed the unlikely spectacle of a three-party contest, but Labour never really had a chance.

The Liberal Democrats, with 23 percent of the vote, won 57 seats in 2010, while Labour, with 29 percent of the vote, won 258 seats and the Conservatives, with 36.1 percent of the vote, won 306 seats. Thus, the Liberal Democrats achieved a share of the vote that was roughly two-thirds that of the Conservatives but won roughly one-fifth of the actual number of seats. Such are the benefits of an electoral system to the victor (as well as to the second major party).

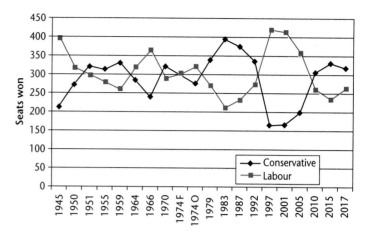

FIGURE 2.5 Comparison of the Number of Seats Won by Conservative Versus Labour in UK General Elections from 1945 to 2017

Source: http://ukpolitical.info

Is there any wonder why, more than anything else, the Liberal Democrats wants what neither major party will give them: a change in the electoral system to proportional representation (PR), where the number of seats allocated to parties in Parliament would closely approximate the proportion of votes cast for a given party? PR would be a game changer, catapulting the Lib Dems into major party status and making them a potential kingmaker, tipping the balance in many close general elections to either the Conservatives or Labour. For that very reason, it is unlikely that such a fundamental change in the electoral system will be introduced any time soon. But parliamentary sovereignty means that any time that there is a political will to change the electoral system, Parliament can change it.

Although the UK has long had a two-party dominant party system, in part thanks to the first-past-the-post electoral system that generally tends to promote stable, single-party governments, in both the 2010 and 2017 elections, no party secured a majority on its own (see Figure 2.5). Although in 2017, the two major parties did significantly increase their total share of votes and seats, the Conservative Party was forced to ally with a small party to obtain a majority. Thus, the future of the UK's traditional pattern of two-party dominance remains quite uncertain.

Gender, Ethnicity, and Representation

The party and electoral systems contribute to the creation of a Parliament that has been and remains a bastion of white men, but it is becoming more diverse with each general election. After the 2015 election, women made up 29 percent of the representation, up from 22 percent in 2010—thanks largely to Labour, whose new MPs made up 43 percent of Labour's share, helped too by the SNP cohort, of whom more than a third (36 percent) were women. However, there is now not one single female Liberal Democrat MP. The United Kingdom also still compares unfavorably with Sweden's parliament, which is 45 percent female and sets the gold standard for gender equality. Britain lags behind many other countries in gender equality, including Belgium (41.3 percent), Iceland (39.7 percent), Argentina (36.6 percent), and Burundi (30.5 percent).

The 2015 election brought more ethnic diversity to the British Parliament as well. According to the Parliamentary Candidates UK Project, cosponsored by the University College London and Birkbeck University, nonwhite MPs made up more than 6 percent of the new Parliament, up from 4.2 percent in 2010—a 56 percent increase—and approximately 42 minority-ethnic MPs were elected to the Commons. This result built on the success of the 2010 election, when 27 nonwhite MPs won seats in Westminster (among them Alan Mak, the first MP of Chinese origin).

Trends in Electoral Behavior

Recent general elections have deepened geographic and regional fragmentation. British political scientist Ivor Crewe has referred to the emergence of two two-party systems: (1) competition between the Conservative and Labour parties dominates contests in English urban and northern seats, and (2) Conservative–center party competition dominates England's rural and southern seats. A third two-party competition has emerged in Scotland, where Labour competes with the SNP.[6]

The national (that is regional) parties have challenged two-party dominance since the 1970s, but with only limited results. The SNP was founded in 1934, and its Welsh counterpart, the Plaid Cymru, in 1925. The 2010 election showed the strength of Labour in Scotland, where it won forty-one seats and 42 percent of the Scottish popular vote, an improvement over 2005. The Lib Dems came in a distant second with eleven seats, and the SNP won six seats. The election demonstrated once more that the Conservatives have very little traction in Scotland (they walked away with a single seat). In Wales, the Conservatives fared better, gaining five more seats than they had won in 2005, for a total of eight seats at Westminster. The Plaid Cymru won three seats, one more than in 2005. Although Labour lost four seats compared to 2005, they walked away with a very strong showing, winning twenty-six out of forty seats.

The right-wing, populist UKIP was the big winner in Britain in the European parliament elections in 2014. Even though it won no seats, it did transform the future electoral map in Britain, winning 27.5 percent of the ballots. In 2015, the Conservative share of the vote held up well across most groups, especially among the 65+ voters, where they picked up 5.5 points from Labour since 2010. The Labour Party failed to make a dent in the Conservative majority, except for young people and renters and BME voters.

While the vote share of the two main parties remains broadly stable, the pattern of voting for other parties has completely changed. The Liberal Democrats' vote share has collapsed across the board. They have fallen sharpest among under 34s (perhaps related to tuition fees) and private renters, who are the most likely to vote Green. Meanwhile, the UKIP takes third place among nearly every group; exceptions include managerial and professional ranks and BME voters. It does best among older, white, working-class voters.

As we have seen in recent elections, the Conservative-Labour swing among the men and women vote overall was very similar. Both vote Conservative in relatively equal proportions, while women are slightly more likely to vote Labour and less likely to vote UKIP. There are more differences, though, if we do not treat men and women as homogenous groups. Most notably, younger women had the biggest swing to Labour of any group, while older women had a small swing back to the Conservatives. The two groups are almost exact opposites of each other: Labour has a 20 point lead among women aged 18-24, while the Conservatives have an 18 point lead among women over 55.

Political Culture, Citizenship, and Identity

In their mid-twentieth century study of the ideals and values that shape political behavior, political scientists Gabriel Almond and Sidney Verba wrote that the civic (or political) culture in Britain was characterized by trust, deference to authority, and pragmatism.[7] But the 1970s became a crucial turning point in British political culture and group identities that challenged this view.

During the 1970s, the long years of economic decline culminated in economic reversals in standard of living for many Britons. Also, the historic bonds of occupational and social class grew weaker for many. Both union membership and popularity declined. At the same time, a growing number of conservative think tanks and mass-circulation newspapers worked hard to erode support for the welfare state. New social movements such as feminism, antinuclear activism, and environmentalism challenged the basic tenets of British political culture. Identities based on race and ethnicity, gender, and sexual orientation gained significance. These trends fragmented the political map and inspired a shift to the right.

Thatcher's ascent reflected these changes in political culture, identities, and values. Thatcherism rejected collectivism, the redistribution of resources from rich to poor, and state responsibility for full employment. It considered individual property rights more important than the social rights claimed by all citizens in the welfare state. Thatcherism set the stage in cultural terms for the new Labour consolidation of neoliberalism and the core political–cultural orientation in Britain.

Social Class

A key change in political culture in the last quarter-century has been the weakening of bonds grounded in the experience of labor. During the Thatcher era, the traditional values of "an honest day's work for an honest day's pay" and solidarity among coworkers were derided as "rigidities" that reduced competitiveness—a perspective that has continued through New Labour and the coalition government.

Being "tough on the unions" was a core premise of New Labour, and the Conservative-led coalition government powerfully reinforced this view. In the context of the aggressive cuts in public spending, tough days remain ahead for unions, particularly public-sector unions, which have become a lightning rod, not only in the United Kingdom, but in the United States as well, for governments looking to cut budgets—and blame somebody for the need to make cuts. Collective bargaining has been largely relegated to declining private-sector industries and the public sector.[8] Strike rates in the United Kingdom have generally been below the average of both the Organisation for Economic Cooperation and Development (OECD) and the European Union in recent decades.

National Identity

Decolonization has created a multiethnic Britain, and national identity has become especially complicated. Questions about fragmented sovereignty in light of Britain's decision to exit the European Union, challenges to the commingled histories of four nations (England, Scotland, Wales, and Ireland/Northern Ireland), and the interplay of race and nationality have created doubts about British identity that run deep. Ethnicity, intra-UK territorial attachments, Europeanization, and globalization are complicating national identity. Can Britain foster a more inclusive sense of British identity, or will it revert to what has historically been called "fortress Britain"?

Nearly 8 percent of the people who live in Britain are of African, African-Caribbean, or Asian descent. The authors of a landmark study of multiethnic Britain explained: "Many communities overlap; all affect and are affected by others. More and more people have multiple identities—they are Welsh Europeans, Pakistani Yorkshirewomen, Glaswegian Muslims, English Jews, and black British. Many enjoy this complexity but also experience conflicting loyalties."[9]

Despite many success stories, ethnic minority communities have experienced police insensitivity, problems in access to the best public housing, hate crimes, and accusations that they are not truly British if they do not root for the English cricket team. In addition, harsh criticism is directed at immigrants and asylum seekers. Since this criticism comes in the wake of intense scrutiny of the Muslim community after 9/11 and 7/7 and more recent terrorist strikes throughout Europe (Paris, Brussels, Berlin, and even London), it contributes to the alienation of the ethnic minority community, particularly among some groups of Muslim citizens, and as in the United States, ordinary law-abiding Muslims in the United Kingdom have experienced intensified mistrust and intimidation. But it is also true that Muslim university graduates are assuming leading roles in a number of white-collar professions, and in 2016, Sadiq Khan, "son of a Pakistani bus driver," was elected mayor of London with more than 1.3 million votes and the largest personal mandate of any politician in British political history.

Interest Groups, Social Movements, and Protest

In recent years, in response to globalization, environmental issues, and the rightward slide of politics throughout Europe, political protest has been on the rise. Protesters demand more accountability and transparency in the operations of powerful international trade and development agencies. In 1999, for example, London became the site of protests timed to correspond with the Seattle meeting of the World Trade Organization (WTO). The London demonstration attracted some 100,000 protesters.

The intensity of environmental activism has taken off with the growing attention to climate change. In 2015, hundreds of thousands of people took to the streets in London ahead of the Paris climate summit at the end of the year. Thousands of students marched through London to protest the rising costs of university and further education in 2012. A stretch of Whitehall was brought to a near-standstill in 2015 by a group outside Downing Street protesting the United Kingdom's plans to bomb

ISIS targets in Syria, and in 2016, thousands of people protested the referendum decision to leave the European Union. Most recently, members of the newly formed Stop Trump Coalition sent a letter to the *Guardian* protesting the prospect of an impending visit to the United Kingdom by U.S. president Donald Trump.

The Political Impact of Technology and the Media

Recent developments have underscored the impact of technology on British politics in the past decade. In a scandal that is still reverberating with global implications, a parliamentary committee released a report in 2012 disclosing that Rupert Murdoch, the Australian media mogul whose companies in 2011 accounted for the second-largest media holdings in the world (including the prestigious *Times of London* and *The Wall Street Journal*), was linked to a major hacking scandal. The hackers used sophisticated electronic technologies to gain access to emails and voice mails for the purpose of breaking major news stories ahead of the competition, creating collateral damage for many news organizations and high-flying politicians. The scandal also implicated Tony Blair at a trial about the hacking incidents, when it was revealed that the former prime minister secretly offered to advise the Murdoch empire as the scandal erupted.

Potentially more significant in this era of governmental use of sophisticated and often secret surveillance of ordinary citizens, it has been revealed that Government Communications Headquarters (GCHQ), the UK surveillance agency, has collected millions of webcam images. Social media, in more recent years, has revealed itself to be an important indicator of Britain's political climate. Twitter, above all else, has become a thermometer depended upon all too often by politicians and other public figures who not too long ago would have relied instead on polls and charts. In the days following Brexit, for example, MP Boris Johnson, the leading orchestrator of the move, was the target of so much ridicule and derision on Twitter and Facebook that many believe this to be the reason that he decided not to run for party leader when Cameron resigned as prime minister. The Internet has become public opinion, regardless of the actual truth about the demographics that it represents.

Not just damaging to the careers of political leaders, the widespread use and abuse of technology poses a threat to the everyday lives of British citizens and under-scores the vulnerabilities of the digital age. In May 2017, an Internet-based black-mail attempt hit computer networks in dozens of countries worldwide and crippled Britain's NHS. Transmitted via email, the malicious software, known as WannaCry, locked British hospitals out of their computer systems and demanded ransom before users could be let back in. Doctors could not call up patient files, and emergency rooms were forced to divert people seeking urgent care. Critics of the Conservative government were quick to suggest that chronic underfunding of the NHS left its computer systems especially vulnerable to cyberattack.

Where Do You Stand?

Is perpetual surveillance too high a price to pay for security?

Has the new age of social media transformed the political culture for better or worse?

BRITISH POLITICS IN TRANSITION

- Is Britain best understood as four nations or one?

- How well is Britain's ancient political system adjusting to contemporary challenges?

Political Challenges and Changing Agendas

Early in her premiership, facing historically high unemployment and division in her cabinet, Margaret Thatcher famously refused to back down from her hard-core conservative policies, famously intoning, "U-turn if you want to, the Lady's not for turning." One might think that Theresa May, Britain's second woman prime minister, elected in the wake of the disarray caused by Britain's unexpectedly sharp break from the European Union, might shape up to be a second Maggie. Britain, an offshore island, has always had a complicated relationship to its European allies, preferring to nurture its special relationship with the United States instead, and while it finally joined the European Union in 1973, it has never fully embraced its European identity. Nevertheless, Britain's decision to leave the European Union came as a shock to both itself and the rest of the world. The referendum roiled global markets and caused the British pound to fall temporarily to its lowest level in decades.

British citizens themselves appeared to be caught by surprise by the results. Prime Minister David Cameron, whose only lukewarm support for the European Union contributed to the success of the referendum, was compelled to step down the very next day, and Theresa May, the longest-serving Home Secretary, was promptly named his successor. The Brexit vote expressed Britain's wish to leave the European Union but said nothing about how to make the break, leaving the brand-new and untested prime minister, who had herself voted against leaving the European Union, facing unprecedented challenges. Rather than acting like a second Maggie Thatcher, however, and marching Britain straight out of the European Union, Prime Minister May has tried to walk the Brexit tightrope, fudging both the terms and the timing of Britain's departure from the European Union and earning criticism from all sides and the unflattering play on her name, "Mrs. Maybe."

Constitutional Reform

Questions about the role of the monarchy and the House of Lords have long been simmering on Britain's political agenda. Why should the House of Commons share sovereignty with the House of Lords? What is the role of the monarchy—a very expensive institution and one subject to periodic scandal—in a modern political system? In addition, the balance of power among constitutionally critical institutions raises important questions about a democratic deficit at the heart of the Westminster model. Britain's executive easily overpowers Parliament. Its strength in relation to the legislature may be greater than in any other democracy.

Add to these concerns the prime minister's tendency to bypass the cabinet on crucial decisions and the bias in the electoral system that privileges the two dominant parties. We have seen these tensions at work most vividly in light of the Brexit referendum. Although a Supreme Court ruling forced Prime Minister May to submit the Brexit bill for parliamentary approval, this step proved to be far from the major hindrance that she appeared to fear it would be. The bill passed both houses of

Parliament with overwhelming support, and in March 2017, May sent a letter to Donald Trusk, president of the European Council, formally invoking Article 50 and beginning the legal process of Britain's withdrawal from the European Union.

Article 50 of the Lisbon Treaty allows a member-state of the European Union to notify the group of its intention to withdraw and obliges the European Union to try to negotiate a "withdrawal agreement" with that state. As that process moves forward, it remains unclear what impact the Brexit vote will have upon the relationships among the four governments within the United Kingdom. Will it increase the chances of Scottish independence? In 2014, Scotland voted fairly convincingly to stay in the European Union, while England and Wales voted to leave—a fact that has led the Scottish Parliament to seek to hold a second referendum on Scottish independence in 2018 or 2019.

Identities in Flux

The relatively small scale of the ethnic minority community limits the political impact of the most divisive issues concerning collective identities. It is probably in this area that rigidities in the British political system most severely challenge the principles of democracy and tolerance. Given Britain's single-member, simple-plurality electoral system, and no proportional representation, minority representation in Parliament remains very low. There are deep-seated social attitudes that no government can easily transform.

The issues of immigration, refugees, and asylum still inspire a fear of multiculturalism among white Britons. Since the 7/7 bombings committed by British Muslims in London, intense scrutiny has been focused on the Muslim community, which faces endless finger-pointing and harassment, and positions are hardening against multiculturalism. In February 2011, Prime Minister Cameron explicitly challenged the long-standing cross-party support for multiculturalism at a high-visibility security conference in Munich. He condemned a culture of "hands-off" tolerance in the United Kingdom and in Europe, and in strong terms, he warned of the dangers of multicultural policy, which made it possible for Islamic militants to radicalize Muslim youth, some of whom were likely to become terrorists. He concluded that Europe had to defeat terrorism at home, not exclusively by the use of force elsewhere (for example, in Afghanistan).

Now as the United Kingdom reels from a post-Brexit surge in racist hate crimes and xenophobia, Prime Minister May appears to be following closely in Cameron's footsteps, driving policies aimed at surveilling, criminalizing, and extraditing Muslims, refugees, and migrants. From the beginning of her tenure as Home Secretary in 2010, May has been a key backer of the controversial "Preventing Violent Extremism" (Prevent) program, which was launched in the aftermath of the 7/7 bombings. Under this strategy, Muslims unconnected to wrongdoing have been subject to surveillance and criminalization.

In November 2014, May proposed the "Counter-Terrorism and Security Act," which was implemented in 2015 and dramatically expands the powers of the government to seize the passports of people suspected of traveling outside the United Kingdom for "terrorist activity" and permits the temporary expulsion of suspected terrorists. More recently, May put herself in a difficult position, in light of her reluctance to condemn U.S. president Donald Trump's ban on refugees and entry to the United States for citizens of seven Muslim-majority nations, as thousands across the world took to the streets in protest. Critics accuse her of putting good relations with President Trump and the hopes of a post-Brexit trade deal between the United Kingdom and the United States ahead of human rights.

Is Demography Destiny?

Britain's young adults, who for much of the twentieth century enjoyed well-above-average living standards, have been displaced by the rise of well-off pensioners, in the most dramatic generational change in decades. Thanks to evaporating jobs, unaffordable property, and rising debt, average twentysomethings in Britain have seen their living standards slip from a position of comparative affluence to well below par over the past 35 years. At the same time, older Britons have enjoyed a rapid rise up the economic ladder, thanks in large part to fiscal policies of the coalition government that aimed to protect pensioners from austerity measures and concentrated fiscal pain instead on young adults.

The 2010 decision to triple university tuition, for example, making the United Kingdom's average undergraduate tuition fees the highest in the industrialized world, was met with angry student protesters outside Parliament. According to a 2016 Ipsos MORI poll, about 54 percent of the country believes that young people's lives will be worse than their own generation's. The population's deep sense of foreboding about the next generation's prospects stands in stark contrast to an overwhelming recognition from those born before World War II, as well as the baby boomers (born between 1945 and 1964), that they have a much better life than their parents'. The Brexit vote also underscored the generational divide that characterizes life in Britain. Almost three-quarters (73 percent) of 18- to 24-year-olds said that they had voted to stay in the European Union, compared with 62 percent of 25- to 34-year-olds and 52 percent of 35- to 44-year-olds.

GLOBAL CONNECTION

Britain and the Legacies of Empire

At its height during the reign of Queen Victoria (1837–1901), the British Empire encompassed fully one-quarter of the world's population and exerted direct colonial rule over some four dozen countries scattered across the globe. In a stunning reversal of Britain's global status and fortunes, the empire fell apart in the half-century of decolonization between the independence of India in 1947 and the return of Hong Kong to China in 1997. The sun finally set on the British Empire (apart from a few scattered dependencies), but the legacies of empire lived on, shaping Britain's relationship to the world in important ways.

The end of empire did not bring the end of Great Power aspirations for Britain, but it shifted its emphasis, as the British role in the globalizing world of states has been shaped by its determination to view its special relationship with the United States as a dominant framework for foreign policy and global leadership, even at the expense of a full commitment to economic integration with and leadership in the European Union. Now that Britain has voted to sever its relations with the European Union, its special relationship with the United States is all the more important.

With the end of empire, it was inevitable that the special relationship between the United Kingdom and the United States would become a relationship between unequal partners. As a result, U.S. interests have tended to exert a tremendous magnetic pull on British foreign policy, to the relative neglect of European partnerships and broader international influences.

Before 9/11, New Labour stood for a coherent and progressive foreign policy framework—one that linked globalization to a growing UK commitment to narrow the development gap, and in the words of Robin Cook, Blair's first foreign secretary, "to be a force for good" in the world. The Kosovo war created the context for Blair's explicit linkage of globalization with foreign and security policy.

Blair's "doctrine of international community" gave new weight to the notion of global interdependence by asserting a responsibility to use military force when necessary to achieve humanitarian objectives and contain catastrophic human rights abuses. This doctrine, as well as Blair's Atlanticist leanings, conditioned his response to 9/11, and subsequently his determination to bring the United Kingdom into the war in Iraq.

(continued)

But in the days following 9/11, the powerful attraction of the Atlantic alliance, with Blair's distinctive inflections, took an irresistible hold on British foreign policy. At this critical juncture, several elements came together to forge the decision to support George W. Bush and the U.S. administration, even when the venue of the war on terror changed from Afghanistan to Iraq: concern about strengthening unilateralist forces in Washington, characterization of the intervention as a humanitarian effort, and a belief that the terms of the special relationship demanded UK support of the U.S. efforts in Iraq as part of a global war on terror.

In Blair's doctrine of international community, the reverberations of empire were unmistakable. The civilizing mission of empire and the right of the metropolitan power to use force against the weaker dependent or failed states were both understood to constitute an exercise of humanitarian intervention. And the use of force, however it was justified, represented an exercise in great power politics.

Part of the challenges facing the Conservative–Liberal government under the leadership of David Cameron was how to reconcile the pro-European orientation of the Liberal Democrats with the Euroskeptical approach of the Tories. Perhaps to allay European concerns, as well as those of his coalition partners, Cameron's first trip abroad as prime minister was to Paris and Berlin, and Afghani president Hamid Karzai was the first foreign leader to meet with him. Cameron's balancing act fell apart, disastrously for his own premiership, with the advent of Britain's unexpected vote to withdraw from the European Union. This turn of events pushed Cameron to resign and forced Theresa May, the next Conservative prime minister, to recalibrate Britain's relationship with Europe, all the while once again reaffirming Britain's special relationship with the United States. May was the first foreign leader to visit Donald Trump after his inauguration, and much to the dismay of many at home, issued an invitation on the spot for Trump to pay a state visit, with all the trimmings.

MAKING CONNECTIONS Does its special relationship with the United States enhance Britain's standing in a globalizing world of states, or does it lock Britain into a set of problems not of its own making, but rather determined in Washington?

British Politics in Comparative Perspective

Positioned off the northwest coast of France, Britain has always preserved its distance from Europe in both nautical and political terms. From the British perspective, Europe is invariably "them, not us." From this point of view, Britain's decision to withdraw from the European Union should not have shocked the world as much as it did. But Britain's challenges to its geopolitical identity do not end at its shores. It must also reaffirm the illusion of unity within the United Kingdom—a challenge that is very real, in light of the 2014 Scottish referendum that very nearly demolished once and for all the precarious assumption that the United Kingdom would remain one state, but four nations – a challenge that remains very much on the horizon. The Scottish parliament voted in March 2017 to seek a second referendum for independence. England, Scotland, Wales, and Northern Ireland are each governed by separate institutions and anchored by different cultural values and incommensurate approaches to economic governance. The question posed long ago remains unresolved and likely to spur greater divisions in the future: Is Britain one nation or four? Stay tuned!

Where Do You Stand?

Is Britain important enough and functioning well enough today to stand alongside the United States as one of the two great models of democratic government?

With Vladimir Putin's Russia on the ascendant, the United States looking inward, and the European Union facing tremendous economic and institutional challenges, is there an opportunity for Britain to play a greater role in a globalizing world of states?

Chapter Summary

Undoubtedly, people in Britain today sense that the nation is experiencing a very un-British moment, in which all that is solid is melting into air and the political firmament is more fractured than it has been in generations. Consider the decline of Britain's historic laissez-faire economic model and the unresolved legacies of empire, reflected in tumultuous debates and recriminations over race, ethnicity, and the meaning of "Britishness." Add to those tensions the surprising constitutional and institutional uncertainty following from Scotland's renewed commitment to seeking independence and the possibility of the breakup of modern Britain occurring within another generation. Perhaps the single most disruptive factor, affecting all four of our core themes, is Britain's unexpected decision to part company with its European allies and leave the European Union behind.

Brexit has reconfigured Britain's role in the world of states in several different dimensions. On the one hand, the British need to find a way to maintain productive economic and political relationships with its European allies in a way that will balance the wishes of those who want to control Britain's borders and political sovereignty against the need to maintain a vibrant economy in a rapidly changing and increasingly globalized context. To this end, the government faces real challenges in negotiating its exit strategy from the European Union. Some ministers favor a "soft" Brexit, under which the United Kingdom would prioritize access to the single market, while others back a "hard" break, which would make immigration control the priority.

At the same time, the split with Europe has made Britain's special relationship with the United States all the more important—an alliance made more complicated in the wake of Donald Trump's 2016 election as U.S. president and mercurial style of leadership. What kind of ally will the United States be to the United Kingdom going forward? Until recently, the use of the referendum has not played a strong role in the British democratic experience, but both the Scottish referendum in 2014 and the Brexit vote in 2016 have provided significant constitutional challenges to Britain's age-old parliamentary system. Both votes have also forced Britain to reevaluate its collective identity.

Going forward, will Britain remain a union of four nations, or will being "British" be replaced with different groups of citizens who identity as Scottish, Welsh, Irish, or English? In addition, will Brexit harden Britain's recent anti-immigrant stance, following in the footsteps of many right-wing nationalist movements in Europe and the United States? For generations, it was common to hear that "the sun never set on the British Empire," but in the contemporary context, it is perhaps more salient to observe that the consequences of empire have never been resolved and continue to shape and bedevil what it means to be British.

Key Terms

cabinet government
constitutional monarchy
foreign direct investment (FDI)
fusion of powers
hegemonic power
hung parliament
Industrial Revolution

judicial review
laissez-faire
macroeconomic policy
monetarism
neoliberalism
parliamentary democracy
parliamentary sovereignty

quango
special relationship
unitary state
welfare state
Westminster model

Suggested Websites

The official UK government website
www.direct.gov.uk

The UK Parliament
www.parliament.uk

BBC
http://www.bbc.com

Ipsos-Market and Opinion Research International (Mori), Britain's leading polling organization
http://www.ipsos-mori.com/

The Scottish Parliament
http://www.parliament.scot

National Assembly for Wales
www.assembly.wales

Prime Minister's Office
https://www.gov.uk/government/organisations /prime-ministers-office-10-downing-street

Suggested Readings

Arnold, Guy. *America and Britain: Was There Ever a Special Relationship?* London: Hurst & Company, 2014.

Eagleton, Terry. *Across the Pond: An Englishman's View of America.* New York: W.W. Norton & Company, 2014.

Goodhart, David. *The British Dream: Successes and Failures of Post-War Immigration.* London: Atlantic Books, 2014.

Heffernan, Richard, Philip Cowley, and Colin Hay, eds. *Developments in British Politics.* Palgrave Macmillan, 2016.

Kumar, Krishan. *The Making of English National Identity.* Cambridge, U.K.: Cambridge University Press, 2003.

Laurence, Jonathan. *The Emancipation of Europe's Muslims: The State's Role in Minority Integration.* Princeton, NJ: Princeton University Press, 2012.

MacShane, Dennis. *Brexit: How Britain left Europe.* London/New York: I. B. Tauris, 2016.

Nairn, Tom. *The Break-up of Britain: Crisis and Neonationalism.* Altona Vic, Australia: Common Ground, 2003.

Parekh, Bhikhu. *A New Politics of Identity: Political Principles for an Interdependent World.* London: Palgrave, 2008.

The Scottish Government. *Scotland's Future: Your Guide to an Independent Scotland.* Edinburgh: the Scottish Government, 2013.

Trilling, Daniel. *Bloody Nasty People: The Rise of Britain's Far Right.* London: Verso, 2013.

France

Mark Kesselman

Official Name: French Republic (*République Française*)

Location: Western Europe

Capital City: Paris

Population (2014): 66.3 million

Size: 634,427 sq. km.; slightly smaller than Texas

THE MAKING OF THE MODERN FRENCH STATE

Politics in Action

Focus Questions ▽

• What are two distinctive features of French history that have led scholars and French politicians to speak of French exceptionalism?

• What explains France's relative economic decline from the nineteenth century until World War II?

In the short space of 17 months, during 2015 and 2016, France experienced three large-scale terrorist attacks carried out by Muslim extremists. The first took place in January 2015, when two brothers with assault rifles stormed the Paris office of *Charlie Hebdo*, a weekly satirical magazine known for its sharp-edged cartoons, including several caricaturing the Prophet Mohammed, and murdered the editor, chief cartoonist, staff members, and a policeman. While the attack was occurring, an accomplice entered a kosher supermarket near Paris, shot dead four customers, and took remaining customers hostage. The police quickly forced their way into the supermarket and killed the gunman.

A series of coordinated attacks in Paris that occurred in November that year proved far more deadly. The first occurred at a concert by an American band called Eagles of Death Metal, when terrorists armed with suicide vests and assault rifles stormed the Bataclan music hall and slaughtered ninety concertgoers. At the same moment, a potentially far more destructive attack was foiled during a soccer match at the Stade de France, attended by 75,000 spectators, including the French president. Three terrorists wearing suicide vests tried to force their way into the stadium. When stopped by police, they blew themselves up without additional loss of life. While this mayhem was occurring, several terrorists roamed around Paris's Left Bank, randomly shooting patrons in outdoor cafés and restaurants. In all, 130 people were killed and more than 350 were wounded in the coordinated attacks that night.

The third terrorist attack occurred the following summer, on Bastille Day, July 14, France's national holiday and the equivalent of Independence Day in the United States. Like July 4 in the United States, it is the occasion for merrymaking, fireworks displays, and other festivities. On July 14, 2016, crowds at the resort city of Nice, on the Mediterranean coast, assembled at a beachfront park to watch the fireworks—and then a Tunisian immigrant living in France slowly drove a large truck into the park, accelerated, and wreaked havoc by driving through the panicked crowd. While police quickly stopped the truck and shot the driver dead, the attack resulted in 86 deaths and 202 wounded.

Following these attacks, the president declared a state of emergency, which grants the government the power to conduct electronic surveillance, conduct house searches without warrants, detain suspects without cause, and order house arrests, all without judicial oversight. The supposedly temporary emergency powers were enshrined into laws passed in 2015 and 2016 and extended for the sixth time in May 2017 by newly elected president Emmanuel Macron. Critics charge that the new laws condone and even encourage executive overreach. The government responded that, partly thanks to these powers, it had thwarted seventeen terrorist attacks in 2016 and arrested 400 people on charges of planning attacks.

Terrorist attacks appear designed to gain maximum publicity, sow feelings of insecurity, and deter foreign tourists from visiting France. Foreign tourism accounts for a hefty 7 percent of France's gross domestic product (GDP), so this could have a devastating effect on the national economy. France appears likely to remain a favorite—perhaps *the* favorite—target of terrorist attacks in the world today, as suggested by

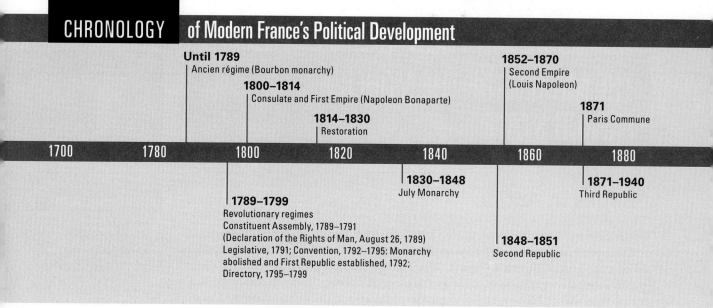

Until 1789
Ancien régime (Bourbon monarchy)

1800–1814
Consulate and First Empire (Napoleon Bonaparte)

1814–1830
Restoration

1852–1870
Second Empire
(Louis Napoleon)

1871
Paris Commune

| 1700 | 1780 | 1800 | 1820 | 1840 | 1860 | 1880 |

1789–1799
Revolutionary regimes
Constituent Assembly, 1789–1791
(Declaration of the Rights of Man, August 26, 1789)
Legislative, 1791; Convention, 1792–1795: Monarchy
abolished and First Republic established, 1792;
Directory, 1795–1799

1830–1848
July Monarchy

1848–1851
Second Republic

1871–1940
Third Republic

two smaller terrorist attacks in early 2017. One was foiled when a man shouting "God is great!" attacked a military patrol at the Louvre museum in Paris and was immediately shot. Another occurred on Paris's famed Champs-Elysées, when a gunman affiliated with ISIS opened fire on police officers, killing one and wounding two others (as well as a civilian bystander) before he was shot and killed. In all, this brought the total of victims killed in terrorist attacks since the *Charlie Hebdo* attack to 239.

The attacks promote a particular level of anxiety because they occur in a context of persistently high unemployment, slow economic growth, and conflicts involving ethnicity, immigration, globalization, and national identity—problems that the political system has failed effectively to address. The result has been a popular mood in France quite at odds with the country's famed reputation for *joie de vivre* (joy of living—quality life). Indeed, long before the recent attacks, the popular mood had soured. The newspaper *Le Monde* reported on March 20, 2007, that France ranked 64th out of 178 countries around the world in an international poll examining citizen happiness. (The United States ranked 23rd; Germany, 35th; and Britain, 42nd.)

There are 5 million Muslims living in France, the largest number in any Western European country; the vast majority are law-abiding. A major challenge confronting the French political system is how to prevent violence by militants inspired by radical Islamic organizations without profiling all Muslims as potential terrorists. Certain elements of French political culture, discussed later in this chapter, increase the difficulty of integrating Muslims into the French political community. The French political system is severely tested by the challenges posed by terrorist attacks, as well as socioeconomic and cultural problems with varying connections to terrorism. This chapter studies how the political system confronts these severe stresses. (See Table 3.1 and Figure 3.1.)

Geographic Setting

France is among the world's favored countries, thanks to a temperate climate, large and fertile land area, rich culture, and prosperous economy. Its natural beauty, superb architecture, vibrant culture, and world-class cuisine explain why it is the world's most popular tourist destination.

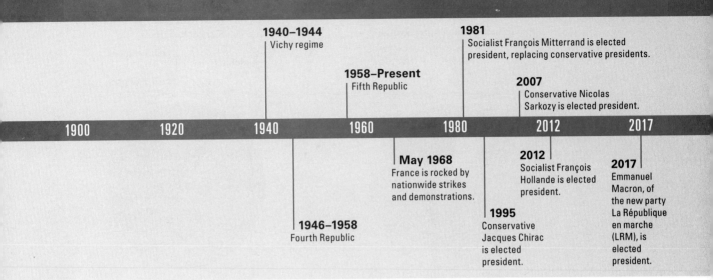

1940–1944
Vichy regime

1981
Socialist François Mitterrand is elected president, replacing conservative presidents.

1958–Present
Fifth Republic

2007
Conservative Nicolas Sarkozy is elected president.

1900 · 1920 · 1940 · 1960 · 1980 · 2012 · 2017

May 1968
France is rocked by nationwide strikes and demonstrations.

2012
Socialist François Hollande is elected president.

2017
Emmanuel Macron, of the new party La République en marche (LRM), is elected president.

1946–1958
Fourth Republic

1995
Conservative Jacques Chirac is elected president.

France occupies a key strategic position in Europe. It borders the Mediterranean Sea in the south and shares borders with Belgium, Switzerland, and Germany on the north and east. Spain lies to the southwest, with Italy to the southeast. With

Table 3.1	Political Organization
Political System	Unitary republic. Semi-presidential system; popularly elected president, bicameral parliament, and prime minister and government ministers are appointed by president: they are formally responsible to National Assembly (lower house of parliament) and informally responsible to the president.
Regime History	Frequent regime changes, including five republics since the French Revolution of 1789. A dictatorial regime based in Vichy collaborated with the Nazis during World War II; the Fourth Republic existed from 1946 to 1958; and the Fifth Republic, originating in 1958, is universally accepted.
Administrative Structure	Unitary, with thirteen mainland regions; and ninety-five mainland departments, Corsica, and five overseas departments.
Executive	Dual executive: president (5-year term); PM appointed by president, generally leader of majority coalition in National Assembly, and formally responsible to National Assembly (as well as informally responsible to president).
Legislature	Bicameral. Senate (upper house) has power to delay legislation passed by lower house and to veto proposed constitutional amendments. National Assembly (lower house) can pass legislation and force government to resign by passing a censure motion.
Judiciary	A system of administrative, criminal, and civil courts. At the top, a nine-member independent Constitutional Council named for nonrenewable 9-year terms; president of republic names three members, president of each house of parliament names three. The Constitutional Council exercises right of judicial review.
Party System	Multiparty. La République en marche (LRM), Les Républicains (LR), Socialist Party (PS), National Front (FN), Left Front, Green Party, others.

France: Demographic Profile

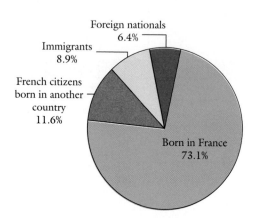

Foreign nationals
6.4%

Immigrants
8.9%

French citizens
born in another
country
11.6%

Born in France
73.1%

France: Religions

Buddhists
0.4%

Folk Religions
0.4%

Other Religions
0.2%

Jews
0.5%

Muslims
7.5%

Christians
63.0%
(Overwhelmingly
Catholic)

Unaffiliated
28.0%

Note: Due to a law dating from 1872, French state authorities are prohibited from collecting data on individuals' ethnicity or religious beliefs. Data on religion comes from private survey research.

French Currency: Euro (€)
International Designation: EUR
Exchange Rate (2017):
- 1€ = 1.15US$
- 1US$ = 0.89€

100 Euro Note Design: European historical Baroque/Rococo style (the 17th and 18th century) arch

© Cengage

Labrador Photo Video/Shutterstock.com

FIGURE 3.1 The French Nation at a Glance

a population of over 66 million, France is among the most populous countries in Western Europe. But its large area—211,000 square miles—means that population density is low (about half that of Britain, Germany, and Italy).

France has a modern and productive economy. Most people work in the industrial and service sectors, although it boasts a large agricultural sector that produces (and exports) world-class products like fine wines and cheese. No other French city rivals Paris, the capital, in size and cultural, political, and financial influence. In fact, Lille, Lyon, and Marseille are the only other relatively large cities. In 2016, the country's GDP was about $2.5 trillion, and per capita income that year was about $42,000. France ranks 21st among all countries of the world in the United Nations Development Program's Human Development Index.

Critical Junctures

Creating Modern France

Historical surveys of modern France often begin with Charlemagne, who became Holy Roman emperor in 800 CE and dominated much of Western Europe, including present-day France. Following his death in 814, the empire disintegrated. Norsemen from Scandinavia established a duchy in Normandy, in northwest France. One of their rulers, William the Conqueror, invaded England in 1066 and defeated English troops at the Battle of Hastings. During the following centuries, French monarchs frequently clashed with powerful provincial leaders. Challenges also came from outside. For example, the

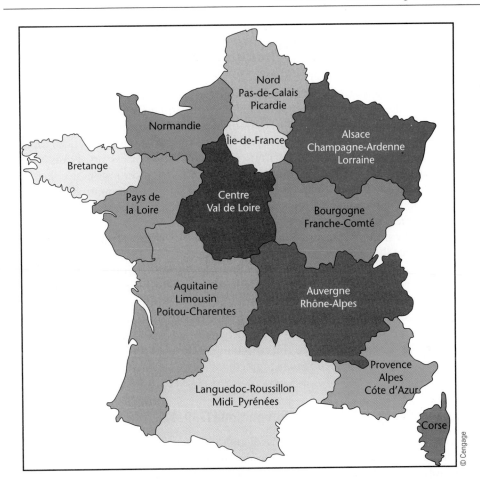

© Cengage

English attempt to conquer France during the Hundred Years' War (1337–1453) was thwarted when Joan of Arc, a peasant who believed she had a divine mission to protect her country, led French forces to defeat the English army. While the English captured and burned Joan at the stake, she remains a symbol of intense national pride.

During the sixteenth century, the French Wars of Religion violently pitted Catholics against Protestants. In 1598, Henry IV helped end religious strife by issuing the Edict of Nantes granting Protestants religious liberty. However, the bitter memory of religious conflict, as well as the powerful Catholic Church's repeated attempts to shape French society and culture, may help explain why France adopted a more militant form of **secularism** in France than was the case in neighboring countries.

The seventeenth through early nineteenth centuries were the high point of France's economic, military, and cultural influence. During this period, France was the richest and most powerful country in continental Europe as well as Europe's artistic and scientific capital. In the eighteenth century, it was the center of the Enlightenment, the philosophical movement that emphasized the importance of scientific reason rather than religious belief or folk wisdom.

The Ancien Régime

A turning point in the struggle between French monarchs and provincial rulers came when Louis XIV (r. 1643–1715) created a powerful, modern state. France began to be centrally administered by state agents, some of whom directed administrative

secularism

The doctrine that mandates maintaining a separation between church and state, and specifies that the state should be neutral in matters of religion. The French conception of secularism holds that religious beliefs and practices should be confined to the private sphere, and should not play a role in public or political life.

departments in Paris while others were posted to the provinces. A uniform legal code began to be applied throughout France.

An informal agreement between the monarchy and powerful landholding nobility promoted political stability. The nobles supported the monarchy; in return, they were lightly taxed. The Catholic Church—itself a large landowner and tax collector—also enjoyed privileged status. On the other hand, historian James Collins notes, the king "had to raise ever more money to feed his military...." The steep costs of foreign wars and the lavish lifestyle of the royal court stretched the monarchy's "financial capacity beyond its limits."[1] The response of Louis XIV and his two successors, Louis XV and XVI, was to raise taxes on the rising middle classes—the most productive sectors of the economy—and on peasants and urban workers, a policy that eventually provoked revolution. These complex arrangements were later described as the *ancien régime*, or old regime.

From the mid-seventeenth to the mid-eighteenth century, France was usually at war. The French economy stagnated while resources were diverted for military purposes. Meanwhile, France's major rival Britain enjoyed the benefits of the Agricultural and Industrial Revolutions. In 1789, Louis XVI convened representative assemblies (the Estates General) that had not met for centuries in order to obtain their support for raising taxes. His decision fueled anti-royal opposition. On July 14, 1789, a Parisian crowd stormed the Bastille, a widely despised prison in Paris, and freed the prisoners. The event symbolized the crumbling of royal authority. Not long after, the monarchy and entire *ancien régime* toppled.

The Two Faces of the French Revolution (1789–1815)

The Revolution of 1789 was a *political* and a *national* revolution. It replaced the monarchy by a **republic**. It was an *international* revolution, inspiring national uprisings, often supported by French armed intervention, throughout Europe. It was *liberal*, and championed individual liberty in the political and economic spheres, as well as secularism and religious freedom. It was *democratic*, and proclaimed that all (male) citizens have an equal right to participate in key political decisions.

Although the revolutionary regime proclaimed liberty, equality, and fraternity, it treated opponents brutally, beheading many at the guillotine. The regime's intolerance and hostility toward the Catholic Church divided French society.

The revolution that toppled the *ancien régime* replaced it with an even more centralized political system. Emperor Napoleon Bonaparte, the brilliant revolutionary general who seized control of the state and ruled from 1799 to 1814, created state institutions that survive to this day, for example, the system of administration in which territorial *départements* or subdivisions are administered by a **prefect** appointed by the central government. Ever since the revolution, France has struggled to forge a satisfactory balance between state autonomy—the state's independence from groups within society—and democratic participation and decision making.

Many Regimes, Slow Industrialization (1815–1940)

Following Napoleon's defeat in 1815, France experienced steady decline through World War II. One cause was chronic political instability, involving a succession of ineffective regimes. The most durable was the Third Republic. Created after France's

---

ancien régime

The monarchical regime that ruled France until the Revolution of 1789, when it was toppled by a popular uprising.

revolution

The process by which an established political regime is replaced (usually by force and with broad popular participation) by a new regime that introduces radical changes throughout society.

republic

In contemporary usage, a political regime in which leaders are not chosen on the basis of their inherited background (as in a monarchy).

prefects

French administrators appointed by the minister of the interior to coordinate state agencies and programs within France's territorial subdivisions known as *départements*.

defeat in the Franco-Prussian War and a civil war that followed in 1871, it ended with France's defeat by Germany in World War II. The Third Republic involved an all-powerful parliament and weak executive—a surefire recipe to prevent decisive state action.

During the nineteenth century, while regimes came and went at a dizzying pace, economic change was slow. Unlike Britain and Germany, France chose economic stability over the dislocations of modernization. In 1800, France was the world's second economic power; by 1900 it slipped to fourth. (However France did embark on the quest for colonies: it amassed the world's second largest colonial empire.) French manufacturers excelled in custom-made luxury goods, like silk and porcelain. But these commodities did not lend themselves to mechanized production. In addition, slow population growth spelled stagnant demand and therefore low investment.

State policies contributed to economic stability. In order to offset political instability, the state shielded farmers, manufacturers, and artisans from foreign competition. France maintained some of the highest tariff barriers in Western Europe throughout this period. However, the state did promote some economic modernization. For example, in the 1860s, it organized an efficient rail network and sponsored an investment bank to finance railway development.

France's decline continued due to the country's participation in World War I. Although France was among the victors, much of the brutal war was fought on French soil, and about 1.4 million soldiers were killed and 4 million wounded during the terrible conflict. Following the war, France's slow economic growth, internal divisions, and poor planning during the 1930s, when Hitler's Germany was rearming following its defeat in World War I, help explain France's crushing defeat by Germany in 1940—the second loss in less than a century. (The first was in 1870, when Germany defeated France in the Franco-Prussian War.)

Vichy France (1940–1944) and the Fourth Republic (1946–1958)

In 1940, at the start of World War II, Germany quickly overran much of France. The French parliament appointed Philippe Pétain, an aged World War I military hero, to be prime minister in this time of dire crisis. Pétain sealed the Third Republic's destruction by signing an armistice with Hitler that divided France in half. Germany occupied and directly administered the North. For several years, until Germany imposed direct rule throughout France, Pétain led an **authoritarian** puppet state in central and southern France. Known as the Vichy regime because its capital was Vichy, a city in central France, it violently sought to repress French opposition to Germany and also sent over 1 million French citizens to Germany to work producing goods for the Nazi war effort. Vichy was the only government not directly under German occupation that actively targeted Jews: it sent 76,000 French and foreign Jews to Nazi death camps.

Most French people passively accepted the Vichy regime and German domination. However, at immense personal risk, some Communists, Socialists, and Catholic activists organized an armed opposition movement. Charles de Gaulle, a general who was appointed a junior cabinet minister in the last Third Republic government before Pétain became prime minister, led the Resistance movement. His brilliant leadership of the Resistance and subsequent performance when he served as president several decades after the war have earned him the reputation as France's most influential politician of the twentieth century.

authoritarian

A system of rule in which power depends not on popular legitimacy, but on the coercive force of the political authorities.

PROFILE

Charles De Gaulle

Bettman/Getty Images

Charles de Gaulle was from a conservative Catholic background. He chose a conventional career path for someone of his milieu by attending St. Cyr, France's equivalent of West Point. However, he soon became a gadfly by proposing a substitute for French reliance on large troop concentrations and fixed fortifications— the strategy that resulted in 1.4 million French casualties in World War I. Instead, he advocated organizing a highly trained, mobile professional army using modern equipment like tanks and swift personnel carriers. Although his proposal was rejected, he so impressed political leaders that in 1940 he was appointed a junior government minister after Nazi forces invaded France.

When the German offensive succeeded, and the Third Republic collapsed, de Gaulle bitterly opposed the decision by Philippe Pétain, leader of the Vichy regime, to sign an armistice dictated by Hitler signifying France's defeat.

During World War II, de Gaulle led most of the Resistance forces combating the Vichy regime and German occupation. When France was liberated by Allied forces in 1944, de Gaulle was the natural choice to lead the newly formed provisional government. However, he resigned within 2 years when he failed to gain sufficient parliamentary support to create the kind of regime he sought, one based on a strong executive—the critical ingredient whose absence, in his view, weakened the Third Republic and facilitated the Nazi military victory.

De Gaulle gambled that, given his stature as wartime leader, he would quickly regain office following his resignation in 1946. When he was not, he sulked from the sidelines as the Fourth Republic, created in 1946 with a constitution very similar to that of the Third Republic, stumbled along without him. However, de Gaulle's opportunity arose when the Fourth Republic failed to overcome the armed struggle by forces seeking independence for Algeria, France's large colony in North Africa. In order to forestall an insurrection by French military officers seeking to topple the Fourth Republic because they feared that political leaders were seeking an agreement with pro-independence Algerian forces, parliament chose de Gaulle as prime minister in 1958 and authorized him to organize a regime to replace the Fourth Republic. De Gaulle oversaw the drafting of a constitution to replace that of the Fourth Republic. Its centerpiece was the strong executive and weak parliament that he had long advocated. In a **referendum** in 1959, voters approved the proposed constitution, and de Gaulle became the Fifth Republic's first president.

De Gaulle amply used the powers granted by the new constitution, along with others not explicitly delegated, to create a strong state and to govern forcefully within France and in actions on the world stage. He was a frequent gadfly in relations with the United States, for example, passionately denouncing American intervention in Vietnam in the 1960s.

In May 1969, 10 years after de Gaulle returned to power, the regime was rocked by weeks of nationwide strikes and demonstrations protesting the prime minister's high-handed leadership. Although he restored control, he emerged much weaker. Attempting to renew his sagging legitimacy, he sponsored a referendum the following year to reform political institutions. When it was defeated, he immediately resigned the presidency and withdrew from political life. However, the Fifth Republic survives to this day and remains de Gaulle's most influential legacy.

MAKING CONNECTIONS Why do some scholars consider Charles de Gaulle as a rebel whereas others regard him as a conservative? Which interpretation is more persuasive, and why?

referendum

An election in which citizens vote on approving (or rejecting) a policy proposal.

It is useful to compare the constitution of the Fourth Republic (1946–1958) with that of the Fifth (1959–present) to understand what de Gaulle hoped to achieve. Created over his opposition, the Fourth Republic embodied an extreme form of parliamentary rule and weak executive. As in the Third Republic, the constitution granted parliament a near monopoly of power—at the same time that it was not able to function effectively. One reason was that members of parliament were elected by **proportional representation (PR),** a procedure that encouraged a large number of parties to be represented in parliament. This made it difficult for a majority to agree on policy initiatives; hence parliament was often deadlocked. Similarly, PR promoted governmental instability because, in order to form a government that could command a majority in parliament, it was necessary to form multiparty coalitions, which sometimes disintegrated due to infighting among coalition partners. Since the constitution required a government to resign if opposed by a majority, governments were voted out of office about once every six months!

The Fourth Republic might have survived despite governmental instability. However, the regime collapsed in 1958 when it failed to resolve a crisis involving Algeria, a French colony in North Africa that the government considered an integral part of mainland France. After the French army failed to crush an insurgent movement seeking Algerian independence, a rumor spread that the government was considering negotiating a peace accord with the insurgents. Rebellious army officers responded by threatening to order troops stationed in Algeria to invade mainland France and overthrow the republic. At this critical moment, de Gaulle emerged from retirement and offered to persuade the dissident officers to scrap plans for a coup—on condition that parliament vote de Gaulle's return to power, with the authority to scrap the Fourth Republic and propose a new regime. Although de Gaulle's bold proposal was illegal, it succeeded.

On regaining power, De Gaulle oversaw the drafting of a new constitution whose centerpiece was a strong executive and weak parliament—the opposite of the Fourth Republic. The Fifth Republic that he sponsored is now among the most durable regimes in modern French history.

The Fifth Republic (1958–present)

Critics of the Fourth Republic charged that it was all talk—that is, debate—and no action. (As we discuss in Section 2, later in this chapter, this overstates the case.) On the other hand, the Fifth Republic can be considered the reverse. It was designed to empower political leaders to act decisively—too decisively, critics claim, because it lacks adequate checks and balances to hold political leaders accountable.

De Gaulle's actions demonstrated both the strengths and flaws of a system lacking adequate channels for expressing legitimate opposition. In May 1968, opposition to his haughty governing style and the regime's **conservative** policies exploded when millions of students, workers, and others brought France to a standstill by engaging in the largest general strike in Western European history.

For weeks, France was immobilized. Although de Gaulle eventually regained control of the situation, he was discredited and resigned the following year. Whatever de Gaulle's failings, no subsequent French president has rivaled his national and international standing.

The conservative forces that supported de Gaulle's return to power in 1958 swept every major election until 1981. However, economic slowdown and divisions in the ruling coalition during the 1970s eventually enabled Socialist Party candidate François Mitterrand to win the 1981 presidential election on a platform promising sweeping economic and social reforms. Despite widespread fears that the dramatic political shift would produce chaos, the peaceful transition that followed demonstrated the ability of Fifth Republic political institutions to accommodate political alternation.

Mitterrand's Socialist government sponsored audacious reforms, including **decentralization**, expanded social benefits, and increased state economic control. The centerpiece involved a state takeover (known as *nationalization*) of many large industrial firms, banks, and insurance companies. The aim of doing so was to boost economic efficiency and social equity. Although the reforms were partially successful,

proportional representation (PR)

A procedure for electing representatives in which political parties sponsor rival lists of candidates within multimember constituencies. Seats are allotted to parties in proportion to the votes that a party's list receives in the district. By contrast, in a single-member district system, such as the one used in the United States and Britain, the party with the most votes in a given district (that is, a plurality) wins the seat, a procedure that favors larger parties and thus reduces the number of parties represented in parliament.

conservative

The belief that existing political, social, and economic arrangements should be preserved.

decentralization

Policies that aim to transfer some governmental decision-making power from higher to lower levels of government.

Students and workers unite in a mass demonstration on the Left Bank of Paris, May 27, 1968.

as described in Section 2 of this chapter, they were costly and controversial. When economic crisis loomed in 1983, Mitterrand reversed course and ordered the reforms scaled back and partially reversed. His decision has been widely interpreted as demonstrating the futility of achieving radical reforms in an industrialized democracy, especially by an isolated country. (At the moment that Mitterrand was embarking on a radical reformist path, Ronald Reagan in the United States and Margaret Thatcher in Britain were sponsoring conservative austerity measures.) Since the Socialist government's right turn, France has resembled other affluent capitalist countries pursuing market-friendly economic policies. However, ideological conflicts have not ended in France. The new axis of conflict does not pit a radical leftist option against moderate center-left or center-right options but, rather, several centrist options against a radical right alternative. The current structure of ideological conflict was dramatically demonstrated in the presidential elections of 2002 and 2017.

2002: The Le Pen Bombshells and Their Aftermath

The 2002 presidential elections promised to be a remake of the usual competition between center-left and center-right coalitions that had become familiar since the Socialist Party's turn toward the center in 1983. Instead, the election revealed a disturbing ideological fissure within French society not reflected in mainstream party competition.

French presidential elections are held according to a two-ballot system. Candidates from many parties compete at the first ballot. If no candidate gains an absolute majority—which is invariably the case—a runoff ballot is held two weeks later between the two front-runners. After the Socialist Party's right turn in 1983, presidential and parliamentary elections usually pitted candidates of center-left parties against those of the center-right. The 2002 election promised to be no different.

Lionel Jospin, the center-left Socialist prime minister, and Jacques Chirac, the center-right conservative president, who was running for reelection, were widely expected to be the runoff candidates. As predicted, Chirac came in first. However, confounding predictions, Jospin was nudged out for second place by Jean-Marie Le Pen, leader of an ultra-nationalist far-right party—the National Front (also known as the FN). The fragmentation of center-left parties enabled Le Pen, a demagogue who targeted Muslim immigrants, Jews, and mainstream politicians, to nudge out Jospin for second place and face Chirac in the runoff.

Chirac crushed Le Pen in the second ballot by adding to his own first-round supporters most of the voters who had supported other center-left smaller party candidates. In addition, most center-left supporters of Jospin reluctantly turned out for Chirac to prevent a Le Pen victory.

The following two presidential elections (in 2007 and 2012) resembled the earlier pattern of domination by mainstream parties, with the FN confined to the sidelines. However, the party achieved a remarkable comeback under the leadership of Le Pen's daughter, Marine Le Pen, who succeeded her father as head of the FN in 2011. In elections to the European Parliament in 2014, the FN achieved the amazing exploit of coming in first among all parties. Marine Le Pen nearly equaled this performance in the 2017 presidential elections, where she trailed front-runner Emmanuel Macron in the first round by merely 2.7 percentage points. Although Macron trounced Le Pen in the runoff, Le Pen ranks among the most influential leaders of Europe's resurgent far-right parties.

The 2017 Presidential Elections: Reshuffling the Deck

No matter what the outcome of the 2017 presidential election, it would have involved a sharp break with the typical pattern of French political life. The candidates of the two major mainstream parties that had dominated the presidency for decades trailed the front-running maverick politicians and outsiders. The latter included the youthful Macron, a relative newcomer who bolted from the Socialist Party to form an independent political movement, La République en marche (LRM), in 2016; Marine Le Pen, the FN candidate; and Jean-Luc Mélanchon, who led a newly formed far-left party. As described in more detail in Section 4, later in this chapter, both candidates from the established parties failed to make the runoff ballot. The results of the 2017 presidential election and the legislative elections the following month have completely upended the French party system.

France after September 11

Since the terrorist attacks of September 11, 2001, against the United States, France has been deeply involved in global conflicts. While the government supported the U.S. military action against al Qaeda and the Taliban regime in Afghanistan in 2001, it strongly opposed the U.S. invasion of Iraq in 2003. In 2011, it took the lead—ahead of the United States—in organizing military intervention in Libya against the regime of Muammar al-Qaddafi. In 2013, it urged President Barack Obama to engage in military action against the regime of Syrian

Anadolu Agency/Getty Images

President Emmanuel Macron

dictator Bashar al-Assad. Further, as described in the beginning of this chapter, France has been a principal target of terrorist attacks by Islamic extremists in recent years.

France's relations with the United States have often been prickly. In the 1960s, Charles de Gaulle roundly opposed the U.S. invasion of Vietnam. He withdrew from the command structure of the North Atlantic Treaty Organization (NATO) and ordered U.S. military bases in France closed, on the grounds that they infringed on France's sovereignty. The French government loudly condemned the U.S. war in Iraq in 2003.

Yet the relationship of France and the United States is not all negative. At the same time that many French warn of an American cultural invasion, as well as oppose the powerful role that the United States exercises internationally, the French flock to theaters screening U.S. films, and branches of McDo (as McDonald's is known in France) are found in towns large and small throughout the country. Indeed, McDonald's highest European sales are in . . . France!

The ties between the governments of France and the United States have varied from hot to cold. Presidents Nicolas Sarkozy and Obama cooperated closely. And when President François Hollande supported American military intervention in Syria in 2013, U.S. secretary of state John Kerry referred to France as "our oldest ally." However, President Macron made clear in 2017 that he did not share President Donald Trump's skepticism regarding globalization and climate change, and the newly elected presidents' first meeting was quite frosty.

The French "Non"—Now or Forever?

France has traditionally been a leader in promoting cooperation among members of the European Union (EU), the association described in Chapter 5 promoting European economic integration and political cooperation. In 2005, France again took the lead—but this time in an opposite fashion—when French citizens voted in a referendum to reject a proposed constitution strengthening the EU. The decision staggered the EU. Many French, especially those with less education and low income, opposed the constitutional change because they blamed the EU for their economic hardship. In hindsight, the "Non" vote set the stage for the far more decisive "Brexit" vote by British citizens in 2016, described in Chapter 2, that mandated Britain's complete exit from the EU. France's membership in the EU proved to be a mixed blessing during the global economic crisis beginning in 2008. When the French government led the effort to provide an EU bailout for several financially strapped member states, the move was both costly and unpopular in France. More generally, attitudes toward EU membership and globalization have recently replaced the traditional left-right cleavage in French politics: Parties on the extreme left and right of the political spectrum are hostile toward EU membership and globalization, while parties on the center-left, center, and center-right support these arrangements.

The Four Themes and France

Analyzing the four themes that frame *Introduction to Comparative Politics* reveals dramatic changes and suggests troubling questions about recent French politics.

France in a Globalized World of States

Although France is a middle-rank power, it is among the world's richest and most powerful countries. It is one of the five permanent members of the UN Security Council, a leader in the EU, and possesses advanced nuclear weaponry.

The French state has helped the country adapt to global economic competition. France is a world leader in telecommunications, aeronautics, and high-speed rail transport. It led the European consortium that developed the Airbus wide-bodied airplane. France has excelled at developing relatively safe and cheap nuclear power. (Three-quarters of all French electricity is generated by nuclear power.) The pattern of state economic guidance that prevailed in France since the end of World War II has been called statism. However, international economic competition, EU and other international commitments, ideological shifts, and citizens' demands for more autonomy have substantially reduced the state's role in economic management in recent decades.

statism

A doctrine advocating extensive state direction of the economy and society.

Governing the Economy

Compared to other industrialized capitalist countries, the French state has been exceptionally active in managing the economy. However, following the brief expansion of the state's economic role after 1981, and the right turn since 1983, the state has assumed a more modest role.

The Democratic Idea

France has passionately embraced two competing conceptions of democracy. The first involves the belief that citizens should participate directly in shaping political decisions rather than merely voting for leaders who make policy decisions. This idea nourishes protest movements like the May 1968 strikes and demonstrations discussed below. The second conception of democracy fears citizen decision-making on the grounds that it produces irresponsible and uninformed policies. This approach favors representative government, in which citizens choose leaders, who are entrusted with making policy decisions.

Politics of Collective Identity

The dominant understanding of French national identity assigns a central position to the republican state and citizenship. In principle, native born and newcomers alike are entitled to be citizens—on condition that they accept that France's republican and secular values trump identities based on religion, ethnicity, or gender. While citizens are free to value these identities in the private sphere, the informal creed dictates that citizens should shed their private group identities and act solely as rational individuals when they enter the public arena. Thus, multiculturalism (or *communitarianism*, as the French term it) is rejected because it clashes with the universalist/secular model of republican unity.

And yet France is deeply divided by social, economic, and cultural cleavages. Recently, ethnic and religious conflict, unemployment, the EU, and globalization have destabilized national identity. Furthermore, the universalist/secular model has been applied in a way that can restrict people's freedom, such as when dress codes legislated in 2004 and 2011 were invoked by some towns in 2016 to prohibit women from wearing the burkini on public beaches. (For an account of this situation, see Section 4, later in this chapter.) An important reason for the success of the National Front is its ability to exploit tensions relating to group identities and interrelations.

Themes and Comparisons

French politics offers rich lessons for comparative politics. Scholars have coined the term *French exceptionalism* to highlight a prevalent belief held both by scholars and citizens that France's cultural patterns and political system are distinctive.

For example, President Jacques Chirac stated in his Farewell Address in 2007, "France is a country unlike any other. It has special responsibilities inherited from its history and the universal values that it has helped forge." [2] One account has identified four elements that comprise French exceptionalism: the state's key role directing economic and social life; extensive political and ideological polarization; the principle that citizens should regard themselves as individuals rather than as members of ethnic or religious groups; and the claim that the dominant elements of French political culture, involving secularism, liberty, equality, and fraternity, have universal value. [3]

Where Do You Stand?

Do you agree—or disagree—with the widespread opposition in French public opinion to the principle of multiculturalism?

To what extent do the elements comprising French exceptionalism endure; to what extent have they declined?

SECTION 2

POLITICAL ECONOMY AND DEVELOPMENT

▽ Focus Questions

- What have been two major changes in the state's role in economic management in the Fifth Republic?

- What is one major strength and one major weakness of the state's approach to economic management since 1983?

Thanks to skill, clever state management, and favorable historical and geographic circumstances, France has the world's sixth-largest economy. For decades after World War II, the French state played a key role in promoting the transition from an agricultural to an industrial economy. However, since 1983 the state has retreated. Although France remains at the high end among affluent countries regarding the extent of state economic steering and regulation, private business firms now operate in less-regulated markets and receive less state financing and guidance. Accompanying the change has been a shift from an inward-looking, protectionist posture to an export orientation. France is now a major global economic actor. However, French economic performance is quite mediocre. For decades, economic growth has been sluggish, unemployment widespread, and economic challenges daunting.

State and Economy

The New French Revolution

During the nineteenth century, when Britain and Germany were engaging in rapid industrialization, the French state chose the conservative course of preserving traditional society and economy. Predictably, France lagged behind her European neighbors and rivals. A turning point in the state's role occurred after World War II. The groups governing the newly created Fourth Republic recognized the need to give highest priority to economic and social modernization. In order to achieve this goal, they created powerful new state agencies. One scholar described the result as "a new French Revolution. Although peaceful, this has been just as profound as that of 1789 because it has totally overhauled the moral foundations and social equilibrium of French society."[4]

French-Style Economic Management

After World War II, a principal tool that was developed to enable the state to transform France's rural, stagnant economy into a modern, urban, industrial economy was **indicative planning**. A national Planning Commission of technocrats established national economic and social goals for the next several years, and provided extensive state assistance to selected industries, sectors, and regions in order to achieve these goals.

In the new scheme, the state was the chief economic player. Newly created state agencies were provided with ample capital to finance and power to supervise key industrial sectors (this is known as **industrial policy**). The state encouraged small and medium firms in important industries, including steel, machine tools, and paper products, to merge to achieve economies of scale. The state created firms, dubbed "national champions," in high-tech sectors so that they could become major competitors in French and world markets. For example, France became a leader in designing, building, operating, and exporting nuclear power installations. While it is often believed that statism is **socialist**, many conservative leaders at the time, beginning with de Gaulle, supported a statist approach as the most effective way to modernize the French economy.

France's Economic Miracle

From 1945 to 1975, France's economic growth rate was among the world's highest (see Figure 3.2). As a result, average yearly income nearly tripled between 1946 and 1962. At the same time that France leapfrogged into the twentieth century, however, the state's heavy-handed direction provoked intense conflicts, strikes, and protest, most notably in May 1968.

New problems developed in the 1970s because the challenges of technological change and global competition required economic flexibility and decentralized economic decision-making—the opposite of statism, with its centralized style. This structural problem, along with economic slowdown in the 1970s, helped produce the electoral defeat of the conservative coalition that had governed France since the creation of the Fifth Republic. In 1981, the dam burst when Socialist candidate François Mitterrand was elected president on an audacious platform proposing to extend statist direction of the economy, increase social benefits, and expand personal liberty.

French Socialism in Practice—and Conservative Aftermath

François Mitterrand's Socialist government sponsored a dizzying array of measures to revive the economy, create jobs, and recapture domestic markets. It substantially extended France's

indicative planning

A term that describes a national plan identifying desirable priorities for economic and social development, as well as the measures needed to promote this development.

industrial policy

A policy that uses state resources to promote the development of particular economic sectors.

socialist

The doctrine stating that the state should direct the economy in order to promote equality and help low-income groups.

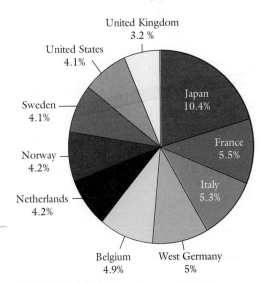

FIGURE 3.2 Average Growth Rates in Gross National Product, 1958–1973

Source: From *The Fifth Republic at Twenty* by William G. Andrews and Stanley Hoffmann (Eds). © 1981 State University of New York.

ÇA ALORS !??
LE PRÉSIDENT EST SOCIALISTE
ET LA TOUR EIFFEL
EST TOUJOURS Ô SA PLACE !??

INCROYABLE !

"What!?? The president's a Socialist and the Eiffel Tower is still standing!??" "Incredible!"

Courtesy Plantu, Cartoonists and Writers Syndicate/Cartoon Arts International, Inc., from Le Monde, May 1981

ample social safety net by boosting the minimum wage, family allowances, old-age pensions, rent subsidies, and state-mandated paid vacations. It promoted cutting edge technological development in biotech, telecommunications, and aerospace. A centerpiece of the program was **nationalization**, involving the state takeover of many privately owned industrial and financial firms. The Socialist reforms promoted social equity and helped modernize the French economy, society, and state in the long run. But in the short run, the high cost of and stiff opposition to the reforms provoked a severe fiscal crisis and drove France to the brink of bankruptcy.

The crisis cruelly demonstrated the limited margin of maneuver for a medium-rank power. In 1983, Mitterrand reluctantly ordered an about-face in economic policy. Political scientist Jonah Levy observes, "A leftist administration that had been elected just 2 years earlier on a campaign to intensify *dirigisme* [that is, statism] began instead to dismantle *dirigisme*."[5] Since 1983, the core elements of statism have been abandoned.

The Socialist government's difficulties in the early 1980s partly resulted from the fact the radical reform programs collided with opposite changes in economic policy occurring elsewhere. Just when President Mitterrand was extending statism, British Prime Minister Margaret Thatcher and American President Ronald Reagan were sponsoring **deregulation** and cutting back social benefits. France did not have the clout to buck the international tide. The failure of the socialist experiment dealt a body blow to France's traditional statist pattern. The result since the mid-1980s has been that governments of the center-left and center-right alike have pursued a contradictory quest both to preserve France's extensive social safety net and to devise cost-saving measures to stimulate economic growth.

France's Neoliberal Modernization Strategy

Since 1983, economic priorities have included **privatization**, deregulation, and liberalization. Privatization involves the sale of publicly owned financial and industrial firms to private investors. Deregulation reduces the state's role in setting prices and wage levels, allocating credit, and hiring and firing employees. Financial liberalization facilitates movements of capital in and out of France. This package of economic policies is often referred to as **neoliberal**. France's approach to governing the economy has now partially converged with that of other rich capitalist countries—at the same time that it retains an ample, costly, and highly popular social welfare sector.

In brief, although many of the more statist features of the Mitterrand era have been reversed, differences with other rich capitalist countries persist. Long after the right turn of 1983, political scientist Vivien Schmidt observed that France has not "abandoned its statist model . . . . Governments have not stopped seeking to guide business . . . even as they engineer the retreat of the state."[6] State spending is currently 57 percent of the GDP, the highest in the Eurozone, compared to 44 percent in Germany and 38 percent in the United States. France and Finland are the two countries in the 28-member Organisation for Economic Development and Co-operation (OECD), the international organization of wealthy capitalist countries,

nationalization

The policy by which the state assumes ownership and operation of private companies.

deregulation

The process of dismantling state regulations that govern business activities.

privatization

The sale of state-owned enterprises or services to private companies or investors.

with the highest proportion of state spending as a share of GDP. Statism therefore remains alive (if not altogether well).

The French economy has not fared well recently. Although France's strong safety net, which boosted consumer demand, enabled it to weather the 2008 economic recession better than Britain and Germany, the economy has stagnated for years. For example, *Le Monde* newspaper reported on February 28, 2017 that, whereas French companies represented 5 percent of the value of companies traded on worldwide stock markets in 2007, this proportion dwindled to 2.8 percent in 2017. In 2007, 32 French companies were among the world's 500 largest; the comparable figure was 22 in 2017. Long after the end of the 2008 recession, French economic growth was an anemic 1 percent annually, and average household purchasing power in 2017 was less than it had been in 2008.

International economic agencies and business groups in France periodically urge the government to reduce social spending, budget deficits, and workers' protections. However, these proposals typically generate massive resistance. For example, in 2016, President Hollande proposed loosening regulations on the scheduling of work. The plan was highly unpopular. It divided Hollande's own Socialist Party and provoked massive strikes and demonstrations. Especially notable (and noticeable!) was a walkout by Paris sanitation workers that left mountains of trash littering neighborhoods throughout the city. In order to pass the reform, the Hollande government was forced to deploy a much-criticized constitutional procedure (described in Section 4). The conflict virtually destroyed the Socialist Party's prospects in the 2017 presidential and parliamentary elections.

Assessing French Economic Performance

Many factors account for France's persistently poor economic performance. France spends less than other leading countries on research and development (R&D). There are chronically large budget deficits, heavy public debt, and high taxes. Social programs are costly and becoming more expensive as the population ages.

Among France's most acute economic problems is unemployment, which has been in the range of 10 percent or more for decades. According to the Institute for Management Development, the French economy is only the 28th most competitive in the world. However, it is highly productive. Although full-time French workers have a shorter workweek than British and German workers, their hourly output is the world's highest.

Society and Economy

According to Nobel Prize–winning economist Paul Krugman, it is misleading to regard France simply as an economic laggard. Rather, the country has chosen a distinctive path. Instead of giving priority to economic efficiency and output, it has sought to balance these goals with concern for citizens' quality of life, as evidenced by policies favoring early retirement, short workweeks, and long vacations.[7] Workers who are laid off are eligible for up to 2 years of unemployment insurance and job retraining. And, despite intense protests, some reforms have been achieved. In recent years, the retirement age has been raised and pension benefits trimmed.

France has among the world's most extensive welfare states. Dubbed the French social model, it reflects a widely held belief that the state should help citizens lead healthy, secure lives. Social services include free prenatal care for pregnant women, generous maternity leave policies, family payments, and subsidies enabling children

neoliberal

A term used to describe government policies that aim to promote private enterprise by reducing government economic regulation, tax rates, and social spending. The term *liberal* in Europe usually refers to the protection of individual political and economic liberty; this is quite different from its meaning in the United States, where it refers to government policies to distribute resources to low-income groups.

to attend preschool. High school students who pass a stiff graduation exam are entitled to attend public universities where tuition is virtually free. Other social benefits include public housing and rent subsidies, and publicly mandated five weeks of paid vacation annually for workers in both the public and private sectors. Special mention should be made of the public health system, which provides nearly universal coverage of medical care and international experts rank among the best in the world.

Yet, if social welfare programs are popular, they are not without problems. For example, access to many social programs is unequal and promotes what the French call *the social fracture*. Stably employed workers and pensioners are on the fortunate side of the divide. (Seventy percent of social spending goes for pensions and other benefits for the elderly.) Youth, part-time workers (who are often young), women, and those from immigrant backgrounds experience higher levels of unemployment and receive fewer social benefits. (However, those most in need are entitled to a minimum yearly income.)

France's social programs are costly: one-third of French GDP is devoted to social spending. And an aging population spells rising medical and retirement costs, along with shrinking revenue to pay the bills. For decades, governments have proposed cutting social benefits—only to encounter intense pushback that often succeeds in blocking change.

Labor Relations

Relations between management and labor have traditionally been conflictual. While employers often view unions as opponents, workers have responded by organizing strikes and enlisting state support for their cause. The labor movement has historically been quite weak: Under 10 percent of employees are currently union members. However, when unions organize demonstrations to protest proposed government social cutbacks, citizens turn out in droves.

Inequality and Ethnic Minorities

France has long prided itself on being inclusive toward ethnic minorities. Public opinion polls find the French less fearful of immigrants compared to citizens in most European countries. Yet, immigrants face daunting obstacles, including an unemployment rate double that of other French citizens. A research project provided dramatic evidence that one reason is racial and ethnic discrimination. Researchers submitted applications for job openings by two groups of fictitious applicants. While "Thomas Lecomte" and "Guillaume Dupont" ("traditional" native-born French names) were invited to one job interview for every 19 applications, "Youssuf Belkacem" and "Karim Brahimi," with identical credentials, were invited to one job interview for every 54 applications.[8]

Inequality and Women

France provides extensive social services enabling women to work outside the home (see Figure 3.3). As a result, about two-thirds of women do so. Government spending for family payments, child care, and maternity benefits is nearly double that in other EU countries. Mothers are entitled to 6 months of paid maternity leave. (It might be noted that only two U.S. states have any provision for paid maternity leave.) Fathers are also entitled to paid paternity leave. Laws mandate gender equality in the workplace and outlaw sexual harassment.

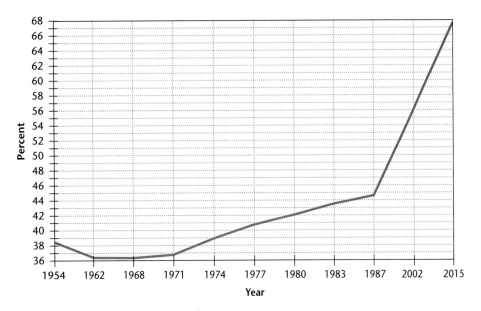

FIGURE 3.3 Women in the Labor Force

Source: INSEE, in Louis Dirn, *La Societe Francaise En Tendances* (Paris: PUF, 1990), p. 108; 2002 data from INSEE, *Tableaux de l'Economie Francaise, 2003–2004* (Paris: INSEE, 2003), p. 77. www.insee.fr/fr/statistiques/2569336sommaire=2587886. Accessed July 27, 2017.

Nevertheless, gender inequalities in employment persist. The proportion of female managers and administrators is among the lowest of all industrialized countries. Women earn about 15 percent less than men for comparable work. The impact of a 2010 law mandating equal pay for equal work can be summed up in a newspaper's bleak headline: "For Women in France, Dim Outlook on Equality."[9] France ranks fifth in terms of gender equality among countries in the OECD.

The Generation Gap

There is a wide generation gap in the French economy. Older workers are more likely to be stably employed and to receive good wages and solid fringe benefits, including protections against layoffs. However, the result is to deter employers from hiring new workers. The result: over one-quarter of young workers are unemployed—double the proportion of older workers. In recent years, government measures to encourage early retirement and ease restrictions on scheduling work and dismissing workers have encouraged job creation. However, two-thirds of newly created jobs are temporary or part-time and provide lower wages and fringe benefits.

Environmental Issues

There is a keen awareness in France of environmental challenges. A constitutional amendment in 2004 banned the adoption of new technology if there is significant uncertainty about its possible environmental risks. (The measure is known as the precautionary principle.) On the other hand, France is firmly committed to nuclear energy, on which it depends for most of its electricity. It is a world leader in developing and exporting nuclear technology, and the French nuclear industry has an excellent safety record.

THE GLOBAL CONNECTION

France and the European Union

France helped create the European Union (EU) in 1957, and has been a leader of the organization ever since. Three devastating wars in less than a century between France and Germany taught both countries about the need to cooperate. The Franco-German tandem has largely shaped the pace and character of European integration. Economic integration fostered by the EU has helped modernize the French and other European economies, contributed to making Europe one of the most prosperous regions of the world.

The French economy and society have been profoundly reshaped by EU membership. The bulk of French international trade and investment are no longer with the country's former colonies in Asia and Africa. Nowadays, over 60 percent of French imports and exports are with other member states of the EU.

The EU provides France with many benefits during good economic times. For example, French farmers receive the largest share of the EU's generous agricultural subsidies. However, when the economy turned sour in the 1980s, many citizens turned against the EU. The proportion of French supporting the EU plummeted from a large majority in the 1980s to less than half in the first decade of the twenty-first century. This was evident when, in 2005, citizens rejected a referendum proposing a revised draft of the EU constitution. The vote also revealed a wide chasm between the majority of French voters, who voted no on the constitution, and leaders of the governing parties, who lobbied for a yes vote.

The 2008 economic crisis created additional strains within the EU. Prosperous members, including France, who shared a common currency, the euro, with distressed members, notably Greece and Portugal, were obliged to provide bailouts. A refusal would have had disastrous consequences for the euro, Eurozone countries, and entire EU. The EU's near implosion illustrated how closely the EU's fate is linked to the economic well-being of its member states. With Britain voting to leave the EU in 2016, and anti-EU sentiment growing elsewhere, including in France, the future of the EU remains uncertain.

MAKING CONNECTIONS Has France's membership in the EU been a blessing or a curse?

France in the Global Economy

For much of the nineteenth and twentieth centuries, France was relatively isolated from the international economy. High tariffs limited foreign competition, protected French industry, and limited technological innovation. In the last half century, however, France has become tightly integrated in the wider international economy and a major global economic player. Imports and exports account for over half of French GDP. Foreign investors, notably American pension funds, own nearly half of all shares traded on the Paris stock exchange. One-third of French workers work for firms partly or wholly foreign-owned. France ranks among the world's largest importers and exporters of capital. Yet participation in the EU and in the global economy has caused intense strains in domestic politics because the costs and benefits of participation are unequally distributed. Citizens with less education and job skills benefit least, which helps explain the popularity of the FN, a party squarely opposed to the EU and globalization. (FN presidential candidate Marine Le Pen in 2017 supported holding a referendum on whether France should exit the EU.) In addition to the fact that the EU and globalization are often blamed for France's economic difficulties, many French cherish what is regarded as distinctively French. For example, in negotiations involving creation of the World Trade Organization (WTO), whose mission is to promote free trade around the world, the French government strenuously (and successfully) lobbied for what was called the cultural exception, that is, a government's right to subsidize and favor its domestic cultural sector, including film and television production. At the same time, the French are avid consumers of American films and popular culture.

Were policy-makers wrong to weaken state capacity by scaling back statism?

Is the French social model an example to be copied—or rejected?

GOVERNANCE AND POLICY-MAKING

Charles de Gaulle designed the Fifth Republic to enable a strong executive to govern without significant checks and balances. He not only lamented the weak political institutions of the Fourth Republic, but also France's great regional and ideological diversity. He bitterly (and half-humorously) lamented, "How can you govern a country that has 246 varieties of cheese?" However, critics suggest that in providing the answer he went too far: the constitution that he designed for his high-handed governing style involves an insufficiently accountable executive and unduly weak parliament.

At the same time, several changes since the creation of the Fifth Republic have resulted in reducing the executive's power and have produced a more balanced regime. The first change involves decentralization of the state. The constitution originally specified that the French Republic is "indivisible." However, beginning in the 1980s, successive governments have transferred substantial governmental powers to subnational government, and a constitutional amendment was added that proclaims: "the organization of the republic is decentralized."

Second, as Section 2 described, the state's relation to the economy has shifted. It now commands less, and consults and persuades more. The third change has limited both the executive and legislature. In the past, French democratic theory claimed that, because governments were elected, they should govern freely and not be constrained by the constitution or unelected authorities. However, the constitution of the Fifth Republic has gradually become accepted as the authoritative source for distributing power among political institutions and, as described below, the Constitutional Council has gained the power of judicial review, that is, the ability to nullify legislation that it judges to be in violation of the constitution.

Focus Questions ❓

- What are two advantages and two disadvantages of France's semi-presidential system?

- What might be the consequences of replacing the present two-ballot procedure for electing the president with a single ballot system?

Organization of the State

The Fifth Republic is a semi-presidential system, a pattern that combines elements of presidential and parliamentary systems. It is a hybrid that combines an independent president and a prime minister responsible to parliament.

Since the 1980s, the constitutional framework has become stronger by overcoming two daunting political challenges. The first involved alternation in power between rival political coalitions. The conservative movement led by Charles de Gaulle and de Gaulle's successor, Valéry Giscard d'Estaing, had ruled the Fifth Republic from its creation in 1958 until 1981. However, in the 1981 presidential election, Socialist François Mitterrand defeated conservative incumbent president

THE U.S. CONNECTION

The American Presidential System and French Semi-Presidential System Compared

The Fifth Republic has what is known as a semi-presidential system. As the term implies, it is a hybrid of classic presidential and parliamentary systems. Thus, in a presidential system, such as in the United States, the executive and the legislature are elected separately and each branch has independent powers. Neither selects the other, is directly accountable to the other, nor can dissolve the other. The legislature can, however, impeach and force the president to resign for treason or other grave misdeeds. The French Fifth Republic has a similar impeachment procedure, but it has never been used.

In a parliamentary system, by contrast, the executive and legislature are fused. The government has substantial control over the parliamentary agenda and can dissolve parliament. On the other hand, the government is accountable to parliament and must resign if parliament votes no confidence.

The Fifth Republic partially resembles a presidential system in that both the president and National Assembly (the more powerful chamber in the bicameral legislature) are directly elected. However, unlike the case in both the presidential and parliamentary systems, the French system is directed by a dual executive—the president and a prime minister who is appointed by the president.

The French constitution distributes powers in ways that strongly favor the executive at the expense of parliament. For example, in a presidential system, legislative leaders control the agenda. However, the constitution of the Fifth Republic authorizes the executive to control parliament's agenda. It also enables the executive to invoke a procedure, described later in this chapter, for approving a legislative text that it sponsors without the need for passage by a parliamentary majority—a procedure not found in either presidential or parliamentary systems. In contrast to a presidential system, the French executive can dissolve the National Assembly. While the National Assembly can force the prime minister to resign by voting a motion of censure, it cannot vote to censure the president.

The most important difference between the presidential and semi-presidential systems involves executive-legislative relations. The American legislature is powerful and fiercely independent. Even when the same party controls both Congress and the presidency, members of Congress have their own base of power. Further, elections to Congress occur at fixed intervals, further reducing the U.S. president's influence. By contrast, the French executive can dissolve the National Assembly and provoke new elections. Because the U.S. Congress is independent, agreement occurs not because the president commands—but because the two branches negotiate a compromise. By contrast, the French constitution renders the president powerful and parliament relatively humble.

MAKING CONNECTIONS Why do you think that many countries adopting new political systems in recent decades have chosen the semi-presidential over the presidential or parliamentary system?

Giscard d'Estaing. Despite dire predictions that the shift in political control (alternation) might produce instability, the system continued to function without disruption.

The second challenge involved divided institutional control, that is, the situation in which the president leads one political coalition and a rival coalition controls the National Assembly. The French call this cohabitation, or power sharing. Many feared that if it occurred, it would produce stalemate and crisis. The test did not arise for decades after the creation of the Fifth Republic. However, in 1986, 5 years into President Mitterrand's presidential term, conservative forces won the elections to the National Assembly. Mitterrand immediately bowed to political realities and appointed Jacques Chirac, leader of the conservative coalition, to be prime minister. Although the two were bitter rivals, despite occasional public jousts they devised workable solutions to dividing the labor of governing. However, cohabitation proved highly unpopular when it occurred again, starting in 1997, during Chirac's presidency, after a Socialist sweep of parliamentary elections forced him to name a Socialist prime minister. This time, the five long years of cohabitation motivated the major political parties to amend the constitution, described below, in order to make cohabitation less likely to recur.

cohabitation

The term used by the French to describe the situation when a president and prime minister belong to opposing political coalitions.

The Executive

France was the first major country to adopt a semi-presidential system. After the fall of communism, Russia and many formerly communist countries in Eastern Europe were so impressed by France's example that they adopted it. Fifty countries have now chosen the semi-presidential system, including Austria, Finland, Iceland, Iraq, Pakistan, Portugal, Sri Lanka, as well as Russia following the end of the Soviet Union, and postcommunist countries in Eastern Europe.

The President

The French president possesses more institutional power than the U.S. president. The French president directs the powerful executive branch. The president is independent of the legislature, and can dissolve it when he (there has never been a female president) so chooses. Especially when able to rely on a political ally as prime minister, the president can control parliament and determine its agenda. When the same party coalition wins the executive and legislative branches, the president is more powerful than the chief executive in virtually any other democratic nation.

The presidential office is so powerful because of (1) the towering personalities of Charles de Gaulle, founder and first president of the Fifth Republic, and François Mitterrand, Socialist president from 1981 to 1995; (2) the ample powers conferred on the office by the constitution; and (3) political practices of the Fifth Republic.

Presidential Personalities Charles de Gaulle was in a class by himself. As the first president in the Fifth Republic, he set the standard for his successors. (Table 3.2 lists the Fifth Republic's presidents and their terms of office.) Thanks to his role as leader of the Resistance in World War II, he initially enjoyed wide popularity. He put his stamp on the presidential office by drafting a constitution endowing the president with ample powers; and, in part thanks to his commanding personality and unique record as a Resistance leader, firmly directed the government, executive, and entire political system. He created a legacy of presidential leadership that continues to this day.

Following de Gaulle, seven presidents have been elected in the Fifth Republic. However, only one so far—François Mitterrand—has come close to compiling a record of strong leadership and bold policy initiatives. Mitterrand sponsored the Socialist government's initial radical reform agenda and later directed its about-face in 1983. By demonstrating that the Left could govern effectively, he facilitated subsequent political alternation in the Fifth Republic. Emmanuel Macron was in considerable measure a successful member of the political and economic establishment: he attended France's most selective school for training the administrative elite, and was also a successful banker and cabinet minister. However, he ran as an outsider because he was not nominated by either mainstream party, and because he promised to break with mainstream ideological orthodoxy. In his words, he was the candidate of neither the

Table 3.2	Presidents of the Fifth Republic
President	**Term**
Charles de Gaulle	1958–1969
Georges Pompidou	1969–1974
Valéry Giscard d'Estaing	1974–1981
François Mitterrand	1981–1995
Jacques Chirac	1995–2007
Nicolas Sarkozy	2007–2012
François Hollande	2012–2017
Emmanuel Macron	2017–present

left nor the right. (He was an outsider in another respect: at age 39, he was the youngest candidate ever to run for president in France.) Macron ran on a platform promising audacious reforms to modernize France, but it is not yet clear how effective he will be in overcoming stiff resistance to implementing his program and, therefore, how influential he will prove to be as president.

The Constitutional Presidency The constitution of the Fifth Republic endows the president with the ceremonial powers of head of state. He resides in the resplendent Élysée Palace and represents France at international diplomatic gatherings. He derives immense power from being the only official elected by the entire French electorate.

A candidate for president must be a French citizen at least 23 years old. Presidential terms are for 5 years, and a constitutional amendment limits presidents to two terms. There is no vice president in France. If a president leaves office before serving out a full term, the president of the Senate (the upper house of parliament) acts as interim president and a new presidential election is held within a short time.

Presidents are elected by a two-ballot procedure. A candidate wins by obtaining an absolute majority of those voting at the first ballot. If no candidate receives a first-ballot majority—which has been the case in every presidential election to date, not surprising given that many candidates compete—a runoff election is held between the two front-runners two weeks later.

The Constitution grants the president the following powers:

- The president names the prime minister, which clearly demonstrates which of the two is dominant within the executive.

- The president approves (or vetoes) the prime minister's choice of cabinet officials and high-ranking civil, military, and judicial officials.

- The president presides over meetings of the Council of Ministers (the government). Note that the constitution entrusts the president, not the prime minister, with this responsibility.

- The president conducts foreign affairs, through the power to negotiate and ratify treaties. He also names French ambassadors and accredits foreign ambassadors to France.

- The president directs the armed forces and, as a 1964 decree specifies, has exclusive control over France's nuclear forces.

- The president may dissolve the National Assembly and call new elections.

- The president appoints three of the nine members of the Constitutional Council, including its president; and also can refer bills passed by parliament to the Council to determine if they violate the constitution.

- Article 16 authorizes the president to assume emergency powers in a grave crisis. This power has been used once, when de Gaulle invoked it to suppress a military uprising. A 2008 constitutional amendment grants the Constitutional Council power to review use of this power after 30 days.

- Article 89 authorizes the president, with the approval of the prime minister, to propose constitutional amendments. An amendment must be approved by both houses of parliament and then ratified either by a national referendum or by a three-fifths vote of both houses of parliament meeting together as a congress.

- Article 11, amended in 1995, authorizes the president to organize a referendum to approve important policy initiatives or reorganize political institutions. (This procedure is distinct from the process of amending the constitution—which, as we have just seen, may also involve calling a referendum.)

- Article 5 directs the president to be an arbiter to ensure "the regular functioning of the governmental authorities, as well as the continuance of the State." While the precise meaning of this phrase is not specified, it endows the president—the sole official delegated this power—with additional authority and legitimacy.

The Political President The constitution grants the president ample powers. But, for such powers to be effective, they must be translated into actual influence. Moreover, the president is not the sole official granted constitutional powers: others include the prime minister, government, and Constitutional Council.

A key political factor that affects the extent of presidential leadership is whether the president's political allies control the government and National Assembly. When they do, presidential supremacy is assured; when they do not (that is, during cohabitation), the president must share power.

The Prime Minister and Government

The constitution authorizes the president to appoint the prime minister. Further, although the constitution is not fully clear on this point, it is generally accepted that the president can dismiss the prime minister. Presidents generally choose as prime minister a senior politician from the party dominating the majority coalition in the National Assembly. This ensures parliamentary support for the prime minister and government. The prime minister in turn nominates, and the president appoints, members of the cabinet or government, a collective body mostly directed by the prime minister.

A key issue is whether the president enjoys a politically friendly parliamentary majority. When this is the case, the president can name an ally as prime minister, thus enabling the president to shape the overall direction of policy. This matters because Article 20 of the constitution authorizes the government, not the president, to "determine and direct the policy of the nation;" and Article 21 authorizes the prime minister to "direct the action of the government." The prime minister is responsible for national defense and ensures "the execution of the laws." Thus, the prime minister accepts the president's leadership because of political, not constitutional, dictates. In other words, the president's preeminence results as much from *political dynamics* as from *constitutional directive*.

Although there is typically some behind-the-scenes jockeying for power between the president and prime minister, prime ministers who are political allies of the president mostly accept presidential primacy. (There was one case when a president dismissed the prime minister for insubordination when he judged that the prime minister had exceeded acceptable limits by promoting his own agenda.) However, the fact that prime ministers accept presidential leadership out of political choice, not constitutional necessity, becomes crystal clear during cohabitation. At these times, the prime minister and government—who are political opponents of the president— have enjoyed considerable autonomy to shape policy.

To summarize the complex relationship between president and prime minister: During periods of unified control, presidents use their formal and informal powers to the hilt, and prime ministers, while powerful and enjoying some autonomy, play second fiddle. At these times, presidents can shape policy in virtually any domain they choose, while the prime minister is delegated responsibility for translating general policies into specific programs and supervising the implementation of policy. The prime minister shepherds government proposals through parliament, drums up popular support for the president, takes the heat on controversial issues, and supervises the bureaucracy. During cohabitation, the balance of power shifts toward the prime minister. While the president retains major responsibility for defense and foreign policy—an area that the constitution explicitly delegates to the president—the prime minister assumes control over domestic policy.

An unpopular experience of cohabitation, which occurred from 1997 to 2002, provoked an important institutional reform. During cohabitation, the frequent sniping between conservative president Jacques Chirac and Socialist prime minister Lionel Jospin provoked an institutional reform devised to discourage a repeat performance. The change involved reducing the president's term from 7 to 5 years, the same length as that of the National Assembly, and holding elections for both several weeks apart. The aim was to increase the likelihood that the same political coalition would win both elections. This was in fact the outcome when Nicolas Sarkozy won the presidency in 2007 and his political allies gained a majority in the National Assembly. A similar outcome occurred in 2012, when François Hollande was elected president and a Socialist Party–led coalition won the parliamentary elections several weeks later. The reform thus achieved its intended goal of producing unified party control.

In the presidential and parliamentary elections of 2017, the situation was complicated considerably by the fact that the newly elected President Macron did not lead a long-established political party. He created La République en marche (LRM), a new party, from scratch in June 2016 while serving in the cabinet. He resigned his cabinet position two months later and shortly thereafter launched his presidential bid. After winning, he scrambled to select loyal supporters, both from within and outside LRM, to run for the National Assembly in elections held the following month. His strategy proved brilliantly effective.

Most cabinet members, also known as "ministers," who direct government departments, are senior politicians from the dominant parliamentary coalition. Cabinet positions are allotted to political parties in rough proportion to their strength in the majority parliamentary coalition. An attempt is also made to ensure regional and, within recent years, gender balance. In 2017, Macron, formerly a Socialist cabinet minister, chose a highly unconventional and visible way to symbolize his determination to choose associates and policies that were anchored neither on the traditional left nor right of the political spectrum. Macron selected Edouard Philippe for prime minister, a deputy of Les Républicains (LR) and mayor of Le Havre at the time of his appointment, and he chose cabinet ministers from across the political spectrum.

The French cabinet is not an important forum for developing or debating policy. Major policies are shaped at the Élysée or Matignon (official residence of the prime minister) or by interministerial committees directed by the president, prime minister, or their staff.

Bureaucracy and Civil Service

The bureaucracy is large and sprawling. An army of civil servants—approximately 2.3 million—performs the day-to-day work of the state. Another 2.7 million staff public hospitals and subnational governmental bureaucracies. About one in five

French jobholders is a civil servant! Members of the personal staffs of the president, prime minister, or cabinet ministers, who assist in formulating and implementing policy, are especially powerful.

The French bureaucracy has extensive power to regulate France's social and economic life. The Fifth Republic bolstered the executive's influence by limiting parliament's legislative power and granting the government authority to issue binding regulations with the force of law.

The top slots in the bureaucracy rank among the most prestigious and powerful positions in France. To qualify for a high-level position, one must graduate from an elite educational establishment called a **grande école**. Over 1 million students are enrolled in French higher education at any given time. Most study at public universities. A small minority—3,000 students—are admitted to the handful of highly competitive *grandes écoles*. The most prestigious are the École Polytechnique, which provides scientific and engineering training, and the École Nationale d'Administration (ENA), which trains top administrators. Children from culturally and economically favored backgrounds have an immense advantage in the fierce competition for admission to the *grandes écoles*.

Top graduates of *grandes écoles* are recruited to an even more select fraternity, a **grand corps**. These small, cohesive networks help direct government departments. Membership in a *grand corps* is for life and provides a fine salary, high status, and considerable power. Members often leave the bureaucracy after several years for plum jobs in the private sector. Membership in a *grand corps* is also a stepping stone to run for parliament or obtain a cabinet appointment. Over half the prime ministers and presidents in the Fifth Republic, including President Emmanuel Macron, were members of *grands corps*.

grandes écoles

Prestigious and highly selective schools of higher education in France that train top civil servants, engineers, and business executives.

grands corps

Elite networks of graduates of *grandes écoles*.

Public and Semipublic Agencies

Public and semipublic agencies play a powerful role in French economic life. However, following the Mitterrand government's turn away from statism, there has been a steep decline in the number of state-owned enterprises. Several giant semipublic agencies remain. For example, Electricity of France, which has a monopoly to distribute electricity throughout the country, has been described as a state within the state. The French national railroad is another enormous public enterprise. Yet many formerly state-owned bastions like France Télécom, Air France, and the Renault automobile company, have been fully or partially privatized.

Other State Institutions

The Judiciary

The French system of Roman law differs substantially from the common law pattern prevailing in Britain and the United States. French courts pay little attention to judicial precedents. What counts are legislative texts and legal codes that regulate specialized fields like industrial relations and local government. Regarding criminal law, a judicial official, the *juge d'instruction*, is responsible for preparing the prosecution's case. Criminal defendants enjoy fewer rights than in the U.S. or British system of criminal justice. In the French trial system, judges actively question witnesses and recommend verdicts to juries. The *Cour de cassation* is the top appeals court for civil and criminal cases; its role is quite technical and apolitical. A separate system of administrative courts hears allegations of wrongdoing by the bureaucracy.

Through much of modern French history, the judiciary was considered an arm of the executive. In the past few decades, however, independent administrative regulatory authorities have gained extensive power in telecommunications, stock market trading, and commercial competition. An additional important initiative was the creation of the Constitutional Council in the Fifth Republic.

The Constitutional Council

The Constitutional Council is the Cinderella of the Fifth Republic. One study observes, "Originally an obscure institution conceived to play a marginal role in the Fifth Republic, the Constitutional Council has gradually moved toward the center stage of French politics and acquired the status of a major actor in the policy-making system."[10] The Constitutional Council has often acted as a check on the legislature and, especially, on the executive. It became more powerful and independent after successfully claiming the right of judicial review. Unlike the U.S. Supreme Court, the council must review a bill within 1 month of its passage, after which it can no longer rule on the constitutional status of the law.

The nine members of the council serve staggered 9-year nonrenewable terms. The presidents of the National Assembly and Senate each appoint three members. The president of the republic names the remaining three members and designates the council's president. A 2008 constitutional amendment gave parliament a limited right to veto nominees to the council. The first woman was appointed to the council in 1992.

In contrast to most constitutional courts, lower court judges in France are rarely appointed to the Constitutional Council. Instead, most members are prominent politicians and public figures. The Constitutional Council is considered a relatively nonpartisan body.

State Council

France has a system of administrative courts that decide cases brought by individuals alleging that administrative actions have violated their rights. Given that the executive and bureaucracy are so powerful, these courts have an important role within the political system. The most important administrative court is the *Conseil d'État* (State Council). It advises the government about the constitutionality, legality, and coherence of proposed laws that the government is drafting, as well as reviews administrative regulations and decrees.

Subnational Governments

France has three levels of subnational elected governments: municipal, departmental, and regional. Until the 1980s, local governments were quite weak. Responsibility for regulating local affairs was in the hands of nationally appointed field officers, such as prefects, civil engineers, and financial inspectors.

The Socialist government elected in 1981 loosened the national government's tight supervision of local governments and created regional governments. Subnational governments were granted increased power to levy taxes and were authorized to formulate education, transportation, social welfare, and cultural policy for their localities. The result helped revitalize local life and bring government closer to citizens. But it also created new problems, such as corruption occurring when local officials receive bribes to award public works contracts to private firms.

The Military and Police

Although a middling-rank power nowadays, France was once a world leader and it continues to wield significant influence. It is one of the five permanent members of the UN Security Council and a member of the nuclear arms club. Although the French military intervened in domestic politics at some key moments in the past, it has remained under civilian control since 1958. France has negotiated military alliances with many of its former colonies in Africa, and its armed forces have often bolstered allied (and dictatorial) regimes.

Within France, the police operate with considerable freedom—too much, according to critics. Alongside local police forces, the ministry of defense directs a national police force. Judges and executive officials rarely rein in the police. The "forces of order," as they are called in France, have a reputation for engaging in brutal tactics, illegal surveillance, arbitrary actions, and racial profiling. These criticisms increased following the 2015 attacks at *Charlie Hebdo* magazine and the Bataclan theater. The government first declared a temporary state of emergency, which expanded its counterterrorist capabilities, then renewed it, and later made the expanded counterterrorism powers permanent by laws passed by large majorities in 2015 and 2016. Security officials have gained the right to conduct surveillance on an individual basis and to mine metadata without judicial authorization; to conduct house raids, obtain personal data, detain suspects, and engage in house arrests—all without judicial authorization and need to provide evidence. Soon after the executive gained the new powers, thousands of house raids were conducted, with little evidence that they produced useful information.

Although many of the new powers have enabled authorities to engage in racial and ethnic profiling of Muslims, they also appear to be aimed at preventing peaceful protest by all French citizens. Critics charge that the expanded powers represent considerable over-reach and endanger liberty. For example, a UN panel of human rights experts charged in 2016 that the new measures represented "excessive and disproportionate" restrictions on civil liberties.

The Policy-Making Process

As discussed previously, the policy-making process differs substantially between periods of unified control and cohabitation. In both cases, however, executive dominance sharply limits legislative and popular participation. As Section 4 will describe, this situation has frequently provoked popular protest.

France's participation in the global economy has deeply affected the policy process. While France's leading role within the EU has enabled it to leverage its power, EU commitments have also limited France's freedom of action and has served as a lightening rod to attract popular opposition.

Where Do You Stand?

Is there an adequate balance in the Fifth Republic between democratic participation and effective policy-making? Suggest one reform that could improve the balance.

Have decentralization reforms strengthened or weakened the state?

REPRESENTATION AND PARTICIPATION

- Why do scholars claim that the French legislature does not adequately represent citizens and hold the executive accountable?

- What are two reforms that might promote checks and balances, empower the legislature, make it more representative, and enable it to hold the executive accountable?

Because Charles de Gaulle believed that political parties and parliament prevented vigorous executive leadership in the Third and Fourth Republics, he designed the constitution of the Fifth Republic to limit popular participation, representation, and legislative autonomy. While he succeeded in muzzling parliament, he failed to curb parties. Indeed, the reform that he sponsored to elect the president by popular suffrage stimulated the development of strong political parties. Thanks to the incentive that winning the all-important presidential contest provides, formerly decentralized parties chose to become centralized, unified organizations. At the same time, the development of strong parties has helped promote energetic executive leadership.

The Legislature

The French parliament consists of the indirectly elected Senate (the upper house) and the more powerful, directly elected, National Assembly. Parliament neither enjoys the independence that legislatures have in presidential systems, nor can it hold the executive fully accountable, as parliaments can in parliamentary systems, since the National Assembly can only censure the prime minister, not the more powerful president.

The Constitution created a revolution in French constitutional law. Rather than providing parliament with an open-ended grant of authority, that is, parliamentary sovereignty, Article 34 enumerates the areas in which parliament is authorized to legislate and prohibits legislation on other matters. The Constitution also authorizes the executive to issue regulations and decrees that do not require parliamentary approval. Further, Article 38 authorizes the government to request parliament to grant the government authority to issue ordinances (regulations) with the force of law. Governments have used this controversial procedure to limit parliamentary debate and prevent unwelcome amendments.

Even within the limited area of lawmaking, parliament lacks autonomy. The government initiates about 90 percent of bills passed into law. Parliament has limited control over the budget. The executive can dissolve the National Assembly before its normal 5-year term ends. Although the executive cannot dissolve the Senate, the Senate is the weaker branch.

The government's control over parliament is further bolstered by Article 44 of the constitution, known as the package or blocked vote, which limits parliament's freedom to propose amendments to legislative proposals. Governments have used (or abused) the package vote to restrict debate on many key legislative bills.

The most controversial weapon the government can deploy to pass legislation is Article 49.3, described by a scholar as "one of the most powerful instruments at the disposal of contemporary democratic government."[11] The procedure authorizes the government to call for a confidence vote on its overall policies or on a specific bill. When it does so, the policies, or bill, are considered approved unless an absolute majority of deputies (as members of the National Assembly are called) pass a censure motion within 24 hours. Deputies who abstain or are absent are, in effect, counted as supporting the government. The Socialist government under President Hollande invoked

Article 49.3 to ram through parliament a reform of the labor code in 2016 despite the intense opposition of many Socialist deputies. This procedure for bypassing parliament proved so unpopular that a constitutional amendment in 2008 limited its use to once in each parliamentary session, and only for matters involving finances or security.

Deputies can also propose censure motions; again, passage requires approval by an absolute majority of deputies. (Only the National Assembly, not the Senate, can pass censure motions.) The constitution limits the number of parliament-initiated censure motions. Further, since governments typically command a parliamentary majority, it is unlikely that the National Assembly will vote for censure. Only one censure motion has ever been voted on in the Fifth Republic.

This discussion suggests why parliament is generally considered a rubber stamp, why its debates are not widely reported, and why opposition parties cannot adequately air grievances. Given this situation, discontented groups are more likely to express opposition in the streets rather than channel demands through parliament.

Parliamentary committees (called *commissions*) are authorized to review and propose amendments to draft legislation. However, because the government can drop amendments that it dislikes before putting the text to a vote, commissions are not very powerful.

The National Assembly is far more powerful than the Senate because it alone can censure the government, and it can pass laws despite the Senate's opposition. The Senate can at most delay approval of legislation voted in by the National Assembly. However, the Senate's approval is required to pass constitutional amendments.

Modest reforms have been enacted in response to widespread calls to strengthen parliament. A constitutional amendment in 2008 empowered parliament to approve nominations to key executive positions. Opposition parties were given control over the parliamentary agenda for 1 day a month. Yet parliament continues to play a limited role in the French political system.

How a Bill Becomes a Law

The Constitution provides two procedures for passing laws. A rarely used provision authorizes the government to propose legislation via a referendum. The typical procedure is for parliament to pass legislation. Following a bill's introduction in one of the two chambers (usually the National Assembly), a commission reviews the bill. The text is then submitted to the full house for debate, possible amendment, and vote. If approved, the same procedure is followed in the second chamber.

A bill becomes law if passed in identical form by both houses (unless later nullified by the Constitutional Council). If the two houses twice vote different versions of a bill (or one time each if the government declares the bill a priority matter), a joint commission of members from both houses seeks to negotiate a compromise. If it succeeds, both houses vote upon the revised text. If they fail to pass the text at this reading, the government can request the National Assembly to vote again. If it passes, the bill becomes law despite the lack of senatorial approval. This method has been used to bypass the Senate on some important legislation.

Once a bill passes, the president of the republic, president of either legislative chamber, or sixty deputies or senators can refer the bill to the Constitutional Council within a month. The council can strike down the entire text or those portions that it judges violate the Constitution. After this period, the law can never be reviewed by the council except in a case where a citizen alleges that a law violates constitutionally protected rights.

Why might the two chambers hold different positions? Mainly because they are elected by different procedures and represent different interests.

Electing the Legislature

The 577 deputies of the National Assembly are elected for a 5-year term by a two-ballot single-member district procedure that resembles the procedure for electing the president. To be elected at the first ballot, a candidate must receive an absolute majority of the votes cast in a district. While a few popular incumbent deputies are reelected at the first ballot, most elections require a runoff the following week. Whereas in presidential elections, only the two front-runners can compete at the runoff ballot, in elections to the National Assembly, any candidate receiving at least 12.5 percent of first round votes can compete in the runoff. However, until the eruption of the National Front, most second-ballot elections pitted a candidate on the left against one on the right. The reason is that center-left and center-right minority candidates typically supported the best-placed major party candidate on their side of the left-right divide. This pattern has been disrupted by the presence of many National Front candidates present in runoff elections. And, as described later in this section, the 2017 elections to the National Assembly presented a very different configuration.

The 348 members of the Senate are elected for 6-year terms by electoral colleges consisting of local elected officials from France's 101 *départements*. Since politicians from rural areas are the largest group in these electoral colleges, the Senate usually has a conservative orientation.

Political Parties and the Party System

Contrary to de Gaulle's fear that political parties would prevent stable leadership, they forcefully promoted it for most of the Fifth Republic. Recently, however, ideological convergence between the two major parties, as well as their failure to resolve major economic, social, and cultural problems, has provoked a backlash. Many French citizens feel disillusioned and unrepresented by the mainstream parties.

The present situation is in strong contrast to the typical pattern of the past several decades, which had involved alternating governing coalitions led by the center-left Socialist Party (PS) and center-right party, renamed Les Républicains (LR) in 2015. When both parties failed to deal effectively with socioeconomic and cultural challenges, as well as experienced intense internal divisions, this created an opportunity for outsiders. The decline of the two formerly dominant parties has been intertwined with a surge in popularity of the far-right National Front (FN), the movement led by ultra-leftist Jean-Luc Mélanchon, and, most dramatically, the meteoric rise and presidential victory of Emmanuel Macron in 2017. In brief, the French party system is currently in a state of intense turbulence and change.

The Major Parties

Despite the recent revolt against the two formerly governing parties, they remain influential, thanks to their control of subnational governments and significant representation in parliament.

Les Républicains Until de Gaulle reached power in 1958, right-wing parties were numerous and fragmented. De Gaulle's allies formed a party that unified many on the moderate right. The social base of the party—business executives, shopkeepers, professionals, elderly, wealthy, religiously observant, rural, and highly educated voters—reflects its conservative orientation.

The Gaullist party (whose name changed periodically—most recently to Les Républicains) was the keystone of the Fifth Republic in the early years. Although the party's fortunes flagged in the 1970s and 1980s, it regained dominance when its leader, Jacques Chirac, was elected president in 1995. Chirac was reelected in 2002 and, when his second term ended in 2007, was succeeded as president by his political ally, Nicolas Sarkozy. However, the party was marginalized when Socialist Party candidate François Hollande defeated Sarkozy's reelection bid in 2012. Thanks to Hollande's dismal performance as president, LR fortunes soon improved and François Fillon, Sarkozy's former prime minister, won the LR's presidential primary in 2016. A seasoned and competent politician, Fillon was the front-runner in the 2017 presidential campaign—until his reputation as a squeaky-clean politician was destroyed by revelations that he had used his public office to create no-show jobs in parliament worth over 800,000 euros for his wife and children. Fillon's electoral prospects plummeted and, although he partially recovered, his third place showing in the first round excluded him from the runoff. The LR partially recouped in the 2017 legislative elections and emerged as the leading opposition party to Macron's LRM.

Parti Socialiste (PS) A perpetual failure in the early years of the Fifth Republic, the Socialist Party (PS) became a vanguard reshaping France under François Mitterrand's leadership in 1981 and a center-left pillar of the Fifth Republic. Until the FN's and LRM's recent rise, the PS and the center-right conservative party (now called the LR) vied for control of French political institutions.

The PS regained control of the presidency in 2012, when Socialist Party candidate François Hollande foiled Sarkozy's bid for reelection. However, Hollande's performance as president proved to be singularly unimpressive thanks to his lackluster manner, questionable personal conduct, and ineffective policies, as well as the dour economic and political climate. As the 2017 presidential elections approached, and Hollande's approval ratings sank to a record low of 4 percent (!), he bowed to reality and announced that he would not seek reelection. The surprise victor in the Socialist presidential primary was Benoît Hamon, a little-known former Socialist cabinet minister, running on a leftist platform calling for a universal income payment. Many PS politicians calculated that Hamon's electoral prospects were poor and switched their support to Emmanuel Macron, the young and dynamic former Socialist who bolted the PS in 2016 to launch an independent campaign. Hamon's miserable performance in the 2017 election—he gained less than 7 percent of the vote—contributed to the rout of the PS in the 2017 legislative elections. Although the party maintains the support of many local elected officials, civil servants, teachers, and educated professionals, it has become virtually a minor party.

Although in recent decades, the LR and PS represented different socioeconomic groups, their supporters mostly occupied secure positions in the mainstream of French society. Unskilled workers, unemployed, school dropouts, and other marginal groups often support fringe parties. This provided an opening for several upstart parties and candidates. Until Macron's election in 2017, the most important was the Front National (FN).

The National Front (FN) For decades, the FN was conventionally classified as a fringe party because of its small size and anti-mainstream ideological stance. It was among the first openly racist parties in Western Europe since World War II on the basis of its bigoted attacks on Muslim immigrants, especially Arabs from North Africa. It advocated—and continues to advocate—withholding social benefits from documented immigrants, and even deporting them. However, ever since the FN came in first in the 2014 European Parliament elections, comfortably ahead of the two mainstream parties in the 2014 European elections, its classification as a fringe party has had to be substantially revised. Although its candidate Marine Le Pen was far outdistanced in the second round of the 2017 presidential election, the FN is now among France's largest parties. The FN continues to campaign as an anti-system party on the ideological fringe by championing positions outside the mainstream. However, the party's steady growth, large size, and recent acceptance of some mainstream republican values mean that it can no longer be considered simply a fringe party. This development, along with the fracturing of the LR and PS, signifies a fundamental reorganization of the French party system.

Jean-Marie Le Pen founded the FN and was its leader for decades. His vulgar and combative style contrasted dramatically with the polished manner of most French politicians. Le Pen blamed the political establishment for rising crime rates, unemployment, and what he charged was the EU's domination of France. He championed traditional far-right themes of Muslim-bashing and anti-Semitism. For example, he repeatedly characterized the Holocaust as an insignificant "historical detail" and claimed that the Nazi occupation of France during World War II was not especially harsh. As a result, he was often criminally prosecuted and convicted of hate speech—which further increased his notoriety.

The FN achieved a dramatic breakthrough in the 2002 presidential election, when a large number of leftist candidates split the left vote and enabled Le Pen to come in second behind incumbent president Jacques Chirac. Le Pen thus qualified to face off against Chirac in the second ballot. However, Le Pen was trounced 82 percent to 18 percent in the runoff, when mainstream voters and parties rallied around Chirac.

Because Le Pen preferred appealing to a narrow base and provoking outrage among most voters to modifying his program in order to achieve broader support, the FN apparently reached the upper limit of support after his major breakthrough in 2002. The party gained a new lease on life, however, when Marine Le Pen succeeded her father as party leader in 2011. She demonstrated brilliant leadership and cleverly broadened the party's appeal—"de-demonizing" it, in her terms—by downplaying the FN's most shocking themes, including anti-Semitism, biologically based racism, and homophobia. Marine Le Pen replaced her father's crude bigotry with an appeal to secular, republican principles. She claimed that because these principles are incompatible with Islamic beliefs and practices, observant Muslims are not legitimate members of the French community. She sought to strengthen the party's image of respectability in 2015 by expelling several openly racist members from the FN—most notably, her father. At the same time, she retained far-rightist support thanks to coded extremist appeals and continued Muslim-baiting, as when she compared Muslims praying in Paris streets to the Nazi occupation of France in World War II.

In addition to moderating her father's culturally reactionary message, Marine Le Pen stressed economic themes that her father had neglected. She reached out to economically vulnerable and less educated voters by echoing a leftist critique of the destruction caused by "*le patronat*"—large employers. She skewered mainstream politicians for being tools of the wealthy and powerful. She embraced economic nationalism, charging that globalization and the EU are responsible for unemployment. And she advocates French withdrawal from the EU and the Eurozone (that is, using the euro as the national currency).

If many elements of the FN's program sound familiar, it is because they are: the party resembles anti-elitist, far-right parties elsewhere in Europe and beyond. Its far-rightist critique of the status quo enabled the FN to become a major alternative to the two formerly dominant mainstream parties.

Marine Le Pen's efforts to broaden the party's appeal has paid off handsomely. She came in third in the 2012 presidential elections and second in the 2017 presidential elections. Although Le Pen and FN are among the most influential forces in French politics, the two-ballot election procedure used in presidential, legislative, and regional elections makes it difficult for the movement to win a majority in these contests. The reason is that most parties and candidates that are rivals at the first ballot typically band together at the second to prevent an FN victory. The 2017 presidential and parliamentary election results conformed to this pattern.

Minor Parties

Minor parties are found throughout the ideological spectrum. Some are vehicles for promoting particular political leaders—for example, La France Insoumise, created by Jean-Luc Mélanchon to support his 2017 presidential run. The most surprising—and successful—is LRM, which Emmanuel Macron hastily organized to promote his 2017 presidential campaign. LRM had virtually no ground troops when Macron launched his candidacy in late 2016—and few more by the time that he was catapulted to the presidency in May 2017. One of Macron's challenges was to mount a ground game for the June 2017 legislative elections that followed his victory. Although these elections occur on the same day and are connected to national swings, they can also be considered 577 local elections, where personal networks, experience, and notoriety count for a lot. Macron scrambled to select sympathetic candidates to obtain sufficient support in the National Assembly to enable him to govern effectively. Macron achieved another astonishing—even unprecedented—exploit when the local politicians and politically inexperienced members of civil society that he hastily recruited to run on the LRM ticket won an absolute majority of seats in the 2017 legislative elections.

Among the many challenges that Macron overcame was to develop a program that would give concrete meaning to his claim to be neither left nor right. One element countered Le Pen's and Mélanchon's antiglobalization and anti-EU messages head on. Macron campaigned on a platform of wholeheartedly embracing globalization. He also advocated policies to modernize France's society and economy. In practice, this meant relaxing restrictions on business and weakening labor rights. Such an approach risks challenging the French statist and social model. The idea has often been proposed—but generally without much success. Time will tell if Macron can formulate proposed reforms that are more effective in gaining popular support.

Other minor parties include several green parties and the French Communist Party (PCF), created after the Russian Revolution to promote revolutionary change in France. Thanks to its important role in the underground Resistance movement during World War II, the PCF became France's largest party after the war. At its heyday, it controlled France's largest trade union and local governments in heavily working class towns. However, the party steadily lost support and become a pale shadow of its former self due to its authoritarian organization and dogmatic ideology.

Elections

France's most important elections are the legislative and presidential elections (see Tables 3.3 and 3.4). The following troubling developments indicate a crisis of political representation and the party system.

- Voting patterns are highly unstable. In all but one of the eight legislative elections between 1981 and 2017, the governing majority shifted among governing coalitions.

- Voter turnout has generally been declining in both presidential and parliamentary elections. It was at historic lows in the 2017 presidential and parliamentary elections.

Table 3.3	Presidential Elections in the Fifth Republic (percentage of those voting)								
December 1965		**June 1969**		**May 1974**		**April–May 1981**		**April–May 1988**	
Candidate	Ballot Percentage	Candidate	Ballot Percentage	Candidate	Ballot Percentage	Candidate	Ballot Percentage	Candidate	Ballot Percentage
Extreme Right								J.M. Le Pen (FN)	14.4
Center Right de Gaulle (Center-Right)	43.7 (54.5)	Pompidou (UNR)	44.0 (57.6)			Chirac (RPR)	18	Chirac (RPR)	19.9 (46.0)
Center Lecanuet (Opposition-Center)	15.8	Poher (Center)	23.4 (42.4)	Giscard	32.9 (50.7)	Giscard	28.3 (48.2)	Barre	16.5
Center Left Mitterrand (Socialist-Communist)	32.2 (45.5)	Defferre (PS)	5.1	Mitterrand (PS)	43.4 (49.3)	Mitterrand (PS)	25.8 (51.8)	Mitterrand (PS)	34.1 (54.0)
Left		Duclos (PCF)	21.5			Marchais (PCF)	15.3	Lajoinie (PCF)	6.8
Abstentions	15.0 (15.5)		21.8 (30.9)	15.1	12.1		18.9 (14.1)		

Note: Numbers in parentheses indicate percentage of vote received in second ballot. Percentages of votes for candidates do not add to 100 because of minor party candidates and rounding errors.

Sources: John R. Frears and Jean-Luc Parodi, *War Will Not Take Place: The French Parliamentary Elections Of March 1978* (London: Hurst, 1976), p. 6; *Le Monde*, L'Election présidentielle: 26 avril-10 mai 1981 (Paris: *Le Monde*, 1981), pp. 98, 136; *Le Monde*, April 28 and May 12, 1988; *Journal Officiel*, May 14, 1995; *Le Monde*, May 5–6, 2002; *Le Monde*, May 7, 2002; www.electionresources.org/fr/president.php?election=2007%region=fr (accessed on June 18, 2007).

- The rise of the FN and of Macron's LRM represent a rejection of the two formerly dominant mainstream governmental parties.

Countless prominent politicians have been convicted of criminal misconduct, including former presidents Jacques Chirac and Nicolas Sarkozy and many former cabinet ministers. LR candidate François Fillon was the clear front-runner in the 2017 presidential campaign until a newspaper exposé revealed that he illegally accepted expensive gifts and arranged payments to family members for fictitious jobs. Although Marine Le Pen has loudly condemned members of the political

	April–May 1995		April–May 2002		April–May 2007		April–May 2012		April–May 2017	
	Candidate	Ballot Percentage	Candidate	Ballot Percentage	Candidate	Ballot Percentage	Candidate	Ballot Percentage	Candidate	Ballot Percentage
	J.M. Le Pen (FN)	15	J.M. Le Pen (FN)	17.0 (17.9)	J.M. Le Pen (FN)	10	M. Le Pen (FN)	17.9	M. Le Pen (FN)	21.3 (33.9)
					De Villiers	2				
	Chirac (RPR)	20.8 (52.6)	Chirac (RPR)	19.9 (82.1)	Sarkozy (UMP)	31 (53)	Sarkozy (UMP)	27.2 (48.4)	Fillon (LR)	20.0
	Balladur (UDF)	18.9	Bayrou (UDF)	6.8	Bayrou (UDF)	19	Bayrou (Mouvement Démocratique)	9.1	Macron (LRM)	24.0 (66.1)
			Saint-Josse (CNPT)	64.3	Nihous (CNPT)	1				
			Madelin (PR)	3.9						
	Jospin (PS)	23.3 (47.4)	Jospin (PS)	16.1	Royal (PS)	26 (47)	Hollande (PS)	28.6 (51.7)	Hamon (PS)	6.4
			Chevènement	5.3	Voynet (Greens)	2		2.3		
			Mamère (Greens)	5.3			Joly (Greens)			
	Hue (PCF)	8.6	Hue (PCF)	3.4	Buffet (PCF)	2	Mélanchon (Front de Gauche)	11.1	Mélanchon (La France Insoumise)	19.6
			3 candidates (Extreme Left)	10.6	4 candidates (Extreme Left)	7				
		20.6		27.9 (19.9)		16 (16)		20.5 (19.7)		22.7 (34.7)

establishment for being corrupt, the EU charged her in 2017 with misappropriating EU funds. The torrent of political scandals helps explain the rising disillusionment with politicians in the country. A 2016 poll found that 60 percent believe that politicians are corrupt (18 percent higher than in 2013).[12]

Political Culture, Citizenship, and Identity

Until the 1980s, two traditional subcultures powerfully shaped French political and cultural life. The first had a strongly working-class flavor and was structured by the parties on the Left, notably the PCF. The other was a conservative subculture linked to the Catholic Church. The subcultures provided members with contrasting political orientations and social identities. Most French citizens identified with one or

Table 3.4	Electoral Results, Elections to National Assembly, 1958–2017 (percentage of those voting)														
	1958	1962	1967	1968	1973	1978	1981	1986	1988	1993	1997	2002	2007	2012	2017
Far Left	2%	2%	2%	4%	3%	3%	1%	2%	0%	2%	2%	3%	2%	1%	5%
PCF	19	22	23	20	21	21	16	10	11	9	10	5	4	7	1
Socialist Party/Left Radicals	23	21	19	17	22	25	38	32	38	21	26	25	26	34	6
Ecology	—	—	—	—	—	2	1	1	1	12	8	4	3	—	0
Center	15	15	18	10	16	21*	19*		19*	19*	15*		8	6	43
Center-Right	14	14	0	4	7			42*				5*	4	—	6
UNR-RPR-UMP-LR	18	32	38	44	24	23	21	—	19	20	17	34	40	27	22
Far-Right	3	1	1	0	3	0	3	10	10	13	15	12	7	14	11
Abstentions	23	31	19	20	19	17	30	22	34	31	32	36	40	43	57

*Number represents the percentage of combined votes for Center and Center-Right parties.
Sources: Françoise Dreyfus and François D'Arcy, *Les Institutions politiques et administratives de la France* (Paris: Economica, 1985), 54; *Le Monde*, March 18, 1986; *Le Monde, Les élections législatives* (Paris: Le Monde, 1988); Ministry of the Interior, 1993, 1997, 2017. *Le Monde*, June 11, 2002; www.electionresources.org/fr/deputies.php?election=2007&region=fr (accessed 6/18/2007).

the other. In recent decades, however, both subcultures have disintegrated. The PCF has collapsed and the number of self-identified Communists and observant Catholics has plummeted. No new, broad-based networks have replaced them. Instead, French society has become both more fragmented—albeit no less conflicted.

Social Class

For centuries, class cleavages produced intense political conflict and polarization. Class identification rapidly declined in the 1970s as a result of structural economic changes and a decline of ideology. Demographic shifts contributed as well, especially a massive reduction in the industrial workforce due to the downsizing of basic industries. This was matched by the rise of service sector employment, which scrambled class boundaries and traditional social identities while no new social anchors have developed. The rise of unemployment beginning in the 1970s and persisting until today has contributed further to a widespread sense of insecurity. These conditions provide fertile soil for political outsiders and newcomers of diverse orientations, including Marine Le Pen, Jean-Luc Mélanchon, and Emmanuel Macron.

Ethnicity and Immigration

France has traditionally been a magnet for immigrants. Indeed, in 1930 it had a higher proportion of immigrants than the United States. A new wave of immigrants arrived after World War II, in part because the government actively recruited workers

Daniel Vernon/Alamy Stock Photo

The "Jungle" at Calais

from Eastern Europe and North and Sub-Saharan Africa to help rebuild the economy. They often remain second-class citizens, occupying apartments in vast housing projects in shabby neighborhoods with few amenities.

When the economy slowed in the 1970s, the government began restricting immigration. New arrivals since then have mostly consisted of family members of immigrants already established in France, those occupying skilled positions, citizens of EU countries in Eastern Europe, and refugees from Afghanistan, Eritrea, the Sudan, and other war-torn regions. Many recent undocumented arrivals are migrants traveling to the northern port city of Calais, where, in search of jobs, they attempt to sneak into cargo trucks crossing through the Channel Tunnel to England. About 10,000 of such migrants congregated for years in a huge, squalid tent city, known as the Jungle, on the outskirts of Calais. The government disbanded the Jungle in 2016 and provided migrants with alternative shelter and assistance, which proved woefully inadequate. Although humanitarian nongovernmental organizations provided help, the plight of migrants remains appalling.

The FN has exploited the combination of economic stagnation, high unemployment, and terrorist attacks to fan the flames of anti-immigrant feeling. Presidents Sarkozy and Hollande partially mimicked the FN's anti-immigrant orientation. President Macron has attempted to counter anti-immigrant sentiment and has called for more inclusiveness and assistance. However, the challenge of promoting social integration remains daunting.

Citizenship and National Identity

The French describe their approach to immigration, citizenship, and national identity as the republican model. On the one hand, it is inclusive. No matter newcomers' race, religion, or national background, all are welcome—on condition that they learn French and adopt prevailing French political values.

However, while the republican model is officially nondiscriminatory, it contains an implicitly exclusionary and potentially repressive aspect by insisting that cultural identities and values—other than republican, secular ones—should remain private and play no role in the public sphere. This aspect of the republican model is illustrated by the adoption of legislation in 2004 and 2010 involving a dress code for Muslim women. (Section 5, later in this chapter, describes a more recent ban on Muslim women's traditional clothing.) The 2004 law banned displaying "conspicuous signs of religious affiliation" in public schools. Although the laws applied to displays of Jewish and Catholic crosses, its main target was the *hijab* (head scarf—or *foulard*, in French). The government claimed that the law sought to preserve religious neutrality in public schools and combat Muslim **fundamentalism**.

The 2010 law extended the ban by prohibiting women from wearing garments concealing the face, such as the *burqa* and the *niqab*, when they appeared in public space, including streets, parks, businesses, government buildings, and public transportation. Although very few of France's Muslim women are veiled, the law's sponsors claimed that the ban was needed to preserve women's dignity and protect secular values. Historian Joan Scott suggests that the clothing ban reflects "the impotence and/or unwillingness of the government to . . . adjust national institutions and ideologies ... to the heterogeneity of [France's] current population . . . ."[13]

The republican model champions the value of individual merit and claims that people's social and cultural identities have no place in the public sphere. However, the policy of ignoring—or banning—the public expression of racial, religious, and ethnic affiliations often functions in practice to marginalize minorities. For example, despite the fact that there are glaring racial and ethnic inequalities in France, the republican model prevents designing affirmative action programs to rectify them. The government has addressed inequality indirectly, such as by directing resources to what it designates as "sensitive areas," that is, impoverished urban neighborhoods that (not coincidentally) are often home to minorities. However, Muslims and people of color are severely underrepresented in top political and economic positions.

The French are intensely proud of their country's cultural heritage. But globalization, economic instability, and ethnic diversity have shaken confidence and pride in France's enviable position in the world and fueled uncertainty about the meaning and value of French identity.

Gender

When French philosopher and novelist Simone de Beauvoir published *The Second Sex* after World War II, that analyzed the social processes assigning women to a secondary role in society, it became a feminist trailblazer. In the 1960s and 1970s, French feminist theorists played a major role in reshaping literary studies around the world. And yet, despite these noteworthy contributions, France lagged in pursuing gender equality in the political sphere.

Women have traditionally been highly underrepresented in the French political system. Although they make up over half the electorate, there has never been a female president and only one prime minister. However, after decades of struggle by the women's movement, France adopted a constitutional amendment in 1999 that mandates gender parity for many elected offices. France was the first country in the world to require political parties to nominate an equal number of men and women for elected positions. Since then, over 100 other countries have followed France's lead.

The **parity laws** require parties to nominate an equal number of male and female candidates for elected offices filled by proportional representation. Parties failing to do so can be disqualified. Further, for offices filled by the plurality system in single-member districts, notably the National Assembly, parties that do not nominate an equal number of men and women receive smaller public subsidies.

fundamentalism

A term used to describe extremist or ultraorthodox religious beliefs and movements.

parity law

A French law passed in 2000, following the adoption of a constitutional amendment in 1999, and subsequently extended, that directs political parties to nominate an equal number of men and women for many elections.

Following passage of the parity law, the number of women elected to town councils skyrocketed, and women now make up about half of these legislative bodies. However, only one-quarter of Senators are female, and women remain highly underrepresented in the National Assembly. France ranks lower than Britain and Germany with respect to the proportion of female members of the legislature. One reason is that parties can circumvent the requirements of the parity law by nominating women in districts where a party has little prospect of winning. Thus, while female representation in the National Assembly recently soared from 12 percent in 2002 to 39 percent after the 2017 elections—it remains far less than the proportion of female voters.

The parity law does not apply to the presidency, the most important elected position. However, pressure for parity may have indirectly helped Ségolène Royal, PS president of a regional council, gain the PS nomination for president in 2007, the first time that a major political party nominated a female presidential candidate. However, Royal ran a lackluster campaign and came in second behind Nicolas Sarkozy. Her defeat may also have partly been due to sexism.

After his election as president in 2012, François Hollande appointed an equal number of men and women to the cabinet. He also created the first ministry of women's rights with full cabinet status. Emmanuel Macron emulated Hollande's example in 2017.

While women have achieved greater political representation, thanks to the parity law, changing values, and pressure from the women's movement, they continue to have unequal political, social, and economic representation.

Interest Groups, Social Movements, and Protest

Compared to Britain, Germany, and the United States, interest groups in France are relatively weak. When developing policy, the French executive has typically kept interest groups at arm's length. There are exceptions, however, notably the farm lobby and the largest business association.

The development of a more modest state since the 1980s has encouraged an explosion of voluntary and advocacy associations in areas like sports, leisure, feminism, environment, and civil liberties. One estimate is that the number of associations has doubled since the 1980s to over 1 million today.

French Trade Unions

The French labor movement is quite weak. Far fewer workers belong to unions than is the case in other industrial democracies: about 8 percent of the labor force, the lowest figure among comparable countries and a steep decline from the period after World War II, when over 30 percent of workers belonged to unions. Most union members are in public sector unions.

The labor movement is further weakened by internal divisions. In many industrialized democracies, including Britain, Germany, and Japan, a single trade union confederation groups all unions located in specific economic sectors. By contrast, France has four confederations, along with several independent unions. Each confederation pursues its own agenda and competes with the others for members. Rival confederations rarely cooperate and sponsor joint activities. When they do, as occurred for example in demonstrations in 2010 opposing reforms of the pension system, and in 2016 opposing labor market reforms, the whole is much greater and more powerful than the sum of the parts.

Despite their small numbers, unions possess three important resources. First, they are represented on the governing boards of powerful public agencies, including the social security, health, pension, and unemployment insurance funds. Second, union agreements are often extended to cover all workers in a given sector. Thus, virtually all paid employees are covered by union-negotiated agreements. Third, unions have repeatedly demonstrated their capacity to mobilize members and nonmembers alike to protest plant closings or proposed cutbacks in social benefits. Such protests can immobilize industries, cities, or the entire economy. At such times, government administrators, business leaders, and union officials may hold feverish meetings, and unions may obtain significant benefits. When calm returns, unions again assume a marginal role—until the next explosion.

Social Movements and Protest

Fifth Republic institutions were designed to discourage citizens from acting autonomously. As mentioned earlier, there are fewer organized interest groups and voluntary associations in France than in comparable countries, and those that exist, such as the trade union movement, are weak. The lack of institutionalized channels of representation helps explain why France has a centuries-old tradition of direct protest. France is among the European countries where the highest proportion of citizens report having participated in demonstrations. A partial list of groups that have engaged in strikes and demonstrations in recent years include farmers, postal workers, teachers and professors, students, truckers, railway workers, industrial workers, sanitation workers, health care workers, retired workers, the unemployed, homeless, immigrants, actors, research workers, petrochemical workers, and opponents of gay marriage!

The Political Impact of Technology and the Media

Like societies around the world, France is powerfully influenced by recent technological change and the increased speed and density of electronic communications. France has traditionally been at the forefront of technological change. However, it has slipped recently, both because it is a middling size country and because it has devoted fewer public and private resources to R&D. One result has been a French brain drain of scientists, engineers, and entrepreneurs who have migrated to California's Silicon Valley. They report moving because of attractive salaries, light government regulation, and the greater availability of financial support for startups. Unless this trend is reversed, it bodes badly for France's future international economic position.

The French are avid consumers of the media, both print and electronic. Countless books are published annually, and the government has promoted the survival of independent bookstores and deterred chain bookstores and Internet sales by prohibiting substantially discounted book sales. There are numerous newspapers and magazines, although, as elsewhere, the print media is severely challenged by online publishing.

The French electronic media, including television and social media, play an important role in the nation's life. Their political impact is complex, diverse, and contradictory. Some of those engaging in terrorist attacks may have been radicalized by the Internet—and a counterterrorism law passed in 2017 went so far as to limit the time that citizens could legally access radical websites, save for purposes of research.

Where Do You Stand?

Is the balance in the values comprising French national identity more inclusive or repressive?

Does popular protest in France demonstrate the vibrancy or weakness of French democracy?

FRENCH POLITICS IN TRANSITION

SECTION

5

A new chapter occurred in the summer of 2016 in the ongoing saga of France's anti-Muslim dress codes. In a country where women often go topless on public beaches, mayors of over thirty French seacoast towns issued ordinances banned women from wearing the "burkini." The term, a playful combination of *burqa* and *bikini,* refers to full-body swimsuits worn by some Muslim women. The rationale for banning the burkini was that it both victimizes women and somehow represents a threat to public order. The prime minister supported the local bans on the grounds that the burkini symbolizes "women's enslavement." Supporters of the campaign to ban the burkini were visibly embarrassed when a photograph posted on the Internet went viral depicting four armed police

Focus Questions ▼

• What are two major challenges facing the French political system? Name one feature of French political institutions or culture that can help meet these challenges, and one feature that makes it difficult to meet the challenges.

• What are two features of French politics that have surprised you after reading this chapter, and why?

Women in bikini and burkini at beach on the Riviera, summer 2016

Fethi Belaid/Getty Images

officers surrounding a woman wearing a burkini and ordering her to remove the top. The bigotry of the burkini ban was made more apparent when another photograph was posted on the Internet of several nuns wearing customary full-body Catholic habit happily wading at the water's edge—quite undisturbed by the forces of law and order! The double standard was hard to miss: while Catholic women in France can wear garb plainly proclaiming their affiliation, it is illegal for Muslim women to do so.

The burkini ban highlights implicit bias in France's ostensibly religiously neutral, secular, universalistic cultural values. Although later overturned by the State Council, the ban suggests the danger that France's hard-edged form of secularism will be applied in a form that discriminates against Muslims.

Political Challenges and Changing Agendas

Reshaping the French Social Model?

France's famed social model is under intense stress. One cause is conflict provoked by the government attempts to cut social spending and loosen regulations on employers hiring and firing workers. When governments propose social reforms, the reaction is immediate and massive. Extensive protests have occurred over proposals to reform the health care system, labor market, cultural institutions, pension benefits, and the electrical power and petrochemical industries.

Opposition has been provoked not only by the actual cutbacks, but also by the high-handed manner in which they have been introduced. When Britain, Germany, and other affluent countries have initiated social cutbacks, organized consultation has smoothed the process of adjustment. In France, reforms have typically been developed in secret by the government and imposed from above. The result has been wholly predictable in a country with a proud tradition of popular protest!

"Oui" to Roquefort Cheese, "Non" to Genetically Engineered Products

France is home to a flourishing antiglobalization movement comprised of far-leftists, intellectuals, farmers, and environmentalists. For years, the movement's best-known leader was José Bové, a former sheep farmer from southwestern France, where Roquefort cheese (made from sheep's milk) is produced. Small farmers like Bové oppose the standardized methods of farming that agribusiness corporations seek to impose, including using genetically modified seed and other products, which the movement opposes as potentially risky and designed to boost corporate profits. Farmers also oppose corporate-controlled food processing and distribution. Bové became a popular hero after he ransacked a McDonald's construction site and served a six-week prison sentence.

Opposition to globalization is a major theme in French political discourse on both the left (Mélanchon) and the right (Le Pen). One reason is that many French citizens regard globalization as threatening French culture and oppose the "invasion" of American companies, products, and values that threatens France's cherished way of life. Globalization and the EU are also blamed for exporting French jobs to low-wage countries. The EU is blamed for allowing workers from low-wage EU member countries like Poland to migrate to France. However, as discussed in Section 2 earlier in this chapter, France is tightly integrated into the global economy, and many jobs in France are devoted to producing goods and services for export.

The Challenge of the FN

The National Front (FN) has reaped a political harvest from warning about globalization, as well as about the threat supposedly posed by the 5 million Muslims in France, the largest number of any country in Western Europe. Political sociologist Pierre Birnbaum observes, "What the National Front proposes to the French people . . . is a magical solution to their distress, to their loss of confidence in grand political visions of the nation."[14]

The FN attracts extensive support from native-born white citizens, many on the margins of French society. Yet, despite the FN's popularity, French attitudes toward immigrants of Muslim backgrounds are more positive than is the case for citizens of neighboring countries. When French, Germans, and British citizens were asked whether "it is a good thing [that] people from the Middle East and North Africa [are] coming to your country," the French were most likely to answer yes. This result suggests yet another dimension on which French society is polarized. The same poll found that French Muslims report feeling far less alienated from the dominant culture compared to Muslims in Britain and Germany.[15] However, others polls report that anti-Muslim sentiment has risen substantially since the 2015 and 2016 attacks described in the opening of this chapter.

France Falling?

France has been wracked by self-doubt in recent years, what the French now call "declinism," as illustrated by books with titles like *France in Free Fall, France's Disarray, Chronicles of French Denial, French Melancholy* and, perhaps the most alarmist: *The French Suicide*, which has sold over 500,000 copies. A newspaper headline cruelly observed, "France, The European Champion of Pessimism."[16] Over two-thirds of respondents in one poll agreed that the country is in decline. Another poll found that only 9 percent of respondents believe their children will be better off than the previous generation, compared to 17 percent in Britain and 28 percent in Germany.[17]

However, might such pessimism be exaggerated? While France's political system is often described as rigid and unable to adapt, political scientist Peter A. Hall observes that "the economy, society and politics of France have changed . . . profoundly during the past 25 years."[18] Examples include important reforms involving decentralization, health care, retirement, and industrial relations. And Emmanuel Macron's election in 2017 dramatically illustrates that the political system is a work in progress.

Another example of adaptation and flexibility involves policies involving sexual orientation. A 1999 law authorized civil unions between unmarried couples, including gay couples, and legislation authorizing gay marriage passed in 2013. However, the measure was heatedly opposed by the conservative parties, who organized massive demonstrations for months.

Have recent changes in economic and social policies and practices promoted a welcome pluralism or a destructive fragmentation of French society? Many French believe that their country's distinctive way of life is under siege, and that French society has been destabilized. A key question is whether the positive features of France's past can be preserved while initiating reforms to address the country's economic, social, political, and cultural problems.

France's Relation to Terrorism

Long before the United States was attacked on September 11, 2001, France had been the target of terrorist violence. In the postwar period, it was often provoked by France's brutal colonial war in Algeria in the 1950s and 1960s. In recent years, numerous violent incidents linked to Muslim extremists have occurred. The most deadly were described in the opening section of this chapter, but smaller ones occur on a regular basis. The government has devoted enormous resources to counterterrorism. Following the major attacks of 2015 and 2016, laws were passed substantially extending the state's powers of surveillance and control. However, critics charge both that there is insufficient accountability and that the campaign has involved human rights abuses as well as religious and ethnic discrimination. One scholar suggests that, rather than pumping more resources into surveillance and police work, there should be greater emphasis "on improving social conditions for the French Muslim population and finding ways of making them feel part of the national community."[19]

Is Demography Destiny?

Protests organized by high school and university students have often dramatically symbolized the existence of a generational divide in France. The May 1968 upheaval was in part provoked by the opposition of young French people to what they regarded as hierarchical, conservative values. (One of the sparks that ignited the uprising was police intervention at a suburban university outside Paris seeking to crush a student protest.)

Young people have legitimate reasons to protest. For example, as discussed in Section 2, legal barriers to dismissing full-time workers may deter employers from hiring new—often young—workers. Youth unemployment, at about 25 percent, is more than double that for older workers.

French Politics in Comparative Perspective

Is French politics becoming less exceptional? Recall the four elements comprising the exceptionalist model identified in the beginning of this chapter: the key role of the state in France's economic and social life; extensive political and ideological polarization; the obligation for citizens to identify in the political sphere as individuals rather than as members of groups based on bonds of race, ethnicity, or religion; and the claim that French political culture, involving secularism, liberty, equality, and fraternity, has universal value. Statism and ideological conflict, the first two features of the exceptionalist model, have markedly declined in recent years. However, as discussed in Section 2, although statism has declined, it persists. And while traditional left-right divisions are less evident, ideological passions remain powerful. The third and fourth elements are also under siege, as evidenced by conflicts involving immigration, as well as declining confidence in the uniqueness and universal value of French political culture.

France lends itself to comparisons along the four dimensions that have framed this book. It can usefully be compared with countries where the state plays a less central role. France's statist style of economic management, even the currently more modest version, offers an interesting contrast to countries in which market forces are less regulated. The French theory and practice of democracy lend themselves to comparison with democracy elsewhere. And the ways that France deals with issues involving collective identity can usefully be compared with regimes adopting a different approach.

A second kind of comparison involves historical comparisons within France. For example, analyzing the impact of the parity law provides an opportunity to study the relationship of political institutions to political and social change.

Where Do You Stand?

The criticism that French political institutions failed overlooks how successful they have been in meeting past challenges.

France's best days are behind it.

Chapter Summary

France is justly celebrated for its natural beauty, rich culture, and quality of life. But the country also has a turbulent past and present, as well as deep socioeconomic and cultural divisions. For centuries, the state structured French political and social life. However, in recent decades, the state has lost its preeminent role.

Following a century of relative economic stagnation, France reinvented itself after World War II. For several decades after the war, the economy soared and most French benefited. The state played a central role in planning the French economic miracle. Eventually, however, the state proved less effective at steering an economy that demands decentralized and flexible decision making. The last attempt at state-sponsored development occurred under the Mitterrand presidency. Despite some positive features of his reformist agenda, the failure of the statist elements shifted the balance toward a more market-based economy. At the same time, the state continues to play a larger role in France than in most other industrialized capitalist countries.

Although the French social model is a source of great pride and great benefits, it carries heavy costs. Additional economic burdens involve high unemployment, especially among youth and ethnic minorities; an aging population, whose costly medical care and pensions pose burdens for social welfare systems; and state budget deficits caused by the high cost of financing social programs. France's close ties to the EU and the international economy more generally have produced great benefits but have also involved economic hardships and dislocations that fall especially hard on youth, immigrants, and the less educated.

France's semi-presidential system has proved highly successful in achieving the goals that President de Gaulle sought when designing the Fifth Republic. However, the Fifth Republic lacks adequate mechanisms for representing citizens' interests. The result is a wide gap between the state and civil society.

While French society is a rich mosaic of many religious, ethnic, and racial groups, those from immigrant backgrounds are often second-class citizens, assigned to less desirable jobs or are not offered jobs at all. They often live in drab housing projects located in suburban slums. The plight of recent migrants from North Africa and the Middle East is even worse.

As a result of design flaws in public institutions and the rigidity of political culture, what may appear as a calm political situation in France has often turned out to be the calm before the storm. At the same time, the Fifth Republic is approaching the Third Republic's record for the longest-lived modern French regime. France occupies an enviable position in the world, and a majority of citizens enjoy a fine quality of life. However, despite these achievements, and the fact that France's political system and society possess ample resources to confront current challenges, the French are divided and troubled about the future. A half century after youthful protesters chanted in May 1968, "The struggle continues," the words have lost none of their relevance.

Key Terms

ancien régime
authoritarian
cohabitation
conservative
decentralization
deregulation
fundamentalism
grandes écoles

grands corps
indicative planning
industrial policy
nationalization
neoliberal
parity law
prefect
privatization

proportional representation (PR)
referendum
republic
revolution
secularism
socialist
statism

Suggested Readings

Bell, David A. *Shadows of Revolution: Reflections on France, Past and Present.* New York: Oxford University Press, 2016.

Brouard, Sylvain, Andrew M. Appleton, and Amy G. Mazur, eds. *The French Fifth Republic at Fifty: Beyond Stereotypes.* New York: Palgrave Macmillan, 2009.

Chafer, Tony, and Emmanuel Godin, eds. *The End of the French Exception?* Basingstoke, Hampshire, UK: Palgrave Macmillan, 2010.

Cole, Alistair, Patrick Le Galès, and Jonah D. Levy, eds. *Developments in French Politics 4.* New York: Palgrave MacMillan, 2008.

Fenby, Jonathan. *The History of Modern France: From the Revolution to the Present Day.* New York: Simon & Schuster, 2015.

Hazareesingh, Sudhir, *How the French Think: An Affectionate Portrait of an Intellectual People.* New York: Basic Books, 2015.

Levy, Jonah, ed. *The State after Statism: New State Activities in the Age of Liberalization.* Cambridge: Harvard University Press, 2006.

Scott, Joan Wallach. *The Politics of the Veil.* Princeton, NJ: Princeton University Press, 2007.

Vail, Mark I. *Recasting Welfare Capitalism: Economic Adjustment in Contemporary France and Germany.* Philadelphia: Temple University Press, 2010.

Weil, Patrick. *How to Be French: Nationality in the Making since 1789.* Durham, NC: Duke University Press, 2008.

Suggested Websites

A blog by Arthur Goldhammer, a keen and insightful observer of French politics and society
http://artgoldhammer.blogspot.com

Embassy of France in the United States
www.ambafrance-us.org

French Ministry of Foreign Affairs
www.diplomatie.gouv.fr/en

French National Assembly
www.assemblee-nationale.fr/english

French government
www.gouvernement.fr/english

Le Monde (centrist newspaper—in French)
www.lemonde.fr

Liberation (center-left newspaper—in French)
www.libération.fr

Le Figaro (conservative French newspaper—English translation)
http://plus.lefigaro.fr/tag/lefigaro-in-english

4 Germany

Wade Jacoby

AP Images/Lionel Cironneau

© Cengage

Official Name: Federal Republic of Germany (*Bundesrepublik Deutschland*)

Location: Central Europe

Capital City: Berlin

Population (2016): 82.8 million

Size: 357,021 sq. km.; slightly smaller than Montana

1806–1871
Nationalism and German Unification

| 1805 | 1806 | 1870 | 1890 | 1900 | 1910 | 1915 |

1871–1918
Second Reich

1919–1933
Weimar Republic

SECTION 1

THE MAKING OF THE MODERN GERMAN STATE

Focus Questions

- Why did German politics take such a disastrous turn in the first half of the twentieth century?

- How successfully have German leaders since World War II provided for their citizens without destabilizing the rest of Europe?

Check MindTap for the most up-to-date coverage on the German elections.

Politics in Action

In August 2015, Germany opened its doors in an unprecedented manner. At the initiative of Chancellor Angela Merkel, close to 900,000 refugees were allowed to enter the country over the span of a few months. Rallying support for her policy decision, Merkel uttered her famous mantra "*Wir schaffen das*," meaning "We can do this." Indeed, many Germans displayed an exceptionally welcoming attitude towards these new arrivals. However, both in Germany and abroad her move was also highly controversial. For instance, the then U.S. presidential candidate Donald J. Trump called it an "utterly catastrophic mistake."

Years of war, famine, and poverty had been pushing growing numbers to flee the Middle East, Central Asia, and Africa and head for Europe. Summer 2015 saw a boiling point as tens of thousands surged northward. In Hungary, thousands were stuck for weeks at the Budapest train station, blocked by Hungarian authorities from proceeding farther. Merkel decided to unilaterally suspend the European Union (EU) procedures for refugee admission, which requires refugees to stay in the first safe country they reach until their case can be adjudicated. Taking Merkel's decision as a sign of welcome, hundreds of thousands more entered the country in subsequent months.

This episode was an unusual moment in German politics—both for the country and for Merkel herself. For decades, Berlin was committed to finding joint solutions to common problems, usually relying on multilateral institutions and international organizations. Here, it acted nearly alone (only Sweden and Austria also took large numbers of refugees). The turn in Germany's refugee policy was also unusual for Merkel. The conservative leader had generally acted cautiously and was committed to rules and established procedures. Here, she turned on a dime and did so without coordinating most of Germany's European partners or even consulting the

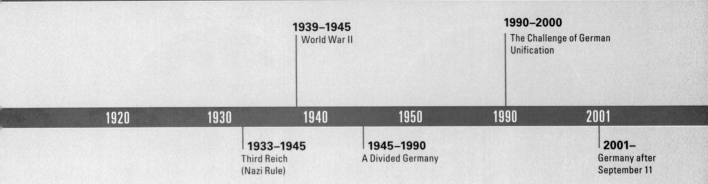

1939–1945 World War II	**1990–2000** The Challenge of German Unification

1920	1930	1940	1950	1990	2001

1933–1945 Third Reich (Nazi Rule)　　**1945–1990** A Divided Germany　　**2001–** Germany after September 11

parliament. Later, she pushed to make a dramatic deal with Turkey's authoritarian government to keep down further refugee flows.

For Germany, this large influx of refugees presents a significant social challenge (see Figure 4.1 for the ethnic and religious composition of Germany prior to the refugees' arrival). Many refugees will stay in Germany for good. In the face of

Table 4.1	Political Organization
Political System	Parliamentary democracy.
Regime History	After the Third Reich's defeat in 1945, the United States, France, Britain, and the Soviet Union partitioned and occupied Germany. In 1949, the Federal Republic of Germany (FRG) was established in the west, and the German Democratic Republic (GDR) was established in the east. The two German states unified in 1990.
Administrative Structure	Federal, with sixteen states, including the city-states of Berlin, Hamburg, and Bremen.
Executive	Dual. Ceremonial president is the head of state, elected for a 5-year term (with a two-term limit) by the Federal Convention. More powerful chancellor (prime minister) is head of government and is a member of the *Bundestag* and the leader of the majority party, which usually rules in a coalition with one other party.
Legislature	Bicameral. *Bundestag* (631 members after 2013 federal election) elected via dual-ballot system combining single-member districts and proportional representation. Upper house (*Bundesrat*) comprised of sixty-nine members who are elected and appointed officials from the sixteen states.
Judiciary	Autonomous and independent. The legal system has three levels: Federal High Court, which is the criminal-civil system; Special Constitutional Court, dealing with matters affecting Basic Law; and Administrative Court, consisting of Labor, Social Security, and Finance courts.
Party System	Multiparty. Major parties are the Christian Democratic Union (CDU), Christian Social Union (CSU) (in Bavaria only), and Social Democratic Party (SPD). Smaller parties include Greens, Left Party (*die Linke*), Free Democratic Party (FDP), and Alternative for Germany (AfD).

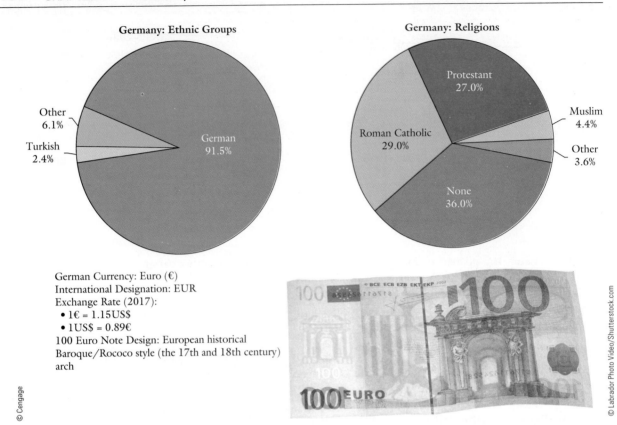

FIGURE 4.1 The German Nation at a Glance

the demographic aging of the German population and growing shortages of skilled labor, this may be an opportunity. Yet how will Germany integrate the hundreds of thousands of people from very different cultures and with very difficult prospects concerning participation in society and the labor market? Some are doctors, engineers, or architects, but others are illiterate. Many will embrace their new home while others are political radicals. Stepping back, this episode shows us that when problems grow large enough, even cautious politicians can make unexpected choices.

Geographic Setting

Located in central Europe, Germany has often been at the heart of the best and the worst of European history. It has an area of 137,803 square miles (slightly smaller than Montana). Its population is 82.8 million, the vast majority of whom are ethnic German. The rest is made up of about 2.4 percent Turks, and a further 6.1 percent are a mixture of Kurds, Italians, Poles, Russians, and other nationalities. Nearly 8 million foreign citizens reside in Germany (about 9.5 percent of the population)—a mix that includes citizens of other EU nations and also asylum seekers from war-shattered countries. The country has roughly even proportions of Roman Catholics, Protestants, and religiously nonaffiliated citizens. Germany has the largest population in Western Europe, second only to Russia in all of Europe. Since the 1960s, ethnic diversity has been increased by several million Turks and Kurds, who came to the Federal Republic as *Gastarbeiter* (guest workers)—foreign workers without

***Gastarbeiter* (guest workers)**

Workers who were recruited to join the German labor force in the 1960s and early 1970s, generally from Italy, Yugoslavia, and especially Turkey.

Germany

DENMARK

Baltic Sea

North Sea

Kiel
SCHLESWIG-
HOLSTEIN

•Rostock

MECKLENBURG-
West Pomerania

HAMBURG
•Hamburg

BREMEN

POLAND

LOWER SAXONY

BERLIN

Berlin ★

•Hannover

BRANDENBURG

NETHERLANDS

SAXONY-
ANHALT

NORTH RHINE-
WESTPHALIA

•Leipzig

Cologne•

Rhine

•Dresden

SAXONY

Bonn•

HESSE

THURINGIA

BELG.

Frankfurt
•

RHINELAND-
PALATINATE

CZECH REPUBLIC

LUX.

SAARLAND

•Nuremberg
BAVARIA

FRANCE

Stuttgart
•

Danube

BADEN-
WÜRTTEMBERG

•Munich

AUSTRIA

0   100 Miles

SWITZERLAND

0   100 Kilometers

© Cengage

citizenship. Over the past decades, immigration by about 6 million EU citizens has further increased cultural heterogeneity. In 2015 and 2016, Germany received close to 1 million refugees, with more than two-thirds of these asylum seekers coming from war-torn Syria, Afghanistan, and Iraq.

For a densely populated country, Germany has a high proportion of land in agriculture (51.6 percent). It consists of large plains in the north, smaller mountain ranges in the center, and the towering Alps at the Austrian and Swiss borders. The absence of natural borders in the west and east has been an important geographic fact, enhancing the possibilities for both commerce and conflict. Indeed, conflicts and wars with its neighbors were a frequent feature of German life until the end of World War II. Inadequate natural resources—aside from scattered iron ore and coal deposits—also shaped German history. Many of Germany's external relationships, both commercial and military, have involved gaining access to resources and markets.

Critical Junctures

The first German empire ("Reich") was the Holy Roman Empire, a loose association of over 300 other entities that lasted until destroyed by the Napoleonic armies in the early nineteenth century. Yet unifying the disparate German territories into a nation-state took until the 1870s, after successful wars by Prussia, the largest of these states, with Denmark (1864), Austria (1866), and France (1870). The Prussian king was made *Kaiser* (emperor), as smaller German states joined Prussia in a Second Empire.

The Second Reich (1871–1918)

A combination of the Ruhr Valley's industrial elites and the landed elites of Prussia controlled the Second Reich. It had some democratic features, like universal male suffrage for the lower house of the legislature (*Reichstag*). However, this mattered little since the upper house (*Landtag*), which Chancellor Otto von Bismarck controlled, made all key decisions.

Where Britain industrialized early and in industries (like textiles) that did not require large amounts of capital, Germany industrialized quite late and required much more capital to construct, for example, enormous steel factories. Bismarck's goal was rapid industrialization, supported by state power and a powerful banking system to foster this large-scale industrial investment. By the time he left office in 1890, these goals had been achieved. The state pushed heavy industries like coal and steel, often at the expense of those producing consumer goods. Lacking a strong domestic consumer-goods economy, Germany had to export a substantial portion of what it produced.

Fast economic growth brought many challenges, including social dislocation as agricultural workers left villages for growing cities. A small middle class of professionals and small-business owners pressured the government—mostly unsuccessfully—to democratize and provide basic liberal rights. Industrialization also created a skilled manual working class and a militant Social Democratic Party (SPD). The SPD's primary goals were economic rights in the workplace and mass participation in politics—democratization. The party was influenced by revolutionary thinkers Karl Marx and Friedrich Engels, whose communist philosophy argued that workers, who produce society's goods and services, should also possess most economic and political power.

As German chancellor, Bismarck banned the SPD to weaken socialism, yet he also created the first welfare state. He used the welfare state to blunt protests against the disruption from rapid economic growth. This "Bismarckian" welfare state included some basic health benefits and the world's first state-sponsored old age pensions. Bismarck also created a powerful and centralized German state. The *Kulturkampf* (cultural struggle) he initiated against the Catholic Church sought to remove educational and cultural institutions from church control and place them under the state.

By 1900, Germany's economic goal was obtaining raw materials and accessing world markets in which to sell its finished goods. Germany joined the imperial "scramble for Africa." But as a latecomer, Germany could colonize only resource-poor southwestern and eastern Africa. This experience pushed German leaders to develop the shipbuilding industry and a navy to protect and expand German economic and geopolitical interests.

Entangled alliances and the resulting rivalries with its European neighbors eventually led to World War I, which Germany bears much responsibility for starting. After Bismarck was dismissed by the new and more jingoist Kaiser Wilhelm II, subsequent

liberal

Basic citizenship rights of speech, assembly, petition, religion, and so forth.

chancellor

An old German title now used by the German head of government and essentially the same as "prime minister."

Kulturkampf

Bismarck's fight with the Catholic Church over his desire to subordinate church to state.

German leaders had been far less skilled. The political system remained undemocratic and the colonies unprofitable. Meanwhile, Germany engaged Britain in a fierce naval rivalry and faced an aggrieved France, still smarting over lost territories. To the south, Germany's alliance with Austria-Hungary exposed it to the nationalist problems of the Balkans. To the east, Germany perceived a threat from a growing Russia with its large army. When a Serb separatist assassinated the Austrian emperor's nephew in July 1914, nationalists of all stripes were inflamed, including those in Germany.

Germany declared war on Russia, France, and Belgium in August 1914. German leaders hoped to gain economic and political benefits from a quick victory in World War I. Instead, the long conflict quickly cost Germany its few colonies and, eventually, its imperial social order. The Second Reich collapsed in November 1918, as Germany suffered a humiliating defeat in the war, leaving a weak foundation for the country's first parliamentary democracy.

The Weimar Republic (1918–1933)

Kaiser Wilhelm II abdicated after Germany's defeat, and the Weimar Republic replaced the Second Reich. The SPD, the only major party not discredited by the war, led Germany's first democracy. Its first task had been to surrender to the Allies. The surrender was later used to discredit the party on the grounds that it had betrayed Germany by accepting defeat, even though, in fact, the war was already lost.

The new government was a **procedural democracy**. However, the Weimar Republic lacked broad public support because both the Conservative forces on the right and the Communists on the left rejected democratic government. Part of the right also accused the Weimar government of "stabbing Germany in the back" by surrendering in a war that was, in their mythology, never truly lost.

Weimar got off to a shaky start. In an attempt to manage the postwar chaos, the new SPD leaders asked the undemocratic military to guarantee order and stability. The next 4 years saw multiple coup attempts. Communists attempted to take control of some cities, and the right, including then little-known Adolf Hitler, attempted the "beer hall putsch." The 1919 Treaty of Versailles ended the war but required Germany to pay heavy reparations to the victorious allies. When the government printed money to pay these reparations, however, the value of the German currency crashed. Inflation raged until, in 1923, a glass of beer cost 4 billion marks, and a pound of meat was 36 billion. Wages were paid several times a day so workers could spend their income before it became worthless. Still, subsequent Weimar governments controlled inflation, and Germany returned to some prosperity for a few years, strengthening its economy (often with loans from the United States) and improving its foreign relations.

Yet the Depression of the 1930s struck Germany especially hard. Trade crashed and German incomes fell. Into this turmoil stepped Adolf Hitler, the leader of the Nazi Party. Exploiting the deepening economic crisis and the purported humiliation of Germany by the allies, the Nazis mobilized large segments of the population by preaching hatred of the left and of "inferior, non-Aryan races"—especially Jews.

The Great Depression thus made Germany even more politically unstable. No parties could win a majority on their own or form lasting coalitions with other parties. Meanwhile, many conservative Germans underestimated Hitler's real intentions and considered his hate-filled speeches merely as political rhetoric. In early 1933, the Nazis pressured President Paul von Hindenburg to appoint Hitler chancellor in a Nazi–Nationalist coalition, which the Nazis's conservative allies saw as way to harness Hitler's popular support for their conservative agenda. Hitler also got Hindenburg to

Weimar Republic

Germany's constitutional system between 1918 and the Nazi seizure of power in 1933. So-named because the assembly to write the constitution occurred in the German city of Weimar.

procedural democracy

A system with formal procedures for popular choice of government leaders (especially free party competition) but that may lack other democratic elements.

Nazi

A German abbreviation for the National Socialist German Workers' Party, the movement led by Hitler.

grant—by emergency executive order—broad powers to the Nazi-dominated cabinet. Hitler then seized on a fire in the Reichstag to claim terrorism required a tougher hand, and the Nazis quickly banned other political parties and repressed the opposition. The Nazi regime quickly consolidated its hold on power.

The Third Reich (1933–1945)

The Nazis used the military, paramilitary, and police to brutally suppress the opposition and used propaganda to mobilize large parts of the population. The Nazis set up the first concentration camps in 1933, populated mostly with their political opponents.

Hitler's forces centralized power and rebuilt an economy devastated by the Depression (although already in recovery by late 1932). They concentrated all political authority in Berlin, limiting regional autonomy. After the regime banned free trade unions, industries forced workers into longer hours and less pay. Although some segments of big business had initially feared Hitler, most of German industry eventually endorsed Nazi economic policies. The Nazis also emphasized massive public works projects and, with the onset of war, gave industrialists access to slave labor from conquered territories.

Extolling a mythically glorious and racially pure German past, Hitler made scapegoats out of political opponents, homosexuals, ethnic and religious minorities, and, especially, Jews. Hitler blamed many political problems on Jews, an "external" international minority. Jews were quickly excluded from many professions, including teaching, law, medicine, and the civil service, and were prohibited from marrying non-Jews. Of course, far worse measures would be adopted during the war.

Hitler strides triumphantly through a phalanx of Nazi storm troopers (SA) in 1934.

ullstein bild/The Granger Collection

Openly defying the Treaty of Versailles (Weimar governments had cheated quietly since the early 1920s), Germany began to produce lots of weapons and remilitarized the Rhineland, Germany's key coal and steel region. Hitler further claimed that a growing Germany needed increased space to live (*Lebensraum*) in eastern Europe. In 1938, he engineered a union (*Anschluss*) with his native Austria, most of whose leaders and citizens supported the pact with enthusiasm. His troops then occupied the German-speaking Sudetenland area of Czechoslovakia. When Poland resisted Nazi territorial claims, Hitler's forces attacked on September 1, 1939, beginning World War II with his soon-to-be famous *Blitzkrieg* tactics. Britain, France, and eventually, the Soviet Union and the United States, formed an alliance to oppose Germany, which was allied with Italy and Japan.

Blitzkrieg

German battle tactics that began with aerial assaults to destroy enemy forces and infrastructure, followed quickly by a massive invasion of armored troops, with ordinary infantry mopping up resistance.

Hitler conquered much of Europe during 1939 and 1940. In 1941, despite a friendship treaty with the Union of Soviet Socialist Republics (USSR), Hitler attacked the Soviet Union, assuming it would fall as easily as his other conquests. The attack was a costly failure and foreshadowed the Third Reich's defeat, although not until after an estimated 40 to 50 million Europeans lost their lives.

The most heinous aspect of the Nazi regime was the systematic extermination of 6 million Jews and the imprisonment in concentration camps of millions of Jews and other civilians. Prisoners were the target of extreme brutality, and many were shot or died from starvation, disease, or overwork. The Nazis also ran "scientific" experiments on camp inmates and the mentally ill and disabled. The Nazis created extermination camps in occupied countries like Poland, equipped with gas chambers for murdering Jews and other inmates. This was the so-called Final Solution. Jews from countries controlled by Nazi allies generally survived in higher numbers than those in countries directly occupied by the Germans, few of whom avoided transport to the death camps.

A fierce Allied bombing campaign killed about 300,000 German civilians and razed major cities to the ground. About 2 million German civilians and 4.5 million German soldiers died from war, in a country whose prewar population was about 70 million.

A Divided Germany (1945–1990)

Following Germany's total defeat in 1945, Cold War tensions led to the formal division of Germany: The Federal Republic of Germany (FRG) emerged in the west out of zones assigned to the western Allies (Britain, France, and the United States). Meanwhile, the communist German Democratic Republic (GDR) was formed out of a zone directed by the Soviet Union in the east. Postwar Germany was soon reshaped by the respective ideological visions of the two victorious sides. Democratic political institutions and a market economy were installed in the west, while the communist political system and command economy in the east was controlled by the Socialist Unity Party (SED), which was dominated by East Germany's Soviet patrons.

The two Germanys became nation-states in 1949, and both formal occupations ended. Yet large foreign military bases remained, and neither half of divided Germany was fully sovereign. The FRG deferred to the United States in international relations, as did the GDR to the Soviet Union. Neither of the two Germanys joined the Cold War's international alliances— the North Atlantic Treaty Organization (NATO) and the Warsaw Pact, respectively—until 1955.

The Federal Republic (West Germany) became a democracy with constitutional provisions for free elections, civil liberties and individual rights, and an independent judiciary (see Table 4.1). The FRG's democratic system produced rapid economic growth and remarkable political stability. The center-right Christian Democrats ruled continuously until 1966 under chancellors Konrad Adenauer (1949–1963) and Ludwig Erhard (1963–1966). In these years, the FRG established a parliamentary regime, extensive social welfare benefits, a politically regulated market economy, and reestablished strong state governments. Germany's first (and for decades only) so-called grand coalition of CDU and SPD was led by CDU chancellor Kurt Kiesinger (1966–1969).

Under center-left Social Democratic chancellor Willy Brandt (1969–1974), West Germany initially had plenty of jobs, increased social services, and pursued a diplomatic opening to the Warsaw Pact. But in the mid and late 1970s, two recessions increased unemployment and forced SPD Chancellor Helmut Schmidt (1974–1982) to trim some benefits. Under Helmut Kohl (1982–1998), the Christian Democrats returned to power as part of a center-right coalition with the market-oriented Free Democratic Party (FDP) (*Time* Magazine's headline was "Germany Changes Helmuts").

As noted, the GDR was established in Soviet-occupied East Germany in 1949, a one-party state controlled by the SED. Although the state provided full employment, housing, and extensive social benefits, it was a rigid, Stalinist regime. The infamous *Stasi*, or secret police, was present everywhere. (At the regime's end, there was a full-time *Stasi* official for every 180 GDR citizens. By comparison, there was one Soviet KGB for every 595 people, and one member of the Nazi Gestapo for every 8,500). The *Stasi* kept close tabs on East Germans and dealt ruthlessly with those suspected of opposing the regime.

Unsurprisingly, many East Germans emigrated west, and in 1961, the GDR built a wall entirely around the city of West Berlin to prevent further emigration. Over the next 40 years, about 5,000 escaped through Berlin (early on, two young boys snuck out several weeks in a row to watch cowboy movies in West Berlin). Over time, sneaking out became very dangerous, and at least 136 people lost their lives trying to flee the GDR through Berlin. Over the years, many creative escapes were tried, including a homemade hot air balloon, zip lines, hiding under carcasses of slaughtered cows, driving under a guard barrier in a sawed-off convertible, and flashing a smuggled membership card from the Munich Playboy Club, which (somewhat) resembled a diplomatic passport.

Although the wall allowed the GDR to hang onto more of its citizens, Western radio and TV signals allowed the GDR population to witness the growing prosperity and freedoms of the FRG. The GDR was the richest state in the Soviet bloc, but that mattered little to East Germans, who measured their material lives and civil liberties against those in the FRG. For example, voting in East Germany consisted of dropping a ballot with a single Communist Party candidate name into the voting box. Those who preferred a different candidate had to use a different (non-private) booth, cross out the printed name, and write in their preferred choice. Most of those who took this step lost privileges and even their jobs. In fact, fraudulent local government elections, in spring 1989, contributed to citizen unrest that ended with the breaching of the Berlin Wall. Emboldened by misleading news reports, GDR citizens surged toward the wall on the evening of November 9, and equally confused border guards chose not to shoot.[1]

The Challenge of German Unification (1990–2001)

When Soviet rule over communist regimes loosened throughout East Central Europe in 1989, the two German states at first envisioned a slow process of increased contacts and cooperation while maintaining separate sovereign states for the medium term.

But German unification came rapidly, primarily because only reunification could convince East Germans not to migrate west. In 1990, the former East Germany was absorbed into the FRG as five new West German states (*Länder*).

Formal unification took place in 1990 to great fanfare. But unification euphoria did not last. The communist-planned economy was much weaker than had been recognized. East German technology was decades behind, and the unified German government spent huge sums just to rebuild communication networks and major roads that, for the first time in many years, allowed unrestricted traffic between East and West.

Aligning East Germany with the FRG was a daunting job and necessitated large tax increases. Unemployment soared, especially in eastern Germany—to approximately 20 percent—fueling ultra-right-wing political movements who blamed foreigners for taking away jobs. Skinheads and other extremist groups often targeted Turkish immigrants.

To win the support of eastern Germans, Chancellor Kohl downplayed the costs of unification. To win the support of western Germans, he had to convince them that steep unification taxes would achieve economic integration. But the longer the unification process remained incomplete, the less patient the German electorate became. Even today, regional income differences for comparable work persist. For instance, a college graduate with a business degree earns an average monthly wage of $4,150 in western Germany, compared to only $3,105 in the five eastern states.

West Germany also extended its currency to East Germany in 1990. As European capital flowed into East Germany, raising the value of the famous Deutsche Mark (DM), German manufacturers nervously observed the price of German exports rising with it. This trend also increased their support for a European solution to national currency fluctuations. Kohl, who had been uncertain about a European currency union, committed Germany to the idea, which France had long supported. Germany's leaders generally have been strong supporters of European integration. When the euro eventually replaced the currency of eleven European countries in 2002, however, many Germans wondered whether the EU and the euro would provide the same stability as the formidable DM and the inflation-fighting *Bundesbank* (Germany's central bank). Many also worried about Germany's loss of domestic control of monetary and, to a lesser extent, fiscal policies (Kohl responded by insisting on limits on each Eurozone member's debts and deficits).

After 16 years of Kohl's leadership, a political tidal wave occurred in the 1998 elections. SPD leader Gerhard Schröder convinced Germans that a change was necessary. He became chancellor, and the SPD formed a coalition government with the environmentalist Green Party that lasted 7 years (1998–2005).

Germany after September 11, 2001

Tension with the United States ratcheted up when, during Schröder's 2002 reelection campaign, he opposed the Bush administration's arguments for war against Iraq. The strong relationship between Germany and the United States was significantly weakened. While Schröder's foreign policy stance was popular with German voters, his government (in coalition with the Greens) lost support in a number of other areas. It was replaced in 2005 by a "grand coalition" of CDU-CSU and SPD. Schröder gave way as chancellor to CDU leader Angela Merkel, who then won reelection in 2009 with her preferred coalition partners, the Free Democrats (FDP). Together, these parties were focused on the economic and financial crisis, often choosing austerity policies that left other European leaders (and, on some occasions, U.S. President Barack Obama) visibly frustrated.

austerity policies

Spending cuts, layoffs, and wage decreases meant to address budget problems.

A particular frustration for the United States has been Germany's very large export surplus. Many observers feel Germans love to sell but refuse to buy; Germany's global surplus of exports over imports reached a whopping 8.1 percent of GDP in 2016. Meanwhile, German frustrations with the United States reached a fever pitch in 2013 when NSA contractor Edward Snowden released material documenting that the United States had tapped Merkel's cell phone (the chancellor is a ferocious texter). Subsequent upheavals in the Ukraine, fears of Russian meddling in European democracy, and worries about European terrors attacks combined to reduce German anger over the NSA scandal.

Overall, Germany's foreign policy has become less predictable. It has broken with its traditional quasi-pacifist stance to send many troops abroad in recent years. By 2017, Germany was contributing around 3,400 soldiers to fourteen multilateral missions from West Africa to the Middle East. And yet it had resisted efforts in 2011 to impose a "no-fly zone" in Libya, abstaining from the vote on UN Resolution 1973. The CDU-FDP government also ruled out military action against Syria in fall 2013, though it later transpired Germany had, under a civilian license, sold chemicals to Syria that could be used to make sarin gas. Russia's policy toward Ukraine has split German opinion. Few support Russia, and most support the West, but a large minority would like to see Germany positioned between the two.[2]

The Four Themes and Germany

Germany in a Globalized World of States

Germany's development can be understood in light of this book's four major themes. Consider the first theme: a globalizing world of states. In the nineteenth century, Germany's war-propelled unification caused anxiety among its neighbors. In the twentieth century, both World War I and the crimes of the Third Reich during World War II intensified this fear. Today, although Germany's foreign policy is constrained by the EU, some Europeans still remain wary of Germany's international role. Is Germany a "normal" state? Should it be normal? Germany's foreign policies still spark some concerns. Many worry that German energy policy cooperates too much with Russia and too little with the rest of Europe or that Germany's remarkable success in economic globalization has made it less sympathetic to its poorer European neighbors.

As for the second theme, governing the economy, late unification and industrialization prevented Germany from starting the race for empire and raw materials until the late nineteenth century. The state's pursuit of fast economic growth and an awakened sense of German nationalism made the state aggressive. During the Third Reich, Hitler then sought to fuse state and economic power. In reaction, policymakers after World War II tried to remove the state from running the economy, but there was a strong consensus in Germany that the economy needs an "order" that can only come from government. Thus, Germans are not as obsessed with "free" markets, as in the United States and the United Kingdom, an attitude reflected in German economic policy (as described in Section 2).

The postwar period saw the development of *Modell Deutschland* (the German model), a term often used to describe the Federal Republic's unusual economy, focused heavily on industrial exports. While successful for decades, it remains an open question whether these economic institutions will continue to function well in a unified Europe. The EU sometimes promotes free market practices faster than Germany can absorb them. Meanwhile, Germany often produces export surpluses faster than the rest of Europe and, increasingly, the rest of the world can absorb them. Both imbalances often spark frustration.

The democratic idea, our third theme, developed late in Germany. Not until 1918, and the shaky Weimar Republic, did Germany attain democracy. And despite a formally democratic constitution, Weimar was a prisoner of forces bent on its destruction. Lacking a stable multiparty political system, Weimar was plagued by a sharp polarization of political parties. Germany's descent into the most brutal form of authoritarianism in the 1930s destroyed every vestige of democracy.

The constitution of the Federal Republic in 1949 was designed to overcome both Weimar shortcomings and Nazi crimes. This was a delicate task since in the Weimar system the state was too weak while in the Nazi system it was far too strong. But postwar constitution-making proved a resounding success. Today, at a time when most Europeans are unimpressed by the quality of their politicians, Germans remain relatively satisfied. Every democratic system needs citizen support, and the Germans are in far better shape than many of their neighbors. And while party systems in many European democracies have eroded, Germany's has remained reasonably stable.

The fourth theme is the politics of collective identity. Compared to other democratic countries, German political institutions, social forces, and patterns of life emphasize collective action rather more than individualism. This does not mean that German citizens have less personal freedom or that there are no political conflicts in Germany. It means that political expression, in both the state and civil society, generally revolves around group representation and cooperative spirit. For example, unions and employer associations continue to shape the workplace culture and practices of German firms in profound ways. Certainly, Germany's history from Prussian militarism through Nazism has led many to worry about the dangers of "collectivist" impulses. However, Germany is unlikely to embrace an individualistic democracy like that of the United States.

Germany's collective identity since 1945 also has been broadened by linking the country's fate to that of Europe. Germany's participation in the EU also produced a more flexible understanding of what it means to be German. For example, many Germans still readily describe themselves as "Europeans," even with all of Europe's recent problems. And Germany's traditionally restrictive immigration law was changed in 1999 to enable those who had lived in Germany for decades to obtain citizenship. A big question going forward is how German voters' identification with Europe will affect their willingness to assist countries—like Greece and Italy— hardest hit by the economic and migrations crises.

Comparisons

Germany differs from many other developed countries. For example, like Japan, Germany was late to industrialize and late to democratize. Yet the Nazi past and the destruction caused by the Third Reich make Germany different from every other industrialized democracy (including Japan). Although concerns about this period persist, they have been substantially allayed by Germany's stable democratic experience since 1949 and its extensive efforts to "make good" the crimes of the Nazi period with states like Israel, Poland, and France.

Germany's political patterns provide rich topics of significance for the study of comparative politics, including the contrast between its nationalistic history and democratization in an integrating Europe; its distinctive form of organized capitalism that is neither state-led nor laissez-faire; its successful representative democracy that combines participation and representation of the entire electorate in a stable parliamentary regime; and a politics of identity that builds on existing groups but leaves some room for newcomers.

Where Do You Stand?

Does the Nazi past still oblige Germans to behave differently from other people?

Was it smart, compassionate, or just naïve for Germany to welcome a million refugees?

SECTION

2

POLITICAL ECONOMY AND DEVELOPMENT

State and Economy

▼ Focus Questions

- In what ways is a "social market economy" different from the kind of market economy found in the United States?

- What are the strengths and weaknesses of the German social market economy, and how are its traditional strengths challenged by the EU, neoliberal ideas, globalization, and economic crisis?

German capitalism is unusual, and its biggest strengths links to its largest vulnerabilities. It tries to capture the benefits of intense competition between firms *and* of close cooperation among firms. This is no easy trick, but Germany has proved highly successful at pursuing this goal: Germans' standard of living is among the highest in Europe, and Germany exports as much as the United States despite having just one-fourth the population. Still, the German economy faces a bevy of challenges, but Germany also has great economic strength in its organized and cooperative form of capitalism and highly competitive firms.[3] At the same time, Germany is over-reliant on one source of growth—exports—to the exclusion of the two other usual sources—consumption and investment. Thus, Germany is heavily dependent on a "liberal international order" that supports trade.

The Social Market Economy

After World War II, German economic policies took a different course from either Anglo-American laissez-faire policies (generally based on "freeing" the market from the state) or state-led capitalism in countries like France and Japan. Germany's state was important, but its role was indirect. It complemented rather than replaced the critical decisions taken by private groups like employers, trade unions, chambers of commerce, churches, and others. Broadly, this remains true today. Although the government sets guidelines, it encourages voluntary associations to play a key role. Subsequent negotiations among employers, banks, unions, and regional governments fill in key details whose aim is to fulfill the government's broad objectives.

The German state allows market forces to work relatively unimpeded within the general framework and rules set by the government. In short, this system regulates not the details, but the general rules of the game under which all actors must play. This pattern, known as **framework regulations**, has enabled German economic policy to avoid the abrupt lurches between laissez-faire and state-led economic policy that have characterized post–World War II Britain.[4] To be sure, some have criticized

framework regulations

Laws that set broad parameters for economic behavior but that require subsequent elaboration, often through formal agreements between employers and employees.

the system as rigid and cumbersome, a charge discussed below.[5] To its advocates, however, German economic policy is flexible and encourages private actors to cooperate to devise their own solutions. As a result, the German system is often able to produce agreement on major policy directions without much social upheaval and protest.

Since the time of Adenauer, the Germans have referred to this broad approach as the **social market economy** (*Soziale Marktwirtschaft*), which attempts to combine a competitive, market-based economy with an extensive social safety net. Ludwig Erhard, Adenauer's Economics Minister and successor as chancellor, was the architect of this hybrid economic order. The social component includes health and unemployment insurance, pensions, and educational and maternity benefits.

The market component of the social market economy is equally critical. There is intense competition in the German economy. German firms are often world leaders in everything from cars and machine tools to kitchen appliances and chocolate bars. The typical pattern of high wages and high benefits has not prevented Germany from maintaining its international market position far better than most of its competitors. Even when the Euro goes up in value, German products remain in high demand.

Semipublic Institutions

Yet classic state instruments are only part of the story. Indeed, by the late 1940s, the idea of a strong German central state was discredited for two reasons: the excesses of Nazism *and* the American occupation authorities' confidence in the private sector. West German authorities faced a dilemma. How could they rebuild society if a strong state sector was prohibited? The answer was to create modern, democratic versions of those nineteenth-century institutions that blurred the boundaries between the public and private sectors (hence "semipublic").[6]

The most influential semipublic institutions include the boards (comprising representatives of employers associations, labor unions, and the state) that manage the health insurance funds, pensions, and unemployment insurance systems, plus the employment agencies, the central bank, and the vocational education and training system. Cooperation between firms and the government encourages moderation. For example, Germany's Chambers of Industry and Commerce are far less partisan (and arguably far more useful) than their openly partisan American counterparts. Similarly, union and employer representatives sit on the boards of the pension and unemployment systems. Another semipublic institution, the **health insurance fund**, brings all major health interests together to allocate costs and benefits through consultation. There is still disagreement, but the politics of health care is far less contentious—yet far more effective—than in the United States.

The social market economy is part of the broader system of **democratic corporatism**, in which national (and state) governments delegate certain policy-making authority to private and semipublic institutions. In countries that had a **guild system** in the Middle Ages, democratic corporatism is common, and similar systems exist in the Netherlands, Belgium, the Scandinavian countries, Switzerland, Slovenia, and Austria. In return for access to power and a role in policy administration, groups representing a particular economic sector are expected to aggregate the interests of their own members and act responsibly. Semipublic institutions differ greatly from "pluralist" representation in countries such as the United States, where interest groups seek benefits from government agencies while keeping the implementation process at arm's length.

social market economy

A system that aims to combine the efficiency of market economies with a concern for fairness for a broad range of citizens.

health insurance fund

A semipublic institution that administers insurance contributions from employees and employers and thus pays for health care for covered participants.

democratic corporatism

A bargaining system in which important policies are established and often carried out with the participation of trade unions and business associations.

guild system

The right of craftsmen to control who can learn, enter, and practice their craft.

The social market economy and the semipublic institutions both require effective labor and business organizations. German trade unions are powerful, representing more than 6 million workers—nearly one-sixth of the labor force and a higher rate of unionization than in most advanced capitalist countries.[7]

German unions negotiate with associations of employers, and this requires less *state* regulation of wages, working conditions, and employment. Even when the government introduced a minimum wage of $9.50 (Germany was one of the last countries in the Organisation for Economic Cooperation and Development to do so), this had only limited impact because, thanks to industry-specific collective bargaining agreements, many German workers already enjoyed higher wages and ample fringe benefits.

The interplay of cooperation and conflict is not limited to the broad economy but also takes place *inside* each German firm through a system known as **codetermination** (*Mitbestimmung*). In the United States and United Kingdom, management makes most business decisions. By contrast, codetermination gives employees the right to participate in major decisions that affect their firms and industries. Although common in northern Europe, including the Netherlands and Scandinavia, codetermination is best known in Germany.

Codetermination allows representatives of workers and trade unions to obtain voting seats on the supervisory boards of directors of firms with 2,000 or more employees. Separate provisions are made for smaller firms. Firm managers sometimes resent having to share management decisions with workers, but they usually acknowledge codetermination helps them reach accommodation with workers. Codetermination also has provided German workers with a broader and deeper knowledge of the goals and strategies of the firms for which they work.

Another German institution providing workers a voice is the **works council**. While the first form of codetermination gives trade unions a voice outside the plant (that is, on the board), the works councils represent workers inside the workplace by addressing shop-floor and firm-level affairs. Whereas unions bargain over wages, hours, and working conditions, works councils concentrate on social, environmental, and personnel matters.

Another useful semipublic institution is the vocational education system. After completing high school, almost half of young Germans complete a 3-year apprenticeship that combines school-based classes with four days a week devoted to working and learning in a company. By combining school and workplace-based learning, apprenticeships resemble a rigorous college internship, except that they usually benefit working class youth and last 3 years rather than three months. Many apprentices are later hired as permanent employees by the firm with which they trained. Long after manufacturing in the United States and Britain languished, about a fifth of the German economy remains engaged in manufacturing.[8]

So long as its trading partners tolerate Germany's large surplus of exports over imports, German firms can focus on raising product quality rather than slashing wages. Germany's highly skilled blue-collar workers can drive expensive cars, obtain high-quality medical care, and enjoy six weeks of paid vacation each year. By contrast, wages and benefits in much of the (non-traded) service sector are far lower, and unemployment rates for the least skilled are 19 percent in West Germany and 32 percent in the East.

Germany's research and development strategy supports these export-based economic policies. Rather than seek breakthroughs in exotic technologies that take years to commercialize, German firms adapt existing technologies to boost already competitive sectors. During the postwar years, this policy enabled Germany to maintain competitiveness and a big trade surplus. Challenges have been, first, to integrate

codetermination

The legal right of employees to elect representatives to help determine the direction of the company in which they work.

works council

A group of firm employees elected by coworkers to represent the workforce in negotiations with management at that specific shop or company.

former GDR workers raised in an East German industrial culture that told workers to follow orders rather than apply initiative; second, to invest in formerly communist countries where high skills and lower wages can be combined; and third, to build a true German competitor to giants like Google, Facebook, or Amazon.

Current Strains on the Social Market Economy

Over time, Germany's social market economy has faced many strains, including the rise of new competitors, the challenge of free market ideas (especially at the EU level and among employers), the difficulties of German unification, and the burden of the financial crisis.

Germany is a trading state, and new competitors now challenge the markets of German firms used to being world leaders. German firms face relatively high costs in wages, taxes, social contributions, and investments in apprenticeships and technology development, so they need high revenues to make a profit. Although making workers more productive is one route, this has not been enough for manufacturing firms facing ferocious competition from Asian auto and machine tool producers. Another solution for German firms is to procure supplies from lower-cost Eastern European countries rather than to maintain long-standing relationships with other domestic firms that were the lynchpin of the German model.

More fundamentally, Germany's social market economy has been increasingly attacked at the level of ideas. For years, free-market proponents from abroad criticized the German model for the "clubby" relationships among its social partners (business associations, labor unions, and federal and state governments). Critics charged that this pattern added costs and reduced flexibility for employers. Yet working with unions has not prevented German firms from maintaining (and often expanding) their competitive positions.

Free market supporters also accuse the social market economy of a failure to create sufficient jobs. However, through much of the postwar period, this too was false: For nearly 25 years, German unemployment hovered around a remarkable 1 to 2 percent. Since the 1970s, however, unemployment has varied from 6 to over 10 percent. Unemployment fell from nearly 12 percent in 2005 to just over to 6 percent by early 2017, the lowest figure since reunification. Since wages are high, employers limit part-time work and hold off hiring until the need for employees becomes acute. During recessions, however, employers tend to hold onto skilled workers. In fact, by keeping skilled workers on the payroll, business was able to get a jump on the economic recovery after the 2009 slump.

Unification in 1990 posed a particular challenge for the social market system. In the early 1990s, the costs of unification were consuming 20 percent of Germany's budget. Moreover, employers and trade unions found their history of cooperation in the west difficult to transfer to eastern Germany. After the government privatized thousands of East German firms, the firms' new owners fired workers in droves. The problems in eastern Germany soon threatened to overwhelm the system.

A decade after reunification, the SPD-Green (left-oriented) government made labor law, pension policy, and unemployment insurance less generous. These "Agenda 2010" reforms sparked furious criticism from trade unions. Finally, the financial crisis compounded anxieties. On the one hand, German voters and politicians were reassured that the German financial system seemed less prone to excesses than those of the United States and the United Kingdom. On the other hand, German banks were burned by risky investments abroad (one bailout cost taxpayers $140 billion, and many bad loans still threaten German banks).

GLOBAL CONNECTIONS

Germany's Global Leadership

The 2016 "Best Countries" ranking, by *US News and World Report,* placed Germany #1 overall. When Germans hear such things about themselves, they are puzzled. Why are they so popular? they wonder. Is it because of what they do? Or because of what they don't do?

British political scientists William Paterson and Simon Bulmer refer to Germany as a "reluctant hegemon." It doesn't want to lead but often feels other states want it to. Leadership is risky and expensive. Germans are cautious and fairly frugal. This was evident in the Eurozone crisis, and also in foreign policy more generally.* Take Germany's military. The *Bundeswehr* is a professional (all-volunteer) army in a country deeply skeptical of the use of force.

Between 2001 and 2014, however, the *Bundeswehr* deployed up to 5,000 soldiers at a time to Afghanistan in support of NATO operations, the largest deployment of German troops since World War II. While the mission began as one of peace building and reconstruction, it turned into a combat mission. As "warlike conditions" were reported, however, public support for the Afghanistan mission fell (from 65 percent in 2005 to under 40 percent by 2011). Around 900 hundred German soldiers remained in Afghanistan to train and advise. Many soldiers gained combat experience, and the *Bundeswehr*

both developed a counterinsurgency doctrine and gained experience with drones, used to target Taliban fighters. But the deployment also revealed inadequate equipment, poor communication between soldiers and political leaders, and political restrictions on the military that often incurred the ridicule of other NATO allies.

Part of Germany's popularity comes from not throwing its weight around. But many of Germany's friends wish it would take a far more active role. Would Germans prefer to be influential or popular? A 2016 *Bundeswehr* "White Paper" outlined Germany's readiness to take on more regional and global responsibility. Small numbers of German troops in Lithuania (part of the NATO "Reassurance" initiative for Baltic states on Russia's borders) and in Mali seem a step in this direction. How far German politicians (and voters) are willing to go is an open question.

MAKING CONNECTIONS If German interests are global, can their politics remain regional (European)? And what of ethics? Can Germans be pacifist and still supply weapons to the rest of the world?

*Simon Bulmer and William Paterson, "Germany as the EU's Reluctant Hegemon?" *Journal of European Public Policy* 20, no. 10 (2013), 1387–1405.

Society and Economy

Booming economic growth after World War II provided a sound foundation for social programs. Until the 1990s, Germany provided generous social benefits to almost everyone, including support for public transit, subsidies for the arts, virtually free higher and vocational education, and a comprehensive welfare state.

But the costs of unification, adjustment to the EU, and globalization all challenge Germany's high standard of living and well-paid workforce. The primary workplace fault line lies between the core of mostly male, high-skilled blue-collar workers in the competitive export industries and less-skilled workers, often employed in smaller firms with lower wages and part-time work. Immigrants and women are over-represented in the latter sector.

Ethnicity and Economy

Until recently, Germany's only large ethnic minority originated in the *Gastarbeiter* program of the 1960s. Temporary workers were recruited from southern Europe (especially Turkey) on the understanding that they would return home if unemployment increased. When the economy did turn down in the mid-1970s, many guest workers stayed. Yet because German citizenship had not been granted to these workers or their children, they were in legal limbo. The clash between German and

Gastarbeiter cultures increased in intensity in the 1980s, particularly in areas where Turkish workers were highly concentrated. However, the SPD-Green government in 1999 allowed some second- and third-generation immigrant descendants to obtain citizenship or maintain dual citizenship.[9]

Currently, just under 3 million people of Turkish or Kurdish background live in Germany, although in recent years more have left Germany than have arrived. While early Turkish migrants supplemented industrial work with niche occupations in Turkish groceries and restaurants, these niches are declining. One partial replacement is caring for the elderly, especially Turkish elderly. Increasingly, some higher-paid service jobs are held by ethnic Turks (many now German citizens). Even so, nearly 40 percent of Turkish families are near or below the poverty line, and Turkish unemployment levels rose well above those for Germans during the economic crisis. More than 50 years after the first *Gastarbeiter* arrived, 51 percent of young Turks in Germany have no professional qualifications. Meanwhile, about a third of the original *Gastarbeiter* now live in poverty.[10]

Racist attacks against Turkish immigrants and other ethnic minorities have shown that nearly 70 years of democracy have not eliminated German xenophobia. Hostility to foreigners prevails particularly among East Germans, who were raised in a closed society that did not value tolerance. Former GDR citizens, raised on a promise of guaranteed lifetime employment, suddenly faced a labor market that did not supply enough jobs. Yet they were expected to embrace a much more ethnically diverse society than they had ever known. Thus, many Germans who were falling through the cracks of the welfare state and were without jobs became susceptible to racist arguments blaming minorities for Germany's economic problems. Some smaller towns and villages in eastern Germany are literally no-go zones for immigrants.

In recent years, immigrants actually had *higher* educational qualifications on average than did native Germans. Germany faced a tech worker shortage in the early 2000s that led the government to recruit software specialists from India. However, this new wave of *Gastarbeiter* was arriving precisely when some Germans were increasingly agitated about the immigration boom, and a backlash quickly occurred. A much bigger question now faces the refugees arriving in recent years from war-torn countries. Some are doctors and engineers, but many are illiterate.

Gender and Economy

As Germany's population falls, higher labor force participation is a must. Until the late 1970s, men monopolized positions of authority in both management and labor (though unions subsequently made greater strides in expanding leadership opportunities for women). Women's participation in the workforce has always been far lower than the male rate. In the wake of the economic crisis, however, rates for women surged a bit more than for men, in part because daycare funding is up (see Table 4.2).

Table 4.2	Labor Force Participation Rates (Ages 20–64)						
	1992	1996	2000	2004	2008	2012	2016
Male	80%	76%	77%	75%	80%	82%	82%
Female	58%	58%	61%	63%	68%	72%	74%

Source: Eurostat (2017).

Historically, women's benefits have been closely tied to their roles as mothers and wives. German women often face job discrimination, and though they are about as likely to work outside the home as American women, they are far more likely to work part-time. It is much harder for German women to achieve positions of power and responsibility than it is for their American counterparts.

Environmental Issues

Germany is a resource-poor but highly industrialized country, which means it must strive for maximum efficiency. Moreover, environmental worries ranked low when the country was poor after World War II. But since the 1970s, most citizens have come to embrace environmental concerns, and most see waste and pollution as big problems. To discourage energy consumption, Germans tolerate some of the highest energy prices in the world. To fill the tank of a Volkswagen Golf at the current price of $5.50 per gallon costs a cool $73 in Germany, compared to about $30 in the United States (at $2.25 per gallon). Driving 150 mph may be *legal* (much of the Autobahn has no speed limit), but at $5.50 per gallon it's very *expensive*.

Energiewende

A policy to shift German energy consumption from fossil fuels and nuclear to sustainable sources such as wind, solar, hydro, and biomass.

Since 2010, Germany has embarked on a major reform of energy policy, known as the *Energiewende*. The objectives are to replace fossil fuels (oil and gas) and nuclear energy with renewable sources like wind, solar, biomass, and ocean power, to increase energy efficiency, and to promote sustainable development. The goal is to reduce fossil fuel consumption by 80 to 95 percent by 2050, by which time at least 60 percent of German energy should come from renewables (currently, it is 30 percent).

The major German parties have roughly similar agendas in many areas of environmental policy, though they disagree a lot about the pace to implement changes. German businesses have complained about rising energy prices, but an even greater concern is the need to build transmission networks from scratch between new (often decentralized) supply sources and the places where energy is consumed. A case in point are the new offshore wind farms in the North Sea, which produce excess energy for the energy-intensive industries in the southern states of Bavaria and Baden Wurttemberg—but the necessary power grid still needs to be built. Finally, new technologies are required, and part of the German motivation is not just to be clean but to be first to the market for greener products. German companies hope to capitalize on these advances by selling them to the rest of the world. If the government can clarify the direction of the *Energiewende* and the necessary investments are made, this idea could still succeed.

Germany in the Global Economy

Germany chooses not to face globalization alone but through the EU. After World War II, many people outside Germany feared a too-powerful Germany since the country had run roughshod over its neighbors for much of the previous 80 years. Yet by the 1990s, Germany contended with an opposite problem: what was widely dubbed an economic giant–political dwarf syndrome in which Germany was accused of benefiting from a strong world economy while taking on too few political and military responsibilities.[11]

Chancellors Kohl, Schröder, and Merkel all hoped an integrated Europe might solve both problems. Germany's postwar political leaders embraced European unity because they welcomed the opportunity that a more united continent would present. Germany remains the economic anchor of the EU, while empowering it to take on political responsibilities that it would be unable to assume on its own, such as UN peacekeeping operations in the Balkans (which had been a site of many of Germany's World War II–era crimes). The EU Single Market helps Germany adapt to globalization by selling to the 500 million consumers in EU member states.

The biggest test of Germany's European leadership came with the euro. For decades, Germany's powerful economy contributed to a strong national currency, the famous Deutsche Mark (DM). Although the DM boosted postwar German economic performance and contributed mightily to German self-confidence, a strong DM also made German exports expensive. Meanwhile, Germany's European partners often struggled to match Germany's low inflation rates and thus to keep their own export products competitive.

Successive German chancellors judged that a common currency would boost economic success for both Germany and Europe. This is where the euro came in. It promised to prevent European neighbors from weakening their currency at Germany's expense. In return, Germany's neighbors hoped to suffer less inflation and attract more investment capital. Kohl insisted that countries that used the euro must promise to control public spending and inflation (a promise many countries—including Germany—would subsequently break on several occasions).

Now used by over 300 million Europeans, the euro was introduced in most EU member countries in 2002. Gone was the redoubtable DM. For most of the time since its emergence, the euro's value has traded above the U.S. dollar. While this has been an advantage for European tourists wanting to visit the United States, it has not been not so high that it prevents the export-oriented German economy from selling its goods in the Americas or Asia.

Between 2010 and 2013, however, Germany came under pressure to help bail out Greece, Ireland, Portugal, and Cyprus—members of the **Eurozone** who got in huge trouble, partly because the euro led capital to flow into their countries well in excess of their borrowing needs. Much larger Spain and Italy also have worrisome debts. In summer 2012, faced with the possibility of the Eurozone breaking apart, Merkel reluctantly agreed to let the European Central Bank finance some state debt, in part to prevent the collapse of the Eurozone and because German banks, who had lent hundreds of billions to the crisis countries, demanded repayment. Germany also backed major reforms to stabilize European financial markets. The euro may yet have to be reconfigured, although blowing it up entirely and going back to national currencies would be expensive and destabilizing.

This dilemma has no easy solution, so watch it carefully. Issues such as trade, economic competition with East Asia and North America, the euro, European economic integration, climate change, and patterns of financial regulation pose daunting challenges. More than most countries, Germany's economic fortunes are tied to globalization, and it worries that U.S. president Trump campaigned against "globalism." The growth in world trade has allowed German firms to export and prosper. When global trade collapsed 2008, Germany suffered badly. However, the recovery of trade boosted German exports into record territory since 2010. The resulting trade surplus has irritated the United States. Both the Obama and Trump administrations pushed Germany to consume more and invest more (the two main sources of growth besides exports).

Eurozone

The nineteen EU members who share a common currency, the euro. Of the nine remaining EU members, all but Denmark (opt-out) and the UK (leaving EU) are obliged to join the Eurozone.

Where Do You Stand?

What can Germany do to best alleviate tensions between immigrants and ethnic Germans?

Have Germany (and Europe) gone too far in efforts to protect the environment? Or not far enough? What case can be made for each position?

SECTION

3

GOVERNANCE AND POLICY-MAKING

▽ **Focus Questions**

- What institutional changes aimed to fix the problems of Weimar fragmentation and Nazi autocracy?

- How does German federalism differ from federalism in the United States?

Basic Law

The 1949 proto-constitution of the Federal Republic, which continues to function today.

German politics is no less rule-driven than the German economy. Each has its own "constitutional order." Most Americans expect a constitution to be a single written document. In Germany, there is a single document, but it is not called a constitution (*Verfassung*). When West Germany was founded in 1949, the Cold War kept East Germany in the communist bloc. Thus, West Germany chose to adopt a more temporary-sounding "Basic Law" (*Grundgesetz*), hoping reunification would come soon and permit the writing of a true constitution. When reunification finally did come—40 years later—the Basic Law had been so successful that both the term and the document itself were kept, while the old GDR was added to the FRG in the form of five new *Länder*.

In what sense did the Basic Law succeed? The primary goals of the young Federal Republic were to avoid repeating the mistakes of the Weimar Republic and to lay to rest the legacy of the Nazi regime. The Basic Law aimed to deal with both failures, and it did.

Two fundamental institutional weaknesses undermined the Weimar government: (1) the fragmented party system prevented stable majorities in the *Reichstag*, and (2) the president's right to exercise emergency powers enabled him to centralize authority and suspend democratic rights. The first weakness (instability) encouraged the second (the use of emergency powers to break legislative deadlocks).

Since Weimar's weakness facilitated the Nazi takeover, the core reform after World War II aimed to minimize the risk of extremism and the abuse of executive power. These problems were dealt with by introducing federalism and a weak presidency, and by reforming electoral procedures to curb instability.

Organization of the State

After flourishing for over 65 years, the Federal Republic has clearly attained its most important goals. It has permitted successful alternations in power, although the Basic Law's provisions for federalism and divided powers tend to keep policy change slow and incremental. Undemocratic parties have received miniscule voter support despite occasional neo-Nazi threats and worrisome incidents of racial violence.

Government Institutions

The German state features a fairly weak president and a much stronger chancellor (prime minister), who is elected by the bicameral parliament's (more powerful) lower house (the *Bundestag*). Germany's parliamentary democracy resembles the parliamentary systems of Britain and Japan in that there is a fusion of powers where the chancellor (the executive or head of government) is also a leader (and generally *the* leader) of parliament's largest party. This contrasts with the separation of powers in the United States. Generally, the German executive dominates the lower house of the legislature (the *Bundestag*). Most parliamentary members of

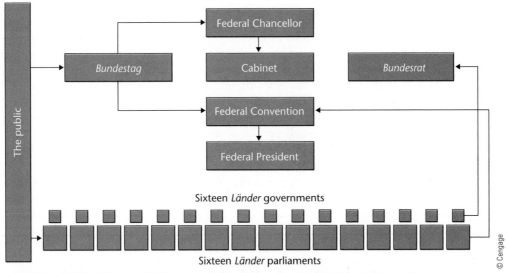

FIGURE 4.2 **Constitutional Structure of the German Federal Government**

the governing parties support the chancellor at all times, since their own positions depend on a successful government. Legislators' party voting rates in Germany are among the highest in Europe. An upper house (the *Bundesrat*) embodies Germany's unique form of federalism where the sixteen states have considerable powers (see Figure 4.2).

The Executive

The division between the head of government (the chancellor) and the head of state (the president) is firmly established, with responsibilities clearly distinguished between the two offices.

The President

The German president's role is largely ceremonial. The president is elected by the Federal Convention (an electoral college of all *Bundestag* members and an equal number of delegates elected by the state legislatures). The presidential term is 5 years, and most presidents serve only one term. No woman has been elected president. German presidents are usually senior politicians who are moderates within their parties and broadly acceptable to the electorate. A case in point is Germany's current president, Frank-Walter Steinmeier, who previously served as foreign minister and is widely respected by Social Democrats and Conservatives. However, if a political crisis were to prevent the chancellor from governing, the president could act as caretaker or help to engineer a new election.

The Chancellor

The Basic Law requires that the chancellor be elected by an absolute majority of the *Bundestag*. Germany has usually had coalition governments because no one party has typically commanded an absolute majority in the *Bundestag* (though Merkel's

CDU-CSU came within five seats of doing so in 2013). The chancellor's ability to be a strong party (and coalition) leader is thus essential to the government's success. However, even weak chancellors can usually count on the majority coalition to support their remaining in office. Only once (1998) has a government been tossed out by German voters and replaced with an entirely new one.

The chancellor sets out the main direction of government, names cabinet ministers (in coordination with leaders of the coalition partner), and can reorganize the number and type of ministries. The chancellor has considerable authority to govern, thanks to the Federal Chancellery (*Bundeskanzleramt*). This "superministry" has wide-ranging powers that enable the chancellor to oversee the entire government and mediate conflicts among other ministries.

Chancellors have a fair opportunity to implement their programs and take responsibility for success or failure because the interval between parliamentary elections is 4 years, and it is difficult to call snap elections. It is also hard to topple a

grand coalition

A government made up of the two largest parties, often in response to outsider parties deemed unfit for governing.

🪪 PROFILE

Thomas Trutschel/Getty Images

Angela Merkel

Angela Merkel was 51 years old in 2005 when she became the first female chancellor. A minister's daughter, a physicist, a latecomer to political life, an eastern German, a Protestant in a party dominated by Catholics, and a woman who does not champion feminist positions, Merkel is hard to predict or pigeonhole.* Like many East Germans, her political awakening came in 1989 when she took part in pro-democracy protests as the Berlin wall came down. Merkel eventually joined the CDU and rose swiftly through the party ranks, winning the confidence of Chancellor Helmut Kohl. Positions as a *Bundestag* member, cabinet minister, and then party leader followed. In 2005, her CDU won a plurality, and Merkel became chancellor in a **grand coalition** with the SPD.

As the new chancellor, her talk of a "new social market economy" combined appeal to tradition with a promise of renewal. Her opposition to Turkish membership in the EU appealed to many voters, as did her suggestion that "multiculturalism" was a poor model for German society. In foreign policy, Merkel helped put climate change on the international agenda and helped rescue the EU's Constitutional Treaty after its rejection by French and Dutch voters. Her government responded to the 2008 economic crisis with two medium-sized stimulus bills and "cash-for-clunker" rebates for purchasing fuel-efficient new cars.

Merkel's second term saw her CDU allied with its preferred coalition partner, the Free Democrats. Her approach to the economic crisis angered many other international leaders. U.S. officials were skeptical at the modest size of the German stimulus package while Greek and Irish leaders chafed at her lectures about fiscal responsibility. Yet Merkel understood the suspicions of German voters, who rewarded her with a huge electoral victory in 2013. A careful and cautious politician, Merkel's "emotional intelligence, communication skills, and cultivation of stakeholders" has made her a "transformational leader" in the eyes of close observers, who note that "politics does not have to be awe-inspiring to be successful. Eventually, they will stop talking about your hair."**

Like Kohl, Merkel sidelined key opponents within her party. Thus, even when her popularity flagged due to economic uncertainty during 2010–2011 and the refugee crisis after 2015, there was no clear alternative CDU leader. Her ability to avoid major political conflict and rebound strongly from temporary setbacks earned her the nickname "Teflon" by U.S. intelligence agents. Merkel remained uncontested up to the September 2017 *Bundestag* elections. Her principal opponent in that race, the SPD's Martin Schulz, showed early promise but soon fell well behind in the polls.

MAKING CONNECTIONS What aspects of German politics helped Angela Merkel, an unlikely political figure, rise to the position of chancellor?

*Sarah Wiliarty, *The CDU and the Politics of Gender: Bringing Women to the Party* (New York: Cambridge University Press, 2010).

**Joyce Marie Mushaben, *Becoming Madam Chancellor: Angela Merkel and the Berlin Republic* (Cambridge, UK: Cambridge University Press, 2017).

„... WENN DU GROß BIST, MUSST DU DAS BOOT DAHINTEN ZIEHEN !"

A working-class figure tows a small boat of retirees upstream while noting to the child, "When you grow up, you get to pull the second boat." See discussion on pages 178–179.

Waldemar Mandzel, www.w-mandzel.de

government. Under the Weimar constitution, disparate forces could band together to unseat the chancellor but were often unable to agree on a replacement. Therefore, the Federal Republic's founders added a twist to the no-confidence vote familiar from most parliamentary systems. A German chancellor cannot be removed unless the *Bundestag* simultaneously elects a new chancellor (usually from an opposition party).

This **constructive vote of no confidence** provision promotes stability and strengthens the chancellor in two ways. First, chancellors can more easily reconcile disputes among cabinet officials because the dispute does not threaten the chancellor's position. Second, because the opposition must agree on concrete and specific alternatives to the existing government, this minimizes opposition for its own sake.

At the same time, chancellors face significant limits on their power. As will be discussed in Section 4, the *Bundesrat* (upper house), not directly under the chancellor's control, has important powers.

constructive vote of no confidence

This measure requires the *Bundestag* to elect a new chancellor by an absolute majority in order to oust the current one.

The Cabinet

Once a majority of the *Bundestag* has elected the chancellor, the new chancellor consults with officials from its agreed coalition partner to form the cabinet. Negotiations on the policies that a coalition will pursue often become heated. The choice of cabinet ministers is made on policy as well as personal grounds. The most significant ministries are those of finance, economics, justice, interior, and foreign policy.

Chancellors often rely on strong ministers, though some chancellors have taken ministerial responsibility themselves in key areas such as economics and foreign policy. The economics and finance ministries always work closely with the European Central Bank (ECB), since the euro adoption has taken over the main functions of the old German Central Bank (the *Bundesbank*).

Ministers (the equivalent of U.S. cabinet secretaries) are important government actors. Where the U.S. presidential system puts a premium on "interagency" coordination, Germany's parliamentary government puts more responsibility on individual minsters. They have broad autonomy to set policy in their ministry, subject to the chancellor's overall authority to guide the government and the coalition agreement between the parties. Ministers are also collectively responsible for cabinet policy: they are expected to support the government's position and not publicly express disagreements or reservations about policy. Campaign seasons give ministers strong temptations to criticize government policy and curry favor with voters. For example, during the 2017 campaign, SPD Foreign Minister Sigmar Gabriel often criticized as excessive the government's plan to spend 2 percent of German GDP on defense.

The Bureaucracy

The national bureaucracy is a key part of the executive branch of the government. In Germany, it is especially powerful, and its members are protected by civil service provisions that give them influence, prestige, and guaranteed employment for life. German **civil servants** believe their work is a profession, not just a "job."

Surprisingly, the federal government employs only about 25 percent of civil servants; the rest are employed by state and local governments. Today, most civil servants are university graduates and/or come from positions within the parties. Top-level federal bureaucrats are primarily policy-makers who work closely with their ministers and the legislature. State and local bureaucrats are the main agents of policy implementation. Under Germany's distinctive form of federalism, the states administer most policies, even those determined at the national level. Because of the close links among the various levels of the bureaucracy, public policies are often more consistent than in countries where federal and state governments are at odds with one another. Indeed, overlapping responsibilities on policy issues make it difficult to identify the exclusive responsibility of the three levels.

The German bureaucracy enjoys respect from the population. German bureaucrats have a well-deserved reputation for competence. Most civil servants are politically neutral. However, a few top federal officials are partisan, consistent with the idea that parties play a critical role in German democracy and so should be represented in society's main institutions. Most civil servants are chosen on the basis of merit, with elaborate licensing and testing for the highest positions. Civil servants can and do run for office. About one-third of the *Bundestag* is typically made up of civil servants. This contrasts with the United States, where few legislators have any experience as administrators.

civil servants

Employees of federal, state, and municipal governments.

Other State Institutions

In addition to the institutions discussed so far, the military, the judiciary, and subnational governments are essential institutions for governance and policy-making.

The Military and Police

From the eighteenth century through World War II, the German military was powerful and aggressive. After 1945, it was disbanded because of its role in the war. Later reconstituted, it was placed under strict civilian control and tightly limited by law and treaty. Germany renounced nuclear weapons and prohibited the armed forces from operating outside Germany. The military was to be used only for European defense and in coordination with NATO authorities. Constitutional changes ended this prohibition, and Germany's *Bundeswehr* participated in peacekeeping and military operations starting in 1995 in Bosnia. After 2014, Germany sent arms to the Kurdish Peshmerga forces fighting the Islamic State (ISIS), and the army had a parliamentary mandate running into 2018 to help train Kurdish and Iraqi forces.

Russia's illegal annexation of the Ukrainian Crimea and its intervention in eastern Ukraine catapulted Germany into a new position of leadership after 2014. Merkel sought to push Russia to cease fire and withdraw any troops and heavy weapons. Western powers have levied economic sanctions on Russia. While these sanctions hurt German industrial and agricultural exporters, the grand coalition stuck to them. German voters are suspicious of Russia and yet divided on how much German pressure can change Russian behavior. Russian hackers stole data from the German *Bundestag* in 2015, and meddling in the 2017 election only increased these suspicions.

Germany's 2011 suspension of the draft made its army an all-volunteer professional force that is easier to deploy abroad. However, the military's role remains limited. Germany spends approximately 1.2 percent of its GDP on the military, less than most other large, industrialized countries like the United States. However, in 2014, Germany pledged with its NATO allies to reach a 2 percent of GDP target by 2024. It also spends less on foreign aid than does the United Kingdom.

German police powers are organized on a *Land* basis and, because of the excesses of the Third Reich, strong provisions are in place to protect human and civil rights. To be sure, there have been exceptions. By far the worst police abuses came not from the West German police forces, however, but from East Germany's notorious secret police, the *Stasi*. The *Stasi* spied on virtually the entire society and arbitrarily arrested and persecuted thousands of citizens. They even had a mole in Chancellor Willy Brandt's office, which helped lead to his resignation in 1974. After unification, *Stasi* archives were opened because the government believed that full disclosure of *Stasi* excesses was essential. Making public the names of informants has often created bitter confrontations. Outstanding German films have treated these topics, including *Goodbye Lenin* in 2003, and *The Lives of Others* (*Das Leben der Anderen*) in 2006. The legacy of *Stasi* spying also helps explain Germans' negative reaction to the NSA surveillance scandal.

German police have faced heightened challenges in the wake of 9/11 and more recently by ISIS-inspired terrorism in Europe. Police gained new powers, including surveillance, but courts later cut back some of these powers. Still, the potential for terrorist attacks has generally increased in Germany in recent years, as the country has seen a number of "near misses," including a 2006 plot by two Lebanese men to explode suitcase bombs on a commuter train. Several other planned attacks were foiled by German security authorities, sometimes working on tips from the NSA. However, in December 2016, a Tunisian terrorist drove a truck into a popular Berlin Christmas market. This attack killed a dozen people and injured more than fifty. Although the attacker had been observed by regional authorities, Germany's decentralized security structure complicated the sharing of information and risk assessments for this particular attack. About 900 German citizens traveled to join ISIS in Syria or Iraq, of which at least 300 made their way back to Germany by 2017.

To date, no attacks are known to have been perpetrated by this group, most of which are under tight surveillance.

The Judiciary

The German judiciary has always been powerful. During the Nazi regime, it issued numerous repressive decisions, banning non-Nazi parties, allowing the seizure of Jewish property, and sanctioning the deaths of millions. The Federal Republic's founders were determined to prevent further judicial abuses. The Basic Law charges the judiciary with safeguarding the democratic rights of individuals, groups, and political parties. In fact, the Basic Law enumerates twenty individual rights—more than exist in the U.S. Constitution or in British common law.

Germany's legal system differs from the legal tradition of Britain and the United States in other ways as well. The Anglo-American common law precedent-based systems are characterized by adversarial relationships between contending parties. The judge merely presides over a clash between opposing lawyers. In continental Europe, including France and Germany, civil law has roots in Roman law and the Napoleonic code. The judiciary acts as an active administrator of the law rather than just an arbiter. In defining the meaning of laws and implementing their administration, German courts go considerably beyond those in the United States and Britain.

The Federal Republic's court system is three-pronged. One branch consists of the criminal-civil system, with the Federal High Court at the top. It is a unified system that tries to apply consistent criteria to cases in the sixteen states. The Federal High Court reviews appeals of lower court decisions, including criminal and civil cases, disputes among the states, and matters viewed as political in some countries, such as the abortion ruling.

The Special Constitutional Court deals with matters directly affecting the Basic Law. A postwar creation, it was built to safeguard the new democratic order. The Constitutional Court is widely respected and has issued many landmark decisions, including one in 2009 that halts any further transfer of German power to the EU unless expressly ratified by the German parliament (not just the government). The Court has also deliberated on (and, so far, generally approved) key Euro-bailout programs of the European Central Bank (though it expressed great skepticism in a 2014 ruling on ECB purchases of government bonds).

The Administrative Court system is the third branch of the judiciary. It can check the bureaucracy's power, an important function since policy is often determined by the bureaucracy. Citizens can use administrative courts to challenge bureaucratic decisions, for example, with respect to labor, welfare, or tax policies.

The courts have sometimes come under fire. In the late 1970s, critics charged that courts did not restrain clandestine searches for leftist terrorists. These searches arguably violated the rights of citizens. More recently, the courts have been criticized for giving undue protection to neo-Nazis and potential al Qaeda terrorists. The judicial system must walk a fine line between maintaining civil rights in a democratic society and preventing extremist violence.

Subnational Government

Like the United States, Canada, Switzerland, and Austria, Germany is a *federal* republic. There are sixteen *Länder* (states); eleven constituted the old West Germany and five additional ones were made from former East Germany. These state governments enjoy considerable autonomy and independent powers. Each state has a regional assembly that functions much as the *Bundestag* does at the federal level. The governor of each *Land* is the leader of the largest party (or coalition) in the regional assembly and forms a state government, just as does the chancellor in the *Bundestag*. State elections are held on independent, staggered 4-year cycles, which generally do not coincide with federal elections. Subnational governments in Germany are powerful, important, and responsible for much national policy implementation, including most laws passed by the federal government. German states must also share a portion of their tax revenues, so states with stronger economies (grudgingly) support those with weaker economies and lower revenues.

The negative side of German federalism is its lack of flexibility. Since the Basic Law did not specify which powers were reserved for the federal level and which for the states, policymaking is cumbersome. Different levels share responsibility, hence conflict often results. At times, opposition parties have used the upper house to "blockade" (that is, stalemate) the lower house. A 2006 reform tried to clarify the policy domains of the federal and state levels and reduce blockades. However, it has not been very effective.[12]

State politics is organized on the same basis as the national parties. The common party names and platforms at all levels let voters see the connection among local, regional, and national issues. Parties adopt platforms for state and city elections, so voters can see the differences among parties and not be swayed solely by personalities. The German party system encourages politicians to begin their careers at the local level. Regional and local party members' careers are tied closely to the national, regional, and local levels of the party. This way, voters can reward ideological and policy continuity across levels.[13]

German local governments employ about 1.2 million people and assume a wide range of tasks, providing social services (often working with semipublic institutions), implementing environmental standards, and managing the transport network. Local governments can raise revenues by owning enterprises. Many Germans believe that publicly owned museums, theater companies, television and radio networks, recreational facilities, and housing complexes improve their quality of life. And yet unlike U.S. cities, German municipalities can't issue bonds (e.g., incur debt). This means they often wait far too long to invest in schools, hospitals, and other vital services that would improve their citizens' lives, increase productivity, and counteract Germany's systematic underinvestment in the future. Similarly, with the *Energiewende*, more localities must urgently develop new energy grids and production facilities.

The Policy-Making Process

The chancellor and cabinet are responsible for policy-making, but the process is largely consensual. Contentious issues are debated within various public, semipublic, and private institutions. Although the legislature has some role in policy-making, the primary drivers are the cabinet departments (and sometimes the experts on whom they call). The upper house is coequal in all areas where state (*Land*) interests and/or administration play a central role. In practice, this means almost any important bill. Recent reforms tried to streamline this, for example, trying (unsuccessfully) to remove the federal government from higher education policy.

Policy implementation is also shared. The *Bundesrat* plays a big role, along with corporatist interest groups and semipublic organizations noted earlier. EU policy is shaped by both national and regional governments and by private sector interests using corporatist institutions. The states are guaranteed a role in shaping EU policies that affect them.

The *Bundesrat's* power translates into a strong role for the opposition, and this means the *Bundestag's* ruling coalition has strong incentives to cooperate with the opposition.[14]

Both unification and the increasing importance of the EU (for example, the adoption of the euro and the rules associated with it) have challenged Germany's generally informal and consensual style of policy-making.[15] Moreover, for all its system-maintaining advantages, the German consensual system is somewhat intolerant of dissent. This tendency helps explain why protest politics occasionally erupts in Germany, seemingly out of nowhere.

Consensual politics often generates distinctive policies. Take Germany's unusual housing policy. Where other rich democracies push homeownership, Germany is a nation of renters. Under half of German households own their homes (compared to two-thirds of United States households). World War II produced housing shortages, so German governments built millions of multifamily rentals. This meant higher residential density and less suburbanization than the United States. Renting remains attractive in Germany because of strong tenant protections, gradual rent increases, and high quality rental units. This consensus was challenged by the refugee crisis, which led to surging house prices due to an influx of immigrants from Europe and refugees from the Middle East. Alarmed by these developments, German policy-makers are currently debating ways of retaining affordable rental housing.[16]

Where Do You Stand?

In light of the German experience, should constitution-writers be more worried about designing too strong a state or too weak a one?

Do you see foiled terror plots as strong evidence of success?

SECTION 4

REPRESENTATION AND PARTICIPATION

Focus Questions

- How has the rise of new parties disrupted traditional parties' ways of doing business?

- How and why do protest politics work differently in Germany and the United States?

German parties represent well many established interests, yet parties and interest groups often neglect other major collective identities and interests. Partly, this is understandable. Incorporating disparate political cultures is a dilemma for any society, and eastern and western Germany still have *very* different cultures. Yet the German party system is not particularly responsive to new interests and values bubbling up from society. New parties, like the libertarian Pirate Party or the Alternative for Germany (AfD), were certainly able to get a toehold, but lasting breakthroughs have been rare.

The Legislature

Like most parliamentary regimes, Germany "fuses" power rather than "separates" it. This means the executive is voted in not directly by voters but by the legislature. Unlike many parliamentary systems that are tightly controlled by the government, however, both the lower house (*Bundestag*) and the upper house (*Bundesrat*) possess important partially independent powers. Both branches of the legislature are broadly representative of the major interests in German society, although some interests such as business and labor are somewhat overrepresented, whereas ecological and noneconomic interests are underrepresented.

The *Bundestag*

The lower house usually consists of around 600 seats. German elections are by a two-ballot system, known as the mixed member system. This system blends the British and United States traditions of a single legislator representing one district and the European tradition of multidistrict proportional representation (PR), in which parties are allotted seats in the legislature in proportion to the percentage of popular votes they receive. In this hybrid system, each voter casts two votes on his or her ballot: the first, for an individual candidate in a voter's local district, the second, for a list of national/regional candidates grouped by party affiliation. In this way, votes can help establish "constituency" relationships with individual representatives and as well as which parties will have the most influence in the *Bundestag*. Are you confused yet? If so, you're in good company! Several studies have shown that many German voters can't tell the difference between the two votes and do not know which one determines the allocation of seats in parliament (spoiler alert: it's the second or proportional vote).

Bundestag seats are allocated among parties by PR—but with a twist produced by the single-member district feature. For every seat won by a party's candidate in an individual district, his or her party is allotted one less seat from the party's slate elected via list voting. In practice, the two large parties, the Social Democrats and the Christian Democrats, win virtually all of the district seats. In this way, the *Bundestag*'s composition is "mixed" between those deputies who are directly elected and those elected from party lists. This mix gives the system both a constituency logic and also a mechanism for parties to incentivize legislators to toe the party line. Once elected, the two groups of legislators sit together and have identical powers.

Until the mid-1980s, the *Bundestag* was heavily male-dominated, with roughly 90 percent of the seats held by men. Today, Germany's legislature is more gender balanced, (see Table 4.3). This result has been achieved partly through some German parties' voluntary use of gender quotas for their electoral lists. The Left Party, Greens, and Social Democrats alternate male and female candidates on their party lists for the *Bundestag*, and the CDU's rules call for at least one of every three list places to be allotted to a women.[17] As of 2017, Germany ranked 23rd of 190 countries worldwide in

mixed member system

An electoral system in which about half of deputies are elected from direct constituencies and the other half are drawn from closed party lists. The *Bundestag*'s form of mixed member system is basically a variant of PR.

Table 4.3	Percentage of Women Members of the *Bundestag*		
Year	Percentage	Year	Percentage
1949	6.8	1983	9.8
1953	8.8	1987	15.4
1957	9.2	1990	20.5
1961	8.3	1994	26.3
1965	6.9	1998	30.2
1969	6.6	2002	32.2
1972	5.8	2005	31.8
1976	7.3	2009	32.8
1980	8.5	2013	37.1

Source: Bundeszentrale für Politische Bildung, 2014.

terms of women's representation in the national parliament. Angela Merkel, a beneficiary of the CDU's gender "quorum," was one of only twenty female Presidents and Prime Ministers in the world. People with what Germans euphemistically call "immigration backgrounds" are increasingly represented in the *Bundestag*, with their number growing from twenty-one (2009) to thirty-five (2013). Only three MPs were Muslim.[18]

The PR list system produces multiple parties, but it also helps strengthen parties. If legislators consistently defy their party, the leadership can punish them by assigning them a low list position in the next election. This greatly reduces their chances of being reelected and thus is a powerful lever to promote party discipline. Party unity contributes to consistency in the parties' positions over a 4-year legislative period and enables the electorate to identify each party's stance on issues.

5 percent clause

A party must get at least 5 percent of the "second votes" for its candidates to get seats in the *Bundestag* (or the state parliaments). This rule depresses votes for "splinter" parties unlikely to meet this threshold.

A key constitutional element of German politics is the so-called **5 percent clause**, which requires parties to obtain at least 5 percent of the party-list vote to enter parliament. In addition, 5 percent of the vote is required in state or municipal elections for representation in those governments. This barrier matters! In 2013, the Free Democrats, who had been in the *Bundestag* since 1949, just missed getting 5 percent (4.8). A new party, the AfD, received 4.7 percent and so also failed to crack the *Bundestag*. Both have subsequently used state elections to stay on voters' minds, and both are quite likely to join the *Bundestag* after 2017. Over time, many smaller parties have simply faded away. Thus, Germany has avoided the wild proliferation of parties that plagues some democracies, such as Italy and Israel. The German Constitutional Court ruled the 5 percent clause unconstitutional for European (not national or state) elections, and this had a big effect on the 2014 elections to the European Parliament. Alongside the usual larger parties, several smaller ones got into the European Parliament: the FDP had 3.5 percent and three seats, while seven other parties got one MEP each, including the far-right National Democratic Party and the Animal Rights Party. Meanwhile, the AfD won seven seats in the European Parliament.

The tradition of strong, unified parties in the *Bundestag* means new members must serve long stints as backbenchers before acceding to leadership, and individual legislators have few chances to make an impact. Many leaders have preferred to serve their political apprenticeship in state or local government, where they have more visibility. This system, in turn, does improve the skills of young politicians.

The executive branch introduces most (but not all) legislation and must initiate all federal budget and tax legislation. There is often a consensus within parties and within coalitions about what legislation should be introduced. When the executive proposes a bill, it first goes to the *Bundesrat* for comment. Thereafter, it has a quick first reading in the *Bundestag*—primarily to identify any contentious issues in the bill. It then goes to a relevant *Bundestag* committee for review, while the upper house is also notified. Most committee deliberations take place privately, and committee members have great latitude to shape the legislation. Committees generally consult with many groups, both pro and con. This makes it more likely that a consensus-oriented outcome will be achieved.

After the committee reports, the bill has two more readings in the *Bundestag*, with debate between governing parties and opposition generally most intense around the second reading. The primary purpose of the debate is to educate the public about the major issues of the bill. Following passage in the *Bundestag*, the *Bundesrat* must approve most bills for them to become law.

The *Bundesrat*

Unlike the upper house in many parliamentary systems, the *Bundesrat* has real power. Made up of sixty-nine members elected by and from the sixteen state governments, it is the arena where the national and state governments interact. When the government initiates a bill, it sends it first to the *Bundesrat* for comment. The *Bundesrat* can also initiate bills; these must get the government's comment before it is sent to the *Bundestag* for consideration.

The *Bundesrat* can exercise an absolute veto on amendments to the constitution as well as all laws that affect the fundamental interests of the states, such as taxes, territorial integrity, and basic administrative functions. Historically, laws of this kind have amounted to slightly over half (53 percent) of bills, although a 2006 constitutional reform subsequently dropped this to around 40 percent. The *Bundesrat* also can exercise a suspensive veto, which slows the passage of legislation. However, the *Bundestag* can override a suspensive veto by passing the measure again by a simple majority.

Note that even when a governing coalition has a staggering majority in the *Bundestag* (e.g., 2013–2017), this majority often is not replicated in the *Bundesrat*. The *Bundesrat's* political composition depends upon which parties control the sixteen state governments, and they are on different electoral calendars. Each state delegation casts its votes on legislation in a unified bloc, reflecting the views of the state's current coalition. Consequently, the parties in the coalitions that direct the majority of state governments affect what legislation is passed, even if they're not in the ruling *Bundestag* coalition. After the 2013 election, the government that held 80 percent of the *Bundestag* seats had only twenty-seven out of sixty-nine votes in the *Bundestag*. The remainder represented governments that included opposition parties, who will often vote "no" (or abstain, which effectively count as a "no"). Because state elections usually take place between *Bundestag* electoral periods, the *Bundesrat* majority often shifts during the *Bundestag's* 4-year legislative period.

The *Bundesrat* introduces comparatively little legislation, but its administrative responsibilities are considerable. Most *Bundesrat* members are also state government officials, experienced in implementing laws. The *Bundesrat* is responsive to the concerns of the entire country and provides a forum for understanding how national legislation affects each state. Its members' expertise is frequently called on in the committee hearings of the *Bundestag*, which are open to all *Bundesrat* members. The *Bundesrat* also administers the world's largest public television network (ARD) and helps coordinate regional and national economic policies.

Finally, the *Bundesrat* plays a significant role in dealing with the EU. It has long advocated representation for the *Länder* in EU institutions, and it represents the German government in Brussels in some negotiations that centrally affect the states.

Political Parties and the Party System

party democracy

The constitutional guarantee that political parties have a privileged place in German politics, including generous subsidies for building party organizations.

Germany's constitution explicitly establishes a "**party democracy**" and intends that parties be central to shaping state policy. Until the early 1980s, Germany had a "two-and-a-half" party system, composed of a moderate-left Social Democratic Party (SPD), a moderate-right Christian Democratic grouping (CDU in all of West Germany except Bavaria, where it is called the CSU), and a small market-oriented Free Democratic Party (FDP).

18th Bundestag 2013
Party Seats and Percentage of the National Vote

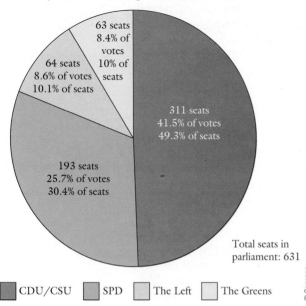

63 seats
8.4% of
votes
10% of
seats

64 seats
8.6% of votes
10.1% of seats

311 seats
41.5% of votes
49.3% of seats

193 seats
25.7% of votes
30.4% of seats

Total seats in
parliament: 631

■ CDU/CSU   ■ SPD   □ The Left   □ The Greens

© Cengage

FIGURE 4.3 Distribution of Seats

In recent decades, three new parties emerged to challenge the "two-and-a-half" major parties. One was the Greens, generally on the left and favoring ecological, environmental, and peace issues. The other was the Party of Democratic Socialism (PDS), the former Communist Party of East Germany. In 2005, the latter formed *Die Linke* (Left Party) with a group of left-wing ex-Social Democrats who believed SPD Chancellor Schröder's Agenda 2010 reforms undermined social democracy. Further, as was noted above, the AfD was launched in 2013 (on anti-Euro-zone stances) and surged in 2015 (on anti-refugee stances). These three small parties, along with the CDU/CSU, SPD, and FDP, make up the current electoral landscape of Germany. Figure 4.3 shows the relative strength of the four parties that passed the 5% hurdle in 2013 and entered the *Bundestag*.

The Christian Democrats

The CDU/CSU (two distinct, but closely allied parties) have dominated postwar German politics, governing, usually in coalitions, from 1949 to 1969, 1982 to 1998, and continually since 2005. The CDU and CSU (Bavaria-only) unite Catholics and Protestants in confessional, catchall parties of the center-right. Christian Democracy champions the social market economy. Their social policies in the decades after World War II were paternalistic, but they sponsored the considerable expansion of the German welfare state. The party alliance has been a consistent advocate of European integration since Konrad Adenauer's leadership in the early postwar period. The most significant accomplishments of the long Kohl regime (1982–1998) are German unification and Germany's determination to deepen EU integration.

CDU leader Angela Merkel became Germany's first female chancellor after the 2005 election, when the CDU/CSU entered into a grand coalition with its main competitor, the SPD. Big FDP gains in the 2009 election enabled Merkel to form her preferred coalition with this more free market liberal party. In the 2013 elections, she then came within five seats of capturing the first absolute majority since Adenauer's in 1957 (for more on Merkel, see the Profile box in Section 3). Instead, she partnered with the Social Democrats again, since, as explained earlier, the FDP failed to gain 5 percent of the nationwide vote. In the run-up to the September 2017 election, Merkel particularly faced pressure from the right. Her controversial refugee policy had disgruntled many traditional conservative voters, driving them into the arms of the AfD, although the 2017 CDU election campaign saw some return to law and order themes.

The Social Democratic Party

The traditional leading party of the left, the SPD, was founded in 1875 in response to rapid industrialization and Bismarck's authoritarianism. Following World War I, it became the leading party—but without having a majority—in the early years of the Weimar Republic. The SPD was the only party in the Weimar parliament to vote against Hitler's rise to power, and the party still takes great pride in its historical opposition to the Nazi dictatorship.

Despite being the second-largest party in postwar Germany, the SPD obtained only about 30 percent of the vote until the early 1960s and never succeeded in joining a national government. In an attempt to broaden its constituency, it altered its program in 1959. By deemphasizing its reliance on Marxism and its working-class base, it sought to recruit voters from throughout the social structure, including the middle class, and among Christians.

In 1969, the SPD was finally elected to office as the leading member of a majority coalition (with the FDP). It remained in power for 13 years under chancellors Willy Brandt and Helmut Schmidt. The SPD brought to the coalition a concern for increased welfare and social spending, as well as an effort to ease strained relations with the USSR and other communist countries (*Ostpolitik*).

The SPD was out of power from 1982 to 1998 when it failed to formulate winning alternative policies and strategies, though it governed many states. In 1998, the exhausted Kohl regime was voted out, and the SPD formed a coalition with the Greens. The early years of the second SPD-led regime were successful, but divisions within the party over economic reforms (particularly Agenda 2010) brought the second term of the SPD-Green government to an early end in 2005. After limping through a grand coalition with the CDU for four more years, the SPD vote plunged to 23 percent in the 2009 elections, its lowest total ever. It rose to 26 percent in the 2013 elections, and given the elimination of the FDP from parliament, this enabled it to enter a grand coalition with the CDU/CSU again.[19] The SPD's 2017 candidate for chancellor, former European Parliament President Martin Schulz, argued that the Agenda 2010 reforms went too far and left many service sector workers with miserable pay and low benefits.

Ostpolitik

The policy developed by the SPD's Willy Brandt to promote contact and commerce with the Soviet Union and its communist allies during the Cold War.

The Greens

The Greens entered the political scene in 1979 and have won seats at national and regional levels ever since. This heterogeneous party drew support from several constituencies in the early 1980s: urban-based **citizen action groups**, environmental activists, farmers, antinuclear activists, the peace movement, and supporters of Marxism-Leninism. After first overcoming the 5 percent hurdle in the 1983 *Bundestag* elections, the Greens went on to win seats in most subsequent state and national elections by stressing noneconomic quality-of-life issues.

Electoral success generated division within this "antiparty party." The *realos* (realists) believed it was important to moderate the party's positions in order to win power; the *fundis* (fundamentalists) opposed any collaboration with existing parties, in order to avoid compromising the party's demands, even if this meant damaging their short-term electoral prospects. The squabbling between *fundis* and *realos* long undercut the party's credibility.

In 1998, the Greens got a chance to govern in a national coalition. But the *fundi-realo* split soon emerged when Green foreign minister, Joschka Fischer, a *realo*, split the party by supporting Germany's participation in the NATO-led bombing of Serbia. Fischer explained that his generation was raised both to say "never again war" *and* "never again Auschwitz." When forced to choose, he insisted Germany must choose the latter in order to prevent Serbian tyrant Slobodan Milosevic from genocidal aggression against Kosovar Albanians.

Back in opposition, the Greens are clearly seen as a serious competitor by both SPD and CDU. Merkel sought to accentuate the CDU's difference with the Greens in her shift toward nuclear energy, a move that backfired after the earthquake-driven Japanese nuclear crisis in 2011. Shortly thereafter, the Greens had their biggest

citizen action groups

Nonparty and often single-issue initiative groups, who focus on concrete problems such as the environment, traffic, housing, or other social and economic issues.

regional success when a Green became governor of a state for the first time (and won reelection in 2016). Nationally, the Greens generally poll a bit above or below the 10 percent mark, which currently puts them in kind of a no man's land: even with a stronger showing by the SPD, the chances seem slight of a renewed SPD-Green coalition for 2017, while the CDU and Greens currently also seem unlikely to reach a combined 50 percent of the *Bundestag*.

The Free Democratic Party

For decades, the FDP specialized in leveraging modest numbers of votes into lots of power. This "swing party" regularly allied with each of the two major parties (SPD and CDU/CSU) at different periods after 1949, often holding both the foreign and economics ministries in those coalitions.

The FDP could "swing" so easily because it contained two ideologies: economic liberalism (in the European sense of free market-oriented) and social liberalism (personal freedoms). Recently, the FDP has become more explicitly free-market, emphasizing deregulation and privatization. The growth of the Green and Left Parties has diminished the "kingmaker" status of the FDP. In 2009, after polling an astonishingly high 15 percent, the FDP replaced the SPD in Merkel's CDU-led government coalition. However, the FDP's standing subsequently plummeted. In 2013, its weak performance in government combined with its voters' worries about German policies to rescue the euro and led many voters to abandon it.

Having missed clearing the 5 percent hurdle, the FDP limped along in (some) state parliaments and the European Parliament, seeking to reverse its fortunes before the 2017 elections. However, by 2016, the party was involved in only a single state-level ruling coalition—in Rhineland-Palatinate, where the "yellow" FDP ruled with the "red" SPD and the Greens in a so-called "traffic light" coalition. The FDP is very weak in the five eastern states, having recently met the 5 percent hurdle in only a single state (Berlin). Yet 2017 saw the FDP re-enter government in Schleswig-Holstein and North Rhein Westphalia, building momentum for a re-entry to the *Bundestag* in 2017.

The Left Party

In 2005, the Left Party was formed when the former East German Communist Party (PDS) merged with a breakaway faction of the SPD that had been alienated by the Agenda 2010 reforms to liberalize the labor market and the welfare state. While officially a new party concentrated in the former East Germany, the PDS had a long and volatile history. Beginning in the late 1940s, the Communist Party (SED) dominated all aspects of life in East Germany. The GDR led by the SED was probably the most repressive regime in eastern Europe. After unification in 1990, the SED demonstrated tactical agility by changing its name to the PDS and moderating its program. It often polled over 20 percent in the five *Länder* of the former East Germany and won seats in the *Bundestag* in each election. The merger with left-wing dissidents from the SPD concentrated in western Germany thus provided the Left Party with electoral support precisely where the old PDS had been weakest.

The Left Party's strong showing is largely due to its opposition to cuts in social spending. With a base in the west of around 5 percent and traditional eastern support of close to 20 percent, it now seems solidly entrenched. The Left Party's durability makes "coalition math" far more complicated than in the simple old days of CDU-FDP, CDU-SPD, or SPD-FDP alliances. The Left Party has been part of several coalitions at the state level and in 2016 joined an SPD-led "red-red-green" government in the state of Berlin. Such a coalition might be numerically possible at the federal level in 2017, although the Left Party's opposition to NATO would be a major stumbling block. The Left Party is the only German party to consistently oppose the German-supported austerity policies in struggling Eurozone states.

Alternative for Germany

Germany is one of the few countries in Western Europe that has not had a far-right and/or neofascist party gain seats in its national legislature since World War II. Because the Left Party's primary support in the east comes from marginalized and/or unemployed people, it has provided a left-wing alternative for many voters who, in other west European countries, have turned to the far right.

In 2013, however, the AfD party formed around opposition to Germany's Eurozone rescue policies, which AfD supporters held to be overly generous, out of step with German traditions of ordo-liberalism, and in violation of European treaties. When the AfD (just) failed to reach the 5 percent hurdle at the 2013 election, the party soon drifted toward insignificance, even as it began stressing a new worry: refugees and other migrants. However, when in 2015 the government decided to open the door to nearly a million refugees, the AfD took the lead in mobilizing opposition outside the parliament. When the party swapped its leadership cadre of economics professors for media-savvy provocateurs, its support jumped rapidly. Its party platform calls for banning burkas, minarets, and the Islamic call to prayer. A March 2016 election in Saxony-Anhalt saw the AfD reach a whopping 24 percent of the vote, becoming the second largest party in that state. By mid-2017, the AfD had members in all five eastern parliaments plus seven of the eleven in western Germany.

Elections

Germany has enjoyed relatively stable voting patterns, despite the ups and downs of unification and European integration. But the entry of new parties in the *Bundestag* in recent decades may now reflect higher volatility among voters and, hence, among parties. The danger is that the multiparty system increases the chances of inconclusive elections, in which no party is a decisive winner. After the vote, it may fall to the parties to haggle amongst themselves to choose among possible coalitions. Will voters then react with even greater frustration? And will parties turn to more and more adventurous coalitions in order to form majorities? These questions featured a lot in the 2017 campaign, whose exact outcome you now know, but I—writing in the summer of 2017—do not! Right now, it seems Merkel's CDU will win the most seats. But will it form another grand coalition with the SPD? Or will the FDP, the Greens, or both join them in the government?

Check MindTap for the most up-to-date coverage on the German elections.

Adding complexity to elections, up to a fifth of German voters seem to vote "strategically," most often by voting for one of the big three parties sure to cross the 5 percent threshold, even if it's not their real favorite. Others vote for their favorite candidate with the first vote and their favorite coalition partner for that candidate's party with the second vote. And while the ballot may confuse some, it doesn't prevent high turnout. Until recently, German voter turnout rates of 80 to 90 percent exceeded those in most other Western European countries. German elections are increasingly marked by the "personal vote," in which the traits of specific leaders count for more than the parties' programs. Figure 4.4 shows the shifting composition of the electorate over time, as well as the slight recent decline in voter turnout.

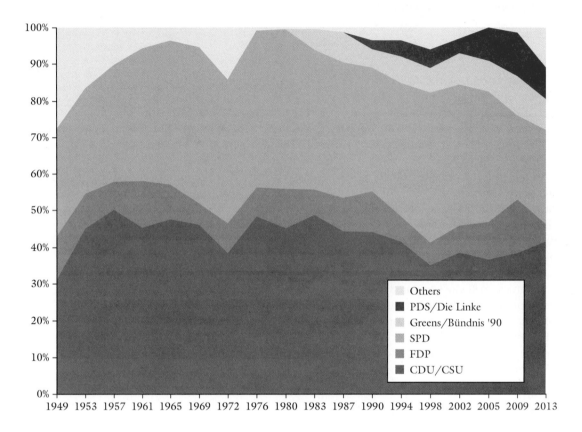

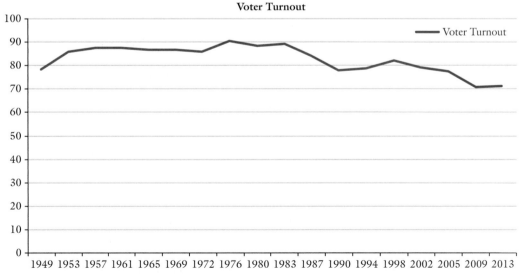

FIGURE 4.4 FRG Election Results, 1949–2013

Sources: German Information Center, 2005; *Bundestagswahl*, 2009, 2013.

Political Culture, Citizenship, and Identity

With parties representing such a broad ideological spectrum, there is wide-ranging political debate. Germany's moderate right parties (CDU/CSU and FDP) have integrated a broad swath of right-wing voters into democratic and even centrist politics. Among the democratic left, there is a strong participatory ethic, fostered by extensive participation at the workplace through the works councils. Moreover, the Greens have placed great emphasis on grassroots democracy—that is, rank-and-file participation. The Greens, and now the Left Party, have forced the two traditional parties to engage in grassroots efforts to mobilize support. Meanwhile, the AfD calls for more referendums and direct democracy, something Germans have used very little.

Germany's educational system is steeped in tradition, though it has changed considerably in recent decades. Traditionally, only a small cohort (from affluent backgrounds) went on to university—most children who eventually enrolled in higher education already began the university prep track in the sixth grade!—while the rest went on to technical or vocational tracks. In recent years, German schools have been disappointingly middle-of-the-pack in comparative analyses.

Postwar universities long remained elitist and restrictive and often provided little critical analysis of Germany's bloody twentieth-century history. But widespread student mobilizations in the 1960s opened up the educational system to a much wider class spectrum and also caused many of the '68 Generation (1968 was the year of the most significant student demonstrations) to challenge their parents about attitudes shaped by the Nazi period and before. Far more Germans now attend universities. In fact, almost 60 percent of young Germans start a degree, but few German universities are in the top rank globally. In the mid-2000s, several German states tried to charge tuition of €500 per semester—up to then, university tuition was free—but stiff student resistance recently ended this experiment. The result is that universities remain underfunded, and faculties teach too many courses to provide much mentoring to students.

Refugees, Immigration, and Migrant Labor

German crimes in the Holocaust and World War II—where many non-Jews also experienced German brutality—led postwar Germany to accept a special responsibility to Jews and other ethnic minorities. The new FRG government made large compensation payments to survivors of the Holocaust, their families, and the state of Israel. It also passed generous asylum laws to enable large numbers of those facing political persecution elsewhere to obtain German residency, although not citizenship. With the end of the Cold War and the opening up of east European borders, the trickle of asylum seekers turned into a flood. In response, the government restricted political asylum in the mid-1990s.

Immigrants to Germany have traditionally had little chance to obtain citizenship. The 1913 Immigration Law stipulated that citizenship was based on blood (*jus sanguinis*) and not naturalization (*jus solis*). Obtaining German citizenship was thus easy for ethnic Germans whose families had lived in Russia or Eastern Europe for generations, but difficult for the *Gastarbeiter* children born in Germany. Until the SPD-Green government eased citizenship rules in 1999, Germany's restrictive definition of identity looked insular and backwards in a Europe rapidly becoming more international.

Every European state faces a version of this dilemma: How can they protect national identity and still respond to the economic and ethical motives to allow some immigration and asylum? While some Germans are fearful immigration will weaken the traditional conception of "German," globalization has opened the country to increasing migration. Economic pressures to increase immigration go together with a demographic trend that, likewise, affects almost all European countries: a shrinking native-born population. The aging native population relies on a welfare and pension system financed by currently employed (that is, younger) workers. One partial solution to the fiscal demands of an aging population is young immigrant workers who could both revitalize economic growth and help fund pension and welfare obligations. To do so, however, requires that Germany—and many of its neighbors—reconsider who can be a citizen. The grand coalition introduced limited dual citizenship (until age 21) for anyone of foreign background who was born in Germany.

Until the 1960s, women had been politically marginalized in the FRG. Taking to heart the traditional slogan *Kinder, Kirche, Küche* (children, church, kitchen), few women held positions in society outside the home. Even with the social explosions of the 1960s and the spread of feminism since the 1970s, German women have generally lagged behind women in many west European countries in obtaining adequate representation in business and civil society. However, as the data in Table 4.3 show, German women have quadrupled their representation in the *Bundestag* from approximately 8 percent in 1980 to 37 percent in 2013.

Following unification, there were controversial differences between the Federal Republic and the former GDR on policy affecting women. Women in the former East Germany had more presence and influence in public life and in the workplace than did their counterparts in West Germany. To be sure, female employment was nearly obligatory in the GDR. Still, East German women enjoyed greater government provision for childcare and family leave. In fact, one of the hottest debates in Germany during the early 1990s was whether to reduce East German-style benefits to women in favor of the more conservative and restrictive ones of the Federal Republic. The West German practices and patterns prevailed after unification, to the frustration of many.

Interest Groups, Social Movements, and Protest

As discussed in Section 2, Germany remains a country of organized groups: major economic producer groups such as the BDI (Federal Association of German Industry), BDA (Federal Association of German Employers), and DGB (German Trade Union Confederation); political parties (in which authentic participatory membership remains higher than in most other countries); and social groups.

Interest groups in Germany operate differently than in the United States and Britain. In Germany, interest groups have a societal responsibility beyond representing the immediate interests of their members. Laws allow private interests to perform some public functions. Thus, interest groups are part of the fabric of society and are virtually permanent institutions. This makes it critical that they can adapt to new issues. Despite the emphasis on negotiation and consensus, strikes and demonstrations do occur. In some cases, strikes and other conflicts pressure institutions to be responsive. Rather than being detrimental to democratic participation, such bottom-up protests contribute to a vibrant civil society.

In the best case, because they aggregate the interests of all their members, groups take a broader view of problems and solutions. The state neither remains distant, as in Britain and the United States, nor intervenes in the intensive fashion typical of France and Japan. Political scientist Peter Katzenstein observes that in Germany, the state is not an actor that "imposes its will on civil society," but rather a series of "relationships" mediated and solidified in semipublic institutions.[20] In other words, organizations that would elsewhere be regarded as "mere interest groups" work with semipublic agencies (as described in section 2) to fill a critical role between state and society.

Many smaller groups fall outside this organized system, including political parties that fail to meet the 5 percent electoral threshold. Since the student mobilizations of the late 1960s, Germany has witnessed considerable protest and mobilization of social forces outside established channels. Among the most significant have been feminists, the peace movement, the antinuclear movement, and church-linked protests in East Germany in 1989 that catalyzed the breakdown of the communist regime. A 1988 Bruce Springsteen concert in East Berlin shocked Communist Party officials by drawing so many people that it overwhelmed the security staff. While not overtly political, Springsteen did open the show with "Badlands" and mused about a day when "barriers would be torn down." A year later, they were.[21]

With the fall of the wall came a surge of xenophobic neo-Nazi activity. Many East Germans felt overwhelmed by the economic and social woes as the country was reunited. This discontent sparked animosity towards foreigners and led to several attacks in the early 1990s. In the 2000s, the neo-Nazi group Nationalist Socialist Underground (NSU) murdered several ethnic Turks and Kurds before their crimes were uncovered in 2011. This "NSU-scandal" created a huge stir, because Germany's domestic intelligence agency allegedly knew of the crimes before they were made public. Thus, right-wing violence not only remains a problem but also is growing: the Ministry of the Interior reported 22,960 right-wing motivated crimes in 2015—an increase of one-third compared to 2014—including over 3,000 violent incidents.

The Iraq war beginning in 2003 produced an increase in social protest, largely among forces to the left of the governing SPD-Green coalition. The Left Party actively opposed German troop deployments to Afghanistan (around sixty German soldiers and police have been killed since being deployed there since 2002). However, most protests on this issue have been limited to hundreds rather than thousands of demonstrators.

ullstein bild/The Granger Collection, NYC

About a year before the wall came down, 300,000 East Germans (about 200,000 without tickets) jammed into a park in East Berlin to hear a free Springsteen concert. For many, it was their first experience of seeing East German security forces back off from a crowd of citizens.

In fall 2016, tens of thousands protested against the proposed EU-U.S. trade treaty, arguing that it would undercut health and environmental standards and unduly benefit foreign investors. Smaller numbers protested the government's refugee policy in 2016.

The Political Impact of Technology and the Media

Germany's press is free, diverse, and vibrant, and it offers an amalgamation of publicity, entertainment, and information. There are three main public TV channels and a variety of private cable and satellite channels. During election campaigns, each major party gets seven free 90-second ads on the public stations. The campaigns spend most of their strictly limited campaign funds on billboards and posters, leaving television viewers largely unmolested by ads. The private lives of German politicians are still generally off-limits and respected by the press. On one occasion, a chancellor and vice-chancellor had a total of nine marriages between the two men, but the press paid little attention to this.

Newspapers appeal to a broad range of political opinion and are in far stronger financial shape than are American newspapers. Befitting a federal and decentralized country, there is no informal national "paper of record" akin to the *New York Times*. The rough-and-tumble tabloid press has a populist tone and is quick to punish any signs of elitism on the part of politicians. The tabloids played a key role in mobilizing opposition to German financing of the Eurozone crisis after 2008.

New media are less well developed in Germany than elsewhere, and there is substantial worry that American-owned new media giants will take on a dominant position in German media. About 28 million Germans have a Facebook account, and nearly half the country uses WhatsApp (owned by Facebook). Google's market share in search engines is above 95 percent. Worries about the proliferation of "fake news"—particularly from Russian sources—led the government to sponsor a law in 2017 that imposes fines for websites that don't actively police such stories and/or move too slowly to remove them.

German politicians use Twitter, Facebook, texting, and blogging to reach out to voters. Yet there have been only limited attempts to emulate Obama's and Trump's online campaigns, which devoted great efforts to using these tools to target swing voters. Such tactics are very difficult in Germany because parties can only legally collect voter data with voters' consent. And unlike parties in the United States, Germany parties are prohibited from combining consumer data with political information. They also have far less money than American parties and cannot afford vast data-collecting operations (German campaign laws severely limit private contributions from individuals and groups.) Door-to-door campaigning is rare, as most Germans are unnerved by the thoughts of campaigners visiting their homes. Parties tread very carefully—including limits on TV ads—lest they turn off voters by too much intrusion.

The relentless search for technological improvements has influenced Germany's leading role in debates over global warming. German politicians from across the political spectrum have pushed for regional (EU) and global action (at Kyoto/Copenhagen/Paris) to limit and possibly reverse climate change. This position reflects a broad consensus among German voters about the reality and dangers of man-made global warming. Most Germans are shocked to hear that many Americans question the existence of global warming and think that it is a matter of opinion rather than scientific evidence. German firms, including those in the all-important auto sector, generally accept regulations requiring cleaner technology. Therefore, they have a keen interest in requiring their competitors in other countries to face the

THE U.S. CONNECTION

Comparing Anti-Nuclear Movements in the United States and Germany

Ever since a tsunami destroyed Japan's Fukushima nuclear plant in 2011 concerns about nuclear safety have increased in the United States and Germany. Both nuclear industries share some important features. Their relative size is roughly equal: the United States gets about 19 percent of its electricity from nuclear power, and Germany's eight remaining plants account for about 14 percent of its electricity. (France's fifty-eight plants produce 76 percent of its electricity). In both countries, there is fierce debate about whether to extend the life of existing plants and general agreement to oppose building new plants. Both governments play a critical role in licensing and inspecting plants, subsidizing R&D, and insuring against risks. In both, private companies produce nuclear power, and the government is responsible for dealing with waste.

Both states also have selected a waste storage site that has never opened because of political opposition. In the United States, it involves tunnels bored into Yucca Mountain in the Nevada desert. In Germany, the potential dump at a salt dome called Gorleben has now been superseded by a search for a site that will be good for "a million years." Finally, in both countries there was an iconic nuclear accident (Three Mile Island in Pennsylvania in 1979 and Chernobyl in Ukraine in 1986) that helped end construction of new nuclear plants. Yet alongside these similarities, there are striking differences in how

the antinuclear movements work in both countries. The German antinuclear movement, which began in the early 1970s, has often been radical, even violent at times. It built on a cultural foundation of ecological activism, and, by forming the Green Party, it eventually "broke through" an electoral system that requires coalition government and has more space for small parties than in the United States.

In the United States, the antinuclear movement has been split, with neither faction resembling its German counterpart. One wing has focused on legal tactics, essentially challenging the nuclear industry (and often the government) in court. The other wing has been confrontational, but nonviolent.*

In Germany, the movement has been highly confrontational. Nuclear waste trains have been disrupted by protestors shooting fireworks and boarding the trains. The Japanese nuclear disaster only deepened skepticism, and Merkel's government eventually decided to phase out all German nuclear plants by 2022.

MAKING CONNECTIONS How do differences in the German and American electoral systems help account for differences in antinuclear movements?

*Christian Joppke, *Mobilizing Against Nuclear Energy: A Comparison of Germany and the United States* (Berkeley: University of California, 1993).

same regulatory conditions. However, even better—as shown by the scandal in which Volkswagen cheated on diesel emissions in 11 million cars worldwide—is to let your competitors meet the regulatory conditions while you sidestep them. However, the scandal cost Volkswagen $15 billion in fines and a considerable loss of reputation. VW subsequently confessed to colluding with the other German car-makers on regulations and prices, both in Europe and abroad.

Notwithstanding this black eye for the "Made in Germany" slogan, German firms and politicians are confident that they can meet bold targets for reductions in CO_2 emissions set by the 2016 Paris Agreement (partly because they got credit for shutting down dirty East German industries that were slated to close anyway). German business is also convinced that it can make money selling green technology to other countries. This is another important motivation for shifting the energy mix towards renewable sources.

Where Do You Stand?

Does democracy work better with larger American-style parties—which form coalitions before elections—or smaller German-style parties—which form coalitions after elections?

Can citizen use of social media improve political decisions? Increase our enjoyment of politics?

SECTION
5

GERMAN POLITICS IN TRANSITION

▽ Focus Questions

- Does the EU require Germany to be especially generous in order for the EU to function properly?

- How durable is the German economic model in the face of new regional and global competitors?

In June 2009, EU officials breathed an enormous sigh of relief as the German Constitutional Court gave its blessing to the Treaty of Lisbon, which reformed the EU. Five years earlier, both French and Dutch voters had decisively rejected an earlier effort (the so-called Constitutional Treaty). In the aftermath, Merkel helped devise a new treaty that was signed and ratified by all EU members, but this new treaty was challenged in Germany's Constitutional Court for harming parliamentary democracy and national sovereignty. If the Court had overturned German ratification, the treaty would be dead. Instead, the Court found that Lisbon was acceptable because the EU's member states would remain in control of the EU. In other words, the Court did not see a federal "United States of Europe" emerging from the Treaty— and the Court warned that such a federal state would violate the German Basic Law. On the other hand, the Court stated there were some policy areas where Germany could delegate no further powers to the EU since this would undermine national democratic and parliamentary control. Seven years later, as described in Chapter 2 of this book, the United Kingdom—a close partner of Germany in many EU matters— voted narrowly to leave the EU by 2019.

These two different outcomes have in common the sense that the EU cannot further limit national sovereignty. Germany must adapt to this new reality and make the best of the EU as it presently exists. Since the 1950s, Germany has depended on European integration to solve many problems, from its inability to run an independent foreign policy to its need for foreign consumers to buy its huge export surpluses. To win support, Germany often made side payments to other states. But both Germany's capacity and its will to do this have waned.

As Europe's leading economic power, Germany has benefited from European integration. It is safer and more prosperous. Behaviors its neighbors might once have seen as a German bid for domination are more acceptable when seen as Germany's participation in the EU. Since the 2008 economic crisis, admirers have even pointed to Germany's impressive employment performance as evidence of the value of Germany's policies and practices. At the same time, some German investments in the rest of Europe have gone spectacularly sour, and Germany has felt obliged to bail out less prosperous Eurozone member states (partly so those states could repay what they owe to Germany's banks).

The EU has reformed its economic rules since 2009, mostly in ways that Germany has supported. Still, the 2009 German Constitutional Court decision that limited any deeper German integration with the EU was not the only warning about the limits of integration. A 2014 decision on central bank rules caused further anxiety by placing strict limits on a key rescue tool. And, of course, Brexit will cost Germany a key ally in many intra-EU debates over economic policy.

Overall, Germany has become far more ambivalent about European integration at the same time that the EU clearly needs further reform. Germans do still have favorable views of the EU—a 2015 Pew poll found 58 percent thought the EU "was a good thing"—but lower than German support in the past. About 64 percent feel the euro is a "good thing" for Germany.[22] East Germans are far more skeptical and perceive less benefit from EU membership. Euro-skepticism is also evident in the parties' behavior. Even the CDU, the party most identified with Europe, has ceased to see further European integration as positive. Many AfD voters want weaker states out of the Eurozone.

Further, given the enlargement of the EU, it becomes harder for the German-French tandem to shape EU integration. Whether the election of Emmanuel Macron changes this remains to be seen. There is more talk of a "multi-speed Europe" in which smaller groups of willing countries move "ahead" (toward more integration with each other), while other states move at their own (slower) pace. This was already the case with both the Eurozone and the Schengen area of free movement, but it could be extended to other domains. Yet multispeed Europe could increase free riding and "cherry picking" in which states take only those policies that bring benefits. Such a "Europe without costs" might be too weak to help its member states solve their problems.

Political Challenges and Changing Agendas

The future of German politics depends on how the country addresses the four themes identified at the outset: the globalizing world of states, governing the economy, the democratic idea, and the politics of collective identity. Germany long enjoyed a spiral of success that enabled it to confront these issues with confidence. For example, problems of collective identities were handled in a much less exclusionary way as women, non-native ethnic groups, and newer political parties and movements contributed to a healthy diversity in German politics. Democratic institutions balanced participation and dissent, offsetting the country's turbulent and often racist past by 70 years of stable multiparty democracy. Germany's economic success has been significant and unique. With the support of its neighbors and allies, Germany has taken a leading role in European integration.

Beginning with the globalizing world of states, Germany is now firmly anchored in western Europe while also shaping the transition of the former communist central and eastern European states toward economic and political modernization and EU membership. After the collapse of communism, some feared German investors would "reconquer" eastern Europe. For a time, these states resisted German investment. But Germany emerged as a forceful advocate of both EU and NATO enlargement, and today Germany has generally friendly and mutually beneficial relations with the countries of the region (although tensions are rising with populist Hungary and Poland). At the same time, most German politicians stress that their state has become a "normal" state that should not be shamed into doing things because of its fascist past.

Germany's approach to governing the economy also faces challenges in the early twenty-first century. For many years, the German economy was characterized as "high everything," in that it combined high-quality manufacturing with high wages, high fringe benefits, high worker participation, and high levels of vacation time. Although the German economy has remained among the world's leaders, the huge costs of unification, globalization, and the fiscal crisis in Europe all challenge the German model anew.

When financial crisis struck the United States in 2008, many Germans first thought this was strictly an American problem. After all, the German economy was much less reliant on soaring profits in the financial sector. This interpretation was further strengthened by the clear problems in Europe's own financial center, London. When the German economy also tanked in 2009, however, it undermined the idea that the financial crisis was strictly a "made in America" problem. When global access to capital dried up, financing for trade dried up with it. Since Germany exports high-quality machinery, chemicals, cars, and electronics, this decline hurt badly. Meanwhile, German banks turned out to be neck-deep in messy investments abroad. Suddenly, the mood shifted, and the fear in Germany was palpable.

As the crisis swept through Europe, falling exports soon threw the German economy into decline. GDP fell by about 5 percent in 2009. Almost as quickly as it crashed, the German economy recovered, starting in 2010, buoyed by state policies that covered some of the wages of skilled workers during the downturn. As Germany boomed, however, other European states sank deeper into economic misery. The German government's subsequent advice to troubled European countries can be summed up as "less risk and less debt." To an extent, this advice made sense. It implied both consumers and governments in struggling countries should spend less. Yet if other European states consume less, to whom will Germany sell its exports?

Once Greece and then Ireland, Portugal, and Cyprus needed emergency financing from the EU, Germany's role became especially difficult. German leaders worried that to bail them out might discourage reforms and enrage German voters. Yet to let these states go bankrupt might threaten the euro, the European currency that benefits Germany. There is no simple way out of this dilemma, then or now. German-favored austerity policy hasn't worked, and it has badly damaged the credibility of democracy (and of the EU) in the eyes of many crisis-state voters.

Meanwhile, German democracy appears well established. It features high (if declining) voter turnout, fairly stable parties, and a healthy civic culture. Many observers believe that broad-based participation is part of the fabric of German political life. Yet the more complex business of forming effective governing coalitions is a big challenge, as is the assimilation of the five eastern states. Can eastern Germans who have lost jobs accept that ethnic minorities are not the main cause of their unemployment? Can tolerance and understanding offset a right-wing movement that preaches distrust and blames scapegoats for the costs of unification? There is reason for optimism. On balance, eastern Germans have shown that they understand and practice democracy amazingly well.

In the area of collective identities, Germany faces many unresolved challenges. Prior and more recent waves of migrants will be essential to Germany's economy. Their long-term acceptance by the CDU/CSU, not to mention the smaller ultra-right parties, will likely be the key to a fundamental change in the concept of who is a German. More than two generations after the end of World War II, young Germans are asking what being German actually means. Changes in citizenship laws will complicate this issue, for although this search for identity can be healthy, and immigrants can help enrich and renew the meaning of German identity, these changes can encourage extremist groups to preach exaggerated nationalism and hatred of foreigners and minorities.

By contrast, religious divides seem manageable: 29 percent of Germans are Catholic and 27 percent Protestant, with about 36 percent unaffiliated or other. Before the arrival of nearly 1 million refugees in recent years, Germany's Muslim population was already at around 4.4 percent. Anti-Muslim sentiment is strongest in eastern Germany.

Is Demography Destiny?

Germany's demographic developments—especially the aging of society—are changing the country in fundamental ways. Young people face a striking disparity between wages in the low end service sector and the much higher wages in industry and the high end of the service sector (like banking and insurance). Earlier generations did not face such large disparities. There are jobs aplenty, but the question is whether one can acquire the skills for the good jobs or build a reasonable life around the bad ones. Youth unemployment is just under 7 percent, higher than adult unemployment but far below the European average of 17 percent. But Germany has become a remarkably unequal society in recent decades, and many low-wage, low-benefit young workers lack the resources to acquire the skills needed to compete for good jobs.[23]

Meanwhile, pensioners and older workers are anxious, too. The German birthrate fell markedly after 1990, particularly in the former GDR but also in the West. The German female fertility rate remains about 1.4 births per woman—well below the 2.1 rate at which a population remains stable. This places great demographic pressure on the German welfare state because the low birthrate and increasing age of baby boomers means fewer younger workers now contribute to the welfare and retirement benefits of an aging population. (See the cartoon on page 157.) Managers worry about worker shortages, and some have called for more immigration to fill the gap. Without additional immigration, Germany's population will fall to about 75 million by 2050, with an extremely low percentage of those under 15 and nearly 40 percent of the population over age 60. Germany is already the second oldest country in the world (after Japan).

To encourage more children, former Family Minister Ursula von der Leyen (herself a physician and mother of seven) instituted policies making it easier for both mothers and fathers to take time off for the birth of a child (roughly, six weeks before and six weeks after birth at full pay, split between the two parents). Either parent can take a further year's parental leave at two-thirds pay, and families get around $200 a month per child to help pay for extra expenses. The ministry also increased federal daycare funding, though daycare access remains difficult for millions of German families. Despite these policy shifts, no major increases in childbirths have occurred so far.

And yet demography is *not* destiny. Rather, it's clear that Germany could—if it chose to—increase its population by allowing in more migrants. It is likely that demographic issues played some role in the 2015 decision to take refugees into Germany. Even if Germany gains 200,000 new residents per year, its population will continue to shrink. And yet to take in more people, Germany will have to do far more integration than with the *Gastarbeiter* of the 1960s and 1970s. If seen only as workers and not as human beings, new arrivals will struggle to feel welcome in Germany's rigid society.

German Politics in Comparative Perspective

Germany offers important insights for comparative politics. First, it shows that an authoritarian past can be put to rest. Germany's impressive democratic experience during the first seventy years of the Federal Republic has clearly exorcised the ghosts of the Third Reich. Yet some critical questions remain. To what extent do the educational system, civil service, and the media bear some responsibility for the recent rise of right-wing violence? Have educational reforms since the 1960s provided a spirit of critical discourse in the broad mainstream of society that can withstand the rise of far-right rhetoric? Can judges effectively punish those who abuse ethnic minorities' civil rights? Will the news media continue to express a wide range of opinion and contribute to a healthy civic discourse? Or will strident, tabloid-style journalism stifle the reasoned debate that any democracy must have to survive and flourish?

Second, Germany's historical development illustrates how being late to achieve political unity and late to industrialize can have negative consequences. These two factors, combined with an unfavorable institutional mix, eventually helped produce a catastrophic first half of the twentieth century for Germany and much of the world. Yet the country's subsequent transition to a successful economy with a solid democracy can provide positive lessons for other countries.

Third, Germany offers a distinctive model for combining state and market. Germany's social market economy blurs the distinction between the public and private sectors. The German state pursues development plans based on its cooperative interaction with a dense network of key social and economic participants, particularly in such areas as climate change or energy policy. This approach is neither as free market as in the United Kingdom nor as statist as in France or Japan. To succeed, it requires both a state with a light touch and an organized and self-confident society.

Fourth, while immigration politics are emotional and deeply rooted, Germany reminds us that countries can make fundamental changes here as well. For decades, German policy essentially said, in the words of a popular CDU slogan, "Germany is not an immigration country." But the Schröder government modified Germany's immigration policies to provide a path for long-time foreign workers to gain citizenship. Again, questions persist. Can remaining ethnic tensions be resolved in a way that enhances democracy?

Finally, Germany shows us that middle-ranked powers can wield lots of clout, especially if they can emerge as regional leaders with attractive policies. For example, Germany has played an important role in debates over climate change, where its approach has broad support in the EU. Germany has led Western policy towards Ukraine in recent years. Nevertheless, Germany could not convince British leadership to avoid a legally unnecessary referendum on EU membership, with the ultimate result that Germany lost an important EU partner.

Germany is facing intense pressures from within its borders and from a complex mix of external influences. Its role as both a major western and an eastern European power puts it in a unique position. What an ironic but inspiring twist if Germany, the country whose virulent nationalism caused the most widespread destruction and destabilization in the twentieth century, took the lead at the head of the supranational EU in promoting democracy, creativity, and stability in the twenty-first century.

Where Do You Stand?

Do you consider low birthrates a "problem" to be fixed? If so, how? Or should Germans accept that their population will decline?

Chapter Summary

Germany's past will never fully go away, but measuring today's Germany exclusively by its past is a big mistake. Germany's turbulent history presented postwar policy-makers with two daunting challenges: the too-strong state and the too-weak one. On the one hand, policy-makers had to avoid recreating a state that could destroy the freedom or indeed the very lives of citizens or critics. On the other hand, policy-makers needed to

avoid re-creating a state so fragmented and weak it could not tackle Germany's problems. There is no doubt that policy-makers handsomely succeeded in both these tasks. Germany is peaceful, democratic, and rich.

In the meantime, plenty of new challenges have arisen. From the ruins of World War II, Germany has built one of the world's strongest economies. With only 80 million people, Germany sometimes exports more goods than the 326 million Americans or nearly 1.4 billion Chinese. Yet absorbing all these exports has led to a backlash in the United States, where Donald Trump has threatened to change the global trading system. Though trade conflicts have the potential to make all countries worse off, "surplus countries" like Germany are more vulnerable than "deficit countries."[24]

All this means globalization can be a rollercoaster for a medium-sized country like Germany. Germany responds with a social market economy that differs from free market economies like the United Kingdom and statist economies like France. Government regulation establishes general framework regulations rather than detailed standards. A key role of the state is to force firms to compete. The government sets broad licensing and performance standards for most professions and industries. Once core state requirements are announced, the government trusts that private actors will respect those broad parameters (and checks to be sure they do).

Germany's indirect approach to regulation is bolstered by the active engagement of unions and employers, in cooperation with state and municipal policy-makers. Semipublic institutions provide a forum in which these social partners help shape the German economy. At the same time, Germany is challenged to provide regional and global leadership on a wide range of issues, from the rescue of financially stressed European governments to border management and refugee inflows to global warming.

Germany's political system still struggles to generate effective policy. Its version of federalism has led to ferocious battles between the center and the states, while the EU has complicated policy-making at both national and subnational levels. Meanwhile, the country's vast investment in the EU suddenly looks to be on much shakier ground than just a few years ago. Germany's fragmenting party system has now generated at least seven parties represented at the state or federal level. When more than one coalition may be mathematically and politically possible, parties will be more inclined to horse trade, a fact that is sure to turn off voters and cause their further alienation from parties. Moreover, German grand coalitions—such as the one that emerged in 2005, and again in 2013—are notorious for boosting in the next round the electoral fortunes of the smaller parties who are left out.

Meanwhile, problems are not getting any simpler to solve. Like all European states, the German state and society must address immigration—in all its positive and negative complexity. It must do so, however, with relatively little experience in treating foreigners as potential citizens. The economic crisis, environmental and energy issues, and increasingly fierce tussles over the role of the EU all crowd the agenda in ways that parties seem increasingly unable to manage. The major advantage Germans have may lie in the remarkable capacity of German society to contribute to joint problem solving. This legacy of the earlier historical periods will be a critical asset as Germany faces the challenges ahead.

Key Terms

5 percent clause
austerity policies
Basic Law
Blitzkrieg
chancellor
citizen action groups
civil servants
codetermination
constructive vote of no
    confidence

democratic corporatism
Energiewende
Eurozone
framework regulations
Gastarbeiter
grand coalition
guild system
health insurance fund
heavy industries
Kulturkampf

liberal
mixed member system
Nazi
Ostpolitik
party democracy
procedural democracy
social market economy
Weimar Republic
works council

Suggested Readings

Herrigel, Gary. *Manufacturing Possibilities: Creative Action and Industrial Recomposition in the U.S., Germany, and Japan.* Oxford, UK: Oxford University Press, 2010.

Jacoby, Wade. *Imitation and Politics: Redesigning Modern Germany.* Ithaca, NY: Cornell University Press, 2001.

MacGregor, Neil. *Memories of a Nation.* New York: Knopf, 2015.

Thelen, Kathleen. *Varieties of Liberalism and the New Politics of Social Solidarity.* New York: Cambridge University Press, 2014.

Snyder, Timothy. *Bloodlands: Europe Between Hitler and Stalin.* New York: Basic Books, 2012.

Streeck, Wolfgang. *Re-Forming Capitalism: Institutional Change in the German Political Economy.* Oxford: Oxford University Press, 2009.

Suggested Websites

American Institute for Contemporary German Studies
www.aicgs.org/

Der Spiegel (in English)
http://www.spiegel.de/international/

Deutsche Welle (in English)
http://www.dw.de/

German Embassy, German Information Center
http://www.germany.info/gic/

German Institute for International and Security Affairs
(SWP)
http://www.swp-berlin.org/en/

German Politics
http://www.tandf.co.uk/journals/fgrp

German Politics and Society
http://journals.berghahnbooks.com/gps/

German Studies Web
**http://wess.lib.byu.edu/index.php/German
_Studies_Web**

Max Planck Institute for the Study of Societies, Cologne
http://www.mpi-fg-koeln.mpg.de/index_en.asp

WZB, Social Science Research Center, Berlin
https://www.wzb.eu/en

5 European Union

George Ross

Official name: European Union

Location: Comprised of 28 countries in Western and Eastern Europe

Capital City: Brussels, Belgium

Population (2016): 510 million

Size: 4,234,782 sq km; less than one-half the size of the United States

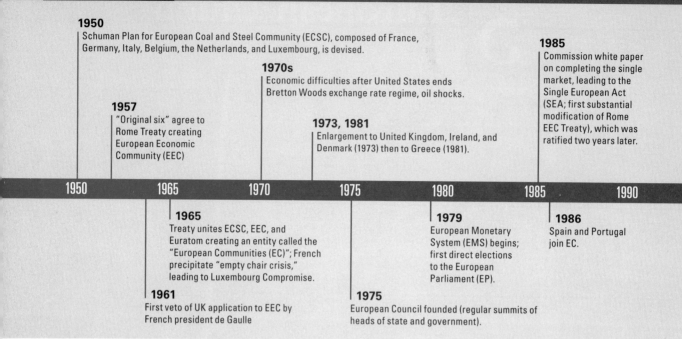

1950
Schuman Plan for European Coal and Steel Community (ECSC), composed of France, Germany, Italy, Belgium, the Netherlands, and Luxembourg, is devised.

1970s
Economic difficulties after United States ends Bretton Woods exchange rate regime, oil shocks.

1985
Commission white paper on completing the single market, leading to the Single European Act (SEA; first substantial modification of Rome EEC Treaty), which was ratified two years later.

1957
"Original six" agree to Rome Treaty creating European Economic Community (EEC)

1973, 1981
Enlargement to United Kingdom, Ireland, and Denmark (1973) then to Greece (1981).

1950   1965   1970   1975   1980   1985   1990

1965
Treaty unites ECSC, EEC, and Euratom creating an entity called the "European Communities (EC)"; French precipitate "empty chair crisis," leading to Luxembourg Compromise.

1979
European Monetary System (EMS) begins; first direct elections to the European Parliament (EP).

1986
Spain and Portugal join EC.

1961
First veto of UK application to EEC by French president de Gaulle

1975
European Council founded (regular summits of heads of state and government).

THE MAKING OF THE EUROPEAN UNION

▼ Focus Questions

- Imagine that it is 1950. You are advising leaders of the "original six" European governments about European integration. Mindful of the problems identified at the beginning of this chapter, what would you recommend they do—and avoid doing—to forestall those problems?

- How did the Cold War shape European integration?

Politics in Action

On May 9, 1950, French foreign minister Robert Schuman proposed that France and Germany, plus any other democratic nation in Western Europe that wanted to join, should establish a transnational "community" to govern the coal and steel industries. For most of the twentieth century, France and Germany had been either at war or preparing for war, at huge cost. Schuman came from Lorraine, an historic battleground area bordering Germany. Konrad Adenauer, who supported Schuman's proposal, was the first chancellor of the new German Federal Republic and had been the mayor of Cologne, just on the other side of the Rhine, before Adolf Hitler put him in Buchenwald prison. The leaders of other European Coal and Steel Community (ECSC) countries, all survivors of horrific war, were determined to change Europe. Schuman's announcement spoke to deeper issues:

> World peace cannot be safeguarded without creative efforts.... The contribution that an organized and vital Europe can bring to civilization is indispensable to the maintenance of peaceful relations.... Europe will not be made all at once, nor... in a single holistic construction: it will be built by concrete achievements that will create solidarity in facts. To assemble European nations first demands that opposition between France and Germany be eliminated.... (first paragraph of the Schuman declaration, of May 9, 1950)

1997
Treaty of Amsterdam—creates European Employment Strategy, movement toward central and eastern European enlargement.

2000
Treaty of Nice—flawed proposal for institutional reform to facilitate eastern enlargement; Lisbon Strategy to confront globalization and make EU the world's leading "knowledge economy" by 2010.

2008
Global financial crisis begins in United States; Great Recession starts.

2009–2017
Eurozone EMU crisis begins; EMU members decide to grant harsh, austerity-producing loans to indebted member-states and reform EMU.

| 1995 | 2000 | 2005 | 2010 | 2014 | 2017 |

1991
Maastricht Treaty on European Union negotiated (ratified 1993), toward Economic and Monetary Union, Common Foreign and Security Policy, Justice and Home Affairs, Codecision by Council and EP; the EC renamed the European Union (EU).

2002–2005
European Convention proposes European Constitutional Treaty (ECT); French and Dutch referendums refuse to ratify it.

2007–2008
Climate change and energy security package, Lisbon Treaty adopted, containing most ECT institutional reforms; is ratified after second Irish referendum.

2014
Massive flows of refugees from Syrian civil war and the refugee crisis in North Africa.

2016
UK referendum votes to leave EU (Brexit).

2017
Sixtieth anniversary of Treaty of Rome

Nearly seven decades later, the European Union (EU), direct descendent of the ECSC, had become something that its creators could never have imagined. Built in peace around democracy and with respect for the rule of law, the EU had become a partial union of most of the states in Europe, each very much alive, with its own institutions, history, and culture.

Geographic Setting

The EU began in 1950 with six members. Today's twenty-eight members (twenty-seven after the UK Brexit takes place in 2019) now cover almost all of Europe, from the Atlantic to Eurasia, and reach from the shores of the Mediterranean to the Arctic Circle. Within this vast area, only Switzerland, Norway, a few small Balkan countries—and, when Brexit negotiations are concluded, the United Kingdom—do not belong to the union. With the United Kingdom, the EU's present population is 510 million; without it, it is 445 million. It is the world's wealthiest and economically largest open market. Its capital is Brussels, Belgium.

Critical Junctures

From the beginning, changes in international conditions were central to the EU's development. World War II destroyed the appeal of antidemocratic regimes, reinforced democratic ideals, and led to sweeping social reforms, but it also left Europe economically devastated. The Soviet Union and the United States, wartime allies, quickly became Cold War enemies—the Soviet Union set up communist-dominated "Peoples' Republics" to the east, while the United States helped jump-start reconstruction in the west with the Marshall Plan. Overwhelming American military power made major conflict between western European countries inconceivable, particularly after the United States formed the North Atlantic Treaty Organization (NATO) at the end of the 1940s.

Economic integration and modernization became the backbone of European integration, however, based on the calculation that, if national markets were tied together, countries might have a stake in peacefully resolving differences. This concept, plus the U.S. desire to end the occupation of western Germany and establish a new German Republic, lay behind the founding of the ECSC, a centrally regulated market for the coal and steel industries between Germany, France, Italy, Belgium, the Netherlands, and Luxembourg. These "original six" nations later signed the 1957 Rome Treaty to create the European Economic Community (EEC, which would become the European Communities—EC—in 1965), a customs union without trade barriers for industrial products that continued the ECSC's institutions in modified form. There was a technocratic executive commission, intergovernmental final decision making, a Court of Justice (which eventually became the European Union Court of Justice, or EUCJ) to adjudicate treaty obligations, and a weak European Parliament (EP). The early years saw jockeying between member-states about the workings of these institutions, but fortunately, the EC was born just as postwar prosperity blossomed—and it contributed to that condition by promoting new trading opportunities amplifying national economic growth and a new Common Agricultural Policy (CAP) stimulating agricultural modernization.

International economic turmoil, oil shocks, rising unemployment, and *stagflation* (a combination of high inflation and low growth) in the 1970s ended this happy situation. Exchange-rate fluctuations following U.S. renunciation in 1973 of its commitment to back the dollar with gold made things worse, as did the divergent ways in which EC members reacted. After a brief flurry of ambitious proposals for new integration (most unimplemented), policy discord among members hindered EC decision making into the 1980s. The EC rebounded energetically after ambitious programs were begun in 1985 to "complete the single market" to remove nontariff protection and to create a European space without borders, where goods, services, capital, and, eventually, people could move without hindrance. The **Single European Act (SEA)**, ratified in 1987, greatly expanded the EC's policy reach, gave new power to the EP, and institutionalized qualified majority decision making in the Council of Ministers, thereby making it easier to pass European-level legislation. The United Kingdom, Denmark, and Ireland joined in 1973. The entry of Greece in 1981 and Portugal and Spain in 1986 added three poorer and formerly authoritarian Mediterranean countries to the EC, which helped these nations modernize and democratize. The period culminated in the Maastricht Treaty on European Union (ratified in 1993), when the EC became the EU, agreed on an **Economic and Monetary Union (EMU)**, and pledged to build a **Common Foreign and Security Policy (CFSP)**, promote new cooperation in **Justice and Home Affairs (JHA)** to facilitate the border-free internal movement of people, and again strengthened the EP.

International conditions again challenged the EU in the 1990s. Fueled by the financial sector and new technologies, globalization engulfed Europe. The United States was more dynamic in the new knowledge economy, while European manufacturing started moving in search of cheaper labor. The end of the Cold War, although it removed the threat of communism from the world, brought troubles as well. The EU, obliged to rethink its security positions, began with a clumsy and ineffective response to warfare in the former Yugoslavia and puzzled over how to deal with the formerly communist countries of Central and Eastern Europe (CEECs). It first sent them aid and negotiated freer trade, but it waited until the later 1990s to begin incorporating them.

Single European Act (SEA)

The first major revision of the Rome Treaty, which facilitated the single-market program, expanded EU prerogatives, and gave new power to the EP.

Economic and Monetary Union (EMU)

The 1991 Maastricht Treaty federalization of EU monetary policy, creating the European Central Bank (ECB), the Eurozone, and the euro.

Common Foreign and Security Policy (CFSP)

The Maastricht Treaty's commitment to deeper EU cooperation in international affairs and defense.

Justice and Home Affairs (JHA)

Changes in the Maastricht Treaty to allow free movement of EU citizens throughout the union's member-states.

To cope with newcomers that would nearly double its membership—Sweden, Finland, and Austria in 1995 and eight CEECs plus Cyprus and Malta in 2005–2007—the EU had to rebuild its institutions. Its first effort, the 2001 Nice Treaty, was unsatisfactory, leading to a European Convention that produced an ambitious European Constitutional Treaty (ECT) in 2004. When it was rejected by French and Dutch referendums in 2005, leaders composed an amended proposal that became the **2009 Lisbon Treaty**.

Lisbon's institutional changes were eclipsed by the 2008 global financial collapse, however. Beginning in 2009, several Eurozone countries, starting with Greece, came close to national bankruptcy, exposing deep flaws in the EMU. EMU and the EU, along with the International Monetary Fund (IMF), responded by imposing harsh austerity as a condition for bailouts, abruptly stopping these countries' economic growth, raising unemployment, lowering living standards, and damaging the EU's legitimacy. Next, the aftermath of the "Arab Spring" uprisings in parts of the Middle East beginning in late 2010 stoked instability in many of the countries that the EU had targeted for outreach in its "neighborhood" foreign policy. Some, like Syria, degenerated into civil war, while others, like Libya, disintegrated altogether. There followed a vast flow of refugees that caught the EU unprepared and divided, while increased terrorism deepened European resistance to outsiders and fed xenophobic, Euroskeptic political movements.

Next, the United Kingdom's approval in 2016 of a "Brexit" referendum on leaving the EU led to long, complicated negotiations about divorce between the British and the EU that were (and continue to be) damaging. It did not help that these events overlapped with Russian president Vladimir Putin's annexation of the Crimea in response to the possibility that Ukraine would sign an association agreement with the EU. The election of the mercantilist and nationalist Donald Trump to the U.S. presidency later the same year was another sign that the international situation around the EU had become more volatile. This rapid-fire succession of serious challenges produced the most daunting crisis that the EU has ever faced.

Four Themes and the European Union

The EU is a regional organization that European countries set up to confront problems that they could not resolve separately. It has created a European economic space of great mobility, prosperity, vitality, and international competitiveness. Europe's states have embraced peace, economic success, and political cooperation, all while maintaining their unique identities. Governing the European economy, the EU's major function, has resulted in a complex division of labor between EU-level market openings, based on the free circulation of goods, services, capital, and people, while member-states retain sovereignty over most taxation, budgeting, and social programs. Changes at the EU level require intense bargaining among EU member-states, but over time, the EU's powers spilled over beyond economic governance into more sensitive political areas.

Once decisions are made, the European Commission, which proposes legislation, then enforces compliance. The **European Court of Justice (EUCJ)** has created coherent European-level law, and the directly elected EP codecides with governments on commission-proposed legislation. The European Council, in regular summits of member-state leaders, provides the EU's general strategy. This EU system bears little resemblance to anything at a national level. By its very nature, the EU is not a state; rather, it is an entity that can do only what its member-states agree to do together when driven to cooperate. So it is unlikely to become a state in any foreseeable future.

Lisbon Treaty 2009

After a decade redesigning EU institutions to fit expansion to Central and Eastern Europe, the treaty created positions of the president of the European Council and the High Representative for Foreign and Security Policy, and increased the powers of the European Council and European Parliament (EP).

European Union Court of Justice (EUCJ)

Originally called the Court of Justice, the EU supreme court that decides the legality of EU legislation and its implementation.

From the immediate postwar period to the present, European integration has helped consolidate European democracy and observe the rule of law. Finally, as it reached beyond its borders in trade promotion, humanitarian aid and peacekeeping, environmental policy, and foreign policy, the EU has acted as a normative Europe, seeking to spread its democratic DNA abroad.

The EU's collective identity is a work in progress because it must combine national loyalties with European ones. Since the 1993 Maastricht Treaty institutionalized the coexistence between national and European citizenships, there has been progress to this end, symbolized by the EU flag, anthem, passport, and programs like Erasmus, which has subsidized millions of European college students to study outside their own countries. In the economic realm, businesses and workers have become more "European." Becoming French, British, German, Italian, Hungarian, and so on took centuries, however, and it is overly optimistic to expect Europeans to embrace dual identities—one national and familiar and one new, European, and unclear—in a few decades. As Jacques Delors, president of the European Commission from 1985–1995, observed, "People do not fall in love with a single market." The EU is difficult to understand, particularly because of its backbone in complicated matters of economic governance. It has also often been a convenient scapegoat for national politicians to attack policies that their citizens might not like. Its moments of popular success have occurred when its policies have provided tangible benefits to citizens.

Comparisons

In comparing the EU with nation-states, we must identify what it does and does not share with them. The EU is committed to democracy, the rule of law, and liberal principles of citizenship, as are its national members. The legal division of labor between the EU and its members is built on international treaties, and the EU, carefully overseen by the EUCJ, can do only what these treaties permit. The EU system has a great deal of power in market-building and economic governance, and member-states retain powers over taxation, economic redistribution, and interior matters of civil law, national citizenship, and social policy. Sovereignty is shared in clearly defined ways— the Maastricht Treaty mandated the obligation for the EU to respect "subsidiarity" (i.e., locating policy authority at the lowest effective level of governance).

The EU's general strategy is mainly decided by the European Council and the Council of Ministers, both representing democratically elected national governments and supported by the directly elected EP. Proposing EU legislation, however, is the exclusive duty of a supranational European Commission, which also is charged with overseeing its implementation. The commission is a uniquely empowered executive, not a government, however, and the EU does not have traditional government-opposition relationships. The EU can be compared with other regional organizations, such as Mercosur in Latin America and the Association of Southeast Asian Nations (ASEAN) in Asia, both also built around trade and economic governance, but is vastly more ambitious economically and politically.

Where Do You Stand?

Being part of a fervent national community is a fundamental part of a person's identity. Is it dangerous to tamper with this, as the EU has done?

Should the EU become a state? What kind of a state?

POLITICAL ECONOMY AND DEVELOPMENT

Post–World War II international politics, national problems, and political creativity launched European integration, with economic governance at its heart. The challenges of dealing with these matters were powerful enough to create the EEC Common Market in industrial and agricultural goods. Delegating sovereignty in economic governance raised large issues, however. What would be delegated? How? What would it change for EEC members? What kinds of new transnational democratic politics, policies, and institutions were needed?

Europe's post-1945 landscape was new. The United States and the United Kingdom, concerned with rebuilding international commerce, helped build the Bretton Woods system, which supported the dollar with gold, underwrote European reconstruction with the World Bank, stabilized trade through the International Monetary Fund (IMF), and promoted trade via the General Agreement on Tariffs and Trade (GATT). This was a great leap forward for multinational economic coordination. But even more was done in this critical period. Because the United States also worried about European political stability, in large part because of growing Cold War polarization– there were strong Communist Parties in both Italy and France—it responded with the Marshall Plan (1947), providing financial aid to help European governments direct economic reconstruction, followed by American and Western European rearmament through NATO. The U.S. occupation of Germany promoted rehabilitating, rather than punishing, Germany, leading in 1949 to the new German Federal Republic, which in 1955 joined NATO.

Postwar European leaders calculated that European integration might help end a centuries-long series of continental bloodbaths, but they disagreed over what that would mean. Some wanted to create a federal United States of Europe, a quasi-state at the European level. In contrast, so-called intergovernmentalists wanted forms of international cooperation that preserved national sovereignty. Both sides also puzzled over what precise policy areas should be integrated. Early debates led to the Council of Europe, an important human rights organization, but not a real instrument of integration. The French initially wanted to break post-Nazi Germany into pieces and dramatically limit its power, despite American insistence on German rehabilitation. Jean Monnet, head of French economic planning at the time and a skilled international political operator, proposed the ECSC, better known as the "Schuman plan," after Robert Schuman, the French foreign minister steered it through a hesitant French government. France, Germany, Luxembourg, the Netherlands, Belgium, and Italy (the British refused to participate)—signed the ECSC treaty in 1951, and the ECSC began in July 1952.

Monnet's insight was that integration would succeed if European institutions proposed practical solutions, particularly to economic problems, but he knew that it had to be built around existing national systems and avoid stirring up nationalist feelings. He also hoped that cooperation beginning in the coal and steel industries might spill over into new areas and eventually impel political integration. France and Germany accepted ECSC because they feared that otherwise the United States would impose a less attractive plan. French public opinion accepted ECSC because it promised to neutralize German economic and political threats. German

Focus Questions ▽

- Discuss the relative weights of international and European-domestic factors in policy orientations of the EU.

- Assess the changing balance between "supranational" and member-state institutions in EU history.

industrial interests needed European markets for growth and the new German government needed new international legitimacy after the Nazi era, so Germany was also willing to go along. Others in the "original six" had their own reasons for signing up, but the United Kingdom refused out of its opposition to supranational arrangements.

Although ambitious proposals for a European Defense Community (EDC) and a European Political Community were rejected, the idea of "functional" European integration had staying power. In Messina, Italy, in 1955, the ECSC six committed to creating a European atomic energy agency (another Monnet idea) and a European Common Market—a free trade area with a common external tariff or customs union among the six member-states. The 1957 Treaties of Rome established Euratom (which thereafter existed very quietly) and the very consequential EEC. Member-states again had different but complementary reasons for signing. The French wanted Euratom but were less enthusiastic about a Common Market, accepting it in exchange for a common agricultural policy that would benefit France's large agricultural sector and an EEC deal for their former colonies. The Germans knew that a trade-liberalizing EEC would help their economy grow and give them new legitimacy. The United Kingdom again stayed out, mistakenly betting that the EEC would fail while its own plans for a parallel European Free Trade Area (EFTA), involving far less cross-national regulation, would succeed.

The EEC's Common Market sought to remove internal trade barriers for industrial goods; aimed to end "obstacles to freedom of movement for persons, services, and capital," in the words of the EEC's founding Rome Treaty; and promised greater trade, growth, and efficiency. Its other objectives included common antitrust, agricultural, and transport policies. Member-states agreed to harmonize their legal systems on Common Market matters. There were also provisions for a European Social Fund, a European Investment Bank to help less prosperous regions, and association arrangements for ex-colonies. Institutionally, there was an appointed European Commission (based on the model of the ECSC High Authority) with exclusive power to propose laws, implement EEC policies, and safeguard the treaty. A council of national ministers, on which all member-states were represented and which was coordinated by a presidency rotating from country to country every six months, acted as the "legislature" that voted on commission proposals. There was also an appointed and weak EP, empowered to bring suits against other EEC institutions for "failure to act" and authorized to pose questions to the commission. Finally, the EUCJ adjudicated in those areas where the Rome Treaty gave EEC precedence over national laws.

The Rome Treaty set up new European institutions to build a transnational market, while national governments retained powers over taxation, budgeting, industrial and social policies, and any areas not explicitly included. The **European Commission**, with an exclusive right to propose new law, was populated with officials pledged to seek "European" rather than national or partisan ends. New policies were to be approved intergovernmentally: the Rome Treaty gave member-states a veto for an initial period, after which decisions would be made by **qualified majority voting (QMV)**, a method of weighting the differential influences of members. After approval, the commission translated general proposals into detailed rules under member-state monitoring.

The underlying philosophy was that shaping transnational policies was best left to expert administrators working with a perspective beyond national and partisan concerns. Because European integration was controversial, technocratic methods might help European decisions fly under national political radars. This strategy has

European Commission

The EU executive, with a monopoly on proposing EU legislation and overseeing its implementation as "guardian of the treaties."

Qualified majority voting (QMV)

The method for the Council of Ministers to decide most EU legislation until the approval of the 2009 Lisbon Treaty. It weighted member-state voting power depending upon size and defined how many votes were needed to constitute a majority.

been generally successful for decades. However, it has provoked periodic opposition that has swelled to a roar in recent years on the grounds that it constitutes a "democratic deficit."

The commission's first job was carving space from member-states' economic governance powers to build a Common Market, and it faced immediate disagreement about what the new EEC should be. French president Charles de Gaulle twice vetoed British application for membership (in 1963 and 1967) on the grounds that the United Kingdom was not sufficiently "European"—meaning that Britain was too close to the United States and also preferred a free trade zone over the EC's customs area approach. A staunch antifederalist champion of national sovereignty, de Gaulle also paralyzed the Council of Ministers in the 1965 "empty chair" crisis, in which France refused to attend Council meetings to block what he saw as Commission power-grabbing on budgetary matters and prevent the scheduled shift from unanimity to QMV in the Council of Ministers. The resulting decision, called the "Luxembourg Compromise," allowed any EEC member to block European proposals for years by claiming that its vital national interests were at stake. And when the Commission proposed an economically liberal CAP, which threatened to prohibit French agricultural subsidies, the French insisted on a plan that subsidized farmers at the expense of consumers and taxpayers. Commission attempts to promote the Rome Treaty's common transport, regional, and industrial policies were unsuccessful.

Despite all this, however, the EC—a new title after a treaty combined the ECSC, Euratom, and the EEC in 1965 into the European Communities—succeeded in creating a Common Market. It was given a powerful boost by buoyant economic conditions plus successful European emulation of U.S. consumerism and mass production. During the 1960s, Western Europeans thrived on an impressive 5 percent average economic growth while internal EC trade grew even faster.

When the obstreperous de Gaulle resigned from the French presidency in 1969 in response to domestic conflicts, EC leaders were freer to propose plans for greater market openings, admitting new members, expanding EC budgetary powers, and promoting regional development (a by-product of enlarging the EU to include the United Kingdom in 1973), intergovernmental foreign policy coordination (European Political Cooperation), and the EMU. The EC, initially dependent on direct contributions by members, also acquired new revenues from agricultural levies, import duties, and national value-added taxes (VATs).

International storm clouds then appeared. In the early 1970s, beset by trade deficits, the United States ended its commitment to the Bretton Woods fixed dollar/gold standard and allowed the dollar to float, causing fluctuating exchange rates that upset the international monetary and trading system. Quickly thereafter, in 1973, an oil price rise engineered by the Organization of Petroleum Exporting Countries (OPEC) spiked inflation in energy-dependent Western Europe, and when OPEC repeated the same gesture in 1979 it had similar results. It then became treacherous to govern European economies. Profits and investments declined, European industry lost comparative advantage, and stagflation undermined public finances. Divergent national responses made things worse. Germany restructured to achieve price stability, France first tried stimulating demand but then shifted to cutbacks and austerity, and British Labour governments floundered in inflation before losing in 1979 to the Conservative Party, led by Margaret Thatcher, who then sponsored stiff neoliberal reforms. In 1981, France's new Socialist Party administration tried inflationary policies again and immediately faced a menacing explosion of rising prices and costs. More generally, EC members tried to protect national producers with nontariff barriers (NTBs).

At the same moment, the CAP, which had rapidly become an enclave of farmers' lobbies backed by member-states encouraging overproduction, ate up more and more of the EC's small budget.

There were nonetheless some solid accomplishments. The first enlargement, involving the United Kingdom, Denmark, and Ireland, came in 1973, bringing with it new regional development policies for economically lagging areas. The EUCJ made landmark rulings about the direct effect of EC law on citizens and on workplace gender equality. Although economic shocks shelved plans for the EMU, the EC set up a more modest European Monetary System (EMS) to control currency fluctuations. Most significant, however, was the inauguration in 1974 of regular summit meetings of EC heads of state and government in the intergovernmental **European Council**, which became the EC's ultimate decision-shaper.

By the early 1980s, European integration was in trouble. The United Kingdom complained incessantly about its budget payments, while Greece, after joining in 1981, demanded more development aid. Both nations blocked EC decision making in order to get concessions. The Commission came to be seen as a meddlesome Brussels bureaucracy. The EP, directly elected for the first time in 1979, drew up far-seeing plans that went nowhere. The EMS sputtered through repeated currency revaluations. Observers and journalists commented more generally about "Eurosclerosis." A turning point occurred when French-German cooperation at the 1984 Fontainebleau European Council settled the British budget dispute, promised aid to Greece, and nominated Jacques Delors to be president of the Commission. Delors, a former French finance minister, then immediately asked the EP in early 1985, "[Is] it presumptuous to . . . remove all the borders inside Europe between now and 1992?"

The Delors Commission quickly produced a *White Paper on Completing the Internal Market* that contained 300 new market-opening measures and sought to eliminate internal border posts, simplify cross-border formalities, develop common European product standards, harmonize VATs and excise taxes and national health and safety regulations, and remove NTBs to implement the "four freedoms" of movement of goods, services, capital, and, citizens. The white paper spawned an intergovernmental conference (IGC) that produced the SEA, ratified in 1987, the first major revision of the Rome Treaty. The SEA tied single-market proposals to qualified majority Council voting (excepting fiscal policy, external border controls, the movement of people, and workers' rights), authorized the EP to propose amendments, expanded EC regional policy prerogatives to promote "economic and social cohesion", and opened new areas in research and development, the environment, and social policy. It also officially institutionalized the European Council and European Political Cooperation (foreign policy coordination) and foreshadowed monetary integration.

The single-market program was responding to changing international conditions. Japan had become a feared manufacturing rival as the United States was forging ahead in electronics. Delors had canvassed other paths, including greater foreign policy and defense cooperation, but members would only agree on changes within the EC's existing economic governance base. Germany wanted greater intra-European trade; France wanted closer European integration to enhance its diplomatic power and prod domestic reforms, Thatcher's British government favored economic liberalization in principle, and European big business had long lobbied for greater market opening. Although organized labor feared "social dumping" (companies relocating to reduce production costs, especially wages), it liked the Commission's promise of a new "social dialogue."

European Council

The EU institution that devises general strategies; made up of member-state heads of state that meets at least twice annually.

The resulting enthusiasm for the single market created political resources that the Commission could reinvest. Following the SEA, it thus proposed combining EC budget changes, limiting CAP costs, and doubling regional development funding for poorer new EC members (Spain and Portugal had joined in 1986). It then launched a quest for social Europe with a social charter listing possible new EC workplace changes, plus European collective bargaining. Most important, it helped resurrect the debate on economic and monetary union.

A blue-ribbon committee led by Delors set out plans to open up capital movements, federalize monetary policy, and establish the European Central Bank. It also proposed creating a single currency that it claimed would make intra-European factor costs more transparent, reduce transaction costs, prod financial sector restructuring, make wages reflect national productivity, bring national budgetary and fiscal policies closer to economic fundamentals, give governments new reasons for domestic reforms, and constitute a reserve alternative to the U.S. dollar.

The drive to EMU culminated in the **Maastricht Treaty** on European Union, ratified in 1993; another name change (the EC to the EU); innovations in economic governance; and new EU prerogatives. Maastricht was conditioned by the fall of the Berlin Wall. The German government, tepid about monetary integration, knew that German reunification frightened others, so it agreed to negotiate the EMU to reassure them. In exchange, it insisted on terms that prioritized strict price stability and commitments to promote greater convergence among their economies. The French had hoped to constrain German monetary power with a European "economic government," but they had to accept a deal built around tough convergence criteria—that is, mandatory ceilings of inflation and budget deficits of 3 percent annually and on longer-term debt of 60 percent of gross domestic product (GDP). EMU would have a politically independent European Central Bank and a single currency, prohibit bailouts of members in trouble, and had to be in place by 1999.

Maastricht was complicated by Belgian and German insistence on "political union" to promote greater EU political legitimacy. The final treaty involved a compromise mandating "subsidiarity" in EU decision making (i.e., matters should be decided at the lowest jurisdiction appropriate to policy goals), a common EU foreign and security policy (CFSP), and a new JHA area to broaden the existing **Schengen area** to all EU members, coordinate police information, facilitate action against "Europeanized" crime, and harmonize parts of civil law. The treaty also established formal EU citizenship and common asylum policies. The most significant institutional result was the creation of codecision that gave the EP equal weight with the Council of Ministers in deciding EU legislation and the right to vote on the membership of the Commission. Finally, negotiators deemed the CFSP and JHA too important for the traditional **Community Method** of Commission proposal, Council and Parliament decisions, and EUCJ review; they insisted that these areas be placed in legally separate intergovernmental "pillars" with unanimity decision rules.

It was hoped that the Maastricht Treaty would promote EU momentum, but what followed was disappointing. Citizens began to worry that the EU was changing too much, too fast. Denmark voted against ratification of the Maastricht Treaty, although a second referendum passed after major concessions, and a French referendum barely passed. Citizen wariness deepened thanks to the recession that occurred after 1992 due to EMS problems connected to German unification. Once this recession eased, EU member-states also had to face the EMU convergence requirement that compressed growth and employment.

Maastricht Treaty

A treaty ratified in 1993 giving the EU its present name, creating the EMU and CFSP, and granting the EP power to codecide EU legislation.

Schengen Area

Named after a town in Luxembourg where five EU members (France, Germany, and the Benelux states) agreed in 1985 to abolish border controls among their countries. The "Schengen acquis"—the accumulated rules and procedures of Schengen prior to Maastricht—was incorporated into the Maastricht Treaty and officially made part of the EU legal framework in the 1997 Amsterdam Treaty. Open internal EU borders have been adopted by all EU members except Romania, Bulgaria, Croatia, and Cyprus, while the United Kingdom and Ireland opted out. Schengen also includes Norway, Iceland, and Switzerland, which are not part of the EU.

Community Method

The EU method of making decisions in which the European Commission proposes, the Council of Ministers and EP decide, and the EUCJ reviews European law.

Then, in 1993, the Delors Commission tried once again to mobilize EU member-states with a new *White Paper on Growth, Competitiveness, and Employment,* which sounded the alarm about globalization and argued for large new changes in EU economic governance. This time, EU members refused the Commission's lead. The white paper's ideas, which circulated for years thereafter, included investments in better basic education, training, lifelong learning, and new programs to help wage-earners manage the difficult transitions spurred by globalization and technological change.

The white paper's failure also marked the end of Delors's quest for a "social Europe." While there had been success at harmonizing health and safety rules and training programs, hopes for European-level collective bargaining fell short. European employers initially refused to bargain, leading the Commission to insert a Social Protocol into the Maastricht Treaty that would turn European-level collective agreements directly into EU law. Although there were deals on European Works Councils, parental leave, and part-time work, progress stopped when employers again stopped negotiating.

Environmental Issues

Environmental issues exploded in the 1960s and 1970s, and because these problems did not respect borders, they were good candidates for EU action, particularly once EU interest had been enhanced by the successes of so-called green movements and parties. A 1972 summit invited the Commission to reflect on European environmental policies, leading to an "action plan" that included the principle of "polluter pays," "green-label" product codes, environmental impact assessments, water safety tests, and regular multiyear environmental action programs that continue to the present day.

The EU's conversion to environmentalism deepened in the SEA, after which it strongly engaged in international environmental initiatives, signing conventions on the Mediterranean and Antarctic and fighting on the front line of the UN Framework Convention on Climate Change (UNFCCC) at Rio in 1992. It was central to creating and implementing the Kyoto Protocol to limit the production of greenhouse gas and then devised a cap-and-trade scheme that was the world's most advanced (albeit not without problems). In 2007–2008, the EU committed to cut greenhouse gas, use more renewable energy, and increase energy efficiency by 20 percent apiece by 2020. The "20-20-20" goal was also meant to help launch a successor to the Kyoto Protocol, but the 2009 Copenhagen UN climate change negotiations ended with a weak deal between the United States and China, with the EU outside looking in.

There was no chance at Copenhagen that the U.S. Congress would accept a treaty modeled on the EU's objectives. Emerging market powers, like China, were willing to act, but they opposed binding commitments in the name of sovereignty. Others, including some African states, refused new constraints unless affluent countries financed them, amid suspicion that measures to limit climate change were meant to deprive economic newcomers of comparative advantages. The 2015 Paris results were better, but once again the United States and China cut the final deal. The 20-20-20 program worked reasonably well within the EU, however, with new efforts scheduled for after 2020. The EU has discussed a coordinated internal energy policy many times, but without success.

Changes in EU economic governance have often been spurred by international events. The EMU, for example, might never have happened had the Cold War not ended, leading to German reunification. After Maastricht, Germany began to worry

GLOBAL CONNECTION

The EU in the Global Economy

The EU is committed to market economics and promoting an open global trading system through the GATT and, more recently, the World Trade Organization (WTO). The EU is the world's largest trading bloc, with 500 million wealthy consumers and 25 percent of the world's GDP. It is also the world's largest recipient and source of foreign direct investment and its leading development aid donor. It has strong environmental and climate change policies, advocates welcoming emerging market newcomers into a peaceful, well-regulated international order, and has recently pursued second-generation trade agreements to liberalize services, public procurement, intellectual property law, and encourage mutual recognition of norms, standards, and regulations. The most successful deal to date has been the Comprehensive Economic and Trade Agreement (CETA) with Canada. However, similar negotiations on a Transatlantic Trade and Investment Partnership (TTIP) became a dead letter after the election of U.S. president Donald Trump. EU optimism about globalization is in decline because of new competition from low-wage countries, declining manufacturing jobs, and the Great Recession–Eurozone disasters.

MAKING CONNECTIONS What dimensions of globalization have most challenged the EU? Why have EU member-states recently become more susceptible to nativist and xenophobic trends?

that the EMU would include free-spending, overborrowing southern European countries, so it insisted that the 1997 Amsterdam Treaty include a Stability and Growth Pact to oblige EMU candidates to observe the criteria after they became Eurozone members.

The EMU began in 1999 with 11 members, with the introduction of euro notes and coins following in 2002. The United Kingdom and Denmark had opted out and Sweden later decided not to join EMU, but initial members included Italy, Spain, Portugal, and in particular Greece, known for its lax fiscal policies, deficits, and debts. EMU's new **European Central Bank (ECB)**, located in Frankfurt, Germany, was charged with maintaining price stability (inflation of 2 percent per year or less), EU monetary policy, managing exchange rates, and holding reserves. Its philosophy was that rule-breaking would most likely come from fiscally imprudent governments and selfish market actors, and that corrections must come from peer pressure and EMU rule enforcement. Many analysts worried, however, about whether EMU was an optimum currency area at all because it lacked strong enforcement powers, its "no-bailout" provision ruled out transnational assistance to confront shocks, and it had low labour mobility because of the large economic divergences among its members. Economic growth after 1998 launched the EMU, but after the turn of the century, over half of EMU countries, including Germany and France, had violated Stability Pact rules, leading to a reform to make the pact more flexible in 2005. These episodes were forgotten in the brief global euphoria that soon gave way to the Great Recession.

Parallel to all this, the Lisbon European Council pledged in 2000 to make the EU "the most competitive and dynamic knowledge based economy in the world" by new technologies, labor market and social policy reforms, education, greater focus on the environment, and sustainable growth. Since these areas were primarily national prerogatives, the so-called Lisbon strategy proposed innovative tactics to prod member-states to reform on their own terms, in particular by a decentralized open method of coordination (OMC). In 2004, as EU national politics shifted to the center-right, the strategy was redesigned to focus on government programs to spur more growth and jobs, and particularly to raise labor market participation levels. The results fell short.

European Central Bank (ECB)

The ECB is the institutional center of the EMU and the Eurozone, located in Frankfurt, Germany. Statutorily independent from politics and having a powerful president, it decides Eurozone monetary policy to produce price stability and economic convergence, enforces EMU rules, and governs EMU exchange rates.

Following the burst of an American housing bubble in 2008, the Great Recession began, bringing huge market losses, credit and liquidity freezes, stalled real economies, company failures, high unemployment, declining government revenues, and an explosion of public debt. Europeans initially hoped to escape the "American crisis," but dubious financial practices had long since crossed the Atlantic. The ECB supplied liquidity and cooperated with the U.S. Federal Reserve, and EU members coordinated national bailouts and stimulus packages, higher bank capital requirements, new accounting techniques, and greater EU supervision of the financial system.

EMU had initially focused on rules about inflation and economic convergence. However, richer northern EMU members quickly learned to export their goods to poorer ones and then use their private banks to recycle the profits through new loans, facilitated by EMU one-size-fits-all interest rates, to finance more imports from poorer countries, operations that strongly encouraged risky development strategies and inflated current account deficits among EMU's peripheral members. Debt problems worsened because of rising national spending on automatic stabilizers such as unemployment insurance. Growth stalled and government revenues declined.

Then, in autumn 2009, a newly elected Greek government announced that its predecessor had lied about its budget deficits that were in fact more than four times the 3 percent Eurozone limit. Bond markets were then shocked into raising interest rates on Greek bonds, and within months, Greece faced national insolvency, presenting huge threats to the German, French, and other banks that were heavily exposed to Greek debt.

It took months of dithering before Eurozone member-states, acting in the Eurogroup (the intergovernmental governing body of the Eurozone) and European Council, decided to try to save the euro. Germany was at the heart of the dithering, and threats to German banks from an eventual Greek bankruptcy were at the heart of this rescue effort. Bailing out the EMU members that were going under (beginning with Greece) began in May 2010. The Eurozone initially set up a temporary European Financial Stability Facility (EFSF), later transformed into the European Stability Mechanism (ESM), to provide conditional loans to threatened EMU members, with IMF help. The loans dictated harsh economic and social reforms and were overseen by a troika of EU, IMF, and ECB officials who de facto suspended the recipients' economic policy sovereignty.

The shock of the first Greek loan produced large public protests, and its interest rates deepened Greek debt, eventually necessitating two more loans and sparking constant bickering between Greece and its creditors. Ireland, whose government had imprudently decided to bail out Irish banks in response to an unsustainable housing bubble that they had created, was next in line to borrow on similar terms. Portugal, Cyprus, and Spanish banks eventually followed. Meanwhile, the ECB lowered interest rates, provided vast sums to keep European banks afloat, and played an important role in Eurozone crisis bargaining. It injected more credit in 2011 via its Long-Term Refinancing Operations (LTRO), helped to begin a new banking union, and intervened at a critical 2012 moment by pledging to do "whatever it takes" through Outright Monetary Transactions (OMT). The sums involved were colossal.

The Eurogroup and European Council also restructured the EMU's rules and practices, initially with a six-pack and two-pack of directives that enhanced the monitoring and enforcement of national budgetary choices and included a new European semester to review member-state budget plans prior to national approval. In 2012, EU members, except for the United Kingdom, agreed to a new European Fiscal Compact that obliged balanced budgets. Next came Banking Union, in which the ECB took on the key role of supervising large, systemically important banks (with national supervisory authorities monitoring the rest). A single-resolution mechanism was also created to deal with failing banks, along with a rulebook of banking practices. Banking Union was unfinished, however, because member-states resisted a common deposit guarantee system and Eurozone control over national purchases of bank debt.

The disastrous Eurozone crisis revealed the EMU's original flaws and the fact that the European financial sector had foolishly adopted perilous risk-taking, pioneered by the United States and United Kingdom. Everyone suffered to some extent, but those EMU members that were forced to borrow from the EU-EMU's conditional loan schemes were devastated. Crisis unemployment levels were extremely high across the EU—well over 20 percent in the hardest-hit countries, with youth employment often double this figure. Austerity involved large spending cutbacks, misery for those receiving public services, and steep declines to living standards.

Among the bailout countries, Ireland recovered first, followed by Spain and Portugal; however, Greece remained for years under "troika" supervision and teetered on the verge of leaving the Eurozone. It took until the end of 2016 before Eurozone GDP returned to its pre-2008 levels, indicating a massive loss of wealth. Crisis decision making was cumbersome and biased toward the preferences of economically stronger northern countries (Germany in particular). Responses involved short-term policy mistakes that regularly rekindled market panics. The events deepened citizen doubts about the EU's capacities as economic manager and its democratic legitimacy, while also feeding national electoral volatility. The EU's newer Mediterranean members, who had joined the union to build more prosperous and democratic societies and had been fervent supporters of European integration, lost some of their initial faith. Euroskepticism gained ground, national elites faced populist rebellions, and extremist political parties gained strength.

Yet another drama with huge implications for EU economic governance was sparked in June 2016, when the United Kingdom voted by 52–48 percent to leave the EU, a development that became known as Brexit. The key issue, beyond British conservatives' traditional complaints about loss of sovereignty, was immigration, which many Britons blamed on the EU's free movement of people among its member-states. Article 50 of the Lisbon Treaty set out processes for negotiating the terms of the "divorce" over two years, and the process began in April 2017. Leading EU members were unwilling to allow the United Kingdom any serious cherry-picking of concessions to stay in the single market, choosing which EU measures to retain and which to abandon (particularly the free moment of people within the EU). Britain thus faced a "hard Brexit" situation, which would leave the British outside the EU seeking new international trading arrangements at a moment when trade deals were losing their appeal and also facing years of complicated work to replace rules, norms, regulations, and habits acquired in 45 years of EU membership. For the EU, the uncertainties were different and serious. Relationships between the post-Brexit United Kingdom and EU economic governance needed to be redefined, with some outcomes likely to cause economic damage to both the United Kingdom and the EU.

WHERE DO YOU STAND?

What are possible ways to manage the political problems caused by the economic challenges of EU-style transnational cooperation? Why have some EU countries done better than others economically, even in crises as threatening as the recent global financial collapse?

EU GOVERNANCE AND POLICY-MAKING

▼ **Focus Questions**

- To what degree does the EU provide promising models for governance on a global scale?

- Why might citizens have trouble identifying with EU institutions?

Organizing a Nonstate: EU Institutions

In 1648, exhausted from the bloody Thirty Years War, Europeans founded the Westphalian state system. European states then rivaled and often fought one another for centuries. Decades ago, some of these states began the EU. The institutions that they built were not statelike; instead, they were designed to govern discrete policy areas where states could agree. These institutions persist in the EU's unique system of multilevel governance (MLG). The EU is the European center of a network of governing structures from Brussels to local councils that is based on intergovernmental treaties and depends on the cooperation of its member-states. For much of its life, the EU was a European Community (EC) working through an **institutional triangle** including the Commission, the Council of Ministers, and the EP. Over time, however, the model has become increasingly complex.

In the 1970s, the European Council, the EU's strategist-in-chief, as well as the EP, won new powers. The 1993 Maastricht Treaty established a CFSP and a JHA competency, areas so much at the core of national sovereignty that national EU leaders initially insisted that they be set as intergovernmental "pillars," separated from the EC. The triangle has incorporated some parts of these areas, but at the same time, institutional power has shifted further to the European Council.

Institutional triangle

A term signifying the interactions between the three most significant EU institutions: the Commission, the Council of Ministers, and the EP.

👤 PROFILE

AP Images/Cornelius Poppe/NTB Scanpix/Pool

José Manuel Barroso, Herman Van Rompuy, and Martin Schulz

The EU won the Nobel Peace Prize in 2012, perhaps because the Nobel Committee hoped to encourage EU leaders to solve the Eurozone crisis. No one initially knew which EU leader should go to Oslo to accept the award, however. Eventually, José Manuel Barroso, Commission president; Martin Schulz, president of the EP; and Herman Van Rompuy, European Council president, mounted the stage together.

Behind this event lay serious questions. What was the true nature of the EU, and where was its institutional heart? Everyone agreed about the EU's centrality in economic governance, and everyone knew that the EU's prerogatives had grown well beyond it, despite arguments about how much, where, and whether this was good. In Oslo, the three presidents stood for the three axes of EU government. The European Commission represented the regulatory governance ideals of Jean Monnet; the EP represented federalist hopes that the EU might eventually become a European state; and the European Council represented the ideal of a confederation of states. The EU was an unsteady mixture of all three.

MAKING CONNECTIONS Think about the reasons behind the complexity of the EU's institutions. What differences have this complexity made?

The European Commission: Executive and Bureaucracy?

The 1957 Rome EEC treaty gave the European Commission three prerogatives. It alone could propose legislation, in the form of regulations, directives, and recommendations (laws binding all members in the same terms, laws to be transposed into national legal codes, and nonbinding "soft" laws, respectively). It also supervised the implementation of EU policies, in particular by turning laws into rules and regulations. Finally, it was the "guardian" of the EU treaties, if necessary bringing member-states and private bodies before the EUCJ to oblige them to follow EU law.

In addition to these responsibilities, its main job has been to help overcome the difficulties that national governments have when cooperating by devising projects that express common European interests and leading toward new collective commitments. It has been most successful when key member-states—above all France and Germany—have agreed. But when member-states have wanted a weak Commission, as they have since 1995, they have appointed weak Commission presidents. Designing policy and getting it through the Council of Ministers and the EP lie at the heart of things, however. Yet the Commission does not always propose creating something from scratch; rather, it often translates the desires of others, particularly those of the European Council and the requirements of international agreements. It is also the object of intense lobbying.

The Commission can initiate proposals only when EU treaties allow it to. It has some strong competencies, as in EU competition (antitrust) policies, the CAP, rules for the **European single market**, and regional development plans to help poorer regions to develop, during which it acts like a federal government. It also plays a key role in European environmental policy and helps design European-level research and development programs. It draws up the first draft of EU budgets, which is then heavily rewritten by member-states. Internationally, it represents the EU in trade matters and, until 2009, when the Lisbon Treaty created the High Representative for Foreign and Security Policy, in some international organizations as well. It manages foreign aid programs and jointly supervises EU diplomatic delegations with the Council of Ministers. Day-to-day implementation of most EU measures is left to the administrations of member-states.

Commissioners are appointed by member-states for five-year terms that coincide with the term of the EP. Since the 2004–2007 enlargement, each member-state has one Commissioner, which will make a total of twenty-seven after Brexit takes effect. The Commission president, nominated by the European Council and approved by the EP, exerts influence from assigning Commissioners specific tasks, presiding over the Commission, and planning its agenda. Since 2014, the EP's leading parties have nominated so-called peak candidates for the job of Commission president, with the expectation that the European Council will choose the candidate from the most successful party in EP elections [for instance, Jean-Claude Juncker, candidate of the center-right European Peoples' Party (EPP) in 2014]. The Commission has several vice-presidents, each overseeing separate clusters of activities.

Commissioners deliberate and decide together in a college in which each one participates equally. They politically supervise one or several of the Commission's General Directorates (DGs), following the Commission's programmatic lines. Despite its reputation as a formidable "Brussels bureaucracy," the total Brussels-EU administration, of which the Commission is the largest part, is only around 40,000 people—the number of civil servants of a mid-sized European city. It top "A-grade" posts are carefully distributed among member-state nationals. Each Commission DG has a general director, the Commission's highest administrative post. Commission jobs are interesting and well paid, with numerous perks, and in addition, are exempt from national taxes.

European single market

The official title of the EU's barrier-free economic space created after 1985.

The Council of Ministers and the European Council

In the Council of Ministers and the European Council, member-states express national preferences and negotiate European cooperation. The Council of Ministers is composed of national ministers empowered to deal with European issues. Its most important job is passing European law by codeciding on Commission proposals with the EP. It legally concludes EU international agreements, approves the EU budget (with the EP), and decides some issues in the areas of CFSP and JHA. The Council is assisted by a Committee of Permanent Representatives (COREPER), composed of member-state ambassadors to the EU, which does much of the preliminary work, relying on preliminary sorting by 150–200 working committees of national civil servants. It also coordinates several high-level functional committees, including the Political and Security Committee that prepares CFSP, a special Agriculture Committee, a trade committee, a committee on JHA matters, and an Economic and Financial Committee.

For two decades after the de Gaulle–initiated "empty chair" crisis, the Council decided unanimously on any measure that any member deemed in its vital national interest. The SEA (1987) opened QMV on almost all single-market matters, however, and the Maastricht, Amsterdam, and Nice treaties extended QMV, although not to everything. The 2009 Lisbon Treaty replaced QMV with a "double majority" formula requiring that a majority (55 percent) of member-states that have at least a majority (65 percent) of the EU population was needed for approval.

The Council of Ministers has traditionally worked behind closed doors and, leaks excepted, the public has rarely known what positions different countries have taken. Worries about legitimacy opened the proceedings to a few television broadcasts and public announcements of certain votes, which is less significant than it seems because the Council usually decides by consensus. Inside knowledge is also limited because much of the Council's work is done in back-corridor discussions, with only final decision making open to the public. The Council is organized by a presidency that rotates among member-states every six months, coordinates Council-Parliament interactions including codecision "conciliation committees," and submits the Council's annual program to the EP. Prior to the Lisbon Treaty, the president also prepared and presided over European Council meetings and spoke for the EU on foreign policy matters (except trade). Because the rotating presidency was not always effective, these jobs are now done by the president of the European Council and the High Representative for Foreign Affairs and Security Policy (who also presides over the Foreign Affairs Council).

Prior to enlargement to the CEECS, the European Council consisted of reunions of heads of state and government plus one other minister (usually the foreign minister), the Council secretary-general, and the Commission president and secretary-general, organized at least twice during each six-month presidency. Summits began with a brief speech by the president of the EP, who then departed, leaving only the leaders and the Commission president to discuss issues. The leaders then held a working lunch to focus on the most difficult problems, while foreign ministers dispatched easier ones. The final hours produced "Presidency Conclusions" that outlined the European Council's thoughts, decisions, and goals.

The Lisbon Treaty created an appointed European Council president, who now serves for a two-and-one-half-year term that can be renewed once. There have been two thus far: Herman Van Rompuy and Donald Tusk, the former prime ministers of Belgium and Poland, respectively. Lisbon also institutionalized the CFSP to represent the EU internationally, consolidate the EU's different foreign policy operations, and establish a new EU External Action (diplomatic) service. The Council of Ministers and the European Council rely on a 2,000-strong secretariat, with staff for

Table 5.1	Major Conclusions of Recent European Councils
Fontainebleau, 1984	Solved "British check" and Spain/Portugal enlargement issues, appointed Jacques Delors
Milan, 1985	Approved a single-market white paper, then called an intergovernmental conference leading to the SEA
Brussels, 1987	Delors 1 budgetary package (reform of EU budgeting, structural funds, and CAP)
Madrid, 1989	Delors Committee report on EMU
Dublin, 1990	East German länder can be part of Germany within the EU
Maastricht, 1991	Maastricht Treaty
Edinburgh, 1992	Opens enlargement to EFTA countries
Essen, 1994	First discussion of enlargement to CEECs
Dublin, 1996	EMU Stability and Growth Pact
Amsterdam, 1997	Amsterdam Treaty
Berlin, 1999	Budgetary package to finance and facilitate enlargement to CEECs
Lisbon, 2000	Lisbon Strategy on competitiveness and knowledge society
Nice, 2000	Nice Treaty
Laeken, 2001	Calls European Convention, which leads to the 2004 European Constitutional Treaty
Brussels, 2003	10 CEECs sign treaty to join the EU
Brussels, 2007	20-20-20 climate change proposals. Lisbon Treaty is agreed upon
2010–2016	Urgent and multiple policy changes made in order to respond to the Eurozone crisis

the secretary-general, legal services, and seven general directorates. The importance of the European Council is clear from the partial list of its conclusions, listed in Table 5.1.

Other Institutions

The European Parliament: A European Legislature?

The European Parliament (EP) was originally a weak consultative assembly whose members were appointed by member-states. Since 1979, however, members of the EP (MEPs) have been directly elected every five years. The EP lives a vagabond existence, shuttling between Strasbourg, France, where it holds its plenary sessions; Brussels, where it meets in political groups and standing committees; and Luxembourg, where its administration is headquartered. It has long been seen as a work in progress that may eventually provide the EU institutional system with the legitimacy that the EU has had trouble engendering. But perhaps the most important thing about the EP is that it cannot propose laws—an exclusive power of the European Commission.

Since the Lisbon Treaty, the EP's 751 seats are distributed across member-states in a system of digressive proportionality, giving voters in smaller member-states more weight than those in larger ones. Elections are by proportional representation and are run nationally: national parties present lists of candidates, and those elected usually join one of seven European-level party groups. These transnational groups are important for promoting broader European perspectives, and they receive institutional incentives in terms of key positions and resources. For much of the EP's recent history, the center-right EPP and center-left Progressive Alliance of Socialists and Democrats (S&Ds) have predominated and often collaborated, with the Alliance of Liberals and Democrats for Europe (ALDE) group in third position.

Elections to the EP are meant to encourage debate between aspiring leaders and voters about future European policies, raise levels of political education about European integration, and reinforce EU solidarity and identity. Up to now, however, votes for the EP have been second-order national elections, treated by national politicians more as important indicators of the relative strength of national parties than as important EU events. EP elections have had lower turnout than their national counterparts, a problem that has progressively been getting worse (well below 50 percent in general). More recently, the growing successes of Euroskeptic parties have also, to a degree, challenged the EP's consensus that the more EU, the better.

The EP elects its president and executive bureau for five-year terms. In practice, the EPP and S&P have agreed to a grand coalition to comanage political matters, which has recently included dividing the five-year presidency between Socialist and EPP leaders, pushing both groups toward consensus and helping make the EP more coherent, if sometimes at the cost of murky compromises. After the 2009 elections, the presidential term was divided between a Polish Christian Democrat and a German Social Democrat. In 2017, however, this coalition broke down when the S&D candidate refused to support the EPP candidate, instead opting to form a "progressive opposition." The EP president presides, sets the agenda for parliamentary sessions, and addresses member-state leaders at the European Council. An EP Bureau comprised of fourteen elected vice-presidents participates in interinstitutional discussions with its Commission and Council counterparts. The bulk of the EP's work is done by seventeen permanent committees, which report and study in their functional areas and try to fend off an army of lobbyists.

In the EP's early years, the Council of Ministers consulted it, so to speak, but it had no obligation to incorporate the EP's suggestions, even though the parliament possessed the so-called nuclear option—dismissing the Commission by a two-thirds vote—which to date has never been used. The EP's roles have since grown as member-states became more concerned to demonstrate the EU's democratic credentials.

In the 1970s, the EP acquired powers over the EC's budget (the right to reject it—another threat not yet used) and to "grant discharge" to Commission spending accounts, and it discovered that it could delay decisions by juggling time limits for delivering its opinions. The Rome Treaty also gave the EP the right to bring the Commission and Council before the EUCJ for "failure to act" where the treaty seemed to oblige it, supplemented later by a right to sue if the Council infringed on EP powers.

The real shift began in 1987, however, when the SEA instituted a "cooperation" (amending) procedure, supplemented by a "codecision" provision in Maastricht in which Parliament and Council codecide Commission proposals as if they were two separate legislative houses. Each reads and may amend Commission proposals twice. If they do not agree, the proposal goes to a conciliation committee of the Council and Parliament. If this committee agrees, the measure returns to the Council and Parliament for a third reading, when it is usually approved. If it does not agree at that point, the proposal is deemed to have failed. Parliament also possesses "assenting" power over applications from prospective new members, international treaties, EMU arrangements, multiyear regional fund programs, and its own electoral procedures. Treaty changes since Maastricht (i.e., Amsterdam and Lisbon) have declared the combination of QMV and codecision the EU's ordinary legislative procedure and given the EP the power to approve new Commission presidents and each Commission member.

The EP can now argue tenaciously with member-states and the Commission and help push European integration forward. For example, when the EC was in its 1980s doldrums, the EP produced a Draft Treaty establishing the European Union, which later helped the Delors Commission propose the single market. At the end of the 1990s, EP inquiries about corruption within the Commission ultimately prompted the Commission's resignation. More recently, in the 2014 EP electoral campaign an EPP-S&D agreement to proclaim their peak candidates as potential Commission presidents helped lead to the appointment of Jean-Claude Juncker. The idea behind this was that EP elections should produce a president from the European-level party with the most seats, thus making the Commission more like a real government.

In general, growing parliamentary influence has been good for an EU whose legitimacy has been a problem. Parliaments are most effective when they debate alternative political platforms, as happens nationally, but the EP still does not have the right of legislative initiative and can only react to Commission proposals. The Lisbon Treaty added new "yellow card" procedures, allowing national parliaments to signal when they believed that EU legislative proposals violate their **subsidiarity**, but this has rarely happened. Lisbon also established a **citizen initiative** procedure, in which at least 1 million citizens across several member-states could petition EU institutions to take up a specific piece of legislation within the remit of EU treaties. Grass-roots campaigns have attempted to launch such initiatives, but thus far with no success.

The European Union Court of Justice

European law is based on treaties agreed by member-states, and all EU action must spring from this treaty basis. European laws become law in EU member-states, superior to, and superseding, their preexisting laws. The EUCJ, born as part of the ECSC, is the ultimate arbiter of the juridical meanings of treaties and laws. Located in Luxembourg, the EUCJ can strike down laws from member-states and EU institutions and, in so doing, it interprets the treaties and defines EU law. Its rulings are binding on member-states and their citizens.

The EUCJ is composed of twenty-eight justices (which will be twenty-seven post-Brexit), one from each member-state. They are appointed for six-year renewable terms. In addition, eight advocates-general review complicated and unprecedented cases and provide legal opinions for the justices, who then rule on fundamental legal matters. The Court can sit in plenary session when it wishes, and it is required to do so when dealing with matters brought before it by an EU institution or member-state. Otherwise, it subdivides its work into chambers (of three and five judges each), which then can refer matters to the full Court.

The Court's huge workload led the SEA to establish a Tribunal of First Instance, renamed the "General Court" in the Lisbon Treaty, with one judge per member-state,

Subsidiarity

The principle, consecrated by the Maastricht Treaty, that the EU should seek to forge decision making at the level of the lowest effective jurisdiction.

Citizen initiative

A clause in the Lisbon Treaty allowing citizens to propose referendums to initiate EU legislation, provided 1 million legal signatures have been obtained in a "significant number" of different EU member-states.

Table 5.2	Significant Decisions of the EUCJ
Decision	**Importance**
Van Gend en Loos v Nederlandse Administratie der Belastingen, 1963	The decision ruled that the EC constituted a new order of international law derived from agreed limitations of sovereignty by member-states.
Costa v. ENEL, 1964	A decision central to establishing the supremacy of EU law over that of member-states.
Van Duyn v. Home Office, 1974	This ruling gave individuals the same right to employment in another state as nationals of that state.
Defrenne v. Sabena, 1976	Based upon Article 119 of the Rome Treaty enjoining equal treatment of men and women in employment, this case opened EU initiatives to attenuate gender discrimination in EU labor markets. A follow-up decision in 1977 decreed that eliminating gender discrimination was a fundamental principle of EC law.
Rewe-Zentral AG v Bundesmonopolverwaltung für Branntwein, 1979	This case dictated that member-states must accept goods from other member-states on the principle of mutual recognition, assuming that all members have reasonable product standards.
Vereniging Bond van Adverteerders v. the Netherlands State, 1988	The decision obliged member-states to open up national telecommunications services to competition.

each serving a six-year term. The General Court rules on complex matters of fact, and its decisions concerning questions of law (but not fact) can be appealed to the full EUCJ. The 2009 Lisbon Treaty established an EU Charter of Fundamental Rights (with the United Kingdom, Poland, and the Czech Republic securing opt-outs), which has led to substantial new litigation, particularly by individuals, implying an extension of EU jurisprudence. Table 5.2 lists some of the EUCJ's most significant rulings.

The Eurogroup, Advisory Committees, Agencies

The EU has many ancillary institutions. Perhaps the most important today is the Eurogroup of EMU finance ministers who oversee the EMU, with a president who serves a two-and-one-half-year term. There are also two advisory committees: an Economic and Social Committee (ECOSOC), with delegates from business, labor, and other professions; and a Committee of the Regions, both of which review and submit opinions on pending EU legislation. There is a Court of Auditors, which systematically reviews EU spending, and the European Investment Bank, which mobilizes investment loans for regional planning and development. The ECB and the European External Action Service will be discussed later in this chapter. There are also community agencies scattered among the member-states, which work on a range of informational and regulatory matters, including fish stocks and plant variety, Europol, maritime security, health and safety at work, disease prevention and control, the environment, food safety, railways, the properties of chemicals, and many more.

Where Do You Stand?

EU institutions are much more difficult to understand than those of most democratic national states, to the detriment of European integration. If true, why?

Imagine you are a European trying to make sense of all this. Would you throw up your hands and revert to your national identity or would you dive headlong into the brave new world of Europe?

THE EU AND ITS POLICIES

SECTION
4

Federal Policies

Building a European Market

The most important task of the EU has been integrating national markets. The Rome Treaties created a Common Market for manufactured goods and a common agricultural policy, but many problems needed to be resolved before the market was truly open. People could not cross borders easily, goods stalled at customs posts while truck drivers filled out endless forms, professionals had difficulty working in other countries, financial and services markets remained national, national sales taxes discouraged trade, and in the 1970s, members erected new nontariff trade barriers. The 1985 single-market program revived European integration by further liberalizing and deregulating national markets into a single one with uniform European standards and norms, competition rules, environmental policies, and some integrated forms of taxation. As the EU enlarged to poorer countries, it also devised new regional development policies to help them. Finally, it worked hard to fulfill pledges to establish the "four freedoms" of movement in goods, services, capital, and people.

Led by the internal market commissioner, the single-market program was developed after wide consultation with interested groups, national-level administrations, COREPER, and other bodies. The EP then examined, and sometimes amended, the proposals, and the Council of Ministers decided by QMV. Member-states then transposed new laws and rules into national legal codes. One of the more daunting challenges was harmonizing technical standards and norms, most often by using "mutual recognition," a principle based on the EUCJ's 1979 *Cassis de Dijon* ruling that goods legally marketed in any member-state should circulate freely throughout the EU, so long as minimum standards were upheld. Last but not least, national VAT taxes had to be harmonized to prevent them from distorting competition. EU laws were general commitments that, in order to work in practice, the Commission had to develop more precise administrative laws (often called "delegated legislation"), a process overseen in "comitology" by committees of national civil servants.

Changes continued past the single-market target date of 1992 involving intellectual property laws, harmonized savings taxes, liberalized public procurement, telecoms, electricity and gas provision, opening air travel to greater competition, and making it easier to set up services. In 1999, the Commission proposed an action

Focus Questions

- To what degree does the EU provide promising models and lessons for governance on a global scale?

- Does the EU have a built-in motor pushing it towards "ever greater union"?

plan to harmonize rules and open markets in securities, banking, and insurance. Opening service markets was controversial, however, and widespread protest about the 2005 Services Directive, which proposed to free up the EU market for services beyond the market for industrial goods that had been the earlier focus, helped defeat the European Constitutional Treaty, which proposed to update EU institutions for enlargement to the CEECs, Cyprus, and Malta.

There had always been recognition that public services in health, education, public transportation, post offices, and utilities were different from grocery stores and law firms, but economic conditions were changing, and with them ideas about public services. Postal services, challenged by FedEx, UPS, and the Internet, have been privatizing. National pricing and access restrictions for what had once been "natural monopolies" (i.e., airlines, electricity, gas, and telecoms) have been lowered. Challenges to public health care, pensions, and education in Europe are on their way.

Finally, single-market progress has sometimes been blocked by special interests, such as national professional associations, banks and financial service firms, employers, and unions. EU enlargement has also made it more difficult to apply market rules and regulations. The free movement of people stirs up deep anxieties about immigration in the public. Corporations are bigger and more powerful. The single market has created one of the largest open markets, but it has not counteracted job insecurity due to international competition and new technologies.

Competition Policy

There would have been little point in having a European single market if companies and countries could limit competition within it. The Rome Treaty thus declared that measures should be taken so that "competition in the internal market is not distorted," making the Commission responsible for developing and enforcing them. Competition policy is one of its federal competencies, subject only to EUCJ review. Anticompetitive firm behavior—cartels, trusts, and monopolies—can be outlawed when judged to be against European interests. Since 1989, the Commission has overseen mergers, and more recently, it has played a key role in deregulating public utilities. It can also prevent "state aid" abuses (i.e., subsidies).

The Commission's antitrust powers are both negative (preventing illegal behavior) and positive (regulating and authorizing). Its Directorate-General for Competition (DG COMP) monitors company conditions, observes market developments, requests information from firms and governments, and investigates possible violations. DG COMP's explorations of potential violations can end informally because the threat of sanctions often leads to negotiation, but if this fails, the Commission may levy substantial fines. Because mergers and acquisitions are often global, DG COMP can have international scope, as demonstrated in its 2004 ruling and fines against Microsoft's practice of "bundling" software programs together in its Windows operating system. Merger control procedures call for proactive judgments about how a proposed merger could restrain trade. Perhaps the most spectacular case occurred in 2001, when the Commission blocked an avionics merger between General Electric and Honeywell after U.S. authorities had already approved it. More often, however, mergers are allowed after company plans are reformulated to meet DG COMP's concerns.

The issue of state aid is especially difficult because jobs and votes are often directly at stake, and some EU members have strong statist traditions. The Maastricht Treaty prevents the EU from disallowing state ownership, for example. Further, even if the Commission can prevent state subsidies that might impair markets, it can also allow one-off restructuring projects for industries and regions hurt by recessions, market shifts, and natural disasters—most often with a proviso that subsidies will be phased out once crisis conditions have ended. DG COMP has also allowed subsidies for large projects that might enhance the European market, like the English Channel tunnel ("Chunnel") between London and Paris.

EU competition policy is constantly evolving, and national and corporate players often push back. The EUCJ has also sanctioned DG COMP when it has done its work badly. In addition, the Commission has decentralized competition policy matters beneath a certain threshold to national authorities that follow European rules. Finally, member-states, within limits, have regained much decision making over state aid.

Agriculture

The Rome Treaty brought a Common Market in both agricultural and manufactured products. The CAP was originally a system of price supports administered on a product-by-product basis by the Commission, which kept EU prices far higher than they might otherwise have been. The system not only encouraged modernization, but also overproduction, overuse of chemical fertilizers, pollution, and damage to water tables. Farmers built powerful interest groups and formed tight alliances with national agriculture ministries, even as CAP incentives produced surpluses, expensive EU-funded storage, and international dumping, and with economies of scale, support went disproportionately to larger producers. In time, DG Agriculture became the Commission's largest unit, classifying carrots and other farm products, renting storage barns, selling surpluses globally, and fixing prices that the Council of Ministers approved by QMV (with the EP marginalized until the 2009 Lisbon Treaty). Each product area had its own management committee, overseen by an intergovernmental agriculture committee, with implementation left largely to member-states, monitored by the Commission.

Reform talk was not long in coming. Net contributor member-states like Great Britain and the Netherlands disliked subsidizing farmers in other places. The CAP's costs threatened to crowd out other EU activities and discredit European integration. Serious cost control began in the 1980s, and land set-asides and direct income support, rather than price subsidies, began in 1992. There has since been a decline in EU international dumping, plus an effort to reshape the CAP to promote sustainable rural development. Fitting the CAP to Eastern European agriculture has been a more recent challenge because making new member-states full CAP participants would have greatly expanded the budget. Tough intergovernmental bargaining dominated by western EU members meant that the CEECS received less, however, and CAP budgets have been slowly declining as a percentage of the overall EU budget.

Regional Development

"Structural funds" constitute the EU's second-largest budget item (after agriculture), as well as an important expression of solidarity between better-off and less prosperous regions. The Rome Treaty initially recognized the need for regional development to help Italy's southern regions. After the EU enlarged in 1973 to the United Kingdom, Denmark, and Ireland, a European Regional Development Fund (ERDF) was created to help distressed and underdeveloped areas. Enlargement to poorer countries in the 1980s called for new efforts, and the SEA made economic and social cohesion a new common policy. The 1988 reform of the funds began a doubling of funding over five years, with another doubling taking place during the 1990s.

EU regional development funding prioritizes specific objectives and promotes "partnership" between the Commission (which vets and administers projects) and national and regional cofinancing, following an "additionality" principle that obliges host countries to contribute 15 percent of project costs. Priorities were assisting underdeveloped regions (75 percent of the fund budget), restructuring deindustrialized regions, enhancing skills, combating long-term and youth unemployment, and aiding rural areas. Funding went to multiannual, multitask, and multiregional programs, mainly in areas where average income was 75 percent or less than that of the EU per capita income. The Maastricht Treaty added a cohesion fund to compensate Greece, Ireland, Portugal, and Spain for their participation in the EU's environmental and transport policies. The CEEC enlargement reshaped policies because the new members were almost all below the 75 percent threshold and should have received most of the money. Older member-states insisted on receiving what they had earlier, and the result created some resentment.

The effects of EU regional programs are difficult to calculate. Amounts going to any particular country are small in absolute terms but can add a substantial 4 percent to a country's GDP, often through infrastructure projects connecting it to the broader EU. Investments in roads, railroads, energy provision, telecommunications, airports, and ports bring rapid returns. The funds also help avoid "races to the bottom" through cheap labor and minimalist social policies. Another bonus is that regional levels of government develop greater stakes in European integration. Funding has also been indirectly positive for richer EU members because increased purchasing power and public spending in poorer countries buys goods and services from the rest of the EU. The structural funds also provide incentives for reform. The CEECs, for example, with incomes of less than 40 percent of the EU average, have had to develop administrative capacity to absorb funds productively. But the biggest payoff is that EU regional development can help consolidate good administrative practices, the rule of law, and greater democracy. Finally, the threat of withholding structural funds when a country strays from desirable paths can be sobering.

The EU Budget

The EU's annual budget in 2015 was 145 billion euros, around 1 percent of its member-states' GDP (in comparison, the average national budget is 44.5 percent of GDP). The EU budget grew through the 1980s and 1990s, then it stabilized, and recently it has been declining slightly. Many EU policies also entail large national spending, however. The EU's funds have three revenue sources—own resources (customs duties on imports to EU and sugar levies), 0.3 percent of member-state VAT taxes, and national transfers to the EU based on members' gross national income (GNI); in 2015, 0.84321 percent of national GNI. Almost all western EU members contribute more to the budget than they get back, with poorer EU countries net beneficiaries of this largesse.

The EU budgetary process has two steps. The first involves tough intergovernmental negotiations every five years to establish multiyear financial perspectives, in which the Commission submits a projected budget that member-states then squeeze out as much as they can for themselves. The second involves annual EP reviews of yearly budgets and discharge (approval) of the accounts once the budget year is completed. Smart and Inclusive Growth (competitiveness policies and economic, social, and territorial cohesion) and Sustainable Growth (agriculture and rural development, fisheries, and climate change policies) consume upward of 80 percent of annual budgets, with administration, JHA, and foreign policies taking up the rest.

EMU and the Euro

Maastricht charged the ECB with maintaining price stability (defined as an inflation rate of less than 2 percent annually), EU monetary policy, foreign exchanges, reserves, and payments systems. The ECB has a powerful president, a six-member executive board, and a governing council of national central bank governors. It is statutorily independent of political influence. All EU members, except those with opt-outs, are required eventually to join the EMU, which in 1999 had 11 members and now has 19 out of 28 EU member-states. Buoyant economies initially allowed the ECB to dispel worries that its dedication to price stability might stifle growth. Its one-size-fits-all interest rates lowered borrowing costs for poorer economies—a windfall encouraging debt-based development strategies. On the negative side, the 1997 Stability and Growth Pact (reformed in 2005) bound EMU members to deficits of less than 3 percent, but in a few short years, half of EMU members had stopped observing the rules.

EMU federalized monetary policy, but its members retained control over national taxing, spending, and budgeting. The Eurogroup of EMU finance ministers tried to promote coherence, but weak enforcement tools contributed to the situation that exploded in the Eurozone crisis. The crisis itself led to the imposition of brutal austerity on some of EMU's poorer members and produced a reconfiguration of rules, including a substantial increase in central oversight of national policies and new enforcement powers, increasing the ECB's policy-making and regulatory powers. During the crisis, the ECB was a significant summit negotiator, implemented nonstandard policies to stabilize the Eurozone economy, provided funds to commercial banks at low interest rates to keep credit open, purchased bank and national debt on secondary markets, and provided vast liquidity that would not have been available otherwise. The 2012 pledge of ECB president Mario Draghi to "do what it takes" was rightfully seen as a turning point toward greater calm.

Shared Policies

In some areas, the EU has more limited, horizontal power to generate ideas, set examples, delineate best practices, provide seed money, and cajole national policy-making. The precise division of shared labor is determined by EU treaties, especially Maastricht's concept of "subsidiarity." A few examples illustrate this, which are covered next (see also the discussion of environmental politics in section 1 of this chapter).

Globalization and Competitiveness

EU policies to promote economic competitiveness began with the ECSC. Since then, the EU has often been involved in helping reconfigure troubled industries and regions through financial aid, education and retraining, and allowing temporary trade protection. Europe was initially far behind the United States, and the Common Market proved a key catching-up tool.

After the economic problems of the 1970s, the United States jumped ahead again, just when Japan and the Asian Tigers brought their own comparative advantage of low-cost labor to the international market. The single market and EMU were proposed to prevent Europe from falling too far behind. The United States moved forward again in the 1990s, propelled by its global financial power and vanguard position in information technology, while China, India, and other low-cost newcomers penetrated the manufacturing markets where Europe had earlier specialized.

Key new areas like research and development (R&D) in technology and industrial policy remain primarily national, but the EU provides many incentives for cooperation. In the early 1980s, the EU began funding high-tech R&D in electronics. The SEA and the Maastricht Treaty allowed more EU activity in R&D to complement member-state efforts. The 2000 Lisbon European Council then proposed a "European Research Area" to raise R&D spending to 3 percent of EU GDP by 2010 (a target not yet met). The flagship vehicles for EU R&D have been multi-year research framework programs drawn up by the Commission, approved by the Council, and designed to work with national policies. They have done well creating Europe-wide networks of researchers.

The 2000 Lisbon strategy also sought greater cooperation and convergence among member-states, usually through the OMC, around goals for education, workplace change, and social program reforms. Budgets have been small and efforts are hindered by national rivalries, but there has been greater European focus, sharing of best practices, and greater coherence. The EU has also invested in areas of immediate trans-European importance—infrastructure, environmental research and programs, and health and food safety, for example—and there have been major European industrial-policy innovations in mobile phones, space technologies, and satellites that have "Europeanized" standards, helped security policy, and supported air transport.

Proposals to open energy markets have come and gone, however, hindered by opposition from national energy monopolies and fears about losing existing energy sources. Brussels has also moved on chemicals regulation (such as the REACH Directive, which required chemical companies to provide detailed definitions of their products, along with information about possible toxicity) and climate change and talked about lightening its regulatory hand in general. The financial crisis of 2009 set things back, however. Unemployment shot up, and the EU remained well behind achieving its goal of becoming the world's leading knowledge economy. By then, the EU was looking forward to a new "2020" strategy, aimed at raising the employment rate, reaching Lisbon's 3 percent R&D target, reducing greenhouse gases, finding new noncarbon energy sources, and reducing school dropout and poverty rates.

Social Policy

Social policy, an area where the EU has influence, but little direct power, illustrates another combination of the union's multilevel governance and subsidiarity. Welfare state and employment policies remain national. The Rome Treaty limited the EU to matters of labor market mobility within the Common Market, occupational training, and equal opportunity for men and women, while creating a European Social Fund with the vague purpose of making "the employment of workers easier, increasing their geographical and occupational mobility within the Community." Today's EU still has a wide variety of social policy regimes, reflecting the variety of its member-states.

Concern with workplace inequality between men and women led to a clause in the Rome Treaty requiring "equal treatment." The EU has since developed programs for advancing women's rights and antidiscrimination policies. The SEA harmonized workplace health and safety and also stated that "the Commission shall endeavor to develop the dialogue between management and labor at [a] European . . . level." The Commission elaborated this concept in the Maastricht Treaty's Social Protocol, leading to directives on working time, European Works Councils, parental leave, and "atypical work" (part-time and short-term contracts).

Later in the 1990s, member-states were losing their enthusiasm for EU social policy, however, and emphasis shifted to decentralized, "soft" procedures and the OMC to promote change in pensions, poverty policy, and other social policy matters. Amsterdam's European Employment strategy may have helped raise work participation rates, but OMC has been sidelined in most other areas. The Commission has since promoted social investment, but results have lagged.

The EU's indirect influence on social policy through market-building and enlargement has been profound, however. National wage-setting and labor market arrangements have had to be adjusted as a result of the single market, for example, contributing to greater labor market segmentation, decentralization of collective bargaining, and the decline of trade unions. Unemployment insurance programs have been reshaped to use carrots and sticks to encourage job searches. There have also been movements to privatize and marketize formerly national public-sector health care programs, retirement pensions, and higher education. Whether these changes are good or bad is a matter of debate. What is clear, however, is that EU-level market-opening actions and EUCJ rulings have significantly helped constrain and change member-state social policies.

Intergovernmental Europe?

With the Maastricht Treaty, the EU entered the new areas of JHA and the CFSP, originally considered intergovernmental "pillars" to allow governments to control the pace of change.

Justice and Home Affairs

The Rome Treaty advocated the "free movement of people," but it took decades before much happened. The single market in the 1980s meant that crime would "Europeanize" along with ordinary citizens and legitimate businesses, and without EU cooperation on visas and border control, asylum policy, and police intelligence, EU members would have been largely unable to know who was on their territory and what they were doing. In addition, without increased legal cooperation, freedom of movement might leave EU citizens baffled about their rights, finding themselves confronted by a bewildering array of civil laws. Even before the EU confronted these issues at Maastricht, ad hoc groups of member-states formed around problems such as drugs and human trafficking. But it was the Schengen Group in the 1980s that first removed restrictions on internal border crossings to permit free movement of their citizens.

Maastricht's JHA clauses brought these many areas into an intergovernmental pillar. Detailed JHA business was done by COREPER and the Council of Ministers, with help from national experts, police, customs, and judicial cooperation on civil and criminal matters. Europol built up police cooperation, there was new information and intelligence gathering and sharing, and new large databases about the Schengen area, customs, asylum-seeking, and stolen property were built. Later, the Amsterdam Treaty incorporated the full Schengen *acquis*.

Because intergovernmental methods were slow and cumbersome, the 1997 Amsterdam Treaty began shifting JHA matters (asylum and immigration, judicial cooperation on civil law) into the Community Method, which also included a *passarelle* clause that allowed member-states, if unanimous, to shift further areas in the future. Sensitive matters of police and judicial cooperation on criminal issues remained intergovernmental, however. Amsterdam also committed to an Area of Freedom, Security, and Justice designed to shift emphasis from intergovernmental police activities to the rights of EU citizens and legal visitors, and proposed more policy harmonization through mutual recognition and international cooperation on civil law matters like divorce, alimony, child visitation, and financial matters like debt and bankruptcy. A broader EU Charter of Fundamental Rights was inserted into the 2009 Lisbon Treaty, with British, Polish, and Czech opt-outs.

There are now several monitoring and information agencies across the EU on issues of drugs, discrimination, and fraud, a European Police College, a European Police Chiefs task force, and Eurojust, an organization of senior justice officials to facilitate cross-border prosecutions. A common European arrest warrant superseded national extradition proceedings in 2004. Europol's antiterrorist coverage and budget were growing prior to the terrorist attacks of September 11, 2001 (9/11), and have grown even more substantially since the terrorist attacks in Madrid in 2004, London in 2005, and Paris and Brussels in 2015–2016. The Lisbon Treaty further integrated border and asylum control issues into the community method of decision making and established minimal rules for certain cross-border crimes (e.g., terrorism, drugs and arms trafficking, money laundering, sexual exploitation of women, and cybercrime), leaving only a few areas to be decided unanimously (such as passports and identity cards, family law, and the Europeanization of criminal law). The Lisbon Treaty also promised to increase the speed and effectiveness of legal cooperation, particularly by mutual recognition.

There are clouds over JHA today, however. Immigration, including internal economic migration from new EU member-states westward and economic migrants from the EU south, has become a heated political issue. EU and national elites now engage in balancing acts between defending the rights of free movement, the human rights of migrants, and political pressure from rising anti-immigrant xenophobia. The aftermath of the Arab Spring in the Middle East and North Africa has turned illegal immigration in the Mediterranean region into a vast refugee exodus overwhelming the EU. Disputes between member-states are rife, often fueled by hard-right parties using refugee issues to increase their support, with further polarization created by terrorist attacks. Objections to free movement and immigration were a major force behind the Brexit vote and led to border closings in the Schengen area. Burden-sharing between EU members on refugee issues has become a toxic issue, and beefing up external EU borders is immensely difficult, leaving some EU members with insufficient resources to confront refugees fleeing intolerable situations. Generous gestures of welcome in Germany, Sweden, and elsewhere have caused political backlashes, and many CEEC member-states are refusing refugees altogether.

Foreign and Security Policy

Jacques Delors, when Commission president, often asked whether the EU was content to be a "big Switzerland"—that is, an economic giant and foreign policy dwarf. From its beginnings, while the EU has been an important international trade actor, U.S. hegemony, NATO, and diverging member-state preferences have kept it away from security matters and reluctant to engage in strong EU diplomatic action, even if larger EU member-states have been important actors on their own. After the Cold War, however, the Maastricht Treaty created an intergovernmental pillar for the new CFSP.

THE U.S. CONNECTION

The EU and the United States have an intimate history. Without U.S. support, European integration might not have happened, even if this has not precluded the occasional American annoyance. For example, when the EU revived in the 1980s, the United States thought it was too slow to copy American neoliberalism and too eager to defend its social programs. The United States was also skeptical about the EMU and worried that the CFSP might threaten NATO. Larger U.S.-EU conflicts, such as the EU's divided response to the Iraq War in 2003, left a bitter aftertaste.

Further, the EU's antitrust policies bothered American corporations, and spying on EU leaders by the U.S. National Security Agency (NSA) annoyed European politicians. Stepping back makes the picture look different, however. The United States and EU have stood side by side on big issues like democracy, the rule of law, liberal freedoms, human rights, and opposition to illiberal regimes. At the same time, there are questions about the future. While Europe remains important, it is wounded by its many crises. Globalization's new actors—particularly China and other emerging market countries—led the Barack Obama administration to talk about a shift of focus to Asia and Obama's successor, President Donald Trump, to predict dour days for the EU.

MAKING CONNECTIONS Why has the close EU-U.S. connection been fraught with controversy? Why has it recently come under greater political pressure?

The EU has been built around a customs union and internal opening of markets, with international trade policy important to its foreign policy. EU trade initiatives begin with intergovernmental agreement on mandates that the Commission then uses to negotiate. In the 1990s, the EU and the United States together replaced GATT with the WTO, with its dispute resolution mechanism and commitments to new issues in health, environment, labor standards, public procurement, intellectual property rights, and lowering NTBs. Private trade diplomacy by European economic interests and a lively European civil society of protest groups and nongovernmental organizations (NGOs) have become very important.

The Doha Development Round, the first WTO multilateral trade round, failed, mainly over differences between developing parts of Asia and Latin America and established northern interests. Trade diplomacy has nonetheless remained central to the EU, which has turned to new bilateral, often-regional, second-generation trade treaties that go beyond borders to minimize barriers in norms, standards, public contracting, and professional certification. The deal concluded in 2015 with Canada (namely, CETA) may be the best example, even if CETA has had problems because EU public opinion has begun to question the desirability of new globalization. CETA was meant to coincide with similar EU negotiations with the United States on the Transatlantic Trade and Investment Partnership (TTIP) which, since the election of Donald Trump, are off the table. International trade policy will doubtless continue to be an essential, if bumpy, road for the EU, however.

EU progress in foreign and security policy has been slow, even if the EU has developed new institutions and practices. Larger EU members, especially the older imperial powers, have had divergent goals, and smaller EU countries have worried about domination by bigger ones. Therefore, common foreign policy in the EU is very unlikely ever to be a single European policy. Maastricht's intergovernmental CFSP ambitions and byzantine decision rules were modest, and even the Lisbon Treaty's "communitization" left large matters for unanimous decision making. After Maastricht, there had been pious hopes that the Western European Union (WEU), a European defense arrangement from the 1940s, might become the EU's defense arm, and the treaty spoke longingly of a future "common defense policy, which might in time lead to a common defense."

Europe's inadequate response to troubles in the former Yugoslavia in the 1990s, in which large differences between key member-states made serious action almost impossible, demonstrated how difficult the issues were. Reflections led to new openings to humanitarian intervention and peacekeeping. The Amsterdam Treaty then proposed a European Security and Defense Identity, which included planning operations in the Council of Ministers, a High Representative for CFSP who would also be Secretary General of the Council of Ministers and support the rotating presidency on CFSP issues, and empowering the Council to develop common strategies.

In 1998, the French and British issued a Joint Declaration on European Defense, to create "capacity for autonomous action, backed up by credible military forces, the means to decide to use them, and a readiness to do so," an initiative prompted by what had happened in Kosovo, where the United States called and fired most of NATO's shots. The 1999 Helsinki European Council then announced headline goals for 2003 of a 60,000-person rapid-reaction force deployable within 60 days for up to a year, supported by warplanes and ships. A Council Politics and Security Committee (COPS) would plan and control this, aided by an EU Military Committee that included military chiefs of EU members and a Brussels general staff. Helsinki also underlined the EU's "determination to develop an autonomous capacity to take decisions and, where NATO as a whole is not engaged, to launch and conduct EU-led military operations in response to international crises." More coordination and integration of the European defense industry was also called for but did not get far. After all this, however, the EU today has only two equipped and supported 1,500-troop battle groups ready to carry out concurrent missions.

EU initiatives in defense and security inevitably engaged the United States. Disputes led to the United States agreeing to give the EU access to some NATO assets for limited actions so long as NATO remained predominant. After 9/11, Europeans expressed massive support for Americans, assisted U.S. intelligence services, beefed up European counterterrorism, and agreed to participate in U.S.-led NATO actions in Afghanistan. The Iraq War in 2003 created bitter disagreement, however, with the French and Germans opposed as the British marched to Baghdad along with Spain, Italy, Portugal, and several CEEC candidates for EU membership.

In recent years, the EU has invested more in "soft-power" areas like environmental politics, development aid, and crisis management, where it can take the lead. EU enlargement itself has constituted soft power, as the prospect of joining pushed many applicants to democratize, commit to the rule of law, and cooperate for the European greater good. The EU has also tried to offer partial benefits, like trade and development aid, to its near neighbors to the East (i.e., Turkey, the Ukraine, and others) and Mediterranean countries, but here, progress has been far from smooth. Progress toward Turkish membership has stopped, and hopes for a so-called Mediterranean Union disappeared in the aftermath of the Arab Spring.

The EU's "Eastern Partnership" policy ran into Russian toughness in Ukraine. The EU played an important role in limiting the Iranian nuclear program and has been the largest supplier of humanitarian aid to Syria, although difficulties in handling refugee flows have been painful. Along with the United States, it has also tried to resolve the Israeli-Palestinian conflict for many years, to little avail.

The EU and its member-states give 50 percent of the world's total development help, which has become more problem-targeted and conditional, seeking out infrastructure projects with efforts to leverage aid into better administration and governance in recipient countries. Regional programs are also directed to the very poorest countries, often used to cofinance NGO activities and sophisticated operations for areas hit by natural disasters, population displacement, and deadly conflict.

The EU is difficult to overlook internationally, and its CFSP institutions have grown larger incrementally. The 2009 Lisbon Treaty created a new High Representative for CFSP, who performs two functions simultaneously—the Commission vice president for external relations and president of the CFSP Council of Ministers. This person is charged to build and then run the European External Action Service.

Judged by the metrics of smart bombs and big battalions, the EU remains a foreign and defense policy weakling, however. Whether this will change in a much perilous and more multipolar world is unforeseeable, even if one hears calls for greater EU defense capacities and even an EU army.

Where Do You Stand?

What are your recommendations for reforming the EU's institutions to make them more effective?

The EU does not appear to have the necessary legitimacy to sustain its policies. What reforms might change this?

REPRESENTATION AND PARTICIPATION IN THE EU

SECTION 5

There are many ways of organizing political representation and participation. Cross-national differences, built upon a variety of histories, cultures, geographies, languages, myths, lore, and legend, continue to loom large. Complicating these issues, the EU is the capstone of a unique European system of multilevel governance and not a state at all. Nonetheless, EU institutions are democratically representative, with liberal values, respect for the rule of law, and multiple checks and balances. They are also full of particularities, as Figure 5.1 shows.

Consider EU citizenship. Consecrated by the 1993 Maastricht Treaty, it supplements national citizenship by conferring a number of new rights—voting in European and municipal elections, accessing EU documents, petitioning the EP and the European Ombudsman, moving, residing and working freely across the union, freedom from discrimination, and consular protection, among others. Citizens in EU member-states are thus "dual" citizens, but relationships among the levels are asymmetrical. In practice, multilevel governance means that citizens live mainly at the national level, national states are the central constituents of the EU, and the EU works "federally" in only a few areas, creating a complicated system of representation and participation.

The European Commission has exclusive rights to propose new EU laws and represent European citizens as a whole. Historically, this has meant defining and disseminating the interests of Europe beyond its member-states. Aside from preaching Europe's causes of peace and prosperity and proclaiming that the EU is a good thing, this can be accomplished only through the persuasiveness and positive results of Commission proposals. Commissions have five-year terms, their members are nominated by national

Focus Questions

- What are the main reasons that the EU's "democratic deficit" has become more visible in recent years?

- The EU is in the midst of confronting a cluster of very serious crises. Are these crises caused by rapid changes in the world around the EU, by the EU's internal deficiencies, or both?

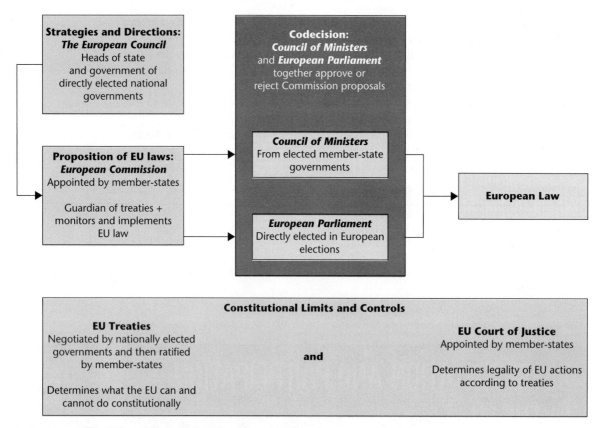

FIGURE 5.1 The EU and Representative Democracy

governments, and their presidents must represent the predominant political "family" emerging from periodic EP elections. Once vetted by the EP, Commission members swear to serve without regard to their country of origin or political beliefs.

The Commission then becomes a collective body whose proposals should, in principle, help advance citizens' belief and trust in the EU. However, because making "more Europe" involves taking powers, importance, and legitimacy away from EU member-states, the Commission has often faced resistance. It represents a partially postnational Europe that it is simultaneously charged with creating. At its best, it can provide ways to help solve the common problems of member-states. Doing so requires having a very talented leadership, however, because the Commission starts with few grass-roots supporters and is not directly responsible to any electorate, even if it consults with many interests and groups. In the last analysis, however, it depends on other EU institutions and member-states.

The European Council shapes the EU's general strategies through multilateral negotiations that generally determine what the Commission will do and what the EP will debate and decide. The Council of Ministers, until 1993 the EU's sole decider, is now, with the EP, its codecider. Practically everything that the EU undertakes is tailored to what the European Council desires and what the Council will accept. Both the Council of Ministers and the European Council are composed of members of nationally elected governments, meaning that the democratic representation supporting them is indirect. Member-states elect leaders from national parties who are concerned mainly with national matters and whose positions on Europe are only vaguely understood by most citizens.

National governments send heads of government and ministers to negotiate with colleagues from other countries to decide Council and European Council positions, and they must try to shape their positions to include what they perceive to be the desires of their citizens, and also be prepared to adjust them to fit specific issues on the EU table and the preferences of other member-states. EU-level bargaining is a diplomatic affair, distant and often secret, with a commitment to reaching consensus that often masks specific national roles. Representation for both of these Councils is unquestionably democratic, but their processes and results are often very distant from citizens.

The European Parliament

The EP plays a key role in codecision making and has become a vibrant forum for scrutinizing Commissions and Councils, proposing new European issues and ideas and debating EU alternatives. It complements the Commission by helping to create an EU public sphere. Direct EP elections have greatly increased the number of parties involved (now totaling more than 150 on national EP ballots), and enlargement has multiplied voices and interests. With codecision, the EP is often characterized as one house in a bicameral legislature, along with the Council of Ministers, but this can be misleading because the prerogative of proposing EU laws rests with the Commission.

Codecision allows the EP to amend Commission proposals, and it can also vet prospective Commissioners and force the Commission to resign in extremis, but it remains a parliament without a real government and opposition. MEPs come from national parties with widely varying attitudes toward the EU, including Euroskeptic groups who believe that the institution should not exist at all. Once elected, MEPs are Europeanized by membership in one of the EP's political groups. No group has ever had an EP majority. Until recently, the center-right EPP and center-left S&D groups usually have cooperated to steer the parliament's course.

Although the EP is not well understood by European citizens, there can be no question about the democratic nature of its representation. But, turnout for EP elections, never as high as in national elections, has been steadily declining. EP elections are typically second-order national elections, contested by national parties and centering on national rather than EU-related issues. The results of EP elections are interpreted mainly for what they indicate about the strength of different national forces. Recently, however, mainstream national parties have been in considerable turmoil. Center-left and center-right parties based on traditional left-right cleavages that anchored national politics throughout much of the post-1945 period have weakened and, more generally, partisan life has been fragmenting around the issues of globalization, Europeanization, and renascent nationalism. "Populism," a term referring to the public mistrust of established elites, has spread widely. The result has been the rise of antisystem parties, many of whom incorporate a heavy dose of Euroskepticism into their platforms.

Political Cultures, Citizenship, and Identities

In theory, EU institutions are democratically representative, and yet there has long been criticism of the so-called democratic deficit in the EU. Why? There is no single answer. Theoretical models of democratic representation are based on national experiences, and today's Europeans still live much more of their political lives in national states, each with its own history, culture, languages, and ways of doing politics. Such foundations create strong national identities, political outlooks, and path-dependent national institutions that shape much of what happens and how it is understood. A key democratic deficit problem is that the EU is distant from the national lives of citizens and difficult for them to understand and identify with. The comparatively unique and complex nature of the EU's institutions adds to this difficulty. All this means that when the EU intervenes tangibly in national lives, it can cause controversy. When EU policies add value, the EU is likely to do well. Public policies are almost invariably valuable to some and costly to others, however, and unlike national states, the EU does not possess a large reservoir of trust, support, and identification to shepherd it through difficult times.

The EU's history provides more answers to the question of democratic deficit. European integration has always had opponents who oppose supranationality and loss of sovereignty. During its initial years in the postwar economic boom, when the EU was limited to matters of trade regulation in industrial goods and agriculture, it benefited from a permissive public consensus. National politics mattered, while the EU remained relatively in the background. Beginning with the single market, however, the EU gained new power in economic governance and beyond. Combined with the more recent effects of globalization and technological change on employment and national systems of social protection, the permissive consensus began to give way to greater skepticism and resistance that have been deepened by recent crises.

An effective system of democratic representation must also respond to different constituent demands and needs—and for the EU, this must mean national constituents and citizens. Successive enlargements have greatly changed the size and composition of the EU. The diverse histories, cultures, stages of development, geographical settings, and problems of its twenty-eight members (soon to be twenty-seven) have remapped the EU's landscape into a collection of regional and national fragments with different hopes, needs, political outlooks, and media. After decades of EU reluctance, the United Kingdom is now on the way out the door.

The 19 members of the EMU live in a different monetary and economic governance world than other EU members outside it. The Eurozone crisis has deflated earlier EU enthusiasm in Greece, Spain, Portugal, Cyprus, and other countries, although when recovery comes, this may be only temporary. Some CEECs, whose backgrounds are very different and who look for different outcomes from the EU than the EU's earlier members, are now restless about the EU's constraints. Indeed, some, like Hungary, now advertise commitments to "illiberal democracy," in direct contradiction to core tenets in the EU's community of values. Faced with such variety, it has become fashionable to advocate a multizone, multispeed EU. Doing so might make sense, but it would create new puzzles as well.

Finally, representation does not only mean definitions drawn from political philosophy. It is also about mutually shared relationships to aggregate citizens' different interests, usually through political parties, to produce governments and widely acceptable policies. What happens, however, if many citizens do not readily accept so-called respectable parties and their offerings? Recent alarms about populism, the relative electoral decline of traditional parties of the social democratic left and center-right, the more general weakening of long-standing left-right cleavages, and the rise of new nationalist and xenophobic parties all bespeak deteriorating representational relationships at national levels, with inevitable consequences for the EU.

Interest Groups, Social Movements, and Protest

Lobbying and interest-group activities are additional forms of political representation involving advantage-seeking by particular groups. Brussels is bustling with interest-group activity—there are more than 30,000 lobbyists registered by the EP, for example. Address plaques around the EU's headquarters in Brussels announce industry associations, chambers of commerce, trade unions, EU regions, NGOs, consultants, lawyers, and other intermediaries, almost all of whom work at linking particular interests and EU institutions. The Commission and the EP are besieged by highly skilled professionals, former EU officials, globalized legal firms plying their trades, social movement entrepreneurs, and countless others.

In today's democratic market societies, interest groups of all kinds congregate where the issues that concern them are decided. Like it or not, given the complex nature of politics, technology, economic organizations, and the law, designing policy nowadays can hardly be done without input from concerned interests. EU Commission officials, almost always talented policy generalists, must devise policies that are highly technical and often need and seek outside help to do so.

Technical expertise is not enough, though. Lobbyists also need to know the Commission's arcane procedures and personnel inside out to know where and when to go and whom to contact. Lobbying the EP, to take another example, not only involves technical and procedural knowledge, but good political connections as well—lobbyists need to know which standing committees are important for their purposes and which political groups are most likely to be influential and open to influence. Member-state governments, which collectively set EU policy agendas and later codecide the fate of proposals, are also targets. To reach them, political, procedural, and technical participants must be supplemented by cultural knowledge and familiarity with national élites.

All democratic political systems strive for transparency and control over interest group and lobbying activities, and the EU is among the more transparent and regulated. But there are limits. Lobbying and interest group influence is murky and difficult to understand everywhere—a frenetic scramble of aggressive actors whose powers are difficult to pin down. Interest-group and lobbying activity in the EU, as in most national states, is shaped by the EU's complicated structures. The EU is not a state, but rather a set of transnational institutions whose actions flow from cooperative agreements between member-states. This implies that interest groups, lobbies, and other civil society organizations, including NGOs, are likely to focus both on EU institutions—the Commission and the EP—and on member-states. The EU has quasi-federal powers in only some areas, and because economic governance is by far the most important of these, it is the center of EU interest-group action. Where policy and influence issues are more narrowly focused on one Commission DG or EP committee, such as in environmental policies, consumer protection, agriculture, regional development, and culture, NGOs and social movements have more favorable terrain. Finally, in those very significant policy areas where the EU has few roles to play and member-states retain their sovereignty, such as national fiscal and budgetary policies, taxation, and social programs, interest-group activity will be primarily national, not only to influence national outcomes but also to influence the European activities of national governments. European-focused interest groups do a great deal of venue-shopping as a result.

Because economic governance is huge and complex, armies of market actors will try to influence national and EU decisions. Although it is unlikely that any specific group will regularly come out on top, the heavyweights will generally be capitalist in one way or another. This tells us little more, however, than that Europeans, like people practically everywhere, live in market societies.

Indeed, lobbying around economic governance involves ferocious, highly strategic combat between different, often opposing business interests, with Commission policy designers, EP Committees and party groups, and member-state governments in the middle. Large interest-group players will also work to influence general EU agenda-setting and the preferences of member-states, and in national policy areas, there will be a host of primarily national actors at work, most of which are less concerned with the EU level.

It is difficult, therefore, to generalize about interest groups and lobbying in the EU. The EU's economic governance focus will tend to favor business interests with large influence resources. This is all the more true because trade union power and resources have been declining and because unions are more focused on national decisions. Add to this the weakening of traditional left-right political cleavages, the fact that the center of political gravity across the EU has shifted farther rightward, and that international economic competitiveness has emerged as the EU's most important economic governance issue, and it is not surprising that big private-sector business lobbies have gained advantage. Finally, business lobbying has sometimes been fundamental and positive. The European Business Round Table of Industrialists, a group backed by a few very large EU corporations, helped promote and define the single-market program in the 1980s, for example.

In areas like environmental policy, consumer protection, regional policies, antidiscrimination matters, humanitarian aid, and, more recently, trade policy, effective NGOs and social justice activists can often advance their positions because the EU, with its chronic problems of legitimacy, is welcoming to civil society mobilization and sometimes has even been eager to help civil society groups to mobilize. The Commission worked hard at different points to promote industrial and economic endeavors (e.g., in electronics in the 1980s) that private interests were neglecting. Later, it fostered workplace training groups and, in the Lisbon strategy, group interactions to help reform social policies. The Delors Commission, in its "social Europe" agenda, tried to bring national trade unions into an effective transnational European Trade Union Confederation. Other examples of such institutional-group sponsoring can be found in regional development, gender relations, environmental policy, and poverty policies.

Finally, there are two large buildings next to the enormous EP edifices in Brussels that house the ECOSOC and the Committee of the Regions. Both represent long-standing EU efforts to bring national and regional interest groups together to focus more on European matters. The ECOSOC, composed of member-state producer group delegates—business, labor, and others—must be consulted on pertinent proposed EU legislation and this process has nourished networks, contacts, and friendships across interest-group lines that can come into play for other purposes. The Committee of the Regions, also consulted on pertinent matters, builds connections between regional delegates and, aided by the financial incentives in structural funds, also creates a greater European focus.

Social movements and protests constitute very different forms of interest representation in all democracies, including the EU, and today are widespread and growing. Recently, grass-roots mobilizations in Europe, with counterparts in regions and countries beyond, have brought new focus to many issues, including feminism, environmental problems, regional grievances, globalization (now often including Europeanization), antidiscrimination rights of all kinds, gay marriage, anti-immigrant xenophobia, growing inequality, and a host of other causes. These rising, ebbing, and often militant undertakings are important to EU institutions, in part because the Commission and EP are open to hearing and sometimes cultivating them, even if such movements and protests tend to grow locally and nationally, with the EU itself less often a target.

There have been exceptions, however. Agricultural organizations long ago developed annual militant rituals of raucously parading their tractors and animals in front of the Commission's Brussels headquarters when agricultural prices were being decided. European labor unions mobilized through the European Trade Union Confederation in the mid-1980s to oppose the Bolkestein Directive on liberalizing the service sector, contributing to the defeat of the European Constitutional Treaty in French and Dutch national referendums. World Social Forums, which flowered in Europe, had prominent anti-EU dimensions. Environmental movements have had EU-level prominence and were important to shaping the REACH directive that now regulates the EU chemical sector.

Nonetheless, protests against EU-imposed austerity policies in the Eurozone crisis were widespread, mixing traditional, often very militant, trade union actions and new mobilizations and protests. "Occupy" and "indignado" type mobilization, in which new social media played significant roles, were important in Greece, Spain, and, to a lesser extent, Portugal and Italy. There have also been strong local and national mobilizations against EU and Commission efforts to promote burden-sharing in the refugee crisis, joining ongoing anti-EU protest against immigration and the free movement of people. Finally, anti-immigrant and free-movement protest anger was perhaps the most important factor in the Brexit referendum.

Elections

Representation and participation in the EU come in many varieties and have been dynamic over recent decades. Its electoral shape, whose EU levels are discussed in Section 3, has also been changing. The traditional center-left and, to a lesser degree, center-right political parties that have long channeled European representation desires and mobilization, have been losing steam, often opening space for newcomers. Interest and lobbying groups and many NGOs have thus focused much more intensely on influencing the EU where it has pertinent prerogatives, particularly in economic governance. The issues and repertoires of political parties, along with social movements and protest mobilization, have broadened from earlier economistic foci into a broad range of more cultural concerns, even if mainly on the national level.

Social movement and protest actions, once they have established themselves, have often sought to form new issue-oriented "movement" political parties and have found openings mainly (but not only) in the proportional representation electoral systems that predominate in most EU member-states. Once they make electoral breakthroughs, as have Syriza in Greece, Podemos in Spain, the Five Star Movement in Italy, various Green Parties, and anti-immigrant nationalist parties like the French Front National, they can build local power and claim positions in multiparty coalition governments where they can defend their issues and positions. Time and again, movement parties have become important national players in recent years.

The Political Impact of Technology and the Media

Real European mass media, beyond a few élite Anglophone publications (the *Financial Times and the Economist* are among the leaders) and websites for EU insiders, are very hard to find, despite the repeated efforts of start-up newspapers and journals plus TV news broadcasts (including "Euronews," largely funded by the EU itself). One result has been that national citizens tend to learn about the EU and its activities through media that are profoundly national in cultural and language terms and deeply embedded into national political cultures. The media thereby provide largely national points of view, with far less focus on European-wide issues. In what remains a strongly fragmented EU, the explosion of new media, where sweeping global technological innovations encourage further fragmentation by siloing national cultural and ideological communities, may complicate things further. One small bright spot, different from the media per se, has been the proliferation in academia of "EU Studies" courses and scholarship.

- Why has adding new members to the EU caused so much difficulty?

- How can we explain the recent retreat of EU member-states from commitment to European integration?

We, the leaders of 27 Member States and of EU institutions, take pride in the achievements of the European Union . . . Sixty years ago, recovering from the tragedy of two world wars, we decided to bond together and rebuild our continent from its ashes. We have built a unique Union with common institutions and strong values, a community of peace, freedom, democracy, human rights and the rule of law, a major economic power with unparalleled levels of social protection and welfare . . .

From the Rome Declaration of member-states and leaders of the European institutions, written for the EU's sixtieth birthday celebration in Rome, March 25, 2017.

Political systems inevitably have their ups and downs. Politics in the EU has thus constantly been in transition—sometimes incrementally, sometimes dramatically, often positively, and sometimes negatively. It is easy to overromanticize the EU's great achievements. It has promoted innovative cooperative relationships among members who had earlier lived in mutual hostility, helped promote decades of peace and prosperity, and established a vast, open market for economies that might otherwise have stagnated in national isolation. The EU has also been a major contributor to opening international trade and been a steadfast advocate of multilateral approaches in international relations. It has advanced the cause of democracy in Europe and pioneered innovative transnational governance by making a plausible case for postnational problem-solving.

The EU's stars are out of line after the Eurozone crisis. Is there a way forward?

AP Photo/Gregorio Borgia

To be sure, it has been blessed with good fortune, received a great deal of help from others, and been supported by friendly postwar international structures in trade, economics, and security. The EU's achievements have not come easily, however. Events have demonstrated repeatedly how complicated it is to persuade proud nation-states to delegate sovereignty to untried transnational processes and institutions. It was also predictable that after more than six decades, European peoples (younger generations in particular) should take the EU's successes for granted and anxiously demand solutions to the new problems confronting today's Europe. The EU has done very well and changed a great deal, but the world around it today may be changing even more rapidly.

Political Challenges and Changing Agendas

In its brief history, it has seemed that each time that the EU succeeded in creating stable institutional and policy conditions, the world around it changed dramatically and demanded that it respond. The EU was an adolescent in the 1970s, when the bottom began to fall out of the postwar transatlantic economic and financial order. If it had difficulty coping at first, by the mid-1980s, it was building the single market, reconfiguring its institutions, and devising new policies in response. It was not long before more challenges came, however. The end of the Cold War reshaped Europe and international affairs, the EU area fell behind the United States in digital technologies, and new emerging-market economic actors appeared, bringing significant comparative advantages with them. As new global institutional structures took shape, the EU and its member-states had to learn how to work within them. The EU hesitantly responded with the Maastricht Treaty (EMU, CFSP, JHA, and other leaps forward), the Amsterdam Treaty, and the 2009 Lisbon Treaty. Then, of late, it has had to deal with the Great Recession, the collapse of stability in its near neighborhood, and, for the first time, one of its member-states deciding to abandon it.

It would be unfair to conclude that the EU has failed to meet these challenges, even if responding has always been politically difficult and the issues larger than most had anticipated—most recently, globalization. On one hand, globalization has been moving the EU at warp speed away from its somewhat controllable economic and social space into a larger system, whose volatile dynamics have made adaptation very hard. On the other hand, the EU, with market opening at its core and trade promotion at the heart of its approach to the rest of the world, has been among the most important actors pushing globalization forward. Indeed, simultaneously promoting and responding to globalization have been among the mainsprings of EU actions for nearly three decades. The EU has thus participated in shaping globalization as a policy-maker and as an oft-perplexed reactor to the processes that it has helped shape.

Globalization has fostered large social and technological changes in all wealthier societies, including most EU member-states. Among its many consequences, globalization has helped dualize industrial labor forces. In the immediate post-1945 era, as the EU helped Europe catch up with the United States, its new order was built around relatively permanent, often unionized, and legally protected manufacturing jobs. In recent years, however, the number of such jobs has dramatically declined, replaced by a plethora of less secure jobs and changing individual life-courses that involve multiple employment transitions.

Among the deep causes of this development have been deindustrialization, helped by European losses in market shares of manufactured goods to emerging economies and the capital intensification and technological changes made by European firms in response. This shift, experienced differently across the EU, has created great uncertainty for industrial workers and youth who would have found manufacturing work in the past. What once was a middle class enjoying rising wages, supportive public policies in education, social protection, and labor market regulation, with good prospects for the young, has been shrinking. A connected consequence has been the expansion of very poor workers, employed, often sporadically, in dead-end, low-paid work and inhabiting ghettolike urban conditions, with little hope of improving their conditions. A third change, connected to prior human capital investment changes in the EU as well as globalization, has been the rise of well-educated, upper-middle-class professionals employed in better-paid positions in burgeoning private- and public-service sectors with postindustrial and cosmopolitan values. Finally, EU countries have seen increases in income and wealth inequality similar to those occurring across the Atlantic world, often with the same unsettling political effects.

Is Demography Destiny?

During this same recent period, Europe's demographic situation has become another challenge. Europe's population, as a relative percentage of the world's population, is in rapid decline, which also correlates with its declining share in global GDP. The median age of Europeans is now 45, the oldest in any of the world's major regions—that is, Europe is rapidly aging. This trend is already straining overloaded public health care and pension programs, while also limiting productivity and GDP growth. Theoretically, Europeans might counteract it were they willing to accept higher levels of immigration from outside, but they have increasingly resisted this.

Politics in Comparative Perspective

Such very large sociological shifts in the EU have coincided with political and ideological changes. In insecure and threatened parts of what was once the working class, there are widespread feelings of having been left behind and abandoned by political elites, creating fertile ground for ambitious populists, whose political stock in trade is scapegoating. Anti-immigrant and nationalist xenophobia and disbelief in the motives and ideas of elites thus abound, challenging the credibility of the democratic representation central to social cohesion.

Political elites, even when they so desire, have difficulty devising successful policies to cope with recent social changes. Perhaps more important, neoliberalism has come to color the outlooks of these elites, including an embrace of strong market fundamentalism, the belief that political interference in market mechanisms, even to anticipate or correct market failure, will limit growth, and the belief that those who win deserve their reward and that those who do not deserve their fate.

Among the most tangible consequences of globalization and social and ideological change in the EU has been energetic advocacy of reform of the social models that EU members painstakingly built after World War II, which brought universal health care, pensions that afforded dignity to older citizens, policies that aided families to thrive, expanded public education, and protected labor markets. These deeply institutionalized social-policy projects have been challenged by leaders who cite the economic problems that they allegedly produce and their programmatic deficiencies.

In particular, leaders often invoke the need for greater flexibility to confront globalization. Liberalizing reforms have made progress in EU member-states, although they have varied widely from place to place; however, many citizens whose lives have been affected by such reforms see them as threatening. Decisions about reforms have mainly been national because the EU division of labor leaves most social policy matters in national hands, and the backlash has been mostly national as a result. The EU has also sometimes taken up the reform cause in progressive ways, as in the Delors and Lisbon strategy years, in anticipation that without such ways, citizens' lives in globalization could prove very difficult indeed.

But more recently, the EU has been less progressive in these areas, while continuing to be a powerful agent promoting globalization. Many regard European integration as responsible for what they experience as security-threatening innovations. This distrust has been reinforced by the sometimes unsettling effects of intra-European immigration following the EU's commitment to the free movement of people within the single market and Europe's more general opening to immigrants and different cultures.

These many challenges help account for the political changes occurring in and around the EU today. At the member-state level, Europe's traditional governing parties have become—indeed, have had to become—economic governance intermediaries for globalization, alienating many, including earlier supporters, and opening space for antiglobalization and anti-EU mobilization. The EU's recent crises have made this already volatile situation much worse.

If the storm of crises lets up, there may be renewed stability, perhaps on different grounds. On the other hand, there also may be even more problems for the EU. The EU's near neighborhood, recently seen as fertile ground for soft-power EU seduction, has become a hotbed of new threats, including the refugee crisis, terrorism, and, on its eastern edges, Russian provocations. Turkey has turned from being a promising candidate for EU membership to authoritarianism, and its deal with the EU to help control refugee flows in exchange for billions of euros and new EU concessions could collapse at any moment. And U.S. president Donald Trump's "America First" position, which he has stated in sharply mercantilist, nationalist, antimultilateral, and occasionally anti-EU, terms, gives comfort to Euroskeptic forces in Europe. The world beyond the EU has become more unpredictable, compounding the challenges facing European integration.

The EU: Summary and Prospects

The EU is unquestionably one of the most creative projects to emerge in the aftermath of World War II. It was designed by farsighted statesmen to reconfigure a Westphalian state system that led to unimaginable bloodbaths in the twentieth century. The approach originally chosen was the transnationalization of key dimensions of economic governance through unique new institutions. One hope was that cooperation on economic matters would be understood by member-states in the midst of postwar reconstruction as necessitated by the otherwise uncompetitive nature of small national markets. A second hope was that cooperation would spread beyond economic matters into broader, more political, areas.

The project, on balance, has been more successful than its founders could have hoped. Economic growth and innovation, in large part stimulated by European cooperation, have led to greater prosperity and positive social change, and its attractiveness has led to today's much-enlarged EU. It has also been controversial because it has repeatedly challenged deep national identities and interests, and because EU institutions have rarely been able to achieve the popularity and legitimacy that the project has needed. In large part, this failure occurred because of the difficult-to-achieve necessity of finding intergovernmental agreement and popular consensus.

The project has also been pursued within larger international systems that are difficult to anticipate and control. This has meant that the EU has repeatedly been challenged to change, like it or not, because of large shifts in the world around it. In recent years, its difficulties have grown, in part because citizens have come to take for granted the EU's past achievements while finding it more difficult to accept its new proposals, and in part because the EU has itself grown larger and more complicated and because politics at the member-state level seem to be changing in ways unfavorable to greater transnational cooperation.

It will take time to understand these deeper trends. In the meantime, a troubled EU must confront its uncertainties. The European Commission, in the thick of the fray and reflecting on Europe's interests, needs, and hopes, prepared a *White Paper on the Future of Europe* for the EU's sixtieth anniversary (EU 2017), one of whose merits is sober recognition that the EU is at a crossroads and faces large new choices. In particular, it discusses possible scenarios for the near future. The first, "Carrying On" (perhaps better titled "Muddling Through"), is not up to the present difficult situation. Even if it would not shake things up, something more (or at least different) is needed. The second, "Nothing But the Single Market," would retreat to core areas because the EU "cannot agree to do anything more in many policy areas." Choosing it would make "decision-making . . . easier to understand but [the] capacity to act collectively is limited," perhaps leading toward increased bilateral negotiating between member-states on many issues. Scenario 4, "Doing Less More Efficiently," involves a clearer division between the responsibilities of the EU and member-states that could help citizens to understand the EU better, help alleviate legitimacy problems, and limit persistent blame-shifting and EU-bashing. The fifth, "Doing Much More Together"—that is, more federalism—includes completing the single markets for energy, digital policy matters, and services, strengthening federal enforcement, consolidating the Eurozone, more social policy, systematic management of borders and asylum, beefed up counterterrorism, greater foreign policy unity, a defense union, and increasing the EU's budget. But these goals are unrealistic because of the obvious absence of member-state and citizen political will to achieve them.

The third scenario, "Those Who Want to Do More," is the one that the Commission prefers (though technically it is supposed to conceal its preferences). In it, EU single-market and trade activities remain more or less the same, but there could be a multi-speed approach in other areas, where shifting groups of EU members coordinate more closely depending on the issue. One involves the EMU, where a group might deepen its cooperation in taxation, budgets, and social policy. Another group might cooperate more fully on security, migration, and justice issues. The Commission suggests the possibility of yet another group deepening cooperation on defense, particularly on military coordination and joint equipment. Finally, it notes that some might make additional budgetary contributions in areas where they want to do more.

Such a multispeed future would make EU decision making more difficult to understand. Unspoken, but underlying the Commission's text, is that there is already some "variable geometry" within the EU. The EMU and the Schengen area have their advantages and disadvantages, for example, but neither contains all member states and the EU treaties already in place allow groups of member-states to move ahead through enhanced cooperation. Given a historically, politically, and economically diverse EU membership of twenty-eight (soon perhaps twenty-seven) countries, multispeed arrangements could make a lot of sense, provided that astute institutional ways to accomplish them could be devised.

Finally, hidden in the white paper is the hope that if and when groups of like-minded member-states agreed to move ahead, holdouts would eventually be eager to jump on the bandwagon. Whether this scenario, or any of the others in this paper, will allow the EU to thrive in the difficult conditions stretching into the future is anyone's guess. The EU will certainly survive because its institutions and policies are so deeply intertwined with those of it member-states. However, it has always had larger ambitions than surviving.

Where Do You Stand?

Enlargement of the EU to include almost all European countries, ex-communist central and eastern European ones in particular, was bound to bring new difficulties. What are the most important of these difficulties, how has the EU responded to them, and how well have these responses worked?

The Eurozone crisis has left the EU in a difficult situation. EU member states are at odds, many citizens are unhappy, and economic conditions are not promising. How might the EU rekindle public enthusiasm for the cause of integration?

Key Terms

Citizen initiative
Common Foreign and Security
  Policy (CFSP)
Community Method
Economic and Monetary Union
  (EMU)
European Central Bank (ECB)

European Commission
European Council
European single market
European Union Court of Justice
  (EUCJ)
Institutional triangle
Justice and Home Affairs (JHA)

Single European Act (SEA)
Lisbon Treaty 2009
Maastricht Treaty
Qualified majority voting
  (QMV)
Schengen Area
Subsidiarity

Suggested Readings

Brunnermeir, Markus K, Harold James, and Jean-Pierre Landau. *The Euro and the Battle of Ideas*. Princeton, NJ: Princeton University Press, 2016.

Cini, Michelle, and Nieves Perez-Solorzano Borragan. *European Union Politics*, 4th ed. Oxford, U.K.: Oxford University Press, 2016.

Dinan, Desmond. *Europe Recast*. 2nd ed. Boulder, CO: Lynne Rienner, 2014.

Dinan, Desmond, Neill Nugent, and William E. Paterson, eds. *The European Union in Crisis*. London: Palgrave, 2017.

European Commission. *White Paper on the Future of Europe: Reflections and Scenarios for the EU 27 by 2025*. Brussels: European Commission, 2017.

Matthijs, Mathias and Mark Blyth, eds. *The Future of the Euro*. Oxford, U.K.: Oxford University Press, 2015.

Ross, George. *The European Union and Its Crises, Through the Eyes of the Brussels Elite*. Houndsmills, U.K.: Palgrave Macmillan, 2011.

Ross, George. *Jacques Delors and European Integration*. Cambridge, U.K.: Polity, 1995.

Ther, Philipp. *Europe Since 1989: A History*. Princeton, NJ: Princeton University Press, 2016.

Tsoukalis, Loukas. *Can the European Union Be Saved?* Oxford, U.K.: Oxford University Press, 2016.

Wallace, Helen, Mark A. Pollack, and Alasdair Young, eds. *Policy-Making in the European Union*, 7th ed. New York: Oxford University Press, 2015.

Suggested Websites

Delegation of the European Commission to the United States
www.eurunion.org

European Union, official Brussels site
www.europa.eu

Bruegel, good source on EU economics
www.bruegel.org

The EUobserver, an excellent daily EU bulletin from a centrist-liberal group in the EP
www.EUObserver.com

Notre Europe-Institut Jacques Delors (Paris); includes many documents in English
www.notre-europe.eu

Japan

Shigeko Fukai and Haruhiro Fukui

Official Name: Japan

Location: Eastern Asia

Capital City: Tokyo

Population (2016): 126.7 million

Size: 377,930 sq. km.; slightly smaller than California

THE MAKING OF THE MODERN JAPANESE STATE

Politics in Action

- How did the timing and circumstances surrounding Japan's entry into the world of modern states influence its domestic politics and foreign policy in the late nineteenth and early twentieth centuries?

- Which watershed events in Japanese history are particularly relevant to understanding government and politics in contemporary Japan?

The 2016 parliamentary election in Japan and presidential election in the United States may have set in motion a chain of events of immense historical significance, both within and outside each country. For Japan, such events include the first-ever revision of its unique constitution.

Every constitution is unique in one respect or another, as is every country. Japan's constitution, however, may be said to be more unique than any other in three respects: First, it was written largely by a few American lawyers while Japan was under the U.S.-led Allied Occupation in the wake of World War II; second, one of its articles (Article 9) denies Japan not only the right to ever use armed force to settle international disputes, but also even the right to maintain military forces or fight a war; and, third, it has never been revised since its enactment seven decades ago. It is thus not only an "Occupation-imposed" constitution, but also the most radically pacifist, and the oldest unamended national charter in the world. Governed by this extraordinary constitution, postwar Japan has enjoyed its own "Long Peace" and prosperity, largely thanks to its alliance with the United States, which, with American preponderant military power, guaranteed its security against potential external threat. Since the 1950s, this unique constitution has nonetheless been subject to sustained attacks by Japan's right-wing nationalists, represented by a group of leaders from the Liberal Democratic Party (LDP), which despite its name is a conservative political party that has governed Japan for most of the postwar period.

As discussed in Section 3, their efforts to amend the document (especially Article 9) have failed so far primarily due to their inability, until the summer of 2016, to win the constitutionally required support of a two-thirds majority in both houses of the Diet, Japan's parliament, and a majority in a subsequent public referendum. The LDP and its conservative allies have had control of well over two-thirds of the House of Representatives (the lower house) since 2012, but won a comparable supermajority in the House of Councillors (the upper house) for the first time only in 2016. Public opinion was generally in favor of amending some articles, except Article 9, or adding some new articles to the constitution. In the second half of 2016, the revisionists were thus on the cusp of attaining part of their decades-old goal, but not their key objective—the amendment of Article 9.

By coincidence, the 2016 U.S. presidential election ended in the surprise victory of Donald Trump, an "America First" businessman, who suggested during his election campaign that Japan was getting a free ride for its own security by depending on U.S. military power, and that if it was unwilling to pay a much higher share of the cost of this valuable benefit, it should be ready to defend itself, perhaps with its own nuclear weapons. To many inside and outside the Japanese government, this implied potential abandonment by Japan's most important trading partner and only military ally, while, to some right-wing nationalists, it must have sounded like a potential godsend for pushing the amendment of Article 9.

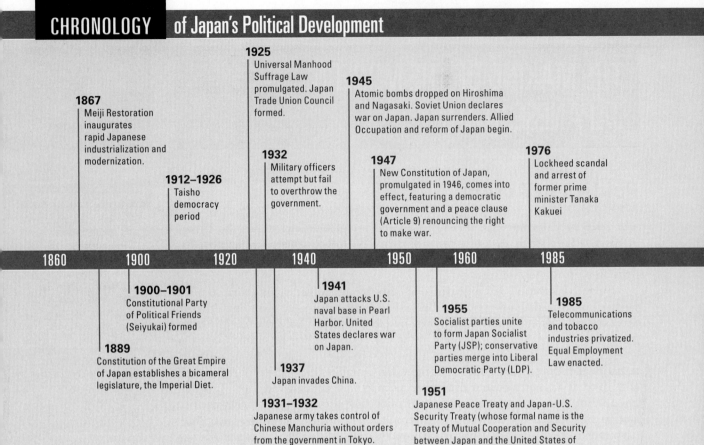

1867 | Meiji Restoration inaugurates rapid Japanese industrialization and modernization.

1912–1926 | Taisho democracy period

1925 | Universal Manhood Suffrage Law promulgated. Japan Trade Union Council formed.

1932 | Military officers attempt but fail to overthrow the government.

1945 | Atomic bombs dropped on Hiroshima and Nagasaki. Soviet Union declares war on Japan. Japan surrenders. Allied Occupation and reform of Japan begin.

1947 | New Constitution of Japan, promulgated in 1946, comes into effect, featuring a democratic government and a peace clause (Article 9) renouncing the right to make war.

1976 | Lockheed scandal and arrest of former prime minister Tanaka Kakuei

1860   1900   1920   1940   1950   1960   1985

1889 | Constitution of the Great Empire of Japan establishes a bicameral legislature, the Imperial Diet.

1900–1901 | Constitutional Party of Political Friends (Seiyukai) formed

1931–1932 | Japanese army takes control of Chinese Manchuria without orders from the government in Tokyo.

1937 | Japan invades China.

1941 | Japan attacks U.S. naval base in Pearl Harbor. United States declares war on Japan.

1951 | Japanese Peace Treaty and Japan-U.S. Security Treaty (whose formal name is the Treaty of Mutual Cooperation and Security between Japan and the United States of America) signed in San Francisco

1955 | Socialist parties unite to form Japan Socialist Party (JSP); conservative parties merge into Liberal Democratic Party (LDP).

1985 | Telecommunications and tobacco industries privatized. Equal Employment Law enacted.

This turn of events may significantly change the current pattern of Japanese politics and foreign relations. (See Table 6.1 on page 234.)

Geographic Setting

Japan is an archipelago of about 6,850 islands lying off the east coast of Eurasia. To its west, across the Sea of Japan, it faces the Russian Far East and North and South Korea, and, across the East China Sea, the central coast of China. To the east, across more than 5,000 miles of the Pacific Ocean, lie the west coasts of the United States and northern Mexico. Japan's northernmost and southernmost cities lie due west of Portland, Oregon, and Isla Margarita Island in Baja California, Mexico, respectively.

The Japanese archipelago covers a land area of about 146,000 square miles. A total of 97 percent of the land area sits within four islands—Honshu, Hokkaido, Kyushu, and Shikoku. The nation is slightly smaller than California and slightly larger than Montana. With about 127 million people, it is the tenth most populous country in the world and about ten times as densely populated as the United States. A little less than two-thirds of the population lives in 260 cities with a population of 100,000 or more, about half of them in eleven cities with 1 million or more residents apiece.

Nearly all Japanese are descendants of immigrants from today's Southeast Asia, South Pacific islands, Siberia, China, and Korea, who arrived in a series of waves and

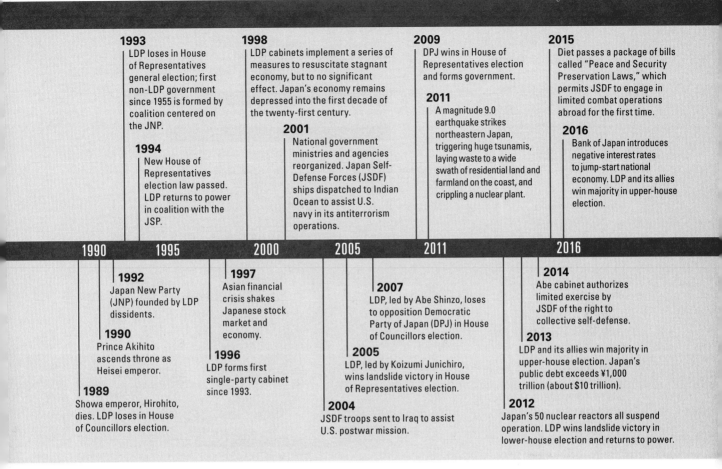

1993
LDP loses in House of Representatives general election; first non-LDP government since 1955 is formed by coalition centered on the JNP.

1994
New House of Representatives election law passed. LDP returns to power in coalition with the JSP.

1998
LDP cabinets implement a series of measures to resuscitate stagnant economy, but to no significant effect. Japan's economy remains depressed into the first decade of the twenty-first century.

2001
National government ministries and agencies reorganized. Japan Self-Defense Forces (JSDF) ships dispatched to Indian Ocean to assist U.S. navy in its antiterrorism operations.

2009
DPJ wins in House of Representatives election and forms government.

2011
A magnitude 9.0 earthquake strikes northeastern Japan, triggering huge tsunamis, laying waste to a wide swath of residential land and farmland on the coast, and crippling a nuclear plant.

2015
Diet passes a package of bills called "Peace and Security Preservation Laws," which permits JSDF to engage in limited combat operations abroad for the first time.

2016
Bank of Japan introduces negative interest rates to jump-start national economy. LDP and its allies win majority in upper-house election.

1990   1995   2000   2005   2011   2016

1992
Japan New Party (JNP) founded by LDP dissidents.

1990
Prince Akihito ascends throne as Heisei emperor.

1989
Showa emperor, Hirohito, dies. LDP loses in House of Councillors election.

1997
Asian financial crisis shakes Japanese stock market and economy.

1996
LDP forms first single-party cabinet since 1993.

2007
LDP, led by Abe Shinzo, loses to opposition Democratic Party of Japan (DPJ) in House of Councillors election.

2005
LDP, led by Koizumi Junichiro, wins landslide victory in House of Representatives election.

2004
JSDF troops sent to Iraq to assist U.S. postwar mission.

2014
Abe cabinet authorizes limited exercise by JSDF of the right to collective self-defense.

2013
LDP and its allies win majority in upper-house election. Japan's public debt exceeds ¥1,000 trillion (about $10 trillion).

2012
Japan's 50 nuclear reactors all suspend operation. LDP wins landslide victory in lower-house election and returns to power.

trickles beginning about 35,000 years ago, mostly during the period when the sea levels were about 300 feet below present levels, and the land that is today's Japan was connected by land with most of its neighboring regions and countries (Figure 6.1). The immigrants from these diverse sources and their descendants have intermingled and interbred to produce the genetically heterogeneous, but culturally largely homogeneous, people of contemporary Japan.

Critical Junctures

Premodern Japan

Recent scientific research, popularly known as "genetic tracking," shows that the Japanese archipelago began to be populated by immigrants from the surrounding areas, originally beachcombers, hunters, and gatherers, as early as 38000 BCE, during the last glacial period. By about 7000 BCE, some inhabitants began to build and live in small settlements and raise livestock. In the third century BCE, newly arrived immigrants from Korea and China began to build much larger settlements, or proto-states, in the southwestern regions of the country. Over the next several centuries, most of these proto-states were unified into a single state led by an "emperor" who claimed to be a descendant of a mythical Sun Goddess, which was obviously derived

Japan: Ethnic Groups

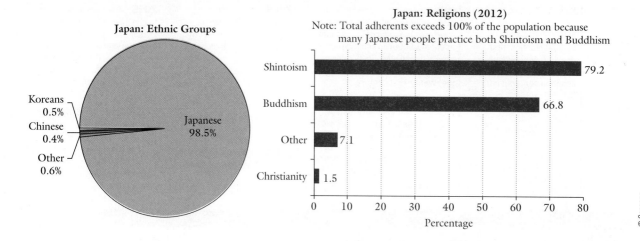

Koreans 0.5%
Chinese 0.4%
Other 0.6%
Japanese 98.5%

Japan: Religions (2012)

Note: Total adherents exceeds 100% of the population because many Japanese people practice both Shintoism and Buddhism

Religion	Percentage
Shintoism	79.2
Buddhism	66.8
Other	7.1
Christianity	1.5

© Cengage

Japanese Currency: Yen (¥)
International Designation: JPY
Exchange Rate (2017):
- US$ 1 = ¥109.4
- ¥1 = US$0.01

10,000¥ Note Design: Fukuzawa Yukichi (1834-1901), Meiji period author, educator, publisher, and translator who was influential in spreading Western ideas to Japan.

© Takeshi Nishio/Shutterstock.com

FIGURE 6.1 The Japanese Nation at a Glance

from the rulers of ancient China. This led to the founding of the world's oldest surviving monarchy.

Early Japanese rulers frequently sent emissaries to China, often via Korea, to pay homage to its emperors, and they returned with a variety of goods and ideas. These included the teachings of the Chinese philosopher, Confucius (551–479 BCE), who exhorted reverence for ancestors and deference to authority—ideas that have had enduring impacts on Japanese society and politics. Buddhism, with its origins in India, also reached Japan via China and Korea in the mid-sixth century. Commingled with the native Japanese religion, Shinto, Confucianism and Buddhism continue to shape Japanese people's everyday life.

A succession of emperors (and a few empresses), or their regents, ruled the ancient and early medieval Japanese state from a capital in a western region of the country, present-day Nara and Kyoto until the late twelfth century, when they began to lose effective control of both the territory and the people to local landlords with armed farmers in their employ, who over time grew into professional warriors. A few of them became powerful warlords, with their own vassals. This gave rise to a Japanese version of medieval feudalism at the same time as, and very similar to, its European counterpart. Over the next few centuries, some of these warlords appropriated the title of **shogun** (general), claiming to be the emperor's military guardians.[1] In the early seventeenth century, one of these shoguns, Tokugawa Ieyasu,* established a

shogun

The title, meaning "general," assumed by a succession of hereditary leaders of the three military dynasties—the Minamotos, the Ashikagas, and the Tokugawas—that ruled Japan from the late twelfth century to the mid-nineteenth century. Their government was called the shogunate.

_____

*In Japanese, the family name comes before the personal or given name.

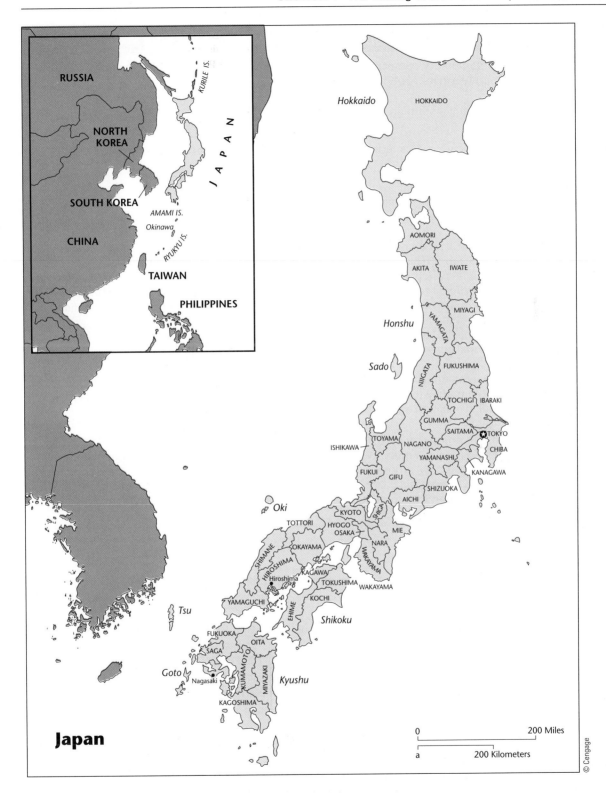

Japan

Table 6.1	Political Organization
Political System	Parliamentary democracy and constitutional monarchy, in which the emperor is merely a symbol of national unity.
Regime History	Current constitution promulgated in 1946 and in effect since 1947.
Administrative Structure	Unitary state, 47 intermediate-level subnational "prefectures," and 1,740 municipalities.
Executive	Prime minister selected by legislature; a cabinet of about twenty ministers appointed by prime minister.
Legislature	Bicameral. The upper house (House of Councillors) has 242 members elected for 6-year terms. Half of the members are elected every 3 years. 146 are elected from multiple-seat, prefecture-wide districts; 96 are elected nationally by a party list proportional representation method. The lower-house (House of Representatives) has 475 members elected for 4-year terms, which may be shortened by the dissolution of the house. 295 lower-house members are elected from single-seat constituencies; 180 are elected by party list proportional representation from eleven regional constituencies.
Judiciary	Supreme Court has fourteen judges appointed by the cabinet and the chief judge nominated by the cabinet and appointed by the emperor; all are eligible to serve until 70 years of age, subject to periodic popular reviews.
Party System	Stable one-party dominant (Liberal Democratic Party) system from mid-1950s to mid-1990s, a quasi-two-party from 2007 to 2012, predominant-party (Liberal Democratic Party-Komeito coalition) since. Major parties: Liberal Democratic Party, Democratic Party of Japan, Clean Government Party, Social Democratic Party, Japan Communist Party, Nippon Ishin no Kai (aka Japan Restoration Party).

military government, or shogunate, in the new capital city of Edo (today's Tokyo), which lasted for the next 265 years. Figurehead emperors were left to reside in the old capital, Kyoto.

These events took place largely in isolation from developments in the rest of the world, thanks to Japan's insular location. The isolation, however, was seriously broken twice in the mid-sixteenth century by the arrivals, first, of a couple of Portuguese sailors in possession of guns on a Chinese ship stranded on an island off the coast of Kyushu, and then, of a Spanish Jesuit missionary, Francis Xavier. The former event introduced the Japanese to the cutting-edge weapon of the era and led to the production of a half million local copies in the next few decades, while the second event ushered in a "Japan's Christian Century," when an estimated 130,000 Japanese were converted to Christianity.

Under the Tokugawa shogunate's iron-fisted rule, however, Japan was closed almost completely to the outside world by government order. The production and possession of guns, a potential source of physical threat to the ruling regime, were strictly regulated, and Christianity, a potential source of spiritual threat to the regime, was banned. The nation was divided into about 300 feudal domains, each under a local lord's rule and all under the shogunate's control. Within each domain, the people were divided into six classes—warriors, farmers, artisans, merchants, "filthy hordes," and "nonhumans." Warriors, called **samurai (or bushi)** in Japanese, made up about 8 percent of the total population and constituted a substratum of the ruling class. The last two classes were "outcast" groups. Members of the several classes were strictly segregated from each other, both occupationally and residentially. Women were treated as inherently inferior and subordinate to men and could not participate in public events. Most children from samurai families—and increasingly those of well-to-do farmers and merchants—received rudimentary school education. In addition to reading, writing, and arithmetic, they learned Confucian teachings about the correct social order and proper personal behavior.[2]

Meiji Restoration and Taisho Democracy (1868–1925)

In 1867, a widespread insurrection toppled the Tokugawa regime, an event triggered by the forced entry in 1853 and 1854 of a small flotilla of U.S. warships under the command of Commodore Matthew C. Perry into the Edo Bay. This violated the centuries-old official ban on the entry of foreigners into the Japanese territory, with the exception of authorized Chinese, Korean, Ryukyuan (Okinawan), and Dutch merchants. The shogun capitulated to Commodore Perry's demand that Japan open its ports to U.S. naval and merchant ships. This gave anti-Tokugawa local lords and their followers an excuse to revolt against the shogunate, ostensibly to defend national honor and integrity.

The rebels installed a young heir to the imperial throne as the nation's new ruler and moved him and his court to Edo, which was renamed Tokyo ("eastern capital"). His reign was named Meiji ("enlightened rule"), and the insurrection came to be known as the "Meiji Restoration." Over the next 50 years, Japan's government was led by a small group of erstwhile rebels and their friends, dubbed the "Meiji Oligarchy," who quickly transformed a feudal state into a modern industrial and military power.

The Meiji government replaced the feudal domains by prefectures and simplified the social class system. The samurai class was nominally retained, while farmers, artisans, and merchants were lumped into a single "commoner" class, and those in the two outcast categories became a "new commoner" class. A national public education system, composed of compulsory primary school and voluntary secondary school and college, was introduced, opening new avenues for all citizens to improve their life opportunities on the basis of knowledge and academic performance regardless of their family background or social status.

The democratic idea was introduced into Japan for the first time and gave rise to a "freedom and people's rights" movement, led by two proto-political parties, the Liberals and the Reformists. In 1889, the oligarchy responded to their demand by issuing a constitution modeled after Prussia's and establishing a bicameral legislature, the Imperial Diet. The upper house, the House of Peers, consisted of hereditary and appointed members, such as adult male members of the imperial family, former feudal lords, and men credited with distinguished service to the state. The lower house, the House of Representatives, was elected by an all-male electorate of top-bracket taxpayers, who initially accounted for only a little over 1 percent of Japan's total population, rising to about 5.5 percent by the early 1920s.

The 1889 constitution guaranteed civil rights and freedoms to the people "subject to the limitations imposed by law" and required every law to be enacted with the

samurai

The warrior class in medieval Japan, also known as "*bushi*." The class emerged around the tenth century, and a dominant band of its members established Japan's first warrior government in the twelfth century. The last samurai government was overthrown in the Meiji Restoration of the mid-nineteenth century.

consent of the Imperial Diet. But the emperor had the right to approve and issue all laws; open, close, and adjourn the Diet; and declare war, make peace, and conclude international treaties. In his name, the oligarchy ruled the nation through several nonelective institutions, such as the Privy Council, the House of Peers, and the civil and military services.

During the reign of the Meiji emperor's successor, the Taisho ("great righteousness") emperor, a period known as **Taisho democracy** (roughly 1912–1926), Japan made significant progress in political liberalization, Two political parties, Seiyukai (Constitutional Party of Political Friends) and Kenseito (Constitutional Government Party), alternately formed a government through electoral competition. A Universal Manhood Suffrage Law was enacted in 1925, removing the tax payment requirement for the vote and quadrupling the size of the electorate (males over the age of 25) to about 20 percent of the total population.

Rise and Fall of Militarist Nationalism (1926–1945)

Despite these important political changes, Taisho democracy was fundamentally superficial and fragile. Sharp class inequalities still divided Japanese society. Rural Japan was dominated by a small class of wealthy landlords and urban Japan by a few giant industrial and financial conglomerates, known as *zaibatsu*. The government bureaucracy was controlled by graduates of a single government-run university, the present-day University of Tokyo. As the Japanese economy became mired in a long recession after World War I, and then was devastated by the Great Depression in the early 1930s, advocates of democracy at home and peace abroad increasingly faced savage attacks by the military and ultranationalist civilian groups.

Japan's victories in the Sino-Japanese War (1894–1895) and the Russo-Japanese War (1904–1905) had substantially boosted the military's political influence. Under the new Showa ("enlightened peace") emperor's reign, which began in 1926, the Japanese army invaded, and then occupied, northern Chinese provinces and created a puppet state called Manchukuo in 1932.[3] In that same year, a group of young naval officers attacked several government offices in Tokyo and shot the prime minister to death in an abortive coup d'état. In a similar attempt in February 1936, bands of army soldiers murdered the finance minister and several others and occupied a whole block in central Tokyo for four days.[4] These events intimidated and silenced most opponents of the military, both inside and outside the government. All political parties were effectively muzzled and then disbanded by government order in 1941.

When the League of Nations condemned the Japanese invasion of China in 1933, Japan walked out of the organization. Faced with growing international isolation, Japan formed a military alliance with Nazi Germany in 1936, joined by fascist Italy the following year. In the summer of 1937, the Japanese army began a full-scale invasion of China and, the following winter, unleashed a murderous rampage against civilians in the capital city, an incident now known as the "Rape of Nanking." The United States responded by nullifying its trade agreement with Japan in 1939. Cut off from a major source of raw materials essential to the survival of its industrial economy, Japan moved its troops into French Indochina (Vietnam, Laos, and Cambodia) in July 1941 in search of alternative sources of supplies. In response, Washington froze Japanese-owned assets in the United States and banned the sale of oil to Japan.

Taisho democracy

A reference to Japanese politics in the period roughly coinciding with Emperor Taisho's reign, 1912–1926. The period was characterized by the rise of a popular movement for democratization of government by the introduction of universal manhood suffrage and the reduction of the power and influence of authoritarian institutions of the state.

zaibatsu

Giant holding companies in pre–World War II Japan, each owned and controlled by a particular family. The largest of these were divided into a number of independent firms during the post–World War II Occupation, but many were later revived as *keiretsu*, although no longer under the control of any of the original founding families.

Faced with the prospect of running out of its limited fuel reserve, the Japanese government, now led by General Tojo Hideki, decided to start a war against the United States. On December 7, 1941, Japanese naval air units executed a carefully planned surprise attack on the U.S. naval base at Pearl Harbor in Hawaii. The United States immediately declared war on Japan.

Japan had some notable military successes early in the war but soon began to lose one major battle after another in the Pacific Ocean. By late 1944, its effort was reduced to a desperate attempt to defend its homeland from increasingly frequent and devastating air raids by U.S. bombers. In August 1945, Japan's resistance ended when the first atomic bombs used in war annihilated two of its major cities, Hiroshima and Nagasaki. On August 15, Japan surrendered unconditionally to the Allied powers.

The Birth and Evolution of a Pacifist Democracy (1945–Present)

The Allied Occupation of Japan transformed an authoritarian militarist state into a pacifist democracy.[5] The occupation, which lasted from 1945 to 1952, was formally a joint undertaking by the major Allies: the United States, the British Commonwealth, the Soviet Union, and China. In practice, the United States, represented by General Douglas MacArthur acting as the **Supreme Commander for the Allied Powers (SCAP)**, played the predominant role.

During the first year and a half of the Occupation, SCAP pursued twin central goals: the complete demilitarization and democratization of Japan. The Japanese armed forces were swiftly dismantled, military production was halted, and wartime

Supreme Commander for the Allied Powers (SCAP)

The official title of General Douglas MacArthur between 1945 and 1951 when he led the Allied Occupation of Japan.

AP Images/Stanley Troutman

Hiroshima in the wake of the atomic bombing in August 1945.

leaders were either arrested or purged from public office. Seven of them, including General Tojo, were executed for war crimes. Militaristic and antidemocratic institutions and practices were banned. At the same time, workers' right to organize was recognized and women were given the vote. Only the government bureaucracy was left largely intact to administer the nation on SCAP's behalf.

The authoritarian Meiji Constitution was replaced by a democratic constitution drafted by a handful of American lawyers. The new constitution granted the emperor a purely symbolic role and transferred all his political powers to the people and their elected representatives. It also made the bicameral Diet the state's sole lawmaking body. All its members, including those in the reorganized and renamed upper house, the House of Councillors, were to be directly elected by the people. Article 9, known as the "peace clause," defined the new Japan as a permanently disarmed pacifist nation.

The Allied powers and Japan signed a peace treaty in September 1951, in the midst of the Korean War. The United States and Japan signed a bilateral security treaty at the same time, which allowed the United States to keep its military bases in Japan, an arrangement renewed in 1960 and still in place today. As an adjunct to the U.S. military, a quasi-military force of Japan's own, originally named the National Police Reserve and subsequently renamed the Japan Self-Defense Forces (JSDF), was created and has since grown into a full-fledged, but so far strictly defensive, military force of some 250,000 troops.

Japan Self-Defense Forces (JSDF)

Inaugurated in Japan as a police reserve with 75,000 recruits in August 1950, following the outbreak of the Korean War. Today, it consists of approximately 250,000 troops equipped with sophisticated modern weapons.

In 1960, the revision and extension of the Japan-U.S. Security Treaty proposed by Prime Minister Kishi Nobusuke's cabinet provoked fierce opposition, both in the Diet and in the streets of Tokyo and other major cities. The opponents warned that the treaty would make Japan a semipermanent military dependency of the United States and an enemy of Japan's closer neighbors, China and the Soviet Union. The government of the LDP nonetheless rammed the revised treaty through the Diet, an action that provoked such a violent public reaction that President Dwight D. Eisenhower's scheduled state visit to Japan was canceled and the Kishi cabinet resigned.

The experience of the 1960 political crisis led Kishi's successors to avoid controversial constitutional and security policy issues and concentrate on economic issues. This change in the LDP's strategy ushered in a quarter-century of political stability and phenomenal economic growth, until, in the late 1980s, a huge speculative bubble in the nation's real estate and stock markets burst, plunging the nation into a deep and long recession. Despite repeated government interventions to jump-start the stagnant economy over the next three decades, the nation remains mired in an interminable slump to this day.

The Four Themes and Japan

Japan in a Globalized World of States

The modern world that Japan joined in the late nineteenth century appeared to its leaders to be divided between economically and technologically advanced and militarily powerful Western imperialist nations on one hand, and less developed, weaker, and often-conquered non-Western nations, on the other. To survive in such a world as an independent nation, Japan had to quickly catch up with and join the first group of states. Meiji Japan did so, emerging by the late 1920s as the first modern Asian power. A little over a decade later, it even felt strong enough to launch a war against the United States. The devastating experience of the war, however, led most Japanese to abandon their faith in military force as a means of their nation's survival and to seek peaceful international cooperation as a better alternative.

Postwar Japan joined the United Nations (UN) in 1956. It has been elected a nonpermanent member of the Security Council eleven times since 1958. It has also been the second-largest contributor, next to the United States, to the operating budgets of not only the United Nations, but also the International Monetary Fund (IMF) and the World Bank. In the Asia-Pacific region, it has been the largest contributor to the Asian Development Bank (ADB) and provided all its presidents. It is a founding member and a major promoter of the Asia-Pacific Economic Cooperation (APEC) forum and an active supporter of the Association of Southeast Asian Nations (ASEAN).

Governing the Economy

Meiji Japan successfully built a modern industrial economy virtually from scratch, thanks importantly to careful and comprehensive strategic planning and guidance by the state, an approach later named **industrial policy**. This approach was spectacularly successful not only in pre–World War II Japan, but also in postwar Japan, and has been copied by many other nations. The policy, however, ceased to work in the increasingly globalized world of the late twentieth and early twenty-first centuries.

industrial policy

A policy that uses state resources to promote the development of particular economic sectors.

The Democratic Idea

Japanese encountered the idea of democracy for the first time during the early Meiji period in the mid-nineteenth century. Once the nation was exposed to the idea, a number of groups around the nation began to call for the creation of political institutions embodying the idea. The Meiji oligarchy responded to their demand by, first, creating a system of partially elective prefectural legislatures (assemblies), then promulgating a Western-style constitution and instituting a partially elective national legislature, the Imperial Diet.

Japan thus entered the twentieth century as a formally constitutional monarchy with national and local legislatures and multiple vocal political parties. Its leaders, as well as most of its people at that time, were far more interested in rapid industrialization and military buildup than in democratic government, and any progress toward democracy was halted when the militarists seized power in the 1930s. Nonetheless, Japan's encounter and experiment with democratic politics in the pre–World War II period prepared the nation for far more serious and successful democratization after the war. The democratic idea has now become a core element of Japanese political culture.

Politics of Collective Identity

Leaders of the ancient Japanese state, all or most of whom had come to the archipelago from Korea, probably due to conflicts back home, claimed their new state to be a land of "the Rising Sun," separate and independent from both Korea and China.

Among common people, however, the sense of a Japanese ethnic or national identity remained weak and poorly articulated until the late thirteenth century, when the nation was attacked twice by naval forces sent via Korea by the Mongolian emperor of China, Kublai Khan. The invasion attempts failed both times, thanks mainly to timely typhoons, which were called "divine winds" and used to create the myth that Japan was a divine and invincible nation. The myth was subsequently systematically and effectively harnessed by leaders of Meiji and early Showa Japan as a means to win popular support for their aggressive foreign and military policies, which eventually led to World War II in the Pacific.

The war devastated the nation not only physically, but also spiritually. However, it did not seriously affect its people's national identity. Despite the presence of a few minority groups with considerable grievances (see Section 4), virtually all Japanese continued to share a deep and strong sense of common national identity and destiny.

Comparisons

In terms of certain geographical features and its historical experiences, Japan shares more with some European nations than with its Asian neighbors. For example, Britain is not only an archipelagic nation like Japan, but also, like Japan, it has been inhabited by humans since about 30,000 years ago. Britain was connected to continental Europe until the end of the Ice Age, as Japan was once connected to mainland Asia. Medieval Japanese feudalism was very similar to medieval Britain's. Both are also old monarchies. Until the eleventh century, however, Britain was repeatedly invaded by peoples from the continent, while Japan was spared such large-scale foreign invasions after the sixth century. These geographical and historical similarities and differences may help explain some aspects of their contemporary political institutions and culture.

Modern Germany, too, resembles modern Japan in some ways. Both entered the modern world at about the same time in the mid-nineteenth century; became a major industrial and military power by the early twentieth century; started and lost World War II; were occupied, disarmed, and democratized by their wartime enemies; and reemerged as two of the postwar world's most economically powerful and politically stable democracies.[6] Postwar Germany has, however, not only made genuine but also durable peace with its neighbors, whom it had invaded, occupied, and brutalized during the war. Postwar Japan, by comparison, has failed to achieve genuine reconciliation with its neighbors, especially China and Korea, whom it had invaded, occupied, and brutalized, and continues to anger and antagonize them to this day. These remarkable similarities and differences may teach us some important lessons about the role of political culture and leadership.

Where Do You Stand?

1. Is Japan an exceptional nation in the modern world? Why or why not?

2. Is Japan a particularly good subject for comparative politics because it is so different from or so similar to some other nations, or both?

POLITICAL ECONOMY AND DEVELOPMENT

State and Economy

Focus Questions ⑦

- In what ways is the historical evolution of the modern Japanese economy unique?

- Why and in what ways has Japan served as a model for other developing nations, particularly for those in East Asia?

The pre–World War II Japanese state with its slogan of "rich country with a strong army" played a central role in achieving rapid industrialization and economic development in the resource-poor nation. The Meiji government founded and operated munitions factories, mines, railroads, telegraph and telephone services, and textile mills, until it sold them at low prices to private entrepreneurs, some of whom later became heads of *zaibatsu* conglomerates.[7] These corporate empires spearheaded the rapid expansion of the Japanese economy, significantly helped by government subsidies, tax breaks, tariff protection, and infrastructure construction.

The Sino-Japanese War (1894–1895) and the Russo-Japanese War (1904–1905) also spurred the growth of Japan's heavy industries. World War I brought about a wartime boom in Japanese exports and left it with a positive trade balance for the first time since the Meiji Restoration in 1868.[8] Thanks also to the entrepreneurial talent and initiative of its business leaders and a highly motivated and increasingly skilled workforce, Japan's economy grew steadily by about 3 percent per year from 1868 through the early twentieth century. In the 1930s, now under nearly total control by the state, it grew at more than 5 percent per year.[9] By the beginning of World War II, Japan had become one of the world's fastest-growing and most competitive economic powers.

Following its defeat in that war, Japan recovered remarkably quickly, thanks largely to the assistance provided by the U.S.-led Occupation in combating the postwar political and social chaos and rebuilding the ruined economy. Such assistance included the donation of a variety of relief goods, policy advice and guidance, and early authorization for the nation to resume foreign trade. Even more important in the long run, however, was a set of economic reforms, including the dissolution of the *zaibatsu* conglomerates and wholesale redistribution of landlord-owned farmland to tenant cultivators. By significantly reducing the concentration of wealth and economic power, these reforms paved the way for a vast expansion of Japan's middle class and domestic consumer markets. The Occupation's demilitarization program freed Japan from the burden of military spending and enabled it to devote its capital, labor, and technology exclusively to the production of civilian goods and services.

After the Occupation ended in 1952, the United States continued to assist Japan's economic recovery by opening its own markets to Japanese exports and granting Japanese firms access to advanced industrial technology developed by U.S. firms. A major reason that the United States was motivated to do this was the shift of the primary objective of U.S. policy toward Japan from its total demilitarization and democratization to its swift incorporation into the anticommunist Cold War bloc in the wake of the communist victory in the Chinese civil war and the outbreak of the Korean War. The World War II archenemy had become a potential key Cold War ally.

The United States also supported Japan's admission to the United Nations, the IMF, the World Bank, and the General Agreement on Tariffs and Trade (GATT), which later became the World Trade Organization (WTO). Membership in these international organizations enabled Japanese manufacturers to gain access to overseas raw materials, merchandise, and capital markets, as well as advanced industrial technologies. Thanks to these circumstances, the Japanese economy grew at an average annual rate of 10 percent from the mid-1950s to the early 1970s, until it became one of the most dynamic and competitive economies in the postwar world.

The Japanese state continued to play the role of patron and guardian for domestic industries, as it had been doing since the Meiji period. Under its wide-ranging industrial policy programs, the government provided investment funds and tax breaks and allocated foreign exchange and foreign technologies to targeted industries. The 1973 oil crisis dealt a severe blow to Japan, which at the time depended on Arab oil for more than three-quarters of its total crude oil imports, and the pace of its economic growth substantially slowed. Prompted by the government, however, the Japanese manufacturing industry shifted its emphasis from the raw materials-intensive sectors, such as chemicals and metals, to the assembly and knowledge-intensive sectors, and managed to substantially reduce its energy consumption.

The production and export of automobiles and electronics subsequently expanded rapidly, thanks importantly to the development of energy-saving and antipollution technologies, such as numerically controlled machine tools and industrial robots. By the 1980s, the surging Japanese exports had made Japan the world's largest creditor nation, and the United States had begun to view Japanese imports as a serious threat to its own industries, leading to "trade war" marked by intense negotiations and often belligerent rhetoric. This led to the 1985 Plaza Accord, a joint decision by representatives of the United States, Japanese, and European finance ministers to bring about a drastic devaluation of the U.S. dollar in order to make Japanese and German exports more expensive and less competitive in international markets.

Alarmed by the potentially crippling effects of the Plaza Accord on the nation's export-driven economy, the Japanese government increased the amount of money in circulation and lowered interest rates, even while trade surpluses continued to increase the money supply. This led many banks and companies to invest in real estate and stocks, giving rise to rampant asset inflation (i.e., a "bubble"). The average price of stocks tripled and the urban land price index quadrupled in the 1985–1989 period. In late 1989, the government belatedly and abruptly tightened lending regulations and raised interest rates. This sudden policy reversal burst the bubble and touched off a protracted recession and deflation, a process in which not only prices decrease (a good thing), but so do profits, production, and wages (bad things)—a situation that continues to this day.

Protection of domestic agriculture is another case of Japan's failed economic policy. Until the early 1990s, Japan maintained a total ban on the import of foreign rice under the pressure of a powerful interest group network, an **iron triangle** (see Section 3) of farmers organized in agricultural cooperatives, Diet members from rural districts, and Ministry of Agriculture bureaucrats. The protection of rice farmers at the expense of crop diversification and changes in people's dietary preferences, such as increased consumption of meat, led to a sharp decline in Japan's calorie-based food self-sufficiency rate from about 80 percent in 1960 to 39 percent in 2015. This is worrisome, as it makes the country vulnerable if international food supplies are for some reason disrupted.

In the financial sector, an informal system of government control known as **administrative guidance** has led the nation's major banks and securities firms to form tight-knit networks of mutual cooperation and assistance, backed by an implicit government commitment to bail out their members in trouble. This so-called convoy system helped weak and uncompetitive financial institutions survive, until many

iron triangle

A term coined by scholars of U.S. politics to refer to the relationships of mutual support formed by particular government agencies, members of congressional committees or subcommittees, and interest groups in various policy areas. Adapted by scholars of Japanese politics, the term refers to similar relationships formed among Japanese ministry or agency officials, Diet members, and special interest groups.

administrative guidance

Informal advice given by a government agency to a private organization, such as a firm, Critics charge that this is a disguised form of collusion between a government agency and a private firm.

of them, saddled with bad loans accumulated in the days of the bubble economy, went bankrupt in the 1990s and early 2000s. Those that survived stopped lending, especially to small businesses, which effectively starved them of investment funds and aggravated the recession. The government set up the Financial Services Agency in 2001 to help banks and securities firms rid themselves of bad loans and begin to lend again. The agency has since mediated a series of bank mergers to create some of the largest financial institutions in the world. These moves, however, have done little to lift Japan out of its recession.

Since being elected in December 2012, the government, led by Prime Minister Abe Shinzo, has been attempting to revive the sick economy through so-called Abenomics, which consists of "three arrows": (1) policies designed to devalue Japan's currency (the yen) and stimulate exports, (2) massive fiscal spending with expanded public works projects and tax breaks for corporations financed with government bonds, and (3) deregulation and structural reforms in wide-ranging areas, including, among others, the labor market, health care, corporate governance, immigration, education, and agriculture. Abenomics thus combines some Keynesian policies, such as expansion of public works, with some neoliberal policies, such as welfare-spending cuts, tax reductions for corporations and the wealthy, and labor market deregulation.

The first arrow seemed to work for a while by driving down the yen's value and boosting exports and big companies' earnings. These gains, however, have not led to an increase in wages or investment in Japan because they were not based on an increase in economic productivity or competitiveness. The second arrow has been shot with the launch of a 30 trillion yen (about $273 billion) fiscal stimulus package, but it has merely repeated the familiar results of the previous stimulus plans tried since the 1990 market crash—few lasting effects on the economy while adding to the already-huge public debt.

A crucial pillar of the third arrow was a ten-nation Trans-Pacific Partnership (TPP) negotiation to create an Asia-Pacific free trade zone. It was hoped that such a regional arrangement would help break the iron triangle of resistance by bureaucrats, politicians, and interest group leaders to structural reform and improve the productivity of Japanese industries by opening them to international competition. The success of the TPP negotiations is far from certain, however, and so is the success of this component of Abenomics, which is particularly susceptible to highly fluid and unpredictable external influences (especially that of the United States).

Thus, as of early 2017, the third arrow is yet to fly, and most consumers still face the rising costs of imported energy and foodstuffs, along with stagnant wages. Critics warn against the danger that public debt may grow to an unsustainable level, while worsening income inequality threatens to undermine social cohesion, and even the legitimacy of the existing institutions and practices of democratic politics and policymaking, as has recently happened elsewhere.

Society and Economy

The private industrial sector of the Japanese economy is characterized by interdependence and networking among a small number of large enterprises, on one hand, and a vast number of small and medium enterprises (SMEs), on the other. In this "dual structure" system, a great deal of critical technological innovation occurs in SMEs, but many of them serve as subcontractors to larger firms and pay their employees as much as 40 percent less and offer much poorer working conditions and job security than the bigger enterprises.

keiretsu

A group of close-knit Japanese firms that have preferential business relationships and, often, interlocking business relationships and stock-sharing arrangements.

Several huge business alliances, known as *keiretsu*, have been formed by some of the large firms. As exemplified by the Mitsubishi Group, a typical *keiretsu* consists of a major bank and several large manufacturing, trading, shipping, construction, and insurance companies that are horizontally linked with one another. There are also vertically structured *keiretsu*, like the Toyota Group, in which one large firm is tied to a number of smaller firms that serve as contractors and subcontractors to provide all or most parts needed to produce final products. A large firm affiliated with a vertical *keiretsu* may also head a horizontal *keiretsu*. While *keiretsu* may have some economic advantages, such as facilitating the flow of supplies needed for production, they also hinder economic competition and efficiency.

Since the late 1990s, both types of *keiretsu* have met increasing challenges from the accelerating process of globalization, such as the overseas relocation of manufacturing bases and cross-border mergers and acquisitions (M&A) and business alliances. This process has weakened some *keiretsu*, but Japanese managers and employees by and large continue to stick with their own firms and *keiretsu* in their selection of the sources of personnel, investment funds, product parts, and other elements.

While the Japanese economy was booming in the 1970s and 1980s, most Japanese regarded themselves as members of the middle class, thanks to a relatively egalitarian pattern of income distribution. This situation began to change in the 1990s as the Japanese economy started to shrink. Although Japan's unemployment rate remains relatively low (at about 3 percent), in 2016, its rate of relative poverty—defined as the percentage of households with incomes lower than 60 percent of the median household income in the given country—rose to one of the highest levels among the members of the Organisation for Economic Cooperation and Development (OECD), which represents the world's wealthiest nations, due notably to an increase in the number of nonregular workers, from about 16 percent in the mid-1980s to 40 percent in 2015. These are part-time or temporary employees who receive few, if any, benefits. Many firms' recession-induced cost-cutting efforts and the deregulation of the Labor Standard Law and other labor-related laws since the late 1990s contributed to the growth of this group of workers. But an underlying long-term cause is the structural change of the Japanese economy from manufacturing-centered to service-centered. As a result, a new cleavage between regular and nonregular employees has added to the traditional division between workers in large firms and those in SMEs. This new labor market duality overlaps gender gaps to compound the inequalities in Japanese society.

Although Japanese women are as highly educated as Japanese men, gender gaps in Japan are among the worst in the world and show few signs of improvement. An Equal Employment Opportunity Law was enacted in 1987, followed by a Women Empowerment Law in 2015, but they have had little impact. Women account for about three-quarters of the nation's nonregular workers, and the average female employee is paid about half as much as the average male employee. The traditional ideal of the "good wife and wise mother" homemaker is still very much alive in Japanese society and corporate employment practices, making it extremely difficult for women to pursue a demanding career and manage child-rearing at the same time. The rapid aging of Japan's population, however, makes it imperative to promote female participation in all fields of life by reforming the tax and social welfare systems, increasing affordable childcare, and ending outdated corporate practices that have the effect of disadvantaging women.

The 1947 Occupation-enforced constitution mandated the development of a comprehensive national social welfare system. Today, the Japanese system is

Japan's New National Symbol

comparable to that of the United States, but not to those in most Western nations, in providing such service to its citizens. While Japan's total public social welfare spending matches the OECD average of 22 percent of gross domestic product (GDP), the redistributive impacts of Japan's tax and social welfare systems are among the lowest in the OECD, and its social welfare spending is concentrated in pensions and health care for the elderly.[10] Although virtually all Japanese are provided with some social welfare benefits, the amounts of these benefits, which in 2017 ranged between the yen equivalent of about $600 and $2,500 per month per household, hardly meet the needs of most families. This situation creates a vicious circle: by depressing household consumption, aggravating the persistent deflation, and prolonging the recession. A key to breaking this pattern would be expansion of the social welfare programs. Social welfare spending, however, is already the largest government budget item. The rapidly aging population automatically ratchets such spending up each year, while tax revenue remains stagnant and barely covers 60 percent of the national government's annual budget. The result has been a huge and growing government debt.

Environmental Issues

As early as the mid-nineteenth century, the government-sponsored development of modern industries—mainly mining, textiles, and iron works—caused considerable environmental damage in Japan. Under a regime committed to building a "rich nation with a strong army," however, most victims silently endured the consequences of the government policy.

Postwar Japan's frantic effort to repair and rebuild its war-ravaged economy, and then to catch up and compete with the leading economies of the postwar world, caused far more serious and widespread environmental problems, as illustrated by the cases known as the **Four Great Pollution Trials**. In the face of widespread public protests, the Diet passed a series of stiff antipollution laws in the late 1960s and early 1970s to prevent recurrence of such disasters,[11] which led to a significant improvement in the environment.

The Four Great Pollution Trials

The Four Great Pollution Trials of the early 1970s include mercury poisoning in Minamata City, thus known as the "Minamata Disease," a similar case in another city, thus known as the "Second Minamata Disease," cadmium poisoning known as the "itai-itai (ouch-ouch) disease," and severe asthma caused by inhalation of airborne sulfur dioxide that occurred in Yokkaichi City (hence the "Yokkaichi Asthma").

In the postbubble so-called lost decades of the 1990s and 2000s, public attention shifted from environmental issues to the more pressing economic problems, and the top priority of the Japanese government became the resuscitation of its stagnant economy. The key to the success of this effort was believed to be a reliable domestic source of energy to fuel the nation's industry. A network of nuclear power plants and a breeder reactor would serve as such a source in theory. On such an assumption, the first Japanese nuclear reactor was built in the mid-1960s and, despite a fatal accident that occurred in 1999 at the hub of the nation's nuclear power industry, Tokai Village, as many as fifty-four had been built and were in operation by 2012, supplying about 30 percent of the electric power used in the nation.

The validity of the assumption, however, was called into question by a catastrophic accident in March 2011 at a nuclear power plant in Fukushima Prefecture on the nation's northeastern coast caused by a large-magnitude undersea earthquake and tsunami. More than 5 years after the event, popularly known as the **Fukushima nuclear disaster**, the level of radiation released by the damaged reactors remains so high that they cannot be directly inspected, much less repaired. More than 100,000 evacuees continue to live away from their homes, waters off the coast remain closed to fishing, and how and where to dispose of the huge amounts of lethal waste are yet to be determined.

After the disaster, the Japanese nuclear reactors were all put offline, but five have since been reactivated, despite opposition by the majority of respondents in most opinion polls. In 2016, the government decided to decommission the prototype Monju breeder reactor, which produces the material needed for a nuclear reaction and which has been beset by recurrent accidents ever since it started operating in 1991 and had cost the taxpayers about 1 trillion yen (roughly $10 billion). The decision to decommission Monju has rekindled a long-standing international concern over Japan's massive stockpile of plutonium produced by the breeder reactor, which could potentially be used for the production of nuclear bombs.

In spite of all the proven risks and costs of nuclear power generation, the government is poised to restart as many of the nuclear reactors currently offline as quickly as possible. Here again, the hands of a powerful iron triangle at work are evident.

Japan in the Global Economy

Following the 1868 Meiji Restoration, Japan pursued rapid industrialization, initially by exporting products of labor-intensive industries, such as textiles, and then increasingly higher-value-added products of more capital-intensive industries, including iron and steel, shipbuilding, and machinery. In the 1960s and 1970s, Japanese exports dramatically increased, thanks to their price competitiveness and, over time, their reputation for high quality, as well as the lowering of trade barriers around the world. Japan's successful export-led strategy of economic growth was followed by its Asian neighbors, such as South Korea and Taiwan, and helped them to achieve similar results.

As Japanese exports to the United States grew, however, Washington began to charge Tokyo with unfair trade practices. The U.S. complaints and criticism focused on Japan's high tariffs on imported goods in the 1950s, which shifted to **nontariff barriers (NTBs)** in the 1960s and then, in the 1980s, to domestic structural impediments to the entry of foreign imports and investments, such as a complex and opaque distribution system and collusive business practices among *keiretsu*-member companies. In response, Japan has removed or significantly reduced

Fukushima nuclear disaster

On March 11, 2011, a magnitude 9 undersea earthquake off the Pacific coast of Fukushima Prefecture triggered a series of tsunami waves of monstrous heights, which in turn caused reactor meltdowns at a local nuclear power plant, as well as destruction of a dozen towns and villages and the deaths of nearly 19,000 people.

nontariff barrier (NTB)

A practice, such as import quotas, health and safety standards, packaging and labeling rules, and unique or unusual business practices, that is designed to limit foreign imports and protect domestic industries; a form of protectionism that does not use tariffs.

GLOBAL CONNECTION

Japan and the Regional Political Economy

The Asia-Pacific region has been of special economic and strategic interest to Japan throughout its history. In the lead-up to and during the Pacific War, the region was the primary target of Japanese imperialism. Today, Japan is a leading partner in the evolving framework of regional cooperation and economic development.

The region was hit by financial crises in 1997 and 2008, the latter triggered by the bankruptcy of a U.S. investment bank, Lehman Brothers. These events led the Japanese government to propose the creation of an Asian Monetary Fund as a mechanism to prevent a recurrence of a similar crisis. Blocked by U.S. opposition, an alternative regional currency swap arrangement, known as the Chiang Mai Initiative, was set up in 2010 by ASEAN and three neighboring nations, Japan, China, and South Korea. This mechanism now provides the member nations financial support for dealing with short-term liquidity problems.

Trading and investment activities by private firms in the region have since steadily increased, giving rise to multiple networks of intraregional cross-border transactions, especially in intermediate goods. These evolving regional production networks have facilitated the growth of automobile, machinery, and electronics industries, among others, and accelerated expansion of the middle class and domestic markets in most nations in the region. Japanese multinationals' foreign direct investment, accompanied by technology transfer, has played a pivotal role in this process of regional economic growth and integration.

Particularly notable progress has been made in the area of environment-related trade, investment, and cooperative projects led by Japan. Since 2013, Japan, China, and South Korea have been conducting a trilateral policy dialogue on the issue of transborder air pollution from sources in China. This type of cooperation also helps reduce the tensions among the three nations over the territorial and history issues.

Now that the TPP negotiation has become defunct with U.S. withdrawal, the attention and interest of the governments and people in the region are likely to shift to the China-led free trade initiative, known as the Regional Comprehensive Economic Partnership (RCEP).

MAKING CONNECTIONS Was the failure of the TPP negotiation good or bad for the Asia-Pacific region, Japan, and/or the United States? Why?

the tariff and nontariff import barriers and other alleged unfair practices. In the meantime, many Japanese manufacturers have moved their plants abroad, including the United States and Europe, where their markets are, to avoid their trade barriers.

Meanwhile, China has replaced Japan as the trading partner with the largest bilateral trade balance surplus with the United States and the largest foreign exchange reserves in the world. Japan's share of the U.S. trade deficit had declined to less than 10 percent by 2016, while China's rose to 46 percent. In fact, Japan has been importing more than it has been exporting since 2011, and its earnings of U.S. dollars and other currencies are now generated mostly by its service industries (such as patent brokerage and tourism) and overseas investments. As a result, the main target of the U.S. concern over its trade deficits has largely shifted from Japan to China.

In the meantime, increasing international competition and rising wage levels at home have led many Japanese manufacturers to relocate their plants to developing countries, especially China and nations in Southeast and South Asia. While contributing to regional economic development and integration, these actions also "hollow out" Japan's own industrial base by transferring both jobs and technology overseas and leave many of its own workers only lower-paid, nonregular, service-sector jobs, similar to what has occurred in the United States.

Foreign direct investment in Japan itself has always been and remains at the lowest level among the OECD nations. The nation's businesses and mainstream media call for faster and deeper integration into the world economy, but they are opposed by groups critical of the current thrust of globalization based on neoliberal ideas.

Many of the opponents share a vision of a more equitable, self-reliant, and ecology-friendly local economy, supported by a more effective system of income redistribution and control of wasteful consumption and energy use. While still fragmented, this type of antiglobalization movement has grown considerably stronger since the 2011 Fukushima disaster.

Where Do You Stand?

1. What factors or circumstances account for the spectacular success of the Japanese model of economic development until the 1980s and its serious failure since?

2. Some Japanese call for actions to accelerate the globalization of the Japanese economy, while others oppose such actions because they believe those actions are based on pernicious neoliberal ideas. Which view do you support, and why?

SECTION 3

GOVERNANCE AND POLICYMAKING

▼ Focus Questions

- Is the influence of powerful iron triangles on policymaking compatible with democratic government and politics in Japan?

- What factors or circumstances encourage or discourage the vigorous exercise of political leadership by Japanese prime ministers and their cabinets?

Organization of the State

Japan is a constitutional monarchy and a parliamentary democracy, much like Britain and Sweden. The monarch (the emperor) is the symbolic head of state, but the people exercise sovereign power through their elected representatives.

Japan is the oldest surviving monarchy in the world with the reign of the first legendary emperor dating back to the mid-seventh century BCE and that of the first documented emperor to the late seventh century CE. According to tradition, Akihito, the present occupant of Japan's Chrysanthemum Throne—named for the flower chosen as the crest of the imperial family in 1868—is the 125th in an unbroken line of Japanese emperors and empresses. His ancestors were Japan's actual rulers from the late seventh through the early tenth centuries and thereafter remained the nation's titular rulers until after the end of World War II. Under the Meiji Constitution (1889–1947), the emperor was not only Japan's sovereign ruler, but also a demigod.

The Japanese imperial family today consists of twenty-two members, most prominently Emperor Akihito and Empress Michiko; the emperor's oldest son and heir apparent, Crown Prince Naruhito, his wife, Masako, and their daughter, Aiko. Succession to the throne is governed by strict traditional rules of patrilineage, and only male heirs are entitled to succeed to the throne. Under these rules, only two—the Crown Prince and his younger brother Akishino—had been eligible for succession until Akishino's son, Hisahito, was born in 2006. This situation had given rise to intense public debates over the need to amend the law to allow a female heir to succeed to the throne—a standard practice among contemporary European monarchies. Once the potential male heir was born, however, the debates ended almost overnight. Once installed as the legal heir to the throne, the emperor keeps his title all his life.

Compared to his aloof and enigmatic father, Hirohito, who at least figuratively led Japan into and out of the disastrous World War II and whose role in that war remains controversial, Emperor Akihito is a far more down-to-earth, liberal, and internationalist monarch. An 11-year-old boy at the war's end, he lived through the austere early postwar years as an impressionable young man, mingled freely with classmates from commoner families, learned English from an American Quaker woman, and married a businessman's daughter.

In his message to the nation in August 2016, on the occasion of the 70th anniversary of the atomic bombing of Hiroshima and Nagasaki and the end of the Pacific War, he suggested, as nobody had ever done, that he, at the age of 82, should be allowed to retire sometime soon. This announcement sent shock waves through the whole nation and has given rise to heated debates, both among the political parties and general public, on the need to change the legal rules of imperial succession. Nearly everybody agrees to let Emperor Akihito retire and change the current rules to let him do so. But the LDP and its supporters want to make the change an exceptional and temporary expediency applicable only to Akihito, while the opposition parties and their supporters want to make it permanent and applicable to his successors as well by changing the Imperial Household Law itself. While the debate over Akihito's retirement raged on, the imperial couple went on a series of memorial and prayer tours of some of the deadliest Pacific War battlegrounds, from Hiroshima and Nagasaki at home to Saipan, Palau, and the Philippines in the South Pacific.

Unlike in a presidential system, such as that of the United States, and like other parliamentary systems, such as Britain, the Japanese constitution allows a considerable degree of fusion of powers between the legislative and executive branches, although the judiciary is an independent third branch, like its American counterpart. The Diet formally nominates the prime minister, enacts laws, approves the government budget, ratifies international treaties, and audits the financial transactions of the state. In practice, however, the cabinet, rather than the Diet, initiates most legislation and makes most laws. Decision-making by the cabinet, in turn, is strongly influenced by the nonelected national bureaucracy. There has long been widely shared concern about the bureaucratic control of Japanese government undermining its democracy.

Japan is divided into forty-seven prefectures (provinces), which are subdivided into about 1,720 municipalities, ranging from large cities like metropolitan Tokyo, with about 9.3 million residents, and Yokohama, with 3.7 million, to half a dozen villages with no more than a few hundred inhabitants. Unlike the United States, Japan is a unitary state where subnational governments exercise only such powers as delegated by the national government. The constitution guarantees autonomy of elected local chief executives (prefectural governors and municipal mayors) and local assemblies, but local governments are subordinate to the national government and enjoy much less effective decision-making power than their counterparts in federal states.

Another important aspect of Japanese politics is its constitutional pacifism (Article 9), introduced under the postwar Allied Occupation regime. In the spirit of this constitutional commitment, the powerful prewar military bureaucracy was dismantled, while its civilian counterpart gained much greater independent power and influence.

Despite persistent controversy over its authorship by the postwar Occupation authorities, the present Japanese constitution has never been amended since its enactment in 1947. The issue of constitutional revision, however, has been around since the beginning. In fact, postwar Japan's most successful political party, the LDP, was founded in 1955 by a group of ardent and articulate advocates of constitutional "reform," including the first three prime ministers of the period immediately following the LDP's birth. Their and their followers' efforts, however, were blocked by the stringent constitutional requirements for an amendment: approval by two-thirds or more of all members of the two houses of the Diet, followed by approval by a majority of voters in a national referendum.

The LDP dominated nearly all subsequent Diet elections and governed the nation, by itself until the mid-1990s and in coalition with another party or parties thereafter, but, until 2016, never controlled two-thirds of members in both houses. Nor did a majority of voters support the LDP's drive to tamper with the constitution, which seemed to most citizens to be working just fine. However, since the 1990s, public opinion, as reflected in periodic polls conducted by government agencies and the major newspapers, has changed, and the majority or near-majority of Japanese voters now support some revision of the constitution. But the changes they support vary and often contradict each other. For example, in addition to the pacifist clause, Article 9, possible revisions include the replacement of the current parliamentary election of the prime minister with direct popular election, so as to strengthen central leadership, and the consolidation of the forty-seven prefectures into ten or so larger regional units in order to promote decentralization of power. Many people also favor the inclusion of new articles related to such issues as the protection of the environment and the role of government in national emergencies.

An amendment of Article 9 has continued to be opposed by the majority of the public, especially since the election of the current prime minister, Abe Shinzo, a grandson of one of the LDP's three constitutional revisionist founders and prime ministers in the 1950s, Kishi Nobusuke, and himself the leader of the current crop of the most committed revisionists in the ruling party and government. This status quo may undergo a significant change in the months and years following the 2016 upper-house election in Japan that gave the LDP a strong majority.

The Executive

Prime Minister and Cabinet

The Japanese prime minister is elected by the Diet and is, in practice, the leader of the dominant party or party coalition in the lower house. Each house elects a candidate for prime minister. If different candidates are elected by the two houses, the one elected by the lower house becomes prime minister. The prime minister must be a current Diet member and retains his or her seat in the Diet while serving as the head of the executive branch. He or she has the constitutional rights to submit bills to the Diet in the name of the cabinet, control and supervise the national civil service, and, in rare cases, suspend a cabinet member's constitutionally guaranteed immunity from an adverse legal action during his or her tenure in office. The prime minister is also the commander-in-chief of Japan's military, the JSDF, and may order, subject to the Diet's consent, JSDF troops to take appropriate action in a national emergency.

If the lower house passes a vote of no confidence against a cabinet, the prime minister must either resign, in which case the ruling party will choose a new party leader and prime minister, or dissolve the house and call a new election. A prime minister may also resign for a variety of other reasons, such as poor health, loss of support from important groups in his or her party, a personal scandal, and, increasingly, loss of support among the general public, as indicated by results of public opinion polls. A prime minister's average tenure in office in postwar Japan has been just a little over 2 years, with several serving for less than a year. The frequent turnover of cabinets seriously impairs their ability to implement their policy plans and also damages public trust in government. The cabinet has often been caricatured as a puppet who simply rubber-stamps decisions made and approved in advance by bureaucrats.

In the period from 1955, when the LDP was founded and formed its first government, to the end of 2013, all but five of Japan's twenty-eight prime ministers were LDP leaders. They were first chosen as the party's president, formally by election, but often by consensus reached behind closed doors among leaders of the several intraparty factions. This practice usually produced a prime minister who had previously held important cabinet and/or party positions, in accordance with the rules of a seniority-based promotion system and the need to maintain balance of power among the factions. All but two of the ten LDP presidents and prime ministers who have served during the last two decades were so-called hereditary Diet members—they were elected to Diet seats inherited from their relatives (typically their fathers). Most turned out to be ineffectual as party and government leaders and served very short terms.

The only notable exception to this rule was Prime Minister Koizumi Junichiro (2001–2006), who inherited his lower house seat from his father but rose to the top party position due mainly to his personal popularity for his aggressive antiestablishment, populist posture. During his unusually long 5-year tenure, he pushed a series of neoliberal reforms under the slogan, "No pain, no gain," which helped to boost the Japanese economy in the short run. In the long run, however, only the ranks of nonregular employees rose sharply, while social welfare programs did not expand to reduce the "pain" of the deregulation. His immediate successor, Abe, lasted only 1 year the first time around, but he was returned to office at the end of 2012 and was still in power in mid-2017. Not only a right-wing nationalist, but also a shrewd and flexible opportunist, he has outlasted Koizumi and become one of Japan's longest-serving prime ministers since its cabinet system was introduced at the end of the nineteenth century.

The National Bureaucracy

The core of the Japanese state is the eleven national government ministries, each with virtually exclusive jurisdiction over a specific area or areas of public policy. A ministry's mandate, as defined by law and practice, includes the exercise of both regulatory and custodial powers over both individuals and organizations. The regulatory power is exercised mainly through the enforcement of legal and quasi-legal requirements for licenses, permits, or certificates for virtually every kind of activity of actual or potential public interest. The custodial power is used to provide various types of public assistance to private citizens and groups, including subsidies and tax exemptions for select industries. There has been persistent criticism of, but no effective remedy for, excessive control of government and society by bureaucrats.

Each ministry is headed by a minister and a small group of his or her deputies with titles variously translated as "administrative vice-minister," "parliamentary vice-minister," and "state minister." Each ministry consists of a secretariat, which oversees its operations; several staff bureaus, concerned mainly with broad policy issues; and several line bureaus, responsible for the implementation of specific policies and programs. Each bureau is subdivided into divisions and departments. These core components are supplemented, as a rule, by several auxiliary agencies, commissions, committees, and institutes. The vertically segmented organization and an entrenched tradition of ministerial autonomy often interfere with policy coordination and cooperation among ministries. Japanese civil servants serve, as a rule, in one particular ministry for their entire career, a practice that further encourages interministerial rivalries and jurisdictional disputes, as well as fostering the tendency for officials to promote ministerial interests at the expense of broad national interests.

The Japanese national civil service examinations are highly competitive, especially in the fast-track or "career" category, officially called Class I. The standard mandatory retirement age for career bureaucrats is 60, a relatively young age in a society boasting the longest life expectancy at birth among the industrial nations. Not surprisingly, many public service retirees seek and find postretirement jobs in the public, semipublic, or private sector, often through their ministry's connections. This practice of gaining sponsored postretirement employment is known as *amakudari* ("descent from heaven"), and serves as an important link in the formation of the powerful "iron triangles" of bureaucrats, politicians, and interest group leaders.

Amakudari

A widespread practice, known as "descent from heaven," for public service retirees to take jobs in public corporations or private firms with which their office has or recently had close ties.

The "descent" is usually arranged in advance between the ministry ("heaven") from which the official is retiring and a public or semipublic organization or private enterprise within the circle of the ministry's clientele. The civil service law forbids employment of a retired civil servant within 2 years of his or her retirement by a private enterprise that has had a close business relationship with the government office where the retired official has been employed in the last 5 years. This restriction, however, may be lifted at the National Personnel Authority's discretion, as it is routinely done for several dozen retiring senior bureaucrats each year. Many more illegally find postretirement jobs the same way. Moreover, there are no legal restrictions on the "descent" of a retired official into a public or semipublic organization.

In the 1970s and 1980s, Japan's government bureaucracy was greatly admired, both at home and abroad, as the exceptionally intelligent, energetic, and dedicated architect of the nation's post–World War II economic miracle. By the end of the 1990s, however, its enviable reputation had largely dissipated. First, the depressed state of the Japanese economy was blamed on bureaucrats. Second, a series of headline-grabbing scandals involving officials in some of the traditionally most powerful and prestigious ministries tainted the reputation of Japanese bureaucrats at large as unselfish, public-minded, and incorruptible mandarins. Third, politicians began to assert a broader and more effective policymaking role, at the expense of bureaucrats. Fourth, diminishing tax revenue and tighter spending discipline spelled shrinking resources for bureaucrats to tap into for greasing their relationships with politicians and special interest groups, thus seriously eroding their influence. Still, bureaucrats continue to exercise enormous power in Japan's policymaking and implementation processes.

In addition to the national government ministries and agencies, there were, as of 2015, over 6,000 public and semipublic enterprises funded wholly or substantially by the central government. Their activities ranged from energy resource development to the promotion of international cooperation and oversight of publicly managed gambling. In practice, however, many have long outlived their original purposes and now serve primarily as destinations of retiring bureaucrats' descent from heaven. They were among the main targets of the short-lived civil service reform campaign of the Democratic Party of Japan (DPJ) when it was in power from 2009 to 2012. This campaign fizzled out as the inexperienced DPJ politicians serving as cabinet ministers were easily and quickly outmaneuvered by formidable veteran bureaucrats.

In 2016, Japan's national government, including its auxiliary organizations and JSDF administrative staff and troops, had on its payroll about 580,000 people, or 1.0 percent of the approximately 58 million gainfully employed people in the country. The Japanese national civil service costs about 5.2 percent of the national government's annual budget and 0.8 percent of Japan's GDP. It is difficult to compare the costs and benefits of different nations' public bureaucracies, but it is probably reasonable to call Japan's relatively well balanced.

Other State Institutions

The Military

Prewar Japan's large and powerful military establishment was totally dismantled by the Allied Occupation authorities after World War II and the nation was forbidden to rearm by the Article 9 peace clause of the 1947 constitution. The outbreak of the Korean War in 1950, however, led the Japanese government, with strong American prompting, to launch a rearmament program. Initially, a national police reserve was created, so called to avoid provoking controversy over its constitutionality. By 1954, this force had evolved into the JSDF. In 1959, the Supreme Court ruled that Article 9 did not forbid Japan to take necessary measures to defend itself as an independent state. The JSDF is now accepted by the Japanese public as a legitimate component of the Japanese state. It is roughly equal, both in physical size and in operational capability, to the armed forces of the major Western European nations. Although Japan spends only about 1 percent of its GDP on defense, its 4.98 trillion yen (about $40.9 billion) defense budget in 2015 was the eighth largest in the world, after those of the United States, China, Saudi Arabia, Russia, Britain, India, and France. Nevertheless, the keystone of Japan's security policy has been its alliance with the United States.

In 1992, the Diet passed an International Peace Cooperation (IPC) Law. Since then, JSDF troops have participated in limited noncombat UN peacekeeping operations around the world. These include medical assistance, refugee repatriation, logistic support, infrastructural reconstruction, election-monitoring, and policing operations. They are, however, forbidden to use weapons except for self-defense and during emergency evacuations. The JSDF has been also active in disaster relief operations both in Japan and abroad. Public support for JSDF has grown dramatically since its search and rescue operations in the 2011 Fukushima nuclear disaster. The majority of Japanese citizens now support the dispatch of JSDF troops abroad for similar activities.

In September 2015, amid heightened public concern about a dispute with China over a tiny group of islands in the East China Sea, called "Senkaku" by Japan and "Diaoyu" by China, and with North Korea over its nuclear program, Prime Minister Abe's coalition government had a pair of security policy bills railroaded through the Diet so as to reduce the legal restrictions on the use of weapons by JSDF troops and lift the ban on their participation in international collective self-defense actions. While the legislation was passed by the Diet, it met with vociferous objections by the opposition members. It also provoked highly charged public protests across the nation and was opposed by a majority of respondents in a series of public opinion polls taken at the time.

The Judiciary

The judicial branch of the Japanese government operates according to the rules set by the Supreme Court, which consists of the chief judge and fourteen other judges. All Japanese judges are appointed by the cabinet, except for the chief judge of the Supreme Court, who is nominated by the cabinet and formally appointed by the emperor. Supreme Court judges are subject to a popular review and potential recall in the first lower-house election following their appointment and every 10 years thereafter. None, however, has ever been recalled as a result of a popular review.

The Supreme Court, eight higher (regional) courts, and fifty district (prefectural-level) courts possess, and occasionally use, the constitutional power of judicial review. But the Supreme Court has been extremely reluctant to declare an existing law unconstitutional. Since it was established in 1947, it has declared only twenty-two

U.S. CONNECTION

U.S.-Japan Alliance and the JSDF

When Japan signed the peace treaty with the Allied powers in 1951 to end their occupation of the nation, it also signed a mutual security treaty with the United States. By virtue of this treaty, which was revised and extended indefinitely in 1960, the United States maintains an extensive network of military bases and troops in Japan. There are currently about 50,000 U.S. troops stationed in Japan, more than in any other foreign country.

In 1978, Japan began to provide monetary support for the upkeep of those bases and, in 1987, to pay the total payroll for their local employees and utilities, as well as sharing part of training, base relocation, and facilities improvement costs, both obligations outside the terms of the Japan-U.S. Status of Forces Agreement concluded in 1960. These host-nation contributions amount to about 75 percent of the total cost for the maintenance of U.S. bases in Japan, as compared to South Korea's and Italy's 40 percent apiece and Germany's 30 percent.

Japan has the eighth-largest defense budget in the world but spends a far smaller portion of its GDP (about 1 percent) for defense than the United States (3.3 percent). (See Figure 6.2.) Not surprisingly, Washington has been demanding a larger defense effort by Tokyo. Japan has responded not by increasing its defense spending, an action both financially and politically difficult, but by expanding JSDF's participation in UN-sponsored and/or U.S.-led, so-called peacekeeping operations abroad.

As tensions have risen between Japan and its neighbors in recent years, over China's military modernization and expansion, territorial disputes with China and South Korea, and, especially, North Korea's nuclear weapons program, Japanese concern about the reliability of the U.S. guarantee to defend its allies with its nuclear weapons, if necessary, a guarantee known as the *nuclear umbrella,* has deepened, fueling the push among conservative politicians and pundits, led by Prime Minister Abe, for the relaxation of the constitutional restrictions on Japanese rearmament. The 2015 security laws were enacted with a view to strengthening the U.S.-Japan alliance. Two helicopter carriers, large enough to be considered as aircraft carriers in disguise, have since been built. The Abe government has also been trying to build a regional security network by providing several Southeast Asian nations with maritime patrol ships and other weapons to help them counter China's expanding military presence.

The uncertainty about the U.S. policy under President Trump, who has accused U.S. allies of "free riding," and the intensifying antibase movement in Okinawa have led many Japanese to reassess the costs and benefits of continuing dependence on the six-decade-old U.S.-Japan alliance versus the development of Japan's own independent defense capability, as right-wing nationalists have long advocated.

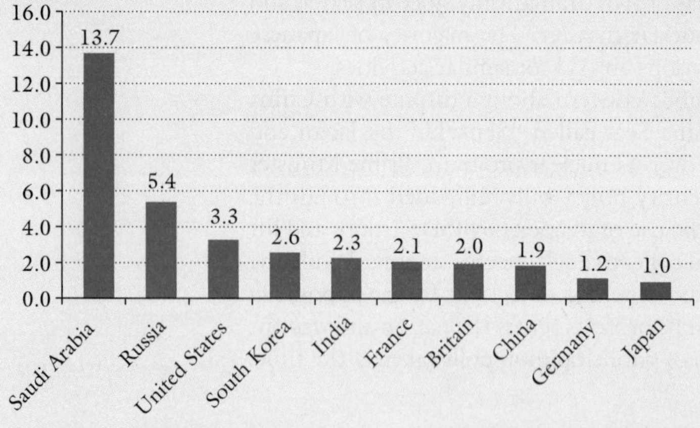

FIGURE 6.2 Military Expenditures as Percentages of GDP, 2015

Source: The Stockholm International Peace Research Institute, *2016 Fact Sheet* (for 2015) April, 2016. http://books.sipri.org/files/FS/SIPRIFS1604.pdf

MAKING CONNECTIONS How have the purpose and role of the U.S.-Japan security alliance changed since the early 1950s as strategic conditions have radically changed in the world and, especially, in the Asia-Pacific region?

existing laws (all politically insignificant) unconstitutional. This apparent proclivity for inaction may be attributed mainly to the influential legal opinion that holds that the judiciary should not intervene in decisions of the legislative or executive branch of government, which represents the people's will more directly than the judiciary.

All court cases used to be handled by professional judges alone until May 2009, when a quasi-jury system was introduced, Under the new system, even a major criminal case is heard and a decision made by a panel composed of three professional judges and six randomly chosen citizens. The introduction of this "Lay Judge System" (*saiban'in-seido*) is one of the most radical political reforms in post–Occupation Japan and a major step toward democratizing the country's legal system.

The Police

The organization and operation of the Japanese police are under the control of prefectural governors and prefectural public safety commissions. The National Police Agency exercises largely nominal supervisory and coordinating authority. This decentralized system was created by the postwar Allied Occupation and has since been maintained, with some modifications, in reaction against prewar Japan's notoriously abusive national police.

Postwar Japan has been one of the world's safest countries. According to the *Numbeo Crime Index by Country*, Japan was the eighth-most crime-free (i.e., safest) country in 2017, ranking far higher than Germany (thirty-first), Britain (fifty-sixth), France (fifty-ninth), and the United States (seventy-third) among the 125 countries included in the annual survey. In terms of the ratio of offenders convicted to those arrested, Japan boasts a virtually 1 to 1 track record.

This extraordinarily high conviction rate is achieved largely by prosecutors' heavy reliance on confessions. But these confessions often result from abusive interrogation methods employed behind closed doors in "substitute prisons" where suspects can be detained, without a specific charge, for up to twenty-two days by police or prosecutors and are allowed very restricted access to legal counsel, in apparent violation of the constitutional guarantee (Article 34) of all citizens' right to counsel and the right of habeas corpus, which requires that a person under arrest be brought before a judge as soon as possible. Japan has been frequently criticized for its alleged abuse of prisoners and suspects, and the arbitrary and often inhumane way that prisons are run.

Along with the introduction of the quasi-jury system in 2009, some efforts have been made to open the judicial system to greater public scrutiny and help reduce human rights abuses. For example, with a view toward increasing the transparency and accountability of the prosecutorial procedures, the National Police Agency introduced in 2016 a new set of guidelines, including mandatory audio and video recordings of entire interrogation sessions.

On the other hand, the Abe government had a state secrets law passed by the Diet in 2013 with a view to curbing leaks of government secrets, despite strong objections by the opposition parties and widespread public protest. In early 2017, the government started pushing for enactment of an anticonspiracy law, ostensibly as a means to combat global terrorism. In the eyes of its opponents, the law is a means to revive abuse of power by the police and restrict civil liberties, especially freedom of thought, a move that is reminiscent of the repressive Peace Preservation Law of the pre–World War II militarist regime.

Subnational Government

The Japanese prefectures and their subdivisions are under the administrative and financial control of the national government and enjoy very limited independent decision-making authority. The national government collects about two-thirds of the taxes levied by all levels of government, pays about one-third of local government administrative costs and special project budgets, and wields decision-making power roughly proportional to the lopsided division of the taxing and funding power.

Lay Judge System (*saiban'in-seido*)

The quasi-jury system for trials of criminal cases introduced in May 2009. In each case, the guilt or innocence of the accused—and, if convicted, the sentence—are determined by a judicial panel composed of three professional judges and six laypersons.

In this respect, Japan differs from most other economically developed democracies, where subnational levels of government enjoy much greater autonomy and power.

Japan's 1947 constitution devotes a full chapter to local self-government and refers to "the principle of local autonomy." There has always been a broad consensus among Japanese scholars and a large segment of the general public that robust local autonomy is an essential element of modern democracy. This academic and public opinion has been increasingly embraced by the national associations of prefectural and local politicians as a variety of local issues, such as social welfare, local economy, and environmental protection, have become too diverse for the central government to deal with adequately on its own. A Local Decentralization Promotion Law was enacted by the Diet in 1995, followed by a series of similar legislative and executive actions under both the LDP and DPJ governments. In 2009, the DPJ government even appointed a blue-ribbon panel with a grandiose title "Local Sovereignty Strategy Conference," which drew up an ambitious plan of reforms to be undertaken.

The enthusiasm for decentralization, however, soon began to wane, and the blue-ribbon panel was abolished by the LDP government in March 2013. Decentralization thus remains more rhetoric than action, due importantly to strong opposition among LDP Diet members, unwilling to lose an important source of funding for their pet local projects, and national bureaucrats, averse to seeing their turfs and perks shrink.

The Policymaking Process

Policymaking in postwar Japan has long been dominated by the dynamics of politics played by and among the iron triangles of LDP politicians, bureaucrats, and interest group leaders. As a rule, draft bills were reviewed and approved by the LDP's Policy Research Council, which operated through a dozen standing committees, each corresponding to a government ministry, and a host of ad hoc committees. The recommendations of these committees were presented to the council's executive committee and then to the party's Executive Council. If approved by both bodies, the recommendations usually became government policies to be implemented through legislative actions of the Diet or administrative actions of the bureaucracy.

Most LDP policy committees were led by veteran Diet members experienced and knowledgeable in specific policy areas. Over the years, they formed close personal relationships with senior bureaucrats and leaders of special interest groups. They also formed close-knit networks among themselves, popularly known as *zoku* ("tribes"), and worked in cooperation with allied bureaucrats and interest groups through an iron triangle. Such tribes and iron triangles dominated policymaking in all major policy areas, but were especially prominent in agriculture, construction, education, telecommunications, and transportation.

Each iron triangle promoted special interests favored by its affiliated politicians and bureaucrats. The bureaucrats had their turfs protected and often expanded by allied politicians, while the politicians had their election campaigns financed by contributions of the allied interest groups. The LDP tribes were the principal actors in Japan's widespread **pork-barrel politics** and the major sources of political corruption. Big businesses, small shop owners, farmers, builders, insurers, and doctors were all represented by their own tribes that protected their interests against those who threatened them, whether they were Japanese consumers, insurance policyholders, medical patients, or foreign businesses.

The power of the vested interests has been vividly illustrated by the activities of a group of nuclear power advocates widely known as the Nuclear Village. This is a

zoku

A group of Diet members with recognized experience and expertise in a particular policy area, such as agriculture, construction, and transportation, and close personal connections with special interests in that area. *Zoku* means "tribes."

pork-barrel politics

A term originally used by scholars of American politics to refer to legislation that benefits particular legislators by funding public works and projects in their districts. More broadly, the term refers to preferential allocation of public funds and other resources to particular districts or regions so as to give electoral advantage to particular politicians or political parties.

network of institutional and individual advocates of nuclear power in the utility and manufacturing industries, the Diet, government bureaucracy, financial institutions, the mass media, and academia. This network has dominated Japan's energy policy-making ever since the LDP government found in nuclear power an answer to the problem of post–oil crisis power supply in the early 1970s, and, since the early 1980s, the best way to reduce greenhouse gas emissions as well. A critical factor in the 2011 Fukushima nuclear disaster was the corruption of the government regulators by the nuclear village, which had provided them with postretirement jobs, as well as generous political funds to allied politicians, for a long time. Despite the intense public criticism that it faced in the wake of the 2011 disaster, the village has survived and is thriving under the pro–nuclear power LDP government.

The actions of the entrenched iron triangles, all working to protect their own interests and often at cross-purposes with each other, make government in Japan look like a downtown intersection in a perennial traffic gridlock. This policymaking stalemate stymies periodic reformist efforts, as illustrated by the failure of the third arrow of Abenomics—government deregulation and wide-ranging socioeconomic reforms—to fly, even with the ruling coalition led by Prime Minister Abe in control of both houses of the Diet. The old and outdated policies, practices, and procedures thus survive and help only to aggravate already bad situations, such as the protracted economic slump and mounting public debt. In the absence of effective political leadership with an inspiring vision of the future, the situation breeds pessimism and political alienation and discourages citizen participation and activism.

Where Do You Stand?

1. When a national disaster occurs as a result of a private firm's action or actions subsidized and supervised by government, such as Japan's 2011 nuclear disaster, who should be held responsible and pay for it—the firm or the government (that is, taxpayers)?

2. What action or actions, done by whom, might bring about effective structural reforms to end the policymaking stalemate in Japan?

REPRESENTATION AND PARTICIPATION

SECTION

4

The Legislature

According to the postwar Japanese constitution, the Diet is the state's highest and sole lawmaking organ. It consists of a House of Councillors (upper house) and a House of Representatives (lower house). The lower house is the larger and more powerful of the two, with the ability to override a decision of the upper house in conflict with itself regarding the government budget, ratification of international treaties, and the election of a new prime minister. The full term of office for the 475 members of the House of Representatives is 4 years, but this house may be, and frequently is, dissolved before its incumbent members' term is up, and a new election then is called at the discretion of the cabinet. The 242 members of the House of Councillors serve a fixed term of 6 years. Their terms are staggered, and half of them are elected every 3 years.

An ordinary session of the Diet lasts for 150 days each year and may be extended only once, but for an indefinite period stretching until the end of the current calendar year. An extraordinary session may be called at any time by the cabinet or by one-quarter or more of the members of either house. As in the U.S. Congress, the bulk of legislative work is done in a number of standing and ad hoc committees in each house.

A bill must be passed by both houses to become a law. An ordinary bill may be introduced either by the cabinet or a group of twenty or more lower-house members or ten or more upper-house members. A budget bill may be introduced either by the cabinet or fifty or more lower-house members or twenty or more upper-house members. Until the early 2000s, far more cabinet bills were introduced and passed than members' bills. During the last decade, the numbers of the two types of bills introduced have become more equal, but a vastly higher percentage (5 to 1 ratio during the 2014 Diet session) of cabinet bills have been passed than members' bills.

A bill approved by a committee of either house is referred to and debated by the whole house and, if approved, transmitted to the other house, where the same process is repeated. An ordinary bill is passed or rejected by a simple majority in a committee of either house, then by the whole house, but an amendment of the constitution requires the consent of two-thirds or more of all members in each house, followed by the approval of a majority of voters in a national referendum.

An ordinary bill already passed by the lower house and then rejected by the upper house may be voted on again and made law by a two-thirds majority of lower-house members present and voting. A budget bill must be introduced first to the lower house and may be passed by that house alone, regardless of the upper house's action. Ratification of an international treaty may be introduced to either house, but, if the two houses disagree, the decision of the lower house prevails. Like their counterparts in most other parliamentary democracies, Japanese Diet members normally vote strictly along party lines.

The overwhelming majority of Japanese legislators are men. At the end of 2016, there were 44 and 50 women members, respectively, in the lower and upper house, accounting for 9 percent and 21 percent of all members in each house. A November 2016 survey by the Inter-Parliamentary Union ranked Japan 156th among 193 nations in the percentage of women in a unicameral (single-house) parliament or the lower house of a bicameral (two-house) parliament.

Political Parties and the Party System

For a decade following the end of World War II, several political parties, mostly formed by surviving members of prewar parties, divided themselves into three loose-knit ideological groupings: the Liberals on the right, the Democrats in the middle, and the Socialists (Japan Socialist Party: JSP) and the Communists (Japan Communist Party: JCP) on the left. The Liberals were in power for the better part of the Allied Occupation of Japan. In 1955, the Liberals and Democrats merged into the LDP. For the next three-and-a-half decades, the conservative LDP dominated Japanese politics both at the national and local levels.

The LDP's de facto one-party rule in a seemingly superstable predominant party democracy began to unravel in the late 1980s, due partly to a series of political corruption scandals, in which a number of party leaders were implicated and over which a group of dissidents deserted the party to form a new Democratic Party of Japan (DPJ) with defectors from the JSP. As a result, the LDP lost the 1993 lower-house election for the first time in its 38-year history and yielded control of government to a coalition of opposition parties. The LDP, however, came back into power in less than a year and stayed in power for the next 14 years in coalition, initially with the JSP—renamed the Social Democratic Party (SDP) in 1996—and, subsequently, with Japan's only religious party, the centrist Buddhist Komeito, founded in the mid-1960s. The LDP-Komeito coalition lost the 2007 upper-house and the 2009 lower-house elections and yielded government to a rival, DPJ-led coalition. However, due partly to its ineffectual response to the 2011 "triple disaster" (i.e., the nuclear power plant accident) and partly to its failure to pull the nation out of the long recession, the DPJ-led coalition was roundly beaten by the LDP and Komeito in the 2012 and 2014 lower-house and 2013 and 2016 upper-house elections (see Table 6.2).

In recent years, a number of minor parties have come and gone. One of them, the right-wing Japan Restoration Party (Nippon Ishin no Kai), won more seats than the leftist SDP in the 2012 and 2014 lower-house elections and the 2013 upper-house election. But prior to the 2016 upper-house election, the Japan Restoration Party split, and about half of its Diet members joined the Democratic

predominant-party democracy

A multiparty democratic political system in which one party or coalition of parties maintains a predominant position in parliament and control of government for a long period of time.

Table 6.2	Japan's Political Parties and Recent Election Results			
			Diet Seats	
Ideology	Party Name	Year Founded	House of Representatives 2014 Election	House of Councillors 2016 Election (Total in House)
Right	LDP	1955	295	55 (120)
	Japan Restoration Party	2015	42	7 (12)
Center	Komeito	1964	31	14 (25)
	Democratic Party (DP; formerly DPJ)	1998	63	32 (49)
Left	SDP	1955	2	1 (2)
	JCP	1945	8	6 (14)
	Other parties		24	1 (9)
	independents		15	5 (11)
Total			480	121 (242)

Party of Japan (DPJ), which then changed its English name to simply the Democratic Party (DP).

The five better-established parties continue to stick to their familiar positions on most domestic and foreign policy issues, but increasingly equivocally. On the issue of changes to the postwar constitution, the LDP remains committed to its revisionist position, especially with regard to Article 9, a position adopted at its founding in 1955 and reaffirmed with renewed urgency by the party's current leadership. The LDP's longtime coalition partner, Komeito, on the other hand, has been antirevisionist, albeit with increasing ambivalence, and so have the DPJ, JCP, and SDP. The Japan Restoration Party is generally eclectic in its policy preferences but aligns with the LDP on the constitutional issue. On another highly controversial issue, the question of whether resident foreigners (mainly Koreans) should be granted the right to vote in local elections, the LDP and the Japan Restoration Party oppose such a change, while the other four parties support their enfranchisement with varying degrees of consistency.

When it comes to territorial disputes with neighboring nations, all parties are agreed on the legitimacy of the Japanese claim to the three island groups in dispute: the Northern Islands with Russia; Senkaku with China; and Takeshima (known as "Dokdo" in Korean) with South Korea. Moreover, all but the SDP implicitly support the LDP's tacit commitment to defend them by force, if necessary. The SDP alone calls for the resolution of all territorial disputes strictly by negotiation. Similarly, all agree that jump-starting the stagnant economy is a more pressing need than curbing the mounting government debt, and they generally support expansionary monetary and fiscal policies. On the future of nuclear power plants in the wake of the 2011 "triple disaster," all but the LDP call for their shutdown by 2030 or sooner.

All Japanese political parties are primarily groups of Diet and prefectural assembly members with token grassroots memberships. In a nation with an electorate of well over 100 million in 2016, the LDP had about 1 million registered grassroots members, Komeito 450,000, the JCP 300,000, the DP 250,000, and the SDP 16,000.

Under a political reform law passed in 1994 with a view to reducing the susceptibility of politicians to corruption due to fund-raising pressures, Japan's national parties are subsidized by the state treasury. Each party receives a share of an amount equal to ¥250 multiplied by Japan's current total population, in proportion to the sum of the number of seats that it currently holds in the two houses of the Diet and the average share of the vote that it has won in the most recent lower-house and the two most recent upper-house elections. According to this complicated formula, the LDP received in 2016 about ¥17.5 billion ($145 million, at $1 = ¥120), the DP ¥9.3 billion ($77.5 million), Komeito ¥3.0 billion ($25 million), Japan Restoration Party ¥780 million ($6.5 million), and the SDP ¥440 million ($3.6 million). The JCP refuses to accept this handout from the government.

Japanese local government and politics are generally nonpartisan. All the current forty-seven prefectural governors and nearly all the 2,161 mayors are independents, and so are over 78 percent of municipal assembly members. The only exception is prefectural assembly members, 75 percent of whom are affiliated with one or another major national party (about half with the LDP). Japanese local elections, even more than Diet elections, are dominated, or monopolized, by men. Women account for a little over 10 percent of the prefectural and municipal assembly members and a little over 1 percent of the governors and mayors.

👤 PROFILE

Koike Yuriko: Shattering Japan's Glass Ceiling

An archaic patriarchy, Japan saw one of its most visible glass ceilings shattered with a single powerful blow in the summer of 2016. A woman won the governorship of Tokyo, a position that always had been held by a man since it was created in 1943, as its antecedent had been ever since the city became Japan's capital in the late nineteenth century.

The ceiling smasher, Koike Yuriko (b. 1952) is a 1976 graduate of Cairo University's sociology department. Upon her return to Japan, she worked first as a professional interpreter in Arabic, and then as a television newscaster for 15 years, before running for and winning an upper-house seat in 1992 as a candidate of a short-lived anti-LDP party. The following year, she gave up that seat to run for and win a lower-house seat. During the next decade, she moved from one short-lived party to another until finally joining the LDP, led by the popular maverick prime minister Koizumi Junichiro, in 2002. Thereafter, she rose rapidly through the ranks in the ruling party, serving in a variety of important party and cabinet positions, including the minister of defense and the minister of the environment. In 2008, she even ran for the party leader-cum-prime minister position against four other senior party officials, all male, but lost, coming in second.

Increasingly frustrated and alienated thereafter in the male-dominated party, Koike ran for governor of Tokyo in 2016 as an independent against twenty other candidates, including one supported by the LDP, and won a landslide victory with 45 percent of the vote, far ahead of her LDP-supported rival's 28 percent. She has since taken up a series of hot-button issues, to the consternation of her predecessors and LDP members of the Tokyo Metropolitan Assembly. Among these have been irregularities in the bidding and budgeting for the 2020 Tokyo Olympics and the proposed move of the famous Tsukiji fish market to a site vacated by a gas-processing plant after contaminating the subsoil with highly toxic substances. Both of these were high-profile, high-cost, taxpayer-funded projects.

Koike was the seventh Japanese female governor and the newest member of an incumbent trio as of early 2017. The first female Japanese governor was elected in 2000 in Osaka, the nation's third-largest city. All those who have followed her have faced and smashed a glass ceiling or two, helping, in Koike's words, "to make the government more open and transparent to citizens."

Source: "Koike metropolitan government gets started: Focus on transparency," Asahi Shimbun, August 2, 2016. (http://www.asahi.com /articles/DA3S12491279.html). Accessed January 10, 2017.

Elections

Diet election campaigns are also partially funded by the state treasury. Candidates receive free posters, stamped postcards, space in the official gazette, free radio and television advertising, use of public halls for campaign rallies and speeches, and prepaid passes for the use of public transportation during the legally limited campaign periods.

Under the system in effect from the mid-1920s to 1994, all lower-house members, as well as some upper-house members, were elected in multimember districts by the **single nontransferable vote (SNTV)** method. This system tended to pit candidates of the same party against each other within each district and led most candidates to focus on constituency services rather than on broader policy issues. Constituency service activities were carried out primarily by the candidate's personal campaign organization, generically known as *koenkai* (support association).

In 1994, the SNTV system for lower-house elections was replaced by a system in which 295 members are elected in **single-member districts (SMDs)** and 180 in eleven regional constituencies by a party-list proportional representation (PR) method. To field a candidate or candidates in a PR district, a party must have at least five incumbent Diet members or have won at least 2 percent of the vote in the most recent Diet election. Each voter casts two ballots—one for a candidate in a single-member district and one for a party in a PR district.

single nontransferable vote (SNTV)

A method of voting used in a multimember election district system. Each voter casts only one ballot for a particular candidate, and that vote may not be transferred to another candidate, even of the same party. Each district is assigned two or more seats, which are filled by the candidates who win the largest numbers of votes.

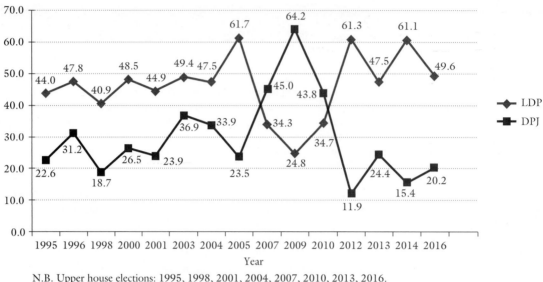

N.B. Upper house elections: 1995, 1998, 2001, 2004, 2007, 2010, 2013, 2016.
Lower house elections: 1996, 2000, 2003, 2005, 2009, 2012, 2014.

FIGURE 6.3 **LDP and DPJ Percentage Shares of Diet Seats, 1995–2016 Elections**

© Cengage

koenkai

A candidate's personal campaign organization, normally based on a network of his or her relatives, friends, fellow alumni, coworkers, and their acquaintances. An effective *koenkai* is expensive to maintain and conducive to political corruption.

single-member district (SMD)

An electoral district in which only one representative is elected, most commonly by the first-past-the-post method (i.e., whoever wins the most votes). In contrast, a proportional representation (PR) system seats in a legislature are allocated to parties according to the percentage of votes that each party receives.

The 242 members of the upper house are elected to 6-year terms. Unlike the lower house, the upper house cannot be dissolved and elections occur every 3 years. A total of 96 members (48 in each triennial election) are elected by a party-list PR method in a nationwide competition. The remaining 146 members (73 every 3 years) are elected from prefectures (between 2 and 10 per prefecture) by the SNTV method.

As mentioned previously, the LDP dominated Diet elections under the pre-1994 lower-house electoral system and continued to do so for a decade under the new system (see Figure 6.3). In the 2007 upper-house election, however, the DPJ-led opposition beat the LDP-led ruling coalition, while the LDP held a two-thirds majority in the lower house. Because, as a rule, a bill must be passed by both houses to become a law, this situation led to a constant legislative gridlock. Then, in the 2009 lower-house election, the DPJ won a landslide victory, forming the first non-LDP government since 1994. In the July 2010 upper-house election, the DPJ won more seats than the LDP, but, when the numbers of seats won by the parties allied with each were counted, it was not enough to keep control of the house. This created a reverse-divided and still gridlock-prone Diet. The LDP won decisive victories both in the 2012 lower-house and 2013 upper-house elections, regaining control of both houses for the first time since 2007. It did nearly as well in the 2014 lower-house and 2016 upper-house elections and, reinforced by the seats won by the two parties allied with it, Komeito and the Japan Restoration Party, consolidated its predominant position.

Until the late 1980s, voter turnout in Diet elections fluctuated between 68 percent and 77 percent in lower-house elections and 57 percent and 75 percent in upper-house elections. Turnout rates hit low points in the mid-1990s, a period characterized by a series of political corruption scandals, at about 60 percent in lower-house elections and 45 percent in upper-house elections. The rates subsequently recovered to 69 percent in the 2009 lower-house election and 58 percent in the 2010 upper-house election, but fell back to 59 percent in the 2012 lower-house election and

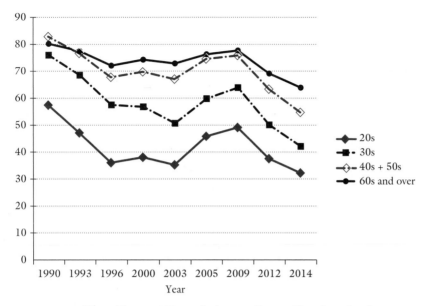

FIGURE 6.4 Voter Turnout Rates in Lower House Elections by Age Cohort, 1990–2014

Source: Akarui Senkyo Kyokai (Association for Promoting Fair Election), *Nendaibetsu Tohyoritsu no Suii* (Changes in Voter Turnout Rates by Age Cohort, http://www .akaruio.or.jp/070various/071syugi/693/

53 percent in the 2013 upper-house election and remained at the same level in the 2014 lower-house and 2016 upper-house elections. These numbers signal a significant rise in recent years in the level of political alienation or disenchantment, if not apathy, among Japanese voters and their tepid support for the current state of party and legislative politics.

As Figure 6.4 shows, nonvoting has been particularly widespread among younger voters. Over the last two decades, the turnout rates of voters under the age of 40, and particularly those under 30, have been conspicuously and consistently lower than that of the older cohorts, especially those in their 60s, potentially a warning sign for the future of representative democracy in the country.

Political Culture, Citizenship, and Identity

Japanese are ethnically and culturally more homogeneous than most other nations, but there are several distinctive minority groups in the nation. These include two ethnic minorities, the Ainu and Okinawans, a class-based minority known as *buraku* (hamlet) people, resident Koreans from Japan's former colony, and other resident foreigners.

The Ainu and Okinawans

The Ainu are descendants of some of the earliest immigrants to the Japanese archipelago, known as the *Jomon* (rope-patterned) people, from the common decorative pattern found on pottery left by them, who once inhabited the greater part of the country. By the end of the Tokugawa period in the mid-nineteenth century, however, they had been virtually wiped out, except in Hokkaido in the far north of the country. With their distinctive language and culture, including the concept of land as communal, as opposed to personal, property, they had been treated as a quasi-foreign people before the Meiji Restoration. As they subsequently began to be treated as members of the Japanese nation, the survivors in Hokkaido were systematically robbed of their land by new immigrants from other regions of the country and, like Native Americans in the United States and Aboriginals in Australia, routinely abused and condemned to abject poverty. As an increasing number of immigrants have arrived in their home territory, intermarriage has increased. According to a 2006 survey, there were about 24,000 self-identified Ainu in Hokkaido in that year. There are no reliable statistics available on the Ainu population in the nation as a whole, but it is estimated to be about 200,000.

Until the late 1990s, the Ainu were, in theory, protected by an 1899 law, titled the Law for the Protection of Former Native People in Hokkaido, but, in practice, nearly totally ignored by the Japanese government and most Japanese citizens. In 1994, an Ainu scholar and author filled a vacancy in the upper house of the Diet left by a deceased JSP member and played a key role in the enactment of a 1997 Law to Promote Ainu Culture, which replaced the old Meiji law and has helped bring more government and public attention to the plight of this minority group. Prompted by the adoption of the Declaration on the Rights of Indigenous Peoples by the UN General Assembly in 2007, the Diet declared the Ainu the indigenous people of Japan in 2008.

Okinawans are also believed to be more direct descendants of the *Jomon* people than most other Japanese. Before the Meiji Restoration, they were subjects of the Kingdom of the Ryukyus, a state under Chinese suzerainty until the early seventeenth century, when it was invaded and occupied by a band of warriors sent by the lord of a Japanese feudal domain in southern Kyushu. As a result, they came under the rule of ambiguous dual suzerainty of Qing China and Tokugawa Japan. The Meiji government unilaterally incorporated the island kingdom into Japan's newly created system of local administration in 1879.

Like the Ainu, Okinawans, with their own distinctive language and culture, have faced widespread prejudice and discrimination. Their average per capita income remains the lowest in the nation to this day. Their identity as an ethnic minority has considerably weakened over the years. Neither their collective historical memories, especially the memories of the tragic experiences that they have been subjected to during and since the end of the Pacific War, nor their grievances over their current living conditions have significantly declined.

Outcast Groups

Discrimination against Japan's outcast people dates back to the pre-Tokugawa era. For centuries, they were condemned to pariah status and lived in ghettos, pejoratively referred to as the *buraku*. The discrimination legally ended in the wake of the Meiji Restoration but persisted in practice.

In 1922, a group of young activists from a "hamlet" in Nara Prefecture, near Kyoto, founded a National Levelers Association, named after the famous egalitarian movement in seventeenth-century England. The original organization was disbanded in 1940, on the eve of the Pacific War, but a successor organization was founded in 1955 called the Buraku Liberation League. Under its pressure, a series of laws was passed by the Diet in the 1970s to help eliminate the approximately 4,600 "hamlets" that still existed and integrate the more than 1 million residents into the broader national community. Since then, considerable improvement has been made in the economic conditions of former outcast communities, but complete equality and full integration into the national community remain ideals yet to be realized, and the Liberation League, with an estimated membership of about 60,000, continues its campaign for elimination of the residual discriminatory practices related mainly to employment and marriages.

Koreans and Other Resident Foreigners

After the Meiji Restoration, especially after Japan annexed Korea in 1910, many Koreans migrated to Japan. Initially, most came voluntarily. By the 1930s, however, many were drafted and brought to Japan as slave labor to work in some of the nation's most poorly equipped and accident-prone factories and mines. At the end of World War II, more than 2 million Koreans were living in Japan. A majority returned to Korea, but approximately 650,000 stayed in Japan.[12]

Unlike the United States, where any person born within its territory is automatically granted citizenship regardless of his or her parents' citizenship status, based on the *jus soli* ("right of the soil") principle, Japan grants citizenship to anyone born of a parent who is a Japanese citizen, regardless of where he or she is born, but to nobody else except through naturalization procedure, based on the *jus sanguinis* ("right of blood") principle. Moreover, Japan does not permit dual citizenship in principle. Most of the half million or so Koreans who currently live in Japan were born of Korean parents and therefore were denied Japanese citizenship at birth. Some of them, especially younger ones, may apply for and acquire Japanese citizenship after they reach the legally required age of 20. About 350,000, or about 70 percent, are recognized as having been colonial Japanese citizens before 1945, or being one of their descendants, and thus are entitled to permanent residence in Japan. Like all other resident foreigners, however, these Koreans cannot vote in Japanese elections, nor can they receive publicly funded social security or pension benefits.

As the process of globalization has intensified in the last few decades, Japanese society, like many others around the world, has become increasingly diversified. Compared with most nations of North America and Western Europe, however, Japan remains far more closed to and insulated from foreign immigrants and their social, cultural, and political influences. The number of resident foreigners in Japan in 2016 was about 2.8 million, or only about 2.2 percent of Japan's total population of about 127 million. Moreover, about a third of these foreigners were Chinese, including some 125,000 from Taiwan, nearly 20 percent were Koreans, and about 8 percent were Japanese Brazilians and Peruvians. In other words, nearly two-thirds of the resident foreigners shared ethnic and cultural backgrounds with native Japanese. They are nonetheless "foreigners" and treated as such, both legally and in their daily lives.

Interest Groups, Social Movements, and Protest

Like other modern democracies, Japan is home to countless interest groups, but only a few peak organizations play or have played a significant political role at the national level. These represent the political interests of big businesses, labor, and farmers. Large and politically effective social movements and protests are also relatively rare in contemporary Japan.

By far the most prominent among the politically significant interest groups is the Japan Business Federation (*Keidanren*). Established in 1961, this peak organization of Japan's major companies is the main conduit of business political contributions to the LDP. Since the early 1990s, its role as the predominant party's major fund-raiser has been suspended from time to time in the face of public outcry against political corruption, but it was resumed in 2014. The largest contributors include Japan's leading automobile, petrochemical, electric, iron and steel manufacturers and trading, real estate, securities, and nuclear power companies. In return for their largesse, they won in 2016, via their peak organization, a reduction of corporate taxes to below 30 percent for the first time. The current *Keidanren* president describes his group's relationship with the LDP, especially under Prime Minister Abe's leadership, as the "two wheels of a vehicle."

There is another politically prominent big business organization, called Japan Association of Corporate Executives (*Keizai Doyukai*). This group, however, is not composed of big companies, as *Keidanren* is, but of individual executives of big companies. Moreover, and unlike the former, it insists on keeping its distance from all political parties, including the LDP. While ideologically conservative and generally pro-LDP, it does not deliberately facilitate political contributions to any party by its members' companies.

On the other side of the coin is the peak labor organization, the Japanese Trade Union Confederation (JTUC: *Rengo*). This organization was formed in the 1980s as a result of the merger of a national federation of left-wing and mainly public service unions, the General Council of Trade Unions of Japan (*Sohyo*), its conservative counterpart of private-sector unions, the Japanese Confederation of Labor (*Domei*), and two other less partisan union organizations.

Sohyo, allied with the JSP and JCP, led the Japanese labor movement in the early postwar years. At the height of its strength in 1949, the organization boasted a membership of 35,000 unions with 6.6 million employees, representing about 55 percent of Japan's total urban labor force. These unions and their members participated in frequent, sometimes violent, actions against management and routinely won major concessions over wages and working conditions. As economic conditions improved, however, the appeal of the militant labor movement, especially the left-wing *Sohyo*, dissipated. Eventually, *Sohyo* was disbanded and merged with the more conservative groups in 1982.

In the meantime, the overall rate of unionization itself had fallen to one-third of the total urban labor force by the mid-1970s, and has kept falling since, to one-quarter by the mid-1990s and to less than one-fifth by 2010. In today's Japan, where 40 percent of the urban labor force consists of nonunion temporary and part-time employees, *Rengo* represents only about 10 percent of the nation's 58 million workers and a little over two-thirds of the unionized workers.

Nearly all of Japan's 25,000 labor unions, which have a total membership of 10 million workers, are company unions. The majority of the unions and their members are, like the majority of Japanese citizens, political independents or conservatives. A recent survey of some 25,000 members of the Japan Federation of Basic Industry Workers Unions (JBU: *Kikanroren*), a *Rengo* affiliate, found 23 percent of respondents supporting the LDP, 18 percent the DP, and 53 percent no particular party. Thus, the political role of Japanese labor in general, and *Rengo* in particular, is not insignificant, but it is far more limited than it used to be in the early postwar period. Above all, labor is not one of a friend, much less an ally, of either of the left-wing parties, the SDP and the JCP.

The political role of peak national organization representing Japan's farmers, known as *Nokyo* (Japan Agricultural Cooperatives: JA), is similar to that of Japanese labor, although the historical patterns of their partisanship are very different. The JA is a well-known pro-LDP group. It was founded in 1948 as the national network of farmers' cooperatives, which served as the official intermediaries between producers and consumers of agricultural commodities (mainly rice) at a time when all kinds of foodstuffs were extremely scarce and the whole nation was on the verge of starvation. Many of its members were beneficiaries of the postwar land reform implemented during the Allied Occupation and the rule of the Japanese conservative party. They have since been staunch supporters of the LDP.

Unlike the role of the business peak organization, *Keidanren*, as the LDP's fund-raiser, JA's contribution has primarily been in mobilizing rural voters for party candidates in Diet elections and LDP-supported candidates in local elections. In recent years, however, the political role of JA has diminished because of the steady decline in the number of cooperative members. Farmers accounted for about one-third of Japan's total workforce in the 1950s and 1960s, but their number has fallen to about 3 percent. JA's total membership grew from about 6.5 million in 1960 to nearly 10 million in 2012, but these numbers include nonfarmer "associate members," whose ranks increased from three-quarters of a million to nearly 5.4 million over the period, while the number of full-time farmer "principal members" decreased from about 5.8 million to 4.6 million. As a small and rapidly aging minority among Japanese voters, farmers are not of much interest to LDP politicians or those of any other party. JA no longer provides a key support base for the LDP, but it is increasingly a dependent constituency for the party and LDP-led government to support.

Women's Movement

A quintessential patriarchal society, pre–World War II Japan nonetheless was home to a movement for gender equality. In fact, the first Japanese women's organization, the Tokyo Women's Temperance Union, was founded as early as in 1886 and campaigned mainly for the abolition of prostitution. The Bluestocking Society, formed in 1911 by a group of younger women writers inspired by the eighteenth-century English organization of the same name, attacked the traditional patriarchal family system and called for the expansion of educational and professional opportunities for women, but with little immediate success.

"Japan Lagging in Gender Equality" (An old Japanese adage says that a good woman walks three steps behind her husband.)

The Taisho Democracy era after World War I saw the birth of women's organizations more explicitly committed to achieving gender equality in politics. The Society of New Women founded in 1920 successfully lobbied the Imperial Diet to amend the Peace and Police Law, a 1900 law that prohibited women's participation in political parties and other political organizations. This was followed by the formation of Japan's first suffragist organization in 1924 and its first openly socialist women's organization in 1929. In the militarist climate of the 1930s, however, all these liberal women's organizations were disbanded and replaced by organizations espousing the traditional status and role of women as good homemakers, wives, and mothers.

The political emancipation of women was one of the central goals of the postwar reforms undertaken by the Allied Occupation. Japanese women were enfranchised for the first time in 1947 and began to participate actively in politics as voters. Informal, but widespread, discrimination against women, however, remains a conspicuous characteristic of contemporary Japanese society and politics. According to the 2015 edition of the UN *Human Development Report* (*HDR*), Japan ranked twentieth among 188 countries in the Human Development Index (HDI), which measures overall quality of economic and physical life. But according to the same year's edition of the World Economic Forum's *Global Gender Gap Report*, which measures degrees of gender equality, Japan ranked 111th among 144 nations. Japan is thus one of the most gender-unequal nations in the world—by far the most gender-unequal among the advanced industrial nations. The Japanese movement for gender equality has a long way to go.

Protest

Today's Japan is a generally peaceful and orderly nation, free from vocal widespread, not to mention violent, organized political protest. The only exceptions are demonstrations against the revision of the constitution, especially Article 9, in Tokyo

A "human chain" formed by opponents of U.S. military bases in Okinawa.

*/Newscom/Kyodo News/

and other major cities around the nation and protests against U.S. military bases in Okinawa. The former attracts tens of thousands of participants each time, but they come and go depending on how serious the prospects of a dreaded amendment of the peace clause appear at the time. As the Abe government has become increasingly wary of provoking a violent public protest that could repeat the 1960 event that brought down his grandfather's government, and as a result toned down its call for an immediate amendment of Article 9, protests, too, have become considerably less frequent and strident, though not dead.

The antibase protest in Okinawa, on the other hand, continues unabated and, in fact, grows more persistent and insistent, and with good reason. In the three-month-long Battle of Okinawa, by far the bloodiest fought between Japanese and U.S. forces within Japanese territory at the end of World War II, about two-thirds of the approximately 190,000 Japanese killed or missing were Okinawans and nearly 80 percent of them were civilians. After the war ended in August 1945, Okinawa was administratively separated from the rest of the country, placed under U.S. military rule, and made a key outpost of U.S. forces in Asia during the Cold War.

The island was returned to Japanese administration in 1972, but it has continued to host more than a quarter of the 135 or so U.S. military bases in Japan. These mostly marine bases take up 10 percent of the island's total land area, which accounts for only 0.6 percent of Japan's territory. The islanders' objections to this obvious inequity in the burden-sharing for national security among the prefectures, reinforced by local residents' outcries against frequent and widely publicized base-related accidents and crimes, led the governments of both nations in 2006 to move the particularly controversial base in the midst of a densely populated city near the prefectural capital, Naha, to the less populated area some 25 miles northeast. The plan, however, did not address the Okinawans' basic objections to the egregious concentration of U.S. bases in Japan on the small island. This situation continues to be opposed both by the prefecture's governor and the mayor of its capital city, as well as a majority of the public as reflected in a poll taken by the prefectural government in April 2016. The pent-up frustration and anger surrounding this issue explodes in large-scale demonstrations from time to time.

The Political Impact of Technology and the Media

A total novice in, but an eager and enthusiastic student of, modern industrial and military technologies as it entered the mid-nineteenth-century Eurocentric world, Japan had grown into a major technological power by the early twentieth century. On the eve of World War II, the nation was capable of building some of the most sophisticated military hardware at the time, including the world's largest warships and most agile warplanes.

Under the Allied powers' control following its surrender in 1945, Japan was stripped of all its military industry, as well as its armed forces and arsenal. Within the next two decades, however, it reemerged as one of the postwar world's leading technological powers. Moreover, its industries soon began to develop potentially **dual-use technologies** in a number of fields, including nuclear power, aerospace, electronics, new materials, and biological engineering. Some began to develop even overtly military technologies, such as missiles and drones, albeit only within the

dual-use technologies

Technology normally used for civilian purposes, but which may have military applications.

framework of joint design and production projects with their U.S. counterparts. Moreover, the Abe government lifted the long-standing ban on arms export in 2014, and major Japanese arms makers have begun to bid for an ethically questionable, but economically lucrative, "merchant of death" role in competition with their U.S. and European counterparts.

The designer, builder, and user of the world's first high-speed rail transport, known as the "bullet train" since its inauguration in 1964, Japan dominated export markets around the world for cutting-edge industrial products, especially automobiles, electronics, and machine tools, over the next two decades, in competition with the United States and a few European nations. However, Japan's technological edge in the civilian goods export market began to be challenged by others (notably South Korea and Taiwan) in the 1990s and China in the 2000s. Once touted as one of the world's most technologically advanced and innovative industrial economies, Japan ranked only twenty-sixth on the 2016 *World Competitiveness Scoreboard* of sixty-one nations, compiled by the International Institute for Management Development (IMD) of Lausanne, Switzerland.

Like other democracies, Japan is inundated with all manners of information purveyed by both print and electronic media. Its mainstream mass media are, however, far less outspoken and contentious than their U.S. counterparts, due importantly to the influence of the *kisha* (reporters) club. A *kisha* club consists of reporters from the nation's major print and electronic media.[13] Each club is provided with office space by the organization that it covers, and its members gather information mainly from the organization's official spokespersons. A reporter who seeks and leaks unofficial information risks losing good standing with the host organization, and even club membership. The system tends to suppress publication of news critical of the organizations concerned, such as a government ministry or a major firm. Moreover, all major Japanese newspapers and privately owned television and radio stations depend heavily on advertisements for revenue and tend to avoid publishing information that might offend and alienate their advertisers.

As has happened in the United States and elsewhere, social media have become an increasingly common mode of communication in Japanese society, replacing the traditional print and electronic media as the main source of information for the average citizen. One of the unforeseen and unintended results of this has been to enable people with shared political views to form virtually instant online networks. According to studies by some Japanese scholars, such networks tend to sharpen and harden partisan divisions among Japanese voters. Since the 2013 House of Councillors election, when the use of social media in election campaigns was legalized for the first time, both the right-wing LDP and the left-wing JCP have made significant gains in Diet elections, while the more moderate DPJ and SDP both have suffered significant losses. The alleged divisive political impact of social media has ominous implications in a nation known for its strong concern for national unity and social harmony.

Where Do You Stand?

1. Is the current Japanese parliamentary election system a good one? If so, in what sense? If not, how might it be improved?

2. Is the current state of interest group politics in Japan good or bad for democracy? Why?

JAPANESE POLITICS IN TRANSITION

Political Challenges and Changing Agendas

Japan is still struggling with both the physical and psychological damage left by the 2011 Fukushima nuclear disaster. It depressed Japan's GDP growth to −0.6 percent in 2011, just as it had achieved an encouraging increase to 4.7 percent in the previous year following more than a decade of lackluster performance. In 2012 and 2013, GDP growth climbed back to about 1.5 percent, but has since fallen to virtually zero percent. In 2017, Japan's GDP per capita on a purchasing power parity (PPP) basis was estimated to be about $40,400, comparable to Britain's and France's, but well below that of the United States ($59,400). Most Japanese, however, are not seriously concerned about postdisaster changes in their personal economic conditions, much less about the rankings of Japan's GDP in general or GDP per capita among the nations of the world, which have not changed much since long before the 2011 disaster. In fact, an October 2013 survey by Japan's public broadcaster, NHK, found 90 percent of respondents satisfied with their current living conditions.

The same survey, however, also found that the most important objective for 45 percent of respondents was to live happily with their family members and close friends; for 25 percent, it was to freely enjoy their private lives, and for a small minority of about 5 percent, it was to contribute to building a better world in cooperation with other people. This apparent surge of self-centeredness is accompanied by, and probably arises from, a surge of a deeply pessimistic view of the future of Japan among its own citizens. An October 2014 survey by the Japanese government's Cabinet Office found that 60 percent of respondents at large, and 65 percent of respondents in their thirties, expected their country to be worse off in the next half-century than at the present time. It is difficult to predict at this point whether this apparent national gloom is going to last or is just passing, but if lasting, it may well be a sign of slow but steady erosion of postwar Japan's democratic political culture.

The mounting government debt is another daunting challenge that the nation faces. Over the period from 1997 to 2015, Japan's GDP grew by 6 percent per year, while its national government spending grew by 22 percent, leaving its government coffer chronically in deficit. The growing deficit has been routinely covered by newly issued government bonds, the accumulated amount of the public debt has steadily increased, and debt service has risen to claim nearly a quarter of the entire budget. The outstanding national government debt in 2016 stood at about 250 percent of Japan's GDP, or about $100,000 per citizen—by far the highest in the world, far surpassing the $60,000-per-citizen level in the United States,

Recent cabinets have tried hard to increase revenue and cut spending. In 1989, the effort led to the introduction of a 3 percent national value-added tax, officially called the "consumption tax". The rate was raised to 5 percent in 1997 and to 8 percent in 2014. It is scheduled to be increased further, to 10 percent, in 2019. A serious effort to cut spending has also been underway since the 1980s but has so far failed to make a tangible dent in the astronomical level of the outstanding government debt. It is small wonder, then, that the largest donor of official development assistance (ODA) funds throughout the 1990s, Japan, had fallen to fourth place by 2015, behind the United States, Britain, and Germany.

These difficult and worsening problems, compounded by the impacts of the Fukushima nuclear disaster, breed a widespread sense of helplessness and doubt about government's ability to solve them, which in turn keeps a large segment of the Japanese electorate from voting in Diet, and also local, elections. This growing nonparticipatory mood poses the most serious challenge and threat to the future of Japanese democracy.

Is Demography Destiny?

On top of the several difficult problems discussed here, Japan also faces an even more intractable challenge: the rapid aging of its population. The nation's average life expectancy at birth of 85 is the longest in the world, and its estimated birthrate of 7.80 per 1,000 persons is the second lowest, after Monaco's. As a result of these two trends, Japan now has a higher percentage of citizens 65 years old and over than any other major advanced industrial nation. This has led to a sharp rise in the cost of health care for the elderly and a significant decline in the number of younger, productive workers.

The October 2013 monthly demographic report of the Japanese Ministry of Internal Affairs and Communications showed that the number of minors under 15 years old was 12.9 percent of Japan's total population. The percentage share of this age group had been steadily declining over the last several decades. Back in 1950, this group accounted for more than one-third of the nation's total population. Its ranks fell below those of 65 years old and over for the first time in 1997. Today, the elderly account for a little over a quarter of the total population, or nearly twice as many as minors. This makes Japan the fastest-aging nation in the world. The question many Japanese ask is: Who will be providing for the rapidly growing ranks of the elderly, and how?

Prompted by a widespread public shock over the fall of the total fertility rate to a historical low of 1.57 in 1990—thus known as the "1.57 shock"—the Japanese government set up a special, cabinet-level task force in 1994 to devise and implement a series of legislative, budgetary, and administrative steps to reverse, or at least halt, the alarming trend. These initially emphasized financial support for the construction and maintenance of local day care centers and nursery schools, but have subsequently been expanded to include a variety of more direct assistance to mothers and would-be mothers, such as providing free or subsidized prenatal and postnatal care and services. Since the turn of the millennium, prefectural and municipal governments have begun to initiate a number of similar programs on their own, such as funding special discounts for pregnant women at designated retail stores. The national government alone now spends nearly $1.5 billion each year on a variety of "birthrate-boosting" programs. All these efforts, however, have failed to stop, much less reverse, the long-term demographic change.

An important related issue is the political behavior of Japanese youth. As noted in Section 4, the turnout rates of Japanese youth under the age of 30 in recent Diet elections have been consistently and significantly lower than that of any older age cohort. There are a number of plausible reasons for this apparent reluctance of Japanese youth to participate in the most basic form of democratic politics. Lack of political interest, however, does not seem to be an important reason, in light of the results of a recent government survey.

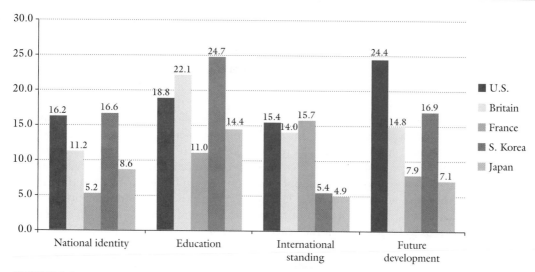

FIGURE 6.5 Percentages of Youth Proud of Four Aspects of Their Own Nation

Data source: Cabinet Office, Government of Japan, Heisei 25-nendo wagakuni to shogaikoku no wakamono no ishiki ni kansuru chosa (2013 survey of views of Japanese and several foreign nations' youth), 2014. http://www8.cao.go.jp/youth/kenkyu/thinking/h25/pdf_index.html

Every 5 years since 1972, the Japanese government has been conducting a survey of the views on wide-ranging social and political issues of some 1,000 randomly chosen youth in Japan and their counterparts in several other nations. In the most recent survey, in 2013, they were asked whether they were interested in the current politics of their nation. A total of 50 percent of Japanese youth answered in the affirmative, as compared to 62 percent of South Korean, 59 percent of U.S., 56 percent of British, and 52 percent of French respondents. The percentage of the Japanese youth satisfied with the current state of their society (32 percent) was marginally higher than that of their French counterparts (31 percent), but lower than their South Korean counterparts (35 percent) and significantly lower than their British (55 percent) and U.S. (45 percent) counterparts.

The most striking findings of this survey, however, were their diverse responses to questions asking whether they were proud of their own country for its strong sense of national identity, high standard of education, international influence and standing, and potential for future development. As Figure 6.5 shows, the percentages of Japanese youth who were proud of their nation for its international standing and potential for future development were the lowest among the respondents from the five nations. Japanese youth are thus politically more pessimistic than apathetic, and this pervasive pessimism lies behind the significantly and consistently low turnout of Japanese youth in recent elections.

The Japanese experience suggests, then, that demography and its political impacts may not be "destiny," but multidimensional, complex, and extremely difficult, if not impossible, for a government or society to control.

Japanese Politics in Comparative Perspective

Japan faces a number of complex and difficult political, economic, and social challenges. In broader comparative perspective, however, few of them are unique to Japan. Its aging population problem is acute, but the same problem is nearly as serious in most advanced and emerging industrial nations, except the United States, but including China. Japan's economic and fiscal problems, such as low and falling growth rates and growing budget deficits, are also widely shared by most high-income nations. Natural disasters such as earthquakes and tsunamis, and even those caused by humans, such as accidents at nuclear power plants, occur in many other nations as well.

Among the nearly 200 nations in today's globalized world, however, Japan is unique, with a pacifist constitution written by foreigners in the wake of the bloodiest war in human history started, in part, by Japan itself. The LDP and LDP governments have been pushing, with increasing vigor in recent years, for the revision of the so-called imposed constitution, but public opposition has so far blocked their move. Whether, and how much longer, Japan will remain the world's only nation with an explicitly and strictly pacifist constitution is the most important and interesting question for us to keep asking in the years to come.

Where Do You Stand?

1. Do you think that today's Japanese youth are understandably pessimistic about the present state and future of their own nation, or unreasonably so? How does this compare to your own feelings about your own country?

2. Should Japan revise its present constitution, fully rearm itself, and become more like most other advanced industrial nations in that regard?

Chapter Summary

We began this chapter with a brief speculative commentary on the potential impacts of the 2016 Diet election in Japan and presidential election in the United States on the future of the postwar Japanese constitution, especially its "peace clause," Article 9. We then touched on the main watershed events in its history, from the arrival of its first human inhabitants some 38,000 years ago to the present; the birth of the Japanese monarchy under the powerful influence of its closest neighbors, China and Korea; the rise of the warrior class and the isolationist Tokugawa shogunate; its fall under U.S. military pressure and the Meiji Restoration, leading to a short period of democratic government followed by the rise of virulent militarism and the plunge into the disastrous Pacific War. We then reviewed the critical junctures in the evolution of the demilitarized and democratized postwar Japan through the phase of an economic "miracle" under the LDP's virtual one-party rule, followed by a period of prolonged recession, in which the nation still remains mired.

Section 2 tracked the trajectory of the development of Japan's modern industrial economy since the Meiji period, nurtured and protected by the state under its industrial policy. We considered in particular the impacts of the demilitarization and democratization reforms on the spectacular performance of postwar Japan's trade-dependent economy in the late 1950s through the early 1970s, and then the effects of the 1985 Plaza Accord, which significantly increased the cost of Japan's exports, and the Japanese government's ill-conceived response, which led, first, to the growth of a bubble economy, and then its bursting and the onset of an ongoing recession. We also considered how and why the so-called Abenomics has failed to solve the conundrum of the Japan's sick economy, compounded by a rapidly aging population and increasingly intense competition with the emerging economies in the region.

Section 3 sketched the characteristics of governance and policymaking in a unitary state where the central government wields a disproportionate amount of political and financial power at the expense of local governments. We pointed out that, apart from the predominant power and role of the central government common to most unitary states, Japan has the world's oldest surviving monarchy, albeit allowed only a symbolic role today, and a military of ambiguous constitutionality. We reviewed the practice of policymaking during the LDP's four-decade-long control of government, effectively under the rule of the iron triangles of politicians, bureaucrats, and interest groups in all major policy areas with a nonassertive judiciary reluctant to use its constitutional power of judicial review against actions of the legislative and executive branches. We saw that the recent changes of government have made no significant difference to the role and power of either the central government or the iron triangles in the basic structure and practice of governance and policy-making in Japan.

Section 4 discussed, first, the structure and operation of the Diet, noting that it resembles the U.S. Congress in some respects, such as its bicameral structure and committee-centered legislative activity, and that it is, also like the U.S. Congress but unlike most other national legislatures in today's world, an exceptionally male-dominated institution. We then described the party system characterized by the conservative LDP's predominant position, pointed out that all Japanese parties are primarily groups of Diet and prefectural assembly members with very small grassroots membership, and explained the extremely complicated rules of Diet elections. Our discussion extended to the important features of Japanese political culture and society, such as the status of the native ethnic minorities and resident Koreans, the current and past political roles of the major interest groups, women's movement, and Okinawan protest against the U.S. military bases in the island. The section ended with a brief overview of the political role and influence of the traditional print and electronic media and, increasingly, newer social media.

Section 5 summarized the main challenges that Japan faces, such as the lingering economic and psychological effects of the 2011 triple disaster, the economic and political costs of the dramatic, and apparently irreversible, demographic change, the pervasive nonparticipatory mood among the Japanese youth, and the prospects of a revision of the 1947 constitution, especially its "peace clause," which has so far set postwar Japan apart from every other nation, present or past.

Key Terms

administrative guidance
Amakudari
dual-use technologies
Four Great Pollution Trials
Fukushima nuclear disaster
industrial policy
iron triangle
Japan Self-Defense Forces
  (JSDF)

keiretsu
koenkai
Lay Judge System
  (*saiban'in-seido*)
nontariff barrier (NTB)
pork-barrel politics
predominant-party democracy
samurai
shogun

single nontransferable vote
  (SNTV)
single-member district (SMD)
Supreme Commander for the
  Allied Powers (SCAP)
Taisho democracy
zaibatsu
zoku

Suggested Readings

Barnhart, Michael A. *Japan Prepares for Total War: The Search for Economic Security, 1919–1941.* Ithaca, NY: Cornell University Press, 1987.

Dower, John. *Embracing Defeat: Japan in the Aftermath of World War II.* London: Penguin Books, 1999.

Haddad, Mary Alice. *Building Democracy in Japan.* Cambridge, U.K.: Cambridge University Press, 2012.

Hall, John Whitney, et al., eds., *The Cambridge History of Japan,* 6 vols. Cambridge, U.K.: Cambridge University Press, 1988–1993.

Hashimoto, Akiko. *The Long Defeat: Cultural Trauma, Memory, and Identity in Japan.* Oxford, U.K.: Oxford University Press, 2015.

Hein, Laura, and Mark Selden, eds. *Islands of Discontent; Okinawan Responses to Japanese and American Power.* Lanham, MD: Rowman & Littlefield, 2003.

Lockwood, William W. *The Economic Development of Japan: Growth and Structural Change, 1868–1938.* Princeton, NJ: Princeton University Press, 1954.

Payliss, Jeffrey Paul. *On the Margin of Empire: Buraku and Korean Identity in Prewar and Wartime Japan.* Cambridge, MA: Harvard University Asia Center, 2013.

Samuels, Richard J. *Securing Japan: Tokyo's Grand Strategy and the Future of East Asia.* Ithaca, NY: Cornell University Press, 2007.

Winkler, Christian G. *The Quest for Japan's New Constitution: An Analysis of Visions and Constitutional Reform Proposals, 1980–2009.* London: Routledge, 2011.

India

Atul Kohli and Amrita Basu

Official Name: Republic of India (Bharat)

Location: South Asia

Capital City: New Delhi

Population (2017): 1.34 billion

Size: 3,287,590 sq. km.; slightly more than one-third the size of the United States

THE MAKING OF THE MODERN INDIAN STATE

Politics in Action

Focus Questions ⑦

• What explains India's ability to maintain democratic institutions for most of its postindependence history?

• What lessons does India hold for the prospects of establishing democracy in multiethnic societies?

On November 8, 2016, at 10.15 p.m., India's Prime Minister Narendra Modi announced on television that two of India's largest currency bills—₹500 and ₹1000 rupees (about $7.50 and $15.00, respectively) –would no longer be honored the next day. All Indians with cash savings in these denominations were given 50 days to exchange them at banks for new, valid bills. In one secretive stroke, Mr. Modi demonetized the Indian economy by some ₹15 trillion rupees ($220 billion), about 10 percent of the Indian GDP. Modi initially claimed that the policy would rid the economy of counterfeit money that terrorists used. To this was soon added another rationale, that demonetization would help eliminate corruption in the broader economy because many corrupt practices require "under the table" cash exchanges.

What followed in India over the next several months was nothing short of chaotic. Most people conduct commercial transactions through cash and a relatively small proportion use credit cards. Furthermore, the policy was implemented poorly. New currency bills turned out to be in short supply. ATM machines had not been adjusted and could not deal with the new currency. People waited in long lines for days on end to exchange their cash savings into the new currency before the 50-day deadline. Demonstrations broke out. Newspaper editorials criticized the government. The foreign press, such as the well-reputed *Economist,* criticized the policy, especially its implementation. The resulting economic slowdown caused the World Bank to significantly lower its estimate of India's GDP growth for the coming year.

When elections were held in some Indian states in early 2017, including in the largest Indian state of Uttar Pradesh (U.P.), it was widely expected that the electorate would punish Modi and the ruling party he heads—the Bharatiya Janata Party (BJP) –for the demonetization fiasco. Much to everyone's surprise, nothing of the sort happened. Modi's party won handsomely in U.P. and in other state elections. Modi is a charismatic politician. Voters apparently agreed with his claim that demonetization would hurt the rich and the corrupt, and was therefore worth some short-term inconvenience for the "common man." The BJP also mobilized along religious nationalist lines, pitching the Hindu majority against the Muslim minority. Rival parties failed to capitalize on the political opportunity provided by demonetization reform. The BJP's superior organization, along with a message that combined populism and anti-Muslim demagoguery, enabled Modi to strengthen his political position.

These political developments underline several interrelated themes that will be discussed later in this chapter. First, democracy in India is highly competitive; political parties use both fair means and foul to achieve power. Second, poor policies often do not turn out to be electoral liabilities, just as good policies do not always turn out to be electoral assets. Electoral outcomes are also swayed by qualities of leadership, how campaign messages are crafted and conveyed, and most of all, by direct or indirect appeals to identity politics. Third, even good policies are often implemented poorly. This policy-gap underlines a central feature of Indian politics: a well-functioning

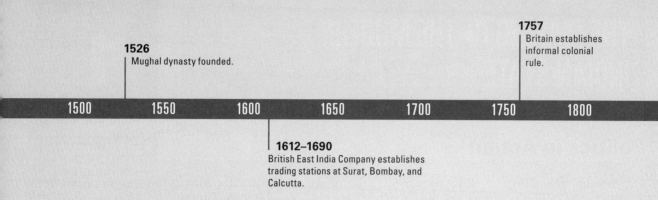

1526
Mughal dynasty founded.

1757
Britain establishes informal colonial rule.

1500   1550   1600   1650   1700   1750   1800

1612–1690
British East India Company establishes trading stations at Surat, Bombay, and Calcutta.

democracy that often fails to provide good government. And finally, policy making in India is becoming more and more centralized. While some secretiveness prior to demonetization is understandable, it is less understandable that the livelihood of more than a billion people was deeply disrupted by a handful of political leaders and officials. (See Figure 7.1 and Table 7.1.)

Geographic Setting

India is the seventh-largest country in the world and the third-largest country in Asia. It is called a subcontinent because of its large and distinct land mass. India's rich geography includes three diverse topographic zones (the mountainous northern zone, the basin formed by the Ganges River, and the peninsula of southern India) and a variety of climates (cold in the northern mountain range; dry and hot in the arid, northern plateau; and subtropical in the south). Along with Pakistan and Bangladesh, India is separated from the rest of Asia by the Himalayas to the north and the Indian Ocean to the east, south, and west. Only the northwest frontier is easily passable and has been used for thousands of years.

With 1.34 billion people, India's population is second only to its neighbor China. Although the Indian economy is growing rapidly, so is its population. Population growth strains physical infrastructure and increases the need for social services, especially because so many children are born into poverty. The Indian government's family planning policies have been meager and ineffective.

India is by far the world's largest democracy and the oldest democracy in Asia, Africa, and Latin America. It has had democratic institutions since it became an independent country in 1947, after nearly two centuries of British colonial rule. The durability of Indian democracy is impressive, considering the country's huge population, extensive poverty, and enormous social and regional diversity. India has twenty-two official national languages. Hindi, the largest, is spoken by about 30 percent of the

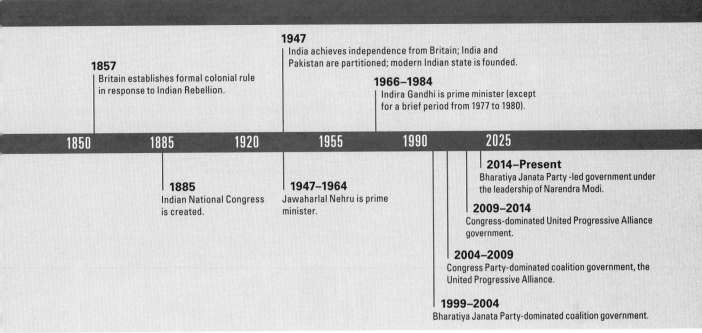

1857
Britain establishes formal colonial rule in response to Indian Rebellion.

1947
India achieves independence from Britain; India and Pakistan are partitioned; modern Indian state is founded.

1966–1984
Indira Gandhi is prime minister (except for a brief period from 1977 to 1980).

1850	1885	1920	1955	1990	2025

1885
Indian National Congress is created.

1947–1964
Jawaharlal Nehru is prime minister.

2014–Present
Bharatiya Janata Party -led government under the leadership of Narendra Modi.

2009–2014
Congress-dominated United Progressive Alliance government.

2004–2009
Congress Party-dominated coalition government, the United Progressive Alliance.

1999–2004
Bharatiya Janata Party-dominated coalition government.

population. There are also numerous regional dialects. India contains many ethnic groups, regionally concentrated tribal groups, and followers of every major religion in the world. While Hindus represent 79.5 percent of the population, India includes Muslims, **Sikhs**, Christians, Jains, Buddhists, and several tiny Jewish communities. India's approximately 172 million Muslims, 14 percent of the Indian population, are the third-largest Muslim population in the world, after Indonesia and Pakistan.

Sikhs

Sikhs, a religious minority, constitute less than 2 percent of the Indian population and 76 percent of the state of Punjab. Sikhism is a monotheistic religion that was founded in the fifteenth century.

Xinhua/Alamy

Queue at ATM machines following demonetization reform.

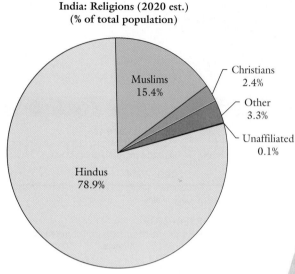

India: Religions (2020 est.)
(% of total population)

Muslims 15.4%

Christians 2.4%

Other 3.3%

Unaffiliated 0.1%

Hindus 78.9%

India: Languages

The Constitution of India recognizes 22 national languages, of which Hindi, the primary tongue of about 40% of the population, is the official language of the country. The Constitution also allows for the use of English for official purposes. There are 844 different dialects practiced in various parts of the country.

Indian Currency:
Rupee (₹)
International Code: INR
Exchange Rate (2017)
• US$1 = ₹64.38
• ₹1 = US$0.02
1000₹ Note Design:
Mahatma Gandhi (1869–1948)

© Cengage

RAMINDER PAL SINGH /Newscom/
European Pressphoto Agency/Amritsar/
Punjab/india

FIGURE 7.1 The Indian Nation at a Glance

caste system

According to the Hindu religion, society is divided into castes. Membership in a caste is determined at birth. The different castes form a rough social and economic hierarchy.

Brahmin

The highest caste in the Hindu caste system.

Indian society, especially the Hindu population, is divided into numerous caste groupings. Mainly based on occupation, castes tend to be closed social groups into which people are born, marry, and die. Historically, the **caste system** compartmentalized and ranked the Hindu population through rules governing daily life, such as eating, marriage, and prayer. Caste hierarchy conceptualizes the world as divided into realms of purity and impurity. Each hereditary and endogamous group (that is, a group into which one is born and within which one marries) constitutes a *jati*, which is itself organized by *varna*, the principle that orders the caste system. The four main *varnas* are the *Brahmin*, or priestly caste; the *Kshatriya*, or warrior and royal caste; the *Vaishyas*, or trading caste; and the *Shudra*, or artisan caste. Each *varna* is divided into many *jatis* that correspond to occupational groups.

Two-thirds of Indians live in far-flung villages in the countryside. However, the major cities, Bombay (renamed Mumbai), Calcutta (renamed Kolkata), and New Delhi, the national capital, are among the largest and most densely populated cities in the world.

Critical Junctures

Indian civilization dates to the Indus Valley Civilization of the third millennium BCE. The subcontinent, comprising present-day Pakistan, India, and Bangladesh, has witnessed the rise and fall of many civilizations and empires. Alexander the Great's invasion of northwestern India in 326 BCE introduced trade and communication with western Asia. The Maurya dynasty (322–185 BCE) under Emperor Ashoka united

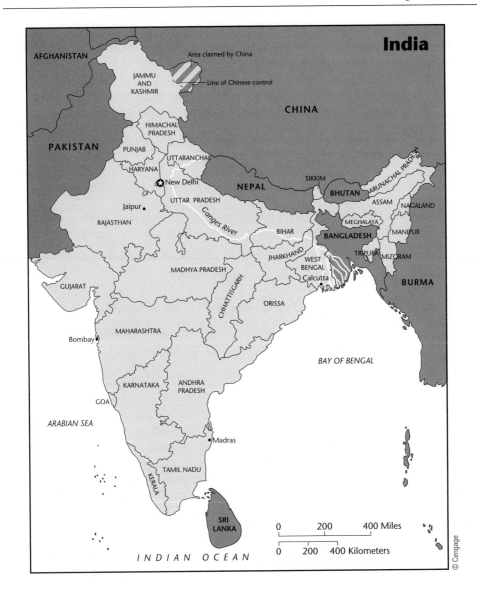

separate kingdoms in northern India into a single empire. The Mughal kingdom (early sixteenth century to mid-nineteenth century) further expanded to include most of the Indian subcontinent and parts of what are now Afghanistan.

As the Mughal Empire declined, several states expanded and new states emerged. The most important formed the Maratha Empire, which, at its height, controlled most of central and northern India. Other important regimes in the post-Mughal period included the Sikh Empire in the north, and the Mysore kingdom and state of Hyderabad in the south.

Precolonial India was mostly divided into princely states. However, the power of princely rulers was limited by a dominant social order that they were unable to change.

The Colonial Legacy (1757–1947)

The British began gaining control of the subcontinent in the late seventeenth century when the East India Company, a large English trading organization, developed

Table 7.1	Political Organization
Political System	Parliamentary democracy and a federal republic.
Regime History	In 2014, the government was formed by the BJP, with Narendra Modi as the prime minister. The BJP and the Congress are two of India's main national parties.
Administrative Structure	Federal, with twenty-nine state governments and seven union territories.
Executive	Prime minister, leader of the party or coalition with the most seats in the parliament.
Legislature	Bicameral, upper house elected indirectly and without much substantial power; lower house, the main house, with members elected from single-member districts, winner-takes-all.
Judiciary	Independent constitutional court with appointed judges.
Party System	Multiparty system. The Bharatiya Janata Party (BJP) is the dominant Party; the Congress Party is the major opposition party.

Indian Rebellion

An armed uprising in 1857 by Indian soldiers against expansion of British colonialism in India.

commercial interests in India. With strong backing from the British Crown, it played off one Indian prince against another. After the **Indian Rebellion** of 1857, also known as the Sepoy Rebellion and the Mutiny of 1857, a large-scale revolt by Indian soldiers, Britain assumed direct control from the East India Company.

The British described India, its most valuable colonial possession, as the "jewel in the [British] crown." India provided Britain with raw materials, notably cotton, and a profitable market for Britain's growing industries, especially textiles. (Britain dismantled India's own textile industry to create demand for British products.) The Indian nationalist movement succeeded in expelling the British and made India an independent country in 1947, shortly after World War II. India was among the first colonies in the developing world to gain independence.

To control the subcontinent, the British created a relatively efficient administrative structure consisting of an all-India civil service, police force, and army. At first, only British nationals were permitted to serve in these institutions. Eventually, some educated Indians were permitted to join. After independence, these institutions continued to be organized along the principles the British colonialists established in the nineteenth and twentieth centuries. Britain started constructing a railway system in east India in the 1840s; by 1880 there were over 9,000 miles of rail lines throughout the country. The rail system continued to expand throughout the twentieth century. It is currently among the largest in Asia and remains an important means for transporting people and freight.

The Nationalist Movement and Partition (1885–1947)

British rulers and traditional rural Indian elites became allies of sorts, squeezing resources from the peasantry to maintain the bureaucratic state and support the luxurious lifestyle of the parasitic landlord class. However, this exploitative pattern generated increasing opposition. The growth of commerce, education, and urbanization gave rise to urban, educated upper-caste Indians who resented being treated as second-class citizens. They formed the Indian National Congress (INC) in 1885.

In its early years, the INC periodically met and petitioned British rulers for a greater voice in administering India's affairs. They sought political equality and access to higher administrative offices. Eventually, their requests turned into demands. Some nationalists resorted to violence; others adopted a strategy of nonviolent mass mobilization. Thanks to the brilliant and inspiring leadership of Mohandas Karamchand Gandhi, the INC preserved a fragile unity. Gandhi led India's nationalist movement for decades, and his strategy of militant but nonviolent protest set a high standard for political activists around the world. In the United States, civil rights leader Martin Luther King, Jr., for example, was deeply inspired by Gandhi, as was Nelson Mandela in South Africa.

As support for the INC grew, the British had to repress it or make concessions. They tried both. The turning point occurred when Britain's struggle against Nazi Germany during World War II increased the costs of maintaining control over India. To gain Indians' support for the war effort, Britain promised to grant India independence. In August 1947, soon after the war ended, India became a sovereign nation.

The euphoria of Indian independence was tempered by the human tragedy that accompanied the partition of the subcontinent. Influential members of India's minority Muslim elite regarded the Hindu-dominated INC with suspicion, in part because of the legacies of colonial divide-and-rule policies. When the INC refused to concede to their demands for separate Muslim political rights, they demanded the creation of an independent Muslim state in northern India, which had a large Muslim population. Britain conceded and divided the subcontinent into two sovereign states in 1947—the Muslim state of Pakistan and the secular state of India, in which most citizens were Hindu. The period following Partition, as it was called, was turbulent and destructive. Millions of Muslims fled from India to Pakistan, and millions of Hindus fled the other way. More than 10 million people migrated and nearly a million died in interethnic violence. The Muslim population of India declined from 24 percent before independence to 10 percent thereafter.

Three features of the nationalist movement greatly influenced Indian state building and democracy. First, the INC created a broad tent within which political, ethnic, and religious conflicts could play out. This helped India form and maintain a relatively stable political system. However, second, Hindu-Muslim tensions, which gave rise to Partition, resulted in enduring hostilities between the neighboring states of India and Pakistan. The two countries have fought three wars since Partition. Although some recent initiatives have defused tensions, there remains the possibility of war between these two nuclear powers.

Third, the nationalist movement laid the foundations for democracy in India. Many of the INC's prominent leaders, like Gandhi and Jawaharlal Nehru, were educated in England and were committed democrats. Moreover, the INC chose its leaders through internal elections, participated in provincial elections, and ran democratic governments, albeit with limited powers, in British-controlled Indian provinces. These pre-independence democratic tendencies were valuable future resources.

The Nehru Era (1947–1964)

After independence, India adopted a Westminster model of British-style parliamentary democracy. The INC transformed itself from an opposition movement into a political party, the Congress Party. It was highly successful at first, both because of its popularity in having led India to independence and because the Congress government created a nationwide **patronage system** that rewarded supporters with posts and resources.

patronage system

A political system in which government officials appoint loyal followers to positions rather than choosing people based on merit.

nonaligned bloc

Countries that refused to ally with either the United States or the USSR during the Cold War years.

Jawaharlal Nehru wanted India to play a global role. Together with other leaders of newly independent countries in Asia and Africa, he initiated what became known as the **nonaligned bloc**, a group of countries seeking autonomy from the two superpowers. He attempted to set India on a rapid road to industrialization by promoting heavy industry. He was also committed to redistributing wealth through land reform. However, much of India's land remained concentrated in the hands of traditional rural elites. Although Nehru and the Congress Party proclaimed pro-poor, socialist commitments, they generally failed to deliver on their promises. To this day, India remains divided between small affluent elites and hundreds of millions of poor peasants and urban workers. In recent years, India's economic growth has created a sizeable middle class between these two extremes. Nonetheless, most Indians in both cities and countryside remain poor. Despite India's amazingly rapid economic growth in the past two decades, the per capita income of its citizens places India among the poorest countries in the world.

An important change in the decade following independence was the creation of states based on the principal language in the region. Many non-Hindi language speakers feared domination by Hindi speakers and demanded that India be reorganized into linguistically defined states. Nehru reluctantly agreed to the creation of fourteen such states in 1957. In later years, additional states were carved out of existing ones, and there are now twenty-nine major states within India.

The Indira Gandhi Era (1966–1984)

When Nehru died in 1964, the Congress Party was divided over the choice of a successor and hastily selected a compromise candidate, mild-mannered Lal Bahadur Shastri, as prime minister. When Shastri died in 1966, rivalry among potential successors broke out. Party elites chose another compromise candidate, Nehru's daughter, Indira Gandhi (no relation to Mohandas Gandhi). They calculated that, as Nehru's daughter, she would help the Congress Party garner sufficient electoral support to remain in power. They also thought that she would be a weak woman whom they could manipulate. Their first calculation was correct; the second was wholly inaccurate.

Indira Gandhi was India's second longest-serving prime minister. Her father was the longest-serving. She held office from 1966 to 1984, for all but three years, 1977 to 1980. She consolidated control over the Congress Party, replacing existing leaders with loyal allies. She adopted a populist rhetoric that appealed to India's poor. However, she did not translate it into real gains. Like her father, she failed to redistribute agricultural land from large landowners to small farmers and agricultural laborers or to generate employment, provide welfare, and broaden access to education and medical services.

Indian politics became increasingly turbulent under Indira Gandhi. As her power grew, she encountered growing opposition. In 1974, the political situation became quite unstable. After the opposition organized strikes and demonstrations in 1975, Gandhi declared a State of Emergency. She suspended many democratic rights, arrested most opposition leaders, and ruled by decree. The **Emergency** lasted nearly two years, the only period since independence that India did not function as a democracy (see Table 7.2 for a list of Indian prime ministers).

Emergency (1975–1977)

The period when Indian Prime Minister Indira Gandhi suspended many formal democratic rights and ruled in an authoritarian manner.

Gandhi ended the Emergency in 1977 and called for national elections, confident that she would be reelected. However, opposition groups hastily united under an umbrella organization, the Janata Party. Gandhi and the Congress Party were soundly defeated. For the first time since independence, a non-Congress government occupied power. Soon after the elections, however, Janata leaders became factionalized, and the government collapsed. Indira Gandhi regained power in the 1980 parliamentary elections.

Table 7.2	Prime Ministers of India, 1947–Present	
	Years in Office	**Party**
Jawaharlal Nehru	1947–1964	Congress
Lal Bahadur Shastri	1964–1966	Congress
Indira Gandhi	1966–1977	Congress
Morarji Desai	1977–1979	Janata
Charan Singh	1979–1980	Janata
Indira Gandhi	1980–1984	Congress
Rajiv Gandhi	1984–1989	Congress
V. P. Singh	1989–1990	Janata
Chandra Shekhar	1990–1991	Janata (Socialist)
Narasimha Rao	1991–1996	Congress
Atal Bihari Vajpayee	1996 (13 days)	BJP and Allies
H. D. Deve Gowda	1996–1997	United Front
I. K. Gujral	1997–1998	United Front
Atal Bihari Vajpayee	1998–2004	BJP and Allies
Manmohan Singh	2004–2014	Congress and Allies
Narendra Modi	2014–Present	BJP and Allies

Indira Gandhi's tenure in power between 1980 and 1984 was marked, as it had been when she governed earlier, by a personal and populist political style, an increasingly centralized political system, failure to implement antipoverty policies, and political turbulence. However, Gandhi departed from her previous approach in two ways. First, she abandoned her earlier socialist commitments and strengthened the private sector to improve India's economic performance. Second, she abandoned secularism and began using religious appeals to mobilize India's Hindu majority. Gandhi contributed to polarization and conflict by misleadingly depicting Sikhs' grievances as religious and secessionists. This encouraged the rise of an extremist faction among Sikhs who took over the holiest Sikh temple, in the city of Amritsar in 1984. Gandhi made the fatal mistake of dispatching troops to root out the militants. Sikhs were outraged when the operation badly damaged the temple and left many dead and injured. Months later, Gandhi was assassinated by her Sikh bodyguards. Immediately after her death, outraged groups of Hindus, led by Congress Party members, killed 2,800 Sikhs in New Delhi and other north Indian cities. Some of the people responsible for the carnage were convicted decades later.

Under Indira Gandhi's leadership, Indian politics became more personalized, populist, and nationalist. While her foreign policies strengthened India's international position, her domestic policies weakened democratic institutions. For example, whereas during the Nehru era, local elites had helped select the Congress Party's higher political officeholders, Gandhi directly appointed national and regional-level party officials. Although this enabled her to gain a firm grip over the party, it also isolated her from broader political forces and eroded the authority of regional leaders.

Indira Gandhi's death ushered in the third generation of the Nehru–Gandhi dynasty, when her son Rajiv Gandhi succeeded her as prime minister (1984-1989). Rajiv Gandhi won a landslide victory in the elections that followed his mother's death because of sympathy for him at his mother's assassination. He came to office promising a clean government, a high-tech economy that would carry India into the next century, and reduced ethnic conflict. He was somewhat successful in easing tensions in the Punjab. But he inflamed relations between Hindus and Muslims by sponsoring a law that sharply limited the rights of Muslim women. His leadership was also marred by allegations of corruption.

Coalition Governments (1989 to the Present)

For the first three decades after independence, many parties competed for office. However, none came close to rivaling Congress, particularly in national politics. The Congress Party led every government from 1947 to 1989, except for one brief interlude (1977–1980). The decline of the Congress Party ushered in an era of instability with no clearly dominant party. In each national election since 1989, coalition governments have depended on the support of state-based parties.

However, in 2004 the Congress coalition government gained a stronger mandate than it had in many years. The leader of Congress was Sonia Gandhi, the Italian-born widow of slain Prime Minister Rajiv Gandhi. Although she had demonstrated her ability to lead Congress, party elites feared that her Italian background made her a risky choice as prime minister. Instead they named Manmohan Singh, a respected former cabinet minister, as prime minister.

For the first time, a politician who was neither leader of his own party nor that of the ruling alliance became prime minister. Although he was not a charismatic figure, Manmohan Singh initially proved to be a highly capable and popular prime minister. He is credited with introducing measures to shake the Indian economy from its torpor and promote rapid economic growth. His Congress-led coalition government was re-elected to power in 2009 by a larger margin than in 2004. However, as described below, his reputation became tarnished when he failed to address widespread corruption by Congress government officials. Narendra Modi of the BJP party was elected as India's prime minister in the 2014 election by a significant majority.

Narendra Modi represents a striking contrast with the soft spoken, self-effacing Oxford educated Sikh leader Manmohan Singh. Modi comes from a Gujarati Hindu family of modest means, and began his ascent to power through a Hindu nationalist organization, the Rashtriya Swayamsevak Sangh (RSS). With RSS backing, Modi joined the BJP and advanced through the ranks to become its general secretary and later chief minister of Gujarat. Many members of the Modi-led BJP administration were convicted of violence against Muslims in Gujarat in 2002 but the court did not find sufficient evidence to prosecute Modi. In contesting the 2014 elections and since becoming prime minister, Modi has generally avoided taking hard line Hindu nationalist positions. However, he retains close ties to the RSS, has placed some of its members in key institutional positions and has promoted some of its policies. He remains a controversial but popular leader.

September 11 and Its Aftermath

India was affected by the September 11, 2001, attacks on the World Trade Center in New York and on the Pentagon in Washington. Although none of the al Qaeda terrorists who hijacked the planes on September 11 was from India or neighboring Pakistan, the global network of violence that flourished after 9/11 cast a shadow over Indo-Pakistan relations. On the Pakistani side, high-level units of Pakistan's powerful and shadowy intelligence organization, the Inter-Services Intelligence (ISI), provided support for groups linked to al Qaeda.

For years before 9/11, these groups carried out attacks on Indian armed forces and civil officials in the part of Kashmir controlled by India but claimed by Pakistan. After 9/11, militants based in Pakistan, supported by the ISI, began to launch attacks on the Indian heartland. Two incidents were especially dramatic. First, on December 13, 2001, militants bombed the Indian Parliament in Delhi, killing fifteen people. India charged that Pakistan was behind the attack and both countries assembled a million troops on the border. The U.S. helped defuse tensions temporarily and relations significantly improved in 2005, when the two countries agreed to initiate a cross-border bus service. However, the second flash point occurred in November 2008, when ten Pakistani members of the terrorist organization Lashkar-e-Taiba stormed Mumbai's iconic Taj Intercontinental Hotel and the Chhatrapati Shivaji Railroad Terminus. They barricaded themselves in the hotel, took hundreds of hostages, and executed scores of guests (selecting Westerners as their prime target). For three horrifying days, television stations around the world portrayed the standoff at the hotel. The crisis ended when Indian elite forces stormed the hotel and killed all but one militant, who was later tried and sentenced to death in May 2010. A total of 164 people were killed and 308 people injured in the attack. Tensions between India and Pakistan dramatically escalated when the surviving militant described ISI's involvement in the massacre. Although Prime Minister Singh avoided a war with Pakistan, the Mumbai attack inflamed relations between the two countries.

AP Images/Lefteris Pitarakis

One hundred and sixty-four people were killed and 308 people were injured in the November 29, 2008, bombing of the Taj Hotel in Mumbai. The Lashkar-e-Taiba claimed responsibility for this attack.

Ties between India and the United States have become closer since 9/11. The United States accorded India an important role in strengthening the Afghan president Hamid Karzai's government (2004–2014) following the United States decision to withdraw troops from Afghanistan and its discovery of Osama bin Laden in Pakistan. The United States has increased weapon sales to India and the Indian government has signed a strategic partnership agreement with Karzai. While the United States–Indian relationship has experienced some ups and downs, for now, India, the United States and the Afghan government are working together to contain militancy in the region.

The Four Themes and India

India in a Globalized World of States

India is well positioned, by its large size, growing wealth, democratic legitimacy, and geographic location, to play a powerful role in world affairs. Yet for this to occur, it is necessary for India to nurture peaceful relations with its powerful neighbors, Pakistan and China.

Governing the Economy

In the years following independence, Indian policy-makers first sought to achieve economic self-sufficiency through state-led industrialization to satisfy the needs of India's large internal market. This economic strategy required protectionist measures (such as high tariffs) to shield India from foreign economic competition. It succeeded in creating some important basic industries but also generated extensive inefficiencies and failed to reduce severe poverty. Like many developing nations, India adjusted its economic strategy to meet the demands of competitive and interdependent global markets. During the 1980s, the government provided incentives to India's private sector to increase production. Since 1991, reforms have opened the Indian economy to the outside world. The results include both rapid economic growth and growing inequalities. Among the daunting challenges facing Indian leaders is how to sustain growth while sponsoring measures to reduce poverty and economic inequalities.

The Democratic Idea

In recent decades, India has become more democratic in some ways but less democratic in others. A larger number of people, with more diverse identities, are participating in politics. The Indian political class is no longer recruited from a single region, caste, and class. However, business leaders wield much more political influence than do the far more numerous poor. The growth of Hindu nationalism has challenged minority rights and resulted in attacks on Muslims and Christians. Prime Minister Modi has also centralized much personal power.

The Politics of Collective Identity

Democracy is supposed to provide a level playing field in which diverse interests and identities seek to resolve their differences. India demonstrates that an incredibly large and diverse country can generally process conflicts peacefully and democratically. However, it also demonstrates the recurrent danger of political forces instigating violence, often for electoral purposes.

Implications for Comparative Politics

India's fascinating profile can deepen our understanding of comparative politics. First, it represents an exceptional case of a poor yet vibrant democracy. Despite widespread poverty and illiteracy, most Indians value their citizenship rights and exercise them vigorously. Against great odds, India became and remains a thriving democracy, an especially striking achievement given the authoritarian fate of most newly independent countries in Asia and Africa.

Second, although the Indian state has remained cohesive and stable at the national level, political violence has occurred in a variety of states and regions. Third, with well over a billion people of diverse cultural, religious, and linguistic identities,

Indian democracy is an excellent arena for analyzing various theories and dilemmas of comparative politics. At its best, India offers instructive lessons in multiethnic democracy. At its worst, it can provide lessons in how democracy can be misused.

Fourth, theorists of democratic change in Latin America and Eastern Europe have puzzled over what constitutes a consolidated democracy and how to achieve it. Here, a comparison between India and Pakistan is instructive. Whereas the two countries were formed at the same moment, India has functioned as a democracy for all but three years since 1947, while Pakistan has been an authoritarian state for most of the same period.

Fifth, comparativists have explored whether democracy and social equity can be achieved simultaneously in poor countries. The case of Kerala, a state in southern India, suggests that the answer is a cautious yes. Although one of the poorest states in India, Kerala has achieved near-total literacy, long life expectancy, low infant mortality, and widespread access to medical care. Kerala's development indicators compare favorably with the rest of India, other low-income countries, and even wealthy countries like the United States.

Finally, comparativists have long engaged in a lively debate about the impact of democracy on economic growth. While cross-national evidence remains inconclusive, India's record of steady economic growth of some 6 percent annually since 1980 powerfully demonstrates how successful economic management can occur within a democratic framework. At the same time, India's failure to adequately redistribute its economic resources provides a more sobering lesson.

Where Do You Stand?

Would India be better off with a more authoritarian system?

Is democracy meaningful for those who do not have enough to eat and may not be able to read and write?

POLITICAL ECONOMY AND DEVELOPMENT

SECTION 2

At independence, India had a poor, largely agricultural economy. Although a large majority of Indians, especially the poor, still work and live in the countryside, India has developed a substantial industrial base, a booming service sector, and a vibrant middle class. During the first three decades following independence, the Indian economy was mainly state-directed. Though the overall economic growth during this period was sluggish, India successfully created an industrial base behind protectionist walls. The more recent rapid growth has built on this base. Since 1980, Indian governments have prioritized economic growth, led by the private sector. Unlike many other developing countries, India has preferred national over foreign investors as agents of economic growth. Both national and regional governments have provided support to investors in the form of access to land, tax relief, and transport and other subsidies. The results have included not only rapid economic growth but also growing inequalities. The Indian economy is now one of the world's fastest growing economies, even faster than that of China. However, India also remains home to the world's largest number of poor and seriously malnourished children.

Focus Questions

- What have been two major achievements and two major failures of Indian economic development strategy?

- How successfully has India managed to balance the goals of promoting economic efficiency and social equity? Suggest one or more ways that the trade-off could be improved.

State and Economy

The Economy after Independence

One of the central tasks that Indian leaders faced after 1947 was to modernize the sluggish economy. During Nehru's rule, India's model of development emphasized the creation of public enterprises and state guidance of private economic activity. Nehru created a powerful planning commission that established government investment priorities. Unlike the planning process in communist states, Indian plans included a large role for private entrepreneurs. Some large, private family-owned firms in industries like steel were a powerful force in the Indian economy. But the government also limited the start-up and expansion of private industries. It imposed high tariffs, arguing that newly created Indian industries required protection from foreign competitors.

This government-planned mixed economy enabled India to create an impressive industrial base but did little to help the poor. The protected industries were quite inefficient by global standards, and were hindered from acting boldly by the mountains of red tape that government bureaucrats generated.

Given the predominantly rural character of India, the highly unequal distribution of agricultural land presented a particularly significant challenge. Although legislation passed in the early 1950s reduced the size of landholdings, little of the reclaimed land was reallocated to poor tenants and agricultural laborers. Most remained in the hands of medium- to large-sized landowners, who became part of the Congress political machine. This weakened the Congress Party's socialist commitment and its ability to assist the rural poor.

Rather than fulfilling its promise to enact substantial land reforms, the government adopted an alternative strategy in the late 1960s. Known as the **green revolution**, it aimed to increase agricultural production by providing farmers with improved seeds, subsidized fertilizer, and irrigation. The green revolution made India self-sufficient in food and even a food exporter. This represented a sharp contrast with the past, when famines resulted in mass starvation.

However, the benefits of the green revolution were highly uneven. While production increased sharply in the Punjab, for example, poor farmers in less favored regions were left behind. The very success of the green revolution created long-term problems. Synthetic fertilizers depleted the soil. The high costs of pesticides, agricultural equipment, and genetically modified seeds forced farmers to borrow large sums at high interest rates from banks and money-lenders. In recent years, the states that were the standard bearers of the green revolution have experienced a severe agricultural crisis. One tragic result has been a wave of suicides by farmers who were unable to repay massive debts.

To summarize, the period between 1950 and 1980 consisted of **state-led economic development** that expanded the public sector, protected the domestic sector from foreign competition and closely supervised private sector activity. Political leaders hoped to strengthen India's international position by promoting self-sufficient industrialization. This policy was somewhat successful. State-led development insulated the Indian economy from global influences. The strategy resulted in modest economic growth, whose main beneficiaries were the business classes, medium and large landowning farmers, and political and bureaucratic elites. A substantial urban middle class also developed. By 1980, India was a significant industrial power that produced its own steel, airplanes, automobiles, chemicals, military hardware, and many consumer goods. Although land reform failed, the green revolution greatly increased food production.

However, state-led development also had substantial flaws. Shielded from foreign competition, industry was often inefficient, and the entire economy grew at a slow

green revolution

A strategy for increasing agricultural (especially food) production, involving improved seeds, irrigation, and abundant use of fertilizers.

state-led economic development

The process of actively promoting economic development through government policy, usually involving indicative planning and financial subsidization of industries.

pace. The elaborate rules and regulations controlling private economic activity encouraged corruption, as entrepreneurs bribed bureaucrats to evade the rules. And the focus on heavy industry meant that most investment involved purchasing machinery rather than creating jobs: 40 percent of India's population, primarily poor tenant farmers and landless laborers, were unable to escape poverty; indeed, the number of desperately poor people increased substantially.

Economic Liberalization

Political and economic elites became increasingly dissatisfied with India's inadequate economic performance compared with that of other Asian countries. For example, during the 1970s, whereas India's economy grew at the rate of 3.4 percent annually, South Korea's grew at 9.6 percent. India's business and industrial classes began to regard government regulation of the economy as a hindrance rather than a help. They became aware that poverty limited the possibility for expanding domestic markets. A turning point occurred in the 1980s and accelerated after 1991, when India moved toward **economic liberalization**. Under the leadership of Finance Minister (and later Prime Minister) Manmohan Singh, the Indian government loosened its tight grip on the economy by eliminating price controls, reducing state intervention in day-to-day economic affairs, easing import regulations, reforming the tax system, and eliminating many state-run monopolies. As a result, the private sector expanded, foreign investment poured into the country, and the economy grew rapidly.

economic liberalization

The removal of government control and regulation over private enterprise.

India's economic performance has been highly impressive since then, with growth rates of 5–7 percent annually. This record is especially noteworthy compared to the dismal performance of many debt-ridden African and Latin American economies. An important reason for this growth is that the Indian government has supported entrepreneurs, often channeling public resources toward supporting private profits instead of investing in education or health. Since 1991, the reduction of tariffs and other restrictions has further integrated India into the global economy.

This pattern of economic growth required borrowing capital from abroad to expand productive equipment. In the 1990s, India was forced to borrow from the International Monetary Fund (IMF) and the World Bank to repay past loans. In return, these international organizations required the Indian government to reduce subsidies to the poor and sell government shares in public enterprises. Government policies reduced the workforce in public enterprises and reduced public spending and deficits.

Reforms in Agriculture

Since the 1990s, governments have limited public spending by reducing subsidized food supplies for the poor. In compliance with the dictates of the World Trade Organization (WTO), the government removed restrictions on imports. Although industrialized countries continue to maintain trade barriers on agricultural products and subsidize their domestic farmers, India's safety net has shrunk as its agricultural economy has been opened to global forces.

There are substantial successes on the positive side of the economic ledger. Some industries, such as information technology, have taken off. The service sector is expanding and contributes significantly to economic growth. The stock of modern technology continues to grow, and the closer relationship between government and business has encouraged substantial domestic and foreign investment. At the same time, India has yet to devise an adequate balance between economic development, environmental protection, and social equity. The booming economy consumes enormous amounts of scarce resources and further burdens the Indian and global ecosystem.

Society and Economy

Inequality and Social Welfare Policy

India is deeply stratified by class and income. At the top of the income pyramid, a small group of Indians have made incredible fortunes in business and industry. The wealth of the Ambanis, Tatas, and Birlas rivals that of the richest corporate tycoons in the world. About 100 million Indians are relatively well off and enjoy a standard of living comparable to that of middle or upper-middle-class people elsewhere. Moreover, thanks to a large pool of low-wage labor, middle-class Indians generally employ at least one full-time domestic worker.

India's lower-middle classes, about half the population, are mainly self-employed business owners, small farmers, and urban workers. Finally, India has the largest number of poor people in the world. According to both Indian government and World Bank figures, about a fifth of Indians are living in poverty. Many observers believe that these numbers seriously underestimate the level of poverty in India. While the proportion of those who the government defines as poor has halved since independence, rapid population growth has increased the absolute number of the poor: from about 200 million in the 1950s to about 300 million currently.

About three-quarters of the poor live in India's thousands of villages. Most are landless laborers. The urban poor are concentrated in giant slums with few public services, such as electricity and indoor plumbing. Although the economic boom has improved conditions for hundreds of millions, many more Indians remain mired in poverty, and their children have little prospect of leading a better life.

The sizable number of poor people encourages many Indian politicians to adopt populist or socialist electoral platforms—although often in name only. However, there are some important exceptions. For example, the states of West Bengal and Kerala have a long history of radical politics; the poor in these states are well organized and periodically elect left-leaning state governments that have redistributed land to the poor and implemented antipoverty programs. The poor have also fueled many social movements. The Naxalite revolutionary movement is an important example. Influenced by Maoist ideals, it organizes the landless poor to engage in land seizures and attacks on the state and dominant classes.

Naxalite

The Naxalite movement emerged as a breakaway faction of the CPM in West Bengal in 1967. It is a radical, often violent, extra-parliamentary movement.

Over the years, Indian governments have pursued various poverty alleviation programs. The last Congress government (2004–2014) initiated the Rural Employment Guarantee Scheme to provide the poor with jobs constructing roads and bridges, and cleaning agricultural waterways. Because the rural poor are unemployed for nearly half the year, when agricultural jobs are not available, off-season schemes have become an important source of jobs and income. To reduce high malnutrition rates, parliament passed a Food Security Bill that provides rice and grain at heavily subsidized prices to the country's poor. Two-thirds of India's population qualifies for subsidized food under the bill.

However, overall, India has a poor record of reducing poverty. Antipoverty programs and land reforms have generally failed to reduce economic inequality and help the poor. India has few Western-style welfare programs, such as unemployment insurance and comprehensive public health programs. Especially noteworthy is that India does not provide universal primary education. Thus, 81 percent of men and only 63 percent of women are literate, which increases the likelihood that poverty will be perpetuated in future generations.

A variety of inequalities in India have increased over the last two decades, notably between regions as well as between cities and the countryside. For example, the average per capita income of a resident of a richer state, such as Gujarat, is four times higher than of an individual living in the poor state of Bihar. The average citizen living in a village is also likely to be much poorer than someone living in a city, while inequalities within cities have also become more skewed.

India's population continues to grow at a rapid pace. Before long it will be the world's largest country. India's democratic government, unlike China's authoritarian system, has generally resisted coercive population control policies. But it has also failed to practice more progressive ways to reduce population growth. For example, although literate women are more likely to marry later in life and have fewer children, the Indian government has failed to make education a priority, and as noted above, women are especially likely to be illiterate. Since India has more people than can be employed productively, the growing population hinders economic growth, though some argue that a youthful population will add to India's economic advantages in the future.

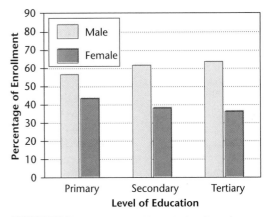

FIGURE 7.2 Educational Levels by Gender

Source: UNESCO Institute for Statistics, www.uis .unesco.org/en/stats/stats.

India is one of the few countries in the world with a lower percentage of females than males. Evidence that Indian society favors boys over girls can be inferred from such social indicators as lower female literacy, nutrition levels, and survival rates of female infants. Prejudice against girls is reinforced through traditions like the dowry system (the Hindu custom of giving the groom and his family substantial money and goods at a daughter's wedding). Although dowries are illegal, they have grown alongside increased materialism and aspirations for upward social mobility, particularly among the urban middle and lower-middle classes.

India has the world's largest population of child labor, although this has been declining in recent years. Children are employed in agriculture, match production, rug weaving, and vending at train stations. They often work long hours at low wages. Because they cannot attend school, they have limited prospects for upward mobility.

The problem of child labor is closely related to the lack of universal primary education (see Figure 7.2). Many Indian elites claim that compulsory primary education is an unaffordable luxury in a poor country like India. However, this argument is false; many poor African countries have higher rates of primary school enrollment than India. The more likely obstacle to universal primary education is poverty and caste inequality. Many poor families see large families as a form of insurance, for they depend on their children's labor for support. And many upper-caste elites do not consider educating lower-caste children a priority. Over the last two decades, however, the government has increased public spending on primary education, and enrollments have increased sharply. The Indian Constitution of 1950 stated that within a ten-year period the state would endeavor to provide free and compulsory education for children. However, not until 2010 did the Right of Children to Free and Compulsory Education Act make education for children between the ages of 6 and 14 a fundamental right. The Act requires elementary schools to improve their infrastructure, teacher qualifications and student–teacher ratio, and requires private schools to reserve 25 percent of seats for poor children (to be reimbursed by the state). Although the Act was a landmark achievement, the government has lagged in its implementation. The quality of education in government schools remains poor.

Those who suffer most are at the bottom of the caste hierarchy. The Indian census classifies nearly 10 percent of India's population as untouchables; the official term is scheduled castes, and the more widely used term is *dalits*. This group engages in occupations such as cleaning and leather work, which are considered "unclean." *Dalits* are subject to discrimination, violence, and exclusion from meaningful participation in social and economic life.

The caste system has a destructive impact on Indian social and economic life. By assigning people to specific occupations at birth, it limits individual choice and impedes social and economic mobility. Although the link between caste and occupation has weakened, especially in urban areas, it remains an important organizing principle in economic and political life. Caste groups sometimes redesignate their caste identities to achieve group mobility without undermining the principles governing caste hierarchies. In the political arena, voting blocs are often organized on a caste basis. Caste divisions among the lower classes in rural India make it difficult for the poor to defend their class-wide interests.

scheduled caste

The lowest caste in India; also known as untouchables.

Dalits

The lowest caste in India's caste system, whose members are among the poorest and most disadvantaged Indians. The term dalit means oppressed. It is widely used today in preference to the terms "scheduled castes" or "untouchables."

Environmental Issues

India faces serious and far-reaching environmental problems. Its lakes and rivers are polluted by sewage and factory waste. Some of the world's most polluted cities are in India. In 2015, India suffered about 1.1 million premature deaths because of air pollution. By the government's own estimates, water from over half of India's rivers is too polluted to drink and more than a quarter of rivers are too polluted to bathe in. Yet rivers remain the main source of drinking water for millions of Indians, with resulting diseases and illnesses. Illegal deforestation and mining cause massive environmental damage. India will likely experience severe consequences from global climate change due to its long coastline and reliance on seasonal monsoons for agricultural production. The emission of carbon dioxide has already created an increase in temperature, rise in sea level, and destruction of coastal croplands and fisheries.

There are many causes of environmental destruction. Rapid urbanization amidst population growth has increased natural disasters like droughts, floods and cyclones. Although these problems require political solutions, the government has for decades failed to anticipate and address environmental degradation. Rather, it has prioritized economic growth over environmental protection. The question of environmental sustainability ranks low on the agendas of political parties.

However, amidst these bleak realities are some positive trends. The first concerns the role of India's Supreme Court in promoting environmental protection by upholding a fundamental constitutional right to a healthy environment. As a result, an individual can approach the Court directly when environmental harm jeopardizes the public interest. The Supreme Court has issued notices and directives to the national and state governments on multiple environmental issues, such as freezing production licenses to manufacturers of toxic pesticides, relocating hazardous industries from the national capital, limiting noise pollution, and requiring civic bodies to manage plastic waste. Under the Environmental Protection Act (1986), various projects require clearance by the state or national environment ministries. The Court also required the national government to appoint a national environment regulator to evaluate the environmental impact of development projects.

Second, the state has become more attentive to the need for environmental protection. In 2010, the government created a special tribunal to expeditiously address environmental problems. The tribunal has taken steps to conserve wildlife, improve air quality in Delhi, clean up the Ganges river, and address off-shore oil spills and the flooding that results from dam construction.

Until recently, the Indian government opposed international pressures to introduce measures limiting climate change, citing the failure of Western countries to implement such measures. Although it remains committed to equity consideration in international climate negotiations, India has pledged to develop a more comprehensive approach to reducing greenhouse gas emissions through reforestation, improving energy efficiency, and introducing cleaner, more efficient, renewable technologies. India has also agreed to submit detailed and regular information to the international community on its domestic climate change efforts.

Achieving environmental progress requires collaboration among domestic and transnational groups, and the state and civil society organizations. It also requires that the government more vigorously monitor compliance and penalize noncompliance. Perhaps the greatest challenge is for the government to reconcile its business-friendly orientation with policies that promote environmental sustainability.

India in the Global Economy

Although for decades, starting in the 1950s, India provided leadership to the nonaligned bloc, it sought to minimize global economic exchange. When India's economy was relatively closed to outside influences, powerful groups had vested interests in preventing change. Many bureaucrats accepted bribes from business executives to issue licenses or evade regulations. Moreover, labor unions, especially in government-controlled factories, supported inefficient operations because this kept employment at high levels. These well-entrenched groups resisted liberalization and threatened to support opposition parties if the government sponsored a decisive policy shift.

By the 1980s, the negative effects of this pattern finally forced a change in government policy. When the government opened the economy, foreign investment soared from $100 million annually in 1992 to nearly $4 billion annually in 1998, to nearly $8 billion annually during 2006–2007. The 2015 amount—$44 billion—is giant in comparison. However, foreign investment in India remains lower than in China and Brazil. Furthermore, it is concentrated in industries producing for the domestic market; it has not facilitated export promotion, a major source of hard currency.

One high-tech sector in which India excels is computer software. Indian firms and multinational corporations employ large numbers of highly skilled, low-cost, English-speaking scientific and engineering talent, making India a world leader in the production of software. India boasts the equivalent of California's Silicon Valley in Bangalore in southern India, home to many software firms. Furthermore, transnational corporations in the West routinely hire graduates of India's superb higher institutions of engineering and technology.

For the same reason, India has become a prime destination for corporate call centers, tech support, and back office operations of banks, insurance companies, and financial firms. Scores of high-rise office buildings, shopping malls, and housing complexes have sprung up outside Delhi and Mumbai, graphic evidence of the new India. However, because they are so cut off from traditional Indian society, they further intensify the country's extreme social fragmentation.

India's integration within the global economy has increased because of a WTO agreement on trade in services, which requires the government to ease restrictions on banking, insurance, and other services. There are more than forty foreign banks in

GLOBAL CONNECTIONS

India in the Global Economy

India's economy has globalized since 1991. Tariffs on trade have come down. India's exports and imports have grown rapidly. Laws on foreign investment have also become more liberal. While direct foreign investment is significantly lower in India than in China, foreign investment into India has continued to grow over the last two decades. Foreign funds, in the form of portfolio investments, have also poured into India, buoying not only the stock markets but also adding volatility. India is not as well integrated into global financial markets as many Latin American and some East Asian economies. While criticisms of this selective integration abound, India suffered a lot less during the 2008 global financial crisis than other developing markets.

MAKING CONNECTIONS What are the pros and cons of a country like India being integrated in the global economy?

India, and the government has also opened the insurance sector to private and foreign investment. This has been a mixed blessing. For example, foreign banks focus on retail banking in profitable urban areas and ignore less lucrative areas. This reduces the possibilities for farmers and small-scale industrialists in rural and poorer regions to obtain loans.

Because India has compiled an enviable growth record over the last few years, it has become an attractive destination for foreign investment. India has catapulted into the first ranks of large developing countries. It is a charter member of the so-called BRIC countries: Brazil, Russia, India, and China—a bloc of developing countries that wields significant clout in the international arena.

Where Do You Stand?

Will economic growth on its own solve the problem of poverty in India?

There is an old argument that democracies are not good at promoting growth. What does the India case teach you about this argument?

GOVERNANCE AND POLICY-MAKING

Organization of the State

The 1950 constitution, adopted soon after India gained independence, created a democratic republic with a parliamentary system and a weak, mostly ceremonial, president. India's political system is federal, and states have substantial autonomy, power, and responsibilities. For much of the period since 1947, India has been a stable, democratic country with universal suffrage and regular local, state, and national elections. This record of democratic stability is remarkable among developing countries. Indian democracy has proved so durable because its political institutions have been able to accommodate many challenges. (See Table 7.1 for an outline of Indian political organization.)

Unlike the British constitution, which it resembles in many respects, the Indian constitution is a written document that has been periodically amended. Because the Indian constitution is highly detailed, it leaves less room for interpretation than many other national constitutions. Three features are worth noting. First, unlike many constitutions, the Indian constitution directs the government to promote social and economic equality and justice. The constitution thus outlines policy goals, rather than simply enumerating formal procedures of decision making and allocating powers among political institutions. Although the impact of these constitutional provisions on welfare and social justice is limited, political parties and social movements have appealed to them when seeking reforms.

Second, the Indian constitution, like the U.S. constitution, provides for freedom of religion and defines India as a secular state. And third, the constitution allows for the temporary suspension of many democratic rights under emergency conditions. These provisions were used, for understandable reasons, during wars with Pakistan and China. But they have also been invoked, more disturbingly, to deal with internal political threats, most dramatically during the national Emergency from 1975 to 1977.

Further, the constitution specifies that, if state governments are unable to function in a stable manner, the national government is authorized to declare President's Rule, which involves suspending the elected state government and administering the state's affairs from Delhi. President's Rule was designed to be used as a last resort to temporarily curb unrest in federal states. However, by 1989 the central government had declared President's Rule sixty-seven times. The Congress

🪪 PROFILE

The Nehru–Gandhi Dynasty

Jawaharlal Nehru was a staunch believer in liberal democratic principles. When India became independent in 1947, Nehru became prime minister and retained that position until his death in 1964. Nehru was a committed nationalist and social democrat. He sought to strengthen India's autonomy and national economy and improve the lives of the Indian poor. He tried to establish a socialist, democratic, and secular state, although India often failed to live up to these lofty ideals. Nehru attempted to set India on a rapid road to industrialization by promoting heavy industry. He advocated redistributing wealth through land reform, although much of India's land remained concentrated in the hands of traditional rural elites. Finally, Nehru championed democratic and individual rights, including the right to private property. Upon his death, India inherited a stable polity, a functioning democracy, an economy characterized by a large public sector, and a complex pattern of state control over the private sector.

Indira Gandhi became prime minister shortly after the death of her father, Jawaharlal Nehru, and dominated the Indian political scene until her assassination in 1984. While her foreign policies strengthened India's international position, her domestic policies weakened democratic institutions. Her tendency to personalize authority within the Congress Party contributed to the erosion of the party. She engaged in repressive measures to curtail growing political opposition. After she ordered the army to invade the Golden Temple, the Sikhs' most revered temple, she was assassinated by her Sikh bodyguards.

MAKING CONNECTIONS Some observers have suggested that having one family dominate Indian politics for many years promoted political stability. Others claim that it weakened Indian democracy. Who is correct?

government, particularly under Indira Gandhi's leadership, often used it to remove opposition governments and strengthen its own control. Under pressure from the opposition, Gandhi created a commission in 1983 to review center-state relations. It reported that President's Rule had been justified only twenty-six of the sixty-seven times that it had been used and urged the central government to exercise restraint in imposing it. A landmark 1994 Supreme Court ruling affirmed the commission's findings, called for judicial review of central government decisions to impose President's Rule, and declared that the courts were authorized to strike it down. The coalition governments that have held office since 1989 have been reluctant to invoke President's Rule. An important reason is that regional parties that participate in national governing coalitions oppose suspending state governments that they may lead.

In India's federal system, the central government controls most essential government functions, such as defense, foreign policy, taxation, public expenditures, and economic planning. State governments formally control agriculture, education, and law and order. However, because states are heavily dependent on the central government for funds to finance programs in these policy areas, their actual power is limited.

The *Lok Sabha*, or House of the People, is the lower chamber of parliament; the *Rajya Sabha* is the upper house. (India's parliament will be described in Section 4.) Following elections to the *Lok Sabha*, the leader of the political party with the most seats becomes the prime minister. Effective power is concentrated in the prime minister's office. The prime minister in turn nominates members of the cabinet, mostly members of parliament belonging to the ruling coalition. The prime minister and cabinet members also head various ministries.

Lok Sabha

The lower house of parliament in India, where all major legislation must pass before becoming law.

Rajya Sabha

India's upper house of parliament; considerably less politically powerful than the *Lok Sabha*.

The Executive

The Prime Minister and Cabinet

The prime minister governs with the help of the cabinet, which periodically meets to discuss important issues, including new legislative proposals. Because the cabinet directs the majority party coalition in parliament, passing a bill is less complicated than it can be in a presidential system. The permanent bureaucracy, especially senior- and middle-level bureaucrats, is responsible for policy implementation. As in most parliamentary systems, such as Britain, Germany, and Japan, there is considerable overlap between the executive and the legislative branches of the government.

The Prime Minister

The prime minister directs India's Council of Ministers, and is therefore in charge of all government ministries. As such, the prime minister is ultimately responsible for all the daily activities of the central government. The prime minister has the power to appoint individuals to various government offices, establish policy on significant issues, and direct the civil service. From 1947 to 1984, except for several brief interludes, India had only two prime ministers: Jawaharlal Nehru and Indira Gandhi (see Table 7.2). This is nearly unique among democracies; it underlines the powerful hold that the Nehru–Gandhi family had on India's political destiny. With the election of Narendra Modi as India's prime minister in 2014, dynastic rule by the Nehru-Gandhi party may have come to an end.

THE U.S. CONNECTION

Comparing Chief Executives in India and the United States

In the U.S. presidential system, the positions of head of state and chief executive are combined in one office: the president. This pattern is quite unusual. In most countries, there are two offices. The head of state is mostly a ceremonial office, occupied by a monarch or president indirectly elected by the legislature or an electoral college and possessing limited powers. In India, the president is elected for a 5-year term by an electoral college composed of elected representatives from the national and state governments. The president symbolizes the unity of India and is expected to rise above partisan conflicts. However, presidential approval is necessary for most parliamentary bills to become laws. Presidents can veto bills by refusing assent or delaying their enactment. Presidents appoint prime ministers routinely and when parliamentary elections do not produce a clear verdict as to which party should lead the new government.

By combining the functions of head of state and head of government, the United States concentrates enormous power in one person. The Indian system assigns the two functions to different officials, thus generally leaving the president above the political fray and making the prime minister a more partisan figure. What are the strengths and weaknesses of each system?

MAKING CONNECTIONS Which is preferable and why: the Indian system in which the functions of head of state (president) and head of government (prime minister) are assigned to different officials? Or the American system of combining the two functions within the single office of the president?

The Cabinet

The prime minister chooses the cabinet, mostly from among the governing party's senior members of parliament. Being named to the cabinet is among the most sought-after prizes in Indian politics. The main criteria guiding a prime minister's choice are seniority, competence, and personal loyalty. Regional and caste representation are also considered. With the advent of coalition governments, representatives from each political party in the coalition must be named to the cabinet. The result is that cabinets nowadays are often large, unwieldy, and divided.

Cabinet ministers have three roles. First, they are members of the government and participate in shaping its general policy orientation. Second, they are leaders of their own parties and must try to maintain party cohesion and support for the government. This may be difficult, especially if the government pursues a policy that is unpopular with the party's members. Third, cabinet ministers direct a ministry responsible for a policy area. They must thus supervise the ministry's civil servants and try to ensure that the department performs competently. Complicating a minister's situation is that what brings success in one area may detract from success in another.

The Bureaucracy

The prime minister and cabinet ministers supervise the bureaucracy in close collaboration with senior civil servants. Each senior minister oversees a sprawling department staffed by some highly competent, overworked, senior civil servants and many not-so-competent, underworked, lowly bureaucrats.

The **Indian Administrative Service (IAS)**, an elite corps of top bureaucrats, constitutes a critically important but relatively thin layer at the top of India's bureaucracy. Recruitment occurs through a highly competitive examination. Many more

Indian Administrative Service (IAS)

India's civil service, a highly professional and talented group of administrators, run the Indian government on a day-to-day basis.

candidates compete than are chosen, since IAS appointments provide lifetime tenure, excellent pay, and great prestige. During 2009 to 2010, for example, out of the nearly 400,000 applicants for IAS civil service posts, just 2,281 were selected for an interview, and only 875 were eventually appointed. Whereas political leaders come and go, senior civil servants stay—and accumulate a storehouse of knowledge and expertise that makes them powerful and competent.

Many of India's most talented young men and women were attracted to the IAS in the decades after independence because of the prestige that came with service in national government. The attraction of the IAS has declined, however, and many of India's most talented young people now go into engineering and business administration, or leave the country for better opportunities abroad. Government service has become tarnished by corruption, and the level of professionalism within the IAS has declined as politicians increasingly prefer loyalty over merit and seniority when making promotions. Nevertheless, the IAS continues to recruit highly talented young people, many of whom eventually become dedicated senior civil servants who constitute the backbone of the Indian government.

Below the IAS, the level of talent and professionalism drops sharply. The national and state-level Indian bureaucracy is infamous for corruption and inefficiency. Civil servants are powerfully organized and, thanks to lifetime tenure, free to resist orders from their superiors. There has been a marked decline in the competence and integrity of the Indian bureaucracy through the years. Its lack of responsiveness and accountability pose a major problem for Indian democracy. These problems contribute to the gap between good policies and their poor implementation at the local level.

Other State Institutions

The Military and the Police

With more than 1.4 million well-trained and well-equipped members, the Indian armed force is a highly powerful and professional organization. It has never intervened directly in politics. Over the years, the continuity of constitutional, electoral politics and a relatively apolitical effective military have come to reinforce and strengthen each other. Civilian politicians provide ample resources to the armed forces and, for the most part, encourage them to function as a professional organization. The armed forces, in turn, accept direction from democratically elected civilian leaders.

The Indian police forces have never been as professionalized as the armed forces. The police come under the jurisdiction of state governments, not the central government. Because state governments are generally less effective and honest than the national government, the Indian police are not neutral civil servants. State-level politicians regularly interfere in personnel issues, and police officers in turn regularly oblige politicians. The police are easily bribed and often allied with criminals or politicians. The police generally favor dominant social groups such as landowners, upper castes, and the majority Hindu religious community. A large, sprawling, and relatively ineffective police service remains a problematic presence in Indian society.

In addition to the national army and the state-level police, the national government controls paramilitary forces that number nearly half a million people. As Indian politics became more turbulent in the 1980s, paramilitary forces steadily expanded. Because the national government calls on the army only as a last resort to manage internal conflicts, and because state-level police forces are generally unreliable, paramilitary forces are often used to maintain order.

The Judiciary

An independent judiciary is another component of India's state system. The major judicial authority is the Supreme Court, comprising a chief justice and seventeen other judges. The president appoints judges on the advice of the prime minister. Once appointed, judges cannot be removed from the bench until reaching the mandatory retirement age of 65.

The main political role of the Supreme Court is to ensure that legislation conforms to the constitution. Thus, like the U.S. Supreme Court, it can strike down legislation that it judges to be in violation of the constitution. The Supreme Court has often challenged state abuses of power in its civil rights judgments. It introduced a system of public interest litigation that allows anyone to file a petition in the High Court alleging that a person or group's legal or constitutional right(s) have been breached. This has resulted in judicial activism against executive wrongdoing.

A principal source of conflict is that the constitution simultaneously protects private property yet also directs the government to pursue social justice. Indian leaders have often promulgated socialist legislation, for example, requiring the redistribution of agricultural land. The Supreme Court has on occasion judged that legislation of this nature violates the right to private property. For instance, during the early years of independence, the courts overturned state government laws to redistribute land from *zamindars* on grounds that the laws violated their fundamental rights. Parliament retaliated by amending the constitution to protect the executive's authority to promote land redistribution. But matters did not end there. The Supreme Court responded by ruling that parliament lacked the power to abrogate fundamental rights.

zamindars

Landlords who served as tax collectors in India under the British colonial government. The *zamindari* system was abolished after independence.

Over the years, the Supreme Court has clashed head-on with parliament because of the contradiction between constitutional principles of parliamentary sovereignty and judicial review. For example, it has required central and state governments to prevent starvation by releasing food stocks and to promote education by providing school lunches and daycare facilities.

Like other Indian political institutions, the judiciary has suffered from institutional decay. The caseload on the Supreme Court, as with much of the Indian legal system, is extremely heavy, and there is a significant backlog of cases. When cases drag on for years, public confidence in the judiciary crumbles. Still the Supreme Court remains a powerful and valuable institution.

Compared to other large, multiethnic democracies, India has generally protected fundamental civil rights, including an independent judiciary, universal suffrage, and a free and lively press. Nevertheless, the tradition of a strong, interventionist state has enabled the government to violate civil liberties. In 2002, the Indian parliament passed the Prevention of Terrorism Act (POTA), which provided a vague definition of terrorism and allowed citizens to be charged without having committed a specific act. Grounds included conspiring, attempting to commit, advocate, abet, advise, or incite terrorism. Penalties included harsh prison sentences and death. Confessions made to police officers were admissible as evidence in courts, contrary to ordinary law, and the police used torture to extract confessions.

Shortly after Manmohan Singh became prime minister in 2004, the cabinet repealed POTA on grounds that it had been misused. Instead, it amended existing laws to tackle terrorism. However, Singh's government did not dismiss charges against those previously arrested under POTA.

Under the current BJP government, Hindu nationalist organizations have engaged in increased violence against women, religious minorities and intellectuals. They have attacked couples from interfaith (namely Hindu-Muslim) backgrounds and Muslims whom they have accused of consuming beef and slaughtering cows. (Hindu religious laws prohibit these practices.) They have called for banning books which criticize Hindu orthodoxy, and have attacked intellectuals who have opposed superstition and religious idolatry.

An infamous example of the Indian state violating a citizen's civil rights involved Kanhaiya Kumar, a doctoral student at India's premiere university, Jawaharlal Nehru University. Mr. Kumar was arrested in 2016 by the Modi government for participating in a peaceful student demonstration. He was charged under a British-era sedition act for conducting "anti-national" activities. The Supreme Court refused to intervene and the arrest led to large student demonstrations in support of Mr. Kumar and against the government's heavy-handed treatment of dissent. Although he was released from prison after 3 weeks, his case remains under investigation.

Subnational Government

The structure of India's twenty-nine state governments parallels that of the national government. Each state has a government, headed by a chief minister who leads the party with most seats in the lower house of the state legislature. The chief minister appoints cabinet ministers who head ministries staffed by a state-level, permanent bureaucracy. The quality of government below the national level is often poor.

Each state also has a governor appointed by the national president. Although governors are supposed to serve under the direction of the chief minister, in practice they often become independently powerful, especially in states that have unstable governments or are at odds with the national government. Governors can dismiss elected state governments and proclaim temporary President's Rule if they determine that the state government is ineffective.

There is an ongoing power struggle between state and central governments. States often demand more resources from the central government, and have also demanded greater power and recognition of the state's distinctive cultural and linguistic identities. When conflicting political parties are in power at the national and state levels, center-state relations can be inflamed by political and ethnic conflicts.

Indian politics has become increasingly regionalized in recent years. States have become more autonomous economically and politically. State parties play an increasingly important role in national governance and, with economic liberalization, have sought foreign investment independent of the national government. One consequence is that regional inequalities are widening.

panchayats

Elected bodies at the village, district, and state levels that have development and administrative responsibilities.

reservations

Jobs or admissions to colleges reserved by the government of India for specific underprivileged groups.

India has an elaborate system of local governance. The *panchayats* are locally elected councils at the local, district, and state levels. They were strengthened in 1992 by a constitutional amendment that stipulated that *panchayat* elections should be held every five years. It further required that one-third of seats on the *panchayats* should be reserved for women and that scheduled castes and tribes should be represented in proportion to their numbers in the locality. Most states have met the 33 percent women's **reservations** at all three levels and several have exceeded it.

The resources and planning capabilities of the *panchayats* are relatively limited. State legislatures determine how much power and authority they can wield. Most *panchayats* are responsible for implementing but not devising rural development schemes. Although *panchayats* have considerable resources, they have little discretion over how to allocate funds. Corruption is common because local political elites, bureaucrats, and influential citizens often siphon off public funds. Thus, many of the funds spent on poverty alleviation programs have been wasted.

The Policy-Making Process

The government in New Delhi formulates major policies. Senior civil servants play an important role identifying problems, collecting and synthesizing data, and presenting political leaders with alternative solutions. Because the prime minister usually commands a majority in parliament, passage of most legislation is ensured.

The real policy drama in India occurs when major bills are debated in parliament and when laws are implemented. Consider the policy shift to economic liberalization. The new course was formulated by a handful of senior ministers and bureaucrats. To reach the decision, however, a complex set of political activities took place. Decision-makers at the highest level of government consulted important interest groups, such as associations of Indian businessmen and representatives of international organizations like the World Bank and IMF. Groups that opposed the reform made their positions known. Organized labor, for example, called a one-day general strike to oppose privatizing the public sector. Newspapers, magazines, and intellectuals weighed in. Political parties announced their positions. Members of the ruling Congress Party did not necessarily support their own leaders at the early stage. Opposition parties highlighted the harm that the reform might inflict. These pressures modified the policy that the government eventually adopted.

After policies have been adopted, their implementation is far from assured. Regarding liberalization, some aspects of the new policy package proved easier to implement than others. Changing the exchange rate was relatively easy because the policy decision and its implementation required the actions of only a handful of politicians and bureaucrats. By contrast, simplifying the procedures for creating new business enterprises proved far more complicated. Implementation required the cooperation of many bureaucrats—whose power would be reduced from the change—and who consequently tried to sabotage the newly simplified procedures.

Where Do You Stand?

Is India too centralized?

The poor quality of local bureaucracy in India is not a problem because active civil society groups can solve local problems. Discuss.

REPRESENTATION AND PARTICIPATION

SECTION
4

The Legislature

The Indian parliament is bicameral, consisting of the more powerful *Lok Sabha*, the lower house, and the weaker upper house, the *Rajya Sabha*. *Lok Sabha* elections are of vital importance. First, the outcome determines which party coalition will control the government. Second, although members of parliament cannot shape policies,

⁇ Focus Questions

- How effectively does India's parliament represent the country's diverse interests?

- What are the causes and consequences of the shift from a one-party system dominated by the Congress Party to the emergence of a multiparty system?

they enjoy considerable status, access to resources, and influence over allocation of government funds.

Elections to the *Lok Sabha* are held at least every five years. However, as in other parliamentary systems, the prime minister may choose to call elections earlier. India is divided into 543 electoral districts of roughly equal population, each of which elects one representative to the national parliament by a first-past-the-post electoral procedure. Since party leaders control nominations, most legislators are beholden to them for securing a party ticket. Given the importance of the party label for nominations, members of parliament support party leaders and maintain strong voting discipline in the *Lok Sabha*.

The main tasks of the *Lok Sabha* are to elect the prime minister (that is, the leader of the winning party coalition), pass legislation, and debate government actions. Although any member of parliament can introduce bills, the government sponsors most of those that are eventually passed and become laws. After bills are introduced, they are assigned to parliamentary committees for detailed study and discussion. The committees report the bills back to the *Lok Sabha* for debate, possible amendment, and preliminary votes. They are then sent to the *Rajya Sabha*, which generally approves bills passed by the *Lok Sabha,* though in recent years the Modi government has found the former to be a significant obstacle as it is controlled by members of the Congress Party.

Most members of the *Rajya Sabha* are elected indirectly by state legislatures. The *Rajya Sabha* is much weaker than the *Lok Sabha* because its assent is not required for the passage of spending measures that the *Lok Sabha* approves, it cannot introduce no-confidence motions, (as the Lok Sabha can) and it is much smaller than the *Lok Sabha*. After the *Rajya Sabha* votes on (and possibly amends) bills, they return to the *Lok Sabha* for a third reading, after which the final text is voted on by both houses. If passed, it is sent to the president for approval.

Although the *Lok Sabha* can make and unmake governments (by voting to bring them down), it does not play a significant role in policy-making. Keep in mind that (1) the government generally introduces new legislation; (2) most legislators are politically beholden to party leaders; (3) all parties maintain tight discipline to ensure voting along party lines; and (4) the government controls the majority party coalition, thus ensuring passage of its legislative proposals.

The Parliament's social composition does not have significant policy consequences. Whether members of parliament are business executives or workers, men or women, or members of upper or lower castes is unlikely to significantly influence policy. Nevertheless, groups in society derive symbolic recognition from having their own members in parliament.

The typical member of parliament is a male university graduate between 40 and 60 years old. Over the years, there have been some changes in the social composition of legislators. For example, legislators in the 1950s were likely to be urban men and were often lawyers and members of higher castes. Today, nearly half of all members come from rural areas, and many have agricultural backgrounds. Members of the middle castes (the so-called backward castes) are also well represented today. These changes reflect some of the broad shifts in the distribution of power in Indian society. By contrast, the proportion of women and of poor, lower-caste individuals in parliament remains low. The representation of women in parliament has gradually increased from 4 percent in the first parliament (1952–1957) to 11 percent in 2014 (see Figure 7.3). The small number of women MPs reflects party biases toward nominating female candidates. Only 7 percent of the candidates in the 2009 general election and 8 percent in 2014 were women.

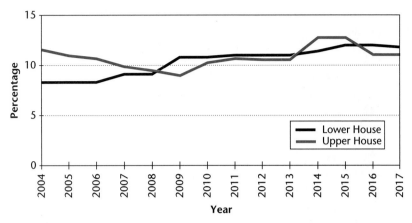

FIGURE 7.3 Women in Parliament

http://www.ipu.org/wmn-e/classif.htm.

Following many years of deliberation and debate, the upper house of parliament approved a constitutional amendment in 2010 reserving at least 33 percent seats in parliament and the legislative assemblies for women; it still awaits approval by the lower house.

Political Parties and the Party System

Political parties and elections are where much of the real drama of Indian politics occurs. Since parties that control most seats in the national and state parliaments form the government and control public resources, parties devote substantial political energy to contesting elections. Since independence, the party system has evolved from being dominated by Congress to one in which Congress is merely one of the major parties. Indeed, following the 2014 election, the Congress is in danger of becoming a minor party (see Table 7.3). What thus began as a virtually one-party system has evolved into a real multiparty system with three main political tendencies: centrist, center-left, and center-right.

India's major national parties are ideologically diverse. The Congress stands for secularism, economic liberalization, and mild redistribution of wealth. It has oscillated between center left and center right positions. The BJP, on the right, favors private enterprise and supports secularism in principle but not in practice. In addition to these two main contenders, other major competitors include the Janata, the all-India Communist Party Marxist (CPM), and forty regional parties.

The Indian party system has changed dramatically since 1989. A multiparty system has emerged following the decline of Congress and growth of state parties. Taken together, the forty officially recognized state parties have significant weight in Indian politics. Some are regional powerhouses and control state governments. State parties have largely determined the outcome of the last three elections and participated in every coalition government since 1989. In the 2014 elections, the BJP won a solid majority of seats with 31 percent of the popular vote. With the Congress and the Communists winning only 22.5 percent of the vote between them, nearly half the popular vote was secured by regional parties. As one would expect, there are feverish negotiations among coalition parties over the allocation of cabinet positions and the policies that the governing coalition will pursue. While the fragmentation

Table 7.3 | Major Party Election Results

	1991		1996		1998		1999		2004		2009		2014	
	%	Seats	%	Seats	%	Seats	%	Seats	%	Seats	%	Seats	%	Seats
Congress	37.3	225	29	143	25.4	140	28.4	112	26.69	145[a]	28.55		19.3%	44
BJP and Allies	19.9	119	24	193	36.2	250	41.3	296	35.9	1.189	24.63		31%	282
Janata	10.8	55	Joined with UF		Joined with UF		1	1	Joined with Congress		0	—	Ran separately	—
United Front	—	—	31	180	20.9	98	—	—	—	—	—	—	—	—
Communists[b]	—	48	Joined with UF		Joined with UF		5.4	32	7.0	53	1.43	—	3.2%	9
Others							23.9	107	19.9	78	34.71			208

[a]The more relevant figures in 2004 for Congress and allies were 35.82 and 219, respectively.
[b]Includes both the CPM and the CPI.
Source: *India Today*, July 15, 1991, March 16, 1998; *Economic Times* website, economictimes.indiatimes.com; and *The Hindu*, May 20, 2004.

of the party system enables the representation of multiple interests, it also deters the government from acting decisively. Cabinets are large, unwieldy, and cautious. If the government acted boldly, it could lose the support of one or more coalition partners, forfeit its parliamentary majority, and be forced to resign.

Although polls have often predicted a "hung Parliament," where no coalition gets a clear majority to form a government on its own, thus far the Congress Party and the BJP have been sufficiently strong to enable them to govern. The fact that the BJP won a clear majority in the 2014 election may well be the beginning of a new trend.

The Congress Party

Following independence, with Nehru at its helm, Congress was the unquestioned ruling party of India. Over the years, especially since the mid-1960s, this hegemony came to be challenged. By the time Indira Gandhi assumed power in 1966, the Congress Party had begun to lose its political sway, and anticolonial nationalism was fading. Soon, many poor, lower-caste citizens became independent from the political guidance of village big men. As a result, numerous regional parties started challenging the Congress Party's monopoly on power.

Indira Gandhi sought to reverse the decline in Congress's electoral popularity by mobilizing the poor, who were India's vast majority. Her promise to end poverty struck a popular chord and propelled Gandhi to the top of India's political pyramid. Her personal success, however, split the party. Indira Gandhi replaced the party's decentralized bottom-up structure with a centralized organization that enabled leaders to control the party, but was a major liability in achieving grassroots support.

Whereas during the 1970s, Congress had a left-of-center, pro-poor political platform, beginning in 1984, it became centrist under Rajiv Gandhi (see Section 2). For much of the 1980s and 1990s, the Congress Party tilted right of center, championing economic efficiency, business interests, and limited government spending on health, education, and welfare. However, its victories in the 2004 and 2009 national elections were based on a platform of secularism and limited redistribution. The lack of ideological clarity hurt the Congress party in the 2014 election, when it lost decisively. The Gandhi family in recent years has sought to portray the Congress as slightly to the left of the ruling BJP.

The Janata Party and Janata Dal

The Janata Party was created in 1977, when several small parties formed an alliance to oppose Indira Gandhi's Emergency. It was not a cohesive political party but a changing coalition of small parties and factions. It had a weak organizational structure and lacked a distinctive, coherent political platform. To distinguish itself from Congress, it claimed fidelity to Mahatma Gandhi's vision of modern India as decentralized and village-oriented. The Janata Party primarily represented small, rural agriculturalists who generally fall in the middle of the rigid caste hierarchy between Brahmins and untouchables.

Much to everyone's surprise, Janata won the 1977 elections and, with support from other parties, formed the national government. This loose coalition lasted only a little over two years, when conflicting leadership ambitions tore it apart. The Janata Party maintained a small presence in a few Indian states. In 2013, it merged with the BJP.

The most important successor to the Janata Party was the Janata Dal, which was formed in 1988. Under the leadership of V. P. Singh, the Janata Dal came to power in 1989 in a coalition known as the National Front. VP Singh took the audacious

Mandal Commission

A government-appointed commission headed by B. P. Mandal to consider seat reservations and quotas to redress caste discrimination.

other backward classes

The middle or intermediary castes in India that have been accorded reserved seats in public education and employment since the early 1990s.

step of supporting a proposal by the **Mandal Commission**, an official government agency, that recommended quotas in government jobs and admissions to universities for what are known **as other backward classes**, generally, the middle, rural castes. The policy is known as reservation, like the policy of reserving seats for women in the *panchayats* described above, and resembles affirmative action programs in the United States. The **other backward classes**, who became beneficiaries of reservations constitute between 32 and 52 percent of the population. Prime Minister Singh's attempt to garner electoral support backfired when upper castes organized demonstrations, riots, and political violence opposing reservations. This contributed to the downfall of Singh's government.

The Janata Dal returned to power briefly in 1996, as head of a United Front coalition, with outside support from the Congress party. However, the government collapsed when Congress withdrew support for the coalition less than a year later. The Janata Dal has since split into many parties, which repeatedly seek to come together as elections approach.

The Bharatiya Janata Party (BJP)

The rise of the BJP, which began as the small and marginal Jan Sangh to become one of the two major national parties and the ruling party between 1999 and 2004, and again in 2014, is among the most important developments in Indian politics in recent decades. The BJP is a right-leaning, Hindu-nationalist party, the first major Indian party to seek support based on religious identity. Unlike Congress and Janata, the BJP is highly centralized and well organized. Its disciplined party members become party cadres only after long apprenticeship.

The BJP differs from Congress and the Janata Party in another respect. It has close ties to a large non-parliamentary organization, the RSS, which recruits young people (especially educated youth in urban areas) by championing a chauvinistic reinterpretation of India's "great Hindu past." The BJP also has close ties with another RSS affiliated group, the Visva Hindu Parishad (VHP), a religious organization.

Until the late 1980s, the Jana Sangh and the BJP were mainly supported by the urban, lower-middle classes, especially small traders and commercial groups. Since their numbers were relatively small, the BJP was a minor actor on the Indian political scene. The party widened its base of support in the late 1980s by appealing to Hindu nationalism. The BJP found in Indian Muslims a convenient scapegoat for the frustrations of various social groups and polarized Hindus and Muslims around elections.

In the 1989 elections, the BJP emerged as the third-largest party after the Congress and Janata parties. In 1991, it gained the second-largest number of seats in parliament. The BJP sought Hindu support by allying with the RSS and VHP to challenge the legitimacy of a Muslim mosque (the *babri masjid*) located at Ayodhya, in northern India. Hindu nationalist leaders claimed that centuries ago, a Muslim ruler destroyed a Hindu temple at the birth place of the Hindu god Ram to construct the mosque. They organized a nationwide campaign, which culminated in the destruction of the mosque on December 6, 1992. Seventeen hundred people, mostly Muslim, were killed in the aftermath of the campaign.

After the BJP was twice defeated in parliamentary elections following the destruction of the mosque at Ayodhya, it shelved contentious issues that favored the interests of Hindus. Its efforts succeeded when it helped form a coalition, the National Democratic Alliance (NDA), which took office briefly (March–April 1999) followed by a full term (October 1999–January 2004). With the formation of the NDA government, the BJP renounced some of its chauvinist positions and publicly distanced itself from the RSS and the VHP at the national level. However, it continued to maintain close ties to the two organizations; all top-ranking BJP leaders are RSS members.

The BJP, in alliance with the VHP, has continued to engage in anti-minority violence in several states. The most important instance was in Gujarat, where a BJP government was in office. From February to March 2002, Hindu nationalists orchestrated a campaign of terror against the Muslim population, which resulted in 2,000 deaths. The BJP capitalized on Hindu electoral support to return to office in Gujarat in 2002 and 2007.

The BJP suffered consecutive defeats in the 2004 and 2009 general elections. Its 2009 defeat revealed its weaknesses in key federal states, where important coalition partners left the NDA fearing they would lose minority votes in the aftermath of the Gujarat violence. Further, the BJP's image of a cohesive and disciplined party was tarnished by conflicts among its leaders.

The 2009 elections also revealed the lack of popular support for Hindutva. The Congress won in part because it rejected sectarian religious appeals and claimed it would improve the socioeconomic conditions of minorities. The BJP's 2014 election campaign combined themes of Hindu nationalism, caste politics and promises to renew India's economic growth and promote development. These appeals, along with support from the business community and business controlled media, contributed to the BJP's handsome electoral victory in 2014.

The Communist Party of India (CPM)

India is one of the few democratic countries in the world with a self-proclaimed communist party. Although the CPM is communist in name, it has evolved into a social democratic (or center-left) party that accepts democracy and a market economy. At the same time, it seeks to obtain greater benefits for the poor. The CPM's political base today is concentrated in two Indian states: West Bengal and Kerala. CPM candidates are often elected to the *Lok Sabha* from these states, and the CPM has frequently run their state governments.

The CPM is a disciplined party, with party cadres and a hierarchical authority structure. Within the national parliament, CPM members often strongly criticize government policies that are likely to hurt the poor. CPM-run state governments in West Bengal and Kerala have provided relatively honest and stable administration. They have sponsored moderate reforms that seek to provide services to shantytown dwellers, channel public investments to rural areas, and ensure the rights of agricultural tenants (for example, by preventing landlords from evicting them).

However, in recent years, the CPM has sought to attract foreign investment through the creation of Special Economic Zones, which offer tax breaks and other subsidies to multinational corporations. The CPM government's heavy-handed acquisition of farmland for one such zone in West Bengal in 2007, provoked widespread protests that the CPM government violently repressed. In 2011 state elections, the CPM lost control of the governments of both Kerala and West Bengal. The performance of the CPM in the 2014 national elections was quite dismal. It returned to power in 2016 in Kerala but not in West Bengal.

The Aam Admi Party

The Aam Aadmi Party (translation: *Common Man Party;* abbreviated as AAP) was created by Arvind Kejriwal, a former bureaucrat and political activist who demanded a crackdown on corruption and the passage of a Right to Information Act, which enables any citizen to request information from a public authority and requires a response to that request within thirty days.

Kejriwal formed the AAP in 2011. Its platform for elections in Delhi included creating an agency to investigate charges of corruption against public officials, decentralization, improving the quality of health care and government schools, rehabilitating slum dwellers, and reducing consumers' electricity bills by 50 percent. The AAP engaged in grassroots organizing to communicate its empathy for popular concerns.

The AAP stunned the political class by placing second in the Delhi elections. The BJP won the largest number of seats. With no party obtaining an overall majority, the AAP formed a minority government with support from the Congress Party and Arvind Kejriwal became Chief Minister (similar to mayor) of Delhi.

Kejriwal made a splash by shunning the trappings of wealth and power. He refused the services of a Personal Security officer and an official residence. His swearing in ceremony took place at the Ram Lila *maidan*, a prior site of protest against corruption. The ministers who attended the ceremony traveled there by metro.

The AAP government quickly implemented some campaign promises. It provided subsidies to reduce electricity bills for low income households and established an antigraft helpline for citizens to report corrupt officials. However, the Delhi government was soon involved in a scandal related to sex trafficking and drug racketeering. Another problem resulted from the AAP lack of a majority in the Legislative Assembly. When Kejriwal failed to pass a bill creating an anticorruption agency, he resigned as Chief Minister only 49 days after assuming office. The poor electoral performance of the AAP party in the 2014 elections suggested that its prior success had been a flash in the pan. However, the AAP made a spectacular comeback in 2015 when it recaptured sixty-seven of the seventy seats in the Delhi government. Using this as a base, Kejriwal and the AAP began trying to expand the party's reach beyond Delhi to other states, especially Punjab.

The major contenders in the 2014 parliamentary elections were the BJP and Congress dominated coalitions. The BJP selected Narendra Modi as its candidate for prime minister, and its electoral campaign highlighted Modi's personal popularity, particularly among youth and the middle classes, who consider him incorruptible and efficient in delivering economic growth. Meanwhile, Congress delayed announcing its candidate for prime minister, perhaps in part because most of its leaders are uncharismatic septuagenarians who lack Modi's charisma. Rahul Gandhi, the young heir of the Nehru-Gandhi dynasty, was not very popular and naming him as candidate for prime minister early would have highlighted the Congress Party's reliance on dynastic politics. He was eventually named but the Congress party fared very poorly. Gandhi is now the party's main public face.

Corruption, inflation, and slowing economic growth rates were the major issues in the 2014 elections. These factors, along with the Congress Party's unimpressive election campaign, resulted in a landslide victory for the BJP. After several decades of coalition governments, India now has a majority government in power.

The BJP's landslide victory in the state assembly elections in U.P. in 2017 suggests that it is well positioned to return to power in the 2019 national elections. The reason is that U.P., India's most populous state, has always played a crucial role in Indian politics. The BJP's victory partly reflected the weakness of opposition parties. More positively, the BJP pursued an effective strategy of combining caste and Hindu nationalist appeals. Narendra Modi's popularity probably also played a role.

The Modi government selected Yogi Adityanath, a Hindu priest, long-time BJP Member of Parliament, and founder of a militant Hindu nationalist youth organization, as U.P.'s chief minister. Adityanath is brazenly anti-Muslim. He was imprisoned in 2007 for provoking anti-Muslim violence and is still facing trial. In U.P., as in the national context, the BJP, is a controversial and polarizing force. While its supporters are clearly ecstatic at its performance, many citizens remain apprehensive, both about its anti-Muslim politics and its pro-business policy preferences.

Elections

Elections in India are a colossal event. Nearly 500 million people are eligible to vote, and close to 300 million cast ballots—a turnout rate far higher than in the United States. Although television plays an important role, campaigning still often involves personal contacts between politicians and voters. Senior politicians fly around the country making speeches at election rallies amid blaring music. Lesser politicians and party supporters travel the dusty streets in tiny villages and district towns. Political messages boom from loudspeakers.

Given India's low literacy rates, pictures of party symbols are critical: a hand for Congress; lotus flower for the BJP; hammer and sickle for the CPM; and broom for the AAP. Illiterate citizens vote by putting a thumb mark on the preferred symbol.

Members of parliament are elected by a single-member district first-past-the-post system. Many candidates compete in each electoral district; the candidate with a plurality wins the seat. This system privileges the major political parties.

A pillar of Indian democracy is the fact that elections are open, competitive, and honest. Much of the credit goes to the independent Election Commission, which has been highly successful in protecting the integrity of the electoral process.

Political Culture, Citizenship, and Identity

Several aspects of Indian political culture are noteworthy. First, the political/public and private spheres are not sharply differentiated. One undesirable result is corruption, since politicians frequently seek personal and family enrichment through public office. A more attractive result is a high level of citizens' political involvement. Second, the Indian elite is extremely factionalized. Personal ambition prevents leaders from pursuing collective goals, such as forming cohesive parties, running stable governments, or giving priority to national development. Unlike many East Asian countries, for example, where consensus is powerful and political negotiations take place behind closed doors, politics in India involves open conflicts.

Third, regions are highly differentiated by language and culture, villages are poorly connected with each other, and communities are stratified by caste. Some observers regard group fragmentation as playing a positive role in promoting political stability. Others believe that it obstructs implementing national reforms to improve the lot of the poor.

India's highly open style of democracy often fuels political conflicts involving identity groups. Ethnic conflicts were minimal when Nehru stressed secular nationalism and Indira Gandhi highlighted the poor-versus-rich cleavage. In the 1980s and 1990s, however, the decline of the Congress Party and developments in telecommunications and transportation accentuated group differences. As a result, identity-based political conflicts have mushroomed. Two are especially significant, First, caste conflicts, that were formerly local and regional, have become national in character.

V. P. Singh initiated this process when he introduced reservations for other backward classes. This gave rise to political parties that sought to advance the interests of lower caste groups and it increased caste-based contestation.

Second, identity-based conflicts pit Hindus against Muslims. For most of the post-independence period, Hindu-Muslim conflicts were confined to the local level. However, in the mid-1980s and 1990s, the BJP provoked anti-Muslim emotions to attract Hindu support. Although anti-Muslim violence has not occurred on a national scale, it has occurred in many regions.

Interest Groups, Social Movements, and Protest

India has a vibrant tradition of political activism that has both enriched and complicated the workings of democracy. Social movements, non-governmental organizations (NGOs), and trade unions have pressured the state to address the interests of underprivileged groups. Recent welfare and civil rights legislation, including the Right to Information, Rural Employment Guarantee Act, Forest Act, and Land Acquisition and Rehabilitations Act, were passed in response to the demands of civil society activists.

Labor has played a significant role. Workers in the formal sector are organized in unions that frequently engage in strikes, demonstrations, and a technique called *gherao*, where workers hold executives of a firm hostage to press their demands. Labor unions are politically fragmented, particularly at the national level. Instead of the U.S. model of one union/one factory, unions allied to different political parties often organize within a single factory. Rival labor organizations compete for workers' support at higher levels as well. The government generally stays out of labor–management conflicts.

Social movements date back to the mid-1970s. Prime Minister Indira Gandhi distrusted voluntary organizations and movements, and sought to restrict their activities. During the national Emergency (1975–1977), the government imprisoned members of the opposition. However, activists reacted by forming political parties and social movements. Socialist leader Jai Prakash Narain organized the most influential movement opposing Emergency rule. It contributed to the downfall of Congress and the election of the Janata Party. A decade later, V. P. Singh resigned from Congress and formed the *Jan Morcha* (Peoples' Front), a movement that brought new groups into politics and helped elect the National Front in 1989. There was a significant growth in NGOs. The government viewed NGOs favorably and regarded them as partners in development activities.

The large number and extensive activities of social movements make India quite distinctive among developing countries. The most significant social movements include the women's movement, the environment movement, the farmers' movement, the *dalit* movement, and the anticorruption movement.

The roots of the *dalit* activism against caste discrimination lie in a reform movement among Hindus that began in 1875. The modern *dalit* movement was inspired by Dr. Bhimrao Ramji Ambedkar, the *dalit* author of the Indian constitution, who formed the Republican Party in the late 1960s. When the party disintegrated, it was succeeded by the Dalit Panthers, a movement that demanded that *dalits* be treated with dignity and provided with better educational opportunities. Today, the *dalit* movement seeks a greater share of electoral power and public office. The biggest *dalit* party is the Bahujan Samaj Party (BSP), created in 1989 with the goal of increasing *dalits'* political representation. The BSP grew rapidly in the 1990s by championing *dalit* empowerment while appealing to a broad cross-caste base of support. It succeeded in forming coalition governments with other political parties in U.P., and independently (2007–2012). Its powerful female leader, Mayavati (known by one name only) was U.P.'s chief minister.

Poor rural groups have organized movements to defend their land and livelihood by protesting deforestation, the construction of hazardous chemical plants, and the creation of large dams. The Chipko movement, which emerged in the early 1970s in the Himalayas, is one of the best-known and oldest movements against deforestation. It has influenced similar forms of activism in other regions. In 1984, a gas leak in a Union Carbide plant in Bhopal caused an explosion resulting in thousands of deaths and injuries; it resulted in a movement demanding adequate compensation for victims and the adoption of environmental regulations to prevent similar disasters in the future. The Narmada Bachao Andolan (Save the Narmada Struggle) has protested the construction of the giant Sardar Sarvodaya dam in western India since 1986. Activists claimed that the dam would benefit prosperous regions to the detriment of poor regions and displace millions of people, mostly tribals, who do not possess land titles.

The 1980s witnessed the formation of many urban women's organizations that were autonomous from political parties and the state. They engaged in campaigns against female feticide (which results from determining the sex of the fetus through amniocentesis), media misrepresentation of women, harmful contraception dissemination, coercive population policies, rape in police custody, and dowry murders.

After a lull in activism around sexual violence, 2012 witnessed massive protests in response to the horrific gang rape and subsequent death of Jyoti Pandey, a 23-year-old student in Delhi. People demonstrated in Delhi and elsewhere in the days that followed, outraged at the brutal crime and more broadly, the question of sexual violence. The protest reflected the same frustration with the state that fueled the anticorruption movement.

The government responded to popular pressure by appointing a judicial committee to recommend amendments to criminal law concerning sexual assault. In response to the committee's recommendations, the government created fast-track courts for prosecuting rape and passed a law in 2013 that increased penalties for sexual offences. However, the law failed to criminalize marital rape and prosecute military personnel accused of sexual offences under criminal law.

Three important developments have influenced the character and trajectory of social movements in recent years. First, many social movements have developed close relationships to the state and electoral politics. In the past, social movements tended to be community-based and issue-specific. Movements would come to an end once they achieved some success, for example, limiting deforestation, stopping the construction of a dam, or obtaining higher agricultural subsidies. Although many social movements remain limited in focus, duration, and geographic reach, some have sought to overcome these limitations by engaging in electoral politics. The *dalit* movement, Hindu nationalist movement, and anticorruption movement are important examples. Other movements have sought to work with the state. The women's movement, for example, has worked closely with the bureaucracy and the courts.

Second, the character of social movements has changed amidst the growth of nationalism and neoliberalism. The growth of the religious right has confronted left-wing social movements with a serious challenge. Although the religious right and

Protest against sexual violence in New Delhi.

Hindustan Times/Newscom/Hindustan Times/New Delhi/Delhi/India

secular left disagree on most issues, they have adopted the same stance on some questions, like opposing economic liberalization and globalization. Furthermore, as the state has abandoned its socialist commitments, social movements have also ceased to focus on poverty and class inequality. The most important exception is the Naxalites. Although they have strong support among some of India's poorest communities, their use of violence has repelled many social activists.

Third, many NGOs and social movements have developed extensive transnational connections. The consequences have been double-edged. On the positive side, funding from foreign sources has been vital to the survival of NGOs and social movements. However, foreign funding has created a division between activists with and without access to foreign donors. Moreover, the Modi government distrusts social change-oriented NGOs, and has restricted their access to foreign funding

The Political Impact of Technology and the Media

The growth of technologies of communication has had important implications for politicians, political parties, and relations between citizens and the state. The cell phone and Internet have revolutionized communications in India. Although only 25 million of 1.3 billion Indians have access to landline telephones, nearly a billion people have cell phones. India has nearly 400 million Internet users, the third largest user base after China and the United States. Urban youth are the primary users of cell phones and the Internet, although a sizable 40 percent of cell phone users live in rural areas.

Political parties and social movements have used the Internet to galvanize support, politicize issues, and raise funds within India and among diasporic groups. Narendra Modi is an ardent proponent of social media and extensively employed Twitter and Facebook in his election campaign. AAP raised over $3 million through the Internet in its first few months of existence. Social movements protesting rape and corruption have used social media to organize protests and disseminate information.

Technological innovations have also influenced India's military weaponry and strategy. It has invested in Unmanned Aerial Vehicles (UAVs) and is planning to bolster its cyber security credentials. Some military analysts have been critical of India's lack of preparedness in combating cyber terrorism, as Indian government websites have been the target of several cyberattacks, probably from China.

Both citizens and the state have employed technology to monitor each other. Citizens have used the Internet to expose government corruption, seek greater transparency and achieve better access to government services. The Indian government plans to provide electronic identity cards to every Indian citizen, which should improve service delivery but might also enable the government to increase surveillance. India began an ambitious cyber surveillance program in 2009. Aside from accessing cell phone records and intercepting phone calls, the program allows the government to access Internet data. In 2012, Research in Motion, the company manufacturing BlackBerrys, provided the Indian government with encryption keys that allowed it to retrieve emails and messages on its phones.

Where Do You Stand?

Since democracy is about preventing the abuse of power, fragmentation of power in India is a good thing. Discuss.

Based on what you have learned about Indian politics and the BJP, do you think the election of Narendra Modi is a positive development for India?

INDIAN POLITICS IN TRANSITION

SECTION 5

Political Challenges and Changing Agendas

India has come a long way in the seven decades since independence. On the positive side of the ledger, Indians can justly be proud of the fact that this large, poor, and incredibly diverse country has survived intact. The fact that India has been fairly well governed during this period represents another achievement. The disturbing record of failed states in far smaller countries provides a reason to celebrate the fact that the Indian state is reasonably effective. A further achievement is that India has been a well-functioning democracy for virtually its entire existence and has generally upheld the rule of law and protected civil rights, notably those of minorities. Finally, despite unevenness, India is leapfrogging into the twenty-first century. By scoring sustained and rapid economic growth for nearly four decades, India has become a leader of the world's emerging economies.

However, these impressive features are but half of the proverbially half-filled glass. We highlight some pressing challenges that India must surmount to fulfill its rich and promising potential.

The Challenge of Ethnic Diversity

The future of Indian democracy is closely bound up with how the country confronts the growing politicization of ethnic identities, that is, the attempt by organized ethnic groups to obtain state power and state-controlled economic resources—and exclude other ethnic groups in the process. Caste, language, and religion are the basis for political mobilization. Democracy can encourage political parties and leaders to manipulate group identities for electoral purposes, as is evident in the rise of the BJP.

Political struggles in India are simultaneously struggles for identity, power, and wealth. Identity politics is characterized by two distinct trends: the tendency for a variety of diverse nonclass-based regional and ethnic groups to make demands on parties and governments; and pressure on political parties to broaden their electoral appeals to the middle and lower strata of Indian society. If India's growth dividend

Focus Questions ▼

• Identify two major challenges confronting India. How well equipped are Indian political institutions to meet these challenges?

• In what ways does India provide a useful model of economic and political development for other countries?

is sufficiently large, it may be possible to satisfy both sets of demands. However, this requires an unusually favorable set of circumstances, including continued economic growth, skillful political leadership, and commitment to distributing economic gains broadly enough to satisfy all significant groups.

Political Violence

In recent years, India has experienced the growth of two forms of violence in addition to Hindu nationalist violence described earlier. The first is fueled by the poor and dispossessed, who have participated in the Naxalite-led insurgency in thirteen out of India's twenty-eight states. Former Prime Minister Singh characterized the "Maoist rebels" as India's major "law-and-order problem." The Naxalite-led insurgency has produced 5,000 deaths since 2009.

Second, India has become a prime site of terrorist violence in recent years. In the 1990s, most attacks were linked to regional conflicts in the Punjab, Kashmir, and the Northeast. While violent attacks continue in Kashmir, they have extended to other parts of the country. The sources of terrorist attacks have also become more varied. Organizations with links to the RSS have planned several of them, while blaming them on Muslim militants. Pakistan's ISI and other transnational Islamic networks have been responsible for many others.

India-Pakistan Tensions

From the moment that India and Pakistan became separate states, their relations have varied from tense to violent, including three wars, simmering tensions over Kashmir, and periodic violence between their armed forces. Indo-Pakistani conflict is a major reason for the two countries' high military expenditures.

Manmohan Singh was responsible for constructive diplomatic overtures to Pakistan. A high point in their relations occurred during the Asian semifinals of the Cricket World Cup tournament in 2011, which pitted India against Pakistan and was played in India. Prime Minister Singh took the unprecedented step of inviting the Pakistani Prime Minister Asaf Ali Zardari to India as his guest and Zardari accepted the invitation. This was followed by additional meetings during 2011–2012, when both countries agreed that they would extend for five years an agreement to reduce the risk of accidents involving nuclear weapons. They also supported measures to enhance cross-border trade and travel across the Line of Control in Jammu and Kashmir. Still, India remains suspicious that Pakistan is harboring terrorist organizations and remains dissatisfied with its refusal to prosecute the perpetrators of the 2008 Mumbai attacks.

Narendra Modi's presidency began auspiciously when he invited the Pakistani head of state to his inauguration. Unfortunately, Modi has not followed through. Tensions increased following two terrorist attacks in India in 2016, for which India blamed Pakistan. The fact that both countries possess nuclear weapons makes the stakes especially high. A key issue is whether India can prevent conflict with Pakistan from spiraling into nuclear war. Moreover, India has tense relations with not one but two nuclear-armed neighbors. Conflict with China, its powerful neighbor to the north and east, is also never far from the surface.

Nuclear Weapons

Soon after the BJP was first elected to power in May 1998, it fulfilled an electoral promise by gate-crashing the nuclear club. Although the BJP government cited threats from China and Pakistan as the key reason to develop nuclear weapons, its decision can also be traced to electoral considerations. The Hindu bomb, as the BJP described it, was an excellent way to mobilize Indians' national pride and thereby deflect attention from domestic, economic, and political problems.

After India detonated a nuclear bomb, Pakistan responded in kind, triggering fears of a nuclear arms race in South Asia. Worldwide condemnation and sanctions on both India and Pakistan swiftly followed. The Manmohan Singh government took a dramatic step toward defusing tensions over the nuclear issue in 2004 by proclaiming India's commitment to preventing the proliferation of weapons of mass destruction. As a result, United States and India signed an agreement in 2005 that provides for cooperation on nuclear issues despite India's continuing violation of nonproliferation norms. (For example, India has refused to sign the Comprehensive Test Ban Treaty and the Nuclear Nonproliferation Treaty.) In a major policy shift in 2012, the United States dropped its demand that India authorize the United States to inspect the weapons that the United States has sold to India.

Kashmir in a World of States

The roots of the conflict over Kashmir go back to its being divided between India and Pakistan. In 1947, the Hindu Maharaja of Kashmir, annexed the part of Kashmir he governed to India. Since the wishes of Kashmiris were unclear, India announced that it would hold a plebiscite, a vote for or against the form of government, to determine whether the residents of Indian-controlled Kashmir wanted to remain part of the Indian nation. That plebiscite was never held. The status of Kashmir—whether it should be part of India, part of Pakistan, or an independent state—was unresolved in 1947 and is still contested. The state's population is roughly 65 percent Muslim and 35 percent Hindus and other minorities. Most of the non-Muslim minorities— Hindus, Sikhs, and Buddhists, concentrated in the areas of Kashmir called Jammu and Ladakh—prefer living under Indian sovereignty. A large proportion of Muslims feel otherwise. The major causes of ethnic and religious tensions are rivaling political interests.

Tensions involving Kashmir have persisted in part because of the different interests and perspectives of the three major regional powers. Mutual distrust between India and Pakistan, tensions between India and China, and a strategic partnership between Pakistan and China have made peaceful resolution on the status of Kashmir all but impossible. China occupies part of a disputed area of Kashmir. Pakistan has escalated hostilities by violating a UN-sponsored ceasefire, refusing to withdraw troops stationed there, and supporting militants who have engaged in terrorist attacks against moderate Kashmiris. India has aggravated the situation by preventing other powers from helping resolve the dispute. Further, the Indian Army routinely employs repression to curb political dissent in Kashmir. In past years, the Indian government installed unrepresentative and unpopular governments in Kashmir favorable to India. On the positive side, the 2014 election in Kashmir, which brought a coalition government led by the People's Democratic Party and the BJP to power, was open and inclusive. The Indian government has increased investments in Kashmir for economic development and job creation.

India's Regional Relations

India's relations with regional powers have been inconsistent historically. Relations with China have been especially tumultuous. The two countries fought a war in 1962, and recurrent border disputes since then reflect their competition for regional and international influence. China continues to claim sizable portions of territory in Kashmir that India considers its own. China has made border incursions into the volatile northeastern border state of Arunachal Pradesh. India has opposed Beijing's growing investments in the Pakistan-occupied portion of Kashmir. Although there have been periodic tensions between India and China over territorial matters, the two countries share interests vis-à-vis the West on global trade, climate change, and other issues. New Delhi and Beijing have signed a series of economic agreements. China is India's major trading partner. Bilateral trade was $70 billion during 2015–2016, although China exported a lot more to India than the other way around.

India's relations with other countries in the region have been mixed. India and Nepal established strong economic and political ties through the 1950 Indo-Nepal Treaty of Peace and Friendship. Although tensions escalated after Nepal became an absolutist monarchy in 2005, relations improved after the king was deposed and democracy reestablished in Nepal in 2008.

India's relations with Sri Lanka and Bangladesh have been deeply influenced by their shared ethnic compositions. India is home to 55 million Tamils, who live in the southern state of Tamil Nadu. The Liberation Tigers of Tamil Eeelam, which waged a secessionist movement in Sri Lanka resulting in a prolonged civil war between 1983 and 2009, received significant support from Indian Tamils. India's attempt to disarm the LTTE by sending troops to Sri Lanka (1987–1990) backfired. Barring disputes between the two countries over water rights, relations between the two countries have improved since the end of the civil war in Sri Lanka.

India supported the creation of Bangladesh as a predominantly Bengali nation that seceded from Pakistan in 1971. India's Bengali population strongly identified with Bangladesh's claims to nationhood, and India's military helped engineer Bangladesh's breakaway from Pakistan. However, Bangladesh has expressed resentment at trade imbalances, India's control over water resources, and Indian army incursions into its territory. Since 2010, the two countries have taken steps toward improving trade relations and resolving border disputes.

Economic Performance

India's economic experience is neither a clear success nor clear failure. India has maintained strong and steady economic growth rates for decades. As a result, from being held up as an example of economic failure, India has recently emerged as a leader of developing countries. Several factors are responsible. The first involves the relationship between political governance and economic growth. India has been fortunate to have enjoyed relatively good government: its democratic system is mostly open and stable, most political leaders are public spirited, and top bureaucrats are well trained and competent.

The second factor concerns India's strategy for economic development. In the 1950s, India chose to insulate its economy from global forces, limiting trade and foreign investment and emphasizing the government's role in promoting self-sufficiency in heavy industry and agriculture. The positive result was that India grew enough food to feed its large and growing population and produced a vast range of industrial goods. This strategy, however, was not without costs. India sacrificed the additional economic growth that might have come from competing effectively in global markets. Moreover, during this period it made little effort to alleviate its staggering poverty: land redistribution failed, job creation by heavy industries was minimal, and investment in the education and health of the poor was limited. In addition to the terrible human and social costs of this neglect, the poor became a drag on economic growth because they were unable to buy goods and stimulate demand for increased production; moreover, a hungry, uneducated and unhealthy labor force is not a productive labor force.

Fortunately, the sluggish phase is now long past, and the Indian economy has grown briskly over the last four decades. However, India's numerous poor are not benefiting sufficiently from growth. Cuts in public spending on education and health services have been especially hard on the poor. The government has not succeeded in distributing the gains of growth to reduce poverty and inequality.

International Power and Domestic Prosperity

India's attempts to become a strong regional and international power are shaped and constrained by the international environment. The increasing interdependence of the global economies was illustrated by the 2008 economic crisis. India's growth rate declined as did the demand for its exports and foreign investments, and the fiscal deficit rose to nearly 7 percent of the GDP (see Figure 7.4). However, the Indian economy quickly regained strength, and has surged since then.

Institutional Decay

Institutional decay is at the root of many of India's challenges. Competent, honest, and responsive institutions are required to deal with the far-ranging problems identified above, including Indo-Pakistan relations, ethnic diversity, and economic performance. Yet such institutions are in short supply. Disturbing evidence periodically surfaces of corruption that tarnishes key sectors of the state, such as the police, civil service, and political parties. Official corruption is not limited to accepting bribes in exchange for favors. For example, in 2010, it became evident that cabinet ministers and their associates had received kickbacks from India's purchase of weaponry and sale of telecommunication rights. India's telecom minister was accused of selling licenses to use Indian airwaves to cell phone operators at extremely low prices, costing the Indian government $40 billion in lost revenues. The incident led

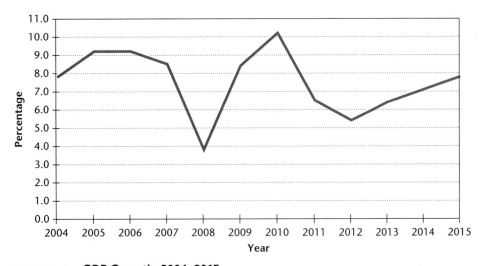

FIGURE 7.4 GDP Growth, 2004–2015

Source: World Bank GDP Growth, http://data.worldbank.org/indicator /NY.GDP.MKTP.KD.ZG/ countries/IN-8s?display=graph.

to investigations revealing corruption at the highest levels of the central government. Although there was no evidence that Prime Minister Singh was directly involved, his refusal for months to launch an official investigation undermined his authority. Without a thorough housecleaning to eliminate institutional decay, India will make little progress in dealing with its many pressing challenges.

In brief, India has an enviable array of resources and a daunting host of challenges. How well it will use its resources to confront these challenges is an open question. Will it be able to capitalize on its positive achievements, such as the long-standing democratic ethos framed by functioning institutions, a vibrant media and civil society, and a growing and ambitious middle class? Or will it be crippled by ethnic hostility resulting in inaction at best and disintegration of the country at worst? The growth of Hindu nationalism has challenged some of India's founding tenets including its commitment to secularism, minority rights, and the protection of civil liberties. India's democracy depends now as in the past on its respect for social and cultural pluralism.

The alleviation of poverty and class inequality remains a pressing challenge. So too does the Naxalite insurgency. The state's repressive response to Naxalism has only contributed to its growth. Tensions with Pakistan and instability in Kashmir continue to simmer. Understanding how India meets—or fails to meet—these challenges will be of enormous interest to students of comparative politics in the years to come. How India reconciles its national ambitions, domestic demands for greater economic redistribution, and global pressures for an efficient economy will affect its ability to influence regional and global trends.

Is Demography Destiny?

India is one of the youngest countries in the world; over half of all Indians are under the age of 25. Young people play an important role in Indian politics. They have been active in struggles against corruption and antiquated rape laws. They significantly influence electoral outcomes. In the 2014 elections, 149 million of the 725-million electorate of India were first-time voters.

Economists believe that when young people join the workforce, it will contribute to significant economic growth. However, this potential requires a major investment in education and the creation of jobs. The government reported that in 2013 the unemployment rate for the population was 4.7 percent whereas for the 15–29 age group it was 13.3 percent.

There are significant differences in the employment opportunities and lifestyles of urban and rural youth. The unemployment rate for high school graduates among 15- to 29-year-olds is 36.6 percent in the rural areas and 26.5 percent in the urban areas.

Inadequate rural employment opportunities have resulted in large-scale youth migration from villages to cities. Youth migrants represent three-quarters of the total internal migrants in India, up from two-thirds two decades ago. Young migrants add pressure to the already weak infrastructure in urban areas. If they lack documents that establish their identity and residency rights, they are not eligible for social benefits and often live in squalor.

By contrast, urban middle-class youth represent the face of globalizing India and often incur the resentment of the lower middle classes. Class tensions have generated social tensions that Hindu nationalists have magnified. For example, some Hindu nationalists have organized campaigns opposing Western influence on gender relations.

Indian Politics in Comparative Perspective

India provides an incredibly interesting and important laboratory for studying issues in comparative politics. Consider the issue of democratic consolidation. Although democracy was introduced to India by its elites, it soon established firm roots within society. A clear example is when Indira Gandhi declared Emergency rule (1975–1977) and curtailed democratic freedoms. In the next election, in 1977, Indian citizens decisively voted Gandhi out of power, registering their preference for democratic rule. Most Indians value democracy and advance their claims within democratic institutions, even when those institutions are flawed.

Comparativists debate whether democracy or authoritarianism is better for economic growth. In the past, India's economic performance did not compare well with the success stories of authoritarian regimes in East Asia and China. However, India's impressive economic growth in recent years suggests that the returns are not yet in. India provides a fine laboratory for studying the relationship between democratic institutions and economic performance.

Another important comparative question concerns the relationship between democratic institutions and multiethnic societies. By studying India's history, particularly the post-1947 period, comparativists can explore how cleavages of caste, religion, and language have been contained and their destructive consequences minimized. Yet, on the other hand, it is also important to study the reasons for the repeated instances of ethnic violence. Comparativists have also puzzled over the conditions under which multiple and contradictory interests within a democratic framework can generate positive economic and distributional outcomes. Here, the variable performance of different regions in India can serve as a laboratory. For instance, what can be learned from studying two communist-ruled states, Kerala and West Bengal, which sponsored land redistribution policies and extensive social welfare programs? Many scholars have praised the Kerala model because it abolished tenancy and landlord exploitation, provided effective public distribution of subsidized rice to low-income households, enacted protective laws for agricultural workers and pensions for retired agricultural laborers, and provided extensive government employment for low-caste communities.

Democracy in India has endured for nearly seven decades. Given the record of democratic failures in the developing world, this is one of India's major achievements. It has been all the more noteworthy because of its multiethnic, federal polity. Countries such as the former Soviet Union and Yugoslavia were unable to hold together their diverse ethnic groups. India's success here merits particular recognition. And finally, on the positive side of the ledger, India's economy has grown at a reasonably impressive rate since 1980. An ethnically plural democracy that can sustain economic growth is a country worth studying.

Against these positive achievements, however, are significant failures, also discussed above. The most glaring is the failure to improve the living conditions of those at the bottom of the society. While India has experienced considerable economic growth, its fruits have not been shared equally. India houses a very large percentage of poor people. Nearly half the children in the country are undernourished and literacy is widespread. The level of rape, as well as women's unequal access to education, health care, and employment underline their precarious position in Indian society. And finally, Indian cities are highly polluted, and lack of planning and organization make them less-than-livable environments.

While India's democracy is vibrant, the quality of governance is often poor. This is at the root of numerous shortcomings in India's development record. The government in India reacts to short-term electoral incentives and often fails to take actions on pressing problems of long run significance. The quality of bureaucracy in India, especially at the lower ranks, is lamentable. As a result, even good intentions and policies do not get implemented. Narendra Modi won the 2014 election by promising to overcome such obstacles and put India on a rapid growth trajectory. Yet his record in this and other respects is not impressive. The demonetization fiasco discussed at the beginning of the chapter highlights the continuing gap between good intentions and poor implementation.

It is not yet clear whether India will be able to build upon and extend its achievements or will fail to cope with many severe challenges in coming years. The results will be of vital importance to over 1 billion Indian citizens. And, given the nature of the challenges it faces, its immense size and strategic importance, what happens in India will have enormous implications for scholars and citizens throughout the world.

Where Do You Stand?

What are the potential economic gains of public investment in education and social welfare?

India's lowest castes have gained in dignity and, even though poor, now feel more included in the Indian political system. Discuss.

Chapter Summary

India is the seventh-largest country in the world and the third-largest country in Asia. It is called a subcontinent because of its large and distinct land mass. With 1.34 billion people, India's population is second only to its neighbor China. Two thirds of Indians live in far-flung villages in the countryside. However, India also has among the largest and most densely populated cities in the world.

India is by far the world's largest democracy and the oldest democracy in Asia, Africa, and Latin America. It has had democratic institutions since it became an independent country in 1947 after nearly two centuries of British colonial rule. Under Mohandas Karamchand Gandhi's brilliant leadership, the Indian National Congress (INC) achieved national independence through peaceful means.

After independence, India adopted a Westminster model of British-style parliamentary democracy. The 1950 constitution created a democratic republic with a parliamentary system and a weak, mostly ceremonial, president. India's political system is federal, and states have substantial autonomy, power, and responsibilities. A pillar of Indian democracy is the fact that elections are open, competitive, and honest. Nearly 500 million people are eligible to vote, and close to 300 million cast ballots.

In recent decades, India has become more democratic in some ways and less in others. Its party system has become more competitive. The Congress Party, which led the anticolonial movement, formed every government from 1947 to 1989, except for one brief interlude (1977–1980). Since 1989, the Congress Party has declined and a true multiparty system has emerged. A larger number of people, with more diverse identities, are participating in politics. However, business leaders wield much more political influence than do the far more numerous poor. Political parties often foster violence for electoral purposes. The ruling Hindu nationalist party has unleashed violence against Muslim and Christian religious minorities, centralized power and challenged civil rights and liberties.

India provides a fine laboratory for studying the relationship between democratic institutions and economic performance. At independence, India had a poor, largely agricultural economy. Although a large majority of Indians, especially the poor, still work and live in the countryside, India has developed a substantial industrial base, a booming service sector, and a vibrant middle class. During the first three decades following independence, the Indian economy was mainly state-directed. The overall economic growth during this period was sluggish. Since 1991, reforms privatized the economy and opened the Indian economy to the outside world. As a result, the economy grew rapidly. However, the daunting challenges facing Indian leaders is how to sustain growth while reducing poverty and economic inequalities.

India is well positioned, by its large size, growing wealth, democratic legitimacy, and geographic location, to play a powerful role in world affairs. Yet for this to occur, it is necessary for India to nurture peaceful relations with its powerful neighbors, Pakistan and China. India's democracy is an excellent arena for analyzing various theories and dilemmas of comparative politics. Its record, of democratic stability since most of its independent history, is remarkable among developing countries.

Key Terms

Brahmin
caste system
dalits
economic liberalization
Emergency (1975–1977)
green revolution
Indian Administrative Service
  (IAS)

Indian Rebellion
Lok Sabha
Mandal Commission
Naxalite
nonaligned bloc
other backward classes
panchayats
patronage system

plebiscite
reservations
sati
scheduled castes
Sikh
state-led economic development
untouchables
zamindars

Suggested Readings

Basu, Amrita. *Violent Conjunctures in Democratic India.* New York: Cambridge University Press, 2016.

Chandra, Kanchan. *Why Ethnic Parties Succeed: Patronage and Ethnic Head Counts in India.* Cambridge: Cambridge University Press, 2007.

Chatterjee, Partha. *Lineages of Political Society: Studies in Postcolonial Democracy.* New York: Columbia University Press, 2011.

Frankel, Francine. *India's Political Economy, 1947–2004: The Gradual Revolution.* New Delhi: Oxford University Press, 2005.

Guha, Ramachandran. *India after Gandhi: The World's Largest Democracy.* New York: Harper Perennial, 2008.

Hasan, Zoya. *Politics of Inclusion: Caste, Minority and Representation in India.* Delhi: Oxford University Press, 2009.

Jayal, Niraja Gopal. *Citizenship and its Discontents: An Indian History.* Cambridge, MA: Harvard University Press, 2013.

Jayal, Niraja Gopal, and Pratap Mehta, eds. *The Oxford Companion to Politics in India.* New Delhi: Oxford University Press, 2010.

Kohli, Atul. *Poverty Amid Plenty in the New India.* Cambridge: Cambridge University Press, 2012.

Panagariya, Arvind. *India: The Emerging Giant.* New York: Oxford University Press, 2008.

Sen, Amartya. *The Argumentative Indian.* London: Allen Lane, 2005.

Varshney, Ashutosh. *Ethnic Conflict and Civic Life: Hindus and Muslims in India.* New Haven: Yale University Press, 2002.

Suggested Websites

Indian National Congress
http://www.inc.in/

Bharatiya Janata Party (BJP)
www.bjp.org

Aam Aadmi Party (AAP)
http://www.aamaadmiparty.org/

Times of India
**http://timesofindia.indiatimes.com
  /international-home**

Economic and Political Weekly, a good source of information on Indian politics
www.epw.in/

Frontline, a magazine with coverage of Indian politics
http://www.frontline.in/

The Hindu, an English daily paper in India
http://www.thehindu.com/

Hindustan Times
www.hindustantimes.com

Directory of Indian government websites
goidirectory.nic.in

Sabrang Communications, providing coverage of human rights issues in India
www.sabrang.com

The United States

Louis DeSipio

Official Name: United States of America

Location: North America, between Canada and Mexico

Capital City: Washington, D.C.

Population (2014): 318.9 million

Size: 9,826,630 sq. km.; about half the size of South America; slightly larger than China

THE MAKING OF THE MODERN AMERICAN STATE

Politics in Action

The election of Donald Trump as U.S. president in 2016 surprised many observers of U.S. politics, Democratic Party leaders, and, quite likely, many of Mr. Trump's senior advisors. Trump had run an unconventional campaign and trailed his opponent, former Sectary of State Hillary Rodham Clinton, in most polls since the party conventions the summer before the November election. Clinton ran a traditional, well-funded campaign that appeared to ensure that she would win a sizeable victory in the Electoral College, the body that formally elects the president, as well as in the popular vote.

The results on election night confounded these expectations. Clinton won the popular vote by nearly 3 million votes. Trump won the presidency by winning most of the so-called battleground states—states where both candidates most actively competed for votes in the general election—and by taking two states thought to be solidly in the Clinton's camp—Wisconsin and Michigan. All but two states allocate all their Electoral College votes to the candidate who wins the most votes in the state. These victories ensured a sizeable Electoral College victory and the presidency for Trump. He won the votes of 306 electors and Clinton won 232.

Thanks to the Trump victory and a Republican sweep of elections to the Senate and House of Representatives, Republicans controlled the presidency and both houses of Congress for the first time since 2006. This unified government is unusual in contemporary U.S. politics. It does not, however, guarantee that the Republican agenda will be implemented. The U.S. Constitution sets the branches of government against each other, so Congress and the president may compete even when they are controlled by the same party. Equally importantly, the Republican Party does not speak with a single voice on many policy issues. Moreover, in areas where Congress and the president do agree and pass laws (or where the Executive Branch uses authority granted by Congress to issue regulations), these new policies can be challenged in the courts or by the states. The Supreme Court may strike down legislation if it judges that a law violates the Constitution. And the Constitution ensures that states have powers independent of the national government. **Federalism** is a system of governance with twin sovereigns—the federal government and state governments.

In his acceptance speech at the Republican National Convention, Donald Trump asserted that "I alone can fix it," referring to a series of crises that he reported that the nation faced. Despite his victory in the 2016 election, he quickly discovered as president that the United States political system does not empower a single omnipotent leader, but instead offers many points of access to political power and influence, and competing institutions that seek a role in fixing national problems. (See Figure 8.1 and Table 8.1.)

federalism

A system of governance in which political authority is shared between the national government and regional or state governments. The powers of each level of government are usually specified in a federal constitution.

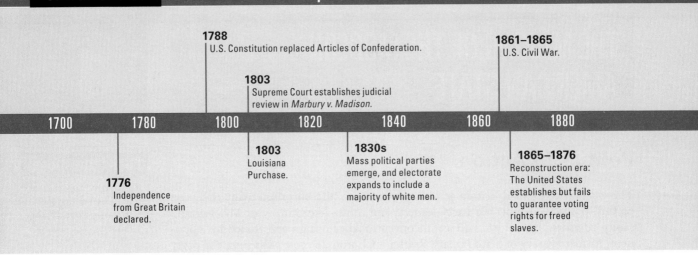

CHRONOLOGY of U.S. Political Development

1788
U.S. Constitution replaced Articles of Confederation.

1861–1865
U.S. Civil War.

1803
Supreme Court establishes judicial review in *Marbury v. Madison*.

| 1700 | 1780 | 1800 | 1820 | 1840 | 1860 | 1880 |

1803
Louisiana Purchase.

1830s
Mass political parties emerge, and electorate expands to include a majority of white men.

1865–1876
Reconstruction era: The United States establishes but fails to guarantee voting rights for freed slaves.

1776
Independence from Great Britain declared.

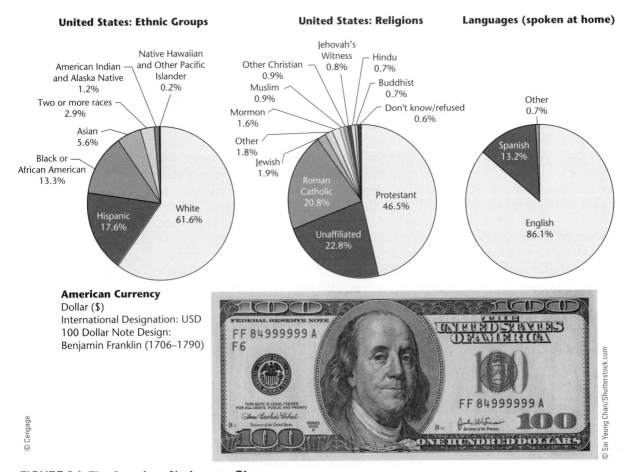

United States: Ethnic Groups

- American Indian and Alaska Native 1.2%
- Native Hawaiian and Other Pacific Islander 0.2%
- Two or more races 2.9%
- Asian 5.6%
- Black or African American 13.3%
- Hispanic 17.6%
- White 61.6%

United States: Religions

- Jehovah's Witness 0.8%
- Hindu 0.7%
- Other Christian 0.9%
- Muslim 0.9%
- Mormon 1.6%
- Buddhist 0.7%
- Don't know/refused 0.6%
- Other 1.8%
- Jewish 1.9%
- Roman Catholic 20.8%
- Protestant 46.5%
- Unaffiliated 22.8%

Languages (spoken at home)

- Other 0.7%
- Spanish 13.2%
- English 86.1%

American Currency
Dollar ($)
International Designation: USD
100 Dollar Note Design:
Benjamin Franklin (1706–1790)

FIGURE 8.1 The American Nation at a Glance

© Cengage

© Sai Yeung Chan/Shutterstock.com

1933–1940
The New Deal responds to the economic distress of the Great Depression.

1974
Richard Nixon resigns the presidency in the face of certain impeachment.

1978
California passes Proposition 13.

2001
The World Trade Center and the Pentagon are targets of terrorist attacks using hijacked civilian airliners.

2010
Republicans win control of the House of Representatives.

2016
Donald Trump elected President of the United States.

| 1900 | 1930 | 1960 | 1980 | 1990 | 2010 | 2016 |

1896
Voter turnout in elections begins century-long decline.

1941–1945
United States participates in World War II.

1964
Tonkin Gulf Resolution authorizes military actions in Vietnam.

2008
Barack Obama elected President of the United States.

1996
Federal government ends the guarantee of social welfare programs to the poor established during the New Deal.

Geographic Setting

The United States occupies nearly half of North America. Its only two neighbors, Mexico and Canada, do not present a military threat and are linked to the United States in a comprehensive trade agreement: the North American Free Trade Agreement (NAFTA). United States territory is rich in natural resources, arable land, navigable rivers, and protected ports. This abundance has led Americans to assume they will always have enough resources to meet national needs. Finally, the United States has always had low population densities and has served as a magnet for international migration.

European colonization and conquest of indigenous inhabitants led to the eventual unification of the territory that became the United States under one government and the expansion of that territory from the Atlantic to the Pacific Ocean. This process began in the early 1500s and reached its peak in the nineteenth century, when rapid population expansion was reinforced by an imperialist national ideology (**manifest destiny**) advocating expansion all the way to the Pacific. Native Americans were pushed aside. The United States experimented with colonialism around 1900, annexing Hawaii, Guam, the Northern Marianas Islands, and Puerto Rico.

Puerto Rico is a colony of the United States with limited autonomy in trade and foreign policy. Puerto Ricans are U.S. citizens by birth and can travel freely to the United States. Although some in Puerto Rico seek independence, most want either a continuation of Commonwealth status or statehood. Guam is an "unincorporated territory" (a U.S. territory that is not on the road to statehood and whose citizens do not have all the protections of the U.S. Constitution).

manifest destiny

The public philosophy in the nineteenth century stating that the United States was not only entitled but also destined to occupy territory from the Atlantic to the Pacific.

Critical Junctures

The first four critical junctures in United States political history appeared at points when popular discontent was sufficiently powerful to change governing institutions or relationships. Each juncture challenged dominant ideas about who should have a

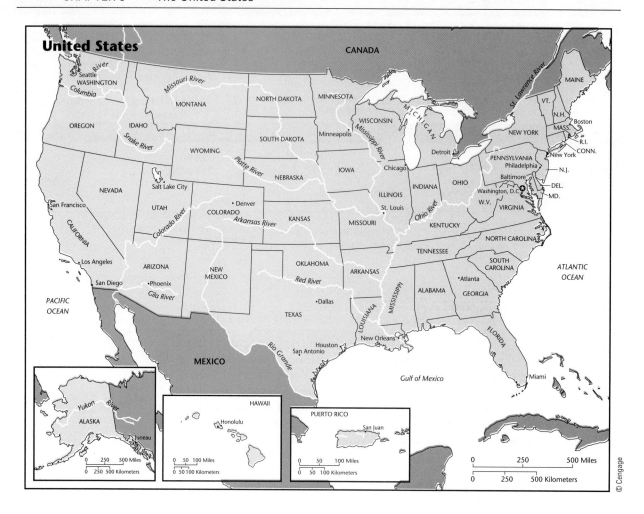

voice in democratic government and what the relationship between government and citizen should be.

The Revolutionary Era (1773–1789)

Popular and elite discontent with British colonial rule sparked the American Revolution, when the thirteen colonies under British rule in North America revolted. The period began with the signing of the **Declaration of Independence**. At the outset, there was a cleavage between popular and elite interests. Popular interests wanted to keep government in each colony close to home and to rank and file citizens, and wanted each colony to have substantial independence from the others. Elite interests advocated a national government with control over foreign policy, national assumption of state Revolutionary War debts, and the ability to establish national rules for commerce.

Popular interests won the first round of this battle. From 1777 to 1788, the **Articles of Confederation** governed the nation. They specified that the national government could not implement foreign or domestic policy, raise taxes, or regulate trade between the states without the cooperation of the individual states. The limited powers of the national government under the Articles rested in a legislature, but the states had to ratify most key decisions. States also established their own foreign

Table 8.1	Political Organization
Political system	**Presidential system.**
Regime history	Representative democracy, usually dated from the signing of the Declaration of Independence (1776) or the Constitution (1787).
Administrative structure	Federalism, with powers shared between the national government and the fifty state governments; separation of powers at the level of the national government among legislative, executive, and judicial branches.
Executive	President, "directly" elected (with Electoral College that officially elects president and vice president) for 4-year term; the cabinet is an advisory group of heads of major federal agencies and other senior officials selected by president to aid in decision making but with no formal authority.
Legislature	Bicameral. Congress composed of a lower house (House of Representatives) of 435 members serving 2-year terms and an upper house (Senate) of 100 members (two from each state) serving 6-year terms; elected in single-member districts (or, in the case of the Senate, states) by simple plurality (some states require a majority of voters).
Judiciary	Supreme Court with nine justices nominated by president and confirmed by Senate, with life tenure; has specified original and appellate jurisdiction and exercises the power of judicial review (can declare acts of the legislature and executive unconstitutional and therefore null and void).
Party system	Essentially a two-party system (Republican and Democrat), with relatively weak and fractionalized parties; more than in most representative democracies, the personal following of candidates remains very important.

policies, often different from each other. They also established their own fiscal policies and financed state budgets through extensive borrowing.

The Constitution maintained most power with the states but granted the federal (or national) government authority over commerce and foreign and military policy. It also gave the federal government the power to levy taxes, thus providing a source of financing independent of the states. It set out the tripartite structure of independent Congress, judiciary, and executive. And, most important, it created a president with powers independent of the legislature.

The Constitution delegated specific, but limited, powers to the national government in Article I, Section 8. These included establishing post offices and roads, coining money, promoting the progress of science, raising and supporting an army and navy, and establishing a uniform rule of naturalization. These powers implicitly granted the federal government the power to create a national economy. Finally, the Constitution limited citizens' voice in government. Presidents were elected indirectly, through the Electoral College, a body of political insiders from each state elected on Election Day and who meet the following month to elect the president. Although the Framers thought the Electoral College would exercise independent judgment about who would make the best president, it eventually became a rubber stamp that ratified the results of popular elections for president held in each state.

Members of the Senate were originally elected by state legislatures. Only members of the House of Representatives were elected by the people, and state legislatures

Articles of Confederation

The first governing document of the United States, agreed to in 1777 and ratified in 1781. The Articles concentrated most powers in the states and made the national government dependent on voluntary contributions of the states.

determined who within the state was entitled to vote for members of the House. At first, in most states only property-holding men held the votes. By the 1840s, suffrage was broadened to include most white adult men. Women did not receive voting rights nationally until 1920, and it goes without saying that slaves could not vote.

As popular support for ratifying the newly drafted Constitution grew, many who supported the Articles of Confederation made a new demand: The new Constitution should include enumerated protections for individuals from governmental power. Meeting this demand for a **Bill of Rights** was necessary to ensure ratification of the Constitution. Among the most important provisions of the Bill of Rights have been freedom of speech, assembly, and the press. Since federal judges interpret these rights, along with the Constitution as a whole, the federal courts played a growing role in the national government. This became particularly evident in the twentieth century.

The Civil War and Reconstruction (1861–1876)

The morality of slavery convulsed the nation before the Civil War, but the war itself began over the question of whether the states or the national government should be dominant. Many states believed they could reject specific federal laws; whenever Congress threatened to pass legislation to restrict slavery in the South, one or more southern state legislatures threatened to nullify it. Many believed that if any state could nullify federal laws, the union would be put at risk. It took the Civil War, the bloodiest war in United States history, to resolve this issue in favor of the indivisibility of the union. The war also established national citizenship to supplement state citizenship, which had existed even before the Constitution.[1] Establishing national citizenship began a slow process that eventually culminated in the New Deal during the Great Depression of the 1930s, as citizens looked to the federal government to meet their basic needs in times of national crisis.

To establish full citizenship for the freed slaves, Congress revisited the question of individual liberties and citizenship. The post-Civil War debates on the relationship of citizens to the national government established several important principles that were codified in the Fourteenth Amendment to the Constitution (1868). First, it extended the citizen rights and protections of the Bill of Rights to cover actions by states as well as by the federal government. Second, it extended citizenship to all persons born in the United States. This made U.S. citizens of freed slaves and also guaranteed that the United States-born children of immigrants were U.S. citizens at birth. Third, Congress sought to establish federal regulation of voting and to grant the vote to African Americans. When the federal government failed to continue enforcing black voting rights in the period after post-Civil War Reconstruction, African Americans, particularly in the South, were routinely prevented (by violence if need be) from exercising the vote until the Voting Rights Act in 1965. The fundamental guarantees that ensure voting rights today limit prerogatives originally recognized in the Constitution as the belonging exclusively to the states.

The New Deal Era (1933–1940)

The third critical juncture in United States political development was the New Deal, the policy package fashioned by President Franklin Delano Roosevelt as a response to the economic crisis of the Great Depression. After constitutional challenges were overcome to expanding the role of the federal government, the Roosevelt administration used its constitutional power to regulate interstate commerce to expand federal

---

Bill of Rights

The first ten amendments to the U.S. Constitution (ratified in 1791), which established limits on the actions of government. Initially, the Bill of Rights limited only the federal government. The Fourteenth Amendment and subsequent judicial rulings extended the provisions of the Bill of Rights to the states.

regulation of business. The New Deal also established a nationally guaranteed safety net, which included such programs as Social Security to provide monthly payments to retired workers, as well as programs to provide housing for the working poor and food subsidies for children in poor households. The federal government also subsidized agriculture and protected farmers against the cyclical nature of demand. Once the legislative and judicial battles waged to establish these policies were won, they represented a fundamental expansion of the role of the federal government.

As a result of the New Deal and subsequent programs in following decades, the federal government now asserted dominance over the states in delivering services to the people. Equally important, during the New Deal the presidency asserted dominance over the Congress in policy-making. Franklin Roosevelt found powers that no previous president had exercised. All post-New Deal presidents are much more powerful than any of their predecessors, except perhaps for Abraham Lincoln. Although the New Deal programs represented a significant change from the policies that preceded the Great Depression, they also reflected underlying American political values (see Section 4).

As the 1930s Depression came to a close, and Nazi Germany under Adolph Hitler launched into war in Europe, along with Japan's aggression in Asia, the United States geared up for war. Although the United States had previously been involved in international conflicts beyond its borders, the experience of World War II was different, both at the beginning and end of United States involvement. The United States entered the war after Germany's ally, Japan, attacked the United States at Pearl Harbor, Hawaii. And after the war, the United States initiated and implemented a multilateral strategy to contain the Soviet Union.

Divided Government, Frequently Shifting Partisan Dominance, and Political Contestation of the Scope of Government (1968 to the Present)

The fourth critical juncture, which began with Richard Nixon's election as president in 1968, is ongoing today. This critical juncture has two dimensions. First, the two political parties have routinely divided control of the presidency and Congress, with dominance of each branch of government shifting regularly. This division exacerbates the inefficiency that was designed into the American constitutional order and the result increases popular distrust of government (see Section 3). One party has replaced the other in the presidency six times since 1968. This division of the federal government, between the parties and the routine shift in party control of the Congress or the presidency, slow government response to controversial policy issues.

The second dimension of the contemporary critical juncture emerges from the apparent inefficiency caused by divided government. Many in the United States began to question the increase in the scope of governmental services that began with the New Deal. The electoral roots of this popular revolt can be found in the passage of Proposition 13 by California voters in 1978, which limited California's ability to increase property taxes. The passage of Proposition 13 began an era that continues today, in which many citizens reject the expansion of government.

Popular discontent in the contemporary era is not limited to taxes; it also focuses on the scope of government. This period saw popular mobilization to reshape government's involvement in "values" issues, such as abortion, same-sex marriage, and the role of religion. Advocates on all sides of these issues want government to protect their interests, while condemning government for allegedly promoting the interests of groups with opposing positions. Ultimately, the courts become the venue to shape government policies on social issues.

Social Security

National systems of contributory and noncontributory benefits to provide assistance for the elderly, sick, disabled, unemployed, and others similarly in need of assistance.

property taxes

Taxes levied by local governments on the assessed value of property. Property taxes are the primary way in which local jurisdictions in the United States pay for primary and secondary education. Because the value of property varies dramatically from neighborhood to neighborhood, the funding available for public facilities like schools—and their quality—also varies from place to place.

A jet crashes into the World Trade Center on September 11, 2001.

AP Images/Moshe Bursuker

While divided government had become the norm in 1968, the division became even more razor thin starting in the late 1990s. Each election raises the possibility of a switch in partisan control of the Senate or the House and the intense focus of both parties and **interest groups** on winning the handful of seats that could switch control of Congress from one party to the other.

September 11, 2001, and Its Aftermath

It is in this environment that the United States responded to the terrorist attacks of September 11 on the World Trade Center in New York and Pentagon in Washington, D.C. Initially, Congress and the populace rallied behind the president to increase the scope of federal law enforcement powers and to provide financial assistance for New York City, the families of the victims of the attack, and the airlines. Popular support for President Bush and his administration's initial efforts to respond to the challenges of September 11 continued as the administration prepared for an invasion of Afghanistan.

interest groups

Organizations that seek to represent the interests of their members in dealings with the government. Important examples are associations representing people with specific occupations, business interests, racial and ethnic groups, or age groups in society.

The initial post-9/11 domestic cohesion and international support for the United States dissipated quickly. United States efforts to extend the war on terrorism to Iraq became the focus of growing opposition to United States power and unilateralism in international affairs.

The Four Themes and the United States

The United States in a Globalized World of States

Until the New Deal and World War II, the United States pursued a contradictory policy toward the rest of the world of states. It sought isolation from international politics but unfettered access to international markets. World War II changed the first of these stances, at least at elite levels (see Section 2). The United States sought to shape international relations through multilateral organizations and military force. It designed multilateral international organizations that enabled it to have a disproportionate voice (for example, in the United Nations Security

Council). With the end of the Cold War, some advocated a reduced role of the U.S. government in the world of states or, at a minimum, a greater willingness to use a unilateral response to international military crises. President Trump voiced similar concerns as a candidate. He has more latitude to change United States foreign policy than other leaders of advanced democracies because foreign policy has rarely been central to the evolution of U.S. politics and governance and Congress is more likely to defer to the executive on the direction of foreign policy than on domestic policy making.

Governing the Economy

The conflict between the president and Congress, the centralization of federal power in the twentieth century, and the growing concern about the cost and scope of government represent the central challenge to predicting the future direction of U.S. politics. Each one of these elements involves questioning how much the federal and state governments should regulate the economy. There will be no quick resolution; the Constitution slows resolution by creating a system of federalism and separation of powers (see Section 3).

The federal and state governments have sought to manage the economy by promoting domestic manufacturing, exploiting the nation's natural resources, and regulating the banking sector, while interfering little in the conduct of business (see Section 2). As discussed below, this hands-off attitude toward economic regulation can come at a price.

separation of powers

An organization of political institutions within the state in which the executive, legislature, and judiciary have autonomous powers and no one branch dominates the others. This is the common pattern in presidential systems. In parliamentary systems, there is a fusion of powers.

The Democratic Idea

The democratic idea in the United States context was one of an indirect, representative democracy with checks on democratically elected leaders. The emergence of a strong national government beginning in the New Deal era meant that national coalitions could often focus their demands on a single federal government, rather than having to target a host of state governments as well. The decline in mediating institutions that can channel these demands reduces the ability of individual citizens to influence the national government (see Section 4). In the contemporary era, however, many in U.S. society challenge the size and scope of the federal government and seek a return to the states-focused polity that characterized the United States before the New Deal.

The Politics of Collective Identity

As a nation of immigrants, the United States must unite immigrants and descendants of immigrants from Europe, Africa, Latin America, and Asia, along with the established U.S. population. Previous waves of immigrants often experienced one or two generations of political and societal exclusion before becoming fully accepted participants in the society. Whether today's immigrants (particularly those who enter the United States without legal immigrant status) experience the same relatively rapid acculturation remains an open question. Preliminary evidence indicates that the process may be even quicker for immigrants who possess skills and education but slower for those who do not.[2] The United States has never fully remedied its longest-lasting difference in collective identities with full economic and political incorporation of African Americans, which was central to the Civil War and Reconstruction era and remains a challenge to today's U.S. politics.

Themes and Comparisons

Scholars of U.S. politics have often grappled with the theme of American exceptionalism—the idea that the United States is unique and cannot easily be compared to other countries. In several respects, the United States *can* be considered exceptional: Its geography and natural resources offer it advantages that few other nations can match; its experience with mass representative democracy is longer than that of other nations; it has been able to expand the citizenry far beyond the descendants of the original citizens; and U.S. society has been much less divided by class than have the societies of other states.[3]

The U.S. Constitution, for all of its limitations, has served as the model for the constitutions of many newly independent nations. Some form of separation of powers has become the norm in democratic states. Similarly, district-based and **single member plurality (SMP) electoral systems** (see Section 4) have been widely adopted to reduce conflict in multiethnic states, of which the United States was the first large-scale example.

single member plurality (SMP) electoral system

An electoral system in which candidates run for a single seat from a specific geographic district. The candidate receiving the most votes, that is, a plurality, wins, whether or not this amounts to a majority. SMP systems, unlike systems of proportional representation, increase the likelihood that two national coalition parties will form.

Where Do You Stand?

The balance between the powers of the federal and state governments has shifted considerably. Can you suggest how different government responsibilities should be distributed between levels of government?

Can the United States afford to continue to be the world's policeman? Should it be the world's policeman?

SECTION 2

POLITICAL ECONOMY AND DEVELOPMENT

Focus Questions

- What principles guide United States governmental decisions about economic regulation?

- How does federalism shape United States decision-making on protections for workers and social welfare programs for citizens?

free market

A system in which government regulation of the economy is limited.

State and Economy

When national leaders highlight the accomplishments of the United States, they often claim that by government regulating the economy less than is the case in other rich democracies, the United States allows the private economy to thrive. In this simplified version of the story, the private sector is the engine of national growth, and economy is most successful when left alone by government. Economic success, then, is tied to the free market—*the absence of government regulation* and the opportunity for entrepreneurs to build the nation's economy. As we will see, however, this picture is oversimplified and therefore misleading.

Relative to other advanced democracies, the U.S. economy is much less regulated. "Less regulated" does not mean that the government's role has ever been minimal. It provided extensive assistance to create the smooth functioning of markets as well as encourage risk-taking, in the form of subsidies, land grants, patents, bank deposit insurance, and subsidies for R&D, to name a few. This pattern of mixed government intervention along with considerable freedom for private initiative encouraged the creation and expansion of many new types of industrial production and technological innovation that subsequently spread throughout the world.

The Constitution reserves for the federal government authority to regulate *inter*state commerce and commerce with foreign nations. As a result, state and local governments are limited in their ability to shape the economy. However, states have established the ability to regulate workplace conditions as part of their **police powers** or of jurisdiction over public health and safety, and they enjoy considerable latitude to provide subsidies and tax incentives to promote economic activity within their borders.

Except for agriculture, higher education, and some defense-related industries, the size of various sectors of the economy is almost entirely the result of the free market. The federal government does try to incubate some new industries, but it primarily uses grants to private agencies—often universities—to accomplish this end. The United States also occasionally supports ailing industries. Defense spending for R&D, aerospace, and electronic communication has also been an important engine of economic innovation and growth.

Since the New Deal, the federal government has guaranteed minimum prices for most agricultural commodities and has sought to protect agriculture by paying farmers to leave some land fallow. It has also considerably reduced the costs of production and risks associated with agriculture by providing subsidized crop insurance, canals and aqueducts to transport water, and flood control projects. It has subsidized the sale of U.S. agricultural products abroad and purchased some surplus agricultural production for storage and distribution in the United States. Although a less explicit form of subsidy, liberal immigration laws and weak regulation of laws restricting immigration have ensured a reliable, inexpensive labor supply.

The federal government has also limited its own ability to regulate the economy. With the formation of the **Federal Reserve Board** in 1913, it removed control of the money supply from elected officeholders. Today, unelected leaders on the Federal Reserve Board, most with ties to the banking industry, control the volume of money in the economy and the key interest rates that determine the rates at which banks lend money to businesses and individuals. Congressional challenges to the Federal Reserve's autonomy raise concerns among other nations that the United States will be less able to act as a global banker and lender of last resort in the future.

The U.S. government does not regulate the flow of capital across borders. As a result, many large United States based firms have evolved into multinational corporations, removing themselves from a great deal of U.S. government regulation and taxation.

In contrast to the idea that government does not intervene in the economy, it is important to recognize that from the nation's earliest days the federal government has promoted agriculture and industry, spurred exports, and (more recently) sought to stabilize the domestic and international economy. These promotional efforts included tariffs, which sought to disadvantage products that competed with United States manufacturers; roads and canals, so that United States-produced goods could be brought to market cheaply and quickly; the distribution of federally owned lands in the West to individuals and to railroads, so that the land could contribute to national economic activity; and large-scale immigration, so that capital would have people to produce and consume goods (see Section 3). Efforts to promote U.S. industry often came at the expense of individual citizens, who are less able to organize and make demands of government. Tariffs, for example, kept prices high for domestic consumers.

Through much of the nation's history, the United States used its diplomatic and military resources to establish and maintain markets for United States-produced commodities and manufactured goods abroad. The United States, for example, uses

police powers

Powers that are traditionally held by the states to regulate public safety and welfare. Police powers are the form of interaction with government that citizens most often experience. Even with the growth in federal government powers in the twentieth century, police powers remain the primary responsibility of the states and localities.

Federal Reserve Board

The United States central bank established by Congress in 1913 to regulate the banking industry and the money supply. Although the president appoints the board of governors (with Senate approval), the board operates largely independently.

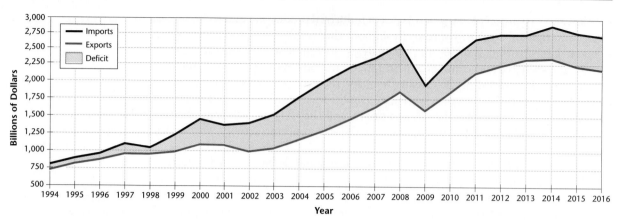

FIGURE 8.2 **U.S. Trade Deficit, 1994–2016**

Source: U.S. Bureau of the Census. 2017. "U.S. Trade in Goods and Services - Balance of Payments (BOP) Basis," https://www .census.gov/foreign-trade/statistics/historical/gands.pdf (accessed March 30, 2017).

its position in the world economy and on multilateral lending institutions to open markets abroad to U.S. imports, provide loans for nations facing economic distress, and protect some United States produced goods from foreign competition. Despite national rhetoric to the contrary, the United States has consistently promoted economic development.

The U.S. economy has increasingly come to rely on two unintentional forms of international subsidy. First, it has built up a steadily increasing international trade deficit. In other words, the United States has bought much more from abroad than it has sold. Although some aspects of these trade deficits reflect a strength in the U.S. economy (for example, the ability to purchase goods produced inexpensively abroad), continuing deficits of this level act as a downward pressure on the U.S. dollar (see Figure 8.2). In the 2016 presidential election, Donald Trump used trade deficits as evidence that other countries were taking advantage of the United States and that existing trade agreements disadvantaged the nation.

Slowing this downward pressure for the time being is the second form of international subsidy: The U.S. dollar serves as the international reserve currency. This means that many nations and individual investors keep their reserves (their savings) in dollars. By doing so, they keep demand for the dollar up, reducing the downward pressure that comes from trade deficits. The long-term stability of the U.S. economy and the value of the dollar as a reserve currency are being challenged by an increasing national debt (discussed later in this chapter) and market concerns about unfunded liabilities in federal and state pension, health care, and insurance programs.

In the twentieth century, the U.S. government took on new responsibilities to protect citizens and to tax businesses, in part, to provide services for workers, the elderly, and the poor. The government also expanded regulation of workplace safety, pension systems, and other worker-management issues (see Section 3). Despite the expansion of the government's role in providing protections to workers, the United States offers fewer guarantees and benefits to its workers than do other advanced democracies.

The public sector has traditionally been smaller in the United States than in other advanced democracies. Some groups advocate increasing government's role, as, for example, occurred when President Barack Obama sponsored the Affordable Care Act (ACA) in 2011 that provided government subsidies to enable lower income citizens to purchase medical insurance. Other groups claim that federal and state government activities could be better conducted by the private sector. The federal government operates hospitals for veterans, provides water and electrical power to Appalachian states, manages lands in the West and Alaska, runs the civilian air traffic control system, and, after September 11, manages passenger and luggage screening at most commercial airports. Roads have traditionally been built and maintained by the state and federal governments, and waterways have been kept navigable by the federal government.

Often left out of the story of the development of the U.S. economy is the important role of its natural resources and the environment. The nation's territory is immensely diverse and abundant in terms of natural resources and environments, stretching from tropical to arctic. The territory includes enough arable land to produce more than enough year round for the domestic market as well as for extensive exports. The United States has protected ports and navigable rivers. For more than a century, it was able to expand trade while not investing in a large standing military to defend its trade routes.

Society and Economy

The United States adheres more strictly to its laissez-faire ideology in terms of the outcomes of the economic system. The distribution of income and wealth is much more unequal in the United States than in other advanced democracies, whose governments' tax and fiscal policies aim to reduce inequalities, and that gap has been steadily widening over the past 30 years. In 2015, the top 5 percent earned more than 22.2 percent of the total amount earned (see Figure 8.3). Wide differences exist between women and men as well as between racial groups. Women, on average, earned $10,000 annually less than men. Non-Hispanic whites earned an average of $63,000 in 2012 compared to $77,000 for Asian Americans, $37,000 for blacks, and $45,000 for Hispanics.

While these conditions have been sharply criticized by liberals, conservatives defend them as a just reward for those who are harder working and more talented. Another defense is the claim that inequality creates the incentive for people at the lower end of the economic spectrum to seek social mobility. Wealth and income

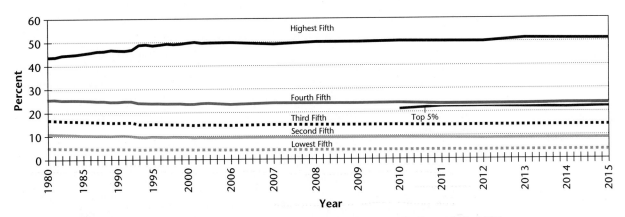

FIGURE 8.3 Share of Aggregate Income Received by Households, Quintiles, 1980–2015

Source: U.S. Bureau of the Census. 2016. "Historical Income Table—Households" Table H-2. Share of Aggregate Income Received by Each Fifth and Top 5 Percent of Households, All Races: 1967 to 2015. https://www.census.gov/data/tables/time -series/demo/income-poverty/historical-income-households.html (accessed March 30, 2017).

have become even more skewed since 1980. The mere mention in an election of the class implications of a policy, particularly tax policy, will usually lead conservatives to charge that this amounts to fomenting class warfare.

Federal income taxation of individuals is progressive, with higher-income people paying a higher share of their income in taxes. Rates range from 0 percent for individuals with annual incomes less than $9,275 to 39.6 percent for individuals with incomes exceeding approximately $415,050. The progressive nature of federal taxes is reduced considerably by two factors. Upper-income taxpayers receive a much higher share of their income from investments, which are taxed at lower rates. Second, all taxpayers with salary income are subject to a regressive tax for Social Security and disability benefits. The tax for Social Security and Medicare is currently 7.65 percent paid by the worker and 7.65 percent paid by the employer. The Social Security share of this tax is imposed only on the first $127,200 of income and not at all on higher incomes.

State and local taxes tend to be much less progressive. Most states levy a sales tax ranging between 2.9 and 7.25 percent (supplemented in some states by a local sales tax). Many states levy a state income tax, but no state has an income tax that is as progressive as the federal income tax. The final major form of individual taxation is property taxes. Governments in the United States have increasingly supplemented taxes with user fees charged for the provision of specific services.

Thus, the gap between rich and poor in the United States is not remedied by progressive taxation. Nor is it significantly reduced by government social programs and policies, for example, a high minimum wage, housing subsidies, or public child care facilities and health care, as is the case in some countries, such as Sweden and Germany.

Labor unions have been a key mechanism elsewhere that has promoted class-wide coalitions representing workers' interests. Although United States labor unions have often focused workers' attentions on income inequalities, they have traditionally been weak in the United States. This weakness reflects individual-level antipathy toward unions, employers' determined opposition to the formation of unions, and state and federal laws that limit the abilities of unions to organize and collectively bargain.

Another factor helping to explain the extent of inequality in the United States involves immigration policy, which has often focused workers' attention away from class and toward cultural differences that reduced the salience of class divisions in U.S. society. The U.S. economy could not have grown without the importation of immigrant labor. The United States has generally sought to remedy labor shortages with policies that encouraged migration. Today, the United States is one of just four countries that allow large-scale migration of those who do not already have a cultural tie to the receiving nation. Immigration to the United States numbers approximately 1 million people annually who immigrate under the provisions of the law to a permanent status that allows for eventual eligibility for U.S. citizenship (see Figure 8.4).[4] The number of unauthorized immigrants in the United States has not increased since 2009.[5]

Although the United States tolerates the unequal distribution of income and wealth, government did intervene in the free market during the twentieth century, to establish protections for workers and, to a lesser degree, guarantee the welfare of the most disadvantaged in the society. The programs for workers, which are primarily **distributive policies**, receive much more public support than do programs to assist the poor, which are primarily **redistributive policies**. Distributive policies allocate resources into an area that policy-makers perceive needs to be promoted without a significant impact on income or wealth distribution. Redistributive policies take

distributive policies

Policies that allocate state resources into an area that lawmakers perceive needs to be promoted. For example, leaders today believe that students should have access to the Internet. In order to accomplish this goal, telephone users are being taxed to provide money for schools to establish connections to the Internet.

redistributive policies

Policies that take resources from one person or group in society and allocate them to a different, usually more disadvantaged, group. The United States has traditionally opposed redistributive policies to the disadvantaged.

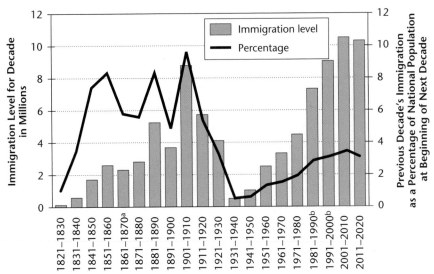

aUntil 1867, the federal government recorded as immigrants only people who arrived at seaports.

bThese figures include recipients of legalization under the Immigration Reform and Control Act of 1986 who immigrated to the United States prior to 1982 but were recorded as having entered in the year in which they received permanent residence.

FIGURE 8.4 Immigration to the United States, 1821–2020

Source: Adapted from DeSipio, Louis, and Rodolfo O. de la Garza, *U.S. Immigration in the Twenty-First Century: Making Americans, Remaking America* (Boulder, CO: Westview Press, 2015), Table 2.2.

resources from one person or group in society and allocate them to a more disadvantaged group in the society. Most worker benefits, such as health insurance, childcare, and pensions, are provided by private employers, if they are provided at all, but are regulated by the government.

Best known among the federal programs aimed toward workers is Social Security, which taxes workers and their employers to pay benefits to retired and disabled workers (and nonworker spouses). In the past, retirees almost always received more than they paid into the system (a form of intergenerational redistribution), but it will take significant reforms to guarantee that this outcome continues when today's workers reach retirement age. The U.S. government faces the dilemma of having to lower benefits for each of these programs, raising taxes, or paying benefits out of general revenues. Changing the tax basis of Social Security and Medicare now (or lowering benefits now) would delay this point of reckoning.

In 2010, in response to growing numbers of uninsured Americans and spiraling health care costs, Congress created a new national health care program for U.S. citizens and permanent residents—the ACA. The ACA is largely distributive in nature, with some additional subsidies (redistribution) for low-income individuals. It builds on the private health insurance that many Americans receive through their employers or unions. The ACA is controversial for several reasons. Some fear that it will undermine the incentive for employers, particularly small employers, to provide insurance. Others prefer that government provide insurance directly fearing that private insurance, with its overhead costs and quest for profits, will absorb health care expenditures that could go to providing better treatments. States are concerned that they will have to provide insurance to residents who are not otherwise able to get private insurance and that they will have to assume much of the cost. Finally, some feel that the new mandate that all Americans have health insurance or be fined violates the Constitution (the Supreme Court rejected this assertion in 2013). In the months after President Trump's inauguration, the House of Representatives passed the American Health Care Act (AHCA), a bill that repealed many provisions of the ACA, including the individual mandate to have insurance and the imposition of taxes to pay for providing health insurance to the working poor. The bill seemed to face immense unpopularity, polling poorly among the public and criticized by many pundits and experts, and Republicans in the Senate responded by indicating that they would draft their own bill. The Senate was not able to find a solution satisfactory to Senate Republicans and the ACA remained in place.

The government also established and administratively enforced a minimum wage. Labor unions and progressive interest groups have waged campaigns in some states and localities to establish higher minimum wages than the federal minimum wage. Opponents argue that high minimum wages deter employers from hiring.

The states regulate worker-employer relations through unemployment insurance and insurance against workplace injuries. Benefits and eligibility requirements vary dramatically by state, as is the case for social programs more generally. The federal government mandates that all workers be eligible for 26 weeks of unemployment benefits (assuming the worker has been employed for more than 6 months).

Welfare Beginning in the 1930s, the United States also established social welfare programs to assist the economically disadvantaged. As one would expect in a system organized around the free market, these programs have never been as broad-based, generous, or widely accepted as in countries with larger labor movements. In the United States, individual states administer these programs—which provide food, health care, housing assistance, some job training, and some cash assistance to the poor—with a combination of federal and state funds.

Conservative governments at the national, state, and local levels have recently aimed to limit public benefits and public employment to U.S. citizens. Over time, the effect of these restrictive policies may create a gap between the non-Hispanic white and black populations, on the one hand, and ethnic groups with large shares of immigrants, such as Latinos and Asian Americans, on the other.

Both the federal and state governments are facing gaps between income and expenditures. The federal government can continue to run a large annual deficit. The cumulative total of these deficits—the national debt—is about $19.9 trillion. Most states do not have this option and must either raise revenues or cut services annually.

Deficits can have a salutary effect on the national economy during weak economic times because government expenditures can stimulate the economy and support individuals who are out of work. In the long run, however, the federal debt absorbs money that could be invested in private sector activities and may slow national economic growth. In 2017, the federal government will pay approximately $266 billion in interest on its debt, an amount that will increase considerably if and when interest rates rise.

Environmental Issues

Another area in which government has taken a limited role in regulating the activities of private actors in the American economy is environmental regulation. When the environment first became an issue in international politics in the 1970s, aggressive government policies sponsored by Republican President Richard Nixon to clean the air and the nation's oceans and navigable waterways had a dramatic impact. Emissions standards have made the air much healthier, even in the nation's most car-focused cities. Waterways that were dangerous to the touch are now open to swimming. New lands were added to the national park system.[6] The visible successes of early environmental **regulations** reduced the salience of environmental issues. However, these 1970s-era environmental regulations have not been followed by a continuing national commitment to environmentalism and an attempt to slow climate change. While President Obama gave priority to these issues, President Trump questioned their utility and economic benefits.

The United States has fewer environmental regulations than other advanced democracies and has been less willing to participate in multilateral agreements on environmental issues than on issues such as international security and economic cooperation. The United States, for example, is a signatory to the Kyoto Protocols to limit climate change (primarily through the reduction of greenhouse gases), but the treaty was never ratified by the U.S. Senate and is nonbinding on the United States. At least nine U.S. states and 740 U.S. cities have passed emissions caps that broadly follow Kyoto guidelines (though often less rapidly than Kyoto would mandate). Unlike an international treaty, however, these state and city efforts can be amended with a majority vote in a legislature and are more difficult to enforce. President Obama committed the United States to join 194 countries in honoring the 2015 Paris Agreements to limit greenhouse gas emissions. As a candidate, Donald Trump indicated that he would "cancel" United States participation in the restrictions established by the Paris Agreements. He followed through on these promises early in his term. Trump used executive orders to limit Obama-era policies encouraging the use of clean (non-fossil fuel) based energy sources and withdrew the United States from the Paris agreements.

Environmental issues are not central to the agendas of either U.S. political party. In an era of routinely divided government (see Section 4), new legislation to protect the environment is unlikely to pass in the U.S. Congress.

President Trump has signaled that environmental protection will not be a central goal of his administration. Scott Pruitt, the Administrator of the Environmental Protection Agency (EPA), is a skeptic of the human influence on climate change. In his previous job, Attorney General of Oklahoma, he frequently sued the EPA to challenge federal regulations. Early in his term, President Trump signed an Executive Order to curb federal enforcement of climate regulations arguing that jobs were a more important challenge for the nation than climate change.

regulations

The rules that explain the implementation of laws. When the legislature passes a law, it sets broad principles for implementation; how the law is actually implemented is determined by regulations written by executive branch agencies. The regulation-writing process allows interested parties to influence the eventual shape of the law in practice.

The United States in the Global Economy

Since colonial times, the United States has been linked to world trade. By the twenty-first century, the United States had vastly expanded its role in international finance and was an importer of goods produced abroad (often in low-wage countries that could produce goods less expensively than in the United States) as well as an exporter of agricultural products and high-tech products like aircraft and software. However, given the intricate and interconnected nature of global supply chains for many products—think the far-flung number of countries in which parts are produced, for example, for an automobile that is assembled in Tennessee—the very meaning of imports and exports has begun to be questionable.

After World War II, the United States reversed its traditional isolationism to take a leading role in regulating the international economy. The increasing interdependence of global economies was the result, in part, of conscious efforts by world leaders at the end of World War II, through the Bretton Woods Agreement, to establish and fund multinational lending institutions. Chief among them were the World Bank and the International Monetary Fund (IMF). Since their creation in the 1940s, they have been supplemented by a network of international lending and regulatory agencies and regional trading agreements.

The United States is a participant in important regional trading networks, such as The North American Free Trade Agreement (NAFTA) with Canada and Mexico and an agreement with neighboring countries in the Caribbean to reduce tariffs on many goods. President Trump argued that multilateral trade deals, especially NAFTA, put the United States at a disadvantage and promised to renegotiate existing agreements.

The U.S. government plays a central role in the international political economy through its domination of international lending agencies, and regional defense and trade organizations. But, as President Trump's election shows, these efforts are ultimately limited by domestic politics. Congress often limits the funding for international organizations. The United States then appears, to many outside the country, as a hesitant and sometimes resentful economic leader.

In recent years, another multilateral institution has emerged that could potentially challenge U.S. economic dominance. The European Union (EU) is an organization of twenty-eight European nations with growing international influence. Eighteen EU members share a common currency, the euro. As the euro came into widespread use, the dollar faced its first challenge in many years as the world's

"Well, they look pretty undocumented to me."

Immigration has been central to the development of the United States economy from its earliest days. Native populations have long been suspicious of newcomers.

dominant trading currency. The future of the European Union as a political and economic union is currently under challenge. In 2016, the United Kingdom voted to leave the European Union, a separation nicknamed "Brexit," which could take place as early as April 2019.

The United States also funds binational international lending through such agencies as the Export-Import Bank and the Overseas Private Investment Corporation. These agencies make loans to countries and private businesses to purchase goods and services from United States owned businesses. The United States also provides grants and loans to allies to further United States strategic and foreign policy objectives or for humanitarian reasons.

The United States has slowly, and grudgingly, adapted to a world where it can no longer simply assert its central role. Thus, the U.S. government and, more slowly, an increasing share of the American public see their problems and needs from a global perspective. The separation of powers between the executive and legislative branches, and the local constituencies of members of Congress, ensures continuing resistance to this international role. Parts of the coalition that elected Donald Trump to the presidency seek a return to a more unilateral foreign policy with the United States routinely asserting its leadership.

GLOBAL CONNECTION

"The Wall": Symbolism and Substance in U.S. Immigration Policy

Throughout his campaign, Donald Trump generated highly enthusiastic responses at campaign rallies by promising to build a wall on the Mexico-U.S. border to limit illegal immigration and, in a frequent addendum, confidently proclaimed that Mexico would pay for it. The chant "Build the wall" was heard at President Trump's inauguration. Trump's anti-immigrant, anti-Muslim, and anti-Mexico message was heard from his campaign's first day. The Trump administration immediately moved to fulfill these promises with expanded immigration enforcement, limits on refugee migrations, promises to reduce legal immigration to the United States, and initial funding to expand the existing border wall with Mexico.

Lost in this conversation is whether a wall, more specifically expansion of the existing walls that cover nearly 700 of the 1,989 miles of the U.S.-Mexico-U.S. border, will further deter unauthorized migration to the United States. Although this question was not asked by the Trump administration, it has long-term implications for the United States domestically and internationally. Mexico strongly opposes an expansion the wall and has stated clearly that it will not pay for its construction. Estimates of the cost of building a wall along the entire Mexico-U.S. border vary from $8 billion to $70 billion. Further expansion of the wall will also have environmental consequences and take land from United States landholders, often against their will. Nearly half of unauthorized migrants do not cross the border illegally. Instead, they enter the United States on short-term visas and overstay their visas. Most importantly, the size of the unauthorized population has not increased since 2009.

Less expensive and less inflammatory policy solutions are available to policymakers to reduce unauthorized migration to the United States; these are harder to implement because they would limit the rights of U.S. citizens. A national identification card and the requirement that it be used for starting a new job or obtaining government services combined with penalties for employers who employ unauthorized workers would reduce the incentives for new authorized migration. Expanded guest worker programs would ensure that employers could fill hard-to-fill jobs. A path to legal status for long-term unauthorized residents of the United States would recognize that people who have resided in the United States for long periods are unlikely to return to their country of origin. Solutions such as these—elements of a comprehensive immigration reform—would be more likely than a symbolic policy like the "Wall" to reduce future unauthorized migration to the United States.

MAKING CONNECTIONS The average unauthorized immigrant resident in the United States has lived in the United States for 12 years. Should the Congress establish a path by which unauthorized immigrants can achieve legal status and eventually U.S. citizenship?

What services and protections should the United States guarantee to each of its citizens?

The United States has seen its national debt grow dramatically over the past twenty years and will probably not be able to rely on borrowing at comparable levels in the future. Should taxes be raised to meet the level of federal expenditures or should programs be cut? If you believe that programs should be cut, which programs should be cut?

SECTION 3

GOVERNANCE AND POLICY-MAKING

Focus Questions

- How have twentieth-century presidents been able to expand these powers of the presidency?

- Can citizens more effectively influence the policy-making process through protest movements like Occupy Wall Street and the Tea Party or through traditional mainstream party mobilization?

Organization of the State

The U.S. Constitution was drafted in 1787 and ratified the following year. The Constitution established a central government with a tripartite institutional organization. The Constitution left the states most of their preexisting powers (particularly police powers and public safety). It granted limited but important powers to the new U.S. government involving commerce and foreign policy that were denied to the states.

The Constitution has been amended twenty-seven times since 1787. The first ten of these amendments (ratified in 1791) make up the Bill of Rights, the set of protections of individual rights that were a necessary compromise to ensure that the Constitution was ratified. The remaining seventeen amendments have extended democratic election practices and changed procedural deficiencies in the original Constitution that came to be perceived as inconsistent with democratic practice. Examples of amendments to extend democratic election practices are the extension of the vote to women and to citizens over the age of eighteen (the Nineteenth and Twenty-Sixth Amendments, respectively) or the prohibition of poll taxes, a tax that had to be paid before an individual could vote (the Twenty-Fourth Amendment). Changes to procedural deficiencies included linking presidential and vice presidential candidates on a single ticket, replacing a system where the candidate with the most votes in the Electoral College won the presidency and the second-place candidate won the vice presidency (the Twelfth Amendment), and establishing procedures to replace a president who becomes incapacitated (the Twenty-Fifth Amendment).

Amendments must first be proposed by a two-thirds vote of members of both the House and Senate or through a convention called by three-quarters of the states. Although the Constitution allows states to initiate amendments through a Constitutional convention, all twenty-seven have resulted from amendments initially proposed by Congress. Once an amendment has been proposed, it must be ratified by three-quarters of the states to be approved.

Two guiding principles anchor the American system of government: federalism and separation of powers.[7]

Federalism is the division of authority between the federal and state governments. Separation of powers is an effort to set government against itself by vesting separate branches with independent powers so that any one branch cannot permanently dominate the others.

These two characteristics of American government—federalism and separation of powers—were necessary compromises to guarantee the ratification of the Constitution. They are more than compromises, however. They reflect a conscious desire by the constitutional Framers to limit the federal government's ability to control citizens' lives. To limit what they perceived as an inevitable tyranny of majorities over numerical minorities, the Framers designed a system that set each part of government against all the other parts. Each branch of the federal government could limit the independent action of the other two branches, and the federal government and the states could limit each other.

Federalism and separation of powers have a consequence that could not be fully anticipated by the Framers of the U.S. Constitution: U.S. government is designed to be slow to act, that is, inefficient. Because each part of government can hinder action by the others, policy-making is difficult. No single leader or branch of government can unequivocally dominate policy-making, as the prime minister can in a parliamentary system. Although a consensus across branches of government frequently appears when the executive and legislative branches are controlled by members of the same party or in times of national challenge, this commonality of purpose is far from guaranteed.

Federalism establishes multiple sovereigns. A citizen of the United States is simultaneously a national citizen and a citizen of one of the states. Each citizen has responsibilities to each of these sovereigns and can be held accountable to the laws of each. Over the nation's history, the balance of power has shifted, with the federal government gaining power relative to the states, but to this day, states remain responsible for many parts of citizens' lives and act in these areas independently of the federal government.

Many powers traditionally reserved to the states have shifted to the federal government. The most rapid shift occurred during the New Deal, when the federal government invoked its commerce regulation powers to create a wide range of programs to address the economic and social needs of the people.

The second organizing principle of American government is separation of powers. Each of the three branches of the federal government—the executive, the legislative (see Section 4), and the judiciary—shares in the responsibilities of governing and has some oversight over the other branches. In order to enact a law, for example, both houses of Congress must pass a proposed law, and the president must sign it. If the president vetoes the proposed law, it is not enacted. However, Congress can override the president's veto through a two-thirds vote in both houses of Congress. Finally, federal courts (and ultimately the Supreme Court) can rule on the constitutionality of a law passed by Congress and signed by the president, and can nullify the law if it judges that it violates the Constitution. However, even this decision is not final, for the Constitution can be amended, according to the procedure outlined above, to authorize whatever the particular law specifies. In sum, separation of powers allows each branch to limit the others and prevents any one branch from carrying out its responsibilities without the others' cooperation. It also allows for the phenomenon of divided government in which different political parties control the executive and legislative branches of government. This complexity encourages an ongoing competition for political power.

The Executive

The Presidency

The American presidency has grown dramatically in power since the nation's first days. The president serves a four-year term and can be reelected for just one additional term as a result of a constitutional amendment ratified in 1951 limiting presidents to two terms. The president is both head of state and head of government.

In terms of formal powers, the president is far weaker than Congress. Through much of U.S. political history, the president was not at the center of the federal government. Quite the contrary: The Constitution establishes Congress as the central branch of government and relegates the president to a secondary role as responsible for administering programs designed and funded by Congress. Even now, the president must receive support from Congress to implement his agenda. And the president cannot dictate Congressional support but must persuade and cajole such support.

The Constitution designates the president as the commander-in-chief of the military who is authorized to grant pardons, negotiate treaties (which require the approval of two-thirds of the Senate), and make senior appointments to the executive branch and judicial posts (with the support of a majority of the Senate). The president is required to provide an annual state of the union report to Congress and may call Congress into special session. Finally, the president manages the bureaucracy, which at the time of the Constitution's ratification was small but has grown immensely in size and responsibility.

With one exception, presidents until the turn of the twentieth century did not add considerably to the delegated powers. The exception was Abraham Lincoln, who dominated Congress during the Civil War. He became a national leader and was able to establish his own power base directly in the citizenry. Lincoln created a national power base for the presidency by presenting himself as the only national political leader, an important position during the Civil War. He had the advantage of being commander-in-chief during wartime; however, the foundation of his power was not the military but his connection to the people.

In the twentieth century, presidents rediscovered that they had a previously untapped resource that Lincoln had initially discovered. Beginning with Theodore Roosevelt, twentieth-century presidents used the office of the president as a bully pulpit (in his words) to speak to the nation and propose public policies that met national needs. No member of Congress or the Senate could claim a similar national constituency.

Later in the twentieth century, presidents found a new power. Beginning with the New Deal, presidents sponsored programs that expanded the federal bureaucracy, provided services to citizens, and, consequently, increased the connection between the people and the president.

Finally, twentieth and twenty-first century presidents learned another important lesson from Lincoln. The president has an authority over the military that places the office at the center of policy-making in military and international affairs. Thus, in the period from World War II to the collapse of the Soviet Union, and beyond (for example including the post 9/11 Iraq war and the War on Terror), the presidency gained strength from the widely perceived need for a single decision-maker.

Although the presidency has grown stronger, the office remains structurally weak relative to Congress, especially in the case of divided government: Presidents have little power over Congresses controlled by the other party. Since Congress retains the power to appropriate funds, the president must ultimately yield to its will on the design and implementation of policy.

PROFILE

Donald Trump

Pool/Getty Images

Donald Trump did not follow the traditional path to the presidency. In contrast to previous presidents, he had never previously served in the military or run for elected office. Instead, Trump had been a businessperson, largely in real estate and resort development, and a reality television host. His personal life was also unusual. At 70, he was the oldest person first elected president, and he was twice divorced (only one previous president—Ronald Reagan—had been divorced). His immigrant roots also made him unique. He traces his ancestry to the second great wave of migration—the period from the 1870s to the early 1920s. With the exception of Barack Obama's immigrant father, all previous presidents traced their ancestry to pre-Civil War migrants (as did Obama's mother's family). Trump's election was also unusual in political terms. He is the fifth president to lose the popular vote. No president since James K. Polk (1844) had lost his home state and won the presidency.

President Trump entered office with Republican majorities in the Senate and House of Representatives. Unified government offers him the opportunity to shape law and policy in areas that he campaigned on—immigration enforcement, tax reform, deregulation, infrastructure improvements, restructuring trade agreements, building the military, and defeating ISIS and other international threats to the United States.

All new presidents take time to find their political footing; President Trump and his advisors, however, appeared particularly ill-prepared to lead early in his term. Appointments to senior posts in the Executive Branch took longer than for other modern presidents and White House advisors often fought among themselves rather than crafting a national agenda. President Trump often disrupted his own agenda by ill-timed and false Twitter posts. Republican Congressional leaders openly expressed their frustration with Trump and his team. Trump was unwilling to work with Democrats who saw little political advantage in working with Trump.

The consequences of this lack of readiness offset the advantages that a newly elected president supported by friendly legislative majorities might have enjoyed. Although Trump experienced an important early victory, when Neil Gorsuch, his nominee to the Supreme Court, was approved, he also suffered an embarrassing early defeat when Congress initially failed to help him fulfill his campaign promise to repeal and replace the ACA. A few weeks later, the House of Representatives passed another version of the act, called the American Health Care Act (AHCA), but Senate Republicans failed to reach a compromise to allow for a repeal or replacement of the ACA.

MAKING CONNECTIONS President Trump's early months in office saw mixed legislative success. What resources did Trump have to achieve his goals? What limits do all presidents, including Trump, face?

Until the election of Barack Obama, all presidents had been white men. All but one (John F. Kennedy) have been Protestant. In today's politics, having served as a governor works to a candidate's advantage. Despite a common assumption, only four vice presidents have been elected to the presidency immediately at the end of their vice presidential term. It is more common for vice presidents to assume the presidency on the death of the president.

The Cabinet and the Bureaucracy

To manage the U.S. government, the president nominates (and the Senate confirms) senior administrators to key executive branch departments. The chief officer (secretary) of the core departments make up the president's cabinet. The cabinet has no legal standing, and presidents frequently use it only at a symbolic level. The president can extend cabinet membership to other senior administrative officials (such as the U.S. ambassador to the United Nations), so the number of cabinet members fluctuates from administration to administration.

The senior officers of the executive branch agencies establish broad policy directions and manage a workforce of approximately 1.8 million civilian civil servants (the bureaucracy). Although part of the executive branch, the bureaucracy is also accountable to Congress, which must vote the budgets for the executive branch and can investigate and punish executive agencies who are unresponsive to congressional demands.

The bureaucracy generally lacks the resources to collect information and shape the laws that guide its operations. Interest groups have eagerly filled this informational role, in order to shape bureaucratic decision-making to serve their interests. Therefore, the information that interest groups provide comes at a cost. Moreover, interest groups are ready to support agencies that favor their interests—and to do battle when an agency acts in ways they oppose. As a general rule, bureaucracies often develop symbiotic relations with the interests that they should be regulating because both sides find cooperation to be in their mutual interest. The resulting pattern is known as an iron triangle (comprising a private interest group, a federal agency implementing a policy, and a congressional committee or subcommittee overseeing the policy in question). The iron triangle often excludes new players who represent alternative views on how policies should be implemented. The pattern also generally serves to bolster the power of the political and economic "haves" against that of the "have-nots."

Other State Institutions

Besides the presidency and the Congress (discussed in Section 4), several other institutions are central to the operation of U.S. government: the judiciary, subnational governments, the military, and national security agencies.

The Judiciary

Of the three branches of federal government, the courts are the most poorly defined in the Constitution. Initially, it was unclear what power the courts possessed vis-à-vis other branches of government. Equally important, the courts were quite dependent on the president, who nominated judges, and on Congress, which approved the nominations and defined the jurisdictional authority of the courts.

In 1803, in perhaps the most important case that the Supreme Court ever decided, it established the foundation for a more substantial role in federal policy-making by ruling in *Marbury v. Madison* that the courts inherently had the right to review the constitutionality of laws. This ruling, although used rarely in the nineteenth century, gave the judiciary a central place in the system of **checks and balances**.

Even with the power of judicial review, the judicial branch remains weaker than the other branches. In addition to Congress's ability to establish court jurisdiction in nonconstitutional cases and the president's ability to nominate people to the courts of his choosing, the courts have other weaknesses. They must rely on Congress to appropriate funds and the executive branch to enforce their decisions. Enforcement proves particularly difficult when a court's rulings are not in line with powerful segments of public opinion, such as when the courts ruled that busing in northern schools should be used to accomplish racial integration in the schools.

Beginning in the second half of the twentieth century, the federal courts gained power relative to the other branches of government because of the expansion of federal regulatory policy. The courts have also gained power because they became a venue for individuals and groups whose interests were harmed by democratically elected

---

Marbury v. Madison

The 1803 Supreme Court ruling that the federal courts inherently have the authority to review the constitutionality of laws passed by Congress and signed by the president—and can strike down a law that the Court judges to violate the Constitution. The ruling, initially used sparingly, gave the courts a central role in the system of checks and balances.

checks and balances

A governmental system of divided authority in which coequal branches can restrain each other's actions.

Supreme Court nominee Sonia Sotomayor prepares to testify before the Senate Judiciary Committee as part of her confirmation process.

institutions and who could press claims based on constitutional guarantees of civil rights or civil liberties. African Americans, for example, received favorable rulings from federal courts before Congress and the president responded to their demands. Since the 9/11 attacks, the courts have played an important role in authorizing the extent to which the executive branch and majorities in Congress can limit individual rights in order to provide collective security. Courts—including the Supreme Court—have been more cautious than the elected branches on this question.

The power of the courts ultimately rests with their ability to persuade the citizenry that their procedures are fair and their judgments based on the Constitution and the law. This may become more difficult in the future with the increasing partisan polarization of the electorate and the elected branches and the commensurate politicization of the judicial appointment process.

The steady increase in judicial power in the twentieth century should not obscure the fundamental weakness of courts relative to the elected branches. The courts are more dependent on the elected branches than the elected branches are on them.

Subnational Government

State governments are an important part of government in the United States, in part because they provide more direct services to people more than does the federal government. The most important is education, which has always been a state and local responsibility in the United States. Others include maintaining law and order, as well as physical infrastructure (roads and bridges).

States and localities are able to experiment with new policies. If a policy fails in a single state, the cost is much lower than if it had been implemented nationally. On the other hand, success in one state can serve as a model to be copied in others or nationally.

In addition to state governments, local governments include counties, cities, and districts for special services, such as water and fire protection. Local entities are statutory creations of the state and can be altered or eliminated by the state (and therefore are not considered a form of federalism).

The Military

The U.S. Army, Navy, Marine Corps, Coast Guard, and Air Force include approximately 1.3 million active-duty personnel plus an additional 800,000 reserve and national guard troops. The president is commander-in-chief of the U.S. military. On a day-to-day basis, U.S. forces serve under the command of a nonpolitical officer corps.

Because of the unique geographic location of the United States, the military has had to dedicate few of its resources to defending U.S. territory. Beginning with the new United States geopolitical role after World War II, the military was given responsibility to support United States multilateral and regional defense agreements.

The United States increasingly looks to its allies to support U.S. military objectives abroad. In preparation for war with Iraq in 2003, U.S. military leaders designed an invasion force of 130,000, with 100,000 ground troops and the remainder in support positions abroad. These troops were supported by at least 15,000 British ground troops and 160,000 contractors.[8]

Many of the traditional responsibilities of the military, such as support of troops and specialized technical activities, have been transferred to reserve units and to private firms who work under contract to the Defense Department. Reserve troops are now called to active duty more frequently.

With the increased expectations for the military came increased reliance on defense technologies. United States nuclear weapons, intelligence technologies, and space-based defense technologies, as well as the maintenance of conventional weaponry and troop support, have significantly raised the cost of maintaining the military. This has led to ongoing national debates about the cost of the military. Industries have emerged to provide goods and services to the military. Proposals to cut defense spending often face opposition from these industries.

National Security Agencies

The 9/11 attacks focused the attention of policy-makers on domestic security. Agencies with responsibility in this area had been dispersed throughout the federal government. Congress concentrated these agencies in the Department of Homeland Security under a single cabinet secretary. Although it took somewhat longer, intelligence-gathering agencies were placed under the administrative control of a director of national intelligence. Funding for domestic security and international intelligence gathering increased by approximately one-third.

Legislation passed in the months after 9/11 also subjected U.S. citizens and permanent residents to greater levels of government scrutiny and to potential violations of civil rights. The Bush administration asserted (and the courts rejected) a position that suspected terrorists could be seized and held indefinitely, without charges.

The Policy-Making Process

Because of separation of powers and constitutional limits on each branch of government, the federal policy-making process is complex and unwieldy and has no clear starting or ending point. As a result, citizens and organized interests have multiple points of entry and can both advocate and try to prevent outcomes through multiple points of attack. Given the lack of centralization, policies often conflict with each other. The United States, for example, subsidizes tobacco cultivation but seeks to hamper tobacco use through high cigarette taxes, health warnings, and limits on advertising. Federalism further complicates policy-making, since states often have contradictory policies. In sum, policy advocates have many venues in which to propose new policies or change existing policies: congressional committees, individual members of Congress, executive-branch regulatory agencies, the courts, state governments, and, in some states, direct ballot initiatives.

With so many entrance points, there are equally many points at which policies can be blocked. Once Congress passes a law, executive-branch agencies must issue regulations specifying how the law will be implemented. Subtle—and significant—changes can be inserted as part of this process. On controversial issues, senior political appointees set policy for the writing of regulations.

Furthermore, people or interest groups that feel disadvantaged by regulations can fight them in the courts. Once a policy is in place, it can be opposed or undermined by creating a competing policy in another agency or at the state level.

The Constitution gives no guidance about the origins and outcomes of policy initiatives. The president must present an annual report to Congress on the state of the nation. This has evolved into an organized set of policy proposals. Without presidential leadership in policy-making, Congress partially filled the void. The Constitution directs Congress to take action in specific policy areas, such as establishing a post office or building public roads. Once Congress established committees to increase its efficiency (see Section 4), these committees offered forums for discussion of narrow policy. These committees, however, are not mandated in the Constitution and are changed to reflect the policy needs of each era. Thus, while presidents can propose policies (and implement them), only Congress has the ability to deliberate about new policies and pass them into law.

Beginning in the 1970s some federal courts experimented with initiating policy as a way of maintaining jurisdiction in cases brought before them. These efforts, such as court-mandated control over state prison or mental health care systems, spurred much national controversy and caused the judiciary to decline in public opinion. Today, the courts are much more likely to block or reshape policies than to initiate them.

Without any clear starting point, individual citizens have great difficulty when they seek to advocate a new policy. Mediating institutions have emerged to represent popular interests in the policymaking process. Political parties organize citizen demands and channel them to political leaders. The parties balance the needs of various interests in society and come as close as any other group in society to presenting comprehensive policy proposals (often summarized in the parties' platforms). Group-based interests also organize to make narrow demands. In the twentieth century, as both federal and state governments began to implement more widespread distributive and redistributive policies, more organized interest groups appeared. These interest groups have become the dominant form of mediating institution in U.S. politics (see Section 4). Unlike political parties, however, interest groups represent only a single issue or group of narrowly related issues. Prominent or wealthy individuals or groups can get Congress's or the president's attention through campaign contributions and other types of influence.

Where Do You Stand?

With the new role assumed by the United States among the globalized world of states after World War II, could the United States be led by the presidency as it was envisioned in the Constitution? Why or why not?

Separation of powers and federalism impede the policy-making process in the United States relative to other nations. However, these arrangements were designed for good reasons. What constitutional changes would you propose to improve the policy-making process in the United States while at the same time preserving the benefits of the two arrangements?

SECTION 4

REPRESENTATION AND PARTICIPATION

▼ Focus Questions

- Which features of Congress's constitutional powers and organizational structure lead some scholars to claim that it is the most powerful branch? Do you agree or disagree that it is in fact the most powerful branch? Why or why not?

- Who votes and who doesn't in U.S. politics? Why?

bicameral

A legislative body with two houses, such as the U.S. Senate and House of Representatives.

The Legislature

The founders envisioned that, of the three branches in the federal government, Congress would be at the center and would be the most powerful. They concentrated the most important powers in it and were most explicit about its responsibilities. For most of the nation's history, their expectations for the powers of Congress have been met. However, as we have seen, developments beginning with the New Deal and continuing through the Cold War to the present have at least partially shifted the balance of power toward the presidency.

Among the most important compromises of the Constitutional Convention involved the structure of Congress. States with large populations naturally wanted seats in the national legislature to be allocated based on population. Also naturally, small states feared they would be at a disadvantage under this system and wanted each state to have equal representation. The resulting compromise sought to satisfy both groups of states by creating a **bicameral** system with two houses, one allocated by population—the House of Representatives—and the other providing equal representation for every state—the Senate. This compromise has remained largely uncontested for the past 225 years despite the growing gap in population between large and small states. Nowadays, each Wyoming resident's senatorial vote counts for sixty-seven times that of each Californian. This structural imbalance is here to stay, since changing it would require replacing the Constitution—and there are a sufficient number of small states to block such a change.

The two legislative bodies are structured differently and are responsive to somewhat different constituencies. The House has 435 members and is designed to be more responsive to the popular will. Terms are short (two years), and the districts are smaller than for the Senate, except in the smallest states. The average House seat has approximately 716,000 constituents and will continue to grow as the U.S. population increases. The Senate has 100 members and is designed to be more deliberative, with six-year, staggered terms. Although unlikely—it has never happened—it is possible to vote out the entire membership of the House of Representatives every two years; the Senate could see only one-third of its members unseated during any election year.

Most members of the Senate and House of Representatives are white male Protestants; the House is modestly more diverse. In the 115th Congress (2017–2019), approximately 19 percent of House members were women, 11 percent were African American, 8 percent were Latino, and 3 percent were Asian American. Most members, regardless of gender, race, or ethnicity, are highly educated professionals. Law is the most common profession. The Senate is less racially diverse: there are three African American, four Latino, and three Asian American senators, with the remaining ninety being white. However, the Senate has a higher share of women than the House: twenty-one women served in the Senate in 2017. Seven openly gay men, lesbians, and bisexuals serve in Congress, one in the Senate and six in the House.

The three central powers of Congress are passing legislation, appropriating funds for the government, and executive oversight. For a bill to become law, it must be passed in the same form by both the House and the Senate and signed by the president. If a bill is passed with different language in the two houses, a conference committee drawn from both sides tries to reach agreement on a text that is resubmitted for a vote to both houses. Equally important, Congress has the power to determine the level of taxes levied on businesses and individuals, as well as the amount of funds provided to the government to pay members of the bureaucracy as well as for government-funded programs. Congress also monitors the implementation of laws and how the funds that it appropriates are spent. By these means, Congress can oversee programs being administered by the executive branch and shape their implementation.

Congress has organized a system of committees and subcommittees on specific areas of public policy to increase its efficiency. Discussion and debate take place primarily in these smaller bodies. The committee system permits members to specialize and have some influence, while not requiring that they know the substance of all facets of government. Committees are organized topically, and members often seek to serve on committees that are of particular interest to their constituencies—for instance, a member of Congress from a rural area may seek to serve on the Agriculture Committee. All members seek to serve on key committees that have broad responsibility for a wide range of government activities, such as the Appropriations Committee, through which all spending bills must pass. Specialization allows each member to have some influence while not requiring that she or he know all aspects of government.

For a bill to become law, it must be reviewed by the committee and subcommittee that have responsibility for the substantive area that it covers. When a member proposes a bill, it goes to a committee based on its subject matter. Most never get any further; few bills receive hearings before a subcommittee or committee. The House and Senate leadership (the Speaker of the House, the Senate Majority Leader, and committee chairs) are central to deciding which bills receive hearings—at which the bill is debated and usually amended. If the bill receives majority support from the committee, it is debated by the body as a whole. However, this may never occur in the House because that institution has another roadblock: the Rules Committee, which determines which bills can be debated on the floor and under what terms. Those not brought to the floor vanish into the dustbin of history—at least for that session of Congress! Senate rules provide for another potential roadblock: bills can be debated for an unlimited time through the use of the filibuster—although it can be ended if sixty senators vote for cloture to limit debate. In 2013 and 2017, the Senate voted to eliminate filibusters when reviewing presidential nominations to executive branch agencies and the courts.

Congress is at the heart of the policy-making process by its ability to pass legislation as well to investigate federal programs (although it does not administer them). There is an inherent tension between the constitutional powers of Congress and the national focus on the president as the national leader. This was evident in the federal government's response to the 9/11 attacks. Initially, President Bush shaped the public policy response. As Bush administration policies evolved and the response came to focus on structural changes in the federal government, however, Congress began to reassert its constitutional prerogatives. Congress also ensured that the National Commission on Terrorist Attacks on the United States, unofficially known as the 9/11 Commission, would be formed, funded, and given sufficient time to conduct its investigation. The commission provided the political pressure necessary to force the Bush administration to create a new federal official—the Director of National Intelligence—who would oversee most United States intelligence-gathering agencies.

Congressional oversight of presidential leadership in the United States response to September 11, the wars in Afghanistan and Iraq, and Russian interference in the 2016 presidential election demonstrate that Congress remains very powerful even as the president's power has increased.

Political Parties and the Party System

The roots of two-party politics can be found both in the nation's political culture and in the legal structures that govern elections. The Democrats can trace their origins to the 1800 election, while the Republicans first appeared in 1854. Despite the fact that today's parties have consistently competed against each other, the regional, demographic, and ideological coalitions that support them (and which they, in turn, serve) have periodically changed considerably.

Today, the Republicans depend on a coalition of upper-income voters, social conservatives, small-business owners, residents of rural areas, and evangelical Christians. The Republican Party receives more support from men than from women and is strongest in the South and the Mountain West. Donald Trump's election in 2016 was made possible because he added to the Republican Party's traditional support base a substantial number of white workers—a group that for decades voted for the Democratic Party.

The Republicans have tried to make inroads in minority communities but have been largely unsuccessful, with the exception of Cuban Americans and some Asian American groups (see Table 8.2). For Republicans to win Latino (or African American) votes on a wider scale, the party would have to be willing to alienate some core Republican constituencies.

The contemporary Democratic coalition includes urban populations, the elderly, racial and ethnic minorities, workers in export-oriented businesses, unionized labor, and, increasingly, working women. Suburban voters have increasingly joined the Democratic coalition. Today's Democrats are concentrated in the Northeast and on the West Coast.

The proportion of Democratic partisans grew steadily over the Bush years and declined slightly in Obama's first term. In 2017, Democrats made up 30 percent of the electorate, Republicans 26 percent, and Independents 42 percent. Although Independents have increased the most over the past two decades, most tend to persistently prefer one party or the other. When these "leaners" are accounted for, the Democrats maintain the advantage—roughly 49 percent to 41 percent. Generally, Democrats, who are more likely to be poor, less educated, and younger than

Table 8.2	Democratic Party Share of Two-Party Vote, Presidential Elections 1992–2016						
	1992 Percent	**1996 Percent**	**2000 Percent**	**2004 Percent**	**2008 Percent**	**2012 Percent**	**2016 Percent**
Whites	49.4	48.3	43.8	41.4	43.9	39	39
Blacks	89.2	87.5	91.8	88.9	96.0	93	92
Hispanics	70.9	77.4	68.4	56.6	68.9	71	69
Asian Americans	36.0	47.3	56.8	56.0	63.9	73	69

Note: These calculations exclude votes for candidates other than Democratic and Republican candidates.
Source: Author's calculations based on *New York Times*. 2016. "Election 2016: Exit Polls" https://www.nytimes.com/interactive/2016/11/08/us/politics/election-exit-polls.html?_r=0 (accessed March 30, 2017).

Republican voters, are less likely to turn out on Election Day, particularly in "off-year" (nonpresidential) elections. After the 2016 election, the Republicans controlled governorships in thirty-four states, and the Democrats controlled fifteen (Alaska's governor is an independent). As a result of the 2016 elections, the Republicans held a majority of seats in the House of Representatives (240 to 194, with one vacancy) and the U.S. Senate (52 to 46, with two independents who caucus with the Democrats).

The electorate is much more evenly divided than the partisan imbalance in the House or governorships suggest; Democrats achieved gains in 2006, 2008, and 2012, while Republicans did so in 2010 and 2014. While both parties are internally divided, splits are greater in the Republican Party and pit moral conservatives against fiscal conservatives. Beginning in the 1990s, each wing wanted the party to give priority to its interests as a way of expanding the party's base of support. In 2010, this division manifested itself in the emergence of the Tea Party activists who sought to move the Republican Party to the right on fiscal issues out of concerns that the federal government was spending too much and usurping powers that should be held by the states (see "U.S. Connection: Populism in U.S. Politics").

Donald Trump's election did not end this division. The inability of Republican members of Congress to reach a compromise on terms to repeal and replace the ACA highlighted the ongoing division within the party.

Divisions within the two parties lead to speculation that new parties might emerge. But the political culture of the United States dampens the likelihood that a faction of one party will bolt and form a new party. Instead, two coalitional parties are the norm, an unusual pattern among advanced democracies.

United States electoral law reinforces this situation. Most elections are conducted under a SMP election system in district-based elections. Single-member district-based elections reward coalitional parties and diminish opportunities for single-issue parties or narrowly-focused parties, such as the Green Party or the Libertarian Party. Broad coalitional parties can contest seats in election after election, while smaller parties in the United States are likely to dissolve after several defeats.

There are more than 600,000 elected offices in the United States. To compete regularly in even a small percentage, a party must have a national presence and a

U.S. CONNECTION

Populism in U.S. Politics

The surprise election of Donald Trump to the presidency reflected Trump's unique and unexpected skills as a candidate, but also a rise in populism in U.S. politics. Populism posits that the interests of the average citizen conflict with those of elites, who are portrayed as corrupt and out of touch with the needs of the common man or woman. Trump presented himself as the voice of average Americans who had been long disadvantaged by a decline in the economy, the failure of political leadership, open borders, and a loss of American status globally. Populist movements have also been on the rise in other advanced democracies in recent years.

Populism has long played a role in U.S. politics. Its current incarnation emerged in the 2010 U.S. elections with the rise of the Tea Party. Despite its name, the Tea Party is a social movement not a party, and is organized within the Republican Party. Tea Party activism emerged in response to popular anger over federal government spending and growing federal budget deficits, Federal Reserve actions to support the banking sector and keep interest rates low, and the enactment of the ACA.

Tea Party organizations and chapters have endorsed candidates for the Senate and House of Representatives in elections since 2010. In several important cases, Tea Party candidates competed in Republican Party primaries and defeated incumbents and/or the preferred candidates of Republican leaders. While several candidates for the Republican nomination for president in 2016 sought to channel the anger and populism of the Tea Party movement, it was Trump who proved most successful at winning Tea Party support, which ensured his nomination. He then won the presidency by mobilizing Tea Party support, along with that of other elements in the Republican coalition—to which he added the votes of some in the white working class who had previously voted Democratic.

Today's Tea Party reflects the latest in a long line of United States populist movements that appear in eras when the national government is perceived to be distant and out of touch. Over time, its energy will likely dissipate and, ironically, the Trump election could speed its demise if his administration comes to be perceived as a failure. The Tea Party's rejection of formal organization and leadership structures make it difficult to sustain the high levels of citizen involvement seen in recent elections. Whether or not the Tea Party survives as an independent movement, its organizing principles of reducing the size and scope of the federal government will likely be part of United States political debates for the foreseeable future.

MAKING CONNECTIONS What groups in the U.S. electorate does the Tea Party movement speak to and mobilize? Are these groups likely to be a larger or smaller share of the overall electorate 20 years from now?

---

national infrastructure. Most third parties fail long before they are able to compete in more than a few hundred races.

Finally, the diversity of the U.S. population and the wide range of regional needs and interests reward parties that can form coalitions prior to elections, thus promoting a system with just two political parties. The Constitution-driven inefficiency of the U.S. government would become all the more dramatic if multiple parties (rather than two that must, by their nature, be coalitions) were competing in legislatures to shape outcomes.

Elections

A key element of the United States commitment to democratic norms is holding frequent elections for a range of national, state, and local offices. Unlike the case in parliamentary systems, national elections are conducted on a regular schedule: presidential elections every four years, Senate elections every six years, and House of Representatives elections every two years. States and localities set the terms of election to their offices, but almost all have fixed terms.

Fundamental to understanding U.S. elections is federalism. States set the rules for conducting elections and for who can participate and how votes are counted. When the country was founded, this authority was almost complete, since the Constitution said little about elections. At that time, most states limited electoral participation to white male landholders. By the 1830s, many states had eliminated the property-holding requirement, in part in response to the emergence of competitive political parties that sought to build membership.

The exclusion of women and African Americans from the suffrage lasted far longer, and required the intervention of the federal government and Constitutional amendments to reduce state authority in determining voter eligibility. The first effort to nationalize electoral rules was initially a failure. It involved extending the franchise to African Americans after the Civil War through the Fourteenth and Fifteenth Amendments. Southern states evaded the constitutional mandate by repressive means and by erecting Jim Crow and other laws that limited voting and other rights of African Americans. The Nineteenth Amendment, ratified in 1920, which extended the vote to women, was more successful.[9] The Civil War amendments finally achieved their stated aim with the passage of the Voting Rights Act (VRA) in 1965, which secured African Americans access to the ballot box. In 1975, Congress extended the VRA to other ethnic and racial groups who had previously seen their right to vote abridged because of their origin or ancestry—Hispanics, Asian Americans, Native Americans, and Alaskan Natives. In 1971, the Twenty-Sixth Amendment gave the vote to all citizens aged eighteen and older.

States continue to regulate participation in elections through their control of voter registration. In most advanced democracies, the national government is responsible for voter registration, and virtually all citizens are therefore registered as a matter of course. In the United States, individuals must take the initiative to register to vote. Registration prescreens potential voters to ensure that they meet the state's requirements for voting: residence in the jurisdiction for a set amount of time and, in many states, the absence of felony convictions. While registering may appear simple and necessary to prevent voter fraud, such as a single voter voting multiple times in the same election, the requirement to register in advance of the election prevents many from being able to vote.[10] Moreover, many states have recently tightened procedures for registering and voting, for example, by requiring potential voters to submit a government-issued ID, such as a driver's license. Since many low income voters do not have a car, they are unable to comply with the requirement. This practice—known as voter suppression—reduces the number of low income voters. Not coincidentally, such requirements are instituted by the elected officials affiliated with party with the most to gain—the Republicans—since low income voters are likely to support the Democrats.

Federalism makes for extensive diversity—and confusion—regarding elections. State governments are responsible for holding elections, deciding which nonfederal offices are filled through elections, and determining the terms of nonfederal office-holders. Thus, a local office that is filled by election in one state may be an appointed office in another. Terms for state and local offices, such as governors, vary. Elections are held at different points throughout the year. Finally, federalism delegates responsibility to the states for determining how votes are collected and counted, even in elections to national office.

What are the consequences of this federalist system of elections? At a minimum, it leads to confusion and burnout among potential voters. Many voters are unaware of elections that are not held on the same schedule as national elections.

One result of this decentralized system with a legacy of group-based exclusion is that increasing numbers of citizens do not vote. In the late 1800s, for example,

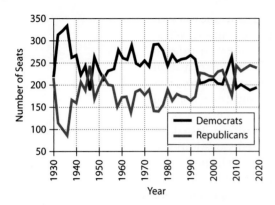

FIGURE 8.5 Party Control of the U.S. House of Representatives, 1930–2017

Source: U.S. House of Representatives, Office of the Clerk. 2017. "Party Divisions of the House of Representatives 1789–Present." http://history.house.gov/Institution/Party-Divisions/Party-Divisions/ (accessed March 30, 2017).

turnout in national elections exceeded 80 percent of those eligible to vote, and the poor participated at rates comparable to the rich. By 1996, turnout in the presidential election dropped below 50 percent (returning to 60 percent in 2016). In state and local races, turnouts in the range of 10 to 20 percent are the norm. Perhaps more important, turnout varies dramatically among different groups in society. The poor are less likely to vote than the rich, the young less likely than the old, and the less educated less likely than the more educated.[11] Because blacks and Hispanics are more likely to be young, poor, and have lower levels of formal education, they are less likely to vote than are whites. They are also more likely to be the target of voter suppression. Hence, political institutions are less likely to hear their demands and respond to their needs.

Class- and age-driven differences in participation are not entirely the result of federalism and variation in electoral rules and the conduct of elections. Declining party competitiveness at the state level also plays a role. Nevertheless, the steady elimination of formal group-based exclusion has been replaced by the marginalization of the majority of some groups, such as Asian Americans and Hispanics. The United States has yet to live up to its democratic ideals.

Declining participation should not obscure the dramatic changes in leadership and issues addressed that result from elections (see Figure 8.5). In 2006, the Democrats regained control of the Senate and House and elected Nancy Pelosi as the first woman to serve as Speaker of the House. In 2010, the Republicans regained control of the House as well as many governorships and state house majorities. These Republican victories enabled the party to shape redistricting—the boundaries of electoral districts that determined congressional and state legislative seats for the remainder of the decade. The Republicans gained a Senate majority in 2014 and the presidency in 2016.

Political Culture, Citizenship, and Identity

The United States is a large country with distinct regional cultures, ongoing immigration leading to distinct languages and cultures, class divisions, and a history of denying many Americans their civil rights. Despite these cleavages, the United States has maintained almost from its first days a set of core political values that has served to unify the majority of the citizenry. These values are liberty, equality, and democracy.

Liberty, as it is used in discussions of United States political culture, refers to liberty from restrictions imposed by government. A tangible form of this notion of liberty appears in the Bill of Rights, whose amendments guarantee the rights of free speech, free assembly, free practice of religion, and the absence of cruel and unusual punishment. Support for liberty takes a second form: support for economic liberty and free enterprise. Property and contract rights are protected at several places in the Constitution. However, since Congress is empowered to regulate interstate commerce this can create collisions between governmental regulation and property rights that courts are called upon to arbitrate.

More generally, the protections contained in the Bill of Rights often conflict with each other: Economic liberties reward some in the society at the cost of economic opportunities for others. Nevertheless, the idea that citizens should be free to pursue their beliefs and their economic objectives with only limited government interference has been a unifying element in United States political culture.

Equality is a second unifying American political value. The Declaration of Independence boldly declares that it is "self-evident" that "all men are created equal." But what is meant by men? At many times in the nation's history, women, Native Americans, African Americans, Mexican Americans, Chinese Americans, Japanese Americans, and naturalized citizens have been excluded from membership in the polity and, consequently, from being treated as equal. However, each of the excluded groups, such as African Americans during the civil rights movement, used the widespread belief in equality to organize and demand that the United States live up to its ideals.

It is important to define what is meant by this belief in equality. In general, what is meant is equality of opportunity, not equality of result. There is support for the notion that people should have an equal opportunity to compete for economic rewards. But in the United States the dominant view is that it is not government's job to promote equality of outcomes. This contrasts with the approach of some democratic countries, in which it is considered legitimate for government policy to seek to minimize inequality of results or outcomes. It is not surprising, given this difference in values and priorities, that economic inequality is greater in the United States than in many other advanced democracies.

The final unifying value is representative democracy. Throughout the nation's history, there has been a belief that government is legitimate only to the degree that it reflects the popular will. As with the notion of equality, the pool of citizens whose voices are considered as worthy of being heard has changed over time, from white male property holders at the time of the founding to most adult citizens today.

The United States has never had a national religion and, at times in the nation's history, conflicts between Protestants and Catholics have been divisive. In contemporary society, political conflicts involving religion usually pit those for whom religion provides routine guidance in politics and social interactions against those for whom religion is a private matter that should not shape political activities.

In 2016, 49 percent of U.S. adults were Protestant, 23 percent were Roman Catholic, 2 percent were Jewish or Mormon, and under 1 percent were Muslim. Eighteen percent of U.S. adults reported no religious preference. However, despite the fact that there is no established religion in the United States, religion plays a more central role in U.S. politics than it does in the politics of European democracies. Moral issues—such as abortion and LGBTQ rights—guide the votes of a sizeable minority of the population. Many elected leaders proclaim their religiosity to a degree that would not be acceptable in European politics (and would not have been in U.S. politics as recently as 30 years ago).

Values are very much at the heart of contemporary political debates. Leaders have marshaled these values throughout the nation's history both to advance their interpretation of how core values shape their policy preferences as well as to reduce potential cleavages in U.S. society. Since the United States cannot look to a common ethnicity of its people (as, for example, Germany can), to a sovereign with a historical tie to the citizenry (as in a monarchy, like the United Kingdom), or to a purported common religion or ideology among its citizens (as does Iran or Cuba), these shared values have been invoked to unify the diverse peoples of the United States.[12]

Interest Groups, Social Movements, and Protest

In the United States, political participation has long included activities other than elections and party politics. In the nation's story about its origins, protest proves central; the Revolution was spurred by acts of civil disobedience such as the Boston Tea

Party. Similarly, protest and social movements have repeatedly demanded that the United States live up to its democratic ideals. From the woman's suffrage movement of the nineteenth century to the civil rights movement of the 1950s and 1960s, people excluded from the democratic community have organized to demand inclusion.

Protest movements have also been able to tap the willingness of Americans to become involved in collective action. This voluntarism and civic involvement have long been identified as stronger in the U.S. democracy than in other advanced democracies.

In recent years, however, observers of U.S. politics have noted a decline in civic involvement, a decline also occurring in other advanced democracies. Although social movements remain, they have become more driven by elites than were their predecessors. The likelihood of civic participation has followed the patterns of voting, with the more educated, wealthier, and older generally more likely to volunteer and be civically engaged.[13] The decline in civic involvement has serious long-term implications for society. As civic involvement declines, Americans talk about politics less with their peers and have a reduced sense that they can shape political outcomes. They are less likely to be part of networks that allow for collective political action. Political scientist Robert Putnam has identified this as the "bowling alone" phenomenon.[14] Americans traditionally had many social venues, such as bowling leagues, where they had an outlet to talk about politics and, potentially, to organize when they were frustrated with political outcomes—what Putnam called social capital. There are fewer of these today (people are busier, have more job responsibilities, and spend more time watching television). The decline in civic engagement has led to reduced political efficacy and greater frustration with the course of politics.

Protest, of course, remains an option for people who feel neglected by the political order. In 2006, for example, as many as 5 million immigrants, along with their families and supporters, took to the streets to protest anti-immigrant legislation in the House of Representatives. In 2017, about 4 million people participated in the National Women's March the day after Donald Trump's inauguration as president. Mass protests such as these, however, are very much the exception. Surveys suggest that no more than 4 percent of the American public have participated in an organized protest in the past year.

The twentieth century saw the rise of a new form of organized political activity: interest groups. Like political parties and candidates for office, these organizations try to influence the outcome of public policy by influencing policy-makers. They differ, however, in that they are usually organized to influence a single issue or a tightly related group of issues. Also unlike social movements, they rely on money and professional staff rather than on committed volunteers. Interest groups increased in prominence as the federal and state governments increasingly implemented distributive and redistributive policies. Beginning in the 1970s, a specialized form of interest group, the **political action committee (PAC)**, were devised to evade legal restrictions on corporations and organized labor making financial contributions to political candidates and political parties.

Interest groups are so numerous in U.S. politics that it is not even possible to venture a guess as to their number. They include national organizations, such as the National Rifle Association, as well as local groups, such as associations of library patrons. They include mass organizations, such as the American Association of Retired Persons, and very narrow interests, such as oil producers seeking to defend tax protections for their industry.

political action committee (PAC)

A narrow form of interest group that seeks to influence policy by making contributions to candidates and parties in U.S. politics.

Although interest groups and PACs are now much more common than social movements in U.S. politics, they do not replace one key function traditionally fulfilled by the social movements: the attempt to establish accountability between citizens and government. Interest groups by definition protect the needs of a cohesive group in the society and demand that government allocate resources in a way that benefits the interests of that group. Their members usually already receive rewards from government or are seeking new benefits. Their membership, then, tends to include more socially, financially, and educationally advantaged members of U.S. society. There is no place in the network of interest groups for individuals who are outside the democratic community or whose voices are ignored by the polity. The key role that social movements and protest have played in U.S. politics is being replaced by a more elite and more government-focused form of political organization.

The Political Impact of Technology and the Media

An open question for scholars of U.S. politics is the degree to which technology, and particularly social media, can serve as a resource to share political information and to mobilize those not fully engaged in civic and political life, in other words, to counter the bowling alone phenomenon. Social media ensure that most Americans are in more frequent contact with friends, family, and colleagues than they have been in the recent past. Just as a bowling league did once, this contact can allow for the easy transfer of political information and the subtle (and, sometimes, not so subtle) encouragement to participate.

Candidates, parties, and interest groups are certainly aware of technology's potential value in generating more popular engagement. The 2008 and 2012 Obama campaigns, for example, focused an unprecedented effort on using social media, both in the Democratic Party primaries and the general election. Analysts credit these efforts with turning out higher than expected turnout from young voters and for the high levels of support they gave to Obama. Donald Trump, both as candidate and as president, used Twitter to shape the news cycle, to disrupt critical news coverage from the traditional media, and to speak directly to voters without the mediation of reporters. Future campaigns (and social movement activism and interest group activity) will find new strategies—and probably more effective ones—to use technology to reach potential supporters.

Technology, however, should not be seen as a panacea for reinvigorating community engagement in U.S. civic and political life. Not all in society have equal access to technologies and those that don't are probably also members of the groups least likely to participate in politics. Ultimately, technology is a means to communicate and it is up to leaders to develop a message that will resonate with potential supporters, however that message is delivered.

Where Do You Stand?

The nation's founders wanted the U.S. Congress at the center of government and the policy-making process. Would you give it the same powers and responsibilities if you were writing the Constitution today? Why or why not?

Should voting in U.S. national elections be made mandatory?

UNITED STATES POLITICS IN TRANSITION

▼ **Focus Questions**

- In what ways can effective mediating institutions overcome the roadblocks to governance built into the U.S. Constitution?

- How has the U.S. role in global governance and global institutions changed in the period since World War II?

The election of Donald Trump surprised many observers of U.S. politics, who had observed the changing composition of the U.S. electorate and predicted that these changes would benefit the Democrats. The electoral influence of white voters was diminishing relative to those of minority voters, whose numbers were growing and who were much more likely to vote for Democratic candidates (Whites split their votes more evenly). President Obama lost the white vote, but won the presidency twice. As President Trump's 2016 victory demonstrated, the U.S. electorate has a dramatically lower share of minority participants than does the population as a whole. Latinos, for example, made up 18 percent of the population in 2016, but just 11 percent of the electorate; Asian Americans made up 6 percent of the population and 4 percent of the electorate.

Some of these gaps will doubtless narrow over time. Minority populations tend to be younger, for example, than non-Hispanic whites, and voting increases with age. The minority voting gap, nevertheless, presents an ongoing challenge for the American democracy, one that will likely grow in the short term. The gap is even greater in the states with large minority populations. At the state level, the pool of regular voters is dominated by older, upper-income white voters; this population is likely to resist paying for the services needed by many minority nonvoters, such as K–12 education, social services, and adult education.

Political Challenges and Changing Agendas

The United States today faces some familiar challenges and some that result from the leading position that the United States assumed in the world of states since World War II. Primary among the continuing challenges is the need to live up to its own definition of the democratic idea and to balance this goal of representative government elected through popular participation with the divergent economic outcomes that result from its laissez-faire approach to governing the economy. The United States must address these challenges with a system of government that was designed to impede the actions of government and a citizenry that expects much of government but frequently does not trust it to serve popular needs.

The United States assumed a new role and set of responsibilities in the world of states, since the end of World War II. United States governing institutions must now respond not just to their own people, but more broadly to an international political order that is increasingly interconnected and seeks rapid responses to international security, political, and economic crises. The institutional arrangements of U.S. government hamper quick responses and increase the likelihood of parochial responses that the rest of the world interprets as isolationism or unilateralism. These institutional arrangements are reinforced by a citizenry that for the most part cares little about foreign policy (except when war threatens), expects quick and often painless solutions to international crises, and has little respect, and sometimes open animosity, for multinational political and economic institutions such as the United Nations and the IMF. Despite the citizenry's continued focus on domestic concerns, U.S. jobs and national economic well-being are increasingly connected to international markets and to the willingness of governments and individuals to buy U.S. Treasury bonds. As the Trump campaign demonstrated, many in the United States have come to resent this economic integration and fear its long-term costs to U.S. industry and jobs.

Economics is not the only element affecting the role that the United States plays in the world of states, as was violently brought home by the 9/11 attacks. Although the citizenry has demonstrated a willingness to pay the financial cost of a global military, it has been much less willing to sacrifice lives. As a result, United States leaders must continually balance their military objectives and responsibilities to allies and international organizations with the difficulty of committing U.S. forces to conflicts that might lead to substantial casualties.

This tension between United States reliance on a global economic order among developed nations and a willingness to pursue a unilateral military and defense policy appeared repeatedly after the 9/11 attacks. The initial approach of national leaders as well as the citizenry was to pursue military actions against Afghanistan and Iraq alone if necessary. Although alliances formed for each military engagement, the threat of unilateral action made the building of long-term multilateral alliances all the more difficult.

In addition to its economic and military roles, the United States exports its culture and language throughout the world. This process also contributes to economic development in the United States; equally important, it places the United States at the center of an increasingly homogenizing international culture. But this process also creates hostility in countries that want to defend their national and local cultures.

The substantial changes in the U.S. connections to the world of states have not been matched by equally dramatic changes in the United States role in governing the economy. The United States tolerates income and wealth disparities greater than those of other advanced democracies. Business is less regulated in the United States than in other democracies.

Since the Great Depression, the United States has seen an expansion of redistributive programs to assist the poor. In the period of divided government, however, the United States has reduced its commitment to assisting the poor. For example, President Bill Clinton established time limits for any individual to collect benefits. The trend has therefore been to reduce the already relatively thin social safety net in the United States, and therefore it seems highly unlikely that the United States will reverse course and develop targeted programs to assist citizens in need on a scale comparable to other advanced democracies.

Distributive programs targeted to the middle class, such as Social Security, Medicare, and college student loans, have much more support among voters and are harder to undermine, even if they challenge traditional laissez-faire approaches. The costs of these programs, however, are putting an increasing long-term burden on the federal budget and, because of deficit spending, on the national economy. There is little political will to deal with these long-term costs. Shifting Democratic and Republican legislative majorities add to this complexity; each party must treat each election as the opportunity to regain the majority.

The U.S. government faces a daunting challenge to its sense of its own democratic idea. One reason is that many citizens are disengaged from the political community. Only 60 percent of the electorate turned out in 2016, and this represented a slight decline from 2012. Turnout in non-presidential-year elections is even lower—approximately 37 percent in 2014. Participation is not spread evenly across the population: older, more affluent, and more educated citizens are much more likely to vote than are the young, the less educated, and the poor.

The breadth of nonelectoral politics is also narrowing. As described above, there has been an erosion of the formerly rich networks of community-based organizations, voluntary organizations, and other forms of nonelectoral political activity. Community politics in the United States began to decline in the 1950s (roughly when electoral turnout began to decline) and is at record lows today.

The politics of collective identities has always been central to U.S. politics because of the large numbers of new immigrants arriving in the country through much of its history. Each wave of immigrants has differed from its predecessors in terms of culture and religion. These differences forced the country to redefine itself. The "old" group of each era often perceived the "new" group as a threat to the political values of the nation, a pattern which appears to be repeating itself in the current period. This nativism was central to the Trump message both to Republican primary voters and to the electorate as a whole in the general election. Early in his term, President Trump used Executive Orders to seek to limit migration from majority-Muslim countries and to target all unauthorized immigrants for deportation.

Since 1965, the United States has experienced a long period of high levels of immigration, primarily consisting of Asian and Hispanic immigrants. Overall immigration has been greater than the previous period of high immigration (beginning after the Civil War and extending to the 1920s). President Trump and many in Congress today are proposing legislation and seeking administrative means to deter undocumented migration and reduce the number of legal immigrants admitted to the United States. The way that this issue is resolved will have weighty consequences for American democracy.

Without strong political parties, mediating institutions, and nonelectoral community politics, the political integration of newly arrived immigrants and their children may stall. Although naturalization rates are increasing, naturalized citizens vote and participate in other forms of politics at lower levels than United States-born citizens. If this pattern continues, the nation faces a new risk: Contemporary immigrants and their children may not be represented in the political order even after immigrants become U.S. citizens.

In the past, institutional arrangements and mediating institutions could partly overcome the weaknesses of the U.S. constitutional system. Congress dominated the executive until the New Deal era, after which the president dominated Congress until Watergate. This institutional dominance reflected the Framers' intent through the Great Depression and after, at least in terms of the dominance of one branch. It is unclear that the Framers envisioned a system where two, and occasionally all three, branches of government would compete for dominance and where the Congress and the presidency would be routinely controlled by different political parties.

Mediating institutions once played a role that they cannot tackle today. Once the political parties formed as mass institutions in the 1830s, they served a necessary role in unifying popular opinion and forcing elite compromise. Today, parties are in decline and have been partially replaced by interest groups—a distinct type of mediating institution that does not seek compromise across issues and instead promotes narrow interests.

The United States faces the same challenges it has always faced, and it is still limited by a governing system that seeks to inhibit government activity. In the past, it has overcome these challenges when citizens participated actively, often working through mediating institutions and mobilizing new groups to active political participation. With citizen participation becoming more selective and mediating institutions less broadly based, the United States will have trouble facing challenges. Because of the United States central position in the world economy, if they cannot meet their challenges, the whole world will suffer with them.

Is Demography Destiny?

Increasingly, the group asked to resolve these tensions in American governance, define the place of the United States in the world, and pay for the long-term costs of underfunded social welfare programs are today's young adults and those not yet of voting age. This youth population is a very different population along many dimensions than today's likely voters. Compared to the entire electorate, the under-30s are more likely to be non-white and either immigrants or the children of immigrants. They are much less likely to live in rural areas and (at least for those in their 20s) are likely to have higher levels of formal education. Perhaps most troubling for a nation that premises its legitimacy on the democratic idea, the youth population has a significant share of unauthorized immigrants who have no way to regularize their immigration status.

The differences between today's youth population and older members of U.S. society are not simply compositional. Today's young adults have come of age in an era of sustained economic uncertainty and geopolitical change, a world in which the United States was attacked on September 11, 2001. The threat of global terror has shaped their understandings of safety and the role of government in their lives. Their likely future participatory and partisan trajectories and their understandings of the United States role in the world are not yet fully formed (particularly for those under 18). It is safe to say that they are very different from today's voters and leaders in terms of the issues that shape their connection to politics and their expectations for what government can realistically deliver.

Ultimately, the position of today's youth in tomorrow's politics will depend on the degree to which they organize (for whatever purpose), the political institutions that mobilize them, and their judgment about whether government is responsive to their needs. Youth are probably most affected by the bowling alone phenomenon; studies find that they have lower than average rates of civic and electoral participation. The Obama campaigns as well as Bernie Sanders 2016 Democratic Primary campaign made clear that youth can mobilize. Even without specific campaigns that encourage such mobilization, today's youth will likely follow the paths of previous generations and become more engaged in civic and political activities as they age. Moreover, while the deep partisan divide and polarization impede governance, this situation creates a huge incentive to educate the citizenry and mobilize supporters. Young adults would be the most likely age cohort to benefit from an expanded national culture of mobilization and participation. Should this occur, in the short-tern, it would likely serve as a resource for the Democrats. Whatever the choices that young people make in coming years, it is a mathematical certainty that those choices will shape the character of the American political system. In brief, this is an invitation to participate!

U.S. Politics in Comparative Perspective

From the perspective of the study of comparative politics, the United States is an enigma. Its size, wealth, unique experiences with immigration, history of political isolation from the world, and reliance on separation of powers and federalism do not have clear parallels among other advanced democracies. This distinctness comes through perhaps most clearly in the way the United States engages its international political responsibilities. The president has traditionally directed the scope of U.S. foreign policy. Congress, as it reasserts power relative to the president, will likely play an increasing role. Members of Congress, who represent narrow geographic districts and are more directly connected to popular interests, are less likely to take an internationalist perspective than the president does. When Congress speaks on international issues, it is often with multiple voices, including some that oppose United States involvement in multilateral organizations. The Trump presidency challenges the post–World War II pattern of presidential support for United States engagement with multilateral organizations. This conflict over control and direction of foreign policy has increased since the end of the Cold War.

The relationship of the United States to Cuba offers an example. Between 1961 and 2015, the United States did not recognize Cuba. Late in his term, President Obama reestablished diplomatic relations, but did not have the authority to reverse the economic sanctions that the United States imposed on Cuba after the Cuban revolution (1959). Travel of U.S. citizens to the island is also highly regulated. Although Obama was able to reduce barriers to travel, he could not eliminate them. Only Congress can eliminate the economic sanctions and end travel restrictions. Interests in the United States across the ideological spectrum (agricultural producers, recent Cuban émigrés, the travel and tourism industry, and liberals who never supported the sanctions) pressured Obama to expand opportunities for trade with Cuba. These efforts were blocked by Cuban American leaders, who threatened electoral reprisals if a candidate were to support a change in policy, and by Cuban American members of Congress, who used their leadership positions to slow policy change. President Trump indicated that he would reverse Obama's actions. U.S. policy toward Cuba will be one of many measures of the degree to which Trump campaign rhetoric is modified by the experiences of serving as president.

The impact of the constitutionally mandated structural and institutional weaknesses of U.S. government is not limited to the American people. The United States plays a dominant role in the world economy, as well as a central political role in international organizations. Thus, the inefficiencies and multiple entry points into U.S. policy-making shape the ability of the United States to respond to crises and develop coherent long-term policies in conjunction with its allies. In 1998, for example, as the world economy declined, President Clinton, with the support of the chair of the Federal Reserve, proposed that the United States increase its contribution to the IMF by $18 billion. Congress initially balked at this request. While intransigence and horse trading between Congress and the president make sense to analysts of U.S. politics, analysts abroad cannot understand the inability of the United States to act in a time of crisis. Eventually, it might be noted, Congress did pass the added IMF appropriation.

In sum, despite its central role in the international economic system and in multilateral organizations, the United States often remains reluctant to embrace fully the international system that it helped shape. The post-9/11 world makes this a much more difficult position to sustain. The challenge of the contemporary era is not only states—the central problem in the Cold War era—but also international non-state-based networks, such as ISIS. These threats cannot be controlled through economic dominance and multilateral political alliances. Nor will this challenge go away if the U.S. withdraws from engagement in the international sphere. Thus, as the United States faces the challenges of a post–9/11 world, it must reexamine the degree to which it is willing to act unilaterally and to pay the price for global concern about its occasional unilateralism.

Where Do You Stand?

Thinking about likely changes in demographic composition of the United States and the electorate over the next 50 years, do you expect the United States to have more or less engagement in the globalized world of states in the future? Why?

Should the United States rely on its geographic isolation and economic power to reduce its leadership role in the multilateral organizations that it helped create after World War II?

Chapter Summary

The U.S. democratic model remains a powerful force in the world of nations. It has flourished for over two centuries and has adapted to the pressures of an increasingly globalized world. It faces the ongoing challenge of meeting the demands of its citizens and other nations with a system of governance designed over two centuries ago to limit government. Reinforcing this challenge is the stark partisan division in the populace that has emerged over the past 20 years. As a candidate for the presidency, Donald Trump seized the rhetoric of economic and political nationalism to win surprise victories in Republican primaries and in three states (Wisconsin, Michigan, and Pennsylvania) critical to his Electoral College victory. Yet, as he quickly learned and ruefully admitted after his election, dealing with domestic and international complexities is much harder than he expected.

Mass organization can significantly change the focus and direction of government. In recent elections, however, victorious coalitions on the left (2008) and the right (2010 and 2016) have each offered a vision of change that resonates with and mobilizes different segments of the electorate. The constitutional system may slow the influence of this mass mobilization on policy-making, but ensures that the citizenry's voice will be periodically heard and that governing institutions will change to partially reflect changing demands among voters and other organized interests in U.S. society.

The internal debate over the size and scope of the U.S. government presents an ongoing challenge for the globalized world of states. The long-term health of the U.S. economy (and consequently U.S. society) significantly influences the health of the global economy. Frequent changes in the United States leadership role and United States reluctance to work with multinational institutions that it created make it harder in the long run for the United States to maintain the role of a global leader that it has occupied since the end of World War II.

Key Terms

Articles of Confederation
bicameral
Bill of Rights
checks and balances
Declaration of Independence
distributive policies
Federal Reserve Board

federalism
free market
interest groups
manifest destiny
Marbury v. Madison
police powers
political action committee (PAC)

property taxes
redistributive policies
regulations
separation of powers
single member plurality (SMP)
   electoral system
social security

Suggested Readings

Amar, Akhil Reed. *The Bill of Rights: Creation and Reconstruction*. New Haven, CT: Yale University Press, 1998.

Dawson, Michael C. *Black Visions: The Roots of Contemporary African-American Political Ideologies*. Chicago: University of Chicago Press, 2002.

The Federalist Papers. Edited by Clinton Rossiter. New York: Mentor, 1961.

Fisher, Louis. *Constitutional Conflicts between Congress and the President*, 6th ed. Lawrence: University of Kansas Press, 2014.

Hartz, Louis. *The Liberal Tradition in America.* New York: Harvest/HBJ, 1955.

Hochschild, Arlie. *Strangers in Their Own Land: Anger and Mourning on the American Right.* New York: The New Press, 2016.

Kupchan, Charles. *The End of the American Era: U.S. Foreign Policy and the Geopolitics of the Twenty-First Century.* New York: Knopf, 2002.

Verba, Sidney, Kay Lehman Schlozman, and Henry Brady. *Voice and Equality: Civic Voluntarism in American Politics.* Cambridge: Harvard University Press, 1995.

Wilson, Woodrow. *Congressional Government: A Study in American Politics.* Baltimore: Johns Hopkins University Press, 1885.

Zolberg, Aristide. *A Nation by Design: Immigration Policy in the Fashioning of America.* Cambridge: Harvard University Press, 2006.

Suggested Websites

The 9/11 Commission Report
https://9-11commission.gov/report/911Report.pdf

Congress.gov—Legislative Information from the Library of Congress
https://www.congress.gov//

Find Law—Cases and Codes: U.S. Constitution
http://caselaw.findlaw.com/

New York Times
https://www.nytimes.com/

U.S. Census Bureau
https://www.census.gov/

White House
https://www.whitehouse.gov/

9 Brazil

Alfred P. Montero

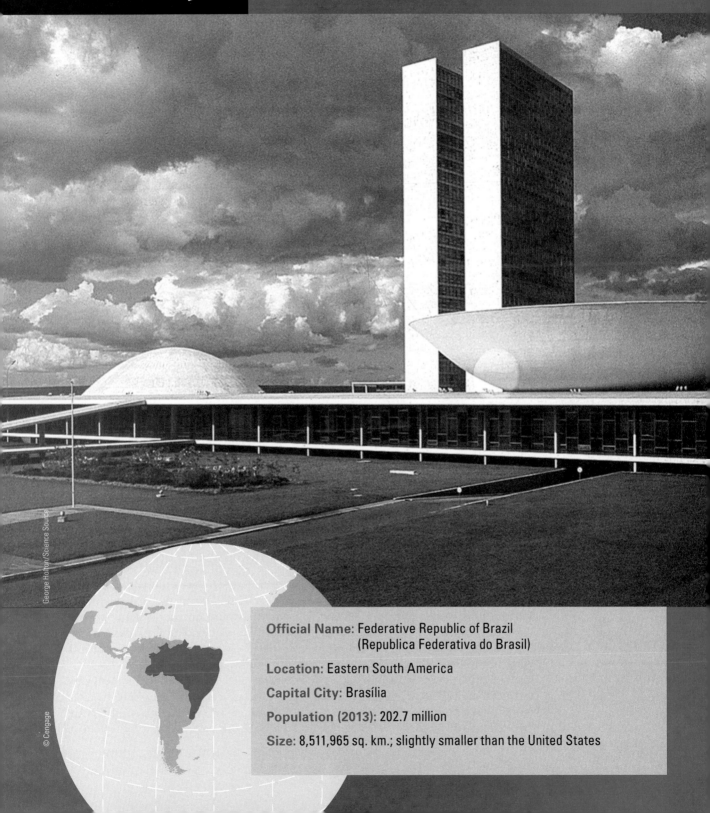

George Holton/Science Source

© Cengage

Official Name: Federative Republic of Brazil
(Republica Federativa do Brasil)

Location: Eastern South America

Capital City: Brasília

Population (2013): 202.7 million

Size: 8,511,965 sq. km.; slightly smaller than the United States

1822
Dom Pedro I declares himself emperor of Brazil, peacefully ending 300 years of Portuguese colonial rule.

1888
Abolition of slavery

1930
Getúlio Vargas gains power after a coup led by military and political leaders. His period of dictatorship (1937–1945) is known as the New State.

1950
Vargas is elected president. Scandals precipitate his suicide in 1954.

1960
Jânio Quadros becomes president.

| 1800 | 1850 | 1900 | 1930 | 1950 | 1960 |

1824
Constitution drafted

1891
A new constitution establishes a directly elected president.

1889
Dom Pedro II, who assumed throne in 1840, is forced into exile; landowning elites establish an oligarchical republic.

1945
Vargas calls for general elections. General Eurico Dutra of the Social Democratic Party wins.

1956
Juscelino Kubitschek becomes president.

SECTION

1

THE MAKING OF THE MODERN BRAZILIAN STATE

Focus Questions

- Why has the authority of government varied between the central state and subnational authorities from independence to the present?

- In what major ways has Brazilian democracy been limited since independence?

Politics in Action

In 2013, four years after the decision of the International Olympic Committee (IOC) to award Rio de Janeiro the 2016 Summer Games, and a year before Brazil prepared to host the prestigious 2014 World Cup of Football (soccer), massive protests on the streets of major Brazilian cities galvanized the world. The protestors, many of whom were young and college educated, directed their anger at the corruption of the political class and big construction firms that were seen as having benefited directly from the large infrastructure projects needed to host both international sporting events. Pressed by these protests, President Dilma Rousseff and the Brazilian congress passed anticorruption legislation during the summer of 2013 to expand the powers of investigatory institutions such as public prosecutors and the Federal Police. Little did they anticipate that they were inadvertently strengthening accountability institutions that would soon train their powers on them. During the next three years, federal prosecutors, judges, and courts of auditors would uncover systemic corruption involving the state oil company, Petrobras, the major political parties, and the largest construction companies in Brazil. Rousseff's own presidency ended abruptly in August 2016, when she was impeached for fudging the federal budget.

Her vice president and immediate successor, Michel Temer, and his cabinet would struggle under the weight of continued investigations, leaks from plea bargained testimony, and numerous search and seize operations against even cabinet ministers and the leaders of congress. As the public was deluged with evidence that their political

1964
A military coup places power in the hands of successive authoritarian regimes.

1984
Diretas Já!, a mass mobilization campaign, calls for direct elections.

1988
A new constitution grants new social and political rights.

1992
Collor is impeached; Vice President Itamar Franco assumes presidency.

1998
Cardoso is reelected.

2002
Lula da Silva is elected president.

2010
Dilma Rousseff, Lula's former chief-of-staff, is elected Brazil's first woman president.

2015
The "car wash" (*Lava Jato*) corruption investigation engulfs much of the political class.

1970   1985   1990   1995   2000   2010   2016

1961
Quadros resigns. João Goulart gains presidency despite an attempted military coup.

1985
Vice-presidential candidate José Sarney becomes president on the sudden death of elected president Tancredo Neves.

1989
Fernando Collor is elected president.

1994
Fernando Henrique Cardoso is elected president after his Real Plan controls inflation.

1999
The Real Plan weathers a financial crisis.

2006
Lula is reelected after surviving a corruption scandal.

2014
Rousseff is reelected president.

2016
Rousseff is impeached and her vice president, Michel Temer, becomes president.

leaders and the executives of some of the most successful companies have benefited from systemic graft, popular revulsion has raised questions concerning the quality of Brazil's democracy. Is Brazilian democracy failing, due to systemic corruption, and is it becoming more ungovernable as so many members of the political class are investigated? Or is Brazilian democracy moving through an important transition in which the strength of accountability-enhancing institutions secure a less corrupt and more responsive form of government in the future?

Geographic Setting

Larger than the continental United States, Brazil occupies two-thirds of South America. Its 206 million inhabitants are concentrated in the urban southern and southeastern regions; the vast northern Amazon region, with 5.3 million, is sparsely populated.

Brazil includes thick rain forest in the Amazon valley, large lowland swamps (the *pantanal*) in the central western states, and vast expanses of badlands (the *sertão*) in the north and northeast. The country is rich in natural resources and arable land. The Amazon has an abundance of minerals and tropical fruit; the central and southern regions provide iron ore and coal; and offshore sources of petroleum are significant and will become even more so as they are exploited. Brazil's farmlands are highly fertile. The Amazon's climate is wet, the *sertão* is dry, and the agricultural areas of the central, southeastern, and southern regions are temperate. Natural resource exploitation make the fragile ecology of the Amazon a matter of international concern.

Immigration of Europeans and Africans has contributed to an ethnically mixed society. Approximately 48 percent of the population is white, 43 percent *mulatto* (brown), 8 percent black, and 0.5 percent Asian.[1] These numbers probably ignore people of mixed race, who are sometimes classified erroneously as being white or *mulatto*. The indigenous people of the Amazon basin are estimated to number 250,000. The Asian population, which numbers just over 1 million, is dominated by people of Japanese descent who immigrated from 1908 through the 1950s.

Brazil: Ethnic Groups

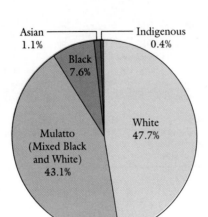

Asian 1.1%

Indigenous 0.4%

Black 7.6%

Mulatto (Mixed Black and White) 43.1%

White 47.7%

Brazil: Religions

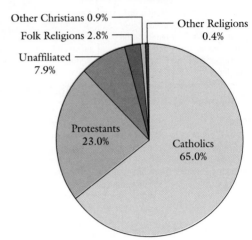

Other Christians 0.9%

Folk Religions 2.8%

Unaffiliated 7.9%

Other Religions 0.4%

Protestants 23.0%

Catholics 65.0%

Brazilian Currency
Real/Reais (R$)
International Designation: BRL
Exchange Rate (2017):
- US$1 = R$3.28
- R$1 = US$0.30

100 Reais Note Design: Effigy of the Brazilian Republic.

© Cengage

© Vinicius Tupinamba/Shutterstock.com

FIGURE 9.1 The Brazilian Nation at a Glance

Brazil is a blend of different cultural influences, although Portuguese as the common language helps keep Brazilians united. Brazilians are not greatly divided over religious differences. About 65 percent of the population professes Roman Catholicism, although the Church plays only a secondary role in politics and society (see Section 4). Evangelical Protestants have recently made inroads. Protestants now compose about 22.2 percent of the population. Afro-Brazilian and indigenous religions also operate alongside the Catholic liturgy (see Figure 9.1 and Table 9.1).

**moderating power
(poder moderador)**

A term used in Brazilian politics to refer to the situation following the 1824 constitution in which the monarchy was supposed to act as a moderating power, among the executive, legislative, and judicial branches of government, arbitrating party conflicts, and fulfilling governmental responsibilities when nonroyal agents failed.

Critical Junctures

The Brazilian Empire (1822–1889)

Brazil was a Portuguese colony, not a Spanish one, and it escaped the violent wars of independence that afflicted the Spanish colonial system. Brazilian independence was declared peacefully by the Crown's own agent in the colony in 1822 after the King of Portugal left his own son to rule. With this monarchical connection, Brazilian independence could be secured without the violent rupture in the Spanish cases.

To control its sprawling territory, Brazil centralized authority in the emperor, who acted as what Brazilians call a **moderating power** *(poder moderador)*, mediating conflicts among the executive, legislative, and judicial branches of government and powerful landowning oligarchy. This centralization contrasted with other

Table 9.1	Political Organization
Political System	Federal republic, presidential with separation of powers.
Regime History	Democratic since 1946 with periods of military authoritarianism, especially 1964–1985.
Administrative Structure	Federal, with twenty-six states plus the Federal District, which also functions as a state. Subnational legislatures are unicameral. State governments have multiple secretariats, the major ones commonly being economy, planning, and infrastructure. The states are divided into municipalities (about 5,570), with mayors and councillors directly elected.
Executive	President, vice president, and cabinet. The president and vice president are directly elected by universal suffrage in a two-round runoff election for 4-year terms. Since 1998, the president and vice president may run for a second term.
Legislature	Bicameral: The Senate is made up of three senators from each state and from the Federal District, elected by plurality vote for an eight-year term; the Chamber of Deputies consists of representatives from each state and from the Federal District, elected by proportional vote for a four-year term.
Judiciary	Supreme Court, High Tribunal of Justice, regional courts, labor courts, electoral courts, military courts, and state courts. Judiciary has financial and administrative autonomy. Supreme Court justices are subjected to mandatory retirement at 75.
Party System	Multiparty system including several parties of the right, center-right, center-left, and left. Elections are by open-list proportional representation. New parties must register with the Superior Electoral Court after having acquired sufficient signatures to meet a minimal threshold in at least nine states.

postcolonial Latin American states, which suffered numerous conflicts among territorially dispersed strongmen (*caudillos*).

Imperial Brazil enjoyed several features of representative democracy: regular elections, alternation of parties in power, and scrupulous compliance with the constitution. Liberal institutions only regulated political competition among rural, oligarchical elites; most Brazilians, who were neither enfranchised nor politically organized, were left out.

The Old Republic (1889–1930)

In 1889, came the peaceful demise of the empire, the exile of Emperor Dom Pedro II, and the emergence of a republic ruled by the landowning oligarchy. The decline of slavery and the rise of republicanism ended the empire. The coffee economy created a growing economy autonomous from the state. The coffee planters, who constituted a wealthy oligarchy, embraced liberal political values to limit centralized political authority. As these elites grew suspicious of attempts to centralize power, they discounted the need for a moderating power in the national state.

The Old Republic (1889–1930) was based on the influence of coffee growers and a small urban industrial and commercial class linked to the coffee trade and a ranch economy that produced meat and hides. The constitution of 1891, inspired by the U.S. model, established a directly elected president, guaranteed separation of church and state, and gave the vote to all literate males (about 3.5 percent of the population before 1930). The legitimacy of the republican political system was established on

governing principles that were limited to a privileged few, but no longer determined by the hereditary rights of the emperor. The states gained greater authority to formulate policy, spend money, levy taxes, and maintain their own militias.

Although the constitution expressed liberal ideas, most Brazilians lived in rural areas, where the landed oligarchy squashed dissent. As in the southern United States and in Mexico, landed elites manipulated local politics. In a process known as *coronelismo*, these elites, or colonels, as they were known, manipulated their poor workers so they would vote to elect officials favored by the elite.

These ties between patron (landowner) and client (peasant) became the basis of modern Brazilian politics. In return for protection and occasional favors, the client did the bidding of the patron. As cities grew, and the state's administrative agencies expanded, the process of trading favors and demanding political support in return became known as **clientelism**.

In contrast to the centralized empire, the Old Republic consecrated the power of local elites. Governors and mayors were empowered to control areas of economic policy delegated by the federal government.

The 1930 Revolution

As world demand for coffee plummeted during the Depression of the 1930s, the coffee and ranch elites faced their worst crisis. Worker demonstrations and the Brazilian

clientelism

An informal aspect of policy-making in which a powerful patron (for example, a traditional local boss, government agency, or dominant political party) offers resources such as land, contracts, protection, jobs, or other resources in return for the support and services (such as labor or votes) of lower-status and less powerful clients. Corruption, preferential treatment, and inequality are characteristic of clientelist politics.

Communist Party challenged the legitimacy of the Old Republic. Among the discontented political elites, a figure emerged who transformed Brazilian politics forever: Getúlio Vargas (see "Profile: Getúlio Dornelles Vargas" in Section 3 of this chapter).

Vargas came to power as the head of a new "revolutionary government," but it favored a dissident elite. That is why Vargas swiftly crushed middle-class and popular dissent. He built a political coalition around a new project of industrialization led by the central government and based on central state resources. Unlike the Old Republic, Vargas controlled regional governments by replacing all governors with handpicked allies (*interventores*). The center of gravity of Brazilian politics swung back to the national state.

Vargas believed he could win the support of landed elites, commercial interests, bureaucrats, and the military by answering their demands in a controlled way. They were allowed to participate in the new political order, but only as passive members of state-created and state-regulated unions and associations. This model of state corporatism rejects the idea of competition among social groups by having the state arbitrate all conflicts. For instance, when workers requested increases in their wages, state agencies determined to what extent such demands would be met and how business would pay for them.

By 1937, Vargas had achieved a position of virtually uncontested power. During the next eight years, he consolidated his state corporatist model by establishing labor codes, creating public firms to produce strategic commodities such as steel and oil, and pursuing paternalistic social policies. These policies were collectively called the New State (*Estado Nôvo*).

The Populist Republic (1945–1964)

The increasing mobilization of segments of the working and middle classes, and U.S. diplomatic pressure forced Vargas to call for full democratic elections to be held in 1945. Three political parties competed in these elections: The Social Democratic Party (PSD) and the Brazilian Labor Party (PTB) were pro-Vargas, while the National Democratic Union (UDN) stood against him. The PSD and the PTB, which operated in alliance, were both creations of the state, while the UDN brought together regional forces that wanted a return to liberal constitutionalism. The campaign was so bitter that the military forced Vargas to resign, two months before the general election.

The turn to democracy in 1946 did not break with the past. The new constitution guaranteed periodic elections, but the most important economic and social policies were still decided by the state bureaucracy, not by the national legislature.

Populism, but not democracy, defined the new political order. In Brazil, the terms *populist* and *populism* refer to politicians, programs, or movements that seek to expand citizenship to previously disenfranchised sectors of society in return for political support. Populist governments grant benefits to guarantee support, but discourage lower-class groups from creating their own organizations. Populists do not consider themselves accountable to the people.

Brazilian workers supported Vargas for his promises to improve the social insurance system, and elected him in 1950. However, economic limitations and opposition claims that he was preparing a new dictatorship made Vargas politically vulnerable. He was soon swept up in a bizarre scandal involving the attempted assassination of a popular journalist. During the crisis, intense accusations of Vargas's complicity in the assassination increasingly wore him down, and he committed suicide on August 24, 1954. Under Vargas's democratic successor, Juscelino Kubitschek (1956–1960), the economy improved due to a post-war boom in manufacturing. Kubitschek was a master of political symbolism and

interventores

In Brazil, allies of Getúlio Vargas (1930–1945, 1950–1952), who were chosen by the dictator during his first period of rulership to replace opposition governors in most states. The *interventores* represented a shift of power from subnational government to the central state.

state corporatism

A system of interest representation in which the constituent units are organized into a limited number of singular, compulsory, noncompetitive, hierarchically ordered, and functionally differentiated categories, recognized or licensed (if not created) by the state. These organizations are granted a representational monopoly within their respective categories in exchange for limiting their demands and allowing the state to recruit their leaders.

nationalism

An ideology seeking to create a nation-state for a particular community; a group identity associated with membership is such a political community. Nationalists often proclaim that their state and nation are superior to others.

nationalism, promoting images of a new, bigger Brazil that could create "fifty years of development in five." This was symbolized by his decision to move the capital from Rio de Janeiro to a planned city called Brasília—a utopian city. The project rallied support for Kubitschek's developmentalist policies.

The presidents who followed Kubitschek proved much less competent. João Goulart, for instance, began an ill-fated campaign for structural reforms, mainly in education and agriculture. In response to what they perceived as threats to their interests, peasant league movements, students, and professional organizations organized protests, strikes, and illegal seizures of land. As right-wing organizations battled leftist groups in the streets of the capital, the military ended Brazil's experiment with democratic populism in March 1964.

The Rise of Bureaucratic Authoritarianism (1964–1985)

bureaucratic authoritarianism (BA)

A term developed by Argentine sociologist Guillermo O'Donnell to interpret the common characteristics of military-led authoritarian regimes in Brazil, Argentina, Chile, and Uruguay in the 1960s and 1970s. According to O'Donnell, bureaucratic authoritarian regimes led by the armed forces and key civilian allies emerged in these countries in response to severe economic crises.

The military government installed what the Argentine political sociologist Guillermo O'Donnell termed **bureaucratic authoritarianism (BA)**.[2] Such regimes are installed to respond to severe economic crises and are led by the armed forces and key civilian allies, most notably professional economists, engineers, and administrators. BA regimes limit civil rights and other political freedoms, sometimes going so far as wholesale censorship of the press, torture of civilians, and imprisonment without trial, all for the sake of economic development.

The military government first planned a quick return to civilian rule and even allowed limited democratic institutions to continue. After being purged in 1964 of the BA's opponents, the national congress continued to function, and direct elections for federal legislators and most mayors (but not the president or state governors) took place at regular intervals. In November 1965, the military replaced all existing political parties with only two: the National Renovation Alliance (ARENA) and the Brazilian Democratic Movement (MDB). ARENA was the military government's party, and MDB was the "official" party of the opposition. Former members of the three major parties joined one of the two new parties.[3]

The powers of these democratic institutions were severely limited. The military government used institutional decrees to legislate the most important matters, preventing the congress from having an important voice. Few civilian politicians could speak out directly against the military for fear of being removed from office.

In economic policy, the military reinforced the previous pattern of state interventionism. The government promoted state-led economic development by creating hundreds of state corporations and investing enormous sums in established public firms. Brazil implemented one of the most successful economic development programs among newly industrialized countries. Termed the "Brazilian miracle," these programs demonstrated that, like France, Germany, and Japan in earlier periods, a developing country could create its own economic miracle.

The Transition to Democracy and the First Civilian Governments (1974–2001)

abertura

In Brazil, *abertura* (as it is known in Portuguese; *aperture* in Spanish) refers to the period of authoritarian liberalization begun in 1974 when the military allowed civilian politicians to compete for political office in the context of a more open political society.

After the oil crisis of 1973 set off a wave of inflation around the world, the economy began to falter. Increasing criticism from Brazilian business led the last two ruling generals, Geisel and Figueiredo, to begin a gradual process of democratization. Initially, these leaders envisioned only a liberalizing, or opening (*abertura*), of the regime to allow civilian politicians to compete for political office. As was later the case with Gorbachev's *glasnost* in the Soviet Union, however, control over the process

George Holton/Science Source

Brazil's capital, Brasília. The planned city was designed by the world-famous Brazilian architect Oscar Niemeyer.

of liberalization gradually slipped from military hands and was captured by organizations within civil society. In elections in 1974, the opposition party, the MDB, stunned the military government by increasing its representation in the Senate from 18 to 30 percent, and in the Chamber of Deputies from 22 to 44 percent. Although the party did not have a majority in congress, it did capture a majority in both chambers of the state legislatures in the most important industrialized southern and southeastern states.

In the following years, the opposition made successive electoral gains and obtained concessions from the government. The most important were the reestablishment of direct election for governors in 1982, political amnesty for dissidents, the elimination of the government's power to oust legislators from political office, and the restoration of political rights to those who had previously lost them. In the gubernatorial elections of November 1982, the opposition candidates won landslide victories in the major states.

The military wanted to maintain as much control over the succession process as possible and preferred to have the next president selected within a restricted electoral college. But mass mobilization campaigns demanded the right to elect the next president directly. The *Diretas Já!* ("Direct Elections Now!") movement, comprising an array of social movements, opposition politicians, and labor unions, expanded in size and influence in 1984. Although the movement failed to achieve its goal of making the founding elections of the new democracy direct, the effort inspired a generation of movement leaders with gender, racial, religious, and issue-based orientations. More immediately, the military lost supporters, who backed an alliance (the Liberal

Front) with Tancredo Neves, the candidate of the opposition PMDB (Party of the Brazilian Democratic Movement, the successor to the old MDB). Neves's victory in 1984, however, was marred by his sudden death on the eve of the inauguration. Vice President José Sarney became the first civilian president of Brazil since 1964.

The process leading to Sarney's presidency disappointed those who had hoped for a clean break with the authoritarian past. Most of the politicians who gained positions of power in the new democracy hailed from the former ARENA or its misleadingly named successor, the Democratic Social Party (PDS). Most of these soon joined Sarney's own PMDB or its alliance partner, the Party of the Liberal Front (PFL). A political transition that should have produced change led to considerable continuity.

A chance for fundamental change appeared in 1987 when the national Constituent Assembly met to draft a new constitution. Given the earlier success of the opposition governors in 1982, state political machines became important players in the game of constitution writing. The state governments petitioned for the devolution of new authority to tax and spend. Labor groups also exerted influence through their lobbying organizations. Workers demanded constitutional protection of the right to strike and the right to create their own unions without authorization from the Ministry of Labor.[4]

Soon after Sarney's rise to power, annual rates of inflation began to skyrocket. The government sponsored several stabilization plans, but without success. Dealing with runaway inflation and the removal of authoritarian politicians became the key issues in the 1989 presidential elections, the first direct contests since the 1960s.

Once again, Brazilians would be disappointed. Fernando Collor de Mello, became president after a grueling campaign against Lula da Silva, the popular left-wing labor leader and head of the Workers' Party (*Partido dos Trabalhadores*, or PT), who would lead the leftist opposition for another decade before rising to the presidency himself. Collor's administration embraced structural reform, such as privatization of state enterprises and deregulation of the economy, but it failed to solve the nagging problem of inflation. Collor was eventually impeached in late 1992 due to his involvement in bribery and influence peddling.

Collor's impeachment brought Itamar Franco to the presidency. Franco's most important decision was naming Fernando Henrique Cardoso, his finance minister. Cardoso, who was a renowned sociologist before entering politics in the 1970s, rose to prominence as one of the key leaders within the PMDB and later the Party of Brazilian Social Democracy (PSDB) during the democratic transition. In July 1994, Cardoso's Real Plan finally stopped inflation by creating a new currency, the *real* that would be managed closely by the Central Bank (see Section 2).

Cardoso rode the success of the Real Plan to the presidency, beating out Lula and the PT in 1994 and again in 1998. He proved adept at keeping inflation low and consolidating some of the structural reforms first started by Collor. But Brazil's budget and trade deficits increased, and financial crises in Asia and Russia in 1997 and 1998 eventually led to a crisis in the Real Plan. In January 1999, although the value of the real collapsed, the currency soon stabilized, and hyperinflation did not return. The Cardoso administration was also able to pass the Law of Fiscal Responsibility in 2000, which limited spending by state and municipal governments and even made it a crime to submit inaccurate budgets to auditors. It was a violation of this law that became the basis for Dilma Rousseff's impeachment in 2016.

Brazil after September 11, 2001

September 11 and the collapse of the Argentine economy, one of Brazil's chief markets, that same year produced a crisis of confidence. Argentina's crisis threatened to destabilize the recovery of the *real*. Meanwhile, Washington's war on terror threatened to displace social and economic priorities in Brazil's relations with the United States. Diplomacy with Washington became particularly bitter over the Bush administration's insistence on going to war with Iraq and its heavy-handed approach to dealing with foreigners.

The election of Lula da Silva as president in October 2002 reflected how far Brazilian democracy had come. This former industrial worker-turned-party organizer and opposition agitator, succeeded in capturing the presidency and then launching an expansion of social welfare and economic promotion policies that produced high growth with lower levels of inequality and poverty. He did so while embracing Cardoso's anti-inflation policies. But like his predecessor, he faced a congress prone to gridlock. Major social security reforms were watered down in 2004. Worse still, PT-led municipal governments, once a model of good governance in Latin America, were accused of procuring kickbacks to fund electoral activities. PT leaders surrounding Lula were implicated in a second scandal (known as the monthly retainer, or *mensalão*) involving the purchase of votes in the congress for reform legislation. However, Lula won reelection in 2006 anyway, and he continued to garner high presidential approval ratings well into his second term. He expanded public expenditures on infrastructure and industry as part of his Plan for the Acceleration of Growth.

Lula's successor in 2010 was his chief of staff, Dilma Rousseff. Rousseff became Brazil's first woman president. A former militant against the authoritarian regime, Rousseff was jailed and tortured in 1970 and 1972. After obtaining her degree in economics, she ventured again into politics during the New Republic but as an appointee in municipal and state government in Rio Grande do Sul and its capital, Porto Alegre. She joined the PT late in her career, in 2000, and was plucked from obscurity by Lula in 2002 to become his Minister of Energy and later his chief of staff. Having no real experience in elected office, her first experience as an elected leader was the presidency.

As much as Rousseff's government sought to build on the successes of Lula, neither the economy nor political institutions proved so accommodating. Growth slowed after 2011 due to decreasing commodity prices and China's own slowdown, plunging Brazil into a near depression with rising unemployment and high interest rates to keep inflation at bay. The euphoria of hosting the 2014 World Cup and the 2016 Summer Olympic Games was squashed by an expanding corruption investigation known as "Operation Car Wash" (*Lava Jato*). As part of a routine investigation focused on a notorious money-launderer and car-wash owner, Alberto Youssef, federal prosecutors uncovered a broader ring involving a cartel of construction companies and the state oil company, Petrobras. Cartel members would overcharge Petrobras for products and services in return for contracts, while proceeds from the extra payments would be laundered and distributed to the professional and personal accounts of political parties and their leaders involved in the graft. Most of these parties were allied to Rousseff's government, including the Workers' Party. Led by the telegenic federal judge, Sérgio Moro, and Deltan Dallagnol, a lawyer for the Federal Public Ministry, the investigations have uncovered the involvement of more than half of the sitting members of congress and scores of executives in the largest construction companies. The top executive of the biggest of these firms, Marcelo Odebrecht of the Odebrecht Company, received a 19-year sentence in 2016. Along with dozens of other executives and former politicians, Odebrecht continues to offer plea-bargained testimony in return for a reduced prison term. Such plea bargaining, which was made legal only in 2013, has provided a treasure trove of evidence sufficient to convict many of the accused politicians before the Supreme Court, the only venue that can try politicians for such crimes.

The Four Themes and Brazil

Brazil in a Globalized World of States

Both international and domestic factors have influenced the Brazilian state's structure, capacity, and relations with society. During the empire, international opposition to slavery forced powerful oligarchs to turn to the state for protection. The coffee and ranch economies provided the material base for the Old Republic and were intricately tied to Brazil's economic role in the world. Even the *Estado Nôvo*, with its drive to organize society, was democratized by the defeat of fascism in Europe. The return to democracy during the 1980s was part of a larger global experience, as authoritarian regimes gave way all over Latin America, Eastern Europe, southern Europe, and the Soviet Union. As Brazil's economy has grown in size, it faces greater responsibilities in the globalized world of states, both in foreign economic and security policy.

Governing the Economy

The entry of the working and middle classes as political actors reshaped the Brazilian state during the twentieth century. Vargas's New State mobilized workers and professionals. Populist democracy later provided them protection from unsafe working environments, the effects of eroding wages, and the prohibitive expense of health care. Public firms employed hundreds of thousands of Brazilians and transformed the development of the country. During the 1980s and 1990s, neoliberal reforms dramatically altered the role of the Brazilian state (see Section 2). Brazil's governance of the economy highlights the strategic role of the state in the maintenance of growth. State-led growth built the foundation for governing the economy, and developmentalism moved Brazil from a predominantly agrarian economy into an industrialized one. With the slowdown in the global economy, state companies find themselves under multiple pressures. Fiscal cutbacks and corruption investigations have limited their expansion in the current development model.

The Democratic Idea

personalist politicians

Demagogic political leaders who use their personal charisma to mobilize their constituency.

Brazil certainly has the formal institutions of a democracy, but patrimonialism, populism, corporatism, and corruption undermine them. Brazilian politicians typically cultivate personal votes (**personalist politicians**) that challenge the creation of strong parties and alliances (see Section 4). But despite its shortcomings, Brazilians appreciate that democracy gives them more say in policy-making. Thousands of new political groups, social movements, civic networks, and economic associations have emerged in recent years. The Brazilian state is highly decentralized into twenty-six states, a federal district, and 5,570 municipalities. Each center of power is a locus of demand-making by citizens and policy-making by elites. Numerous judicial, auditing, investigatory, and prosecutorial authorities have proven crucial to deepening democracy and rooting out corruption.

The Politics of Collective Identity

In assessing the politics of collective identity, the first question to answer is who are the Brazilians? This has always been a vexing issue, especially because heavy flows of international commerce, finance, and ideas have made Brazil's borders obsolete. One common answer is that the symbols of the Brazilian nation still tie Brazilians together:

carnival, soccer, samba, bossa nova, and a common language. Even though these symbols have become more prevalent, they have lost some of their meaning because of commercialization. Catholicism is a less unifying force today, as Pentecostalism and evangelism have eaten into the church's membership. Women have improved their social position and political awareness as gender-based organizations have become important resources of civil society. Yet even here, Brazil remains extremely patriarchal: women are expected to balance motherhood and other traditional roles in the household, even while economic needs pressure them to produce income.

Race remains the most difficult issue to understand. Racial identity continues to divide Brazilians, but not in the clear-cut manner it divides blacks and whites in the United States. Categories are multiple, with nonwhites adopting variations of racial identities, including white. Afro-Brazilians see themselves in complex ways as members of different classes, status groups, and mixed races that are neither strictly white or black.

Class continues to separate Brazilians due to high income inequality. Like India, Brazil's social indicators consistently rank near the bottom in the world, although these indicators are improving. Income disparities mirror racial differences. The poor are mostly blacks and mulattos while the rich are mostly white.

Themes and Comparisons

As a large, politically decentralized, and socially fragmented polity, Brazil presents several extraordinary challenges to the study of comparative politics. First, the Brazilian state has varied in its degree of centralization, producing distinct capacities for promoting development, democracy, and social distribution. Although political centralization has made the French state strong, decentralized states such as the United States and Germany have proven successful as well. The Brazilian case provides lessons for how other large, decentralized states in the developing world, such as India, might reconcile the needs of development and democracy.

The challenges posed by Brazil's democratic institutions provide rich material for comparative analysis. Along with Russia, Brazil demonstrates how the lack of a coherent party system can endanger democracy. Yet unlike Russia, Brazilian democracy is relatively protected by a network of judicial and legal institutions that are largely autonomous from politics and that have proven adept at rooting out corruption and enhancing accountability. Although high social inequality cuts against even these democratic strengths, it is reassuring to see the powerful come to justice. The complex divisions afflicting Brazilians' collective identities challenge attempts to address the country's problems. In this regard, Brazil presents an interesting puzzle for theories about collective identities: How has such a socially fragmented society remained a coherent whole while sustaining democracy?

Where Do You Stand?

The *Estado Nôvo* and the bureaucratic authoritarian periods were associated with the industrial development of Brazil. Do you think that this suggests that economic development may sometimes require authoritarian rule?

Supporters of Cardoso and Lula disagree on which leader did the most for Brazil. Which one would you say did more to address the needs of democracy, the economy, and social development?

SECTION

2

POLITICAL ECONOMY AND DEVELOPMENT

▼ **Focus Questions**

- How did the Brazilian state's role in promoting development change as the country moved from import-substitution to market-oriented reform?

- Identify some of the persisting problems of Brazilian economic development and how progress has been made during the New Republic in addressing them.

export-led growth

Economic growth generated by the export of a country's commodities. Export-led growth can occur at an early stage of economic development, in which case it involves primary products, such as the country's mineral resources, timber, and agricultural products; or at a later stage, when industrial goods and services are exported.

interventionist

An interventionist state acts vigorously to shape the performance of major sectors of the economy.

import substitution industrialization (ISI)

Strategy for industrialization based on domestic manufacture of previously imported goods to satisfy domestic market demands.

Like most developing countries, Brazil's politics has always been shaped by the quest for economic and social development. Two processes have left enduring legacies: the pattern of state intervention in the domestic market and the effects of external economic change. External economic crises have compelled the state to intervene through protection, subsidies, and even the production of goods it previously imported. These policies made Brazil one of the faster-growing newly industrialized countries of the world, alongside India and China, during the first decade of the twenty-first century. Yet changes in commodity prices and globalization trends have also slowed the country's growth in recent years, bedeviling its political leaders and promoting social and economic dislocation.

State and Economy

Brazil's economic development prior to the New State depended on **export-led growth**, that is, on the export of agricultural products. During the Old Republic, international demand for coffee gave Brazil a virtual global monopoly. Cotton, sugar, and cereals also continued to be important export products.

Coffee linked Brazil to the world market with minimal state involvement in the period before the Great Depression. Export receipts provided a reservoir of capital to build railroads, power stations, and other infrastructure. These investments then spurred the growth of light industries, mostly in textiles, footwear, and clothing. Public finance had a minor role.

The state became far more **interventionist** during the 1930s, when international demand for coffee declined. As exports fell, imports of manufactured goods also declined. These forces prompted **import substitution industrialization (ISI)**, a model of development that promoted domestic production of previously imported manufactured goods. At first, Brazil did not need large doses of state intervention. This so-called light, or easy, phase of ISI focused on products that did not require much capital or sophisticated technology such as textiles and footwear. Most of these industries were labor intensive and created jobs.

At the end of World War II, the ISI model expanded through the promotion of heavy industry and capital-intensive production. A new generation of **state technocrats**, inspired by the United Nations Economic Commission for Latin America (ECLA), sought to "deepen" ISI by promoting capital-intensive sectors through industrial policies including planning, subsidies, and financial support. State agencies promoted the quick growth of these industries.

During the 1950s, Brazil was a prime example of ECLA-style **developmentalism**, the ideology and practice of state-sponsored growth. The state promoted private investment by extracting and distributing raw materials for domestic industries at prices well below the international market. Other firms that were linked to sectors of the economy receiving these supports would benefit in a chain reaction.

Growth rates achieved impressive levels, especially during the 1970s (see Table 9.2), but the first serious contradictions of ISI emerged by this time. Protection led to noncompetitive, inefficient production, in which growing industries depended too heavily on public subsidies. ISI also became import-intensive. Businesses used subsidized finance to import technology and machinery, since the government overvalued the currency to make import prices cheaper. But this overvaluation hurt exports, by making them more expensive. Because the export sector could not supply much-needed revenues to sustain growth, the government printed money, which in turn led to inflation.

The failures of ISI during the 1960s inspired many Brazilian academics to adopt the view, then popularized as the "dependency school," that underdeveloped or "peripheral" countries could not achieve sustained levels of industrialization and growth in a world dominated by "core" economies in North America and Western Europe. ISI's failures, it was argued, were due to the ill-fated attempt to adjust marginally the inherently exploitative structure of world markets. In order to confront this situation, the dependency school advocated delinking Brazil from the world economy. While this view was widely popular among leftist economists in Brazil and elsewhere, it did not become a basis for policy.

Table 9.2	Governing the Economy: Average GDP Growth Rates
1940–1949	5.6%
1950–1959	6.1%
1960–1969	5.4%
1970–1979	12.4%
1980–1989	1.5%
1990–1996	2.1%
1997–2000	0.8%
2001–2003	1.0%
2004–2007	3.2%
2008–2010	5.7%
2011–2013	1.9%
2014–2015	–2.0%

Source: IBGE and the World Bank.

From 1964 to 1985, the state continued to promote industrialization, especially durable consumer goods for the domestic market. Multinational firms also invested and transferred technology. Industry accounted for 40 percent of Brazil's GDP by 1980.

Parastatals (public or state firms) played a crucial role in the ISI development model. Large-scale projects were financed and managed by bureaucratic agencies, state firms, and foreign companies. Peter Evans characterized these complex relations among the state, foreign investors, and domestic capitalists as a "triple alliance."[5] But the state remained the dominant partner.

Partially due to the slowing down of ISI and the accumulation of debt and higher inflation, the democratic governments after 1985 turned to a more market-oriented or market-friendly approach, dubbed neoliberal policies. These involved reducing tariffs on imports, deregulating parts of the economy, and privatizing some large companies in sectors such as steel, telecommunications, and transport. As export prices for commodities such as soy, oil, and iron ore increased during the 2000s, Brazil became flush with capital, allowing the Lula and Rousseff presidencies to pursue a hybrid model of export growth that combined openness of the domestic market to foreign investment along with large investments by the state in infrastructure and energy. The end of this commodity boom after 2011 coincided with low growth and corruption investigations involving many of the private and public firms that benefited the most during the boom period.

The Fiscal System

As the Brazilian economy became more complex after the 1960s, new opportunities for evading taxes emerged. An **informal economy** of small firms, domestic enterprises, street vendors, and unregistered employees proliferated, outside the taxable economy.

state technocrat

A career-minded bureaucrat who administers public policy according to a technical rather than a political rationale. In Mexico and Brazil, these are known as the *técnicos*.

developmentalism

An ideology and practice in Latin America during the 1950s in which the state played a leading role in seeking to foster economic development through sponsoring vigorous industrial policy.

parastatals

State-owned, or at least state-controlled, corporations, created to undertake a broad range of activities, from control and marketing of agricultural production to provision of banking services, operating airlines, and other transportation facilities and public utilities.

informal economy

That portion of the economy largely outside government control, in which employees work without contracts or benefits and employers do not comply with legal regulations or pay taxes. Examples of those working in the informal economy include casual employees in restaurants and hotels, street vendors, and day laborers in construction or agriculture.

Economists estimate that the informal economy could be as large as 20 percent of Brazil's gross domestic product ($420 billion). It may employ 40 to 60 million people, and may represent a loss of $70 billion annually in forgone tax revenues.

The new constitution of 1988 allowed states and municipalities to expand their collection of taxes and to receive larger transfers of funds from Brasília. Significant gaps then emerged in tax collection responsibilities and public spending. Although the central state spent less than it collected in taxes between 1960 and 1994, Brazil's 5,570 municipal governments spent several times more than they collected. Subnational governments also gained more discretion over spending, since the federal government required few earmarks. State governors also used public banks held by the state governments to finance expenditures, thus expanding their debt.

The Cardoso administration had the most success in recovering federal tax revenues and reducing the fiscal distortions of Brazil's federal structure. The Fiscal Responsibility Law of 2000 set strict limits on federal, state, and municipal expenditures. A combination of improved tax collection and an expansion of economic growth during the 2000s kept public debt in check, but debt exploded with the end of the commodity boom, pressuring the post-impeachment presidency of Michel Temer to pursue more austere fiscal policies (see Figure 9.2).

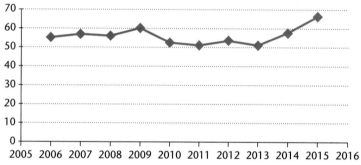

FIGURE 9.2 Governing the Economy: Brazilian Public Debt to GDP, 2006–2015

Source: Based on numbers produced by the Central Bank of Brazil.

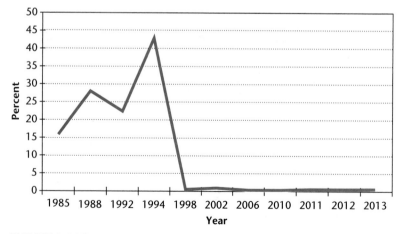

FIGURE 9.3 Governing the Economy: Monthly Rates of Inflation, 1985–2013

Source: Author's design based on Brazilian Central Bank figures.

The Problem of Inflation

Inflation accompanied state-led development because the state, business, and unions all distorted the value of goods and services by manipulating prices, interest rates, and wages. Successive attempts to control inflation fell apart as different interest groups attempted to retain these controls. No fewer than seven "stabilization" plans between 1985 and 1994 collapsed, sometimes generating "hyperinflation" (600 percent or more annual inflation). Figure 9.3 illustrates this terrible track record.

Only Cardoso's Real Plan proved successful. The Real Plan anchored the real, allowing it to float within a range set by the Central Bank. The exchange rate rose and fell, generating an acute but not lasting crisis in 1999. However, hyperinflation never returned, and the government moderated public spending growth. Renewed growth during the Lula administration kept the public debt under control. But the Rousseff government raised public spending, jeopardizing this record of fiscal and price stability. Average annual inflation became 6 percent, which is slightly worse than the average in developing countries. Low and even negative growth combined with high interest rates kept inflation in check.

Society and Economy

Between 1950 and 1980, employment in industry jumped from 14 percent to 24 percent, while employment in agriculture declined from 60 percent to 30 percent. Nevertheless, the jobs created in industry did not begin to absorb the huge number of unemployed. Many new jobs required skilled and semiskilled specialized labor. In the late 1980s and 1990s, even skilled workers faced losing their jobs because of intense industrial restructuring that caused manufacturing to employ 48 percent fewer workers. With the rapid expansion of the economy during the 2000s, urban unemployment fell dramatically from 18 percent to 5.4 percent by 2012, but it has doubled since then as growth has stalled.

Industrialization also failed to eradicate the racial inequalities inherited from slavery. Despite the impressive industrial development of Brazil, Afro-Brazilians continued to make less than their white colleagues and had fewer opportunities for upward mobility. According to one study, nonwhite men and women in Brazil have made real gains in their income because of improvements in education and occupation, but the gap separating nonwhite income from white income remains significant.[6] On average, blacks make 41 percent and mulattos make 47 percent of what whites make.

Women make up 28 percent of the economically active population and continue to enter the labor market in record numbers. Working women typically have more years of schooling than men, but they still receive lower salaries for the same job. Brazilian women make only 70 percent of what men make, and black women do even worse at 40 percent. In rural areas, women are substantially disadvantaged in the granting of land titles. Female heads of families are routinely passed over by official agencies distributing land titles to favor oldest sons, even when these are minors. Thirty-four percent of illiterate women earn the minimum wage or less, versus 5 percent of illiterate males. Although recent economic growth and rising median incomes have begun to reverse decades of worsening inequality, income remains more unequally distributed in Brazil than it is in most other developing countries (see Table 9.3).

The Welfare System

In a country of startling social inequalities, welfare policy plays a remarkably small role, even though expenditures on health care and education stand at 25 percent of GDP. The effects of this spending are uneven. Salaried formal sector workers receive most benefits, including pensions and the best access to both private and public health care. Workers in the informal sector generally do not collect welfare benefits since the federal government does not consider them employed. Corruption, clientelism, and outright waste prevent benefits from going to the people who need them the most.[7]

More people need welfare than actually contribute to the welfare state. That means the government must finance the shortfall. More serious is the unevenness of the system. More than 70 percent of all income transfers are retirement benefits that go to middle-class and upper-class individuals. The indigent receive only 1.5 percent of these funds. Informal workers and the unemployed must use public health services, while formal sector workers access the public health care system for expensive procedures and retain private insurance for less expensive care.

The Cardoso administration laid some of the groundwork for reversing poverty and inequality. In addition to several programs to provide grants directly to poor families

Table 9.3	Governing the Economy: Brazilian Income Distribution in Comparative Perspective			
Country	**10% Richest**	**20% Richest**	**20% Poorest**	**10% Poorest**
Brazil	41.8	57.4	3.3	1.0
Mexico	38.9	54.1	4.9	1.9
Chile	41.5	56.7	4.6	1.7
China	31.4	47.9	5.2	2.1
Nigeria	32.7	49.0	5.4	2.0
India	29.8	44.0	8.3	3.6
United States	30.2	36.4	5.1	1.7
United Kingdom	24.7	40.1	7.5	2.9
France	26.8	41.2	7.8	3.1
Russia	32.2	48.3	5.9	2.3

Source: World Bank, *World Development Indicators 2016* (Washington, DC: World Bank, 2016).

to improve their health and the education of their children, Cardoso also targeted the rural poor. The Family Health Program, for instance, provides community health workers for areas that have historically been underserved. Some studies have shown that this program accelerated the decline in infant mortality and improved prenatal care and family reproductive medicine, including reductions in the rates of HIV/AIDS.[8]

The Lula administration focused even more on social reform. In the fall of 2003, the government passed a social security reform that raised the minimum retirement age, placed stricter limits on benefit ceilings, reduced survivor benefits, and taxed pensions and benefits. Issues including the taxation of social security benefits for judges and military officers and the reduction of survivor benefits for the latter group became stumbling blocks in cross-party negotiations. The government made concessions on these and other issues, but the total annual savings were less than half of the original target.

The most notable social reform is *Bolsa Família* (the Family Grant Program), which consolidated three programs started by the Cardoso government. Lula expanded the funding of *Bolsa Família*, which grants modest monthly sums to families that keep their children in school and see the doctor for regular vaccinations and checkups. Since 2003, 11.1 million families or 20 percent of the Brazilian population (46 million people) have benefited from *Bolsa Família*, both in terms of improved household incomes and legal certifications of births, and the program consumes less than 3 percent of total social spending.[9] Poverty rates have fallen as a result and both incomes and literacy have improved. Low growth, higher unemployment in recent years, and the Temer government's embrace of fiscal austerity with proposed deep cuts to social programs threaten this track record.

Agrarian Reform

Landownership is highly concentrated in Brazil with only 1 percent of landowners (about 58,000 individuals) holding an amount of land equal to the size of Venezuela and Colombia combined; that is half of all arable land in Brazil. The poorest farmers survive on 2 percent of the country's land, but these number over 3 million people.

The Cardoso administration expropriated some unproductive estates and settled 186,000 families on them. Despite Lula's earlier rhetoric concerning land reform, his administration failed to initiate anything close to a land reform. The issue was one that energized the presidential campaign in 2010 of a former PT member, Marina Silva, of the small Green Party, whose 19 percent share of the first-round vote dramatically suggested that neglected social issues involving land and ecology still remain salient issues in Brazilian politics. If Silva returns as a major candidate in 2018, these issues may become salient again.

The landless poor have swelled the rings of poverty around Brazil's major cities. During the 1950s and 1960s, the growth of industry in the south and southeast enticed millions to migrate in the hopes of finding new economic opportunities. By 2015, 86 percent of Brazil's population was living in urban areas. The pressures on Brazilian cities for basic services and limited housing have overwhelmed local budgets and led to extensive squatting on public land. In the largest cities, squatters have built huge shantytowns called *favelas* that house a majority of the poor, most of whom work formally and informally in the metropolitan economy.[10]

Regional disparities in income have remained stark. The nine states of the Northeast have a per capita GDP half of the national average. The Northeast has 28 percent of the national population but accounts for only 13.8 percent of the GDP. By contrast, the Southeast has 42.6 percent of the population and 55.2 percent of the GDP. The agglomeration of industry in the South and Southeast and the persistence of poverty in the Northeast have created pressures for land reform or at least poverty-alleviating policies.

Environmental Issues

The environmental limits of Brazil's development model have only become more apparent over time. During the height of the ISI period, the central and southern states of São Paulo, Minas Gerais, Rio de Janeiro, and Rio Grande do Sul became sites of environmental degradation. In the 1970s, Guanabara Bay and the Paraiba do Sul River basin, both in Rio de Janeiro state, approached the brink of biological death. Urban pollution in São Paulo devastated the Tietê River, threatening the health of millions. In Cubatão, an industrial city east of metropolitan São Paulo, pollution became so bad that by 1981, one city council member reported that he had not seen a star in twenty years.

Big development projects invaded the Amazon River basin beginning in the 1970s. These industrial projects threatened the tropical forests, as did cattle ranching, timber extraction, and slash-and-burn agriculture by poor farmers. By the 1980s, it was clear that the primary result of these practices was the deforestation of the Amazon. The annual rate of deforestation during the 1990s approached alarming levels, with 11,216 square miles lost in 1995 alone. After a decline during the late 1990s, the rate shot up again to 10,588 square miles in 2004, after which it leveled off at a much lower point of an average of 1,930 square miles per year after 2011.

favelas

A Portuguese-language term for the shantytowns that ring many of the main cities in Brazil. The *favelas* emerge where people invade unused land and build domiciles before the authorities can remove them. Unfinished public housing projects can also become the sites of *favelas*. They expanded after the 1970s as a response to the inadequate supply of homes in urban centers to meet the demand caused by increasing rural to urban migration.

AP Images/Victor R. Caivano

Brazilian president Luiz Inacio Lula da Silva is shown in this photo attending a reelection campaign wearing a cap of the Landless Peasant Movement (MST). As the largest rural movement in Latin America, the MST campaigns for land rights for poor farmers and organizes land invasions to settle landless rural workers and their families.

Partly due to the return to democracy in 1984, new environmental movements within and outside Brazil began to influence official and public opinion. The national environmental movement in Brazil initially gained its strongest attention when ecological groups mobilized at the United Nations Earth Summit, hosted in Rio de Janeiro in 1992. In the years that followed, international advocacy networks established a presence in Brazil, led by the World Wildlife Fund and Greenpeace. These organizations and domestic groups pressured the government to make commitments to reduce carbon emissions and to reduce deforestation, which undermines the capacity of the planet to absorb excess CO_2. By clamping down on illegal natural resource extraction and unsustainable slash-and-burn agriculture, the Brazilian state was able to slow the deforestation rate to its lowest levels in decades. Yet sustained commitment, as well as improved policing via satellite and follow-up on the ground, are necessary to keep these rates low.

Under the Lula and Rousseff administrations, Brazil made substantial commitments to address environmental problems. Brazil signed and ratified all of the major multilateral conventions on species depletion, climate change, toxic waste, as well as the environmental framework agreement for Mercosul, making the customs union a notable presence in international environmental legislation. Brazil has also agreed to reduce its carbon dioxide emissions by 36.1 to 38.9 percent below what they would otherwise be in 2020. Conservation efforts also increased, with a total of over 60 million hectares under legal protection from exploitation. It is uncertain if the Temer government will preserve Brazil's ratification of the Paris climate agreement of 2016 in the wake of U.S. president Donald Trump's decision in mid-2017 to pull the United States out of the accord.

However, these commitments may also be undermined by the dominant economic development model with its emphasis on extraction of natural resources, and especially off-shore oil. Dilma Rousseff's government was enthusiastic about the most environmentally questionable projects, including the massive Belo Monte Dam in Pará. Governmental and nongovernmental environment impact statements note that the project will cause loss of habitat, affect fish migration routes, disrupt water supply on the Xingú river, and violate the cultural and human rights of indigenous groups in the area. By the time the Belo Monte Dam is finished, it will be the second largest in Brazil, behind Itaipú, and the world's third largest after China's Three Gorges Dam.

Brazil in the Global Economy

Brazil has maintained strategic relations with the global market. The financing needs of state-led industrialization required Brazil to pursue international sources of credit, making it the largest debtor country in Latin America during the 1980s.[11] When soaring inflation in the industrialized countries ratcheted up interest rates on the debt, Brazilian growth slowed under the weight of higher interest payments.

Unlike the other large Latin American countries, Brazil initially rejected the reform agenda proposed by the International Monetary Fund (IMF). Although the

GLOBAL CONNECTION

Governing the Economy in a World of States: The Rise of China and Brazilian Trade

Although no more than 14 percent of Brazil's GDP is represented by exports, the roles of trade and foreign economic policy have become more central elements of Brazil's development. Soon after China joined the World Trade Organization (WTO) in October 2001, it became Brazil's largest trade partner, surpassing the United States and the European Union. Brazilian exports of soy, oil, and iron ore have proven strategic to China's economic boom and Chinese demand, in turn, helped sustain the longest period of economic growth in Brazil since the 1970s. Total Brazilian exports to China increased from $7.7 billion in 2005 to $46.5 billion by 2011 or 18 percent of Brazil's total exports, though that has leveled down to $35 billion in 2015 as Chinese growth has slowed and the real has lost value during the current recession.

The expansion of trade with China coincided with a reorientation of Brazil's foreign economic policy. During the 1990s, Brazil led its neighbors, Argentina, Paraguay, and Uruguay, to create the Common Market of the South (MERCOSUL). Under the Treaty of Asunción (1995), the partners agreed to reduce tariffs on imports from signatories and impose a common external tariff (CET) ranging from 0 to 23 percent of imports by nonmembers. As Brazil's trade with China and other parts of the world have increased, trade with MERCOSUL partners declined after 2006. This strengthened Lula's and Rousseff's efforts to diversify trade relations by cultivating more South–South trade in South Asia, Africa, and East and Southeast Asia. Brazil currently supplies 37 percent of all Latin American exports to Asia.

MERCOSUL remains active, but the signatories have failed to deepen it into a more effective common market along the lines of the European Union due, in part, to Brazil's greater interest in cultivating ties to Asia. This strategy has also made Brazil more likely to defend its own interests in trade disputes before the WTO against hemispheric partners such as the United States.

MAKING CONNECTIONS Does the linkage between Brazilian growth and the rise of China empower or limit the capacity of the Brazilian government to control the economy?

Source: Alfred P. Montero, *Brazil: Reversal of Fortune* (Cambridge: Polity Press, 2014), Chapter 7.

Collor and Cardoso governments implemented some of this agenda by reducing tariffs and privatizing some state companies, Brazil's economy retained much of its autonomy in the global market. Tariff rates are among the highest in the developing world, the state still owns golden shares in several large, privatized firms, and the state engages in industrial policy, particularly through the National Development Bank (BNDES). As its trade relations have changed, Brazil has even turned away from some of its commitments to hemispheric trade agreements (see Global Connection: Governing the Economy in a World of States: The Rise of China and Brazilian Trade).

Nevertheless, Brazil's commitment to the international free-trade system will likely expand with the continued importance of its export sector. Maintaining a healthy trade surplus will continue to be a major component in the country's formula for growth, especially as commodity prices for soy, oranges, wheat, coffee, and other products recover. At the same time, Brazil cannot depend on the occasional "commodity boom" to sustain growth. It is becoming one of the major manufacturing and agrindustry nodes in the globalized system of production and consumption with ties to East Asia becoming more important as a target market for exports and also outward-oriented Brazilian companies such as the airplane manufacturer, Embraer. A frequent user of the WTO dispute resolution apparatus, Brazil will increasingly employ the rules governing international trade to protect these interests and secure market access.

SECTION 3

GOVERNANCE AND POLICY-MAKING

Organization of the State

politics of the governors

In Brazil, this term refers to periods of history in which state governors acquire extraordinary powers over domains of policy that were previously claimed by the federal government. The term refers most commonly to the Old Republic and the current state of Brazilian federalism.

Brazilian state institutions have changed significantly since independence. Even so, a number of institutional legacies continue to shape Brazilian politics. The most important is the centralization of state authority in the executive. This process began with the rise of Getúlio Vargas and the New State during the 1930s (see "Profile: Getúlio Dornelles Vargas"). Yet old tendencies such as the **politics of the governors** helped shape the constitution of 1988, not to preserve the centralization of presidentialism but to reestablish the decentralization of federalism.

The Brazilian state has traditionally placed vast power in the hands of the executive. The directly elected president is the head of state, head of government, and commander in chief of the armed forces. Although the executive is one of three branches of government (along with the legislature and the judiciary), Brazilian presidents have traditionally been less bound by judicial and legislative constraints than most of their European or North American counterparts. Brazilian constitutions have granted more discretion to the executive than to the other branches in enforcing laws or making policy.

Brazil's executive and the bureaucracy manage most of the policy-making and implementation functions of government. Both the Brazilian federal legislature and state governments look to the president and to the minister of the economy for leadership on policy. The heads of the key agencies of the economic bureaucracy—the ministers of the economy and of planning, the president of the Central Bank, and the head of the national development bank—have more discretion over the details of policy than the president does. Recent presidents have also had little choice but to delegate authority to the bureaucracy since the presidency cannot control the entire state but the president retains ultimate authority over cabinet ministers, the heads of bureaucratic agencies.

Although the Brazilian president is the dominant player among the three branches of government, the legislature and the judiciary have become stronger. The 1988 constitution gave many oversight functions to the legislature and judiciary, so that much presidential discretion in economic and social policy is now subject to approval by one or both (see Table 9.1).

📇 PROFILE

Getúlio Dornelles Vargas

Getúlio Vargas as president in 1952.

Keystone/Getty Images

Getúlio Dornelles Vargas (1883–1954) came from a wealthy family in the cattle-rich southernmost state of Rio Grande do Sul. Vargas's youth was marked by political divisions within his family between federalists and republicans, conflicts that separated Brazilians during the Old Republic. Political violence, which was common in the state's history, also affected Vargas's upbringing. His two brothers were both accused of killing rivals. After a brief stint in the military, Vargas attended law school in Porto Alegre, where he excelled as an orator.

After graduating in 1907, he became a district attorney. Later, he served as majority leader in the state senate. In 1923, Vargas was elected federal deputy for Rio Grande do Sul, and in 1924, he became leader of his state's delegation in the Chamber of Deputies. In 1926, he became finance minister. He served for a year before winning the governorship of his home state. Never an ideologue, Vargas practiced a highly pragmatic style of governing that made him one of Brazil's most popular politicians.

Vargas's position as governor of Rio Grande do Sul catapulted him into national prominence in 1929. The international economic crisis forced several regional economic oligarchies to unite in opposition to the coffee and pro-export financial policies of the government and in favor of efforts to protect their local economies. The states, including the state of São Paulo, divided their support between two candidates for the presidency: Julio Prestes, who was supported by President Luis, and Vargas, head of the opposition. The two states of Minas Gerais and Rio Grande do Sul voted as a bloc for Vargas, but he lost the 1930 election. Immediately afterward, a coup by military and political leaders installed Vargas in power.

The reforms of Vargas's corporatist and authoritarian New State after 1937 established the revised terms that linked Brazilian society to the state. Even today, his political legacy continues in the form of state agencies designed to promote economic development and laws protecting workers and raising living standards for families to prevent suffering from poverty and hunger.

MAKING CONNECTIONS In what ways did the rise of Vargas respond to the perils of fragmented power in Brazil?

Source: Robert M. Levine, *Father of the Poor? Vargas and His Era* (New York: Cambridge University Press, 1998).

The Executive

Although the adoption of a parliamentary regime was briefly considered following the 1987 National Constituent Assembly, Brazil remained a presidential system. Even so, rules designed to rein in the federal executive found their way into the 1988 constitution. Partly in reaction to the extreme centralization of executive authority during military rule, the delegates restored some powers to congress from before 1964, and they granted congress new ones, including oversight of economic policy and the right to be consulted on executive appointments. Executive decrees, which allowed the president to legislate directly, were replaced by "provisional measures" (also known as "emergency measures"). Provisional measures authorized the president to legislate for sixty days, at the end of which congress can pass, reject, or allow the provisional law to expire. But consistent with the assertion of congressional power, new restrictions on provisional measures passed both houses of congress in 2001. Especially since Fernando Henrique Cardoso's presidency, presidents and the leaders of the largest parties in the congress have haggled over the details of legislation, with each branch demanding patronage from the other to secure passage. Nevertheless, Brazilian presidents, through their prerogative in initiating annual budgets and employing provisional measures for other legislation, retain considerable powers to legislate.[12]

The president is elected for a four-year term with the opportunity to stand for reelection in a consecutive term and the right to run for a nonconsecutive term afterward. The major presidential candidates since the Cardoso presidency have tended to be prominent government ministers or governors. These elites often capture party nominations with the help of organizations with which they are already affiliated, making national conventions nothing less than coronations. Political allies then shift resources to those candidates whom they calculate are most likely to win and shower patronage on supporters once in government. Though there are parallels with the U.S. presidency, Brazilian presidents have different institutional powers (see "The U.S. Connection: The Presidency").

U.S. CONNECTION

The Presidency

Along with the U.S. president, the Brazilian president is the only executive directly elected by all voters throughout the country, making him or her the head of government and head of state. The Brazilian president has powers that exceed those of the U.S. president. Over 85 percent of all bills before congress emerge from the Palácio do Planalto, the president's offices in Brasília. The most important bill is the annual budget, which is crafted by the chiefs of the economic bureaucracy and the presidency and then sent to congress. The Senate and the Chamber of Deputies may amend legislation, but that is usually done with an eye to what the president will accept. Like the U.S. president, the Brazilian president maintains a pocket veto and, like forty-four U.S. state governors but not the U.S. president, also has a line-item veto. Brazilian presidents may also impound approved funds, which makes legislators mindful of enacting policies in ways not favored by the president. Brazilian presidents can issue executive orders with the force of law, but they expire if they are not taken up by the congress within 60 days. "Provisional measures," as they are called in Brazil, are employed regularly and with little judicial oversight, though they are often the focus of negotiations with congressional leaders who, since 2001, have more of a say in their ratification.

The president has the power to appoint upward of 48,000 civil servants, eight times more than the 6,000 appointed by U.S. presidents. Of these, only ambassadors, high court justices, the solicitor general, and the president of the Central Bank are subject to Senate approval.

Similar to the U.S. president, the Brazilian president is the commander-in-chief of the armed forces. In practice, however, the military branches have retained some prerogatives over internal promotion, judicial oversight, and development of new weapons systems. Brazilian presidents since Collor have exerted their authority over the military, restricting the autonomy of the armed forces in some of these areas.

U.S. presidents can be removed from office by Congress through the process of impeachment, which requires the House of Representatives to approve articles of impeachment by a majority vote and the Senate to convict the president by a two-thirds majority. The impeachment process in Brazil is similar. First the Chamber of Deputies initiates the process with a two-thirds vote to accept the charges of impeachment. Then the Senate tries the president, with the chief justice of the Supreme Court overseeing the procedures. The president must step down for up to 180 days during the trial and, if impeached on a two-thirds vote of the Senate, must do so permanently. Collor stepped down before the Senate trial, but Rousseff was convicted in 2016 and removed from office for a "crime of responsibility" involving a violation of the Law of Fiscal Responsibility that requires the president to submit a balanced budget. Rousseff used loans from public banks to cover shortfalls, violating the spirit of the law at the very least. Michel Temer then replaced her.

MAKING CONNECTIONS How is the Brazilian presidency stronger than the U.S. presidency and in what ways is it weaker?

Since the beginning of the military governments, the ministry of economy has had more authority than any other executive agency. These powers grew in response to the economic problems of the 1980s and 1990s. As a result of their control of the federal budget and the details of economic policy, recent ministers of the economy have had levels of authority typical of a prime minister in a parliamentary system. This power is shared somewhat with the Central Bank, which coordinates monetary authority and financial regulations with the presidency.

The Bureaucracy: State and Semipublic Firms

Bureaucratic agencies and public firms have played a key role in Brazilian economic and political development. After 1940, the state created a large number of new agencies and public enterprises. Many of these entities were allowed to accumulate their own debt and plan development projects without undue influence from central ministries or politicians. Public firms became a key part of the triple alliance of state, foreign, and domestic capital that governed the state-led model of development. By 1981, the federal government owned ten of the top twenty-five enterprises in Brazil, and state governments owned eight others. Public expenditures increased from 16 percent of GDP in 1947 to over 32 percent in 1969, far higher than in any other Latin American country except socialist Cuba.

Much of this spending (and the huge debt that financed it) was concentrated on development projects, many of gigantic proportions. Key examples include the world's largest hydroelectric plant, Itaipú; Petrobras's petroleum processing centers; steel mills such as the now-private National Steel Company in Volta Redonda, Rio de Janeiro, and Vale do Rio Doce (today known only as Vale), which maintains interests in sectors as diverse as mining, transport, paper, and textiles. On the eve of the debt crisis in 1982, the top thirty-three projects accumulated $88 billion in external debt, employed 1.5 million people, and contributed $47 billion to the GDP.

Managing the planning and financing of these projects calls for enormous skill. Recruitment into the civil service is by competitive exams, with advanced degrees required for those seeking management positions in the more technical economic and engineering agencies. The National Bank for Economic and Social Development (BNDES) remains the most important financier of development projects in Brazil. Founded in the early 1950s, the BNDES plays a key role in channeling public funds to industrial projects such as the automobile sector and domestic suppliers of parts and labor. The experience of the BNDES demonstrated that, despite Brazil's clientelist legacies, the Brazilian bureaucracy could function effectively. Meritocratic advancement and professional recruitment granted these agencies some autonomy from political manipulation.[13] BNDES's technocracy took on larger responsibilities during the Cardoso, Lula, and Rousseff presidencies. At present, the bank's array of investment and development projects make it a larger development bank than the World Bank.

Juridical changes represent some of the most important ways in which the role of the bureaucracy has changed. The 1988 constitution initially reinforced certain bureaucratic monopolies, for example, the state's exclusive control over petroleum, natural gas, exploration of minerals, nuclear energy, and telecommunications. But this began to change with the adoption of structural reforms during the 1990s, beginning with the Collor government's National Destatization Program (*Programa Nacional de Destatização*; PND). Under the PND, public firms, amounting to a total value of $39 billion, were sold ($8.5 billion in the steel sector alone). The Cardoso administration went even further. It persuaded congress to amend the constitution to remove the public monopoly on petroleum refining, telecommunications, and infrastructure, making these sectors available for auction or licensing arrangements with private firms. In 1998, much of the public telecommunications sector was privatized, bringing in about $24 billion. Under Lula and Rousseff, state-controlled entities such as Petrobras and BNDES reasserted their role in the economy, with the latter as the primary source of long-term finance and venture capital.

Other State Institutions

The Judiciary

Brazil has a network of state courts, with jurisdiction over state matters, and a federal court system, not unlike the one in the United States, which maintains jurisdiction over federal crimes. A supreme court (the Supreme Federal Tribunal or STF), similar in jurisdiction to the U.S. Supreme Court, acts as the final arbiter of court cases. The Supreme Federal Tribunal's eleven justices are nominated by the president and confirmed by an absolute majority of the Senate. The Superior Court of Justice (STJ), with thirty-three justices, operates beneath the Supreme Federal Tribunal as an appeals court. The Supreme Federal Tribunal decides constitutional questions. The military maintains its own court system.

The judiciary adjudicates political conflicts as well as civil and social conflicts. The Electoral Supreme Tribunal (*Tribunal Supremo Eleitoral*, TSE) has exclusive responsibility to organize and oversee all issues related to elections. The TSE has the power to investigate charges of political bias by public employees, file criminal charges against persons violating electoral laws, and validate electoral results. In addition to these constitutional provisions, the TSE monitors the legal compliance of electoral campaigns and executive neutrality in campaigns. Political candidates with pending charges are allowed to run for office, but they are prohibited from taking their elected seats if they do not resolve the charges. Dozens of "dirty record" (*ficha suja*) candidates have been prevented from running for office, reinforcing the power that the TSE and its regional electoral courts have to oversee all elections.

As in the rest of Latin America, penal codes established by legislation govern the powers of judges. This makes the judiciary less flexible than in North America, which operates on case law, but it provides a more effective barrier against judicial activism—the tendency of the courts to render broad interpretations of the law. The main problem in the Brazilian system has been the lack of judicial review. Lower courts do not have to follow the precedents of the STF or STJ, though a comprehensive judicial reform act in 2004 strengthened the capacity of the STF and STJ to set precedent and reduce the number of appeals. The reform established a National Judicial Council to regulate the lower courts, where judges are more tolerant of nepotism and conflict of interest.

These and other reforms since 2013 have also strengthened the role and professionalization of prosecutorial and investigatory offices, especially the Public Ministry, the federal and state prosecutors, and the auditing agencies of the federal and state treasuries. Strict civil service guidelines, meritocratic admission and advancement, and much oversight provided by these agencies explain the unveiling of systemic corruption in Brazilian politics. *Lava Jato* is the largest of several major corruption investigations that have upended the political establishment. These investigations brought down the president of the Chamber, Eduardo Cunha, who oversaw Rousseff's impeachment. Some of the largest political figures in Brazil, including Lula and Michel Temer, remain in the crosshairs of prosecutors.

Subnational Government

Like Germany, Mexico, India, and the United States, the Brazilian state has a federal structure. The country's twenty-six states are subdivided into 5,564 municipal governments. The structure of subnational politics in Brazil consists of a governor; his or her chief advisers, who also usually lead key secretariats such as economy and planning; and a unicameral legislature often dominated by supporters of the governor. Governors serve 4-year terms and are limited to two consecutive terms in office.

By controlling patronage through their powers of appointment and spending, governors and even some mayors can wield extraordinary influence.[14] The 1982 elections were the first time since the military regime when Brazilians could elect their governors directly. This lent legitimacy to the governors' campaign to decentralize fiscal resources. In recent years, key elements of reforms have been watered down in order to curry favor with this influential constituency. Political decentralization further fragmented the Brazilian polity, but it also empowered some subnational governments to sponsor innovative new policies.[15] The 1988 constitution accelerated this process by giving the states and municipalities a larger share of tax revenues. During the early to mid-1990s, this process went too far, and it allowed states and cities to go deeply into debt. The Cardoso administration went the farthest to halt this unsustainable process of debt-led subnational spending. The federal government required states and municipalities to finance a larger share of social spending. The Central Bank took over bankrupt state banks and privatized most of them. The Fiscal Responsibility Law of 2000 introduced new penalties for profligacy by subnational governments.

Nevertheless, governors and mayors remain significant actors in policy-making. These politicians remain party leaders as they are key hubs for distributing patronage to lower-ranked politicians. At the same time, these leaders have sometimes demonstrated the capacity for good government. A study of one state demonstrated that even the most underdeveloped subnational governments can promote industrial investment, employment, and social services.[16]

The Military and the Police

Like many other South American militaries, the Brazilian armed forces retain substantial independence from civilian presidents and legislators. Brazil has suffered numerous coups; those in 1930 and 1964 were critical junctures, while others brought in caretaker governments that eventually yielded to civilian rule. The generals continue to maintain influence in Brazilian politics, blocking policies they do not like and lobbying on behalf of those they favor.

The military's participation in Brazilian politics became more limited, if still quite expansive, following the transition to democracy in 1985. Several laws gave the military broad prerogatives to "guarantee internal order" and play a "tutelary role" in civilian government. During the Sarney administration, members of the armed forces retained cabinet-level rank in areas of importance to the military, such as the ministries of the armed forces and the nuclear program. Most important, the military succeeded in securing amnesty for its human rights abuses committed during the preceding authoritarian regime. In an effort to professionalize the armed forces, the Collor government slashed the military budget, thereby reducing the autonomy that the military enjoyed during the authoritarian period. Collor also replaced the top generals with officers who had few or no connections to the authoritarian regime and were committed to civilian leadership. Cardoso introduced a new security strategy that thoroughly professionalized the armed forces, leaving them out of civilian processes controlling the defense budget.

In recent years, there has been a militarization of local police forces. The state police consists of two forces: the civil police force, which acts as an investigative unit, and the uniformed military police force, which maintains order. The military police do not regulate only military personnel but civilians as well. They often partake in specialized commando-type operations in urban areas, especially in the *favelas*, and they engage in riot control. These forces are only nominally controlled by state governors; they are, in fact, trained, equipped, and managed by the armed forces, which also maintain a separate judicial system to try officers for wrongdoing.

Rising urban crime rates produced a movement to "pacify" and control areas that had once been ceded de facto to drug gangs. "Pacification units" of specialized police forces routinely invade and patrol *favelas* in Rio, São Paulo, Recife, and other major cities with destitute urban rings. The specter of criminal violence has shocked Brazilians into voting for politicians who promise better police security. But voters have learned that police forces themselves are often part of the problem. Despite official oversight of police authorities, the military and civil police forces in many cities of the northeast, São Paulo, and Rio de Janeiro often act abusively. Cases of arbitrary detention, torture, corruption, and systematic killings by Brazilian police have been the focus of human rights investigations.[17] The police are also targets of violence, as organized crime syndicates, especially in São Paulo, have become more brazen in their attacks on police installations.

The federal police force is a small unit of approximately 3,000 people. It operates like a combined U.S. Federal Bureau of Investigation, Secret Service, Drug Enforcement Agency, and Immigration and Naturalization Service. Despite its limited size, the federal police force has been at the center of every national investigation of corruption. Thanks to the federal police and the Public Ministry, the official federal prosecutor with offices in each of Brazil's states and the federal district, the federal government's capacity for investigation and law enforcement has expanded considerably.

The Policy-Making Process

Although policy-making continues to be fluid and ambiguous, certain domains of policy are clearly demarcated. Foreign policy, for example, is exclusively the responsibility of the executive branch. Political parties and the congress still have only inconsistent power over investment policies. Bureaucratic agencies retain command over the details of social and economic policies.

Clientelism injects itself at every stage of policy-making, from formulation and decision making to implementation. Personal contacts often shape who benefits from policy-making. Quid pro quos, nepotism, and other kinds of favoritism, if not outright corruption, regularly obstruct or distort policy-making.[18] Complex formal and informal networks link the political executive, key agencies of the bureaucracy, and private interests. These networks are the chief players in clientelist circles. Cardoso described these clientelistic networks as **bureaucratic rings**. He considered the Brazilian state to be highly permeable, fragmented, and therefore easily colonized by private interests that make alliances with midlevel bureaucratic officers to shape public policy to benefit themselves. The *Lava Jato* and other corruption scandals illustrate how the sustained influence of private interests, such as the construction companies who won bids for Petrobras projects, influence the bidding process and pay bribes to politicians and the campaign coffers of the main parties. Odebrecht, the largest construction company, paid a reported $800 million in bribes on 100 projects in twelve different countries and received $3.34 billion in new business due to these bribes.

Among the key sources of influence outside the state is organized business. Unlike business associations in some Asian and West European countries, Brazilian business groups have remained independent of corporatist ties to the state. Business associations have also remained aloof from political parties. Lobbying by Brazilian entrepreneurs is common, and their participation in bureaucratic rings is legendary. Few major economic policies are passed without the input of the Federation of São Paulo Industries (*Federação das Industrias do Estado de São Paulo*, or FIESP).

The country's labor confederations and unions have had less consistent access to policymaking. Although unions were once directly organized and manipulated by the corporatist state, they gained autonomy in the late 1970s and the 1980s. From then on, they sought leverage over policy-making through outside channels, such as the link between the *Central Única dos Trabalhadores* (CUT, Workers' Singular Peak Association) and Lula da Silva's Workers' Party. Attempts to bring labor formally into direct negotiations with business and the state have failed, in part due to widening cleavages within the union movement due to their sector's orientation toward trade, technology, and remuneration.

Debate and lobbying do not stop in Brazil once laws are enacted. Policy implementation is a subject of perpetual bargaining. One salient example is "the Brazilian way" (*o jeito brasileiro*)—a social convention that allows any Brazilian to ask for a temporary suspension of a rule for the sake of expediency. Although *jeito* is used only for relatively minor rules, it delivers the message that the rule of law is not to be entirely respected either by the rich or by the poor.

bureaucratic rings

A term developed by the Brazilian sociologist and president Fernando Henrique Cardoso that refers to the highly permeable and fragmented structure of the state bureaucracy that allows private interests to make alliances with midlevel bureaucratic officers. By shaping public policy to benefit these interests, bureaucrats gain the promise of future employment in the private sector.

Where Do You Stand?

Would you consider the Brazilian state "strong"?

How does clientelism in policy-making make it easier for even massive corruption to occur?

REPRESENTATION AND PARTICIPATION

▼ **Focus Questions**

• In what ways do Brazilian political institutions impede representation and elite accountability?

• How does the mobilization of civil society in Brazil enhance the country's democratic governance?

The fragmentation of legislative politics, the weaknesses of political parties, and the interests of particular politicians and their clientelistic allies make enacting reform on behalf of the national interest extremely difficult. Those politicians and parties that dispense the most patronage and cultivate clientele networks are the most successful. More often than not, the main beneficiaries are a small number of elite economic and political interests who develop ongoing relationships with legislators, governors, and presidents.

The transition to democracy, however, coincided with an explosion of civil society activism and mobilization. The expansion of voting rights and the involvement of gender and ethnic groups, urban social movements, and environmental and religious organizations in Brazilian politics have greatly expanded the range of political participation. Just the same, political institutions have failed to harmonize the demands of conflicting forces.

The Legislature

The national legislature is composed of an upper house, the Senate, with 81 members, and a lower house, the Chamber of Deputies, with 513 members. Every state and the federal district elect three senators by simple majority. Senators serve for eight-year terms and may be reelected without limit. Two-thirds of the Senate is elected at one time, and the remaining one-third is elected four years later. Senatorial elections are held at the same time as those for the Chamber of Deputies, all of whose members are elected on a four-year cycle. Federal deputies may be reelected without limits. Each state is allowed a minimum of eight and a maximum of seventy deputies, according to population. This procedure introduces severe malapportionment in the allocation of seats. Without the ceiling and floor on seats, states with large populations, such as São Paulo, would have more than seventy deputies, and states in the underpopulated Amazon, such as Roraima, would have fewer than eight.

The two houses of the legislature have equal authority to make laws, and both must approve a bill for it to become law. Each chamber can propose or veto legislation passed by the other. When the two chambers pass bills on a given topic that contain different provisions, the texts go back and forth between houses without going through a joint conference committee, as in the United States. Once a bill is passed by both houses in identical form, the president may sign it into law, reject it as a whole, or accept some parts of it and reject others. The legislature can override a presidential veto by a majority vote in both houses during a joint session, but such instances are rare. Constitutional amendments must be passed twice by at least three-fifths of the votes in each house of congress. Amendments may also be passed by an absolute majority in a special constituent assembly proposed by the president and created by both houses of congress. The Senate is empowered to try the president and other top officials, including the vice president and key ministers and justices, for impeachable offenses. It also approves the president's nominees to high offices, including justices of the high courts, heads of diplomatic missions, and directors of the Central Bank.

Most legislators view their service primarily as a means to enhance their own income, thanks to generous public pensions and kickbacks earned from dispensing political favors. Election to the federal legislature is often used as a stepping stone to even more lucrative, especially executive, posts. After the presidency, the most coveted positions are the governorships of industrialized states. Most members of congress come from the middle or upper-middle classes; they have much to gain if they can step into well-paid posts in the executive and the parastatal enterprises following their congressional service. A mere 3 percent of seats in congress are held by Afro-Brazilians. Only 9 percent of the seats in the Chamber and 14 percent of those in the Senate are held by women.

The deficiencies of the Brazilian legislature were highlighted in recent years by several corruption scandals. Partly due to the fragmentation of the party system (see below), the Lula government bought the votes of deputies in smaller parties. Kickback schemes from public contracts are a common way of financing these forms of political coordination. The *Lava Jato* investigation unveiled the largest such scheme in Brazilian history, with indictments and leaks from plea bargaining testimony leading the news each day.

Congress is often criticized for its lack of accountability. One response to legislative corruption has been to use parliamentary commissions of inquiry to review allegations of malfeasance by elected officials. Although these temporary committees have demonstrated some influence, they have rarely produced results. The temporary committees work alongside sixteen permanent legislative committees that treat issues as diverse as taxation and human rights. These committees, however, are not nearly as strong as committees in the U.S. Congress. Legislative committees, both temporary and permanent, often fail to conclude an investigation or find solutions to persistent dilemmas in policy.

Political Parties and the Party System

Many of the traditional weaknesses of the party system were reinforced after the transition to democracy. The result was to make parties anemic. Politicians switched parties nearly at will to increase their access to patronage, sometimes during their terms in office. A Supreme Court decision in 2007 ruled against this practice but allowed switching prior to elections. Other rules of the electoral system create incentives for politicians to ignore party labels. Brazil's experience with proportional representation (PR), which is used to elect federal and state deputies, is particularly important in this regard. Proportional representation may be based on either a closed-list or an open-list system. In closed-list PR, the party selects the order of politicians, and voters cannot cross party lines. Because voters are effectively choosing the party that best represents them, this system encourages party loyalty among both the electorate and individual politicians. In an open-list PR system, the voters have more discretion and can cross party lines. Brazil's PR system is open-list. Voters cast their ballots for individuals not parties by inputting the candidate's electoral number. The geographic boundaries of electoral districts in Brazil for state and federal deputies are entire states. There are few limits on how many individuals and parties may run in the same electoral district. Crowded fields discourage party loyalty and emphasize the personal qualities of candidates. Worse still, the open-list PR system creates incentives for politicians to ignore party labels, because voters can cross party lines with ease.

With so much emphasis on the personal qualities of politicians, ambitious individuals often ignore established party hierarchies while achieving elected office. As a result, Brazil has the most fragmented party system in Latin America and one of the most fragmented in the world. This makes parties extremely poor vehicles for representing political alternatives. Brazil's electoral system further fragments power because state, not national, parties select legislative candidates, with governors exerting tremendous influence over nominations.

Given the political fragmentation of the legislature and the weakness of the party system, presidents struggle to maintain majority alliances in congress. Since the Cardoso presidency, the distribution of cabinet ministries to leaders or notables of parties other than the president's has been a primary means of crafting congressional alliances. While it may be the case, as some political scientists have claimed, that this system of "coalitional presidentialism" is stable and has enabled the political system to become more governable, the system is confusing and can easily invite corruption.

Fundamental to the confusing nature of the Brazilian political system is the number of political organizations that have emerged over the last few years. These parties can be defined ideologically, although the categories are not as internally consistent or cut and dry as they might seem (see Table 9.4).

Political parties on the right currently defend neoliberal economic policies designed to shrink the size of the public sector, as well as support the reduction and partial privatization of the welfare state. Right-wing parties are fairly united in favor of rolling back social spending; they also advocate electoral reform—specifically, the establishment of a majority or mixed, rather than purely proportional, district voting system.

A loose set of conservative parties currently struggles for the mantle of the right. Leading the pack is the PFL, which was refounded in 2007 as the Democrats (DEM). PFL/DEM is one of the larger parties in the congress and has generally opposed center-left presidents Lula and Rousseff. Many small parties have allied with right-wing and center-right parties or advocated right-wing issues, such as the Brazilian Labor Party (PTB), the Progressive Party (PP), the evangelistic Liberal Party/Party of the Republic (PL/PR), and the hard-right Social Christian Party (PSC).

The two other largest parties in congress are the PMDB and the PSDB. These parties, while having disparate elements, tend to dominate the center and center-right segments of the ideological spectrum. Along with the PFL/DEM, these have been the key governing parties during the democratic era. There is agreement that these parties have become more solidly in favor of neoliberal reform, so they can be characterized as being on the right or center-right.[19] They are also the parties that led the impeachment process against Dilma Rousseff after PMDB broke its allegiance with her government in March 2016.

Political parties on the left not only advocate reducing deficits and inflation but also maintaining the present size of the public sector and improving the welfare state. Left-oriented parties want to expand the state's role in promoting and protecting domestic industry. On constitutional reform, they support the social rights guaranteed by the 1988 constitution.

The Workers' Party (PT) has been the most successful of the leftist parties, having elected Luiz Inácio "Lula" da Silva twice to the presidency, followed by Dilma Rousseff. The PT was founded by workers who defied the military government and engaged in strikes in São Paulo's metalworking and automobile industries in 1978 and 1979. Although the PT began with a working-class message and leftist platform, its identity broadened and moderated during the 1980s and early 1990s. Under Lula's leadership the party increasingly sought the support of the middle class, rural and urban poor, and even segments of business and the upper classes. In the years preceding Lula's presidency, the party moderated its criticism

Table 9.4	The Democratic Idea: The Major Parties in Brazil
Conservative/Right-Wing Parties	
PFL/DEM	*Partido da Frente Liberal* (Party of the Liberal Front) [refounded as the *Democratas* (Democrats) in 2007]
PL/PR	*Partido Liberal* (*Liberal Party;* refounded as the Party of the Republic in 2007)
PP	*Partido Progressista* (Progressive Party)
Centrist Parties	
PMDB	*Partido do Movimento Democrático Brasileiro* (Party of the Brazilian Democratic Movement)
PSDB	*Partido da Social Democracia Brasileira* (Party of Brazilian Social Democracy)
Populist/Leftist Parties	
PT	*Partido dos Trabalhadores* (Workers' Party)
PSB	*Partido Socialista Brasileiro* (Brazilian Socialist Party)
PCdoB	*Partido Comunista do Brasil* (Communist Party of Brazil)
PDT	*Partido Democrático Trabalhista* (Democratic Labor Party)
PPS	*Partido Popular Socialista (ex-Partido Comunista Brasileiro)* (Popular Socialist Party)

of capitalism, ultimately accepting many of the economic reforms that Cardoso implemented. During Lula's presidency, the PT moved further to the center. After Rousseff's impeachment and Lula's deepening problems with prosecutors, PT militants began to imagine refounding the party by abandoning politicians under investigation and cultivating younger leadership. Yet if Lula survives legal scrutiny, he may still gain the party's nomination for a third presidential run in 2018.

Currently, no party has more than 25 percent of the seats in either house of congress (see Figures 9.4 and 9.5). Cardoso's multiparty alliance of the PSDB-PFL-PTB-PPB controlled 57 percent of the vote in the lower house and 48 percent in the upper house. Lula failed to organize a similar "governing coalition;" his government depended on enticing centrist and center-right parties to vote for his proposals. His successor, Dilma Rousseff, enjoyed a larger support base in congress than Lula or even Cardoso, but

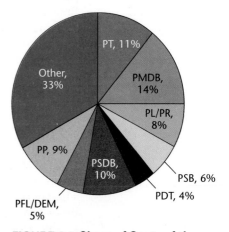

FIGURE 9.4 Share of Seats of the Major Parties in the Chamber of Deputies, as of February 2016

Source: Data from final TSE numbers.

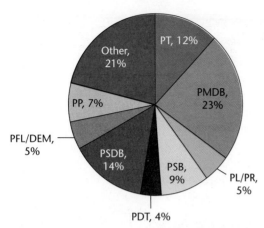

FIGURE 9.5 Share of Seats of the Major Parties in the Senate, as of February 2016

Source: Data from final TSE numbers.

this failed to protect her when the economy slowed and *Lava Jato* encouraged some parties to end their support of the government.

Elections

The Brazilian electorate stands at 142 million with an average turnout of about 80 percent. These figures make it the largest and most participatory electorate in Latin America. Compulsory voting, improved literacy, and efforts by political parties, especially on the left, to educate citizens on the value of participation have expanded the electorate impressively.

Yet given the multiplicity of parties, unbalanced apportionment of seats among the states, and sheer size of some state-sized electoral districts, candidates often have few incentives to be accountable to their constituencies. In states with hundreds of candidates running in oversized electoral districts, the votes obtained by successful candidates are often widely scattered, limiting the accountability of those elected. In less-populated states, there are more seats and parties per voter; the electoral and party quotients are lower. As a result, candidates often alter their legal place of residence immediately before an election in order to run from a safer seat, compounding the lack of accountability.

With the *abertura*, political parties gained the right to broadcast electoral propaganda on radio and television. All radio stations and TV channels are required to carry, at no charge, two hours of party programming each day during a campaign season. The parties are entitled to an amount of time on the air proportional to their number of votes in the previous election. But some candidates gain more access through private channels and community radio stations that family members may own.

Despite the shortcomings, Brazilians have voted in larger numbers and have avoided the kinds of antisystem protests seen in other Latin American countries. Nevertheless, participation is not enough. Relatively few Brazilians identify with a political party. (The vast majority of those who do are aligned to the PT). Most Brazilians have no clear left-right ideology, so there is little to align political representatives and voters other than material interests.

Not surprisingly, Brazilians remain disappointed with the results of democracy. The weakness of political parties, coupled with the persistence of clientelism and accusations of corruption against even previously squeaky clean parties such as the PT, have disillusioned average Brazilians and have generated support for occasional protests that call attention to systemic problems without calling for a change of the regime itself.

Political Culture, Citizenship, and Identity

The notion of national identity describes a sense of national community that goes beyond mere allegiance to a state, a set of economic interests, regional loyalties, or kinship affiliations. A national identity gains strength through a process of nation building during which a set of national symbols, cultural terms and images, and shared myths consolidate around historical experiences that define the loyalties of a group of people.

Several developments made Brazilian nation building possible. Unlike nation formation in culturally, linguistically, and geographically diverse Western Europe, Africa, and Asia, Brazil enjoyed a homogeneous linguistic and colonial experience. As a result, Brazilian history largely avoided the ethnic conflicts that have posed obstacles to nation building in Eastern Europe, Nigeria, and India. Immigrants added their ideas and value systems at the turn of the century, but they brought no compelling identities that could substitute for an overarching national consciousness. Regional secessionist movements were uncommon in Brazilian history and were short-lived episodes when they did emerge in the twentieth century.

Despite Brazil's rich ethnic makeup, racial identities in Brazil have seldom been the basis for political action. Brazilians often agreed on the specious idea that Brazil was a racial democracy. Even in the face of severe economic and political oppression of native peoples, Afro-Brazilians, and Asians, the myth of racial democracy has endured in the national consciousness.

Like the myth of racial democracy, the major collective political identities in Brazilian history have sought to hide or deny the real conflicts in society. For example, the symbols and images of political nationalism tended to boost the quasi-utopian visions of the country's future development. Developmentalists under the military governments and democratic leaders such as Kubitschek espoused optimism that "Brazil is the country of the future." (More cynical Brazilians quipped that Brazil is the country of the future, and always will be.)

Luiz Inácio "Lula" da Silva, founder of the Workers' Party and Brazilian president (2002–2006).

The persistence of optimistic myths about the country in the face of socioeconomic and political realities often leads to angry disengagement from politics. Slow improvements in primary and secondary education have not been enough to produce a more engaged and knowledgeable electorate. Yet avenues for participation have proliferated in the democratic period, creating the hope that new and more empowering identities might develop.

During the redemocratization process, new trends in Brazilian political culture emerged. Most segments of Brazilian society came to embrace "modernization with democracy," even if they would later express doubts about its benefits. One prominent example is the role played by the Catholic Church in promoting democracy. During the transition, a number of Catholic political organizations and movements aided by the church organized popular opposition to the military governments. After the transition, archbishops of the Catholic Church helped assemble testimonials of torture victims. The publication of these depositions in the book *Nunca Mais* (*Never Again*) incited condemnation of the authoritarian past. In this way, an establishment that previously had been associated with social conservatism and political oppression became a catalyst of popular opposition to authoritarianism. One well-known outcome of these changes was the development of liberation theology, a doctrine that argued that religion should seek to free people not only from their sins but also from

T photography/Shutterstock.com

Carnival in Brazil, the world's largest floor show, is also an insightful exhibition of allegories and popular myths about the country, its people, and their culture.

social injustice. By organizing community-based movements to press for improved sanitation, clean water, basic education, and, most important, freedom from oppression, Catholic groups mobilized millions of citizens. Among the Brazilian church's most notable accomplishments was the development of an agrarian reform council in the 1970s, the Pastoral Land Commission. The commission called for extending land ownership to poor peasants. The Brazilian church also created ecclesiastical community movements to improve conditions in the *favelas*. Pentecostal and other evangelical movements have fed off of the demand for such action, providing an alternative for Brazilians who choose not to turn to Roman Catholicism.

These trends have coincided with a growing but still tempered distrust of the state. Early during the regime transition, business groups assailed the failures of state-led development, while labor unions claimed that corporatist management of industrial relations could not advance the interests of workers. But such distrust was never taken too far. The democratic period has enjoyed a consensus among journalists, economists, politicians, intellectuals, and entrepreneurs that national institutions can be adjusted incrementally to strengthen democracy and promote economic growth. Constitutional, administrative, and economic reforms are the focus of those who call for change, including the street protestors that commanded the attention of the world preceding the World Cup.

Those who see Brazilian democracy as holding promise can take comfort from the fact that political transitions since Cardoso's election have been without institutional disruption. There is even some evidence that voters reward good policies. The fact that Rousseff won a narrow reelection in 2014 largely because she maintained popular social policies such as the *Bolsa Família* is an example. Yet just as easily, the positive regard of the voters can be squandered, as popular support for Rousseff's impeachment demonstrates. Widespread corruption investigations, which are likely to continue for some time, may strengthen long-term accountability in Brazilian democracy but reduce the public's confidence in democratic leadership and institutions.

Unlike the situation in the United States, the events of 9/11 did not fundamentally change Brazilian political culture or increase the nation's sense of vulnerability. Having suffered the military regime's torture and arbitrary killings—a kind of state terrorism—in their own country, Brazilians are well aware that democracy and decency have enemies capable of the greatest cruelty. Many Brazilians also live with everyday terrors—poverty, hunger, disease, and violence—that they regard as far more dangerous than terrorism.

Interest Groups, Social Movements, and Protest

Despite much disengagement from and distrust of politics, Brazil has a highly participatory democracy. In the mid-1970s, Brazil witnessed an explosion of social and political organization: grassroots popular movements; new forms of trade unionism; neighborhood movements; professional associations of doctors, lawyers, and journalists; entrepreneurial associations; and middle-class organizations. At the same time, a host of nongovernmental organizations (NGOs) became more active in Brazil; among them were Amnesty International, Greenpeace, and native Brazilian rights groups. Domestic groups active in these areas increasingly turned to the NGOs for resources and information, adding an international dimension to what was previously an issue of domestic politics.

By the 1980s, women were participating in and leading popular initiatives on a wide variety of issues related to employment and the provision of basic services. Many of these organizations enlisted the support of political parties and trade unions in battles over women's wages, birth control, rape, and violence in the home. Although nearly absent in employers' organizations, women are highly active in rural and urban unions. In recent years, Brazilian women have created more than 3,000 organizations to address issues of concern to women. A good example includes special police stations (*delegacias de defesa da mulher*, DDMs) dedicated to addressing crimes against women, adolescents, and children. The DDMs have been created in major Brazilian cities, and particularly in São Paulo state.

Women's groups have been given a boost as more women have joined the workforce. More than 20 percent of Brazilian families are supported exclusively by women. Social policies such as *Bolsa Família* reinforce the importance of women in society by focusing their resources on women as the heads of households. Women have also made strides in representative politics and key administrative appointments. Ellen Gracie Northfleet became the first woman to head the Supreme Court until her retirement in 2011; Cármen Lúcia, who was appointed by Lula in 2006 and is the second woman on the court, is now president of the STF. Women in formal politics have in recent years become mayors of some major cities, such as São Paulo, and Marina Silva, who heads her own party, Rede, regularly figures into national conversations about candidates for 2018. Although in recent years, the number of women with seats in congress has nearly doubled, the rate remains one of the lowest in Latin America.

In contrast to the progress of women's movements, a movement to address racial discrimination has not emerged. Only during the 1940s did some public officials and academics acknowledge that prejudice existed against blacks. At that time, the problems of race were equated with the problems of class. Attacking class inequality was thus considered a way to address prejudice against blacks. This belief seemed plausible because most poor Brazilians are either mulatto (mixed race) or black. But it might be just as logical to suggest that they are poor because they are black. In any case, the relationship between race and class in Brazil is just as ambiguous as it is in the United States and other multiethnic societies.

Both gender and race are often encompassed in organizational politics that take on social and class-based issues. Conflicts over housing policy, sanitation, transport, health, and education involve not only movements but also nongovernmental organizations and municipal government. Thousands of Brazilian towns and cities sponsor popular councils and policy-specific conferences that involve a variety of civil societal organizations. Health councils have become the most common, with local citizens debating with organizations and their elected representatives how resources for medical care should be spent. Such processes are said to undercut clientelism by investing in pluralism.

The strength of Brazilian civil society is evident in urban settings, but it has been only sporadically available in the more sparsely populated areas of the Amazon basin. Over the past half century, large-scale and poorly regulated economic development of the Amazon has threatened the cultures and lives of Indians. Miners, loggers, and land developers typically invade native lands, often with destructive consequences for the ecology and indigenous people. For example, members of the Ianomami, a tribe living in a reserve with rich mineral resources, are frequently murdered by miners. During the military government, the National Indian Foundation, FUNAI, turned a blind eye to such abuses, claiming that indigenous cultures represented "ethnic cysts to be excised from the body politic."[20] With the *abertura*, many environmental NGOs defended the human rights of indigenous people as part of their campaign to defend the Amazon and its people. As the matter of global warming and the importance of the Amazon as the "green lung of the planet" has focused attention on the region, transnational movements and NGOs have become more involved in publicizing the plight of indigenous peoples and the ecological costs of development.

The Political Impact of Technology and the Media

Technology has fundamentally affected the way that Brazilians interact with the political system. The organized media fundamentally affects the choices that voters make. Beyond the large national broadcasters, 2,168 community radio stations, many owned by politicians or family members, exert influence over how citizens think about the issues. More than 78 percent of all towns in Brazil have no other source of radio. In poor areas, such as the Northeast, 35 percent of all stations are controlled by politicians who use them to mobilize their own voters. This form of manipulation of the ideas citizens hear has been dubbed by journalists as *coronelsimo eletrônico* (electronic clientelism)—a high-tech form of the old clientelist networking.

In other ways, technology has improved elite accountability to voters. Electronic voting was adopted nationally a few years after the transition to democracy. The technology, which provides a paper trail, has been effective in eliminating ballot-stuffing, miscounting, and other forms of electoral fraud and incompetence. The creation of an electronic record of voting has also facilitated the work of the National Electoral Court as it investigates cases of attempted fraud around the country.

Social media and politics have mixed in Brazil like in no other country. Brazil maintains the largest population of Facebook and Twitter users outside of the United States. These social media played a fundamental role in the protests that affected 430 cities throughout the country in June 2013. Organizers coordinated their planning and selected timing and location using social media. Like protests such as the various Occupy movement events, these events were leaderless and non-partisan with various groups employing competing Twitter feeds and Facebook pages to take ownership of the protests. The technological inflections of the protests fit neatly with the youthful element of largely educated, middle-class, white Brazilians that formed much of the vanguard. These participants used social media not only to coordinate the events themselves but also to gather video footage and share tips on dealing with tear gas (vinegar was a key ingredient of the anti-dote). Rousseff's impeachment and the continuing corruption investigations have galvanized protests that seem to grow and spread with each major revelation of wrongdoing. Technology has helped coordinate these protests, but it is only with the salience of corruption that the politics of these movements has become more focused on enhancing the accountability of the political class.

Brazil has the world's fastest rate of Internet user growth. The government, through its efforts to deepen the quality of education through modified curricula and the use of standardized tests to identify schools in need, has redoubled its efforts to expand Internet access and computer literacy to the poorest Brazilians. At the same time, the federal government and the states and many cities have made ample use of the Internet to disseminate information and interact with their citizens, especially through social policies in health care, poverty alleviation, and pensions. Brazil presently has perhaps the most transparent system of access to data on government expenditures and policies than any Latin American country. And recent freedom of information legislation has legally empowered regular citizens to open up access to government data even further.

Where Do You Stand?

Supporters of "coalitional presidentialism" see the Brazilian political system as progressively more governable. Do you agree?

Are strong parties necessary in order to make civil societal groups in Brazil more influential in policy-making?

BRAZILIAN POLITICS IN TRANSITION

SECTION

5

Political Challenges and Changing Agendas

During the Brazilian winter (the North American summer) of 2016, as the world became transfixed on the Olympic Summer Games, the Senate was preparing to convict President Dilma Rousseff of "crimes of responsibility" for her mismanagement of the federal budget. During the same weeks, Marcelo Odebrecht, the scion of one of the most powerful business families in Brazil, was preparing his plea-bargained testimony to federal prosecutors as part of the *Lava Jato* investigation. After being sentenced to nineteen years in federal prison, Odebrecht was prepared to tell all about a decades-old system of bribery, kickbacks in public procurement, and how his own company,

Focus Questions ?

- What are some of the legacies of Brazil's struggles with corruption for the country's democracy?

- Is Brazil prepared to be considered a global power?

Odebrecht, participated for years in a cartel of some thirteen corrupt companies. Many of the very politicians who had voted for Rousseff's impeachment in the Chamber and many who were trying her in the Senate had prominent roles in Odebrecht's tale of corruption and abuse of power. Eventually, both the Olympic Games and the impeachment would reach their conclusion, with the latter dissolving a presidency. By contrast, *Lava Jato* has continued, and in its wake, it has revealed far more serious crimes than those that led to Rousseff's dismissal. The uncovering of massive corruption in Brazilian politics by constitutionally-protected investigatory and prosecutorial bodies is reshaping the country's democracy. To illustrate how fundamental these revelations are, the press dubbed the release of the testimony of 77 Odebrecht executives in 2017 as simply "The End of the World." The release implicated most of the political class, from President Temer downward. Later, Temer himself was caught on audiotape playing a role in a bribe. Calls for his impeachment and new elections resonated loudly soon afterward.

The causes of this level of systemic corruption are deeply imbedded in the nature of policy-making and political coalition-formation. The Brazilian state has long had "pockets of efficiency" such as Petrobras and BNDES, but even these agents of the state have long been connected to the political class through formal and informal channels. Political clientelism and Fernando Henrique Cardoso's concept of "bureaucratic rings" describe well the nature of exchange of political favors, patronage, and campaign finance that have undermined the responsiveness of Brazilian representatives to the voters and have made them more keen to follow their own individual and group interests. The injection of private interests—and few sectors of the private market are more powerful in Brazil than the largest construction companies, like Odebrecht—explains the extensive nature of the graft and why it could be hidden for so long. Both state and private interests were in on it and many made millions from it.

Political institutions also reinforced these tendencies. The open-list electoral system creates strong incentives for politicians to cultivate personal votes. The lack of ideological cohesion and internal organizational discipline causes party leaders to rely on the dispensation of patronage to rank-and-file members to secure their votes. Party leaders and presidents have, during the democratic period, bargained continually to craft alliances based on promises of patronage. Budgetary allotments were only the visible tip of the iceberg. The systemic graft represented in the *mensalão* and *Lava Jato* scandals are the submerged part of the iceberg that observers have only gleaned through what prosecutors and the Public Ministry have been able to show the public in recent years. Some of the accused have revealed in stunning detail through plea-bargained testimony how such systemic corruption was central, not marginal, to how the most important business of the congress and the presidency has been done.

The lack of accountability and democratic responsiveness that the corruption scandals and Rousseff's impeachment reveal, map onto the larger socio-economic inequalities that are evident in Brazil. Although the most recent phase of economic and social development in Brazil under the presidencies of Lula and Rousseff expanded the household incomes of the poorest and somewhat reduced wealth inequalities, the slowdown of the economy, rising unemployment, and continued political instability risk overshadowing this positive track record in recent years. The gains achieved through *Bolsa Família* and more equitable access to health care and public education may be reversed as the Temer government scales back welfare policy to address yawning deficits and rising public debt.

Even if the economy stabilizes, the environmental limits of Brazil's economic growth model present other structural concerns. The fact that many of Brazil's exports are still extractive (such as iron ore and lumber), or agricultural commodities (such as soy), place ever more pressure on the country's ecology. Deforestation of the Amazon and international climate change are intricately linked. A key issue is whether Brazil can help preserve the rain forest and reduce its own production of greenhouse gases. These issues of global importance, however, have not received the attention they merit by any of the Brazilian governments of the democratic period.

It is difficult to imagine reforms of the state, the economy, and welfare, or improved environmental regulations without first reorienting the political class in the wake of corruption scandals. Fortunately, Brazilian democracy is reinforced by powerful accountability mechanisms in the judiciary, the Public Ministry, and the Federal Police. Critics have charged, with some justification, that these entities often go too far with preventive detention, search and seize operations, and violations of privacy by the frequent use of wire-tapping. Supporters note that Brazilian democracy is in crisis and defend these abuses as a small price to pay for rooting out corrupt politicians and bureaucrats. Judging from the record of the earlier *mensalão* scandal that eventually led to trials and imprisonment of top government officials eight years after the initial revelations, the *Lava Jato* investigations will take a long time. In the interim, voters may begin to reject the same old political faces and parties in favor of antisystem and populist candidates who are untarnished by previous involvement. The result may be "cleaner" candidates but less experienced ones with agendas that may make the political system less governable.

Brazilian democracy might succumb to the same trend of antisystem and populist politics seen elsewhere, including in the United States, France, and increasingly in Germany. Most Brazilian voters are poor and they already feel isolated from politics and the fruits of economic development. For many, this sense of disengagement has turned into open doubt about the utility of democracy itself. Annual polls continue to show that Brazilians have one of the weakest levels of support for democracy in Latin America.

Although Brazil is one of the world's key platforms for agricultural production and manufacturing, Brazilian firms and workers (not to mention the public sector) struggle to become competitive in a rapidly changing global marketplace. Brazilian exports may yet improve as demand for natural resource exports recovers, but a return to an unsustainable commodity boom as the basis for growth would be a mistake. This model of growth cannot guarantee employment, equity, or environmental sustainability.

As globalization and democratization have made Brazilian politics less predictable, older questions about what it means to be Brazilian have reemerged. Brazil highlights the point made in the Introduction that political identities are often reshaped in changed circumstances. What it means to be Brazilian has become a more complex question. While democracy has given ordinary Brazilians more of a voice, they have become active mostly on local issues, not at the national level. Women, nongovernmental organizations, Catholics, Pentecostals, blacks, landless peasants, and residents of *favelas* have all organized in recent years around social and cultural issues. As anticorruption protests continue, these various local- and issue-based movements may come together to call for greater accountability of the political system.

Brazilians might also unite behind a renewed commitment to having Brazil pursue its own independent foreign policy in the world. Under Lula, Brazil pursued a policy of "benign restraint" of the United States, which included opposing the United States on issues such as the war in Iraq, although it cooperated with Washington in the war against terrorism and regional integration. Under Rousseff, Brazil pursued a less conflictual policy that focused more on access to natural resources and foreign markets. But the presidency of Donald Trump in the United States may cause Brazil to become more assertive. It is not clear if that will be in response to a more aggressive and nationalist American foreign policy in Latin America or in reaction to a vacuum of leadership left by a more isolationist Washington, D.C.

Is Demography Destiny?

Many of those protesting corruption on the streets of Brazil's largest cities belong to a generation of young people in their late teens and twenties that has no memory of the dictatorship of the 1964–1985 period and the hyperinflation of the late 1980s and early 1990s. They have only known a Brazil with an established democracy, abundant resources in which perennial problems of poverty, inequality, and poor governance are the key challenges facing public policy. This clash of youthful expectations and lingering problems is at the center of the protests. With the doubling of the national population of university students over the past decade, young Brazilians, frustrated with corruption and a tightening labor market, have taken matters into their own hands by using social media to coordinate sustained contentious movements.

Young Brazilians have proven to be far from apathetic about politics. They vote and mobilize often, though the degree of engagement is a function of the level of education with the college educated acting most consistently. Access to technology and available time are two other factors that facilitate the activism of middle-class youth. Although college students do not often feel the problems of workers and informal sector employees because they tend not to use public health care and other government services, they do use public transport. This is one reason why a sudden spike in transport costs sparked the protests of 2013. Reactions to systemic corruption have galvanized Brazilians across race, class, and geographic boundaries.

Demographically, Brazil remains a young country that is not aging as rapidly overall as countries such as China or Japan. The Brazilian pension system, for example, remains on a sound demographic footing. Improvements in educational quality and access mean that workers will be more productive over time. If these benefits are distributed more equally to include more women and Afro-Brazilians, they promise to transform society over the long term.

Brazilian Politics in Comparative Perspective

The most important lesson that Brazil offers for the study of comparative politics is that fragmented polities threaten democracy, social development, and nation building. The Brazilian political order is fragmented on several levels. The central state is fragmented by conflicts between the executive and the legislature, divided alliances and self-interested politicians in congress, decentralized government, pockets of efficient and professional state agencies and others that are open to graft and bureaucratic rings. Political parties are fragmented by clientelism and electoral rules that create incentives for politicians and voters to ignore party labels. Finally, civil society itself is fragmented into numerous, often conflictual, organizations, interest groups, professional associations, social movements, churches, and, most important, social classes and ethnic identities.

In some socioeconomically fragmented societies, such as the United States and India, institutions have been more successful in bridging the gap between individualistic pursuits and the demand of people for good government. Political parties, parliaments, and informal associations strengthen democracy in these countries. Where these institutions are faulty, as they are in Brazil, fragmentation exacerbates the weakness of the state and the society.

A weak state deepens the citizenry's sense that all politics is corrupt. Police brutality, human rights violations, judicial incompetence, and the unresponsiveness of bureaucratic agencies further discourage citizens from political participation. These problems reinforce the importance of creating systems of accountability. Unfortunately, the English word *accountability* has no counterpart in either Portuguese or Spanish. Given Brazil's (and Latin America's) long history of oligarchical rule and social exclusion, the notion of making elites accountable to the people is so alien that the languages of the region lack the required vocabulary. Systems of accountability must be built from the ground up; they must be nurtured in local government and in community organizations, and then in the governments of states and the central state. The judiciary, political parties, the media, and organizations of civil society must be able to play enforcement and watchdog roles. These are the building blocks of accountability that are the fulcrum of democracy. As Brazil works through the revelations of massive corruption scandals over the next few years, its democracy may become stronger as long as these accountability mechanisms remain constitutionally protected and effective.

Without a system of elite accountability, representation of the citizenry is impossible. In particular, the poor depend on elected officials to find solutions to their problems. Brazilian politicians have shown that through demagoguery and personalism, they can be elected. But being elected is not the same as representing a constituency. For this to occur, institutions must make political elites responsive and accountable to the people who elected them.

The notable successes of social policy under Cardoso, Lula, and Rousseff have made substantial changes in the lives of millions of poor Brazilians, but sustaining these efforts requires great political unity. Collective identities, by definition, require mechanisms that forge mutual understandings among groups of people. Fractured societies turn to age-old ethnic identities that can produce destructive, internecine conflict, as the India–Pakistan and Nigerian experiences demonstrate. In Brazil, such extreme conflict has been avoided, but the divisive effects of a fragmented polity on collective identities are serious nonetheless. Divided by class, poor Brazilians continue to feel that politics holds no solutions for them, so they fail to mobilize for their rights. Blacks, women, and indigenous peoples share many interests. Yet few national organizations have been able to assemble a coalition of interest groups to change destructive business practices. Finally, all Brazilians (not to mention people the world over) are harmed by the clearing of rain forests, pollution of rivers and lakes, and destruction of species; yet the major political parties and congress seem incapable of addressing these issues consistently.

Perhaps the most serious effect of political fragmentation on Brazil has involved the struggle to defend the country's interests in an increasingly competitive, global marketplace. While globalization forces all countries, and particularly developing countries, to adapt to new technology, ideas, and economic interests, it also provides states with the opportunity to attract investment. Given the weakness of the Brazilian state, the social dislocation produced by industrial restructuring (such as unemployment), and the current instability of the international investment climate, Brazil maintains only an ambiguous vision of its role in the global capitalist order. Although Brazilian business, some unions, and key political leaders speak of the need to defend Brazil's interests in the international political economy, the country has few coherent strategies. But dealing with these issues requires a consistent policy created by a political leadership with clear ideas about the interests of the country. In Brazil's fragmented polity, developing such strategies is difficult.

In the world since September 11, 2001, issues of security outpaced matters of equity and development. The Lula and Rousseff governments proved that a sustained commitment to social policy can reduce both poverty and inequality. But the end of the PT presidencies during a sharp economic and political crisis challenges the Temer government and its successor with finding sustainable solutions to economic malaise and structural change without losing sight of Brazil's social and environmental problems. If the political system can rid itself of erstwhile practices of clientelism and corruption while addressing these problems, Brazil can be an influential model for other developing countries. As a large and resource-rich country, Brazil presents a useful case for comparison with other big developing countries such as Mexico, Russia, India, and China that are dealing with similar challenges.

As a transitional democracy, Brazil can provide insights into governance systems. As a negative example, Brazil's ongoing experiment with presidentialism, multiparty democracy, and open-list PR may well confirm the superiority of alternative parliamentary systems in India and Germany or presidentialism in France and the United States. As a positive example, Brazil's ability to keep a diverse country united through trying economic times has much to teach Russia and Nigeria, since these countries too are weighed down by the dual challenges of economic reform and nation building.

Within Latin America, Brazil continues to consolidate its position as the preeminent economy of the region. Brazil exercises regional leadership on commercial questions, and with its continued dominance of the Amazon basin, the country commands the world's attention on environmental issues in the developing world. Brazil's experiences with balancing the exigencies of neoliberal economic adjustment with the sociopolitical realities of poverty will keep it at center stage. Brazil may not be "the country of the future," but it is a country with a future. None of the problems of Brazilian politics and social development are immune to improvement. If political reform is consolidated in the next few years, the groundwork will have been laid for transforming Brazil into a country that deserves the respect of the world.

Where Do You Stand?

Should Brazil exert its influence in the world even if it means growing conflicts with the United States?

Do you think that Brazil is "the country of the future"?

Chapter Summary

Brazil is a country of continental size with a long history of building a national state and, in recent decades, a more democratic system of government. Both processes have been shaped at different points by presidents such as Vargas, Cardoso, and Lula. Central characteristics of Brazilian politics such as clientelism, personalism, and corporatism have endured and adapted to the modernization of the state and the economy. Brazilian democracy has survived and prospered since 1985, and it now does so in the context of heightened expectations concerning development and its role in the world.

During the past three decades, Brazil has emerged from being an inward-oriented industrializer dependent on the state and foreign credit to becoming a market-oriented industrialized country that has achieved an enviable new competitive position in the world. Old problems of inflation and runaway government debt have been brought under control, though public debt has increased in recent years.

Persistent social inequalities and poverty have improved due to more efficiently targeted social policies. The ecological and land-ownership dimensions of development will require reform to improve the quality of life for more of Brazil's people. The economy is now more interconnected with other markets than at any other time in the country's history.

The Brazilian state is a mixture of professionalism and clientelism, and both of these dimensions have persisted even as the country has democratized and developed. Brazilian democracy has strengthened law enforcement as the prosecutorial, oversight, and investigative functions of the state have become more adept at detecting corruption. The historical injection of private interests into public policy coupled with improved oversight mechanisms have enhanced political accountability by revealing unprecedented levels of official and private-sector corruption in recent years. Brazilian democracy will be challenged by how well the judiciary and the political class continue to bring the guilty to justice and remove impunity from those who have it enjoyed it far too long.

The Brazilian political system suffers from weak partisan identities among voters, low discipline within political parties, and inconsistent relations between the presidency and congress. The open-list PR electoral system makes these tendencies worse, and further confuses voters. At the same time, civil society remains actively engaged in politics, often in sustained and organized ways. Despite Dilma Rousseff's difficulties in maintaining a congressional coalition, her impeachment and the ascendance of former vice president Michel Temer to the presidency have not removed the tendency to rely on ad hoc alliances with congress. The continuity of mass protests and increasing pressure from a more participatory citizenry fired up by almost-daily revelations of corruption will continue to exert pressure on Temer's fiscal and political reforms.

If the Temer government is able to survive corruption investigations, it may succeed in keeping the political system governable before the next presidential election in 2018. If commodity prices improve, growth rates increase, and the unemployment rate falls, Brazil may return to making progress on its social deficits. Much depends on the quality of the country's new leadership in the next few years. The passing of former giants of Brazilian politics such as Lula and Cardoso, may open new opportunities for younger leaders from the PT, the PSDB, and other established parties. These leaders' most important ally will be the Brazilian people, who will continue to demand cleaner government with a stronger interest in reform.

Key Terms

abertura
bureaucratic authoritarianism (BA)
bureaucratic rings
clientelism
developmentalism
export-led growth
favelas

import substitution industrialization (ISI)
informal economy
interventionist
interventores
legitimacy
moderating power *(poder moderador)*

nationalism
parastatals
personalist politicians
politics of the governors
proportional representation (PR)
state corporatism
state technocrat

Suggested Readings

Ames, Barry. *The Deadlock of Democracy in Brazil: Interests, Identities, and Institutions in Comparative Politics.* Ann Arbor: University of Michigan Press, 2001.

Hochstetler, Kathryn, and Margaret Keck. *Greening Brazil: Environmental Activism in State and Society.* Durham, NC: Duke University Press, 2007.

Hunter, Wendy. *The Transformation of the Workers' Party in Brazil, 1989–2009.* New York: Cambridge University Press, 2010.

Kingstone, Peter R., and Timothy J. Power, eds. *Democratic Brazil Revisited.* Pittsburgh: University of Pittsburgh Press, 2008.

Mainwaring, Scott. *Rethinking Party Systems in the Third Wave of Democratization: The Case of Brazil.* Stanford, CA: Stanford University Press, 1999.

Montero, Alfred P. *Brazil: Reversal of Fortune.* Cambridge, UK: Polity Press, 2014.

Samuels, David J. *Ambition, Federalism, and Legislative Politics in Brazil.* New York: Cambridge University Press, 2003.

Skidmore, Thomas E. *The Politics of Military Rule in Brazil, 1964–85.* New York: Oxford University Press, 1988.

Stepan, Alfred. *Rethinking Military Politics: Brazil and the Southern Cone.* Princeton, NJ: Princeton University Press, 1988.

Weyland, Kurt. *Democracy Without Equity: Failures of Reform in Brazil.* Pittsburgh: University of Pittsburgh Press, 1996.

Suggested Websites

LANIC database, University of Texas—Austin, Brazil
Resource page
lanic.utexas.edu/la/brazil/

YouTube, President Lula da Silva's 2007 address at Davos
http://www.youtube.com/watch?v=RqsDMU3ASgo

SciELO Brazil, Searchable Database of Full-Text Articles
on Brazil
www.scielo.br

National Development Bank of Brazil, Searchable
Database of Documents on Brazilian Economy and
Development (many in English)
**http://www.bndes.gov.br/SiteBNDES/bndes
/bndes_en/**

10 Mexico

Halbert Jones

Official Name: United Mexican States (Estados Unidos Mexicanos)

Location: Southern North America

Capital City: Mexico City

Population (2016): 123.2 million

Size: 1,972,550 sq. km.; slightly less than three times the size of Texas

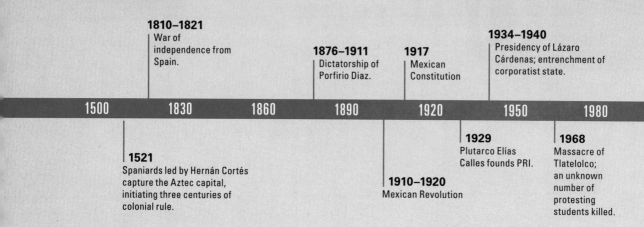

1810–1821
War of independence from Spain.

1876–1911
Dictatorship of Porfirio Diaz.

1917
Mexican Constitution

1934–1940
Presidency of Lázaro Cárdenas; entrenchment of corporatist state.

| 1500 | 1830 | 1860 | 1890 | 1920 | 1950 | 1980 |

1521
Spaniards led by Hernán Cortés capture the Aztec capital, initiating three centuries of colonial rule.

1910–1920
Mexican Revolution

1929
Plutarco Elías Calles founds PRI.

1968
Massacre of Tlatelolco; an unknown number of protesting students killed.

THE MAKING OF THE MODERN MEXICAN STATE

▼ Focus Questions

- In what ways have the critical junctures of Mexican history grown out of the country's relations with other countries, especially the United States?

- What factors contributed to Mexico's democratic transition at the end of the twentieth century?

Politics in Action

During the summer of 2016, Mexican President Enrique Peña Nieto faced a dilemma. Across the border in the United States, a presidential election was approaching, and the candidates of the two major U.S. political parties were adopting positions that caused growing concern in Mexico. Seeking to appeal to voters who believed that American jobs were being lost to other countries, Democrat Hillary Clinton and Republican Donald Trump both took a critical stance toward the North American Free Trade Agreement (NAFTA), a pact that had created close links between the U.S. and Mexican economies. Trump was especially hostile to the accord, calling it a "disaster" and the "worst trade deal ever signed in the history of our country." For Mexican leaders who had spent a quarter-century pursuing an economic strategy based largely upon the access to the U.S. market provided by NAFTA, Trump's insistence that he would demand "total renegotiation" of the agreement caused considerable alarm.

Even more upsetting to many Mexicans was the derogatory language used by candidate Trump when referring to their country and its people. The real estate mogul had made immigration control and the fortification of the Mexico–U.S. border central themes of his campaign. He alleged that Mexican immigrants were "bringing drugs" and "bringing crime" into the United States, and he pledged that he would force Mexico to pay for the construction of a "beautiful wall" between the two countries. Such statements made the Republican nominee a reviled figure in Mexico—paper-mache piñatas in his image that could be beaten with sticks at

Timeline

1982 — Market reformers come to power in PRI.

1988 — Carlos Salinas is elected amid charges of fraud.

1997 — Opposition parties advance nationwide; PRI loses absolute majority in congress for first time in its history.

2009 — PRI makes major gains in congressional elections as the country faces a wave of drug-related violence.

1985 1990 1995 2000 2005 2010 2020

1978–1982 — State-led development reaches peak with petroleum boom and bust.

1989 — First governorship is won by an opposition party.

1994 — NAFTA goes into effect; uprising in Chiapas; Colosio assassinated.

2000 — PRI loses presidency; Vicente Fox of PAN becomes president, but without majority support in congress.

2006 — Felipe Calderón of PAN takes office as president; no party has a majority of seats in congress.

2012 — Enrique Peña Nieto of the PRI elected to the presidency; his administration pursues an ambitious reform program.

children's parties had become a popular item—but the Mexican government had to confront the possibility that Donald Trump might be the next president of the United States. President Peña Nieto therefore invited both U.S. candidates to visit Mexico to begin a dialogue prior to the elections in November. Trump accepted, landing in Mexico City on August 31, 2016.

From the Mexican perspective, the meeting between Peña Nieto and Trump was not a success. Much of the Mexican public was outraged not just that their president had received such an offensive visitor but also that he had boosted Trump's bid for the presidency by giving him the opportunity to meet with a foreign leader. There was a widespread feeling, too, that Peña Nieto had not defended Mexico's interests or upheld the country's dignity sufficiently forcefully and effectively in his meeting with Trump. Indeed, immediately after his visit to Mexico, the Republican candidate traveled on to a campaign stop in Arizona, where he reiterated his hard line on immigration and the border wall. The negative reaction in Mexico was so strong that the cabinet minister viewed as responsible for arranging the visit, Treasury Secretary Luis Videgaray, was forced to resign.

When Donald Trump unexpectedly won the U.S. presidency in November, there were important reverberations in Mexico. The value of the Mexican peso—which had fluctuated throughout the campaign based on the markets' assessment of Trump's prospects—immediately fell by 11 percent. And before Trump took office in January 2017, Peña Nieto brought Videgaray back to the cabinet, this time as foreign secretary, in the hope that he would be able to engage productively with the new U.S. administration. Nonetheless, Peña Nieto found it necessary to cancel a visit to Washington that would have made him one of the first foreign leaders to meet with the new president after Trump reiterated his commitment to the building of a border wall that would be paid for by Mexico.

The difficulties faced by Peña Nieto in his early dealings with Donald Trump reflect both the fundamental importance to Mexico of its relationship with the United States and some of the significant changes that have taken place in Mexican politics in recent decades. In light of the strong influence that the United States has historically exercised on Mexico, Peña Nieto must have felt he had little choice but

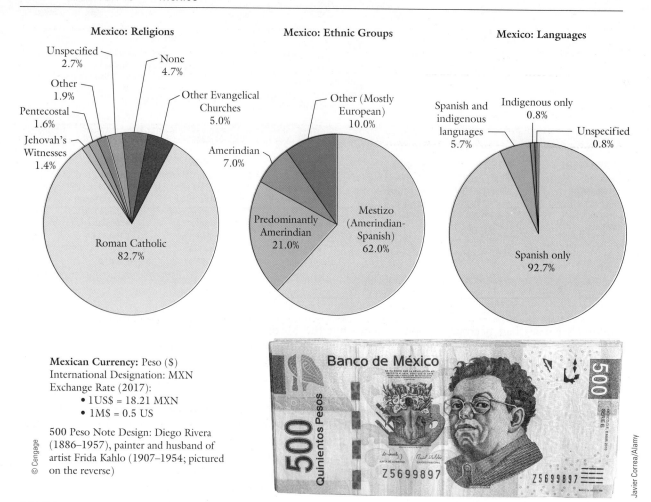

FIGURE 10.1 **The Mexican Nation at a Glance**

to seek to engage with Trump, despite—or, indeed, precisely because of—the candidate's troubling views on issues important to his country. And while in an earlier age the first instinct of a Mexican leader might have been to strike a nationalist pose in response to hostility or criticism from the United States, the partnership that has developed between the two countries since NAFTA came into force in 1994 has arguably made it more difficult for Mexico to adopt a confrontational stance towards Washington, as to do so might jeopardize political and economic links that have become much more extensive over the past quarter-century.

At the same time, the negative reaction that Peña Nieto faced from within Mexico is something that would not have been expected a generation ago, when the country's political landscape was dominated by a single party, and overt criticism of the president was rare. Today, Mexico is a multiparty democracy with a free press and a citizenry that is able to engage in politics in a variety of ways. Opposition parties, investigative journalists, and the general public can and do voice their displeasure with the performance of the government. As the country faces new uncertainties in its relationship with the United States, Mexican leaders must therefore tread carefully to safeguard their national interests while maintaining the support of the Mexican people. This will no doubt be among the greatest challenges facing not just President Peña Nieto, but

Table 10.1	Political Organization
Political System	Federal republic
Regime History	Democratic since 1946 with periods of military authoritarianism, especially 1964–1985.
Regime History	Current constitution in force since 1917
Administrative Structure	Federal system with thirty-one states and a capital city (Mexico City)
Executive	President, elected by direct election with a 6-year term of office; reelection not permitted
Legislature	Bicameral Congress. Senate (upper house) and Chamber of Deputies (lower house); elections held every three years. There are 128 senators: 3 from each of the thirty-one states, 3 from the capital city, and 32 elected nationally by proportional representation for six-year terms. The 500 members of the Chamber of Deputies are elected for three-year terms from 300 electoral districts, 300 by simple majority vote, and 200 by proportional representation.
Judiciary	Independent federal and state court system headed by a Supreme Court with eleven justices appointed by the president and approved by the Senate.
Party System	Multiparty system. One-party dominant (Institutional Revolutionary Party) system from 1929 until 2000. Major parties: National Action Party, Institutional Revolutionary Party, Party of the Democratic Revolution, and National Regeneration Movement.

also his successor, due to be chosen in federal elections in 2018, in a contest in which a constitutional prohibition on reelection will make the incumbent ineligible to stand. (See Figure 10.1 and Table 10.1.)

Geographic Setting

Mexico includes coastal plains, high plateaus, fertile valleys, rain forests, and deserts within an area slightly less than three times the size of Texas. Two imposing mountain ranges run the length of Mexico: the Sierra Madre Occidental to the west and the Sierra Madre Oriental to the east. Mexico's geography has made communication and transportation between regions difficult and infrastructure expensive. Mountainous terrain limits large-scale commercial agriculture to irrigated fields in the north, while the center and south produce a wide variety of crops on small farms. The country is rich in oil, silver, and other natural resources, but it has long struggled to manage those resources wisely. Mexico is the second-largest nation in Latin America after Portuguese-speaking Brazil in terms of population and the most populous Spanish-speaking nation in the world. Sixty percent of the population is *mestizo,* or people of mixed indigenous and Spanish ancestry. About 30 percent of the population claims descent from Mexico's original inhabitants, although only 6.5 percent speak an indigenous language. The largest **indigenous groups** are the Maya in the south and the Nahua in the central regions, with well over 1 million members each. Although Mexicans take great pride in their nation's pre-Columbian heritage, issues of race and class divide society.

mestizo

A person of mixed white, indigenous, and sometimes African descent.

indigenous groups

Population descended from the original inhabitants of the Americas, present prior to the Spanish Conquest.

Mexico became a largely urban country in the second half of the twentieth century, and Mexico City is one of the world's largest metropolitan areas, with about 20 million inhabitants. Migration both within and beyond Mexico's borders has become a major issue. Greater economic opportunities in the industrial cities of the north lead many women and men to seek work there in the *maquiladoras*, or assembly industries. Many job seekers continue on to the United States. On Mexico's southern border, many thousands of Central Americans look for better prospects in Mexico and beyond.

maquiladoras

Factories that produce goods for export, often located along the Mexico–U.S. border.

Critical Junctures

Independence, Instability, and Dictatorship (1810–1910)

After a small band of Spanish forces led by Hernán Cortés toppled the Aztec Empire in 1521, Spain ruled Mexico for three centuries. Colonial policy was designed to extract wealth from New Spain, as the territory was known, ensuring that economic benefits flowed to the mother country.

caudillos

Charismatic populist leaders, usually with a military background, who use patronage and draw upon personal loyalties to dominate a region or a nation.

In 1810, a parish priest in central Mexico named Miguel Hidalgo began the first of a series of wars for independence. Although independence was gained in 1821, Mexico struggled to create a stable government for decades afterward. Liberals and conservatives, monarchists and republicans, and federalists and centralists were all engaged in the battle to shape the new nation's future. Between 1833 and 1855, thirty-six presidential administrations came to power, and in many regions, local strongmen, or *caudillos*, exercised more authority than the national government.

Mexico

© Cengage

During this chaotic period, Mexico lost half of its territory. Central America rejected rule from Mexico City in 1823, and the northern territory of Texas won independence in 1836. After Texas became a U.S. state in 1845, a border dispute led the United States to declare war on Mexico in 1846. U.S. forces invaded the country and occupied Mexico City. An 1848 treaty recognized the loss of Texas and gave the United States title to what later became the states of New Mexico, Utah, Nevada, Arizona, California, and part of Colorado for about $18 million, leaving a legacy of deep resentment toward the United States.

After the war, liberals and conservatives continued their struggle over issues of political and economic order. The Constitution of 1857 incorporated many of the goals of the liberals, such as a somewhat democratic government, a bill of rights, and limitations on the power of the Roman Catholic Church. In 1861, Spain, Great Britain, and France occupied Veracruz to collect debts owed by Mexico. The French army continued on to Mexico City, where it installed a European prince as the Emperor Maximilian (1864–1867). Conservatives welcomed this respite from liberal rule. Benito Juárez returned to the presidency in 1867 after defeating and executing Maximilian. Juárez is still hailed in Mexico today as an early proponent of more democratic government.

In 1876, a popular retired general named Porfirio Díaz came to power. He established a dictatorship—known as the *Porfiriato*—that lasted thirty-four years and was at first welcomed by many because it brought sustained stability to the country.

Díaz imposed an authoritarian system to create political order and economic progress. Over time, he relied increasingly on a small clique of advisers, known as *científicos* (scientists), who wanted to adopt European technologies and values to modernize the country. Díaz and the *científicos* encouraged foreign investment and presided over a

GLOBAL CONNECTION

Conquest or Encounter?

The year 1519, when the Spanish conqueror Hernán Cortés arrived on the shores of the Yucatán Peninsula, is often considered the starting point of Mexican political history. The land that was to become Mexico was home to extensive and complex indigenous civilizations that were advanced in agriculture, architecture, and political and economic organization. By 1519, diverse groups had fallen under the power of the militaristic Aztec Empire, which extended throughout what is today central and southern Mexico.

Cortés and the colonial masters who came after him subjected indigenous groups to forced labor; robbed them of gold, silver, and land; and introduced flora and fauna from Europe that destroyed long-existing ecosystems. They also brought alien forms of property rights and authority relationships, a religion that viewed indigenous practices as the devil's work, and an economy based on mining and cattle—all of which soon overwhelmed existing structures of social and economic organization. Within a century, wars, exploitation, and the introduction of European diseases reduced the indigenous population from an estimated 25 million to 1 million or fewer. Even so, the Spanish never constituted more than a small percentage of the total

population, and massive racial mixing among the indigenous groups, Europeans, and to a lesser extent Africans produced a new *raza*, or *mestizo* race.

What does it mean to be Mexican? Is one the conquered or the conqueror? While celebrating indigenous achievements in food, culture, the arts, and ancient civilization, middle-class Mexico has the contradictory sense that to be "Indian" nowadays is to be backward. But perhaps the situation is changing, with the upsurge of indigenous movements from both the grassroots and the international level striving to promote ethnic pride, defend rights, and foster the teaching of Indian languages.

The collision of two worlds still resonates. Is Mexico colonial or modern? Third or First World? Southern or Northern? Is the United States an ally or a conqueror? Many Mexicans at once welcome and fear full integration into the global economy, asking themselves: Is globalization a new form of conquest?

MAKING CONNECTIONS How does Mexico's experience as a colony of Spain compare with the history of other countries that once were part of European empires?

period of rapid growth and development. Social tensions grew, however, as many poorer Mexicans found themselves forced off their lands, and as many members of the middle and upper classes came to resent the Porfirians' monopoly on political power.

The Mexican Revolution and the Sonoran Dynasty (1910–1934)

The most formative event in the country's modern history was the Revolution of 1910, which ended the *Porfiriato* and was the first great social revolution of the twentieth century. The revolution was fought by a variety of forces for a variety of reasons, which made the consolidation of power that followed as significant as the revolution itself.

Díaz had promised an open election for president, and in 1910, Francisco Madero presented himself as a candidate. Madero and his reform-minded allies hoped that a new class of politically ambitious citizens would move into positions of power. When this opposition swelled, Díaz tried to repress growing dissent, but the clamor for change forced him into exile. Madero was elected in 1911, but he was soon using the military to put down revolts by reformers and reactionaries alike. When Madero was assassinated during a **coup d'état** in 1913, political order collapsed.

At the same time that middle-class reformers struggled to displace Díaz, a peasant revolt that focused on land claims erupted in central and southern regions. This revolt had roots in legislation that made it easy for wealthy landowners and ranchers to claim the lands of peasant villagers. Villagers joined forces under a variety of local leaders. The most famous was Emiliano Zapata. His manifesto, the Plan de Ayala, became the cornerstone of the radical agrarian reform that became part of the Constitution of 1917.

In the north, the governor of Coahuila, Venustiano Carranza, placed himself at the head of an army that pledged to restore constitutional governance after Madero's murder, while Francisco (Pancho) Villa's forces combined military maneuvers with banditry, looting, and warlordism. In 1916, troops from the United States entered Mexico to punish Villa for an attack on U.S. territory. The presence of U.S. troops on Mexican soil resulted in increased hostility toward the United States.

The Constitution of 1917 was forged out of the diverse and often conflicting interests of the various factions that arose during the 1910 Revolution. It established a formal set of political institutions and guaranteed citizens a range of progressive social and economic rights: agrarian reform, social security, the right to organize in unions, a minimum wage, an eight-hour workday, profit sharing for workers, a secular public education system, and universal male suffrage. Despite these socially advanced provisions, the constitution did not provide suffrage for women, who had to wait until 1953 to vote in local elections and 1958 to vote in national elections. To limit the power of foreign investors, restrictions were placed on the ability of non-Mexicans to own land or exploit natural resources. Numerous articles severely limited the power of the Catholic Church, long a target of liberals who wanted Mexico to be a secular state. Despite such noble sentiments, violence continued as competing leaders sought to assert power and displace their rivals.

Power was gradually consolidated in the hands of a group of revolutionary leaders from the north of the country. Known as the Sonoran Dynasty, after their home state of Sonora, these leaders were committed to a capitalist model of economic development. Eventually, one of the Sonorans, Plutarco Elías Calles, emerged as the *jefe máximo,* or supreme leader. After his presidential term (1924–1928), Calles managed to select and dominate his successors from 1929 to 1934.

In 1929, Calles brought together many of the most powerful contenders for leadership to create a political party. The bargain he offered was simple: Contenders for power would accommodate each other's interests in the expectation that without

coup d'état

A forceful, extra-constitutional action resulting in the removal of an existing government.

political violence, the country would prosper and they would be able to reap the benefits of even greater power and economic spoils. For the next seven decades, Calles's bargain ensured nonviolent conflict resolution among elites and the uninterrupted rule of the Institutional Revolutionary Party (PRI) in national politics.

PRI elitist

Lázaro Cárdenas, Agrarian Reform, and the Workers (1934–1940)

In 1934, Calles handpicked Lázaro Cárdenas as the official candidate for the presidency. He fully anticipated that Cárdenas would go along with his behind-the-scenes management of the country. To his surprise, Cárdenas executed a virtual coup that established his own supremacy.[1] Even more unexpectedly, Cárdenas mobilized peasants and workers in pursuit of the more radical goals of the revolution. During his administration, more than 49 million acres of land were distributed, nearly twice as much as had been parceled out by all the previous postrevolutionary governments combined. Most of these lands were distributed in the form of *ejidos* (collective land grants) to peasant groups. Recipients of these grants provided an enduring base of support for the government. Cárdenas also encouraged workers to form unions to demand higher wages and better working conditions. In 1938, he wrested the petroleum industry from foreign investors and placed it under government control.

ejido

Land granted by Mexican government to an organized group of peasants.

During the Cárdenas years (1934–1940), the bulk of the Mexican population was incorporated into the political system. Organizations of peasants and workers, middle-class groups, and the military were added to the official party. In addition, Cárdenas's presidency witnessed a great expansion of the role of the state as the government encouraged investment in industrialization, provided credit to agriculture, and created infrastructure.

growth

The Politics of Rapid Development (1940–1982)

In the decades that followed, Cárdenas's successors used the institutions he created to counteract his reforms. Gradually, the PRI developed a huge patronage machine, characterized by extensive chains of personal relationships based on the exchange of favors. These exchange relationships, known as clientelism, became the cement that built loyalty to the PRI and the political system.

This kind of political control reoriented the country's development away from the egalitarian social goals of the 1930s toward a development strategy in which the state actively encouraged industrialization and the accumulation of wealth. Growth rates were high from the 1940s through the 1960s, but protests against the regime's authoritarian tendencies were beginning to arise by 1968, when government forces brutally suppressed a student movement in the capital's Tlatelolco district. Moreover, by the 1970s, Mexico's economic strategy was faltering.

Just as the economy faced a crisis in the mid-1970s, vast new amounts of oil were discovered in the Gulf of Mexico. Soon, extensive public investment programs were fueling rapid growth in virtually every sector of the economy. The boom was short-lived, however. International petroleum prices plunged in the early 1980s, forcing Mexico to default on its national debt in 1982 and plunging the country into a deep economic downturn.

Crisis and Reform (1982–2000)

This crisis led two presidents, Miguel de la Madrid (1982–1988) and Carlos Salinas (1988–1994), to introduce the first major reversal of the country's development strategy since the 1940s. New policies were put in place to limit the government's role in

---

📇 **PROFILE**

Lázaro Cárdenas

As president from 1934 to 1940, Lázaro Cárdenas arguably did more than any other Mexican leader to make possible the longevity of the political system that emerged from the Revolution of 1910. Through his reforms, Cárdenas won the loyalty and admiration of many Mexicans, convincing them of the legitimacy of the revolutionary regime.

Cárdenas was very much a product of the Revolution. Born in 1895 in the small town of Jiquilpan, Michoacán, he was only 15 years old when fighting broke out in 1910. As armed groups marched across west-central Mexico, the young Cárdenas joined the revolutionary forces, leaving behind the printshop where he had been working to support his widowed mother and seven siblings. Thanks to his literacy and penmanship, he received a commission as an officer on the staff of a local commander, and he rose quickly through the ranks. As part of the Constitutionalist Army, Cárdenas served under General Plutarco Elías Calles, a mentor who would later become a rival.

While on campaign, Cárdenas became deeply aware of the hardships endured by Mexico's indigenous and rural populations and of their struggles for land. Later, in the 1920s, as the regional military commander in the country's most important oil-producing zone, he saw how foreign companies disregarded local regulations and flouted Mexican sovereignty. These experiences played a significant role in shaping his political outlook.

After serving as governor of his native state (1928–1932) and in the cabinet as defense minister (1933), Cárdenas was selected by his old patron Calles as the ruling party's presidential candidate in the 1934 elections. After taking office, however, Cárdenas shook off his predecessor's influence and launched wide-ranging reforms. His policies made him unpopular with business leaders, landowners, and social conservatives, but many more Mexicans felt that he was the first president to concern himself with their well-being. Cárdenas also won widespread admiration for his personal honesty and morality.

After stepping down from the presidency, Cárdenas watched with concern as subsequent administrations turned to the right, adopting more conservative policies even as they continued to claim to represent the ideals of the Revolution. The venerable ex-president sought to use his standing within the PRI and in Mexican society to press for more progressive policies. In the early 1960s, for example, he praised Fidel Castro's Cuban Revolution and signaled his support for renewed reform within Mexico. Nonetheless, he ultimately remained loyal to the system he had played such an important role in constructing.

Although Lázaro Cárdenas died in 1970, his name continues to carry great weight. Political leaders—including his son Cuauhtémoc, a founder of the Party of the Democratic Revolution (PRD)—still invoke his legacy, and countless Mexicans identify Cárdenas as the president they admire most.

MAKING CONNECTIONS How would Cárdenas's role in the expropriation of the oil industry and as a staunch defender of national sovereignty be seen as relevant in contemporary political debates in Mexico?

---

the economy and to reduce barriers to international trade. This period marked the beginning of a new effort to integrate Mexico into the global economy. In 1993, President Salinas signed the North American Free Trade Agreement (NAFTA), which committed Mexico, the United States, and Canada to the elimination of trade barriers between them. These economic reforms were a turning point for Mexico and meant that the country's future development would be closely tied to international economic conditions.

After a "lost decade" of stagnant growth following the 1982 default, the economic volatility that continued to afflict the country through much of the 1990s came to be accompanied by worrying signs of political instability. In 1994, a guerrilla movement, the Zapatista Army of National Liberation (EZLN), seized four towns in the southern state of Chiapas. The group demanded land, democracy, indigenous rights, and the immediate repeal of NAFTA. Many citizens throughout the country openly supported the aims of the rebels. Following close on the heels of the rebellion came the assassination of the PRI's presidential candidate, Luis Donaldo Colosio, an event that shocked all citizens and shook the political elite deeply.

With the election of replacement candidate Ernesto Zedillo in August 1994, the PRI remained in power, but these shocks provoked widespread disillusionment and frustration with the political system. At the same time, reforms to the country's electoral processes and institutions made it easier for opposition groups to challenge the ruling party and gave the public greater confidence in the fairness of elections. In 1997, for the first time in modern Mexican history, the PRI lost its majority in the lower house of the national congress. The 2000 election of Vicente Fox as the first non-PRI president in seven decades was the culmination of this electoral revolution.

Since 2000: Mexico as a Multiparty Democracy

After taking office in December 2000, Vicente Fox found it difficult to bring about the changes that he had promised to the Mexican people. Proposals for reform went down to defeat, and the president was subjected to catcalls and heckling when he made his annual reports to the congress. The difficulties faced by Fox as he attempted to implement his ambitious agenda arose in part because he and his administration lacked government experience. However, a bigger problem for the president was that he lacked the compliant congressional majority and the close relationship with his party that his PRI predecessors had enjoyed.

With his legislative agenda stalled, Fox hoped that achievements in international policy would enhance his prestige at home. He was particularly hopeful that a close connection with the U.S. president, George W. Bush, would facilitate important breakthroughs in relations with the United States. The events of September 11, 2001, dramatically changed the outlook, however. The terrorist attacks on the United States led officials in Washington to seek to strengthen border security and to shift much of their attention away from Mexico and Latin America and toward Afghanistan and the Middle East. As a result, Mexican hopes for an agreement under which a greater number of their citizens would legally be able to migrate to and work in the United States were dashed. Thus, Fox found both his domestic and international policy priorities largely blocked.

As Fox's term in office came to a close, his National Action Party (PAN) turned to Felipe Calderón as its candidate in the 2006 presidential election. His main opponent was Andrés Manuel López Obrador of the Party of the Democratic Revolution (PRD). When Calderón won by a small margin, López Obrador refused to concede defeat. This defiant response had the unintended effect of dividing the opposition and allowing Calderón to consolidate his hold on power.

By far the greatest challenge Mexico faced as Calderón took office was the increasing cost of fighting the war on drugs and organized crime. The new president relied on the army and federal police to launch military offensives against drug cartels throughout the country. Calderón secured the support of the United States for his strategy through the Mérida Initiative, which offered U.S. security assistance to Mexico and to Central American countries fighting transnational criminal organizations. The offensive resulted in the apprehension or killing of many leading drug traffickers, but it also touched off a wave of violence that has claimed tens of thousands of lives, damaged the country's image abroad, and undermined the confidence of many Mexicans in the ability of their government to maintain order and assure their safety.

OMAR TORRES/Getty Images

In recent years, Mexican authorities have moved forcefully against the country's drug-trafficking organizations, using the military to pursue cartel kingpins like Joaquín "El Chapo" Guzmán.

In the 2012 presidential election, Mexicans turned to the PRI in the hope that the party that had maintained stability in the country for so many years would be able to control the violence and govern effectively. Voters chose Enrique Peña Nieto, the young former governor of the state of Mexico, over the PRD's López Obrador and Josefina Vázquez Mota of the PAN (the first female presidential candidate nominated by a major party). López Obrador again made allegations of electoral fraud, but in contrast to the situation after the very close election of 2006, official results showed that Peña Nieto had won by a clear margin. Another orderly and peaceful transfer of power between parties, this time from the PAN back to the PRI, took place on December 1, 2012.

The return of the formerly dominant party to the presidency did not amount to a restoration of the old political system, however. Unlike his PRI predecessors, Peña Nieto faced a divided legislature and a citizenry that had become accustomed to questioning presidential authority and to having its say. To overcome the partisan divisions in congress that had created so many problems for Fox and Calderón, Peña Nieto moved quickly to capitalize on his mandate, entering into a "Pact for Mexico" with the major party leaders to press ahead on needed reforms. The agenda included an overhaul of the education system, a revamping of tax policy, and—perhaps most controversially in a country in which Cárdenas's expropriation of the oil industry is remembered as a national triumph—the opening of the energy sector to foreign investment.

Although the Peña Nieto administration was initially largely successful in steering many of its initiatives through the legislative process, it has also faced intense protests and mounting criticism. A dissident faction of the teachers' union has resisted the proposed reform of the education system, and widespread protests against a rise in gasoline prices at the beginning of 2017 reflected a broader dissatisfaction with the government. Allegations of corruption have tarnished the image of the president and his party. Concerns have also resurfaced not just about the persistence in some regions of criminal violence, but also about possible official complicity in it. For example, the 2014 disappearance, under murky circumstances, of forty-three students from Ayotzinapa, in the southern state of Guerrero, generated outrage around the world. The inability, or unwillingness, of federal investigators to offer a credible resolution to the case left many Mexicans deeply disillusioned. Against this difficult backdrop, the election in 2016 of a U.S. president who has pledged to build a wall on the Mexican border, and threatened to tear up a free trade agreement that is vital to the Mexican economy, represented a daunting additional challenge for President Peña Nieto as he entered his final months in office.

The Four Themes and Mexico

Mexico in a Globalized World of States

Mexico's history has been deeply marked by its place in the world economy, its interactions with foreign powers, and its weakness relative to its powerful neighbor to the north. Through much of the nineteenth century, it faced pressure and intervention not just from the United States but also from European powers seeking to dominate the country. When stability was finally achieved under Porfirio Díaz, it was foreign investment that fueled development and growth, even as foreign domination of some sectors of the economy contributed to the resentments that would explode in the Revolution of 1910. Through much of the twentieth century, Mexico sought to protect its interests by developing its own industries to serve a domestic market and by asserting its economic and ideological independence from the world's great powers. After the early 1980s, the government rejected this position in favor of rapid integration into the global economy.

Global economy

Since taking the strategic decision to open its economy, Mexico has embraced the opportunities and confronted the challenges presented by globalization. Mexican leaders calculated that by securing access to the vast U.S. and Canadian markets, they would allow the country to maintain a competitive position in an increasingly interconnected global economy. NAFTA did lead to a dramatic rise in the level of trade between Mexico and its North American neighbors, but the increased exposure to the world economy also left Mexico more vulnerable to abrupt shifts in international capital flows and to financial crises. After one such crisis hit at the end of 1994, for example, the Mexican economy contracted sharply, inflation soared, and taxes rose while wages were frozen. Mexico was likewise deeply affected by the global economic crisis of 2008, largely because of its strong links with the hard-hit U.S. economy.

Governing the Economy

Mexico's development from the 1930s to the 1980s was marked by extensive government engagement in the economy. During this period, the country industrialized and became primarily urban. At the same time, the living conditions of most Mexicans improved, and standards of health and education rose significantly. Yet, along with these achievements, development strategies gave rise to industrial and agricultural sectors that were often inefficient and overly protected by government, inequalities in the distribution of income and opportunities increased, and growth was threatened by a combination of domestic policies and international economic conditions. In the 1980s, the earlier model of development collapsed in crisis, and more market-oriented policies have significantly reduced the role of government in the economy while opening the country up to global economic forces. Yet growth has been slow under the new policies and inequalities have increased further. The larger questions of whether the current development strategy can generate growth, whether Mexican products can find profitable markets overseas, whether investors can create job opportunities for millions of unemployed and part-time workers, and whether the confidence of those investors can be maintained over the longer term continue to challenge the country.

The Democratic Idea

The Mexican people's pursuit of the ideal of democratic governance has been another important historical theme. Indeed, Madero launched the Revolution of 1910 with a call for "effective suffrage" and competitive elections, and his slogans were adopted by the postrevolutionary regime. Under the PRI, however, the country opted not for true democracy but for representation through government-mediated organizations within a **corporatist state**, in which interest groups became an institutionalized part of state structure rather than an independent source of advocacy. Although the democratic forms specified in the constitution were observed, the ruling party dominated the electoral process at all levels of government, and opposition groups were co-opted, marginalized, or (as a last resort) repressed. The system was referred to as a "perfect dictatorship," because of its ability to perpetuate itself and maintain stability, generally without having to resort to violence.

Over the last several decades of the twentieth century, however, the legitimacy of PRI rule was increasingly called into question. Demands for a more democratic system led to electoral reforms and the emergence of a more open political landscape. In the more competitive political environment that developed as a result, opposition parties won governorships, seats in congress, and, in 2000, the presidency. Although the PRI returned to power (via the ballot box) in 2012, democratic practices are now well established. However, many Mexicans are frustrated that democratic governance has not delivered security and sustained growth. The country's future stability depends on the ability of a more democratic system to guarantee public safety and provide economic opportunities.

corporatist state

A state in which interest groups become an institutionalized part of the state structure.

The Politics of Collective Identity

A fundamental underlying strength of the Mexican nation is a strong sense of identity forged through more than two centuries of resistance to foreign interventions and invasions and through the shared experience of the Mexican Revolution. Mexico's identity is also strongly reinforced by the country's proximity to the United States. Although commercial links, migration, popular culture, and many other forces tie Mexico closely to the "colossus of the north," Mexicans are keenly aware of what sets them apart from their North American neighbors, and they are determined to maintain their own traditions and values.

While patriotism and a common cultural background bind together citizens from all walks of life, Mexican society is also marked by deep divisions. The 1994 Zapatista rebellion reflected the fact that rural Mexico in general, the south of the country in particular, and indigenous groups most of all had been left behind by policies promoting industrial development and integration into the world economy. Huge disparities in the distribution of wealth and income also create potentially explosive divisions between economic and social classes throughout the country. Although the PRI was able to maintain stability by using patronage and clientelism to mediate among a diverse range of interest groups for decades, in a more democratic system political appeals directed at particular classes could become increasingly effective.

Comparisons

Mexico's modern history resembles that of Russia and China in that it has been framed by a social revolution that overturned the preexisting order, but the ideology that drove the Mexican revolutionary process was not communism. Instead, the Revolution of 1910 reflected concerns that arose from social conditions and historical experiences that were particular to Mexico. A diverse, often fractious revolutionary coalition called for democratic government, social justice, and national control of the country's resources. In the years after the revolution, the state created conditions for political and social peace. By incorporating peasants and workers into party and government institutions, by providing benefits to low-income groups during the 1930s, and by presiding over considerable economic growth after 1940, the regime became widely accepted as legitimate. In a world of developing nations wracked by political turmoil, military coups, and regime changes, the PRI established a strong state with enduring institutions. The party presided over decades of political stability and sustained (if unequally distributed) growth. Only in the face of economic crisis did this system begin to crumble toward the end of the twentieth century.

By moving since the 1980s to develop a more open and competitive political system, while embracing globalization as a development strategy, Mexico has followed a path chosen by a number of other Latin American nations, such as Brazil and Chile. In contrast to those countries, however, Mexico made a transition away from civilian authoritarian rule rather than military dictatorship, and the democratic nature of the institutions provided for in the 1917 constitution meant that no major reform was required to bring about a change in regime. In the twenty-first century, the Mexican government is more transparent and accountable to its citizens than it was in the past, and there is much greater scope than before for civil society activism and for independent political activity. Mexicans value the new opportunities for political participation that they have won, but they have discovered that democratic institutions do not necessarily provide more efficient and effective governance. The rise of drug cartels as a significant threat to public security in recent years has also shaken Mexicans' confidence in their institutions. Although these criminal organizations do not pursue explicitly political ends in the way that guerrilla insurgencies and terrorist groups in other nations might, their wealth and the powerful economic forces that sustain them make them in some ways harder to fight. Given the capacity that these groups have to corrupt public officials and to carry out acts of violence, Mexicans fear the influence they might have on their country's politics. Finally, although Mexico has achieved an impressive degree of industrialization and economic development, it continues to face the challenge of overcoming deep inequalities between regions and social classes and of providing opportunities for millions of citizens living in poverty.

civil society

Refers to the space occupied by voluntary associations outside the state, for example, professional associations (lawyers, doctors, teachers), trade unions, student and women's groups, religious bodies, and other voluntary association groups.

POLITICAL ECONOMY AND DEVELOPMENT

State and Economy

In light of the central role played by the Mexican state in the development of the national economy over the course of more than a century, a more thorough discussion of that history is necessary to understand the relationship between state and economy today.

During the *Porfiriato* (1876–1911), policy-makers believed that Mexico could grow rich by exporting raw materials. Their efforts to attract international investment encouraged a major boom in the production and export of products such as henequin (for making rope), coffee, cacao (cocoa beans), cattle, oil, silver, and gold. Soon, the country had become so attractive to foreign investors that large amounts of land, the country's petroleum, its railroad network, and its mining wealth were largely controlled by foreigners. Nationalist reaction against these foreign interests played a significant role in the tensions that produced the Revolution of 1910.

After the revolution, this nationalism combined with a sense of social justice inspired by revolutionary leaders such as Zapata. The country adopted a strategy in which the government guided industrial and agricultural development. This development strategy, often called state capitalism, relied heavily on government actions to encourage private investment and reduce risks for private entrepreneurs. At the same time, many came to believe that Mexico should begin to manufacture the goods that it was then importing.

state capitalism

An economic system that is primarily capitalistic but in which there is some degree of government ownership of the means of production.

Import Substitution and Its Consequences

Between 1940 and 1982, Mexico pursued a form of state capitalism and a model of development known as import substitution industrialization (ISI). Like Brazil and other Latin American countries during the same period, the government provided incentives and assistance to promote industries that would supply the domestic market.

Between 1940 and 1950, GDP grew at an annual average of 6.7 percent, while manufacturing increased at an average of 8.1 percent. In the 1950s, manufacturing achieved an average of 7.3 percent growth annually, and in the 1960s, that figure rose to 10.1 percent. Agricultural production also grew as new areas were brought under cultivation and new technologies were adopted on large farms. Even the poorest Mexicans believed that their lives were improving, and key statistical indicators reflected a real rise in standards of living (see Table 10.2). So impressive was Mexico's economic performance that it was referred to internationally as the "Mexican Miracle."

During this period, business elites, unionized workers, and wealthy commercial farmers benefitted from state policies and provided a strong base of support for the apparently successful ISI model. Government policies eventually limited the potential for further growth, however. Industrialists who received subsidies and were protected from competition had few incentives to produce efficiently. The domestic market was

Table 10.2	Mexican Development, 1940–2010						
	1940	1950	1960	1970	1980	1990	2010
Population (millions)	19.8	26.3	38.0	52.8	70.4	88.5	117.9
Life expectancy (years)	—	51.6	58.6	62.6	67.4	68.9	76.7
Infant mortality (per 1,000 live births)	—	—	86.3	70.9	49.9	42.6	14.7
Illiteracy (% of population age 15+)	—	42.5	34.5	25.0	16.0	12.7	6.9
Urban population (% of total)	—	—	50.7	59.0	66.4	72.6	77.8
Economically active population in agriculture (% of total)	—	58.3	55.1	44.0	36.6	22.0	13.1
	1940–1949	1950–1959	1960–1969	1970–1979	1980–1989	1990–1999	2000–2009
GDP growth rate (average annual %)	6.7	5.8	7.6	6.4	1.6	3.4	1.3
Per capita GDP growth rate (average annual %)	—	—	3.7	3.3	−0.1	1.6	0.3

Source: World Bank, World Development Indicators; Central Intelligence Agency.

also limited by poverty; many Mexicans could not afford the sophisticated manufactured products the country would need to produce in order to keep growing under the import substitution model.

Indeed, as the economy grew, many were left behind. The ranks of the urban poor grew steadily, particularly from the 1960s. By 1970, a large proportion of Mexico City's population was living in inner-city tenements or squatter settlements surrounding the city.[2] Mexico developed a sizable informal sector—workers who produced and sold goods and services at the margin of the economic system and faced extreme insecurity.

Also left behind in the country's development after 1940 were peasant farmers. Their lands were often the least fertile, plot sizes were minuscule, and access to markets was impeded by poor transportation and exploitive middlemen. Increasing disparities in rural and urban incomes, coupled with high population growth rates, contributed to the emergence of rural guerrilla movements and student protests in the mid- and late 1960s.

Sowing the Oil and Reaping a Crisis

In the early 1970s, Mexico faced the threat of social crisis brought on by rural poverty, chaotic urbanization, high population growth, and the questioning of political legitimacy. The government responded by investing in infrastructure and public industries, regulating the flow of foreign capital, and increasing social spending. It was spending much more than it generated, causing the public debt to grow rapidly.

Just as the seriousness of this unsustainable economic situation was being recognized, vast new finds of oil came to the rescue. Between 1978 and 1982, Mexico became a major oil exporter. The government embarked on a policy to "sow the oil" in the economy and "administer the abundance" with vast investment projects in virtually all sectors and with major new initiatives to reduce poverty and deal with declining agricultural productivity.

Oil accounted for almost four-fifths of the country's exports, causing the economy to be extremely vulnerable to changes in oil prices. And change they did. Global overproduction led to a steep drop in petroleum prices in 1982. At the same time, access to foreign credit dried up. In August 1982, the government announced that the country could not pay the interest on its foreign debt, triggering a crisis that reverberated around the world.

The economic crisis had several important implications for structures of power and privilege in Mexico. The crisis convinced even the most diehard believers that import substitution created inefficiencies in production, failed to generate sufficient employment, cost the government far too much in subsidies, and ultimately increased dependency on industrialized countries. In addition, the power of privileged interest groups and their ability to influence government policy declined.

A wide variety of interests began to organize outside the PRI to demand that government do something about the situation. Massive earthquakes in Mexico City in September 1985 proved to be a watershed for Mexican society. Severely disappointed by the government's failure to respond to the disaster, hundreds of communities organized rescue efforts, soup kitchens, shelters, and rehabilitation initiatives. A surging sense of political empowerment developed, as groups long accustomed to dependence on government learned that they could solve their problems better without it.[3]

The elections of 1988 became a focus for protest against the economic disloca-tion caused by the crisis and the political powerlessness that most citizens felt. For the first time in decades, the PRI was challenged by the increased popularity of opposi-tion political parties, one of them headed by Cuauhtémoc Cárdenas, the son of the country's most revered president. When the votes were counted, it was announced that Carlos Salinas, the PRI candidate, had received a bare majority of 50.7 percent, as opposition parties claimed widespread electoral fraud.

New Strategies: Structural Reforms and NAFTA

Between 1988 and 1994, the mutually dependent relationship between industry and government was weakened as new free-market policies were put in place. Deregulation gave the private sector more freedom to pursue economic activities and less reason to seek special favors from government. The private sector also came to control much more of the economy as the government sold off state enterprises as part of its reform program. In the countryside, a constitutional revision made it possible for *ejidos* to be divided into individually owned plots; this made farmers less dependent on govern-ment but more vulnerable to losing their land.

Among the farthest-reaching initiatives was the North American Free Trade Agreement (NAFTA). This agreement with Canada and the United States created the basis for gradual introduction of free trade among the three countries. However, the liberalization of the Mexican economy and opening of its markets to foreign competition increased Mexico's vulnerability to changes in international economic conditions. These factors, as well as mismanaged economic policies, led to another major economic crisis for the country at the end of 1994, and profound recession in 1995. NAFTA has meant that the fate of the Mexican economy is increasingly linked to the health of the U.S. economy.

The Mexican Economy Today

Under the influence of NAFTA, the Mexican economy has become increasingly ori-ented toward production for the North American market, and the manufacturing sector in particular has grown in importance. In addition to the traditional *maqui-ladora* industries along the northern border, Mexico is taking advantage of the large number of engineers trained by its universities to develop more advanced industries. Querétaro, in central Mexico, for example, is emerging as a center for the aerospace industry. The country also plays an integral part in a manufacturing process for auto-mobiles that has become continental in scale, with parts from the United States, Canada, and Mexico moving between plants in the three countries as new cars are assembled. These developments give the country an economic profile that is quite distinct from that of many of its Latin American neighbors, many of which still rely more heavily on exports of agricultural products and raw materials.

Remittances reflect another close economic link with the United States. Mexican migrants in the United States sent some $27 billion home to relatives in 2016 (see The U.S. Connection: Mexican Migration to the United States). Representing more than 2 percent of Mexico's GDP, these transfers provide a vital economic lifeline to many communities in central and southern Mexico, some of which send almost all of their adult men to the United States to work.

Oil production also remains important to the economy, particularly since the national petroleum company, PEMEX, continues to provide a substantial propor-tion of government revenues. However, the government's reliance on oil revenues

remittances

Funds sent by migrants working abroad to family members in their home countries.

has starved the state oil monopoly of the capital it would need to invest in new technologies and seek out new deposits. As the output of existing oilfields has begun to decline, the politically sensitive question of reform in the energy sector became unavoidable. President Peña Nieto's energy reform has allowed foreign companies to enter into joint ventures in Mexico with PEMEX, a development that could revitalize the sector but could also inflame nationalist resentments if Mexico is not seen to benefit from new discoveries.

U.S. CONNECTION

Mexican Migration to the United States

Mexicans began moving to the United States in substantial numbers late in the nineteenth century, and their ranks grew as many fled the conditions created by the Revolution of 1910. Most settled in the border states of California and Texas, where they joined preexisting Mexican communities that had been there since the days when the American southwest had been part of Mexico. Even greater numbers of migrants began to arrive during World War II, when the U.S. government allowed Mexican workers, known as *braceros*, to enter the country to help provide much-needed manpower for strategic production efforts. After the *bracero* program came to an end in 1964, Mexicans continued to seek work in the United States, despite the fact that most now had to enter the country illegally.

To a large extent, the U.S. government informally tolerated the employment of undocumented migrants until the 1980s, when policy-makers came under pressure to assert control over the border. The 1986 Immigration Reform and Control Act (IRCA) allowed migrants who had been in the United States for a long period of time to gain legal residency rights, but it called for tighter controls on immigration in the future. An unintended effect of IRCA, and of subsequent efforts to deter illegal immigration, was to turn what had been a pattern of seasonal migration into a flow of migrants that settled permanently north of the border. Before 1986, most Mexican migrant workers left their families at home and worked in the United States for only a few months at a time before returning to their country with the money they had earned. The "amnesty" granted by IRCA encouraged its beneficiaries to remain in the United States and to bring their relatives from Mexico to join them. Moreover, as increased vigilance and new barriers made crossing of the border more difficult, more of the migrants who arrived in the United States decided to remain there rather than risk apprehension by traveling back and forth between the two countries.

In the 1990s and 2000s, growing Mexican communities spread into areas such as North Carolina, Georgia, Arkansas, and Iowa, where few Mexicans had lived before. They also became increasingly mobilized politically as they organized to resist anti-immigrant voter initiatives such as Proposition 187 in California in 1994 and Proposition 200 in Arizona in 2004, both of which threatened to cut off social services for undocumented migrants. At the same time, their political importance in Mexico has reached unprecedented heights as officials at all levels of government there recognize the critical importance to the Mexican economy of the remittances received from migrants working abroad. Mexican governors, mayors, and federal officials now regularly visit representatives of migrant groups in the United States, often seeking their support and funding for projects at home. Moreover, a 1996 law allowing Mexicans to hold dual citizenship makes it possible for many Mexican migrants to have a voice in the governance of both the country of their birth as well as the country where they now reside. In 2005, Mexican legislators finally approved a system under which registered Mexican voters living abroad could participate in federal elections. Although levels of electoral participation by Mexicans abroad have so far been relatively modest, this huge group could play a decisive role in future contests.

Since the economic downturn caused by the financial crisis of 2008, the volume of Mexican migration to the United States has diminished considerably. Indeed, in recent years the net flow of migrants has been negative, meaning that more Mexicans have returned home from the United States than have moved north in search of work. Nonetheless, migration will continue to represent both a close connection and a source of tension between Mexico and the United States.

MAKING CONNECTIONS How might debates over immigration policies in the United States affect the politics and foreign relations of Mexico?

Society and Economy

Mexico's economic development has had a significant impact on social conditions in the country. Overall, standards of living and quality of life rose markedly after the 1940s. Provision of health and education services expanded until government cutbacks on social expenditures in the early 1980s, and has been extended further in recent years as modest economic growth has resumed. Among the most important consequences of economic growth was the development of a large middle class, most of whom live in Mexico's numerous large cities.

These achievements reflect well on the ability of the economy to increase social well-being in the country. But in terms of standard indicators of social development—infant mortality, literacy, and life expectancy—Mexico fell behind a number of Latin American countries that grew less rapidly but provided more effectively for their populations. Costa Rica, Colombia, Argentina, Chile, and Uruguay had lower overall growth but greater social development in the period after 1940. These countries paid more attention to the distribution of the benefits of growth than did Mexico.

In part, because of the specific way in which Mexico has pursued economic growth, there is also a regional dimension to disparities in social development. The northern areas of the country are significantly better off than the southern and central areas. In the north, large commercial farms using modern technologies grow fruits, vegetables, and grains for export. Moreover, urban industrial centers such as Monterrey and Tijuana provide steady employment for skilled and unskilled labor. Along the border, *maquiladoras* provide many jobs, particularly for young women who are seeking some escape from the burdens of rural life or the constraints of traditional family life.

In the southern and central regions of the country, the population is denser, the terrain more difficult, and the number of farmers eking out subsistence greater. Investment in irrigation and transportation infrastructure has been lacking in many areas. Most of the 26 million Mexicans who continue to live in rural areas, and most of the country's remaining indigenous groups, live in the south of the country, often in remote zones where they have been forgotten by government programs and exploited by regional bosses for generations.

The general economic crisis of the 1980s had an impact on social conditions in Mexico as well. Wages declined by about half, and unemployment soared as businesses collapsed and the government laid off workers. The informal sector expanded rapidly. Here, people manage to make a living by hawking chewing gum, umbrellas, candy, shoelaces, and many other items in the street; jumping in front of cars at stoplights to wash windshields and sell newspapers; producing and repairing cheap consumer goods; and selling services on a daily or hourly basis. The economic crisis also reduced the quality and availability of social services, as the government imposed austerity measures. Although economic recovery has been slow and fitful in recent decades, the Mexican government has begun to fill the void left by cuts in social spending during the depths of the crisis. Recent years have seen the launch of successful programs that provide vastly expanded access to basic health care and cash grants to poor families that keep their children in school.

Environmental Issues

With its varied landscapes, including long coastlines, extensive coral reefs, towering mountain peaks, tropical rain forests, and arid deserts, Mexico is a country of tremendous biodiversity, with many fragile ecosystems that have been badly damaged by insensitive economic development. Although a tradition of conservation stretches back at least to the 1930s, when Lázaro Cárdenas established a national park system, for many years the pursuit of economic development and industrialization was given priority over the enforcement of environmental regulations. One result was that Mexico City became one of the most polluted cities in the world, and in some rural areas oil exploitation left devastating environmental damage.[4]

When residents of Mexico City and other parts of the country began to mobilize outside of the PRI in the 1980s to pressure the government to address the issues that mattered most to their communities, environmental concerns were an important item on their agenda, and much stricter controls on automobile and industrial emissions have helped to make the capital's air more breathable since that time. As Mexico has sought a place in the global economy since the late 1980s, pressure from abroad also played a vital role in bringing about a strengthening of the state's commitment to environmental protection. When critics of NAFTA threatened to block the agreement in the United States on the grounds that Mexico failed to live up to international environmental standards, the Mexican government signed onto side agreements providing for greater environmental oversight in order to secure the ratification of the free-trade accord. The government also signaled that it was assigning greater importance to environmental concerns by creating a ministry for the environment and natural resources in 1994; more than coincidentally, the new cabinet department came into existence in the same year that NAFTA went into effect.

Although many concerns remain, the will and the capacity of the Mexican state to act to protect the environment have been significantly enhanced over the past two decades. Moreover, in an increasingly interconnected world, Mexican civil society organizations with an interest in these issues have benefitted greatly from the connections they have developed with international networks of environmental groups.

Mexico in the Global Economy

The crisis that began in 1982 altered Mexico's international economic policies. In response to that crisis, the government relaxed restrictions on the ability of foreigners to own property, reduced and eliminated tariffs, and did away with most import licenses. Foreign investment was courted in the hope of increasing the manufacture of goods for export. The government also introduced a series of incentives to encourage the private sector to produce goods for export. In 1986, Mexico joined the General Agreement on Tariffs and Trade (GATT), a multilateral agreement that sought to promote free trade among countries and that later became the basis for the World Trade Organization (WTO). In the 1990s and 2000s, Mexico signed trade pacts with many countries in Latin America, Europe, and elsewhere.

The government's effort to pursue a more outward-oriented development strategy culminated in the ratification of NAFTA in 1993, with gradual implementation beginning on January 1, 1994. The agreement signaled a new period in U.S.–Mexican relations and led to the much closer integration of the two countries' economies. Since NAFTA entered into force, domestic and foreign investors in the Mexican economy have come to value their access to the U.S. market very highly, and the United States is Mexico's most important trading partner by a wide margin.

In 2015, 81.2 percent of Mexico's exports were sent to its northern neighbor, and 47.4 percent of its imports came from that country.[5]

NAFTA has helped to attract investment and has contributed to impressive growth in some sectors of the economy, but it also entails risks for Mexico. Critics have argued that embracing free trade with Canada and the United States represents a surrender of sovereignty. Certainly, Mexico's economic situation is now more vulnerable to the ebb and flow of economic conditions in the U.S. economy. After the United States plunged into a deep recession in 2008, Mexico's economy contracted by more than 7 percent, despite the fact that the crisis was not of its own making. Moreover, having adopted an economic model based on free trade with the United States, Mexico now faces vulnerability to the growing unpopularity of NAFTA there. If the United States were to withdraw from the agreement, or if it forced a significant renegotiation of its terms, the Mexican economy would be badly hurt.

Furthermore, some domestic producers worry that NAFTA exposes them to competition from powerful U.S. firms. Farmers fear that Mexican crops cannot compete effectively with those grown in the United States; for example, peasant producers of corn and beans have been hard hit by the availability of lower-priced U.S.-grown grains.[6] Also, some in Mexico are concerned with evidence of "cultural imperialism" as U.S. movies, music, fashions, and lifestyles increasingly influence consumers. Indeed, for Mexico, which has traditionally feared the power of the United States in its domestic affairs, internationalization of political and economic relationships poses particularly difficult problems of adjustment.

On the other hand, the United States, newly aware of the importance of the Mexican economy to its own economic growth and concerned about instability on its southern border, hammered together a $50 billion economic assistance program composed of U.S., European, and IMF commitments to support its neighbor when economic crisis struck in 1994. The Mexican government imposed a new stabilization package that contained austerity measures, higher interest rates, and limits on wages. Remarkably, by 1998, Mexico had paid off all of its obligations to the United States.

Globalization is also stripping Mexico of some of the secrecy that traditionally surrounded government decision making, electoral processes, and efforts to deal with political dissent. International attention increasingly focuses on the country, and investors want clear information on what is occurring in the economy. The government can no longer respond to events such as the peasant rebellion in Chiapas, alleged electoral fraud, or the management of exchange rates without considering how such actions will be perceived in Tokyo, Frankfurt, London, or Washington.

Where Do You Stand?

Mexico is recognized by investors as an important emerging economy, but can its development strategy be considered a success when some regions of the country and some economic sectors are being left behind? What can be done to address the disparities being exacerbated by uneven growth?

Taking into account the full range of effects that NAFTA has had on Mexico, do you think the free trade agreement has been good or bad for the country?

GOVERNANCE AND POLICY-MAKING

- In what ways does the actual exercise of state power in Mexico differ from the model outlined in the constitution? What are the main reasons for these discrepancies?

- To what extent is federalism a reality in Mexico today? How is power divided between administrations at the national, state, and local levels?

sexenio

The 6-year term in office of Mexican presidents, governors, and senators.

Organization of the State

Under the Constitution of 1917, Mexico's political institutions resemble those of the United States. There are three branches of government, and a set of checks and balances limits the power of each. The congress is composed of the Senate and the Chamber of Deputies. A total of 128 senators are elected: 3 from each of the country's thirty-one states; 3 from Mexico City; and another 32 elected nationally by proportional representation (PR). The 500 members of the Chamber of Deputies are elected from 300 electoral districts—300 by simple majority vote and 200 by proportional representation. State and local governments are also elected. The president, governors, and senators are elected for six-year terms, an important institutional feature of Mexican politics referred to as the *sexenio*. Congressional deputies (representatives in the lower house) and municipal officials are elected for three years.

In practice, the Mexican system is very different from that of the United States. The constitution is a long document that can be easily amended. It lays out the structure of government and guarantees a wide range of human rights, including familiar ones such as freedom of speech and protection under the law, but also economic and social rights such as the right to a job and the right to health care. In practice, these rights do not reach all of the population. Although there has been some decentralization, the political system is still much more centralized than that of the United States. Since the democratic transition of 2000, the congress has become more active as a decision-making arena and as a check on presidential power, but the executive remains central to initiating policy and managing political conflict.

The Executive

The President and the Cabinet

The presidency is the central institution of governance and policy-making in Mexico. Until the 1990s, the incumbent president always selected who would run as the PRI's next presidential candidate, appointed officials to all positions of power in the government and the party, and often named the candidates who almost automatically won elections as governors, senators, deputies, and local officials.[7] Even after the transition to a more competitive political system, the president continues to set the broad outlines of policy for the administration and has numerous resources to ensure that those policy preferences are adopted. Until the mid-1970s, Mexican presidents were considered above criticism in national politics and revered as symbols of national progress and well-being. While the crises of the 1980s and 1990s diminished presidential prestige, the extent of presidential power remains a legacy of the long period of PRI dominance.

Mexican presidents have a set of formal powers that allows them to initiate legislation, lead in foreign policy, create government agencies, make policy by decree or through

AP Images/Alexandre Meneghini

President Enrique Peña Nieto (left) is congratulated by his predecessor, Felipe Calderón, at his inauguration on December 1, 2012.

administrative regulations and procedures, and appoint a wide range of public officials. More importantly, informal powers allow them to exert considerable control. The president manages a vast patronage machine for filling positions in government and initiates legislation and policies that were, until recently, routinely approved by the congress.

Mexican presidents, although powerful, are not omnipotent. They must, for example, abide by a deeply held constitutional norm by stepping down at the end of their term, and they must adhere to tradition by removing themselves from the political limelight to allow their successors to assume full presidential leadership. All presidents, regardless of party, must demonstrate their loyalty to the myths and symbols of Mexican nationalism, and they must make a rhetorical commitment to social justice and sovereignty in international affairs.

In the 1990s, President Zedillo gave up a number of the traditional powers of the presidency. He announced, for example, that he would not select his PRI successor but would leave it up to the party to determine its candidate. This created considerable tension as the PRI had to take on unaccustomed roles and politicians sought to fill the void left by the "abandonment" of presidential power. Fox, Calderón, and Peña Nieto inherited a system in which the president is expected to set the policies and determine the priorities for a very wide range of government activity, yet needs a strong party in congress and experienced people in his administration to enact legislation and implement policies.

Until the democratic transition of 2000, presidents were almost always members of the outgoing president's cabinet. With the victory of the PAN in 2000, this long tradition came to an end. Prior to running for president, Vicente Fox had been in business and had served as the governor of the state of Guanajuato. Calderón, although he had served briefly as energy minister, was not the candidate within the PAN that Fox had initially favored. In this respect, Calderón's victory in 2006 continued a trend toward greater independence of parties from presidential preferences. As the PRI candidate in 2012, Peña Nieto obviously had not served in the cabinets of Fox or Calderón; instead, he had just completed a term as the governor of the populous state of Mexico, which includes many of the suburbs of Mexico City. His candidacy reflected the prominence that state governors had attained in the PRI during the years that the party had been out of power at the national level.

Mexican presidents since the mid-1970s have generally had impressive educational credentials and have tended to be trained in economics and management rather than in the traditional field of law. Most presidents since López Portillo have had postgraduate training at elite institutions in the United States. By the 1980s, a topic of great debate in political circles was the extent to which a divide between *políticos* (politicians) and *técnicos* (**technocrats**) had emerged within the national political elite. Having studied law and attended Mexican universities, Peña Nieto's educational background differs from that of his immediate predecessors.

Once elected, the president moves quickly to name a cabinet. Before 2000, he usually selected those with whom he had worked over the years as he rose to political prominence. He also used cabinet posts to ensure a broad coalition of support; he might, for example, appoint people with close ties to the labor movement, business interests, or some of the regional strongholds of the PRI. Only in rare exceptions were cabinet officials not active members of the party. When the PAN assumed the presidency, the selection of cabinet members became more difficult. Until then, the PAN had elected officials only to a few state and local governments and to a relatively small number of seats in congress. As a consequence, the range of people with executive experience to whom Fox could turn was limited. He appointed U.S.-trained economists for his economic team and business executives for many other important posts. Few of these appointees had close ties to the PAN or prior experience in government. By contrast, Calderón filled his cabinet positions with longtime members of the PAN who had a longer history of political engagement, but after so many years in opposition, many of these appointees also lacked extensive experience in government.

Peña Nieto has followed the traditions of the PRI by naming a number of aides from his term as governor of the state of Mexico, as well as allies from key regions, to his cabinet. At the same time, he has looked beyond his party to fill some posts; his appointees have included a former president of the left-of-center Party of the Democratic Revolution (PRD) and a former member of Felipe Calderón's cabinet.

Over the years, few women have been selected for ministry-level posts. Initially, they only presided over agencies with limited influence over decision making, such as the ministries of tourism and fisheries. More recently, however, women have served as foreign minister and as attorney general.

The president has the authority to fill numerous other high-level positions, which allows him to provide policy direction and keep tabs on what is occurring throughout the government. The range of appointments that a chief executive can make means that the beginning of each administration is characterized by extensive turnover of positions. Progress on the president's policy agenda can therefore be slow toward the beginning of each *sexenio* as newly appointed officials learn the ropes and assemble their staff. The president's power to make appointments allows him to build a team of like-minded officials in government and ensure their loyalty.

The Bureaucracy

Mexico's executive branch is large and powerful. Almost 1.5 million people work in the federal bureaucracy, most of them in Mexico City. An additional 1 million work in state-owned industries and semiautonomous agencies of the government. State and local governments employ over 1.5 million people.

---

technocrat

A career-minded official who administers public policy according to a technical rather than a political rationale.

Officials at lower levels in the bureaucracy are unionized and protected by legislation that gives them job security and a range of benefits. At middle and upper levels, most officials are called "confidence employees"; they serve as long as their bosses have confidence in them. These officials have been personally appointed by their superiors at the outset of an administration. Their modest salaries are compensated for by the significant power that they can have over public affairs. For aspiring young professionals, a career in government is often attractive because of the challenge of dealing with important problems on a daily basis. Some employees also benefit from opportunities to take bribes or use other means to promote their personal interests.

The Parastatal Sector

The parastatal sector—composed of semiautonomous or autonomous government agencies, many of which produce goods and services—was extremely large and powerful in Mexico prior to the 1990s. As part of its post-1940 development strategy, the government engaged in numerous activities that in other countries are carried out by the private sector. Thus, until the Salinas administration, the country's largest steel mill was state-owned, as were the largest fertilizer producer, sugar mills, and airlines. In addition, the Federal Electricity Commission still produces energy, which it supplies to industries at subsidized prices. The state-owned petroleum company, PEMEX, grew to enormous proportions in the 1970s and 1980s under the impact of the oil boom. NAFIN, a state investment corporation, provides a considerable amount of investment capital for the country. At one point, a state marketing board called CONASUPO was responsible for the importation and purchase of the country's basic food supplies, and in the 1970s, it played a major role in distributing food, credit, and farm implements in rural areas.

This large parastatal sector was significantly trimmed by the economic policy reforms that began in the 1980s. Concerted efforts were then made to privatize many of these enterprises, including the telephone company, the national airlines, and the nationalized banks. Many strategic industries thus passed into a small number of private hands, and much of the banking sector came under the control of foreign corporations. However, some core components of the parastatal sector will likely remain in government hands for the foreseeable future because an influential bloc of nationalist political actors insists on the symbolic importance of public ownership of key industries. For example, even with reforms taking effect to allow foreign investment in the energy sector, PEMEX is likely to remain a state enterprise with a key position in the petroleum industry.

Other State Institutions

The Military

Mexico is one of only a few countries in the developing world, particularly in Latin America, to have successfully marginalized the military from centers of political power. Although former military leaders dominated Mexican politics during the decades immediately after the Revolution of 1910, Calles and Cárdenas laid the groundwork for civilian rule by introducing the practice of rotating regional military commands so that generals could not build up geographic bases of power. In addition, postrevolutionary leaders made an implicit bargain with the military leaders by providing them with opportunities to engage in business so that they did not look to political office as a way of gaining economic power. After 1946, the military no longer had institutional representation within the PRI and became clearly subordinate to civilian control. No military officer has held the presidency since that time.

This does not mean that the military has always operated outside politics. It has been called in from time to time to deal with domestic unrest: in rural areas in the 1960s, in Mexico City and other cities to repress student protest movements in 1968, and in Chiapas beginning in 1994. When the PAN government made it possible for citizens to gain greater access to government information, it was discovered that the military had been involved in political repression, torture, and killing in the 1970s and 1980s. The scandal created by such revelations lowered its reputation, although polls show that Mexicans continue to have more confidence in the armed forces than many other institutions, including the police forces, which are widely regarded as corrupt and ineffective.

In recent years, the military has been heavily involved in efforts to combat drug trafficking and organized crime. In some regions particularly hard hit by drug-related violence, the military took over many policing functions. Although the army is seen as less corrupt than many of the local police forces that they have replaced, concerns about their ongoing presence on the streets of Mexican cities have arisen, particularly as allegations of civil and human rights violations by soldiers have emerged in some areas, and as rumors have arisen about deals struck between military officials and drug barons.

Whenever the military is called in to address domestic security concerns, some Mexicans worry that the institution is becoming politicized and may come to play a larger role in political decision making. Thus far, such fears have not been realized, and many believe that as long as civilian administrations are able to maintain the country's tradition of stability, the military will not intervene directly in politics.

The Judiciary

Unlike Anglo-American legal systems, Mexico's law derives from the Roman and Napoleonic tradition and is highly formalized. Because Mexican law tends to be very explicit and because there are no punitive damages allowed in court cases, there are fewer lawsuits than in the United States. One important exception to this is the *amparo* (protection), whereby individual citizens may ask for a writ of protection, claiming that their constitutional rights have been violated by specific government actions or laws.

There are both federal and state courts in Mexico. The federal system is composed of the Supreme Court, which decides the most important cases; circuit courts, which take cases on appeal; and district courts, where cases enter the system. Following the same system as in the United States, Supreme Court justices are nominated by the president and approved by the Senate. Since most of the important laws in Mexico are federal, state courts have played a subordinate role. This is changing, however. As Mexican states become more independent from the federal government, state law has been experiencing tremendous growth. In addition, there are many important specialized federal courts, such as labor courts, military courts, and electoral courts.

Like other government institutions in Mexico, the judiciary was for many decades politically, though not constitutionally, subordinate to the executive. The courts occasionally slowed the actions of government by issuing *amparos*; however, in almost every case in which the power of the state was at stake, the courts ruled on the side of the government. The Zedillo administration tried to change this by emphasizing the rule of law over that of powerful individuals. Increasing interest in human rights issues by citizens' groups and the media added pressure to the courts to play a stronger role in protecting basic freedoms.

Although the judicial system remains the weakest branch of government, reforms continue to be proposed. In 2008, in response to concern for the rights of defendants who fall victim to police and prosecutorial misconduct, constitutional amendments called for the introduction of public trials with oral testimony and the presumption of innocence. When fully implemented, the reforms will represent one of the most significant changes to the judiciary in modern Mexican history. The northern state of Chihuahua was the first to adopt the new system, but the new procedures have been controversial there, and progress elsewhere in the country has been slow.

Subnational Government

As with many other aspects of the Mexican political system, regional and local government in Mexico is quite different from what is described in the constitution. Under Mexico's federal system, each state has its own constitution, executive, unicameral legislature, and judiciary. Municipalities (equivalent to U.S. counties) are governed by popularly elected mayors and councils. But most state and municipal governments are poor. Most of the funds they command are transferred to them from the central government, and they have little legal or administrative capacity to raise their own revenue. States and localities also suffer greatly from the lack of well-trained and well-paid public officials. As at the national level, many jobs in state and local governments are distributed as political patronage, but even officials who are motivated to be responsive to local needs are generally ill equipped to do so. In light of these weaknesses, it is not surprising that local governments have been particularly susceptible to the ability of wealthy, heavily armed drug cartels to corrupt and intimidate public officials, especially in poor and remote regions.

Since the early 1990s, the government has made several serious efforts to decentralize and devolve more power to state and local governments. At times, governors and mayors have resisted such initiatives because they meant that regional and local governments would have to manage much more complex activities and be the focus of demands from public sector workers and their unions. Local governments were also worried that they would be unable to acquire the budgetary resources necessary to carry out their new responsibilities.

Until 1989, all governors were from the PRI, but since then, politics at the state level has become competitive in almost every region of the country. Since the first PAN governor took office in Baja California almost three decades ago, more than four-fifths of Mexico's states have had at least one non-PRI administration. Municipalities have also increasingly been the focus of authentic party competition. As opposition parties came to control these levels of government, they were challenged to improve services such as police protection, garbage collection, sanitation, and education. PRI-dominated governments have also tried to improve their performance because they are now more threatened by the possibility of losing elections.

The Policy-Making Process

The Mexican system is very dependent on the quality of its leadership and on presidential understanding of how economic and social policies can affect the development of the country. As indicated throughout this chapter, the president's single six-year term of office, the *sexenio*, is an important fact of political life in Mexico. New presidents can introduce extensive change in positions within the government. They are able to bring in "their" people, who build teams of "their" people within ministries, agencies, and party networks. This generally provides the president with a group of high- and middle-level officials who share the same general orientation toward public policy and are motivated to carry out his goals. When the PRI was the dominant party, these officials believed that in following presidential leadership, they enhanced their chances for upward political mobility. In such a context, even under a single party, it was likely that changes in public policies could be introduced every six years, creating innovation or discontinuity, or both.

Together with the bureaucracy, the president is the focal point of policy formulation and political management. Until 1997, the legislature always had a PRI majority and acted as a rubber stamp for presidentially sponsored legislation. Since then, the congress has proven to be a more active policy-maker, blocking and forcing the negotiation of legislation, and even introducing its own bills. The president's skills in negotiating, managing the opposition, using the media to acquire public support, and maneuvering within the bureaucracy can be important in ensuring that his program is fully endorsed.

Significant limits on presidential power occur when policy is being implemented. At times, policies are not implemented because public officials at the lower levels disagree with them or make deals with affected interests in order to benefit personally. This is the case, for example, with taxes that remain uncollected because individuals or corporations bribe officials to overlook them. In other cases, lower-level officials may lack the capacity to implement some policies, such as those directed toward improving education or rural development services. For various reasons, Mexican presidents cannot always deliver on their intentions. Traditionally, Mexican citizens have blamed lower-level officials for such slippage, but exempting the president from responsibility for what does or does not occur during his watch has become much less common since the 1970s.

Where Do You Stand?

Should Mexico lift its constitutional ban on presidential reelection, as a number of other Latin American countries have done in recent years? Would having to face the voters for reelection make officials more accountable, or might allowing them to stay in office for more than one term open the door to a return to authoritarianism?

With the decline in the deference given to presidential preferences in recent years, more voices have been heard and taken into account as policies have been formulated, but the process has become more contentious and less efficient. On balance then, is it good for Mexico that the authority of the president has diminished over the past two decades?

REPRESENTATION AND PARTICIPATION

How do citizen interests get represented in Mexican politics, given the high degree of centralization, presidentialism, and, until recently, single-party domination? Is it possible for ordinary citizens to make demands on government and influence public policy? In fact, Mexico has had a relatively peaceful history since the Revolution of 1910, in part because the political system offers some channels for representation and participation. Throughout this long history, the political system has emphasized compromise among contending elites, behind-the-scenes conflict resolution, and distribution of political rewards to those willing to play by the formal and informal rules of the game. It has also responded, if only reluctantly and defensively, to demands for change.

Often, citizens are best able to interact with the government through a variety of informal means rather than through the formal processes of elections, campaigns, and interest group lobbying. Interacting with government through the personal mechanisms of clientelism usually means that the government retains the upper hand in deciding which interests to respond to and which to ignore. For many interests, this has meant "incorporation without power."[8] Increasingly, however, Mexican citizens are organizing to alter this situation, and the advent of truly competitive elections has increased the possibility that citizens who organize can gain some response from government.

Focus Questions ▼

- Since the early 1980s, how has the balance of power in Mexico shifted between the legislative and executive branches of government? How do these shifts correspond to changes in the overall political landscape?

- What are the power bases of the main political parties in Mexican politics? What factors made it possible for the PAN to unseat the long-dominant PRI in 2000? What accounts for the success of the PRI in returning to power in 2012?

The Legislature

Students in the United States are frequently asked to study complex charts explaining how a bill becomes a law because the formal process of lawmaking affects the content of legislation. Under the old reign of the PRI in Mexico, while there were formal rules that prescribed such a process, studying them would not have been useful for understanding how the legislature worked. Because of the overwhelming dominance of the ruling party, opposition to presidential initiatives by Mexico's two-chamber legislature, the Senate and the Chamber of Deputies, was rarely heard. If representatives did not agree with policies they were asked to approve, they counted on the fact that policy implementation was flexible and allowed for after-the-fact bending of the rules or disregard of measures that were harmful to important interests.

Representation in congress has become more diverse since the end of the 1980s. Between 1988 and 2006, the PRI's grip on the legislature steadily weakened. By the end of that period, the party had fewer representatives in the Chamber of Deputies than either of its two main rivals. The PRI subsequently made large gains in mid-term legislative elections in 2009, and it is once again the largest party in the both houses of congress, but today the legislature is divided between strong PRI, PAN, and PRD blocs, with no single party able to dominate proceedings (see Figure 10.2). In large part because the PRI has lost its stranglehold on congressional representation, the

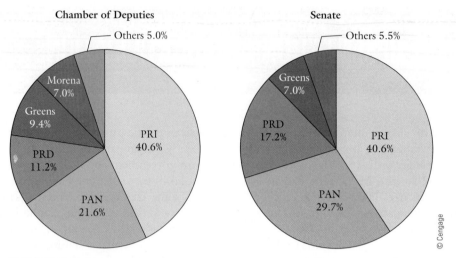

FIGURE 10.2 Congressional Representation by Party, 2016

Source: CIA World Factbook, https://www.cia.gov/library/publications/resources /the-world-factbook/geos/mx.html.

role of the legislature in the policy process has been strengthened considerably since the late 1990s.[9] The cost of greater power-sharing between the executive and the legislature, however, has been a slow-down in the policy process. The biggest change, therefore, has been that the congress has evolved from a rubber-stamp institution to one that must be negotiated with by the executive branch.

Political Parties and the Party System

Even under the long reign of the PRI, a number of political parties existed in Mexico. By the mid-1980s, some of them were attracting more political support, a trend that continued into the 1990s and 2000s (see Table 10.3). Electoral reforms introduced by the PRI administrations between the 1970s and the 1990s made it easier for opposition parties to contest and win elections. In 1990, an electoral commission was created to regulate campaigns and elections, and in 1996 it became fully independent of the government. Now all parties receive funding from the government and have access to the media.

The PRI

Mexico's Institutional Revolutionary Party (PRI) was founded by a coalition of political elites who agreed that it was preferable to work out their conflicts within an overarching structure of compromise than to continue to resort to violence. In the 1930s, the forerunner of the PRI (the party operated under different names until 1946) incorporated a wide array of interests, becoming a mass-based party that drew support from all classes in the population. Over seven decades, its principal activities were to generate support for the government, organize the electorate to vote for its candidates, and distribute jobs and resources in return for loyalty to the system.

Until the 1990s, party organization was based largely on the corporatist representation of class interests. Labor was represented within party councils by the

Table 10.3	Voting for Major Parties in Presidential Elections, 1934–2012			
Year	Votes for PRI Candidate	Votes for PAN Candidate	Votes for PRD Candidate	Voter Turnout (% of eligible adults)
1934	98.2	—	—	53.6
1940	93.9	—	—	57.5
1946	77.9	—	—	42.6
1952	74.3	7.8	—	57.9
1958	90.4	9.4	—	49.4
1964	88.8	11.1	—	54.1
1970	83.3	13.9	—	63.9
1976	93.6	—	—	29.6
1982	71.0	15.7	—	66.1
1988	50.7	16.8	31.1	51.6
1994	48.7	25.9	16.6	77.3
2000	36.1	42.5	16.6	64.0
2006	22.3	35.9	35.3	58.6
2012	38.2	25.4	31.6	63.1

Source: From *Comparative Politics Today: A World View*, 4th ed., Gabriel Almond and G. Bingham Powell, Jr. © 1988. Reprinted by permission of Addison-Wesley Educational Publishers, Inc. For 1988: Dieter Nohlen, ed., *Elections in the Americas: A Data Handbook*, vol. 1 (Oxford, UK: Oxford University Press). For 1994–2012: Instituto Nacional Electoral, www.ine.org.mx.

Confederation of Mexican Workers (CTM), which included industry-based unions at local, regional, and national levels. Peasants were represented by the National Peasant Confederation (CNC), an organization of *ejido* and peasant unions and regional associations. The so-called popular sector, comprising small businesses, community-based groups, and public employees, had less internal cohesion but was represented by the National Confederation of Popular Organizations (CNOP). Of the three, the CTM was consistently the best organized and most powerful. Traditionally, the PRI's strongest support came from the countryside, where *ejidatarios* and independent small farmers were dependent on rewards of land or jobs. As the country became more urbanized, the support base provided by rural communities remained important to the PRI, but produced many fewer votes than were necessary to keep the party in power.

Within its corporatist structures, the PRI functioned through extended networks that distributed public resources—particularly jobs, land, development projects, and access to public services—to lower-level activists who controlled votes at the local level. In this system, those with ambitions to hold public office or positions within the PRI put together networks of supporters from above (patrons), to whom they delivered votes, and supporters from below (clients), who traded allegiance for access to public resources. For well over half a century, this patron-client system worked extremely well. PRI candidates won by overwhelming majorities until the 1980s. Of course, electoral fraud and the ability to distribute government largesse are central explanations for these numbers, but they also attest to an extremely well-organized party.

By the 1980s, new generations of voters were less beholden to patronage-style politics and much more willing to question the party's dominance, and the PRI began to be challenged by parties to the right and left. Outcomes were hotly contested by the opposition, which claimed fraudulent electoral practices. As the PRI faced greater competition from other parties and continued to suffer from declining popularity, efforts were made to restructure and reform it. Party conventions were introduced in an effort to democratize the internal workings of the party, and some states and localities began to hold primaries to select PRI candidates, a significant departure from the old system of selection by party bosses.

After the PRI lost the presidency in 2000, the party faced a difficult future. At the dawn of the twenty-first century, Mexico's voters were younger, better educated, and more middle-class than they were during the period of PRI dominance. They were also more likely to live in urban areas than they were in the days of the party's greatest success. With the vast majority of the country's population living in cities, the PRI faced the challenge of winning the support of more urban voters.

Nonetheless, the PRI remained a strong political force. It did not, as some predicted, dissolve once it lost control of the presidency. As one of the largest blocs in a divided congress between 2000 and 2012, PRI representatives could often exercise significant influence over the legislative agenda. Just as importantly, the party continued to control most subnational governments, and state governors emerged as some of the most influential figures in the party. The PRI is still the only party that has a significant presence in every region of the country. When they returned the PRI to power in 2012, many Mexicans clearly hoped that the party would be able to draw upon its long experience in government to offer a greater degree of order and stability after the violence and gridlock of recent years.

As the 2018 presidential elections approach, however, it seems that voters' feelings towards the PRI are largely negative. A variety of corruption allegations surrounding the president and other PRI officials at all levels of government have reminded Mexicans of some of the more negative aspects of the party's legacy. President Peña Nieto of the PRI entered the last year of his presidency with some of the lowest approval ratings ever recorded, and the party's candidates performed unexpectedly poorly in gubernatorial elections in 2016 that were seen as a key indicator of its standing with the electorate in the run-up to 2018. Recent history shows, however, that the PRI is a resilient organization, and it will certainly remain an important actor in Mexican politics.

The PAN

The National Action Party (PAN) was founded in 1939 to represent interests opposed to the centralization and **anticlericalism** of the PRI. It was established by those who believed that the country needed more than one strong political party and that opposition parties should oppose the PRI through legal and constitutional actions.

anticlericalism

Opposition to the power of churches or clergy in politics. In countries such as France and Mexico, this opposition has focused on the role of the Catholic Church in politics.

Historically, this party has been strongest in northern states, where it has drawn upon a regional tradition of resistance to central authority. It has also been primarily an urban party of the middle class and is closely identified with the private sector. The PAN has traditionally campaigned on a platform endorsing greater regional autonomy, less government intervention in the economy, reduced regulation of business, clean and fair elections, rapprochement with the Catholic Church, and support for private and religious education. When PRI governments of the 1980s and 1990s moved toward market-friendly and export-oriented policies, the policy differences between the two parties were significantly reduced. Nevertheless, a major difference of perspectives about religion continued to characterize the two parties.

For many years, the PAN was able to elect only about 10 percent of all deputies to the national congress and to capture control of just a few municipal governments. Beginning in the 1980s, it was able to take advantage both of the damage done to the PRI by economic crises and the opportunities provided by political reforms to increase its power. A PAN candidate was elected as the first opposition state governor in many years in 1989, and the party built up a sizeable bloc in both houses of congress during the 1990s. The PAN's victory in the 2000 presidential election was a historic breakthrough. Its triumph that year and in 2006 made the PAN the nation's governing party for twelve years.

In nominating Vicente Fox for the presidency in 2000, the party was taking an unusual step, for Fox was not a long-standing member of the party. Many party insiders considered him to be an opportunistic newcomer. Although Fox won the presidential election, the PAN organization was weak and not at all united in backing him. His inability to capitalize on his electoral victory and push forward a more ambitious package of reforms allowed the party insiders to regain control of the nominating process and advance the candidacy of Felipe Calderón in 2006. Unlike Fox, he was a lifelong member of the PAN and was the son of one of the PAN's founding members. In 2012, the party nominated a former education and social development minister, Josefina Vázquez Mota, as its presidential candidate. Her third-place showing indicated the country was ready for a change, and although the party continues to hold several governorships and the second-largest number of seats in both houses of congress, the PAN has struggled since its defeat to overcome internal divisions over its future.

The PRD and Morena

Another group that has played a key role in the construction of a more competitive political system in Mexico is the Party of the Democratic Revolution (PRD), which emerged in the late 1980s as a populist, nationalist, and leftist alternative to the PRI. Its candidate in the 1988, 1994, and 2000 elections was Cuauhtémoc Cárdenas, the son of Mexico's most revered president. In the 1988 elections, Cárdenas was officially credited with winning 31.1 percent of the vote. He benefited from massive political defection from the PRI and garnered support from workers disaffected with the boss-dominated unions, as well as from peasants who remembered his father's concern for the welfare of the poor.

Even while the votes were being counted, the party began to denounce widespread electoral fraud and claim that Cárdenas would have won if the election had been honest. The party challenged a number of vote counts in the courts and walked out on the inaugural speech given by the PRI's Salinas. Considerable public opinion supported the party's challenge. After the 1988 elections, then, it seemed that the PRD was a strong contender to become Mexico's second-most-powerful party. It was expected to have a real chance in future years to challenge the PRI's "right" to the presidency.

However, in the aftermath of these elections, the party was plagued by internal divisions over its platform, leadership, organizational structure, and election strategy. By 1994, it still lagged far behind the PRI and the PAN in establishing and maintaining the local constituency organizations needed to mobilize votes and monitor the election process. In addition, the PRD found it difficult to define an appropriate left-of-center alternative to the market-oriented policies carried out by the government. In the 1994 and 2000 elections, Cárdenas won less than 17 percent of the vote.

Under the leadership of a successful grassroots mobilizer named Andrés Manuel López Obrador, who was elected to head the party in 1996 and who subsequently served as mayor of Mexico City, the PRD began to stage a turnaround. PRD administrations in several states, many municipalities, and, most important, in Mexico City showed that the party could take on the challenges of governance. Under López Obrador, the PRD's prospects for the 2006 elections looked good. Indeed, for most of 2005, polls indicated that López Obrador was the clear favorite to win the presidency. In early 2006, however, the PAN's Calderón was able to shift the focus of his campaign and raise fears that a López Obrador presidency would threaten the stability of Mexico's economy. The election was hard-fought and characterized by growing animosity. In the end, Calderón was able to win by a narrow margin. López Obrador refused to concede defeat and staged several protests, including a shadow inauguration where he declared himself the "legitimate" president of Mexico.

López Obrador's response to the outcome of the 2006 election split public opinion and created another debilitating divide in the PRD, this time between those who supported their candidate's claims and more pragmatic party leaders who favored looking to the future. These divisions deepened in the aftermath of the 2012 elections, when López Obrador again claimed fraud in the wake of his defeat. With some in the party signaling a willingness to work with the incoming Peña Nieto administration as a constructive opposition party, López Obrador broke away from the PRD and formed a new party, the National Regeneration Movement (Morena). Although he did not follow López Obrador into a new political organization, Cuauhtémoc Cárdenas also demonstrated his unhappiness with the state of the PRD by resigning in 2014 from the party he had helped to establish.

Although the PRD remains the third-largest force in congress and continues to govern Mexico City and a few states, the factionalism that has characterized the party make its future prospects uncertain. Meanwhile, Morena won seats in the Chamber of Deputies in mid-term congressional elections in 2015, and its leader, Andrés Manuel López Obrador, is again seen as a leading contender for the presidency in 2018.

Other Parties

There are a number of smaller parties that contest elections in Mexico. In 2017, the most important small parties were the Citizens' Movement, the Labor Party (PT), the Green Party (PVEM), and the New Alliance Party (PANAL). Since Mexican law requires parties to receive at least 2.5 percent of the vote to be able to compete in future elections, the long-term viability of some of these organizations is doubtful, but several of these organizations have been successful in attracting sufficient votes to maintain their registration (and access to public funding for political parties) over several electoral cycles. Small parties usually do win a few of the seats in the Chamber of Deputies and the Senate that are filled by proportional representation.

Smaller parties sometimes have an impact on national politics by forming alliances with the larger parties, either endorsing their candidates in national and state elections or backing a single slate of candidates for congress. For example, in 2012, the Citizens' Movement and the PT formed an alliance with the PRD to support the presidential candidacy of Andrés Manuel López Obrador, and the PRI and the PVEM jointly backed Peña Nieto. For its part, the New Alliance Party, generally seen as the political arm of the powerful national teachers' union, withdrew from the coalition supporting Peña Nieto and sought to influence the electoral process by nominating its own presidential candidate (who won just over 2 percent of the vote). The Green Party also holds a state governorship, and the Citizens' Movement has held one in the past, though in both cases their members were elected to office thanks to alliances with larger parties.

Elections

The main political parties draw voters from a wide and overlapping spectrum of the electorate. Nevertheless, a typical voter for the PRI is likely to be from a rural area or small town, to have less education, and to be older and poorer than voters for the other parties. A typical voter for the PAN is likely to be from a northern state, to live in an urban area, to be a middle-class professional, to have a comfortable lifestyle, and to have a high school or even a university education. A typical voter for the PRD or Morena is likely to be young, to be a political activist, to have an elementary or high school education, to live in one of the central states, and to live in a small town or an urban area. As we have seen, the support base for the PRI is the most vulnerable to economic and demographic changes in the country, although disillusionment with the status quo under the PAN allowed the party to overcome this challenge in 2012.

Since 1994, elections have been more competitive and much fairer than they were during decades of PRI dominance, and subsequent congressional, state, and municipal elections reinforced the impression that electoral fraud is on the wane in many areas. The PAN's victory in 2000 substantially increased this impression. When López Obrador claimed in 2006 and 2012 that he had been robbed of victory, the legitimacy of the federal electoral authorities was questioned, but no evidence of wide-scale fraud or election tampering was uncovered. Concerns remain, however, about the impact of media bias, unlawful campaign spending, and vote buying on the outcomes of some elections.

Political Culture, Citizenship, and Identity

Most Mexicans have a deep familiarity with how their political system works and the ways in which they might be able to extract benefits from it. They understand the informal rules of the game in Mexican politics that have helped maintain political stability despite extensive inequalities in economic and political power. Clientelism has long been a form of participation in the sense that through their connections, many people, even the poorest, are able to interact with public officials and get something out of the political system. This kind of participation emphasizes how limited resources, such as access to health care, can be distributed in a way that provides maximum political payoff. This informal system is a fundamental reason that many Mexicans continued to vote for the PRI for so long. However, new ways of interacting with government are emerging, and they coexist along with the clientelistic style of the past. An increasing number of citizens are seeking to negotiate with the government on the basis of citizenship rights, not personal patron–client relationships.

Interest Groups, Social Movements, and Protest

accommodation

An informal agreement or settlement between the government and important interest groups in response to the interest groups' concerns about policy or program benefits.

The Mexican political system has long responded to groups of citizens through pragmatic accommodation to their interests. This is one important reason that political tensions among major interests have rarely escalated into the kind of serious conflict that can threaten stability. Where open conflict has occurred, it has generally been met with efforts to find some kind of compromise solution. Accommodation has been particularly apparent in response to the interests of business. Mexico's development strategy encouraged the growth of wealthy elites in commerce, finance, industry, and agriculture.

Labor has been similarly accommodated within the system. Wage levels for unionized workers grew fairly consistently between 1940 and 1982, when the economic crisis caused a significant drop in wages. At the same time, labor interests were attended to through concrete benefits and limitations on the rights of employers to discipline or dismiss workers. Union leaders controlled their rank and file in the interest of their own power to negotiate with government, but at the same time, they sought benefits for workers who continued to provide support for the PRI. The power of the union bosses has declined, partly because the unions are weaker than in the past, partly because union members are demanding greater democratization, and also because the PRI no longer monopolizes political power. Likewise, in the countryside, rural organizations have gained greater independence from the government. Indigenous groups have also emerged to demand that government be responsive to their needs and respectful of their traditions.

Mexicans are accustomed to making demands on their leaders, and protest is an established feature of Mexican political culture. Here, protesters march into Mexico City's central square, the Zócalo.

AP Images/Gregory Bull

Despite the strong and controlling role of the PRI in Mexico's political history, the country also has a tradition of civic organizations that operate at community and local levels with considerable independence from politics. Urban popular movements, formed by low- and modest-income (popular) groups, gained renewed vitality in the 1980s.[10] When the economic crisis resulted in drastic reductions of social welfare spending and city services, working- and middle-class neighborhoods forged new coalitions and greatly expanded the national discussion of urban problems. The Mexico City earthquake of 1985 encouraged the formation of unprecedented numbers of grassroots movements in response to the slow and poorly managed relief efforts of the government. Subsequent elections provided these groups with significant opportunities to press candidates to respond to their needs.

Urban popular movements bring citizens together around needs and ideals that cut across class boundaries. Neighborhood improvement, the environment, local self-government, economic development, feminism, and professional identity have been among the factors that have forged links among these groups. Women have begun to mobilize in many cities to demand community services, equal pay, legal equality, and opportunities in business that have traditionally been denied to them.

Traditionally, much activism has focused on questions of economic redistribution rather than divisive social issues, but this has recently begun to change. Political issues that are commonly discussed in the United States, such as abortion and gay rights, have recently begun to be debated publicly in Mexico. In April 2007, the PRD-controlled legislative assembly of Mexico City voted to decriminalize abortions in the first trimester (in the rest of Mexico abortion continues to be illegal except in cases of rape or severe birth defects, although in fact gaining access to a legal abortion even under these circumstances is difficult). And in November 2006, the capital city's PRD-led government legalized gay civil unions. Reflecting its background as a largely Catholic, socially conservative party, the PAN remains vehemently opposed to these measures. For example, in 2000, the PAN-dominated legislature of Guanajuato voted to ban abortion even in the case of rape, and established penalties of up to three years in prison for women who violated the law.

Although President Fox was opposed to abortion, he did attempt to distance himself from the Guanajuato law and for the most part avoided discussing contentious social and cultural subjects. But under his administration, condom use was encouraged and a campaign against homophobia was launched. In 2004, he caused a furor within his own party when his administration approved the distribution of the morning-after pill in public clinics. These policies were denounced by Calderón, who came from a more traditionalist wing of his party. He vowed in his 2006 campaign to ban the use of this pill and openly expressed his opposition to abortion and gay rights. President Peña Nieto has largely sought to avoid confronting these contentious social issues. He has described himself as personally opposed to abortion but opposed to its criminalization, and he has said that the question of same-sex unions should be left to Mexico's states.

The Political Impact of Technology and the Media

As politics and elections have became more open and competitive in Mexico in recent decades, the roles of public opinion and the mass media have become more important. Today, the media play an important role in forming public opinion in Mexico. As with other aspects of Mexican politics, the media began to become more independent in the 1980s, enjoying a "spring" of greater independence and diversity of opinion.[11] There are currently several major television networks in the country, and many citizens have access to global networks. The number of newspapers and news magazines is expanding, as is their circulation. There is some concern, however, that many of the most important and influential media outlets in the country are controlled by a small number of individuals and corporations. Also, violence against and intimidation of Mexican journalists by drug trafficking organizations has limited the ability of the press to report on the important issues raised in the context of the fight against organized crime in recent years. Nonetheless, citizens in Mexico today hear a much wider range of opinion and much greater reporting of debates about public policy and criticism of government than at any time previously.

As in other countries, changes in communications technology over the past two decades or so have had a major impact on the ways in which citizens organize themselves and on the ways in which politicians and political parties seek to reach their constituents. Young, highly educated, and urban groups in particular are heavy users of social media, and even many poorer Mexicans and residents of smaller towns and rural areas have mobile telephones and some degree of access to the Internet. During the 2012 presidential campaign, therefore, all of the major candidates actively sought to attract Twitter followers and to project a positive image on Facebook. They also found themselves subject to embarrassment when footage of their gaffes on the campaign trail was circulated widely on social media. A viral video in which Peña Nieto struggled to name three books that had influenced him reinforced some voters' suspicion that the PRI candidate was not a deep thinker, and footage of the PAN's Vázquez Mota stumbling over prepared remarks damaged her efforts to make up ground in the polls.

Social media even gave rise to a movement that changed the narrative of the 2012 campaign for a time. After candidate Peña Nieto was confronted by protesters during an appearance at a Mexico City university in May 2012, the media reported that the protesters had been agitators from outside the campus rather than students at the institution, prompting 131 of the protesters to post a video online in which they displayed their university identification cards. Thousands of other social media users who also saw television and other media coverage of the campaign as biased toward Peña Nieto expressed their support by posting, "Yo soy 132," or "I am the 132nd [student]." The online movement led to marches and rallies, calling for a deepening of democracy in Mexico.

Communications technology has also taken on political significance in Mexican citizens' response to the drug-related violence that has affected the country in recent years. In regions in which local journalists were effectively silenced by threats from the cartels, some users of social media relied on that outlet to broadcast information on the danger posed by criminal activities in specific locations. When Twitter users in Veracruz circulated what turned out to be an inaccurate report of a shootout at a school, state authorities prosecuted them for terrorism. Although the governor issued a pardon in that case, the state legislature proceeded to pass a new law to make it a crime to use social media to undermine public order. Thus, the place of new communications technologies in Mexican politics and society continues to be negotiated and to evolve.

Where Do You Stand?

Through public funding and guaranteed broadcasting airtime, political parties in Mexico are given a privileged position as recognized vehicles for the representation of citizens' interests, but increasingly Mexicans are mobilizing for political change outside of party structures, through civil society organizations, popular movements, and social media. How should government policies respond to these developments?

Should public funding of political parties be curtailed, or would that simply create an opening for wealthy private interests to exert greater influence in politics?

MEXICAN POLITICS IN TRANSITION

SECTION
5

The Mexican political landscape has been transformed over the past twenty years, as a long period of dominance by a single party has given way to a competitive multiparty system. The country's institutions, leaders, and citizens are still adjusting to this ongoing process of change. While most Mexicans are proud that their political system has become more democratic, many also lament that the division of power between political parties and branches of government at times seems to make the state less efficient and possibly less able to address effectively the challenges of development and governance faced by Mexico.

One particularly dramatic illustration of how much Mexican politics has changed can be seen on September 1 of each year, when, in accordance with Article 69 of the Constitution, the executive branch delivers a report on the state of the nation to congress at the opening of its annual session. For decades, this date was known informally as the "Day of the President," as the ritual surrounding the address highlighted the prestige and authority of the chief executive. The president would don his ceremonial red, white, and green sash before traveling to the legislative chambers from the National Palace, the symbolic seat of power in Mexico since the days of the Spanish viceroys. While delivering his *informe* (report), the president could count on a respectful hearing from an attentive audience of deputies and senators who were overwhelmingly drawn from the ranks of his own party. Although the spectacle of the *informe* during the heyday of PRI dominance excluded dissenting voices, it projected an image of a strong, stable political system. Even in 1982, when President José López Portillo broke into tears while reporting on his failure to avert a debt crisis that sent the country into an economic tailspin, legislators dutifully applauded.

That deference to the president began to break down in 1988, however. After a contentious presidential election marred by allegations of fraud, a legislator who had broken away from the PRI to support opposition candidate Cuauhtémoc Cárdenas dared to interrupt President Miguel de la Madrid's speech. More recently, after members of the PRD charged that Felipe Calderón's election in 2006 was illegitimate, the outgoing president, Vicente Fox, was prevented from even reaching the rostrum when he arrived to give his address on September 1 of that year. He complied with his

Focus Questions

- What challenges does the process of globalization pose to Mexicans' strong sense of national identity?

- How successful has Mexico been in confronting the legacy of authoritarian rule? To what extent have recent administrations been able to make the government more accountable and transparent?

constitutional mandate by submitting a printed copy of his report and then left the building without delivering his speech. In 2007, President Felipe Calderón likewise appeared before a deeply divided legislature only long enough to hand over a printed version of his *informe*, and new rules introduced in 2008 eliminated the requirement that the president deliver his report in person. Since then, the annual report of the executive branch has been transmitted by a government minister to the legislature, where representatives of the parties represented in Congress deliver a response. In 2013, plans for Peña Nieto to make a public presentation of his first *informe* at a large military parade ground had to be scaled back in the face of massive protests by a dissident teachers' union that had paralyzed Mexico City. Instead the president shared his report with a much smaller audience at his official residence. These incidents show how many more voices, besides the president's, are heard on important national issues in Mexico today, although to many the fact that the chief executive is no longer able to find a respectful audience for his report suggests that the capacity of the state has been diminished.

Political Challenges and Changing Agendas

As Mexicans adjust and adapt to the dramatic political transition of recent years, they are conscious that their nation faces many challenges, and they are struggling to build a political system that will be both democratic and effective. They are calling upon the state to be open about abuses of authority in the past and to protect citizens from such abuses in the future. They seek to address long-standing inequalities in Mexican society, in part by ensuring that women and ethnic minorities have access to economic opportunities and social services. They also hope to preserve Mexican identity while realizing the economic benefits of integration into global networks.

Mexico today provides a testing ground for the democratic idea in a state with a long history of authoritarian institutions. The democratic ideas of citizen rights to free speech and assembly, free and fair elections, and responsive government are major reasons that the power of the PRI came under so much attack beginning in the 1980s. As part of its commitment to delivering a sharp change from the practices of the past, the PAN administration of Vicente Fox (2000–2006) pledged to make government more transparent and to improve the state of human rights in Mexico. In the past, the government had been able to limit knowledge of its repressive actions, use the court system to maintain the political peace, and intimidate those who objected to its actions. Fox appointed human rights activists to his cabinet and ordered that secret police and military files be opened to public scrutiny. He instructed government ministries to supply more information about their activities and about the rights that citizens have to various kinds of services. The government also sought to protect the rights of Mexicans abroad, and the United States and Mexico established a working group to improve human rights conditions for migrants.

The results of these actions have been dramatic. For the first time, Mexicans learned of cases of hundreds of people who had "disappeared" as a result of police and military actions. In addition, citizens have come forward to announce other disappearances, ones they were unwilling to report earlier because they feared reprisals. In 2002, former PRI president Luis Echeverría was brought before prosecutors and questioned about government actions against political dissent in 1968 and 1971, a kind of accountability unheard of in the past. The National Human Rights Commission has been active in efforts to hold government officials accountable and to protect citizens from repetitions of the abuses of the past.

Yet challenges to human rights accountability remain. Opening up files and setting up systems for prosecuting abusers needs to be followed by actions to impose penalties on abusers. The Mexican judicial system is weak and has little experience in human rights cases. In addition, action on reports of disappearances, torture, and imprisonment has been slowed by disagreement about civil and military jurisdictions. Human rights activists claimed that police and military personnel, in particular, still had impunity from the laws, and human rights concerns have grown as the military has taken a more direct role in law enforcement since the Calderón administration launched its effort to dismantle drug trafficking organizations. Human rights advocates point to recent alleged abuses by members of the armed forces and call for greater accountability from an institution that is still shielded from much civilian scrutiny. Although human rights are much more likely to be protected than in the past, the government still has a long way to go in safeguarding the rights of indigenous people, political dissidents, migrants, the lesbian, gay, bisexual, and transgender (LGBT) community, and poor people whose ability to use the judicial system is limited by poverty and lack of information.

Human rights

Mexico is also confronting major challenges in adapting newly democratic institutions to reflect ethnic and religious diversity and to provide equity for women in economic and political affairs. The past two decades have witnessed the emergence of more organized and politically independent ethnic groups demanding justice and equality from government. These groups claim that they have suffered for nearly 500 years and that they are no longer willing to accept poverty and marginality as their lot. The Catholic Church, still the largest organized religion in the country, is losing members to Protestant sects that appeal particularly to the everyday concerns of poor Mexicans. Women are becoming more organized, but they still have a long way to go before their wages equal those of men or they have equal voice in political and economic decisions.

Another significant challenge for Mexico today is reconciling its strong sense of national identity with the strains placed on a country's sovereignty by the process of global economic integration. Mexicans define themselves in part through a set of historical events, symbols, and myths that focus on the country's troubled relationship with the United States. The myths of the Revolution of 1910 emphasize the uniqueness of the country in terms of its opposition to the capitalists and militarists of the northern country. This view stands in strong contrast to more recent perspectives touting the benefits of an internationally oriented economy and the undeniable post-NAFTA reality of information, culture, money, and people flowing back and forth across borders.

The country's sense of national identity is also affected by international migration. Every year, large numbers of Mexicans enter the United States as workers. Many return to their towns and villages with new values and new views of the world. Many stay in the United States, where Hispanics have become the largest ethnic minority population in the country. Although they may believe that Mexico is a better place to nurture strong family life and values, they are nevertheless strongly influenced by U.S. mass culture, including popular music, movies, television programs, fast food, and consumer goods.

The inability of the Mexican economy to create enough jobs pushes additional Mexicans to seek work in the United States, and the cash remittances that migrants abroad send home to their families and communities are now as important a source of income for Mexico as PEMEX's oil sales. However, the issues surrounding migration have become even more complex since the attacks of September 11, 2001. Hopes for a bilateral accord that would permit more Mexicans to enter and work in the United States legally evaporated after U.S. officials suddenly found themselves under greatly increased pressure to control the country's borders. The recent election of Donald Trump to the U.S. presidency on a platform calling for the construction of a border wall shows that the politics of immigration control will remain an important issue in U.S.-Mexican relations. Whether or not the U.S. government approves, the difference in wages between the United States and Mexico will persist for a long time, which implies that migration will also persist.

There is disagreement about how to respond to the economic challenges that Mexico faces. Much of the debate surrounds the question of what integration into a competitive international economy really means. For some, it represents the final abandonment of Mexico's sovereignty. For others, it is the basis on which future prosperity must be built. Those who are critical of the market-based, outwardoriented development strategy are concerned about its impact on workers, peasants, and national identities. They argue that the state has abandoned its responsibilities to protect the poor from shortcomings of the market and to provide for their basic needs. They believe that U.S. and Canadian investors have come to Mexico only to find low-wage labor for industrial empires located elsewhere. They see little benefit in further industrial development based on importation of foreign-made parts, their assembly in Mexico, and their export to other markets. Those who favor closer integration with Canada and the United States acknowledge that some foreign investment does not promote technological advances or move the workforce into higher-paying and more skilled jobs. They emphasize, however, that most investment will occur because Mexico has a relatively well-educated population, the capacity to absorb modern technology, and a large internal market for industrial goods.

Inequality represents another daunting challenge for Mexican society. While elites enjoy the benefits of sumptuous lifestyles, education at the best U.S. universities for their children, and luxury travel throughout the world, large numbers of Mexicans remain ill-educated, poorly served with health care, and distant from the security of knowing that their basic needs will be met. As in the United States, some argue that the best solutions to these problems are economic growth and expanded employment. They believe that the achievement of prosperity through integration into the global economy will benefit everyone in the long run. For this to occur, however, they insist that education will have to be improved and made more appropriate for developing a well-prepared workforce. From their perspective, the solution to poverty and injustice is fairly clear: more and better jobs and improved education.

For those critical of the development path on which Mexico embarked in the 1980s and 1990s, the problems of poverty and inequity are more complex. Solutions involve understanding the diverse causes of poverty, including not only lack of jobs and poor education but also exploitation, geographic isolation, and discriminatory laws and practices, as well as the disruptive impact of migration, urbanization, and the tensions of modern life. In the past, Mexicans looked to government for social welfare benefits, but their provision was deeply flawed by inefficiency and political manipulation. Thus, although many continue to believe that it is the responsibility of government to ensure that citizens are well educated, healthy, and able to make the most of their potential, the populace is deeply suspicious of the government's capacity to provide such conditions fairly and efficiently.

Is Demography Destiny?

Young people currently account for a very high proportion of the country's population, making them a fundamentally important factor in Mexican politics. Unlike China, Japan, or many European countries, Mexico is not a rapidly aging country, with a large share of its population over 65. Instead, more than half of the population is under 30. This means that very many voters in the 2012 elections cast their ballots with little memory of the PRI's "perfect dictatorship." Having grown up in a democratic Mexico with a competitive political environment, these voters are perhaps unlikely to be interested in a return to the PRI's old style of politics, but the party preferences and affiliations of younger Mexicans remain to be defined.

Young people have long played a central role in driving political change in Mexico. The student movement of 1968 helped to begin the process of questioning the legitimacy of PRI rule, and younger voters played a disproportionally important part in bringing about the democratic transition of 2000. The younger generation is also heavily overrepresented in the social media world from which future political campaigns and initiatives are likely to arise, as the "Yo soy 132" movement did in 2012. Given the demographic significance of Mexico's younger population, the development of those preferences will shape Mexican politics for a long time to come.

young people impact

Mexican Politics in Comparative Perspective

Mexico faces many of the same challenges that beset other countries: creating equitable and effective democratic government, becoming integrated into a global economy, responding to complex social problems, and supporting increasing diversity without losing national identity. The legacies of its past, the tensions of the present, and the innovations of the future will no doubt evolve in ways that continue to be uniquely Mexican.

Mexico represents a pivotal case of political and economic transition for the developing world. If it can successfully bridge the gap between its past and its future and move from centralization to effective local governance, from regional vulnerability to global interdependence, and from the control of the few to the participation of the many, it will set a model for other countries that face the same kind of challenges.

Where Do You Stand?

Does Mexico offer lessons for other countries moving from authoritarian forms of governance to more democratic ones? What might Mexico learn from the experience of some of the other countries you are studying?

If you were a young person in Mexico today, what issues do you think would be most important to you? Which political party (if any) would you support, and why?

Chapter Summary

The Mexican political system is unique among developing countries in the extent to which it managed to institutionalize and maintain civilian political authority for a very long time. The country's development has been shaped by the revolutionary ideals that arose from its distinctive historical experience, by its proximity to the United States, and by its ongoing efforts to find a place in an interconnected global economy. Currently, Mexico is undergoing significant political change, transforming itself from a corporatist state to a democratic one. At the same time, Mexican society is experiencing high levels of violence as the state confronts drug trafficking organizations that represent a challenge to its authority and to the rule of law.

While Mexico's development from the 1930s to the 1980s was marked by extensive government engagement in the economy, since that time the country has opened its economy and pursued prosperity through market reforms and free trade. But while links with the U.S. economy have deepened, growth has been slow under the new policies. Industry and oil give the country a per capita income higher than those of most other developing nations, but the country suffers from great inequalities in how wealth is distributed, and poverty continues to be a grim reality for millions. The way the country promoted economic growth and industrialization is important in explaining why widespread poverty has persisted and why political power is not more equitably distributed.

On paper, Mexico's government resembles that of the United States, with three branches of government, checks and balances among them, and federalism defining the relationship between national, state, and local governments. In practice, however, the country developed a political system that concentrated most power in the hands of the president and the executive branch and managed political conflict through a dominant party. Much of the power of the president and the PRI was based on their capacity to use patronage to respond to political conflicts. This system is undergoing rapid change, as the legislature and court systems develop more independent roles, state and local governments acquire more independence, and multiple parties compete for power.

Mexico's democratic transition took place gradually, as Mexican citizens developed the capacity to question the dominance of the PRI regime and as the government introduced important changes that opened up opportunities for opposition parties to develop and for people to vote more easily for these parties. Since the election of 2000 demonstrated that a transition of power from a civilian authoritarian regime to a more democratic one could take place peacefully, Mexico has had considerable experience with democratic politics. This experience has been marked both by pride in the country's democratic path and frustration that democratic institutions have not been able to pass needed reforms, to create jobs, and to guarantee security.

What will the future bring? How much will the pressures for change affect the nature of the political system? In 1980, few people could have foreseen the extensive economic policy reforms and pressures for democracy that Mexico would experience in the next three decades. Few would have predicted the defeat of the PRI in the elections of 2000, much less its return to power in 2012. In considering the future of the country, it is important to remember that Mexico has a long tradition of relatively strong institutions. It is not a country that will easily slip into sustained political instability. Despite real challenges faced as Mexico confronts criminal organizations and seeks to reform its police forces and judicial system, the country is not in danger of collapse, as some outside observers have been tempted to suggest. A tradition of constitutional government, a strong presidency, a political system that has incorporated a wide range of interests, little military involvement in politics, and a deep sense of national identity—these are among the factors that need to be considered in understanding the political consequences of democratization, economic integration, and greater social equality in Mexico.

Key Terms

accommodation
anticlericalism
caudillos
civil society
corporatist state

coup d'état
ejidos
indigenous groups
maquiladoras
mestizo

remittances
sexenio
state capitalism
technocrats

Suggested Readings

Beezley, William and Michael Meyer, eds. *The Oxford History of Mexico*. New York: Oxford University Press, 2010.

Call, Wendy. *No Word for Welcome: The Mexican Village Faces the Global Economy*. Lincoln: University of Nebraska Press, 2011.

Camp, Roderic Ai., ed. *The Oxford Handbook of Mexican Politics*. New York: Oxford University Press, 2012.

Délano, Alexandra. *Mexico and its Diaspora in the United States: Policies of Emigration since 1848*. New York: Cambridge University Press, 2011.

Edmonds-Poli, Emily, and David A. Shirk, *Contemporary Mexican Politics*, 3rd ed. Lanham, MD: Rowman & Littlefield Publishers, 2015.

Eisenstadt, Todd A. *Politics, Identity, and Mexico's Indigenous Rights Movements* (Cambridge Studies in Contentious Politics). New York: Cambridge University Press, 2011.

Henderson, Timothy J. *Beyond Borders: A History of Mexican Migration to the United States*. New York: Wiley-Blackwell, 2011.

Langston, Joy K. *Democratization and Authoritarian Party Survival: Mexico's PRI*. New York: Oxford University Press, 2017.

Preston, Julia, and Samuel Dillon. *Opening Mexico: The Making of a Democracy*. New York: Farrar, Straus and Giroux, 2004.

Selee, Andrew, and Jacqueline Peschard. *Mexico's Democratic Challenges: Politics, Government, and Society*. Stanford, CA: Stanford University Press, 2010.

Suggested Websites

Office of the President
www.gob/mx/presidencia/en

Secretariat of Foreign Relations
www.gob.mx/sre/en

Mexican Embassy to the United States
https://embamex2.sre.gob.mx/eua/index.php/en/

Office of Mexican Affairs, U.S. Department of State
http://www.state.gov/p/wha/ci/mx/

The Mexico Project, National Security Archive
http://nsarchive.gwu.edu/mexico/

South Africa

Tom Lodge

REUTERS/Alamy

Location: Southern Africa, at the southern tip of the continent of Africa

Capital City: Pretoria (administrative capital); Cape Town (legislative capital); Bloemfontein (judicial capital)

Population (2016): 55.6 million

Size: 1,219,090 sq. km.; nearly twice the size of Texas

© Cengage

THE MAKING OF THE MODERN SOUTH AFRICAN STATE

Politics in Action

- Why did institutionalized racism become such a central characteristic of South African social life in the twentieth century?

- In which ways does racial inequality persist in South Africa?

For nearly a century, the statue of Cecil Rhodes, mining millionaire and key architect of British imperialist expansion in Southern Africa, sat heavily upon its granite base on Table Mountain, a short walk from South Africa's ivy-covered elite campus, the University of Cape Town (UCT). Not any more, though. On March 9, 2015, UCT's Black Student Society held a protest meeting by the statue. The group was dispersed by security officials after one student daubed the effigy with excrement. The incident prompted a series of escalating campus confrontations that swiftly spread to other campuses. Networks proliferated through social media, and then came together as the #FeesMustFall movement. To the activists on Table Mountain, Rhodes's brooding presence was only a symbol of their deeper concerns. Despite the university authorities' removal of the sculpture the following month, the protests escalated, engulfing all of South Africa's universities in an insurrectionary tide which continued throughout 2016.

Between 2000 and 2015, South African universities doubled their intake but government financing remained static. College authorities made up the difference by increasing student fees. Certain universities now charge fees that exceed many people's wages. Larger classes are also now common and meant less attentive teaching and higher failure rates, especially for students from "disadvantaged" backgrounds; mainly black students. Protest coalesced around the demand for free or at least cheaper education, but students also raised more difficult issues about ideology and content. Universities needed to be "decolonized," they demanded, there needed to be fewer white staff and less "Western science." Change shouldn't stop at the campus gates, charged student leaders, government should also cease taking orders "from white monopoly capital," and its members should stop acting like white "puppets." Amongst the protestors, there is a new political iconoclasm: on campuses today you are much more likely to see the red berets of the radical Economic Freedom Front than the Congress regalia that used to configure the dress code at political events. That is not the only code the students are ready to break. One of the early leaders of the movement, ex-Wits Student Council leader Mcebo Dlamini, confided on Twitter his admiration for Hitler, and blamed his dismissal from the university on Jewish "devils" who were "uncircumcised at heart."

The government ignored the protest at first; it was a matter for the universities, the minister explained, but 18 months later, in October 2016, President Jacob Zuma appointed a ministerial task team to address what he now admitted to be a crisis. His action came after a week of clashes between heavily armed police and students at Wits University in Johannesburg. After all, for the generation leading the African National Congress (ANC), student protest is not inconsequential. Many of South Africa's political leaders are veterans of the student rebellions that inspired a national

CHRONOLOGY of South Africa's Political Development

1779
First Frontier War in the Eastern Cape between settlers and Xhosa kingdoms.

1834
Abolition of slavery.

1836
Great Trek and subsequent establishment of Afrikaner republics of the Orange Free State and the Transvaal (South African Republic).

1899–1902
Anglo-Boer War and British occupation of Afrikaner republics.

1913
Land Act

1923
Native Urban Areas Act codifies urban racial segregation.

1650	1780	1810	1840	1870	1900	1920

1652
Establishment of settlement at Cape Town by Dutch East India Company.

1806
Incorporation of Cape Colony in British Empire.

1820
Arrival of British settlers in Eastern Cape.

1860
Arrival of first Indian indentured laborers in Natal.

1912
Formation of the African National Congress (ANC).

1910
Act of Union

1922
Rand Rebellion by white mineworkers.

Table 11.1	Political Organization
Political System	Parliamentary democracy and federal republic.
Regime History	Governed by an African National Congress–led coalition from 1994. Between 1910 and 1994 governments were formed by parties representing a white minority and were elected through racially restricted franchises.
Administrative Structure	Nine regional governments sharing authority with a national administration. Regional governments can be overridden on most significant issues by national legislatures.
Executive	President elected by parliament. President selects cabinet.
Legislature	National assembly and regional legislatures elected on the basis of party list proportional representation. National Council of Provinces made up by delegations from each regional government serves as a second chamber.
Judiciary	Independent constitutional court with appointed judges.
Party System	Multiparty system. African National Congress predominates.

uprising against the ruling white regime during the 1980s. But today's revolt is an uprising of the "born frees," the children who have grown up in a democratic South Africa and are beginning to question the moral authority of the ruling party's most venerated elders. (See Table 11.1.)

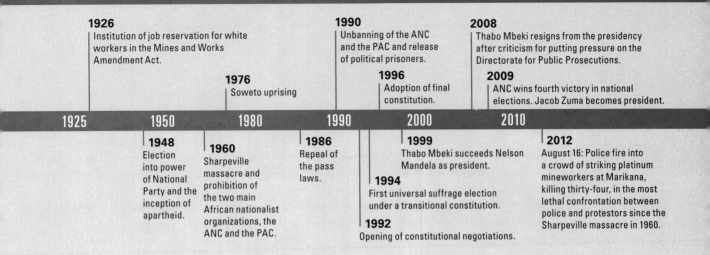

1926
Institution of job reservation for white workers in the Mines and Works Amendment Act.

1976
Soweto uprising

1990
Unbanning of the ANC and the PAC and release of political prisoners.

1996
Adoption of final constitution.

2008
Thabo Mbeki resigns from the presidency after criticism for putting pressure on the Directorate for Public Prosecutions.

2009
ANC wins fourth victory in national elections. Jacob Zuma becomes president.

1925　1950　1980　1990　2000　2010

1948
Election into power of National Party and the inception of apartheid.

1960
Sharpeville massacre and prohibition of the two main African nationalist organizations, the ANC and the PAC.

1986
Repeal of the pass laws.

1999
Thabo Mbeki succeeds Nelson Mandela as president.

1994
First universal suffrage election under a transitional constitution.

1992
Opening of constitutional negotiations.

2012
August 16: Police fire into a crowd of striking platinum mineworkers at Marikana, killing thirty-four, in the most lethal confrontation between police and protestors since the Sharpeville massacre in 1960.

Geographic Setting

South Africa is about twice the size of Texas. In the 2016 interim census, the population totaled 55.6 million. Two-thirds of this population is urban. Government statistics divide the population into four main race groups: nearly 45 million Bantu-language-speaking *Africans*, who are descended from migrants from Central Africa. The first European settlers arrived in the seventeenth century. Their descendants make up 4.5 million *Whites*, a slight decline since the last census as a consequence of white emigration. The 4.9 million *Coloureds* (the term used universally in South Africa) represent a group whose ancestry includes the earliest indigenous hunter-gatherers, as well as Indonesian slaves and offspring from unions between white settlers and these groups. A fourth group is the nearly 1.4 million Indians who are mostly descendants of indentured laborers brought from India.

Under the apartheid regime (1948–1993) of racial segregation, each group had a different legal status. While racial segregation is outlawed today, the communal identities created by official racial classification still influence social life. Most blacks still live in historically segregated ghetto-like neighborhoods, and most whites live in the more comfortable suburbs. (See Figure 11.1 for the South African nation at a glance.) However, a rapidly expanding black middle class is joining whites to live in the suburbs. Realtors in Johannesburg and Pretoria reported in 2012 that around half the home buyers in historically white suburbs were middle-class Africans. In 2016, researchers found that the black middle class had trebled in size since 2004.

Africans

This term, in South African usage, refers to Bantu language speakers, the demographic majority of South African citizens.

Critical Junctures

In 1652, the Dutch East India Company established a reprovisioning station at the southern tip of Africa. The Dutch settlers were not the first to arrive. Africans had

South Africa: Ethnic Groups

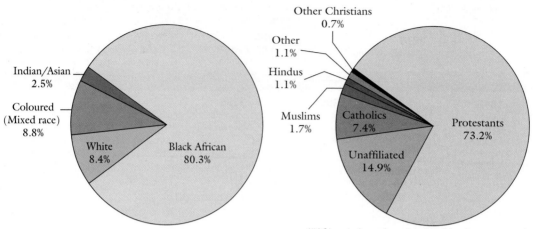

Indian/Asian 2.5%

Coloured (Mixed race) 8.8%

White 8.4%

Black African 80.3%

South Africa: Religions

Other Christians 0.7%

Other 1.1%

Hindus 1.1%

Muslims 1.7%

Catholics 7.4%

Protestants 73.2%

Unaffiliated 14.9%

("African independent churches," local groups constituted around charismatic preachers and prophets that blend African and Western religious beliefs and practices, including healing.)

South Africa: Languages*
*spoken at home

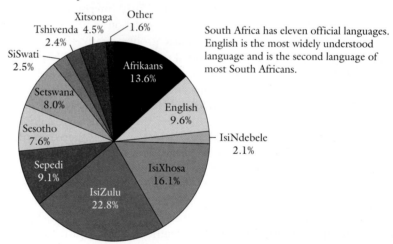

Xitsonga 4.5%

Other 1.6%

Tshivenda 2.4%

SiSwati 2.5%

Setswana 8.0%

Sesotho 7.6%

Sepedi 9.1%

IsiZulu 22.8%

IsiXhosa 16.1%

Afrikaans 13.6%

English 9.6%

IsiNdebele 2.1%

South Africa has eleven official languages. English is the most widely understood language and is the second language of most South Africans.

South African Currency

Rand (R)
International Designation: ZAR
Exchange Rate (2017):
- 1 US$ = 12.86 R
- 1 R = 0.08 US$
- 100R Note Design: Cape Buffalo

© Cengage

© Jonathan Noden-Wilkinson/Shutterstock.com

FIGURE 11.1 The South African Nation at a Glance

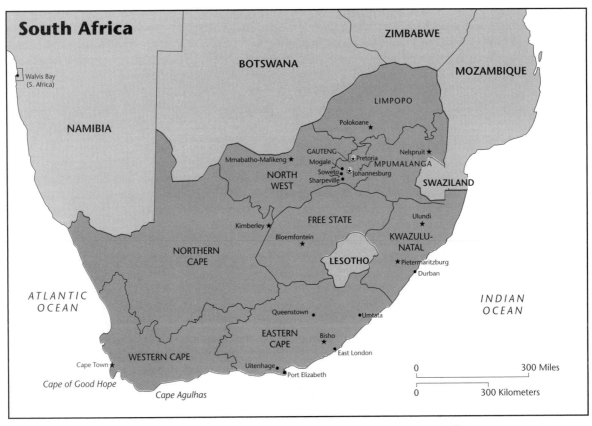

Source: From Tom Lodge, *South African Politics Since 1994*, pp. vi–vii. Reprinted with permission.

settled in the region at least 2,000 years previously, when Bantu speakers drove away or merged with earlier San, and/or the Khoikhoi hunter-gatherers and pastoralists.

By the eighteenth century, Dutch settlers in South Africa called themselves **Afrikaners** because they spoke a Dutch dialect called Afrikaans. In 1806, Britain took over the territory and added it to its empire. Because they resented British policies (including Britain's abolition of slavery), about one-tenth of the Afrikaner population—the *Voortrekkers*—migrated northwards between 1836 and 1840. The *Voortrekkers* established the Orange Free State in 1852, and the Transvaal in 1854.

Dynamics of the Frontier, 1779–1906

White settlement quickly and often violently overwhelmed the Khoisan. The settlers encountered tougher adversaries among Xhosa-speaking Africans along the eastern coast. The frontier wars between 1779 and 1878 fixed the boundaries between white farmers and the Xhosa kingdoms.

The strongest African resistance arose in the militarized Zulu Kingdom. The wars that created the Zulu state in the early nineteenth century forced other indigenous peoples to migrate. They based their own states on the Zulu model. But huge areas had been depopulated, available for white settlers. While white settlers usually preserved precolonial African kingdoms and chieftaincies after invading them, these played a subordinate role in colonial administrations.

In 1843, Britain annexed Natal, which had been part of the Zulu kingdom. From 1860, British immigrants established sugar plantations and began recruiting Indian

Afrikaners

Descendants of Dutch, French, German, and Scots settlers speaking Afrikaans. They were politically mobilized as an ethnic group throughout the twentieth century.

Voortrekkers

Pastoralist descendants of Dutch settlers in South Africa who moved north from the British-controlled Cape in 1836 to establish independent republics; later regarded as the founders of the Afrikaner nation.

labor, easier to discipline then local Africans who still retained pastures and were reluctant to work for the starvation wages offered by the sugar barons. Today, about 80 percent of South Africa's Indian population lives in this province, known as KwaZulu-Natal.

Imperialists Against Republicans, 1867–1910

After gold was discovered in the Witwatersrand region of the Transvaal in 1886, a massive mining industry grew up. By 1898, the mine owners, mainly British, increasingly objected to the Afrikaner government in Pretoria, the Transvaal capital, mostly because the government tended to favor local farmers in official programs to recruit African labor. By the late 1890s, the British government had become receptive to the mine owners, or "Randlords," since global rivalries had increased the strategic value of Transvaal's gold. War between Britain and the Afrikaner republics was declared on October 11, 1899. The savage Anglo-Boer War (1899–1902) was prolonged by the guerrilla campaign launched against the British by Afrikaner farmers, called Boers.

Boer

Literally "farmer"; modern usage is a derogatory reference to an Afrikaner.

Britain prevailed. Casualties included 28,000 Afrikaner civilians who died in concentration camps. Africans served in armies on both sides and 14,000 Africans died in internment camps. Voting was already color-blind in the British Cape Colony region, and Africans hoped that after the war they would be able to vote throughout the country. But during the peace negotiations, the British prioritized good relations between the Afrikaners and English over Africans. While an African elite retained the vote in the Cape, the agreement denied the franchise to Africans elsewhere.

Britain's ascendency in South Africa was confirmed by its victory in the Anglo-Boer War. Under the new British administration, officials constructed an efficient bureaucracy. A customs union between the four territories—the Cape, Natal, Transvaal, and Orange Free State—eliminated tariffs. A Native Affairs Department reorganized labor recruitment. In 1910, under the Act of Union, the four territories became provinces of the Union of South Africa, a self-governing dominion of the British Empire. In deference to Afrikaner sensitivities, the functions of a capital city were divided between the old Republican centers and Cape Town. A more important feature of the settlement was that Africans outside the Cape were excluded from voting.

The Origins of Modern Institutionalized Racism, 1910–1945

These arrangements confirmed the essentials of racist order. The need to coerce African labor—in order to control African workers and keep wages low—guided policy. In gold mining, profits depended on very cheap labor. The mine managers housed the workers in walled and guarded "compounds," originally developed to stop smuggling in the diamond fields, but on the Witwatersrand a totalitarian system of control. Given low wages and harsh conditions, additional measures to recruit workers needed to be repressive. Beginning with the 1913 Land Act, new laws enforced racial discrimination. They were designed to meet the needs of a mining economy, which required cheap labor that could not rebel. The Land Act allowed Africans to own land only inside a patchwork of native reserves. Land shortage compelled young men to work on the mines.

In the 1880s, Afrikaner nationalists constructed a heroic historic narrative about how their ancestors had created a frontier community united by a common language and Calvinist Protestantism. This community attracted white people who had been forced off the land during the Anglo-Boer War. During a white miners' armed insurrection in 1922, Afrikaner workers resurrected a Boer commando system.

The miners protested because employers were giving semiskilled jobs to Africans previously reserved for whites. One hundred fifty-three people were killed during the suppression of the rebellion. Two years later, a coalition government of the Labour Party and the (Afrikaner) National Party set up a "civilized labor" policy. It specified that all whites, even unskilled ones, should earn enough to maintain "civilized" standards. To ensure this, better-paid unskilled jobs were reserved for whites. The new government also invested in public industries. The pace of industrialization accelerated after 1933 when currency devaluation prompted fresh waves of foreign investment.

Apartheid and African Resistance, 1945–1960

In 1934, a United Party was created by a fusion between the National Party and the pro-British South African Party led by Jan Smuts, who became prime minister in 1939. The United Party favored a broader conception of white South African nationhood than was held by many Afrikaner nationalists. With respect to Africans, its leaders were generally segregationist, although a minority were more liberal. Social tensions prompted two different sets of political challenges to Smuts's United Party administration.

After moderate Afrikaner nationalists joined Jan Smuts in the United Party, hardliners formed a Purified National Party. Meanwhile, Afrikaner nationalism became a mass movement under the direction of a secret *Broederbond* (Brotherhood) that sponsored savings banks, trade unions, and voluntary organizations. From 1940, the National Party developed a program around the idea of apartheid (separateness) that emphasized even stricter racial separation than already existed. Apartheid dictated restricting Indians and Coloureds, and confining Africans to menial labor. This appealed to white workers who feared African competition. The National Party also drew support from farmers, who found it difficult to recruit labor. The National Party won a narrow electoral victory in 1948, marking the formal beginning of the apartheid era in South African history. More racist legislation followed. Pass laws required all Africans to carry internal passports at all times. Blacks needed special permits to travel to or live in towns. Interracial sex was banned.

African politics also became a mass movement in the 1940s. Although the African National Congress (ANC) was founded in 1912, it had not been very active. In 1945, the Natal Indian Congress, an organization first formed in 1894 by Mohandas Gandhi to protest discrimination against Indians, led a nonviolent resistance movement that inspired ANC leaders.

The Sharpeville Massacre and Grand Apartheid, 1960–1976

In the 1950s, African politicians reacted to fresh restrictions and segregation with civil disobedience, general strikes, and consumer boycotts. After the Communist Party was prohibited in 1950, the ANC and allied Indian and Coloured organizations became more radical, as communists began to play a more assertive role in their leadership. White communists remained active in black trade unions.

On March 21, 1960, South Africa police killed approximately eighty people who had peacefully assembled outside a police station at the township of Sharpeville to protest the pass laws. After the Sharpeville massacre, the authorities banned the ANC and a more militant offshoot, the Pan-Africanist Congress (PAC), which had organized the anti-pass protests.

apartheid

A term in Afrikaans meaning "separateness." It was first used in 1929 to describe Afrikaner nationalist proposals for strict racial separation and "to ensure the safety of the white race."

pass laws

Laws in apartheid South Africa that required Africans to carry identity books in which officials stamped the permits required for Africans to travel between the countryside and cities.

township

In South Africa, a segregated residential area reserved for Africans; during apartheid, tightly controlled and constituted mainly by public housing.

homelands

Areas reserved for exclusive African occupation, established through the 1913 and 1936 land legislation and later developed as ethnic states during the apartheid era.

migrant laborers

Laborers who move to another location to take a job, often a low-paying, temporary one.

While the African liberation movements reorganized in exile and prepared for guerrilla warfare, National Party governments under Hendrik Verwoerd and John Vorster ratcheted up a program of racial separation in what became known as "Grand Apartheid."[1] The 1970 Black Homeland Citizenship Act specified that all Africans would become citizens of supposedly sovereign states within the territory of South Africa; in fact, they remained financially dependent upon Pretoria and no other government recognized them diplomatically. Blacks would no longer be citizens of South Africa. The ten **homelands** became increasingly overcrowded as 1.4 million farm workers were resettled within them. In addition, several hundred thousand city dwellers were deported to the homelands. African urban workers would become permanent **migrant laborers**, forced to renew their contracts every year and leave their families in the homelands.

PROFILE

Nelson Mandela

Colin McConnell/Toronto Star/Getty Images

Born in a Transkei village in 1918, Nelson Mandela claimed royal lineage. After he rebelled against an arranged marriage and was suspended from Fort Hare University, he moved to Johannesburg to work as a legal clerk. He joined the ANC in 1942 and helped to establish the Youth League. This group wanted to radicalize the ANC's outlook in favor of a militant, racially exclusive nationalism. By 1951, however, after he became friends with Indian activists and white Communists, Mandela abandoned his belief that African nationalists should not cooperate across race lines. That year, he helped plan a "defiance campaign" against "unjust laws." Thereafter, as the ANC's deputy president, Mandela played a major role as an ANC strategist. In 1952, he founded a law firm with his comrade Oliver Tambo.

Following the Sharpeville massacre in March 1960, Mandela was detained for 5 months and the ANC was outlawed. These events prompted him to join the Communist Party briefly while retaining his leadership in the ANC. In May 1961, he led a nationwide general strike and in October that year he helped form *Umkhonto-we-Sizwe* (the armed wing of the ANC). Mandela left South Africa in January 1962 to seek support for the ANC abroad. When he returned in July, he was arrested, convicted of sabotage, and sentenced to life in prison after a well-publicized trial which confirmed his popular martyr status.

During nearly thirty years of imprisonment, often involving hard labor that permanently damaged his vision, Mandela maintained his authority over successive generations of convicted activists. Beginning in 1985, he began meeting secretly with government leaders to urge constitutional negotiations with the ANC.

On February 11, 1990, Mandela was released to tumultuous popular acclaim. As ANC president from 1991, his leadership was crucial in curbing the expectations of his organization's often unruly followers, preparing them for the compromises inevitable in a negotiated settlement. He shared the Nobel Peace Prize in 1993 with President F. W. De Klerk. After the ANC's electoral victory in 1994, he served as South African president until 1999. His personal achievements during this period included symbolic acts of reconciliation with the Afrikaner minority. He continued to play an elder statesman role within the ANC and appeared at an ANC rally before the 2009 election, his final political act. He died on December 5, 2013.

Nelson Mandela contributed significantly to the ANC's ideological formation in the 1950s. He was a powerful proponent of the multiracial Congress Alliance. Although influenced by Marxism, he maintained an admiration for British parliamentary democracy. Maintaining his social connections with the rural aristocracy, Mandela skillfully balanced his pronouncements to the various constituencies within the ANC's following. After 1960, his personal courage and theatrical style were vital in keeping rank-and-file militants loyal to the ANC. He pioneered the ANC's transformation to a clandestine insurgent body and led its second transformation into an electoral political party. His speech at his trial in 1964, in which he declared that he was "prepared to die" for his "ideal of a democratic and free society," increased his stature making him, in the words of the *London Times*, "a colossus of African nationalism."

MAKING CONNECTIONS In which ways did Mandela contribute to the making of the modern South African state?

Aiming to limit migration into the towns, the central government took control of the administration of the African townships in the cities. Construction of family housing for Africans in the major cities was halted. Instead, the authorities built huge dormitory-like hostels for "bachelor" workers. "Bantu Education," stressing menial training, was introduced into primary schools in 1954, and was later extended to African secondary schooling. Restrictions were placed on African, Indian, and Coloured enrollment in the major universities, and special segregated colleges were established. New laws allowing detention without trial facilitated the torture of prisoners. Through their informer network, the police located the cells responsible for the sabotage and insurgency that had been undertaken by the ANC and the PAC. By 1965, most significant African leaders who had not fled the country were serving life sentences on Robben Island, a prison offshore from Cape Town. These leaders included Nelson Mandela, ANC deputy president and commander-in-chief of its armed wing, *Umkhonto-we-Sizwe* (Spear of the Nation).

During this era of Grand Apartheid, foreign capital and public investment built up strategic industries such as armaments and synthetic fuels, in anticipation of international sanctions that were beginning to be imposed on South Africa because of its racist policies. The country experienced substantial economic growth and modernization.

As Africans moved into semiskilled manufacturing jobs created by the expanding economy, they obtained new leverage. Wildcat strikes broke out in 1973 as a combative trade union movement gained strength. Daily tabloid newspapers aimed at township readers began to appear in the mid-1960s, responding to mass literacy. They publicized a new generation of political organizations influenced by the U.S. black power movement and influenced by the expanding numbers of graduates from the segregated universities.

Umkhonto-we-Sizwe

Zulu and Xhosa for "Spear of the Nation," the armed wing of the African National Congress, established in 1961.

sanctions

International embargos on economic and cultural contracts with a particular country; applied selectively to South Africa by various governments and the United Nations (UN) from 1948 until 1994.

Antonio Muchave/Sowetan/Gallo Images/Getty Images

Armed police stand by their Nyala (antelope) armored vehicle awaiting orders to disperse the striking mineworkers assembled in front of them, on Nkaneng Hill, on August 12, 2012.

Generational Revolt and Political Reform, 1976–1990

In the mid-1970s, the collapse of Portuguese colonial power in Angola and Mozambique inspired South African anti-apartheid activists. The ideas of the racially assertive black consciousness movement percolated down to secondary schools, quickly finding followers in an educational system that discriminated terribly against Africans.

The Education Ministry rashly ordered that half the curriculum in black schools should be taught in Afrikaans. This provoked demonstrations on June 16, 1976, in the townships around Johannesburg. After the police fired into a crowd of 15,000 children, the revolt quickly spread. The next year saw street battles, strikes, and classroom boycotts. More than 575 protesters died. Several thousand volunteers from outside the country crossed into South Africa to join the liberation organizations.

By the mid-1970s, Afrikaner nationalism had changed. Two-thirds of Afrikaners were now white-collar workers and hence less likely to be worried by African competition for their jobs. Afrikaner firms were now among the most advanced manufacturers. Their directors were increasingly bothered by apartheid regulations that restricted the mobility of black labor. Reflecting this change, African workers gained collective bargaining rights. Black trade unions won legal recognition. The year 1986 saw the repeal of the pass laws and other means of **influx control** that had been used to regulate black migration to the cities.

influx control

A system of controls that regulated African movement between towns and the countryside, enforcing residence in the homelands and restricting Africans' choice of employment.

In 1983, the United Democratic Front (UDF) was formed by anti-apartheid organizations drawn from the student movement, trade unions, and township-based civic associations. They proclaimed their loyalty to the ANC's "nonracial" ideology. UDF affiliates were conspicuous in the insurrectionary protest that developed in the townships in late 1984 in response to rent hikes. Township rioting, military repression, guerrilla warfare, and conflict between supporters of liberation movements and the adherents of homeland regimes all contributed to a new bloody phase of South Africa's political history. Between 1984 and 1994, politically motivated killings claimed 25,000 lives.

The South African Miracle, 1990–1999

On February 12, 1990, a new president, F. W. De Klerk, created a bombshell when he proclaimed the repeal of prohibitions on the ANC and other proscribed organizations, and announced that Nelson Mandela would be released. Although De Klerk was a conservative, he was alarmed by tightening economic sanctions and encouraged by the collapse of the Eastern European communist governments, which had been important supporters of the ANC. He hoped that by abandoning apartheid and beginning negotiations for power-sharing, the National Party could build black support. He also believed that an anti-ANC coalition could prevail, built around a powerful African political movement based on the KwaZulu homeland authority, the Inkatha Freedom Party (IFP), led by a Zulu prince, Chief Mangosuthu Buthelezi. ANC leaders, in turn, were willing to make concessions because they calculated that, while they could not seize power through revolution, opinion polls assured them that they enjoyed growing public support.

At the time, it seemed miraculous that such bitter adversaries could be ready to collaborate so closely in designing a new political system. Their success was even more remarkable because political hostilities continued between their supporters. Between 1990 and 1994, 14,000 people died in violent conflicts between the ANC, Inkatha, and various state-sponsored vigilante groups. By 1993, two years of bargaining had produced a transitional constitution in which the main parties would hold cabinet positions in accordance with their shares of the vote in proportional representation elections. All participants in politically motivated violence, including torture of prisoners and terrorist attacks, could obtain immunity from prosecution. Even senior public servants (mostly white) would keep their jobs. Power would be divided between a national assembly and nine provincial legislatures. These legislatures would absorb the homeland bureaucracies. Parliament would sit as a constitutional assembly to draw up a final constitution in 1996, which would have to follow the fundamental principles agreed to in the 1993 document.

Nelson Mandela walks through the gates of Pollsmoor Prison on the day of his release, hand in hand with his wife, Winnie. Mandela insisted on leaving the prison on foot, rather than being driven.

On April 27, 1994, with just over 62 percent of the ballot, the ANC achieved an overwhelming majority among black voters except in KwaZulu-Natal, where Inkatha obtained a narrow victory. With 20 percent of the national vote, De Klerk's National Party received substantial support from Coloureds and Indians, as well as most white voters. Eight more parties achieved parliamentary representation. On May 10, the Government of National Unity (GNU) took office, led by Nelson Mandela and including representatives of the ANC, the National Party, and the IFP. For many observers, South Africans had achieved an astonishing historical turnaround, nearly unprecedented in terms of the relatively peaceful transformation from the white-dominated repressive regime to a multiracial democracy.

In office, the GNU began the Reconstruction and Development Programme (RDP), a plan drawn up by the ANC's labor ally, the Congress of South African Trade Unions (COSATU). The RDP emphasized "people-driven development" including fairer allocation of public spending on education, health, and welfare between blacks and whites. But the government's actual policies were surprisingly moderate. Under both Mandela and his successor, Thabo Mbeki, while ANC-led administrations attempted to address the basic needs of poor people, social expenditure was limited by tight budgets. The ANC leadership went even further by adopting the Growth, Employment, and Redistribution (GEAR) policy in 1996, which involved embracing free-market reforms, including privatization and tariff reduction. The policy change was enacted despite stiff objections from trade unionists. In 2007, Mbeki's opponents succeeded in electing his deputy Jacob Zuma to replace him as the ANC's party leader and shortly thereafter, Mbeki resigned from the state presidency. His resignation followed the dismissal of corruption charges against Zuma that the judge suggested were instigated from the president's office.

Jacob Zuma became South Africa's head of state in 2009 after the ANC's fourth electoral victory. He rewarded his left-wing allies with key cabinet positions. Rising public investments in roads and railway renewal, together with the construction of stadiums for the soccer World Cup, held in South Africa in 2010, and an oil pipeline from Maputo helped raise the fiscal deficit and increase foreign borrowing by 2012 to four times the level inherited from apartheid. Construction expanded employment between 2009 and 2011 but unemployment began rising again in 2012. By the beginning of 2017 the official unemployment rate was 26.5 percent, 3.5 percent more than in 2009; among school dropouts, joblessness was much higher.

Rising public social spending partially offset the resulting poverty, but it has also contributed to the fiscal deficit, a problem which now divides the government. The efforts of Zuma's finance minister, Nhlanhla Nene, to rein in government spending prompted the president to replace him in 2015 with his "economic comrade," David van Rooyen. An immediate fall in the Rand's exchange value caused him to reconsider, and van Rooyen was replaced within a week by the vastly more experienced Pravin Gordhan, a former communist who had headed up South Africa's tax collection before Zuma appointed him as his first finance ministry in 2009. Market reaction was favorable, for Gordhan was highly regarded as a tough pragmatist. At the end of 2016, however, he was charged with fraud in a case brought by his opponents within President Zuma's entourage; the charges were withdrawn within a few days. Unfazed, Gordhan immediately applied to the courts to take action over seventy-two "suspicious transactions" by companies belonging to close friends and financial backers of Jacob Zuma.

South Africa has lived with high levels of unemployment and acute social inequality for decades. But visible displays of wealth by venal politicians have accentuated political resentments. Various expressions of public anger at the decision to spend $25 million on fortifying the president's luxurious homestead at Inkandla led to a court judgment compelling President Zuma to repay some of the money and extracted from him a public apology in April 2016.

The Four Themes and South Africa

South Africa in a Globalized World of States

Ever since the Anglo-Boer War, South Africa has attracted international attention. The war itself drew in troops from all over the British Empire and the Afrikaner republics attracted sympathy throughout Europe. More recently, of course, anti-apartheid became a movement of global solidarity with black South Africans. Since its formation, South Africa's political economy has been shaped by inflows of capital and population. Throughout the twentieth century, the economy depended on imported technology, making it vulnerable to international pressure. Hence, the sanctions imposed when the country's institutionalized racial segregation attracted near-unanimous censure within the post–World War II world of states proved quite effective, when combined with internal pressure, in ending apartheid.

settler state

Colonial or former colonial administrations controlled by the descendants of immigrants who settled in the territory.

External influences have complicated South Africa's relationship with the rest of Africa. As a settler state, South Africa was perceived by pan-African politicians as a colonial leftover, a perception reinforced by apartheid South Africa's alignment with Western powers during the Cold War. Even after democracy's advent, South Africa's status as the most developed country in Africa excited resentment as much as admiration. As the continent's leading economy in 1999, South Africa became the only African member of the G20 grouping, an annual convention of finance ministers and heads of reserve banks from the world's biggest economies.

Governing the Economy

State-directed industrialization was encouraged with the establishment in 1928 of the Iron and Steel Corporation. Expansion of public enterprise accelerated during apartheid. The threat of foreign trade embargoes prompted protective trade tariffs to encourage import substitution industrialization during the 1960s. However, between 1993 and 2001, South Africa removed about two-thirds of these tariffs to qualify for membership in the World Trade Organization (WTO). Tariff reform affected some industries very harshly. During the 1990's, the government sold off twenty-six state-owned enterprises, mainly fairly minor concerns. Although this was less than 10 percent of the state's assets, trade union resistance to "privatization" led to halting further privatization in 2004. Today, public corporations still control electricity, telecommunications, railways, and several defense manufacturers.

The Democratic Idea

South African democracy is the product of many traditions. Immigrants contributed key features of South African political culture. In the twentieth century, this included the militant socialism that accompanied the arrival of English workers before World War I. Baltic Jewish refugees included veteran Russian revolutionaries. Communists, working with African nationalists, helped ensure that black opposition to apartheid was multiracial. Nonracial themes in South African politics were also shaped by the liberal institutions promoted by earlier arrivals from Europe, for example, the influential network of Methodist schools attended by ANC leaders. Modern South African democratic thought reflects each of these legacies, as well as social ethics derived from indigenous African statecraft, with its traditions of consensual decision making and the etiquette of kinship.[2]

Modern democracy in South Africa is also influenced by the ideas of an African trade union movement that emphasized accountable leadership. South Africa's adoption of a constitutionally entrenched bill of rights was partially influenced by other countries. The negotiators who devised a path from apartheid to democracy were inspired by the succession of transitions from authoritarian regimes that unfolded in many parts of the world in the 1980s and 1990s.

Collective Identity

In ten parliamentary and municipal elections since 1994, post-apartheid South African voters continue to appear to be influenced by feelings of racial identity. Africans overwhelmingly support African nationalist parties. Despite the conspicuous presence of whites in the ANC's leadership, the vast majority of white South Africans support the Democratic Alliance (DA), the ANC's chief opponent. Among all groups, material interests reinforce notions of racial community. Virtually all very poor South Africans are African; they find it difficult to feel any sense of shared social identity with generally affluent white South Africans. The prospects for democratic progress are limited when racial solidarities are so decisive.

Themes and Comparisons

democratization

Transition from authoritarian rule to a democratic political order.

Most comparative analyses of South African politics emphasize its significance as a relatively successful example of democratization. Post-apartheid politics in South Africa offers useful insights into the factors that build and consolidate democratic life: These factors include a pattern of economic growth in which the construction of a modern economy happened before universal enfranchisement; the role played in making democracy work by a vigorous civil society; as well as the effects of a set of state institutions carefully designed to promote social inclusion and reward consensus. South Africa also offers an encouraging model of a racially segmented society that has succeeded in nurturing stable and democratic political institutions.

Where Do You Stand?

What accounts for the fact that the South African system of apartheid was such an exceptionally oppressive system before 1994?

From what you have read so far, how significant have been the changes brought about by South Africa's democratic transition?

POLITICAL ECONOMY AND DEVELOPMENT

▽ Focus Questions

- In what ways has the state's role in the economy changed since 1970 and especially since the end of apartheid?

- How did international sanctions affect the South African apartheid economy and what role did they play in hastening the end of apartheid?

State and Economy

Apartheid Economics

For over half a century, economic and social policy was directed to promoting the apartheid regime. From 1952, laws prohibited Africans from living in any town unless they had been born there or had worked for the same employer for 10 years. Migrant workers without urban residential rights had to live in tightly controlled hostels. By the mid-1960s, repression had eliminated most of the militant African trade unions. In 1968, the Armaments Development and Manufacturing Corporation (Armscor) was created. This greatly expanded the scope of public industrial enterprise.

Apartheid economics was buttressed by a welfare state, although one that functioned in a racially discriminatory fashion. Public construction of African housing began on a significant scale with the inception of a vast township—later named Soweto (the acronym for southwestern township) outside Johannesburg during the 1930s. The need for African labor during wartime industrialization led the government to suspend pass laws. During the 1940s, as Africans rapidly moved to the cities, illegal shanty settlements mushroomed on city fringes. Although after 1948, governments restricted African urbanization, they funded a rapid expansion of public housing to accommodate Africans who already lived in towns. In 1971, African public housing totaled more than 500,000 family dwellings. During the 1960s, official policy favored single workers' hostel construction instead of family housing. Most townships included bleak barracks-like hostels in which African migrant workers slept in bunks using communal bathrooms and kitchens.

In the 1960s, the state extended its control over African educational institutions. But it also increased school enrollment massively. By the end of the decade, most children were at school, although there were huge inequalities per capital pub-lic spending on white and black children. Pension payments between the races were equalized only in 1993. South Africa's universal public pension, together with its range of welfare payments, remain unusual in sub-Saharan African states today.

Liberalization and Deregulation

The dismantling of apartheid was accompanied by economic deregulation. By 1984, most official employment discrimination had ended. In the mid-1980s, the govern-ment began to dismantle the protections and subsidies for white agriculture. Parallel to these developments, the Iron and Steel Corporation was privatized. In the late 1980s, rising defense spending and expanding public debt brought fresh reasons to deregulate and privatize. When the government abolished the restrictive pass laws in 1986, this should have opened up the labor market. But by this time, the main labor shortages were in skilled sectors because generations of Africans had not received industrial training and technical education. Once Africans were allowed to move to the cities, urban growth escalated and since 1990, most South African towns' popu-lations have doubled.

Since 1994, ANC governments have expanded the liberal economic policies of the late apartheid era. Redistributive policies attempt to expand the scope of private ownership rather than broaden the public sector. For instance, between 1994 and 2013, the government helped to finance the construction of more than 3.3 million low-cost houses through grants to impoverished families that enable them to buy their own houses. This vast number of homes was built by private contractors on cheap public land. For many township residents, home ownership was more expen-sive than rented housing or the payments they had made to "shacklords" in squatter camps; the housing subsidies usually did not cover construction costs, and poor fami-lies who moved into the houses often ended up paying more on mortgage repayments than they had paid on rents. Moreover, rural urban migration and demographic pres-sure combined to increase the figures for the "housing backlog"; in 2016, at least another 2.2 million houses were needed to meet the needs of shanty dwellers. At the present rate of construction of government-funded low cost houses—140,000 a year—many of the shanty settlements that surround South African cities will remain for at least another decade.

In 1994, the government agreed to reduce industrial tariffs by two-thirds within a decade, as a condition for joining the World Trade Organization. In 1997, indus-tries stopped receiving export incentive subsidies. Currency exchange controls were substantially relaxed as well to promote foreign investment.

Since 1994, privatization policies have had their most profound effect on munici-pal administration. Heavily indebted local authorities now contract out basic services such as water supply and garbage collection to private companies. To put the railroad network on a commercial footing, most smaller rural stations were closed. Effectively, the state mostly abandoned its former duty to provide cheap, subsidized public trans-port. Even so, the transport corporation remains wholly state-owned after successive failures to attract foreign investors and local black empowerment groups. Indeed, since 2004, government has stopped selling public assets partly because of difficulties in selling the telephone utility. Telkom's sale made it obvious that black South Africans would not be the main beneficiaries of any further "core" privatization. Black busi-nessmen cannot mobilize sufficient capital by themselves to purchase major stakes, and in most of the privatizations up to 2004, they assumed a junior partnership.

economic deregulation

The lifting or relaxation of government controls over the economy, including the reduction of import taxes and the phasing out of subsidized prices.

Society and Economy

South Africa remains one of the most unequal societies in the world despite efforts to alleviate poverty. Measured through the Gini coefficient statistical measure of income inequality in which 0 is "perfectly equal" income and 1 is "perfectly unequal," South Africa inequality in 2011 (the last year for which reliable census data is available) was a disturbingly high .69—slightly higher than at the end of the apartheid level (.67 in 1995). To be sure, large numbers of Africans have been joining the richer population: Those living in the top fifth of income earners rose from 400,000 in 1994 to 1.9 million in 2008, although this also means that income inequality among Africans has increased dramatically. Unemployment, chiefly affecting Africans, remains very high at more than 26 percent at the beginning of 2017, compared to 23.4 percent in 1996.[3] School-leaver or youth unemployment is much higher, at 54 percent in 2016.

South African inequality is, to a large extent, the historic product of apartheid policies. Racial inequities in government expenditure were especially obvious in education. In the 1950s, more whites than Africans were trained as teachers, even though five times as many African children were of school-going age. The 1960s saw a swift expansion of African enrollment, but as late as 1984, only a fraction of Africans compared to most white students completed high school. In 1985, although there were five times more African than white students, the government was still spending half its educational budget on white schools.

After elections ushered in an African-controlled government in 1994, public policies attempted to equalize entitlements and allocations as well as broaden access to public goods, but without dramatic expansion in public spending. Today, public expenditure on education has become equitable. Africans now constitute nearly 70 percent of university students, up from 55 percent in 1994. More people receive welfare grants, 16 million today, up from 3 million in 1994. Measures to alleviate poverty include providing running water for about a third of the rural population. In 1999, municipalities began to implement free water and electricity allowances. During the 1990s, the electricity network expanded massively to embrace poorer rural communities. In addition, 1,300 new clinics have given free public health care to millions of pregnant women and children. However, hospitals in the main urban centers have deteriorated.

Have these efforts resulted in less poverty? Certainly since 1994, poor people have benefited from government services and public support. However, their absolute numbers have not changed much. Between 2006 and 2012, poverty slightly declined by 20 percent, although in 2012, 41 percent of the population was still living below the poverty line. Expanding provision of welfare grants certainly alleviated poverty.[4] However, a dramatic increase in economic growth is needed to reduce poverty significantly.

Unemployment has undermined the government's efforts to address poverty. The manufacturing workforce shrank by 400,000 in ten years after 1988, a 25 percent fall. At the same time 500,000 workers left farms. More recently, however, the number of manufacturing jobs has stabilized, and the numbers employed on commercial farms have increased. Public sector employment shrank only slightly, a reflection of the leverage exercised by public sector trade unions. By the late 1990s, they were the major players in the still powerful union movement. Despite unemployment, union membership has expanded. In 2015, overall union membership was 3.7 million. Unemployment is concentrated among school dropouts and rural people. Africans are still much more likely to be unemployed than other groups.

Between 2002 and 2016, as a consequence of child support grants, more immunization and less malnutrition, under-five infant mortality fell from 77 per 1,000 to 44 per 1,000. However life expectancy also fell: from 64 in 1996 to 51 in 2007, although in 2014 it had risen to 61. Falling life expectancy reflected the devastating impact of HIV/AIDS, which, according to South Africa's Medical Research Council, was responsible for 25 percent of deaths in 2000. Rising life expectancy reflects the government's efforts to expand the treatment of AIDS since 2007. Official statistics indicate that between 1990 and 2010, around 4.5 million South Africans died of AIDS. South Africa's rate of HIV/AIDS infection remains among the highest in the world, with 7 million HIV-positive in 2016. In the late 1980s and early 1990s, accelerating urbanization combined with structural unemployment, political violence, and labor migration loosened social cohesion in poor communities, accentuating their vulnerability to the illness.[5]

Black Empowerment

Enlarging the share of black ownership in the economy remains a policy priority. In the words of Thabo Mbeki, "the struggle against racism in our country must include the objective of creating a black bourgeoisie [that is, middle class]." A series of laws enacted since 1999 promote black business. The Preferential Procurement Act that regulates the awarding of government contracts requires winning companies to allocate shares to "previously disadvantaged" people. The Promotion of Equality Act set up a monitoring system to record how well companies were "deracializing" their managements. The National Empowerment Fund Act reserves 2 percent of the proceeds from the sale of public corporations to finance black shareholding in these concerns, although as we have seen, since 2004, privatization has largely halted because of the absence of black business groups who can purchase majority stakes. In mining and energy, though, traditionally reliant on public subsidies, the government has extracted corporate commitments to black empowerment and has been providing black entrepreneurs about 2.5 billion rand ($375 million) a year of start-up capital.

How successful has been the program to "deracialize" South African capitalism? Measured by the proportion of black-owned companies on the Johannesburg stock exchange, the share of the economy owned by a "black bourgeoisie" remains quite modest. In 2012, 23 percent of the shares of the top 100 companies traded on the Johannesburg Stock Exchange were held by black South Africans mainly through pension funds, roughly the same proportion as owned by white South Africans (the rest are owned by foreign investors), according to the Exchange's own research.

However, black participation in the economy is not limited to black share ownership. Political pressure has prompted all major companies to appoint black people to their boards: In 2010, for example, just under 30 percent of South African company directors were black, though in the same year only 9 percent of chief executive officers in companies were black. In the real estate business, the number of black realtors was almost nonexistent in 1990; it now matches the numbers of white realtors—a telling instance of the proliferation of property ownership in black communities. Within companies, the proportion of black people in management has also been rising steadily. By 2015, the number of black millionaires (in U.S. dollars) had reached 17,000 (compared to the white total of 21,000)—three times the figure in 2007.

Has black empowerment made South Africa more socially stable? Given the rising black share of economic ownership, the government certainly has more incentives to maintain business-friendly policies. Certainly, many who have benefited most from these measures have been politically well-connected, especially former activists.

However, it is also true that political pressure has prompted companies to promote black managers, and this helped a rapid expansion of a black middle class. But black empowerment by itself has not reduced black poverty; what reduction has occurred has been an effect of extending social welfare. Indeed black empowerment may have promoted inefficiencies that have curbed growth and job creation. To most poor black South Africans, wealth still appears predominantly white.

Environmental Issues

The government is also expanding its authority over environmental issues. By the beginning of the 1990s, trade union opposition to unsafe working conditions had evolved into broader concerns about the effects of industrial pollution. The environmental movement acquired a popular base as it embraced "brown" issues of the urban landscape, such as poor access to clean water and unsafe waste disposal by the mining industry.

In 1993, ANC negotiators insisted on including clauses on environmental health and ecological sustainability in the constitution. Since 1994, government policies have attempted to integrate ecological concerns with the requirements of social justice. A series of court cases have produced settlements in which historically dispossessed communities have signed "co-management" agreements with the National Parks Board. The 1998 Marine Living Resources Act opened up fishing grounds to impoverished villagers. In return, villagers are expected to keep the size of their catches sustainable.

More ambitious measures are needed, though, to cope with the scale of today's environmental hazards. Key features of South Africa's political economy make the country and its inhabitants especially vulnerable in a context in which climate change is generating tough challenges. This became evident after a series of severe floods devastated crowded settlements on marginal land. The Department of Health estimated that nearly 2,000 people died as a consequence of floods between 1980 and 2010, and more than 18 million were affected in other ways. For example, flooding is believed to have caused upsurges in malaria and cholera. In South Africa's main industrial region, poor regulation of the mining industry has generated huge quantities of acidic waste, which poses a major threat to national water supplies as the waste pollutes reservoirs. Water demand in an arid country is stressed by increasing reliance on coal-fired power stations to match rising electricity consumption. Because of the need to cool these power stations, the Electricity Supply Commission is now South Africa's biggest water purchaser.

In response, the government adopted bolder measures to curb industrial pollution. In 2012, the government committed itself to capping emissions and to ensuring that half of new power supplies developed by 2030 would be from renewable energy sources. Domestic solar water heating units are increasingly visible features in low-cost housing schemes. Meanwhile, environmental protests have increasingly attracted mass participation. In Johannesburg, a busy local chapter of Earthlife Africa has helped make acid mine drainage a policy concern, although politicians continue to maintain that the risks are "exaggerated." By the 2000's, activists could claim key victories. For example protests and lobbying by the South Durban Community Environmental Alliance against industrial air pollution helped prompt the enactment of Air Quality Management legislation in 2004. However, powerful polluters, including the state owned Electricity Supply Commission, were able to persuade the government to weaken its provisions when regulations under the air quality law were finally decided in 2015, after a decade of "horse-trading."

Activists also encounter public opposition. When nongovernmental organizations oppose industrial development, they sometimes provoke strong hostility from local people suffering from unemployment. This happened in Saldanha Bay in 1998, when environmentalists opposing building a new steel factory were accused of elevating the welfare of penguins over the livelihoods of people.

Environmental groups object to plans to build an additional nuclear reactor at the existing facility at Koeberg, just 30 kilometers from Cape Town. It is the only nuclear power station on the entire continent of Africa. To date, efforts to halt the building of the second reactor have been confined to relatively decorous public meetings. Greenpeace activists did scale the walls of the Koeburg compound to post a placard in 2002, but since then, there has been no militant protest. However, there remains evident public anxiety, particularly as residential settlement has extended closer to the power station. In 2011, a government-sponsored "Green Paper" addressing climate change pledged construction of a new "nuclear power station fleet," which would make nuclear power the source of 13 percent of South African electrical power by 2030. Critics believe that the government's commitment to using renewable sources has weakened as a consequence of contracts for nuclear reactors awarded in 2014 to the Russian agency, Rosatom, contracts in which people within the ruling circle have benefited.

South Africa in the Global Economy

From the mid-1940s, protectionist policies promoted manufacturing for the domestic market. These policies, together with restrictions on the use of black labor, caused growing inefficiencies, which economists believe constrained growth by the early 1970s.[6]

Protectionist policies favored the manufacture of consumption rather than capital goods. This helps explain why, in contrast to other middle-income developing countries, South Africa lagged behind in producing machines and equipment. In comparison to most primary commodity producers, high gold prices and well-diversified markets for exports helped South Africa maintain a trade surplus throughout most of the apartheid era, despite the rising cost of oil imports.

One important consequence of the international sanctions campaign was that the government began to invest in local branches of production, fearing that sanctions might become more effective. For example, during the 1960s, threats of an oil embargo stimulated a petrochemical industry that remains one of South Africa's more competitive export sectors.

More significant in its political effect than trade sanctions on South African policy-makers was the impact of divestment and credit denial by companies and banks, principally from the United States, in reaction to the state of emergency that was imposed in 1985. Divestment resulted from threats by U.S. colleges as well as state and local governments to sell their holdings in companies with South African interests. The divestment campaign culminated in the passage by the U.S. Congress of the Comprehensive Anti-Apartheid Act in October 1986. Divestment did not directly hurt South African economic activity since South African domestic capital was the major source of investment in the economy. However, the prospect of future limitations on the country's ability to secure foreign loans was extremely alarming to the government. By 1987, South African industrialists were dismayed about the difficulties they anticipated in obtaining access to advanced technology.[7]

Traditionally, South Africa dominated its regional economy through such arrangements as the South African Customs Union (which linked South Africa and its neighbors in a free-trade and revenue-sharing zone). During the 1980s, however, the region's economic significance as a trading partner with South Africa substantially increased at the same time that labor migration from the region into South Africa slackened. In the early 1980s, at a time of balance-of-payments difficulties, regional annual trade surpluses in South Africa's favor reached $1.8 billion. South Africa's regional trading partners bought 40 percent of its manufacturing exports. By the end of the decade, however, regional trade was contracting because of the warfare that intensified when South Africa sponsored insurgencies against Marxist governments in neighboring Angola and Mozambique.

The effects of South Africa's post-1994 reintegration into the international economy were initially disheartening. Throughout the rest of the decade, growth levels remained modest—2.3 percent increases in GDP—while foreign investors remained wary. The ending of sanctions helped to increase South African trade with other African countries, but also prompted an outflow of South African investment into countries with lower labor costs. WTO-mandated tariff reductions exposed hitherto protected industries to foreign competition with heavy job losses resulting in textiles and clothing factories. After 2000, however, growth began to accelerate, reaching levels above 5 percent from 2005 until 2008, but then dipping to around between 2.5 and 3.5 percent from 2008 to 2014, and falling again to around 1 percent in 2016. South African economists attribute the most recent decline to contracting Chinese demand for South African minerals after 2009, as well as the effects of drought in 2015 and breakdowns in electricity supply, following two decades of under-investment in power stations.

GLOBAL CONNECTION

South Africa in BRICS

BRICS stands for Brazil, Russia, India, China, and South Africa, an alliance of the world's largest developing economies. The foreign ministers of four of these countries formed a formal association in 2008. At China's urging, South Africa was invited to join the group in 2010. The association seeks to use its members' combined economic strength to shift the distribution of global economic power. Accordingly the group has called for a new reserve currency and the creation of a development bank to rival the International Monetary Fund. After a BRICS meeting in 2013, Jacob Zuma and Vladimir Putin announced their support for a Russian–South African "strategic partnership" that would promote a succession of trading and investment agreements.

For Jacob Zuma's administration, BRICS membership is a welcome recognition of South Africa's status as Africa's most advanced economy. In reality, South Africa is a small power. Its economy is less than a quarter the size of India's and an even smaller fraction of China's. Its importance to the group is a consequence of its mining industry as well as

its sophisticated infrastructure that enables it to perform gateway functions for the African continent. South Africa takes its BRICS membership very seriously. At World Trade Organization summits, South Africa aligns with its partners in arguing that developing countries should be able to maintain protectionist tariffs. Similarly, South Africans joined the Chinese, Brazilians, and Indians in opposing the cuts to energy emissions that are needed to limit global warning.

Meanwhile South African trade with the BRICS group is five times larger since 2005, although, in contrast to its still larger trade with the European Union, South Africa's trade balance with the BRICS group is negative. China has become the biggest export market for South Africa and its fastest-growing investor, especially in banking and mining. Earnings from Chinese exports were critical in helping South Africa weather the 2008 to 2009 global recession.

BRICS cooperation is intended to reach beyond global flows of trade and finance. As already noted, South Africa has aligned itself with its partners in international negotiations about climate change. Such diplomatic alignments

(continued)

have engendered anxiety among human rights activists. In 2011, the Dalai Lama was denied a visa to visit South Africa after being invited to speak at a conference in Pretoria because of Chinese opposition to any kind of recognition of an independent Tibet. In global forums nowadays, South Africa generally takes its cues from its BRICS partners. For example, during South Africa's second term on the UN Security Council, it sided with China and abstained in a vote on a Western powers-sponsored resolution on Syria.

MAKING CONNECTIONS South African policy-makers argue that diplomatic and economic alignment with developing countries as in BRICS is in their national interest. Are they right?

Where Do You Stand?

South African social inequality has increased since 1994. Why does this matter politically?

Is poverty in today's South Africa mainly an effect of apartheid?

GOVERNANCE AND POLICY-MAKING

SECTION 3

Organization of the State

South Africa's modern state organization emerged from protracted bargaining between 1992 and 1996 as apartheid crumbled. A transitional constitution settled how South Africa would be governed after the first democratic elections, which were held in 1994. Parliament, acting as a constitutional assembly, drafted a document that incorporated key principles adopted at the earlier multiparty talks. This ensured that certain minority concerns would receive enduring protection. A bill of rights supplies safeguards ranging from traditional civil liberties to environmental protections and sexual choice. Most clauses of the constitution can be changed through a two-thirds vote in the National Assembly, the lower house of parliament. However, an opening section of the Constitution lists a set of key values that require a 75 percent majority for amendment.

Since 1994, the South African state has been a quasi-federal system. The national government has the power to override laws passed by nine provincial regional legislatures. The provincial administrations depend on funds allocated by the central government.

Between 1994 and 1999, the transitional constitution specified that the executive of the Government of National Unity had to be composed of a coalition of party representatives, with posts being distributed proportionately among parties that achieved more than 5 percent of the popular vote. The National Party, the former ruling group during apartheid, withdrew from the GNU in 1996, partly because of its failure to persuade the drafters of the 1996 constitution to retain **power sharing** after 1999.

Focus Questions

- Why is the executive branch of government so powerful in South Africa?

- Why is public confidence in the legal system so limited?

power sharing

Constitutional arrangements to ensure that the major political parties share executive authority. These can include mandatory coalitions and allocation of senior official positions between parties.

The Executive

Although the South African system of government has inherited many features of the Westminster model, the South African president is considerably more powerful than the British prime minister. South African governments are formed by the president, who must be a member of the National Assembly. After being elected by the Assembly, the president vacates his or her parliamentary seat and appoints and subsequently chairs a cabinet of ministers. The president, who can only serve two 5-year terms, also chooses a deputy president.

South Africa's first president after elections in 1994 was Nelson Mandela, who served one term and declined to serve another on grounds of age. His single term was decisive in establishing the prestige of the new government. His successor, Thabo Mbeki, followed Mandela's example in taking care to cultivate strong personal relationships with members of the Afrikaner elite. Prior to becoming president of the Republic, both Mandela and Mbeki had been elected at ANC conferences to head the party. The president can be impeached or removed from office by a two-thirds vote of the National Assembly, but only on grounds of disability or serious misconduct.

As Mandela's deputy president, Mbeki was largely responsible for the day-to-day management of the administration. After he became president in 1999, the office accumulated new functions. Although he was elected to a second term in 2004, Mbeki lost his party's support in ANC leadership elections at the end of 2007, a consequence both of unpopular economic policies and personal animosities. He resigned the following year, to be replaced by his deputy, Kgalema Motlanthe. After the 2009

Dressed in his warrior kilt (Ishebu), Jacob Zuma demonstrates his mastery of traditional dance steps while his supporters sing his anthem from the Umkhonto camps, "Umshini Wami" (My Machine Gun).

AP Images

election, the new National Assembly elected Jacob Zuma as president and Motlanthe reassumed his former role as deputy.

To his opponents within the ANC, Jacob Zuma's lack of formal education and tangles with the law made him unsuited for office. In truth, however, even Zuma's legal difficulties helped to generate public approval. In 2007, he faced charges for accepting bribes offered during the negotiation of weapons purchases. The previous year, he was acquitted in a rape case in which his defense was that his accuser, a houseguest, had signaled her availability, by wearing a short skirt and failing to cross her legs, wanton behavior from the standpoint of decorous Zulu convention. If he was mistaken, Zuma told the court, he would "have his cows ready" if his accuser agreed to marry him. The judge found him not guilty for other reasons, but Zuma's explanation of his actions resonated with the honor code of many of his supporters—socially marginalized young men who remained rooted in a rural patriarchal culture.

However, these were not his only supporters. Zuma's one-time Communist Party membership encouraged trade unionists to think that he was their champion. More generally, his warm manner and down-to-earth style endeared him to ordinary ANC members. His efforts in the early 1990s to broker peace in KwaZulu Natal earned him respect and trust outside the ANC.

Yet the corruption charges against Zuma were serious. In the 2005 trial of Shabir Shaik, Zuma's former financial adviser, prosecutors demonstrated that Shaik had negotiated a bribe from a French contractor on Zuma's behalf. According to the evidence accepted by the court in Shaik's trial, Jacob Zuma was an active accomplice in corrupt practices. However, the Directorate of Public Prosecutions made various procedural errors in its efforts to prosecute him. As a result, a high court dismissed the case against Zuma in 2008 on technical grounds. His election as president in 2009 was now inevitable. In office, however, Zuma's political support base, which consisted of an uneasy alliance between different disaffected groups within the ANC, began to fragment and various scandals weakened his personal authority.

Unlike the president, cabinet ministers remain members of parliament and are accountable to it through question-time sessions. These are regularly scheduled occasions, in which ministers must reply to queries from backbenchers. Ministers are also accountable to various parliamentary standing committees. Parliamentarians lose office if they are expelled from membership by their parties. This gives the executive great power. Elected by a parliamentary majority, the president will normally be a party leader, enjoying a controlling influence over the makeup of parliamentary representation. Given the president-as-party-leader's de facto power over parliamentary office-holding, a revolt by ruling party backbenchers is extremely unlikely. In 1999, Thabo Mbeki could appoint his cabinet without any restrictions. He chose, however, to include members of the IFP, which had been a fierce rival of the ANC. In 2004, Mbeki made room in his cabinet for Marthinus van Schalwyk, the leader of the National Party, who became Minister for the Environment and Tourism. Since 2009, however, all full ministerial positions have been filled by ANC members. In Jacob Zuma's 2014 government, of thirty-five cabinet ministers fifteen were women, a reflection of the ANC's commitment to gender equity, which has also ensured that at least one-third of ANC parliamentarians are female.

There are few checks other than constitutional restraints on the leadership of the ruling party. Certainly, Thabo Mbeki attempted to impose his personal authority more frequently than his predecessor. For example, he dictated the choice of the leaders of the provincial governments to the ANC regional organization. In 1998, an ANC "deployment committee" was set up. This was intended to decide on key appointments in parastatal organizations, as well as to have the final say over the makeup of the party's electoral lists. Since Zuma's accession to the presidency, however, the management of political patronage has become increasingly personalized, and the party's deployment committee has been sidelined by the president's office.

Unlike Mandela's charismatic and unquestioned authority within the ANC, the accession of both Mbeki and Zuma to the party leadership was contested. Accordingly, leaders are now expected to reward their political allies. Both Mbeki and Zuma used their powers of appointment to favor trusted associates and displace rivals. Such political patronage has resulted in a proliferation of factionalism within the ANC, impeding the development of competent public administration and feeding corruption. Estimates of the annual cost of public corruption suggest that as much as $600 million a year is lost through corruption and waste, much of it through procurements in which politically well-connected suppliers cooperate with officials in charging inflated prices. In 2010, investigators discovered that 6,000 civil servants failed to disclose their business interests, often involving companies with government contracts. Corruption is perceived to be especially concentrated among elected office holders whereas certain branches of the administration, notably the judiciary, are believed to be corruption-free.

In contrast to previous administrations, Zuma's government expanded deficit-funded expenditure, partly because of increasingly generous social welfare provisions, but also through employing more public servants, mainly nurses and teachers as well as policemen, half a million of whom have been added to a bureaucracy of around 21 million in 2014. The government now spends more than double on salaries as it did in 2007. Certain departments—defense, security, justice, finance, trade and industry, and home affairs—are administered in a centralized fashion by national government ministries. For other departments—education, social services, and health—provincially elected governments enjoy considerable discretion. Certain central ministries are extremely efficient—finance, for example, especially with respect to tax collection; but others have a reputation for corruption and incompetence.

U.S. CONNECTION

South African U.S. relations

The schedule for Barack Obama's 2013 visit to sub-Saharan Africa included a weekend stay in South Africa, time for a quick conversation with President Zuma, a "town hall meeting" at the University of Johannesburg, and a visit to Nelson Mandela's prison cell at Robben Island. In fact, locally, a terminally ill Nelson Mandela stole the headlines. Indeed Obama would be back nearly six months later to attend Mandela's funeral. Media focus on Mandela's health may have reduced the impact of Obama's upbeat messages about U.S.–South African partnership, but as one commentator observed, despite all the decorous protocols, officials on both sides had the appearance of merely "going through the motions."

Although diplomatically "cordial," relations between the two governments have been unusually bad tempered recently. In 2011, South Africa denounced the bombing of Muammar Gaddafi's airfields in Libya by North Atlantic Treaty Organization (NATO) members, condemning Anglo-American promotion of "regime change." In 2012, rejecting U.S. calls, South Africa not only refused to reduce its oil imports from Iran, but actually doubled them. South African trade with Iran was already a source of tension with Washington because of undertakings supposedly made by a South African cell phone company to help the Iranians obtain South African weapons in return for local operating rights. Meanwhile, South Africa's BRICS policy prompted its diplomatic alignment with China and more annoyingly, as far as Washington was concerned, with Russia at the United Nations during its second term on the UN Security Council, between 2011 and 2013.

Obama's two brief visits to South Africa in 2013—he spent barely 12 hours in the country attending Mandela's

(continued)

funeral in December—might have been expected to have injected new warmth into the two countries' dealings with each other. Instead, in mid-2014, President Obama threatened South Africa with suspension from the African Growth and Opportunity trading scheme, through which African countries have been able to secure tax-free access to U.S. markets since 2002. South Africa had failed to reciprocate by removing duties on poultry from the United States. The issue was finally sorted out, after conciliatory negotiation by South African officials from the Department of Trade and Industry. Even so, relations remain fractious, colored as they are by the ANC's hostile rhetoric. For example, in 2016, the ANC's secretary general, Gwede Mantashe, announced that the U.S. government-funded "Young African Leadership Initiative" had as its purpose local "regime change." Jacob Zuma's cabinet allies routinely accuse his South African critics and opponents of being "CIA agents."

All this irascibility may just be surface froth. South Africa seems to have collaborated fully with American security agencies in the aftermath of the 9/11 attacks, especially in deporting suspected terrorists under the CIA's "extraordinary rendition" program. And with respect to trade, although China may have displaced the U.S. in its importance as a trading partner, the balance in U.S.–South African trade is more equitable than is the case with China, and crucially, the United States is much more significant than China as a market for South African manufactures. So, to date, despite disagreements, pragmatism has prevailed. Things might be different, though, in future under an American administration headed by people with no sentimental regard for Mandela's legacy.

MAKING CONNECTIONS What are the key considerations that determine foreign policy between South Africa and the United States?

Other State Institutions

The Judiciary and the Police

All judges are appointed through a constitutional process that limits executive discretion. Court judgments demonstrate robust independence, despite complaints by cabinet ministers about judges interfering in policy-making.

Judicial independence has been especially obvious with respect to the Constitutional Court. In a key judgment in 2002, the court ruled on how the government should provide antiretroviral medication for HIV/AIDS patients. The Court continues to demonstrate freedom from executive influence. In March 2016, its judges ruled that President Zuma should repay the state for improvements to his home at Nkandla that were paid from public funds.

Public respect for legal institutions needs to be based on more than their autonomy and integrity, however. For most citizens, courts are inaccessible. Huge caseloads make legal proceedings extremely slow. Nearly half of South Africa's prisoners are awaiting trial. Several thousand cases a year do not reach trial because criminal syndicates bribe court officials to destroy dockets.

South Africa has one of the highest crime rates in the world, a consequence of gross social inequalities, a violent political history, and a general disrespect for the law that apartheid engendered.

Overall, murder conviction rates in South Africa, at 10 percent in 2013, represent one of the lowest levels in the world. This is a reflection of poor police work. Up to the 1990s, judges tolerated routine use of torture to extract confessions, even in petty criminal cases. Today, although judges are much more discerning, reports suggest that the police still routinely torture suspects. Between March 2008 and April 2009, the Independent Complaints Directorate investigated 828 cases of assaults by police officers on people held in their custody; many were sufficiently severe to rate as torture. In 2011 and 2012, nearly 500 people were killed in armed police operations, according to the Independent Complaints Directorate.

Since 1994, despite efforts at reform, police competence remains patchy. Policy choices since the mid-1990s have downgraded the detective services in favor of public order and patrol policing and placed detectives under local uniformed station managers.[8] Rapid expansion of the force—between 2008 and 2013, its size doubled—accentuated inefficiencies. One reason that conviction rates are low is that semiliterate constables ignore basic rules of evidence. Pay scales for rank-and-file police officers are the lowest in the public sector, which makes the force exceptionally prone to corruption. In 2010, Jackie Selebi, former head of Interpol (International Criminal Police Organization), and South Africa's most senior police officer, was convicted on corruption charges and sentenced to fifteen years in prison. His successor, General Bheki Cele, also lost his position after corruption accusations in 2011—but not before he had presided over an aggressive "shoot-to-kill" approach, supported by many politicians.

Combative public order policing had especially lethal consequences at the Marikana platinum mine in North West Province in 2012. On August 16, 500 police fired on a crowd of striking miners, killing thirty-four, some of whose bodies were found handcuffed, evidently finished off by the police after falling wounded. The brutality of the confrontation was partly attributable to events in the preceding week in which nine people had died, including policemen and security guards attacked by the mineworkers. The workers were asking for a 200 percent pay rise and belonged to a new union that had broken away from the National Union of Mineworkers, a key ANC ally. The mining company was well connected politically, with the ANC's deputy president, Cyril Ramaphosa, on its board, and the police command was under

In February 2013, Mido Macia, a Mozambican taxi driver, was arrested by police for a minor traffic violation. Spectators filmed on their cell phone images that were subsequently broadcast. They showed policemen handcuffing Macia to the back of their van and then driving away dragging him along the road. Macia later died of his injuries in a police cell. Eight officers were imprisoned for Macia's murder in 2015.

pressure to deal with the strikers decisively. But other, more day-to-day, incidents indicate that for many policemen, brutal behavior is normal, not an exceptional reaction to stress. In 2013, police were filmed by journalists handcuffing to their vehicle a Mozambican taxi driver arrested for a parking violation. After dragging him along the ground for a few hundred yards, the police took him to the police station, where he subsequently died.

National Security Organizations

The South African military is not in better shape. The South African National Defence Force (SANDF) employed 70,000 soldiers, sailors, and airmen in 2016; less than half the size of the police force. Critics complain that the army has too many generals, and its soldiers are generally too old and too fat. One reason that South Africa is reluctant to play a major role in continental peacekeeping operations is the poor quality of its armed forces. In 1998, the government committed itself to ambitious expenditures on military aircraft, submarines, and light destroyers for the navy, while recruitment was to be increased by 10,000 annually. Today, the Defence Force remains too underequipped and undermanned to play even the confined defensive role envisaged for it in the 2009 Defence White Paper. Half the combat pilot positions in the air force are unfilled. In any case, even if there were enough pilots to fly aircraft, the air force is unable to provide basic supplies. Press reports in 2013 cited internal SANDF documentation indicating that 60 percent of the helicopter fleet and all new fighter-trainers were grounded. One consequence of the helicopter groundings was that aerial anti-poaching operations in the Kruger Park were halted. The army continues to use obsolete 30-year-old equipment. Budgetary increases in 2009 intended for recruitment and material were absorbed in a major pay increase awarded when soldiers joined civil servants in striking for a 10 percent pay raise. Expenditure on the SANDF equals 1.3 percent of GDP and most of this is spent on salaries.

Subnational Government

A more serious limitation on the power of the South African state than its military weakness is shortcomings of the subnational governments, both in provincial administrations and in municipal authorities.

The nine provincial governments are led by premiers, who are limited to two terms in office. In principle, premiers are elected by their legislatures, but in the eight provinces in which the ANC predominates, such elections are formalities. Premiers are in reality appointed and dismissed by the president.

Each premier appoints a mini-cabinet, called an executive council. Provincial revenues derive mainly from central government. In addition, provinces receive conditional grants for particular projects from the national ministries. Provincial administrations are supposed to allocate their expenditure between departments in accordance with national budgetary guidelines. In practice, they enjoy considerable financial discretion, for example, in contracting for services and equipment.

In the beginning, provinces had to amalgamate several civil services from different homelands or from the separate establishments that existed for white, Coloured, and Indian people. The new provincial boundaries brought together rival elites who sometimes remained jealous of each other's influence. In many of the former homelands, bureaucratic systems had suffered considerable degeneration; because governments did not have strong accountability mechanisms, provincial administrations

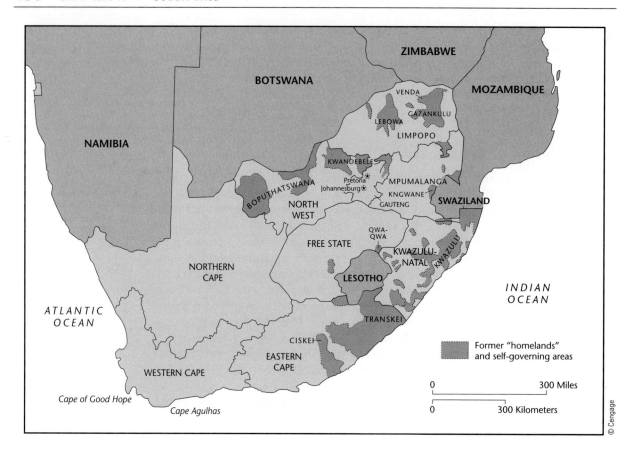

© Cengage

were often short of key skills such as financial record keeping, and civil servants were as a consequence often very corrupt.

Reforming such administrations was extremely difficult, particularly because it was impossible to dismiss public servants during the Mandela era—a consequence of the transition guarantees in the 1993 constitution. Additionally, militant public service unions affiliated to COSATU, the ANC's ally, often protect corrupt officials. Most of the new provincial governments lacked even basic information about the number of their employees or the location of public property. Finally, South Africa's current public administration inherited hierarchical and authoritarian traditions from the apartheid regime, which in practice have proved very difficult to change.

In any case, as social reforms have expanded citizen entitlements—including free prenatal health care, abortions on demand, housing subsidies, and a wider range of welfare grants—the bureaucracy has acquired a whole range of new tasks, even though it was already badly managed and poorly qualified. Public service managers in regional departments often find it difficult to interpret and understand policy designed in national ministries.

Partly because of the failings of the provincial administrations, from 1999 onwards national policy-makers increasingly turned to municipal government as the key agency for the delivery of development projects. Because of their taxation powers, local governments in many respects have greater discretionary power than provincial administrations, especially in the case of the metropolitan councils in South Africa's six main cities. Although big cities derive most of their revenues from local taxes, smaller local authorities remain heavily dependent on government grants. Up until recently, most of South Africa's big cities and smaller centers were locally governed by ANC-dominated administrations.

However, there has been very low voter turnout in local elections, and heavy criticism of the way local councils were performing. The public was clearly disappointed with the first two decades of democratic local government. The Ministry of Provincial and Local Government has invested considerable effort to train councillors as well as to set up a system of ward committees to improve accountability and public participation in planning. But reforms do not seem to have improved the quality of representation in local government. Corruption is especially entrenched in local government, and municipal administration personnel also lack basic skills. For example, in 2007, one-third of city governments employed no engineers, an effect of the exodus during the preceding decade of white apartheid-era officials. As the cabinet minister responsible for municipalities conceded in 2010, outside the big cities, local government was "not working." The extent to which weak local government can be blamed on the ANC will become clearer in the next few years. In the 2016 local elections, the main opposition party, the Democratic Alliance (DA), received 27 percent of the national vote and secured control of four of the major metropolitan councils, Cape Town (where it had governed previously) and in the ANC's former strongholds, Pretoria, Johannesburg, and Port Elizabeth. Independent monitoring agencies rated the twenty-six DA-led municipalities between 2009 and 2014 as amongst South Africa's best for efficient services and clean audits. So, perhaps, fresh political direction will make a difference. Johannesburg's new mayor, Herman Mashaba, millionaire proprietor of hair care cosmetics brand "Black like Me," is "unapologetically" pro-business and promises to curb corruption and waste. One of his first actions was to end an expensive project to construct bicycle lanes: "There are people in Johannesburg who don't have toilets—how can you justify building cycle lanes in wealthy neighborhoods?" he asked.

The Policy-Making Process

Before it came to power in 1994, the ANC appeared to be committed to participatory ways of making policy. This was reflected in the post-apartheid government's rhetoric about "stakeholder" consultation in development planning and institutional accountability, and in the way the post-apartheid Reconstruction and Development Programme (RDP) was adopted.

The early Mandela administration seemed to put this approach into practice when it came to making policy. Assertive parliamentary committees and ministers who were prepared to work closely with these committees made the process more open to interest groups and the infant lobbying industry. Departments conscientiously circulated Green Papers and White Papers (successive drafts of policy proposals) to all interested parties, and they encouraged public feedback at policy presentations up and down the country.

The announcement by the minister of finance of the essential tenets of an official GEAR policy in 1996 represented an abrupt turnaround. From then on, the minister warned, macroeconomic management would stress deficit reduction, the removal of tariff protection, government downsizing, privatization, exchange control relaxation, and setting wage increases below rates of productivity growth. After a currency crisis in late 1995, the government announced that the private sector would henceforth be the main engine for job creation and social progress. The government itself, the minister warned, was not in the business of creating jobs.

The minister announced, immediately after GEAR's publication, that its content was nonnegotiable. This made it different from any other official policy announcements. The announcement of GEAR set the tone for the new style of policy-making. Since 1996, policy shifts have typically occurred in sudden fashion, without elaborate consultative procedures. The surest way to influence policy from outside government has become through direct access to the president's office and the informal networks that surround it.

Successive ANC governments, including Jacob Zuma's, have retained rhetorical commitment to fiscally conservative policies, although Zuma has expanded public employment. This has put economic issues at the center of political conflict. COSATU hostility to GEAR and what it views as subsequent "disastrous neo-liberal policies" has been expressed in several national strikes, most recently in October 2016. Other kinds of dissent, both by unions and the broader public, involve opposition to official financial policies. Trade unions joined with civic associations to mobilize popular protest against contracting out municipal services to private firms as well as to challenge the right of municipalities to evict delinquent tenants and withdraw services from payment defaulters. The austerity produced by GEAR's economies has had an especially severe effect on municipalities, which have received less and less funding from the central government. At the beginning of the Mandela government, ANC leaders hoped to maintain their activist traditions in the ways in which they made decisions and exercised power. In South African democracy's third decade, the worlds of policy decision making and popular political activism have become increasingly insulated from each other.

Where Do You Stand?

The changes in 1994 were a compromise. Did they leave South Africa's administration stronger or weaker?

Did the ANC make unwise concessions during the negotiations? If so, what were they and why were they made? If not, why do you reject the criticisms made of the compromise?

SECTION 4

REPRESENTATION AND PARTICIPATION

Focus Questions

- Why has the South African National Assembly been so ineffective in checking executive power?

- What factors encourage parties to take up moderate positions during elections?

The Legislature

South Africa's legislature consists of a 400-member National Assembly located in Cape Town, as well as the National Council of Provinces, an upper house of parliament. Parliamentarians can take the initiative in drafting and enacting laws but in practice most legislation since 1994 has been drafted by government ministers and officials, not by ordinary members of parliament. After draft laws are introduced into the National Assembly, they are reviewed by specialized "portfolio" committees. These committees usually call for public comments on the bill before recommending either revision, acceptance, or rejection of the law. Once a bill has received its second reading in the National Assembly, it is subject to a final up or down vote. Parliamentary committees also review the work of different government departments. Standing Committees on Public Accounts and Public Finance monitor general public spending, and they can summon ministers and public servants to appear before them.

The second chamber, the National Council of the Provinces, has ninety members made up of nine equal-size delegations drawn from the provincial legislatures. To encourage consensus within provincial delegations, each province can cast only one vote within the Council. Although the National Council for the Provinces reviews all legislation, its functions are only advisory for most laws.

Much of what happens in parliament depends on the ANC caucus, which represents nearly two-thirds of the votes in the National Assembly. On the whole, ANC parliamentarians tend to defer to the executive. This is partly because of the country's electoral system. In general elections, parties compete for National Assembly seats by offering single lists of candidates rather than by running candidates in individual districts or constituencies. How parties choose their lists is up to them. The main parties use electoral procedures in which the resulting nominations are then ranked or "tweaked" by their leaderships. In the case of the ANC, according to its own rules, every third position on their list must be occupied by a woman. In practice, then MPs hold their seats at the will of party leadership, not through being personally elected. The list system through which MPs hold their seats at the discretion of party leaders means that MPs who defy party policy or leadership directives risk incurring heavy penalties, including losing their seat in parliament at the next election.

During the Mandela presidency, ANC MPs were occasionally willing to confront the executive branch. During the Mbeki administration, parliamentary committees became much less assertive, and government ministers treated committees scornfully. In any case, ANC parliamentarians may have other priorities than ensuring executive accountability. The fact that in 2007, 40 percent of the ANC caucus listed themselves as company directors suggests that many ANC MPs devote significant time to private business pursuits. More than half the members of President Zuma's cabinet in 2014 registered major business interests.

Parliament's most important committee, in theory is the Select Committee on Public Accounts (SCOPA) which monitors public expenditure. In 2001, SCOPA began investigating allegations of corrupt arms contracting by a former defense minister, a senior ANC leader. SCOPA contained a majority of ANC members. Initially SCOPA followed its investigation energetically but after clashing with the President's office the leader of the ANC group within SCOPA, Andrew Feinstein resigned, complaining of ministerial efforts to circumscribe the inquiry.[9] Following Feinstein's departure, SCOPA ceased to play any further role in the efforts to identify bribe-takers and the incident is still viewed as a key moment in the government's rejection of parliamentary oversight. To be fair, on several occasions since the arms inquiry, over the last ten years, SCOPA and various other committees have occasionally attempted to challenge the executive, but usually without much support from the ANC contingent on each committee.[10] For example in August 2015, ANC parliamentarians were unanimous in rejecting the recommendations of the Public Protector that President Zuma should repay the money spent on his house at Nkandhla.

Political Parties and the Party System

Today, South Africa's party system is partly shaped by old racial divisions. The main parties that emerged as the leading groups in the 1994 election were well-established organizations during the apartheid era: the African National Congress founded in

1912 and supported by most Africans, and the (Afrikaner) National Party founded in 1914, were voted for by a majority of whites. In 1994, most of the parties competing in the election drew support mainly from a different ethnic or racial group. Even after apartheid, the pattern of racial or ethnic bloc voting has changed only slightly. This has helped to ensure the ANC's predominance.

The African National Congress

The ANC began in a conference of African notables that assembled in 1912 to protest the impending South African Land Act. During World War II, the ANC began to build a mass membership. By this time, several of its leaders were also members of the Communist Party. Within the ANC, both Communists and Africanists (racially assertive African nationalists) who formed the Youth League influenced the ANC to embrace more aggressive tactics. The Communist Party was banned in 1950; its members then worked within the ANC and allied organizations. Communist influence and older liberal traditions nurtured by Methodist schools, which trained most African political leaders, ensured that although the ANC's membership remained exclusively African, it broadened its program. In 1956, the ANC's Freedom Charter proposed a democratic future which all races would enjoy. A "Defiance Campaign" of civil disobedience against new apartheid laws swelled membership.

A breakaway movement, the Pan-Africanist Congress (PAC), formed in 1959 as a more radical alternative to the ANC. After the uproar that followed the Sharpeville massacre in March 1960, the government banned both the ANC and the PAC. Moving underground and into exile, they began planning armed insurgencies.

During its thirty years in exile, the ANC strengthened its alliance with the Communist Party. Partly because of this alliance, it opened its ranks to whites, Indians, and Coloureds. Because survival in exile required discipline and authority, the ANC patterned its internal organization on the centralized model of communist parties.

After 1976, ANC guerrillas attracted attention with attacks on symbolic targets. A charismatic cult developed around the ANC's imprisoned leaders on Robben Island, especially Nelson Mandela. Mandela's stature helped the ANC achieve international recognition and acceptance. By the late 1980s, meetings between its leaders and Western statesmen underlined its status as a government-in-waiting. The ANC established secret contacts with South African officials in the mid-1980s. After the party was unbanned and Mandela was released from prison in 1990, the ANC used foreign contributions to build a sophisticated mass organization in South Africa.

Today, the ANC's overwhelming predominance in South African political life is partly a result of the legitimacy resulting from its role in the struggle against apartheid. Its political authority also results from an extensive political organization, represented through local branches throughout the country. In every parliamentary election since 1994 it has enjoyed a large majority of voter support. In 2014, the ANC's 62.15 percent share of the vote resulted in an allocation of 249 of the 400 seats in the National Assembly.

Even in its first terms in office, authoritarian tendencies within the ANC hardened. In 1997, amendments to the party constitution endorsed centralism and prohibited factionalism. This was supposed to make it difficult for caucuses to emerge around different policy positions. Party officials also tried to promote authoritarian patterns of party discipline by appealing to a supposedly Africanist advocacy of deference for elders in society. However, rebellion against Thabo Mbeki's effort to secure a third term as party president at the ANC's national conference in 2007 may have helped strengthen its commitment to internally democratic procedures.

Smaller Parties

In the most recent general election, in May 2014, twelve opposition parties won seats. Of these, only two represent significant challenges to the ANC's parliamentary predominance. The DA continued its steady expansion of support by obtaining over 22 percent of the ballot and eighty-nine seats. A new formation, positioning itself to the left of the ANC, the Economic Freedom Front, obtained twenty-five seats with 6 percent of the vote. Meanwhile Inkatha, the ANC's old rival among Zulu-speaking voters in KwaZulu-Natal, continued its decline, losing support to a breakaway group, the National Freedom Party. The eight other parties that won seats in parliament each received less than one percent of the votes. Since 1994 the most conspicuous trend in opposition politics has been the expansion of the Democrats as well as the disappearance of the old ruling party during apartheid, the National Party. The National Party obtained more than 20 percent of the vote in 1994. In the next two polls, most of its support was captured by the Democrats. The National Party disbanded in 2006 and some of its leaders joined the ANC. The IFP's support also declined from its 1994 high point of 10 percent of the vote. Over the years other parties have included right-wing Afrikaner groups, parties drawing upon political networks established in the ethnic homelands during apartheid, and various fringe socialist and "black conscious" or "Africanist" nationalist groupings.

A common perception about South African elections is that their results reflect a racial or ethnic "census," with racial and ethnic identity supplying the main consideration in promoting voter choice. From this perspective, the ANC as the historic agency of black South African political emancipation can count on the loyalty of most black voters. Correspondingly, in this view, the ANC's main opponent, the DA, draws its most firm adherents from middle-class voters in the white minority. However, this is changing. Black politics is not monolithic and the Democrats' electoral base includes significant shares of African and Coloured voters. Moreover, voters no longer identify quite so emotionally with parties. People are less likely to believe that they "belong" to a party or that it is "theirs," considerations that used to favor the ANC.[11] Analysis of comments on Facebook during the 2016 local elections suggest that in the main cities a large proportion of voters were making up their minds at the last moment, to the ANC's detriment. In this poll, the ANC's share of the national vote was its lowest ever in an election, 54 percent, down from 61 percent in the 2011 municipal elections.

In 1994, the ANC's main competitor for African votes was the IFP. Inkatha was established ostensibly as a Zulu cultural organization in 1975 by the KwaZulu homeland chief minister, Chief Mangosuthu Buthelezi. It won all the seats in the KwaZulu legislative assembly elections in 1978 and thenceforth ruled the homeland until KwaZulu's incorporation into the province of KwaZulu-Natal in 1994. Although, unlike other homeland parties, Inkatha projected itself as a militant liberation movement and enjoyed mass support among Zulu migrant communities around Johannesburg. It secured control of the KwaZulu-Natal provincial administration in 1994 and 1999, losing its dominance in 2004, although its members continue to serve in a coalition administration with the ANC. Indeed, programmatically, it shares many of the ANC positions except with respect to what it considers to the rights and prerogatives of "traditional leaders." Inkatha lost more ground in the 2014 election. Very much an organization constructed around the charismatic qualities of its founder and president, Mangosuthu Buthelezi, its reluctance to renew its leadership is one ingredient in its decline. Chief Buthelezi, now in his eighties, remains the movement's leader. Divisions over the leadership issue contributed to the breakaway of the National Freedom Party. IFP's electoral support is mainly in rural districts within the Zulu royal kingdom but even here it is challenged by the ANC, particularly as Jacob Zuma's public persona is constructed around the same "traditionalist" Zulu values that Inkatha claims to defend: patriarchy, deference to age, martial virtues, and cattle-based pastoralism.

The DA can trace its origins to an opposition group in the all-white parliament who supported African enfranchisement and formed the Progressive Party in 1959. Only one survived the 1961 election, Helen Suzman, and she became a lonely parliamentary opponent of apartheid until she was joined by six other MPs who were elected in 1974. Thereafter, the renamed Progressive Federal Party (PFP) became increasingly influential.

The PFP was criticized by black anti-apartheid groups for supporting an educational requirement for voting eligibility. But from 1984 onwards, it began to recruit and form political alliances within the black and Coloured communities. The PFP renamed itself the Democratic Party (DP) in 1987. Campaigning principally around human rights issues in 1994, the DP performed badly, winning only seven seats with 1.73 percent of the vote. Five years later, the DP's "Fight Back" campaign capitalized on white, Indian and Coloured voters' anxieties arising from rising crime rates and affirmative action in favor of black people. The party won thirty-eight seats, capturing much of the National Party's former support. In 1995, the DP joined forces with the National Party to form the DA in order to contest local elections. A merger was agreed upon, but then in 2001, the NP leadership announced its decision to support and participate in the government. Not all National Party members followed their leaders, and the DA continued to claim that it represented most of the National Party's branches and fought the 2004 elections under the same name.

In the 2014 elections, by the party's own calculations, 750,000 Africans voted for the DA. The Democrats are now led in parliament by Mmusi Maimane, very representative of the younger black middle-class achievers who are the prime target of the DA's efforts to expand its vote. Maimane was born in Soweto in 1980. Educated at private Catholic secondary schools he obtained two master's degrees before lecturing at a business school. Helen Zille, the party's senior leader, serves as premier of the Western Cape. For a decade now, the DA has exercised executive power running one of South Africa's wealthiest regional governments. In this province in which black Africans still constitute a minority, the DA enjoys majority support. The party also controls Cape Town's metropolitan administration.

Zille is white but she speaks Xhosa fluently and since the inception of her premiership, the Democrats even began making modest inroads into the core ANC urban bases in the Western Cape and elsewhere. In fact, the DA has been trying since 2000 to cross the racially segmentary lines that appeared to confine party support in the 1994 election. In the area around Johannesburg, the DA had established, by 2003, thirty-two branches in what it termed "emergent areas," that is, black townships or squatter camps. In 2003, DA and ANC local leaders traded accusations in newspaper letter columns that their opponents were disrupting their party's activities in Alexandra, traditionally an ANC stronghold. This indirectly confirmed that the DA was expanding into fresh territory. Since then, though, DA strategy has changed. Rather than concentrating on building organization in black townships, undertakings that in any case invite aggressive attention from ANC activists, DA planners now favor "relying on public relations as the primary driver of the party's popularity with voters" and they assign a low priority to the task "of establishing membership structures on the ground."[12] What has changed, of course, since the early 2000s, is the introduction of electronic social media as an instrument in communicating political messages. This is a medium in which the DA has played a pioneering role in South Africa.

What are its messages? Programmatically, the DA is somewhat to the right of the ANC, maintaining a firm commitment to free market economics. Hence, it is critical of the ANC's restrictive management of the economy, especially with respect to contractual rights accorded to workers that in its view curb job growth. It also opposes the government's enforcement of affirmative action, although this is an issue on which there is disagreement within the party leadership between older white leaders and younger African middle-class democrats. But the party's appeal to voters probably derives from two main considerations. First, its often highly experienced parliamentarians have been in the forefront of efforts to exercise oversight with respect to official corruption and this has helped to make the party popular at a time when the ANC's venality has become much more conspicuous. The DA has exploited President Zuma's vulnerability on this score with relish. Helen Zille led a delegation to his ostentatious homestead at Inkandla "to inspect the project," a move that provoked outrage from local chiefs, who told reporters that "we have arrived at a point where we say enough of this disrespectful white girl."[13]

The second source of the DA's electoral appeal and a consideration that differentiates it from any other opposition group is that the DA itself commands executive power, for it runs administrations in one provincial government and in several municipalities. In office, it has gained a reputation for honesty and effectiveness in the provision of public services both to middle-class households and to poorer communities. It was in the Western Cape under a DA administration that the first mass provision of antiretroviral medication was made available for HIV/AIDS patients at a time when the ANC national government was opposing such treatment. Incumbency in government also brings to the DA the power of patronage. Its ability to allocate funding and resources as well as make public appointments may well enhance its appeal to new supporters as well as help it to recruit plausible black leaders.

In the 2014 election, it is likely that most of the DA's million or so new votes came from Africans. The DA's gains were concentrated in Gauteng and Western Cape. Geographical analysis of the DA vote's distribution indicates that it is finally making significant inroads into certain African "township" neighborhoods; in the more middle-class districts in Soweto, for example. Here its emphasis on its own black leadership as well as invective directed at corrupt ANC leaders appeared to have paid off.

The other main contender for African votes are the Economic Freedom Fighters. The Economic Freedom Fighters purport to represent a left-wing alternative to the ANC. They advocate industrial nationalization and land seizures, although its left-wing credentials are belied by the lavish lifestyle and habits of its founder, Julius Malema, a millionaire beneficiary of preferential public contracting. Malema was expelled from the ANC in 2012, after attacking what he called the "imperialist puppet" government of Botswana. As the president of the ANC's Youth League he had been very popular. Surveys indicate that his new movement attracts a significant proportion of younger, better-educated Black South Africans, university students for example, especially those frustrated by the continuing predominance White South Africans exercise over the professions. In the 2014 election, EFF did comparatively well in Malema's home province, in Limpopo. But they also drew support from the shanty settlements around Johannesburg, amongst the poorest and most recently urbanized. Between now and the next general election, if the EFF holds together and strengthens its organization, it may well block the DA's advance toward becoming a major force within the ANC's traditional heartland. In the 2016 local elections, the EFF maintained its vote share, and unlike earlier breakaway groups from the ANC, it seems to have consolidated its support.

Elections

South African elections are generally judged to be free and fair, and in certain respects they have become more so. All the available evidence suggests that voters are confident about ballot secrecy as well as the integrity of the count. Most importantly, it has become easier for candidates of all parties to canvass voters outside the areas where their core supporters live. In 1994, there were "no go" areas in which canvassers from certain parties were forcibly excluded by their competitors; although by 2004, each of the main parties were routinely deploying door-to-door canvassers in the same neighborhoods, sometimes at the same time. Voter registration, however, remains an issue. In 2014, 7 million eligible citizens remained unregistered as voters, many of whom would be young first time voters. (See Table 11.2.) The considerations that dissuade younger voters will be discussed in Section 5.

In recent elections, a disturbing development has been an increased tendency for ruling party speakers at mass meetings to suggest that electoral support will be rewarded with grants or other benefits. In 2014, on one or two occasions, the official agency responsible for distributing welfare benefits allocated food packages at ANC rallies. Moreover in the run-up to formal campaigning, observers have noted an increased incidence of brutal electioneering, including attacks on rival activists. There were twelve politically motivated killings between January 2013 and February 2014, mostly in KwaZulu-Natal as a result of conflict in workers' hostels between Inkatha and the breakaway group, the National Freedom Party. The election season itself featured no real violence, although in their campaigning, leaders occasionally used inflammatory or threatening language. The DA's Helen Zille told one meeting that the ANC was "like a snake," and a DA leaflet suggested that the ANC wanted to stop Coloured people getting jobs in the Western Cape. The ANC's Fikile Mbalula characterized the DA government in the Western Cape as "witches" that were "oppressing us." Not to be outdone, ANC deputy president Cyril Ramaphosa warned villagers in Limpopo, his home region, that a vote for the DA would be a vote for the return of the "Boers" and apartheid. Such lapses are exceptional, however. In the 2016 municipal election, the IEC was asked to investigate just one complaint about ANC leaders making threatening remarks to voters. The weight of evidence, then, suggests that the ANC continues to win victories through persuasive campaigning rather than as a consequence of threats or untoward inducements.

Arguably, South Africa's electoral system promotes the formation of socially inclusive political parties and civil electioneering. South Africa uses a national list system of proportional representation. In national and provincial elections, parties nominate lists of candidates for the National Assembly and for each of the nine provinces. Seats are allocated in proportion to each party's share of the votes. The fact that the nation serves as a single national constituency for the parliament contains strong incentives for moderation because the electorate is so spread out. All parties are encouraged to seek votes outside their core support, a consideration that helps to encourage them to adopt programs with broad social appeal. Party leaders put people on their lists who might not win electoral contests if they ran as individual candidates: members of racial minorities or women, for example. As we have noted, however, the drawback is that parliamentarians hold their seats at the will of party leaders and this can make them unduly deferential towards the executive.

Table 11.2	South African General Elections, 1994–2014				
Party	**1994**	**1999**	**2004**	**2009**	**2014**
African Christian Democratic Party	88,104 (0.45%)	228,976 (1.43%)	250,272 (1.60%)	142,658 (0.81%)	104,039 (0.57%)
African Independent Congress	–	–	–	–	97,642 (0.53%)
AgangSA	–	–	–	–	52,350 (0.28%)
African National Congress	12,237,655 (62.55%)	10,601,330 (66.35%)	10,880,915 (69.69%)	11,650,748 (65.90%)	11,650,000 (62.15%)
African People's Convention	–	–	–	–	30,076 (0.17%)
Congress of the People	–	–	–	1,311,027 (7.42%)	123,235 (0.67%)
Democratic Party/ Alliance	338,426 (1.73%)	1,527,337 (9.56%)	1,931,201 (12.37%)	2,945,829 (16.66%)	4,091,584 (22.23%)
Freedom Front	424,555 (2.17%)	127,217 (0.80%)	139,465 (0.89%)	146,796 (0.83%)	165,715 (0.90%)
Inkatha	2,058,294 (10.94%)	1,371,477 (8.58%)	1,088,664 (6.97%)	804,260 (4.55%)	441,854 (2.40%)
National Freedom Party	–	–	–	–	288,742 (1.57%)
New National Party	3,983,690 (20.39%)	1,098,215 (6.87%)	257,824 (1.65%)	–	–
Pan-Africanist Congress	243,478 (1.25%)	113,125 (0.71%)	113,512 (0.35%)	48,530 (0.27%)	37,784 (0.21%)
United Democratic Movement	–	546,790 (3.42%)	355,717 (2.28%)	149,680 (0.85%)	184,636 (1.00%)
Others	149,296 (0.81%)	362,676 (2.19%)	595,101 (3.80%)	480,416 (2.73%)	176,389 (0.96%)
Total Votes	**19,533,498**	**15,977,142**	**15,612,671**	**17,680,729**	**18,654,457**
Turnout of registered voters	–	89.30%	76.70%	77.30%	73.43%
Turnout of voting age population	86%	71.80%	57.80%	59.80%	59.3%

Political Culture, Citizenship, and Identity

Relatively high turnout rates in four out of five national elections were encouraging signs of strong citizenship identity among South Africans. During the Mandela administration, there were rising levels of approval and satisfaction with democracy, although opinion polls suggest such sentiments are less widely shared today.

Opinion polls continue to indicate that South Africans tend to believe that race relations have improved since 1994. For example, in 2015, the South African Institute of Race Relations found a majority of respondents agreeing that race relations had improved, and more remarkably, that job recruitment should be based on merit, not racial background.[14] But racial divisions continue to affect patterns of political support. Although public schools and middle-class neighborhoods have become desegregated, most black people still live in ghetto-like townships or in the historical homeland areas; racial distinctions remain very conspicuous in South African social geography. However, since 1994, new patterns of public behavior seem to have created more conciliatory attitudes among South Africans. Even so, there remain sources of racial tension. The government is critical of what it takes to be the slow progress of black business, and ANC leaders routinely blame the absence of quicker social change on "white economic selfishness" (Thabo Mbeki's phrase). Class-based politics was generally quite comfortably accommodated within the ANC's fold during the anti-apartheid struggle, since most of its active followers were working class, and the war against apartheid could be considered an offensive against capitalism. Even today, union leaders hold back from organizing a workers' party separately from the ANC, recognizing that many workers are likely to retain the loyalties fostered by decades of nationalist politics. However, populist racial invective directed against white privilege and wealth remains politically compelling, especially for leaders of the ANC's Youth League, with a constituency of unemployed school dropouts. As has been evident in the language used by the #FeesMustFall leaders, the same is true for university students, even on elite campuses.

In the 1950s, a powerful women's movement developed within the ANC to oppose extending the pass laws to African women. More and more women were heading single-parent households, and many women were moving into industrial occupations and higher education, which led to feminist movements. One of the first major social reforms enacted by Mandela's government was legalizing abortion on demand. In general, the ANC's female members have forced the party to pay at least some attention to women's rights and entitlements.

Interest Groups, Social Movements, and Protest

Social movements continue to be unusually well-organized for a developing country. Although participation at union meetings may have dwindled, labor unions have extensive financial resources, since dues are automatically deducted from workers' wages, and unions often organize entire economic sectors. In 2017, 3.7 million workers belonged to trade unions, a growth in absolute numbers since 1994, but a smaller proportion of the overall workforce. Unions are now mainly concentrated in the public sector. But the labor movement is increasingly divided, politically and for other reasons. The Marikana mineworkers union was led by a breakaway group, the Association of Mineworkers and Construction Union (AMCU). It accused the National Union of Mineworkers (NUM), a loyal ANC ally, of being a pro-management "sweetheart." At Marikana and elsewhere, the AMCU recruited among underground miners, whereas the NUM was increasingly led by white collar surface workers, better paid and more likely to be urban and well educated. It is not only mineworkers who have broken ranks with the historically entrenched alliance between the ANC and labor. In 2014, the National Union of Metalworkers (NUMSA), COSATU's most important industrial affiliate announced it would not mobilize its members in electioneering for the ANC and subsequently withdrew from COSATU, the trade union federation allied to the ANC.

In townships, residents' associations have created an impressive associational network. Surveys suggest that more people participate in civic associations than in political parties. From 2002, a new generation of local single-issue movements began to address problems of landlessness, electricity cut-offs, and evictions of bond or municipal tax defaulters. Around these concerns a strong vein of assertive protest has gathered momentum. The activist repertoire often borders on the violent: damage to public buildings, tire-burning, and skirmishing with police. The frequency of "major service delivery protests" as monitored by the authorities has risen for a decade. Between 2007 and 2012, the number of protests quintupled, peaking in 2012 with nearly 250 protests.[15] Participants tend to be young, often unemployed school dropouts. The focus of their anger is often the venality of local politicians, but the aggression can direct itself at more vulnerable targets. In 2008, sixty immigrants, mainly from Mozambique and Zimbabwe, were killed by xenophobic rioters in incidents around Johannesburg. The murders were spurred by the widely shared conviction that foreigners were depriving local people of their jobs. Protest tends to be concentrated in poor neighborhoods in bigger cities. But they may not be the poorest neighborhoods; and protest often occurs in areas supporting the ruling party. This suggests that forceful and even violent protest has become part of a bargaining repertoire in which citizens "alternate the brick (protest) and the pro-ANC ballot."[16] Official responses to such protests have recently included heavily armed police ready to fire into crowds. As noted above, Marikana was an extreme version of confrontational public order enforcement favored by Jacob Zuma's police commanders.

Such behavior contrasts with gentler predispositions that seem to prevail in South African associational life. For example, surveys confirm that about half the population does voluntary work for charitable organizations. The proportion is higher among younger people.[17] With the exception of COSATU, which invites white participation, associational life remains racially segregated, however. Business organizations, for example, continue to represent white and black firms separately. The larger corporations are still perceived to represent white privilege. Churches may have racially integrated hierarchies, but most South Africans worship in racially exclusive congregations. Only black South Africans attend soccer games in significant numbers to watch the multiracial teams in the Premier Soccer League. Rugby and cricket fans remain predominantly white despite efforts within the sports administrations to make the teams more diverse. South African democracy is still weakened by divisions between ethnic groups that prevent people from recognizing common interests and shared enthusiasms.

The Political Impact of Technology and the Media

Most South Africans possess cell phones. This means that a majority of the population can access online information through using mobile phones, despite the uneven spread of broadband services. South Africa usage of social media and social networks is the highest on the continent. South Africans are among the top thirty nations signed up to Facebook.

This is beginning to have the transformative political impact that information and communications technology (ICT) is believed to have achieved in other African political settings. In the "Arab Spring" of 2011, Facebook and other online networks played a key role in assembling people without previous activist experience.

In South Africa, political parties have been swift to open Facebook and Twitter accounts as well as draw upon a local social media network, Mxit, which can be accessed by people without smart phones. All parties tried to communicate with supporters through social media during the 2009 campaigning, but the networks had a more telling effect in 2014. For the DA in particular, Facebook has become a major channel of communication with potential supporters, whereas the ANC still depends heavily on face-to-face canvassing, demonstrating its physical presence within core support localities. Election monitoring in South Africa is now facilitated by tablets and mobile phone communication, and development agencies have been using social media networks to reach vulnerable groups. For example, the *UmNyango* project in KwaZulu-Natal has encouraged rural women to report and challenge domestic violence. New social movements that seek to mobilize the "militant poor," such as the shack dwellers' *Abahlali baseMjondolo,* use Facebook. And in the #FeesMustFall movement we have in South Africa the first national insurgent activism that is networked through social media.

Where Do You Stand?

What have been the ANC's main achievements as the ruling party since 1994?

What are the benefits and what are the shortcomings of one party predominating politically for such a long time?

SOUTH AFRICAN POLITICS IN TRANSITION

Focus Questions

- What are likely to be the long-term effects of HIV/AIDS in South Africa?

- In certain respects it has been easier to institute and consolidate democracy in South Africa than in many other developing countries that underwent democratic transitions in the 1980s and 1990s. Why?

Political Challenges and Changing Agendas

The impact of AIDS on South African society is hard to overestimate. More that 12 percent of the population is currently HIV-positive, 7 million people, according to Statistics South Africa. Nearly 5 million South Africans have already died of HIV/AIDS, though the number of deaths at 162,000 in 2015 is down. Its victims tend to be between the ages of fifteen and fifty—the most economically active members of the population. Poor households that support AIDS patients can spend up to two-thirds of their income on the cost of care.[18]

South Africa's initial efforts to combat the spread of AIDS and deal with its effects were tentative and confused. Belatedly, a public education program, including the distribution of free condoms, began to promote awareness of the disease toward the end of the Mandela presidency. At the beginning of the program, however, education was presented as an alternative to medical treatment. Surveys suggested that AIDS awareness was not enough. It did not reduce the sexual behavior that spreads the disease.

In October 1998, the minister of health announced that the government would cease supplying antiretroviral drugs to hospitals that until then had prescribed them to pregnant women to prevent mother-to-child transmission of AIDS. The 80 million rand ($12 million) saving would be used instead for distributing 140 million contraceptives. One month later, Thabo Mbeki, who then was chairman of a ministerial committee on AIDS, defended the minister's decision by claiming that the drug concerned, azidothymidine (AZT), was "dangerously toxic." This was patently false.

Hostility to the public prescription of drugs stemmed from more complicated considerations, however. President Mbeki began expressing doubts about the scientific status of the disease in late 1999. He believed that conventional explanations about the disease's causes stemmed from racial prejudice. In 2001, Mbeki referred to the "insulting" theory that AIDS originated in Africa. In reality, Mbeki contended, South Africans who were dying of the illnesses that immune deficiency exposed them to (tuberculosis for example) were not victims of a virus; they were instead the casualties of poverty. Mbeki was aligning himself with a tiny minority of dissident scientists who have denied AIDS' existence. In 2000, the president established a panel to investigate the scientific evidence about the causes of AIDS.

Mbeki's skepticism about AIDS certainly undermined attempts to combat the pandemic. Between 1998 and 2001, public hospitals were prevented from using antiretroviral drugs, including nevirapine, a much cheaper alternative to AZT—even for treating rape victims. Taking their cue from the president, cabinet ministers began questioning AIDS statistics and projections, suggesting that these derived from faulty sampling procedures. After the Treatment Action Campaign successfully obtained a Constitutional Court judgment compelling the government to use nevirapine, ANC nominees on the Medical Control Council began warning that the drug might need to be deregistered on grounds of toxicity. Although in August 2002, in response to internal pressures within the ANC, the cabinet appeared to commit itself to provision of antiretroviral treatment, the health ministry resisted. The Treatment Action Campaign organized a civil disobedience protest during 2003 against the delay.

Full compliance with the Court's decision only began after Mbeki's fall from power. By 2009, with a new health minister in charge, 850,000 patients were receiving medication and around 3 million are today, about half of those who will need it soon, at an annual cost of 19 billion rand ($1.9 billion). Today the major challenge is administrative: to manage the scale of the treatment required, the health service has recruited 10,000 new nurses and health spending increased from 11.9 percent of the budget in 2009/10 to around 13.1 today. Treatment and the necessary counseling that ensure patient adherence to the drugs regime depends on the services of 73,000 auxiliary community health workers. They are paid token gratuities of between 500 and 1,500 rand (US$50–150) a month and have become increasingly disaffected. But after Zuma himself publicly underwent an AIDs test, the leadership's support for an effective program to counter the pandemic is no longer in doubt. This political turnaround has apparently helped change public behavior; within one year, 10 million people had undergone testing. Infection rates have been on the decline, especially among younger South Africans, a consequence, experts believe, of increased condom usage and more successful preventive education. The 3,000 clinics that dispense the antiretroviral medicines have become more effective in other areas of public health care as well, and, indeed, official South African efforts to address the AIDS epidemic have prompted impressive improvements in primary health facilities. This is just as well. Three hundred thousand additional people every year become HIV-positive, and millions of South Africans will remain acutely dependent on effective public health care for decades to come.

Economic Challenges

Every year, half a million students leave high school without graduating. When they enter the labor market without skills, they ensure that unemployment will remain at high levels for a long time.

Modern governments are not in the business of creating jobs. Mbeki's ministers used to claim that the removal of subsidies and tariffs would encourage more competitive industries. In their view, South Africa had adopted the "correct macro financial policy fundamentals." Critics replied that one factor that deterred investors—high crime rates—was partly the result of the government's failure to undertake thorough police reform. Fairly modest levels of public debt compared to that of most other developing countries prompted left-wing economists to suggest that heavier foreign borrowing might finance higher levels of public investment in services and fighting poverty, as well as stimulate the kinds of growth rates needed to reduce unemployment significantly. This advice may have had some impact. After 2004, during Mbeki's second term, foreign loan–funded investment in infrastructure did help to expand employment, although mainly in short-term construction jobs.

Government social expenditure has helped to soften the effects of poverty, but social inequality is more acute than it was in 1994. Absolute poverty has probably receded a little, given the construction of nearly 3 million houses now inhabited by poor people, and the much wider distribution of welfare grants.

Agricultural landownership is one domain, however, in which white privileges remain especially visible, and so far the government has made only gradual progress to change racial patterns of landholding. By 2012, the government had redistributed 7.5 percent of what had historically been white farmland, two-thirds of South Africa's land mass. Since 2000, a succession of illegal land occupations has underlined how volatile landlessness can be as a political issue, especially when many Africans bitterly remember being forced off the land. In 2016, the Economic Freedom Front began a series of symbolic land seizures, targeting urban wasteland outside Western Cape towns and unused farms in Limpopo. Official South African land reform was based on a principle of "willing seller-willing buyer," in other words, voluntary sales based on the land's commercial value, its "market price," which is a principle the EFF opposes. In 2016, the parliament approved the Land Expropriation Act that was intended to speed up reform, although compulsory purchases of white farms would have to be at fair market prices. Land taken from Africans after 1913 can be restored to the affected communities through the 1994 Restitution of Land Rights Act. But even when historically dispossessed communities win back their original land rights, the process of restitution is subject to protracted negotiations over compensation.

The prospects for South Africa's transitional democracy will be fragile if its political institutions continue to be used, as they are too frequently, to protect property rights. On the other hand, it is also possible that constitutional arguments help the poor and vulnerable as they have been when, for example, in 2001 Constitutional Court judges have upheld homeless people's rights to shelter. Defending and extending democracy may become much more challenging, however, if resources available for public services become scarcer and it becomes more difficult to decide who should receive them. Polls confirm that the South African public's ideas of democracy emphasize improvements in living conditions. In other words, people associate democracy with the provision of livelihoods and basic necessities. They attach less importance to its institutional and political dimensions. In this sense, the challenges of governing the economy and deepening the democratic idea come together in ways that define politics in South Africa today.

Is Demography Destiny?

Young South Africans are becoming better educated: the 2016 interim census indicated that the proportion of population aged 20 years and older with no schooling had more than halved since 1996 and those completing secondary education had doubled. Overall, about half the population is below the age of 24, although the youngest group—those under 14—has proportionately decreased, which suggests a slowing population growth rate that has been evident for more than a decade. For the last decade the proportion of young people aged 15 to 24 seeking work is steadily increasing, totaling around 53 percent in 2011. South Africa has one of the highest rates of youth unemployment in the world. Recent opinion polls show higher rates of distrust of politicians and lower levels of party identification among the youngest South Africans who are eligible for voting. For example, nearly two-thirds of youth believed corruption had increased sharply during 2012.[19]

As noted at the beginning of this chapter, this is South Africa's first "born free" generation, that is, the first cohort entering adulthood who grew up in the decades following the democratic transition. They attach less political significance to anti-apartheid history and, if we are to take seriously the rhetoric of the #FeesMustFall movement they are less predisposed to accept the political compromises with white privilege that were a condition for the 1994 political settlement. Electoral registration statistics suggest that the 18 to 24 age group is the least inclined to vote. When members of this group do vote, they are especially likely to change their support from one party to another between elections.

Contradicting the more general trend of disengagement with organized politics among young people has been the expansion within the ANC of its Youth League's influence. Much of its membership is young men in their early 20s who live in the poorest districts, often in the countryside. The League supported Jacob Zuma's ascendency but it turned against Zuma when top ANC leaders opposed its calls for mining nationalization and land redistribution, the most important demands in the Economic Freedom Fighters' program. The EFF's Facebook page is reported to have the largest impact of any party.

Young people are conspicuously in the forefront of a new mass-based shack dwellers movement, *Abahlali baseMjondolo*, based in the townships around Durban, which claims a following of 10,000; there is certainly potential space to the left of the ANC for youth activism. Meanwhile, the ANC itself relies increasingly heavily on the votes of older people, particularly in the countryside where so many of its base supporters, old-age pensioners, reside. This is a group whose numbers will expand as better health services make the older population proportionately bigger. A major future political division in South Africa is likely to pit younger against older people, with generational identity replacing race as the political fault line.

South African Politics in Comparative Perspective

Unlike many of the countries that moved from authoritarian regimes to democratic governments in the late 1980s and early 1990s, South Africa's political economy was developed through a settler minority that became a permanent part of its population. This made the transition to democracy both easier and more challenging.

Between two world wars, a politically independent settler state could invest the revenues from the local production of primary commodities to develop a relatively diversified industrial economy. It expropriated land from its African subjects and recruited some of their members to create a modern working class. Later, unlike many former colonial countries in Africa, well-organized social forces could mobilize to support democratization, in particular the African trade unions, whose members worked on industrial assembly lines even under apartheid. Democratic politics within the white settler minority prompted wider kinds of political organization across the population almost from the beginning of South Africa's Act of Union in 1910. Today, the political parties in the South African parliament are among the oldest in the developing world. Ironically, despite its often brutal efforts during the apartheid era to promote ethnic division, the South African state probably was a more decisive influence in stimulating a national identity throughout most of the twentieth century than was the case for many more benign governments elsewhere in the colonial and postcolonial world. This was for two reasons. Because of its system of intrusive and overarching controls in their lives, apartheid prompted a nationally unified political response among Africans. Meanwhile the industrialization the state promoted compelled rural people to leave their homes and become workers in the cities forging new kinds of solidarity and joining wider communities.

Nevertheless, South African society was deeply divided in the 1990s, at the beginning of democratization. Except for the churches, most institutions and organizations were segmented, separated, or stratified by race. In addition, economic inequalities between rich and poor were among the most extreme in the world, and this injustice was reinforced by the fact that inequalities ran along racial lines.

In certain respects, South African democratization represents a success story. The national government has created trust among citizens. Its political procedures are recognized to be fair, and political leaders have generally observed its rules. A constitution that was designed to be socially inclusive has fostered broadly representative institutions. Popular support of the government is partly a result of its efforts to extend services to poor people, distribute resources fairly, and expand and improve infrastructure and education. Relatively well-managed public finance encouraged a revival of GDP growth, earning recognition for South Africa as one of the most important emerging economies.

One reason that democratization, since 1994, has brought about more effective governance is that it was preceded by a long process of political and economic reform. The dismantling of the tariffs and subsidies that nurtured and protected industry and commercial agriculture began more than a decade before the universal right to vote. Unlike in the countries of the post-communist world, the coming of democracy did not bring sudden exposure to the harsh shocks of international competition. Economic liberalization has continued at a relatively measured pace compared to the experience of many Third World countries, which have been compelled to undergo very rapid structural adjustment of their economies. The welfare state created under apartheid has maintained many of its provisions and even extended some of them, in sharp contrast to the shrinking scope of social services offered by most governments in the developing world.

Similarly, political liberalization preceded universal enfranchisement over a relatively long period. Industrial relations reform at the beginning of the 1980s, a decade before the political negotiations began, enabled black trade unions to participate in institutionalized collective bargaining. This encouraged the growth of well-structured associational life, both inside and outside the workplace, which reinvigorated older political organizations. Elsewhere, new democracies have been fragile because they have not had strong representative movements and parties. In South Africa, constitutional negotiations did not take place in a political vacuum or in a situation of near state collapse. Until the 1994 elections, the apartheid state retained effective authority, and because the negotiations that moved the country toward democracy unfolded over several years, the settlement elicited a high degree of consensus.

Will South Africa manage to deal with its economic challenges under democratic conditions? To redress poverty and reduce inequality significantly, the state will have to make much more serious inroads into minority privileges. Although the constitution obligates government to meet basic needs of citizens, it was also designed to reassure economically dominant groups that their interests would be safeguarded under democracy. It is likely that the constitution will become increasingly challenged if the government attempts to address inequality through expanding the scope of administrative regulation, for example, or through compulsory purchases to accelerate land reform. Meanwhile, increasing social inequality supplies a setting in when poor people confront authority, officials can respond with extreme violence, as was so evident at Marikana.

Where Do You Stand?

What are the prospects for South African political stability?

Why does South Africa's social inequality matter?

Chapter Summary

A unified South Africa was established in the aftermath of the Anglo-Boer War of 1899–1902. A modern administration was geared to providing cheap labor to the gold mining industry and restricted African access to land. In the decades following Union, white workers succeeded in gaining privileges as citizens, but the status of black South Africans deteriorated. Afrikaner nationalists held office from 1948 and established a strict regime of racial apartheid. Popular African resistance was suppressed in 1960. In exile, the main African movements embraced guerrilla warfare. From 1976 onwards, urbanization, industrialization, and mass literacy prompted powerful challenges to white minority rule. In 1990, in response to insurgency and international pressure, the South African political leadership lifted the ban on the main African political organizations and began to negotiate a political settlement. In 1994, a democratically elected government began attempting to reduce poverty and inequality while also encouraging economic regeneration.

Racial segregation required considerable state intervention in the economy. In particular, until 1986, the state restricted Africans' mobility, in order to ensure adequate supplies of cheap black labor for mining and agriculture. State-owned enterprises, however, helped to develop a substantial manufacturing sector. From the 1970s, external anti-apartheid pressures as well as shortages of crucial skills began to prompt liberalization. Even before the advent of universal suffrage in 1994, most apartheid restrictions had been dismantled. Since then, democratic governments have continued to expand economic liberalization, reduce tariffs, and sell public enterprises. Rising unemployment, partly a consequence of market reform, constrains the government's efforts to reduce poverty.

For the post-apartheid transition period, between 1994 and 1999, a power-sharing coalition helped to reassure racial minorities. Nine provincial governments give South African politics a quasi-federal character and offer smaller political parties the possibility of executive office. Despite such safeguards, the ruling party and its leaders are very powerful because of large ANC majorities in the National Assembly. Presidential authority gains strength from an electoral system that makes members of parliament dependent on the party leadership. Continuing shortcomings in the police, the judicial system, and the provincial administrations effectively limit executive power. Meanwhile policy-making has become increasingly centralized.

On the whole, members of the ruling party in the post-apartheid parliament have failed to exercise formal oversight. The ANC inherited, from an eighty-year liberation struggle, a tightly centralized organizational structure and a mass following that was grouped into an extensive network of branches. It remains the predominant organization among black South Africans. Any effective challenge to its authority will require smaller parties, historically based among racial or ethnic minorities, to draw away significant numbers of the ANC's core support. This is only now beginning to happen. South Africa may represent a racially divided dominant-party democracy, but elections are fair, and strong social movements increase the prospects of democratic consolidation.

The four main challenges to South Africa's political leadership are HIV/AIDS, unemployment, social inequality, and political disaffection among young people. Extreme social inequality as well as official venality may reduce public support for democracy and open up opportunities for populist authoritarian politics. Government efforts to alleviate poverty with high social spending may be difficult to sustain if growth levels remain modest.

Key Terms

Africans
Afrikaners
apartheid
Boer
democratization
economic deregulation

homelands
influx control
migrant laborers
pass laws
power sharing
sanctions

settler state
township
Umkhonto-we-Sizwe
Voortrekkers

Suggested Readings

Beresford, Alexander. *South Africa's Political Crisis: Unfinished Leadership and Fractured Class Struggles*, Basingstoke: Palgrave Macmillan, 2016.

Booysen, Susan. *Dominance and Decline. The ANC in the Time of Zuma*, Johannes-burg: Wits University Press, 2015.

Brown, Julian. *The Road to Soweto: Resistance and the Uprising of 16 June 1976*, Rochester, NY: Boydell & Brewer, 2016.

Bundy, Colin. *Short-Changed. South African Since Apartheid*, Athens, Ohio: Ohio University Press, 2015.

Dubow, Saul. *Apartheid, 1948–1994*, Oxford: Oxford University Press, 2014.

Fourie, Pieter. *The Political Management of HIV and AIDS in South Africa*. New York: Palgrave Macmillan, 2006.

Gready, Paul. *The Era of Transitional Justice: the Aftermath of the Truth and Reconciliation Commission in South Africa and Beyond*, New York: Routledge, 2011.

Gumede, William. *South Africa in BRICS: Salvation or Ruination?* Cape Town: Tafelberg, 2013.

Lodge, Tom. *Mandela. A Critical Life*, Oxford: Oxford University Press, 2006.

Mbali, Mandisa. *South African AIDS Activism and Global Health Politics*, New York: Palgrave Macmillan, 2013.

Suggested Websites

Electoral Institute for Sustainability of Democracy in Africa
http://www.eisa.org.za

Institute of Security Studies (Pretoria)
http://issafrica.org

South African Institute of Race Relations
http://www.sairr.org.za

Statistics South Africa
http://beta2.statssa.gov.za/

12 Nigeria

Darren Kew and Peter M. Lewis

Official Name: Federal Republic of Nigeria

Location: Western Africa

Capital City: Abuja

Population (2016): 186.1 million

Size: 923,768 sq. km.; slightly more than twice the size of California

CHRONOLOGY of Nigerian Political Development

1960
Independence. Nigeria consists of three regions under a Westminster parliamentary model. Abubakar Tafawa Balewa, a northerner and a Hausa, is the first prime minister.

1967–1970
Biafran civil war

1976
Murtala Muhammed assassinated in a failed February coup led by Middle Belt minorities. Muhammed's second-in-command, General Olusegun Obasanjo, a Yoruba, assumes power.

1983
Military coup led in December by General Muhammadu Buhari, a Hausa.

1985
Buhari is overthrown in August by General Ibrahim B. Babangida, a Middle Belt Muslim, in a palace coup. Babangida promises a return to democracy by 1990, a date that he delays five times before being forced from office in late 1993.

| 1960 | 1965 | 1970 | 1975 | 1980 | 1985 | 1990 |

1966
Civilian government deposed in a January coup. General Aguiyi Ironsi, an Igbo, becomes head of state.

A countercoup is led in July by General Yakubu Gowon (an Anga, from the Middle Belt) with aid from northern groups.

1975
Military coup deposes Gowon in July, led by General Murtala Muhammed, a Hausa from the north.

1979
Elections restore civilian rule in October under the Second Republic, featuring the U.S. presidential model in a federation with 19 states. A majority is won by the National Party of Nigeria (NPN), led by northern/Hausa-Fulani groups. Shehu Shagari is elected Nigeria's first executive president.

1993
Moshood Abiola wins presidential elections on June 12 to start the Third Republic, but Babangida annuls the election eleven days later.

Defense Minister General Sani Abacha seizes power in a November coup. Two years later, he announces a three-year transition to civilian rule, which he manipulates to have himself nominated for president in 1998.

1998
General Abacha dies in June and is succeeded by General Abdulsalami Abubakar, a Middle Belt Muslim from Babangida's hometown. Abubakar releases most political prisoners and initiates a new transition program. Parties are allowed to form unhindered.

2007
The ruling PDP again takes a vast majority of election victories across the nation in April and May, amid a deeply compromised process. Yar'Adua becomes president and promises reform, but spends his first year trying to solidify his tenuous hold on power.

2010
President Yar'Adua dies in office in May, after several months of being incapacitated in a Saudi hospital. Vice President Goodluck Jonathan assumes the presidency.

2016
A militant insurgency reignites in the Niger Delta, led by the Niger Delta Avengers, a new group that launched attacks against oil and gas infrastructure in the Niger Delta region, reducing oil production from 2.2 million to 1.65 million barrels per day. As a result of this and the drop in global oil prices, Nigeria slips into recession as its gross domestic product (GDP) drops 1.51 percent.

1995	2000	2005	2010	2015	2017

2002
The Supreme Court passes several landmark judgments, overturning a PDP-biased 2001 electoral law and ruling on the control of offshore oil and gas resources. In November, the Court opens the legal door for more parties to be registered.

2006
In May, President Obasanjo tries to amend the constitution to allow himself a third term in office, but his gambit is thwarted by the National Assembly.

2017
Amid an ongoing recession, President Buhari returns to Nigeria in March, after a two-month absence in London for an undisclosed illness. He flys again to London in May for another lengthy hospital stay, leaving Vice President Osinbajo as acting president.

2015
Former military head of state Muhammadu Buhari and the APC win presidential elections and majorities in the National Assembly and state governments in March and April, marking the first time that an incumbent president or party is removed by elections at the federal level in Nigeria.

2014
Boko Haram kidnaps more than 250 schoolgirls in Chibok, Borno, in April, sparking worldwide outrage. A military counteroffensive in March 2015, supported by neighboring countries and South African mercenaries, pushes the group back into two small pockets of Borno state. Boko Haram splits into two factions in 2016, but it continues a terror bombing offensive and at least 150 of the Chibok schoolgirls remain in captivity. In May 2017, 81 of the abducted girls are released by the insurgents.

2013
The four main opposition parties merge to form the All Progressives Congress (APC), creating the first major challenge to PDP rule since the start of the Fourth Republic in 1999. Six PDP governors defect, giving the APC control of nearly half the state governments and federal House seats, and a majority in the federal Senate.

2012
Massive public demonstrations, which civil society activists call "Occupy Nigeria," peacefully fill the streets of Lagos, Kano, Abuja, and other major urban areas in January to protest the president's removal of a fuel price subsidy. Social media plays a key role for the organizers, many of whom are from the nation's growing middle class professionals. Trade unions, however, form the foundation for strikes that bring the nation to a standstill for two weeks, and when the unions agree to a partial restoration of the fuel subsidy, the demonstrations collapse.

2011
Jonathan wins the presidential election in April, despite opposition from northern factions for violating an informal ethnic rotation principle. The PDP again takes the majority of contests, but improved elections under a reformist chairman allow opposition parties to make some inroads.

An Islamist sect, dubbed "Boko Haram" by the media, resurfaces with greater tactical sophistication in the northeast after being suppressed by the military in 2009, and launches a stunning bombing campaign across the northeast, even striking the headquarters of the United Nations (UN) in Abuja. President Jonathan declares a state of emergency in three northeast states in 2013, and a military counteroffensive hems the insurgency inside its core area of operations around Borno and Yobe states, though military scorched-earth tactics result in heavy civilian casualties.

1999
The Fourth Republic begins in May, as former military head of state Olusegun Obansanjo and his party, the People's Democratic Party (PDP), sweep the presidential and National Assembly elections, adding to their majority control of state and local government seats. The federation now contains thirty-six states.

Zamfara state, in the north, is the first of twelve to institute the *shari'a* criminal code, in November, resulting in Muslim-Christian communal conflicts in several of these states over the next two years. That same month, President Obasanjo sends the army to the Niger Delta to root out local militias. The military remains engaged in regular skirmishes with Niger Delta militias throughout the next decade, until President Umaru Musa Yar'Adua reaches an agreement with the militants and offers them amnesty in 2009.

THE MAKING OF THE MODERN NIGERIAN STATE

▽ **Focus Questions**

- What are some of the key impacts that colonialism and military rule left on the development of the Nigerian state?

- What role has ethnicity played in the development of Nigeria's political parties, and in the collapse of Nigeria's First Republic and descent into civil war?

Politics in Action

In late November 2009, President Umaru Musa Yar'Adua collapsed, for at least the third time since coming to office in 2007, from an ailment that he had never fully explained to the nation. He was rushed unconscious to a hospital in Saudi Arabia, and only his wife and a handful of his closest advisors saw him directly. For over three months, Nigerians had no direct evidence that their president was conscious, or even alive, and even his own ministers and a delegation of senators were refused access. Government activity at the federal level ground to a halt.

Shockingly, for the first two months, neither the National Assembly nor the cabinet raised any public concern that the nation in effect had no president. The First Lady and the president's inner circle released occasional statements that the president was recovering, but prevented any direct contact with him and blocked all attempts to have Vice President Goodluck Jonathan step in as acting president, as the constitution directs. Finally, under both international pressure and concerns about a military coup, the National Assembly declared Jonathan acting president in February 2010. President Yar'Adua returned to the country shortly thereafter, but he was clearly too ill to govern, and he passed away in May 2010. Jonathan then was sworn in as president.

In early 2017, Nigerians were subjected to political déjà vu when President Muhammadu Buhari remained in London on two separate occasions, for months at a time, for medical treatment for an illness that has yet to be fully disclosed to the public. Both times, however, the president dutifully handed power temporarily to Vice President Yemi Osinbajo, though the government remained largely paralyzed in Buhari's absence, amid the nation's worst recession in decades.

The fact that Nigeria could exist for months without a functioning president, during which time Yar'Adua's wife and a few advisors could seek to run the country themselves and go largely unchallenged, or that Buhari could remain incommunicado in London for months for a major illness that he refuses to explain, speaks volumes about the state of the nation's politics. Democratization in Nigeria—18 years after the exit of the military from power—has yet to produce effective, accountable governance. Instead, authoritarian rule has given way to competitive **oligarchy**, in which an increasingly self-interested, oil-rich political elite fights to expand its power, while roughly 85 percent of Nigerians struggle to survive on less than two U.S. dollars per day. This impoverished majority is so disenfranchised that their president could disappear for months without much public outcry.

Under the surface of this fiasco, however, were some important signs that two decades of democracy have had at least some impact. First and foremost, throughout the 2010 crisis, a growing opposition insisted on using the constitution as the framework for resolving the dispute. Ultimately, elites turned to the National Assembly, not the military, and military leaders rejected pressure from some junior officers to stage a coup. Mindful of these events, President Buhari handed temporary power during his absence in 2017 to the vice president, as the law requires.

oligarchy

A political system in which power is in the hands of only a few people.

Nigeria thus encapsulates many characteristics that more broadly identify Africa, as the young democracy faces the challenge of managing the country's contentious communal diversity in conditions of economic scarcity and weak institutions. Nigerians have navigated parallel struggles between **authoritarian** and democratic governance, the push for development amid persistent underdevelopment, the burden of public corruption, and pressures for accountability. Like most other African countries, Nigeria has sought to create a viable nation-state out of the social divisions and mergers created by its colonial borders. More than 250 competing ethnic groups, crosscut by two major religious traditions, have repeatedly clashed over economic and political resources. The result: a Nigeria with low levels of popular legitimacy and **accountability**, and a persistent inability to meet the most basic needs of its citizens. Nigeria today remains an **unfinished state**, characterized by societal instability and political uncertainty. Will Nigeria return to the discredited path of authoritarianism and economic stagnation, or will the civilian leadership rise to achieve a workable democracy and sustainable growth? (See Figure 12.1 and Table 12.1.)

Geographic Setting

Nigeria, with 186 million people inhabiting 356,669 square miles, is the most populous nation in Africa. A center of West African regional trade, culture, and military strength, Nigeria borders four countries—Benin, Niger, Chad, and Cameroon. Independent Nigeria, like nearly all African states, is over a half-century old.

Nigeria, in its present form, was a British colony from 1914 until 1960. Its colonial boundaries had little to do with the borders of the precolonial African societies and

authoritarian

A system of rule in which power depends not on popular legitimacy but on the coercive force of the political authorities.

accountability

A government's responsibility to its population, usually by periodic popular elections, by transparent fiscal practices, and by the legislature having the power to dismiss the government by impeachment or passing a motion of no confidence. In a political system characterized by accountability, the major actions taken by government must be known and understood by the citizenry.

unfinished state

A state characterized by institutional instability and political uncertainty that may render it dysfunctional as a coherent ruling entity.

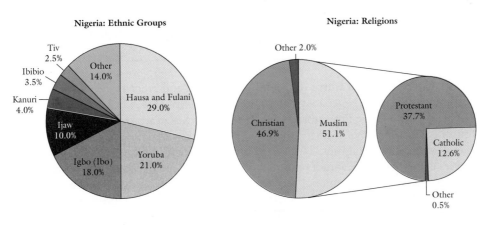

Nigeria: Ethnic Groups

- Tiv 2.5%
- Ibibio 3.5%
- Kanuri 4.0%
- Ijaw 10.0%
- Igbo (Ibo) 18.0%
- Yoruba 21.0%
- Hausa and Fulani 29.0%
- Other 14.0%

Nigeria: Religions

- Other 2.0%
- Christian 46.9%
- Muslim 51.1%
- Protestant 37.7%
- Catholic 12.6%
- Other 0.5%

Nigerian Currency: Naira (₦)

International Designation: NGN
Exchange Rate (2017):
- 1 US$ = 314.75 ₦
- 1 ₦ = 0.0032 US$

500 Naira Note Design: Dr. Nnamdi Azikiwe (1904–1996), first President of Nigeria from 1963 to 1966.

© Cengage

© iStockphoto.com/Johnny Greig

FIGURE 12.1 The Nigerian Nation at a Glance

Table 12.1	Political Organization
Political System	Federal republic
Regime History	Democratic government took office in May 1999, after sixteen years of military rule. The most recent national elections were held in 2015.
Administrative Structure	Nigeria is a federation of thirty-six states, plus the Federal Capital Territory (FCT) in Abuja. The three tiers of government are federal, state, and local. Actual power is centralized under the presidency and the governors.
Executive	A U.S.-style presidential system, currently under Muhammadu Buhari
Legislature	A bicameral civilian legislature was elected in March 2015. The 109 senators are elected on the basis of equal representation: 3 from each state, and 1 from the FCT. The 360 members of the House of Representatives are elected from single-member districts.
Judiciary	Federal, state, and local court system, headed by the Federal Court of Appeal and the Supreme Court, which consists of fifteen appointed associate justices and the chief justice. States may establish a system of Islamic law (*shari'a*) for cases involving only Muslims in customary disputes (divorce, property, etc.). Most Nigerian states feature such courts, which share a Federal Court of Appeal in Abuja. Non-Muslim states also may set up customary courts, based on local traditional jurisprudence. Secular courts retain supreme jurisdiction if conflict arises between customary and secular courts.
Party System	Nearly fifty parties have been registered by the Nigerian electoral commission since 2002. The largest are the All Progressives Congress (APC) and the People's Democratic Party (PDP), which together control all but one state of the federation. The APC won the presidency, a majority of governorships, and the National Assembly in 2015 after sixteen years of PDP rule.

merely marked the point where British influence ended and French began. Britain ruled northern and southern Nigeria as two separate colonies until 1914, when it amalgamated its Northern and Southern Protectorates. In short, Nigeria was an arbitrary creation reflecting British colonial interests, which subdivided some local cultures and compelled others into a common political unit. This forced union of myriad African cultures and ruling entities under one political roof remains a central feature of Nigerian political life today.

Nigeria is a hub of regional activity. Its population is nearly 60 percent of West Africa's total. Nigeria's gross domestic product (GDP) typically represents more than half of the total GDP for the entire subregion and vies with South Africa for the largest on the continent. It is one of the few countries in the world that is evenly divided religiously, half Muslim and half Christian.

Nigeria includes six imprecisely defined geopolitical "zones." The Hausa, Nigeria's largest ethnic group, dominate the northwest (or "core North"). The northeast consists of minority groups, the largest of whom are the Kanuri. Both northern regions are predominantly Muslim. The Middle Belt (or "north central" zone) includes minority groups, both Muslim and Christian. The southwest is dominated by the country's second-largest ethnic group, the Yoruba, who are approximately 40 percent Muslim, 50 percent Christian (primarily Protestant), and 10 percent practitioners of Yoruba traditional beliefs, although many people practice traditional beliefs alongside either Christianity or Islam. The southeast is the Igbo homeland, Nigeria's third-largest group, who are primarily Christian (particularly Catholic). Between the Yoruba and Igbo regions is the southern minority ("south-south") zone, which stretches across the Niger Delta areas and east along the coast as far as Cameroon.

Critical Junctures

Nigeria's recent history has been shaped by legacies from the precolonial period, the crucial changes caused by British colonialism, the postcolonial alternation of military and civilian rule, and the economic collapse from 1980 to 2000, caused by political corruption and overreliance on the oil industry.

The Precolonial Period (800–1900)

In contrast to the forest belt to the south, the more open savanna terrain in the north, with its need for irrigation, encouraged the early growth of centralized states in West Africa. Such states from the eighth century included Kanem-Bornu and the Hausa states. Another attempt at state formation led to the Jukun kingdom, which by the end of the seventeenth century was a subject state of the Bornu Empire.

Trade across the Sahara Desert with northern Africa shaped developments in the savanna areas of the north. Trade brought material benefits, as well as Arabic education and Islam, which gradually replaced traditional spiritual, political, and social practices. From 1804–1808, the Fulani, from lands west of modern Nigeria, fought a religiously inspired war (*jihad*), and established the Sokoto Caliphate, which used Islam and a

jihad

Literally "struggle." Although often used to mean armed struggle against unbelievers, it can also mean to fight against sociopolitical corruption or to struggle for spiritual self-improvement.

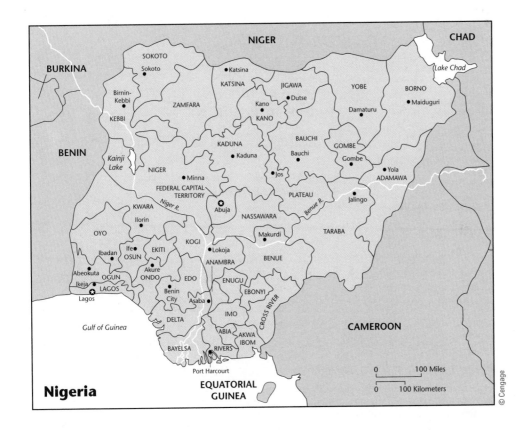

Nigeria

common language, Hausa, to unify the disparate groups in the north. The Fulani Empire held sway until British colonial authority was imposed on northern Nigeria by 1900.

Toward the southern edge of the savanna, politics generally followed kinship lines and was organized among communities. Political authority was so diffuse that later, Western contacts described them as "stateless," or **acephalous societies.** Because such groups as the Tiv lacked complex political hierarchies, they escaped much of the upheaval experienced under colonialism by the centralized states, and retained much of their autonomy.

Southern Nigeria included the highly centralized Yoruba empires and the kingdoms of Oyo and Ife; the Edo kingdom of Benin in the Midwest; the acephalous societies of the Igbo to the east; and the trading city-states of the Niger Delta and its hinterland, peopled by a wide range of ethnicities.

Several precolonial societies had democratic elements that might have led to more open and participatory polities had they not been interrupted by colonialism. Governance in the Yoruba and Igbo communities involved principles of accountability and representation. Among the Islamic communities of the north, political society was highly structured, reflecting local interpretations of Qur'anic principles. Leadership structures were considerably more hierarchical than those of the south, and women were typically consigned to subordinate political status. The Islamic Fulani Empire was a confederation in which the rulers (known as *emirs*) owed allegiance to the sultan, who was the temporal and spiritual head of the empire. The sultan's powers, in turn, were limited by his duty to observe Islamic principles.

acephalous societies

Literally "headless" societies. A number of traditional Nigerian societies, such as the Igbo in the precolonial period, lacked executive rulership as we have come to conceive of it. Instead, these villages and clans were governed by committee or consensus.

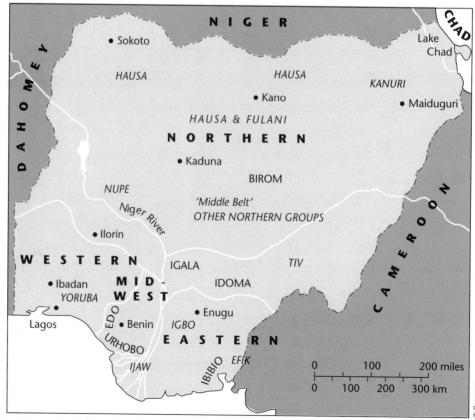

Nigeria under the First Republic, divided into four regions, with the massive Northern Region encompassing two-thirds of the nation's territory and more than half its population.

Colonial Rule and Its Impact (1860–1945)

Competition for trade and empire drove the European imperial powers farther into Africa. Colonial rule deepened the extraction of Nigeria's natural resources and the exploitation of Nigerian labor. Colonialism left its imprint on all aspects of Nigeria's political and economic systems.

Where centralized monarchies existed in the north, the British governed through indirect rule, which allowed traditional structures to persist as subordinates to the British governor and a small colonial administrative apparatus. With more dispersed kingships, as among the Yoruba, or in acephalous societies, particularly among the Igbo and other groups in the southeast, the colonizers either strengthened the authority of traditional chiefs and kings or appointed warrant chiefs (who ruled by appointment by the British Crown), weakening the previous practices of local accountability and participation.

The British played off ethnic and social divisions to keep Nigerians from developing organized political resistance to colonial rule. When resistance did develop, the colonizers were not afraid to employ repressive tactics, even as late as the 1940s. Yet the British also promoted the foundations of a democratic political system. This dual standard left a conflicted democratic idea in Nigeria: formal democratic institutions within an authoritarian political culture. Colonialism also strengthened the collective identities of Nigeria's multiple ethnic groups by fostering political competition among them, primarily among the three largest: the Hausa, Yoruba, and Igbo.

Divisive Identities: Ethnic Politics Under Colonialism (1945–1960)

Based on their experience under British rule, leaders of the anticolonial movement regarded the state as an exploitative instrument. Control of the state was seen as an opportunity to pursue personal and group interests rather than broad national interests. When the British began to negotiate a gradual exit from Nigeria, the semblance of unity among the anticolonial leaders soon evaporated. Intergroup political competition became increasingly fierce.

Nigerian leaders quickly turned to ethnic appeals to build support. Although each one is a numeric minority, the three largest ethnic groups, the Hausa, Igbo, and Yoruba together comprise approximately two-thirds of Nigeria's population. They have long dominated the political process. By pitting ethnic groups against each other for the purposes of divide and rule during colonialism, and by structuring the administrative units of Nigeria based on these three largest ethnic groups, the British ensured that ethnicity would be the main vehicle of political identification and mobilization after independence.

With the encouragement of ambitious leaders, however, these groups took on a more political character. Nigeria's first political party, the National Council of Nigeria and the Cameroons (later the National Convention of Nigerian Citizens, NCNC), initially drew supporters from across Nigeria. As independence approached, however, elites began to divide along ethnic lines to mobilize support for their differing political agendas.

In 1954, the British divided Nigeria into a federation of three regions, each with an elected government. Each region soon fell under the domination of one of the major ethnic groups and its respective party. The Northern Region came under the control of the Northern People's Congress (NPC), dominated by Hausa-Fulani elites. In the southern half of the country, the Western Region was controlled by the Action Group (AG), which was controlled by Yoruba elites. The Igbo, the numerically dominant group in the Eastern Region, were closely associated with the NCNC, which became the ruling party there.

indirect rule

A term used to describe the British style of colonialism in Nigeria and India, in which local traditional rulers and political structures were surrogates of the colonial governing structure.

warrant chiefs

Leaders employed by the British colonial regime in Nigeria, a system in which chiefs were selected by the British to oversee certain legal matters and assist the colonial enterprise in governance and law enforcement in local areas.

Chief Obafemi Awolowo, leader of the AG, captured the sentiment of the times when he wrote in 1947, "Nigeria is not a nation. It is a mere geographical expression. There are no 'Nigerians' in the same sense as there are 'English,' 'Welsh,' or 'French.' The word 'Nigerian' is merely a distinctive appellation to distinguish those who live within the boundaries of Nigeria from those who do not."[1]

The First Republic (1960–1966)

The British granted Nigeria independence in 1960. Nigerians adopted the British Westminster model at the federal and regional levels, with the prime minister chosen by the majority party or coalition in parliament. Northerners came to dominate the federal government by virtue of their greater population. The ruling coalition for the first two years quickly turned into a northern-only grouping when the NPC achieved an outright majority in the legislature. Having benefited less from the economic, educational, and infrastructural benefits of colonialism, the northerners who dominated the First Republic set out to redistribute resources to their

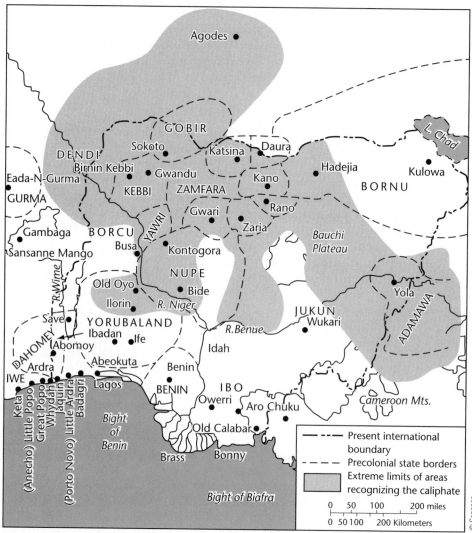

Precolonial Nigeria, showing the Sokoto Caliphate at its greatest extent in the early nineteenth century. The British conquest brought many nations under one roof.

benefit. This NPC policy of "northernization" brought them into direct conflict with their southern counterparts, particularly the Yoruba-based AG and later the Igbo-dominated NCNC.

Rivalries intensified as the NPC sat atop an absolute majority in the federal parliament, with no need to accommodate its former coalition partner, the NCNC. Nnamdi Azikiwe, the NCNC leader who was also president during the First Republic (then a largely symbolic position), and Tafawa Balewa, the NPC prime minister, separately approached the military to ensure that if conflict erupted, they could count on its loyalty. Thus, "in the struggle for personal survival, both men, perhaps inadvertently, made the armed forces aware that they had a political role to play."[2]

Civil War and Military Rule (1966–1979)

With significant encouragement from contending civilian leaders, a group of largely Igbo officers seized power in a violent coup in January 1966. The new leader, General Aguiyi Ironsi, an Igbo, was subsequently killed in a second coup in July 1966, which brought Yakubu Gowon, a Middle Belt Christian, to power as a consensus head of state among the non-Igbo coup plotters.

Because many northern officials had been killed in the initial coup (including Prime Minister Balewa and the premier of Northern Nigeria, Ahmadu Bello), a tremendous backlash against Igbos flared in several parts of the country, especially the north. Ethnic violence sent many Igbos fleeing to their home region in the east. By

1967, the predominantly Igbo population of eastern Nigeria attempted to secede and form its own independent country, named Biafra. Gowon built a military-led government of national unity in what remained of Nigeria (the north and west) and, after a bloody three-year war of attrition and starvation tactics, defeated Biafra in January 1970. The conflict claimed at least a million deaths, with some estimates twice as high.

After the war, Gowon presided over a policy of national reconciliation, which proceeded fairly smoothly with the aid of growing oil revenues. Senior officers reaped the benefits of the global oil boom in 1973–1974, however, and corruption was widespread. Influenced by the unwillingness of the military elite to relinquish power and the spoils of office, Gowon postponed a return to civilian rule, and he was overthrown in 1975 by Murtala Muhammad. General Muhammad ruled for less than seven months and was assassinated before he could achieve a promised democratic transition. General Olusegun Obasanjo, Muhammad's second-in-command and successor, peacefully ceded power to an elected civilian government in 1979, which became known as the Second Republic. Obasanjo retired but would later reemerge as a civilian president in 1999.

Olusegun Obasanjo ruled Nigeria first as military head of state from 1976 to 1979, and then as civilian president from 1999 to 2007. As president, he instituted a number of important reforms, but also tried—and failed—to change the constitution to extend his term in office.

ISSOUF SANOGO/Getty Images

The Second and Third Republics, and Predatory Military Rule (1979–1999)

The president of the 1979–1983 Second Republic, Shehu Shagari, and his ruling National Party of Nigeria (NPN, drawn largely from the First Republic's northern-dominated NPC), did little to reduce the mistrust between the various parts of the federation or to stem the rampant corruption in the country. The NPN captured outright majorities in the 1983 state and national elections through massive fraud and violence. The last vestiges of popular tolerance dissipated, and a few months later the military, led by Major-General Muhammadu Buhari, seized power. General Buhari's tough anticorruption policies won him an initial popularity that would help propel him to the presidency much later, in 2015.

When Buhari refused to pledge a rapid return to democratic rule and failed to revive a plummeting economy, however, his popular support wavered, and in August 1985, General Ibrahim Babangida seized power. Babangida and his cohort quickly announced a transition to democratic rule, then stalled it for several years, and subsequently annulled the presidential election of June 1993. In stark contrast to all prior elections, the 1993 election was relatively fair and was evidently won by a Yoruba businessman, Chief Moshood Abiola. The annulment provoked angry reactions from a population weary of postponed transitions, lingering military rule, and the deception of the country's rulers. Babangida resigned, and his handpicked successor, Ernest Shonekan, led a weak civilian caretaker government. General Sani Abacha, who had been installed by Babangida as defense minister, soon seized power, cracked down on opposition and civil liberties, and fomented corruption on a massive scale. He later attempted to install himself as president in a rigged transition. Only Abacha's sudden death in June 1998 saved the country from certain crisis. General Abdulsalami Abubakar, Abacha's successor, quickly established a new transition program and promptly handed power to an elected civilian government led by President Olusegun Obasanjo and the PDP in May 1999.

The Fourth Republic (1999–Present)

Obasanjo was called out of retirement by the leaders of the PDP to run for president. Obasanjo, although a Yoruba, had handed over power as military head of state in 1979 to the northerner Shehu Shagari at the dawn of the Second Republic, winning the trust of the northern political establishment. In addition, many perceived that an ex-military leader could better manage to keep the armed forces in the barracks once they left power.

Obasanjo claimed a broad mandate to halt Nigeria's decline by reforming the state and economy. Within weeks, he electrified the nation by retiring all the military officers who had held positions of political power under previous military governments, seeing them as the most likely plotters of future coups.

Obasanjo targeted the oil sector for new management and lobbied foreign governments to forgive Nigeria's massive debts. The minimum wage was raised significantly, and a so-called truth and reconciliation commission was set up to address past abuses. Civil society groups thrived on renewed political freedom. Corruption, however, returned with a vengeance, and Obasanjo secured renomination from his party, the PDP, in the 2003 elections by cutting deals with party barons, such that the PDP political machine prevailed while public confidence plummeted and reform was stymied. Obsanajo made an unsuccessful attempt to extend term limits so that he could govern past 2007. Failing this, he chose a little-known, reclusive governor from the north with health problems to be his successor: Umaru Musa Yar'Adua of Katsina state, who along with the PDP won massively fraudulent elections in 2007.

Instead of focusing on his campaign promises, Yar'Adua spent most of his dwindling energies solidifying his control of the PDP. The president's sudden collapse and evacuation to Saudi Arabia in November 2009 indicated that he was dying. Normal government activity all but ceased while a small circle of advisors usurped presidential powers and secured government contracts for their supporters. Amid international pressures and coup threats, Vice President Goodluck Jonathan, from the oil-rich Niger Delta, moved cautiously to assure Northern power brokers that they could work with him. His deft political efforts, backed in part by support from former President Obasanjo, ensured a smooth transition when President Yar'Adua passed away in May 2010.

Like Obasanjo and Yar'Adua, President Jonathan came to office without control of his own party, the PDP, and moved quickly to establish leverage using the largesse of Nigeria's massive, state-controlled oil wealth. Within several months, he made clear his intention to run for president in April 2011. In stark contrast to his predecessors, however, President Jonathan pressed for electoral reform.

The 2011 elections were much improved from the disastrous 2007 contests, but the PDP still utilized its massive resource advantages to buy votes. Frustrations over continued election fraud sparked riots, leading to over 800 deaths.

Many northern factions also remained antagonistic over the shift of power back to a southerner. This antagonism soon led to a massive struggle within the PDP, which the president eventually won, but at great cost. Six governors—five from the disgruntled northern bloc—decamped in 2013 for a new opposition party, the All Progressives Congress (APC). The APC had formed earlier that year, when leaders of the four main opposition parties recognized the limits of their smaller, largely regional parties and sensed an opportunity in the PDP's internal battles.

Jonathan took the oath of office in 2011 promising reforms, but his administration soon fell victim to massive corruption. A growing Islamist insurgency in the northeast by a group called the Congregation of the People of Tradition for Proselytization and Jihad (dubbed "Boko Haram" by the Western media) drew attention away from reform and development and toward increased security concerns and expenditures, which leaders of the Jonathan administration stole in shocking amounts. When Boko Haram militants kidnapped over 250 schoolgirls in 2014—capturing worldwide media attention—and the government could not free them, and with daily corruption scandals racking his administration, President Jonathan saw his public support crumble. The collapse of global oil prices in late 2014 threw Nigeria's oil-dependent economy into recession and doomed the president's and the PDP's chances of reelection in 2015. A well-organized APC, led by 73-year-old Muhammadu Buhari and propelled by his anticorruption and military credentials, swept the 2015 elections, marking the first time in Nigeria's history that an opposition party peacefully took power.

President Buhari took office in May 2015 with popular goodwill and a mandate for sweeping change. Shockingly, he took little advantage of these benefits. He has placed more military pressure on Boko Haram, which by 2017 remained a diminished yet persistent threat, and his administration also has increased anticorruption efforts, mostly targeting the PDP and members of the Jonathan administration. Despite Nigeria suffering its worst recession in thirty years, however, the president took over six months to get his cabinet in place, and economic policies have been lackluster. His seven-week stay in London on medical leave in early 2017, without public explanation, fueled speculation regarding his health and further paralyzed his government.

The Four Themes and Nigeria

Nigeria in a Globalized World of States

Economically, Nigeria was thrust into the world of states in a position of weakness, first as a British colony and later as an independent but poor nation. Despite its resources and the potential of oil to provide the capital needed to build a modern economy, Nigeria remains in a vulnerable and dependent position in the global system. It lost much of its international clout, and in place of the international respect that it once enjoyed as a developing giant within Africa, the country became notorious throughout the 1990s for corruption, human rights abuses, and failed governance. The return of democracy and soaring oil prices have restored some of Nigeria's former stature, but violent ethnic conflicts in parts of the country undermine this trend, while economic vulnerability and persistent corruption keep it a secondary player in the world of states.

Governing the Economy

The south of Nigeria experienced greater burdens—and benefits—from colonial occupation. The coastal location of Lagos, Calabar, and their surrounding regions made them important hubs for trade and shipping activity, around which the British built the necessary infrastructure—schools (which also promoted Christianity), roads, ports, and the like—and a large African civil service to facilitate colonialism. In northern Nigeria, the British used indirect rule through local power structures, left intact Islamic institutions, and prohibited Christian missionary activity. The north consequently received few infrastructural benefits, but its traditional administration was largely preserved. Thus, at independence, the south possessed the basis of a modern economy, but the north remained largely agricultural.

Nigeria's economy has largely depended on unpredictable oil revenues, sporadic international investment, loans, and aid. Owing to neglect of agriculture, Nigeria moved from self-sufficiency in basic foodstuffs in the mid-1960s to heavy dependence on imports less than twenty years later. Following a surge of investment by government and foreign firms in the 1970s, manufacturing suffered from disinvestment for decades. High oil and gas prices spurred growth but did little to reduce poverty. Since 2003, however, this decline has reversed in the south—particularly Lagos—and many areas of the economy outside of oil also began to expand rapidly until recession hit in 2015.

The Democratic Idea

interventionist

An interventionist state acts vigorously to shape the performance of major sectors of the economy.

The Nigerian colonial state was conceived and fashioned as **interventionist**, with far-reaching administrative controls. After independence in 1960, Nigeria's civilian and military rulers alike expanded the interventionist state. Although colonial rulers left Nigeria with the machinery of parliamentary democracy, they socialized the population to be passive subjects rather than active citizens. Colonialism bequeathed an authoritarian legacy to independent Nigeria.

Military rule continued this pattern from 1966 to 1979, and again from 1983 to 1999. When the military gave up power and returned to the barracks in 1999, it left a dominant executive arm at all levels of government—federal, state, and local—at the expense of legislative and judicial institutions. Unchecked executive power has encouraged the arbitrary exercise of authority and patronage politics, which sap the economy and undermine the rule of law, a crucial part of any democracy.

The lack of accountability by the colonial state and postcolonial governments, combined with Nigerian leaders' politicization of ethnicity, reinforced communal identities and stunted the growth of a shared public civic ethic. Nigerians often came to view the state as the realm where resources were plundered by those with power. The democratic idea in Nigeria has also been undermined by deep regional divisions.

Collective Identities

The Nigerian state is overlaid with hundreds of ethnic divisions that military and civilian governments have manipulated for their own selfish ends. These many cultural divisions have been exacerbated by clientelism, corruption, and authoritarian governing structures, which together stir up ethnic group competition and hinder economic potential. *Clientelism* is the practice by which particular individuals or segments receive special policy benefits or political favors from a political patron. In Nigeria, patrons are often linked to clients by ethnic, religious, or other cultural ties, though these ties have generally benefited only a small elite. By fostering political competition along cultural lines, clientelism tends to undermine social trust and political stability, which are necessary conditions for economic growth.

Nevertheless, the idea of Nigeria has taken root among the country's diverse groups nearly 60 years after independence. Most Nigerians enjoy many personal connections across ethnic and religious lines, and elites in both the north and the south have significant business activities throughout the country. Even so, ethnicity remains a critical flash point.

Comparisons

Nigeria is by far the largest country in Africa and among the ten most populous countries in the world. One out of every five black Africans is Nigerian. Unlike most other African countries, Nigeria has the human and material resources to overcome the vicious cycle of poverty and autocracy. Hopes for a breakthrough, however, have been regularly frustrated over six decades of independent rule.

autocracy

A government in which one ruler or a few rulers has absolute power—thus, a dictatorship.

Nigeria remains the oldest surviving federation in Africa, and it has managed through much travail to maintain its fragile unity. That cohesion has come under increasing stress, however, and a major challenge is to ensure that the Nigerian state does not ultimately collapse. Nigeria's past failures to sustain democracy and economic development also render it an important case illustrating the failure to use abundant resources to strengthen national unity and improve the well-being of all citizens. It also illustrates how pervasive corruption can undermine both democracy and development, which depend on the quality of leadership, the adaptation of political culture, the strength of public institutions, and external economic forces. Nigeria has much to teach us on all these topics.

Where Do You Stand?

Many Nigerians feel that the British bringing together so many ethnicities and religions under one political roof was a terrible mistake because the diversity of modern Nigeria is just too great for it to hold together as a single nation. Do you agree?

After all the problems caused by military rule, do you see any advantages to it? Why might it have been, or continue to be, appealing to some Nigerians?

POLITICAL ECONOMY AND DEVELOPMENT

▼ **Focus Questions**

- What were some of the key impacts of the oil boom on Nigeria's political economy?

- What efforts has Nigeria made to try to address poverty and spur development?

Colonialism bequeathed Nigeria an interventionist state, and governments after independence continued this pattern. Following some early developmental interventions, the public sector became the central fixture of the Nigerian economy, to the detriment of the private sector, especially manufacturing and commerce. As the state began to unravel in the late 1980s and 1990s, leaders grew more predatory, plundering the petroleum sector and impeding the nation's vast economic potential.

State and Economy

The Nigerian state plays the central role in economic decision making. Most of the nation's revenues, and nearly all its hard currency, are channeled through the government, which controls these earnings, known as **rents**. Elites gain lucrative results from government contracts and connections. The majority survive by working in the informal sector of the economy, which includes very small-scale commerce, services, and subsistence agriculture in which taxes and regulations rarely reach. The informal economy accounts for about one-fifth of the entire Nigerian GDP.

rents

Economic gains that do not compensate those who produced them and do not contribute to productivity, typically associated with government earnings that are not channeled back into investments or production. Pursuit of economic rents (or "rent-seeking") is profit-seeking that takes the form of nonproductive economic activity.

Origins of Economic Decline

In the colonial and immediate postcolonial periods, Nigeria's economy was centered on agricultural production for domestic consumption and export. The nation was self-sufficient in terms of food production. In the 1960s, emphasis shifted to the development of nonfood export crops through large-scale enterprises.

Small farmers received scant government support. Food production suffered. The Biafran War (1967–1970), severe drought, and the development of the petroleum industry reduced agricultural production, which plummeted from 80 percent of exports in 1960 to just 2 percent by 1980.[3] External debt skyrocketed and corruption increased. The economic downturn of the 1980s created even greater incentives for government corruption. Within three years of seizing power in 1993, General Abacha allowed all of Nigeria's oil refineries to collapse, forcing this giant oil-exporting country into the absurd situation of having to import petroleum. Scam artists proliferated, especially on the Internet, earning perhaps $100 million annually.

structural adjustment program (SAP)

A program established by the World Bank with the intent to alter and reform the economic structures of highly indebted Third World countries as a condition for receiving international loans. SAPs call for privatization, trade liberalization, and fiscal restraint, which often lead to the dismantling of social welfare systems.

From 1985 to the Present: Deepening Economic Crisis and the Search for Solutions

The year 1985 marked a turning point for the Nigerian state and economy. Within a year of wresting power from General Buhari in August 1985, the Babangida regime developed an economic **structural adjustment program (SAP)** with the active support of the World Bank and the IMF (also referred to as the **international financial institutions (IFIs)**). The decision to embark on the SAP was made against a background of economic decline arising from waning oil revenues, a growing debt burden, **balance of payments** difficulties, and lack of fiscal discipline.[4]

The large revenues arising from the oil windfall enabled the state to increase its direct involvement in the economy. Beginning in the 1970s, the government created a number of state-owned enterprises, including large shares in major banks and other financial institutions, manufacturing, construction, agriculture, public utilities, and various services. Although the government has since sold many of its companies, the state remains the biggest employer, as well as the most important source of revenue, even for the private sector.

Privatization, a central feature of Nigeria's adjustment program, intended that state-owned businesses would be sold to private investors to generate revenue and improve efficiency. For many years, however, domestic and foreign investors were hesitant to enter the Nigerian market, in light of persistent political instability, unpredictable economic policies, and endemic corruption. More recently, attractive areas such as telecommunications, utilities, and oil and gas are drawing significant foreign capital.

President Obasanjo utilized the post-2003 oil boom to focus on economic reform and development. Nigeria stabilized its macroeconomic policy, restructured the banking sector, and established a new anticorruption agency, the Economic and Financial Crimes Commission (EFCC). Unfortunately, many of these ambitious goals were followed by lackluster implementation, and President Jonathan continued this trend. President Buhari reinvigorated the EFCC, although his efforts have been directed primarily against members of the Jonathan government and the PDP, and he has yet to implement a consistent economic policy. Buoyant oil revenues helped to spur the economy from 2003 to 2014, including a modest reduction in poverty.

Perhaps Obasanjo's greatest economic achievement was paying off most of Nigeria's large foreign debt (see Table 12.2). Upon taking office in 1999, he urged governments in Europe, Asia, and the United States to forgive most of Nigeria's obligations. After persistent international lobbying, along with progress on economic reforms during Obasanjo's second term, Nigeria secured an agreement in June 2005 with its creditors. The package included debt repayments, discounted buybacks, and write-offs that reduced Nigeria's external debt by 90 percent.

In the early 1990s, a number of larger Nigerian businesses and multinational corporations that were concerned with the nation's economic decline supported the first Economic Summit, a high-profile conference that advocated numerous policies to move Nigeria toward becoming an emerging market that could attract foreign investment along the lines of the high-performing states in Asia.

Through the subsequent Vision 2010 initiative, the government outlined a package of business-friendly economic reforms, while businesses pledged to work toward certain growth targets consistent with governmental priorities in employment, taxation, community investment, and the like. Along with government and business leaders, key figures participated from nearly all sectors of society, including the press, nongovernmental organizations (NGOs), youth groups, market women's associations, and others. Although Vision 2010 was promoted by the Abacha military regime, which generated skepticism, many themes of the plan have persisted. Vision 2010's final report called for the following:

- Restoring democratic rule
- Restructuring and professionalizing the military
- Lowering the population growth rate
- Raising the standard of living
- Rebuilding education
- Meaningful privatization
- Diversifying the export base beyond oil
- Central bank autonomy

international financial institutions (IFIs)

This term generally refers to the International Bank for Reconstruction and Development (the World Bank) and the International Monetary Fund (IMF), but can also include other international lending institutions.

balance of payments

An indicator of international flow of funds that shows the excess or deficit in total payments of all kinds between or among countries. Included in the calculation are exports and imports, grants, and international debt payments.

Table 12.2	Nigeria's External Debt	
Years	Total Debt (as % of GDP)	Total Debt Payments (as % of Exports)
1977	8.73	1.04
1986	109.9	38.04
1995	129.5	14.0
1996	88.97	14.75
1997	78.54	8.71
1999	83.76	7.61
2000	80.45	8.76
2003	66.43	5.93
2005	28.64	15.4
2006	11.79	10.98
2010	9.45	1.50
2011	10.23	0.52
2012	10.42	1.34
2013	10.50	0.49
2014	10.6	0.31
2015	6.23	2.88

Source: World Bank

In 2003–2007, the government of President Obasanjo implemented a National Economic Empowerment Development Strategy (NEEDS), that echoed many of the core goals of Vision 2010. In 2009, President Jonathan proposed his own plan, Vision 20:2020. Yet these programs have repeatedly fallen short of implementation. Two intractable problems that have been binding constraints on growth have been privatization and restructuring of the energy sector. A Petroleum Industry Bill to reform and restructure the critical oil and gas industry languished in the legislature for over a decade, as different interests and factions squabble over key provisions. A segment of the bill passed in May 2017.

Although President Buhari has vowed to restructure the oil industry and tame massive corruption, his administration has made little progress owing to his poor health, a weak strategy, and legislative neglect. Nonetheless, Nigeria's modest private sector has been quietly expanding. While political leaders have left much of the

GLOBAL CONNECTION

Oil Wealth: Blessing or Curse?

Shortly after the 1973–1974 global oil crisis drove up the price of petroleum, Nigeria's petroleum wealth was perceived by the Nigerian elite as a source of strength. By the 1980s, however, petroleum had become a global buyers' market. Thereafter, it became clear that Nigerian dependence on oil was a source of vulnerability because of the sharp fluctuations in petroleum prices (see Figure 12.2). The depth of Nigeria's international weakness became more evident with the adoption of structural adjustment in the mid-1980s. Given the enormity of the economic crisis, Nigeria was compelled to seek IMF/World Bank support to improve its balance of payments and facilitate economic restructuring and debt rescheduling, and it has had to accept direction from foreign agencies ever since.

FIGURE 12.2 Crude Oil Prices 1970–2017

As in Venezuela, Russia, and Iran, oil has been a **resource curse** for Nigeria, in the sense that reliance on income from oil has made it possible for the government to ignore promoting the development of other sectors of the economy that are less vulnerable to global price fluctuations.

Nigeria remains a highly visible and influential member of the Organization of Petroleum Exporting Countries (OPEC), selling on average more than 1.4 million barrels of petroleum daily on world markets. Nigeria's oil wealth and its great economic potential sometimes have tempered the resolve of Western nations to challenge human rights and other abuses, notably during the Abacha period from 1993 to 1998.

Nigeria's oil-dependent economy has mirrored the rise and fall of global oil prices—booming during periods of high prices and tipping into recession when they fall drastically, as they did in 2014. (The numbers shown here have been adjusted for inflation.)

Source: http://www.macrotrends.net/.

MAKING CONNECTIONS How does Nigeria's reliance on oil income affect both its economy and its politics?

---

private sector to its own devices, there has been a boom in innovative segments of the economy, including telecommunications, media, and finance, along with significant government-supported infrastructure development.

Society and Economy

Despite its considerable oil resources, Nigeria's economic development profile is discouraging. Nigeria is listed very close to the bottom of the UN's Human Development Index (HDI), 152 out of 174, behind India (131), the other lower-middle-income country included in this book. GDP per capita has been rising rapidly; in 2016, it was

resource curse

A paradoxical situation that affects some countries rich in natural resources, wherein other sectors of the economy are neglected and a high concentration of wealth and power exists, thus impairing sustainable economic development and encouraging authoritarianism.

at $2,823 ($6,432 purchasing power parity), but wealth is very unequally distributed, and less than 1 percent of GDP was recorded as public expenditures on education and health each. Look at the data in Figure 12.3 and Table 12.3 to get a sense of how the Nigerian economy has developed over the last three decades.

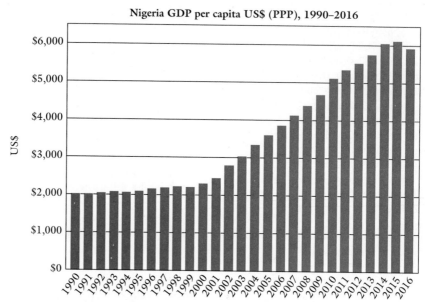

FIGURE 12.3 Nigeria GDP Per Capita US$ (PPP) 1990–2016

Sources: International Monetary Fund, World Economic Outlook

Table 12.3	Selected Socioeconomic Indicators, 1967–2016				
Year	GDP Annual Growth (%)	GDP Per Capita Annual Growth (%)*	Life Expectancy at Birth (Years)	Mortality Rates per 1,000 Live Births	
				Infant	Under-5
1967	−15.7	−17.6	39.3	182.6	307.0
1975	−5.2	−7.8	43.4	144.4	244.3
1980	4.2	1.3	45.5	127.0	214.4
1985	8.3	5.6	46.3	124.3	209.5
1990	12.8	9.9	46.1	125.9	212.5
1995	−0.3	−2.8	46.1	123.4	207.8
2000	5.3	2.7	46.6	112.0	186.8
2005	3.4	0.8	48.7	96.6	158.1
2010	7.8	5	51.3	81.5	130.3
2016	−1.7	−2.7	53.4	71.2	108.8**

*GDP annual growth % – annual population growth %

** 2015

Sources: World Bank World Development Indicators; IMF World Economic Outlook; CIA World Factbook. Some data compiled by Hannah Brown.

In terms of social welfare, Nigeria's overall weak economic performance since the early 1980s has caused great suffering, and recent economic gains have yet to alleviate poverty for the majority of Nigerians. Since 1986, there has been a marked deterioration in the scope of social services, paralleled by declining household incomes, at least through the mid-2000s. The SAP agenda and subsequent austerity measures emphasizing the reduction of state expenditures forced cutbacks in spending on social welfare. Consequently, Nigeria's provision of basic education, health care, and other social services—water, education, food, and shelter—remains woefully inadequate. In addition to the needless loss of countless lives to preventable and curable maladies, the nation is fighting to keep AIDS in check.

Because the central government controls access to most resources and economic opportunities, the state has become the major focus for competition among ethnic, regional, religious, and class groups. Nigeria's ethnic relations have generated tensions that undermine economic advancement. The dominance of the Hausa, Igbo, and Yoruba in the country's national life, as well as the conflicts among ethnic elites, impede a common economic agenda and aggravate the diversion of resources through distributive politics.

Growing assertion by Christian and Muslim communities also have heightened conflicts. Christians have perceived previous northern-dominated governments as being pro-Muslim in their management and distribution of scarce resources, some of which jeopardized the secular nature of the state. These fears have increased since 1999, when several northern states instituted expanded versions of the Islamic legal code, *shari'a*. For their part, Muslims feared that Presidents Obasanjo and Jonathan, both Christians, tilted the balance of power and thus the distribution of economic benefits against the north. Economic decline has contributed to the rise of fundamentalism among both Christians and Muslims, which have spread among unemployed youths and others in a society suffering under economic stagnation.

shari'a

Islamic law derived mostly from the Qur'an and the examples set by the Prophet Muhammad in the Sunnah.

Although the Land Use Act of 1978 stated that all land in Nigeria is ultimately owned by the government, land tenure in the country is still governed by traditional practice, which is largely patriarchal. Despite the fact that women, especially from the south and Middle Belt areas, have traditionally dominated agricultural production and form the bulk of agricultural producers, they are generally prevented from owning land, which remains the major means of production. Trading, in which women feature prominently, is also controlled in many areas by traditional chiefs and local government councilors, who are overwhelmingly male.

Women's associations in the past tended to be elitist, urban based, and mainly concerned with issues of trade, children, household welfare, and religion.[5] Although these groups initially focused generally on nonpolitical issues surrounding women's health and children's welfare, they are now also focusing on explicit political goals, such as getting more women into government and increasing funds available for education. Women are grossly underrepresented at all levels of the governmental system; only 27 of 469 national legislators (or about 5.75 percent) are women.

Environmental Issues

Northern Nigeria is located on the edge of the Sahel, the vast, semiarid region just south of the Sahara Desert that is arable, yet fragile. Although much of the north enjoys seasonal rains that come from the tropical southern part of Nigeria, the northern edges of the country have been suffering the growing effects of climate change as water supplies diminish.

Most dramatic has been the drying of Lake Chad in the northeast, which has shrunk to roughly a fifth of its size in the 1960s. As desertification pressures spread in the north, nomadic Fulani herdsman have been forced to move their cattle toward the more temperate south, increasingly causing violent local conflicts with farmers. These disputes can take on religious tones when the Fulani, who are predominantly Muslim, move into lands settled by Christian farmers.

The environment is also a major issue in the Niger Delta, but for a different reason. Here, years of pollution from the oil industry has killed off much of the local fish stock that communities in the region have depended upon for their livelihoods, and gas flaring from the oil wells lights up the night and makes the air toxic. A small ethnic group in one of the oil-producing communities, the Ogoni, formed an environmental rights organization in 1990 that pushed for peaceful action to clean up the damage and give the Ogoni greater control over the oil wealth. The military, however, clamped down on the movement and executed its key leaders. Thereafter, protests across the region increased, and many turned violent, devolving into the militant insurgency that plagues the Niger Delta today.

Finally, Nigeria's environment faces growing pressures from the nation's population explosion. Sprawling megacities stretch across Nigeria's urban areas, especially from the commercial hub of Lagos, whose expanse has absorbed as far as Ibadan to the north and is estimated to include over 20 million people. At the same time, Lagos is rapidly losing its coastline to the rising sea levels, putting increased pressure on limited space.

Nigeria in the Global Economy

The Nigerian state has remained substantially dependent on foreign industrial and financial interests. The country's acute debt burden was dramatically reduced in 2005, but started growing again by 2014, and Nigeria is still reliant on more advanced industrial economies for finance capital, production and information technologies, basic consumer items, and raw materials. Mismanagement, endemic corruption, and the vagaries of international commodity markets have squandered the country's economic potential. Apart from its standing in global energy markets, Nigeria receded to the margins of the global economy. The recent economic boom centered in Lagos has attracted growing international investment, but this regional hub has not been complemented by effective development initiatives from the federal government or most states, nor has there been a serious effort to attack the grand corruption that depletes resources and undermines investment.

Economic Community of West African States (ECOWAS)

A West African regional organization, including fifteen member countries from Cape Verde in the west to Nigeria and Niger in the east.

Nigeria's aspirations to be a regional leader in Africa have not been dampened by its declining position in the global political economy. The country was a major actor in the formation of the **Economic Community of West African States (ECOWAS)** in 1975 and has carried a disproportionately high financial and administrative burden for keeping the organization afloat. Under President Obasanjo's initiative, ECOWAS voted in 2000 to create a parliament and a single currency for the region as the next step toward an integration similar to the European Union. The currency was never implemented, but ECOWAS citizens are able to travel and trade across member-state borders relatively freely.

U.S. CONNECTION

Much in Common

Since the 1970s, Nigeria has had a strong relationship with the United States. Most of Nigeria's military governments during the Cold War aligned their foreign policies with the West, although they differed over South Africa, with Nigeria taking a strong anti-apartheid stance. Beginning with the 1979 Second Republic constitution, Nigeria closely modeled its presidential and federal systems on those of the United States, and Nigerian courts will occasionally turn to American jurisprudence for legal precedents. Since the 1970s, Washington has supported Nigerian efforts to liberalize and deepen democratic development.

Overwhelmingly, however, the key issue in U.S.–Nigerian relations has been oil. The United States currently sources only 2.6 percent of its petroleum imports from Nigeria, though as recently as 2010, Nigeria supplied close to 10 percent of U.S. imports. Washington traditionally pushed the Nigerian government to increase production of its "sweet crude," the high-quality oil that Nigeria offers. Nigeria also discovered massive gas reserves off its coasts. Nigeria's military governments sometimes used American oil dependence to moderate its pressure on Nigeria's leaders to democratize. Civilian governments since 1999 have often ignored U.S. complaints over declining election quality, and the Yar'Adua administration cultivated ties with China

after the United States downgraded diplomatic relations over the farcical 2007 elections in Nigeria.

Shortly thereafter, the George W. Bush administration welcomed President Umaru Musa Yar'Adua to Washington. President Jonathan initially benefited from U.S. insistence on constitutionalism and election reform. Ironically, he also accepted his 2015 loss to President Buhari in part due to quiet diplomacy from the Barack Obama administration for a peaceful transition of power.

Nigeria and the United States share strong societal ties. Since the 1960s, Christian Nigerians have been attracted to American Pentecostalism, sprouting thousands of new churches over the years and infusing them with a uniquely Nigerian flair; many of these churches are now opening satellites in the United States and around the globe. In addition, a growing number of Nigerians have migrated to the United States, and nearly 300,000 are now U.S. citizens. Since 2000, this diaspora has begun to exercise some influence over U.S. policy, and they also have used their financial resources to support development projects and exercise political influence in Nigeria.

MAKING CONNECTIONS Does the U.S. oil addiction give Nigeria an important influence on U.S. foreign policy?

Nigeria was also the largest contributor of troops to the West African peacekeeping force to Liberia from 1990 to 1997, for the purpose of restoring order and preventing the Liberian civil war from destabilizing the subregion. Nigeria under President Obasanjo also sought to mediate crises in Guinea-Bissau, Togo, and the Ivory Coast, and outside the ECOWAS region in Darfur (Sudan), Congo, and Zimbabwe. President Jonathan continued to support Nigerian peacekeeping commitments abroad, taking a particularly strong stand against the 2012 coup and Islamist rebellion in Mali through ECOWAS. The growing Boko Haram insurgency within Nigeria, however, has absorbed much of the country's military resources since 2011, leaving less for its international commitments. President Buhari, however, led West African leaders in pressuring Gambia's military president to respect his election loss and hand power over to the opposition in 2016.

Where Do You Stand?

Has oil been a blessing or curse for the Nigerian economy?

Many Nigerians feel they have ample natural resources to develop the nation, but that they have been plagued with poor leadership to make it happen. Do you see evidence of this?

GOVERNANCE AND POLICY-MAKING

▽ **Focus Questions**

• What is the "National Question," and how have Nigerians tried to resolve it?

• What is prebendalism, and how has the "Big Man" problem played out in the civilian governments since 1999?

The rough edges of what has been called the "unfinished Nigerian state" appears in its institutions of governance and policy-making. President Obasanjo inherited a government after decades of military rule that was close to collapse, riddled with corruption, unable to perform basic tasks of governance, and yet facing high public expectations to deliver rapid progress. He delivered some important economic reforms over his eight years as president, but he gradually succumbed to the "Big Man" style of corrupt clientelist networks of the military years, and he tried to change the Constitution to extend his stay in power. The Nigerian public, however, rejected his ambitions, providing his political opponents, civil society, and the media with political leverage to compel his departure in May 2007. Presidents Yar'Adua and Jonathan, like Obasanjo, came to power without extensive client networks of their own and immediately set out to build them. President Buhari, interestingly, does not appear to be doing the same himself, but his government and the ruling APC party are suffused with patronage relations.

Organization of the State

The National Question and Constitutional Governance

After almost six decades as an independent nation, Nigerians are still debating basic political structures, the geographic balance of leadership, and in some quarters, if the country should even remain united. This fundamental governance issue is the National Question, and includes the following issues: How is the country to be governed given its great diversity? What should be the institutional form of government? How can all sections of the country work in harmony and none feel excluded or dominated by the others? Without clear answers to these questions, Nigeria has struggled since independence between democracy and constitutionalism, on the one hand, and military control on the other. The May 2006 rejection of President Obasanjo's third-term gambit, the fact that most elites insisted on a constitutional solution to the crisis over President Yar'Adua's demise, and President Jonathan's acceptance of his electoral defeat in 2015 are notable examples suggesting that Nigeria may have turned a corner toward growing respect for constitutional rule.

The Nigerian military in power, and even some civilian leaders, have often been unwilling to observe legal and constitutional constraints. Governance and policy-making in this context are swamped by personal and partisan considerations, and institutions are fragile.

Federalism and State Structure

Nigeria's First Republic experimented with the British-style parliamentary model, in which the prime minister is the chief executive and chosen directly from the legislative ranks. The First Republic was relatively decentralized, with more political power vested in the federal units: the Northern, Eastern, and Western Regions. The Second Republic constitution, which went into effect in 1979, adopted a U.S.-style presidential model. The Fourth Republic continues with the presidential model: a system with a strong executive who is constrained by a system of formal checks and balances on authority, a bicameral legislature, and an independent judicial branch charged with matters of law and constitutional interpretation.

Like the United States, Nigeria also features a federal structure comprising 36 states and 774 local government units empowered, within limits, to enact their own laws. The judicial system also resembles that of the United States, with a network of local and appellate courts, as well as state-level courts. Unlike the United States, however, Nigeria also allows customary law courts to function alongside the secular system, including *shari'a* courts in Muslim communities. Nigerian citizens have the right to choose which of these court systems that they wish to use, but if the disputants cannot agree, then the case goes to the secular courts by default.

In practice, however, military rule left an authoritarian political culture that remains despite the formal democratization of state structures. The control of oil wealth by this centralized command structure has further cemented economic and political control in the center, resulting in a skewed federalism in which states enjoy nominal powers, but in reality, most are highly dependent on the central government. Another aspect of federalism in Nigeria has been the effort to arrive at some form of elite accommodation to moderate some of the more divisive aspects of cultural pluralism. The domination of federal governments from 1960 to 1999 by northern Nigerians led southern Nigerians, particularly Yoruba leaders, to demand a "power shift" of the presidency to the south in 1999, leading to the election of Olusegun Obasanjo. Northerners then demanded a shift back to the north in 2007 and 2015, propelling Umaru Yar'Adua, a northern governor, and later Muhammadu Buhari into office. This ethnic rotation principle is not found formally in the constitution, but all the major political parties recognize it as a necessity. Most parties practice ethnic rotation at the state and local levels as well.[6]

The ethnic rotation principle was interrupted due to political developments in 2010–2011. President Yar'Adua, a northerner, died in May 2010 and was succeeded by Vice President Goodluck Jonathan, a southerner from the Niger Delta. Jonathan was then elected to a full four-year presidential term in April 2011. Northern political factions argued that under the ethnic rotation rule, the presidency should have stayed with them for two terms until 2015. These factions were, however, unable to unite and block Jonathan from winning the PDP nomination and election in 2011, and public anger over this break with rotation was partly responsible for election riots that killed 800 people. Consequently, northern groups tried to wrest control of the PDP in 2012 from the president, and when they failed, they turned to the opposition APC in order to bring the presidency back to their region in 2015.

This informal norm of ethnic rotation has built upon an older, formal practice, known as *federal character*. Federal character, which calls for ethnic quotas in government hiring practices, was introduced into public service by the 1979 constitution. Although this principle is regarded by some as a positive Nigerian contribution to governance in a plural society, its application has also intensified some intergroup rivalries and conflicts. Critics have argued that it is antidemocratic, encouraging elite bargaining at the expense of public voting.

The Executive

President Obasanjo's early months in office were marked by initiatives to reform the armed forces, revitalize the economy, address public welfare, and improve standards of governance. The president sought to root out misconduct and inefficiency in the public sector. Soon, however, familiar patterns of clientelism and financial kickbacks for oil licenses resurfaced. Obasanjo proposed a new anticorruption body, the Economic and Financial Crimes Commission (EFCC), which since its founding in 2003 has generally had an impressive record of indictments.

Nonetheless, a major impediment to reform came from the ruling party itself. The PDP was initially run by a collection of powerful politicians from Nigeria's early governments, many of whom grew rich from their complicity with the Babangida and Abacha juntas. With a difficult reelection bid in 2003, these fixers again delivered a victory for the president and the PDP, accomplished through massive fraud in a third of Nigeria's states and questionable practices in at least another third of the country.

After the 2003 election, President Obasanjo appeared convinced that he needed to build his own clientelist network if he were to govern and extend his tenure in office. He and his supporters soon moved to gain control of the PDP, offering benefits for loyalty, and removing allies of rival Big Men in the party. The EFCC then focused on investigating presidential opponents, arresting some and forcing others into compliance. When Obasanjo's attempted constitutional amendment for a third term was quashed by the National Assembly in May 2006, the president then had himself named "Chairman for Life" of the PDP, with the power to eject anyone from the party.

Not surprisingly, President Yar'Adua spent his first year in office trying to gain control over the PDP. He halted many of the last-minute privatizations of state assets to Obasanjo loyalists and replaced the chairman of the EFCC. The Yar'Adua administration did not impede the National Assembly from a series of investigations into the Obasanjo administration that unearthed massive corruption. By 2009, Yar'Adua had greater leverage over the PDP and Obasanjo was on the decline. Yar'Adua's incapacitation later that year shifted Obasanjo's fortunes, as he supported Jonathan's ascent to acting president against obstruction from Yar'Adua loyalists.

With Obasanjo's support, Jonathan moved to build other alliances to gain influence in the PDP, particularly with the powerful state governors. Their support, bought with the massive resources of the presidency, won him the PDP nomination and swept him to victory in April 2011. As President Jonathan moved to take control of the ruling party, however, his relationship soured with President Obasanjo, who then turned his support to Jonathan's opponents in the PDP. Within months, the party had divided, as six governors defected in 2013 to the newly formed opposition party, the APC, which broke the PDP's lock on power in 2015. The politicians of the APC either come from the PDP or from old opposition parties that functioned in the same fashion. Upon taking office in 2015 as the majority party in the National Assembly, the APC immediately fell to infighting over control of the Senate presidency and other leadership positions and was rocked by several major corruption scandals. Only a handful of bills (mostly budgets) were passed into law in the APC's first two years in power.

These developments demonstrated the continuing deficits of legitimacy for the government. As Nigeria's political elites continue to flout the rules of the democratic system, it is inevitable that patronage, coercion, and personal interest will drive policy more than the interests of the public. President Jonathan followed this pattern of

"Big Man" prebendal politics, but with one important exception—he appointed a credible chairman of the nation's electoral commission, Professor Attahiru Jega, in 2010. Jega moved quickly to implement reforms, assuring a more credible outcome in the 2011 elections, and charted a path for the momentous change of the 2015 polls. In the most recent national elections, not only was the incumbent (Jonathan) defeated, but also the opposition APC ousted the PDP, which had won every election since the start of the Fourth Republic in 1999.

Muhammadu Buhari's electoral victory in 2015, after three previous attempts, was a watershed in Nigerian politics. The former military ruler achieved a peaceful party turnover, raising hopes of a reform-minded government that would attack corruption and stem the raging northeastern Boko Haram insurgency. His presidency to date has produced mixed results. On one side, a new offensive and sharply reduced corruption in the military has produced significant battlefield successes against Boko Haram, though they are hardly a spent force. Additional anticorruption measures have stemmed some of the excesses of the political class.

However, Buhari's managerial capacity has also been lacking. He delayed months in selecting a cabinet, at a time when the economy was in steep economic decline. His administration has been equally slow to address the deepening recession, with severe consequences for social welfare. Despite Buhari's personal restraint, his APC party is riven with factionalism and patronage struggles. In addition, President Buhari is evidently burdened by declining health, and the public has little information on his

---

⧉ PROFILE

Muhammadu Buhari: From General to President

Drew Angerer/Getty Images

President Muhammadu Buhari was born into a Muslim Fulani family in the far northern state of Katsina in 1942, and lost his father at 4 years old. He enrolled in a military academy at age 18 and was commissioned as a second lieutenant in the Nigerian army in 1964. He was a junior participant in the July 1966 northern officers' coup that overthrew the Igbo-led military government of General Aguiyi Ironsi. He then commanded several brigades during the 1967–1970 Biafran Civil War and was instrumental in the 1975 coup that overthrew General Yakubu Gowon. Buhari then served as Petroleum Minister in General Olusegun Obasanjo's military government and commanded several divisions during the Second Republic. At various stages of his career, he received military training in England, India, and the United States, where he attended the Army War College in Carlisle, Pennsylvania, from which he received a master's degree in strategic studies.

Buhari helped to lead the December 1983 coup that ended the Second Republic, and he became military head of state, justifying his takeover based on the massive corruption of the former civilian government. His anticorruption policies won many admirers, but they were conducted amid heavy human rights violations under decrees that gave the military vast, arbitrary powers. These abuses, and his inability to deal with an economic recession produced by low oil prices, enabled General Ibrahim Babangida to remove him in a palace coup in 1985.

After years on the margins of national politics, Buhari re-emerged to run for president four times beginning in 2003, labeling himself a "converted democrat" and banking upon his reputation as a foe of corruption. In March 2015, he was elected president of Nigeria as the candidate of the opposition APC party, winning about 54 percent of the vote. In November 2016, his administration launched a "Change Begins with Me" campaign that was aimed not only at social and economic reform, but also at mobilizing and motivating individual citizens to bring about much-needed changes. It remains to be seen how much real change will happen, especially as the president's health deteriorates.

MAKING CONNECTIONS What impediments to major reform in Nigeria might inhibit the "Change Begins with Me" campaign from having an important effect?

condition. Only his willingness to delegate authority to Vice President Yemi Osinbajo has preserved some continuity of government.

The Bureaucracy

As the Nigerian colonial government was increasingly "Africanized" before independence, the bureaucracy became a way to reward individuals in the clientelist system. Individuals were appointed on the basis of patronage, ethnic group, and regional origin rather than on merit.

It is conservatively estimated that the number of federal and state government personnel increased from 72,000 at independence to well over 1 million by the mid-1980s. The salaries of these bureaucrats presently consume roughly half of government expenditures. Progressive ministers have at times implemented extensive reforms within their ministries, but bureaucratic resistance is pervasive. President Buhari initiated some civil service reforms in 2015–2016 that removed "ghost workers"—fake names on the payroll so that individuals can collect multiple salaries—that helped to save roughly $70 million annually.

Corruption and inefficacy in Nigeria's immense bureaucracy is largely the result of the pervasive influence of **prebendalism**, a form of clientelism that involves the disbursing of public offices and government revenues to one's supporters from the same ethnic group.[7] Prebendalism is an established pattern of political behavior in Nigeria that justifies the pursuit of and the use of public office for the personal benefit of officeholders and their clients. The official public purpose of the office becomes a secondary concern. As with all types of clientelism, the officeholders' clients comprise a specific set of elites to which they are linked, typically by ethnic or religious ties. Thus, clients or supporters perpetuate the prebendal system in a pyramid fashion, with a "Big Man" or "godfather" at the top and echelons of intermediate Big Men and clients below.

prebendalism

Patterns of political behavior that rest on the justification that official state offices should be utilized for the personal benefit of officeholders, as well as of their support group or clients, particularly of the same ethnicity or religion.

Other State Institutions

The Military

Leadership styles among Nigeria's seven military heads of state varied widely, though generally under military administrations, the president or head of state made appointments to most senior government positions.[8] Because the legislature was disbanded, major executive decisions (typically passed by decrees) were subject to the approval of a ruling council of high-level military officers, although by Abacha's time in the 1990s, this council had become largely a rubber stamp for the ruler. Regardless of the degree of autocracy, nearly all juntas spoke of moving to democracy in order to gain legitimacy.

Given the highly personalistic character of military politics, patron-client relationships flourished. The military pattern of organization, with one strongman at the top and echelons of subordinates below in a pyramid of top-down relationships, spread throughout Nigerian political culture.

Having been politicized and divided by these patron–client relationships, the military itself was structurally weakened during its long years in power. While there have been reports of coup plots on a number of occasions during the current Fourth Republic, especially during President Yar'Adua's final days, the military establishment has so far remained loyal and generally within its constitutional security role.

President Obasanjo paid close attention to keeping the military professionally oriented—and in the barracks. U.S. military advisers and technical assistance were invited to redirect the Nigerian military toward regional peacekeeping expertise and to keep them busy outside of politics. So far, this strategy has been effective, but the military remains a concern. Junior and senior officers threatened coups over the farcical 2007 elections and the refusal of Yar'Adua's advisors to hand power to Jonathan in 2009–2010, and they could do so again in future political crises. Importantly, however, the military refused overtures from rogue PDP leaders in the Jonathan government to step in after his election defeat in 2015.

The Judiciary

At one time, the Nigerian judiciary enjoyed relative autonomy from the executive arm. Aggrieved individuals and organizations could take the government to court and expect a judgment based on the merits of their case. This situation changed as successive military governments demonstrated a profound disdain for judicial practices, eventually undermining not only the autonomy, but also the integrity of the judiciary as a third branch of government.

The Buhari, Babangida, and Abacha military regimes, in particular, issued a spate of repressive decrees disallowing judicial review. Through the executive's power of appointment of judicial officers to the high bench, as well as control of judicial budgets, the government came to dominate the courts. In addition, the once highly competent judiciary was undermined by declining standards of legal training and by bribery. The decline of court independence reached a low in 1993, when the Supreme Court placed all actions of the military executive beyond judicial review. The detention and hanging of Ken Saro-Wiwa and eight other Ogoni activists in 1995 underscored the politicization and compromised state of the judicial system.

With the return of civilian rule in 1999, however, the courts slowly regained some independence and credibility. In early 2002, for instance, the Supreme Court passed two landmark judgments on election law and control of the vast offshore gas reserves. After the compromised 2007 elections, the courts overturned twelve gubernatorial races and a host of legislative contests, and the Supreme Court reviewed the 2007 and 2011 presidential elections as well.

Judiciaries at the state level are subordinate to the Federal Court of Appeal and the Supreme Court. Some of the states in the northern part of the country with large Muslim populations maintain a parallel court system based on the Islamic system of *shari'a* (religious law). Similarly, some states in the Middle Belt and southern part of the country have subsidiary courts based on customary law. Each of these maintains an appellate division. Otherwise, all courts of record in the country are based on the English common law tradition, and all courts are ultimately bound by decisions handed down by the Supreme Court.

How to apply *shari'a* law has been a source of continuing debate in Nigerian politics. For several years, some northern groups have participated in a movement to expand the application of *shari'a* in predominantly Muslim areas of Nigeria, and some even have advocated that it be made the supreme law of the land. Prior to the establishment of the Fourth Republic, *shari'a* courts had jurisdiction only among Muslims in civil proceedings and in questions of Islamic personal law. In November 1999, however, the northern state of Zamfara instituted a version of the *shari'a* criminal code that included cutting off hands for stealing and stoning to death for those (especially women) who committed adultery. Eleven other northern states adopted the criminal code by 2001, prompting fears among Christian minorities in these states that the code might be applied to them. A total of 2,000 people were killed in communal strife in Kaduna state in 2000, when the government installed the *shari'a* criminal code despite a population that is half Christian.

Since then, however, northern political and legal systems time have largely adjusted. In fact, the *shari'a* systems in these states have opened up new avenues for public action to press government for accountability and reform. In addition, women's groups mobilized against several questionable local *shari'a* court decisions to challenge them at the appellate level, winning landmark decisions that helped to extend women's legal protections under the code.

Subnational Government

Nigeria's centralization of oil revenues has fostered intense competition among states and local communities for access to federal patronage. Most states would be insolvent without substantial support from the central government. About 90 percent of state incomes are received directly from the federal government, which includes a lump sum based on oil revenues, plus a percentage of oil income based on population. In all likelihood, only the states of Lagos, Rivers, and Kano could survive on their own. Despite attempted reforms, most local governments have degenerated into patronage outposts for the governors to dole out to loyalists. For the most part, they do little to address their governance responsibilities.

The federal, state, and local governments have constitutional and legal powers to raise funds through taxes. However, Nigerians share an understandable reluctance to pay taxes and fees to a government with such a poor record of delivering basic services. The result is a vicious circle: government is sapped of resources and legitimacy and cannot adequately serve the people. Communities, in turn, are compelled to resort to self-help measures to protect their welfare and thus withdraw further from the reach of the state. Few individuals and organizations pay taxes, which means that the most basic government functions are starved of resources.

The Policy-Making Process

Nigeria's prolonged experience with military rule left indelible marks on policy-making in Nigeria. This is reflected in a policy process based more on top-down directives than on consultation, political debate, and legislation. Democratic government has seen important changes, as the legislatures, courts, and states have begun to force the president to negotiate his policy agenda and work within a constitutional framework. Nevertheless, prebendalism and corruption undermine the working of government at all levels of the political system and distort all stages of the policy-making process from formulation to implementation.

Where Do You Stand?

While Nigeria's presidents since 1999 have all promised reform, they have typically succumbed to prevalent patterns of corruption and clientelism, or they have been unable to stem corruption in their parties. Is corruption just too ingrained in Nigeria for any politician to resist its lure?

Does Nigeria's parallel system of *shari'a* and customary courts alongside its secular ones seem like a good idea to accommodate the nation's diversity, or does it perpetuate ethnic and religious differences that divide the country?

REPRESENTATION AND PARTICIPATION

Representation and participation are two vital components of modern democracies. Nigerian legislatures have commonly been sidelined or reduced to subservience by the powerful executive, while fraud, elite manipulation, and military interference have marred the formal party and electoral systems. Thus, we also emphasize unofficial, informal methods of representation and participation through the institutions of civil society.

Focus Questions ⍰

• What have been the benefits and costs of the move from ethnic parties under the early republics to the multiethnic parties of the Fourth Republic?

• What role has civil society played in resisting military rule and voicing the public interest under civilian governments?

The Legislature

Nigeria's legislature has been buffeted by political instability. Legislative structures and processes historically were manipulated, neglected, or suspended outright by the executive. Until the first coup in 1966, Nigeria operated its legislature along the lines of the British Westminster model, with an elected lower house and a smaller upper house composed of individuals selected by the executive. For the next thirteen years of military rule, a Supreme Military Council performed legislative functions by initiating and passing decrees at will. During the second period of civilian rule, 1979–1983, the bicameral legislature was introduced similar to the U.S. system, with a Senate and House of Representatives (together known as the National Assembly) consisting of elected members, which is the model still in use.

Election to the Senate is on the basis of equal state representation, with three senators from each of the thirty-six states, plus one senator from the federal capital territory, Abuja. The practice of equal representation in the Senate is identical to that of the United States, with a slightly different senate formula. Election to Nigeria's House of Representatives is also based on state representation, but weighted to reflect the relative size of each state's population, again after the U.S. model. Only eight women were elected in 1999 to sit in the Fourth Republic's National Assembly; by 2015, this number rose slightly to twenty-seven, yet still constituting only 6 percent of the legislature's membership.

Political Parties and the Party System

An unfortunate legacy of the party and electoral systems after independence was that political parties were associated with particular ethnic groups. The three-region federation created by the British, with one region for each of the three biggest ethnic groups (Hausa, Yoruba, and Igbo), created strong incentives for three ethno-regional parties to gain dominance. This in turn fostered a strong perception of politics as an ethnically zero-sum (or winner-take-all) struggle for access to scarce state resources. The ensuing political and social fragmentation ultimately destroyed the First Republic (1963–1966) and the Second Republic (1979–1983), both of which were overthrown by military coups.

In addition to the original three-region structure of the federation, Nigeria's use of a first-past-the-post plurality electoral system produced legislative majorities for the regional, ethnically identified parties. During subsequent democratic experiments, many of the newer parties could trace their roots to their predecessors in the first civilian regime. Consequently, parties were more attentive to the welfare of their ethnic groups than to the development of Nigeria as a whole. In a polity as volatile as Nigeria, these tendencies intensified political polarization and resentment among the losers.

In the Second Republic, the leading parties shared the same ethnic and sectional support, and often the same leadership, as the parties that were prominent in the first civilian regime. In his steps toward creating the civilian Third Republic, General Babangida announced a landmark decision in 1989 to establish only two political parties by decree.[9] The state provided start-up funds, wrote the manifestos of the parties, and designed them to be, as Babangida described them, "a little to the right and a little to the left," respectively, on the political–ideological spectrum. Interestingly, the elections that took place under these rules from 1990 to 1993 indicated that the two parties cut across the cleavages of ethnicity, regionalism, and religion, demonstrating the potential to move beyond ethnicity.[10] The center-left Social Democratic Party (SDP), which emerged victorious in the 1993 national elections, was an impressive coalition of politicians from several Second Republic parties. The opposing conservative National Republican Convention (NRC) drew on elites from the former NPN, which had dominated the Second Republic.

Nigerians generally reacted with anger to General Abacha's 1993 coup, which overthrew the very short-lived Third Republic, and his subsequent banning of the SDP and NRC. With the unions crushed and President Abiola in jail, the Abacha government registered only five parties,[11] all of which endorsed Abacha as president shortly before his death in July 1998.

The G-34, a prominent group of civilian leaders who had condemned Abacha's plans to remain in power, created the PDP in late August 1998, minus most of their Yoruba members, who joined the Alliance for Democracy (AD). At least twenty more parties applied for certification to the Independent National Electoral Commission (INEC); many of them were truly grassroots movements, including a human rights organization and a trade union party.

To escape the ethnic-based parties of the First and Second Republics, INEC required that parties earn at least 5 percent of the votes in twenty-four of the thirty-six states in local government elections in order to advance to the later state and federal levels. This turned out to be an ingenious way of reducing the number of parties while obliging viable parties to broaden their appeal. The only parties to meet INEC's requirements were the PDP, AD, and the All People's Party (APP).

The parties of the Fourth Republic are primarily alliances of convenience among Big Men from across Nigeria. Their agenda has been to gain power and control over resources. They have few differences in ideology or policy platforms, and politicians who lose in one party will frequently shift to another.

Yet these contemporary parties do feature an important innovation that distinguishes them from those of earlier Republics: they are multiethnic rather than parochial associations based on different collective identities. They rely on elite-centered structures established during previous civilian governments, reflecting cross-ethnic alliances that developed over the last thirty years. The PDP includes core members of the northern establishment NPN, the northern progressive PRP, and the Igbo-dominated NPP of the Second Republic, as well as prominent politicians from the Niger Delta. The APP, later the All Nigerian People's Party (ANPP), was also a multiethnic collection, drawing from the Second Republic's Great Nigeria People's Party (GNPP), a party dominated by the northeastern-based Kanuri and groups from the Middle Belt. The party featured other politicians who had prominent roles in the Abacha-sponsored parties from the northwest, the Igbo southeast, and southern minority leaders. The AD was as Yoruba-centered as its predecessors, the UPN in the Second Republic and the AG in the First Republic. The party would later pay at the polls for its lack of national appeal, however, and joined with breakaway factions of the PDP to form the Action Congress (AC, later the Action Congress of Nigeria, ACN; see the following discussion). In 2013, the ANPP and ACN would join two other opposition parties and six defecting governors from the PDP to form the All Progressives Congress (APC), a truly multiethnic, national party to rival the PDP.

This rise of multiethnic political parties is one of the most significant democratic developments of the Fourth Republic. There is a strong incentive for politicians to bargain and bridge their ethnic differences *within* the party so that they may then compete with the other parties in the system, which would preferably be multiethnic as well. In Nigeria, ethnic divisions—supported by prebendal networks—still dominate national politics, but diversified parties have done fairly well at bridging these many divides during election periods and fostering a climate of compromise amid divisive national debates.

Elections

Historical electoral trends since 1960 show that northern-based parties dominated the first and second experiments with civilian rule. Given this background, it is significant that Moshood Abiola was able to win the presidency in 1993, the first time in Nigeria's history that a southerner electorally defeated a northerner. Abiola, a Yoruba Muslim, won a number of key states in the north, including the hometown of his opponent. Southerners therefore perceived the decision by the northern-dominated Babangida military regime to annul the June 12 election as a deliberate attempt by the military and northern interests to maintain their decades-long domination of the highest levels of government.

In other African countries, like Ghana, the path away from political oligarchy and toward democracy is through the rise of a unified, viable political opposition. This has been slow to happen in Nigeria. For most of the years of the Fourth Republic, the main opposition parties never organized a working relationship or a serious policy challenge to the dominant PDP, except just prior to elections, which didn't translate into enough votes to win.

The PDP was reelected to power in 2011 with a massive majority across Nigeria, controlling the presidency, twenty-three governorships and twenty-six state assemblies, as well as more than half of the seats of the National Assembly. Yet it was also a party in disarray, with its northern segments outraged over President Jonathan's break with the ethnic rotation principle, and southern leaders like former PDP President Obasanjo angered by Jonathan's efforts to seize control of the PDP. Sensing both the limits of their small parties and opportunity in the growing rebellion within the PDP, leaders of the major opposition parties agreed in 2013 to merge to form the APC. The historic 2015 elections looked like the reverse of 2011, with the APC winning the presidency and a majority in both houses of the National Assembly (see Table 12.4). Yet the APC, like the PDP, is largely an alliance of convenience among the powerful personal networks of its "Big Men" politicians, and it will likely hold

Table 12.4	Election Results in Nigeria, 2011 and 2015

Presidential Elections (% of Popular Vote)

2011	Goodluck Jonathan, PDP (58.9%)	Mohammadu Buhari, CDC (32.0%)
2015	Muhammadu Buhari, APC (53.9%)	Goodluck Jonathan, PDP (44.9%)

Other Federal and State Elections

Party	House Votes (%)	House Seats (No.)	Senate Votes (%)	Senate Seats (No.)	Governorships	State Assemblies Controlled (No.)
2011						
PDP	54.4	152	62.4	53	23	26
ACN	19.0	53	21.2	18	6	5
CDC	11.1	31	7.1	6	1	0
Others	15.4	43	9.4	8	6	5
2015						
PDP	34.7	125	45.0	49	11	12
APC	62.5	225	55.0	60	24	24
Others	2.8	10	0	0	1	0

ACN–Action Congress of Nigeria; APC–All Progressives Congress; CDC–Congress for Democratic Change; PDP–People's Democratic Party

together only so long as it serves the interests of these power brokers. Already by 2017, the APC has faced intense internal conflicts that President Buhari refused to mediate, and elders voiced fears that the party could collapse. Nonetheless, the PDP faced similar internal struggles prior to 2003, 2007, and 2011, and, yet in the end, leaders papered over their differences to win elections and maintain national dominance. APC leaders may well do the same.

Political Culture, Citizenship, and Identity

Military regimes left Nigeria with strong authoritarian influences in its political culture. Most of the younger politicians of the Fourth Republic came of age during military rule and learned the business of politics from Abacha and Babangida and their military governors. Still, Nigeria's deep democratic traditions remain vibrant among the larger polity, but they are in constant tension with the values imbibed during years of authoritarian governance when political problems were often solved by military dictate, power, and violence rather than by negotiation and respect for law. Nearly twenty years of civilian rule, however, have seen a growing shift in Nigerian political culture away from its authoritarian past toward a culture of negotiation and law, though corruption patterns continue to flourish.

Modernity Versus Traditionalism

The interaction of Western (colonial) elements with traditional (precolonial, African) practices created the conundrum of a modern sociopolitical system that rests uneasily on traditional foundations. Nigerians straddle two worlds, each undergoing constant evolution. On the one hand, the strong elements in communal societies that promoted accountability have been weakened by the intrusion of Western culture, oriented toward individuality, and exacerbated by urbanization. On the other hand, the modern state has been unable to free itself fully from rival ethnic claims organized around narrow collective identities.

As a result, exclusivist identities continue to dominate Nigerian political culture and to define the nature of citizenship.[12] Individuals tend to identify with their immediate ethnic, regional, and religious groups rather than with state institutions, especially during moments of crisis. Entirely missing from the relationship between state and citizen in Nigeria is a fundamental reciprocity—a working social contract—based on the belief that a common interest binds them together.

Religion

Religion has been a persistent source of community and a basis for conflict throughout Nigerian history. Islam began to filter into northeast Nigeria in the eleventh and twelfth centuries and greatly expanded in subsequent centuries. In the north, Islam first coexisted with, then gradually supplanted, indigenous religions. Christianity arrived in the early nineteenth century and spread rapidly through missionary activity in the south. The amalgamation of northern and southern Nigeria in 1914 brought together the two regions and their belief systems.

These religious cultures have consistently clashed over political issues such as the secular character of the state. The application of the *shari'a* criminal code in the northern states has been a focal point for these tensions. For many Muslims, *shari'a* represents a way of life and supreme law that transcends secular and state law; for many Christians, the expansion of *shari'a* law threatens the secular nature of the Nigerian state and their position within it. The pull of religious versus national identity becomes even stronger in times of economic hardship.

The nation is now evenly divided between Muslims and Christians, and the Middle Belt states where the fault line runs have often been particularly volatile. Communal conflicts frequently erupt in these areas, often between Fulani herdsmen, who are Muslim, and farmers, who in some instances may be Christian, or between farmers of the two religions over control of land or access to public funds. In most of these instances, religion is not the source of the conflict, but once disputes ignite, they can quickly involve religious identity.

A handful of violent Islamist and Christian fundamentalist groups, however, have become active in recent years, particularly in the northeast and the Middle Belt. The most violent of these has been the *Congregation of the People of Tradition for Proselytization and Jihad*, dubbed "Boko Haram" by the media, meaning "Western education is sinful" in Hausa, for the movement's rejection of the Western pedigrees of the Nigerian elite and the Western-created Nigerian state, manifest in its secular education system that it views as corrupt and immoral.

Boko Haram seeks to establish its idiosyncratic vision of an Islamist state in Nigeria and in 2015 pledged its allegiance to the Islamic State in Iraq and Syria (ISIS). Much of its activities were focused in Borno and Yobe states in the northeast until 2011, at which point it received technical assistance from Al-Qaeda's Algerian affiliate and expanded its scope of operations across the northeast and north-central region, attacking police stations and setting off bombs, including at the UN headquarters in Abuja. Boko Haram gained world attention when it kidnapped more than 250 schoolgirls from Chibok in Borno state in 2014—in May

2017, 81 of the abducted girls were released, but the other two-thirds remain in captivity. Counteroffensives by the Nigerian military in 2015–2017 reduced Boko Haram to small pockets in Borno, and the group split into two factions, although it has continued to launch suicide attacks in Nigeria and neighboring countries.

Interest Groups, Social Movements, and Protest

Historically, labor has played a significant role in Nigerian politics, as have student groups, women's organizations, professional associations, and various radical and populist organizations. Business groups have frequently supported and colluded with corrupt civilian and military regimes. In the last year of the Abacha regime, however, even the business class began to suggest an end to such arbitrary rule through mechanisms like Vision 2010. Civil society groups flourished across Nigeria after the end of military rule in 1999.

Organized labor has played an important role in challenging governments during both the colonial and postcolonial eras in several African countries, Nigeria among them. Continuous military pressure throughout the 1980s and 1990s forced a decline in the independence and strength of organized labor in Nigerian politics. The Babangida military regime implemented strategies of state corporatism designed to control and coopt various social forces such as labor. When the leadership of the Nigeria Labour Congress (NLC), the umbrella confederation, took a vigorous stand against the government, the regime deposed its leaders and appointed conservative replacements. Petroleum unions launched prodemocracy strikes in the 1990s and income-focused strikes after 1999, which significantly reduced oil production and nearly brought the country to a halt on multiple occasions.

The Nigerian labor movement has been vulnerable to reprisals by the state and private employers. The government has always been the biggest single employer of labor in Nigeria, as well as the recognized arbiter of industrial relations between employers and employees. Efforts by military regimes to centralize and coopt the unions caused their militancy and impact to wane. Moreover, ethnic, regional, and religious divisions have often hampered labor solidarity, and these differences have been periodically manipulated by the state. Nevertheless, labor unions still claim an estimated 5 million members across Nigeria and remains one of the most potent forces in civil society. The unions have a great stake in the consolidation of constitutional rule in the Fourth Republic and the protections that allow them to organize and act freely on behalf of their members. The NLC has called national strikes on a number of occasions since 2000, typically over wages and fuel price hikes, including the Occupy Nigeria demonstrations of 2012 (discussed next).

Nigeria has a long history of entrepreneurialism and business development. This spirit is compromised by corruption both within the government and business. Members of the Nigerian business class have been sometimes characterized as "pirate capitalists" because of their corrupt practices and collusion with state officials.[13] Many wealthy individuals have served in the military or civilian governments, while others protect their access to state resources by sponsoring politicians they see as favorable to their interests or entering into business arrangements with bureaucrats.

Private business associations have proven surprisingly resilient as an important element of civil society. Organized groups have emerged to represent the interests of the business class and to promote general economic development. There are numerous associations throughout Nigeria representing a broad variety of business activities and sectoral interests. National business associations, such as the Nigerian Association of Chambers of Commerce, Industry, Mines, and Agriculture (NACCIMA), the largest in the country, have taken an increasingly political stance, expressing their determination to protect their interests by advocating for better governance.

Student activism also continues to be an important feature of Nigerian political life, and student unions have been major players in Nigerian politics since the 1960s. Since the 1990s, however, many universities have seen the rise of what are called "cults"—gangs of young men, typically armed, who use rituals associated with their groups. Many of these cultists "graduated" to join the militias that became political thugs and the cults are also often employed by elites for their power plays. In partial response to the cult phenomenon, religious movements have proliferated across Nigerian universities, providing students with an alternative to these violent groups as a way of life. Yet religious groups on campus have also provided vehicles for encouraging and recruiting both Christian and Muslim fundamentalists.

Overall, civil society groups are making substantial contributions to consolidating democracy in Nigeria. In particular, many groups have built good working relationships with the National Assembly and state legislatures, from which both sides have benefited. Their relationships with the political parties, however, remain distant. Nigeria's prospects for building a sustainable democracy during the Fourth Republic will depend, in part, on the willingness of many of these advocacy groups to increase their collaboration with the political parties, while avoiding cooptation and maintaining a high level of vigilance and activism in support of democracy.

The Political Impact of Technology and the Media

The Nigerian press has long been one of the liveliest and most irreverent in Africa. The Abacha and Babangida military regimes moved to stifle its independence, with limited success. Some democratic presidents sought to constrain the press but were generally blocked by the courts. Significantly, much of the Nigerian press is based in a Lagos-Ibadan axis in the southwestern part of Nigeria and has frequently been labeled "southern." Recently, however, independent television and radio stations have proliferated around the country, and after 2000, Nigeria grew rapidly in cellular and Internet connectivity. Internet-based investigative journalists such as SaharaReporters.com have utilized the uncensored medium of the Internet to print stories that the mainstream newspapers have been afraid to publish, exposing the corrupt activities of some of Nigeria's biggest politicians. New technologies are affecting politics, as cellular phones are now everywhere, including the latest models, and intense competition among service providers has produced ample coverage and one of the most efficient and lucrative industries in the country. The doubling of Nigeria's service sector during roughly the same period, as the nation's GDP grew on average over 6 percent annually since 2003, signals that the small but rapidly rising middle class is using this technology extensively.

Although middle-class professionals were using new technologies to monitor elections as early as 2003, the 2011 and 2015 elections saw civil society activists use social media extensively to track and report election violations across the country. Most

Christians and Muslims protest together, and protect each other at prayer times, during Occupy Nigeria in 2012.

impressive, however, were the protests that followed President Jonathan's removal of fuel subsidies in January 2012. In a movement inspired by the Arab Spring and Occupy Wall Street, thousands of Nigerians took to the streets for two weeks in what became known as "Occupy Nigeria." Largely and loosely organized by concerned professionals working through social media sites like Facebook and Twitter, Occupy Nigeria generated peaceful demonstrations in cities across the nation, with the largest in Lagos, Abuja, and Kano, and within days attracted the attention of the NLC, which in solidarity called for a general strike that brought economic activity to a halt.

Most impressively, the movement showed none of the ethnic, religious, or sectional elements so present in Nigerian politics. In fact, interfaith cooperation was evident throughout, with breathtaking pictures of Christians forming a human shield around Muslims while they performed their required daily prayers, and Muslims escorting Christians to church. What united the protesters was a common frustration with the massive corruption throughout the Nigerian establishment—a progressive agenda that seeks sweeping reform and broad-based development. The demonstrations collapsed after the NLC called off the strike as it reached a bargain with the Jonathan administration that restored half of the fuel subsidy. Many of these same organizers, however, turned their skills and virtual networks to mobilize again in support of the opposition APC in the 2015 elections.

Where Do You Stand?

What can the United States or other foreign nations do to support civil society groups and social media-based movements like Occupy Nigeria so they can transform Nigeria?

Do you agree that multiethnic parties are a good idea for political development? Can you think of examples from other countries that prove or disprove the point?

NIGERIAN POLITICS IN TRANSITION

Despite the slow progress of the Fourth Republic, Nigerians overwhelmingly favor democratic government over military rule. About 70 percent of respondents in a recent survey said that they still prefer democracy to any other alternative, although popular frustration is growing with the slow pace of reform and continued corruption in politics. This growing anger with massive, rampant corruption is the one constant across the nation, featuring strongly in the motives of groups as widely variant as Boko Haram, the Niger Delta militias, and the peaceful Occupy Nigeria. Will democracy in Nigeria be consolidated sufficiently to meet minimal levels of public satisfaction, or could the nation again succumb to authoritarian rule?

Nigerian politics must change in fundamental ways for democracy to become more stable and legitimate. First and foremost, the nation must turn away from a system of politics dominated by Big Men—for all intents and purposes, a competitive oligarchy—to a more representative mode of politics that addresses the fundamental interests of the public. Second, Nigerians must conclusively settle the National Question and commit to political arrangements that accommodate the nation's diversity. In short, Nigeria's Fourth Republic must find ways of moving beyond prebendal politics and develop a truly national political process in which mobilization and conflicts along ethnic, regional, and religious lines gradually diminish, and which can address Nigeria's true national crises: poverty and underdevelopment.

Political Challenges and Changing Agendas

Nigeria's fitful transition to democratic rule between 1985 and 1999 was inconclusive, largely because it was planned and directed from above. This approach contrasts sharply with the popular-based movements that unseated autocracies in Central and Eastern Europe or South Africa. The Nigerian military periodically made promises for democratic transition as a ploy to stabilize and legitimate their governments. General Abubakar dutifully handed power to civilian leaders in 1999, but only after ensuring that the military's interests would be protected under civilian rule and creating an overly powerful executive that reinforces prebendalism and its patronage system. The military's rapid transition program produced a tenuous, conflicted democratic government that faces daunting tasks of revitalizing key institutions, securing social stability, and reforming the economy. The continuing strength and influence of collective identities, defined on the basis of religion or ethnicity, are often more binding than national allegiances. The parasitic nature of the Nigerian economy is a further source of instability. Rent-seeking and other unproductive, often corrupt, business activities remain accepted norms of wealth accumulation.

Nonetheless, Nigerians are sowing seeds of change in all these areas. Attitudes toward the military in government have shifted dramatically. Military attitudes themselves have changed significantly as well, as evidenced by the restraint shown by the armed forces during President Yar'Adua's incapacitation and the 2015 election transition in power from the PDP to the APC. The appeal of military rule declined markedly after the abysmal performances of the Babangida and Abacha regimes. Nonetheless,

Focus Questions ▽

- What role can political opposition and civil society play in reversing prebendalism and the politics of the "Big Men"?

- What other reforms can help to settle the National Question and harness the strong democratic yearnings of the Nigerian public?

growing frustrations with corruption and poor governance under nearly twenty years of civilian rule have fostered pockets of renewed interest in the military as a possible solution, which could have serious consequences. With the nation's massive youth demographics—two-thirds of Nigerians are under the age of 25—fewer now have any living memory of military rule and its abuses. If, however, the armed forces remain in their barracks, as still seems more likely than not, then the struggles among civilian political elites will decide the direction of political and economic change. Thus, democratic development may be advanced in the long run if stable coalitions appear over time in a manner that balances the power among contending groups, and if these key elites adapt to essential norms and rules of the political game.

Under the Fourth Republic, members of the political class have sometimes pursued their struggles within the constraints of the democratic system: using the courts, media, legislative struggles, and even legal expediencies such as impeachment. Progress has been made when political actors work through formal institutions, contending openly and offsetting the power of a single group or faction. Frequently, however, the political elite have also shown a willingness to use extra-systemic measures to forward their interests through election rigging, corruption, and militia-led violence. The Niger Delta has been particularly violent, with increasingly well-armed militias that in some cases have shown a measure of independence from their political patrons. The rise of Boko Haram in the northeast created an additional threat for the Nigerian state, which politicians have also been using for political gain.

The next critical step down the long road of democratic development for Nigeria is the creation of a viable, multiethnic opposition party that is committed to peaceful political competition. Opposition parties can help to reduce corruption in the system because they have an interest in exposing the misconduct of the ruling party, which in turn pressures them to restrain their own behavior. Furthermore, in order to unseat the ruling party and win elections, opposition parties need to engage the public to win their votes. In this manner, issues of interest to the public are engaged by the parties. This is the basis of the social contract: elites gain the privilege of power, but only so long as they use it to promote the public interest.

The introduction of so many new parties after 2002 slowed the development of a viable, unified opposition, with the result that the PDP was able to govern largely unchecked for more than a decade and to absorb or coopt opposition leaders when possible. The rise of the APC in 2013 presented a chance for Nigeria to develop two national, multiethnic parties that can check and balance each other and offer the Nigerian public a serious alternative at the ballot box. If the two parties actually reach out to civil society for support and vie for the public's attention by offering truly competitive development policies, then Nigeria might turn the corner toward stability and growth, joining Ghana and other regional democratic states. The 2015 elections that brought the APC to power were some of the most credible in Nigerian history, precisely because the two parties checked and balanced each other and the APC reached out to civil society and the public for support to offset the PDP's incumbency advantages and massive war chest.

Yet the political bargains holding the APC together remain tenuous and have come under tremendous strain as factions have contended over control of the spoils of office. If the APC falls apart into ethnic blocs, and if the PDP is unable to expand from its stronghold in the southeast, then Nigeria runs the risk of a return to the ethnic-based parties of the First and Second Republics and the tragedies that they produced. On the other hand, if the APC holds together or even strengthens its advantage, then Nigeria could return to the problem of an unchecked dominant party, with the APC substituting for the PDP. Nigeria will be better served with a vibrant APC and PDP in relative balance, competing vigorously—and legally—for the public's support.

PIUS UTOMI EKPEI/Getty Images

Protests over federal exploitation of the oil-producing Niger Delta sparked a regionwide insurgency by 2003, with heavily armed militias engaged in both political disputes and criminal activities, cutting Nigeria's oil production by more than a quarter.

In addition, the project of building a coherent nation-state out of competing nationalities remains unfinished. Ironically, because the parties of the Fourth Republic generally do not represent any particular ethnic interest—indeed, they do not represent anyone's interests except those of the leaders and their clients—ethnic associations and militias have risen to articulate ethnic-based grievances. While ethnic consciousness will remain significant, ethnicity should not be the main basis for political competition. If current ethnic mobilization can be contained within ethnic associations arguing over the agenda of the parties, then it can be managed. If, however, any of the ethnic associations captures one of the political parties or joins with the militias to foment separatism, instability will result. The same is true if the PDP comes to be seen as the Christian party of the south and the APC the Muslim party of the north, which happened in both 2011 and 2015 in the election contests between Jonathan and Buhari. Meanwhile, the Niger Delta militias and Boko Haram have both threatened to divide the country, and Igbo separatists have begun to organize demonstrations calling for the restoration of an independent Biafra in the southeast, a claim that previously had led to the 1967–1970 civil war.

Democratic development also requires further decentralization of power structures in Nigeria. The struggle on the part of the National Assembly and the state governors to wrest power from the presidency has advanced this process, as have the growing competence and role of the judiciary. A larger, diversified private sector could also reduce the power of the presidency over time by diminishing government control over important sectors of the economy. A more decentralized system allows local problems to be solved within communities rather than involving national institutions and the accompanying interethnic competition. Decentralization also lowers the stakes for holding national offices, thereby reducing destructive pressures on political competition and political office. The devolution of power and resources to smaller units, closer to their constituents, can substantially enhance the accountability of leaders and the transparency of government operations.

Civil society groups are the final link in democratic consolidation in Nigeria. These groups are critical players in connecting the Nigerian state to the Nigerian people. They aggregate and articulate popular interests into the policy realm, and they advocate on behalf of their members. If the political parties are to reflect anything more than elite interests and clientelist rule, they must reach out and build alliances with the institutions of civil society. For opposition parties to become a viable movement capable of checking the power of ruling parties, they will have to build alliances with diverse elements of civil society in order to mobilize large portions of the population, particularly labor unions.

Foreign pressure also plays an important role in maintaining the quest for democracy and sustainable development. In recent years, major external forces have been more forthright in supporting civil society and democratization in Nigeria. The United States, Britain, and some member-states of the European Union quite visibly exerted pressure on Babangida and Abacha to give up power and applied modest sanctions in support of true democracy. These same governments pressed Nigerian leaders to smooth the transition of power after Yar'Adua's incapacitation and then pressed Jonathan to respect the will of the voters in 2015. Nevertheless, the Western commitment to development and democracy in Africa has been limited by the industrial powers' petroleum interests, which blunted the impact of such pressure on Nigeria, and is exacerbated by growing competition from China for energy resources.

Much of the initiative for Africa's growth, therefore, needs to emerge from within. In Nigeria, such initiatives will depend on substantial changes in the way that Nigerians do business. It will be necessary to develop a more sophisticated and far less corrupt form of capitalism and the promotion of an entrepreneurial middle class within Nigeria who will see their interests tied to the principles of democratic politics and economic initiative. Occupy Nigeria and the 2015 election offer hope in this regard, signifying a rising progressive, multiethnic movement of professionals seeking to change the corrupt system fundamentally.

Nigerian politics has been characterized by turmoil and periodic crises ever since the British relinquished colonial power. Nearly sixty years later, the country is still trying to piece together a fragile democracy, and yet key signs of economic growth and political reform are at last on the horizon. Despite these positive trends, the nation continues to wrestle with overdependence of its economy on oil, enfeebled infrastructure and institutions, heightened sociopolitical tensions, an irresponsible elite, and an expanding mass culture of despondency and rage. Only responsible government combined with sustained civil society action can reverse this decline and restore the nation to what former president Obasanjo called "the path to greatness."

Is Demography Destiny?

Much of this momentous choice between development or collapse may well be decided by Nigeria's youth. With women averaging over five births each and yet a life expectancy of only 53 years, Nigeria's population is widely skewed toward the younger age groups, such that nearly 65 percent of Nigerians are under the age of 25 and over half are under the age of 19. At current growth rates, Nigeria's population is predicted to top 400 million by 2050, making it the fourth-largest nation in the world, with approximately 280 million or more youths under age 30.

The vast majority of these youths are extremely poor, with more than half trying to eke out a living on less than a dollar per day. At least a fifth of them are officially unemployed, but the real unemployment statistics are much worse, especially in the northern half of the country. A few are, however, wired into the global economy through cellular and Internet technology, and their numbers are growing alongside their political sophistication and organizing skills, which they demonstrated during Occupy Nigeria and the 2015 election.

Yet the fact that Nigeria is a youth-majority country underlines another massive political divide: the domination of its elders. Septuagenarian politicians still play powerful roles in both the PDP and APC, and wealthy men in their 50s and 60s dominate the presidency, National Assembly, and governorships. On the other hand, Boko Haram, the Niger Delta militias, and other antistate actors are dominated by the young. Which way will Nigeria's younger faces turn? Much will depend upon the ability of the political parties to engage youth in their ranks and to produce serious policies that foster broad-based development offering opportunity and hope to the massive younger generation that is now rising.

Nigerian Politics in Comparative Perspective

The study of Nigeria has important implications for the study of African politics and, more broadly, of comparative politics. The Nigerian case embodies a number of key themes and issues that can be generalized. We can learn much about how democratic regimes are established and consolidated by understanding Nigeria's pitfalls and travails. Analysis of the historical dynamics of Nigeria's ethnic conflict helps to identify institutional mechanisms that may be effective in reducing such conflict in other states. We can also learn much about the necessary and sufficient conditions for economic development, and the particular liabilities of oil-dependent states.

The future of democracy, political stability, and economic renewal in other parts of Africa, and certainly in West Africa, will be greatly influenced (for good or ill) by unfolding events in Nigeria, the giant of the continent. Beyond the obvious demonstration effects, the economy of the West African subregion could be buoyed by substantial growth in the Nigerian economy. In addition, President Obasanjo conducted active public diplomacy across Africa, seeking to resolve major conflicts, promote democracy, and improve trade. His successors have been less active but still have taken generally strong stances to support democracy and combat terror groups across the region.

Nigeria provides important insights into the political economy of underdevelopment. At independence in 1960, Nigeria was stronger economically than its Southeast Asian counterparts, Indonesia and Malaysia. Independent Nigeria appeared poised for growth, with a wealth of natural resources, a large population, and the presence of highly entrepreneurial groups in many regions of the country. Today, Nigeria is among the poorest countries in the world in terms of human development indicators, while many of its Asian counterparts have joined the ranks of the wealthy countries. One critical lesson that Nigeria teaches is that a rich endowment of resources is not enough to ensure economic development. In fact, it may encourage rent-seeking behavior that undermines more productive activities.[14] Sound political and institutional development must come first.

Other variables are critically important—notably, democratic stability and a capable **developmental state**. A developmentalist ethic, as well as an institutional structure to enforce it, can set limits on corrupt behavior and constrain the pursuit of short-term personal gain at the expense of national economic growth. Institutions vital to the pursuit of these objectives include a professional civil service, an independent judiciary, and a free press. Nigeria has had each of these, but they were gradually

developmental state

A nation-state in which the government carries out policies that effectively promote national economic growth.

undermined and corrupted under military rule. The public "ethic" that has come to dominate Nigerian political economy has been prebendalism. Where corruption is unchecked, economic development suffers accordingly.

Nigeria also demonstrates that sustained development requires sound economic policy. Without export diversification, commodity-exporting countries are buffeted by the price fluctuations of one or two main products. Nigeria, by contrast, has substituted one form of commodity dependence for another, and it has allowed its petroleum industry to overwhelm all other sectors of the economy, and only recently has the nonoil sector begun to revive. Nigeria even became a net importer of products (e.g., palm oil and palm nuts) for which it was once a leading world producer. The country is in the absurd position of being unable to feed its people, despite its rich agricultural lands.

Many African countries have experienced full or partial transitions toward democracy. But decades of authoritarian, single-party, and military rule in Africa left a dismal record of political repression, human rights abuses, inequality, deteriorating governance, and failed economies. A handful of elites acquired large fortunes through wanton corruption. The exercise of postcolonial authoritarian rule in Africa has contributed to economic stagnation and decline. The difficulties of such countries as Cameroon, Togo, and Zimbabwe in achieving political transitions reflects, in large part, the ruling elites' unwillingness to cede control of the political instruments that made possible their self-enrichment.

Nigeria's history exemplifies the harsh reality of unaccountable, authoritarian governance. Nigerians endured six military regimes, countless attempted coups, and a bloody civil war that claimed more than a million lives. They have also seen a once-prospering economy reduced to a near shambles and then partially rebuilt. Today, democracy has become a greater imperative because only such a system provides the mechanisms to limit abuses of power and render governments accountable.

Nigeria also presents an important case in which to study the dangers of communal competition in a society with deep cultural divisions. How can multiethnic countries manage diversity? What institutional mechanisms can be employed to avert collective identity–based tragedies such as the 1967–1970 civil war or the conflicts that have brought great suffering to Rwanda and Syria? This chapter has suggested institutional reforms such as multiethnic political parties, decentralization, and a strengthened federal system that can contribute to reducing tensions and minimizing conflict.

Insights from the Nigerian experience may explain why some federations persist, while identifying factors that can undermine them. Nigeria's complex social map, as well as its varied attempts to create a nation out of its highly diverse population, enhance our understanding of the politics of cultural pluralism and the difficulties of accommodating sectional interests under conditions of political and economic insecurity. Federal character and ethnic rotation in Nigeria have become important, but controversial tools for ethnic conflict management and the creation of state and local governments have given people in different regions a sense of being stakeholders in the entity called Nigeria.

Where Do You Stand?

Are you convinced that a viable political opposition supported by civil society could put Nigeria on the path to development, or do you think that Boko Haram, the Niger Delta militias, and prebendal Big Man politics will eventually push Nigeria to collapse?

Should the United States and other countries be pushing for more and deeper democracy in Africa, or does the example of Nigeria suggest that it is too difficult?

Chapter Summary

Nigeria is a creation of British colonialism, which brought many previously independent nations under one political roof and forced them to live together. Thus, when the British left in 1960, Nigerians continued to struggle with the National Question: who will govern, and how can Nigeria be governed in a manner that makes its many ethnic groups wish to belong to a single entity? Nigerians have struggled to answer this question in two ways: through democracy and through authoritarianism. At independence, Nigeria began as a three-state federation under a parliamentary system dominated by ethnic-based parties reflecting the three largest ethnic groups: Hausa, Yoruba, and Igbo. As each group sought to control the system, it deadlocked, prompting two military coups that escalated into civil war from 1967 to 1970.

After the war, the military broke the federation into more states—eventually, thirty-six of them—which gave more voice to ethnic minorities and broke the unitary nature of political leadership of the Hausa, Yoruba, and Igbo. Military rule, however, grew increasingly corrupt and predatory, especially after the 1970s oil boom brought in massive revenues to the government. Coups in the 1980s and 1990s ended two more experiments with democracy and ushered in military governments under two generals, Babangida and Abacha, which solidified prebendelism—a form of corrupt ethnic clientelism—as the predominant political culture in Nigeria.

The military at last exited power in 1999, handing power to the People's Democratic Party (PDP), a diverse coalition of prebendel "Big Men" and their networks, who came to dominate the politics of the Fourth Republic for sixteen years and swept subsequent elections in 2003, 2007, and 2011. PDP governance was characterized by massive corruption and election rigging in 1999, 2003, and especially 2007. President Jonathan, however, did install a reformist election chief who delivered more credible elections in 2011 and 2015, the latter resulting

in a historic transfer of power to the opposition All Progressives Congress (APC).

In addition, skyrocketing oil prices from 2003 to 2014 fueled an average GDP growth rate of 6 percent, spurring modest growth in the small middle class, who took advantage of the cell phone revolution and vibrant civil society groups to push for more progressive politics in Occupy Nigeria in 2012 and the 2015 elections. The PDP era also saw other institutions begin to exercise more power and begin to check and balance the overly dominant presidency: the Supreme Court and elements of the judiciary demonstrated increased independence, the National Assembly showed occasional signs of leadership, and many state governors charted their own courses.

Despite these gains, the PDP never implemented a sustained, comprehensive development strategy that affected the nation's poor majority—the 80 to 90 percent of Nigerians living on less than two dollars per day. Outrage over this poverty and the massive corruption of the ruling elites spurred growing religious and ethnic conflicts nationwide, and the rise of insurgencies in the Niger Delta and the northeast under Boko Haram. Muhammadu Buhari and the opposition APC rode this wave of public frustration to power in the 2015 elections, but President Buhari's slow pace in policy-making and health problems have left little of his reform agenda implemented by 2017.

To reach democratic consolidation and answer Nigeria's National Question, the country needs to develop viable political opposition, supported by clean elections and anticorruption efforts, and a sustained, broad-based development policy from government that lifts a majority of Nigerians out of poverty. If Nigeria cannot reverse the corrupt, prebendal status quo, however, then the specter will remain of the military or ethnic and religious extremists plunging Nigeria into another cycle of coups, decline, and possibly collapse.

Key Terms

accountability
acephalous societies
authoritarian
autocracy
balance of payments
clientelism
developmental state
Economic Community of West
   African States (ECOWAS)

indirect rule
international financial institutions (IFIs)
jihad
legitimacy
oligarchy
prebendalism
rents
resource curse

shari'a
structural adjustment program
   (SAP)
unfinished state
warrant chiefs

Suggested Readings

Achebe, Chinua. *There Was a Country: A Memoir.* New York: Penguin Books, 2015.

Achebe, Chinua. *Things Fall Apart.* New York: W. W. Norton, 2009 (first edition, 1958).

Falola, Toyin. *Violence in Nigeria: The Crisis of Religious Politics and Secular Ideologies.* Rochester, NY: University of Rochester Press, 1999.

Joseph, Richard A. *Democracy and Prebendal Politics in Nigeria: The Rise and Fall of the Second Republic.* Cambridge, UK: Cambridge University Press, 1987.

Kew, Darren. *Civil Society, Conflict Resolution, and Democracy in Nigeria.* Syracuse, NY: Syracuse University Press, 2016.

Kew, Darren. "Nigerian elections and the neopatrimonial paradox: In search of the social contract," *Journal of Contemporary African Studies* 28, no. 4 (2010): 499–521.

Lewis, Peter M. "Nigeria: Cycles of Crisis, Sources of Resilience," in Peter Lewis and John W. Harbeson, eds., *Coping with Crisis in African States,* Boulder, CO: Lynne Rienner Publishers, 2016.

Kew, Darren, and Peter M. Lewis. "Nigeria's Hopeful Election," *Journal of Democracy,* vol. 26, no. 3 (2015): 94–109.

Lewis, Peter M. "Endgame in Nigeria? The Politics of a Failed Democratic Transition." *African Affairs,* vol. 93 (1994): 323–340.

Obadare, Ebenezer. "Perspective: A Nigerian President's Disappointing Return" *Current History,* no. 116 (2017): 194–197.

Suggested Websites

BBC News about Nigeria
http://www.bbc.com/news/topics/3d5d5e30 -dd50-4041-96d5-c970b20005b9/nigeria

Embassy of the Federal Republic of Nigeria in the United States
http://www.nigeriaembassyusa.org/

Freedom House Reports on Nigeria
https://freedomhouse.org/report/freedom -world/2017/nigeria

Gamji: A collection of news stories from Nigerian newspapers, as well as opinion pieces and other news links
www.gamji.com

The Guardian, Nigeria's leading daily newspaper
www.ngrguardiannews.com

13 The Russian Federation

Joan DeBardeleben

Official Name: Russian Federation (Rossiiskaia Federatsiia)

Location: Eastern Europe/Northern Asia

Capital City: Moscow

Population (2016): 144.2 million (without Crimea)

Size: 17,098,242 sq. km. (excluding Crimea); approximately 1.8 times the size of the United States

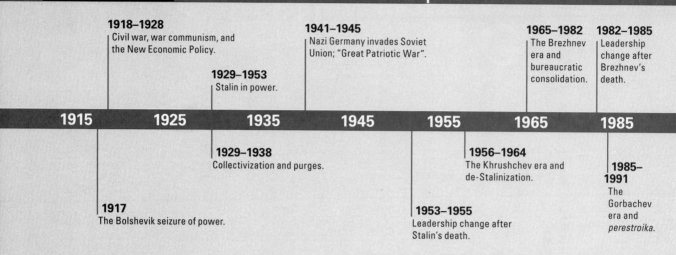

1918–1928
Civil war, war communism, and the New Economic Policy.

1941–1945
Nazi Germany invades Soviet Union; "Great Patriotic War".

1965–1982
The Brezhnev era and bureaucratic consolidation.

1982–1985
Leadership change after Brezhnev's death.

1929–1953
Stalin in power.

| 1915 | 1925 | 1935 | 1945 | 1955 | 1965 | 1985 |

1929–1938
Collectivization and purges.

1956–1964
The Khrushchev era and de-Stalinization.

1985–1991
The Gorbachev era and *perestroika*.

1917
The Bolshevik seizure of power.

1953–1955
Leadership change after Stalin's death.

SECTION

1

THE MAKING OF THE MODERN RUSSIAN STATE

Focus Questions

- What are the most important critical junctures in recent Russian history? In what ways was each juncture a reaction to a recurring problem in Russian history?

- What were Russia's principal challenges in the 1990s and how have they changed since the year 2000?

Politics in Action

A court decision in February 2017, in the city of Kirov, Russia, made international headlines because of its potential impact on the Russian presidential election scheduled for March 2018. In that decision, 40-year-old Alexei Navalny, an outspoken critic of Russian president Vladimir Putin and his structure of power, was convicted of having defrauded a state company four years earlier. The decision, upheld by a higher court in May 2017, could block Navalny's intended run for the presidency because Russian law excludes those with criminal convictions.

Navalny gained visibility first as an anticorruption critic, whose internet blogs became well-known in the context of mass demonstrations that occurred in Russian cities during the 2011–2012 election cycle; his depiction of the dominant United Russia party as a "party of crooks and thieves" became an opposition rallying call. He was then arrested and convicted in 2013 on the same charges as in the 2017 case and sentenced to five years in prison. Surprisingly, Navalny was released pending an appeal and permitted to stand on the ballot in the Moscow mayoral race in October 2013, where he won 27 percent of the vote. Navalny appealed the 2013 conviction to the European Court of Human Rights, which concluded that his right to a fair trial had been violated. The retrial in Kirov, in 2017, was in response to that judgment, but the outcome was similar. Navalny vowed to fight

1991
Collapse of the USSR and establishment of the Russian Federation as an independent state.

1998
Financial crisis and devaluation of the ruble.

2000–2008
Putin presidency, with recentralization of state power.

2007–2008
Parliamentary and presidential elections establishing dominance of United Russia and smooth transition to the presidency of Dmitry Medvedev.

September 2016
State Duma elections, return clear majority for United Russia.

1990   **1995**   **2000**   **2005**   **2010**   **2015**

1993
Adoption of the new Russian constitution by referendum; first (multiparty) parliamentary elections in the Russian Federation (December).

2004
Hostage-taking in Beslan, southern Russia; Putin announces new centralizing measures.

March 2014–
Russia takes control of the Ukrainian region of Crimea and annexes it to Russia.

March 2012–
Vladimir Putin elected as president, after a four-year break.

1991–1999
Yeltsin presidency, with market and democratic reforms.

December 2011–March 2012
State Duma elections and Presidential elections, and protest demonstrations.

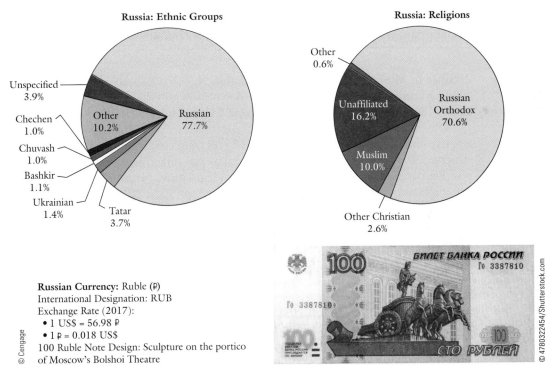

Russia: Ethnic Groups

- Russian 77.7%
- Other 10.2%
- Unspecified 3.9%
- Chechen 1.0%
- Chuvash 1.0%
- Bashkir 1.1%
- Ukrainian 1.4%
- Tatar 3.7%

Russia: Religions

- Russian Orthodox 70.6%
- Unaffiliated 16.2%
- Muslim 10.0%
- Other Christian 2.6%
- Other 0.6%

Russian Currency: Ruble (₽)
International Designation: RUB
Exchange Rate (2017):
- 1 US$ = 56.98 ₽
- 1 ₽ = 0.018 US$
100 Ruble Note Design: Sculpture on the portico of Moscow's Bolshoi Theatre

FIGURE 13.1 The Russian Nation at a Glance

the decision and stated his intention of standing in the presidential vote the next year. Shortly thereafter, in March 2017, Navalny's Anti-Corruption Foundation demanded an inquiry into alleged corruption involving Russian prime minister Dmitry Medvedev, triggering public demonstrations across the country. Navalny himself was

Table 13.1	Political Organization
Political system	Constitutionally a semi-presidential republic.
Regime history	Re-formed as an independent state with the collapse of communist rule in December 1991; current constitution since December 1993.
Administrative structure	Constitutionally a federal system, with eighty-three subnational governments, plus two regions annexed from neighboring Ukraine in 2014 that are not recognized by most Western countries as being part of Russia; politically centralized.
Executive	Dual executive (president and prime minister). Direct election of president; prime minister appointed by the president with the approval of the lower house of the parliament (State Duma).
Legislature	Bicameral. Upper house (Federation Council) appointed by heads of regional executive and representative organs. Lower house (*State Duma*) chosen by direct election, with mixed electoral system involving single-member districts and proportional representation for a total of 450 deputies. Powers include proposal and approval of legislation, approval of presidential appointees.
Judiciary	Independent constitutional court with nineteen justices, nominated by the president and approved by the Federation Council, holding 12-year terms with possible renewal.
Party system	Dominant establishment party (United Russia) within a multiparty system.

detained in Moscow for participation in an unauthorized "walk" in central Moscow, after authorities refused to approve the downtown rally location; he was arrested again in June 2017 for his role in organizing an unauthorized rally.

Observers interpreted the authorities' continued harassment of Navalny as a preemptive move to block any real opposition forces from challenging the current power structure. (See Table 13.1.) Notably, Navalny is not linked to any of the 'loyal' opposition parties that hold seats in the Russian legislature. Navalny's ability to mobilize public support against alleged leadership corruption in 2017 suggested that the extra-parliamentary opposition might be hard to silence.

Geographic Setting

After the Soviet Union broke up in 1991, fifteen newly independent states emerged on its territory. This section focuses on the Russian Federation, in area the largest country in the world, spanning eleven time zones. Russian official sources gave a population figure of 146.5 million for 2016, due to the inclusion of the recently annexed territory of Crimea. Without Crimea, Russia's population would be 144.2 million.[1] (See Figure 13.1.)

Russia underwent rapid industrialization and urbanization under Soviet rule. Only 18 percent of Russians lived in urban areas in 1917, at the time of the Russian Revolution; this has now increased to 74 percent. Less than 8 percent of Russia's land is arable, while 45 percent is forested. Russia is rich in natural resources, concentrated in western Siberia and northern Russia. These include minerals (even gold and diamonds), timber, oil, and natural gas, which now form the basis of Russia's economic wealth.

Before the communists took power in 1917, Russia's czarist empire extended east to the Pacific, south to the Caucasus Mountains and the Muslim areas of Central Asia, north to the Arctic Circle, and west into present-day Ukraine, eastern Poland, and the

Baltic states. In the Soviet Union, the Russian Republic formed the core of a multiethnic state. Russia's ethnic diversity and geographic scope have made it a hard country to govern. Currently, Russia faces pockets of instability on several of its borders, most notably in eastern Ukraine (since early 2014), in Tajikistan and Afghanistan in Central Asia, and in Georgia and Azerbaijan in the south. Besides Ukraine, Russia's western neighbors include Belarus, and several member states of the European Union (EU), namely Finland, Estonia, Latvia, Lithuania, and Poland. Located between Europe, the Islamic world, and Asia, Russia's regional sphere of influence is now disputed.

Critical Junctures

The Decline of the Russian Tsarist State and the Founding of the Soviet Union

Until 1917, an autocratic system headed by the czar ruled Russia. Russia had a **patrimonial state** where the majority of the peasant population was tied to the nobles, the state, or the church (through serfdom). The serfs were emancipated in 1861 as a part of the czar's effort to modernize Russia and to make it militarily competitive with the West.

The key impetus for industrialization came from the state and from foreign capital. Despite some reforms, workers became increasingly discontented, as did liberal intellectuals, students, and, later, peasants, in the face of Russia's defeat in the Russo-Japanese war and continued czarist repression. Revolution broke out in 1905. The regime maintained control through repression and economic reform until March 1917, during the height of World War I, when revolution deposed the czar and installed a moderate provisional government. In November, the Bolsheviks, led by Vladimir Lenin, overthrew that government.

patrimonial state

A system of governance in which the ruler treats the state as personal property (patrimony).

The Bolshevik Revolution and the Establishment of Soviet Power (1917–1929)

The Bolsheviks, which, in 1918, became the Russian Communist Party (Bolsheviks), were Marxists who believed their revolution reflected the political interests of the proletariat (working class). Most revolutionary leaders, however, were not workers, but came from a more educated and privileged stratum, the intelligentsia. Their slogan, "Land, Peace, and Bread," appealed to both the working class and the discontented peasantry—over 80 percent of Russia's population.

The Bolshevik strategy was based on two key ideas: democratic centralism and vanguardism. **Democratic centralism** mandated a hierarchical party structure in which leaders were, at least formally, elected from below, but strict discipline was required in implementing party decisions once they were made. The centralizing elements of democratic centralism took precedence over the democratic elements, as the party tried to insulate itself from informers of the czarist forces and later from real and imagined threats to the new regime. The concept of a **vanguard party** governed the Bolsheviks' relations with broader social forces. Party leaders claimed to understand the interests of working people better than the people did themselves. Over time, this philosophy was used to justify virtually all actions of the party and the state it dominated.

In 1922, the Bolsheviks formed the Union of Soviet Socialist Republics (USSR), which was the formal name of the Soviet Union; they were the first communist party to take state power. Prior to this, the Bolsheviks had faced an extended civil war (1918–1921), when they introduced war communism, which involved state control of key economic sectors and forcible requisitioning of grain from the peasants.

democratic centralism

A system of political organization developed by Vladimir Lenin and practiced, with modifications, by most communist party-states. Its principles include a hierarchical party structure.

vanguard party

A political party that claims to operate in the "true" interests of the group or class that it purports to represent, even if this understanding doesn't correspond to the expressed interests of the group itself.

The *Cheka*, the security arm of the regime, was strengthened, and restrictions were placed on other political groups. By 1921, the leadership had recognized the political costs of war communism. In an effort to accommodate the peasantry, the New Economic Policy (NEP) was introduced in 1921 and lasted until 1928. Under NEP, state control over the economy was loosened so that private enterprise and trade were revived. The state, however, retained control of large-scale industry.

Gradually, throughout the 1920s, the authoritarian strains of Bolshevik thinking eclipsed the democratic elements. Lacking a democratic tradition and bolstered by the vanguard ideology of the party, the Bolshevik leaders were plagued by internal struggles following Lenin's death in 1924. These conflicts culminated in the rise of Joseph Stalin and the demotion or exile of other prominent figures such as Leon Trotsky and Nikolai Bukharin. By 1929, all open opposition, even within the party itself, had been silenced.

The Bolshevik revolution also initiated a period of international isolation. Western countries were hardly pleased with the revolutionary developments, which led to expropriation of foreign holdings, and which represented the first successful challenge to the international capitalist order. Some of Russia's former Western allies from World War I sent material aid and troops to oppose the new Bolshevik government during the civil war of 1917 to 1922.

The Stalin Revolution (1929–1953)

From 1929 until his death in 1953, Joseph Stalin consolidated his power as Soviet leader. He brought changes to every aspect of Soviet life. The state became the engine for rapid economic development, with state ownership of virtually all economic assets. By 1935, over 90 percent of agricultural land had been taken from the peasants and made into state or collective farms. Collectivization was rationalized as a means of preventing the emergence of a new capitalist class in the countryside. It actually targeted the peasantry as a whole, leading to widespread famine and the death of millions. Rapid industrialization favored heavy industries, and consumer goods were neglected. Economic control operated through a complex but inefficient system of central economic planning, in which the state planning committee (Gosplan) set production targets for every enterprise in the country. People were uprooted from their traditional lives in the countryside and catapulted into the rhythm of urban industrial life. Media censorship and state control of the arts strangled creativity as well as political opposition. The party-state became the authoritative source of truth; anyone deviating from the authorized interpretation could be charged with treason.

Gradually, the communist party became subject to the personal whims of Stalin and his secret police. Overall, an estimated 5 percent of the Soviet population was arrested at one point or another under the Stalinist system, usually for no apparent cause. Forms of resistance were evasive rather than active. For example, some peasants killed livestock to avoid giving it over to collective farms.

Isolation from the outside world was a key tool of the Stalinist system of power. But the policy had costs. While it shielded Soviet society from the Great Depression of the 1930s, the Soviet economy, protected from foreign competition, also failed to keep up with the rapid economic and technological transformation in the West.

In 1941, Nazi Germany invaded the Soviet Union, and Stalin joined the Allied powers. Casualties in the war were staggering, about 27 million people, including 19 million civilians. War sacrifices and heroism have remained powerful symbols of pride and unity for Russians up to the present day. After the war, the other Allied powers allowed the Soviet Union to absorb new territories into the USSR itself (these became the Soviet republics of Latvia, Lithuania, Estonia, Moldavia, and

collectivization

A process undertaken in the Soviet Union under Stalin from 1929 into the early 1930s, and in China under Mao in the 1950s, by which agricultural land was removed from private ownership and organized into large state and collective farms.

portions of western Ukraine). The Allies also implicitly granted the USSR free rein to shape the postwar governments and economies in East Germany, Poland, Hungary, Czechoslovakia, Yugoslavia, Bulgaria, and Romania. Western offers to include parts of the region in the Marshall Plan were rejected under pressure from the USSR. Local communist parties gained control in each country. Only in Yugoslavia were indigenous Communist forces sufficiently strong to hold power largely on their own and thus later to assert their independence from Moscow.

The USSR emerged as a global superpower as the Soviet sphere of influence encompassed large parts of Central and Eastern Europe. In 1947, the U.S. president Harry Truman proclaimed a policy to contain further Soviet expansion (later known as the Truman Doctrine). In 1949, the North Atlantic Treaty Organization (NATO) was formed involving several West European countries, the United States, and Canada, to protect against potential Soviet aggression. In 1955, the Soviet Union initiated the Warsaw Pact in response. These events marked the beginning of the Cold War, characterized by tension and military competition between the two superpowers, leading to an escalating arms race that was particularly costly to the Soviet Union.

The Soviet Union isolated its satellite countries in Central and Eastern Europe from the West and tightened their economic and political integration with the USSR. Some countries within the Soviet bloc, however, had strong historic links to Western Europe (especially Czechoslovakia, Poland, and Hungary). Over time, these countries served not only as geographic buffers to direct Western contacts but also as conduits for Western influence.

Attempts at De-Stalinization (1953–1985)

Even the Soviet elite realized that Stalin's terror could be sustained only at great cost. The terror destroyed initiative and participation, and the unpredictability of Stalinist rule inhibited the rational formulation of policy. From Stalin's death in 1953 until the mid-1980s, Soviet politics became more regularized and stable. Terror abated, but political controls remained in place, and efforts to isolate Soviet citizens from foreign influences continued.

In 1956, Nikita Khrushchev, the new party leader, embarked on a bold policy of de-Stalinization, rejecting terror as an instrument of political control. The secret police (KGB) was subordinated to the authority of the Communist Party of the Soviet Union (CPSU), which became the name of the ruling party in 1952, and party meetings resumed on a regular basis. However, internal party structures remained highly centralized, and elections were uncontested. Khrushchev's successor, Leonid Brezhnev (party head 1964–1982) partially reversed Khrushchev's de-Stalinization efforts. Controls were tightened again in the cultural sphere. Individuals who expressed dissenting views through underground publishing or publication abroad were harassed, arrested, or exiled. However, unlike in the Stalinist period, the political repression was predictable. People generally knew when they were transgressing permitted limits of criticism.

From the late 1970s onward, an aging political leadership was increasingly ineffective at addressing mounting problems. Economic growth rates fell, living standards improved only minimally, and opportunities for upward career mobility declined. To maintain the Soviet Union's superpower status, resources were diverted to the military sector, gutting the consumer and agricultural spheres. High pollution levels and alcoholism contributed to health problems. At the same time, liberalization in some Eastern European states and the telecommunications revolution made it increasingly difficult to shield the Soviet population from exposure to Western lifestyles and ideas. Among a certain critical portion of the population, aspirations were rising just as the capacity of the system to fulfill them was declining.

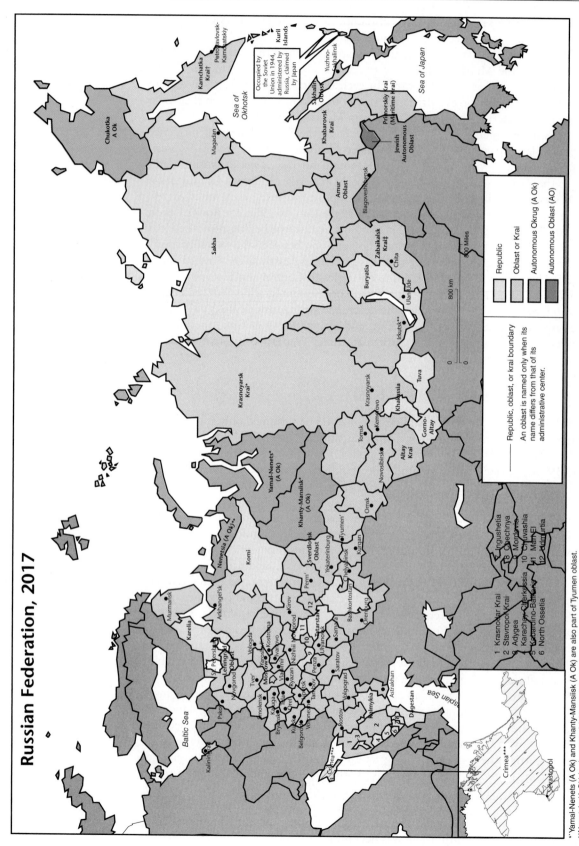

Russian Federation, 2017

Legend:
- Republic
- Oblast or Krai
- Autonomous Okrug (A Ok)
- Autonomous Oblast (AO)

——— Republic, oblast, or krai boundary

An oblast is named only when its name differs from that of its administrative center.

800 Miles

800 km

Note: Hatching indicates that these regions are contested, as their inclusion in Russia is not recognized by large parts of the international community.

1 Krasnodar Krai
2 Stavropol Krai
3 Adygea
4 Karachay-Cherkessia
5 Kabardino-Balkaria
6 North Ossetia
7 Ingushetia
8 Chechnya
9 Mordovia
10 Chuvashia
11 MariEl
12 Udmurtia

*Yamal-Nenets (A Ok) and Khanty-Mansiisk (A Ok) are also part of Tyumen oblast.
**Nenetsia (A Ok) is also part of Arkhangel'sk oblast.
****Note: Hatching indicates that these regions are contested, as their inclusion in Russia is not recognized by large parts of the international community.

© Cengage

Perestroika and Glasnost (1985–1991)

Mikhail Gorbachev took office as the leader of the CPSU in March 1985. He endorsed a reform program that centered around four important concepts intended to spur economic growth and bring political renewal. These were *perestroika* (economic restructuring), *glasnost* (openness), *demokratizatsiia* (a type of limited democratization), and "New Thinking" in foreign policy. Gorbachev's reform program was designed to adapt the communist system to new conditions rather than to usher in its demise.

The most divisive issues were economic policy and demands for republic autonomy. Only about half of the Soviet population was ethnically Russian in 1989. Once Gorbachev opened the door to dissenting views, demands for national autonomy arose in some of the USSR's fifteen union republics. This occurred first in the three Baltic republics (Latvia, Lithuania, and Estonia), then in Ukraine, Georgia, Armenia, and Moldova, and finally in the Russian Republic itself. Gorbachev's efforts failed to bring consensus on a new **federal system** that could hold the country together.

Gorbachev's economic policies failed as well. Half-measures sent contradictory messages to enterprise directors, producing a drop in output and undermining established patterns that had kept the Soviet economy functioning, although inefficiently. To protect themselves, regions and union republics began to restrict exports to other regions, despite planning mandates. In "the war of laws," regional officials openly defied central directives.

Just as his domestic support was plummeting, Gorbachev was awarded the Nobel Peace Prize, in 1991. Under his New Thinking, the military buildup in the USSR was halted, important arms control agreements were ratified, and many controls on international contacts were lifted. In 1989, Gorbachev refused to prop up unpopular communist governments in Hungary, Poland, the German Democratic Republic (East Germany), and Czechoslovakia; pressure from below pushed the communist parties out of power. To Gorbachev's dismay, the liberation of these countries fed the process of disintegration of the Soviet Union itself.

Collapse of the USSR and the Emergence of the Russian Federation (1991 to the Present)

In 1985, Mikhail Gorbachev drafted Boris Yeltsin into the leadership team as a nonvoting member of the USSR's top party organ, the Politburo. Ironically, Yeltsin later played a key role in the final demise of the Soviet Union. In June 1991, a popular election confirmed Yeltsin as president of the Russian Republic of the USSR (a post he had held since May of the previous year). In August, a coalition of conservative figures attempted a coup d'état to halt Gorbachev's program to reform the Soviet system. While Gorbachev was held captive at his summer house (*dacha*), Boris Yeltsin climbed atop a tank loyal to the reform leadership and rallied opposition to the attempted coup. In December 1991, Yeltsin and the leaders of Ukrainian and Belorussian Republics declared the end of the Soviet Union, proposing to replace it by a loosely structured entity, the Commonwealth of Independent States.

As leader of the newly independent Russian Federation, Yeltsin took a more radical approach to reform than Gorbachev had done. He quickly proclaimed his commitment to Western-style democracy and market economic reform. However, that program was controversial and proved hard to implement. The executive and legislative branches of the government also failed to reach consensus on the nature of a new Russian constitution; the result was a bloody showdown in October 1993, after Yeltsin disbanded what he considered to be an obstructive parliament and laid siege

glasnost

Gorbachev's policy of "openness," which involved an easing of controls on the media, arts, and public discussion.

federal system

A political structure in which subnational units have significant independent powers; the powers of each level are usually specified in the federal constitution to its premises, the Russian White House. The president mandated new parliamentary elections and a referendum on a new constitution, which passed by a narrow margin in December 1993.

Yeltsin's radical economic reforms confronted Russians with an increasingly uncertain future marked by declining real wages, high inflation, and rising crime. Yeltsin's initial popularity was also marred by an extended military conflict to prevent Chechnya, a southern republic of Russia, from seceding from the country. Concern that separatism could spread to other regions was an important motivation for the military intervention. Despite these problems, with the help of an active public relations effort, Yeltsin was reelected president in 1996, winning 54 percent of the vote against the candidate of the Communist Party of the Russian Federation, Gennady Zyuganov. During his second term in office, Yeltsin was plagued by poor health and continuing failed policies. In 1998, a major financial crisis added to his problems.

In 1999, Yeltsin appointed Vladimir Putin prime minister and when Yeltsin resigned as president in December 1999, Putin became acting president. In presidential elections that followed in March 2000, Putin won a resounding victory. Putin benefited from auspicious conditions. In 1999, the economy began a period of sustained economic growth that lasted until the 2008–2009 global financial crisis. High international gas and oil prices fed tax dollars into the state's coffers.

Just as economic growth revived, worries about security increased. Instability associated with the Chechnya problem underlay a string of terrorist attacks, beginning in 1999. One particularly tragic event involved a hostage-taking on the first day of school (September 1, 2004) in the town of Beslan in southern Russia, which ended in tragedy, with more than 300 hostages killed—the majority children. Meanwhile, in March 2003, Russian authorities tried to set Chechnya on a track of normalization, holding a referendum that would confirm Chechnya's status within the Russian Federation. However, intermittent violence continued.

Despite these problems, Putin has recorded consistently high levels of popular support throughout his tenure. His position as president was only briefly interrupted by the 4-year term of Dmitry Medvedev (2008–2012), as the Russian constitution

Opposition supporters stand in front of the stage during the "March of Millions" protest rally in Moscow, September 15, 2012.

includes a limit of two consecutive presidential terms. However, during Medvedev's presidency, Putin served as prime minister and remained the de facto leader of the government.

Elections in March 2012 reinstated Putin as president, and legislative elections in 2011 and 2016 reinforced the position of the United Russia party. Charges of election fraud and unfair electoral conditions led to mass protests in 2011–2012 in major Russian cities throughout the country, but Russia's annexation of the Ukrainian region of Crimea in 2014 reinforced popular support for Putin's leadership, as he was seen by many Russians to be effectively representing Russia's international interests.

Beginning in 2004, and continuing upon his return to office in 2012, Putin's leadership produced a drift to soft authoritarianism, involving increased political centralization, restrictions on the political opposition, and reinforcement of the dominance of the United Russia party. However, from 2014, Russia also saw an economic downturn, spurred by a fall in global gas and oil prices and by Western economic sanctions put in place in response to the Crimean annexation. In the lead-up to the Russian presidential election scheduled for March 2018, observers wondered whether economic problems might begin to undermine Putin's popular support.

soft authoritarianism

A system of political control in which a combination of formal and informal mechanisms ensure the dominance of a ruling group or dominant party, despite the existence of some forms of political competition and expressions of political opposition.

The Four Themes and Russia

Russia in a Globalized World of States

Following the collapse of the USSR in 1991, international support for the new reform-oriented government in Russia surged, with the proliferation of aid programs and international financial credits. However, in the 1990s, Russia's status as a world power waned, and the expansion of Western organizations (NATO, EU) to Russia's western border undermined its sphere of influence in Central and Eastern Europe. However, Russia's economic recovery following 1998, the rise of energy prices, and Europe's dependence on imports of Russian energy resources fuelled Russia's renewed international influence. Over time, tensions have reasserted themselves between Russia and the West. These have included differing positions on the Syrian crisis, U.S. intentions to install a missile shield in Central Europe to guard against a potential Iranian attack, the eastward expansion of NATO, and policies toward Russia's neighbors such as Ukraine, Moldova, and Georgia.

Shortly after the Winter Olympics were held in Sochi, Russia, in February 2014, a political crisis in neighboring Ukraine led to the removal of the Russian-leaning president, Victor Yanukovych, and put in place a pro-Western interim government; these changes elicited a Russian military takeover and quick annexation of Ukraine's southern region of Crimea, undoing much of the goodwill that Russia had won in hosting the Olympics. Western governments refused to recognize Russia's annexation of Crimea, and instituted sanctions to deter Russia from further violations of Ukraine's territorial sovereignty. In August 2014, Russia announced countersanctions that would restrict imports of some Western food products. The annexation of Crimea and continuing tensions in Ukraine have proven to be intractable obstacles to an improvement in relations between Russia and the West. In an effort to assert Russia's regional influence, in 2015, Russia and neighboring Kazakhstan and Belarus officially launched a new regional integration scheme, the Eurasian Economic Union, as a counterpoint to the EU; Russia's efforts to reinforce cooperation with other rising powers such as China also increased.

Governing the Economy

For nearly a decade after the collapse of the Soviet system, the Russian Federation was mired in a downward spiral of economic decline. After 1998, however, growth rates recovered, budget surpluses became routine, and the population experienced a marked increase in economic confidence. As revealed during the 2008 global financial crisis and ensuing recession, Russia's economic strategy, which relies heavily on the export of natural resources to support the state budget, makes the country vulnerable to fluctuations in the international economy, with declining growth rates since 2014. Although many important policy problems have been addressed, others remain unresolved, including inadequate levels of foreign investment, capital flight, and continuing high levels of inequality.

The Democratic Idea

Concerns about the fate of Russian democracy have also become widespread in the West and have elicited intermittent public protests within Russia. While the constitution adopted in 1993 has gained a surprising level of public acceptance, domestic opponents express intensified concern that increasing centralization of power and institutional changes adopted after 2004 have undermined real political competition. The regime justifies these changes as necessary to ensure state capacity to govern and to secure continuing economic growth, but critics see Russia as moving in the direction of electoral authoritarianism, where political competition is "managed" by the president's office through a dominant political party, United Russia. High levels of corruption still pervade the Russian political and economic system, despite the proclaimed commitment of the political leadership to curtail them.

The Politics of Collective Identity

Finally, Russians continue to seek new forms of collective identity. The loss of superpower status, doubts about the appropriateness of Western economic and political models, and the absence of a widely accepted ideology all have contributed to uncertainty about what it means to be Russian. Differing visions of collective identity emerged in some of Russia's ethnic republics, particularly in Chechnya and other Muslim areas. Since 2013, a new narrative of national identity has emerged, strongly pushed by Russian state elites. Russia is increasingly depicted as representing traditional European cultural values and as a bridge between Europe and Asia. This narrative challenges Western understandings of terms such as democracy, human rights, and rule of law, as well as tolerance toward diverse definitions of sexual identity and orientation. A particular focus of international criticism relates to a Russian law passed in 2013 that imposes fines for "propagandizing" minors about nontraditional sexual relations.

Comparisons

Many countries have attempted a transition from authoritarian rule to democratic governance. In Russia's case, one of the most important factors affecting this process is the tradition of strong state control, stretching from czarist times through the Soviet period, and now influencing present developments. In addition, the intertwined character of politics, economics, and ideology in the Soviet Union has made reform difficult. In effect, four transition processes were initiated simultaneously in the early 1990s: democratization, market reform, a redefinition of national identity, and integration into the world economy. Whereas other democratizing countries may have undergone one or two of these transitions simultaneously, Russia initially tried to tackle all four at once. Because the former communist elites had no private wealth to fall back on, corrupt or illegal methods were sometimes used by Russia's emerging capitalist class to maintain former privileges. Citizens, confronted with economic decline and an ideological vacuum, have been susceptible to appeals to nationalism and for strong state control. No doubt, past economic and political uncertainty has made the Russian public willing to accept strong leadership and limits on political expression that would be resisted in many Western countries. Russia's current "backsliding" from democratic development may, in part, reflect the difficulties of pursuing so many transitions at once.

Some countries rich in natural resources, such as Norway, have achieved sustained economic growth and stable democratic systems. In other cases, and this perhaps applies to Russia, such dependence on natural resource wealth has produced a "resource curse" that leaves other economic sectors underdeveloped and uncompetitive, with the country highly vulnerable to global economic fluctuations. In the Russian case, the concentration of economic power associated with the natural resource sector has also fed high levels of inequality and corruption.

Where Do You Stand?

Mikhail Gorbachev was awarded the Nobel Peace Prize in 1991, and is credited in the West with having brought a peaceful end to Soviet rule. However, most Russians today hold Gorbachev in low regard. How do you evaluate the historical significance of Gorbachev?

Is the centralization of power that has occurred under President Vladimir Putin justified in order to foster economic stability and stable government?

POLITICAL ECONOMY AND DEVELOPMENT

SECTION

2

The collapse of the Soviet Union in late 1991 ushered in a sea change, radically reducing the state's traditionally strong role in economic development and opening the Russian economy to foreign influence. However, the process of market reform that the Russian government pursued after 1991 brought with it an immediate dramatic decline in economic performance as well as fundamental changes in social relationships. After experiencing an unprecedented period of economic depression from 1991 to 1998, Russia experienced renewed economic growth, but this growth was built largely on the country's wealth of energy and natural resources. With the economic/financial crisis of 2008–2009, a decline in oil prices since 2013, Western economic sanctions, and Russian counter-sanctions, the Russian economy has not been able to sustain continued economic growth. Russia's dependence on natural resource exports introduces long-term economic risks because of exposure to global price fluctuations. Under Vladimir Putin, the role of the state in key government sectors has been strengthened so that Russia's market economic system has distinctive features compared to Western systems. Extreme levels of social inequality and corruption also characterize the system.

Focus Questions ▽

- What were Russia's most difficult problems in moving from the Soviet command economy to a market economy?

- What challenges does the Russian economy face now if it is to meet the expectations of its citizens?

State and Economy

In the Soviet period, land, factories, and all other important economic assets belonged to the state. Short- and long-term economic plans defined production goals, but these were frequently too ambitious. Except in the illegal black market and parts of the rural economy, prices were controlled by the state and production was unresponsive to demand.

The Soviet economic model registered some remarkable achievements: rapid industrialization, provision of social welfare and mass education, relatively low levels of inequality, and advances in key economic sectors such as the military and space industries. Nonetheless, over time, top-heavy Soviet planning could neither sustain rising prosperity at home nor deliver competitive products for export. Gorbachev's efforts to adapt Soviet economic structures to meet these challenges were largely unsuccessful.

Following the collapse of the USSR, Russian president Boris Yeltsin endorsed a more radical policy of **market reform**. Four main pillars of his program were (1) lifting price controls, (2) encouraging small private businesses and entrepreneurs, (3) privatizing most state-owned enterprises, and (4) opening the economy to international influences. In January 1992, price controls on most goods were loosened or removed entirely. As a result, the consumer price index increased by about 2,500 percent between December 1991 and December 1992. Real wages declined by 50 percent. Economic troubles continued throughout most of the 1990s.

Privatization in Russia was rapid compared to most other post-communist countries. By early 1994, 80 percent of medium-sized and large state enterprises in designated sectors of the economy had been privatized; however, they often did not achieve the desired result of improving efficiency and competitiveness. The most widely adopted method, called **insider privatization**, hampered reform of business operations and reduced the expected gains of privatization. Managers, many of whom did not have the skills needed to operate in a market environment, were reluctant to lay off excess labor or resisted overtures by outside investors who might gain control of the enterprise. Some managers extracted personal profit from enterprise operations rather than investing available funds to improve production. Productivity and efficiency did not increase significantly; unprofitable firms continued to operate. When the sale of shares was opened to outside investors, many firms were unattractive because backward technology would require massive infusions of capital. Some of the more attractive enterprises fell into the hands of developing financial–industrial conglomerates that had acquired their wealth through positions of power or connections in the government. At the same time, new ventures, which were generally more efficient than former state firms, faced obstacles: confusing regulations, high taxes, lack of capital, and poor infrastructure (transport, banking, and communications).

Reform of agriculture was even less satisfactory. Large companies and associations of individual households were created on the basis of former state and collective farms. These privatized companies operated inefficiently, and agricultural output declined. Foreign food imports also undercut domestic producers, contributing to a downward spiral in agricultural investment and production.

A key obstacle to the success of the market reform agenda, in the 1990s, was the weakness of the early post-Soviet state institutions. Without an effective tax collection system, for instance, the government could not acquire revenues necessary to pay its own bills on time, provide essential services to the population, and ensure a well-functioning economic infrastructure (such as transportation, energy, and public utilities). A weak state meant inadequate regulation of the banking sector and poor

---

market reform

A strategy of economic transformation that involves reducing the role of the state in managing the economy and increasing the role of market forces.

---

insider privatization

The transformation of formerly state-owned enterprises into private enterprises or other types of business entities in which majority control is in the hands of employees and/or managers.

enforcement of health, safety, and labor standards. As the state failed to carry out these functions, businesses took matters into their own hands, for example, by hiring private security services for protection, or by paying bribes. Ineffective government fed corruption and criminality.

The central government in Moscow also had difficulty exerting its authority in relation to regional officials and in the face of increasing power of business oligarchs. These wealthy individuals benefited from privatization and often wielded significant political influence. Diverse methods of laundering money to avoid taxes became widespread. Corruption involving government officials, the police, and operators abroad fed a rising crime rate. Rich foreigners, Russian bankers, and outspoken journalists became targets of the Russian mafia.

A financial crisis in August 1998 brought the situation to a head. Following a sharp upturn in 1996 and 1997, the Russian stock market lost over 90 percent of its value in August 1998. The government defaulted on its bonds. Many Russian banks, holders of the government's short-term bonds, faced imminent bankruptcy. The government began to print more of the increasingly valueless rubles, threatening to undermine the ruble's value further and thus intensify the underlying financial crisis.

The government finally allowed a radical devaluation of the ruble. Within a 2-week period, the ruble lost two-thirds of its value against the U.S. dollar, banks closed or allowed only limited withdrawals, supplies of imported goods decreased, and business accounts were frozen—forcing some firms to lay off employees and others to close their doors. However, despite these effects, the 1998 financial crisis ushered in positive changes. First, the devalued ruble made Russian products more competitive with foreign imports. Firms were able to improve their products, put underused labor back to work, and thus increase productivity. The state budget benefited from improved tax revenues, and economic growth revived, beginning in 1999 (See Figure 13.2.)

When Vladimir Putin became president, in 2000, he set about strengthening the capacity of the state to maintain the growth impetus. He introduced a set of

oligarchs

A small group of powerful and wealthy individuals who gained ownership and control of important sectors of Russia's economy in the context of privatization of state assets in the 1990s.

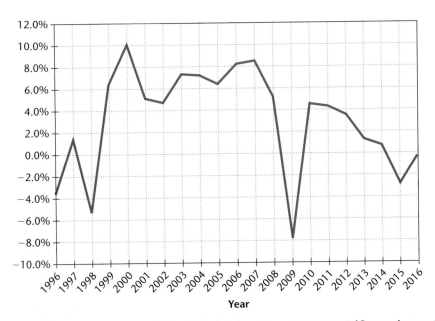

FIGURE 13.2 Russia: Economic Decline and Recovery, 1996–2016 (Gross domestic product percent change over previous year)

Source: Data is from the Russian State Statistics Service.

legislative reforms to spur recovery. A 13 percent flat income tax, deemed easier to enforce, was one very visible aspect of the package. A budget surplus replaced a deficit. By 2007, the Russian government had lowered its debt burden to 3 percent of GDP. Foreign reserves grew from just $12 billion (U.S.) in 1998, to above $500 billion (U.S.) in 2012, and down to just above $325 billion in 2015.[2]

Putin also took measures to limit the power of economic oligarchs who used their financial positions to criticize the government or to affect political outcomes. A prominent case involved Mikhail Khodorkovsky, the chief executive officer and major shareholder of the giant Russian oil company, Yukos. In 2003, Khodorkovsky was placed under arrest for fraud and tax evasion, and in May 2005, he was sentenced by a Russian court to nine years in prison. In December 2013, Khodorkovsky was pardoned and released from prison, a move that many observers interpreted as attempt to gain Western approval in the lead up to the February 2014 Winter Olympics in Sochi, Russia. Since that time, Khodorkovsky has promoted oppositional activity from abroad.

Despite Putin's successes in securing a revival of economic growth, corruption has remained a major obstacle to effective economic management. Transparency International's annual Corruption Perceptions index, based on a compilation of independent surveys, ranked Russia 131th out of the 177 countries surveyed in 2016,[3] indicating continuing high levels of corruption.

Society and Economy

The communist party's social goals also produced some of the most marked achievements of the Soviet system. Benefits to the population in the Soviet period included free health care, low-cost access to essential goods and services, maternity leave (partially paid), child benefits, disability pensions, and mass education. In a short period of time, universal access to primary and secondary schooling led to nearly universal literacy under Soviet rule. Postsecondary education was free of charge, with state stipends provided to university students. Guaranteed employment and job security were other priorities. Almost all able-bodied adults, men and women alike, worked outside the home. Citizens received many social benefits through the workplace, and modest pensions were guaranteed by the state, ensuring a stable but minimal standard of living for retirement.

The Soviet system, however, was plagued by shortages and low-quality service. For example, advanced medical equipment was in limited supply. Sometimes under-the-table payments were required to prompt better quality service. Many goods and services were scarce. Housing shortages restricted mobility and forced young families to share small apartments with parents. Productivity was low by international standards, and work discipline was weak.

As a matter of state policy, wage differentials between the best and worst paid were lower than in Western countries. While this approach had social benefits, it also reduced the incentive for outstanding achievements and innovation. Due to state ownership, individuals could not accumulate wealth in real estate, stocks, or businesses. Although political elites had access to scarce goods, higher quality health care, travel, and vacation homes, these privileges were largely hidden from public view.

The Soviet experience led Russians to expect the state to ensure a social welfare network, but in the 1990s budget constraints necessitated cutbacks, just when social needs were greatest. Although universal health care remained, higher quality care and access to medicine depended more obviously on ability to pay. Benefits provided through the workplace were cut back, as businesses faced pressures to reduce costs. At the same time, some groups benefited from market reforms, including those with Western language skills and those employed in the natural resources, banking, and financial sectors. At the top of the scale are the super-wealthy, including people who appropriated benefits during the privatization process or engaged in successful business activity afterwards. However, losers have been more numerous. Poverty is highest among rural residents, the unemployed, children, the less educated, pensioners, and the disabled. As a result of low wage levels, the majority of those in poverty are the working poor.

Following the economic upturn that began in 1999, large differentials in income and wealth have persisted. While the portion of the population living below the subsistence level declined after 1999, it has risen again since 2014. In the first half of 2016, 14.6 percent of the population was recorded as being below the poverty line; overall, real incomes fell as well, particularly for the less well-off.[4] Many individuals still hold two to three jobs just to make ends meet. Social indicators of economic stress (such as a declining birthrate, suicide rate, and murder rate) began to correct themselves after 2002, but only slowly. The economic-financial crisis of 2008–2009 introduced new economic uncertainties just when many Russians were beginning to feel that life was returning to normal.

In recent years, maintenance of existing levels of state support for social programs has been a contentious issue. Massive street demonstrations occurred in several Russian cities in early 2005 to protest changes to social welfare policy. Called "monetization of social benefits," the reforms involved replacing certain services (such as public transport) that had been provided free to certain groups (pensioners, veterans, and the disabled) with a modest monetary payment to the individual. Many Russians viewed the measures as involving direct reductions in social welfare benefits. After large-scale demonstrations, the government agreed to accompany the reforms by a modest increase in pensions and to restore subsidized transport. Learning from this experience, the government has attempted to avoid cuts in social welfare measures and pensions since, including during the economic-financial crisis of 2008 and the economic downturn since 2014.

Russia saw a steady decline in population until 2009, mitigated to some extent by a positive inflow of immigrants, particularly from other former Soviet republics. Life expectancy in 2016 was estimated at 65 years for Russian men and 77 years for women, an improvement over the 1990s, but still lower than in Western societies. Primary factors contributing to the high mortality rates include stress related to social and economic dislocation and unnatural causes of death (accidents, murders, and suicides).

The government has introduced policies to encourage a rising birthrate, such as higher child support payments, and monetary and other benefits for women having two or more children. Birthrates had begun to rise already in 1999, so it is hard to know how much of the continuing increase is due to government policy. Although declining birthrates often accompany economic modernization, the extraordinary economic stresses of the 1990s exacerbated this tendency; the restoration of economic growth in the late 1990s may have reduced the reluctance of many couples to have children, but the birthrate is still well below the levels of the 1980s. Women continue to carry the bulk of domestic responsibilities while also working outside the home to boost family income. Many women take advantage of the permitted three-year maternity leave, which is only partially paid, but difficulties in reconciling home and work duties no doubt contribute to low birthrates as well.

Russia's ethnic and regional diversity also has economic implications. Levels of development vary greatly across the country's federal units, with major cities (such as Moscow and St. Petersburg), as well as regions rich in natural resources, being the most affluent.

Environmental Issues

In the Soviet period, an emphasis on economic growth at the expense of environmental protection resulted in high levels of air and water pollution, with associated health problems. Inadequate technological safeguards and an insufficient regulatory structure led to the disastrous nuclear accident at Chernobyl (now in Ukraine) in 1986, which produced long-lasting contamination of immense areas of agricultural land in Ukraine and neighboring Belarus, as well as in some areas of Russia. Following the Chernobyl accident, under Gorbachev's *glasnost* policy, citizen environmental awareness and activism increased, often associated with assertions of national identity in the various republics of the USSR, including Russia. In 1988, under Gorbachev's leadership, a specific environmental protection agency was created.

Following the collapse of the USSR, the newly independent Russian state was preoccupied with other problems, in the face of the major economic downturn of the 1990s. The country's heavy economic reliance on resource-extraction industries brought with it higher than average environmental impacts. In May 2000, the State Committee for Environmental Protection (the successor to the environmental agency created in 1988) was abolished with most of its responsibilities moved to a new ministry (now called the Ministry of Natural Resources and Ecology). This model of mixing oversight of use and protection of nature in a single agency may be an indicator of the low priority assigned to environmental protection, as compared to resource use.

A particular priority for the EU was to gain Russian ratification of the Kyoto Protocol, an international agreement to reduce greenhouse gas emissions and to address the dangers of climate change. Given the failure of the United States to support the agreement, Russia's signature was needed to put the agreement into effect. Russia ratified the Kyoto Protocol in 2004. However, this involved minimal commitment since Russia's greenhouse gas emission levels had decreased as a result of production downturns of the 1990s. In 2015, Russia submitted its nationally determined contribution related to the Paris Agreement of the United Nations Framework Convention on Climate Change; the commitment involved a reduction to 70 to 75 percent of 1990 levels by 2030, which, in light of the economic recession of the 1990s, is modest.[5] However, like countries such as China, the proportion of global carbon emissions from Russia (4.53 percent) exceeds it relative share of the global population (1.98 percent) and GDP (3.18 percent), based on 2016 data.[6] The relatively low utilization of renewable energy sources and highly inefficient use of energy in Russia suggest that the country's environmental performance has clear avenues for improvement, and the Russian government has expressed support for such measures, even if their implementation has so far been weak.

Russia in the Global Economy

During the Soviet period, the economy was largely isolated from outside influences, as foreign trade was channeled through central state organs. However, things changed after 1991. Over time, the ruble was allowed to respond to market conditions, and firms were permitted to conclude agreements directly with foreign partners. Western governments and international organizations such as the World Bank, the International Monetary Fund (IMF), and the European Union (EU) contributed substantial amounts of economic assistance, often in the form of repayable credits. After the August 1998 crisis, the Russian government defaulted, first on the ruble-denominated short-term debt, and then on the former Soviet debt. Since then, debt repayments have been made on time. In 2001, the government decided to forgo additional IMF credits. By 2005, it had paid off its IMF debt.

Russia has also become more open to foreign investment. However, levels still remain low compared to many other East European countries, despite improvements since 2004. The inflow of West European investment capital was negatively affected by the financial and economic crisis of 2008, and by Western sanctions against Russia associated with the annexation of Crimea. Major sources of foreign direct investment, since 2000, have been Germany, the United States, and Cyprus (mainly recycled Russian capital, previously exported for tax reasons), but foreign investors are, since 2006, prevented from gaining a majority share in certain sectors of the economy that are identified as of strategic importance. After an extended accession process, involving compliance with rules regarding free trade, in 2012 Russia was admitted to the World Trade Organization (WTO). Initial adaptation costs have included difficulties in some sectors, such as the agricultural and food industries, due to increased competition, as well as lost tariff revenue. However, it is expected that in the medium to long run, WTO membership will contribute significantly to economic growth in Russia. Several trade disputes between the EU and Russia have been taken to the WTO by one or the other of the parties for adjudication since Russia joined the organization.

The geographic focus of Russia's foreign trade activity has shifted markedly since the Soviet period. Whereas in 1994 neighboring Ukraine was Russia's most important trading partner, in 2014 the top spots were filled by China (17.7 percent of imports to Russia and 7.5 percent of exports), the Netherlands (receiving 13.7 percent of Russian exports), and Germany (providing 11.5 percent of imports and 7.5 percent of exports).[7] Overall, in 2016, the EU was Russia's largest trading partner, making up 42.8 percent of the total (down from 44.8 percent in 2015)[8]; meanwhile, Russia was the EU's fourth-largest trading partner, with imports from Russia constituting only 7 percent of the EU's total, and exports to Russia making up 4.1 percent. A substantial portion (about two-thirds) of Russia's export commodities to Europe are mineral resources (including energy resources), while about two-thirds of the EU's exports to Russia are manufactured goods, machinery, and transport equipment, resulting in an asymmetrical trade relationship.[9] In the face of increased tensions with the West, Russia is seeking to increase energy exports to China.

Russia's position in the international political economy remains uncertain. With a highly skilled workforce, high levels of educational and scientific achievement, and a rich base of natural resources, Russia has many of the ingredients necessary to become a competitive and powerful force in the global economy. However, Russia's natural resource and energy wealth has proven to be a mixed blessing. If the country's industrial capacity is not restored, Russia will continue to be vulnerable to shifts in world energy prices and to fluctuations in supply and demand. Since the hydrocarbon sector provides a significant portion of trade (see Figure 13.3) and of revenue for the Russian state budget, any threat to profits in this sector can reverberate through the economy and society at large. Accordingly, in 2004, during the economic upturn, the Russian government established a Stabilization Fund to hold a portion of revenues from export duties generated from the energy sector and from federal budget

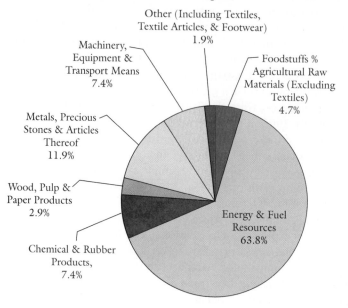

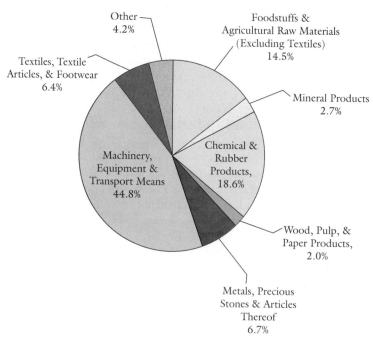

FIGURE 13.3 Structure of Russian Foreign Trade, 2015

Source: Adapted from *Russia in Figures: Statistical Handbook* (Moscow, Federal State Statistics Services of the Russian Federation, 2016), p. 506.

surpluses. In 2008, the fund was split into two parts, a Reserve Fund and National Welfare Fund. The decline in global oil and gas prices, which began in 2014, contributed to a fall in the value of the ruble and threatened state budget revenues, forcing the Russian government to dip into the Reserve Fund to ensure fiscal resources for the state. This led to a dramatic decline in its size, as well as to a lesser decline in the size of the National Welfare Fund, which is, in part, intended to cover future pension obligations.

Levels of capital investment and technological innovation also have not been adequate to fuel increased productivity; even in the lucrative energy sector, experts doubt whether, without significant foreign involvement, Russian firms will be able to develop new reserves adequate to meet both domestic needs and contractual obligations to foreign (at this point mainly European) consumers. At the same time, its wealth in natural resources has given Russia advantages compared to its neighbors, since these expensive materials do not need to be imported. Ultimately, Russia's position in the global economy will depend on the ability of the country's leadership to address domestic economic challenges and to facilitate differentiation of the country's export base.

GLOBAL CONNECTIONS

Russia and International Organizations

Russia has achieved membership in many international organizations such as the World Bank, the International Monetary Fund, and the World Trade Organization. In other cases, Russia has forged partnerships with organizations for which membership is currently not foreseen. Relations with three regional organizations are profiled here:

The European Union (*EU*). In 1999, the EU and Russia established a "strategic partnership," and in 2003 agreed on four "Common Spaces" of cooperation, relating to economic relations, borders, external security, and research, education, and culture. In 2007, the EU and Russia initiated a process to simplify the issuance of visas by both sides, with an eventual goal of lifting visa requirements for short-term visits. In 2010, they announced a Modernization Partnership. The conflict over Ukraine in 2014 introduced a setback as many aspects of the relations were frozen by the EU, placing in question the strategic partnership itself.

The Council of Europe (which is distinct from the EU) is the major vehicle in Europe for the defense of human rights, enforced through the European Court of Human Rights (ECtHR) in Strasbourg, France. Russia acceded to the organization in 1996, and ratified the European Convention on Human Rights in 1998. Thousands of human rights cases involving Russia have been brought to the ECtHR, many related to the Chechnya conflict, and most judgments have gone against Russia. In 2015, Vladimir Putin signed a law allowing the Russian Constitutional Court to block enforcement of an ECtHR decision if it is deemed unconstitutional; the power was first applied in January 2017.

The North Atlantic Treaty Organization (*NATO*) was formed after World War II to safeguard its members on both sides of the Atlantic from the Soviet threat. Following the collapse of the communist system, NATO redefined its mandate to include crisis management, peacekeeping, combatting international terrorism, and prevention of nuclear proliferation. Since 1999, Russia has consistently objected to the expansion of NATO as it took in several new members, specifically countries of Central and Eastern Europe. Nonetheless, the NATO-Russia Founding Act on Mutual Relations of 1997, and the formation of the NATO-Russia Council in 2002, provided a basis for cooperation. In reaction to Russian actions in Crimea and Ukraine in 2014, NATO suspended cooperation with Russia and reemphasized its commitment to collective defense of its members, including those bordering Russia. At the same time, meetings of the NATO-Russia Council recommenced in 2016.

MAKING CONNECTIONS How has NATO enlargement affected Russia's relations with the West?

Where Do You Stand?

Do you think that a strong role for the state in economic affairs makes sense in Russia, given the country's history?

What measures do you think could be taken to bring corruption under control in Russia?

SECTION

3

GOVERNANCE AND POLICY-MAKING

☒ Focus Questions

• Why has the Russian leadership viewed political centralization as necessary and what centralizing measures have been taken since 2000?

• What is the relationship between the prime minister and the president in Russia? How have the particular individuals who have filled these posts helped to shape this relationship?

In the 1990s, the Russian leadership, under Boris Yeltsin, endorsed liberal democratic principles, and subsequent Russian presidents, both Vladimir Putin and Dmitry Medvedev, have reaffirmed their commitment to democracy. However, over time, the manner in which democratic governance should be interpreted to make it compatible with Russia's unique political tradition has become contested. Skeptics see Putin's measures to strengthen presidential power as moving Russia in an authoritarian direction. Protests reached a high point in late 2011 and early 2012, when large public demonstrations in Moscow, and other major cities, questioned the fairness of the legislative and presidential elections. In response, Vladimir Putin, reelected as president in March 2012 after a four-year interlude, endorsed a mix of concessions and heightened controls that elicited continuing debate about the fate of Russia's democratic experiment. Unlike 2011, in 2016 legislative elections occurred without major protests; commentators wondered whether this reflected support for the system or hopelessness about changing it.

Organization of the State

In the Soviet period, before Gorbachev's reforms, top organs of the Communist Party of the Soviet Union (CPSU) dominated the state. The CPSU was hierarchical. Lower party bodies elected delegates to higher party organs, but elections were uncontested, and top organs determined candidates for lower party posts. The Politburo, the top party organ, was the real decision-making center. A larger body, the Central Committee, represented the broader political elite, including regional party leaders and representatives of various economic sectors. Alongside the CPSU were Soviet state structures, which formally resembled Western parliamentary systems but had little decision-making authority. The state bureaucracy had day-to-day responsibility in both the economic and political spheres but followed the party's directives in all matters. The Supreme Soviet, the parliament, was a rubber-stamp body, meaning it only passed legislation that had been approved by the CPSU.

The Soviet constitution was primarily symbolic, since many of its principles were ignored in practice. The constitution provided for legislative, executive, and judicial organs, but separation of powers was considered unnecessary because the CPSU claimed to represent the interests of society as a whole. When the constitution was violated (frequently), the courts had no independent authority to enforce or protect its provisions. Likewise, the Soviet federal system was phony, since all aspects of life were overseen by a highly centralized communist party. Nonetheless, the various subunits that existed within the Russian Republic of the USSR were carried over into the Russian Federation in an altered form.

Gorbachev introduced innovations into the Soviet political system: competitive elections, increased political pluralism, reduced communist party dominance, a revitalized legislative branch of government, and renegotiated terms for Soviet federalism. He also tried to bring the constitution into harmony with political reality. Likewise, even before the collapse of the USSR in December 1991, political institutions began to change in the Russian Republic, which was only one of fifteen federal units that made up the Soviet Union. A new post of president was created, and on June 12, 1991, Boris Yeltsin was elected by direct popular vote as its first incumbent. Once the Russian Federation became independent in December 1991, a crucial turning point in its development was the adoption by referendum of a new Russian constitution in December 1993. This constitution provides the legal foundation for current state institutions (see Figure 13.4) and by now seems to have acquired broad-based popular legitimacy.

The document affirms many established principles of liberal democratic governance—competitive multiparty elections, separation of powers, an independent judiciary, federalism, and protection of individual civil liberties. At the same time, the president and executive branch are granted strong powers. Despite this, in the 1990s, the state demonstrated only a weak capacity to govern, involving dysfunctional conflict between major institutions of government. Subnational governments demanded increased autonomy, even sovereignty, generating a process of negotiation and political conflict between the center and the regions that sometimes led to contradictions between regional and federal laws. The constitution made the executive dominant but still dependent on the agreement of the legislative branch to realize its programs. Under President Yeltsin, tension between the two branches of government was a persistent obstacle to effective governance. In addition, establishing real judicial independence remained a significant political challenge.

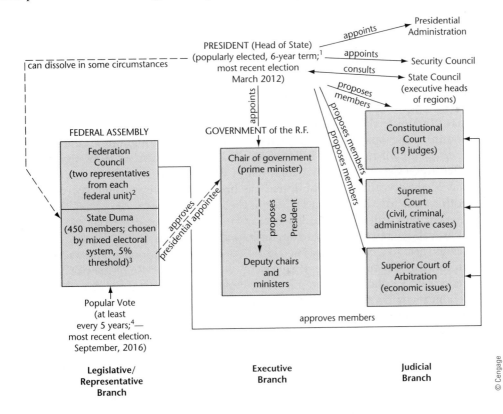

[1]Before 2012 the term was 4 years.
[2]One representative appointed by the regional legislature and one by the regional excutive.
[3]Was a nationwide proportional representation system from 2007–2013, with 7% threshold. Until 2007 half of seats were chosen in single-member-districts and half by proportional representation with a 5% threshold.
[4]Prior to 2011–2012 the term was 4 years.

FIGURE 13.4   Political Institutions of the Russian Federation (R.F.) 2017

During Vladimir Putin's first term (2000–2008) the power of the presidency was augmented further in an effort to address the weakness of central state authority. Many observers feel, however, that Putin's centralizing measures have undermined the very checks and balances that were supposed to protect against reestablishment of authoritarian control.

The Executive

The constitution establishes a semi-presidential system, formally resembling the French system but with stronger executive power. As in France, the executive itself has two heads (the president and the prime minister), introducing a potential context for intrastate tension. The president is also the head of state and holds primary power, except for the periods between 1998 to 2000, and 2008 to 2012. The prime minister, appointed by the president but approved by the lower house of the parliament (the State Duma, hereafter Duma), is the head of government. As a rule of thumb, the president has overseen foreign policy, relations with the regions, and the organs of state security, while the prime minister has focused his attention on the economy and related issues. However, with Yeltsin's continuing health problems in 1998 and 1999, operative power shifted in the direction of the prime minister. In December 1999, Yeltsin resigned from office, making the prime minister, Vladimir Putin, acting president until he was himself elected president in March 2000. Between 2008 and 2012, Dmitry Medvedev served as president, with Putin as prime minister. In the view of most observers, Putin had more effective power than Medvedev, though their relationship was a cooperative one.

One of the president's most important powers is the authority to issue decrees, which Yeltsin used frequently for contentious issues. Although presidential decrees may not violate the constitution or specific legislation passed by the bicameral legislature, policy-making by decree allows the president to ignore an uncooperative or divided parliament. Yeltsin's decision in 1994, and again in 1999, to launch the offensive in Chechnya was not approved by either house of parliament. Under Putin and Medvedev, the power of decree has been used more sparingly, partly because both leaders have had strong support in the legislature.

The president can also call a state of emergency, impose martial law, grant pardons, call referendums, and temporarily suspend actions of other state organs if he deems them to contradict the constitution or federal laws. Some of these actions must be confirmed by other state organs (such as the upper house of the parliament, the Federation Council). The president is commander-in-chief of the armed forces and conducts affairs of state with other nations. Impeachment of the president involves the two houses of the legislative body (the Duma and the Federation Council), the Supreme Court, and the Constitutional Court. If the president dies in office or becomes incapacitated, the prime minister fills the post until new presidential elections can be held.

The Russian government is headed by the prime minister, flanked by varying numbers of deputy prime ministers. The president's choice of prime minister must be approved by the Duma. During his first two full terms in office (2000–2004 and 2004–2008), Putin had three prime ministers (and one acting prime minister). The first of these, Mikhail Kasyanov (May 2000–February 2004) later became an outspoken opposition figure. As noted above, following his election as president in 2008, Medvedev selected Putin as his prime minister, with the roles reversed when Putin returned as president in 2012.

The prime minister can be removed by the Duma through two repeat votes of no confidence passed within a 3-month period. Even in the 1990s, when there was tension with President Yeltsin, the Duma was unable or unwilling to exercise this power, presumably in part because this action could lead to dissolution of the Duma itself. Until 2008, the prime minister was never the leader of the dominant party or coalition in the Duma. This changed when Putin became prime minister in 2008 because he was also elected as chairperson of the dominant party, United Russia, in that year and Dmitry Medvedev, the Russian prime minister, is the current chairman of the party.

The National Bureaucracy

The state's administrative structure includes twenty-one ministries, and some sixteen federal services and agencies (as of March 2017). Based on an administrative reform adopted in 2004, ministries are concerned with policy functions, such as economic development, energy, agriculture, sport, or education and science, whereas other state organs undertake monitoring functions or implementation, as well as providing services to the public. Many observers agree that these administrative reforms have not improved bureaucratic efficiency or government responsiveness.

Some government bodies (such as the Foreign Affairs Ministry, the Federal Security Service, and the Defense Ministry) report directly to the president. The president has created various advisory bodies that solicit input from important political and economic actors and also co-opt them into supporting government policies. The most important are the Security Council and the State Council. Formed in 1992, the Security Council, chaired by the president, provides input in areas related to foreign policy and security (broadly conceived); its membership and size have varied over time, but the body has generally included heads of the so-called power ministries such as Defense and the Federal Security Service, as well as other key ministers and government officials. The State Council, also chaired by the president, was formed in September 2000 as part of Putin's attempt to redefine the role of regional leaders in federal decision making (see below) and includes the heads of Russia's constituent federal units. A smaller presidium of the State Council meets monthly.

Ministers other than the prime minister do not require parliamentary approval. The prime minister makes recommendations to the president, who appoints these officials. Ministers and other agency heads are generally career bureaucrats who have risen through an appropriate ministry, although sometimes more clearly political appointments are made. Many agencies have been reorganized, often more than once. Sometimes restructuring signals particular leadership priorities. For example, in May 2008, Putin created a new Ministry of Energy, splitting off these functions from those of the Ministry of Industry and Trade. This move reflected the growing importance of this sector to Russia's economy.

Top leaders have also used restructuring to place their clients and allies in key positions. For example, Putin drew heavily on colleagues with whom he worked earlier in St. Petersburg or in the security establishment, referred to as *siloviki*, in staffing a variety of posts in his administration. **Clientelistic networks** continue to play a key role in both the presidential administration and other state organs. These linkages are similar to "old-boys' networks" in the West; they underscore the importance of personal loyalty and career ties between individuals as they rise in bureaucratic or political structures. While instituting a merit-based civil service system has been a state goal, it has not yet been achieved in reality. The Russian state bureaucracy continues to suffer low levels of public respect and continuing problems with corruption.

siloviki

Derived from the Russian word *sila*, meaning "force," this refers to Russian politicians and governmental officials drawn from the security and intelligence agencies, special forces, or the military, many of whom were recruited to important political posts under Vladimir Putin.

clientelistic networks

Informal systems of asymmetrical power in which a powerful patron (e.g., the president, prime minister, or governor) offers less powerful clients resources, benefits, or career advantages in return for support, loyalty, or services.

PROFILES

Vladimir Putin

President Vladimir Putin (right) with Prime Minister (and former president) Dmitry Medvedev (left).

AP Images/ITAR-TASS, Presidential Press Service, Vladimir Rodionov

Vladimir Putin is no doubt the most powerful person in Russia. He has enjoyed a consistently high level of public support since his first election as president in March 2000, but he is also reviled by his critics for moving Russia in an authoritarian direction. For many ordinary Russians, Putin represents a reassertion of Russia's potential after painful years of economic decline and loss of international stature in the 1990s. Projecting an image of masculine prowess, Putin has been captured in numerous alluring poses that contribute to his image of strength, for example while executing impressive judo moves, driving a three-wheeled Harley Davidson, and fishing topless in one of Russia's far-flung regions.

Putin was born in October 1952 in what is now St. Petersburg, Russia's second largest city. In the Soviet period, Putin pursued a career in the security services (the KGB), in East Germany, where he remained until 1990 when the communist state there collapsed. While in political office, Putin has drawn many of his staff from the security forces.

Upon returning to his home city of St. Petersburg in 1990, Putin became involved in municipal government before moving to take up a political post in Moscow in 1996. In 1999, Russian president Boris Yeltsin appointed Putin prime minister; shortly afterwards Putin became acting president when Yeltsin resigned from the post for health reasons. In 2000 and 2004 Putin won the presidential election with 56.7 and 71 percent of the vote, respectively. Since the constitution limits the president to two consecutive terms, Putin hand-picked Dmitry Medvedev as the presidential candidate to succeed him for a four-year term from 2008 until 2012. In September 2011, Putin and Medvedev announced that Putin, with Medvedev's support, would again seek the presidency in 2012. While parts of the Russian public did not react well to this preplanned "leadership swap," Putin was again elected president, this time for a six-year term, winning 63.6 percent of the vote.

Putin's domestic public approval rating has remained above 60 percent since the 2012 election, rising to around 80 percent since April 2014 following the Russian annexation of Crimea. Some consider Putin to be a master tactician, who has managed to achieve a pragmatic mix of control and flexibility, weaving a political narrative that is contentious but persuasive to large parts of his domestic audience.

MAKING CONNECTIONS Why is Putin so popular with large parts of the Russian population?

Efforts to reduce the size of the state bureaucracy during Putin's terms of office have had mixed results, with some reduction evident since 2008, following previous increases. In December 2010, as an apparent cost cutting measure, Medvedev issued a presidential decree mandating further cuts in the size of the federal bureaucracy, which apparently led to some further reductions until 2013, but subsequent data make the results hard to assess. However, it appears that the size of Russia's federal bureaucracy is not excessive on a comparative basis.[10]

Public and Semipublic Institutions

In limited sectors of the economy, partial or complete state ownership has remained intact or even been restored after earlier privatization was carried out. Public or quasi-public ownership may take the form of direct state or municipal ownership of assets or majority control of shares in a "privatized" firm. Economic sectors more likely to involve public or semipublic ownership include telecommunications (the nonmobile telephone industry in particular), public transport (railways, municipal transport), the electronic media (television), and the energy sector. Prime examples from the energy sector are Gazprom, a giant natural gas company, and Rosneft, an oil company, in which the federal government, directly or indirectly, controls just over 50 percent of the shares. Several television channels are publicly owned. Indirect state influence is also realized through the dominant ownership share in many regional TV channels by Gazprom-Media, a subsidiary of the state-controlled natural gas company.

In other areas, such as education and health care, while some private facilities and institutions have emerged in recent years, these services are still primarily provided through tax-supported agencies. Some prestigious new private universities, often with Western economic support, have cropped up in major urban areas, but Russia's large historic universities remain public institutions. Likewise, a state-run medical care system assures basic care to all citizens, although private clinics and hospitals are increasingly servicing the more affluent parts of the population. In public transport, smaller private companies that provide shuttle and bus services have grown up alongside publicly owned transport networks. In general, public or semipublic agencies offer services at a lower price, but often also with lower quality.

Significant parts of the social infrastructure remain under public or semipublic control. In the Soviet period, many social services were administered to citizens through the workplace. These services included daycare, housing, medical care, and vacation facilities, as well as food services and some retail outlets. During the 1990s a process of divestiture resulted in the transfer of most of these assets and responsibilities to other institutions, either to private owners or, often, to municipalities. For example, while many state- or enterprise-owned apartments were turned over to private ownership by their occupants, an important part of the country's housing stock was placed in municipal ownership.

Political authorities, including the president, are responsible for appointing executive officials in many public and semipublic institutions. This situation indicates a continuing close relationship between major economic institutions and the state, likely to remain in the future due to the Russian tradition of a strong state and also due to the dismal economic results associated with privatization in the 1990s. Indicative of this trend, the overall share of GDP created in the nonstate sector increased from 5 percent in 1991 to 70 percent in 1997, then fell from 70 percent in 1997 down to 65 percent during 2005 to 2006.[11]

Other State Institutions

The Judiciary

Concepts such as judicial independence and the rule of law were poorly understood in both pre-revolutionary Russia and the Soviet era. These concepts have, however, been embedded in the new Russian constitution and are, in principle, accepted both by the public and political elites. However, their implementation has been difficult and not wholly successful.

A Constitutional Court was formed in 1991. Its decisions were binding, and in several cases even the president had to bow to its authority. After several controversial decisions, Yeltsin suspended the operations of the court in late 1993. However, the 1993 Russian constitution provided for a Constitutional Court again, with the power to adjudicate disputes on the constitutionality of federal and regional laws, as well as jurisdictional disputes between various political institutions.

Judges are nominated by the president and approved by the Federation Council, a procedure that produced a political stalemate after the new constitution was adopted, so that the new court became functional only in 1995. Since 1995, the court has established itself as a vehicle for resolving conflicts involving the protection of individual rights and conformity of regional laws with constitutional requirements.

The court has, however, been cautious in confronting the executive branch, and questions have been raised not only by critics but also by some justices themselves about the independence of the court from presidential influence.

Alongside the Constitutional Court is an extensive system of lower and appellate courts, with the Supreme Court at the pinnacle. These courts hear ordinary civil and criminal cases. In 1995, a system of commercial courts was also formed to hear cases dealing with issues related to privatization, taxes, and other commercial activities. The Federation Council must approve nominees for Supreme Court judgeships, and the constitution also grants the president power to appoint judges at other levels. Measures to shield judges from political pressures include criminal prosecution for attempting to influence a judge, protections from arbitrary dismissal, and improved salaries for judges. One innovation in the legal system has been the introduction of jury trials for some types of criminal offenses.

Subnational Governments

The collapse of the Soviet Union was precipitated by the demands of some union republics for more autonomy within the Soviet federal system, and then for independence. After the Russian Federation became an independent state, the problem of constructing a viable federal structure resurfaced within Russia itself. (See the box feature, "The US Connection".) Some of Russia's sub-national units, especially those that had a distinct ethnic population, were very assertive in putting forth claims for autonomy or even sovereignty within the newly independent Russian Federation. The most extreme example is Muslim-majority Chechnya, whose demand for independence led to a protracted civil war. The ethnic dimension complicates political relations with some other republics as well, particularly Tatarstan and Bashkortostan, which occupy relatively large territories in the center of the country and are of Islamic cultural background.

power vertical

A term used by Vladimir Putin to describe a unified and hierarchical structure of executive power ranging from the national to the local level.

Putin's most controversial initiatives relating to Russia's regions were part of his attempt to strengthen what he termed the **power vertical**. This concept refers to an integrated structure of executive power from the presidential level down through to the local level. Critics have questioned whether this idea is consistent with federal principles, and others see it as undermining Russia's fledgling democratic system. A first step in creating the power vertical was the creation of seven, now nine, federal districts on top of the existing federal units. Although not designed to replace regional governments, the districts were intended to oversee the work of federal offices operating in these regions and to ensure compliance with federal laws and the constitution.

A second set of changes to create the power vertical involved a weakening of the independence of governors and republic heads (hereafter called governors). Beginning in 1996, the governors, along with the heads of each regional legislative body, sat as members of the upper house of the Russian parliament, the Federation Council. This arrangement gave the governors a direct voice in national legislative discussions and a presence in Moscow. In 2001, Putin gained approval for a revision to the composition of the Federation Council, removing regional executives. The State Council was formed to try to assure the governors that they would retain some role in the federal policy-making arena.

Following the Beslan terrorist attack in 2004, Putin identified corruption and ineffective leadership at the regional level as culprits in allowing terrorists to carry out the devastating school hostage taking. Accordingly, Putin proposed an additional reform that created the decisive element of central control over regional politics. This change eliminated the popular election of governors; rather, the president nominated them for approval by the regional legislature. The president's nominees were approved by the regional legislature in every case, usually with an overwhelming

U.S. CONNECTION

Federalism Compared

Russia is a *federal system* according to its constitution. This means that, at least in theory, powers are divided between the central government and Russia's constituent units. Russia claims to have eighty-five regions, including two regions in Crimea (Republic of Crimea and the city of Sevastopol), forcibly annexed from Ukraine in March 2014. However, most Western countries do not recognize the validity of the annexation.

In comparison to the U.S. federal system, the Russian structure seems complicated. Russia's federal units include twenty-one republics, (twenty-two including the Republic of Crimea), forty-nine *oblasts* (regions), six *krais* (territories), one autonomous republic, four autonomous *okrugs* and two cities of federal status (Moscow and St. Petersburg, or three with Sevastopol). Russia's size and multiethnic population underlie this complexity. Because many ethnic groups are regionally concentrated in Russia, unlike in the U.S., these groups form the basis for some federal units.

In the 1990s, Russia's federal government had difficulty controlling what happened in the regions. Regional laws sometimes deviated from federal law. Bilateral treaties with the federal government granted some regional governments special privileges. During his term as president, Vladimir Putin put measures in place to ensure a greater degree of legal and political uniformity throughout the country.

Russia's federal units are represented in the upper house of the national legislature, the Federation Council. Just as the U.S. Senate includes two representatives from each state, in Russia each region also has two delegates in this body; however, their method of selection has varied over time. In 1993, they were elected directly. From the mid-1990s, the governor and the head of each regional legislature themselves sat on the Federation Council. Now the members of the Federation Council are appointed, one by the region's governor and the other by the region's legislature.

Russia's federal units depend on funding from the central government to carry out many of their functions, especially regarding social welfare. Other informal mechanisms, such as use of political patronage through the dominant United Russia party, reduce the independence of the regional executives. Although Russia does have a constitutional court to resolve disputes over the jurisdictions of the federal government and the regions, unlike in the U.S. the constitution does not provide a strong basis for regional power, since it places many powers in the hands of the central government while most others are considered "shared" jurisdictions.

MAKING CONNECTIONS Have centralizing measures in Russia undermined the federal nature of Russia's political system?

---

majority or even unanimously. Following the public protests against alleged fraud in the 2011 and 2012 national elections, Medvedev proposed legislation reinstating gubernatorial elections, but with a "municipal filter" that requires a candidate's nomination to be supported by a certain number of local deputies or officials. Elections held since October 2012, under this law, have resulted in victories for the candidates of the dominant party, United Russia, in almost all cases. This outcome reflects restrictive features of the new law, informal mechanisms of influence exercised by the incumbent, and the failure of opposition forces to unite in support of viable candidates.

The distribution of tax revenues among the various levels of government has been another contentious issue. The Soviet state pursued a considerable degree of regional equalization, but regional differences have increased in the Russian Federation. Putin created a more regularized system for determining the distribution of revenues, taking account of both the regional tax base and differences in the needs of various regions (for instance, northern regions have higher expenses to maintain basic services). However, in fact, an increasing proportion of tax revenues are now controlled by Moscow, and regional governments are constantly faced with shortfalls in carrying out their major responsibilities, for example, in social policy. Economic disparities between rich and poor regions have reached dramatic proportions, with Moscow and areas abundant in natural resources being the best off. Transfers from the federal budget to regions reduce these disparities to a limited degree.

The Military and Security Organs

Because of Vladimir Putin's career background in the KGB, he drew many of his staff from this arena. Thus, while the formal status of the Federal Security Service (the successor to the KGB) has not changed, the security establishment has acquired increasing importance under Putin. A justification for the increasing role for security forces was a series of terrorist attacks, with targets including apartment buildings, schools, a popular Moscow theatre, public transport, and a Moscow airport. Attacks in Russia initially had indigenous roots in the separatist region of Chechnya, as terrorism was used by Chechen militants to counter Russian military efforts to defeat separatist forces. Over time, linkages between Russian terrorist groups and international Islamic fundamentalist organizations have become increasingly important.

Because many Russians are alarmed by the crime rate and terrorist bombings in the country, restrictions on civil liberties justified as guarding against the terrorist threat have not elicited strong popular concern. At the same time, there is widespread public cynicism about the honesty of the ordinary police. Many believe that payoffs can buy police cooperation in overlooking crimes or ordinary legal infractions such as traffic tickets.

The Soviet military once ranked second only to that of the United States. Russian defense spending declined in the 1990s, then increased again after 2000, but is still below Soviet levels. In 2016, military spending represented about 5.3 percent of GDP, the highest level in the post-Soviet period. This compares to 3.3 percent for the United States and 1.9 percent for China.[12] The Soviet and Russian military have never usurped civilian power. The communist party controlled military appointments and, during the August 1991 coup attempt, troops remained loyal to Yeltsin and Gorbachev, even though the Minister of Defense was among the coup plotters. Likewise, in October 1993, despite some apparent hesitancy in military circles, military units defended the government's position, this time firing on civilian protesters and shocking the country.

The political power and prestige of the military suffered as a result of its failure to deal effectively with Chechnya, however in recent years, public confidence in the ability of the Russian military to protect the nation has increased.[13] The Russian Federation still maintains universal male conscription, but noncompliance and draftees rejected for health reasons have been persistent problems. In 2008, mandatory service was reduced from two years to one year; women have never been subject to the military draft. A law to permit alternative military service for conscientious objectors took effect in 2004. The Defense Minister has indicated that a military draft will remain necessary, alongside a professional army. In 2014, sporadic criticism surfaced from relatives of soldiers suspected of being secretly sent to Ukraine and killed.

High crime rates indicate a low capacity of the state to provide legal security to its citizens. Thus, in addition to state security agencies, sometimes businesses and individuals turn to private security firms to provide protection. A network of intrigue and hidden relationships can make it hard to determine the boundaries of state involvement in the security sector, and the government's inability to enforce laws or to apprehend violators may create an impression of state involvement even where there may be none. A prominent example is the case of a former agent of the Russian Federal Security Service, Alexander Litvinenko, an outspoken critic of the Russian government, who took political asylum in the United Kingdom. In November 2006, Litvinenko was fatally poisoned in London with a rare radioactive isotope. On his deathbed, Litvinenko accused the Kremlin of being responsible for his death, an undocumented accusation. The United Kingdom's efforts to extradite Andrei Lugovoi, an ex-KGB agent and Russian politician, to stand trial for the murder were refused by the Russian government, citing a constitutional prohibition. The issue sparked tension between the two countries, including expulsion of diplomats on both sides. These kinds of incidents have generated an atmosphere reminiscent of Cold War spy novels.

The Policy-Making Process

Policy-making in Russia occurs both formally and informally. According to the constitution, the federal government, the president and his administration, regional legislatures, individual deputies, and some judicial bodies may propose legislation. In the Yeltsin era, conflict between the president and State Duma made policy-making contentious and fractious; under Putin and Medvedev, the State Duma has generally gone along with proposals made by the president and the government, and the proportion of legislation initiated by the executive branch has increased significantly.

In order for a bill to become law, it must be approved by both houses of the parliament in three readings and signed by the president. If the president vetoes the bill, it must be passed again in the same wording by a two-thirds majority of both houses in order to override the veto. Many policy proclamations have been made through presidential or governmental decrees, without formal consultation with the legislative branch. This decision-making process is much less visible and may involve closed-door bargaining rather than an open process of debate and consultation.

Informal groupings also have an important indirect impact on policy-making. During the Yeltsin period, business magnates were able to exert behind-the-scenes influence to gain benefits from the privatization of lucrative firms in sectors such as oil, media, and transport. Putin has attempted to reduce the direct political influence of these powerful economic figures, but at the cost of also reducing political competition.

A continuing problem is weak policy implementation. Under communist rule, the party's control over political appointments enforced at least some degree of conformity to central mandates. Under Yeltsin, fragmented and decentralized political power gave the executive branch few resources to ensure compliance. Pervasive corruption, including bribery and selective enforcement, hindered enforcement of policy decisions. Although Putin and Medvedev both have stated their commitment to restrict these types of irregularities, they continue to persist. However, the commitment to reestablishing order and a rule of law has been an important justification for the centralization of power.

Where Do You Stand?

Do you think a strong presidency, such as exists in Russia, is compatible with democracy? If the public supports such an arrangement, does that itself give it democratic legitimacy?

In a country as wide and diverse as Russia, is federalism a good idea, or is it likely to increase the risk of separatism and disunity?

REPRESENTATION AND PARTICIPATION

▽ **Focus Questions**

- To what extent are elections and political parties effective tools for holding leaders accountable in Russia?

- What kinds of social movements have emerged in Russia and what influence do they have?

civil society

A term that refers to the space occupied by voluntary associations outside the state, for example, professional associations, trade unions, and student groups.

mixed electoral system

A system of electoral representation in which a portion of the seats are selected in winner-take-all single-member districts, and a portion are allocated according to parties within multimember constituencies, roughly in proportion to the votes each party receives in a popular election.

As the last leader of the Soviet Union, Mikhail Gorbachev implemented policies in the 1980s that brought a dramatic change in relations between state and society when *glasnost* sparked new public and private initiatives. Most restrictions on the formation of social organizations were lifted, and a large number of independent groups appeared. Hopes rose for the emergence of **civil society**. However, in post-Soviet Russia, only a small stratum of Russian society has been actively engaged; the demands of everyday life, cynicism about politics, and increasing controls on political opposition have led many people to withdraw into private life. Following a spike in public protests between 2011 and 2012, citizen engagement again decreased. However, a new outburst of protest against government corruption erupted in March 2017, with high youth participation. This raised questions about possibilities for renewed activism in the lead up to the presidential election, scheduled for 2018.

The Legislature

The Federal Assembly came into being after the parliamentary elections of December 12, 1993, when the referendum ratifying the new Russian constitution was also approved. The upper house, the Federation Council, represents Russia's constituent federal units. The lower house, the State Duma (hereafter the Duma), has 450 members and involves a **mixed electoral system**.

Within the Duma, factions unite deputies from the same party. The most recent Duma elections, in September 2016, resulted in four party factions gaining representation; 343 of 449 deputies (76.4 percent) were in the faction of the dominant party, United Russia, compared to 53 percent previously. The remaining representation was made up of forty-two Communist Party of the Russian Federation deputies, thirty-nine Liberal Democratic Party of Russia deputies, and twenty-three deputies from A Just Russia. Two deputies were unaffiliated. Compared to the communist period, deputies reflect less fully the demographic characteristics of the population. For example, in 1984, 33 percent were women, but only 16 percent in early 2017. The underrepresentation of women, as well as of workers, in the present Duma indicates the extent to which Russian politics is primarily the domain of male elites.

The upper house of the Federal Assembly, the Federation Council, has two members from each of Russia's federal regions and republics, for a total of 170 members. This includes many prominent businessmen; in some cases, the posts may be granted in exchange for political loyalty. Party factions do not play a significant role in the Federation Council. Deputies to the Federation Council, as well as to the Duma, are granted immunity from criminal prosecution.

The constitution grants the Federal Assembly powers in the legislative and budgetary arenas, but if there is conflict with the president or government, these powers can be exercised effectively only if the legislative branch operates with a high degree of unity. In practice, the president can often override or bypass the legislature through the veto of legislation or use of decrees. Each house of parliament has the authority to confirm certain presidential appointees. The Federation Council must also approve presidential decrees relating to martial law and state emergencies, as well as to deploying troops abroad.

Following electoral rebuffs in the 1993 and 1995 legislative elections, Yeltsin confronted a body that obstructed many of his proposed policies; but the legislature did not have the power or unity to offer a constructive alternative. Since 2003, however, the Duma has cooperated with the president, since a majority of the deputies have been tied to the United Russia faction, closest to the president, and deputies from other parties have also often supported the president's initiatives. In general, the process of gaining Duma acceptance of government proposals has depended more on the authority of the president than on the presence of disciplined party accountability such as exists in some European countries.

Society's ability to affect particular policy decisions through the legislative process is minimal. Political parties are isolated from the public at large, suffer low levels of popular respect, and the internal decision-making structures of parties are generally elite-dominated.

Political Parties and the Party System

One of the most important political changes following the collapse of communism was the shift from a single-party to a multiparty system. In the USSR, the Communist Party (CPSU) not only dominated state organs but also oversaw social institutions, such as the mass media, trade unions, youth groups, educational institutions, and professional associations. It defined the official ideology for the country and ensured that loyal supporters occupied all important offices. Approximately 10 percent of adults in the Soviet Union were party members, but there were no effective mechanisms to ensure accountability of the party leadership to its members.

As part of Gorbachev's reforms, national competitive elections were held in 1989, but new political parties were not formal participants until 1993. Since then, a confusing array of political organizations has emerged. For the December 2011 Duma elections, seven parties met conditions of legal registration. A change in the law governing political parties was adopted as a concession to popular protests after those elections; this change loosened requirements for party registration. In the 2016 Duma elections, 22 parties took part, resulting in a fragmentation of opposition to United Russia.

In the 1990s, many parties formed around prominent individuals, making politics very personalistic. Most parties were newly established, so deeply rooted political identifications have not been built easily or quickly. Also, many citizens do not have a clear conception of how parties might represent their interests. Image making is often as important as programmatic positions, so parties appeal to transient voter sentiments. Nonetheless, there has been a relative stabilization of competition among major contenders in the most recent decade.

While individual leaders play an important role in political life in Russia, some key issues have divided opinions in the post-1991 period. One such issue is economic policy. Nearly all political parties have mouthed support for creation of a market economy. However, communist and socialist parties have argued for a stronger state role in providing social protection for vulnerable parts of the population. The liberal parties, on the other hand, have advocated more rapid market reform, while United Russia charts a middle ground, appealing to voters from a wide ideological spectrum.

Another dividing line relates to national identity. Nationalist parties emphasize the defense of Russian interests: a strong military establishment and protection from foreign economic influence. Liberal parties, on the other hand, have favored adoption of Western economic and political principles, but they have lost public support and are no longer represented in the Duma. Despite its name, the Liberal Democratic Party of Russia is an ultra-conservative nationalist organization.

The United Russia party has articulated an intriguing combination of these viewpoints. Although traditionally identifying Europe as the primary identity point for Russia, more recently the party's leaders have advocated Russia's pursuit of its own unique path of development, based in a conservative interpretation of European values and emphasizing Russia's role as a bridge between Europe and Asia.

Because nationalist sentiments cut across economic ideologies, Russian political parties do not fit neatly on a left–right spectrum, but produce the following tendencies:

- The traditional left, critical of market reform and often mildly nationalistic
- Centrist "parties of power"
- Nationalistic forces, primarily concerned with identity issues, patriotism, and national self-assertion
- Liberal forces, supporting Western-type reforms and values

The most important parties in the first three groupings have been able to work within the existing structure of power. Since 2000, liberal parties have lost influence in mainstream political institutions, with key figures emerging as prominent oppositionists outside of the legislative party system. Of the four parties represented in the State Duma, two are centrist (United Russia and A Just Russia), one is traditional leftist (the Communist Party of the Russian Federation), and a fourth (Liberal Democratic Party of Russia) is nationalist.

The Dominant Party: United Russia

dominant party

A political party that manages to maintain consistent control of a political system through formal and informal mechanisms of power, with or without strong support from the population.

Since 2003, United Russia has clearly been the **dominant party** in Russian politics. Its predecessor, the Unity Party, rose to prominence, together with Vladimir Putin, in the elections of 1999 and 2000. United Russia's vote total rose from 23.3 percent in the 1999 Duma elections up to 64 percent in 2007. In 2016, the party got 54.2 percent of the Duma party vote, and its membership was over 2 million.[14] In April 2008, at a party congress, United Russia's delegates unanimously approved creation of a custom-made post for Vladimir Putin as party chairman, but with his return to the presidency in 2012, Dmitry Medvedev, who became prime minister, took over that position, keeping the presidency formally distinct from the party leadership. In fact, United Russia has served as a major source of political support for Putin. (See Table 13.2.)

What explains United Russia's success? An important factor is the association with Putin, but the party has also built a political machine to generate persuasive incentives for regional elites. The party is focused on winning to its side prominent people, including heads of Russia's regions, who then use their influence to further bolster the party's votes. The party program emphasizes the uniqueness of the Russian approach to governance, a strong state role within a market economy, improvement in socio-economic conditions for the population, law and order, and conservative social values. An important question is to what degree the party would be able to maintain its dominant role without Vladimir Putin in power.

Other Parties Represented in the State Duma

Many consider the Communist Party of the Russian Federation (CPRF) to be the only party in the Duma that could be a real opposition force. The CPRF was by far the strongest parliamentary party after the 1995 elections, winning over one-third

KIRILL KUDRYAVTSEV/Getty Images

Campaign poster of the dominant political party in Russia, United Russia.

of the Duma seats. Its strength declined, however, to just 11.6 percent of the Duma vote in 2007, before rising slightly to 13.4 percent in the 2016 elections. The party defines its goals as democracy, justice, equality, patriotism and internationalism, a combination of civic rights and duties, and socialist renewal. Primary among the party's concerns are the social costs of the market reform process.

The CPRF represents people who have adapted less successfully to the radical changes of recent years, as well as some individuals committed to socialist ideals. Support is especially strong among older Russians, the economically disadvantaged, and rural residents. The party has failed to adapt its public position to attract significant numbers of new adherents, particularly among the young, and its leader since the early 1990s, Gennady Zyuganov (now in his 70s), has not been able to give the party an attractive new face. Although one might expect Russia to offer fertile ground for social democratic sentiments like those that are evident in the Scandinavian countries of Western Europe, the CPRF has neither expanded its base of support, nor has it made room for a new social democratic party that could be more successful.

Two other parties are represented in the State Duma. Like the CPRF, the Liberal Democratic Party of Russia (LDPR) has won seats in every election since 1993. The LDPR is neither liberal nor particularly democratic; as noted above, it is conservative, nationalist, and populist. Its leadership openly appeals to anti-Western sentiments, which are now closer to the mainstream position since the eruption of the Ukraine crisis in 2014 and the imposition of sanctions on Russia by the United States and the EU. Concern with the breakdown of law and order seems to rank high among

Table 13.2 Election Results and Seats in the Russian State Duma, 2007–2017 (in percent)

Party	Percent of 2007 Party List Vote*	Percent of Party List Vote 2011*	Percent of Party List Vote 2016*	Percent of Duma Seats, March 2017*	Current Party Leader
Centrist					
United Russia	64.3	49.3	54.2	76.4	Dmitri Medvedev (since 2012) Vladimir Putin (2007–2012)
A Just Russia	7.7	13.3	6.2	5.1	Sergey Mironov
Communist					
Communist Party of the Russian Federation	11.6	19.2	13.3	9.4	Gennady Zyuganov
Communists of Russia (formed 2012)			2.3	0	Maksim Suraikin
Nationalist					
Liberal Democratic Party of Russia	8.1	11.7	13.1	8.7	Vladimir Zhirinovksy
Patriots of Russia	0.9	1.0	.6	0	Gennady Semigin
Liberal					
Yabloko	1.6	3.4	2.0	0	Sergey Mitrokhin

*Column percentages may not add up to 100 percent because some smaller parties are not listed or due to rounding.

its priorities. The party's leader, Vladimir Zhirinovsky, has garnered support among working-class men and military personnel. However, most often this party has not challenged the political establishment on important issues.

Finally, A Just Russia, founded in 2006, espouses moderate support for social-ist principles, placing it to the left of United Russia on the political spectrum and offering a political magnet for dissatisfied supporters of the CPRF. Many observers consider that A Just Russia was formed with the Kremlin's support to demonstrate the competitive nature of Russia's electoral system, while undermining opposition parties that might pose a real threat to United Russia. In highly exceptional cases, A Just Russia has been able to win mayoral elections in smaller cities; however, the party does not pose a real challenge to the political establishment and has generally supported the president and government.

While these three parties, singly or combined, cannot challenge the power of United Russia, they have on occasion issued protests over what they consider to be unfair electoral procedures. For example, in October 2009, deputies from all three factions abandoned a session of the Duma as a sign of protest against the results of regional elections, accusing United Russia of infringement of proper electoral pro-cedures and demanding that the results be nullified. After consultations with the president, the demands were withdrawn.

Western-Oriented Liberal Parties and Kremlin Critics: Marginalized

The liberal/reform parties have become marginalized since 2003, when they won a handful of seats in the Duma. Prominent figures, such as Boris Nemstov and Grigory Yavlinksy, were influential advocates of reform policies in the 1990s, but they have not been able to build a stable and unified electoral base since. These groups have organized under a variety of transient party names since 1993, including the Union of Rightist Forces, Democratic Choice, and, most recently, Just Cause. The Yabloko party (formed by Yavlinksy) has endured throughout the entire period, but last won seats on the Duma's party list ballot in 2004; in the 2016 elections it won only 2% of the vote, putting it below the threshhold for representation. The liberal/reform parties have espoused a commitment to traditional liberal values, such as a limited economic role for the state, free-market principles, and the protection of individual rights and liberties. Many Russians hold their policies, such as rapid privatization and associated price increases, as responsible for Russia's economic decline in the 1990s. Their support has generally has been stronger among the young, the more highly educated, urban dwellers, and the well-off. Thus, ironically, those with the best pros-pects for succeeding in the new market economy have been the least successful in fashioning an effective political party to represent themselves.

In recent years, Boris Nemstov emerged as an outspoken critic of Putin's leader-ship, helping to organize protest marches and issuing reports revealing corruption and, most recently, providing evidence of Russian support for separatist fighters in eastern Ukraine. In February 2015, Nemtsov was assassinated on a street in cen-tral Moscow. Based on the official investigation, five Chechen men were placed on trial for the murder, but speculation about who was behind this and other politi-cal murders (such as the death of former Duma deputy and Kremlin critic Dennis Voronenkov, in Kiev in March 2017) has been rife.

Kremlin critics have continued to try to gain support through the electoral process. Mikhail Prokhorov, a Russian businessman and billionaire owner of the Brooklyn Nets basketball team, won support from a part of the liberal electorate in his bid for the presidency in 2012 (winning about 8 percent of the vote). He

Memorial to opposition figure, Boris Nemstov.

SERGEI SUPINSKY/Getty Images

subsequently formed the party Civic Platform, which won less than 1 percent (.22 percent) of the Duma party list vote in 2016. The attempt of Alexei Navalny, another opposition figure (although not in the liberal camp), to gain inclusion of his newly created Progress Party in the 2016 Duma elections was denied, on technical grounds.

Elections

Under the Russian constitution, presidential elections were initially held every four years, but beginning with the 2012 election the term is six years; the Duma mandate was extended from four to five years. Turnout in federal elections remains respectable, but declining. It stood at 60 percent in the 2011 Duma election, dropping to about 48 percent in 2016. Turnout in the presidential vote, although somewhat higher than in Duma elections, fell from about 70 percent in 2008 to close to 65 percent in 2012. Particularly for presidential votes, the political leadership has actively encouraged voter turnout, to give elections an appearance of legitimacy. From 1991 until 2003, national elections were generally considered to be reasonably fair and free. Since then, international observers have expressed serious concerns about electoral fairness, pointing to slanted media coverage as well as electoral irregularities.

Until 2007, the electoral system for selecting the Duma combined proportional representation (with a 5 percent threshold) with winner-take-all districts (somewhat similar to the German system for Bundestag elections). In addition, voters were given the explicit option of voting against all candidates or parties; 4.7 percent chose this in 2003. In an interlude from 2007 until 2014, the single-member districts were abolished, so that all 450 deputies were elected on the basis of one national proportional representation district, with a minimum threshold for party representation raised to 7 percent.

In February 2014, the electoral system was revised again, returning to a system similar to that in place prior to 2007; however, there are some additional requirements for registration of candidates in the winner-take-all contests. Parties are required to include regional representatives on their lists from across the country. A 2001 law on political parties created difficult thresholds for party participation in elections, but these were relaxed in April 2012, so that now only 500 members are needed to register a party, but with branches in half of Russia's federal regions. In 2006, national legislation removed the "against all" option from the ballot; it is now available only in municipal elections.[15]

With the rapid ascent of United Russia since 1999, opposition parties have had difficulty offering an effective challenge to the dominant party. Reasons include genuine popular support for Putin and the failure of the opposition parties to develop appealing programs or field attractive candidates. Media coverage has also strongly favored United Russia and the president. Administrative control measures and selective enforcement of laws have provided pretexts to disqualify opposition forces. In addition, the carrot-and-stick method has wooed regional elites, producing a bandwagon effect that builds on rewards for political loyalty. Russia has yet to experience a real transfer of power from one political grouping to another, which some scholars consider a critical step in consolidating democratic governance.

Political Culture, Citizenship, and Identity

Political culture can be a source of great continuity in the face of radical political upheavals. Some attitudes prevalent in the Soviet period have endured with remarkable tenacity. These include acceptance of strong political leadership and centralized power, as well as a belief in science and technology as key national priorities. When communism collapsed, other aspects of Soviet ideology, such as guaranteed employment, were discredited, and in the early 1990s, the government embraced Western political and economic values. However, over time, many citizens and political leaders have become skeptical of this "imported" culture, which conflicts, in some regards, with traditional civic values such as egalitarianism, collectivism, traditional gender roles, and a broad scope for state activity. During Putin's presidency, the leadership espoused the concept of **sovereign democracy**, emphasizing the importance of adapting democratic principles to the Russian context.

In 1989, just over 50 percent of the population of the USSR was ethnically Russian, but now many ethnic minorities reside in other Soviet successor states. According to the 2010 census, Russians now make up 77.7 percent of the population of the Russian Federation. The largest minority group is the Tatars (3.7 percent), a traditionally Muslim group residing primarily in Tatarstan, one of Russia's republics. Other significant minorities are the neighboring Bashkirs (1.1 percent), various indigenous peoples of the Russian north, the many Muslim groups in the northern Caucasus region, and ethnic groups (such as Ukrainians and Armenians) of other former Soviet republics. There are over fifty languages spoken in the Russian Federation, although Russian is clearly the lingua franca. Some 25 million ethnic Russians reside outside of the Russian Federation in other former Soviet republics, which at times has provided a pretext for Russian intervention in regions adjacent to the country, including in Crimea, where nearly 70 percent of the population is ethnically Russian.

Because Russia is a multiethnic state, one important aspect of the state's search for identity relates to what it means to be Russian. The Russian language itself has two distinct words for Russian people: *russkii*, which refers to an ethnicity, and *rossiianin*,

Political culture

Fundamental values, beliefs, and orientations that are held by the population of a country and that can affect the manner in which citizens view their government, participate in politics, or assess policies.

sovereign democracy

A concept of democracy articulated by President Putin's political advisor, Vladimir Surkov, to communicate the idea that democracy in Russia should be adapted to Russian traditions and conditions rather than based on Western models.

a broader civic concept referring to people of various ethnic backgrounds who make up the Russian citizenry. While the political foundation of the Russian Federation is based on a civic rather than ethnic definition of "Russianness," both anti-Semitic and anti-Muslim sentiments surface in everyday life. In recent years, there have been increasing concerns about the rise of an exclusionary form of Russian nationalism. Official state policy, while explicitly opposing ethnic stereotypes, may, in some cases, have implicitly fed them.

At the same time, Putin has acknowledged the difficulty Russia faces in finding a clear sense of national identity that encompasses the country's diversity. In 2013, Putin appealed to traditional Russian values as a basis of national unity, contrasting this with "Euro-Atlantic countries" that are "denying moral principles and all traditional identities: national, cultural, religious, and even sexual."[16] The Russian Orthodox Church appeals to citizens who are looking to replace the discredited values of the communist system. However, religion has not emerged as a significant basis of political cleavage for ethnic Russians.

Attitudes toward gender relations in Russia largely reflect traditional family values. Women carry the primary responsibility for child care and a certain standard of "femininity" is expected of women both inside and outside the workplace. Feminism is not popular in Russia, as many women consider it inconsistent with traditional notions of femininity or with accepted social roles for women.

At the same time, a number of civil society organizations have sprung up to represent the interests of women. Some of them advocate traditional policies to provide better social support for mothers and families, while others challenge traditional gender roles. A law enacted in 2017 decriminalizes some forms of domestic violence that do not cause serious bodily harm (making them subject only to fines or minor penalties); the law has been sharply criticized abroad and by Russian activists. Equally contentious was a 2013 law that imposes fines for promoting ideas about nontraditional sexual relations to youth. The measure was condemned by human rights advocates inside and outside Russia, and elicited strong international protests in the lead up to the 2014 Olympic Games in Sochi, Russia.

Social class was a major theme of collective identity in the Soviet period. The Bolshevik revolution was justified in the name of the working class, and the Communist Party of the Soviet Union claimed to be a working-class party. Because social class was a major part of the discredited Soviet ideology, in the post-communist period many Russians remain skeptical of claims made by politicians to represent the working class, and trade unions are weakly supported. Even the Communist Party of the Russian Federation does not explicitly identify itself as a working-class party.

Interest Groups, Social Movements, and Protest

After the collapse of the USSR, numerous political and social organizations sprang up, representing the interests of groups such as children, veterans, women, environmental advocates, pensioners, and the disabled. Many observers saw such blossoming activism as the foundation for a fledgling civil society that would nurture the new democratic institutions established after 1991. However, there have been many obstacles to realizing this potential, including inadequate resources and restrictions on their activities.

In January 2006, Putin signed legislation amending laws on public associations and noncommercial organizations. These controversial changes, protested widely by Western governments, created new grounds for denying registration to such organizations, established additional reporting requirements (particularly for organizations receiving funds from foreign sources), and increased government supervisory functions. The law reflects concern that foreign influence may spur political activism in the country that could challenge stability or the current structure of power.

A 2012 law requires nongovernmental organizations (NGOs) that engage in political activity on the basis of foreign financing to register as "foreign agents" and submit to strict reporting requirements, as well as public stigma. Several Russian organizations have refused to comply; some NGOs also filed a complaint with the European Court of Human Rights, including the Levada Center, a leading Russian independent public opinion polling organization, which the government declared to be a foreign agent just before the 2016 Russian Duma elections.

At the same time, the government has attempted to channel public activism through official forums. These have included the Civic Forum, organized with government support in 2001, and more recently, the Public Chamber, created in 2005 by legislation proposed by the president. Based on voluntary participation by presidential appointees and representatives recommended by national and regional societal organizations, these bodies are presented as a mechanism for public consultation and input, as well as a vehicle for creating public support for government policy. This likely involves an effort to co-opt public activists from more disruptive forms of self-expression, and also to mobilize the assistance of citizens' groups in delivering social services.

A variety of mass-based political organizations protest the current political direction of the government, but since 2007 the authorities have periodically tried to restrict the use of public demonstrations and protests. The widespread protests that followed the 2011 Duma elections represented the most dramatic evidence of significant opposition sentiment in major urban centers. On December 10, 2011, an estimated 50,000 protesters participated, followed by equally large demonstrations leading up to the presidential election in March 2012. Just before a planned demonstration on June 12, 2012 (named the "march of millions"), Putin signed a new law that imposed high fines for participating in demonstrations that undermine public order or destroy public property; the homes of leading opposition figures were also searched. The law was used to charge hundreds of protesters in March and June 2017, including the sentencing of anti-corruption activist Alexei Navalny to 15 days detention.

An earlier high prolife protest occurred on February 21, 2012, when an unusual performance occurred in Christ the Savior Church in central Moscow. The female punk rock group known as Pussy Riot displayed what it called a "punk prayer," protesting the Russian Orthodox Church's support for Vladimir Putin in the upcoming presidential election. Formed in 2011, the group's 2012 performance elicited particular objection from the authorities, leading to the arrest and 2-year sentencing of some members for "hooliganism, motivated by religious hatred." The ruling became a cause célèbre, interpreted as symbolic of the Kremlin's lack of tolerance of political opposition.

In December 2013, in a well-publicized move, the Russian State Duma passed an amnesty law, supported by President Putin, widely interpreted as an effort to bolster the government's tarnished human rights reputation in the lead up to the Sochi Winter Olympics the following February. Since then, former members of Pussy Riot have taken up various protest causes including prisoner rights in Russia, using songs and a website called MediaZona to counter the Kremlin "misinformation."

More traditional public organizations also continue to exist in Russia. The official trade unions established under Soviet rule have survived under the title of the Federation of Independent Trade Unions (FITU). However, FITU has lost the confidence of large parts of the workforce. In some sectors, such as the coal industry,

The feminist rock group, Pussy Riot, undertakes a protest performance in Christ the Saviour Church, Moscow, in February 2012.

new independent trade unions have formed, mainly at the local level. Labor actions have included spontaneous strikes, transport blockages, and even hunger strikes. Immediate concessions are often offered in response to such protests, but the underlying problems are rarely addressed. Protest actions, especially in times of economic downturn, have most often focused on nonpayment of wages or low wage levels. Official statistics indicated overall unpaid wages of 2,725 million rubles (or about US$48 million) at the beginning of 2017,[17] concentrated in construction and manufacturing. However, local protests over such issues seem to be only weakly linked to the national political protests, referred to above.

Unemployment, low wages, and the breakdown in traditional social linkages have also intensified some social problems. Increasing numbers of young women have turned to prostitution to make a living. HIV/AIDS rates are also increasing at a rapid rate, fueled by intravenous drug use, prostitution, and low levels of sexual health information. Alcohol abuse continues to be a cause of premature death, especially among Russian men, which is one reason why the gap between male life expectancy in Russia (65 years) and female life expectancy (77 years) is high compared to almost any country in the world.

The Political Impact of Technology and the Media

In the post-Soviet period, television has been the main source of news and political information for Russian citizens. Article 29 of the Russian constitution guarantees "freedom of the mass media" and prohibits censorship. However, Russia ranked 148th out of 179 countries in 2016 in terms of press freedom, according to *Reporters without Borders*.[18] A 2014 recent survey, by a respected Russian independent public opinion agency, revealed that 69 percent of respondents acknowledged government censorship in the main Russian TV channels and 77 percent felt that a greater diversity of views in TV media would be desirable. However, suspicion of the media seems to have decreased since 2014 when the Ukraine crisis erupted. In 2016, 35 percent of those polled indicated that TV, radio, and newspaper very or rather often provide obviously false information, compared to 45 percent in 2012.[19] While much of the television coverage is subject to more or less direct influence by the government, some newspapers and independent journalists, as well as Internet sources, do offer a critical perspective on political developments.

As in other countries, Internet usage has increased rapidly in the Russian Federation. In fall 2015, about 67 percent of Russians over age eighteen used the internet at least once a month and about 54 percent daily.[20] However, the major uses of the Internet are social media and entertainment; the Russian corollary of Facebook, called vk.com, is particularly popular with young people. Internet use, as in other countries, is more widespread among the young. Contacts through social media and other Internet sources were important in mobilizing participation in demonstrations surrounding the 2011 and 2012 elections and in March 2017. However, the Internet has not provided a medium for creation of a sustained and unified opposition movement. Furthermore, the state has apparently made effective use of both television and Internet communications to disseminate its interpretations of the news, as well as creating relatively effective e-portals for government services.

The Russian government has also effectively used electronic media to project a positive image abroad through vehicles such as the global TV channel, RT (formerly Russia Today), and its associated Internet site (rt.com). In August 2013, Russian authorities granted asylum to Edward Snowden, for whom the United States sought extradition in connection with his alleged release of classified security documents. Nongovernmental sources in Russia have launched successful cyberattacks; it is often difficult for foreign intelligence agencies to determine whether such attacks are connected to government authorities. Possible Russian state support for the hacking of emails of the U.S. Democratic National Committee, preceding the U.S. presidential election in 2016, was the subject of U.S. congressional and FBI investigations following the election. Russian leaders have rejected any connection with the attacks. Russian hackers were also suspected of being behind a cyberattack against the German national parliament in 2015.

Until recently, government restrictions on domestic Internet usage have been minimal. In early 2014, new legislation created instruments for closer monitoring of bloggers with large followings. Reinforced by a 2016 amendment to previous anti-terrorism legislation, Russian law grants security services the authority to access citizens' online activities and requires Internet service providers to facilitate the collection and 6-month storage of email and text messaging. As yet, this capacity has not been utilized in a systematic way to control opposition activities. The Internet still provides the attentive Russian public with access to a broad range of domestic and foreign opinion, even if most citizens do not utilize this opportunity to its full potential.

Where Do You Stand?

Is the Russian government justified in trying to limit the influence of foreign governments or international organizations on Russian domestic politics?

In a country with a history of radical political ruptures, is it reasonable for the government to put limits on opposition protests in the name of stable government?

RUSSIAN POLITICS IN TRANSITION

▼ Focus Questions

• What types of strategies has Russia pursued in trying to reestablish itself as a regional and global power? How effective have these strategies been?

• What are the main challenges to political stability in Russia?

On March 1, 2014, the Russian Duma authorized President Putin to deploy military forces in Crimea, an autonomous region of the neighboring independent state of Ukraine, justified in order to protect the rights of ethnic Russians residing there. In the preceding days, Crimea had already effectively been brought under Russian military control due to the mobilization of personnel of Russia's Black Sea Fleet based in Crimea under a long-term lease agreement with Ukraine. Russian control of the region was reinforced by the introduction of additional troops. A self-appointed pro-Russian regional government in Crimea held a contested referendum on March 16, with Russia's blessing, proposing that Crimea be annexed to Russia. Russia accepted Crimea into the Russian Federation the same week.

The Russian intervention was in response to a power turnover in Ukraine in late February 2014, which resulted from 3 months of massive popular demonstrations in Ukraine's capital, Kiev, against the incumbent president, Victor Yanukovych. Those protests were triggered by Yanukovych's decision, under heavy Russian pressure, to back away from signing long-awaited free trade and association agreements with the EU. When violence erupted, the crisis culminated in the collapse of Yanukovych's government as he fled Ukraine. Moscow said it was a coup d'état by pro-European Ukrainian political forces. In fact, the new interim Ukrainian government made a sharp turn towards Europe, and presidential elections in May 2014 produced a clear victory for Petro Poroshenko, a pro-Western businessman.

The United States and the EU reacted strongly to Russia's annexation of Crimea, which they said was a violation of Ukraine's territorial sovereignty and a breach of international law. In March 2014, Western governments and the EU instituted sanctions against Russia, not only for the takeover of Crimea, but also because, they claimed, Russia was continuing to foment unrest in eastern Ukraine by covertly encouraging seizures of public buildings by armed separatist forces. Shortly thereafter, Russia implemented counter-sanctions involving a ban on certain food imports from countries that had instituted sanctions against Russia. In February 2015, a compromise to solve the crisis was thrashed out between the leaders of Ukraine, Russia, Germany, and France, called the Minsk II agreement; however, it has not been implemented, with Ukraine and Russia both attributing blame to the other. As of August 2017, Western sanctions against Russia and Russian counter-sanctions remained in place, marking the lowest point in relations between Russia and the West since the end of the Cold War.

Political Challenges and Changing Agendas

Russia's future path continues to remain unclear. While recent years have seen Russia move in an authoritarian direction, some analysts believe that, in the face of economic challenges and continuing high levels of corruption, the current structure of power is vulnerable. When the first edition of this book was published in 1996, five possible scenarios for Russia's future were presented:

1. A stable progression toward democratization
2. The gradual introduction of "soft authoritarianism"
3. A return to a more extreme authoritarianism of a quasi-fascist or communist variety
4. The disintegration of Russia into regional fiefdoms
5. Economic decline, civil war, and military expansionism

At the time of this writing, the "soft authoritarian" scenario seems to have taken hold; however, there are still significant forces that may move Russia back to a more democratic trajectory. Major questions also linger over Russia's regional and international aspirations in the wake of the 2014 events in Ukraine.

In the international sphere, post-Soviet Russia's flirtation with Westernization in the early 1990s produced ambiguous results, leading to a severe recession and placing Russia in the position of a supplicant state requesting international credits and assistance from the West. Russia's protests against unpalatable international developments, such as NATO enlargement and NATO's bombing of Yugoslavia in 1999 during the Kosovo War, revealed Moscow's underlying resentment against Western dominance, as well as the country's sense of powerlessness in affecting global developments. The events of September 11, 2001, however, provided an impetus for cooperative efforts in the battle against international terrorism, and Russia's economic revival imparted to the country a sense of greater power. Evidence of warmer relations included the formation of a NATO-Russia Council in May 2002. But new tensions arose around the U.S. withdrawal from the Anti-Ballistic Missile Treaty in 2002, Russian objections to the U.S. incursion into Iraq in March 2003, U.S. proposals to erect a missile defense system in Central Europe, a 2008 Russian incursion into the neighboring nation of Georgia, Russia's annexation of Crimea in 2014, and most recently, accusations of Russian meddling in the 2016 U.S. presidential election.

One of Russia's main challenges has been to reestablish itself as a respected regional leader, particularly among those states that were formerly part of the Soviet Union. The relationship to Ukraine has been fraught with particular difficulties. Ukraine's own internal political divisions between pro-European and pro-Russian groups have provided Russia with an opportunity to exert political leverage. After the Russian annexation of Crimea in February 2014, Ukraine signed an Association Agreement and comprehensive free trade agreement with the EU, which placed Ukraine more clearly on a Western trajectory. Accordingly, trade with Russia has declined and Ukraine's leaders continue to espouse a desire to join NATO, an objective unlikely to be achieved, but highly offensive to Russia. While the events in Ukraine bolstered the domestic popularity of Vladimir Putin inside Russia, by reigniting a sense of national identity and pride, they also have imposed considerable costs in terms of the rupture with the West, a consequent decline in foreign direct investment and economic ties, and the economic burden associated with integrating Crimea into the Russian Federation.

Russia has struggled to establish itself as a positive role model in the region. Efforts to form regional organizations to strengthen ties between these countries and Russia have taken a variety of forms. The largely ineffective Commonwealth of Independent States, formed in 1991 when the Soviet Union collapsed, was joined later by the Collective Security Treaty Organization (CSTO), the Eurasian Economic Forum, and the Shanghai Cooperation Organization (SCO), including China and the post-Soviet Central Asian states. Each of these organizations included a subset of countries from the former Soviet space as members, but without Ukraine or Georgia. In 2011, Vladimir Putin announced the formation of the Eurasian Economic Union (EEU), building on the Eurasian Customs Union formed in 2010. Launched in 2015, and initially involving only Russia, Belarus and Kazakhstan, the Eurasian Economic Union has since acquired two new members—Kyrgyzstan and Armenia. Putin's vision is for the EEU to lead to more comprehensive regional integration, uniting several of the non-EU countries in the post-Soviet space under Russian leadership. However, concerns about Russian dominance create hesitancy both among current and potential member countries.

Driving Russia's self-assertion is a sense of failure in realizing a primary goal of Russian foreign policy in the post-Soviet period, namely achieving the status of an equal partner with the United States and Europe. At the same time, popular attitudes toward Western countries remain ambivalent. (See Table 13.3). Russia has joined a number of international organizations such as the Council of Europe, the International Monetary Fund, the G7 (renamed the G8 when Russia was added) and the World Trade Organization, while inheriting the Soviet Union's permanent seat on the United Nations Security Council. Other achievements include negotiation of a new Strategic Arms Reduction Treaty with the United States, which took effect in January 2011. However, the decision of the United States to pursue installation of a missile defense system in Central Europe (in response to a potential Iranian attack) irritated Russia. Compared to U.S.-Russian relations, progress in relations between Russia and the EU was more substantial, with a broad range of negotiating platforms, and movement toward eased visa regulations and enhanced trade; however, this process was largely halted in 2014, when the crisis erupted over Crimea and eastern Ukraine.

Russia remains the most important source of Europe's gas imports. However, experts believe that without increased Western investment and technological know-how, Russia will not be able to develop untapped deposits quickly enough to meet both domestic demands and export commitments. A major agreement regarding future Russian gas exports to China, signed in May 2014, is an indicator of Russia's intention of reducing its dependence on exports to Europe.

The 2008–2009 global financial-economic crisis sent a warning to Russia about the dangers of an economy dependent on energy exports. A sharp drop in gas and oil prices temporarily undercut the foundation of Russia's economic motor. From positive growth rates in the previous ten years, Russia moved to a dramatic fall by the first quarter of 2009. Because energy prices recovered fairly quickly and Russia had reserve funds to fall back on, the crisis did not push Russia back to the disastrous economic situation of the 1990s, but the dramatic shift in economic performance may have reminded both the Russian public and its leaders of the potential fragility of the economic recovery.

In November 2009, President Medvedev published a much-discussed article entitled "Go Russia" in which he called for a modernization program, primarily through the development of high-technology sectors. However, with Putin's return to the presidency in 2012, the modernization program proved to be stillborn. Furthermore, hopes that political liberalization might accompany efforts to diversify the economy were also dashed. The continuing disjuncture between a high level of public support for Putin, alongside a continuing lack of confidence in the ability of government institutions to address the country's problems, suggests that the legitimacy of Russia's political system is still on thin ice. The more positive working relationship between the executive and legislative branches that emerged under the Medvedev-Putin tandem has been at the cost of permitting a real parliamentary opposition to function.

Table 13.3	Russian Attitudes Toward Relations with Foreign Countries					
	Jan. 2008	Jan. 2011	Jan. 2014	May 2014	Jan. 2017	Mar. 2017
With the United States						
Very good/good	51.0%	60.0%	43.0%	18.0%	28.0%	37.0%
Negative/very negative	39.0%	27.0%	44.0%	71.0%	56.0%	51.0%
Hard to say	11.0%	13.0%	13.0%	11.0%	16.0%	12.0%
With the EU						
Very good/good	70.0%	69.0%	51.0%	25.0%	40.0%	35.0%
Negative/very negative	17.0%	16.0%	34.0%	60.0%	47.0%	53.0%
Hard to say	13.0%	15.0%	15.0%	15.0%	14.0%	12.0%
With Ukraine						
Very good/good	59.0%	72.0%	65.0%	35.0%	34.0%	33.0%
Negative/very negative	30.0%	19.0%	26.0%	49.0%	54.0%	56.0%
Hard to say	11.0%	9.0%	9.0%	17.0%	13.0%	11.0%

Source: Levada Center, http://www.levada.ru/2017/04/10/rossiya-i-mir-3/. Columns may not add up to 100% due to rounding.

Failed efforts to contain corruption, mechanisms to exert control over the newly reinstated gubernatorial elections, and efforts to dissuade political opposition already show signs of producing poor policy choices that may themselves reinforce public cynicism about the motives of politicians and the trustworthiness of institutions.

Despite changes in social consciousness, the formation of new political identities in Russia also remains unfinished business. (See Table 13.4.) Many people are still preoccupied by challenges of everyday life, with little time or energy to engage in new forms of collective action to address underlying problems. Under such circumstances, the appeal to nationalism and other basic sentiments can be powerful. The weakness of Russian intermediary organizations (interest groups, political parties, or citizen associations) means that politicians can more easily appeal directly

Table 13.4	Russian Views of Different Types of Political Systems								
	Nov. 1997	Mar. 2000	Mar. 2003	Dec. 2006	Feb. 2008	Feb. 2010	Jan. 2012	Jan. 2014	Jan. 2016
The Soviet one, which we had until the 1990s	38%	42%	48%	35%	24%	34%	29%	39%	37%
The current system	11%	11%	18%	26%	36%	28%	20%	19%	23%
Democracy like Western countries	28%	26%	22%	16%	15%	20%	29%	21%	13%
Other	8%	4%	6%	7%	7%	7%	7%	8%	8%
Hard to say	16%	17%	7%	16%	18%	12%	15%	13%	19%

"What type of political system seems the best to you: The Soviet, the present system, or democracy of the type in Western countries?"

Source: http://www.levada.ru/2016/02/17/predpochtitelnye-modeli-ekonomicheskoj-i-politicheskoj-sistem/. Columns may not add up to 100% due to rounding.

to emotions because people are not members of groups that help them to evaluate the claims made by those in power or seeking power. These conditions reduce safeguards against authoritarian outcomes.

Nevertheless, the high level of education and increasing exposure to international media and the Internet may work in the opposite direction. Many Russians identify their country as part of Europe and its culture, an attitude echoed by the government, despite current tensions. Exposure to alternative political systems and cultures may make people more critical of their own political system and seek opportunities to change it. Russia remains in what seems to be an extended period of transition. In the early 1990s, Russians frequently hoped for "normal conditions," that is, an escape from the shortages, insecurity, and political controls of the past. Now, "normality" has been redefined in less glowing terms than those conceived in the initial post-Soviet period, as some political freedoms have been restricted and economic conditions have fluctuated, the standard of living still lags behind most Western countries, and Russia's relations with the United States and the EU have soured. Russians seem to have a capability to adapt to change and uncertainty that North Americans find at once alluring, puzzling, and disturbing.

Is Demographic Destiny?

Young people in Russia have grown up in political circumstances that differ dramatically from those that affected their parents. Whereas individuals born before 1970 (now middle-aged or older) were socialized during the period of communist rule, Russians between the ages of 18 and 30 had their formative experiences during a period of rapid political change following the collapse of the USSR. Whereas their elders were drawn into communist youth organizations and influenced by the dominance of a single party-state ideology, young people today are exposed to a wider range of political views, have greater freedom to travel abroad, and also have freer access to international contacts and viewpoints. These tendencies are reinforced even further by increased access to information through the Internet.

Generational experience also affects the ability to adapt. In the Soviet period, the weak material incentives of the socialist system encouraged risk avoidance, low productivity, poor punctuality, absenteeism, lack of personal initiative, and a preference for security over achievement. However, young people in Russia are adapting to a new work environment. They are more flexible, in part due to their age, and also because of differing socialization experiences that have resulted in altered expectations. Consequently, they are more oriented toward maximizing self-interest and demonstrating initiative. Nevertheless, many Russians of all age groups still question values underlying market reform, preferring an economy that is less profit driven and more oriented to equality and the collective good.

Despite generational differences, young people represent a wide range of political views in Russia, as elsewhere. On one side of the spectrum is the controversial youth group, Nashi (Ours), formed in 2005. While Nashi claims to oppose fascism in Russia, some observers see the group as nurturing intolerance and extremist sentiments. Nashi's goals include educating youth in Russian history and values, and forming volunteer groups to help maintain law and order. The group has been highly supportive of Putin, seeing him as a defender of Russia's national sovereignty. On the other end of the spectrum, those who initially participated in anti-government demonstrations in 2011 and 2012, and more recently in March and June 2017, have been disproportionately young; in 2011 and 2012, young activists were, over time, joined by many middle-aged protesters. While support for Putin in the lead-up to the presidential election of 2012 was relatively similar across age groups, those older than 40 were more likely to support the Communist Party, and more young people supported the nonestablishment candidate, Mikhail Prokhorov. These indicators suggest that age does affect political orientations, but not strongly or reliably enough to predict a generational shift in voting patterns and widespread political protest in the foreseeable future.

Demographic factors can also affect Russia's future. Following the collapse of the USSR, birthrates declined, as did the size of the Russian population. Only since 2009 has the population decline been reversed, but the level (144.2 million in 2016, without Crimea) has still not returned to that of 1991 (148.7 million). Only inward migration has prevented a further fall in Russia's overall population. As in other European countries, this demographic pattern can herald future problems for the social security system, as the population ages. By far the largest number of immigrants to Russia have come from former republics of the Soviet Union, especially the Central Asian states and, most recently, Ukraine. Russia has accepted a relatively small number of refugees in recent years, mainly from Afghanistan and Ukraine, but a large number of people have received temporary asylum from Ukraine since 2015 (over 300,000 in 2016) and a smaller number from Syria (about 1,300 in 2016).

Russian Politics in Comparative Perspective

The way in which politics, economics, and ideology were intertwined in the Soviet period has profoundly affected the nature of political change in all of the former Soviet republics and generally has made the democratization process more difficult.

How has Russia fared compared to some of the other post-communist systems that faced many of these same challenges? The countries of Central Europe that were outside the USSR (Poland, Hungary, Czech Republic, and Slovakia), as well as the Baltic states (Estonia, Latvia, and Lithuania), were able to accede to the EU in 2004, with Bulgaria and Romania also joining in 2007; joining the EU produced a strong motivation to embark on fundamental political and economic reform. This illustrates the potentially powerful impact of international forces on domestic political developments, if domestic actors are receptive. These countries were also under communist rule for a shorter period of time. In addition, most had a history of closer ties and greater cultural exposure to Western Europe; ideas of liberalism, private property, and individualism were less foreign to citizens there than in regions farther east, including Russia. Historical legacies and cultural differences do matter.

Russia's experience demonstrates the importance of strong political institutions if democracy is to be secured. Institutional weakness in the 1990s contributed to high levels of social dislocation, corruption, and personal stress, as well as to demographic decline and poor economic adaptation to the market. However, Russia's rich deposits of natural resources have sheltered it from difficulties facing some neighboring countries like Ukraine. However, this natural resource wealth has made it difficult to untangle economic and political power, reducing political accountability to the public. Heavy reliance on income from natural resource exports has also made Russia vulnerable to global economic trends.

In all of the post-Soviet states (except the Baltic states), the attempt to construct democratic political institutions has been characterized by repeated political crises, ineffective representation of popular interests, corruption, and faltering efforts at civil service and administrative reform. In Russia, terrorist attacks persist, reinforcing a sense of insecurity and producing fertile ground for nationalist sentiments and a strong role for the security forces. Nonetheless, with the exception of the Chechnya conflict and its spillover into the neighboring areas in Russia's European south, Russia has escaped major domestic violence and civil war, unlike parts of the former Yugoslavia, Georgia, Moldova, the Central Asian state of Tajikistan, and, most recently, eastern Ukraine.

Will Russia be able to find a place for itself in the world of states that meets the expectations of its educated and sophisticated population? Prospects are still unclear. One thing is certain: Russia will continue to be a key regional force in Europe and Asia by virtue of its size, its rich energy and resource base, its large and highly skilled population, and its nuclear arsenal. However, Russia's leaders have had an ambivalent attitude toward accepting crucial international norms that would underlie an effective and enduring partnership with the West.

If the Russian leadership gradually moves Russia on a path closer to liberal democratic development, then this may provide an example to other semi-authoritarian countries in Russia's neighborhood. But, if the continuation of existing authoritarian trends is associated with renewed economic growth and stability that benefits the majority of the population, then Russia may settle into an extended period of soft authoritarianism that reinforces the East–West divide. And, then there is the possibility that the Russian leadership's insulation from public accountability could generate unpopular and ineffective policy outcomes, or that the continuation of low world energy prices could trigger a further economic downslide. Such a turn of events could stimulate a new process of reflection on Russia's future path and offer an opportunity for democratic forces to reassert themselves and find resonance among the Russian people.

Where Do You Stand?

Is Russia justified in taking strong action to assure that a neighboring country, such as Ukraine, stays within its "sphere of influence"?

Should Western countries make greater efforts to promote liberal democratic opposition groups in Russia?

Chapter Summary

Russian history has been characterized by a series of upheavals and changes that have often made life unpredictable and difficult for the citizen. The revolutions of 1917 replaced czarist rule with a political system dominated by the communist party in the Soviet Union. In the Stalinist period, communist rule involved a process of rapid industrialization, collectivization of agriculture, and purges of the party, followed by large losses of population associated with World War II. With the death of Stalin in 1952 came another important transition, as Soviet politics was transformed into a more predictable system of bureaucratic authoritarianism, characterized by relative stability but without political competition or democratic control. The most recent transition, ushered in by the collapse of the Soviet Union in 1991, resulted in the emergence of the Russian Federation as an independent state. When the Russian Federation was formed, new political structures needed to be constructed. A constitution was adopted in 1993, which involves a directly elected president with strong political powers.

Russia's political course since 1991 has been profoundly influenced by the fact that the country underwent simultaneous and radical transformations in four spheres: politics, economics, ideology, and geopolitical position in the world. Managing so much change in a short time has been difficult and has produced mixed results. Efforts to democratize the political system have been only partially successful, and experts disagree both about whether the political controls initiated by Putin were needed to ensure stability and under what conditions they might be reversed.

In the economic sphere, after recovering from a period of deep economic decline in the 1990s, Russia's renewed growth depends largely on exports of energy and natural resources, making the country vulnerable to external shocks such as the 2008–2009 global financial crisis and the downturn in world energy prices since 2014. The country faces the challenge of effectively using its natural resource wealth to rebuild other sectors of the economy.

In terms of ideology, nationalism threatens to reinforce intolerance and undermine social unity. Continuing high levels of corruption also undermine popular confidence in state institutions. Whereas most former communist countries that have joined the EU have enjoyed greater success in establishing viable democratic systems with functioning market economies, other post-Soviet states in Eastern Europe and Central Asia face similar challenges to Russia's in consolidating democracy and market reform. Russia has sought to reassert its role as a regional and global force, but a revival of tension with the West in the face of Russia's 2014 annexation of Crimea and conflict over Ukraine threatens stability in Russia's neighborhood, which could affect Russia itself.

Key Terms

civil society	*glasnost*	political culture
clientelistic networks	insider privatization	power vertical
collectivization	market reform	*siloviki*
democratic centralism	mixed electoral system	soft authoritarianism
dominant party	oligarchs	sovereign democracy
federal system	patrimonial state	vanguard party

Suggested Readings

Forsberg, Tuomas, and Hiski Haukkala, *The European Union and Russia*. Houndsmill, Basingstoke: Palgrave Macmillan, 2016.

Gel'man, Vladimir, *Authoritarian Russia: Analyzing Post-Soviet Regime Changes*. Pittsburgh: University of Pittsburgh Press, 2015.

Hough, Jerry, and Merle Fainsod. *How the Soviet Union Is Governed*. Cambridge: Harvard University Press, 1979.

Kanet, Roger E. ed, *Power, Politics, and Confrontation in Eurasia: Foreign Policy in a Contested Region*. Hampshire, UK: Palgrave Macmillan, 2015.

Ledeneva, Alena V. *Can Russia Modernize? Sistema, Power Networks and Informal Governance*. Cambridge: Cambridge University Press, 2013.

Mickiewicz, Ellen, *No Illusions: The Voices of Russia's Future Leaders*. Oxford: Oxford University Press, 2017.

Pipes, Richard. *Russia under the Old Regime*. New York: Scribner, 1974.

Tsygankov, Andrei P., *Russia's Foreign Policy: Change and Continuity in National Identity*, 2nd ed. Lanham, MD: Rowman and Littlefield, 2016.

Suggested Websites

Russian Analytical Digest
http://www.css.ethz.ch/en/publications/rad.html

The Carnegie Moscow Center
www.carnegie.ru/?lang=en

Johnson's Russia List
http://www.russialist.org/

Radio Free Europe/Radio Liberty
http://www.rferl.org/p/5547.html

The Moscow Times
https://themoscowtimes.com/

Center on Global Interests
http://globalinterests.org/

Russia Today (Russian news source, consider bias)
rt.com

14 Iran

Ervand Abrahamian

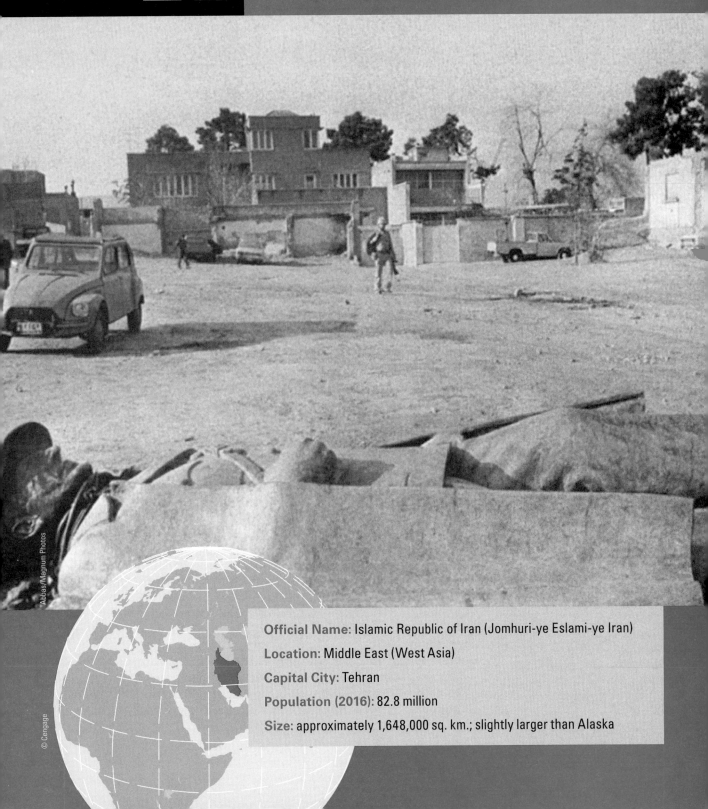

Abbas/Magnum Photos

© Cengage

Official Name: Islamic Republic of Iran (Jomhuri-ye Eslami-ye Iran)

Location: Middle East (West Asia)

Capital City: Tehran

Population (2016): 82.8 million

Size: approximately 1,648,000 sq. km.; slightly larger than Alaska

1925
Reza Khan establishes the Pahlavi dynasty.

1941–1945
Allied occupation of Iran during World War II.

1953
A coup supported by the U.S. Central Intelligence Agency (CIA) overthrows Mossadeq.

1975
Shah establishes the Resurgence Party.

1920   1940   1950   1960   1965   1970   1975

1921
Colonel Reza Khan's military coup.

1941
Muhammad Reza Pahlavi becomes Shah of Iran.

1951
Nationalization of the oil industry by government of Prime Minister Muhammed Mossadeq.

1963
Shah launches "White Revolution."

1905–1911
Constitutional Revolution

SECTION 1

THE MAKING OF THE MODERN IRANIAN STATE

Focus Questions

- To what extent does geography, language, history, religion, and religion give Iran a distinct identity?

- How did Muhammad Reza Shah come to power, and to what role did the United States play in supporting him? How was the Shah overthrown and how did that change Iran's political system?

ayatollah

Literally, "sign of God." A high-ranking cleric in Iran.

Politics in Action

In 2013, Iran with a resounding vote elected Dr. Hassan Rouhani president of the Islamic Republic. Rouhani is a middle-ranking religious cleric, not an ayatollah, and prefers to be addressed as Dr.—a title he has from a university in Scotland where he obtained a Ph.D. in constitutional law. He won the election running on a reform platform, promising to remedy a "sick economy," strengthen the rule of law, and, most important of all, improve relations with the West, especially over the nuclear stand-off with the United States. The 2013 election was in many ways a replay of previous ones. In 1997, Muhammad Khatami, another middle-ranking reform cleric, had been elected president in a landslide victory. He was reelected in 2001, again with a landslide victory, but in 2005, after deteriorations of relations with the United States, he had been replaced by an ultraconservative populist named Mahmoud Ahmadinejad. Ahmadinejad had retained the presidency in 2009, after a hotly disputed election. Iran may lack many features of a true democracy, but it certainly does not lack fiercely contested elections. In May 2017, Rouhani was reelected with a much larger majority.

These very different electoral outcomes illustrate the contradictory political forces at work in the Islamic Republic of Iran. Iran is a mixture of theocracy and democracy. Its political system is based on both clerical authority and popular sovereignty, on the divine right of the clergy and the rights of the people, on concepts

1979
Islamic Revolution; Shah forced into exile; Iran becomes an Islamic Republic; Ayatollah Khomeini becomes Leader.

1979–1981
Hostage crisis—fifty-two U.S. embassy employees held by radical students.

October 1981
Ayatollah Ali Khamenei elected president.

1980–1988
War with Iraq.

1997
Muhammad Khatami elected president on reform platform (reelected in 2001).

2005
Ultraconservative Mahmoud Ahmadinejad elected president.

2013
Dr. Hassan Rouhani elected president on reform platform.

| 1979 | 1980 | 1985 | 1990 | 2000 | 2005 |

December 1979
Referendum on the Islamic constitution.

March 1980
Elections for the First Islamic *Majles* (parliament). Subsequent Majles elections every four years.

1989
Khomeini dies; Khamenei appointed Leader; Rafsanjani elected president (reelected in 1993).

2009
Ahmadinejad reelected; large-scale protests against alleged electoral fraud take place in Tehran and other cities.

2015
UN-Iran Nuclear Agreement.

2017
Rouhani reelected president in May.

June 1981
President Bani-Sadr ousted by Khomeini, replaced by Muhammad Ali Rajai.

January 1980
Abol-Hassan Bani-Sadr elected president.

derived from early Islam and from modern democratic principles. Iran has regular elections for the presidency and the *Majles* (parliament), but the clerically dominated Guardian Council determines who can run. The president is the formal head of the executive branch. But he can be overruled, even dismissed, by the chief cleric, the Leader known in the West as the Supreme Leader. The president appoints the minister of justice, but the whole judiciary is under the supervision of the chief judge, who is appointed directly by the Leader. The *Majles* is the legislature, but bills do not become law unless the Guardian Council deems them compatible with Islam and the Islamic constitution. Thus, the Guardian Council—formed of twelve senior judges with six appointed by the Leader and six jointly by the Majles and the chief judge—has considerable judicial as well as legislative authority. (See Table 14.1.)

Geographic Setting

Iran is three times the size of France, slightly larger than Alaska, and much larger than its immediate neighbors. Most of its territory is inhospitable to agriculture. Rain-fed agriculture is confined mostly to the northwest and the provinces along the Caspian Sea. Only pastoral nomads can survive in the semiarid zones and in the high mountain valleys. Thus, 67 percent of the total population of a little over 80 million is concentrated on 27 percent of the land—mostly in the Caspian region, in the northwest provinces, and in the cities of Tehran, Mashed, Isfahan, Tabriz, Shiraz, and Qom.

Iran is the second-largest oil producer in the Middle East and the fourth-largest in the world, and oil revenues have made Iran an urbanized and partly industrialized country. Over 70 percent of the population lives in urban centers; 84 percent of the labor force is employed in industry and services; 86 percent of adults are literate; life expectancy has reached over 71 years; and the majority of Iranians enjoy a standard of living well above that found in most of Asia and Africa. Iran can no longer be described as a typically poor developing country. It is a middle-income country with

theocracy

A state dominated by the clergy, who rule on the grounds that they are the only interpreters of God's will and law.

Majles

The Iranian parliament, from the Arabic term for "assembly."

Guardian Council

A committee created in the Iranian constitution to oversee the *Majles* (the parliament).

Leader/Supreme Leader

A cleric elected to be the head of the Islamic Republic of Iran.

Table 14.1	Political Organization
Political System	A mixture of democracy and theocracy (rule of the clergy) headed by a cleric with the title of the Leader.
Regime History	Islamic Republic since the 1979 Islamic Revolution.
Administrative Structure	Centralized administration with 30 provinces. The interior minister appoints the provincial governor-generals.
Executive	President and his cabinet. The president is chosen by the general electorate every four years and is limited to two terms. The president chooses his cabinet ministers, but they need to obtain the approval of the *Majles* (parliament).
Legislature	Unicameral. The *Majles*, formed of 290 seats, is elected every four years. It has multiple-member districts with the top runners in the elections taking the seats. Bills passed by the *Majles* do not become law unless they have the approval of the clerically dominated Council of Guardians.
Judiciary	A Chief Judge and a Supreme Court independent of the executive and legislature but appointed by the Leader.
Party System	Multiparty system, but the ruling clergy restricts most party and organizational activities.

Farsi

The Persian word for the Persian language. Fars is a province in south Iran.

a GDP per capita above that of Brazil and South Africa. Recent UN economic sanctions have caused considerable hardship but have not reduced its general standing.

Iran lies on the strategic crossroads between Central Asia and Turkey, between the Indian subcontinent and the Middle East, and between the Arabian Peninsula and the Caucasus Mountains, which are often considered a boundary between Europe and Asia. This has made the region vulnerable to invaders.

The population today reflects these historic invasions. Some 58 percent speak Persian (Farsi), an Indo-European language, as a first language; the remainder of the population primarily speaks eight other languages. Use of Persian, however, has dramatically increased in recent years because of successful literacy campaigns. Over 90 percent of the population can now communicate in Persian, the national language. Although Iran shares many religious and cultural features with the rest of the Islamic Middle East, its Persian heritage gives it a national identity distinct from that of the Arab and Turkish world. Iranians by no means consider themselves part of the Arab world. (See Figure 14.1.)

Islam, with over 1 billion adherents, is the second-largest religion in the world after Christianity. Islam means literally "submission to God," and a Muslim is someone who has submitted to God—the same God that Jews and Christians worship. Islam has one central tenet: "There is only one God, and Muhammad is His Prophet." Muslims, in order to consider themselves faithful, need to perform the following four duties to the best of their ability: give to charity; pray every day facing Mecca, where Abraham is believed to have built the first place of worship; make a pilgrimage at least once in a lifetime to Mecca, which is located in modern Saudi Arabia; and fast during the daytime hours in the month of Ramadan to commemorate God's revelation of the Qur'an (Koran, or Holy Book) to the Prophet Muhammad. These four, together with the central tenet, are known as the Five Pillars of Islam.

From its earliest days, Islam has been divided into two major branches: Sunni, meaning literally "followers of tradition," and Shi'i, literally "partisans of Ali."

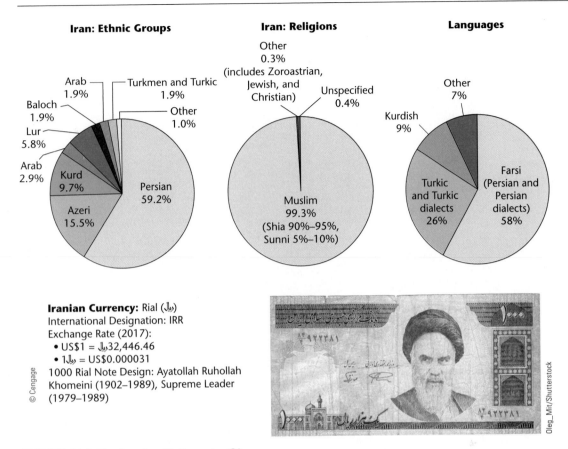

Iran: Ethnic Groups

Arab 1.9%
Turkmen and Turkic 1.9%
Baloch 1.9%
Other 1.0%
Lur 5.8%
Arab 2.9%
Kurd 9.7%
Azeri 15.5%
Persian 59.2%

Iran: Religions

Other 0.3% (includes Zoroastrian, Jewish, and Christian)
Unspecified 0.4%
Muslim 99.3% (Shia 90%–95%, Sunni 5%–10%)

Languages

Other 7%
Kurdish 9%
Turkic and Turkic dialects 26%
Farsi (Persian and Persian dialects) 58%

Iranian Currency: Rial (ریال)
International Designation: IRR
Exchange Rate (2017):
- US$1 = ریال32,446.46
- 1ریال = US$0.000031

1000 Rial Note Design: Ayatollah Ruhollah Khomeini (1902–1989), Supreme Leader (1979–1989)

© Cengage

Oleg_Mit/Shutterstock

FIGURE 14.1 The Iranian Nation at a Glance

Sunnis are by far in the majority worldwide. Shi'is constitute less than 10 percent of Muslims worldwide and are concentrated in Iran, southern Iraq, Bahrain, eastern Turkey, Azerbaijan, and southern Lebanon. There are also concentrations of Shi'i offshoots elsewhere: Zaydis in northern Yemen and Alawis on the Mediterranean coast of Syria.

Although both Sunni and Shi'i branches accept the Five Pillars, they differ mostly over who should have succeeded the Prophet Muhammad (d. 632). The Sunnis recognized the early dynasties that ruled the Islamic empire with the exalted title of caliph ("Prophet's Deputy"). The Shi'is, however, argued that as soon as the Prophet died, his authority should have been passed on to Imam Ali, the Prophet's close companion, disciple, and son-in-law. They further argue that Imam Ali passed his authority to his direct male heirs, the third of whom, Imam Husayn, had been martyred fighting the Sunnis in 680, and the twelfth of whom had supposedly gone into hiding in 941.

The Shi'is are also known as Twelvers since they follow the Twelve Imams. They refer to the Twelfth Imam as the *Mahdi*, the Hidden Imam, and believe him to be the Messiah who will herald the end of the world. Furthermore, they argue that in his absence, the authority to interpret the *shari'a* (religious law) should be in the hands of the senior clerical scholars—the ayatollahs. Thus, from the beginning, the Shi'is harbored ambivalent attitudes toward the state, especially if the rulers were Sunnis or lacked genealogical links to the Twelve Imams. For Sunnis, the *shari'a* is based mostly on the Qur'an and the teachings of the Prophet. For Shi'is, it is based also on the teachings of the Twelve Imams.

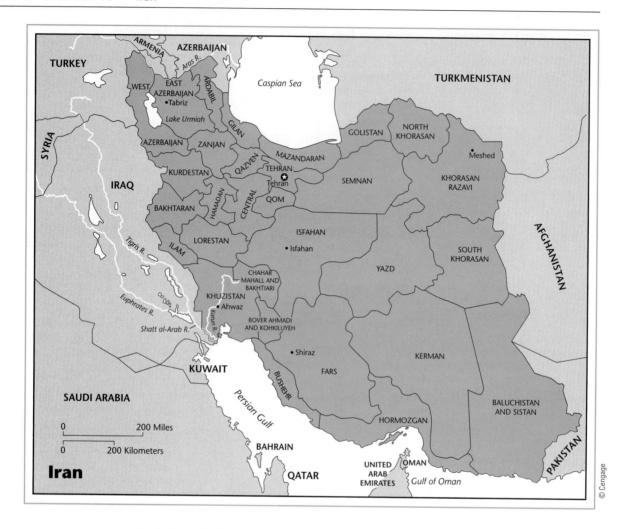

Iran

Critical Junctures

The Safavids (1501–1722)

The Safavid dynasty conquered the territory that is now Iran in the sixteenth century and forcibly converted their subjects to Shi'ism, even though the vast majority had been Sunnis. By the mid-seventeenth century, Sunnism survived only among the tribal groups at the periphery.

Safavid Iran also contained small communities of Jews, Zoroastrians, and Christians. The Safavids tolerated religious minorities as long as they paid special taxes and accepted royal authority. According to Islam, the Christian, Jewish, and Zoroastrian people were to be tolerated as legitimate **People of the Book**, because they were mentioned in the Holy **Qur'an** and possessed their own sacred texts: the Bible, the Torah, and the Avesta.

The Safavids governed through Persian scribes and Shi'i clerics as well as through tribal chiefs, large landowners, city merchants, guild elders, and urban ward leaders. Their army was formed mostly of tribal cavalry led by tribal chieftains. Safavid revenues came mostly from land taxes levied on the peasantry. The Safavids claimed absolute power, but they lacked a central state and had to cooperate with many semi-independent local leaders.

People of the Book

The Muslim term for recognized religious minorities, such as Christians, Jews, and Zoroastrians.

Qur'an

A book of the sacred text of revelations made to Muhammad by Allah.

The Qajars (1794–1925)

In 1722, Afghan tribesmen invaded the capital. After a half-century of civil wars, the Qajars—a Turkic-speaking Shi'i tribe—reconquered much of Iran. They moved the capital to Tehran and re-created the Safavid system of central manipulation and court administration. They also declared Shi'ism to be the state religion, even though they, unlike the Safavids, could not boast of genealogical links to the Twelve Imams. Since these new shahs, or kings, did not pretend to wear the Imam's mantle, Shi'i clerical leaders could claim to be the main interpreters of Islam.

Qajar rule coincided with the peak of European imperialism in the nineteenth century. The Russians seized parts of Central Asia and the Caucasus region from Iran and extracted major economic concessions. The British Imperial Bank won the monopoly to issue paper money. The Indo-European Telegraph Company obtained a contract to extend communication lines throughout the country. Exclusive rights to drill for oil in the southwest were sold to a British citizen. Iranians increasingly felt their whole country had been auctioned off.

These resentments led to a constitutional revolution from 1905 to 1909. The 1906 constitution introduced elections, separation of powers, a legislative assembly, and the concepts of popular sovereignty and the nation (*mellat*). It retained the monarchy, but centered political power in a national assembly called the *Majles*.

The constitution gave the *Majles* extensive authority over all laws, budgets, treaties, concessions, and the makeup of the cabinet. The ministers were accountable to the *Majles*, not to the shah. The constitution also included a bill of rights guaranteeing equality before the law, protection of life and property, and freedom of expression and association.

Shi'ism was declared Iran's official religion. Clerical courts continued to implement the *shari'a*. The constitution also included a clause setting up a Guardian Council of senior clerics elected by the *Majles* with the power to veto parliamentary bills deemed to be un-Islamic. This clause, however, was never implemented.

The initial euphoria of revolution soon gave way to deep disillusionment. Pressures from the European powers continued, and a devastating famine after World War I took some 1 million lives, almost 10 percent of the total population. Internal conflicts polarized the *Majles* into warring liberal and conservative factions. Liberals, mostly members of the intelligentsia, championed social reforms, especially the replacement of the *shari'a* with a modern legal code. Conservatives, led by landlords, tribal chiefs, and senior clerics, vehemently opposed such reforms, particularly land reform, women's rights, and the granting of full equality to religious minorities.

The central government, without any real army, bureaucracy, or tax-collecting machinery, could not administer the provinces. During World War I, Russia and Britain formally carved up Iran into three zones. Russia occupied the north, Britain the south. Iran was left with a small middle "neutral zone."

By 1921, Iran was in complete disarray. According to a British diplomat, the propertied classes, fearful of communism, were anxiously seeking "a savior on horseback."[1]

The Pahlavis (1925–1979)

In February 1921, Colonel Reza Khan carried out a coup d'état. He replaced the cabinet and consolidated power in his own hands. Four years later, he deposed the Qajars and crowned himself Shah-in-Shah—King of Kings—and established the Pahlavi dynasty. This was the first nontribal dynasty to rule the whole of Iran. During the next 16 years, he systematically modernized the country by building almost from scratch a highly-centralized state with a standing army and a large administrative bureaucracy.

Reza Shah ruled with an iron fist until 1941, when the British and the Soviets invaded Iran to stop Nazi Germany from establishing a foothold there. Reza Shah promptly abdicated in favor of his son, Muhammad Reza Shah, and went into exile, where he soon died. In the first 12 years of his reign, the young Shah retained control over the armed forces but had to tolerate a free press, an independent judiciary, competitive elections, assertive cabinet ministers, and boisterous parliaments. He also had to confront two vigorous political movements: the communist Tudeh (Masses) Party and the National Front, led by the charismatic Dr. Muhammad Mossadeq (1882–1967).

The Tudeh drew its support mostly from working-class trade unions. The National Front drew its support mainly from the salaried middle classes and campaigned to nationalize the British company that controlled the petroleum industry. Mossadeq also wanted to sever the Shah's links with the armed forces. In 1951, Mossadeq was elected prime minister and promptly nationalized the oil industry. The period of relative freedom, however, ended abruptly in 1953, when royalist army officers overthrew Mossadeq and installed the Shah with absolute power. This coup was orchestrated and financed by the U.S. Central Intelligence Agency (CIA) and the British. This intensified anti-British sentiment and created a deep distrust of the United States. It also made the Shah appear to be a foreign puppet.

The Pahlavi dynasty continued to build a highly-centralized state. The armed forces grew from 40,000 in 1925 to 124,000 in 1941, and to 410,000 in 1979. The armed forces were supplemented by a pervasive secret police known as SAVAK.

Iran's bureaucracy expanded to twenty-one ministries employing over 300,000 civil servants in 1979. The Education Ministry grew twentyfold. The powerful Interior Ministry appointed provincial governors, town mayors, district superintendents, and village headmen; it could even rig *Majles* elections and create rubber-stamp parliaments.

The Justice Ministry supplanted the *shari'a* with a European-style civil code and the clerical courts with a modern judicial system culminating in a Supreme Court. The Transport Ministry built an impressive array of bridges, ports, highways, and railroads known as the Trans-Iranian Railway. The Ministry of Industries financed factories specializing in consumer goods. The Agricultural Ministry became prominent in 1963 when the Shah made land reform the centerpiece of his "White Revolution." This White Revolution was an effort to promote economic development and such social reform as extending the vote to women. It also created a Literacy Corps for the countryside. This White Revolution from above—encouraged by the United States—was a concerted attempt to forestall a communist-led Red Revolution from below. Thus, by the late 1970s, the state had set up a modern system of communications, initiated a minor industrial revolution, and extended its reach into even the most outlying villages.

The state also controlled the National and the Central Banks; the Industrial and Mining Development Bank; the Plan Organization in charge of economic policy; the national radio-television network; and most important, the National Iranian Oil Company.

The dynasty's founder, Reza Shah, had used coercion, confiscation, and diversion of irrigation water to make himself one of the largest landowners in the Middle East. This wealth transformed the Shah's imperial court into a large military-based complex, providing work for thousands in its numerous palaces, hotels, casinos, charities, and beach resorts. This patronage system grew under his son, particularly after he established his tax-exempt Pahlavi Foundation, which eventually controlled 207 large companies.

The Pahlavi drive for secularization, centralization, industrialization, and social development won some favor from the urban propertied classes. But arbitrary rule; the 1953 coup that overthrew a popular prime minister; the disregard for constitutional liberties; and the stifling of independent newspapers, political parties, and professional associations produced widespread resentment. The Pahlavi state, like the Safavids and the Qajars, hovered over, rather than embedded itself into, Iranian society.

In 1975, the Shah formed the Resurgence Party. He declared Iran a one-party state and threatened imprisonment and exile to those refusing to join the party. The Resurgence Party was designed to create yet another organizational link with the population, especially with the bazaars (traditional marketplaces), which, unlike the rest of society, had managed to retain their independent guilds and thus escape direct government control. The Resurgence Party promptly established its own bazaar guilds as well as newspapers, women's organizations, professional associations, and labor unions. It also prepared to create a Religious Corps to teach the peasants "true Islam."

bazaar

An urban marketplace where shops, workshops, small businesses, and export-importers are located.

The Islamic Revolution (1979)

The grievances against the Pahlavi regime are best summed up by an opposition newspaper in Paris on the very eve of the 1979 revolution. In an article entitled "Fifty Years of Treason," it charged the Shah and his family with establishing a military dictatorship; collaborating with the CIA; trampling on the constitution; creating SAVAK, the secret police; rigging parliamentary elections; organizing a fascistic one-party state; taking over the religious establishment; and undermining national identity by disseminating Western culture. It also accused the regime of inducing millions of landless peasants to migrate into urban shantytowns; widening the gap between rich and poor; funneling money away from the middle-class bourgeoisie into the pockets of the wealthy entrepreneurs linked to foreign companies and multinational corporations; wasting resources on bloated military budgets; and granting new capitulations to the West.

These grievances took sharper edge when a leading opposition cleric, Ayatollah Ruhollah Khomeini—exiled in Iraq—formulated a drastically new version of Shi'ism. His version of Shi'ism has often been labeled Islamic fundamentalism. It would be better to call it political Islam or even more accurately as Shi'i populism. The term *fundamentalism*, derived from American Protestantism, implies religious dogmatism, intellectual inflexibility and purity, political traditionalism, social conservatism, rejection of the modern world, and the literal interpretation of scriptural texts. While Khomeinism shares some of these characteristics, Khomeini was not so much a social conservative as a political revolutionary who used populist rhetoric to rally the population against a decadent elite.

political Islam

A term for the intermingling of Islam with politics and often used as a substitute for Islamic fundamentalism.

Khomeini was born in 1902 into a landed clerical family in central Iran. During the 1920s, he studied in the famous Fayzieh Seminary in Qom with the leading theologians of the day, most of whom were scrupulously apolitical. He taught at the seminary from the 1930s through the 1950s, avoiding politics even during the mass campaign to nationalize the British-owned oil company. His entry into politics did not come until 1963, when he, along with most other clerical leaders, denounced the White Revolution. Forced into exile, Khomeini taught at the Shi'i center of Najaf in Iraq from 1964 until 1978. During these years, Khomeini developed his own version of Shi'i populism by incorporating socioeconomic grievances into his sermons and denouncing not just the Shah but also the whole ruling class.

Khomeini denounced monarchies in general as part of the corrupt elite exploiting the oppressed masses. Oppressors were courtiers, large landowners, high-ranking military officers, wealthy foreign-connected capitalists, and millionaire palace dwellers. The oppressed were the masses, especially landless peasants, wage earners, bazaar shopkeepers, and shantytown dwellers.

Khomeini gave a radically new meaning to the old Shi'i term *velayat-e faqih* (jurist's guardianship). He argued that jurist's guardianship gave the senior clergy all-encompassing authority over the whole community, not just over widows, minors, and the mentally disabled (the previous interpretation). Only the senior clerics could understand the *shari'a;* and the divine authority given to the Prophet and the Imams had been passed on to their spiritual heirs, the clergy. He further insisted the clergy were the people's true representatives, since they lived among them, listened to their problems, and shared their everyday joys and pains. He furthermore claimed that the Shah secretly planned to confiscate all religious endowment funds and replace Islamic values with "cultural imperialism."

Between 1977 and 1978, the Shah tried to deal with a 20 percent rise in consumer prices and a 10 percent decline in oil revenues by cutting construction projects and declaring war against "profiteers," "hoarders," and "price gougers." Shopkeepers suspected the Shah was diverting attention from court corruption and planning to replace them with government-run department stores. They protested that he was out to destroy the bazaar.

The Shah was also subjected to international pressure on the sensitive issue of human rights—from Amnesty International, the United Nations, and the Western press, as well as from the recently elected Carter administration in the United States. In 1977, the Shah gave the International Red Cross access to Iranian prisons and permitted political prisoners to have defense attorneys. This international pressure allowed the opposition to "breathe" again after decades of suffocation.[2]

This slight loosening of the reins began to unravel the regime. Political parties, labor organizations, and professional associations—especially lawyers, writers, and university professors—regrouped after years of being banned. Bazaar guilds regained their independence. College, high school, and seminary students took to the streets— with each demonstration growing in size and vociferousness. On September 8, 1978, remembered in Iran as Black Friday, troops shot and killed a large but unknown number of unarmed civilian protesters in central Tehran. This dramatically intensified popular hatred for the regime. By late 1978, general strikes throughout the country were bringing the whole economy to a halt. Oil workers vowed that they would not export petroleum until they had got rid of the "Shah and his forty thieves."[3]

Meanwhile, neighborhood committees in urban centers, attached to the mosques and financed by the bazaars, were distributing food to the needy, supplanting the police with militias known as *pasdaran* (Revolutionary Guards), and replacing the judicial system with ad hoc courts applying the *shari'a.* Anti-regime rallies were now attracting as many as two million protesters. Protesters demanded the abolition of the monarchy, the return of Khomeini from exile, and the establishment of a republic that would preserve national independence and provide the downtrodden masses with decent wages, land, and a proper standard of living. The revolution was in full swing.

Although led by pro-Khomeini clerics, these mass rallies drew support from a broad variety of organizations: the National Front; the Lawyer's, Doctor's, and Women's associations; the communist Tudeh Party; the Fedayin, a Marxist guerrilla group; and the Mojahedin, a Muslim guerrilla group formed by lay intellectuals. The rallies also attracted students, from high schools and colleges, as well as shopkeepers and craftsmen from the bazaars. A secret Revolutionary Committee in Tehran co-ordinated protests throughout the country. This was one of the first revolutions to be televised worldwide. Many later felt that these demonstrations helped inspire the 1989 revolutions that overthrew the communist regimes in Eastern Europe.

---

jurist's guardianship

Khomeini's concept that the Iranian clergy should rule on the grounds that they are the divinely appointed guardians of both the law and the people.

---

pasdaran

Persian term for *guards,* used to refer to the army of Revolutionary Guards formed during Iran's Islamic Revolution.

Confronted by this opposition and by increasing numbers of soldiers who were deserting to the opposition, the Shah decided to leave Iran. A year later, when he was in exile and dying of cancer, many speculated that he might have mastered the upheavals if he had been healthier, possessed a stronger personality, and received full support from the United States. But even a man with an iron will and full foreign backing would not have been able to deal with millions of angry demonstrators, massive general strikes, and debilitating desertions from his own armed forces.

On February 11, 1979, a few hours of street fighting provided the final blow to the 54-year-old dynasty that claimed a 2,500-year-old heritage.

The Islamic Republic (1979–Present)

Returning home triumphant in the midst of the Iranian Revolution after the Shah was forced from power, Khomeini was declared the Imam and Leader of the new Islamic Republic. In the past, Iranian Shi'is, unlike the Arab Sunnis, had reserved the special term *Imam* only for Imam Ali and his eleven direct heirs, whom they deemed infallible, and, therefore, almost semidivine. For many Iranians in 1979, Khomeini was charismatic in the true sense of the word: a man with a special gift from God. Khomeini ruled as Imam and Leader of the Islamic Republic until his death in 1989.

Seven weeks after the February revolution, a nationwide referendum replaced the monarchy with an Islamic Republic. Liberal and lay supporters of Khomeini, including Mehdi Bazargan, his first prime minister, had hoped to offer the electorate the choice of a *democratic* Islamic Republic. But Khomeini overruled them. He declared the term was redundant since Islam itself was democratic. Khomeini was now hailed as the Leader of the Revolution, Founder of the Islamic Republic, Guide of the Oppressed Masses, Commander of the Armed Forces, and most potent of all, Imam of the Muslim World.

A new constitution was drawn up in late 1979 by the Assembly of Experts (*Majles-e Khebregan*). Although this seventy-three man assembly was elected by the general public, almost all secular organizations as well as clerics opposed to Khomeini boycotted the elections because the state media were controlled, independent papers had been banned, and voters were being intimidated by club-wielding vigilantes known as the *Hezbollahis* ("Partisans of God"). The vast majority of those elected were pro-Khomeini clerics, including forty *hojjat al-Islams* (middle-ranking clerics) and fifteen ayatollahs. They drafted a highly theocratic constitution vesting much authority in the hands of Khomeini in particular and the clergy in general—all this over the strong objections of Prime Minister Bazargan, who wanted a French-style presidential republic that would be Islamic in name but democratic in structure.

When Bazargan threatened to submit his own constitution to the public, television controlled by the clerics showed him shaking hands with U.S. policy-makers. Meanwhile, Khomeini denounced the U.S. embassy as a "den of spies" plotting a repeat performance of the 1953 coup. This led to mass demonstrations, a break-in at the embassy, the seizure of dozens of U.S. hostages, and eventually the resignation of Bazargan. Some suspect the hostage crisis had been engineered to undercut Bazargan.

A month after the embassy break-in, Khomeini submitted the theocratic constitution to the public and declared that all citizens had a divine duty to vote; 99 percent of those voting endorsed it.

In the first decade after the revolution, a number of factors helped the clerics consolidate power. First, few people could challenge Khomeini's overwhelming

Assembly of Experts

Group that nominates and can remove the Leader. The assembly is elected by the general electorate, but almost all of its members are clerics. A term for the intermingling of Islam with politics and often used as a substitute for Islamic fundamentalism.

Hezbollahis

Literally "partisans of God." In Iran, the term is used to describe religious vigilantes. In Lebanon, it is used to describe the Shi'i militia.

hojjat al-Islam

Literally, "the proof of Islam." In Iran, it means a medium-ranking cleric.

charismatic leadership. Second, the invasion of Iran in 1980 by Saddam Hussein's Iraq rallied the Iranian population behind their endangered homeland. Third, international petroleum prices shot up, sustaining Iran's oil revenues. The price of a barrel of oil, which had hovered around $30 in 1979, jumped to over $50 by 1981. This enabled the new regime, despite war and revolution, to continue to finance existing development programs.

The second decade after the revolution brought the ruling clerics serious problems. Khomeini's death in June 1989 removed his decisive presence. His successor, Ali Khamenei, lacked not only his charisma but also his scholastic credentials and seminary disciples. The 1988 UN-brokered cease-fire in the Iran–Iraq War ended the foreign danger. A drastic fall in world oil prices, which plunged to less than $10 a barrel by 1998, placed a sharp brake on economic development. Even more serious, by the late 1990s, the regime was facing a major ideological crisis, with many of Khomeini's followers, including some of his closest disciples, now stressing the importance of public participation over clerical hegemony, of political pluralism over theological conformity, and of civil society over state authority—in other words, of democracy over theocracy.

Iran after 9/11

The terrorist attacks in the United States on September 11, 2001, and the subsequent U.S. invasions of Afghanistan in October 2001 and Iraq in March 2002, had profound consequences for Iran. At first, the U.S. war on terror brought Iran and the United States closer together since Iran for years had seen both the Afghan Taliban and Iraq's Saddam Hussein as its own mortal enemies. Saddam Hussein was hated for the obvious reason; he had waged an eight-year war on Iran. The Taliban was hated in part because it had massacred a large number of Shi'i Afghans; and in part because it was financed by Sunni Wahhabi fundamentalists in Saudi

Abbas/Magnum Photos

The Shah's statue on the ground, February 1979.

Arabia who consider Shi'ism as well as all innovations since the very beginnings of Islam to be unacceptable heresies. In fact, these Sunni fundamentalists consider Shi'is to be as bad if not worse than non-Muslim infidels. Not surprisingly, Iran helped the United States depose the Taliban in 2001. It also used its considerable influence among the Iraqi Shi'is to install a pro-United States government in Baghdad in 2003. It offered the United States in 2003 a "grand bargain" to settle all major differences, including those over nuclear research, Israel, Lebanon, and the Persian Gulf.

These hopes, however, were soon dashed—first, because in his State of the Union address in January 2002, President George W. Bush named Iran (along with Iraq and North Korea) as part of an "Axis of Evil" supporting terrorism and developing weapons of mass destruction. Moreover, after the occupation of Iraq, the United States surrounded Iran with military bases in the Persian Gulf, Turkey, Azerbaijan, Georgia, Afghanistan, and Central Asia. Bush also refused to enter serious negotiations until Iran unconditionally stopped nuclear research. These hard-line actions played a major role in both undermining the Iran's liberal President Khatemi and paving the way for the electoral victory of the bellicose Ahmadinejad in 2005. Reformers did not want to be associated with a U.S. administration that not only insisted Iran should not have a nuclear program but also aggressively advocated regime change in Tehran. For most Iranians, this again resurrected memories of the 1953 CIA-supported coup. These issues increased tensions and brought Iran and the United States closer to a diplomatic, if not military, stand-off. The United States insisted—at least, until the election of President Obama—that it would not negotiate with Iran unless it stopped its nuclear enrichment program. Iran, in turn, insisted that its nuclear program had no military purpose and that it conformed to guidelines set by international treaties.

The Four Themes and Iran

Iran in a Globalized World of States

By denouncing the United States as an "arrogant imperialist," canceling military agreements with the West, and condoning the taking of U.S. diplomats as hostages, Khomeini asserted Iranian power in the region but also inadvertently prompted Saddam Hussein to launch the Iran–Iraq War in 1980.

Khomeini's policies made it difficult for his successors to normalize relations with the West. Khomeini had called for revolutions throughout the Muslim world, denouncing Arab rulers in the region, particularly in Saudi Arabia, as the "corrupt puppets of American imperialism." He strengthened Iran's navy and bought nuclear-powered submarines from Russia. He launched a research program to build medium-range missiles and nuclear power—possibly even nuclear weapons. He denounced the proposals for Arab-Israeli negotiations over Palestine. He sent money as well as arms to Muslim dissidents abroad, particularly Shi'i groups in Lebanon, Iraq, and Afghanistan. He permitted the Islamic Republic's intelligence services to assassinate some one hundred exiled opposition leaders living in Western Europe. These policies isolated Iran not only from the United States but also from the European Community, human rights organizations, and the United Nations. Reforming presidents, especially Khatami and Rouhani, did their best to rectify this damage.

The Islamic Republic is determined to remain dominant in the Persian Gulf and to play an important role in the world of states. It has one of the biggest, but outdated,

THE GLOBAL CONNECTION

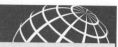

The Nuclear Power Issue

For Iran, nuclear technology—always defined as a "civilian program"—is a non-negotiable right of an independent nation, essential not only for its long-term energy needs but also to attain the hallmark of a developed country. It insists it has no plans to develop atomic weapons having signed the Nuclear Non-Proliferation Treaty (NPT).

For the United States and the other Western powers, any nuclear technology—even for peaceful purposes—in the hands of Iran is fraught with many risks. They argued that such technology could be expanded into a weapons program, and nuclear weapons could then be used on Israel or passed on to "terrorist organizations." It seemed that the only way to resolve the issue is for the West to accept Iran's civilian program, and Iran, in return, to provide verifiable guarantees that its program would not trespass into the military realm. Under the George W. Bush administration, negotiations broke down since the United States demanded that Iran cease forthwith all uranium enrichment.

Under the Obama administration, the United States implicitly accepted Iran's right to enrich uranium so long as it provided verifiable guarantees that it would not enrich

to the point of producing weapons. To pressure Iran to provide such guarantees, the Obama administration persuaded the UN to place dire economic sanctions on Iran. In 2014, the Obama and the Rouhani administrations began serious negotiations to resolve these differences. After a full year of intense negotiations, the two reached agreement. This was formalized as the Joint Comprehensive Plan of Action between, on one side, Iran, and, on the other side, the six main UN representatives—the United States, Britain, France, Russia, China, and Germany. The UN agreed to lift sanctions. Iran, in return, agreed to close down its plutonium plant, drastically reduce its centrifuges as well as amount and degree of enriched uranium, and open up its nuclear installations to intrusive inspections. Critiques complained that the agreement was limited to 15 years. But proponents countered that at the end of this period, Iran would still be restricted by the earlier Nuclear Non-Proliferation Treaty.

MAKING CONNECTIONS What are the main differences between Shi'i and Sunni Islam?

---

conventional armies in the region, a large land mass, considerable human resources, a respectable gross domestic product (GDP), and vast oil production. Moreover, it has potential allies outside Iran—especially the Alawis in Syria, the Zaydis in Yemen, and Shi'is in Lebanon, Bahrain, and Afghanistan.

Governing the Economy

In the first decade of the Islamic Republic, peasants continued to migrate to the cities because of the lack of both agricultural land and irrigation. Industry suffered from lack of investment capital. Inflation and unemployment were high. The population steadily increased, and real per capita income fell due to forces outside state control. To deal with these problems, some leaders favored state-interventionist strategies. Others advocated laissez-faire market-based strategies. Such differences over how to govern the economy are still being debated in Iran and are the source of much political contention.

The Democratic Idea

Khomeini had argued that Islam and democracy were compatible since the vast majority of people in Iran respected the clerics as the true interpreters of the *shari'a*, and wanted them to oversee state officials. Political Islam and the democratic idea, however, appear less reconcilable now that much of the Iranian public has lost its enthusiasm for clerical rule. Khomeinism has divided into two divergent branches: political liberalism and clerical conservatism. These ideological currents, which will be discussed later in this chapter, are at the heart of Iranian politics today.

Democracy is based on the principles that all individuals are equal, especially before the law, and that all people have inalienable natural rights. The *shari'a* is based on inequalities—between men and women, between Muslims and non-Muslims, between legitimate minorities, known as the People of the Book, and illegitimate ones, known as unbelievers. Moderate clerics, however, advocate reforming the *shari'a* to make it compatible with individual freedoms and human rights.

The Politics of Collective Identity

The state emphasis on Shi'ism has to some extent alienated the 10 percent of Iranians who are Sunnis. In addition, the regime's insistence on a theocratic constitution antagonized some important clerics as well as lay secular Muslims, who lead most of the political parties. Similarly, the strong association of Shi'ism with the central, Persian-speaking regions of the country could alienate the important Turkic minority in Azerbaijan province. All of these trends put some strain on Iran's collective national identity.

Comparisons

The Khomeinist movement culminating in the 1979 revolution helped expand Islam from a personal religion concerned with the individual's relations with God into an all-encompassing ideology that dealt with political, legal, social, and economic matters as well as personal ones. The slogan of the revolution was "Islam is the Solution."

This expanded interpretation of Islam became known as Islamism and political Islam. The direct product of this Islam is the creation of an Islamic Republic that is theocratic—a regime in which the clergy claim special authority on grounds that as experts on theology they have a better understanding of religion and therefore greater expertise than laymen in supervising the running of the state. This authority is based not on the claim they enjoy direct communications with God—they do not claim such privilege—but that they have scholarly knowledge of the scriptures and God's laws—the *shari'a*. This makes the Islamic Republic a unique political system in the modern world, although it has been an inspiration for other Islamist movements that have become an important force in the contemporary world.

Islamism

The use of Islam as a political ideology. Similar to political Islam and Islamic fundamentalism.

Although this was the main contribution of the Islamic Republic to comparative politics, the reform movement of the 1990s and early 2000s did its best to counter it. The leading reformers, who label themselves the new Muslim intellectuals, argue that their intellectual fathers, the revolutionary generation, had mistakenly "bloated religion" and expanded it from personal ethics into an all-encompassing political ideology. In other words, they had turned faith into a total system of thought similar to twentieth-century European totalitarian ideologies—the other major isms. The new Muslim intellectuals set themselves the task of slimming down, narrowing, and lightening this bloated system of thought. In short, they have turned away from Islamism back to a more conventional understanding of Islam.

It is these two contrasting interpretations of Islam that help explain the bitter conflict in contemporary Iran between reformers and conservatives, between so-called fundamentalists and liberal pragmatists, between supporters of Khatami-Rouhani and those of Ahmadinejad, and between the generation that made the 1979 revolution and the new generation that came of age during the same revolution. They both consider themselves Islamic but have sharply different interpretations of Islam—especially when it comes to politics, including the relations with the West and the United States.

SECTION 2

POLITICAL ECONOMY AND DEVELOPMENT

State and Economy

British prospectors struck oil in Iran's Khuzistan province in 1908, and the British government in 1912 decided to fuel its navy with petroleum rather than coal. It also decided to buy most of its fuel from the British-owned Anglo-Iranian Oil Company. Iran's oil revenues increased modestly in the next four decades, reaching $16 million in 1951. After the nationalization of the oil industry in 1951 and the agreement with a consortium of U.S. and British companies in 1954, oil revenues rose steadily, from $34 million in 1955 to $5 billion in 1973 and, after the quadrupling of oil prices in 1974, to over $23 billion in 1976. Between 1953 and 1978, Iran's cumulative oil income came to over $100 billion.

Oil financed over 90 percent of imports and 80 percent of the annual budget and far surpassed total tax revenues. Oil also enabled Iran not to worry about feeding its population. Instead, it could undertake ambitious development programs that other states could carry out only if they squeezed scarce resources from their populations. In fact, oil revenues made Iran into a **rentier state**, a country that obtains a lucrative income by exporting raw materials or leasing out natural resources to foreign companies. Iran as well as Iraq, Algeria, Saudi Arabia, and several small Persian Gulf states received enough money from their oil wells to be able to disregard their internal tax bases. The Iranian state thus became relatively independent of society. Society, in turn, had few inputs into the state. Little taxation meant little representation.

From the 1950s through the 1970s, Muhammad Reza Shah tried to encourage other exports and attract foreign investment into non-oil ventures. Despite some increase in carpet and pistachio exports, oil continued to dominate. In 1979, on the eve of the Islamic Revolution, oil still provided 97 percent of the country's foreign exchange. Foreign firms invested no more than $1 billion in Iran—and much of this was not in industry but in banking, trade, and insurance. In Iran, as in the rest of the Middle East, foreign investors were deterred by government corruption, labor costs, small internal markets, potential instability, and fear of confiscation.

Despite waste and corruption, there was significant growth in many modern sectors of the economy under the Shah. (See Table 14.2.) GNP grew at an average rate

rentier state

A country that obtains much of its revenue from the export of oil or other natural resources and is doesn't have to rely on its internal tax base.

of 9.6 percent per year from 1960 to 1977. This made Iran one of the fastest-growing economies in the world. Land reform created over 644,000 moderately prosperous farms. The number of modern factories tripled. The Trans-Iranian Railway was completed. Roads were built connecting most villages with the provincial cities. Iran was seen as having started an economic "take-off" into modernization.

Iran's Economy under the Islamic Republic

Iran's main economic problem has been instability in the world oil market. Oil revenues, which continued to provide the state with much of its income, fell from $20 billion in 1978 to less than $10 billion in 1998. They did not improve until the early 2000s increasing to $17 billion in 2000, $44 billion in 2005, and over $55 billion per year by the late 2000s. This increase was due not to a rise in production—in fact, total production in 2005 was a third less than in 1975—but to the dramatic rise in the price of oil in the international market. A barrel of oil jumped from $14 in 1998 to $30 in 2000, $56 in 2005, and over $100 during 2013–14. Recently, it has mostly been in the $50–60 range. At their price peak, oil revenues enabled the government to allocate as much as $100 billion a year subsidizing essential goods such as bread, heating fuel, gasoline, sugar, rice, milk, and cooking oil. Between 2011 and 2014, it made bold moves trimming these subsidies, and, instead, gave cash directly to the poor. Ironically, the impressive growth in private cars and public transport has strained the refineries and forced Iran to become more dependent on imported gasoline

Although contemporary Iran has been awash in oil money, the country's economic situation has been complicated by a population explosion, the Iran–Iraq War, and the emigration of over 2 million. The annual population growth rate, which was 2.5 percent in the late 1970s, jumped to over 4 percent in the early 1980s, one of the highest rates in the world. The war with Iraq wrought on Iran as much as $600 billion in property damage and over 218,000 dead. The Islamic Revolution itself frightened many professionals and highly skilled technicians, as well as wealthy entrepreneurs, and industrialists into fleeing to the West. Over a quarter million settled in the United States.

The overall result was a 20-year economic crisis lasting well into the late 1990s. The value of real incomes, including salaries and pensions, dropped by as much as 60 percent. Unemployment hit 20 percent; over two-thirds of entrants into the labor force could not find jobs, and peasants continued to flock to urban shantytowns. Tehran grew from 4.5 million to 12 million people. The total number of families living below the poverty level increased, and by the late 1990s, over 9 million urban dwellers lived below the official poverty line.[4] Shortages in foreign exchange curtailed vital imports, even of essential manufactured goods. What is more, the regime that came to power advocating self-sufficiency now owed foreign banks and governments over $30 billion, forcing it to renegotiate foreign loans constantly. In the 2005 presidential elections, these problems helped explain the strong victory of Ahmadinejad, the conservative populist candidate. But the U.S.-imposed sanctions on the Ahmadinejad administration compounded these economic problems, causing spiraling inflation, shortage of imported goods, and increasing a brain drain to the West.

Table 14.2	Industrial Production	
Product	**1953**	**1977**
Coal (tons)	200,000	900,000
Iron ore (tons)	5,000	930,000
Steel (tons)	0	275,000
Cement (tons)	53,000	4,300,000
Sugar (tons)	70,000	527,000
Tractors (no.)	0	7,700
Motor vehicles (no.)	0	109,000

Source: E. Abrahamian, "Structural Causes of the Iranian Revolution," *Middle East Research and Information Project*, no. 87 (May 1980), p. 22.

Nevertheless, the Islamic Republic has over the years scored some notable economic successes. The Reconstruction Ministry built 30,000 miles of paved roads, 40,000 schools, and 7,000 libraries. It brought electricity and running water to more than half of the country's 50,000 villages. The number of registered vehicles on the roads increased from 27,000 in 1990 to over 3 million in 2009. More dams and irrigation canals were built, and the Agricultural Ministry distributed some 630,000 hectares of confiscated arable land to peasants and gave farmers more favorable prices.

The government has exercised control over most of Iran's economy for the entire history of the Islamic Republic. Reformist presidents Khatami and Rouhani took steps to reduce the role of the state in the economy by allowing privatization in some sectors of the economy (including banking) and relaunching a stock market to sell shares of government businesses to private investors. Even Ayatollah Khamenei, the chief religious leader, and former conservative president Ahmadinejad have endorsed privatization. Ahmadinejad initiated a program to give "justice shares" of state-owned industries to low-income citizens. Nevertheless, about 70 percent of the Iranian economy continues to be under state control.

Society and Economy

During the Shah's reign, a huge amount of state investment went into social welfare. Enrollment in primary schools grew from fewer than 750,000 to over 4 million; in secondary schools from 121,000 to nearly 740,000; in vocational schools from 2,500 to nearly 230,000; and in universities from under 14,000 to more than 154,000. Between 1963 and 1977, the number of hospital beds increased from 24,126 to 48,000; medical clinics from 700 to 2,800; nurses from 1,969 to 4,105; and doctors from 4,500 to 12,750. These improvements, together with the elimination of epidemics and famines, lowered infant mortality and led to a population explosion.

The Shah's approach to development, however, increased his unpopularity with many sectors of Iranian society. The Shah believed that if economic growth benefited those who were already better off, some of the wealth would gradually trickle down to the lower levels of society. But these benefits invariably failed to trickle down and got stuck at the top among the better off segments of the population.

In fact, wealth trickled up: In 1972, the richest 20 percent of urban households accounted for 47.1 percent of total urban family expenditures; by 1977, it accounted for 55.5 percent. In 1972, the poorest 40 percent accounted for 16.7 percent of urban family expenditures; by 1977, this had dropped to 11.7 percent. In Iran's cities, in particular, the rich were getting richer, and the poor were getting poorer.

The new factories drew criticism that they were mere assembly plants that used inexpensive labor and were poor substitutes for real industrial development that would benefit the nation. The Shah's public health programs still left Iran with one of the worst doctor–patient ratios and child mortality rates in the Middle East. The per capita income in the richest provinces was ten times more than in the poorest ones. The ratio of urban to rural incomes was five to one. Land reform created a small layer of prosperous farmers but left the vast majority of peasants landless or nearly landless (see Table 14.3). By the mid-1970s, Iran was one of the most unequal countries in the world.[5]

These inequalities created a dual society—on one side the modern sector, headed by elites with close ties to the oil state, on the other side the traditional sector, the clergy, the bazaar middle class, and the rural masses. Each sector, in turn, was sharply stratified into unequal classes (see Figure 14.2).

The upper class—the Pahlavi family, the court-connected entrepreneurs, the military officers, and the senior civil servants—made up less than 0.01 percent of the population.

dual society

A society and economy that are sharply divided into a traditional, usually poorer, and a modern, usually richer, sector. There are also significant inequalities within the traditional and modern sectors.

In the modern sector, the middle class—professionals, civil servants, salaried personnel, and college students—formed about 10 percent of the population. The bottom of the modern sector—the urban working class, factory workers, construction laborers, peddlers, and unemployed—constituted over 32 percent. In the traditional sector, the middle class—bazaar merchants, small retailers, shopkeepers, workshop owners, and well-to-do family farmers—made up 13 percent; the rural masses totaled 45 percent.

These inequalities fueled resentments, which were initially expressed more in cultural and religious terms than in economic and class terms. Among the fiercest critics was Jalal Al-e Ahmad (1923–1969). He argued that the ruling class was destroying Iran by mindlessly imitating the West; neglecting the peasantry; showing contempt for popular religion; worshipping mechanization, regimentation, and industrialization; and flooding the country with foreign ideas, tastes, luxury items, and mass-consumption goods. He stressed that developing countries such as Iran could survive this "plague" of Western imperialism only by returning to their cultural roots and develvoping a self-reliant society, especially a fully independent economy. Al-e Ahmad is deemed to be not only the main intellectual critic of the old order but also the founder of the "back to roots" movement that eventually led to the Islamic Revolution.

Al-e Ahmad's ideas were developed further by another young intellectual named Ali Shariati (1933–1977). Studying in Paris during the 1960s, Shariati was influenced by Marxist sociology, Catholic liberation theology, the Algerian revolution, and, most important, Frantz Fanon's *Wretched of the Earth* (1961), which urged colonial peoples to use violence to liberate themselves from imperial rule.

Shariati argued that history was a continuous struggle between oppressors and oppressed. Each class had its own interests, its own interpretations of religion, and its own sense of right and wrong. God periodically sent down prophets, such as Abraham, Moses, Jesus, and Muhammad. Muhammad had been sent to launch a dynamic community in "permanent revolution" toward the ultimate utopia: a perfectly classless society. Although Muhammad's goal, claimed Shariati, had been betrayed by his illegitimate successors, his radical message had been preserved by the

Table 14.3	Land Ownership in 1977
Size (hectares)	Number of Owners
200+	1,300
51–200	44,000
11–50	600,000
3–10	1,200,000
Landless	700,000

Note: One hectare is equal to approximately 2.47 acres.
Source: E. Abrahamian, "Structural Causes of the Iranian Revolution," *Middle East Research and Information Project*, no. 87 (May 1980).

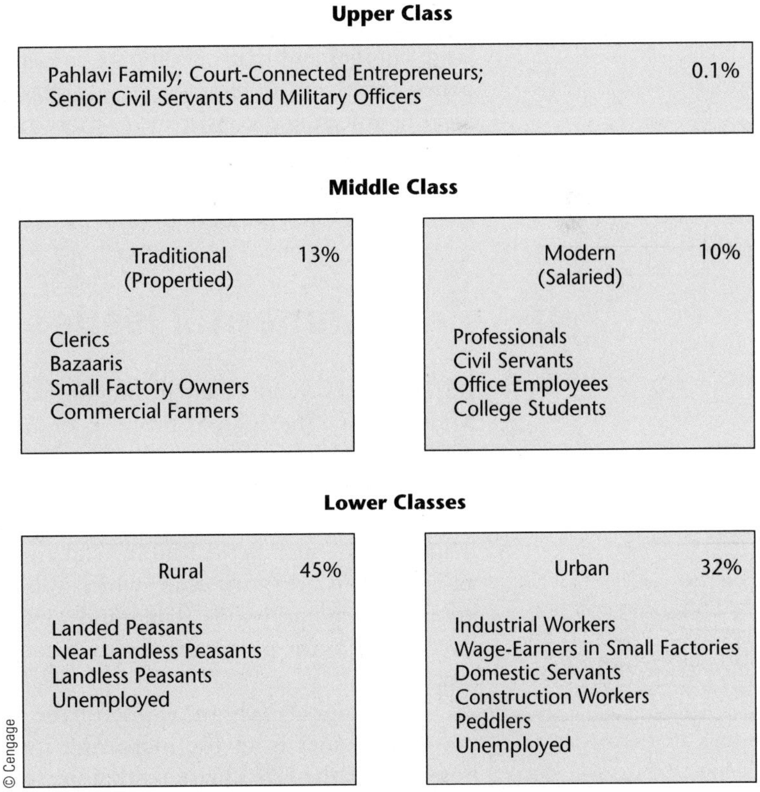

Upper Class

Pahlavi Family; Court-Connected Entrepreneurs; Senior Civil Servants and Military Officers	0.1%

Middle Class

Traditional (Propertied) 13%	Modern (Salaried) 10%
Clerics Bazaaris Small Factory Owners Commercial Farmers	Professionals Civil Servants Office Employees College Students

Lower Classes

Rural 45%	Urban 32%
Landed Peasants Near Landless Peasants Landless Peasants Unemployed	Industrial Workers Wage-Earners in Small Factories Domestic Servants Construction Workers Peddlers Unemployed

© Cengage

FIGURE 14.2 Iran's Class Structures in the Mid-1970s
Iranian society was divided sharply not only into horizontal classes, but also into vertical sectors—the modern and the transitional, the urban and the rural. This is known as a *dual society*.

Shi'i Imams, especially by Imam Husayn, who had been martyred to show future generations that human beings had the moral duty to fight oppression in all places at all times. According to Shariati, the contemporary oppressors were the imperialists, the modern-day feudalists, the corrupt capitalists, and their hangers-on. He criticized the conservative clerics who had tried to transform revolutionary religion into an apolitical public opiate. Shariati died on the eve of the revolution, but his prolific works were so widely read and so influential that many felt that he, rather than Khomeini, was the true ideological inspiration for the Islamic Revolution.

Despite setbacks in the 1980s, life improved for most Iranians in the 1990s. On the whole, the poor in Iran are better off now than their parents had been before the founding of the Islamic Republic. By the late 1990s, most independent farmers owned radios, televisions, refrigerators, and pickup trucks. The extension of social services narrowed the gap between town and country and between the urban poor and the middle classes. The adult literacy rate grew from 50 percent to 83 percent, and by 2000, the literacy rate among those in the 6–29-year-old age range hit 97 percent. The infant mortality rate has fallen from 104 per 1,000 in the mid-1970s to 37 per 1,000 in 2016. Life expectancy climbed from 55 years in 1979 to 68 in 1993 and to 71 in 2016—one of the best in the Middle East. The UN estimates that by 2000, 94 percent of the population had access to health services and safe water.

The Islamic Republic also made major strides toward population control. At first, it closed down birth control clinics. But it reversed direction once the ministries responsible for social services felt the full impact of this high rate of population growth. In 1989, the government declared that Islam favored healthy rather than large families and that one literate citizen was better than ten illiterate ones. It reopened birth control clinics, cut subsidies to large families, and announced that the ideal family should consist of no more than two children. It even took away social benefits from those having more than two children. The current population growth rate is 1.2 percent. The government is now toying with the idea of reversing policy and again encouraging population growth.

Environmental Issues

Iran faces a horrendous environment problem similar to most other countries in the Middle East. The age-old problem of aridity and lack of regular rainfall has been compounded in recent years by a series of droughts and dry winters—most probably caused by climate change and global warming. Rainfall fell by as much as 47 percent in some provinces in the mid-2010s. Consequently, water levels have fallen; major rivers—such Sefid Rud in Isfahan—have turned into streams; and lakes such as Urmiah in northeast Iran, which was once the largest lake in the Middle East, are drying up into ponds. The impressive numbers of dams built in the last 50 years have added to the problem since such concentrations of water inadvertently increase evaporation.

Iran's capital, Tehran, is one of the world's most polluted cities. Much of this pollution comes from the increasing use of private cars. This problem was compounded by the UN sanctions that prevented Iran from importing properly refined gasoline. Furthermore, Tehran is flanked by a high mountain range that blocks the air currents and thus traps the polluted air. Iran's Department of Environment revealed that in 2013, some 45,000 deaths were directly or indirectly caused by air pollution. On a number of days, the municipality has warned citizens not to venture out unless they had to.

Iran's liberal reform movement, especially educated youth, have taken up environmental issues as an important cause. It is significant that the supporters of failed 2009 presidential reformist candidate Mir-Hossein Mousavi named their organization the Green Movement, giving it a double meaning since green is traditionally the color of Shi'i Islam as well as being identified with environmentalism. There have also been public protests against the plight of Lake Urmiah.

Various administrations—both reform and conservative—have taken some measures to address environmental problems. They have placed a moratorium on dam building. They have channeled considerable resources into solar and nuclear energy—the avowed rational for the latter is that it will provide cleaner energy for industrial and home electrical use. They have supported reforestation and water conservation in the cities. They have encouraged citizens in Tehran to use public transportation, especially city buses, rather than private cars and taxis. Moreover, an extensive subway network has been built in Tehran linking many of the suburbs—even the distant ones—to the central city. Tehran now has a modern metro system on a par with the best ones in the world. Furthermore, farmers have been encouraged to cultivate crops that need less water and adopt more efficient methods of irrigating their fields.

The core environmental problems, however, are harder to tackle. Car pollution will not diminish until the traffic problem is tackled head on. Even more serious, the dire problems of increasing aridity and global warming can only be addressed on a global scale. When it comes to the environment, Iran, like other countries, is intimately interconnected with the rest of the world—whether it likes it or not.

Iran in the Global Economy

The integration of Iran into the world of states began in the latter half of the nineteenth century. Several factors account for this integration: concessions granted to the European powers; the Suez Canal and the Trans-Caspian railway; telegraph lines across Iran linking India with Britain; the outflow of capital from Europe after 1870; and, most important, the Industrial Revolution in Europe and the subsequent export of European manufactured goods to the rest of the world. In the nineteenth century, Iran's foreign trade increased tenfold.

The result of Iran's integration into the international system was economic dependency, a situation common in much of the developing world. Less-developed countries become too reliant on developed countries; poorer nations are vulnerable to sudden fluctuations in richer economies and dependent on the export of raw materials, whose prices often stagnate or decline, while prices for the manufactured products they import invariably increase.

Cash crops, especially cotton, tobacco, and opium, reduced the acreage for wheat and other edible grains in Iran. Many landowners stopped growing food and turned to commercial export crops. This led to disastrous famines during 1860, 1869–1872, 1880, and 1918–1920.

Furthermore, many local merchants, shopkeepers, and workshop owners in the bazaars became a propertied middle class aware of their common interests against both the central government and foreign powers. This new class awareness played an important role in Iran's constitutional revolution of 1905.

Under the Shah, Iran became the second-most-important member (after Saudi Arabia) of the **Organization of Petroleum Exporting Countries (OPEC)**; Iran could cast decisive votes for raising or moderating oil prices. At times, the Shah curried Western favor by moderating prices. At other times, he pushed for higher prices to finance his ambitious projects and military purchases. These purchases rapidly escalated once President Richard Nixon began to encourage U.S. allies to take a greater role in policing their regions. Moreover, Nixon's secretary of state, Henry Kissinger, argued that the United States should finance its ever-increasing oil imports, by exporting more military hardware to the Persian Gulf. Arms dealers joked that the Shah read their technical manuals the same way that some men read *Playboy*. The Shah's arms buying from the United States jumped from $135 million in 1970 to a peak of $5.7 billion in 1977. In addition to these vast military expenditures, the oil revenues had other unforeseen consequences: high labor costs; lack of incentives for competing industries; and the easy import of agricultural and manufactured goods. It is for this reason that some economists often describe oil as a resource curse (see page 527).

This military strength gave the Shah a reach well beyond his immediate boundaries. Iran occupied three small but strategically located Arab islands in the Strait of Hormuz, thus controlling the oil lifeline through the Persian Gulf but also creating distrust among his Arab neighbors. The Shah talked of establishing a presence well beyond the Gulf on the grounds that Iran's national interests reached into the Indian Ocean.

The clerical regime relies on two crutches of power: the bayonet and the oil well.

Courtesy Mojahed (in exile)

Organization of Petroleum Exporting Countries (OPEC)

An organization dedicated to achieving stability in the price of oil, avoiding price fluctuations, and generally furthering the interests of the member states.

In the mid-1970s, the Shah dispatched troops to Oman to help the local sultan fight rebels. He offered Afghanistan $2 billion to break its then close ties with the Soviet Union, a move that probably prompted the Soviets to intervene militarily in that country. A U.S. congressional report declared: "Iran in the 1970s was widely regarded as a significant regional, if not global, power. The United States relied on it, implicitly if not explicitly, to ensure the security and stability of the Persian Gulf sector and the flow of oil from the region to the industrialized Western world of Japan, Europe, and the United States, as well as to lesser powers elsewhere."[6]

These vast military expenditures, as well as the oil exports, tied Iran closely to the industrial countries of the West and to Japan. Iran was importing millions of dollars' worth of rice, wheat, industrial tools, construction equipment, pharmaceuticals, tractors, pumps, and spare parts; the bulk of which came from the United States. Trade with neighboring and other developing countries was insignificant.

The oil revenues thus had major consequences for Iran's political economy, all of which paved the way for the Islamic Revolution. They allowed the Shah to pursue ambitious programs that inadvertently widened class and regional divisions within the dual society. They drastically raised public expectations without necessarily meeting them. They made the rentier state independent of society. Economic slow-downs in the industrial countries, however, led to a decline in their oil demands, which diminished Iran's ability to buy such essential goods as food, medicine, and industrial spare parts.

One of the major promises made by the Islamic Revolution was to end this economic dependency on oil and the West. The radical followers of Ayatollah Khomeini, the founder of the Islamic Republic, once denounced foreign investors as imperialist exploiters and waxed eloquent about economic self-sufficiency.

But in 2016, Iran announced a dramatic new law permitting foreigners to own as much as 100 percent of any firm in the country, to repatriate profits to their home country, to be free of state meddling, and to have assurances against both arbitrary confiscations and high taxation. To maintain oil production, Iran needs deep-drilling technology that can be found only in the West. This goes a long way toward explaining why the regime now is eager to attract foreign investment and to rejoin the world economy.

Where Do You Stand?

Some see Iran as divided into socioeconomic classes. Others see it as a dual society divided into a modern and a traditional sector. How would you describe it?

Some see abundant oil revenues as a resource curse; others as a means for rapid development. Which description do you find more apt?

GOVERNANCE AND POLICY-MAKING

SECTION

3

Organization of the State

The political system of the Islamic Republic of Iran is unique. It is a theocracy with important democratic features. It is a theocracy (from the Greek, "divine rule") because the religious clerics control the most powerful political positions. But the system also contains elements of democracy with some high government officials, including the president, elected directly by the general public. All citizens, both male and female, over the age of 18 now have the right to vote.

The state rests on the Islamic constitution implemented immediately after the 1979 revolution and amended between April and June 1989 during the last months of Khomeini's life by the Council for the Revision of the Constitution, which was handpicked by Khomeini himself. The final document is a highly complex mixture of theocracy and democracy.

The preamble affirms faith in God, Divine Justice, the Qur'an, the Day of Judgment, the Prophet Muhammad, the Twelve Imams, the eventual return of the Hidden Imam (the Mahdi), and, of course, Khomeini's doctrine of jurist's guardianship that gives supreme power to senior clergy. All laws, institutions, and state organizations must conform to these "divine principles."

Focus Questions

- In what ways do the clergy have extraordinary powers in Iran?

- How do they control the government of the Islamic Republic?

The Executive

The Leader and Major Organizations of Clerical Power

The constitution named Khomeini to be the Leader for Life on the grounds that the public overwhelmingly recognized him as the "most just, pious, informed, brave, and enterprising" of the senior clerics—the grand ayatollahs. It further described him as the Leader of the Revolution, the Founder of the Islamic Republic, and, most important, the Imam of the Muslim Community. It stipulated that if no single Leader emerged after his death, then all his authority would be passed on to a leadership council of senior clerics.

After Khomeini's death in 1989, however, his followers distrusted the other senior clerics so much that they did not set up such a council. Instead, they elected one of their own, Ali Khamenei, a middle-ranking cleric, to be the new Leader.

Khamenei was born in 1939 in Mashed, Iran's second largest city, into a minor clerical family originally from Azerbaijan. He studied theology with Khomeini in Qom and was briefly imprisoned by the Shah's regime in 1962. Active in the anti-Shah opposition movement in 1978, he was given a series of influential positions immediately after the revolution, even though he held only the rank of *hojjat al-Islam*. He became Friday prayer leader of Tehran, head of the Revolutionary Guards, and, in the last years of Khomeini's life, president of the republic. After Khomeini's death, he was elevated to the rank of Leader even though he was neither a grand ayatollah nor a recognized senior expert on Islamic law. He had not even published a theological treatise. The government-controlled media, however, began to refer to him as an ayatollah. Some ardent followers even referred to him as a grand ayatollah qualified to guide the world's whole Shi'i community. After his elevation, he built a constituency among the regime's more diehard elements: traditionalist judges, conservative war veterans, and anti-liberal ideologues.

The Islamic Republic has often been described as a regime of the ayatollahs (high-ranking clerics). It could be more aptly called a regime of the *hojjat al-Islams* (middle-ranking clerics), since few senior clerics wanted to be associated with it. None of the grand ayatollahs, and few of the ordinary ayatollahs, subscribed to Khomeini's notion of jurist's guardianship. In fact, most disliked his radical populism and political activism.

The constitution gives wide-ranging powers to the Leader, who is elected now by an eighty-six member Assembly of Experts. As the vital link among the three branches of government, the Leader can mediate between the legislature, the executive, and the judiciary. He can "determine the interests of Islam," "supervise the implementation of general policy," and "set political guidelines for the Islamic Republic." He can eliminate presidential candidates and dismiss the duly elected president, and he can grant amnesty. As commander-in-chief, he can mobilize the armed forces, declare war and peace, and convene the Supreme Military Council. He can appoint and dismiss the commanders of Revolutionary Guards as well as those of the regular army, navy, and air force.

The Leader has extensive power over the judicial system. He can nominate and remove the chief judge, the chief prosecutor, and the revolutionary tribunals. He can dismiss lower court judges. He also nominates six clerics to the powerful twelve-man Guardian Council, which can veto parliamentary bills. This Council has also obtained (through separate legislation) the right to review all candidates for elected office, including the presidency and the national legislature, the *Majles*. The other six members of the Guardian Council are jurists nominated by the chief judge and approved by the *Majles*. Furthermore, the Leader appoints more than two-thirds of

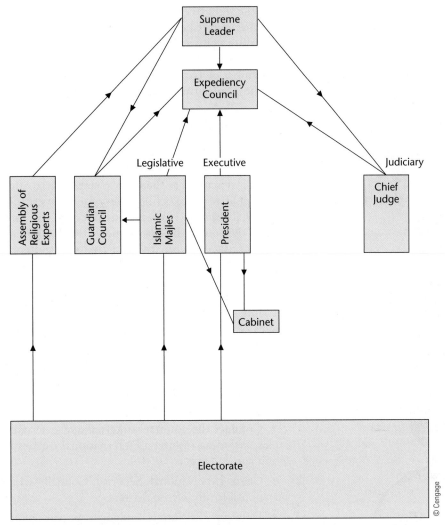

FIGURE 14.3 The Islamic Republic of Iran
The general public elects the *Majles*, the president, and the Assembly of Experts. But the Leader and the Guardian Council decide who can compete in these elections.

the **Expediency Council,** which has the authority to resolve differences between the Guardian Council and the *Majles* (the legislature) and to initiate laws on its own. This Council includes the most important personages in the Islamic Republic—the Guardian Council, the heads of the three branches of government, representatives of the cabinet, and individuals chosen by the Leader. (See Figure 14.3.)

The Leader also fills a number of important non-government posts: the preachers (*Imam Jum'ehs*) at the main city mosques, the director of the national radio-television network, and the heads of the main religious endowments, especially the **Foundation of the Oppressed** (see below). By 2001, the Office of the Leader employed over 600 people in Tehran and had representatives in the most important institutions throughout the country. The Leader has more constitutional powers than ever dreamed of by the Shah.

The Assembly of Experts is elected every 8 years by the general public. Its members must have an advanced seminary degree, so it is packed with clerics. The Assembly

Expediency Council

A committee set up in Iran to resolve differences between the *Majles* (parliament) and the Guardian Council.

Imam Jum'ehs

Prayer leaders in Iran's main urban mosques.

Foundation of the Oppressed

A clerically controlled foundation set up after the revolution in Iran.

has the right to oversee the work of the Leader and to dismiss him if he is found to be "mentally incapable of fulfilling his arduous duties." It has to meet at least once a year. Its deliberations are closed. In effect, the Assembly of Experts has become a second chamber to the *Majles*, the parliament of the Islamic Republic.

The Government Executive

The constitution of the Islamic Republic reserves important executive power for the president. The president is described as the highest state official after the Leader. The office is filled every four years through a national election. If a candidate does not win a majority of the vote in the first round of the election, a run-off chooses between the top two vote-getters. The president cannot serve more than two terms.

The constitution stipulates that the president must be a pious Shi'i faithful to the principles of the Islamic Republic, of Iranian origin, and between the ages of 25 and 75. The president must also demonstrate "administrative capacity and resourcefulness" and have "a good past record." There has been some dispute about whether the language used in the constitution restricts the presidency to males.

The president has the power to

- Conduct the country's internal and external policies, including signing all international treaties, laws, and agreements;

- Chair the National Security Council, which is responsible for defense matters;

- Draw up the annual budget, supervise economic matters, and chair the state planning and budget organization;

- Propose legislation to the *Majles*;

- Appoint cabinet ministers, with a parliamentary stipulation that the minister of intelligence (the state security agency) must be from the ranks of the clergy;

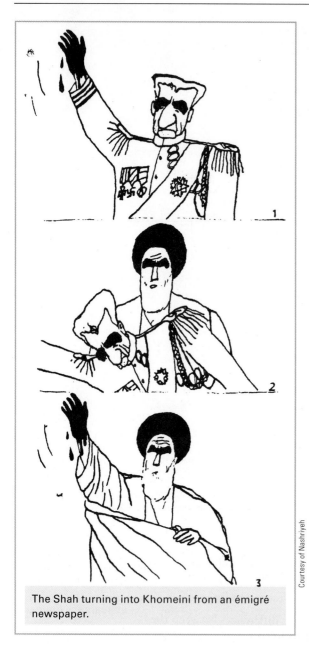

The Shah turning into Khomeini from an émigré newspaper.

Courtesy of Nashriyeh

- Appoint most other senior officials, including provincial governors, ambassadors, and the directors of some of the large public organizations, such as the National Iranian Oil Company, the National Electricity Board, and the National Bank.

Iran has no single vice president. Instead the president may select "a first vice President" and a number of "deputies" to oversee such affairs as veteran's, women's, or energy issues.

During the revolution, Khomeini often stressed that in his Islamic Republic trained officials and not clerics—also known as mullahs or akhunds—would administer the state. But in actual fact, four of the six presidents in the Islamic Republic have been clerics: Khamenei, Rafsanjani, Khatami, and now Rouhani. The first president, Abol-Hassan Bani-Sadr, a lay intellectual, was ousted in 1981 precisely because he denounced the regime as "a dictatorship of the mullahtariat," comparing it to a communist-led "dictatorship of the proletariat." Mahmoud Ahmadinejad (in office 2005–2013), the last lay president, was an urban planner, and was elected initially because of strong support from ultra-conservative clerics. But he eventually lost this support and was eased out of influence. He jeopardized this support by stressing the evangelical rather than the academic-theological side of Shi'i Islam. He insinuated that as a true believer he had privileged access to the hidden knowledge of the Hidden (Absent) Imam.

The Bureaucracy

As chief of the executive branch of the government, the president heads a huge bureaucracy. In fact, this bureaucracy continued to proliferate after the revolution, even though Khomeini had often criticized the Shah for having a bloated government. It expanded, for the most part, to provide jobs for the many college and high

---

PROFILE

President Dr. Hassan Rouhani with his foreign minister at the General Assembly meeting of the United Nations in 2013.

Bloomberg/Getty Images

President Dr. Hassan Rouhani

Hassan Rouhani, a consummate regime insider but running on a clearly moderate ticket, won an easy victory in the 2013 presidential elections. Born in 1948, he had grown up in a non-clerical household in a village a hundred miles east of Tehran. His father, surnamed Fereydun, was a carpenter-turned-farmer who had moved out of Tehran after World War II. At the age of 12, Hassan enrolled in a seminary in Qum where he soon participated in anti-Shah activities and to confuse the police adopted the name Rouhani (literally meaning "Clerical"). Graduating from the seminary, he performed his military service and then enrolled in the Faculty of Law in Tehran University where he specialized in criminal justice. As the revolution began to unfold, he was one of the first young clerics to rush off to Paris to vow allegiance to Khomeini.

After the revolution, Rouhani held a series of high posts: as parliamentary deputy from his home province; as clerical representative on committees to reorganize the chiefs of staff and the radio-television network; as member of the Assembly of Experts and Expediency Council; as long-standing member of the National Security Council; as trouble-shooting ambassador to France, Syria, and North Korea; and, most important of all, President Khatami's chief nuclear negotiator with the United Nations and the United States. He had offered the UN a compromise solution that had been acceptable to most of the other parties, especially the United Kingdom, but had been rejected by the George W. Bush administration. After the Khatami

era, he had headed the main think tank for foreign policy named the Centre for Strategic Studies; had written a number of book on Islamic law; and somehow had managed to find time to complete a doctorate in law from Caledonian University in Glasgow.

He ran the 2013 election on a reform platform. He emphasized the need for "cautious realism," "moderation," "prudence," and "hope"; "economic well-being" and a higher standard of living; greater interaction with the outside world and "normalization of relations," especially with the United States and the West; as well as the importance of citizen's rights and gender equality. He took the previous Ahmadinejad administration to task—sometimes implicitly, sometimes explicitly—for "extremism;" for weakening the economy through mismanagement, inflation, and high unemployment; and bringing down on the nation the horrendous U.S.–UN sanctions by refusing to be more transparent on the nuclear program, by denying the Holocaust, and therefore unnecessarily antagonizing the West. He was clearly courting voters who in previous elections had overwhelmingly supported political liberals like Khatami and economic reformers such as Rafsanjani. Not surprisingly, both Khatami and Rafsanjani enthusiastically endorsed Rouhani. For his part, the Leader remained above the fray—unlike the previous election when he had endorsed Ahmadinejad. He had probably concluded that the economic sanctions necessitated a more compromising foreign policy. His refusal to back the conservative candidates ensured that the revolutionary guards and the conservative clerical institutions would not interfere with the elections.

MAKING CONNECTIONS Why did Rouhani win the presidential elections in 2013?

school graduates. On the eve of the revolution, the state ministries had 300,000 civil servants and 1 million employees. By the early 1990s, they had over 600,000 civil servants and 1.5 million employees.

Among the most important ministries of the Islamic Republic are Culture and Islamic Guidance, which has responsibility for controlling the media and enforcing "proper conduct" in public life; Intelligence, which has replaced the Shah's dreaded SAVAK as the main security organization; Heavy Industries, which manages the nationalized factories; and Reconstruction, which has the dual task of expanding social services and taking "true Islam" into the countryside. Its main mission is to build bridges, roads, schools, libraries, and mosques in the villages so that the peasantry will learn the basic principles of Islam. "The peasants," declared one cleric, "are so ignorant of true Islam that they even sleep next to their unclean sheep."[7]

The clergy dominate the bureaucracy as well as the presidency. They have monopolized the most sensitive ministries—Intelligence, Interior, Justice, and Culture and Islamic Guidance—and have given posts in other ministries to relatives and protégés. These ministers appear to be highly trained technocrats, sometimes with advanced degrees from the West. In fact, they are often fairly powerless individuals dependent on the powerful clergy—chosen by them, trusted by them, and invariably related to them.

Other State Institutions

The Judiciary

The constitution makes the judicial system the central pillar of the state, overshadowing the executive and the legislature. It also gives the Leader and the clergy wide-ranging powers over the judiciary. Laws are supposed to conform to the religious law, and the clergy are regarded as the ultimate interpreters of the *shari'a*. Bills passed by the *Majles* are reviewed by the Guardian Council to ensure that they conform to the *shari'a*. The minister of justice is chosen by the president but needs the approval of both the *Majles* and the chief judge.

The judicial system itself has been Islamized down to the district-court level, with seminary-trained jurists replacing university-educated judges. The Pahlavis purged the clergy from the judicial system; the Islamic Republic purged the university educated.

The penal code, the Retribution Law, is based on such a narrow reading of the *shari'a* that it prompted many modern-educated lawyers to resign in disgust, charging that it contradicted the United Nations Charter on Human Rights. It permits injured families to demand blood money on the biblical and Qur'anic principle of "an eye for an eye, a tooth for a tooth, a life for a life." It mandates the death penalty for a long list of "moral transgressions," including adultery, homosexuality, apostasy, drug trafficking, and habitual drinking. It sanctions stoning, live burials, and finger amputations. It divides the population into male and female and Muslims and non-Muslims and treats them unequally. For example, in court, the evidence of one male Muslim is equal to that of two female Muslims. The regime also passed an "anti-usury banking law" to avowedly implement the *shari'a* ban on all forms of interest taking and interest giving.

Although the law was Islamized, the modern centralized judicial system established under the Shah was not dismantled. Before coming to power, Khomeini argued that in a truly Islamic society, the local *shari'a* judges would pronounce final verdicts without the intervention of the central authorities. Their verdicts would be swift and decisive. This, he insisted, was the true spirit of *shari'a*. After the revolution, however, he discovered that the central state needed to retain ultimate control over the justice system, especially over life-and-death issues. Thus, the revolutionary regime retained the appeals system, the hierarchy of state courts, and the power to appoint and dismiss all judges. State interests took priority over the spirit of the *shari'a*—although religious authorities have ultimate control over the state. Moreover, Revolutionary Courts headed by clerics and introduced as emergency measures in 1979, continue to function even to the present day.

Practical experience led the regime to gradually broaden the narrow interpretation of the *shari'a*. To permit the giving and taking of interest, without which modern economies would not function, the regime allowed banks to offer attractive rates as long as they avoided the taboo term *usury*. To meet public sensitivities as well as international objections, the courts have rarely implemented the harsh penalties stipulated by the *shari'a* and in 2014, formally dropped the death penalty for "apostasy, witchcraft, and heresy." They also relied more on the modern method of punishment, imprisonment, rather than the traditional one of corporal public punishment. By the early 1990s, those found guilty of breaking the law were treated much as they would be in the West: fined or imprisoned rather than flogged in the public square. Those found guilty of serious crimes, especially murder, armed violence, terrorism, and drug trafficking (the leading reason for capital punishment), were often hanged. Iran, after China, has the highest number of executions in the world. This created an embarrassment for Iran at the United Nations, which led the country to cut in the number of executions from about 1,000 in 2015 to fewer than 600 in 2016. In April 2017, the Iranian parliament abolished the death penalty for drug-related crimes, replacing it with life imprisonment. Iran, however, still has the highest per capita number of annual executions.

The Military

The clergy have taken special measures to control Iran's armed forces—both the regular army of 370,000, including 220,000 conscripts, and the forces formed of 120,000 Revolutionary Guards established immediately after 1979, and 200,000 volunteers in the Mobilization of the Oppressed (*Basej-e Mostazafin*), a volunteer militia created during the Iraqi war, which is now under the authority of the Revolutionary Guards. The Leader, as commander-in-chief, appoints the chiefs of staff as well as the top commanders and the defense minister. He also places chaplains in military units to watch over regular officers. These chaplains act very much like the political commissars who once helped control the military in the Soviet Union and still do in China's People's Liberation Army.

After the revolution, the new regime purged the top ranks of the military, placed officers promoted from the ranks of the Revolutionary Guards in command positions over the regular divisions, and built up the Revolutionary Guards as a parallel force with its own uniforms, budgets, munitions factories, recruitment centers, and even a small air force and navy. According to the constitution, the regular army defends the external borders, whereas the Revolutionary Guards protect the republic from internal enemies.

Although the military, especially the Revolutionary Guards, form a key pillar of the Islamic Republic, they consume only a small percentage of the annual budget. In fact, the republic spends far less on the armed forces than did the Shah. In the last years of the Shah's rule, military purchases accounted for 17 percent of the GDP; they now account for less than 5 percent. In 2015, Iran spent $15.2 billion on arms, whereas Saudi Arabia spent $81 billion, and the small Gulf sheikhdoms as much as $25 billion. It is this change of priorities that helps to explain how the Islamic Republic has been able to extend social services to the general population, which is one important reason why it enjoys widespread popular support.

Subnational Government

Although Iran is a highly centralized unitary state, it is divided administratively into provinces, districts, subdistricts, townships, and villages. Provinces are headed by governors-general, districts by governors, subdistricts by lieutenant governors, towns by mayors, and villages by headmen.

The constitution declares that the management of local affairs in every village, town, district, and province will be under the supervision of councils whose members would be elected directly by the local population. It also declares that governors-general, governors, and other regional officials appointed by the Interior Ministry have to consult local councils.

Because of conservative opposition, no steps were actually taken to hold council elections until 1999, when Khatami, the new reformist president, insisted on holding the country's very first nationwide local elections. Over 300,000 candidates, including 5,000 women, competed for 11,000 council seats—3,900 in towns and 34,000 in villages. Khatami's supporters won a landslide victory taking 75 percent of the seats, including twelve of the fifteen in Tehran. The top vote-getter in Tehran was Khatami's former interior minister, who had been impeached by the conservative *Majles* for issuing too many publishing licenses to reform-minded journals and newspapers. Conservatives did well in the 2003 local elections, due largely to widespread voter abstention, but moderates and reformers made a comeback in 2006 when the turnout was about 60 percent of voters. With the 2009 crackdown on the reforms by conservative president, Ahmadinejad, the conservatives won. But with Rouhani's victory in 2013, the reformers succeeded in making a limited comeback in local elections.

Semipublic Institutions

The Islamic Republic has set up a number of semipublic institutions. They include the Foundation of the Oppressed, the Alavi Foundation (named after Imam Ali), the Martyrs Foundation, the Pilgrimage Foundation, the Housing Foundation, the Foundation for the Publication of Imam Khomeini's Works, and the Fifteenth of Khordad Foundation, which commemorates the date (according to the Islamic calendar) of Khomeini's 1963 denunciation of the Shah's White Revolution. Although supposedly autonomous, these foundations are directed by clerics appointed personally by the Leader. According to some estimates, the annual income of the foundations may be as much as half that of the government.[8] They are exempt from state taxes and are allocated foreign currencies, especially U.S. dollars, at highly favorable exchange rates subsidized by the oil revenues. Most of their assets are property confiscated from the old elite.

The largest of these institutions, the Foundation for the Oppressed, administers over 140 factories, 120 mines, 470 agribusinesses, and 100 construction companies. It also owns the country's two leading newspapers, *Ettela'at* and *Kayhan*. The Martyrs Foundation, in charge of helping war veterans, controls confiscated property that was not handed over to the Foundation for the Oppressed. It also receives an annual subsidy from the government. These foundations together control $12 billion in assets and employ over 400,000 people. The recent moves to "privatize" state enterprises have tended to strengthen these foundations since these semipublic organizations are well placed and well enough financed to be able to buy shares in these new companies. Their main competitors in winning government contracts and buying privatized enterprises have been the Revolutionary Guards. Indeed, "privatization" is a misleading term in the Iranian context since it invariably means transfer of state enterprises to semi-state foundations.

The Policy-Making Process

Policy-making in Iran is highly complex in part because of the cumbersome constitution and in part because factionalism within the ruling clergy has resulted in more amendments, which have made the original constitution even more complicated. Laws originate in diverse places and may be modified by pressures from numerous directions. They can also be blocked by a wide variety of state institutions. In short, the policy-making process is highly fluid and diffuse, often reflecting the regime's factional divisions.

The clerics who destroyed Iran's old order remained united while building the new one. They were convinced that they alone had the divine mandate to govern. They followed the same leader, admired the same texts, cited the same potent symbols, remembered the same real and imaginary indignations under the Shah, and, most important, shared the same vested interest in preserving the Islamic Republic. Moreover, most had studied at the same seminaries and came from the same lower-middle-class backgrounds. Some were even related to each other through marriage and blood ties.

But once the constitution was in place, the same clerics drifted into two loose but identifiable blocs: the Society (*Majmu'eh*) of the Militant Clergy, and the Association (*Jam'eh*) of the Militant Clergy. The former can be described as reformers or populists, and the latter as laissez-faire (free-market) conservatives. The reformers hoped to consolidate lower-class support by using state power for redistributing wealth, eradicating unemployment, nationalizing enterprises, confiscating large estates, financing social programs, rationing and subsidizing essential goods, and placing price ceilings on essential consumer goods. In short, they espoused the creation of a comprehensive welfare state. The conservatives hoped to retain middle-class support, especially in the bazaars, by removing price controls, lowering business taxes, cutting red tape, encouraging private entrepreneurs, and balancing the budget, even at the cost of sacrificing subsidies and social programs. In recent years, the statist reformers have begun to emphasize the democratic over the theocratic features of the constitution, stressing the importance of individual rights, the rule of law, and government accountability to the electorate. In many ways, they resemble the liberals and social democrats of European countries. Since Khomeini had vehemently denounced liberalism as anti-Islamic, few describe themselves as liberals. They prefer the label reformers or progressives.

The conservatives in the Islamic Republic were originally labeled middle-of-the-roaders and traditionalists. The reformers were labeled progressives, seekers of new ideas, and Followers of the Imam's Line. The former liked to denounce the latter as extremists, leftists, and pro-Soviet Muslims. The latter denounced the free-marketers as medievalists, rightists, capitalists, mafia bazaaris, and pro-American Muslims. Both could bolster their arguments with apt quotes from Khomeini.

This polarization created a major policy-making gridlock between, on one hand, the early *Majles* dominated by the reformers, and, on the other hand, the Guardian Council controlled by the conservatives. Between 1981 and 1987, over one hundred

U.S. CONNECTION

Conservatives versus Liberals

In both the United States and Iran, conservative politicians—calling themselves "compassionate conservatives" in the United States and "principalists" in Iran—have a core base limited to less than 30 percent of the electorate. To win national elections, they have to reach out to others while continuing to energize their supporters to vote. To reach out, they both resort to patriotic and populist language—stressing "national security," accusing "weak-kneed liberals" for not standing up to foreign enemies, claiming to represent the "ordinary folks" and appealing to cultural values.

In 2005, the conservative candidate, Ahmadinejad, won the presidential elections in part because he presented himself as a "man of the people." He also won partly because his liberal opposition was badly divided. But the biggest reason for the conservative victory was probably because he projected himself as a tough patriot who could better defend the nation from foreign threats—especially after 2002 when President George W. Bush named Iran as a member of the "Axis of Evil."

Conversely, the reformist Rouhani won the 2013 elections by arguing that the conservative administration had stifled economic aspirations by unnecessarily antagonizing the United States, by underestimating the costs of UN sanctions, and by grossly mismanaging finances, especially through printing of money and thus causing of inflation. He held out the hope that normalization of relations with the United States would lead to improved standard of living.

MAKING CONNECTIONS What similarities are there between conservative and liberal politicians in Iran and the United States? How do they differ in the two countries?

---

bills passed by the reformer-dominated *Majles* were vetoed by the Guardian Council on the grounds that they violated the *shari'a*, especially the sanctity of private property. The vetoed legislation included a labor law, land reform, nationalization of foreign trade, a progressive income tax, control over urban real estate transactions, and confiscation of the property of émigrés whom the courts had not yet found guilty of counterrevolutionary activities. Introduced by individual deputies or cabinet ministers, these bills had received quick passage. Some ultraconservatives had countered by encouraging the faithful not to pay taxes and instead to contribute to the grand ayatollahs of their choice. After all, they argued, one could find no mention of income tax anywhere in the *shari'a*.

Both sides cited the Islamic constitution to support their positions. The conservative free-marketers referred to the long list of clauses protecting private property, promising balanced budgets, and placing agriculture, small industry, and retail trade in the private sector. The reformers referred to an even longer list promising education, medicine, jobs, low-income housing, unemployment benefits, disability pay, interest-free loans, and the predominance of the public sector in the economy.

maslahat

Arabic term for "expediency," "prudence," or "advisability," now used in Iran to refer to reasons of state or what is best for the Islamic Republic.

To break the gridlock, Khomeini boldly introduced into Shi'ism the Sunni Islamic concept of *maslahat*—that is, "public interest" and "reasons of state." Over the centuries, Shi'i clerics had denounced this as a Sunni notion designed to bolster illegitimate rulers. Khomeini now claimed that a truly Islamic state could safeguard the public interest by suspending important religious rulings, even over prayer, fasting, and the pilgrimage to Mecca. He declared public interest to be a primary ruling and the others mere secondary rulings. In other words, the state could overrule the views of the highest-ranking clerics. In the name of public interest, it could destroy mosques, confiscate private property, and cancel religious obligations. Khomeini added that the Islamic state had absolute authority, since the Prophet Muhammad had exercised absolute (*motalaq*) power, which he had passed on to the Imams and thus eventually to the Islamic Republic. Never before had a Shi'i religious leader claimed such powers for the state, especially at the expense of fellow clerics.

As a follow-up, Khomeini set up a new institution named the Expediency Council for Determining the Public Interest of the Islamic Order (known as the Expediency Council for short). He entrusted it with the task of resolving conflicts between the Islamic *Majles* and the Guardian Council. He packed it with thirteen clerics, including the president, the chief judge, the Speaker of the *Majles*, and six jurists from the Guardian Council. The Expediency Council eventually passed some of the more moderate bills favored by the reformers. These included a new income tax, banking legislation, and a much-disputed labor law providing workers in large factories with a minimum wage and some semblance of job security.

Constitutional amendments introduced after Khomeini's death institutionalized the Expediency Council. The new Leader could now not only name its members but also determine its tenure and jurisdiction. Not surprisingly, Khomeini's successor Khamenei, packed it with his supporters—none of them prominent grand ayatollahs. He also made its deliberations secret and allowed it to promulgate new laws rather than restrict itself to resolving legislative differences between the Guardian Council and the *Majles*. The Expediency Council is now a secretive body accountable only to the Leader. It stands above the constitution. In this sense, it has become a powerful policy-making body rivaling the Islamic *Majles*, even though it did not exist in the original constitution of the Islamic Republic.

Where Do You Stand?

Iran is often described as a theocracy. Would you agree?

Khomeini claimed there were no contradictions between democracy and Islam. Would you agree?

REPRESENTATION AND PARTICIPATION

SECTION 4

Although the Islamic Republic is a theocracy, it incorporates some features of a democracy. According to the constitution, the voters directly choose the president and the Assembly of Experts, which in turn chooses the Leader. What is more, the elected legislature, the *Majles*, exercises considerable power. According to one of the founders of the regime, the *Majles* is the centerpiece of the Islamic constitution.[9] Another architect of the constitution has argued that the people, by carrying out the Islamic Revolution, implicitly favored a type of democracy confined within the boundaries of Islam and the guardianship of the jurist.[10] But another declared that if he had to choose between democracy and power of the clergy as specified in the concept of jurist's guardianship, he would not hesitate to choose the latter, since it came directly from God.[11] On the eve of the initial post-revolution referendum, Khomeini himself declared: "This constitution, which the people will ratify, in no way contradicts democracy. Since the people love the clergy, have faith in the clergy, want to be guided by the clergy, it is only right that the supreme religious authority oversees the work of the [government] ministers to ensure that they don't make mistakes or go against the Qur'an."[12]

Focus Questions

- What are the powers and limitations of Iran's parliament?

- What social groups are most likely and least likely to support the Islamic Republic?

The Legislature

According to Iran's constitution, the *Majles* "represents the nation" and possesses many powers, including making or changing ordinary laws (with the approval of the Guardian Council), investigating and supervising all affairs of state, and approving or ousting the cabinet ministers. In describing this branch of government, the constitution uses the term *qanun* (statutes) rather than *shari'a* (divine law) so as to gloss over the fundamental question of whether legislation passed by the *Majles* is derived from God or the people. It accepts the reasoning that God creates divine law (*shari'a*) but elected representatives can draw up worldly statutes (*qanuns*).

The *Majles* has 290 members and is elected by citizens over the age of 18. It can pass *qanuns* as long as the Guardian Council deems them compatible with the *shari'a* and the constitution. It can choose, from a list drawn up by the chief judge, six of the twelve-man Guardian Council. It can investigate at will cabinet ministers, affairs of state, and public complaints against the executive and the judiciary. It can remove cabinet members—with the exception of the president—through a parliamentary vote of no confidence. It can withhold approval for government budgets, foreign loans, international treaties, and cabinet appointments. It can hold closed debates, provide members with immunity from arrest, and regulate its own internal workings, especially the committee system.

The *Majles* plays an important role in everyday politics. It has changed government budgets, criticized cabinet policies, modified development plans, and forced the president to replace some of his ministers. In 1992, 217 deputies circulated an open letter that explicitly emphasized the powers of the *Majles* and thereby implicitly downplayed those of the Leader. Likewise, in 2002, the Speaker of the House threatened to close down the whole *Majles* if the judiciary violated parliamentary immunity and arrested one of the liberal deputies.

Political Parties and the Party System

Iran's constitution guarantees citizens the right to organize political parties, and a 1980 law permits the Interior Ministry to issue licenses to parties. But political parties were not encouraged until Khatami was elected president in 1997. Since then, three major parties have been active: the Islamic Iran Participation Front and the Islamic Labor Party, both formed by Khatami reformist supporters, and the more centrist Servants of Reconstruction created by *Hojjat al-Islam* Ali-Akbar Hashemi Rafsanjani, the former president and chairman of the Expediency Council who died in 2017.

In general, formal parties are less important in Iranian politics than reformist and conservative coalitions and groups that form along ideological and policy lines. For example, former president Ahmadinejad had his initial power base in the Alliance of Builders of Islamic Iran, a coalition of several conservative political parties and organizations that delivered votes very effectively in local (2003), parliamentary (2004), and presidential (2005) elections.

According to the Interior Ministry, licenses have been granted to some seven hundred political, social, and cultural organizations, but all are led by individuals acceptable to the regime. Real political opposition has been forced into exile, mostly in Europe. The most important opposition groups are:

The Liberation Movement

Established in 1961 by Mehdi Bazargan, the Islamic Republic's first prime minister. Bazargan had been appointed premier in February 1979, by Khomeini himself, but had resigned in disgust 10 months later when the Revolutionary Guards permitted students to take over the U.S. embassy. The Liberation Movement is a moderate Islamic party. Despite its religious orientation, it is secular and favors the strict separation of mosque and state.

The National Front

Originating in the campaign to nationalize the country's oil resources in the early 1950s, the National Front remains committed to nationalism and secularism, the political ideals of Muhammad Mosaddeq, the prime minister who was overthrown in the CIA-supported coup in 1953. Because the conservative clergy feel threatened by the National Front's potential popular appeal, they have banned it.

The Mojahedin

Formed in 1971 as a guerrilla organization to fight the Shah's regime, the Mojahedin tried to synthesize Marxism and Islam. It interpreted Shi'i Islam as a radical religion favoring equality, social justice, martyrdom, and redistribution of wealth. Immediately after the revolution, the Mojahedin opposed the clerical regime and attracted a large following among students. The regime retaliated with mass executions forcing the Mojahedin to move their base of operations to Iraq. Not unexpectedly, the Mojahedin became associated with a national enemy and thereby lost much of its appeal.

The Fedayin

Also formed in 1971, the Fedayin modeled itself after the Marxist guerrilla movements of the 1960s in Latin America, especially those inspired by Che Guevara and the Cuban revolution. Losing more fighters than any other organization in the struggle against the Shah, the Fedayin came out of the revolution with great mystique and popular urban support. But it soon lost much of its strength because of massive government repression and a series of internal splits.

The Tudeh (Party of the Masses)

Established in 1941, the Tudeh is a mainstream, formerly pro-Soviet communist party. Although the Tudeh initially supported the Islamic Republic as a "popular anti-imperialist state," it was banned, and most of its organizers were executed during the 1980s. Some members now call for the overthrow of the regime; other call for its reform.

Elections

The constitution promises free elections. In practice, however, *Majles* elections, which are held every 4 years, have varied from relatively free but disorderly in the early days of the Islamic Republic to controlled and highly unfair in the middle years; back to relatively free, but orderly in the late 1990s; and back again to highly controlled in 2009. Ballot boxes were invariably placed in mosques with Revolutionary Guards supervising the voting. Neighborhood clerics were on hand to help illiterates complete their ballots. Club-wielding gangs assaulted regime opponents. The government controlled most of the mass media. The Interior Ministry banned dissident organizations, especially their newspapers on the grounds they are anti-Islamic. Moreover, the electoral law, based on a winner-take-all majority system rather than on proportional representation, was designed to minimize the voice of the opposition.

The 2013 presidential elections, however, were surprisingly free and resulted in the victory of the reform candidate Rouhani. He won 52 percent of the vote, thus avoiding a run-off. His main rival, the well-known mayor of Tehran, obtained only 17 percent. The other four candidates—all well-known conservatives—mustered together no more than 30 percent. The candidate supported by the outgoing conservative president, Ahmadinezad, received a mere 11 percent. Rouhani's carried all the main cities with the exception of Qom with its large seminaries. He also carried the Sunni provinces as well as in his home Caspian region. Over 72 percent of the some 50 million eligible voters participated. The Islamic Republic needs such elections, especially with high voter turnout, to retain a modern form of political legitimacy.

The 2017 elections were in some ways a repeat of 2013. Rouhani received 57 percent of the 41 million votes cast. This was one of the largest turnouts in the republic's twelve presidential elections. His conservative opponent—tacitly supported by the Leader—mustered only 38 percent of the vote. Rouhani's supporters also won almost all the council seats in the main cities.

The main obstacle to fair elections has been the Guardian Council with its powers to approve all candidates. For example, the Council excluded some 3,500 candidates (nearly half of the total) from running in the parliamentary elections of 2004 by questioning their loyalty to the concept of jurist's guardianship. The purge of reformers was facilitated both by President George W. Bush's labeling of Iran as a member of the global "Axis of Evil" in 2002 and by the U.S. military occupation of Afghanistan and Iraq. Reluctant to rock the boat at a time of apparent and imminent "national danger," most reformers restrained themselves and withdrew from active politics. Not surprisingly, the conservatives won a hollow victory in the 2004 *Majles* elections. They received a clear majority of the seats, but the voter turnout was less than 51 percent, and in Tehran only 28 percent. This was the worst showing since 1979. For a regime that liked to boast about mass participation, this was seen as a major setback—even as a crisis of legitimacy. There was some increase, to about 60 percent, in the turnout in both rounds of the presidential election of 2005. Still this was a sharp downturn from the more than 80 percent that had voted in the 1997 contest that brought Khatami to power. The 2009 elections, by reactivating the reform movement, may well have produced another record turnout, but because of government interference in tallying the vote, the facts remain unclear.

The Majles elections in 2012 and 2016 tended to lack luster in part because the Guardian Council continued to bar candidates, especially reformers, with name recognition; in part because both reformers and conservatives, now known as Principalists, ran often as "independents," and once elected preferred to lobby for local bread-and-butter issues such as state investments in their constituencies; and in part because the nuclear dispute with the United States increasingly dominated the national scene persuading even the conservatives to tacitly support President Rouhani's negotiations with Washington. With many free-floating votes, Rouhani could put together a cabinet only by striking deals with moderate conservatives and back-benchers from the provinces.

Political Culture, Citizenship, and Identity

In theory, the Islamic Republic of Iran should be a highly viable state. After all, Shi'ism is the religion of both the state and the vast majority of the population. Shi'ism is the central component of Iranian popular culture. Also, the constitution guarantees basic rights to religious minorities, as well as to individual citizens.

All citizens, regardless of race, language, or religion, are promised the rights of free expression, worship, and organization. They are guaranteed freedom from arbitrary arrest, torture, and police surveillance.

The constitution extends additional rights to the recognized religious minorities: Christian Armenians, Christian Assyrians, Jews, and Zoroastrians. Although they form just 1 percent of the total population, they are allocated five *Majles* seats. They are permitted their own community organizations, including schools, their own places of worship, and their own family laws. The constitution, however, is ominously silent about Sunnis and Baha'is. Sunni Muslims are treated in theory as full citizens, but their actual status is not spelled out. Bahai'is, followers of a nineteenth-century preacher in Iran who emphasized the spiritual unity of all humankind, are considered heretics because their founder had proclaimed his own teachings to supersede that of not only the Old and New Testaments but also of the Qur'an and the Shi'i Imams. Moreover, some ultraconservative Shi'is deem Baha'is to be part of the "international Zionist conspiracy" on the grounds their main shrine is located in modern-day Israel. In fact, the shrine long predates the establishment of the state of Israel.

The constitution also gives guarantees to non-Persian speakers. Although over 90 percent of the population understands Persian, thanks to the educational system, some 50 percent continue to speak non-Persian languages at home. The constitution promises them rights unprecedented in Iranian history. It states: "local and native languages can be used in the press, media, and schools." It also states that local populations have the right to elect provincial, town, and village councils. These councils can watch over the governors-general and the town mayors, as well as their educational, cultural, and social programs.

These generous promises have often been honored more in theory than in practice. The local councils—the chief institution that protected minorities—were not held until 20 years after the revolution. Subsidies to non-Persian publications and radio stations remain meager. Jews have been so harassed as "pro-Israeli Zionists" that more than half—40,000 out of 80,000—have left the country since the revolution. Armenian Christians had to end coeducational classes, adopt the government curriculum, and abide by Muslim dress codes, including the veil. The Christian population has declined from over 300,000 to fewer than 200,000.

The Baha'is, however, have borne the brunt of religious persecution. Their leaders have been executed as "heretics" and "imperialist spies." Adherents have been fired from their jobs, had their property confiscated, and been imprisoned and tortured to pressure them to convert to Islam. Their schools have been closed, their community property expropriated, and their shrines and cemeteries bulldozed. It is estimated that since the revolution, one-third of the 300,000 Baha'is have left Iran. The Baha'is, like Iranian Jews and Armenians, have migrated mostly to Canada and the United States.

The Sunni population, which forms as much as 10 percent of the total, has its own reasons for being alienated from Iran's Islamic Republic. The state religion is Shi'ism, and high officials have to be Shi'i. Citizens must abide by Khomeini's concept of jurists' guardianship, a notion derived from Shi'ism. Few institutions cater to Sunni needs. There is not a single Sunni mosque in the whole of Tehran. It is not surprising that the newborn republic in 1979 faced most stiff opposition in regions of the country inhabited by Sunni Kurds, Arabs, Baluchis, and Turkmans. It crushed the opposition by sending in Revolutionary Guards from the Persian Shi'i heartland of Isfahan, Shiraz, and Qom. Sunnis invariably now vote for reform candidates. For example, Rouhani won 81 percent of the vote in the Kurdish region of Baneh.

Azeris, who are Shi'i but not Persian speakers, are well integrated into Iran. In the past, the Azeris, who form 24 percent of the population and dwarf the other minorities, have not posed a serious problem to the state. They are part of the Shi'i community, and have prominent figures in the Shi'i hierarchy—most notably the current Leader, Khamenei. What is more, many Azeri merchants, professionals, and workers live and work throughout Iran.

But the 1991 creation of the Republic of Azerbaijan on Iran's northeastern border following the disintegration of the Soviet Union has raised new concerns, since some Azeris on both sides of the border have begun to talk of establishing a larger unified Azerbaijan. It is no accident that in the war between Azerbaijan and Armenia in the early 1990s, Iran favored the latter. So far, the concept of a unified Azerbaijan appears to have limited appeal among Iranian Azeris.

Interest Groups, Social Movements, and Protest

In its first two decades, the Islamic Republic often violated its own constitution. It closed down newspapers, professional associations, labor unions, and political parties. It banned demonstrations and public meetings. It imprisoned tens of thousands without due process. It systematically tortured prisoners to extract false confessions and public recantations. And it executed some 25,000 political prisoners, most of them without due process of law. The United Nations, Amnesty International, and Human Rights Watch all took Iran to task for violating the UN Human Rights Charter as well its own Islamic constitution. Most victims were Kurds, military officers from the old regime, and leftists, especially members of the Mojahedin and Fedayin.

Although the violation of individual liberties affected the whole population, it aroused special resentment among three social groups: the modern middle class, educated women, and organized labor. The modern middle class, especially the intelligentsia, has been secular and even anticlerical ever since the 1905 revolution. Little love is lost between it and the Islamic Republic. Not surprisingly, the vast majority of those executed in the 1980s were teachers, engineers, professionals, and college students.

Educated women in Iran also harbor numerous grievances against the conservative clerics in the regime, especially in the judiciary. Although the Western press often dwells on the head scarf, Iranian women consider this as one of their less important problems. Given a choice, most would probably continue to wear it out of personal habit and national tradition. More important are work-related grievances: employment, job security, pay scales, promotions, maternity leave, and access to prestigious professions. Despite patriarchal attitudes held by the conservative clergy, educated women have become a major factor in Iranian society. In recent years, they have made up 47 percent of university students, 68 percent of medical students, and 36 percent of government employees. However, overall just 16 percent of Iranian women are actively employed, which is one of the lowest female labor force participation rates in the world.

Women have established their own organizations and journals reinterpreting Islam to conform to modern notions of gender equality. Their main organization is known as the Women's One Million Signature Campaign. One grand ayatollah has even argued that they should be able to hold any job, including president, court judge, and even Leader. Women do serve on local councils and in the *Majles*. There are seventeen women in the current Majles, just 5.9 percent of the total 290 members, which puts the Islamic Republic at 177 out of 193 countries ranked by the percentage female legislators by the Interparliamentary Union.

Factory workers in Iran are another significant social group with serious grievances. Their concerns deal mostly with high unemployment, low wages, declining

Executions in Kurdestan, 1979.

incomes, lack of decent housing, and an unsatisfactory labor law, which, while giving them mandatory holidays and some semblance of job security, denies them the right to call strikes and organize independent unions. Since 1979, wage earners have had a Workers' House—a government-influenced organization—and its affiliated newspaper, *Kar va Kargar* (*Work and Worker*), and since 1999 the Islamic Labor Party has represented their interests. In most years, the Workers' House flexes its political muscle by holding a May Day rally. In 1999, the rally began peacefully with a greeting from a woman reform deputy who had received the second-most votes in the 1996 Tehran municipal elections. But the rally turned into a protest when workers began to march to parliament denouncing conservatives who had spoken in favor of further watering down of the Labor Law. On May Day 2006, an estimated 10,000 workers marched demanding the resignation of the labor minister. Bus drivers in Tehran, who had been active in earlier protests, went on strike in January 2006 to protest the arrest and maltreatment of one of their leaders. Workers also protested the contested presidential elections of 2009 by participating in the mass demonstrations. In the run-up to the May 2017 presidential elections, worker protests against the incumbent Rouhani led him to pledge to reform the labor laws if he is reelected.

The Political Impact of Technology and the Media

The regime places great importance on scientific, especially technological, education. It channels the top high school graduates into scientific fields, and generously nourishes Sharif University, the MIT of Iran—so much so that its top students are often recruited by North American universities even before graduating.

This interest is driven in part by security concerns and in part by deep-seated cultural values. Such education provides not only the physicists needed for the nuclear projects and the lesser known space program, but also technicians to monitor the Internet and prevent cyberattacks on Iran's nuclear installations. The desire to monitor the Internet and cell phones was greatly intensified after the 2009 mass protests over the presidential elections during which the opposition made full use of social media. The authorities countered by employing technology to monitor and disrupt the opposition. Once the opposition had been crushed, many reformist journalists emigrated abroad where they started websites and blogs—often with the help of Western governments and nongovernmental organizations. The security services in Iran have done their best to prevent citizens from gaining easy access to these sites.

Iranian culture also places great value on scientific education. Ever since the state set up an educational system, the top high school graduates have gravitated toward the sciences—not the arts and humanities. Science—and now nuclear science—is seen as the cutting edge of modernity. What is more, the prevalent view in Iran is that the Muslim Civilization had flourished in the distant past because of its scientific achievements, and, therefore, the key to recapturing the lost grandeur is through technology. When Reza Shah abolished traditional titles, college graduates with science-orientated degrees became generally known as "Engineers." Those with nonscientific ones became known as "Doctors." In recent years, a new title has appeared—that of Engineer Hojjat al-Islam—signifying the person has a science degree as well as a seminary education. We may well soon hear of His Excellency Engineer Grand Ayatollah.

Where Do You Stand?

The government in Iran is known as the Islamic Republic. Would you describe it as more Islamic or republican, which implies a prominent role for the public in political matters and public accountability of those with power?

The regime places great emphasis on elections. Why do you think it does so?

SECTION 5

IRANIAN POLITICS IN TRANSITION

Focus Questions

- What are the most important challenges facing the Islamic Republic?

- In what ways is Iran different from other developing countries?

The mass demonstrations of the Arab Spring of 2010–2011, which brought down the presidents of Tunisia, Yemen, and Egypt, have had repercussions in Iran. The Leader, Ali Khamenei, praised them, claiming that they replicated the Islamic Revolution of 1979 in Iran. The reform movement countered that these demonstrations had been inspired by the 2009 protests in Iran against the rigged elections and that they showed such protests—if continued for length of time—could bring down other autocratic regimes. The Leader categorized Mubarek of Egypt and Bin Ali of Tunisia as versions of the Shah of Iran who was deposed by the Islamic Revolution of 1979. The reformers categorized Mubarek and Bin Ali as typical autocrats who rigged and manipulated elections.

Despite these polemics, there are two major differences between Iran and the countries where the Arab Spring led to the downfall of autocrats. First, in those cases, the dictators ultimately fell from power because of the defection of their armed forces, as happened with the Shah. The Islamic Republic of Iran has survived in part because it retains the critical support of the military. Second, the Islamic Republic—despite its democratic shortcomings—does hold regular elections. In contrast, Mubarak and Bin Ali had tried to transform republics into "hereditary republics"—an oxymoron that enflamed public outrage.

Political Challenges and Changing Agendas

Contemporary Iran faces both major internal and challenges. Internally, the Islamic Republic continues to struggle with the troubling question of how to combine theocracy with democracy, and clerical authority with mass participation. After several years, when Iran's reformers seemed to be on the political rise, the conservative clerics and their supporters, who already controlled the judiciary, took over the *Majles* in 2004 and the executive in 2009. Between 2012 and 2013, however, they lost the presidency and the *Majles* to reformers. And the election results of 2016 and 2017 confirmed this trend of growing popular support for reform.

Many observers feel that the conservatives have lost touch with the grassroots of Iranian society and that their political base is probably less than 30 percent of the electorate. It is estimated that some 70 percent of the public favors the reformers, and that much of this majority, if not offered real choices, will, at a minimum, protest by staying home on election days. In fact, conservatives do best when the turnout is low, reformers benefit when it is high. The conservatives, including the Leader Khamenei, now face the challenge of how to maintain some semblance of legitimacy in the face of declining public support.

This challenge is troubling to the clerical leadership since the country has in recent decades gone through a profound transformation in political values, with much of the population embracing key aspects of the democratic idea including political pluralism, mass participation, civil society, human rights, and individual liberties. Even conservatives have begun to use such terms, openly describing themselves as "neoconservatives," "constructivists," and "pragmatists."

Meanwhile, those in the general public who feel excluded from national politics remain active in influential non-governmental organizations that make up an important part of Iranian civil society. The most visible of these is a human rights group headed by Shirin Ebadi, the winner of the Nobel Peace Prize in 2003. Ms. Ebadi has been a lawyer, judge (until the Islamic Republic barred women from holding such positions), writer, teacher, and prominent activist in the struggle to protect the rights of women and children. She fled into exile in London 2009 due to increased repression of regime critics. Even if excluded from the political arena, such activists will remain committed to using legal, nonviolent means to promote change. But they do not want to be associated with U.S. projects for "regime change."

The development of the democratic idea in Iran has been constricted by theocracy. Some argue that Islam has made this inevitable. But Islam, like the other major religions, can be interpreted in ways that either promote or hinder democracy. Some interpretations of Islam stress the importance of justice, equality, and consultation as political principles. Islam also has a tradition of tolerating other religions, and the *shari'a* explicitly protects life, property, and honor. In practice, Islam has often separated politics from religion, government legal statutes from holy laws, spiritual affairs from worldly matters, and the state from the clerical establishment. There are several contemporary examples of Muslim-majority countries, such as Indonesia and Tunisia, where democratic institutions have been successful and the democratic idea may be taking root.

Moreover, theocracy in Iran originates not in Islam itself but in the very specific concept of the jurist's guardianship as developed by Khomeini. On the whole, Sunni Islam considers clerics to be theological scholars, not a special political class. This helps explain why the Iranian regime has found it difficult to export its revolution to other parts of the Muslim world. The failure of the democratic idea to take deeper root in Iran should be attributed less to anything intrinsic in Islam than to the combination of crises between 1979 and 1981 that allowed a particular group of clerics to come to power. Whether they remain in power depends not so much on Islamic values, but on how they handle socioeconomic problems and especially the demands for political participation.

Politics in the Islamic Republic of Iran is sharply divided over the question of how to govern an economy beset by rising demands from its people, wildly fluctuating petroleum revenues, and the nightmarish prospect that in the next two generations, the oil wells will run dry. Most clerics favor a rather conventional capitalist road to development, hoping to liberalize the market, privatize industry, attract foreign capital, and encourage the propertied classes to invest. Others envisage an equally conventional state-led road to development, favoring central planning, government industries, price controls, high taxes, state subsidies, national self-reliance, and ambitious programs to eliminate poverty, illiteracy, slums, and unemployment. Some are hoping to find a third way, combining elements of state intervention with free enterprise.

Economic problems like those that undermined the monarchy could well undermine the Islamic Republic, particularly if there was another sharp drop in oil prices. The country's collective identity, although strong in religious terms, has also come under great strain in recent years. The emphasis on Shi'ism has antagonized Iran's Sunnis as well as its non-Muslim citizens. The emphasis on clerical Shi'ism has further alienated all secularists, including lay liberals and moderate nationalists, to say nothing of a large majority of Iranians who live abroad. Furthermore, the official emphasis on Khomeini's brand of Shi'ism has alienated those Shi'is who reject the whole notion of jurist's guardianship. The elevation of Khamenei as the Leader has also antagonized many early proponents of jurist's guardianship on the grounds that he lacks the scholarly qualifications to hold the position that embodies the sacred and secular power of the Islamic Republic.

Iran's ruling clerical regime has gradually eroded the broad social base that brought it to power in the Islamic Revolution nearly three decades ago. The country's collective identity has been further weakened, by class, ethnicity, gender, and political differences. Growing discontent may be expressed through apolitical channels, such as apathy, emigration, inward-looking religion, or even drug addiction. There is also a possibility that those seeking change may turn to radical action if they cannot attain their goals through a legal reformist movement. Those who want to understand the possibilities for political change in Iran would do well to remember that the country produced two popular upheavals in the twentieth century that fundamentally transformed the political system: the constitutional (1905) and the Islamic (1979) revolutions.

The Islamic Republic's first attempt to enter the world of states as a militant force to spread its theocratic version of Islam proved counterproductive. This effort led to the disastrous war with Iraq. It drove Saudi Arabia and the Gulf sheikdoms into a closer relationship with the United States. It prompted the United States to isolate Iran, discouraged foreign investment, and prevented international organizations from extending economic assistance. It also alarmed nearby secular Islamic states such as Turkey, Tadzhikistan, and Azerbaijan. During the Khatami presidency (1997–2005), however, the regime tried to repair some of this damage. It won over many Arab states and established cordial relations with its neighbors. It also managed to repair some bridges to the European Community. This repair work, however, was seriously undone by the conservative Ahmadinejad administration. The Rouhani administration is now trying to again repair the damage, and, if possible, normalize relations with the Gulf states, especially Saudi Arabia. This repair work, however, received a major setback in 2017 when new leadership in Saudi Arabia—encouraged by U.S. president Donald Trump—launched a much-publicized political offensive against Qatar for not fully siding with it against Iran.

The major external challenge to the Islamic Republic comes from the United States. The George W. Bush administration, by naming Iran as a member of the "Axis of Evil" in 2002 and openly calling for "regime change" (and promoting such change by military means in neighboring Afghanistan and Iraq) dramatically increased pressures on Iran beyond those that already existed because of U.S. economic sanctions, lack of diplomatic relations, and the successful barring of Iran from the World Trade Organization (WTO). The Bush administration further accused Iran of sabotaging the Arab–Israeli peace process, helping terrorist organizations, especially Hamas in Palestine and Hezbollah in Lebanon, and "grossly violating" democratic and human rights of its own citizens. It furthermore accused Iran of transforming its nuclear program into a nuclear weapons program and thus violating the UN Non-Proliferation Treaty.

The conservatives who then dominated Iranian politics were able to transform this external threat into a political asset. They intimidated many reformers into toning down their demands for domestic change, even silencing them, by declaring that the country was in danger, that the enemy was at the gates, and that any opposition to the government in such times would play into the hands of those who wanted to do harm to Iran.

President Obama launched a new policy offering an olive branch. He implicitly made it clear that he would accepted Iran's right to enrich uranium and have a nuclear program so long as it gave verifiable guarantees it would not produce atomic weapons. At the same time, he—unlike his predecessor—succeeded in rallying the UN to impose dire economic sanctions on Iran to bring the latter to serious negotiations. Such negotiations started in 2013—immediately after Rouhani's elections. Rouhani, who, as chief nuclear negotiator under Khatami, had himself earlier offered olive branches to Washington, quickly took up Obama's offer.

Both the Obama and the Rouhani administrations were eager for compromise: the former because it did not want another war and was eager to wind down its entanglements in the Middle East; the latter in part because of the sanctions, in part because it had always favored transparency, and in part because its aim had always been not to develop actual nuclear weapons, but instead to attain the theoretical capacity to be able to develop such weapons in the long-term future if necessity ever required it—such as another Saddam Hussein invading Iran and unleashing weapons of mass destruction. To have such a capacity, Iran needs the scientific knowledge, the centrifuges, and the ability to enrich uranium to a high level required for weapons.

The negotiations were formally between Iran and the Permanent Five Members of UN Security Council plus 1 (United States, United Kingdom, France, Russia, and China, plus Germany). But in reality, they were between Iran and the United States. Behind closed doors negotiators tackled the hard technical issues of how much uranium Iran would be permitted to enrich, how many centrifuges it could retain, whether it could experiment with plutonium as well as uranium, and how much it would open up its facilities to UN inspections.

After months of intense negotiations, an agreement was signed by all parties in January 2016. The so-called Joint Comprehensive Plan of Action (JCPOA) imposes strict limits—to be verified by on-site inspection—on Iran's nuclear program to ensure it does not lead to the production of weapons in exchange for the removal of economic sanctions that have crippled the Iranian economy. During the 2016 presidential campaign in the United States, candidate Donald J. Trump denounced the agreement as "the worst deal ever." It remains to be seen whether the Trump administration will renounce the deal or find ways to continue with its implementation.

Is Demography Destiny?

Iran's youth, especially college students, are a force to be reckoned with: Over half the current population was born after 1979 and as many as 1.15 million are enrolled in higher education. In 1999, eighteen different campuses, including Tehran University, erupted into mass demonstrations against the chief judge, who had closed down a reformist newspaper. Revolutionary Guards promptly occupied the campuses, killing or seriously injuring an unknown number of students. Again in late 2002, thousands of students protested the death sentence handed down to a reformist academic accused of insulting Islam. But in 2004, when the Guardian Council barred thousands of reformers from the parliamentary elections, the campuses remained quiet, partly out of fear, partly out of disenchantment with the reformers for failing to deliver on their promises, and partly because of the concern about the looming danger from the United States military presence in Iraq. Students, however, returned to active politics in large numbers during the 2009 presidential elections between conservative Ahmadinejad and the reform candidates, and even more so in the mass demonstrations protesting these contested elections. Of course, they played an important role in the 2013 election of reformer Rouhani. Youth's major concern is the lack of jobs for the college educated. The "Brain Drain"—an international term coined to describe the exodus of professions from Iran in the 1960s—continues to plague twenty-first century Iran.

Unemployment in Iran for youth (age 15–24 years old) is more than 25 percent. Many college graduates have to settle either for work less suited to their level of education or emigrate to the West. They have difficulty buying or renting homes. They consequently delay leaving their parents and getting married. But Iran so far has not shown the typical symptoms of the generational conflict—conflicts over bread-and-butter issues as such pensions, medical benefits, and old-age care. Such concerns are easily alleviated by the abundant income coming from oil and the anticipated revenue expected from the untapped gas reserves. Oil—not youth—is expected to carry the "burden" of the older generation.

Iranian Politics in Comparative Perspective

Unlike most developing countries, Iran was never formally colonized by the European imperial powers and has always been independent. It is, in many ways, an old state with many institutions that date back to ancient times. Furthermore, while many other developing world states have weak connections with their societies, Iran has a religion that links the elite with the masses, the cities with the villages, the government with the citizenry. Shi'ism, as well as Iranian national identity, serves as social and cultural cement, which gives the population a strong collective identity.

Although Shi'ism gives Iran this asset, it also helps explain why the county is unique in the world in that it has a semi-theocratic state. Despite these theocratic features, Iran still has much in common with many other modernizing countries in Asia and Latin American—especially Brazil, Mexico, Venezuela, India, and Indonesia. In some ways, it is better off. It no longer fits the stereotype of the Third World. It has overcome the worst aspects of underdevelopment—dire poverty, hunger and malnutrition, illiteracy, highly infant mortality, high death rates, and low life expectancy. It has an impressive educational system, and with it a burgeoning middle class that feels quite at home in the modern world. It has huge hydrocarbon resources but unlike many other oil states—such as Nigeria and Venezuela—also has a functioning state capable of effectively governing the whole country. The Islamic Republic is by no means a failed state. Although it is facing many major challenges that will shape its political future, Iran should be seen as a strong, thriving state.

The Islamic Republic could meet its internal challenges by becoming more flexible, liberalizing, giving greater scope to civil society, and allowing more public participation and competitive elections—in short, strengthening the democratic as opposed to the theocratic features of the constitution. If it did so, it could transform itself in the direction of a fuller democracy. If it does not, it could become more rigid, alienate a large segment of the public, lose legitimacy, and thereby make itself vulnerable to overthrow.

Iran could also meet its external challenge by continuing to follow a cautious foreign policy, adhering to the 2016 nuclear agreement, toning down its rhetoric, and assuring its neighbors as well as the United States that it is a "normal state" by conforming to international norms and making it clear that it has no intention to export Islamist revolution to other countries. If it does not, it could well remain a pariah state, isolated both economically and diplomatically from the global community. On the other hand, the West—especially the United States—could do more to understand and accommodate Iran's legitimate desire to be respected as an important regional power. If some middle ground can't be found, it would be a dangerous situation for both Iran and the world.

failed state

a country whose political or economic system has become so weak that the government is no longer in control.

pariah state

a nation considered to be an outcast in the international community and often subjected to isolation and various sanctions

Where Do You Stand?

Iran is often described with it neighboring countries, especially the Arab countries, as part and parcel of the Middle East. What does it have in common with its neighbors? How is it unique among Middle Eastern countries?

Iran's nuclear program has been very controversial in the international community. How do you feel about the 2016 agreement in which Iran would be allowed to continue non-weapon related nuclear development in exchange for removing economic sanctions?

Chapter Summary

The Iranian state—unlike many others in the Middle East—is viable and well established. It has a long history. Its official religion—Shi'ism—binds the elite with the masses, the government with the governed, the rulers with the ruled. Its ministries are embedded deep into society, providing multiple social services. It has substantial oil revenues, which, although fluctuating, provide the government the means to finance the ever-growing social program. What is more, the Islamic Revolution and the eight-year war with Iraq has helped create a sense of national solidarity against the outside world—not just against the West but also much of the Sunni Muslim world.

It has often been said that oil is a resource curse of the producing countries. It has been blamed for creating "rentier states," "dual societies," autocratic governments, unpredictable budgets, and retardation of other economic

activities. Although this may be true in some parts of the world, in Iran, oil has been the main engine driving economic development and social modernization. It is mainly due to oil that Iran entered the twenty-first century with a strong state and a fairly modernized society in which almost all citizens have access to schools, medical clinics, modern sanitation, piped water, electricity, radios, televisions, and basic consumer goods.

The clergy exercise authority over elected officials in three separate ways: the Leader, a cleric, supervises the three branches of government; the Guardian Council can veto legislation passed by parliament; and the same Council can vet all candidates running for high office. Despite these restrictions, the constitution—in theory—has the possibility of moving away from theocracy toward democracy. After all, the constitution enshrines the public with the right to amend the fundamental laws and to elect parliament, president, and Leader.

The political system of the Islamic Republic of Iran contains both theocratic (rule by religious clergy) and democratic elements. The clergy, despite opposition from the intelligentsia, continue to rule in part because they still enjoy considerable legitimacy—especially among the bazaars, rural population, and urban poor; in part because they have brought economic benefits to the wider population; and in part because they have left some room for civil society and have permitted interest groups to function so long as they do not cross certain red lines and directly question the clergy's legitimacy to rule the country. They have also been helped by the perceived notion that the nation has been under siege—even under imminent threat—from the United States.

Internally, the biggest challenge facing the Islamic Republic comes from the tension between theocracy and democracy in the country's politics. How the ruling clerics responds to the growth of the democratic idea among much of the citizenry will profoundly shape Iran's political future. Iran's major external challenge is finding a way to integrate itself more fully into the international economy and diplomatic community. This would require not only changes in the rhetoric and foreign policy of the Islamic Republic, but also a willingness on the part of the United States to accommodate Iran's legitimate demands for respect and acknowledge its role as a major power in the Middle East.

Key Terms

Assembly of Experts
ayatollah
bazaar
dual society
Expediency Council
failed state
Farsi
Foundation of the Oppressed
Guardian Council

Hezbollahis
hojjat al-Islam
Imam Jum'ehs
Islamism
jurist's guardianship
Leader/Supreme
Leader
Majles
maslahat

Organization of Petroleum
Exporting Countries (OPEC)
pariah state
pasdaran
People of the Book
political Islam
Qur'an
rentier state
theocracy

Suggested Readings

Abrahamian, Ervand. *A History of Modern Iran.* New York: Cambridge University Press, 2008.
_____. *The Coup: 1953, The CIA, and the Roots of Modern U.S.–Iranian Relations.* New York: The New Press, 2013.
Ebadi, Shirin, and Azadeh Moaveni. *Iran Awakening: A Memoir of Revolution and Hope.* New York: Random House, 2006.
Gheissari, Ali, and Vali Nasr. *Democracy in Iran: History and the Quest for Liberty.* New York: Oxford University Press, 2006.
Keddie, Nikki. *Modern Iran: Roots and Results of Revolution*, updated ed. New Haven, CT: Yale University Press, 2006.

Moin, Baqer. *Khomeini: Life of the Ayatollah.* New York: Thomas Dunne Books, 2000.
Nafisi, Azar. *Reading Lolita in Tehran: A Memoir in Books.* New York: Random House, 2003.
Parsa, Misagh. *Democracy in Iran: Why it Failed and How it Might Succeed.* Cambridge: Harvard University Press, 2016.
Pollack, Kenneth. *The Persian Puzzle: The Conflict between Iran and America.* New York: Random House, 2005.
Satrapi, Marjaneh. *Persepolis.* New York: Pantheon, 2003.

Suggested Websites

University of Texas—Iran Maps
www.lib.utexas.edu/maps/iran.html

Columbia University—The Gulf/2000 Project's Map Collection
gulf2000.columbia.edu/maps.shtml

The Story of the Revolution, British Broadcasting Corporation
www.bbc.co.uk/persian/revolution

Iranian Mission to the United Nations
www.un.int/iran

Iran Report, Radio Free Europe
www.rferl.org/reports/iran-report

News Related to Iran
www.farsinews.net

www.onlinenewspapers.com/iran.htm

15 China

William A. Joseph

China Photos/Getty Images

© Cengage

Official Name: People's Republic of China
(Zhonghua Remin Gongheguo)

Location: East Asia

Capital City: Beijing

Population (2016): 1.4 billion

Size: 9,596,960 sq. km.; slightly smaller than the United States

1911–1912
Revolution led by Dr. Sun Yat-sen overthrows 2,000-year-old imperial system and establishes the Republic of China.

Sun Yat-sen founds the Nationalist Party (*Kuomintang*) to oppose warlords who have seized power in the new republic.

1934
Mao Zedong becomes a top leader of the CCP; formally elected chairman in 1943.

1945
Japan surrenders, marking the end of the Sino-Japanese War and World War II.

1966–1976
Great Proletarian Cultural Revolution.

1976
Mao Zedong dies.

1920　　　1930　　　1940　　　1950　　　1960　　　1970

1921
Chinese Communist Party (CCP) is founded.

1927
Civil war between Nationalists (now led by Chiang Kai-shek) and Communists begins.

1937
Japan invades China, marking the start of the Sino-Japanese War.

1949
Chinese Communists win the civil war and establish the People's Republic of China (PRC).

1958–1960
Great Leap Forward.

THE MAKING OF THE MODERN CHINESE STATE

Focus Questions
- How did the Communist Party come to power in China?

- How has China changed—and remained the same—since the founding of the People's Republic?

Politics in Action

In the early morning hours of June 4, 1989, Chinese soldiers began an assault to clear pro-democracy demonstrators from Tiananmen Square in Beijing. One of the protestors described what happened when he and others joined hands on the outskirts of the square to form a human chain to halt the army's advance:

> . . . without warning, the troops opened fire on us. People cursed, screamed and ran. In no time, seventy or eighty people had collapsed all around me. Blood spattered all over, staining my clothes.

At a nearby intersection, he saw "several hundred bodies, mostly young people, including some children." He went on:

> As the army continued to move toward the square, an angry crowd of over ten thousand surged forward to surround the troops. This time the soldiers turned on the people with even greater brutality. The fusillades from machine guns were loud and clear. Because some of the bullets used were the kind that explode within the body, when they struck, the victims' intestines and brains spilled out. I saw four or five such bodies. They looked like disemboweled animal carcasses.[1]

By the time dawn broke, Tiananmen Square had indeed been cleared. An unknown number of civilians had been killed. In the days that followed, a wave of government repression spread throughout the country. Thousands of Chinese citizens

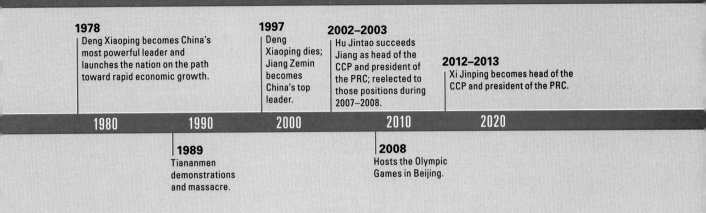

were arrested for their participation in the demonstrations in Beijing and other cities, and there were several well-publicized executions.

The People's Republic of China (PRC) has changed dramatically in many ways in the nearly three decades since so much blood was spilled on the streets of the country's capital. The country is much more prosperous and more deeply integrated into the global economy. Its stature as a rising world power had increased enormously. The Chinese people enjoy greater economic, social, and cultural freedoms. In 1989, fewer than 10,000 Chinese students were studying abroad; by 2016, there were more than 545,000, more than half of which are in the United States.

But much has not changed. The Chinese Communist Party (CCP) still rules China with an iron political grip. Most people do not feel the coercive weight of that grip in their daily lives, but the party still crushes individual or collective action it judges as a challenge to the party's authority. For all of its truly remarkable economic progress, the PRC remains one of the world's harshest dictatorships. The rift between China's authoritarian political system and its increasingly modern and globalized society remains deep and ominous.

And what happened in Tiananmen in 1989, cannot be mentioned in the press. It cannot be publicly commemorated in any way. It is not taught in schools. The Internet police scrub any reference to it in blogs and tweets. No official accounting of the number of dead has ever been given.

Geographic Setting

China is located in the eastern part of mainland Asia, at the heart of one of the world's most strategically important regions. It is slightly smaller than the United States in land area, and is the fourth-largest country in the world, after Russia, Canada, and the United States.

North China is much like the U.S. plains states in its weather and topography. This wheat-growing area is also China's industrial heartland. South China has a much warmer climate. In places it is even semitropical, which allows year-round agriculture and intensive rice cultivation. The vast, sparsely populated western part of the country is mostly mountains, deserts, and high plateaus.

China is the most populous nation in the world with about 1.4 billion people. The PRC has nearly 150 cities with a population of a million or more. Beijing, the capital, has nearly 21.5 million residents, while Shanghai, the economic heart of the country, has 24.1 million. Nevertheless, 560 million people still live in the countryside, which continues to play a very important role in China's economic and political development. (See Figure 15.1 and Table 15.1.)

In 1997, the former British colony of Hong Kong, one of the world's great commercial centers, became a Special Administrative Region (SAR) of the PRC. Hong Kong and China's other SAR, Macau, a one-time Portuguese colony with a thriving casino economy that became part of the PRC in 1999, have a significant degree of autonomy from the government in Beijing in matters other than foreign relations and defense. Beijing also ultimately controls the government in both SARs.

About 92 percent of China's citizens are ethnically Chinese. The remaining 8 percent is made up of fifty-five ethnic minority groups. Most of these minority

China: Ethnic Groups

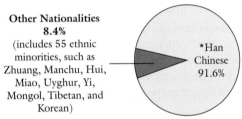

Other Nationalities 8.4%
(includes 55 ethnic minorities, such as Zhuang, Manchu, Hui, Miao, Uyghur, Yi, Mongol, Tibetan, and Korean)

*Han Chinese 91.6%

*Han is the dominant ethnic group in China. The name is derived from the Han Dynasty (206 BCE–220 CE), which is considered the first Golden Age of Chinese civilization.

China: Religions

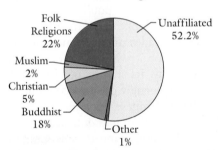

Folk Religions 22%
Muslim 2%
Christian 5%
Buddhist 18%
Unaffiliated 52.2%
Other 1%

Chinese Currency
Renminbi (RMB) ("People's Currency"); also called yuan
International Designation: RMB
Exchange Rate (2017):
• US$1 = RMB6.79
• RMB1 = US$0.15
100 RMB Note Design: Mao Zedong (1893–1976), Chairman of Chinese Communist Party (1943–1976)

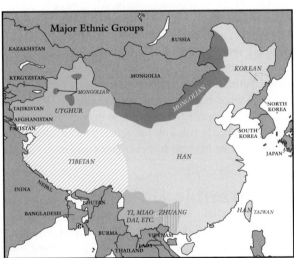

Languages: Standard Chinese (Mandarin) based on the Beijing dialect; other major dialects include Cantonese and Shanghaiese. Also various minority languages, such as Tibetan and Mongolian.

Religions: Officially atheist; Buddhist 18.2%, Christian 5.1%, Muslim 1.8%, folk religion 21.9%, other .08%, unaffiliated 52.2%

FIGURE 15.1 The Chinese Nation at a Glance

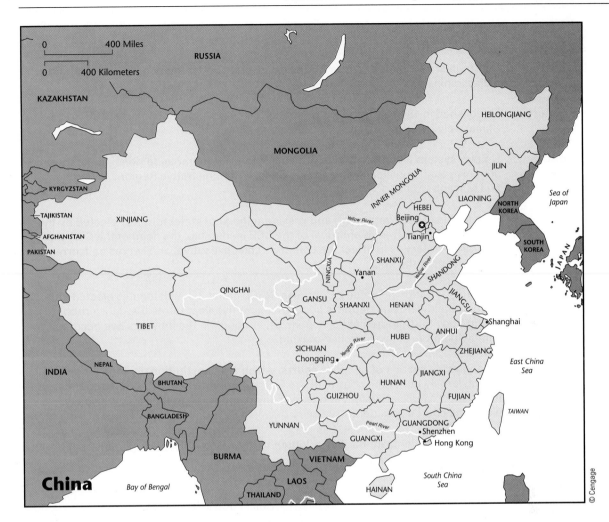

peoples live in the country's geopolitically sensitive border regions, including Tibet and Xinjiang, which has a large Muslim population. The often uneasy relationship between some of China's minorities and the central government in Beijing is a crucial and volatile issue in Chinese politics today.

Critical Junctures

From 221 BCE to 1912 CE, China was ruled by a series of family-based dynasties headed by an emperor. The Chinese empire went through extensive geographic expansion and other significant changes during this time. But its basic political and social organization remained remarkably consistent. One of its most distinctive aspects was a national bureaucracy chosen on the basis of merit, which developed much earlier and on a much larger-scale than similar government institutions in Europe. Imperial officials were appointed by the emperor only after they had passed a series of very difficult examinations that tested their mastery of the teachings of Confucius (551–479 BCE), a philosopher who emphasized obedience to authority, respect for superiors and elders, and the responsibility of rulers to govern benevolently.

Table 15.1	Political Organization
Political System	Communist party-state; officially, a socialist state under the people's democratic dictatorship.
Regime History	Established in 1949 after the victory of the Chinese Communist Party (CCP) in the Chinese civil war.
Administrative Structure	Unitary system with twenty-two provinces, five autonomous regions, four centrally administrated municipalities, and two Special Administrative Regions (Hong Kong and Macao).
Executive	Premier (head of government) and president (head of state) formally elected by the legislature, but only with approval of the CCP leadership; the head of the CCP, the general secretary, is in effect the country's chief executive, and serves concurrently as president of the PRC.
Legislature	Unicameral National People's Congress (NPC); about 3,000 delegates elected indirectly from lower-level people's congresses for five-year terms. Largely a rubber-stamp body for Communist Party policies, although in recent years has become somewhat more active in policy-making.
Judiciary	A nationwide system of people's courts, which are constitutionally independent but, in fact, largely under the control of the CCP; a Supreme People's Court supervises the country's judicial system and is formally responsible to the NPC, which also elects the court's president.
Party System	A one-party system, although in addition to the ruling CCP, there are eight politically insignificant "democratic" parties.

The Chinese empire was fatally weakened in the nineteenth century by an unprecedented combination of poor governance, a population explosion that led to economic stagnation and deepening poverty, internal rebellions, and external aggression by European powers, including the Opium War (1839–1842), which was fought over British demands that they be allowed to sell the narcotic in China. Many efforts were made to reform the imperial government. But these efforts were not enough to save the 2,000-year-old imperial system, and in 1912, a revolution toppled the ruling dynasty and established the Republic of China.

Warlords, Nationalists, and Communists (1912–1949)

Dr. Sun Yat-sen*, who was partly educated in Hawaii, became the first president of the Republic. But he was unable to hold on to power, and China quickly fell into a lengthy period of conflict and disintegration. Rival military leaders, known as warlords, ruled large parts of the country. Sun founded the Nationalist Party, which he hoped would be able to reunify the country.

In 1921, a few intellectuals, inspired by the 1917 Russian revolution, established the Chinese Communist Party. They were looking for a more radical solution to China's problems than that offered by the Nationalist Party. They initially joined with the Nationalists to fight the warlords. But in 1927, Chiang Kai-shek, who had

---

* In Chinese, the family name comes first, followed by the personal or given name.

become the head of the Nationalist Party after Sun's death in 1925, turned against the communists, who were nearly wiped out in a bloody purge. Chiang then unified the Republic of China under his personal and increasingly authoritarian rule.

The CCP relocated its headquarters deep within the remote countryside. This retreat created the conditions for the eventual rise to power of Mao Zedong, who led the communists to nationwide victory two decades later. Mao had been one of the junior founders of the Communist Party. Coming from a peasant background, he had strongly urged the Chinese revolutionaries to pay more attention to China's suffering rural masses. "In a very short time," he wrote in 1927, "several hundred million peasants will rise like a mighty storm, like a hurricane, a force so swift and violent that no power, however great, will be able to hold it back."[2] While the CCP was based in the rural areas, Mao began his climb to the top of the party leadership largely based on his forceful and prescient advocacy that China's rural poor would be the leading force in the revolution.

Under pressure from Chiang Kai-shek's army, in 1934 the communists were forced to embark on a year-long, 6,000-mile journey called the Long March, which took them across some of the most remote parts of China. Although only about 8,000 of the original 80,000 Long Marchers finished the trek, the communists were able to establish a base in an impoverished area of northwest China in October 1935. It was there that Mao consolidated his control of the CCP. He was a brilliant political and military leader, but he sometimes used ruthless means to gain power. He was elected party chairman in 1943, a position he held until his death in 1976.

Japan's brutal invasion and occupation of China beginning in 1937 had a major impact on the Chinese civil war. Chiang Kai-shek's government fled into the far southwestern part of the country, which effectively removed them as an active combatant against the Japanese occupation of the northern and eastern parts of the country. In contrast, the CCP base in the northwest was on the front line against Japan's troops. The Communists successfully mobilized the peasants to use **guerrilla warfare** to fight the invaders. This resistance to Japan gained the CCP a strong following among broad sectors of the Chinese people.

After Japan surrendered in 1945, the Chinese civil war quickly resumed. Communist forces won a decisive victory over the U.S.-backed Nationalists who were plagued by poor leadership, faulty military strategy, and corruption. Chiang Kai-shek and his supporters retreated to the island of Taiwan, 90 miles off the Chinese coast. On October 1, 1949, Mao Zedong declared the founding of the PRC.

Mao Zedong in Power (1949–1976)

The Communist Party came to power in China on a wave of popular support because of its reputation as social reformers and patriotic fighters. The CCP quickly turned its attention to some of the country's most glaring problems. A radical land reform campaign redistributed property from the rich landlords to the poor peasants and increased agricultural production. Highly successful drives eliminated opium addiction and prostitution from the cities. A national law greatly improved the legal status of women. The CCP often used violence to achieve its objectives and silence opponents. Nevertheless, the party gained considerable legitimacy among many parts of the population because of its successful policies during the early years of its rule.

Between 1953 and 1957, the PRC, with aid from the Soviet Union, implemented a **centrally planned economy** and took decisive steps toward **socialism**. Private property was almost completely eliminated through the takeover of industry by the

guerrilla warfare

A military strategy based on small, highly mobile bands of soldiers (the guerrillas, from the Spanish word for war, *guerra*) who use hit-and-run tactics like ambushes to attack a better-armed enemy.

centrally planned economy

An economic system in which the state directs the economy through bureaucratic plans for the production and distribution of goods and services. The government, rather than the market, is the major influence on the economy. Also called a *command economy*.

socialism

A system in which the state plays a leading role in organizing the economy, owns most productive resources and property, and actively promotes equality.

GLOBAL CONNECTION

The Republic of China on Taiwan

After the Nationalists fled to Taiwan, communist forces would probably have taken over the island if the United States had not intervened to prevent an invasion. More than six decades later, Taiwan remains politically separate from the PRC and still formally calls itself the Republic of China.

Chiang Kai-shek and the Nationalists imposed a harsh dictatorship on Taiwan. This deepened the sharp divide between the Mainlanders who had arrived in large numbers with Chiang in 1949, and the native Taiwanese majority, whose ancestors had settled there centuries before and who spoke a distinctive Chinese dialect.

With large amounts of U.S. aid and advice, the Nationalist government promoted rural development, attracted foreign investment, and presided over impressive economic growth by producing globally competitive exports. Health and education levels were quickly raised and now are among the best in the world. Taiwan's GDP per capita ($46,600) is higher than that of Britain or Japan.

After Chiang died in 1975, his son, Chiang Ching-kuo, became president of the Republic of China and head of the Nationalist Party. He permitted some political opposition and gave important government and party positions, previously dominated by Mainlanders, to Taiwanese. When he died in 1988, the Taiwanese vice president, Lee Teng-hui, became president.

Under President Lee, Taiwan made great strides toward democratization. Laws used to imprison dissidents were revoked, the media was freed of all censorship, and multiparty elections were held. There are now more than 200 political parties in Taiwan, although the two major ones, the Nationalists and the Democratic Progressive Party (DPP), have dominated elections since 2000. In 2016, Tsai Ing-wen of the DPP became the first female president of the ROC.

The most controversial political issue in Taiwan is whether the island should work toward reunification with the mainland or declare independence from China. Most people in Taiwan prefer the status quo in which the island is, for all intents and purposes (including its own strong military), independent of the PRC, but is not formally recognized as an independent country by most other countries, nor does it belong to the United Nations.

The PRC regards Taiwan as a rightful part of China and has refused to renounce the use of force if the island moves toward independence. Nevertheless, the two have developed extensive economic relations and other connections. The Taiwan Straits—the ocean area between the island and the mainland—is still considered one of the world's most volatile areas in terms of the potential for military conflict.

MAKING CONNECTIONS Why would Taiwan be reluctant to reunify with the PRC?

---

government and the collectivization of agriculture. The Chinese economy grew significantly during this period. But Mao disliked the expansion of the government bureaucracy and the persistence of inequalities, especially those between the urban and rural areas.

These concerns led Mao to launch the Great Leap Forward (1958–1960). The Great Leap was a utopian effort to speed up the country's development so rapidly that China would catch up economically with Britain and the United States in just a few years. It also aimed to propel China into an era of communism in which there would be almost complete economic and social equality. These goals were to be achieved by mobilizing the labor power and revolutionary enthusiasm of the masses under the leadership of the CCP.

communism

According to Marxism, the stage of development that follows socialism and in which all property is publically owned, economic production is coordinated for the common good, and a radical degree of equality has been achieved.

But irrational policies, wasted resources, poor management, and the suppression of any criticism, combined with bad weather to produce a famine in the rural areas that claimed 30–40 million lives. An industrial depression followed the collapse of agriculture. China suffered a severe setback in economic development.

In the early 1960s, Mao took a less active role in day-to-day decision making. Two of China's other top leaders at the time, Liu Shaoqi and Deng Xiaoping, were put in charge of reviving the economy. They completely abandoned the radical strategy of the Great Leap and used a combination of government planning and market-oriented policies to stimulate production.

This approach did help the Chinese economy. But by the mid-1960s, Mao had reached the conclusion that the policies of Liu and Deng had led to a resurgence of elitism and inequality. He thought they were threatening his revolutionary goals by setting the country on the road to capitalism rather than continuing to build socialism. China also broke relations with its one-time close ally, the Soviet Union, which Mao had concluded was no longer a truly socialist country because of the special privileges that its communist leaders enjoyed.

The Great Proletarian Cultural Revolution (1966–1976) was Mao's ideological crusade designed to jolt China back towards his vision of true socialism. Its main objective was the political purification of the nation through the purging of alleged class enemies in the CCP itself and throughout Chinese society. Using his unmatched political clout and charisma, Mao put together a potent coalition of radical party leaders, loyal military officers, and student rebels (called Red Guards) to support him and attack anyone thought to be guilty of betraying his version of communist ideology, known as Mao Zedong Thought. The Cultural Revolution led to widespread destruction of historical monuments, the psychological and physical persecution of millions of people, and a series of disruptive power struggles within the top leadership of the CCP. As many as 2 million people lost their lives. Among the victims was China's president, Liu Shaoqi, who was subjected to harsh criticism and beaten by the Red Guards, imprisoned without a trial, and died in solitary confinement after being denied timely medical treatment.

Mao passed away in September 1976 at age 82. A month later, a group of relatively moderate leaders arrested their radical rivals, the so-called Gang of Four, led by Mao's widow, Jiang Qing, before they could seize power. This marked the end of the Cultural Revolution.

Deng Xiaoping and the Transformation of Chinese Communism (1977–1997)

To repair the damage caused by the Cultural Revolution, China's new leaders restored to power many veteran officials who had been purged by Mao and the radicals. These included Deng Xiaoping. By 1978, Deng had clearly become the country's most powerful leader, although he never took for himself the formal positions of head of either the Communist Party or the Chinese government. Instead he appointed younger, loyal men to those positions.

Deng's policies were a profound break with the Maoist past. State control of the economy was significantly reduced, and market forces were allowed to play an increasingly important role. After decades of stagnation, the Chinese economy began to experience high levels of growth in the 1980s. Chinese artists and writers were allowed much great freedom. Better-educated officials were recruited to modernize the PRC government. Deng Xiaoping gathered global praise for his leadership of the reforms that were transforming nearly every aspect of life in China.

Then came Tiananmen Square. Large-scale demonstrations began in Beijing in the early spring of 1989 and quickly spread to other cities. Most of the initial protesters were university students who were expressing their discontent about inflation, corruption, and slow pace of political reform. Over time, they became more vocal in their demands for democratization, although they never called for the overthrow of the Communist Party. At one point, more than a million people from all walks of life gathered in and around Tiananmen Square to show support for the students.

For a while, the CCP leadership did little more than denounce the demonstrators as troublemakers and issue vague warnings about dire consequences. But a small group of mostly elderly leaders, including Deng Xiaoping, who was 85 at the time, ran out of patience. The army was ordered to end the "counterrevolutionary rebellion" and restore order in Beijing. It did so with brutal violence on June 4, 1989. The PRC government continues to insist that it did the right thing in the interests of national stability.

Following the Beijing massacre, China went through a period of intense political crackdown and slowdown in the pace of economic change. In early 1992, Deng Xiaoping took bold steps to accelerate reform of the economy. He did so partly because he hoped economic progress would enable China to avoid the collapse of the **communist party-state** such as had happened just the year before in the Soviet Union.

communist party-state

A type of nation-state in which the communist party attempts to exercise a complete monopoly on political power and controls all important state institutions.

From Revolutionaries to Technocrats (1997–Present)

In mid-1989, Deng Xiaoping had promoted Jiang Zemin, the mayor and Communist Party leader of Shanghai, to become the head of the CCP. Although Deng remained the power behind the throne, he gradually turned over greater authority to Jiang, who also became president of the PRC in 1993. When Deng Xiaoping died in February

---

▣ PROFILES

A Tale of Two Leaders

Chinese Communist leaders Mao Zedong and Deng Xiaoping in 1959.

Bettmann/Getty Images

Mao Zedong (1893–1976) and Deng Xiaoping (1904–1997) had much in common. They were both born in rural China and joined the CCP in their early 20s. Both participated in the CCP's Long March during 1934–1935, to escape annihilation by Chiang Kai-shek's Nationalist army. When Mao consolidated his power as the undisputed leader of the CCP in the 1940s, Deng became one of his most trusted comrades. After the founding of the PRC, Deng rose to the highest levels of party leadership. And both men transformed China in ways that mark them as two of the most important figures in all of Chinese—and perhaps world—history.

But, in some ways, Mao and Deng were very different. Most importantly, Deng was a pragmatist—someone who acts to get things done rather than dwelling on abstract ideas. Mao was an idealist who thought about the future in utopian terms and then tried to find ways to make reality fit his vision. Mao twice removed Deng from power during the Cultural Revolution because he concluded that Deng's economic pragmatism was taking

China down "the capitalist road" and away from his communist ideals.

Less than a year after Mao died, and his radical followers were purged in the fall of 1976, Deng made his way back to the inner circle of power. By 1978, he was clearly China's most powerful leader. Deng used his power to lead the country toward spectacular economic growth by taking the PRC in a very un-Maoist capitalist direction.

But another thing that Mao and Deng had in common was an unshakeable belief that communist party leadership of China should not be challenged. Mao initiated a number of ruthless movements to squash dissent. The brutal crackdown on the Beijing pro-democracy protests in June 1989 was Deng's response to those he thought were questioning party rule.

Today, both Mao Zedong and Deng Xiaoping are revered in China. Mao's legacy is tarnished by the tragic human cost of his utopian campaigns. But he is lauded for restoring China's sovereignty and dignity after more than a century of humiliation at the hands of foreign powers. Deng is seen as the architect of China's economic miracle. Few people associate him with the 1989 Beijing massacre, since that remains a forbidden topic in the PRC.

MAKING CONNECTIONS How do you think history will judge the achievements and shortcomings of Mao Zedong and Deng Xiaoping?

1997, Jiang was secure in his position as China's top leader.

Under Jiang Zemin's leadership, China continued its economic reforms and remarkable growth. The PRC became an even more integral part of the global economy through its exports and imports. But the country also faced widening gaps between the rich and the poor, environmental degradation, and pervasive corruption. Overall, China was politically stable during the Jiang era. But the CCP still repressed any individual or group it perceived as challenging its authority.

Jiang Zemin was succeeded as head of the CCP in November 2002, and PRC president in March 2003, by Hu Jintao. The transfer of power from Jiang to Hu was remarkably predictable and orderly. Jiang had retired after two terms in office, as required by new party rules, and Hu had, for several years, been expected to succeed Jiang.

This cartoon captures the contradiction between economic reform and political repression that characterized China under the leadership of Deng Xiaoping and his successors.

Both Jiang and Hu also represented a new kind of leader for the PRC. Mao and Deng had been involved in communist politics almost their whole adult lives. They had participated in the CCP's long struggle for power dating back to the 1920s. They were among the founders of the communist regime in 1949. In contrast, Jiang and Hu were technocrats. They had technical university training (as engineers) before working their way up the ladder of success in the party bureaucracy by a combination of professional competence and political loyalty.

Another smooth and predictable leadership transition took place when Xi Jinping (b. 1953) ascended to the top party position in November 2012, and the presidency of the PRC in March 2013. Xi is also a technocrat (with a degree in chemical engineering). He has not deviated significantly from the combination of economic reform and political repression that has been the CCP's formula for retaining power since the days of Deng Xiaoping. He has, however, taken steps to consolidate more personal power than his two immediate predecessors and weakened the pattern of collective leadership in the CCP's highest organizations that has been in effect for the last two decades. Xi is slated to be "reelected" to a second five-year term as party leader in the fall of 2017, and as China's president in March 2018, which would keep him in power until 2022–2023, when, *if* he follows the term limits precedent set by Jiang and Hu, he would step down from both positions.

collective leadership

A type of political decision-making in which major decisions are reached by consensus or voting among top leaders even when one of those leaders may have more power and influence than the others.

The Four Themes and China

China in a Globalized World of States

When the PRC was established in 1949, China occupied a very weak position in the international system. For more than a century, its destiny had been shaped by interventions from abroad that it could do little to control. Mao made many tragic and terrible blunders during his years in power. But one of his great achievements was to build a strong state able to affirm and defend its sovereignty. Although still a relatively poor country by many per capita measures, the sheer size of its economy makes the PRC an economic powerhouse. Its foreign trade policies have a significant effect on many other countries and on the global economy. China is a nuclear power with the world's largest conventional military force. It is an active and influential member of the world's most important international organizations, including the United Nations, where it sits as one of the five permanent members of the Security Council. China has become a major player in the world of states.

Governing the Economy

Throughout its history the PRC has experimented with a series of very different approaches to governing the economy: a Soviet-style planning system in the early 1950s, the radical egalitarianism of the Maoist model, and the market-oriented policies implemented by Deng Xiaoping and his successors. Ideological disputes over these development strategies were the main cause of the ferocious political struggles within the CCP during the Mao era. Deng began his bold reforms in the late 1970s with the hope that improved living standards would restore the legitimacy of the CCP, which had been badly tarnished by the economic failings and political chaos of much of the previous three decades. The remarkable success of China's recent leaders in governing the economy has sustained the authority of the CCP at a time when most of the world's other communist regimes have disappeared.

The Democratic Idea

Any hope that the democratic idea might take root in the early years of communist rule in China quickly vanished by the mid-1950s with the building of a one-party communist state and Mao's unrelenting campaigns against alleged enemies of his revolution. The Deng era brought much greater economic, social, and cultural freedom, but time and again the CCP has strangled the stirrings of the democratic idea, most brutally in and around Tiananmen Square in 1989. Deng's successors have been faithful disciples. They have vigorously championed economic reform in China. They have also made sure that the CCP retains its firm hold on political power.

The Politics of Collective Identity

Because of its long history and ancient culture, China has a very strong sense of collective national identity. Memories of past humiliations and suffering at the hands of foreigners still influence the international policies of the PRC. The CCP places great emphasis on nationalism as a means to rally the Chinese people behind the government, especially because faith in communist ideology has weakened as the country embraces capitalist economic policies. The enormous inequalities between those that have benefited from these policies and those left behind have led to the emergence socioeconomic class as a growing source of collective identity in contemporary China. China's cultural and ethnic homogeneity has also spared it the widespread communal violence that has plagued so many other countries. The exception has been in the border regions where there is a large concentration of minority peoples, including Tibet and Xinjiang.

In an act of outrage and protest, an unarmed citizen stood in front of a column of tanks leaving Tiananmen Square the day after the Chinese army had crushed the prodemocracy demonstration in 1989. This "unknown hero" disappeared into the watching crowd. Neither his identity nor his fate is known.

AP Images/Jeff Widener

Comparisons

The PRC can be compared with other past and present communist party-states with which it shares many political and ideological features. This raises several intriguing questions: Why has China's communist party-state proven more durable than that of the Soviet Union and nearly all other similar regimes? By what combination of reform and repression has the CCP held on to power? What signs are there that it is likely to hold power for the foreseeable future? What signs suggest that communist rule in China may be weakening? What kind of political system might emerge if the CCP were to lose or relinquish power?

China is also part of the developing world as measured by the average standard of living of its population, but its record of growth in the past several decades has far exceeded that of almost all other developing countries. Furthermore, the educational and health levels of the Chinese people are quite good for a country at its level of development. How has China achieved such relative success in its quest for economic development? By contrast, much of the developing world has become more democratic in recent decades. How and why has China resisted this wave of democratization? What does the experience of other developing countries say about how economic modernization might influence the prospects for democracy in China?

SECTION

2

POLITICAL ECONOMY AND DEVELOPMENT

State and Economy

When the CCP came to power in 1949, China's economy was suffering from over 100 years of rebellion, invasion, civil war, and bad government. The country's new communist rulers almost immediately seized most property from wealthy landowners, rich industrialists, and foreign companies. They then set up a centrally planned economy based on the Soviet model. The state owned or controlled most economic resources. Government planning and commands, not market forces, drove economic activity, including setting prices for almost all goods.

China's planned economy yielded impressive results in terms of increased production. But it also created huge bureaucracies and new kinds of inequalities, especially between the heavily favored industrial cities and the investment-starved rural areas. Both the Great Leap Forward (1958–1961) and the Cultural Revolution (1966–1976) embodied the unique and radical Maoist approach to economic development that was intended to be less bureaucratic and more egalitarian than the Soviet model.

Under Mao, the PRC built a strong industrial base. The people of China became much healthier and better educated. But the Maoist economy was plagued by political interference, poor management, and ill-conceived projects. This led to wasted resources of truly staggering proportions. Overall, China's economic growth rates, especially in agriculture, barely kept pace with population increases. The average standard of living, though much better than before the PRC was founded, changed little between the mid-1950s and Mao's death in 1976.

China Goes to Market

In a 1962 speech about how to recover from the Great Leap Forward famine, Deng Xiaoping had remarked, "It doesn't matter whether a cat is white or black, as long as it catches mice."[3] He meant that the CCP should not be overly concerned about whether a particular policy was socialist or capitalist if it helped the economy. Such sentiments got Deng in trouble with Mao and made him one of the principal targets of the Cultural Revolution.

Once he emerged as China's foremost leader in the aftermath of Mao's death in 1976, Deng let the cat loose. He launched what is referred to as the "Reform and

Opening Up" program to transform the Chinese economy. "Reform" meant letting market forces play a greater role, while reducing government control, whereas "Opening Up" meant dramatically increasing China's engagement with the global economy. Authority for making economic decisions passed from bureaucrats to families, factory managers, and even the owners of private businesses. Individuals were encouraged to work harder and more efficiently to make money rather than to "serve the people" as had been the slogan during the Maoist era.

In most sectors of China's economy today, the state no longer dictates what to produce and how to produce it. Almost all prices are now set according to supply and demand, as in a capitalist economy, rather than by administrative decree. Most government monopolies have given way to fierce competition between state-owned and non-state-owned firms. But there are still several thousand **state-owned enterprises (SOEs)** with more than 60 million employees in China. Although vastly outnumbered by private businesses that account for about 60 percent of the PRC's gross domestic product (GDP) and employ 80 percent of the workforce, SOEs still dominate critical sectors of the economy such as steel, petroleum, banking, telecommunications, and transportation.

But even SOEs must now respond to market forces. Some have become very profitable, modern enterprises with global reach. But many others are overstaffed economic dinosaurs with outdated facilities and machinery. The state-owned sector remains a severe drain on the country's government-owned banks, which are still sometimes required to bail out financially failing SOEs or lend massive amounts of money to even profitable SOEs to allow them expand their business. These large loans are rarely, if ever, paid back. Many economists think that even more drastic SOE reform is needed. But the country's leaders have been unwilling to relinquish control of these important industries. They also fear the political and social turmoil that could boil up from a massive layoff of industrial workers.

The results of the PRC's move, from a planned toward a market economy, have been phenomenal (see Figure 15.2). From 1986 to 2006, the Chinese economy grew at an average of 10.0 percent per year. During the same period, the growth rate in India was 6.1 percent, in the United States 3.2 percent, and Brazil, 2.7 percent. In 2007, the Chinese economy grew 14.2 percent. Then the global recession hit, and economic growth in China plummeted nearly five points, and by 2017, it had slowed to 6.5 percent. By post-recession world standards, that was quite enviable, and China weathered the global financial crisis and its aftermath far better than any other major economy, largely because of a huge government stimulus package.

China's GDP per capita (a measure of the average standard of living) is still very low when compared to that of more developed countries. In 2016, GDP per capita in the United States was $57,300. In the PRC, it was $15,400 (comparable to Brazil); but in 1980, it was only a little over $300, which again reflects how spectacular China's economic growth has been in recent decades.

Rising incomes have also led to a consumer revolution in China. In the late 1970s, people in the cities could only shop for most consumer goods at state-run stores. These carried a very limited range of often shoddy products. Today, China's urban areas are shopping paradises. There are privately owned stores of all sizes, gigantic malls, fast-food outlets, and a great variety of entertainment options. A few decades ago, hardly anyone owned a television. Now most households have a color TV. Cell phones are everywhere. In the cities, a new middle class is starting to buy houses, condominiums, and cars. China is even developing a class of "super-rich" millionaires and billionaires.

Despite these changes, economic planning by the government has by no means disappeared. Officially, the PRC says it has a **socialist market economy**.

state-owned enterprises (SOEs)

Companies in which a majority of ownership control is held by the government.

socialist market economy

The term used by the government of China to refer to the country's current economic system that mixes elements of both socialism and capitalism.

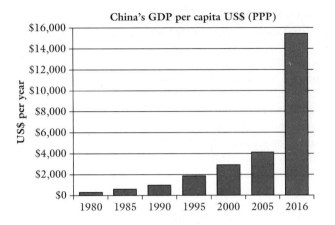

China's GDP per capita US$ (PPP)

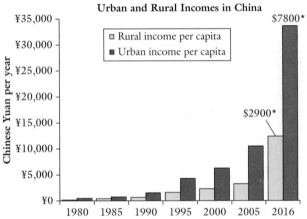

Urban and Rural Incomes in China

*These are rough estimates of rural and urban per capita incomes in 2016 at purchasing power parity.

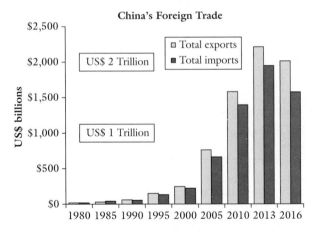

China's Foreign Trade

FIGURE 15.2 The Transformation of the Chinese Economy since 1980
These charts illustrate China's phenomenal economic development over the last three decades. The second chart also shows the growing inequality between the urban and rural areas.

Source: China Statistical Yearbooks.

While allowing a considerable degree of capitalism, national and local bureaucrats continue to exercise a great deal of control over the production and distribution of goods, resources, and services. Market reforms have gained substantial momentum that would be nearly impossible to reverse. But the CCP still ultimately determines the direction of China's economy.

Remaking the Chinese Countryside

One of the first revolutionary programs launched by the CCP when it came to power in 1949, was land reform that confiscated the property of landlords and redistributed it as small private farms to the poorer peasants. But in the mid-to late 1950s the state reorganized peasants into increasingly large collective farms in which the village, not individuals, owned the land, and local officials directed all production and labor. Individuals were paid according to how much they worked on the collective land. Most crops and other farm products had to be sold to the state at low fixed prices. Collectivized agriculture was one of the weakest links in China's command economy because it was very inefficient in the way it used resources, including labor, and undermined incentives for farmers to work hard to benefit themselves and their families. Per capita agricultural production and rural living standards were stagnant from 1957 to 1977.

After Mao's death in 1976, some local officials experimented with giving farmers more freedom to plant what they wanted, consume or sell what they produced, and engage in other private economic activities, such as raising poultry, in order to increase their incomes. China's top leaders not only allowed these experiments, but embraced them as national policy to be implemented throughout the country. Collective farming was abolished. It was replaced by the **household responsibility system**, which remains in effect today. Under this system, the village still owns the farmland. But it is contracted out by the local government to individual families, who take full charge of the production and marketing of crops and are also free to find jobs away from the farm. As a result, both agricultural productivity and rural incomes (see Figure 15.2) have sharply increased in most parts of the countryside.

Economic life in the rural China has also been transformed by the expansion of rural industry and commerce. Rural factories and businesses range in size from a handful of employees to thousands. They employ many tens of millions of people and have played a critical role in absorbing the vast pool of labor that is no longer needed in agriculture. Nearly half the income of rural households now comes from nonfarm employment.

Society and Economy

Economic reform has made Chinese society much more diverse and open. People are vastly freer to choose jobs, travel about the country and internationally, practice their religious beliefs, join nonpolitical associations, and engage in a wide range of other activities that were prohibited or severely restricted during the Maoist era. But economic change has also caused serious social problems.

Economic reform has created significant changes in China's basic system of social welfare. The Maoist economy provided almost all workers with what was called the **iron rice bowl**. As in other communist party-state economies, such as the Soviet Union, the government guaranteed employment and basic cradle-to-grave benefits to most of the urban and rural labor force. The workplace was more than just a place to work and earn a living. It also provided housing, health care, day care, and other services.

China's economic reformers believed that guarantees like these led to poor work motivation and excessive costs. They implemented policies designed to break the iron rice bowl. Income and employment are no longer guaranteed. They are now directly tied to individual effort.

An estimated 45 million workers have been laid off from state-owned enterprises since the late 1990s. Many of these are too old or too unskilled to find good jobs in the modernizing economy. They are now the core of a very large stratum of urban poor that has become a fixture in even China's most glittering cities. The PRC has very little unemployment insurance or social security for its displaced workers.

Economic changes have opened China's cities to a flood of rural migrants. After agriculture was decollectivized in the early 1980s, many peasants, no longer held back by the strict limits on internal population movement enforced in the Mao era, headed to the urban areas to look for jobs. This so-called **floating population** of about 250 million people is the biggest human migration in history. In Shanghai, more than 40 percent of the population of 24.1 million is made up of migrants. Migrant workers are mostly employed in low-paying jobs and live in substandard housing, but fill a crucial niche in China's changing labor market, particularly in boom areas like export industries and construction.

The benefits of economic growth have reached most of China. But the market reforms and economic boom have created sharp class differences, and inequalities between people and parts of the country have risen significantly. A huge gap separates the average incomes of urban residents from those in the countryside (see Figure 15.2). There is also a wide gap between the prosperous coastal regions and most inland areas. In the Maoist era, China was one of the world's most egalitarian countries; today it ranks with Brazil and South Africa as among the most unequal. Surveys show that most Chinese don't resent such inequality as long as their lives are improving and they believe their children's lives will be even better.[4] But if economic growth slows significantly and people find their rising

household responsibility system

The system put into practice in China beginning in the early 1980s in which the major decisions about agricultural production are made by individual farmers based on the profit motive rather than by local officials.

iron rice bowl

A feature of China's socialist economy during the Maoist era (1949–1976) that provided guarantees of lifetime employment, income, and basic cradle-to-grave benefits to most urban and rural workers.

floating population

Migrants from the rural areas who have moved to the cities to find employment.

Ivan Nesterov / Alamy Stock Photo

The futuristic skyline of Shanghai's Pudong district reflect the spectacular modernization of China's most prosperous areas in recent decades.

expectations dashed, glaring socioeconomic inequalities could become a source of discontent and instability.

Significant steps have been taken to improve the lot of the less well-off. In 2006, the government abolished taxes on agriculture, which had been in effect in some form in China for 2,600 years. There are still many very poor people in the Chinese countryside, but hundreds of millions have been lifted out of extreme poverty in the last three decades because of expanded economic opportunities and government antipoverty programs. By 2012, health insurance had been expanded to cover more than 90 percent of the population. But for most people the coverage is pretty minimal, and out-of-pocket expenses can be financially ruinous or deter the sick from seeking care.

China's economic boom and mixed state-private economy have also created enormous opportunities for corruption. Officials still control numerous resources and retain power over many economic transactions from which large profits can be made. Xi Jinping launched a major anticorruption campaign shortly after he came to power in 2012 that has become one of his signature political initiatives. Its targets are so-called "tiger and flies," powerful officials and minor bureaucrats in the party-state hierarchy. Harsh punishments have been doled out to major offenders. In mid-2015, Zhou Yongkang, once one of the top seven leaders of the party and head of China's domestic police force, was found guilty of facilitating the payment of $20 million in bribes to his wife and son and was sentenced to life in prison. Some analysts see Xi's anticorruption campaign as being directed at political foes who might threaten his efforts to consolidate more political power in his own hands. In any case, official graft remains a serious problem in the PRC.

The social status, legal rights, employment opportunities, and education of women in China have improved enormously since the founding of the PRC in 1949.

Women have also benefited from rising living standards and economic modernization in the post-Mao era. But the trend toward a market economy has not benefited men and women equally. Although China has one of the world's highest rates of female participation in the labor force (70 percent), "[w]omen's incomes are falling relative to men's; traditional attitudes are relegating women to the home; and women's net wealth may be shrinking." [5] In 1990, women's annual income was about 77.5 percent of men's in urban areas; by 2010 it had dropped to 67.3 percent. In the rural areas, the gap had become even wider: from 79 percent in 1999 to 56 percent in 2010.

In the early 1980s, China implemented a policy that limited couples to having just a single child. The government claimed that this one-child policy was necessary for the country's economic development. The population growth rate was, indeed, sharply reduced, but the means used to achieve this goal were sometimes coercive, including forced abortions and sterilization. The strong preference for sons in Chinese culture also led to female infanticide and the abandonment of girl babies. In recent years, the availability of inexpensive ultrasound screenings has given rise to widespread gender specific abortions. In 2016, the policy was amended to allow couples to have a second child, but the fact is that the state still claims the right to determine individual reproductive decisions.

Environmental Issues

One of the biggest downsides of China's spectacular economic growth has been the serious damage caused to the environment. Industrial expansion has been fuelled primarily by highly polluting coal. The air in China's cities is among the dirtiest in the world. The tops of ultra-modern skyscrapers are frequently obscured by dense smog. The pollution is so bad in Beijing that breathing the air is equivalent to smoking two packs of cigarettes per day. Many residents wear industrial-strength facemasks as they go about their daily business. Pollution has been linked to lower life expectancy in northern China. Private automobile use is just starting to take off and is expanding rapidly, which will greatly add to urban pollution in addition to further snarling already horrendous traffic.

Soil erosion, wetland destruction, deforestation, and desertification (the loss of arable land to deserts) from unsustainable farming practices are at crisis levels. Roughly 70 percent of China's rivers and lakes are badly polluted. The government does little to regulate the dumping of garbage and toxic wastes. Nearly a quarter of the population (300 million people) does not have access to safe drinking water.

Northern China also faces a severe water shortage due to decreased rainfall, industrial expansion, and urbanization. To remedy this situation, the PRC has undertaken a multi-decade project to divert water from the Yangtze River in central China to the Yellow River and two other rivers in the north. At a current estimated cost of over $60 billion, it is one of most expensive engineering projects in history. It has also raised concerns among environmentalists that the diverted water will be so polluted by factories along its route that it will be unfit for use.

The water diversion project is an example of what one scholar has called PRC's preference for an "engineering fix" to its energy needs and environmental problems.[6] So, too, is the Three Gorges Dam on the Yangtze River, the world's largest and most costly ($28 billion) hydroelectric dam. The dam generates electric power equivalent to fifteen nuclear reactors and has also greatly expanded commercial shipping navigation of the river deep into China's southwest region. But the project resulted in significant ecological damage and over 1.5 million people had to be relocated.

The PRC is critical of rich countries that press it (and other developing countries) to slow down economic growth or invest in expensive pollution controls when those countries paid little heed to the environmental damage caused by their own industrial revolutions. Nevertheless, the Chinese government realizes that environmental degradation is so severe that it could threaten its modernization drive and has been paying more attention to environmental protection. China has also become a world leader in the development of alternative clean energy, including wind and solar power.

China in the Global Economy

At the end of the Maoist era in 1976, the PRC was not deeply involved in the global economy. Total foreign trade was less 10 percent of GDP. Foreign direct investment (FDI) in China was minuscule. Mao's policy of "self-reliance" was intended to make sure that the PRC was not economically dependent on any foreign country. Furthermore, the stagnant economy, political instability, and heavy-handed bureaucracy were not attractive to potential investors from abroad.

In the early 1980s, as part of its "Reform and Opening Up" program, China embarked on a strategy of using trade to promote economic development. This followed the model of export-led growth pioneered by Japan, South Korea, and Taiwan, which takes advantage of low-wage labor to produce goods that are in demand internationally. It then uses the export earnings to modernize the economy.

The PRC is now the world leader in exports and is, after the United States, the second largest importer of goods and services. On average, foreign trade accounted for about half of the PRC's GDP between 2005 and 2015, with a relatively equal balance between imports and exports. As Table 15.2 shows, China is much more economically dependent on trade than is the United States or Japan; but, in comparison with other major economies, it is less or comparably dependent. Trade as a percentage of China's GDP has dropped by about a quarter as the global economy has slowed in the wake of the 2008 recession.

China is often referred to as the "factory to the world," because so many countries import large quantities of products made in the PRC. What makes these products competitive is the low cost of production, particularly wages. In 2009, according the U.S. Bureau of Labor Statistics, the average factory job in China paid $1.34 per hour compared with $32.00 per hour in

Table 15.2	Trade Dependency (2005–2015 Average)		
	Imports (% of GDP)	Exports (% of GDP)	Total Trade (% of GDP)
Germany	37.3	43.1	80.4
South Africa	31.0	30.2	61.2
Britain	29.9	27.6	57.5
China	23.7	28.4	52.1
Russia	21.1	29.7	50.8
India	26.6	22.4	49.0
Japan	15.7	15.7	31.4
United States	16.2	12.3	28.5
Brazil	12.7	12.5	25.2

Source: World Bank World Development Indicators

the United States. By 2019, those numbers are projected to rise to $4.79 per hour in China and $42.82 in the U.S.[7] But Vietnam, Indonesia, Bangladesh, and other developing countries with even lower labor costs are competing with China to attract foreign investment in manufacturing. Long-term economic growth in the PRC will depend on a combination of exporting more sophisticated, less labor-intensive products and shifting the production of goods and services more towards the domestic market.

Where Do You Stand?

There are those who say that China's economy under Mao Zedong was better in some ways than that under Deng Xiaoping and his successors. In what ways might this be true?

Do you see the rise of China as an economic power as a threat to U.S. interests or as mutually beneficial?

U.S. CONNECTION

U.S.-China Relations

Shortly after the founding of the People's Republic, the United States and China fought each other to a stalemate in the Korean War (1950–1953). From then until the early 1970s, the two countries had very little contact because of the Cold War.

In 1972, Richard Nixon became the first U.S. president to visit China. Formal diplomatic relations between Washington and Beijing were established in 1979. Since then ties have deepened, despite some disruptions, such as following the Tiananmen massacre in 1989, and recurring tensions over trade, human rights, cyberattacks, and increasing power competition in East Asia. Many believe that the U.S.–China relation is the most important bilateral diplomatic relationship in the world.

China now trades with the United States more than with any other country, while China is America's second-largest trading partner (after Canada). Many in the United States think that cheap Chinese imports means lost jobs for Americans and that U.S. firms can't compete with Chinese companies because labor costs in China are so much lower. They also say that the PRC engages in unfair trade practices, exploits sweatshop labor, and suppresses independent union activity. Some see the fact that China owns a little over $1.0 trillion of U.S. government debt (which it bought with part of the vast reserves of U.S. dollars earned from exports) as having made the United States dangerously dependent on the PRC. Critics of Sino-American economic relations want the U.S. government to put more restrictions on trade and financial dealings with China.

On the other side, many say that the benefits of U.S. trade with China far outweigh the negative impacts. First of all, consumers benefit greatly by the availability of a large variety of less-expensive products. In fact, although most of the things sold by companies like Walmart and Target are made in China, overall, only 2.7 percent of consumer spending in 2010 by Americans was on goods and services from China; 88.5 percent were from the United States. Furthermore, some argue that the United States should focus on developing more high-tech businesses to create jobs rather than trying to compete with China and other countries in "old-fashioned" labor-intensive industries. They also make the case that many U.S. firms have huge investments in China, which will grow—as will demand for U.S. products—as that country becomes more prosperous. And they point out that U.S. government debt is the result of U.S. overspending. Furthermore they note that China's share of total U.S. debt is only about 5 percent and that Japan, in fact, owns more U.S. debt than does China. Finally, those who oppose restrictions on Sino-American economic engagement see it as one important way to promote not only the free market in China but also a more open society and democracy.

MAKING CONNECTIONS Why and how have U.S.–China relations improved since the end of the Cold War?

GOVERNANCE AND POLICY-MAKING

▽ **Focus Questions**

• What are the most powerful institutions and positions in China's communist party-state?

• What are the differences and connections between the government of the PRC and the CCP?

Organization of the State

In the early 1980s, about two dozen countries in Africa, Asia, Europe, and Latin America, with more than one-third of the world's population, were ruled by communist parties. Today, China, Cuba, Vietnam, North Korea, and Laos are the only remaining communist party-states. The political systems of these countries are characterized by the existence of an official state ideology based on Marxism-Leninism, communist party domination of all government and social institutions, and the suppression of all opposition parties and movements. Ruling communist parties claim that only they can govern in the best interests of the entire nation and therefore have the right to exercise the "leading role" throughout society.

Communist ideology is much less important in China today than it was during the Mao era when there was a great emphasis on enforcing ideological correctness. But even though the PRC has moved sharply toward a market economy in recent decades, the CCP still asserts that it is building socialism with the ultimate objective of creating an egalitarian and classless communist society. Ideology also sets the boundaries for what is permissible in politics since the party does not allow open opposition to its doctrines.

The preamble of the PRC's constitution states that the country is under "the leadership of the Communist Party of China." Article 1 defines the PRC as "a socialist state under the people's democratic dictatorship." It also declares that "disruption of the socialist system by any organization or individual is prohibited." Such provisions imply that the Chinese "people" (implicitly, supporters of socialism and the leadership of the Communist Party) enjoy democratic rights and privileges under CCP guidance. But the constitution also gives the CCP authority to exercise dictatorship over any person or organization that, it believes, opposes socialism and the party.

The Executive

The government of the PRC (the "state") is organizationally and functionally distinct from the CCP. Each has an executive branch, although the Communist Party exercises direct or indirect control over all government organizations and personnel. The government of the PRC acts as the administrative agency for enacting, implementing, and enforcing policies made by the party. In order to fully understand governance and policy-making in China, it is necessary to look at the structure of both the CCP and the government of the PRC and the relationship between the two.

CCP Organization

National Party Congress

The symbolically important meeting, held every 5 years for about 1 week, of about 2,100 delegates representatives of the CCP, who endorse policies and the allocation of leadership positions that have been determined beforehand by the party's much smaller executive bodies.

Central Committee

The top 370 or so leaders of the CCP. It meets annually for about two weeks and is charged with carrying on the business of the National Party Congress when it is not in session.

According to the CCP constitution (a wholly different document from the constitution of the PRC), the "highest leading bodies" of the party are the **National Party Congress** and the **Central Committee** (see Figure 15.3). But neither is as powerful as the much smaller CCP executive organizations.

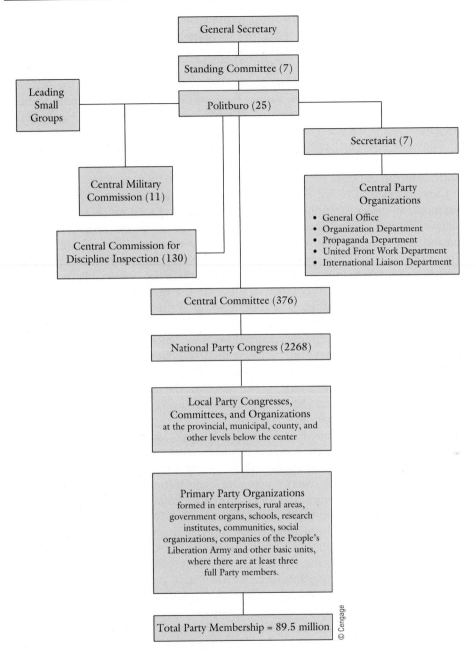

FIGURE 15.3 Organization of the CCP

Note: Numbers in parentheses indicate the number of members as of 2016–2017

The National Party Congress meets for only one week every five years, and it has more than 2,200 delegates. This reflects the fact that the role of the Congress is more symbolic than substantive. The essential function of the National Party Congress is to approve decisions already made by the top leaders and to provide a showcase for the party's current policies. There is little debate and no seriously contested voting of any consequence.

The Central Committee (with 376 full and alternate members) consists of CCP leaders from around the country who meet annually for about a week in the late fall. Members are elected for a five-year term by the National Party Congress by secret ballot, with a very limited choice of candidates. The overall composition of the Central Committee is closely controlled by the top leaders to ensure compliance with their policies.

In principle, the Central Committee directs party affairs when the National Party Congress is not in session. But its size and short, infrequent meetings (called plenums) greatly limit its effectiveness. However, the plenums do represent significant gatherings of the party elite and can be an important forum for discussion.

The most powerful political organizations in China's communist party-state are two small executive bodies at the very top of the CCP's structure: the Politburo (or Political Bureau), and its even more exclusive Standing Committee. These bodies are formally "elected" for five-year terms by the Central Committee from among its own members under carefully controlled conditions and with no choice among candidates. The slate of candidates is determined through a secretive process of negotiation and bargaining within the party elite. The first that most Chinese citizens know of the full composition of the Politburo and the Standing Committee is when they are presented on stage in rank order at the conclusion of the National Party Congress every five years. The current Politburo has twenty-five members, seven of whom also sit on the Standing Committee, the apex of power in the CCP.

Before 1982, the leading position in the party was the chairman of the Politburo's Standing Committee, which was occupied by Mao Zedong (hence Chairman Mao) for more than three decades until his death in 1976. The title of chairman was abolished in 1982 to symbolize a break with Mao's highly personal and often arbitrary style of rule. Since then, the party's leader has been the general secretary, who presides over the Politburo and the Standing Committee. Xi Jinping was elected to his first term as general secretary in 2012.

The Politburo and Standing Committee are not accountable to the Central Committee or any other institution in any meaningful sense. Although there is now somewhat more openness about the timing of and subjects covered in their meetings, the operations of the party's executive organizations are generally shrouded in secrecy. Top leaders work and often live in a huge walled compound called Zhongnanhai ("Middle and Southern Seas") on lakes in the center of Beijing adjacent to Tiananmen Square. Zhongnanhai is not only heavily guarded, as any government executive headquarters would be, but it also has no identifying signs on its exterior other than some party slogans, nor is it identified on public maps.

Two other executive organizations of the party deserve brief mention. The Secretariat manages the day-to-day work of the Politburo and Standing Committee and coordinates the party's complex and far-flung structure with considerable authority in organizational and personnel matters. The Central Commission for Discipline Inspection (CCDI) is in charge of investigating corruption within the party and other violations of party rules. Its investigations and hearings are conducted behind closed doors. If someone is found guilty, they may be demoted or even expelled from the party and, in some cases, turned over to the state judicial system for trial and, if appropriate, for punishment.

The Communist Party has an organized presence throughout Chinese society. CCP organizations in provinces, cities, and counties are headed by a party committee. There are also about 4.5 million primary party organizations, usually called branches. These are found, for example, in workplaces, government offices, schools, urban neighborhoods, rural towns, villages, and army units. Local and primary organizations extend the CCP's reach throughout Chinese society. They are also designed to ensure coordination within the vast and complex party structure and subordination to the central party authorities in Beijing.

Politburo

The committee made up of the two dozen or so top leaders of the CCP.

Standing Committee

A subgroup of the Politburo, currently with seven members. The most powerful political organization in China.

general secretary

The formal title of the head of the CCP. From 1942 to 1982, the position was called "chairman" and was held by Mao Zedong until his death in 1976.

Under Mao and Deng, power within the CCP was highly concentrated in one individual. No important policy decision was made without their consent. Since then, no party leader has had the personal authority or charisma of Mao or Deng, and they have tended to rule through collective leadership in which there is an emphasis on making decisions through consensus within the Standing Committee and Politburo. But Xi Jinping has taken steps that suggest he is breaking with that style of leadership and is consolidating power in his own hands. For example, he is now referred to as the "core leader" of the CCP and has taken control of several key **leading small groups**, ad hoc organizations that coordinate policymaking and implementation across party-state agencies. He is likely doing this in order not only to ensure that his agenda for the country is put into place, but also to be able to exert influence over who will be promoted to succeed him as party leader when (and if) he steps down in 2022.

Party politics at the top has become more institutionalized in some important ways. Not only are the leaders limited to two five-year terms, they are also ineligible to be reelected if they will reach the age of 68 while in office. Term and age limits have added considerable predictability to the leadership succession. But these are norms, not rules, and therefore could be jettisoned if the top leaders decided to do so for political reasons.

The route to the very top has also become more predictable. In 2007, when Xi Jinping was not only elevated to the Standing Committee, but was also given other positions, including vice president of the PRC and head of the school for training up-and-coming party leaders, it was clear that he had been anointed to become general secretary in 2012 and would be reelected in 2017. His predecessor, Hu Jintao, followed the same political trajectory.

In the Mao and Deng eras, few CCP leaders had an education beyond high school. Today, twenty of the twenty-five members of the Politburo (and six of the seven who sit on the Standing Committee) have a university-level degree. Two members of the Standing Committee have a BA in engineering, including Xi Jinping; others studied law, history, economics, and statistics. Almost all of China's leaders have also gained decades of experience working in party and government posts outside the capital. In fact, the only way to rise to the high echelons of power in the CCP is through the provinces. Prior to being elevated to the central leadership, Xi Jinping held key positions in four different provinces and Shanghai, where he served as both mayor and party secretary.

PRC Organization

State authority in China is formally vested in a system of people's congresses that begins at the top with the **National People's Congress (NPC)**, which is a completely separate organization from the National Party Congress (see Figure 15.4). The NPC is China's national legislature and is discussed in more detail in Section 4.

The NPC elects the president and vice president of China. But there is only one candidate, chosen by the top leadership of the Communist Party, for each office. The president's term is concurrent with that of the congress (five years). The constitution sets a two-term limit. As China's head of state, the president meets and negotiates with other world leaders. But the office of president is largely ceremonial and has little executive power.

The president of the PRC has always been a high-ranking CCP leader. Since the early 1990s, the general secretary of the Communist Party has served concurrently as the country's president. Thus, Xi Jinping is both General Secretary Xi and President Xi, although the source of his power clearly lies in the former position.

leading small groups

Ad hoc organizations that report to the CCP Politburo and Standing that have been created to coordinate policy-making and implementation across party-state agencies in the PRC.

National People's Congress (NPC)

The legislature of the PRC. It is under the control of the CCP and is not an independent branch of government.

State Council

The highest organization in the state administration of the PRC, directed by the premier. It also includes several vice premiers, the heads of government ministries and commissions, and a few other senior officials.

The premier (prime minister) of the People's Republic has authority over the government bureaucracy and policy implementation. The premier is formally appointed by the president with the approval of the NPC. But in reality, the Communist Party leadership decides which of its members will serve as premier.

The premier directs the **State Council**, which is something like the cabinet in a presidential or parliamentary system. In addition to the premier, the State Council includes several vice premiers, the heads of government ministries and commissions, and a few other senior officials. Most State Council members run functionally specific departments, such as the Ministry of Foreign Affairs and the National Health and Family Planning Commission.

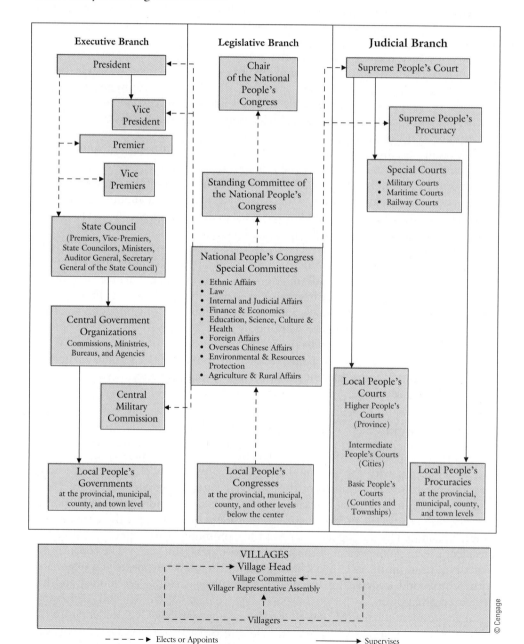

FIGURE 15.4 Organization of the PRC

The CCP uses a weblike system of organizational controls to make sure that the government complies with the party's will in policy implementation. In the first place, almost all key government officials are also party members, which means their first loyalty is to the party. Furthermore, the CCP exercises control over the policy process through party organizations that parallel government agencies at all levels of the system. For example, each provincial government works under the watchful eye of a provincial party committee. In addition, the Communist Party maintains an effective presence inside every government organization through a "leading party group" that is made up of key officials who are also CCP members.

Through its Organization Department, the CCP also exercises control over the state through its power to decide who is appointed to important positions in the government. In fact, this power extends to thousands of jobs in many other areas, including university administrators, trade union leaders, and newspaper editors, to name just a few.

The equivalent of the Organization Department in the United States "would oversee the appointment of the entire US cabinet, state governors and their deputies, the mayors of big cities, the heads of all federal regulatory agencies, the chief executives of GE, ExxonMobil, Wal-Mart and about fifty of the remaining largest US companies, the justices on the Supreme Court, the editors of the *New York Times,* the *Wall Street Journal* and the *Washington Post,* the bosses of the TV networks and cable stations, the presidents of Yale and Harvard and other big universities, and the heads of think-tanks like the Brookings Institution and the Heritage Foundation."[8]

Personnel decisions are based not only on experience and ability, but also on political reliability. The Organization Department and its branches throughout China's political system provide one of the major instruments by which the CCP tries to "ensure that leading institutions throughout the country will exercise only the autonomy granted to them by the party."[9]

Organization Department

A department of the CCP that controls personnel decisions affecting a vast number of jobs in the government and other major institutions in the PRC.

Other State Institutions

The Judiciary

China has a four-tiered system of "people's courts" that reaches from a Supreme People's Court down through higher (provincial-level), intermediate (city-level), and grassroots (county- and township-level) people's courts. The Supreme People's Court supervises the work of lower courts and the application of the country's laws, but it does not exercise judicial review over government (and certainly not party) policies. It also does not interpret the country's constitution as it applies to laws or legislation.

At the end of the Maoist era, there were only 3,000 (poorly trained) lawyers in China; now there are about 300,000 (compared to more than a million lawyers in the United States), with an increasingly high level of professionalism. Chinese courts can provide a real avenue of redress to the public for a wide range of nonpolitical grievances, including loss of property, consumer fraud, and even unjust detention by the police. Citizen mediation committees based in urban neighborhoods and rural villages play an important role in the judicial process by settling a majority of civil cases out of court.

China's criminal justice system is swift and harsh. Great faith is placed in the ability of an official investigation to find the facts of a case. The outcome of cases that actually do come to trial is pretty much predetermined. The conviction rate is 98 to 99 percent for all criminal cases. Prison terms are long and subject to only cursory appeal. A variety of offenses in addition to murder—including, in some cases, rape and major cases of embezzlement and other "economic crimes"—are subject to capital punishment. The number of annual executions is considered a state secret in China, but it is certainly in the thousands, and the PRC executes more people each year than the rest of the world combined.

Although the PRC constitution guarantees judicial independence, China's courts and other legal bodies remain under Communist Party control. The appointment of all judicial personnel is subject to approval by the Organization Department. At all levels of the system, party political and legal committees keep a close watch on the courts. Lawyers who displease officials are often harassed in various ways, their licenses to practice law might not be renewed, and they themselves are sometimes arrested. Like the legislature, the judiciary in the PRC is not an independent branch of the government that can serve as a check on executive power.

China has become a country where there is rule *by* law, which means that the party-state uses the law to carry out its policies and enforce its rule. But it is still far from having established the rule *of* law, in which everyone and every organization, including the Communist Party, is accountable and subject to the law.

Subnational Government

China (like France and Japan) is a unitary state in which the national government exercises a high degree of control over other levels of government. It is not a federal system (like the United States and India) that gives subnational governments considerable policy-making and financial autonomy.

Under the central government, the PRC has twenty-two provinces, four very large centrally administered cities (Beijing, Shanghai, Tianjin, and Chongqing), and five autonomous regions, which are areas of the country with large minority populations (such as Tibet).

Each level of subnational government has a people's congress that meets infrequently and plays a limited, but increasingly active, role in supervising affairs in its area. In theory, these congresses (the legislative branch) are empowered to supervise the work of the "people's governments" (the executive branch) at the various levels of the system. But in reality, subnational government executives (such as provincial governors and city mayors) are more accountable to Communist Party authority than to the people's congresses.

Despite considerable economic decentralization, the central government retains the power to intervene in local affairs when and where it wants. This power of the central authorities derives not only from their ability to set binding national priorities, but also from their control over the military and the police, the tax system, critical energy resources, and construction of major infrastructure projects.

Under the formal layers of state administration are China's 640,000 or so rural villages, which are home to a little less than half of the country's population. These villages, with an average population of 1,000, are technically self-governing and are not formally responsible to a higher level of state authority. In recent years, village leaders have been directly and competitively elected by local residents, and village representative assemblies have become more vocal. However, the most powerful organization in the village is the Communist Party committee, and the single most powerful person is the local Communist Party leader (the party secretary).

The Military, Police, and Internal Security

China's **People's Liberation Army (PLA)**, which encompasses all of the country's ground, air, and naval armed services, is, according to the PRC Ministry of Defense, "a people's army created and led by the Communist Party of China."

autonomous region

A territorial unit that is equivalent to a province and contains a large concentration of ethnic minorities. These regions, for example, Tibet, have some autonomy in the cultural sphere but in most policy matters are strictly subordinate to the central government.

People's Liberation Army (PLA)

The combined armed forces of the PRC, which includes land, sea, air, and strategic missile forces.

The PLA is the world's largest military force, with about 2.0 million active personnel (down from nearly 4 million in 1989). On a per capita basis, the PRC has 1.5 active military personnel per 1,000 of its population, compared with the U.S. ratio of 4.6 per 1,000. The PLA also has a formal reserve force of about 500,000. A people's militia of 8 million minimally trained civilians can be mobilized and armed by local governments in the event of war or other national emergency.

The key organization in charge of the Chinese armed forces is the **Central Military Commission (CMC)**. There are currently eleven members of the CMC, ten of whom are military officers. The one civilian is CCP general secretary and PRC president, Xi Jinping, who chairs the committee. The chair of the CMC is, in effect, the commander-in-chief of China's armed forces and has always been the most powerful leader of the communist party.

China's security apparatus consists of several different organizations. The Ministry of Public Security (MPS) is the main policing organization in the PRC. It also engages in some domestic intelligence gathering. Local public security bureaus, which carry out day-to-day police work, are under the command of the central ministry in Beijing. This would be like having local police forces in the United States under the jurisdiction of the Federal Bureau of Investigation (FBI). The Ministry of State Security (MSS) is the main organization responsible for gathering foreign intelligence and countering espionage in China, although it also carries out domestic spying. In many ways, it combines some of the functions of the FBI and the Central Intelligence Agency (CIA) in the United States. The distinction between intelligence gathering and maintaining internal security is minimal in both the MPS and the MSS. This makes these organizations not just part of the process of providing information to the government or preserving law and order, but also "an integral tool for the preservation of the power of the Chinese Communist Party."[10]

The People's Armed Police (PAP), a paramilitary force of more than 650,000, is the world's largest internal security organization. It responds to riots, terrorist attacks, and other emergencies, protects government buildings, carries out border patrols, and provides prison guards. With units stationed throughout the country, the PAP has been called in to quell worker, peasant, and ethnic unrest.

Central Military Commission (CMC)

The most important military organization in the PRC, headed by the general secretary of the CCP, who is the commander-in-chief of the PLA. On paper, there is both a CCP and PRC Central Military Commission. In fact, the membership is the same and both are chaired by the General Secretary/President.

The Policy-Making Process

At the height of Mao Zedong's power from the 1950s through much of the 1970s, many scholars described policy-making in China as a simple top-down "Mao-in-command" system. Since the late 1980s, terms such as "fragmented authoritarianism"[11] have been used to convey that, although power is still highly concentrated in the top leadership organizations of the CCP, there are now many other sources of influence in the policy-making process. This model sees policy as evolving not only from commands from above, but also as a complex interplay of cooperation, conflict, and bargaining among political actors at various levels of the system. The focus on economic development has also led to the growing influence of nonparty experts, the media, and nongovernmental organizations (NGOs) within the policy-making loop.

At the national level, flexible issue-specific task forces called "leading small groups" bring together top officials from various party and state organizations in order to coordinate policy-making and implementation on matters that cross the jurisdiction of any single organization. Some groups, such as the Central Leading Group on Foreign Affairs, are more or less permanent fixtures in the party-state structure, while others may be convened on an ad hoc basis to deal with short-term matters like a natural disaster or an epidemic. Since most of the members are high-ranking CCP officials, they are also a means to ensure party supervision of policy in that particular area.

China's parliament, the NPC, formally passes legislation that gives policy the force of law. But it takes its cues from the Communist Party leadership and cannot be considered an independent actor in the policy-making process.

Because the PRC is a unitary system, subnational levels of government have little policy-making autonomy. The central authorities pass along policy guidelines through a network of party leadership teams to be found in every locality and important government offices, and those teams closely monitor compliance with party directives. Nevertheless, the decentralization of power that has accompanied economic reform has given local governments considerable clout in policy implementation.

The policy process in China is much more institutionalized and smoother as well as less personalized and volatile than it was in the Maoist era. But it is still highly secretive, and leaders of the People's Republic are not accountable to the people of China. As in most other authoritarian regimes, there is no real system of checks and balances in the policy-making process. The unchallengeable power of the Communist Party is still the most basic fact of political life in the PRC.

Where Do You Stand?

One of the characteristics of a communist party-state is its commitment to Marxism-Leninism as the official ideology. Does the United States have an ideology?

Because of the dominant role of a single political party, China's policy-making process certainly doesn't suffer from political paralysis. Do you think that's a good thing?

SECTION 4

REPRESENTATION AND PARTICIPATION

▽ Focus Questions

- What are the powers and limitations of China's NPC as the legislative branch of government?

- What kinds of protests take place in China, and how does the party-state respond?

The CCP claims that it represents the interests of all the people of China and describes the People's Republic as a socialist democracy. In the CCP's view, this is superior to democracy in capitalist countries where wealthy individuals and corporations dominate politics and policy-making despite multiparty politics. China's *socialist* democracy is based on the unchallengeable role of the CCP as the country's only ruling party and should not be confused with the *social* democracy of Western European center-left political parties, which is rooted in a commitment to competitive politics.

The Legislature

The Chinese constitution grants the National People's Congress the power to enact and amend the country's laws, approve and monitor the state budget, and declare and end war. The NPC is also empowered to elect (and recall) the president and vice president, the chair of the state Central Military Commission, the head of China's

Supreme Court, and the procurator-general (in charge of national-level investigation and prosecution of crime). The NPC has final approval over the selection of the premier and members of the State Council. On paper, China's legislature certainly looks to be the most powerful branch of government. In fact, these powers, are exercised only as allowed by the Communist Party.

The NPC is a unicameral legislature with nearly 3,000 members (called "deputies") who meet only for about two weeks every March. When the NPC is not in session, its powers are exercised by a 175-member Standing Committee (not to be confused with the CCP Standing Committee), which convenes every other month. A council of about fifteen members conducts the day-to-day business of the NPC. The chair of the NPC is always a high-ranking Communist Party leader.

NPC deputies are elected for five-year terms. Except for those from the PLA, they are chosen from lower-level people's congresses in China's provinces, autonomous regions, major municipalities, and a few other constituencies.

Deputies are not full-time legislators, but remain in their regular jobs and home areas except for the brief time when the congress is in session. A large majority of NPC deputies are members of the CCP, while the others belong to one of China's eight noncommunist (and powerless) political parties (see below) or have no party affiliation. Workers and farmers make up about 15 percent of NPC deputies; the remainder are government and party officials, military personnel, intellectuals, professionals, celebrities, and business people.

Despite great fanfare in the press as examples of socialist democracy in action, most legislation is passed and all state leaders are elected by the NPC by overwhelming majorities and with little substantive debate. The annual sessions are largely taken up by the presentation of very long reports by the premier and other state leaders. The NPC never deals with sensitive political issues. The CCP also monitors the election process to make sure that no outright dissidents are chosen as deputies.

Nevertheless, some deputies have become a bit more assertive on issues like corruption and environmental problems. Minor government legislative initiatives have occasionally been defeated or tabled. Major bills may take years to draft and be amended as a result of committee hearings, consultation with experts, and discussion among deputies. The media is not allowed to cover the legislative process in any detail or to print editorial opinions on the issues.

socialist democracy

The term used by the CCP to describe the political system of the PRC. The official view is that this type of system, under the leadership of the Communist Party, provides democracy for the overwhelming majority of people and suppresses (or exercises dictatorship over) only the enemies of the people.

Political Parties and the Party System

The CCP

With 89.5 million members at the end of 2016, the CCP is by far the largest political party in the world. But its membership makes up a very small minority of the population (less than 10 percent of those over 18, the minimum age for joining the party). This is consistent with the CCP's view that it is a "vanguard" party that admits only those who are truly dedicated to the communist cause. Joining the Communist Party is a time-consuming process that can last as long as two years and involves a lengthy application, interviews, references, a background check, and a probation period.

The social composition of CCP membership has changed profoundly since the party came to power in 1949. In the mid-1950s, peasants made up nearly 70 percent of party members. Figure 15.5 shows the composition of the CCP as of late 2015. The party now claims that rather than representing just workers and peasants, it represents the interests of the overwhelming majority of people in China and is open

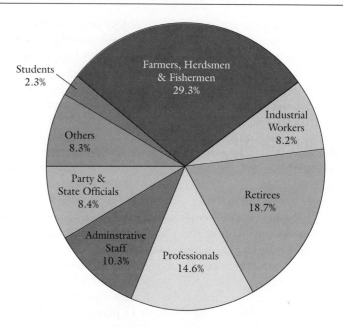

FIGURE 15.5 Occupation of CCP Members (2015)
The percentage of CCP members made up of farmers and workers is much lower than during the Mao years and continues to decline. The category of "Others" in this chart includes private entrepreneurs. Although students represent a small percentage of current CCP members, they are the fastest-growing segment of new members.

Source: Beijing Review, http://www.bjreview.com/Nation/201606/t20160630_800061070.html

to all those who are committed to promoting national development and are willing to accept party leadership in achieving that goal. The membership of the CCP has also become more educated in recent decades, with about 45 percent having a college education or above.

The CCP welcomes members from what it calls the "new social stratum" that has emerged in the process of market reform and globalization of the Chinese economy. The new social stratum includes private business owners ("entrepreneurs") and managerial-level staff in private or foreign-funded companies. This is a dramatic change from the Maoist era when any hint of capitalism was crushed.

Women make up only 25.7 percent of the CCP membership as a whole and just 4.9 percent of the full members of the Central Committee elected in 2012. The Politburo has two female members. No woman has ever served on the party's most powerful organization, the Politburo Standing Committee.

About 2 million people join the CCP each year, the largest number (35 percent) being university students. Even though many Chinese believe that communist ideology is irrelevant to their lives and the nation's future, being a party member remains a prerequisite for advancement in many careers, particularly in government.

China's Noncommunist "Democratic Parties"

China is rightly called a one-party system because the country's politics are so thoroughly dominated by the CCP. But, in fact, China has eight political parties in addition to the CCP. These are officially referred to as China's "democratic parties," which is said to be another example of socialist democracy in the PRC. Each noncommunist party represents a particular group in Chinese society such as intellectuals and professionals, But these parties, all of which were established before the founding of the PRC in 1949 and accept the "guidance" of the CCP, have a total membership of only a little over half a million. They provide advice to the CCP on nonpolitical matters and generate support within their particular constituencies for CCP policies. Individual members of these parties may assume important government positions. But politically, these parties are relatively insignificant and function as little more than "a loyal non-opposition."[12]

New political parties are not allowed to form. When a group of activists who had been part of the 1989 Tiananmen protests tried to establish a China Democracy Party in 1998 to promote multiparty politics, they were arrested or forced into exile abroad, and the party was banned.

Elections

Most elections in the PRC are mechanisms to give the communist party-state greater legitimacy by allowing large numbers of citizens to participate in the political process under very controlled circumstances. But elections, especially at the grassroots level, are becoming somewhat more democratic and more important in providing a way for citizens to express their views and hold some local officials accountable.

Most elections in China are *indirect*. In other words, the members of an already elected body elect those who will serve at the next highest level in the state structure. For example, the deputies of a provincial people's congress—not all the eligible citizens of the province—elect deputies to the NPC. A comparable situation would exist in the United States if members of the Senate were selected by state legislatures rather than by popular vote (as was the case before the Seventeenth Amendment to the Constitution was enacted in 1907).

Direct elections, in which all voters in the relevant geographic area cast ballots for candidates, are held for local people's congresses in urban districts and county towns. But they are most extensive and consequential in rural villages. Elections for village head and other leaders are generally multicandidate with a secret ballot. Villagers have used elections to remove leaders they think are incompetent or corrupt. The village CCP committee closely monitors such grassroots elections. In many cases, the local Communist Party leader has been chosen to serve simultaneously as the village head in a competitive election. This is often because the Communist Party leader is a well-respected person who has the confidence and support of the villagers. Some observers believe direct elections at the village-level could be the seeds of real democracy that will spread to higher levels of the political system. Others see them as a façade to appease international critics and give the rural population a way to express discontent without challenging the country's fundamental political organization. In any case, village elections have given residents some measure of meaningful input into local governance.

Many direct and indirect elections in China now have multiple candidates and open nominations, with the winner chosen by secret ballot. A significant number of independently nominated candidates have defeated official nominees, although even independent candidates also have to be approved by the CCP. And the most powerful positions in the government, such as city mayors and provincial governors, are appointed via the CCP's Organization Department, not elected. Recent electoral reform has certainly increased popular representation and participation in China's government. But elections in the PRC still do not give citizens a means by which they can hold accountable those who have the most power to affect their lives.

Top Chinese communist leaders, from Mao to now, have repeatedly claimed that multiparty democracy is unsuited to China's traditions, present conditions, and socialist principles.

Political Culture, Citizenship, and Identity

From Communism to Consumerism

Marxism-Leninism is still important in Chinese politics, since the Communist Party proclaims that it is China's official ideology. Serious challenges to that ideology are not permitted. The CCP also tries to keep communist ideology viable and visible by efforts to influence public opinion and values through its control of the media, the arts, and education. Political study is still a required but now relatively minor part of the curriculum at all levels of the school system. More than 80 percent of China's students between the ages of 7 and 14, belong to the Young Pioneers, an organization designed to promote good social behavior, community service, patriotism, and loyalty to the party. The Communist Youth League, which serves to foster commitment to socialist values and generate support for party policies, has about 90 million members between the ages of 14 and 28.

Alternative sources of socialization and belief are growing in importance in China. These do not often take expressly political forms, however, because of the threat of repression. In the countryside, peasants have replaced portraits of Mao and other Communist heroes with statues of folk gods and ancestor worship tablets. The influence of extended kinship groups such as clans often outweighs the formal authority of the party in the villages. In the cities, popular culture, including gigantic rock concerts, shapes youth attitudes much more profoundly than party propaganda. Consumerism ("buying things") is probably the most widely shared value in China today. Many observers have spoken of a moral vacuum in Chinese society, which is not uncommon in countries undergoing such rapid, multifaceted change.

Freedom of religion is guaranteed by the PRC constitution (as is the freedom not to believe in any religion). Organized religion, which was ferociously suppressed during the Mao era, is attracting an increasing number of adherents, though a large majority of the population are atheists or practice traditional folk religions. Buddhist temples, Christian churches, and other places of worship operate more freely than they have in decades. The most widely practiced religion is Buddhism, with an estimated 250 million practitioners or 18 percent of the population. The government says there are 23 million Catholics and Protestants in China (less than 2 percent of the population). But unofficial estimates of Christians put the figure at several times that and as high as 70–100 million.

Religious life is strictly controlled and limited to officially approved organizations and venues. Clergy of any religion who defy the authority of the party-state are still imprisoned. The Chinese Catholic Church is prohibited from recognizing the authority of the pope and appoints its own bishops and cardinals.

Unofficial Christian communities, called *house churches,* have sprung up in many areas among people who reject the government's control of religious life. These range from tiny groups that literally meet in private homes to quite large mega-churches. Although local officials generally tolerate these churches, in numerous cases, house church leaders and laypeople have been arrested and the facilities where services are held have had their crosses torn down or have even been bulldozed.

China's media is much livelier and more open than during the Maoist period when it did little other than convey party messages. There is now much greater leeway to publish more entertainment news, human-interest stories, and some nonpolitical investigative journalism in areas that are consistent with party objectives. But all media outlets are under direct or indirect party control, and the state does shut down those that provoke its political displeasure. In 2016, China was ranked 176 out of 180 countries (just a few notches ahead of North Korea) in the Press Freedom Index compiled annually by Reporters Without Borders.

In terms of political restrictions, the arts are the area of life that has seen the greatest change in China in recent years. Books, movies, plays, and other art forms are sometimes banned, but much of the artistic censorship is now self-imposed by creators who know the limits of what is acceptable to the party-state.

The views of Chinese citizens about what makes them part of the PRC—their sense of national identity—are going through a profound and uncertain transformation. Party leaders realize that most citizens are skeptical or dismissive of communist ideology and that appeals to socialist goals and revolutionary virtues no longer inspire loyalty. The CCP has turned increasingly to patriotic themes to rally the country behind its leadership. The official media put considerable emphasis on the greatness and antiquity of Chinese culture. They send the not-so-subtle message that it is time for China to reclaim its rightful place in the world order—and that only the CCP can lead the nation in achieving this goal.

In the view of some scholars and others, such officially promoted nationalism could lead to a more aggressive foreign and military policy. The party-state has fanned nationalist sentiment among Chinese citizens to garner support for its disputes with nearby countries over claims to uninhabited islands in the strategically important Sea of Japan and the potentially oil-rich South China Sea.

Of course, it is the cultural tie of being "Chinese" that is the most powerful collective identity that connects citizen to the nation. The Chinese people are intensely proud of their ancient culture and long history. Their enthusiasm for hosting the 2008 Olympics in Beijing reflected this cultural pride. They can also be very sensitive about what they consider slights to their national dignity. Many Chinese feel that Japan has not done enough to acknowledge or apologize for the atrocities its army committed in China during World War II. This has been a strain in relations between the two countries and has sometimes led to spontaneous anti-Japanese demonstrations by Chinese students.

China's Non-Chinese Citizens

The PRC calls itself a multinational state with fifty-six officially recognized ethnic groups, one of which is the Chinese majority, called the Han people (Han being the name of one of China's earliest dynasties). The Han make up 91.6 percent of the total population. The defining elements of a minority group involve some combination of language, culture (including religion), and race that distinguish it from the Han. The fifty-five non-Han minorities number a little more than 100 million, or about 8.4 percent of the total population. These groups range in size from 17 million (the Zhuang of southwest China) to about 3,700 (the Lhoba in the far west). Most of these minorities have come under Chinese rule over many centuries through the expansion of the Chinese state rather than through migration into China.

China's minorities are highly concentrated in the five autonomous regions of Guangxi, Inner Mongolia, Ningxia, Tibet, and Xinjiang. Only in the latter two, however, do minority people outnumber Han Chinese—who are encouraged to migrate to the autonomous regions. The five autonomous regions are sparsely populated, yet they occupy about 60 percent of the total land area of the PRC. Some of these areas are resource rich. All are located on strategically important borders of the country, including those with Vietnam, India, and Russia.

The Chinese constitution grants autonomous regions the right of self-government in certain matters. But they remain firmly under the control of the central authorities. Minority peoples enjoy some latitude to develop their local economies as they see fit. The use of minority languages in the media and literature is encouraged, as is, to a certain extent, bilingual education. Minority religions can only be practiced, however, through state-approved organizations.

The most extensive ethnic conflict in China has occurred in Tibet. Tibet is located in the far west of China and has been under Chinese military occupation since the early 1950s. Tibetans practice a unique form of Buddhism, and most are fiercely loyal to the Dalai Lama, a monk who they believe is the incarnation of a divine being. China has claimed authority over Tibet since long before the Communist Party came to power. Tibetans have always disputed that claim and resisted Chinese rule, sometimes violently, including in 1959, when the Dalai Lama fled to exile in India following the failure of a rebellion by his followers.

During the Maoist era, traditional Tibetan culture was suppressed by the Chinese authorities. Since the late 1970s, Buddhist temples and monasteries have been allowed to reopen, and Tibetans have gained a significant degree of cultural freedom; the Chinese government has also significantly increased investment in Tibet's economic development. However, China still considers talk of Tibetan political independence to be treason, and Chinese troops have crushed several anti-China demonstrations in Lhasa, the capital of Tibet.

There are about 23 million Muslims in China. They live in many parts of the country and belong to several different ethnic minority groups. The highest concentration of Muslims is in the far west of China in the Ningxia Hui and Xinjiang Uyghur autonomous regions.

The more secular Hui (about 10.5 million) are well assimilated into Han Chinese society. But there continues to be unrest among Uyghurs (about 10 million) in Xinjiang, which borders several Islamic nations, including Pakistan and Afghanistan. Tensions between Uyghurs and Han Chinese exploded in Xinjiang in mid-2010, resulting in about 150 deaths and 1,000 injuries. The government forcefully restored order and then arrested more than 1,500 people (almost all Uyghurs) in connection with the riots, twelve of whom were sentenced to death.

The Chinese government also has clashed with Uyghur militants who want to create a separate Islamic state of "East Turkestan" and have sometimes used violence, including bombings and assassinations, to press their cause. In March 2014, Uyghur separatists used knives to attack people in a train station in southwest China, killing 29 and injuring more than 140 before being killed or captured by police. The government referred to this attack as "China's 9/11" but also urged that the public not blame Uyghurs as a whole for the mayhem. Later that same year, Ilham Tohti, a Uyghur professor at a Beijing university who had raised questions about China's policies in Xinjiang, was sentenced to life in prison for allegedly inciting ethnic hatred between the Han and Uyghur peoples.

China's minority population is relatively small and geographically isolated. Ethnic unrest has been sporadic and easily quelled. Therefore, the PRC has not had the kind of intense identity-based conflict experienced by countries with more pervasive religious and ethnic cleavages, such as India and Nigeria. But it is possible that domestic and global forces will make ethnic identity a more visible and volatile issue in Chinese politics.

Interest Groups, Social Movements, and Protest

Truly independent interest groups and social movements are not permitted to influence the political process in the PRC in any significant way. The CCP supports official **mass organizations** as a means to provide a way for interest groups to express their views on policy matters—within strict limits.

Total membership of mass organizations in China is in the hundreds of millions. Two of the most important are the All-China Women's Federation, the only national organization representing the interests of women in general, and the All-China Federation of Trade Unions (ACFTU), to which more than 250 million Chinese workers belong. Neither constitutes an autonomous political voice for the groups they are supposed to represent. But they sometimes do act as an effective lobby in promoting the nonpolitical interests of their constituencies. For example, the Women's Federation has become a strong advocate for women on issues ranging from domestic violence to economic rights. The Trade Union Federation successfully pushed for legislation to reduce the standard workweek from six to five days. The ACFTU also represents individual workers with grievances against management, although its first loyalty is to the communist party.

Since the late 1990s, there has been a huge increase in the number of NGOs less directly subordinate to the CCP than the official mass organizations. There is an enormous variety of national and local NGOs. These include ones that deal with the environment, health, charitable work, and legal issues. NGOs must register with the government, but they have considerable latitude to operate within their functional areas without direct party interference *if* they steer clear of politics and do not challenge official policies. On January 1, 2017, a new law went into effect imposing much tighter restrictions on the over 7,000 foreign NGOs that operate in China, such as Greenpeace and the American Bar Association, and their local partners

China has certainly loosened up politically since the days of Mao Zedong, and the spread of private enterprises, increasing labor and residential mobility, and new forms of informal association and communication are just some of the factors that are making it much harder for China's party-state to control its citizens as closely as in the past. But it is still very effective in monitoring dissent and preventing the formation of organizations that might challenge the CCP's authority. For example, in 2013, leaders of the New Citizens Movement, which has protested official corruption and advocated for constitutional government, were arrested on charges of illegal assembly in order to stop the movement from spreading.

mass organization

An organization in a communist party-state that represents the interests of a particular social group, such as workers or women, but which is controlled by the communist party.

Protest and the Party-State

The Tiananmen massacre of 1989 showed the limits of protest in China. The party leadership was particularly alarmed at signs that several autonomous student and worker organizations were emerging from the demonstrations. The brutal suppression of the democracy movement was meant to send a clear signal that neither open political protest nor the formation of independent interest groups would be tolerated.

In the aftermath of Tiananmen, the Falun Gong (FLG), a spiritual movement with philosophical and religious elements drawn from Buddhism and Taoism along with traditional Chinese physical exercises (similar to *tai chi*) and meditation, have carried out the largest and most continuous demonstrations against the party-state. The movement claims 70 million members in China and 30 million in more than seventy other countries. Its promise of inner tranquility and good health have proven very appealing to a wide cross section of people in China as a reaction to some of the side effects of rapid modernization.

The authorities began a crackdown on the FLG in 1999, which intensified after approximately 10,000 of its followers staged a peaceful protest in front of CCP headquarters in the center of Beijing. The authorities have destroyed FLG books and tapes, jammed websites, and arrested thousands of practitioners. Despite a few small FLG demonstrations, the crackdown seems to have been successful, with the movement driven deep underground.

Each year, China experiences tens of thousands of so-called "mass incidents" that involve anywhere from a few dozen to more than a thousand people protesting against a wide range of grievances. These are almost always directed against local targets, not the party-state as a whole, and are often accommodated by higher-levels who see them as a way to find out about and address problems before they become even more explosive.

Strikes and demonstrations by retired industrial workers protesting the nonpayment of pensions or severance packages are among the most common type of mass incident in the urban areas. Employees at some foreign-owned enterprises have gone on strike against unsafe working conditions or low wages. Such actions at plants that produce most of the world's iPhones and iPads led Apple to enhance its initiative that monitors working conditions at its supplier plants in China and elsewhere.

The countryside has also seen an upsurge of protests over corruption, exorbitant taxes and extralegal fees, and environmental damage that impairs both human health and agricultural production. Illegal land seizures by greedy local officials working in cahoots with developers who want to build factories, expensive housing, or even golf courses is one of the major sources of rural mass incidents.

Urban and rural protests in China have not spread beyond the locales where they started. They have focused on the protestors' immediate concerns, not on grand-scale issues like democracy, and most often are aimed at corrupt local officials or unresponsive employers, not the Communist Party. By responding positively to citizen concerns, the party-state can win support and turn what could be regime-threatening activities into regime-sustaining ones.

The Political Impact of Technology and the Media

Party-state censors closely monitor print and broadcast media in the PRC, so their political impact is largely limited to promoting official policy. But new technologies are proving to be somewhat more of a challenge to control. Internet access is exploding, with more than 730 million users in China at the end of 2016. That represents 53.3 percent of the population. The vast majority of those users (95.1 percent) access the Internet through their phones.

The Chinese party-state knows that cutting-edge technology is critical to its modernization plans and wants citizens to become computer literate. But, as with so much else in the PRC, the party-state wants to dictate the rules about how such knowledge is used. Web access in China is tightly controlled by the licensing of a small number of Internet Service Providers who are responsible for who uses their systems and how. The government has invested huge sums to develop the Golden Shield Project, which is charged with monitoring and censoring the Internet, including shutting out what it deems as objectionable foreign websites such as *The New York Times*. In early 2011, the authorities moved quickly to stifle social networking calls for peaceful gatherings in several Chinese cities to show support for the democracy movements in the Middle East and North Africa during the Arab Spring. In 2014, the Cyberspace Administration of China was established as the central agency for coordinating Internet oversight and control. Foreign firms, including Amazon and Apple, have been criticized by some for cooperating with party-state censors in restricting online content in China.

Nevertheless, the rapid spread of the Internet and social media—especially the Twitter equivalent, Weibo—has empowered citizens by providing a forum for communication and a flow of information that is difficult for the party-state to proactively control. There have been numerous large-scale online postings that have exposed corrupt officials, environmental problems, and child labor exploitation—and even poked fun at the heavy-handed government control of the Internet. The Internet has also been a means of mobilizing citizen action as in the aftermath of the hugely destructive and deadly earthquake that struck Sichuan province in May 2008 when relief funds were raised and blood drives organized online.

Where Do You Stand?

China claims it is a socialist democracy. Can socialism and democracy coexist?

Do you think the Internet and social media can promote democracy in China?

CHINESE POLITICS IN TRANSITION

Political Challenges and Changing Agendas

Focus Questions ▽

- What are the major economic and political challenges facing the CCP?

- Why has the Chinese communist party-state been more durable than other regimes of its type?

In late 2011, China passed a milestone in its history. For the first time, more people lived in cities than in the countryside. At the end of the Maoist era in the late 1970s, the rural areas accounted for over 80 percent of the population; in 2016, that was down to about 43 percent. The pace of migration is expected to accelerate, and by 2030, nearly three-quarters of China's population—a billion people—will live in cities, more than 200 of which will have a million or more inhabitants. The flow of farmers to the cities in search of better job opportunities—the "floating population"—has been and will continue to be the major source of the new urban population.

Rapid urbanization is a measure of China's progress in modernization, but it also presents the country's leadership with monumental challenges. Migrants mostly work in very low-paying jobs, including export industries, hotels and restaurants, and construction, that offer no security or benefits. They live in substandard housing, often hastily constructed and jam-packed dwellings called "urban villages" located on former farmland that has been incorporated into the municipality.

Perhaps their greatest vulnerability is that their presence in the cities is technically illegal. Beginning in the late 1950s, all Chinese were given either a rural or an urban household registration (*hukou*) that was pegged to a specific location. They were not permitted to live or work in any other area. This system prevented the kind

household registration (*hukou*)

In China, the system that registers each citizen as entitled to work and to live in a specific urban or rural location.

of uncontrolled rural flight that occurred in many other developing countries and led to the establishment of vast urban slums. But, by limiting the mobility of farmers, it also became the basis of deeply entrenched inequality between city and countryside.

The authorities allowed the recent wave of migrants to move to the cities despite their rural *hukous* because their labor was crucial to economic expansion. But the migrants have no formal rights in the urban areas, including access to public health care or education for their children, and can be evicted if the government chooses to do so.

The current leadership of the PRC, under Xi Jinping, has given high priority to promoting what is called "people-centered" urbanization. The government has announced that urban registration will be extended to 100 million migrants currently living in cities while another 100 million will be moved to smaller urban areas by 2020. The government will also invest heavily in housing, schools, hospitals, and public transportation to meet the needs of the new city dwellers. This is a hugely ambitious undertaking that will have an enormous impact the country's economic development. But China's leaders are well aware of the political implications of a project that will profoundly affect the lives of hundreds of millions of people.

China's planned urbanization is just one part of the multifaceted challenge that its leaders face in trying to sustain and effectively manage the economic growth that has not only significantly improved the lives of most of citizens, but also is the strongest basis of public support for the ruling Communist Party. The CCP is gambling that continued solid economic performance will literally buy it legitimacy and that most citizens will care little about democracy or national politics if their material lives continue to get better. So far this gamble seems to have paid off.

As noted in Section 2, the global financial crisis of 2008 brought a significant slowdown to China's GDP annual growth rate. If it continues to drop, the party-state could face the specter of seriously dashed expectations among a population that had grown accustomed to rapidly improving standards of living. That might spell political trouble for the CCP.

The government of the PRC needs to find ways to restructure the economy so that it is less dependent on export-led growth, which is very vulnerable to shifts in the global market. This will involve promoting industries that produce for the domestic economy and its huge untapped consumer market. At the same time, the Chinese government is encouraging its citizens to spend more and save less (in a way, the opposite of the U.S. dilemma) in order to stimulate the domestic economy. Increasing consumer spending would also allow China to rely less heavily on massive government spending and mounting public debt as an engine of economic growth.

Another major economic challenge for the PRC is to deepen reform of the country's banking system, which is still almost entirely state-owned and largely immune from market forces, by allowing more room for both private and foreign investors. But such a step towards capitalism in the financial sector has been resisted by entrenched bureaucratic and economic interests as well as by conservatives in the CCP leadership. And, if China is to truly become a mature, modern, and globally competitive economy, it must move beyond being the "factory of the world" and become a more innovative economy that produces international-caliber, cutting-edge products of its own design.

So far, the enormous class, regional, and urban-rural inequalities that clearly mark modernizing China have not become the source of major social instability. But that could change, particularly if there is further economic contraction, which would hurt the less well-off much more than the wealthy, who are increasingly sending their assets—and their children—abroad.

Corruption affects the lives of most people much more directly than political repression. Despite well-publicized anticorruption campaigns, corruption is still so blatant and widespread that it is probably the single most corrosive force eating away at the legitimacy of the CCP. Environmental problems may not be far behind as a source of dissatisfaction with the political status quo.

China and the Democratic Idea

The PRC has evolved in recent decades toward a system of what has been called "Market-Leninism,"[13] a combination of increasing economic openness (a market economy) and continuing political rigidity under the leadership of a Leninist ruling party that adheres to a remodeled version of communist ideology. The major political challenges now facing the CCP and the country emerge from the sharpening contradictions and tensions of this hybrid system.

As the people of China become more secure economically, better educated, and more connected to the outside world, they will also likely become more politically active. Business owners may want political clout to match their rising economic and social status. Scholars, scientists, and technology specialists may become more outspoken about the limits on intellectual freedom. The many Chinese who travel or study abroad may find the political gap between their party-state and the world's democracies to be increasingly intolerable.

What are the prospects for democratization in China? On the one hand, China's long history of bureaucratic and authoritarian rule and the hierarchical values of still-influential Confucian culture seem to be heavy counterweights to democracy. And, although some aspects of its political control have weakened, the coercive power of China's communist party-state remains formidable. The PRC's relatively low per capita standard of living, large rural population and vast areas of extreme poverty, and state-dominated media and means of communications also impose some impediments to the spread of the democratic idea. Finally, many in China are apathetic about politics or fearful of the violence and chaos that radical political change might unleash. They are quite happy with the status quo of economic growth and overall political stability of the country under the CCP.

On the other hand, the impressive success of democratization in Taiwan in the past decade, including free and fair multiparty elections from the local level up to the presidency, strongly suggests that the values, institutions, and process of democracy are not incompatible with Confucian culture. And though it is still a developing country, China has a high literacy rate, extensive industrialization and urbanization, and a burgeoning middle class—conditions widely seen by social scientists as favorable to the development democracy.

Despite the CCP's continuing tight hold on power, there have been a number of significant political changes in China that could be harbingers of democracy: the enhanced political and economic power of local governments; the setting of a mandatory retirement age and term limits for most officials; the rise of younger, better educated, and more worldly leaders; the increasingly important (if still minor) role of the NPC in the policy-making process; the introduction of competitive elections in rural villages; the strengthening and partial depoliticization of the legal system; tolerance of a much wider range of artistic, cultural, and religious expression; and the important freedom (unheard of in the Mao era) for individuals to be apolitical.

Furthermore, the astounding spread of the democratic idea around the globe has created a trend that could be increasingly difficult for China's leaders to resist. The PRC has become a major player in the world of states, and its government must be more responsive to international opinion in order to continue the country's deepening integration with the international economy and growing stature as a responsible and mature global power.

One of the most important political trends in China has been the resurgence of civil society, a sphere of independent public life and citizen association, which, if allowed to thrive and expand, could provide fertile soil for future democratization. The development of civil society among workers in Poland and intellectuals in Czechoslovakia, for example, played an important role in the collapse of communism in East-Central Europe, in the late 1980s, by weakening the critical underpinnings of party-state control.

The 1989 Tiananmen demonstrations reflected the stirrings of civil society in post-Mao China. But the brutal crushing of that movement showed the CCP's determination to thwart its growth before it could seriously contest the party's authority. But as economic modernization and social liberalization have deepened in the PRC, civil society has begun to stir again. Some stirrings, like the Falun Gong movement, have met with vicious repression by the party-state. The proliferation and growing influence of NGOs that deal with *nonpolitical* matters such as the environment, can be seen as a sign of a vibrant civil society. However, Xi Jinping's policies restricting the activities of NGOs with foreign connections perhaps suggest caution about civil society becoming a source of democratization in the PRC. On the other hand, the relatively new and rapidly growing phenomenon of online activism by China's netizens also suggests the emergence of a "digital civil society" that may well become a source of pressure for democratization.[14]

At some point, the leaders of the CCP will face the fundamental dilemma of whether to accommodate or, as they have done so often in the past, suppress organizations, individuals, and ideas that question the principle of party leadership. Accommodation would require the party-state to cede some of its control over society, and allow more meaningful citizen representation and participation. But repression could derail the country's economic dynamism and is likely to take a toll on China's international reputation.

netizens

A combination of the words *Internet* and *citizen*, as in "citizen of the net." Particularly refers to those who use the Internet to express their political opinions.

Is Demography Destiny?

In most developing countries, the under-30 age group is the fastest-growing segment of the population. By contrast, in China, the over-60s constitute the most rapidly expanding age group. This group numbered about 185 million (13.7 percent of the population) in 2010, and is estimated to grow to 284 million (21.0 percent) by 2025 and 440 million (34.6 percent) by 2050. According to the United Nations, China is aging more rapidly than almost any country in recent history. This demographic trend is the result of a combination of factors, including longer life expectancy and, especially, the one-child policy that was introduced in the early 1980s and changed to a two-child policy only in 2016.

China's "graying population" presents the country with the challenge of supporting this growing cohort of senior citizens. The burden will fall particularly heavily on the shrinking younger generation, which will bear much of the responsibility for caring for elderly parents. Since both the husband and wife in a married couple are likely to be only-children, they will wind up caring for both sets of parents for what could be a decade or two. Other countries face a similar dilemma, but almost all of them (e.g., Japan) have a much higher per capita income and much more developed pension and health care systems. In other words, China's intra-generational challenge is complicated by the fact that it is "getting old before getting rich."[15]

The shift of the demographic balance towards an older population also means that, despite, its huge population, the labor force in China is actually shrinking, which will probably drive up wages. That's a good thing for workers, but it's even more reason for the economy to move towards less dependency on exports since Chinese produced goods will become more expensive on the global market.

Higher education has expanded rapidly in the PRC over the last three decades, but still only about 20 percent of the age-relevant population is in college. Most of that population doesn't even apply since they lack the necessary high school education. For those who do want to apply, admission is extremely competitive, with just three out of five prospective students passing the required national college entrance examination. For jobs other than in the low-wage sectors of the economy, a college degree is a necessity, and, even for a substantial portion of China's 7.6 million college graduates each year (compared to 1.5 million in the United States), finding suitable employment has become a challenge. These unemployed or underemployed college-educated youth have become a fixture in many Chinese cities. They've come to be known as the "Ant Tribe" because they often share crowded apartments and pass the time by hanging out together. If China's economy were to slow down even more, the ranks of the Ant Tribe could grow in size and become increasingly unhappy about their situation. Unemployed educated youth have been a source of social unrest and political protest in many countries and were a major factor in launching the Arab Spring revolutions that began in 2011.

Chinese Politics in Comparative Perspective

China as a Communist Party-State

The fact that the Chinese Communists won power through an indigenous revolution with widespread popular backing and did not depend on foreign military support for their victory sets China apart from the situation of most of the now-deposed Eastern European communist parties. Despite some very serious mistakes over the six decades of its rule in China, the CCP still has a deep reservoir of historical legitimacy among large segments of the population.

The PRC has also been able to avoid the kind of economic crises that greatly weakened other communist systems, including the Soviet Union, through its successful market reforms that have dramatically improved the lives of most Chinese. CCP leaders believe that one of the biggest mistakes made by the last Soviet communist party chief, Mikhail Gorbachev, was that he went too far with political reform and not far enough with economic change, and they are convinced that their reverse formula is a key reason that they have not suffered the same fate.

But China also has much in common with other communist party-states past and present, particularly the insistence on the unchallengeable principle of party leadership in any way that the party chooses to exert that leadership. Stalinist Russia and Maoist China were classified as examples of totalitarianism because of the communist party's claim to exercise nearly total control of not just politics and ideology, but the economy, culture, and society as well. Under totalitarian regimes (which also included Nazi Germany), the distinction between public and private pretty much disappears, and the party-state enforces its authority through a combination of propaganda (extended to education and the media), coercion, and terror.

China is much less totalitarian than it was during the Maoist era. To promote economic development, the CCP has relaxed its grip on many areas of life. Citizens

totalitarianism

A political system in which the state attempts to exercise total control over all aspects of public and private life, including the economy, culture, education, and social organizations, through an integrated system of ideological, economic, and political control. Totalitarian states rely on extensive coercion, including terror, as a means to exercise power.

can generally pursue their private interests without interference by the party-state as long as they avoid sensitive political issues and are not seen as challenging the Communist Party's right to rule.

The PRC can now be considered a "consultative authoritarian regime" that "increasingly recognizes the need to obtain information, advice, and support from key sectors of the population, but insists on suppressing dissent … and maintaining ultimate political power in the hands of the Party."[16] By moderating, if not totally abandoning some its Maoist totalitarian features, the CCP has shown remarkable adaptability that so far has allowed it to both carry out bold economic reform and sustain a dictatorial political system.

China as a Developing Country

The development of the PRC raises many issues about the role of the state in governing the economy. It also provides an interesting comparative perspective on the complex and much-debated relationship between economic and political change in the developing world.

When the CCP came to power in 1949, China was a desperately poor country, with an economy devastated by a century of civil strife and world war. It was also in a weak and subordinate position in the post–World War II international order. Even at the end of the Maoist era in the late 1970s, the PRC was among the poorest nations in the world and little more than a minor regional power. Measured against these starting points, China has made remarkable progress in improving the well-being of its citizens, building a strong state, and enhancing the country's global role.

Why has China been more successful than so many other nations in meeting some of the major challenges of development? Those with political power in the developing world have often served narrow class or foreign interests more than the national interest. The result is that governments of many developing countries have become **predatory states** that prey on their people and the nation's resources to enrich the few at the expense of the many. They become defenders of a status quo built on extensive inequality and poverty rather than agents of needed change. In contrast, and despite extensive corruption in the party-state, the PRC's recent rulers have been quite successful in creating a **developmental state**, in which political power and public policy are used effectively to promote national economic growth. In this very important way, China has become a leader among developing nations.

But, in an equally important way, China is lagging many other countries in Africa, Asia, and Latin America. Whereas much of the developing world has been heading toward democracy, the PRC has stood firm against the wave of democratization. According to several well-respected surveys, China ranks among the world's most authoritarian countries. (See Chapter 1 for more information on this point.)

There is a sharp and disturbing contrast between the harsh political rule of the Chinese communist party-state and its remarkable accomplishments in improving the material lives of the Chinese people. The CCP's tough stance on political reform is in large part based on its desire for self-preservation. But in keeping firm control on political life while allowing the country to open up in other important ways, CCP leaders also believe they are wisely following the model of development pioneered by the newly industrializing countries (NICs) of East Asia, such as South Korea and Taiwan.

The lesson that the CCP draws from the NIC experience is that only an authoritarian government can provide the political stability and social peace required for rapid economic growth. According to this view, democracy—with its open debates about national priorities, political parties contesting for power, and interest groups

predatory state

A state in which those with political power prey on the people and the nation's resources to enrich themselves rather than using their power to promote national development.

developmental state

A nation-state in which the government carries out policies that effectively promote national economic growth.

squabbling over how to divide the economic pie—is a recipe for chaos, particularly in a huge and still relatively poor country. They have recently pointed to political turbulence in the United States and Western Europe as indications that their type of political system offers more stability.

But another of the lessons from the East Asian NICs—one that most Chinese leaders have been reluctant to acknowledge—is that economic development, social modernization, and global integration also create powerful pressures for political change from below and abroad. In both South Korea and Taiwan, authoritarian governments that had presided over economic miracles in the 1960s and 1970s, gave way in the 1980s and 1990s to democracy.

China is in the early to middle stages of a period of growth and modernization that are likely to lead it to NIC status within two or three decades. In terms of the extent of industrialization, per capita income, the strength of the private sector of the economy, and the size of the middle and professional classes, China's level of development is still below the level at which democracy succeeded in Taiwan and South Korea. Before concluding that China's communist rulers will soon yield to the forces of democratization, it is important to remember that "authoritarian governments in East Asia pursued market-driven economic growth for decades without relaxing their hold on political power."[17]

But economic reform in China has already created social groups at home and opened up the country to ideas from abroad that are likely to grow as sources of pressure for more and faster political change. And the experiences of many developing countries suggest that such pressures will intensify as the economy and society continue to modernize. At some point in the not-too-distant future, the CCP is likely to again face the challenge of the democratic idea. How China's new generation of leaders responds to this challenge is perhaps the most important and uncertain question about Chinese politics in the coming decades of the twenty-first century.

Where Do You Stand?

Do you think that the CCP will still be in power in 2049, a century after the founding of the People's Republic?

Do you think China is ready for democracy? Would democracy be good for China?

Chapter Summary

For more than 2,000 years, China was a hereditary monarchy headed by an emperor until it was overthrown by a revolution in 1912. From then until 1949, it was known as the Republic of China, but the central government was never in full control. Warlords ruled various parts of the country, a civil war broke out between the American-backed Nationalist Party government and the CCP, and Japan occupied almost all of eastern China during World War II. In 1949, the civil war ended with the victory of the Communist Party under Mao Zedong and the establishment of the People's Republic of China (PRC). From then until his death in 1976, Mao launched

several radical campaigns that had a disastrous political and economic impact on China. Deng Xiaoping became China's most powerful leader in 1978. He implemented major reforms that helped make China the fastest-growing major economy in the world. But he also made it very clear that he would not tolerate any challenges to the authority of the Communist Party. Deng's successors have largely followed his model of economic reform and political repression.

During the Maoist era (1949–1976), the state thoroughly dominated the economy through a system of central planning in which government bureaucrats determined economic policies. Any kind of private economic activity was suppressed. This approach achieved some success in promoting industrialization and raising the educational and health standards of the Chinese people. But, overall, it left China as a very poor country with little involvement in the global economy. Under Deng Xiaoping and his successors, the state has given up much of its control of the economy and encouraged free-market forces, private ownership, international trade, and foreign investment. Living standards, modernization, and globalization have all increased dramatically. But serious problems, such as socioeconomic inequality and pollution, are a challenge for China's current leaders.

China is one of the few remaining countries in the world still ruled by a communist party. Even though the CCP has moved China in the direction of a capitalist economy, it still proclaims it is following communist ideology. The CCP insists that it is the only political party that can lead the country toward economic development and maintain stability, and it prohibits any serious challenge to its authority. Power is highly concentrated in the top two dozen or so leaders of the CCP, who are chosen through secretive inner-party procedures. The government of the PRC is technically separate from the CCP, and political reform in China has brought some autonomy to government institutions, such as the national legislature and the judiciary. But, in fact, the government and policy-making operates under the close supervision of the Communist Party and almost all high-ranking government officials are also members of the Communist Party.

Representation of citizen interests and political participation in China are carried out under the watchful eye of the CCP. The NPC, the legislature of the PRC, has become more active as the country's focus has shifted from revolutionary politics to economic development. Elections, particularly at the local level, have become more democratic. The Communist Party has also changed significantly, not just welcoming workers,

peasants, and political activists into its ranks, but even recruiting members from among China's growing capitalist class of private business owners. Although they are much more open than during the Maoist era, the media, the arts, and education are still ultimately under party supervision. Communist ideology is declining as a unifying force for China's citizens, and the ability of the communist party-state to control and influence its citizens is weakening. The Internet, religion, consumerism, and popular culture are growing in influence. These all present a challenge to the CCP, which now emphasizes Chinese nationalism as a source of citizen identity. Some of the greatest political tensions in China are in parts of the country with high concentrations of non-Chinese ethnic minorities, such as in Tibet and among Muslims in Xinjiang. Protests by farmers and industrial workers with economic grievances have been on the increase, but these have not become large-scale or widespread.

The legitimacy of the CCP to rule China rests heavily on the fact that it has presided over three decades of phenomenal economic growth that have dramatically improved the lives of most people in the country. Party leaders face major challenges in continuing to manage the economy, especially in light of the global financial crisis of 2008. These challenges include rapid urbanization, reform of the banking system, and the transition from an export-led model of growth to one that depends more on domestic consumption and innovation. The CCP is also very likely to face increasing demands for a political voice from different sectors of society as its citizens become more prosperous, well educated, and worldly. In comparative perspective, China has proven more economically successful and politically adaptable than other communist party-states, including the Soviet Union, which collapsed in 1991. China has also been much more successful than most other developing countries in promoting economic growth, but so far resisted the wave of democratization that has spread to so many other parts of the world.

Key Terms

autonomous region	household registration (*hukou*)	Politburo
Central Committee	household responsibility system	predatory state
Central Military Commission (CMC)	iron rice bowl	socialism
centrally planned economy	leading small groups	socialist democracy
collective leadership	mass organizations	socialist market economy
communism	National Party Congress	Standing Committee
developmental state	National People's Congress (NPC)	State Council
floating population	netizens	state-owned enterprises (SOEs)
general secretary	Organization Department	totalitarianism
guerrilla warfare	People's Liberation Army (PLA)	

Suggested Readings

Davin, Delia. *Mao: A Very Short Introduction*. New York: Oxford University Press, 2013.

Gao Yuan. *Born Red: A Chronicle of the Cultural Revolution*. Stanford, CA: Stanford University Press, 1987.

Joseph, William A., ed. *Politics in China: An Introduction*, 2nd edition. New York: Oxford University Press, 2014.

Kraus, Richard Curt. *The Cultural Revolution: A Very Short Introduction*. New York: Oxford University Press, 2012.

Nathan, Andrew J., Larry Diamond, and Marc F. Plattner, eds. *Will China Democratize?* Baltimore, MD: The Johns Hopkins University Press, 2013.

Pomfret, John. *The Beautiful Country and the Middle Kingdom: America and China, 1776 to the Present*. New York: Henry Holt, 2016.

Schell, Orville, and John Delury. *Wealth and Power: China's Long March to the Twenty-First Century*. New York: Random House, 2013.

Shambaugh, David. *China's Future?* New York: Polity, 2016.

Walder, Andrew G. *China Under Mao: A Revolution Derailed*. Cambridge, MA: Harvard University Press, 2015.

Wasserstrom, Jeffrey. *China in the 21st Century: What Everyone Needs to Know*, 2nd ed. New York: Oxford University Press, 2013.

Suggested Websites

The Central Government of the People's Republic of China
http://www.gov.cn/english/

China Brief (The Jamestown Foundation)
https://jamestown.org/programs/cb/

China Digital Times (University of California at Berkeley)
http://chinadigitaltimes.net/

China in the News
http://chinapoliticsnews.blogspot.com/

China Leadership Monitor (Hoover Institution)
http://www.hoover.org/publications /china-leadership-monitor

International Department of the Communist Party of China
http://www.idcpc.org.cn/english/

News of the Communist Party of China
http://english.cpc.people.com.cn/

Endnotes

Chapter 1

[1] Francis Fukuyama, "The End of History?" *The National Interest*, Summer 1989, pp. 3–18. In 1992, Fukuyama published a book, *The End of History and the Last Man* (New York: Free Press), which expanded on his argument.

[2] *Freedom in the World 2017: Populists and Autocrats: The Dual Threat to Global Democracy*, https://freedomhouse.org/report/freedom-world/freedom-world-2017.

[3] See Philippe Schmitter, "Comparative Politics," in Joel Krieger, ed., *The Oxford Companion to Comparative Politics* (New York: Oxford University Press, 2013), pp. 223–231. For a collection of articles in the field of comparative politics, see Mark Kesselman, ed., *Readings in Comparative Politics*, 2nd ed. (Boston: Wadsworth, 2010).

[4] See, for example, David M. Farrell, *Electoral Systems: A Comparative Introduction*, 2nd ed. New York: Palgrave, 2011.

[5] See, for example, Merilee S. Grindle, *Despite the Odds: The Contentious Politics of Education Reform* (Princeton, NJ: Princeton University Press, 2004), which compares education policies in several Latin American countries; and Paul F. Steinberg and Stacy D. VanDeveer, *Comparative Environmental Politics: Theory, Practice, and Prospects* (Cambridge, MA: MIT Press, 2012).

[6] See, for example, Benedict Anderson, *Imagined Communities: Reflections on the Origins and Spread of Nationalism*, rev. ed. (London: Verso, 1991); and James DeFronzo, *Revolutions and Revolutionary Movements*, 5th ed. (Boulder, CO: Westview Press, 2014).

[7] Peter A. Hall, *Governing the Economy: The Politics of State Intervention in Britain and France* (New York: Oxford University Press, 1986); and Mark Blyth, *Great Transformations: Economic Ideas and Institutional Change in the Twentieth Century* (Cambridge, UK: Cambridge University Press, 2002).

[8] See, for example, most of the chapters in William A. Joseph, ed., *Politics in China: An Introduction*, 2nd ed. (New York: Oxford University Press, 2014).

[9] For discussions in the popular press of rational choice theory, see "Political Scientists Debate Theory of 'Rational Choice,'" in *The New York Times*, February 26, 2000, B11; and Jonathan Cohn, "Irrational Exuberance: When Did Political Science Forget About Politics?" *The New Republic*, October 25, 1999, 25–31.

[10] On democratic transitions, see, for example, Samuel P. Huntington, *The Third Wave: Democratization in the Late Twentieth Century* (Norman: University of Oklahoma Press, 1993); Larry Diamond, Marc F. Plattner, and Philip J. Costopoulos, eds., *Debates on Democratization* (Baltimore: Johns Hopkins University Press, 2010); and Barbara Wejnert, *Diffusion of Democracy: The Past and Future of Global Democracy* (Cambridge, UK: Cambridge University Press, 2014).

[11] See Joel Krieger, ed., *Globalization and State Power: A Reader* (New York: Pearson/Longman, 2006).

[12] This term is borrowed from Hall, *Governing the Economy*.

[13] Peter A. Hall and David Soskice, eds., *Varieties of Capitalism: The Institutional Foundations of Comparative Advantage* (New York: Oxford University Press, 2001). See also David Coates, ed., *Varieties of Capitalism, Varieties of Approaches* (Basingstoke, UK: Palgrave/Macmillan, 2005).

[14] See, for example, Chalmers Johnson, *MITI and the Japanese Miracle: The Growth of Industrial Policy* (Stanford, CA: Stanford University Press, 1982); Meredith Woo-Cummings, ed., *The Developmental State* (Ithaca, NY: Cornell University Press, 1999); Robert Wade, *Governing the Market: Economic Theory and the Role of Government in East Asian Industrialization* (Princeton, NJ: Princeton University Press, 2003); Dwight H. Perkins, *East Asian Development: Foundations and Strategies* (Cambridge, MA: Harvard University Press, 2013); and Linda Yueh, *China's Growth: The Making of an Economic Superpower* (New York: Oxford University Press, 2013).

[15] Adam Przeworski et al., *Democracy and Development: Political Institutions and Well-Being in the World, 1950–1990* (Cambridge, UK: Cambridge University Press, 2000).

[16]Amartya Sen, "Democracy as a Universal Value," *Journal of Democracy* 10, no. 3 (July 1999): 3–17. This article is included in Kesselman, *Readings in Comparative Politics.* For a study that finds a positive correlation between democracy and economic growth, see Daron Acemoglu, Suresh Naidum, Pascual Restrepo, and James A. Robinson, "Democracy Does Cause Growth," Working Paper 2004 (Cambridge, MA: National Bureau of Economic Research, 2014).

[17]Freedom House's annual Freedom in the World reports are available at www.freedomhouse.org.

[18]Sen, "Democracy as a Universal Value," 3.

[19]Andrew Roberts, "Review Article: The Quality of Democracy," *Comparative Politics* 37, no. 3 (April 2005), 357.

[20]For contrasting views on this debate, see Samuel P. Huntington, *Political Order in Changing Societies* (New Haven, CT: Yale University Press, 1968); and Mark Kesselman, "Order or Movement? The Literature of Political Development as Ideology," *World Politics* 26 (1973), 139–154.

[21]Przeworski et al., *Democracy and Development.*

[22]Alfred Stepan, *Arguing Comparative Politics* (New York: Oxford University Press, 2001), 184.

[23]Chuck Collins and Josh Hoxie, "Billionaire Bonanza: The Forbes 400 and the Rest of Us," Institute of Policy Studies, December 2015; and Jesse Bricker et al., "Measuring Income and Wealth at the Top Using Administrative and Survey Data," Brookings Institution, March 2016.

[24]Fareed Zakaria, *The Future of Freedom: Illiberal Democracy at Home and Abroad.* New York: W. W. Norton, 2007.

Chapter 2

[1]Katrin Bennhold, "Gary Lineker, Soccer Hero, Dips a Toe into Post-Brexit British Politics," *The New York Times,* January 27, 2017.

[2]Richard Heffernan, Philip Cowley, and Colin Hay (eds.), *Developments in British Politics Bk. 9.* Basingstoke, U.K.: Palgrave Macmillan, 2011.

[3]Philip Norton, *The British Polity,* 3rd ed. (New York: Longman, 1994), p. 59.

[4]Stephen Haseler, "Britain's Ancient Régime," *Parliamentary Affairs* 40, no. 4 (October 1990): 418.

[5]See Bill Jones and Philip Norton, *Politics UK,* 7th ed. (New York: Longman, 2010), pp. 475–476.

[6]Ivor Crewe, "Great Britain," in I. Crewe and D. Denver, eds., *Electoral Change in Western Democracies* (London: Croom Helm, 1985), p. 107.

[7]See Gabriel A. Almond and Sidney Verba, *The Civic Culture: Political Attitudes and Democracy in Five Nations* (Princeton, NJ: Princeton University Press, 1963); Almond and Verba, eds., *The Civic Culture Revisited* (Boston: Little, Brown, 1980); and Samuel H. Beer, *Britain Against Itself: The Political Contradictions of Collectivism* (New York: Norton, 1982), pp. 110–114.

[8]See Chris Howell, *Trade Unions and the State* (Princeton, NJ: Princeton University Press, 2005), esp. Ch. 6.

[9]Bhiku Parekh et al., *The Future of Multi-Ethnic Britain: The Parekh Report* (London: Profile Books, 2000), p. 10.

Chapter 3

[1]James B. Collins, *The State in Early Modern France,* 2d ed. (New York: Cambridge University Press, 2009), pp. 211, 209.

[2]Chirac's Farewell Address was broadcast on television March 11, 2007. It was recorded and can be seen at www.youtube.com/watch?v=_1QfD2pJ+5U. Accessed May 26, 2017.

[3]Tony Chafer and Emmanuel Godin (eds.), *The End of the French Exception?* (New York: Palgrave Macmillan, 2010), p. 2.

[4]Henri Mendras with Alistair Cole, *Social Change in Modern France: Towards a Cultural Anthropology of the Fifth Republic* (Cambridge: Cambridge University Press, 1991), p. 1.

[5]Jonah D. Levy, "The Return of the State? French Economic Policy under Nicolas Sarkozy," Unpublished paper presented at the 106th Annual Meeting of the American Political Science Association, Washington, D.C., September 2–5, 2010, p. 5.

[6]Vivien A. Schmidt, *From State to Market? The Transformation of French Business and Government* (Cambridge: Cambridge University Press, 1994), p. 442.

[7]See Paul Krugman's columns in *The New York Times,* November 11, 2013, and January 16, 2014, as well as his *New York Times* opinion blog posted March 9, 2014.

[8]*Métro,* March 15, 2007.

[9]Karen Bennhold, "For Women in France, Dim Outlook on Equality," *The New York Times,* October 12, 2010.

[10]John T. S. Keeler and Alec Stone, "Judicial-Political Confrontation in Mitterrand's France: The Emergence of

the Constitutional Council as a Major Actor in the Policy-making Process, "In Stanley Hoffmann, George Ross, and Sylvia Malzacher, eds., *The Mitterrand Experiment: Continuity and Change in Mitterrand's France* (New York: Oxford University Press, 1987), p. 176.

[11]Emiliano Grossman, "Governments under the Fifth Republic: The Changing Instruments/Weapons of Executive Control," in Sylvain Brouard, Andrew M. Appleton, and Amy G. Mazur, eds., *The French Fifth Republic at Fifty: Beyond Stereotypes* (New York: Palgrave Macmillan, 2009), p. 51.

[12]*Le Monde*, April 28, 2016.

[13]Joan Wallach Scott, *The Politics of the Veil* (Princeton, N.J.: Princeton University Press, 2007), p. 40.

[14]Pierre Birnbaum, *The Idea of France* (New York: Hill & Wang), 2001), pp. 278–79.

[15]Data from the Pew Research Center, cited by Marin A. Schain, *The Politics of Immigration in France, Britain, and the United States: A Comparative Study* (New York: Palgrave Macmillan 2008), pp. 19–20.

[16]*Le Monde*, May 6, 2013.

[17]Jonathan Fenby, *The History of Modern France: From the Revolution to the Present Day* (N.Y.: Simon & Schuster, 2015), p. 478.

[18]Peter A. Hall, "Introduction: The Politics of Social Change in France," in Pepper D. Culpepper, Peter A. Hall, and Bruno Palier, eds., *Changing France: The Politics That Markets Make* (New York: Palgrave Macmillan 2006), p. 1.

[19]David A. Bell, *Shadows of Revolution: Reflections on France, Past and Present* (New York: Oxford University Press, 2016), p. 408.

Chapter 4

[1]Mary Sarotte, *The Collapse: The Accidental Opening of the Berlin Wall* (New York: Basic Books, 2014).

[2]Stephen Szabo, *Germany, Russia, and the Rise of Geo-economics*, (London: Bloomsbury, 2015).

[3]Peter Hall and David Soskice, *Varieties of Capitalism: The Institutional Foundations of Comparative Advantage* (New York: Oxford University Press, 2001).

[4]Christopher Allen, "Trade Unions, Worker Participation, and Flexibility: Linking the Micro to the Macro," *Comparative Politics vol.* 22, no. 3 (1990), pp. 253–272.

[5]Hans-Werner Sinn, *Can Germany Be Saved? The Malaise of the World's First Welfare State* (Cambridge: MIT Press, 2009).

[6]Peter Katzenstein, *Policy and Politics in West Germany: The Growth of a Semi-Sovereign State* (Philadelphia: Temple University Press, 1987).

[7]Steven Silvia, *Holding the Shop Together* (Ithaca, NY: Cornell University Press, 2013).

[8]Kathleen Thelen, *How Institutions Evolve: The Political Economy of Skills in Germany, Britain, the United States and Japan* (New York: Cambridge University Press, 2004).

[9]Marc Morjé Howard, *The Politics of Citizenship in Europe* (New York: Cambridge University Press, 2009); and Simon Green, *The Politics of Exclusion: Institutions and Immigration Policy in Contemporary Germany* (Manchester, UK: Manchester University Press, 2004).

[10]Günter Brückner, "Bevölkerung mit Migrationshinter-grund," in Datenreport 2016 (Bundeszentrale für politische Bildung, 2016).

[11]Hans Kudnani, *The Paradox of German Power* (Oxford, UK: Oxford University Press, 2015).

[12]Carolyn Moore and Wade Jacoby, eds., *German Federalism in Transition: Reforms in a Consensual State* (London: Routledge, 2009).

[13]Jonathan Rodden, *Hamilton's Paradox: The Promise and Peril of Fiscal Federalism* (New York: Cambridge University Press, 2006).

[14]Manfred Schmidt, "Germany: The Grand Coalition State." 2015. http://www.uni-heidelberg.de/md/politik/personal/schmidt/schmidt_grand_coalition_state_4th_edition.pdf

[15]Daniel Kelemen, *Eurolegalism: The Transformation of Law and Regulation in the European Union* (Cambridge, MA: Harvard University Press, 2011).

[16]Alexander Reisenbichler. "The Politics of Entrenchment: Growth Models and Housing Finance Policy in the United States and Germany." Ph.D. Dissertation (George Washington University, 2017).

[17]Louise Davidson-Schmich, *Gender Quotas and Democratic Participation* (Ann Arbor: University of Michigan Press, 2016).

[18]Christiane Lemke and Helga Welsh, *Remapping Germany* (Boulder: Rowman & Littlefield, 2018).

[19]Wade Jacoby, "Grand Coalitions and Democratic Dysfunction," *Government and Opposition* vol. 52, no. 2 (2017), pp. 329–335.

[20]Katzenstein, *Policy and Politics in West Germany*, p. 372.

[21]Erik Kirschbaum, *Rocking the Wall: Bruce Springsteen: The Untold Story of a Concert in East Berlin That Changed the World* (Berlin: Berlinica, 2013).

[22]http://www.pewglobal.org/2015/06/02/2015-eu
-survey-presentation/

[23]Marcel Fratzscher, *Verteilungskampf* (Munich: Hanser, 2016).

[24]Michael Pettis, *The Great Rebalancing* (Princeton, NJ: Princeton University Press, 2013).

Chapter 6

[1]George Sansom, *A History of Japan, 1334–1615* (Stanford, CA: Stanford University Press, 1961); A. L. Sadler, *A Short History of Japan* (Sydney: Angus & Robertson, 1963), chs. 4–6.

[2]Ronald P. Dore, *Education in Tokugawa Japan* (London: Athlone, 1965).

[3]Sadako N. Ogata, *Defiance in Manchuria: The Making of Japanese Foreign Policy, 1931–1932* (Berkeley: University of California Press, 1964), pt. II; Yoshihisa Tak Matsusaka, The Making of Japanese Manchuria, 1904–1932. (Cambridge, MA: Harvard University Press, 2003).

[4]Ben-Ami Shillony, *Revolt in Japan: The Young Officers and the February 26, 1936 Incident* (Princeton, NJ: Princeton University Press, 1973).

[5]Robert E. Ward and Sakamoto Yoshikazu, eds., *Democratizing Japan: The Allied Occupation* (Honolulu: University of Hawaii Press, 1987); John Dower, *Embracing Defeat: Japan in the Aftermath of World War II* (London: Penguin Books, 1999).

[6]Bernd Martin, *Japan and Germany in the Modern World* (Providence, RI: Berghahn Books, 1995).

[7]William W. Lockwood, *The Economic Development of Japan: Growth and Structural Change, 1868–1938* (Princeton, NJ: Princeton University Press, 1954), pp. 14–15.

[8]Lockwood, *Economic Development of Japan*, pp. 38–39.

[9]Hugh Patrick and Henry Rosovsky, "Japan's Economic Performance: An Overview," in *Asia's New Giant: How the Japanese Economy Works*, ed. Hugh Patrick and Henry Rosovsky (Washington, DC: Brookings Institution, 1976), pp. 7–9; Takafusa Nakamura, "'Yakushin nihon' no uraomote" (The appearance and reality of the 'advancing Japan'), in *Showa keizaishi* (An economic history of the Showa period), ed. Hiromi Arisawa (Tokyo: Nihon keizai shimbunsha, 1976), pp. 108–111; Hugh Borton, *Japan's Modern Century: From Perry to 1970*, 2nd ed. (New York: Ronald Press Co., 1970), p. 305, Table 5.

[10]Organisation of Economic Co-operation and Development (OECD), *OECD Economic Surveys Japan Overview* 2015, p. 29. http://www.oecd.org/eco/surveys/Japan-2015-overview.pdf

[11]Frank K. Upham, *Law and Social Change in Postwar Japan* (Cambridge, U.K.: Harvard University Press, 1987), ch. 2.

[12]George Hicks, *Japan's Hidden Apartheid: Korean Minority and the Japanese* (Brookfield, VT: Ashgate, 1997).

[13]Susan J. Pharr and Ellis S. Krauss, eds., *Media and Politics in Japan* (Honolulu: University of Hawaii Press, 1996); Laurie Anne Freeman, *Closing the Shop: Information Cartels and Japan's Mass Media* (Princeton, NJ: Princeton University Press, 2000).

Chapter 8

[1]Rogers Smith, *Civic Ideals: Conflicting Visions of Citizenship in U.S. History* (New Haven, CT: Yale University Press, 1997).

[2]Philip Kasnitz, John H. Mollenkopf, Mary C. Waters, and Jennifer Holdaway, *Inheriting the City: The Children of Immigrants Come of Age* (New York: Russell Sage Foundation Press, 2008); Frank D. Bean, Susan K. Brown, and James D. Bachmeier, *Parents Without Papers: The Progress and Pitfalls of Mexican American Integration* (New York: Russell Sage Foundation Press, 2015).

[3]Louis Hartz, *The Liberal Tradition in America* (New York: Harvest/HBJ, 1955).

[4]Nadwa Mossaad, *U.S. Legal Permanent Residents: 2014* (Washington, DC: Office of Immigration Statistics, U.S. Department of Homeland Security, 2016).

[5]Jeffrey S. Passel and D'Vera Cohn, *Overall Number of U.S. Unauthorized Immigrants Holds Steady Since 2009* (Washington, DC: Pew Research Center, 2016).

[6]Gary C. Bryner, *Blue Skies, Green Politics: The Clean Air Act of 1990 and Its Implementation* (Washington, DC: CQ Press, 1995).

[7]See *The Federalist Papers*, ed. Clinton Rossiter (New York: Mentor, 1961), particularly *Federalist* Nos. 10 and 51.

[8]Deborah Avant, *The Market for Force: The Consequences of Privatizing Security* (New York: Cambridge University Press, 2005).

[9]Kristi Anderson, *After Suffrage: Women in Partisan and Electoral Politics Before the New Deal* (Chicago: University of Chicago Press, 1996), chapters 2 and 3.

[10]Tova Wang, *The Politics of Voter Suppression: Defending and Expanding Americans' Right to Vote* (New York: Cornell University Press, 2012).

[11]Jan Leighley and Jonathan Nagler, *Who Votes Now?: Demographics, Issues, Inequality, and Turnout in the United States* (Princeton: Princeton University Press. 2013).

[12]Sanford Levinson, *Constitutional Faith* (Princeton, NJ: Princeton University Press, 1988).

[13]Sidney Verba, Kay Lehman Schlozman, and Henry Brady, *Voice and Equality: Civic Voluntarism in American Politics* (Cambridge: Harvard University Press, 1995).

[14]Robert D. Putnam, *Bowling Alone: The Collapse and Revival of American Community* (New York: Simon & Schuster, 2000).

Chapter 9

[1]Instituto Brasileiro de Geografia e Estatística (IBGE), *Censo 2010 (2010 Census)*, http://censo2010.ibge.gov.br/en/, (accessed November 26, 2013).

[2]Guillermo O'Donnell, *Modernization and Bureaucratic Authoritarianism: Studies in South American Politics* (Berkeley: Institute of International Studies, University of California, 1973).

[3]Thomas E. Skidmore, *The Politics of Military Rule in Brazil, 1964–1985* (New York: Oxford University Press, 1988), p. 49.

[4]Margaret Keck, "The New Unionism in the Brazilian Transition," in Alfred Stepan, ed., *Democratizing Brazil* (New York: Oxford University Press, 1989) p. 284.

[5]Peter B. Evans, *Dependent Development: The Alliance of Multinational, State, and Local Capital in Brazil* (Princeton, NJ: Princeton University Press, 1979).

[6]E. Morsch, N. Chavannes, M. van den Akker, H. Sa and G. J. Dinant, "The Effects of the Family Health Program on Child Health in Ceará State, Northeastern Brazil," *Arch Public Health*, vol. 59 (2001), pp. 151–165.

[7]Wendy Hunter and Natasha Sugiyama, "Democracy and Social Policy in Brazil: Advancing Basic Needs, Preserving Privileged Interests," *Latin American Politics and Society*, vol. 49 (2009), pp. 29–58.

[8]Morsch et al., "The Effects of the Family Health Program."

[9]Wendy Hunter and Robert Brill, "'Documents, Please:' Advances in Social Protection and Birth Certification in the Developing World," *World Politics* vol. 68, no. 2, (April 2016): 191–228.

[10]Janice Perlman, *Favela: Four Decades of Living on the Edge in Rio de Janeiro* (Oxford University Press, 2010).

[11]Jeffry A. Frieden, *Debt, Development, and Democracy: Modern Political Economy and Latin America, 1965–1985* (Princeton, NJ: Princeton University Press, 1991), pp. 54–65.

[12]David Samuels, *Ambition, Federalism, and Legislative Politics in Brazil* (New York: Cambridge University Press, 2003).

[13]Peter B. Evans, "Predatory, Developmental, and Other Apparatuses: A Comparative Political Economy Perspective on the Third World State," *Sociological Forum*, vol. 4, no. 4 (1989), 561–587.

[14]See Samuels, *Ambition, Federalism, and Legislative Politics in Brazil.*

[15]Alfred P. Montero, *Shifting States in Global Markets: Subnational Industrial Policy in Contemporary Brazil and Spain* (University Park: Pennsylvania State University Press, 2002).

[16]Judith Tendler, *Good Government in the Tropics* (Baltimore: Johns Hopkins University Press, 1997).

[17]Amnesty International, *You Killed My Son: Homicides by Military Police in the City of Rio de Janeiro* (London and Rio: Amnesty International, 2015).

[18]Ben Ross Schneider, *Politics within the State: Elite Bureaucrats and Industrial Policy in Authoritarian Brazil* (Pittsburgh: University of Pittsburgh Press, 1991).

[19]Timothy J. Power, *The Political Right in Postauthoritarian Brazil: Elites, Institutions, and Democratization* (University Park: Pennsylvania State University Press, 2000).

[20]Terrence Turner, "Brazil: Indigenous Rights vs. Neoliberalism," *Dissent Magazine* (Summer 1996), https://www.dissentmagazine.org/article/brazil-indigenous-rights-vs-neoliberalism

Chapter 10

[1]Wayne A. Cornelius, "Nation-Building, Participation, and Distribution: The Politics of Social Reform Under Cárdenas," in Gabriel A. Almond, Scott Flanagan, and Robert J. Mundt (eds.), *Crisis, Choice and Change: Historical Studies of Political Development* (Boston: Little, Brown, 1973).

[2]Oscar Lewis, *The Children of Sánchez: Autobiography of a Mexican Family* (New York: Random House, 1961).

[3]Joe Foweraker and Ann L. Craig (eds.), *Popular Movements and Political Change in Mexico* (Boulder, CO: Lynne Rienner, 1989).

[4]Roger Hansen, *The Politics of Mexican Development* (Baltimore: Johns Hopkins University Press, 1971), p. 75.

[5]World Trade Organization, *Trade Profiles: Mexico*, http://stat.wto.org/CountryProfile/WSDBCountryPFView.aspx?Language=E&Country=MX.

[6]Timothy A. Wise, "Agricultural Dumping Under NAFTA: Estimating the Costs of U.S. Agricultural Policies to Mexican Producers," *Mexican Rural Development Research Report No. 7* (Washington, DC: Woodrow Wilson International Center for Scholars, 2010).

[7]Jorge G. Castañeda, *Perpetuating Power: How Mexican Presidents Were Chosen* (New York: New Press, 2000).

[8]Daniel Levy and Gabriel Székely, *Mexico: Paradoxes of Stability and Change* (Boulder, CO: Westview Press, 1983), p. 100.

[9]Luis Carlos Ugalde, *The Mexican Congress: Old Player, New Power* (Washington, DC: Center for International and Strategic Studies, 2000).

[10]Susan Eckstein (ed.), *Power and Popular Protest: Latin American Social Movements* (Berkeley: University of California Press, 1989).

[11]Chapell H. Lawson, *Building the Fourth Estate: Democratization and the Rise of a Free Press in Mexico* (Berkeley: University of California Press, 2002).

Chapter 11

[1]David Welsh, *The Rise and Fall of Apartheid* (Charlottesville: University of Virginia Press, 2009), pp. 67–85.

[2]Andrew Nash, "Mandela's Democracy," *Monthly Review* (April 1999): 18–28.

[3]Most statistics used in this chapter are from the official census agency, *Statistics South Africa*. Its three monthly *Labour Force Surveys* enable comparisons over time.

[4]Servaas van der Berg, "Current poverty and income-distribution in the context of South African history," *Economic History of Developing Regions,* vol. 26, no.1, (2011): pp. 120–140.

[5]Pieter Fourie, *The Political Management of HIV and AIDS in South Africa* (Basingstoke: Palgrave-Macmillan, 2006), 50–64.

[6]Terence Moll, "Did the Apartheid Economy fail?" *Journal of Southern African Studies,* vol. 17, no. 2 (1991): 289–291.

[7]Neta Crawford and Audie Klotz, *How Sanctions Work: Lessons from South Africa* (New York: St Martin's Press, 1999).

[8]Antony Altbeker, *A Country at War with Itself: South Africa's Crisis of Crime* (Johannesburg: Jonathan Ball, 2007), 142–143.

[9]Andrew Feinstein, *After the Party: Corruption, the ANC and South Africa's Uncertain Future* (London and New York: Verso, 2009), 180–184.

[10]Richard Calland, *The Zuma Years: South Africa's Changing Face of Power* (Cape Town: Zebra Press, 2013), 139–149.

[11]Robert Mattes, "Public Opinion since 1994" in Jessica Piombo and Liz Nijzink, eds., *Electoral Politics in South Africa: Assessing the First Democratic Decade* (New York: Palgrave-Macmillan, 2005), p. 55.

[12]Setumo Stone, "DA not creating home-grown members," *Business Day* (Johannesburg), November 5, 2012.

[13]Mandla Zuma, "Zille told: We will defend Zuma's home," *Sunday Times* (Johannesburg), November 4, 2012.

[14]Frans Cronje, "Race: What South Africans Really Think," *Politicsweb*, February 26, 2016, http://www.politicsweb.co,za/news-and-analysis/race-what-south-africans-really-think

[15]Multi-Level Government Initiative, Service Delivery Barometer, Community Law Centre, University of the Western Cape, 2012, http://www.mlgi.org.za/baromters/service-delivery-protest-barometer

[16]Susan Booysen, *The African National Congress and the Regeneration of Political Power* (Johannesburg: Wits University Press, 2011) p. 485.

[17]"Volunteer Statistics in South Africa," *The Star* (Johannesburg), December 11, 2004.

[18]Jeffrey Lewis, "Assessing the Demographic and Economic Impact of HIV/AIDS," in Kyle Dean Kaufmann and David L. Lindauer, eds., *AIDS and South Africa: The Social Expression of a Pandemic* (Basingstoke, UK: Palgrave Macmillan, 2004), p. 111.

[19]Ryland Fisher, "The ANC and South Africa's Youth Vote," *SA Reconciliation Barometer Blog*, Institute for Justice and Reconciliation, Cape Town, January 21, 2013.

Chapter 12

[1]Obafemi Awolowo, *Path to Nigerian Freedom* (London: Faber and Faber, 1947), pp. 47–48.

[2]Billy Dudley, *An Introduction to Nigerian Government and Politics* (Bloomington: Indiana University Press, 1982), p. 71.

[3]Michael J. Watts, *State, Oil and Agriculture in Nigeria* (Berkeley: University of California Press, 1987), p. 71.

[4]Tom Forrest, *Politics and Economic Development in Nigeria,* 2d ed. (Boulder, CO: Westview Press, 1995), pp. 207–212.

[5]Pat A. Williams, "Women and the Dilemma of Politics in Nigeria," in Crawford Young and Paul Beckett, eds., *Dilemmas of Democracy in Nigeria* (Rochester, NY: University of Rochester Press, 1997), pp. 219–241.

[6]Rotimi Suberu, *Federalism and Ethnic Conflict in Nigeria* (Washington, DC: U.S. Institute of Peace, 2001), pp. 119–120.

[7]Richard Joseph, *Democracy and Prebendal Politics in Nigeria: The Rise and Fall of the Second Republic* (Cambridge, UK: Cambridge University Press, 1987).

[8]Henry Bienen, *Armies and Parties in Africa* (New York: Africana Publishing, 1978), pp. 193–211.

[9]Babafemi Badejo, "Party Formation and Party Competition," in Larry Diamond, Anthony Kirk-Greene, and Oyeleye Oyediran, eds., *Transition without End: Nigerian Politics and Civil Society under Babangida* (Boulder, CO: Lynne Rienner Publishers, 1997), p. 179.

[10]Eghosa Osaghae, *Crippled Giant: Nigeria since Independence* (Bloomington: Indiana University Press 1999), pp. 233–239.

[11]Peter M. Lewis, Barnett Rubin, and Pearl Robinson, *Stabilizing Nigeria: Pressures, Incentives, and Support for Civil Society* (New York: Council on Foreign Relations, 1998), p. 87.

[12]Rotimi Suberu, *Public Policies and National Unity in Nigeria*, Research Report No. 19 (Ibadan: Development Policy Centre, 1999), pp. 9–10.

[13]Sayre Schatz, "'Pirate Capitalism' and the Inert Economy of Nigeria," *Journal of Modern African Studies* 22, no. 1 (March 1984): 45–57.

[14]See Terry Lynn Karl, *The Paradox of Plenty* (Berkeley: University of California Press, 1997); and Michael Ross, "The Political Economy of the Resource Curse," *World Politics* 51 (January 1999), 297–322.

Chapter 13

[1]State Statistical Service of the Russian Federation, http://www.gks.ru/wps/wcm/connect/rosstat_main /rosstat/ru/statistics/population/demography/

[2]The Economist Intelligence Unit, *Country Profile Russia* (London, 2008), pp. 49–50; *Country Report Russia*, January 2015, p. 11.

[3]Transparency International, http://www.transparency .org/news/feature/corruption_perceptions _index_2016

[4]World Bank, "Russian Economic Report," no. 36, November 9, 2016, http://www.worldbank.org/en /country/russia/publication/rer

[5]Government Decisions, http://government.ru/en /docs/23015/.

[6]Jan Burck, Franziska Marten, and Christoph Bals, *The Climate Change Performance Index: Results 2017* (Bonn: Germanwatch, 2014), p. 34, https://germanwatch.org /en/download/16484.pdf

[7]Russian Statistical Agency, *Torgovlia v Rossii: Ofitsial'noe izdanie*, Moscow, 2015, p. 171, http://www.gks.ru /free_doc/doc_2015/torg15.pdf

[8]Russian statistical agency, http://trade.ec.europa.eu /doclib/docs/2006/september/tradoc_122530.02 .2017.pdf

[9]European Commission, http://trade.ec.europa.eu /doclib/docs/2006/september/tradoc_122530.02.2017 .pdf, http://ec.europa.eu/trade/policy/countries-and -regions/countries/russia/

[10]Federal State Statistical Service, http://www.gks.ru /wps/wcm/connect/rosstat_main/rosstat/ru/statistics /state/; Mikhail Zherebtsov, "Public Administration Reform and Building of the 'Vertical of Power'" in *Russia: Exploring Incommensurablity*, PhD dissertation, Carleton University, Ottawa Canada, 2014, pp. 164, 335.

[11]*EBRD Transition Report*, 2006.

[12]Stockholm International Peace Research Institute, SIPRI Military Expenditures Database, https://www .sipri.org/sites/default/files/Milex-share-of-GDP.pdf

[13]VTsIOM, "Armiia Rossii: boegotovnost', sposobnost' zashchitit' stranu, vliianie na obshchestvo i ekonomiku," *Press-vypusk* no. 3287, January 17, 2017, https://wciom .ru/index.php?id=236&uid=116030

[14]"Vserossiiskaia politicheskaia partiia 'Edinaia Rossiia'. Dos'e," *TASS*, 4 February 2016, updated 27 June 2016, http://tass.ru/info/2640831

[15]"Est' li grafa 'protiv vsekh' v biulleteniakh na vyborakh v gosdumu 2016 goda?" *Komsomol'skaia pravda*, July 29, 2016, http://www.kp.ru/daily/26565/3581857/

[16]Vladimir Putin, Novgorod oblast, Sept 19, 2013, http://russialist.org/transcript-putin-at-meeting-of-the -valdai-international-discussion-club-partial-transcript/

[17]Russian State Statistical Agency, http://www.gks.ru /bgd/free/B04_03/IssWWW.exe/Stg/d01/8.htm

[18]Reporters Without Borders, World Press Freedom Index 2016, https://rsf.org/en/ranking

[19]Levada Center, "Rossiiane o SMI," February 18, 2014, http://www.levada.ru/2014/02/28/rossiyane -o-smi/ ; and " Doverie SMI i tsenzura," November 18, 2016, http://www.levada.ru/2016/11/18/doverie -smi-i-tsenzura/

[20]"Auditoriia internet i rezervy rosta," Yandex, Spring 2016, https://yandex.ru/company/researches/2016/ya _internet_regions_2016#auditorijainternetairezervyrosta

Chapter 14

[1]British Financial Adviser to the Foreign Office in Tehran, *Documents on British Foreign Policy, 1919–39,* First Series, XIII (London: Her Majesty's Stationery Office, 1963), pp. 720, 735.

[2]M. Bazrgan, "Letter to the Editor," *Ettela'at*, February 7, 1980.

[3]*Iran Times*, January 12, 1979.

[4]Cited in H. Amirahmadi, *Revolution and Economic Transition* (Albany: State University of New York Press, 1960), p. 201.

[5]International Labor Organization, "Employment and Income Policies for Iran" (unpublished report, Geneva, 1972), Appendix C, 6.

[6]U.S. Congress, *Economic Consequences of the Revolution in Iran*, p. 5.

[7]Cited in *Iran Times*, July 9, 1993.

[8]J. Amuzegar, *Iran's Economy under the Islamic Republic* (London: Taurus Press, 1994), p. 100.

[9]A. Rafsanjani, "The Islamic Consultative Assembly," *Kayhan*, May 23, 1987.

[10]S. Saffari, "The Legitimation of the Clergy's Right to Rule in the Iranian Constitution of 1979," *British Journal of Middle Eastern Studies* 20, no. 1 (1993): pp. 64–81.

[11]Ayatollah Montazeri, *Ettela'at*, October 8, 1979.

[12]O. Fallaci, "Interview with Khomeini," *New York Times Magazine*, October 7, 1979.

Chapter 15

[1]Timothy Brook, *Quelling the People: The Military Suppression of the Beijing Democracy Movement* (Stanford, CA: Stanford University Press, 1999), p. 129.

[2]"Report on an Investigation of the Peasant Movement in Hunan Province," *Selected Works of Mao Zedong*, Vol. 1 (Beijing: Foreign Languages Press, 1965), p. 23.

[3]"Restore Agricultural Production," *Selected Works of Deng Xiaoping (1938–1965)* (Beijing: Foreign Languages Press, 1984), p. 293.

[4]Martin King Whyte, "China's Dormant and Active Social Volcanoes," *China Journal*, 75(2016), pp. 9–37.

[5]Isabelle Attané, "Being a Woman in China Today: A Demography of Gender," *China Perspectives*, 4(2012), pp. 5–15.

[6]Katherine Morton, "Environmental Policy," in William A. Joseph, ed., *Politics in China: An Introduction*, 2nd ed. (New York: Oxford University Press, 2014), p. 360.

[7]Sharon Chen, "Manufacturing wages in Indonesia, Vietnam, and the Philippines will rise quickly, while staying well below China's," *Bloomberg.com*, April 5, 2015.

[8]Richard McGregor, *The Party: The Secret World of China's Communist Rulers* (New York: HarperCollins, 2012), p. 72.

[9]John P. Burns, *The Chinese Communist Party's Nomenklatura System: A Documentary Study of Party Control of Leadership Selection, 1979–1984* (Armonk, NY: M. E. Sharpe, 1989), pp. ix–x.

[10]Peter Mattis, "The Analytic Challenge of Understanding Chinese Intelligence Services," *Studies in Intelligence*, Vol. 56, No. 3 (2012), Central Intelligence Agency, p. 1.

[11]See Kenneth Lieberthal and Michel Oksenberg, *Policy Making in China: Leaders, Structures, and Processes* (Princeton, NJ: Princeton University Press, 1988); and Andrew Mertha, "'Fragmented Authoritarianism 2.0': Political Pluralization in the Chinese Policy Process," *China Quarterly*, 200(December 2009), pp. 995–1012.

[12]James D. Seymour, *China's Satellite Parties* (Armonk, NY: M. E. Sharpe, 1987), p. 87.

[13]Nicholas D. Kristof, "China Sees 'Market-Leninism' as Way to Future," *New York Times*, September 6, 1993, http://www.nytimes.com/1993/09/06/world/china-sees -market-leninism-as-way-to-future.html?pagewanted=all.

[14]Guobin Yang, "Internet and Civil Society," in William Tay and Alvin So, eds., *Handbook of Contemporary China* (Singapore: World Scientific, 2011), p. 443.

[15]"China's Predicament: 'Getting Old before Getting Rich,' " *The Economist*, June 25, 2009, http://www .economist.com/node/13888069.

[16]Harry Harding, *China's Second Revolution: Reform After Mao* (Washington, DC: Brookings Institution, 1987), p. 200.

[17]Nicholas Lardy, "Is China Different? The Fate of Its Economic Reform," in Daniel Chirot (ed.), *The Crisis of Leninism and the Decline of the Left* (Seattle: University of Washington Press, 1991), p. 147.

Glossary

5 percent clause A party must get at least 5 percent of the "second votes" for its candidates to get seats in the *Bundestag* (or the state parliaments) as a party. This rule depresses votes for "splinter" parties unlikely to meet this threshold.

A

abertura In Brazil, *abertura* (as it is known in Portuguese; *aperture* in Spanish) refers to the period of authoritarian liberalization begun in 1974 when the military allowed civilian politicians to compete for political office in the context of a more open political society.

accommodation An informal agreement or settlement between the government and important interest groups in response to the interest groups' concerns about policy or program benefits.

accountability A government's responsibility to its population, usually by periodic popular elections, by transparent fiscal practices, and by the legislature having the power to dismiss the government by impeachment or passing a motion of no confidence. In a political system characterized by accountability, the major actions taken by government must be known and understood by the citizenry.

acephalous societies Literally "headless" societies. A number of traditional Nigerian societies, such as the Igbo in the precolonial period, lacked executive rulership as we have come to conceive of it. Instead, these villages and clans were governed by committee or consensus.

administrative guidance Informal advice given by a government agency to a private organization, such as a firm, Critics charge that this is a disguised form of collusion between a government agency and a private firm.

Africans This term, in South African usage, refers to Bantu language speakers, the demographic majority of South African citizens.

Afrikaners Descendants of Dutch, French, German, and Scots settlers speaking Afrikaans. They were politically mobilized as an ethnic group throughout the twentieth century.

Amakudari A widespread practice, known as "descent from heaven," for public service retirees to take jobs in public corporations or private firms with which their office has or recently had close ties.

ancien régime The monarchical regime that ruled France until the Revolution of 1789, when it was toppled by a popular uprising.

anticlericalism Opposition to the power of churches or clergy in politics. In countries such as France and Mexico, this opposition has focused on the role of the Catholic Church in politics.

apartheid A term in Afrikaans meaning "separateness." It was first used in 1929 to describe Afrikaner nationalist proposals for strict racial separation and "to ensure the safety of the white race."

Articles of Confederation The first governing document of the United States, agreed to in 1777 and ratified in 1781. The Articles concentrated most powers in the states and made the national government dependent on voluntary contributions of the states.

Assembly of Experts Group that nominates and can remove the Leader. The assembly is elected by the general electorate, but almost all of its members are clerics. A term for the intermingling of Islam with politics and often used as a substitute for Islamic fundamentalism.

austerity policies Spending cuts, layoffs, and wage decreases meant to address budget problems.

authoritarian A system of rule in which power depends not on popular legitimacy, but on the coercive force of the political authorities.

authoritarian regime A form of government in which power is highly concentrated at the top, political freedom is limited, and those with authority are not accountable to those they govern.

autocracy A government in which one ruler or a few rulers has absolute power—thus, a dictatorship.

autonomous region A territorial unit that is equivalent to a province and contains a large concentration of ethnic minorities. These regions, for example, Tibet, have some autonomy in the cultural sphere but in most policy matters are strictly subordinate to the central government.

ayatollah Literally, "sign of God." A high-ranking cleric in Iran.

B

balance of payments An indicator of international flow of funds that shows the excess or deficit in total payments of all kinds between or among countries. Included in the calculation are exports and imports, grants, and international debt payments.

Basic Law The 1949 proto-constitution of the Federal Republic, which continues to function today.

709

bazaar An urban marketplace where shops, workshops, small businesses, and export-importers are located.

bicameral A legislative body with two houses, such as the U.S. Senate and House of Representatives.

Bill of Rights The first ten amendments to the U.S. Constitution (ratified in 1791), which established limits on the actions of government. Initially, the Bill of Rights limited only the federal government. The Fourteenth Amendment and subsequent judicial rulings extended the provisions of the Bill of Rights to the states.

Blitzkrieg German battle tactics that began with aerial assaults to destroy enemy forces and infrastructure, followed quickly by a massive invasion of armored troops, with ordinary infantry mopping up resistance.

Boer Literally "farmer"; modern usage is a derogatory reference to an Afrikaner.

Brahmin The highest caste in the Hindu caste system.

bureaucracy An organization structured hierarchically, in which lower-level officials are charged with administering regulations codified in rules that specify impersonal, objective guidelines for making decisions.

bureaucratic authoritarianism (BA) A term developed by Argentine sociologist Guillermo O'Donnell to interpret the common characteristics of military-led authoritarian regimes in Brazil, Argentina, Chile, and Uruguay in the 1960s and 1970s. According to O'Donnell, bureaucratic authoritarian regimes led by the armed forces and key civilian allies emerged in these countries in response to severe economic crises.

bureaucratic rings A term developed by the Brazilian sociologist and president Fernando Henrique Cardoso that refers to the highly permeable and fragmented structure of the state bureaucracy that allows private interests to make alliances with midlevel bureaucratic officers. By shaping public policy to benefit these interests, bureaucrats gain the promise of future employment in the private sector.

C

cabinet The body of officials (e.g., ministers, secretaries) who direct executive departments presided over by the chief executive (e.g., prime minister or president).

cabinet government A system of government in which most executive power is held by the cabinet, headed by a prime minister.

caste system According to the Hindu religion, society is divided into castes. Membership in a caste is determined at birth. The different castes form a rough social and economic hierarchy.

caudillos Charismatic populist leaders, usually with a military background, who use patronage and draw upon personal loyalties to dominate a region or a nation.

causal theory An influential approach in comparative politics that involves trying to explain why "if X happens, then Y is the result."

Central Committee The top 370 or so leaders of the CCP. It meets annually for about two weeks and is charged with carrying on the business of the National Party Congress when it is not in session.

Central Military Commission (CMC) The most important military organization in the PRC, headed by the general secretary of the CCP, who is the commander-in-chief of the PLA.

centrally planned economy An economic system in which the state directs the economy through bureaucratic plans for the production and distribution of goods and services. The government, rather than the market, is the major influence on the economy. Also called a *command economy*.

chancellor An old German title now used by the German head of government and essentially the same as "prime minister."

checks and balances A governmental system of divided authority in which coequal branches can restrain each other's actions.

citizen action groups Nonparty and often single-issue initiative groups, who focus on concrete problems such as the environment, traffic, housing, or other social and economic issues.

Citizen initiative A clause in the Lisbon Treaty allowing citizens to propose referendums to initiate EU legislation, provided 1 million legal signatures have been obtained in a "significant number" of different EU member-states.

civil servants Employees of federal, state, and municipal governments.

civil society Refers to the space occupied by voluntary associations outside the state, for example, professional associations (lawyers, doctors, teachers), trade unions, student and women's groups, religious bodies, and other voluntary association groups.

clientelism An informal aspect of policy-making in which a powerful patron (for example, a traditional local boss, government agency, or dominant political party) offers resources such as land, contracts, protection, jobs, or other resources in return for the support and services (such as labor or votes) of lower-status and less powerful clients. Corruption, preferential treatment, and inequality are characteristic of clientelist politics.

clientelistic networks Informal systems of asymmetrical power in which a powerful patron (e.g., the president, prime minister, or governor) offers less powerful clients resources, benefits, or career advantages in return for support, loyalty, or services.

codetermination The legal right of representatives of employees to elect representatives to help determine the direction of the company in which they work.

cohabitation The term used by the French to describe the situation when a president and prime minister belong to opposing political coalitions.

Cold War The hostile relations that prevailed between the United States and the Soviet Union from the late 1940s until the demise of the latter in 1991.

collective identities The groups with which people identify, including gender, class, race, region, and religion, and which are the "building blocks" for social and political action.

collective leadership A type of political decision-making in which major decisions are reached by consensus or voting among top leaders even when one of those leaders may have more power and influence than the others.

collectivization A process undertaken in the Soviet Union under Stalin from 1929 into the early 1930s, and in China under Mao in the 1950s, by which agricultural land was removed from private ownership and organized into large state and collective farms.

Common Foreign and Security Policy (CFSP) The Maastricht Treaty's commitment to deeper EU cooperation in international affairs and defense.

communism According to Marxism, the stage of development that follows socialism and in which all property is publically owned, economic production is coordinated for the common good, and a radical degree of equality has been achieved.

communist party-state A type of nation-state in which a communist party exercises a complete monopoly on political power and controls all important state institutions.

Community Method The EU method of making decisions in which the European Commission proposes, the Council of Ministers and EP decide, and the EUCJ reviews European law.

comparative politics The field within political science that focuses on domestic politics of countries and analyzes patterns of similarity and difference among countries.

comparativist A political scientist who studies the similarities and differences in the domestic politics of various countries.

conservative The belief that existing political, social, and economic arrangements should be preserved.

consolidated democracy A democratic political system that has been solidly and stably established for an ample period of time and in which there is relatively consistent adherence to core democratic principles.

constitutional monarchy A system of government in which the head of state ascends by heredity but is limited in powers and constrained by the provisions of a constitution.

constructive vote of no confidence This measure requires the *Bundestag* to elect a new chancellor by an absolute majority in order to oust the current one.

corporatist state A state in which interest groups become an institutionalized part of the state structure.

Corruption Perceptions Index A measure developed by Transparency International that ranks countries in terms of the degree to which corruption is perceived to exist among public officials and politicians.

country A territory defined by boundaries generally recognized in international law as constituting an independent nation.

coup d'état A forceful, extra-constitutional action resulting in the removal of an existing government.

critical juncture An important historical event when political actors make critical choices that shape institutions and future outcomes in both individual countries and the international system.

D

Dalits The lowest caste in India's caste system, whose members are among the poorest and most disadvantaged Indians. The term

dalit means oppressed. It is widely used today in preference to the terms "scheduled castes" or "untouchables."

decentralization Policies that aim to transfer some governmental decision-making power from higher to lower levels of government.

Declaration of Independence The document asserting that the British colonies in what is now the United States declared themselves independent from Great Britain. The Declaration of Independence was signed in Philadelphia on July 4, 1776.

democracy From the Greek *demos* (the people) and *kratos* (rule), a political system featuring selection to public offices through free and fair elections; the right of all adults to vote, political parties that are free to compete in elections, government that operates by fair and relatively open procedures, political rights and civil liberties, an independent judiciary (court system), and civilian control of the military.

democratic centralism A system of political organization developed by Vladimir Lenin and practiced, with modifications, by most communist party-states. Its principles include a hierarchical party structure.

democratic corporatism A bargaining system in which important policies are established and often carried out with the participation of trade unions and business associations.

democratic transition The process of a state moving from an authoritarian to a democratic political system.

democratization Transition from authoritarian rule to a democratic political order.

dependent variable The variable symbolized by Y in the statement that "If X happens, then Y will be the result;" in other words, the dependent variable is the outcome of X (the independent variable).

deregulation The process of dismantling state regulations that govern business activities.

developmentalism An ideology and practice in Latin America during the 1950s in which the state played a leading role in seeking to foster economic development through sponsoring vigorous industrial policy.

developmental state A nation-state in which the government carries out policies that effectively promote national economic growth.

developmental state patrimonial state A system of governance in which the ruler treats the state as personal property (patrimony).

dictatorship A form of government in which power and political control are concentrated in one ruler or a few rulers who have concentrated and nearly absolute power.

distributional politics The use of power, particularly by the state, to allocate valued resources among competing groups.

distributive policies Policies that allocate state resources into an area that lawmakers perceive needs to be promoted. For example, leaders today believe that students should have access to the Internet. In order to accomplish this goal, telephone users are being taxed to provide money for schools to establish connections to the Internet.

dominant party A political party that manages to maintain consistent control of a political system through formal and informal mechanisms of power, with or without strong support from the population.

dual-use technologies Technology normally used for civilian purposes, but which may have military applications.

dual society A society and economy that are sharply divided into a traditional, usually poorer, and a modern, usually richer, sector. There are also significant inequalities within the traditional and modern sectors.

E

Economic and Monetary Union (EMU) The 1991 Maastricht Treaty federalization of EU monetary policy, creating the European Central Bank (ECB), the Eurozone, and the euro.

Economic Community of West African States (ECOWAS) A West African regional organization, including fifteen member countries from Cape Verde in the west to Nigeria and Niger in the east.

economic deregulation The lifting or relaxation of government controls over the economy, including the reduction of import taxes and the phasing out of subsidized prices.

economic liberalization The removal of government control and regulation over private enterprise.

Economist Intelligence Unit Democracy Index An index compiled by the Economist Intelligence Unit (EIU), based in the United Kingdom, that measures and rank the state of democracy in 167 countries. It classifies the world's states as Full Democracies, Flawed Democracies, Hybrid Regimes, and Authoritarian Regimes.

ejido Land granted by Mexican government to an organized group of peasants.

Emergency (1975–1977) The period when Indian Prime Minister Indira Gandhi suspended many formal democratic rights and ruled in an authoritarian manner.

Energiewende A policy to shift German energy consumption from fossil fuels and nuclear to sustainable sources such as wind, solar, hydro, and biomass.

Environmental Performance Index Developed by Yale University and Columbia University, a measure of how close countries come to meeting specific benchmarks for national pollution control and natural resource management.

European Central Bank The ECB is the institutional center of the EMU and the Eurozone, located in Frankfurt, Germany. Statutorily independent from politics and having a powerful president, it decides Eurozone monetary policy to produce price stability and economic convergence, enforces EMU rules, and governs EMU exchange rates.

European Commission The EU executive, with a monopoly on proposing EU legislation and overseeing its implementation as "guardian of the treaties."

European Council The EU institution that devises general strategies; made up of member-state heads of state that meets at least twice annually.

European single market The official title of the EU's barrier-free economic space created after 1985.

European Union Court of Justice (EUCJ) Originally called the Court of Justice, the EU supreme court that decides the legality of EU legislation and its implementation.

Eurozone The nineteen EU members who share a common currency, the euro. Of the nine remaining EU members, all but Denmark (opt-out) and the UK (leaving EU) are obliged to join the Eurozone.

executive The agencies of government that implement or execute policy. The chief executive, such as a prime minister or president, also plays a key policy-making role.

Expediency Council A committee set up in Iran to resolve differences between the *Majles* (parliament) and the Guardian Council.

export-led growth Economic growth generated by the export of a country's commodities. Export-led growth can occur at an early stage of economic development, in which case it involves primary products, such as the country's mineral resources, timber, and agricultural products; or at a later stage, when industrial goods and services are exported.

F

failed state a country whose political or economic system has become so weak that the government is no longer in control.

Farsi The Persian word for the Persian language. Fars is a province in south Iran.

favelas A Portuguese-language term for the shantytowns that ring many of the main cities in Brazil. The *favelas* emerge where people invade unused land and build domiciles before the authorities can remove them. Unfinished public housing projects can also become the sites of *favelas. They* expanded after the 1970s as a response to the inadequate supply of homes in urban centers to meet the demand caused by increasing rural to urban migration.

Federal Reserve Board The United States central bank established by Congress in 1913 to regulate the banking industry and the money supply. Although the president appoints the chair of the board of governors (with Senate approval), the board operates largely independently.

federal system A political structure in which subnational units have significant independent powers; the powers of each level are usually specified in the federal constitution

federalism A system of governance in which political authority is shared between the national government and regional or state governments. The powers of each level of government are usually specified in a federal constitution.

floating population Migrants from the rural areas who have moved to the cities to find employment.

foreign direct investment (FDI) Ownership of or investment in cross-border enterprises in which the investor plays a direct managerial role.

Foundation of the Oppressed A clerically controlled foundation set up after the revolution in Iran.

framework regulations Laws that set broad parameters for economic behavior but that require subsequent elaboration, often through formal agreements between employers and employees.

free market A system in which government regulation of the economy is limited.

Fukushima nuclear disaster On March 11, 2011, a magnitude 9 undersea earthquake off the Pacific coast of Fukushima Prefecture triggered a series of tsunami waves of monstrous heights, which in turn caused reactor meltdowns at a local nuclear power plant, as well as destruction of a dozen towns and villages and the deaths of nearly 19,000 people.

fundamentalism A term used to describe extremist or ultraorthodox religious beliefs and movements.

fusion of powers A constitutional principle that merges the authority of branches of government, in contrast to the principle of separation of powers.

G

Gastarbeiter (guest workers) Workers who were recruited to join the German labor force in the 1960s and early 1970s, generally from Italy, Yugoslavia, and especially Turkey.

general secretary The formal title of the head of the CCP. From 1942 to 1982, the position was called "chairman" and was held by Mao Zedong until his death in 1976.

glasnost Gorbachev's policy of "openness," which involved an easing of controls on the media, arts, and public discussion.

Global Gender Gap A measure developed by the World Economic Forum of the extent to which women in 58 countries have achieved equality with men.

globalization The intensification of worldwide interconnectedness associated with the increased speed and magnitude of cross-border flows of trade, investment and finance, and processes of migration, cultural diffusion, and communication.

grand coalition A government made up of the two largest parties, often in response to outsider parties deemed unfit for governing.

grandes écoles Prestigious and highly selective schools of higher education in France that train top civil servants, engineers, and business executives.

grands corps Elite networks of graduates of *grandes écoles*.

green revolution A strategy for increasing agricultural (especially food) production, involving improved seeds, irrigation, and abundant use of fertilizers.

gross domestic product (GDP) The total of all goods and services produced within a country that is used as a broad measure of the size of its economy.

gross national product (GNP) GDP plus income earned by the country's residents; another broad measure of the size of an economy.

Guardian Council A committee created in the Iranian constitution to oversee the *Majles* (the parliament).

guerrilla warfare A military strategy based on small, highly mobile bands of soldiers (the guerrillas, from the Spanish word for war, *guerra*) who use hit-and-run tactics like ambushes to attack a better-armed enemy.

guild system The right of craftsmen to control who can learn, enter, and practice their craft.

H

health insurance fund A semipublic institution that administers insurance contributions from employees and employers and thus pays for health care for covered participants.

hegemonic power A state that can control the pattern of alliances and terms of the international order and often shapes domestic political developments in countries throughout the world.

Hezbollahis Literally "partisans of God." In Iran, the term is used to describe religious vigilantes. In Lebanon, it is used to describe the Shi'i militia.

hojjat al-Islam Literally, "the proof of Islam." In Iran, it means a medium-ranking cleric.

homelands Areas reserved for exclusive African occupation, established through the 1913 and 1936 land legislation and later developed as ethnic states during the apartheid era.

household registration (*hukou*) In China, the system that registers each citizen as entitled to work and to live in a specific urban or rural location.

household responsibility system The system put into practice in China beginning in the early 1980s in which the major decisions about agricultural production are made by individual farmers based on the profit motive rather than by local officials.

Human Development Index (HDI) A composite number used by the United Nations Development Programme (UNDP) to measure and compare levels of achievement in health, knowledge, and standard of living.

hung parliament A situation after an election when no single party comprises a majority in the Commons.

hybrid state A country whose political systems exhibit some democratic and some authoritarian elements.

I

illiberal democracy A state where the government has been brought to power (and perhaps reelected) by democratic election, but then takes steps to seriously limit political competition, undermine the rule of law, and deprive citizens of their basic rights.

Imam Jum'ehs Prayer leaders in Iran's main urban mosques.

import substitution industrialization (ISI) Strategy for industrialization based on domestic manufacture of previously imported goods to satisfy domestic market demands.

independent variable The variable symbolized by X in the statement that "If X happens, then Y will be the result;" in other words, the independent variable is a cause of Y (the dependent variable).

Glossary

Indian Administrative Service (IAS) India's civil service, a highly professional and talented group of administrators who run the Indian government on a day-to-day basis.

Indian Rebellion An armed uprising in 1857 by Indian soldiers against expansion of British colonialism in India.

indicative planning A term that describes a national plan identifying desirable priorities for economic and social development, as well as the measures needed to promote this development.

indigenous groups Population descended from the original inhabitants of the Americas, present prior to the Spanish Conquest.

indirect rule A term used to describe the British style of colonialism in Nigeria and India, in which local traditional rulers and political structures were surrogates of the colonial governing structure.

industrial policy A policy that uses state resources to promote the development of particular economic sectors.

Industrial Revolution A period of rapid and destabilizing social, economic, and political changes caused by the introduction of large-scale factory production, originating in England in the middle of the eighteenth century.

influx control A system of controls that regulated African movement between towns and the countryside, enforcing residence in the homelands and restricting Africans' choice of employment.

informal economy That portion of the economy largely outside government control, in which employees work without contracts or benefits and employers do not comply with legal regulations or pay taxes. Examples of those working in the informal economy include casual employees in restaurants and hotels, street vendors, and day laborers in construction or agriculture.

insider privatization The transformation of formerly state-owned enterprises into private enterprises or other types of business entity in which majority control is in the hands of employees and/or managers.

institutional design The institutional arrangements that define the relationships between executive, legislative, and judicial branches of government and between the national government and subnational units, such as states in the United States.

Institutional triangle A term signifying the interactions between the three most significant EU institutions: the Commission, the Council of Ministers, and the EP.

interest groups Organizations that seek to represent the interests of their members in dealings with the government. Important examples are associations representing people with specific occupations, business interests, racial and ethnic groups, or age groups in society.

international financial institutions (IFIs) This term generally refers to the International Bank for Reconstruction and Development (the World Bank) and the International Monetary Fund (IMF), but can also include other international lending institutions.

International Monetary Fund (IMF) The International Monetary Fund (IMF) is a global institution whose mandate is to "foster global monetary cooperation, secure financial stability, facilitate international trade, promote high employment and sustainable economic growth, and reduce poverty." It has been particularly active in helping countries that are experiencing serious financial problems. In exchange for IMF financial or technical assistance, a country must agree to conditions and policies that promote economic liberalization.

interventionist An interventionist state acts vigorously to shape the performance of major sectors of the economy.

interventores In Brazil, allies of Getúlio Vargas (1930–1945, 1950–1952), who were chosen by the dictator during his first period of rulership to replace opposition governors in most states. The *interventores* represented a shift of power from subnational government to the central state.

iron rice bowl A feature of China's socialist economy during the Maoist era (1949–1976) that provided guarantees of lifetime employment, income, and basic cradle-to-grave benefits to most urban and rural workers.

iron triangle A term coined by scholars of U.S. politics to refer to the relationships of mutual support formed by particular government agencies, members of congressional committees or subcommittees, and interest groups in various policy areas. Adapted by scholars of Japanese politics, the term refers to similar relationships formed among Japanese ministry or agency officials, Diet members, and special interest groups.

Islamism The use of Islam as a political ideology. Similar to political Islam and Islamic fundamentalism.

J

Japan Self-Defense Forces (JSDF) Inaugurated in Japan as a police reserve with 75,000 recruits in August 1950, following the outbreak of the Korean War. Today, it consists of approximately 250,000 troops equipped with sophisticated modern weapons.

jihad Literally "struggle." Although often used to mean armed struggle against unbelievers, it can also mean to fight against sociopolitical corruption or to struggle for spiritual self-improvement.

judicial review The capacity of a high court to nullify actions by the executive and legislative branches of government that in its judgment violate the constitution.

judiciary The political institutions in a country responsible for the administration of justice, and in some countries, for determining the constitutionality of state decisions.

jurist's guardianship Khomeini's concept that the Iranian clergy should rule on the grounds that they are the divinely appointed guardians of both the law and the people.

Justice and Home Affairs (JHA) Changes in the Maastricht Treaty to allow free movement of EU citizens throughout the union's member-states.

K

keiretsu A group of close-knit Japanese firms that have preferential business relationships and, often, interlocking business relationships and stock-sharing arrangements.

Keynesianism Named after British economist John Maynard Keynes, an approach to economic policy in which state policies are used to regulate the economy to achieve stable economic growth.

koenkai A candidate's personal campaign organization, normally based on a network of his or her relatives, friends, fellow alumni, coworkers, and their acquaintances. An effective *koenkai* is expensive to maintain and conducive to political corruption.

Kulturkampf Bismarck's fight with the Catholic Church over his desire to subordinate church to state.

L

laissez-faire A term taken from the French, which means "to let do," it refers to the pattern in which state management is limited to such matters as enforcing contracts and protecting property rights, while private market forces are free to operate with only minimal state regulation.

Lay Judge System (*saiban'in-seido***)** The quasi-jury system for trials of criminal cases introduced in May 2009. In each case, the guilt or innocence of the accused—and, if convicted, the sentence—are determined by a judicial panel composed of three professional judges and six laypersons.

Leader/Supreme Leader A cleric elected to be the head of the Islamic Republic of Iran.

leading small groups Ad hoc organizations that report to the CCP Politburo and Standing that have been created to coordinate policy-making and implementation across party-state agencies in the PRC.

legislature The political institutions in a country in which elected or appointed members are charged with responsibility for making laws and usually for authorizing the taxation and expenditure of the financial resources enabling the state to carry out its functions.

legitimacy A belief by powerful groups and the broad citizenry that a state exercises rightful authority.

liberal Basic citizenship rights of speech, assembly, petition, religion, and so forth.

liberal democracy A democratic system of government that officially recognizes and legally protects individual rights and freedoms and in which the exercise of political power is constrained by the rule of law.

Lisbon Treaty 2009 After a decade redesigning EU institutions to fit expansion to Central and Eastern Europe, the treaty created positions of the president of the European Council and the High Representative for Foreign and Security Policy, and increased the powers of the European Council and European Parliament (EP).

Lok Sabha The lower house of parliament in India, where all major legislation must pass before becoming law.

M

Maastricht Treaty A treaty ratified in 1993 giving the EU its present name, creating the EMU and CFSP, and granting the EP power to codecide EU legislation.

macroeconomic policy A policy intended to shape the overall economic system by concentrating on policy targets such as inflation and growth.

Majles The Iranian parliament, from the Arabic term for "assembly."

Mandal Commission A government-appointed commission headed by B. P. Mandal to consider seat reservations and quotas to redress caste discrimination.

manifest destiny The public philosophy in the nineteenth century stating that the United States was not only entitled but also destined to occupy territory from the Atlantic to the Pacific.

maquiladoras Factories that produce goods for export, often located along the Mexico–U.S. border.

Marbury v. Madison The 1803 Supreme Court ruling that the federal courts inherently have the authority to review the constitutionality of laws passed by Congress and signed by the president—and can strike down a law that the Court judges to violate the Constitution. The ruling, initially used sparingly, gave the courts a central role in the system of checks and balances.

market reform A strategy of economic transformation that involves reducing the role of the state in managing the economy and increasing the role of market forces.

maslahat Arabic term for "expediency," "prudence," or "advisability," now used in Iran to refer to reasons of state or what is best for the Islamic Republic.

mass organization An organization in a communist party-state that represents the interests of a particular social group, such as workers or women, but which is controlled by the communist party.

mestizo A person of mixed white, indigenous, and sometimes African descent.

middle-level theory A theory that seeks to explain phenomena in a limited range of cases, such as countries with particular characteristics, such as parliamentary regimes, or particular types of political institution (such as political parties) or activities (such as protest).

migrant laborers Laborers who move to another location to take a job, often a low-paying, temporary one.

mixed electoral system A system of electoral representation in which a portion of the seats are selected in winner-take-all single-member districts, and a portion are allocated according to parties within multimember constituencies, roughly in proportion to the votes each party receives in a popular election.

mixed member system An electoral system in which about half of deputies are elected from direct constituencies and the other half are drawn from closed party lists. The *Bundestag*'s form of mixed member system is basically a variant of PR.

moderating power (*poder moderador***)** A term used in Brazilian politics to refer to the situation following the 1824 constitution in which the monarchy was supposed to act as a moderating power, among the executive, legislative, and judicial branches of government, arbitrating party conflicts, and fulfilling governmental responsibilities when nonroyal agents failed.

monetarism An approach to economic policy that assumes a natural rate of unemployment, determined by the labor market, and rejects the instruments of government spending to run budgetary deficits for stimulating the economy and creating jobs.

N

nation-state A distinct, politically defined territory in which the state and national identity (that is, a sense of solidarity and shared values based on being citizens of the same country) coincide.

nationalism An ideology seeking to create a nation-state for a particular community; a group identity associated with membership is such a political community. Nationalists often proclaim that their state and nation are superior to others.

nationalization The policy by which the state assumes ownership and operation of private companies.

National Party Congress The symbolically important meeting, held every 5 years for about 1 week, of about 2,100 delegates representatives of the CCP, who endorse policies and the allocation of leadership positions that have been determined beforehand by the party's much smaller executive bodies.

National People's Congress (NPC) The legislature of the PRC. It is under the control of the CCP and is not an independent branch of government.

Naxalite The Naxalite movement emerged as a breakaway faction of the CPM in West Bengal in 1967. It is a radical, often violent, extra-parliamentary movement.

Nazi A German abbreviation for the National Socialist German Workers' Party, the movement led by Hitler.

neoliberal A term used to describe government policies that aim to promote private enterprise by reducing government economic regulation, tax rates, and social spending. The term *liberal* in Europe usually refers to the protection of individual political and economic liberty; this is quite different from its meaning in the United States, where it refers to government policies to distribute resources to low-income groups.

neoliberalism A term used to describe government policies aiming to promote free competition among business firms within the market, including reduced governmental regulation and social spending.

netizens A combination of the words *Internet* and *citizen*, as in "citizen of the net." Particularly refers to those who use the Internet to express their political opinions.

nonaligned bloc Countries that refused to ally with either the United States or the USSR during the Cold War years.

nontariff barrier (NTB) A practice, such as import quotas, health and safety standards, packaging and labeling rules, and unique or unusual business practices, that is designed to limit foreign imports and protect domestic industries; a form of protectionism that does not use tariffs.

North American Free Trade Agreement (NAFTA) A treaty among the United States, Mexico, and Canada implemented on January 1, 1994, that largely eliminates trade barriers among the three nations.

O

oligarchs A small group of powerful and wealthy individuals who gained ownership and control of important sectors of Russia's economy in the context of privatization of state assets in the 1990s.

oligarchy A political system in which power is in the hands of only a few people.

Organization Department A department of the CCP that controls personnel decisions affecting a vast number of jobs in the government and other major institutions in the PRC.

Organization of Petroleum Exporting Countries (OPEC) An organization dedicated to achieving stability in the price of oil, avoiding price fluctuations, and generally furthering the interests of the member states.

Ostpolitik The policy developed by the SPD's Willy Brandt to promote contact and commerce with the Soviet Union and its communist allies during the Cold War.

other backward classes The middle or intermediary castes in India that have been accorded reserved seats in public education and employment since the early 1990s.

P

panchayats Elected bodies at the village, district, and state levels that have development and administrative responsibilities.

parastatals State-owned, or at least state-controlled, corporations, created to undertake a broad range of activities, from control and marketing of agricultural production to provision of banking services, operating airlines, and other transportation facilities and public utilities.

pariah state a nation considered to be an outcast in the international community and often subjected to isolation and various sanctions.

parity law A French law passed in 2000, following the adoption of a constitutional amendment in 1999, and subsequently extended, that directs political parties to nominate an equal number of men and women for many elections.

parliamentary democracy System of government in which the chief executive is answerable to the legislature and may be dismissed by it.

parliamentary sovereignty The doctrine that grants the legislature the power to make or overturn any law and permits no veto or judicial review.

party democracy The constitutional guarantee that political parties have a privileged place in German politics, including generous subsidies for building party organizations.

pasdaran Persian term for *guards*, used to refer to the army of Revolutionary Guards formed during Iran's Islamic Revolution.

pass laws Laws in apartheid South Africa that required Africans to carry identity books in which officials stamped the permits required for Africans to travel between the countryside and cities.

patrimonial state A system of governance in which the ruler treats the state as personal property (patrimony).

patronage system A political system in which government officials appoint loyal followers to positions rather than choosing people based on merit.

People of the Book The Muslim term for recognized religious minorities, such as Christians, Jews, and Zoroastrians.

People's Liberation Army (PLA) The combined armed forces of the PRC, which includes land, sea, air, and strategic missile forces.

personalist politicians Demagogic political leaders who use their personal charisma to mobilize their constituency.

police powers Powers that are traditionally held by the states to regulate public safety and welfare. Police powers are the form of interaction with government that citizens most often experience. Even with the growth in federal government powers in the twentieth century, police powers remain the primary responsibility of the states and localities.

Politburo The committee made up of the two dozen or so top leaders of the CCP.

political action committee (PAC) A narrow form of interest group that seeks to influence policy by making contributions to candidates and parties in U.S. politics.

Political culture Fundamental values, beliefs, and orientations that are held by the population of a country and that can affect the manner in which citizens view their government, participate in politics, or assess policies.

political economy The study of the interaction between the state and the economy in a country; that is, how politics influences the economy and how the organization and performance of the economy influence the political process.

political Islam A term for the intermingling of Islam with politics and often used as a substitute for Islamic fundamentalism.

politics of the governors In Brazil, this term refers to periods of history in which state governors acquire extraordinary powers over domains of policy that were previously claimed by the federal government. The term refers most commonly to the Old Republic and the current state of Brazilian federalism.

populism A style of mobilization by a political party or movement that seeks to gain popular support by emphasizing antiestablishment rhetoric, decrying elite concentrations of power as the source of national decline, and promising to be responsive to the needs of ordinary people.

pork-barrel politics A term originally used by scholars of American politics to refer to legislation that benefits particular legislators by funding public works and projects in their districts. More broadly, the term refers to preferential allocation of public funds and other resources to particular districts or regions so as to give electoral advantage to particular politicians or political parties.

power sharing Constitutional arrangements to ensure that the major political parties share executive authority. These can include mandatory coalitions and allocation of senior official positions between parties.

power vertical A term used by Vladimir Putin to describe a unified and hierarchical structure of executive power ranging from the national to the local level.

prebendalism Patterns of political behavior that rest on the justification that official state offices should be utilized for the personal benefit of officeholders, as well as of their support group or clients, particularly of the same ethnicity or religion.

predatory state A state in which those with political power prey on the people and the nation's resources to enrich themselves rather than using their power to promote national development.

predominant-party democracy A multiparty democratic political system in which one party or coalition of parties maintains a predominant position in parliament and control of government for a long period of time.

prefects French administrators appointed by the minister of the interior to coordinate state agencies and programs within France's territorial subdivisions known as *départements.*

privatization The sale of state-owned enterprises or services to private companies or investors.

procedural democracy A system with formal procedures for popular choice of government leaders (especially free party competition) but that may lack other democratic elements.

property taxes Taxes levied by local governments on the assessed value of property. Property taxes are the primary way in which local jurisdictions in the United States pay for primary and secondary education. Because the value of property varies dramatically from neighborhood to neighborhood, the funding available for public facilities like schools—and their quality—also varies from place to place.

proportional representation (PR) A procedure for electing representatives in which political parties sponsor rival lists of candidates within multimember constituencies. Seats are allotted to parties in proportion to the votes that a party's list receives in the district. By contrast, in a single-member district system, such as the one used in the United States and Britain, the party with the most votes in a given district (that is, a plurality) wins the seat, a procedure that favors larger parties and thus reduces the number of parties represented in parliament.

purchasing power parity (PPP) A method of calculating the value of a country's currency based on the actual cost of buying goods and services in that country rather than how many U.S. dollars the currency is worth.

Q

Qualified majority voting (QMV) The method for the Council of Ministers to decide most EU legislation until the approval of the 2009 Lisbon Treaty. It weighted member-state voting power depending upon size and defined how many votes were needed to constitute a majority.

quango The acronym for *quasi-nongovernmental organization,* the term used in Britain for a nonelected body that is outside traditional governmental departments or local authorities.

Qur'an A book of the sacred text of revelations made to Muhammad by Allah.

R

Rajya Sabha India's upper house of parliament; considerably less politically powerful than the *Lok Sabha*.

rational choice theory A largely quantitative approach to analyzing political decision making and behavior that assumes that individual actors rationally pursue their aims in an effort to achieve the most positive net result.

redistributive policies Policies that take resources from one person or group in society and allocate them to a different, usually more disadvantaged, group. The United States has traditionally opposed redistributive policies to the disadvantaged.

referendum An election in which citizens vote on approving (or rejecting) a policy proposal.

regulations The rules that explain the implementation of laws. When the legislature passes a law, it sets broad principles for implementation; how the law is actually implemented is determined by regulations written by executive branch agencies. The regulation-writing process allows interested parties to influence the eventual shape of the law in practice.

remittances Funds sent by migrants working abroad to family members in their home countries.

rentier state A country that obtains much of its revenue from the export of oil or other natural resources and is doesn't have to rely on its internal tax base.

rents Economic gains that do not compensate those who produced them and do not contribute to productivity, typically associated with government earnings that are not channeled back into investments or production. Pursuit of economic rents (or "rent-seeking") is profit-seeking that takes the form of nonproductive economic activity.

republic In contemporary usage, a political regime in which leaders are not chosen on the basis of their inherited background (as in a monarchy).

reservations Jobs or admissions to colleges reserved by the government of India for specific underprivileged groups.

resource curse A paradoxical situation that affects some countries rich in natural resources, wherein other sectors of the economy are neglected and a high concentration of wealth and power exists, thus impairing sustainable economic development and encouraging authoritarianism.

revolution The process by which an established political regime is replaced (usually by force and with broad popular participation) by a new regime that introduces radical changes throughout society.

S

samurai The warrior class in medieval Japan, also known as "*bushi*." The class emerged around the tenth century, and a dominant band of its members established Japan's first warrior government in the twelfth century. The last samurai government was overthrown in the Meiji Restoration of the mid-nineteenth century.

sanctions International embargos on economic and cultural contracts with a particular country; applied selectively to South Africa by various governments and the United Nations (UN) from 1948 until 1994.

scheduled caste The lowest caste in India; also known as untouchables.

Schengen Area Named after a town in Luxembourg where five EU members (France, Germany, and the Benelux states) agreed in 1985 to abolish border controls among their countries. The "Schengen acquis"—the accumulated rules and procedures of Schengen prior to Maastricht—was incorporated into the Maastricht Treaty and officially made part of the EU legal framework in the 1997 Amsterdam Treaty. Open internal EU borders have been adopted by all EU members except Romania, Bulgaria, Croatia, and Cyprus, while the United Kingdom and Ireland opted out. Schengen also includes Norway, Iceland, and Switzerland, which are not part of the EU.

secularism The doctrine that mandates maintaining a separation between church and state, and specifies that the state should be neutral in matters of religion. The French conception of secularism holds that religious beliefs and practices should be confined to the private sphere, and should not play a role in public or political life.

separation of powers An organization of political institutions within the state in which the executive, legislature, and judiciary have autonomous powers and no one branch dominates the others. This is the common pattern in presidential systems. In parliamentary systems, there is a fusion of powers.

settler state Colonial or former colonial administrations controlled by the descendants of immigrants who settled in the territory.

sexenio The 6-year term in office of Mexican presidents, governors, and senators.

shari'a Islamic law derived mostly from the Qur'an and the examples set by the Prophet Muhammad in the Sunnah.

shogun The title, meaning "general," assumed by a succession of hereditary leaders of the three military dynasties—the Minamotos, the Ashikagas, and the Tokugawas—that ruled Japan from the late twelfth century to the mid-nineteenth century. Their government was called the shogunate.

Sikhs Sikhs, a religious minority, constitute less than 2 percent of the Indian population and 76 percent of the state of Punjab. Sikhism is a monotheistic religion that was founded in the fifteenth century.

siloviki Derived from the Russian word *sila*, meaning "force," this refers to Russian politicians and governmental officials drawn from the security and intelligence agencies, special forces, or the military, many of whom were recruited to important political posts under Vladimir Putin.

single-member district (SMD) An electoral district in which only one representative is elected, most commonly by the first-past-the-post method (i.e., whoever wins the most votes). In contrast, a proportional representation (PR) system seats in a legislature are allocated to parties according to the percentage of votes that each party receives.

Single European Act (SEA) The first major revision of the Rome Treaty, which facilitated the single-market program, expanded EU prerogatives, and gave new power to the EP.

single member plurality (SMP) electoral system An electoral system in which candidates run for a single seat from a specific geographic district. The candidate receiving the most votes, that is, a plurality, wins, whether or not this amounts to a majority. SMP systems, unlike systems of proportional representation, increase the likelihood that two national coalition parties will form.

single nontransferable vote (SNTV) A method of voting used in a multimember election district system. Each voter casts only one ballot for a particular candidate, and that vote may not be transferred to another candidate, even of the same party. Each district is assigned two or more seats, which are filled by the candidates who win the largest numbers of votes.

social class A group whose members share common worldviews and aspirations determined largely by occupation, income, and wealth.

social market economy A system that aims to combine the efficiency of market economies with a concern for fairness for a broad range of citizens.

social movement Large-scale grassroots action that demands reforms of existing social practices and government policies.

Social Progress Index (SPI) A composite measurement of social progress in countries that takes into account basic needs, their food, shelter and security; access to health care, education, and a healthy environment; and the opportunity for people to improve their lives.

Social Security National systems of contributory and noncontributory benefits to provide assistance for the elderly, sick, disabled, unemployed, and others similarly in need of assistance.

socialism A system in which the state plays a leading role in organizing the economy, owns most productive resources and property, and actively promotes equality.

socialist The doctrine stating that the state should direct the economy in order to promote equality and help low-income groups.

socialist democracy The term used by the CCP to describe the political system of the PRC. The official view is that this type of system, under the leadership of the Communist Party, provides democracy for the overwhelming majority of people and suppresses (or exercises dictatorship over) only the enemies of the people.

socialist market economy The term used by the government of China to refer to the country's current economic system that mixes elements of both socialism and capitalism.

soft authoritarianism A system of political control in which a combination of formal and informal mechanisms ensure the dominance of a ruling group or dominant party, despite the existence of some forms of political competition and expressions of political opposition.

sovereign democracy A concept of democracy articulated by President Putin's political advisor, Vladimir Surkov, to communicate the idea that democracy in Russia should be adapted to Russian traditions and conditions rather than based on Western models.

special relationship A unofficial term, first used by Winston Churchill, to describe the unusually close political, cultural, economic, and historical relations between the United States and the United Kingdom.

Standing Committee A subgroup of the Politburo, currently with seven members. The most powerful political organization in China.

state The most powerful political institutions in a country, including the executive, legislative, and judicial branches of government, as well as the police and armed forces.

state capitalism An economic system that is primarily capitalistic but in which there is some degree of government ownership of the means of production.

state corporatism A system of interest representation in which the constituent units are organized into a limited number of singular, compulsory, noncompetitive, hierarchically ordered, and functionally differentiated categories, recognized or licensed (if not created) by the state. These organizations are granted a representational monopoly within their respective categories in exchange for limiting their demands and allowing the state to recruit their leaders.

State Council The highest organization in the state administration of the PRC, directed by the premier. It also includes several vice premiers, the heads of government ministries and commissions, and a few other senior officials.

state formation The historical development of a state, often marked by major stages, key events, or turning points (critical junctures) that influence the contemporary character of the state.

state-led economic development The process of actively promoting economic development through government policy, usually involving indicative planning and financial subsidization of industries.

state-owned enterprises (SOEs) Companies in which a majority of ownership control is held by the government.

state technocrat A career-minded bureaucrat who administers public policy according to a technical rather than a political rationale. In Mexico and Brazil, these are known as the *técnicos*.

statism A doctrine advocating extensive state direction of the economy and society.

structural adjustment program (SAP) A program established by the World Bank with the intent to alter and reform the economic structures of highly indebted Third World countries as a condition for receiving international loans. SAPs call for privatization, trade liberalization, and fiscal restraint, which often lead to the dismantling of social welfare systems.

Supreme Commander for the Allied Powers (SCAP) The official title of General Douglas MacArthur between 1945 and 1951 when he led the Allied Occupation of Japan.

Subsidiarity The principle, consecrated by the Maastricht Treaty, that the EU should seek to forge decision making at the level of the lowest effective jurisdiction.

T

Taisho democracy A reference to Japanese politics in the period roughly coinciding with Emperor Taisho's reign, 1912–1926. The period was characterized by the rise of a popular movement for democratization of government by the introduction of universal manhood suffrage and the reduction of the power and influence of authoritarian institutions of the state.

technocrat A career-minded official who administers public policy according to a technical rather than a political rationale.

The Four Great Pollution Trials The Four Great Pollution Trials of the early 1970s include mercury poisoning in Minamata City, thus known as the "Minamata Disease," a similar case in another city, thus known as the "Second Minamata Disease," cadmium poisoning known as the "itai-itai (ouch-ouch) disease," and severe asthma caused by inhalation of airborne sulfur dioxide that occurred in Yokkaichi City (hence the "Yokkaichi Asthma").

theocracy A state dominated by the clergy, who rule on the grounds that they are the only interpreters of God's will and law.

totalitarianism A political system in which the state attempts to exercise total control over all aspects of public and private life, including the economy, culture, education, and social organizations, through an integrated system of ideological, economic, and political control. Totalitarian states rely on extensive coercion, including terror, as a means to exercise power.

township In South Africa, a segregated residential area reserved for Africans; during apartheid, tightly controlled and constituted mainly by public housing.

typology A method of classifying by using criteria that assign cases to categories whose members share common characteristics.

U

Umkhonto-we-Sizwe Zulu and Xhosa for "Spear of the Nation," the armed wing of the African National Congress, established in 1961.

unfinished state A state characterized by institutional instability and political uncertainty that may render it dysfunctional as a coherent ruling entity.

unitary state In contrast to a federal system, a system of government in which no powers are reserved for subnational units of government.

V

vanguard party A political party that claims to operate in the "true" interests of the group or class that it purports to represent, even if this understanding doesn't correspond to the expressed interests of the group itself.

Voortrekkers Pastoralist descendants of Dutch settlers in South Africa who moved north from the British-controlled Cape in 1836 to establish independent republics; later regarded as the founders of the Afrikaner nation.

W

warrant chiefs Leaders employed by the British colonial regime in Nigeria, a system in which chiefs were selected by the British to oversee certain legal matters and assist the colonial enterprise in governance and law enforcement in local areas.

Weimar Republic Germany's constitutional system between 1918 and the Nazi seizure of power in 1933. So-named because the assembly to write the constitution occurred in the German city of Weimar.

welfare state A set of public policies designed to provide for citizens' needs through direct or indirect provision of pensions, health care, unemployment insurance, and assistance to the poor.

Westminster model A form of democracy based on the supreme authority of Parliament and the accountability of its elected representatives; named for the Parliament building in London.

works council A group of firm employees elected by coworkers to represent the workforce in negotiations with management at that specific shop or company.

World Bank An international financial institution (IFI) comprising over 180 member-states that provides low-interest loans, policy advice, and technical assistance to developing countries with the goal of reducing poverty.

World Trade Organization (WTO) A global international organization that oversees the "rules of trade" among its member-states. The main functions of the WTO are to serve as a forum for its members to negotiate new agreements and resolve trade disputes. Its fundamental purpose is to lower or remove barriers to free trade.

Z

zaibatsu Giant holding companies in pre–World War II Japan, each owned and controlled by a particular family. The largest of these were divided into a number of independent firms during the post–World War II Occupation, but many were later revived as *keiretsu*, although no longer under the control of any of the original founding families.

zamindars Landlords who served as tax collectors in India under the British colonial government. The *zamindari* system was abolished after independence.

zoku A group of Diet members with recognized experience and expertise in a particular policy area, such as agriculture, construction, and transportation, and close personal connections with special interests in that area. *Zoku* means "tribes."

About the Editors and Contributors

Ervand Abrahamian is Distinguished Professor of History at Baruch College and the Graduate Center of the City University of New York. He was elected a fellow of the American Academy of the Arts and Sciences. His publications include *Khomeinism: Essays on the Islamic Republic* (University of California Press, 1993), *Tortured Confessions: Prisons and Public Recantations in Modern Iran* (University of California Press, 1999), *A History of Modern Iran* (Cambridge University Press, 2008), and *The Coup: 1953, The CIA, and the Roots of Modern U.S.-Iranian Relations* (New Press, 2013).

Amrita Basu is the Paino Professor of Political Science and Sexuality, Women's, and Gender Studies at Amherst College. Her main areas of interest are social movements, religious nationalism, and gender politics in India. She is the author of *Two Faces of Protest: Contending Modes of Women's Activism in India* (University of California Press, 1994), *Violent Conjunctures in Democratic India* (Cambridge University Press, 2014), and six edited or coedited books.

Joan DeBardeleben is Chancellor's Professor in the Institute of European, Russian, and Eurasian Studies (EURUS) and codirector of the Centre for European Studies at Carleton University in Ottawa, Canada. Her research deals with EU-Russian relations, the EU's policy toward its eastern neighbors, and electoral politics in Russia. Her recent publications include *EU-Russia Relations in Crisis: Understanding Diverging Perceptions*, coeditor and contributor (with Tom Casier) (Routledge, forthcoming); and "Backdrop to the Ukraine Crisis: The Revival of Normative Politics in Russia's Relations with the EU?" in *Power, Politics, and Confrontation in Eurasia: Foreign Policy in a Contested Area*, Matthew Sussex and Roger E. Kanet, eds. (Palgrave Macmillan, 2015).

Louis DeSipio is a professor in the Departments of Political Science and Chicano/Latino Studies at the University of California, Irvine, chair of the Department of Chicano/Latino Studies, and director of the Jack W. Peltason Center for the Study of Democracy. His research interests include Latino politics, the process of political incorporation of new and formerly excluded populations into U.S. politics, and public policies shaping immigrant incorporation, such as immigration, immigrant settlement, naturalization, and voting rights. DeSipio is the author of *Counting on the Latino Vote: Latinos as a New Electorate* (University Press of

Virginia, 2016) and the coauthor, with Rodolfo O. de la Garza, of *U.S. Immigration in the 21st Century: Making Americans, Remaking America* (Westview Press, 2015) and the coauthor, with Todd Shaw, Dianne Pinderhughes, and Toni-Michelle Travis, of *Uneven Roads: An Introduction to U.S. Racial and Ethnic Politics* (Washington, DC: CQ Press, 2015). He is also the author and editor of an eight-volume series on Latino political values, attitudes, and behaviors. His journal articles include "A Return to a National Origin Preference? Mexican Immigration and the Principles Guiding U.S. Immigration Policy" (*Perspectives on Politics*, 2011) and "Immigrant Incorporation in an Era of Weak Civic Institutions: Immigrant Civic and Political Participation in the United States" (*American Behavioral Scientist*, 2011). He is also a past president of the Western Political Science Association (WPSA).

Shigeko N. Fukai is professor emeritus of Okayama University and a visiting professor at Chiba University (Japan). She has written a book in Japanese on a sustainable world order, as well as a series of articles and chapters in both English and Japanese on sustainability, Japan's land problems, and land policy-making; Japan's role in the emergent regional economic order in East Asia; and Japanese electoral and party politics.

Haruhiro Fukui is professor emeritus in the Department of Political Science, University of California, Santa Barbara. His most recent publications include "Japan: From Deterrence to Prevention," in Emil J. Kirchner and James Sperling (eds.), *National Security Cultures: Patterns of Global Governance* (Routledge, 2010), "Japan," in Joel Krieger (ed.), *The Oxford Companion to Comparative Politics* (Oxford University Press, 2013), and "East Asian Studies: Politics," in James D. Wright (ed.), *The International Encyclopedia of Social and Behavioral Sciences*, 2d ed. (Elsevier Science, 2015).

Wade Jacoby is Mary Lou Fulton Professor of Political Science at Brigham Young University, where he also directs the Center for the Study of Europe. He teaches classes on European and comparative politics. He is coeditor of the journal *German Politics* and the author of *Imitation and Politics: Redesigning Modern Germany* (Cornell University Press, 2001) and *The Enlargement of the European Union and NATO: Ordering from the Menu in Central Europe* (Cambridge University Press, 2006).

Halbert Jones is director of the Rothermere American Institute at the University of Oxford. His research interests include U.S.–Latin American relations, the international relations of North America, and twentieth-century Mexican political history. He is the author of *The War Has Brought Peace to Mexico: World War II and the Consolidation of the Post-Revolutionary State* (University of New Mexico Press, 2014). He wishes to acknowledge the role of Professor Merilee S. Grindle of Harvard University in the development of the chapter on Mexico in previous editions.

William A. Joseph is professor of political science and chair of the department at Wellesley College. He is also an associate in research at the John King Fairbank Center for Chinese Studies at Harvard University. His major areas of academic interest are contemporary Chinese politics and ideology, comparative revolutionary movements, and the Vietnam War. He is the editor of and a contributor to *Politics in China: An Introduction*, 2d ed. (Oxford University Press, 2014).

Mark Kesselman is professor emeritus of political science at Columbia University and was senior editor of the *International Political Science Review* from 2009–2017. His research focuses on the political economy of French and European politics. His publications include *The Ambiguous Consensus: A Study of Local Government in France* (Knopf, 1967), *The French Workers Movement: Economic Crisis and Political Change* (HarperCollins, 1984), *The Politics of Globalization: A Reader* (Houghton Mifflin, 2012), and *The Politics of Power: The Politics of Power: A Critical Introduction to American Government* (with Alan Draper and Ira Katznelson), 7th ed. (W.W. Norton, 2013). His articles have appeared in the *American Political Science Review*, *World Politics*, and *Comparative Politics*. He was the recipient in 2017 of the Charles A. McCoy Career Achievement Award of the American Political Science Association's Caucus for a New Political Science.

Darren Kew is an associate professor of conflict resolution and executive director of the Center for Peace, Democracy, and Development at the University of Massachusetts, Boston. He studies the relationship between conflict resolution methods and democratic development in Africa. Much of his work focuses on the role of civil society groups in this development, as well as Muslim-Christian dialogue processes and methods in Nigeria. He also monitored the last three Nigerian elections and the 2007 elections in Sierra Leone. He is the author of numerous works on Nigerian politics and conflict resolution, including *Civil Society, Conflict Resolution, and Democracy in Nigeria* (Syracuse University Press, 2016).

Atul Kohli is the David Bruce Professor of International Affairs at Princeton University. He specializes in the study of development, with a special interest in India. His most recent book is *Poverty amid Plenty in the New India* (Cambridge University Press, 2012).

Joel Krieger is the Norma Weilenz Hess Professor of Political Science Emeritus at Wellesley College. He is the author of *Reagan, Thatcher, and the Politics of Decline* (Oxford University Press, 1986) and *British Politics in the Global Age* (Oxford University Press, 1999). He is the editor-in-chief of *The Oxford Companion to Comparative Politics* (Oxford University Press, 2013) and *The Oxford Companion to International Relations* (Oxford University Press, 2014).

Peter M. Lewis is director of African studies and associate professor at the Johns Hopkins University, School of Advanced International Studies (SAIS). He has written extensively on questions of economic adjustment, democratization, and civil society in Africa; democratic reform and political economy in Nigeria; public attitudes toward reform and democracy in West Africa; and the comparative politics of economic change in Africa and Southeast Asia. His book *Growing Apart: Politics and Economic Change in Indonesia and Nigeria* (University of Michigan Press, 2007) is concerned with the institutional basis of economic development. Most recently, he has coedited *Coping with Crisis in African States* (Lynne Rienner Publishers, 2016).

Tom Lodge is dean of the arts faculty at the University of Limerick (Ireland). He taught politics at the University of the Witwatersrand in Johannesburg, South Africa, between 1978 and 2005. He has written extensively about South African developments, and his most recent book is *Sharpeville: An Apartheid Massacre* (Oxford University Press, 2011).

Alfred P. Montero is the Frank B. Kellogg Chair of Political Science at Carleton College. His main research areas are the political economy of South American countries and the quality of democracy. He is the author of *Shifting States in Global Markets: Subnational Industrial Policy in Contemporary Brazil and Spain* (Penn State University Press, 2002), *Brazilian Politics: Reforming a Democratic State in a Changing World* (Polity Press, 2006), and *Brazil: Reversal of Fortune* (Polity Press, 2014). He is also coeditor (with David J. Samuels) of *Decentralization and Democracy in Latin America* (University of Notre Dame Press, 2004). His research has been published in several scholarly journals, and he is the editor of the refereed journal *Latin American Politics and Society*.

George Ross, Jean Monnet *ad personam* Chair, Université de Montréal, Canada. He is the author of *The European Union and Its Crises* (Palgrave-Macmillan, 2011) and *Jacques Delors and European Integration* (Oxford University Press, 1995), and coeditor of *Euros and Europeans* (Cambridge University Press, 2004) and *What's Left of the Left?* (Duke University Press, 2011).

Index

Note: **Boldface** page numbers indicate definitions of key terms.

A

Aam Admi Party (AAP), 309–311
AAP. *See* Aam Admi Party (AAP)
Abacha, Sani, 520
Abe, Shinzo, 243, 250
Abenomics, 243
abertura, **376**, 406
Abiola, Moshood, 520, 541
abortion, 453, 500, 671
absolute monarchies, 25
Abubakar, Abdulsalami, 520, 547
ACA. *See* Affordable Care Act (ACA)
accommodation, **452**
accountability, 411, 456–457, **513**, 523
acephalous societies, **516**
activism. *See* social movements and protest
Act of Union (1707), 42
Adenauer, Konrad, 142
Adityanath, Yogi, 310–311
administrative courts, France, 112
administrative guidance, **242–243**
administrative structure
    Brazil, 373
    Britain, 43
    China, 658
    France, 87
    Germany, 135
    India, 282
    Iran, 611
    Japan, 234
    Mexico, 419
    Nigeria, 514
    Russian Federation, 558
    United States, 329
advisory committees, EU, 204
AfD. *See* Alternative for Germany (AfD)
Affordable Care Act (ACA), 7, 336, 339–340
African Americans, 330, 333, 349, 357, 359
African National Congress (ANC), **469**, 470, 472–473, 475, 491, 493–495
Africans, **465**
Afrikaners, **467**
agencies, EU, 204
aging population
    China, 694–695
    EU, 224
    Germany, 179
    Japan, 272–273
agrarian reform
    Brazil, 387, 404
    China, 668–669
    Mexico, 422, 423
    Russian Federation, 568
    South Africa, 504

agribusiness, 128
Agricultural Revolution, 90
agriculture policy
    China, 660, 668–669, 670
    EU, 207
    India, 290, 291
    Iran, 627
    Nigeria, 524
    United States, 335
Ahmadinejad, Mahmoud, 608, 633, 638
Ainu, 263–264
air pollution, 56, 480, 626–627
A Just Russia, 591
Akihito (emperor), 248–249
Albania, 17
alcohol abuse, 596
Al-e Ahmad, Jalal, 625
Alexander the Great, 280
Algeria, 92, 130
All-China Federation of Trade Unions (ACFTU), 689
Alliance for Democracy (AD), 540
Allied powers, in World War II, 2
All Nigerian People's Party (ANPP), 540–541
All People's Party (APP), 540
All Progressives Congress (APC), 521, 541
Alternative for Germany (AfD), 169
amakudari, **252**
Amazon, 406
American culture, 103, 363
American exceptionalism, 334
American Health Care Act, 7, 340, 347
American Revolution, 328–330
Amsterdam Treaty, 211, 214, 223
ancien régime, **89–90**
Anglican Church, 43
Anglo-Boer War, 468
Angola, 472
anticlericalism, **448**
antiglobalization movement, 128
anti-nuclear movements, 175
apartheid, **469**
apartheid regime, 465, 468–471, 476–477
APEC. *See* Asia-Pacific Economic Cooperation (APEC)
Arab Spring, 11, 14, 187, 212, 502, 546, 646–647
Aristotle, 6
Article 49.3, 114–115
Articles of Confederation, 328, **329**
ASEAN. *See* Association of Southeast Asian Nations (ASEAN)
Asian Development Bank (ADB), 239
Asian Monetary Fund, 247
Asia-Pacific Economic Cooperation (APEC), 239
Asia-Pacific region, 247
al-Assad, Bashar, 96
Assembly of Experts, **617**
Association of Southeast Asian Nations (ASEAN), 239

atomic bombs, 237
austerity policies, **143**
    Brazil, 384, 386
    Britain, 53
    EU, 221
    Germany, 143
Australia, 48
authoritarian, **91**, **513**
authoritarianism, 4, 17–18, 24
authoritarian regime, 24–25
autocracy, **523**
autonomous region, **680**
"Axis of Evil," 619
Axis powers, in World War II, 2
ayatollah, **608**
Azeris, 643–644
Aztec Empire, 420

B

BA. *See* bureaucratic authoritarianism (BA)
Babangida, Ibrahim, 520, 540
Bahrain, 17
Bahujan Samaj Party (BSP), 313
balance of payments, 524, **525**
Bangladesh, 318
Banking Union, 196–197
Barroso, José Manuel, 198
Basic Law, **154**
Battle of Hastings, 41, 88
Battle of Okinawa, 269
bazaar, **615**
Bazargan, Mehdi, 617, 640–641
Berlin Wall, 1, 4, 142, 193
Bharatiya Janata Party (BJP), 277, 308–309
Biafran War, 524
bicameral, **352**
Big Society, 46
Bill of Rights (1689), 58
Bill of Rights (U.S.), 330, 344, 358
bin Laden, Osama, 287
birthrate
    Germany, 179
    Japan, 272
    Russian Federation, 571, 603
Bismark, Otto von, 138–139
BJP. *See* Bharatiya Janata Party (BJP)
black empowerment, 479–480
Blair, Tony, 45, 47, 60, 64, 70, 77, 80–81
Blitzkrieg, **141**
BNDES. *See* National Bank for Economic and Social Development (BNDES)
Boers, **468**
Boko Haram, 543–544
Bolsa Familia, 386, 404, 405
Bolshevik Revolution, 559–560
Bonaparte, Napoleon, 90
Bové, José, 128

"bowling alone" phenomenon, 360
braceros, 434
Brahmin, **280**
Brandt, Willy, 142
Brasilia, Brazil, 377
Brazil, 369–414
    1930 revolution in, 374–375
    administrative structure, 373
    after 9/11, 378–379
    agrarian reform in, 387, 404
    bureaucracy, 393–394
    bureaucratic authoritarianism in, 376
    citizenship, 402–405
    civil service, 393
    civil society, 406
    collective identity in, 380–381, 402–405, 411
    comparative politics, 410–412
    constitution of, 378
    critical historical junctures in, 372–379
    democracy in, 380, 403–404, 409
    democratic transition in, 376–378
    demographic trends, 410
    economic growth in, 382–383, 408–409
    economic policy, 380, 384–385
    economy of, 378–379, 380, 382–387
    education system, 410
    elections in, 402
    environmental issues, 387–388
    ethnic groups in, 371–372, 403
    executive in, 373, 391–393
    facts and statistics, 30, 32, 34, 369, 372
    fiscal system, 383–384
    foreign policy, 409–410
    geographic setting, 371–372
    global economy and, 388–390
    globalization and, 380, 388–390, 409, 411–412
    governance, 390–397
    Great Depression, 374–375
    immigration to, 403
    industrialization in, 385
    inflation in, 384–385
    interest groups in, 405–406
    judiciary in, 373, 394–395
    legislature in, 373, 398–399
    making of modern, 370–381
    map of, 374
    media in, 406–407
    military, 395–396
    nationalism in, **376**
    New State, 375
    party system in, 373, 399–402
    police, 395–396
    policy-making process in, 396–397
    political challenges and changing agendas in, 381, 407–410
    political culture in, 402–405
    political development of, 370–371
    political economy in, 382–385
    political impact of technology in, 406–407
    political organization of, 373
    political parties in, 375, 376, 399–402
    political system of, 25, 373
    politics in action, 370–371, 407–412
    populism in, 375
    Populist Republic, 375–376
    president of, 391–393
    regime history, 373
    religion in, 381
    religions in, 372, 403–404
    representation and participation in, 398–407
    semipublic institutions in, 393–394
    social class in, 381
    social movements and protest in, 370, 405–406

social welfare programs in, 385–386
society and economy in, 385–387
state and economy in, 382–385
state institutions, 390, 393–396
state organization, 390
subnational government, 395
taxation in, 384
trade between China and, 389
United States and, 379
women in, 381, 385, 405
youth in, 410
Brazilian Empire, 372–373
Brazilian Labor Party (PTB), 375
Bretton Woods system, 189, 191, 341–342
Brexit, 3, 5, 39, 47, 49, 59, 78–79, 96, 187, 197, 343
BRICS (Brazil, Russia, India, China, and South Africa), 482–483
Britain, 38–83
    administrative structure, 43
    Anglo-Boer War, 468
    Brexit in, 3, 5, 39, 47, 49, 59, 78–79, 96, 187, 197, 343
    bureaucracy in, 60–62
    cabinet government, 59–61
    citizenship in, 75
    civil service, 60–62
    collective identity in, 49
    collectivist consensus in, 45
    comparative politics, 81
    consensus era, 51–52
    Conservative-Liberal coalition in, 46–47, 51, 52, 81
    Conservative Party, 46, 70–71
    constitutional reform in, 78–79
    constitution of, 58
    critical historical junctures in, 41–47
    currency of, 41
    decolonization and, 48, 49, 76, 80
    demographic trends in, 80
    economic policy, 51–53
    economy of, 50–52, 57
    elections in, 72–73
    electoral trends in, 74–75
    environmental issues, 56
    ethnic minorities in, 41, 54–55, 76, 79
    executive in, 59
    facts and statistics, 30, 32, 34, 38
    FDI in, 56–57
    foreign policy of, 80–81
    gender equality in, 55, 73–74
    generation gap in, 80
    geographic setting, 39–40
    globalization and, 48–49, 56–57
    Glorious Revolution, 43
    governance in, 58–66
    Great Recession, 46, 51, 54, 57
    income inequality in, 39, 53
    industrial change in, 44
    Industrial Revolution in, 43–44, 49
    inequality in, 54–55
    interest groups in, 76–77
    Japan and, 240
    judiciary in, 43, 65
    Labour Party, 39, 47, 51, 52–53, 69–70
    legislative process in, 67–68
    legislature in, 43, 67
    Liberal Democrats, 71–72, 73
    map, 42
    media in, 77
    military, 64
    monarchy in, 78
    National Health Service, 53
    national identity in, 76, 79
    New Labour Party, 45–46, 50, 52–54, 57, 70
    Old Republic, 373–374

Parliament, 42–43, 50, 58, 66, 67–69
party system in, 43, 69–75
police, 64–65
policymaking process in, 66
political challenges for, 78–79
political culture in, 75
political development of, 40–41
political economy in, 50–52
political impact of technology in, 77
political organization of, 43
political parties in, 69–72, 74
politics in action, 39
politics in transition in, 78–81
public institutions, 63–64
regime history, 43
religion in, 41, 49
representation and participation in, 67–77
semipublic institutions, 63–64
seventeenth-century settlement of, 43
social class in, 75
social movements and protest in, 76–77
social policy in, 53–54
society and economy in, 53–55
state and economy in, 50–52
state institutions, 64–65
state organization, 58–64
subnational government, 65–66
terrorist attacks in, 46
U.S. relationship with, 49, 80
voting rights in, 44, 45
women in, 55
world wars and, 44–45
British Empire, 44, 48, 80–81, 281–282
British Isles, 39, 41
British Telecom (BT), 63
Brown, Gordon, 45–46, 51, 52, 70, 72
BSP. *See* Bahujan Samaj Party (BSP)
BT. *See* British Telecom (BT)
Buhari, Muhammadu, 512, 520, 521, 526, 535, 542
Bundesrat, **165**
Bundestag, 155–157, 161–166
bureaucracy, 9, **10**
    Brazil, 393–394
    Britain, 60–62
    France, 110–111
    Germany, 158
    India, 299–300
    Iran, 633–634
    Japan, 251–252
    Mexico, 440–441
    Nigeria, 536
    Russian Federation, 579–580
    United States, 347–348
bureaucratic authoritarianism (BA), **376**
bureaucratic rings, **397**
burkini, 127–128
Bush, George W., 425, 619, 649
bushi, **235**

C

cabinet, **10**
cabinet government, **59**
    Britain, 59–61
    France, 110
    Germany, 157–158
    India, 298–299
    Japan, 250–251
    Mexico, 438–440
    South Africa, 485
    United States, 347–348
Calderon, Felipe, 425, 439, 455–456
Calles, Plutarco Elías, 422–423
Cameron, David, 46, 47, 64, 70, 78, 79

Canada, 48
CAP. *See* Common Agricultural Policy (CAP)
capitalism, state, 430
carbon emissions, 572
Cárdenas, Cuauhtémoc, 449, 455
Cárdenas, Lázaro, 423, 424
Cardoso, Fernando Henrique, 378, 384, 386, 387, 391, 397
caste system, **280**, 294
Catholic Church, 89, 90, 121, 138, 403–404, 421, 422, 449
Catholicism, 381
caudillos, **420**
causal theories, 11–12, **11**
CDU. *See* Christian Democrats (CDU/CSU)
cell phones, 314–315, 501, 646, 690
Central and Eastern Europe, 186, 208, 218, 561, 563
Central Committee, **674**, 675–676
centrally planned economy, **659**
Central Military Commission (CMC), 681
CETA. *See* Comprehensive Economic and Trade Agreement (CETA)
CFSP. *See* Common Foreign and Security Policy (CFSP)
chancellor, **138**
    Germany, 155–157, 158
Charlemagne, 88
Chechnya, 564, 566, 584
checks and balances, **348**
Chiang Kai-shek, 658–659, 660
Chiang Mai Initiative, 247
childhood poverty, 54
child labor, 293
China, 653–699
    administrative structure, 658
    aging population, 694–695
    Brazil and, 389
    citizenship, 687–688
    civil society in, 694
    collective identity in, 664
    as communist party-state, 695–696
    comparative politics, 665, 695–697
    constitution of, 680
    critical historical junctures in, 657–663
    Cultural Revolution in, 661, 666
    democracy in, 664, 693–694
    demographic trends, 694–695
    Deng Xiaoping and, 661–662
    as developing country, 696–697
    dynastic era, 657–658
    economic development in, 15, 16
    economic growth in, 667–668, 669–670
    economic policy, 664
    economy of, 661, 664, 666–671, 692
    elections, 685–686
    environmental issues, 671–672
    ethnic groups in, 656–657
    ethnic minorities in, 687–688
    executive in, 658, 674–679
    facts and statistics, 30, 32, 34, 653, 656
    geographic setting, 656–658
    globalization and, 663–664, 672–673
    governance, 674–681
    India and, 317–318
    inequality in, 669, 692
    interest groups, 689–690
    Japanese invasion of, 236
    judiciary, 679–680
    judiciary in, 658
    Kashmir conflict and, 317
    legislature in, 658, 682–683
    making of modern, 655–666
    Mao Zedong and, 659–661, 663–664, 666
    map of, 657
    market reform in, 666–668

media in, 687, 690–691
military, 680–681
one-child policy, 671
Opium War, 658
party system in, 658, 683–685
police, 680–681
policy-making process, 681–682
political challenges and changing agendas in, 691–694
political culture, 686–688
political development of, 654–655
political economy in, 666–671
political impact of technology in, 690–691
political organization of, 658
political parties in, 683–685
political suppression in, 17
political system of, 25, 658
politics in action, 655–656
politics in transition, 691–697
regime history, 658
religions in, 656, 686
representation and participation in, 682–691
Republic of, 658–659
return of Hong Kong to, 48, 80
rural reforms in, 668–669
social movements and protest in, 655–656, 661–662, 689–690
social welfare programs, 670
society and economy in, 669–671
state and economy in, 666–669
state institutions, 679–681
state-led development in, 3–4
state organization, 674
subnational government, 680
Taiwan and, 660
technocratic reforms in, 662–663
Tiananmen Square, 655–656, 661, 665
trade balance, 247
urbanization in, 691–692
U.S. relations with, 247, 673
women in, 670–671
youth in, 694
Chinese Communist Party (CCP), 656, 658–659, 663, 664, 674–677, 679, 683–685, 693
Chirac, Jacques, 95, 98, 106, 107, 110, 117, 120
Christian Democrats (CDU/CSU), 165, 166
Church of England, 43
citizen action groups, **167**
citizen initiative, **203**
citizenship
    Brazil, 402–405
    Britain, 75
    China, 687–688
    EU, 217–218
    France, 97, 121, 123–124
    Germany, 171–172
    India, 311–312
    Iran, 642–644
    Japan, 263–264, 265
    Mexico, 451
    Nigeria, 542–543
    Russian Federation, 593–594
    South Africa, 500
    United States, 330, 358–359
civic participation, decline in, 360
civil rights movement, in United States, 359
civil servants, **158**
civil service
    Brazil, 393
    Britain, 60–62
    France, 110–111
    Germany, **158**
    India, 299–300
    Japan, 251–252
civil society, **429**, **586**, 694
    Brazil, 381, 406

China, **694**
    European, 213, 218–221
    Germany, 172–174
    Iran and, 647
    Japan, 265–269
    Mexico, 429, 453
    Nigeria, 544–545, 550
    Russian Federation, 586, 594–596
    United States, 364
civil war
    China, 659
    Liberia, 531
    Nigeria, 519
    Russia, 559
Civil War, U.S., 330
Clegg, Nick, 71, 73
clientelism, **374**, 397, 402, 410, 451, 523, 532, 534, 536
clientelistic networks, **579**
climate change, 56, 194, 341
    Germany and, 174–175
    India and, 294
    Russian Federation and, 572
climate change policy, 174–175
Climategate, 56
Clinton, Bill, 363
Clinton, Hillary, 3, 325, 416
coalitional presidentialism, 400
codetermination, **148**
coffee, 382
cohabitation, **106**, 110
Cold War, **2**, 4, 185–186, 189, 223, 561
    end of, 186, 333
collective bargaining, 75
collective identities, **5**, 20–22
    Brazil, 380–381, 402–405, 411
    Britain, 49
    China, 664
    EU, 188, 217–218
    France, 97
    Germany, 145, 178
    India, 288
    Iran, 621, 642–644
    Japan, 239–240
    Mexico, 428–429, 451
    Nigeria, 523, 542–544
    Russian Federation, 566, 593–594
    South Africa, 475, 500
    United States, 333, 358–359, 364
collective leadership, **663**
collectivism, 45
collectivization, **560**, 660
Collor de Mello, Fernando, 378
colonialism
    Brazil, 372–373
    India, 281–282
    Mexico, 420
    Nigeria, 517–518
    North America, 326
Colosio, Luis Donaldo, 425
Committee of the Regions, 204
Common Agricultural Policy (CAP), 186
Common Foreign and Security Policy (CFSP), **186**
common law, 111
Common Market, 190, 191
Common Market of the South (MERCOSUL), 389
communications technology, 314
communism, **660**
    in China, 659–662, 686–687
    in Eastern Europe, 2, 15, 185
    in Soviet Union, 560–561
Communist Party of India (CPM), 305, 309
Communist Party of the Russian Federation (CPRF), 588–589

Communist Party of the Soviet Union (CPSU), 2, 561, 576, 587
communist party-state, 16, 695–696
communitarianism, 97
Community Method, 193
community party-states, 24, 662
comparative politics, 4
  approaches to, 6–12
  Brazil and, 410–412
  Britain and, 81
  China and, 665, 695–697
  EU and, 224–225
  France and, 130
  Germany and, 179–180
  global challenges and, 2–5
  India and, 288–289
  vs. international relations, 7
  Internet and, 8
  introducing, 1–37
  Iran and, 621, 650–651
  Japan and, 273–274
  level of analysis in, 9–10
  Mexico and, 429, 459
  Nigeria and, 523, 551–552
  Russian Federation and, 566–567, 603–604
  South Africa and, 475–476, 505–507
  themes for, 13–22
  in turbulent times, 5–6
  United States and, 365–366
comparative rankings, 36
comparativist, 7
competition policy, EU, 206–207
competitiveness, EU and, 209–210
Comprehensive Economic and Trade Agreement (CETA), 195, 213
CONASUPO, 441
concentration camps, 141
Confucius, 657
Congress, U.S., 325, 329–330, 345, 351, 352–354, 366
Congress Party, 305, 307
conservative, 93, 638
Conservative Party, 46, 70–71
consolidated democracy, 23
constitution
  Brazil, 378
  Britain, 58
  China, 680
  France, 108–109
  India, 296–297, 301
  Iran, 617, 629, 643
  Japan, 229, 235–236, 238, 249–250, 274
  Mexico, 421, 438
  Russian Federation, 577
  South Africa, 483
  Soviet, 576
  United States, 325, 329, 334, 344–345
constitutional amendments, 344
Constitutional Council, 112
constitutional monarchy, 59
constitutional reform, Britain, 78–79
Constitutional Treaty, 176
constructive vote of no confidence, 157
consumerism, 686–687
Corbyn, Jeremy, 3, 47, 51, 53, 56, 70
core-periphery model, 383
corporatist state, 428
corruption
  Brazil, 370–371, 379, 397, 399, 404–405, 407–408, 409
  China, 670, 693
  India, 319–320
  Iran, 616
  Mexico, 427
  Nigeria, 524, 532, 547

Russian Federation, 557–558, 567, 569, 570
  South Africa, 485
Corruption Perceptions Index (CPI), 8, 9, 36
Cortés, Hernán, 420, 421
Costa v. ENEL, 204
Council of Europe, 189, 575
Council of Ministers, 200–201, 216–217
Council Politics and Security Committee (COPS), 214
counter-terrorism, in Britain, 79
country, 9
coup d'état, 422
Court of Auditors, 204
court system. *See* judiciary
CPI. *See* Corruption Perceptions Index (CPI)
CPM. *See* Communist Party of India (CPM)
CPSU. *See* Community Party of the Soviet Union (CPSU)
crime
  Brazil, 396
  China, 670
  Mexico, 425, 427, 429
  Russian Federation, 584–585
  South Africa, 487
Crimea, 4, 159, 187, 565, 573, 593, 598, 599
critical junctures, 5
  Brazil, 372–379
  Britain, 41–47
  China, 657–663
  European Union, 185–187
  France, 88–96
  Germany, 138–144
  India, 280–287
  Iran, 612–619
  Japan, 231–238
  Mexico, 420–427
  Nigeria, 515–521
  Russian Federation, 559–565
  South Africa, 465–474
  United States, 326–332
crude oil prices, 527
CSU. *See* Christian Democrats (CDU/CSU)
Cuba, 366
Cultural Revolution (China), 661, 666
culture
  American, 103, 363
  political. *See* political culture
currency
  Britain, 41
  reserve, 336
cyberterrorism, 314

D

Dalai Lama, 483
dalits, 294, 312–313
decentralization, 93
Declaration of Independence, 328, 359
decolonization, 48, 49, 76, 80
Defrenne v. Sabena, 204
de Gaulle, Charles, 91–93, 96, 105, 107, 114, 116, 191
deindustrialization, 223
De Klerk, F. W., 472
Delors, Jacques, 188, 212
Delors Commission, 192, 194, 203, 220
democracy, 17, 18
  in Brazil, 380, 403–404, 409
  in China, 664, 693–694
  as comparative theme, 17–20
  consolidated, 19, 23
  economic performance and, 16
  European, 188, 215–216
  in France, 97
  in Germany, 145

illiberal, 24, 218
  in India, 19, 277–278, 288, 296–297, 321–322
  in Iran, 620–621, 647–648
  in Japan, 235–236, 237–238, 239
  liberal, 3, 24
  meaning of, 23
  in Mexico, 425–427, 428
  in Nigeria, 512, 522–523, 548–550
  parliamentary, 58
  party, 165
  political stability and, 20
  procedural, 139
  racial, 403
  representative, 215–216, 359
  in Russia, 566
  socialist, 682, 683
  in South Africa, 475, 504, 506
  sovereign, 593
  in United States, 333
Democracy Index, 8, 9, 24, 26, 36
Democratic Alliance (DA), 491, 495, 496–497
democratic centralism, 559
democratic corporatism, 147
Democratic Party, 354–356, 362, 365
Democratic Party of Japan (DPJ), 259–260, 262
Democratic Republic of the Congo, 17
democratic transition, 12, 19
  in Brazil, 376–378
democratization, 475
demographic trends
  Brazil, 410
  Britain, 80
  China, 694–695
  EU, 224
  France, 88, 130
  Germany, 178–179
  India, 293, 320
  Iran, 650
  Japan, 272–273
  Mexico, 458–459
  Nigeria, 550–551
  Russian Federation, 602–603
  South Africa, 505
  United States, 365
demonetization, India, 277
Deng Xiaoping, 661–662, 666–667
Department of Homeland Security, 350
dependent variable, 11
deregulation, 100, 433, 477
developmentalism, 383
developmental state, 551, 696
devolution, 65, 66
DG COMP. *See* Directorate-General for Competition (DG COMP)
Díaz, Portofino, 421–422
dictatorship, 12, 25
Diet (Japan), 234, 257–258, 261–263
Directorate-General for Competition (DG COMP), 206–207
discrimination, in Japan, 264–265
distributional politics, 21
distributive policies, 338, 363
doctrine of international community, 80–81
Doha Development Round, 213
dominant party, 588
DPJ. *See* Democratic Party of Japan (DPJ)
dual society, 624
dual-use technologies, 269–270
Dutch East India Company, 465

E

Eastern Europe, 2, 15, 141–142, 185, 561, 563
East Germany, 141–142
East India Company, 281–282

Ebadi, Shirin, 647
ECB. *See* European Central Bank (ECB)
ECHR. *See* European Convention on Human Rights (ECHR)
ECJ. *See* European Court of Justice (ECJ)
ECLA. *See* Economic Commission for Latin America (ECLA)
Economic and Financial Crimes Commission (EFCC), 525, 534
Economic and Monetary Union (EMU), **186**, 195, 196, 209, 226
Economic and Social Committee (ECOSOC), 204
Economic Commission for Latin America (ECLA), 382
Economic Community of West African States (ECOWAS), **530**, 531
economic deregulation, 477
economic development
    India, 318–319
    measurement of, 16–17
economic equality, 23
Economic Freedom Fighters (EFF), 497–498
economic growth
    Brazil, 382–383, 408–409
    China, 667–668, 669–670
    comparative, 1958-1973, 99
    France, 99
    India, 289, 290–291, 318–319
    Iran, 622–623
    Japan, 241–242, 246
    Mexico, 428, 431, 435
    Russian Federation, 567, 571
economic liberalization, 291, **291**, 303
economic policy
    Brazil, 380, 384–385
    Britain, 51–53
    China, 664
    EU, 205–207
    France, 99–100
    Germany, 144–145
    India, 288, 290–291
    Iran, 620
    Japan, 239, 242–243
    Mexico, 427–428, 430–432
    Nigeria, 522
    Russian Federation, 563, 566, 568–570
    South Africa, 475, 477, 481
    United States, 333
Economist Intelligence Unit (EIU), 24
Economist Intelligence Unit Democracy Index, 8, **9**, 24, 26, 36
economy
    Brazil, 378–379, 380, 382–387
    Britain, 50–52, 57
    China, 3–4, 16, 661, 664, 666–671, 692
    France, 88, 90, 97, 99, 101
    Germany, 146–149, 150–152, 177–178
    India, 288, 289–294, 318–319
    informal, 383–384
    Iran, 620, 622–626, 648
    Japan, 15, 241–245, 271
    Mexico, 423, 424–425, 427–428, 430–435, 457–458
    Nigeria, 522, 524–529
    political, 15–16
    Russian Federation, 567–575
    South Africa, 473–474, 475, 476–483, 504
    South Korea, 15
    United States, 333, 334–340
ECOSOC. *See* Economic and Social Committee (ECOSOC)
ECOWAS. *See* Economic Community of West African States (ECOWAS)
ECT. *See* European Constitutional Treaty (ECT)

EDC. *See* European Defense Community (EDC)
Edict of Nantes, 89
education system
    Brazil, 410
    Germany, 148, 171
    India, 293
    Iran, 624, 645–646
    Mexico, 426–427
    South Africa, 471, 472, 476–477
EEC. *See* European Economic Community (EEC)
EFSF. *See* European Financial Stability Facility (EFSF)
EIU. *See* Economist Intelligence Unit (EIU)
ejido, **423**
elderly population. *See* aging population
elections
    Brazil, 402
    Britain, 72–73
    China, 685–686
    EU, 221
    European Parliament, 202
    France, 94–95, 110, 116, 119–121, 122
    Germany, 169–170
    India, 277, 306, 310, 311
    Iran, 608, 641–642
    Japan, 229, 259, 261–263
    Mexico, 439–440, 447, 451
    Nigeria, 541–542
    Russian Federation, 592–593
    South Africa, 498–499
    United States, 325, 329, 355–358
Electoral College, 329, 344
electoral system, Britain, 72–73
electoral trends, Britain, 74–75
Emergency (1975-1977), **284**
EMS. *See* European Monetary System (EMS)
EMU. *See* Economic and Monetary Union (EMU)
Energiewende, **152**
energy prices, 152
energy sector, 573–575, 600
England, 42
Enlightenment, 89
environmental activism, Britain, 76
environmental issues
    Brazil, 387–388
    Britain, 56
    China, 671–672
    European Union, 194
    France, 102
    Germany, 152
    India, 294–295
    Iran, 626–627
    Japan, 245–246
    Mexico, 435–436
    Nigeria, 529–530
    Russian Federation, 572
    South Africa, 480–481
    United States, 340–341
Environmental Performance Index (EPI), **8**, 36
Environmental Protection Agency (EPA), 341
EPA. *See* Environmental Protection Agency (EPA)
EPI. *See* Environmental Performance Index (EPI)
equality, 359
Equal Pay Act (1970), 55
ERDF. *See* European Regional Development Fund (ERDF)
Erhard, Ludwig, 142
ESM. *See* European Stability Mechanism (ESM)
ethnic conflicts, 21
ethnic groups
    Brazil, 371–372, 403

China, 656–657, 687–688
    Iran, 611
    Mexico, 418, 457
    Nigeria, 513, 514–515
    Russian Federation, 557, 593
    South Africa, 466
    United States, 327
ethnic identity, 21
ethnicity
    Britain, 41
    France, 122–123
ethnic minorities
    Britain, 54–55, 76, 79
    China, 687–688
    France, 102, 113, 123–124
    Germany, 150–151
    India, 278–279, 315–316
    Iran, 643–644
    Japan, 263–265
    Nigeria, 517–518, 529
    United States, 362
ethnic profiling, 113
ethnonationalist conflicts, 11
EU. *See* European Union (EU)
EUCJ. *See* European Union Court of Justice (EUCJ)
Eurasion Economic Union (EEU), 600
euro, 103, 153, 193, 209, 342–343
Eurogroup, 204
European Central Bank (ECB), 153, 193, **195**, 196
European Coal and Steel Community (ECSC), 184, 189–190
European Commission, 187, 188, **190**, 191, 199–201, 215–216, 226
European Constitutional Treaty (ECT), 187
European Convention on Human Rights (ECHR), 65
European Council, 188, 192, 198, 200–201, 216–217
European Court of Justice (ECJ), 65, 186
European Defense Community (EDC), 190
European democracy, 188
European Economic Community (EEC), 58, 186
European External Action Service, 204
European Financial Stability Facility (EFSF), 196
European Investment Bank, 204
European market, 205–207
European Monetary System (EMS), 192
European Parliament (EP), 186, 199, 201–203, 217
European Regional Development Fund (ERDF), 207
European single market, **199**
European Stability Mechanism (ESM), 196
European Union (EU), 5, 13, 23, 183–227
    agriculture policy, 207
    Brexit from, 39, 47, 49, 59, 78–79, 96, 187, 197, 343
    budget of, 208
    chronology of, 184–185
    citizenship, 217–218
    collective identities in, 188, 217–218
    comparative politics, 224–225
    comparisons with, 188
    competition policy, 206–207
    competitiveness and, 209–210
    critical historical junctures in, 185–187
    deindustrialization in, 223
    demographic trends, 224
    development of, 189–194
    Eastern Partnership policy, 214
    economic policy, 205–207
    elections, 221

European Union (EU) (*Continued*)
environmental issues, 194
facts and statistics, 183
federal policies of, 205–207
foreign policy of, 187, 212–215
France and, 96, 103, 113
geographic setting, 185
Germany and, 152–153, 176–177, 189–190
global economy and, 195, 342–343
globalization and, 209–210, 223, 224–225
governance, 194–195, 198–205
Great Recession in, 187, 196–197
institutions, 198–205
interest groups, 218–221
justice and home affairs, 211–212
making of, 184–188
media in, 221–222
monetary policy, 209
Nobel Peace Prize for, 198
political challenges and changing agendas in, 223–224
political culture in, 217–218
political economy in, 189–194, 195–197
political impact of technology in, 221–222
politics in action, 184–187
politics in transition, 222–226
prospects for, 225–226
refugee issues and, 212
regional development, 207–208
representation and participation in, 215–222
Russia and, 573, 575, 600
security policy, 212–215
shared policies, 209–211
social movements and protest in, 218–221
social policy, 210–211, 224–225
U.S. and, 213
European Union Court of Justice (EUCJ), 186, **187**, 203–204
Eurozone, **153**
Eurozone crisis, 196–197, 218
exchange rates, 191
executive, 9, **10**
Brazil, 373, 391–393
Britain, 43, 59
China, 658, 674–679
France, 87, 107
Germany, 135, 155–158
India, 282, 298–300
Iran, 611, 630–633
Japan, 234, 250–251
Mexico, 419, 438–440
Nigeria, 514, 534–536
Russian Federation, 558, 578–579
South Africa, 464, 484–486
United States, 329, 346–347
Expediency Council, **631**, 639
Export-Import Bank, 343
export-led growth, **382**
exports
Brazil, 382, 389, 408–409
Germany, 144
Iran, 622
Japan, 242, 246–247, 270
Mexico, 430
Nigeria, 524
Russia, 573, 574

F

Facebook, 502, 546
failed state, **651**
Falun Gong (FLG), 689–690
Fanon, Frantz, 625
Farage, Nigel, 46–47
Farsi, **610**

favelas, **387**, 396, 404
Fedayin, 641
federal character, 533
federalism, **325**, 583
Germany, 160–161
Nigeria, 532–533
United States, 345, 351, 357, 358
federal republics, 160
Federal Reserve Board, **335**
federal system, **563**, 583
Federation of Independent Trade Unions (FITU), 595–596
fertility rate
Germany, 179
Japan, 272
Fifteenth Amendment, 357
Fifth Republic, France, 93–94, 105, 106
fiscal system, Brazil, 383–384
5 percent clause, **164**
Fixed-Term Parliament Act (2011), 72
FLG. *See* Falun Gong (FLG)
floating population, **669**
FN. *See* National Front (NF)
foreign direct investment (FDI), **56**
Britain, 56–57
China, 672
India, 295
Japan, 247
Russia, 573
foreign policy
Brazil, 409–410
Britain, 80–81
EU, 187, 212–215
Germany, 144
Russian Federation, 600, 601
U.S., 332–333, 366
foreign tourism, France, 85–86
Foundation for the Oppressed, 636
Foundation of the Oppressed, **631**
Four Great Pollution Trials, **245**
Fourteenth Amendment, 330, 357
Fourth Republic, France, 92–93
Fox, Vincente, 425, 439, 449, 453, 455–456
framework regulations, **146**
France, 84–132
administrative structure, 87
ancien régime, 89–90
bureaucracy, 110–111
citizenship in, 97, 121, 123–124
civil service in, 110–111
collective identity in, 97
comparative politics, 130
Constitutional Council, 112
constitution of, 108–109
critical historical junctures in, 88–96
declinism in, 129
democracy in, 97
demographic trends, 88, 130
economic policy, 99–100
economy of, 88, 90, 97, 99, 101
elections in, 94–95, 110, 116, 119–121, 122
environmental issues, 102
ethnicity in, 122–123
ethnic minorities in, 102, 113
EU and, 96, 103, 113
executive in, 87, 107
facts and statistics, 30, 32, 34
Fifth Republic, 105, 106
Fourth Republic, 92–94
gender equality, 102–103
generation gap in, 102
geographic setting, 86–88
globalization and, 96–97, 103, 128
governance in, 105–111
immigration in, 122–123
industrialization in, 90–91, 98–99

inequality in, 102–103
interest groups, 125–126
judiciary, 87, 111–112
labor relations in, 102
law making in, 115
legislature in, 87, 114–116, 124–125
map of, 89
media in, 126
military, 113
minor parties in, 119
monarchy in, 89–90
Muslims in, 86, 113, 123–124, 127–128
National Front, 129
national identity in, 121, 123–124
neoliberal modernization strategy in, 100–101
parity law in, 124–125
party system in, 87, 116
police, 113
policy-making process, 113
political culture, 121
political development of, 86–87
political economy in, 98–105
political impact of technology in, 126
political organization of, 87
political parties in, 94–95, 116–119
political system of, 87
politics in action, 85–86
politics in transition, 127–130
president of, 107–110
prime minister of, 109–110
public and semipublic agencies, 111
regime history, 87
semi-presidential system of, 106
social class in, 122
socialism in, 99–100
social model, 128
social movements and protest in, 126
society and economy in, 101–102
state and economy in, 98–105
state institutions, 111–114
state organization in, 105–106
subnational government, 112–113
terrorist attacks in, 85–86, 96, 129–130
Third Republic, 90–91
tourism in, 85–86
trade unions in, 125–126
U.S. relations with, 96
Vichy, 91–93
welfare state in, 101–102, 128
women in, 102–103, 124–125
World War I and, 91
World War II and, 91–92
Franchise Act (1884), 44
Franco, Itamar, 378
Franco-Prussian War, 91
Free Democratic Party (FDP), 165, 168
Freedom House, 17
Freedom in the World rankings, 8, 18
Freedom of the World report (2017), 4
free markets, 15, 149, **334**, 335
free trade, 243, 326, 389, 424, 433, 436–437
French culture, 128
French exceptionalism, 97–98, 130
French Revolution, 90
French Wars of Religion, 89
Fukushima nuclear disaster, 175, **246**, 257, 271
Fukuyama, Francis, 2–3
fundamentalism, **124**
fusion of powers, **59**

G

G-34, 540
Gaddafi, Muammar, 64
Gandhi, Indira, 284–286, 297, 298, 307, 321

Gandhi, Mohandas, 283, 469
Gandhi, Rajiv, 286, 307
Gandhi, Sonia, 286
Gang of Four, 661
Gastarbeiter, **136**
GATT. *See* General Agreement on Tariffs and Trade (GATT)
GCHQ. *See* Government Communications Headquarters (GCHQ)
GDI. *See* Gender-Related Development Index (GDI)
GEM. *See* Gender Empowerment Measure (GEM)
Gender Empowerment Measure (GEM), 8
gender equality/inequality, 23
    Britain, 55, 73–74
    France, 102–103, 124–125
    Germany, 151–152, 163–164, 172
    India and, 304–305
    Iran, 644
    Japan, 244, 261, 267–268
    Russian Federation, 594
    United States, 337
gender pay gap, 55, 102, 337
Gender-Related Development Index (GDI), 8
General Agreement on Tariffs and Trade (GATT), 189, 195, 436
General Directorates (DGs), 199
general secretary, **676**
generation gap
    Britain, 80
    France, 102
geographic area, by country, 30
geographic setting
    Brazil, 371–372
    Britain, 39–40
    China, 656–658
    European Union, 185
    France, 86–88
    Germany, 136–137
    India, 278–280
    Iran, 609–610
    Japan, 230–231
    Mexico, 419–420
    Nigeria, 513–515
    Russian Federation, 558–559
    South Africa, 465
    United States, 326
Germany, 133–182
    administrative structure, 135
    after 9/11, 143–144
    Basic Law, 154
    bureaucracy, 158
    cabinet, 157–158
    chancellor of, 155–157, 158
    citizenship in, 171–172
    collective identities in, 145, 178
    comparative politics, 179–180
    comparisons with, 145–146
    critical historical junctures in, 138–144
    democracy in, 145
    demographic trends, 178–179
    division of, 141–142
    economic policy, 144–145
    economy of, 146–152, 177–178
    education system, 148, 171
    elections in, 169–170
    environmental issues, 152
    ethnic minorities in, 150–151
    EU and, 152–153, 176–177, 189–190
    executive in, 135, 155–158
    export surplus, 144
    facts and statistics, 30, 32, 34, 133, 136
    foreign policy of, 144
    gender equality in, 151–152, 163–164, 172
    geographic setting, 136–137

globalization and, 144–145, 152–153
global leadership of, 150
governance, 154–161
Great Depression in, 139
Great Recession in, 153, 177–178
immigration to, 134–137, 150–151, 171–172
interest groups, 172–173
Japan and, 240
judiciary in, 135, 160
legislature in, 135, 162–165
map of, 137
media in, 174–175
military, 159
national identity, 171–172
Nazi, 19, 91, 140–141, 145, 283
party system in, 135, 165–169
police, 159–160
policy-making process in, 161–162
political challenges for, 177–178
political culture, 171–172
political development, 134–135
political economy in, 146–149
political impact of technology in, 174–175
political organization, 135
political parties in, 162, 165–169
political system of, 135
politics in action, 134–136
politics in transition, 176–180
president of, 155
refugee policy, 134–135, 137, 171–172
regime history, 135
relations with U.S., 143–144
representation and participation in, 162–175
Second Reich, 138–139
semipublic institutions, 147–149
social market economy, 146–149
social movements and protest in, 172–174
society and economy in, 150–152
state and economy in, 144, 146–149
state institutions, 154–155
state organization in, 154–158
subnational government, 160–161
Third Reich, 140–141, 145
trade unions in, 148
unification of, 142–143, 149, 193
U.S. occupation of, 189
Weimar Republic, 139–140, 145
women in, 151–152, 163–164, 172
World War I and, 138–139
World War II and, 141, 171
Giddens, Anthony, 45
Gini index, 32–33
Giscard d'Estaing, Valery, 107
glasnost, **563**, 572, 586
global economy
    Brazil and, 388–390
    Britain in, 56–57
    China and, 672–673
    EU and, 195, 342–343
    France and, 103
    Germany and, 152–153
    India and, 295–296
    Iran and, 627–629
    Japan and, 246–248
    Mexico and, 436–437
    Nigeria and, 530–531
    Russia and, 572–575
    South Africa and, 481–482
    United States and, 341–343, 366
Global Gender Gap, 7, 36
globalization, 7, 13–15, 46
    Brazil and, 380, 388–390, 409, 411–412
    Britain and, 48–49
    China and, 663–664, 672–673
    EU and, 209–210, 223, 224–225
    France and, 96–97, 103, 128

Germany and, 144–145, 152–153
India and, 288, 295–296
Iran and, 619–620, 627–629
Japan and, 246–248, 265
Mexico and, 427, 436–437
Nigeria and, 522, 530–531
opposition to, 128
Russia and, 565, 572–575
South Africa and, 474, 481–482
United States and, 332–333, 341–343
Glorious Revolution, 43
Gorbachev, Mikhail, 2, 563, 572, 576, 586, 587
governance
    Brazil, 390–397
    Britain, 58–66
    China, 674–681
    European Union, 194–195, 198–205
    France, 105–111
    Germany, 154–161
    India, 296–302
    Iran, 629–637
    Japan, 248–257
    Mexico, 438–441
    Nigeria, 532–538
    Russian Federation, 576–585
    South Africa, 483–492
    United States, 344–350
Government Communications Headquarters (GCHQ), 77
government institutions. *See* state institutions
government surveillance, 23
    Britain, 77
    India, 314–315
Gowon, Yakuba, 519
Grand Apartheid, 470–471
grand coalition, **156**
grandes écoles, **111**
grands corps, **111**
Great Britain. *See* Britain
Great Depression
    in Brazil, 374–375
    in Britain, 45
    in Germany, 139
    in Japan, 236
    in United States, 330–331
Great Leap Forward, 660, 666
Great Recession of 2008, 3, 46, 51, 54, 57, 153, 177–178, 187
    in Asia-Pacific region, 247
    in Europe, 196–197
    in Russia, 600
Great Smog (1952), 56
Greece, economic crisis in, 196, 197
Green Party
    Britain, 72
    Germany, 166, 167–168, 171
    Mexico, 451
green revolution, **290**
gross domestic product (GDP), **16–17**
    China, 667, 668
    India, 319
    Mexico, 431
    Nigeria, 514, 528
gross national product (GNP), **16–17**
    comparative, 1958–1973, 99
    by country, 32–33
    Japan, 271
Guardian Council, **609**
guerrilla warfare, **659**
guest workers, **136**, 343
guild system, **147**

H

hacking scandal, Britain, 77
Hamon, Benoit, 117

hate crimes, 53, 79
health care system
    Brazil, 386
    Britain, 53
    Iran, 626
    Russian Federation, 570–571
    South Africa, 502–503
health insurance, 339–340, 670
health insurance fund, **147**
hegemonic power, **44**
Henry IV, 89
Hezbollahis, **617**
Hidalgo, Miguuel, 420
higher education
    China, 695
    EU, 223–224
    Germany, 171
    Iran, 645–646
    South Africa, 463–464
high-speed rail, 270
hijab, 124
Hindenburg, Paul von, 139–140
Hiroshima, 237
history, end of, 2–3
Hitler, Adolf, 91, 139–141, 144, 331
HIV/AIDS, 479, 502–503, 596
hojjat al-Islam, **617**
Hollande, François, 96, 101, 107, 117, 125
Holocaust, 141, 171
Holy Roman Empire, 138
homelands, **470**
Hong Kong, 14
    return of, to China, 48, 80
house churches, 686
household registration, **691**
household responsibility system, 668, **669**
House of Commons, 58, 59, 60, 67, 78
House of Lords, 59, 60, 68, 78
House of Representatives, 329–330,
    352–354, 358
housing policy, Germany, 162
Hu Jintao, 663
Human Development Index (HDI), 7, 8, 36
Human Development Report (UN), 29
human rights, 456–457, 616
Human Rights Act (1998), 65
Hundred Years' War, 88–89
Hungary, 134
hung parliament, **72**
Husayn, Imam, 626
Hussein, Saddam, 618
hybrid state, **24**, 25–26

I

IAS. *See* Indian Administrative Service (IAS)
identity-based conflict, 20–21
    India, 311–312, 315–316
illiberal democracy, **24**, 218
illiteracy, 431
Imam Jum'ehs, **631**
IMF. *See* International Monetary Fund (IMF)
immigration
    Brazil, 403
    France, 122–123
    Germany, 134–137, 150–151, 171–172
    illegal, 212, 338
    Japan, 265
    Mexico, 420, 434, 457–458
    United States, 333, 338–339, 343, 364,
        457–458
Immigration Reform and Control Act
    (IRCA), 434
impeachment, 392
import substitution industrialization (ISI),
    382–383, 430–432

INC. *See* Indian National Congress (INC)
income inequality
    Brazil, 385
    Britain, 39, 53
    by country, 386
    EU, 223–224
    India, 292–294
    Iran, 624–625
    Japan, 244
    Nigeria, 527–528
    Russian Federation, 570–571
    South Africa, 478
    United States, 337–338
indigenous groups, **419**
independent variable, **11**
Index of Economic Freedom, 8
India, 276–323
    administrative structure, 282
    after 9/11, 287
    agriculture policy, 290, 291
    anti-terrorism efforts in, 301
    bureaucracy, 299–300
    cabinet in, 298–299
    caste system in, 280, 294
    child labor in, 293
    China and, 317–318
    citizenship, 311–312
    coalition governments in, 286
    collective identity in, 288, 311–312
    colonial legacy in, 281–282
    comparative politics, 321–322
    comparative politics and, 288–289
    constitution of, 296–297, 301
    critical historical junctures in, 280–287
    democracy in, 19, 277–278, 288, 296–297,
        321–322
    demographic trends, 293, 320
    demonetization in, 277
    development of, 277–278
    economic policy, 288, 290–291
    economy of, 288, 289–294, 318–319
    education system, 293
    elections in, 277, 306, 310, 311
    Emergency (1975-1977), 284
    environmental issues, 294–295
    ethnic groups in, 278, 315–316
    ethnonationalist conflicts in, 11, 21
    executive in, 282, 298–300
    facts and statistics, 30, 32, 34, 276, 280
    geographic setting, 278–280
    globalization and, 288, 295–296
    governance, 296–302
    independence for, 48
    Indira Gandhi era, 284–286, 298, 321
    inequality in, 292–294
    institutional decay in, 319–320
    interest groups in, 312–314
    as international power, 319
    judiciary in, 282, 301–302
    Kashmir conflict, 317
    legislature in, 282, 303–305
    making of modern, 277–289
    map of, 281
    media in, 314–315
    military, 300
    nationalist movement in, 282–283
    Nehru era, 283–284, 290
    nuclear weapons of, 316–317
    Pakistan and, 316–317
    partition of, 283
    party system in, 282, 305–311
    police, 300
    policy-making process in, 303
    political challenges and changing agendas in,
        315–320
    political culture in, 311–312

political economy in, 288, 289–291
political impact of technology in, 314–315
political parties in, 305–311
political system of, 25, 282
political violence in, 316
politics in action, 277–278
politics in transition, 315–322
poverty in, 289, 292, 318–319
president of, 299
prime ministers of, 285, 298
regime history, 282
regional relations, 317–318
religions in, 279
representation and participation in, 304–315
social movements and protest in, 312–314
social welfare programs, 292–294
society and economy in, 292–294
state and economy in, 290–291
state institutions, 299–302, 319–320
state organization, 296–298
subnational government, 302
terrorist attacks in, 316
U.S. and, 287
women in, 304–305
Indian Administrative Service (IAS), **299**–300
Indian National Congress (INC), 282–283
Indian Rebellion, **282**
indicative planning, **99**
indigenous groups, **419**
    Mexico, 421
indirect rule, **517**
industrialization
    Brazil, 385
    France, 90–91, 98–99
    Germany, 138
    import substitution, 382–383, 430–432
    Japan, 246
    Russia, 558, 559
    Soviet Union, 2
industrial policy, **99, 239**
Industrial Revolution, **43**–44, 49, 90
industries, nationalized, 63
inequality
    See also gender equality/inequality; income
        inequality
    Brazil, 385
    Britain, 54–55
    China, 669, 692
    France, 102–103
    Germany, 179
    India, 292–294
    Japan, 236
    Mexico, 458
    Nigeria, 527–528
    South Africa, 478
    United States, 337–338
    workplace, 210
infant mortality
    by country, 35
    Iran, 624, 626
    Mexico, 431
    Nigeria, 528
    South Africa, 479
inflation
    in Brazil, 384–385
    stagflation, 186, 191
influx control, **472**
informal economy, 383–**384**
Inkatha (IFP), 495–496
insider privatization, **568**
institutional decay, in India, 319–320
institutional design, **13**, 19
    European Union, 198–205
Institutional Revolutionary Party (PRI), 423,
    425, 426, 428, 433, 445–448, 452–453
institutional triangle, **198**

interest groups, **332**
  Brazil, 405–406
  Britain, 76–77
  China, 689–690
  EU, 218–221
  France, 125–126
  Germany, 172–173
  India, 312–314
  Iran, 644–645
  Japan, 265–267
  Mexico, 452–453
  Nigeria, 544–545
  Russian Federation, 594–596
  social movements and protest in, 500–501
  South Africa, 500–501
  United States, 332, 351, 359–361
intergovernmental Europe, 211–215
International Corruption Perceptions Index
  (CPI), 8, **9**, 36
international financial institutions (IFIs),
  524, **525**
International Monetary Fund (IMF), 13, **14**,
  187, 189, 239, 291, 342, 388, 573
international organizations, 13, 575
international relations, vs. comparative
  politics, 7
international trade
  Brazil and, 389
  British Empire and, 44
  China and, 247, 672–673
  EU and, 213
  Germany and, 149
  Japan and, 242, 246–247
  Russian Federation and, 573, 574
  U.S. and, 336
Internet, 8, 314, 407, 454, 501–502, 597, 602,
  646, 690–691
interventionist, **382**, **522**
interventores, **375**
inverse correlation, 11
Iran, 607–652
  administrative structure, 611
  after 9/11, 618–619
  bureaucracy, 633–634
  citizenship, 642–644
  civil society in, 647
  collective identity in, 621, 642–644
  comparative politics, 621, 650–651
  conservatives vs. liberals in, 638
  constitution of, 617, 629, 643
  critical historical junctures in, 612–619
  democracy in, 620–621, 647–648
  demographic trends, 650
  economic crisis in, 623
  economic policy, 620
  economy of, 620, 622–626, 648
  education system, 624
  elections, 641–642
  elections in, 608
  environmental issues, 626–627
  ethnic groups in, 611
  executive in, 611, 630–633
  facts and statistics, 30, 32, 34, 607, 611
  foreign relations, 648–649
  gender equality in, 644
  geographic setting, 609–610
  globalization and, 619–620, 627–629
  governance, 629–637
  income inequality in, 624–625
  interest groups in, 644–645
  Islamic Republic of, 617–618, 621,
    623–624, 631, 646–647, 647–650
  Islamic Revolution in, 615–617, 628–629
  judiciary in, 611, 634–635
  land ownership in, 625
  languages in, 611

  legislature in, 611, 640
  making of modern, 608–622
  map of, 612
  media in, 645–646
  military, 635–636
  nuclear issue and, 620, 649–650
  Pahlavis in, 613–615, 616–617
  party system in, 611, 640–641
  policy-making process in, 637–639
  political challenges and changing agendas in,
    647–650
  political culture in, 642–644
  political development of, 608–609
  political economy in, 622–626
  political impact of technology in, 645–646
  political organization, 611
  political parties in, 640–641
  political system of, 25, 611
  politics in action, 608–609
  politics in transition, 646–651
  president of, 630–633
  Qajars in, 613
  religion in, 610, 611, 642–643
  representation and participation in, 639–646
  Safavids in, 612
  semipublic institutions, 636–637
  social welfare programs, 624–626
  society and economy in, 624–626
  state and economy, 622–624
  state institutions, 634–637
  subnational government, 636
  terrorism and, 618–619
  U.S. relations with, 614, 615, 619, 628,
    649–650
  women in, 644
  youth in, 650
Iran-Iraq War, 618, 619, 623, 648
Iraq War, 47, 64, 80–81, 95, 173
Ireland, economic crisis in, 196, 197
iron rice bowl, **669**
iron triangle, **242**, 256–257, 348
ISI. *See* import substitution industrialization
  (ISI)
ISIS. *See* Islamic State (ISIS), 64, 86
Islam, 610, 647–648, 650–651
Islamic Republic of Iran, 617–618, 621,
  623–624, 631, 646–647, 647–650
Islamic Revolution, 615–617, 628–629
Islamic State (ISIS), 159, 366
Islamism, 3, **621**
isolationism, 64

J

JA. *See* Japan Agricultural Cooperative (JA)
James II (king), 43
Janata Dal, 307–308
Janata Party, 307–308
Japan, 192, 228–275
  administrative structure, 234
  Allied Occupation of, 229, 237–238, 241,
    253
  Britain and, 240
  bureaucracy, 251–252
  cabinet in, 250–251
  citizenship, 263–264, 265
  civil society in, 265–269
  collective identity in, 239–240, 263–264
  comparative politics, 273–274
  comparisons with, 240
  constitution of, 229, 235–236, 238, 249–250,
    274
  critical historical junctures in, 231–238
  democracy in, 239
  demographic trends, 272–273

  economic growth in, 241–242, 246
  economic policy, 239, 242–243
  economy of, 15, 241–245, 271
  elections in, 229, 259, 261–263
  environmental issues, 245–246
  ethnic minorities in, 263–265
  executive in, 234, 250–251
  facts and statistics, 31, 33, 35, 228, 232
  Fukushima nuclear disaster, 175, 246,
    257, 271
  geographic setting, 230–231
  Germany and, 240
  globalization and, 246–248, 265
  governance, 248–257
  Great Depression in, 236
  industrialization in, 246
  industrial policy, 239
  interest groups, 265–267
  judiciary in, 234, 253–255
  labor unions in, 266
  legislature in, 234, 257–258
  making of modern, 229–240
  map of, 233
  media in, 269–270
  Meiji Restoration, 235, 239, 241
  militarist nationalism in, 236–237
  military, 237–238, 253, 254
  monarchy in, 248–249
  outcast groups in, 264–265
  pacifist democracy in, 237–238, 249, 274
  party system in, 234, 258–260
  police, 255
  policy-making process in, 256–257
  political challenges and changing agendas in,
    271–272
  political culture in, 263–264
  political development of, 230–231
  political economy in, 241–243, 247
  political impact of technology in, 269–270
  political organization, 234
  political parties in, 258–260
  political system of, 234
  politics in action, 229–230
  postwar, 239
  prime minister of, 250–251
  regime history, 234
  representation and participation in, 257–270
  resident foreigners in, 265
  settlement of, 231
  social movements and protest in, 267–269
  social welfare programs in, 244–245
  society and economy in, 243–245
  state and economy in, 241–243
  state institutions, 251–256
  state organization, 248–250
  subnational government, 255–256
  Taisho democracy, 235–236
  taxation in, 271
  territorial disputes, 260
  United States and, 241–242
  U.S. and, 229, 254, 269
  women in, 244, 261, 267–268
  World War II and, 229, 236–237, 240
  youth in, 272–273
Japan Agricultural Cooperative (JA), 266–267
Japan Association of Corporate Executives, 266
Japan Business Federation, 265–266
Japanese Trade Union Confederation (JTUC),
  266
Japan Restoration Party, 259
Japan Self-Defense Forces (JSDF), **238**
Jews, Holocaust and, 141
Jiang Zemin, 662–663
jihad, **515**
Jim Crow laws, 357
Joan of Arc, 89

John (king), 42
Johnson, Boris, 47
Jonathan, Goodluck, 521, 532, 533, 534–535
Jospin, Lionel, 95
JSDF. *See* Japan Self-Defense Forces (JSDF)
JTUC. *See* Japanese Trade Union Confederation (JTUC)
Juárez, Benito, 421
judicial review, **65**
judiciary, 9, **10**
    Brazil, 373, 394–395
    Britain, 43, 65
    China, 658, 679–680
    EU, 211–212
    France, 87, 111–112
    Germany, 135, 160
    independent, 23
    India, 282, 301–302
    Iran, 611, 634–635
    Japan, 234, 253–255
    Mexico, 419, 442–443
    Nigeria, 514, 537–538
    Russian Federation, 558, 581–582
    South Africa, 464, 487–489
    United States, 329, 348–349
jurist's guardianship, **616**
Justice and Home Affairs (JHA), **186**

K

Karzai, Hamid, 287
Kashmir, 317
keiretsu, **244**
Kejriwal, Arvind, 309–310
Kerry, John, 96
Keynes, John Maynard, 51
Keynesianism, 9, 51
Khamenei, Ali, 630, 646
Khan, Reza, 613–614
Khan, Sadiq, 56
Khatami, Muhammad, 608
Khodorkovsky, Mikhail, 570
Khomeini, Ayatollah Ruhollah, 615–620, 629, 630, 632, 638–639
Khrushchev, Nikita, 561
Kissinger, Henry, 628
koenkai, 261, **262**
Kohl, Helmut, 142–143
Koike, Yuriko, 261
Koizumi, Junichiro, 251
Korean immigrants, in Japan, 265
Korean War, 238, 253
Kosovo, 14, 64
Krugman, Paul, 101
Kubitschek, Juscelino, 375–376
Kulturkampf, **138**
Kumar, Kanhaiya, 302
Kurdish migrants, 151
Kurdistan, 11
Kurds, 10–11
Kyoto Protocol, 194, 341, 572

L

labor force, women in, 102, 151, 644
labor force participation rates, Germany, 151
labor market
    Brazil, 385
    Britain, 57
    India, 293
    Iran, 623
    Japan, 244
labor movement
    France, 125–126

Iran, 645
Nigeria, 544
labor productivity, world trade and, 44
labor relations, France, 102
labor unions
    Brazil, 397
    Britain, 75
    China, 689
    France, 125–126
    Germany, 148
    India, 295, 312
    Iran, 614
    Japan, 266
    Mexico, 446–447, 452
    Nigeria, 544
    Russian Federation, 595–596
    South Africa, 500–501
    United States, 338, 340
Labour Party, 39, 47, 51, 52–53, 69–70
laissez-faire, 45, **49**, 337
Lake Chad, 530
Landless Peasant Movement (MST), 388
land reform
    Brazil, 387
    India, 290
    Nigeria, 529
La République en marche (LRM), 110, 119
large N analysis, 11
law making
    See also legislature
    France, 115
    Japan, 258
    Russian Federation, 585
Lay Judge System, **255**
Leader/Supreme Leader, **609**
leading small groups, **677**
League of Nations, 236
Lee Teng-hui, 660
Left Party, 168–169, 171
legislative process, Britain, 67–68
legislative reform, Britain, 68–69
legislature, 9, **10**
    Brazil, 373, 398–399
    Britain, 43, 67–69
    China, 658, 682–683
    France, 87, 114–116, 124–125
    Germany, 135, 162–165
    India, 282, 303–305
    Iran, 611, 640
    Japan, 234, 257–258
    Mexico, 419, 445–446
    Nigeria, 514, 539
    Russian Federation, 558, 586–587
    South Africa, 464, 492–493
    United States, 325, 329–330, 351, 352–354
legitimacy, 10, **11**
Lehman Brothers, 247
Le Pen, Jean-Marie, 94–95, 118
Le Pen, Marine, 3, 95, 103, 117–119, 120
Les Républicains (LR), 116–117
level of analysis, in comparative politics, 9–10
liberal, **138**
liberal democracy, **3**, 24
Liberal Democratic Party (LDP), Japan, 229, 249–251, 256, 258–260, 262, 266
Liberal Democratic Party of Russia (LDPR), 589, 591
Liberal Democrats, 71–72, 73
liberals, 638
Liberation Movement, 640–641
liberation theology, 403–404, 625
Liberia, 531
liberty, 358
Libya, 14, 17, 64, 95
life expectancy
    by country, 34

Iran, 626
Japan, 272
Mexico, 431
Nigeria, 528
Russian Federation, 596
South Africa, 479
Lineker, Gary, 39, 40
Lisbon Treaty (2009), 79, **187**, 197, 200–201, 204, 215, 223
Litvinenko, Alexander, 584–585
lobbying
    Brazil, 397
    EU, 218–221
local government. *See* subnational government
Lok Sabha, 298
London, England, 66
London bombings, 46, 79
Long-Term Refinancing Operations (LTRO), 196
López Obrador, Andés Manuel, 450
Louis XIV, 89–90
Louis XV, 90
Louis XVI, 90
LRM. *See* La République en marche (LRM)
Lula da Silva, Luiz Inácio, 379, 387, 388, 400–401
Luxembourg Compromise, 191

M

Maastricht Treaty, 186, 188, **193**, 194, 198, 212, 223
MacArthur, Douglas, 237
Macia, Mido, 488
macroeconomic policy, **51**
Macron, Emmanuel, 3, 85, 95, 107–108, 110, 119, 125
Madrid, Miguel de la, 423
Magna Carta, 42
Majles, **609**, 613, 637–638, 639, 640, 647
Major, John, 45, 52, 60
Manchukuo, 236
Mandal Commission, **308**
Mandela, Nelson, 470, 472, 473, 484, 491, 493, 494
manifest destiny, **326**
Mao Zedong, 659–661, 662, 663–664, 666, 676
maps
    Brazil, 374
    Britain, 42
    China, 657
    France, 89
    Germany, 137
    India, 281
    Iran, 612
    Japan, 233
    Mexico, 420
    Nigeria, 515, 516, 518
    Russian Federation, 562
    South Africa, 467, 490
    United States, 328
maquiladoras, **420**
Maratha Empire, 281
Marbury v. Madison, **348**
market reform, **568**
Marshall Plan, 185–186, 189, 561
maslahat, **638**
mass organization, **689**
maternity leave, 102, 179, 571
Maurya dynasty, 280–281
Maximilian (emperor), 421
May, Theresa, 3, 47, 48, 53, 55, 57, 60, 71, 78, 79, 81
Mbeki, Thabo, 473, 479, 484, 486, 503

media, 14
 in Brazil, 406–407
 in Britain, 77
 in China, 687, 690–691
 in EU, 221–222
 in France, 126
 in Germany, 174–175
 in India, 314–315
 in Iran, 645–646
 in Japan, 269–270
 in Mexico, 453–454
 in Nigeria, 545–546
 in Russia, 596–597
 in South Africa, 501–502
 in United States, 361
Medicare, 339, 363
Medvedev, Dmitry, 564, 578–579, 600
Meiji restoration, 235, 239, 241
MERCOSUL. *See* Common Market of the
 South (MERCOSUL)
Mérida Initiative, 425
Merkel, Angela, 134, 143, 144, 153,
 155–156, 167
mestizo, **419**
Mexican Revolution, 422–423
Mexico, 415–461
 administrative structure, 419
 agrarian reform in, 422, 423
 bureaucracy in, 440–441
 cabinet, 438–440
 citizenship, 451
 civil society in, 429
 collective identity in, 428–429, 451
 colonialism in, 420
 comparative politics, 429, 459
 conquest of, 421
 constitution of, 421, 438
 crisis and reform in, 423–425
 critical historical junctures in, 420–427
 democracy in, 428
 demographic trends in, 458–459
 development, 1940-2010, 431
 drug trafficking in, 425, 429
 economic crisis in, 432–433, 435
 economic policy, 427–428, 430–432
 economy of, 423–425, 427–428, 430–435,
 457–458
 education system in, 426–427
 elections, 439–440, 447, 451
 environmental issues, 435–436
 ethnic groups in, 418, 457
 executive in, 419, 438–440
 facts and statistics, 31, 33, 35, 415, 418
 geographic setting, 419–420
 globalization and, 427, 436–437
 governance, 438–441
 import substitution in, 430–432
 independence for, 420–421
 interest groups in, 452–453
 judiciary in, 419, 442–443
 languages in, 418
 legislature in, 419, 445–446
 making of modern, 416–427
 map of, 420
 media in, 453–454
 military, 441–442
 as multiparty democracy, 425–427
 parastatal sector in, 441
 party system in, 419, 446–451
 policy-making process in, 444
 political challenges and changing agendas in,
 456–458
 political culture in, 451
 political development of, 416–417
 political economy in, 430–434
 political impact of technology in, 453–454

political organization of, 419
political parties in, 446–451
politics in action, 416–418
politics in transition, 455–459
politics of rapid development, 423
poverty in, 432, 458
president of, 438–440, 444, 455–456
regime history, 419
religions in, 418
representation and participation in, 445–455
revolution in, 422–423
social movements and protest in, 452–453
social welfare programs in, 458
society and economy in, 435
Sonoran Dynasty, 422–423
state and economy in, 430–434
state institutions, 441–443
state organization, 438–441
structural reforms in, 433
subnational government, 443
U.S. border with, 343
U.S. relations with, 416–418, 421, 427,
 457–458
women in, 440
Mexico City, 420, 432, 436
middle class, 223, 244, 290, 292, 320,
 625, 627
Middle East
 Arab Spring in, 11, 14
 conflicts in, 4
middle-level theory, **12**
migrant laborers, **470**, 669
migrants
 See also immigration
 China, 692
 France, 122–123
 Germany, 136, 171–172
 Mexico, 434, 457–458
Miliband, David, 70
Miliband, Ed, 52, 70
military
 Brazil, 395–396
 Britain, 64
 China, 680–681
 France, 113
 Germany, 159
 India, 300
 Iran, 635–636
 Japan, 237–238, 253, 254
 Mexico, 441–442
 Nigeria, 536–537
 Russian Federation, 584–585
 South Africa, 489
 United States, 350
 U.S., 254
military governments, 25
 Brazil, 376–378
 Japan, 236–237
 Mexico, 421–422
 Nigeria, 519–520, 522–523, 533, 547–548
Milosevic, Slobodan, 64
minimum wage, 340
Minsk II agreement, 598
Mitterrand, François, 93–94, 99, 105, 106, 107
mixed electoral system, **586**
mixed member system, **163**
moderating power, **372**
Modi, Narendra, 277, 286, 310–311, 322
Mojahedin, 641
monarchy
 British, 78
 France, 89–90
 Japan, 248–249
monetarism, **52**
monetary policy, EU, 209
Mosaddeq, Muhammad, 614, 641

Mozambique, 472
MST. *See* Landless Peasant Movement (MST)
Mughal Empire, 281
Muhammad, Murtula, 519
multiculturalism, 79, 97
multilateral organizations, 332–333
multinational corporations, 7, 335
Murdoch, Rupert, 77
Muslims
 in Britain, 76, 79
 in France, 86, 113, 123–124, 127–128
 in India, 283
 in Iran, 610
 in Nigeria, 529, 537–538, 543

N

NAFIN, 441
NAFTA. *See* North American Free Trade
 Agreement (NAFTA)
Nagasaki, 237
Napoleon, 44
Natal Indian Congress, 469
National Action Party (PAN), 425, 448–449
National Assembly, 114–115, 125
National Bank for Economic and Social
 Development (BNDES), 393
National Front (FN), 95, 97, 117–119, 129
National Front (NF), 641
National Health Service (NHS), 53
national identity
 See also collective identities
 Brazil, 402–403
 Britain, 76, 79
 France, 121, 123–124
 Germany, 171–172
 India, 311–312
 Japan, 239–240, 263–264
 Mexico, 457
 Russian Federation, 587–588, 593–594
 United States, 358–359
nationalism, **376**
nationalist movements, 10–11
 India, 282–283, 313–314
Nationalist Socialist Underground (NSU), 173
nationalization, 93, **100**
nationalized industries, Britain, 63
National Party Congress, **674**, 675
National People's Congress (NPC), **677**, 682–683
National Regeneration Movement
 (Morena), 450
National Republican Convention (NRC), 540
nationhood, 10
nation-state, **5**, 10
nativism, 364
NATO. *See* North Atlantic Treaty Organization
 (NATO)
natural disasters, 14
natural resources, 337, 573, 609
natural sciences, 11
Navalny, Alexei, 556–558
Naxalite, **292**, 314, 316, 320
Nazi Party, 19, 91, **139**, 140–141, 145, 283
NDPBs. *See* nondepartmental public bodies
 (NDPBs)
Nehru, Jawaharlal, 284, 290, 297, 298, 307
Nemstov, Boris, 591, 592
neoliberal, **101**
neoliberalism, 9, **50**, 51
 Brazil, 383
 France, 100–101
 India, 313–314
neo-Nazis, 173
Nepal, 318
netizens, **694**

Neves, Tancredo, 378
New Alliance Party, 451
New Deal, 330–331, 345
New Economic Policy (NEP), 560
New Labour Party, 45–46, 50, 52, 53–54, 57, 70, 346
newly industrializing countries (NICs), 696–697
news organizations, 8, 174, 596–597
  See also media
New Zealand, 48
NGOs. *See* nongovernmental organizations (NGOs)
NHS. *See* National Health Service (NHS)
Nice Treaty, 187
Nigeria, 509–554
  administrative structure, 514
  bureaucracy, 536
  citizenship, 542–543
  civil war in, 519
  collective identities, 542–544
  collective identity in, 523
  colonial rule of, 517–518
  comparative politics, 523, 551–552
  critical historical junctures in, 515–521
  democracy in, 512, 522–523, 548–550
  demographic trends in, 550–551
  economic crisis in, 524–525
  economic policy, 522
  economy of, 522, 524–529
  elections, 541–542
  environmental issues and, 529–530
  ethnic groups in, 513, 514–515
  ethnic minorities in, 529
  ethnic politics in, 517–518
  ethnonationalist conflicts in, 11, 21
  executive in, 514, 534–536
  facts and statistics, 31, 33, 35, 509, 513
  First Republic, 518–519, 532–533, 539
  Fourth Republic, 520–521, 533, 541, 547, 548
  geographic setting, 513–515
  globalization and, 522, 530–531
  governance, 532–538
  inequality in, 527–528
  interest groups in, 544–545
  judiciary in, 514, 537–538
  legislature in, 514, 539
  making of modern, 512–523
  map of, 515, 516, 518
  media in, 545–546
  military, 536–537
  military rule of, 519–520, 522–523, 533, 547–548
  modernity vs. traditionalism in, 542–543
  party system in, 514, 539–541
  policy-making process in, 538
  political challenges and changing agendas in, 547–550
  political culture, 542–543
  political development, 510–511
  political economy, 524–529
  political impact of technology in, 545–546
  political organization, 514
  political parties in, 539–541, 548
  political system of, 514
  politics in action, 512–513
  politics in transition, 547–552
  poverty in, 529, 550–551
  precolonial period, 515–516
  president of, 534–536
  regime history, 514
  religions in, 513, 514–515, 531, 543–544
  representation and participation in, 539–546
  Second and Third Republics, 520, 539–540
  social movements and protest in, 544–545
  social welfare programs in, 529
  society and economy in, 527–529
  state and economy in, 524–527
  state institutions, 536–538
  state organization, 532–533
  structural adjustment program in, 524–525
  subnational government, 538
  U.S. relations with, 531
  women in, 529
  youth in, 550–551
Nigeria Labour Congress (NLC), 544
Nineteenth Amendment, 357
Nixon, Richard, 331, 340, 628, 673
nonaligned bloc, 284
nondepartmental public bodies (NDPBs), 63–64
nongovernmental organizations (NGOs), 13, 406
  Brazil, 405
  China, 681, 689
  India, 312, 314
  Russian Federation, 595
nontariff barriers (NTBs), 191, **246**
nonviolent resistance, 283
Normandy, 88
North Africa, Arab Spring in, 11, 14
North American Free Trade Agreement (NAFTA), 13, **14**, 326, 342, 416, 424, 427, 433, 436–437, 575, 599
North Atlantic Treaty Organization (NATO), 64, 96, 141, 186, 189, 214, 561
Northern Ireland, 39, 59, 65
North Korea, 4
NSU. *See* Nationalist Socialist Underground (NSU)
NTBs. *See* nontariff barriers (NTBs)
Nuclear Non-Proliferation Treaty (NPT), 620
nuclear power
  France, 97, 102
  Germany, 175
  Iran, 620, 649–650
  Japan, 246, 256–257, 271
  South Africa, 481
nuclear weapons
  India, 316–317
  nonproliferation of, 317

O

Obama, Barack, 7, 95–96, 143, 336, 341, 346, 361, 366, 486–487, 619, 649
Obasanjo, Olusegun, 519, 520–521, 525, 532, 534, 537
Occupy movement, 407, 546
Odebrecht, Marcelo, 407–408
oil crisis (1973), 242
oil industry, **567**
  Iran, 609, 622, 623, 628–629
  Mexico, 432–434
  Nigeria, 522, 524–525, 527, 530, 531
oil wealth, 527
Okinawans, 263–264, 269
Old Republic (Brazil), 373–374
oligarchs, **569**, 570
oligarchy, **512**
OMC. *See* open method of coordination (OMC)
OMT. *See* Outright Monetary Transactions (OMT)
one-child policy (China), 671
OPEC. *See* Organization of Petroleum Exporting Countries (OPEC)
open method of coordination (OMC), 195
Opium War, 658
Organisation for Economic Development and Co-operation (OECD), 100–101, 244
Organization Department, **679**
Organization of Petroleum Exporting Countries (OPEC), 191, **628**
Ostopolitik, **167**
other backward classes, **308**
outcast groups, in Japan, 264–265
Outright Monetary Transactions (OMT), 196
outsourcing, to India, 295
Overseas Private Investment Corporation, 343

P

PAC. *See* political action committee (PAC)
pacifist democracy, 249, 274
Pahlavis, 613–615, 616–617
Pakistan, 283, 289
  after 9/11, 287
  independence for, 48
  India and, 316–317
Palestine, 619, 649
PAN. *See* National Action Party (PAN)
Pan-Africanist Congress (PAC), 494
panchayats, **302**
parastatals, **383**, 441
pariah state, **651**
Paris Agreement (2016), 175, 341, 388, 572
parity law, **124**–125
parliament
  See also legislature
  Britain, 42–43, 50, 58, 66, 67–69
  European, 186, 199, 201–203, 217
  France, 114–115
  India, 303–305
  Russian Federation, 586–587
  South Africa, 492–493
parliamentary committees, 69
parliamentary democracy, **58**
parliamentary sovereignty, **58**, 65, 66
parliamentary system, 19
  Britain, 58–63
  compared with presidential system, 62, 106
  Germany, 162–165
party democracy, **165**
Party of Democratic Socialism (PDS), 166
Party of the Democratic Revolution (PRD), 449–450
party system
  Brazil, 373, 399–402
  Britain, 43, 69–75
  China, 658, 683–685
  France, 87, 116
  Germany, 135, 165–169
  India, 282, 305–311
  Iran, 611, 640–641
  Japan, 234, 258–260
  Mexico, 419, 446–451
  Nigeria, 514, 539–541
  Russian Federation, 558, 587–592
  South Africa, 464, 493–498
  United States, 329, 354–356
pasdaran, **616**
pass laws, **469**
paternity leave, 102, 179
patrimonial state, **559**
patronage system, **283**
Pearl Harbor, 237, 331
Pelosi, Nancy, 358
PEMEX, 441
Peña Nieto, Enrique, 416, 417–418, 426–427, 439–440, 453, 456
pensioners, 80, 102, 179
People Act (1918), 44
People of the Book, **612**
People's Liberation Army (PLA), **680**–681
People's Republic of China. *See* China

perestroika, 563
peripheral countries, 383
Perry, Matthew C., 235
personalist politicians, **380**
Pétain, Philippe, 91
PFI. *See* private finance initiative (PFI)
Plan de Ayala, 422
Plaza Accord (1985), 242
police
    Brazil, 395–396
    Britain, 64–65
    China, 680–681
    EU, 212
    France, 113
    Germany, 159–160
    India, 300
    Japan, 255
    South Africa, 487–489
police powers, **335**
policy-making process
    Brazil, 396–397
    Britain, 66
    China, 681–682
    European Union, 209–211
    France, 113
    Germany, 161–162
    India, 303
    Iran, 637–639
    Japan, 256–257
    Mexico, 444
    Nigeria, 538
    Russian Federation, 585
    South Africa, 491–492
    United States, 350–351
Politburo, **676**
political action committee (PAC), **360**
political activism. *See* social movements and
    protest
political challenges
    in Brazil, 381, 407–410
    in Britain, 78–79
    China, 691–694
    in EU, 223–224
    in Germany, 177–178
    in India, 315–320
    Iran, 647–650
    in Japan, 271–272
    Mexico, 456–458
    Nigeria, 547–550
    Russian Federation, 598–602
    in South Africa, 502–504
    in United States, 362–364
political culture, **593**
    Brazil, 402–405
    Britain, 75
    China, 686–688
    EU, 217–218
    France, 121
    Germany, 171–172
    India, 311–312
    Iran, 642–644
    Japan, 263–264
    Mexico, 451
    Nigeria, 542–543
    Russian Federation, 593–594
    South Africa, 500
    United States, 358–359
political development
    Brazil, 370–371
    Britain, 40–41
    China, 654–655
    France, 86–87
    Germany, 134–135
    Iran, 608–609
    Japan, 230–231
    Mexico, 416–417

Nigeria, 510–511
Russian Federation, 556–557
South Africa, 464–465
United States, 326–327
political economy, **15–16**
    Brazil, 382–385
    Britain, 50–52
    China, 666–671
    European Union, 189–197
    France, 98–105
    Germany, 144, 146–149
    India, 288, 289–291
    Iran, 622–626
    Japan, 241–243, 247
    Mexico, 430–434
    Nigeria, 524–529
    Russian Federation, 567–570
    South Africa, 476–483
    United States, 334–337
political identity, 10
political Islam, 3, **615**
political legitimacy, 10
political organization
    Brazil, 373
    Britain, 43
    China, 658
    France, 87
    Germany, 135
    India, 282
    Iran, 611
    Japan, 234
    Mexico, 419
    Nigeria, 514
    Russia, 558
    South Africa, 464
    United States, 329
political parties
    Brazil, 375, 376, 399–402
    Britain, 69–72, 74
    China, 683–685
    France, 94–95, 116–119
    Germany, 162, 165–169
    India, 305–311
    Iran, 640–641
    Japan, 258–260
    Mexico, 446–451
    Nigeria, 539–541, 548
    Russian Federation, 587–592
    South Africa, 493–498
    United States, 354–356
political representation. *See* representation and
    participation
political science, discipline of, 6–7
political stability, democracy and, 20
political system
    Brazil, 373
    Britain, 43
    China, 658
    classification of, 22–26
    France, 87
    Germany, 135
    India, 282
    Iran, 611
    Japan, 234
    Nigeria, 514
    Russian Federation, 558, 602
    South Africa, 464
    United States, 329
political violence, in India, 316
politics
    of collective identities, 20–22
    comparative. *See* comparative politics
    distributional, 21
    pork-barrel, **256**
politics in action
    Brazil, 370–371

Britain, 39
China, 655–656
European Union, 184–187
France, 85–86
Germany, 134–136
India, 277–278
Iran, 608–609
Japan, 229–230
Mexico, 416–418
Nigeria, 512–513
Russian Federation, 556–558
South Africa, 463–464
United States, 325
politics in transition
    Brazil, 407–412
    Britain, 78–81
    China, 691–697
    EU, 222–226
    France, 127–130
    Germany, 176–180
    India, 315–322
    Iran, 646–651
    Mexico, 455–459
    Nigeria, 547–552
    Russian Federation, 598–605
    South Africa, 502–507
    United States, 362–366
politics of the governors, **390**
pollution
    Britain, 56
    Iran, 626–627
    Nigeria, 530
    South Africa, 480
    United States, 340–341
Pompidou, Georges, 107
population
    See also demographic trends
    Brazil, 371
    China, 656
    by country, 31
    EU, 224
    France, 88
    India, 278
    Iran, 623, 626
    Mexico, 431
    Nigeria, 530
    Russian Federation, 571, 603
populism, **3**, 356, 375
pork-barrel politics, **256**
Portugal, 197
POTA. *See* Prevention of Terrorism Act (POTA)
poverty
    Brazil, 385–386, 387
    childhood, 54
    India, 289, 292, 318–319, 320
    Mexico, 432, 458
    Nigeria, 529, 550–551
    rural, 320, 432
    South Africa, 474, 478, 504
    urban, 432
power sharing, **483**
power vertical, **582**
PPP. *See* purchasing power parity (PPP)
prebendalism, **536**
predatory state, **696**
predominant-party democracy, **259**
prefects, **90**
president
    Brazil, 391–393
    compared with prime minister, 62
    France, 107–110
    Germany, 155
    impeachment of, 392
    India, 299
    Iran and, 630–633
    Mexico, 438–440, 444, 455–456

president (*Continued*)
    Nigeria, 534–536
    Russian Federation, 576–579
    South Africa, 484–486
    U.S., 299, 331, 346–347, 392
presidential elections
    France, 94–95, 110, 120–121, 122
    Mexico, 447, 451
    Nigeria, 541–542
    Russian Federation, 592–593
    Russian interference in, 4
    South Africa, 498–499
    United States, 325
presidential systems, 19
    compared with parliamentary system, 62
    compared with semi-presidential system, 106
    in U.S., 299
Press Freedom Index, 8
Prevention of Terrorism Act (POTA), 301
PRI. *See* Institutional Revolutionary Party (PRI)
prime minister
    Britain, 59, 60
    compared with president, 62
    France, 109–110
    India, 285, 298
    Japan, 250–251
    Russian Federation, 578–579
privacy rights, 23
private finance initiative (PFI), 64
privatization, **100**, 525, 568
procedural democracy, **139**
prodemocracy movements, 14
Progressive Federal Party (PFP), 496
Prokhorov, Mikhail, 591–592
property rights, 358, 504
property taxes, **331**
proportional representation (PR), **92**, 399, 438
Proposition 13, 331
prostitution, 596
protectionism, 481
protests. *See* social movements and protest
Pruitt, Scott, 341
Przeworski, Adam, 16
PSD. *See* Social Democratic Party (PSD)
PT. *See* Workers' Party (PT)
PTB. *See* Brazilian Labor Party (PTB)
public agencies, France, 111
public debt
    Japan, 271
    Nigeria, 525, 526
    Russian Federation, 573
public institutions
    Brazil, 393–394
    Britain, 63–64
    Russian Federation, 580–581
purchasing power parity (PPP), 16–**17**
    by country, 33
Pussy Riot, 596
Putin, Vladimir, 4, 24, 25, 187, 482, 556, 564–565, 567, 569–570, 576, 577, 579, 580, 584, 593, 598

Q

al-Qaddafi, Muammar, 95
Al-Qaeda, 3, 21, 95, 287
Qajars, 613
Qatar, 649
QMV. *See* qualified majority voting (QMV)
qualified majority voting (QMV), **190**
quango, **63**
quasi-governmental organizations, 63
Qur'an, **612**

R

racial democracy, 403
racial discrimination, 405–406
    South Africa, 468–469
racial identity, 475
racial profiling, 113
radical Islamism, 3
Rajya Sabha, 298
Rape of Nanking, 236
rational choice theory, 11–12, **11**
RDAs. *See* regional development agencies (RDAs)
REACH Directive, 210
Reagan, Ronald, 94, 100
Reconstruction, in U.S., 330
redistributive policies, **338**–339, 363
Reform Act of 1832, 44
refugees, 79, 123, 134–135, 137, 171–172, 212
regime history
    Brazil, 373
    China, 658
    France, 87
    Germany, 135
    India, 282
    Iran, 611
    Japan, 234
    Mexico, 419
    Nigeria, 514
    South Africa, 464
regional development, EU, 207–208
regional development agencies (RDAs), 66
regulations, **341**
religion
    Brazil, 372, 381, 403–404
    Britain, 41
    China, 656, 686
    collective identity and, 21
    freedom of, 23
    India, 279
    Iran, 610, 611, 642–643
    Mexico, 418
    Nigeria, 513, 514–515, 531, 543–544
    Russian Federation, 557
    South Africa, 466
    United States, 327, 359
religious conflicts, Britain, 43
religious right, India, 313–314
remittances, **433**
rentier state, **622**
rents, **524**
representation and participation
    Brazil, 398–407
    Britain, 67–77
    China, 682–691
    ethnicity and, 74
    EU, 215–222
    France, 114–127
    gender and, 73–74, 163–164
    Germany, 162–175
    India, 304–315
    Iran, 639–646
    Japan, 257–270
    Mexico, 445–455
    Nigeria, 539–546
    Russian Federation, 586–597
    South Africa, 492–502
    United States, 352–361
Representation of the People Act (1867), 44
representative democracy, 359
    EU and, 215–216
republic, **90**
Republican Party, 354–356
Republic of Ireland, 39, 65

research and development (R&D), 101, 148, 210
reservations, **302**
reserve currency, 336
resource curse, **527**, 567
Resurgence Party, 615
revolution, **90**
    American Revolution, 328–330
    Brazil, 374–375
    Iran, 615–617, 628–629
    Mexico, 422–423
    Russian, 559–560
Rewe-Zentral AG v Bundesmonopolverwaltung fur Branntwein, 204
Rhodes, Cecil, 463
Roman law, 111
Rome Treaty, 186, 190, 206, 207, 210
Roosevelt, Franklin Delano, 330–331
Rouhani, Hassan, 608, 633, 642, 649
Rousseff, Dilma, 370, 379, 401–402, 404, 407–408
rural poverty, 432
    India, 292, 320
Russia
    annexation of Crimea, 159, 187
    authoritarianism in, 4
    facts and statistics, 31, 33, 35
    as illiberal democracy, 24
    interference in U.S. election by, 4
    political system of, 25–26
Russian Empire, 558–559
Russian Federation, 555–606
    administrative structure, 558
    Bolshevik Revolution, 559–560
    bureaucracy, 579–580
    citizenship, 593–594
    civil society in, 586, 594–596
    collective identity in, 566, 593–594
    comparative politics, 566–567, 603–604
    constitution of, 577
    critical historical junctures in, 559–565
    decline of Tsarist state, 559
    democracy in, 566
    demographic trends, 602–603
    economic crisis in, 569
    economic growth in, 567, 571
    economic policy, 563, 566, 568–570
    economy of, 567–575
    elections in, 592–593
    emergence of, 563–565
    environmental issues, 572
    ethnic groups in, 557, 593
    EU and, 573, 575, 600
    executive in, 558, 578–579
    facts and statistics, 555, 557
    federalism in, 583
    foreign policy, 600, 601
    gender equality in, 594
    geographic setting, 558–559
    globalization and, 565, 572–575
    governance, 576–585
    Great Recession and, 600
    inequality in, 570–571
    interest groups in, 594–596
    international organizations and, 575
    judiciary in, 558, 581–582
    legislature in, 558, 586–587
    making of modern, 556–567
    map of, 562
    media in, 596–597
    military, 584–585
    party system in, 558, 587–592
    policy-making process in, 585
    political challenges and changing agendas in, 598–602
    political culture of, 593–594

political development of, 556–557
political dissent in, 591–592
political economy in, 567–570
political impact of technology in, 596–597
political institutions of, 576–577
political organization, 558
political parties in, 587–592
political system of, 558, 602
politics in action, 556–558
politics in transition, 598–605
president of, 576–579
prime minister oo, 578–579
public and semipublic agencies, 580–581
regime history, 558
religions in, 557
representation and participation in, 586–597
social class in, 594
social movements and protest in, 586, 594–596
social problems in, 596
social welfare programs, 570–572
society and economy in, 570–572
under Stalin, 560–561
state and economy in, 568–570
state institutions, 581–585
state organization, 576–577
subnational government, 582–583
terrorist attacks in, 582, 584
women in, 594
youth in, 602–603
Russian Revolution, 1
Russo-Japanese War, 236, 241
Rwanda, 14

S

Safavids, 612
Sahara Desert, 529
Salinas, Carlos, 423, 424
samurai, **235**
sanctions, **471**
Sanders, Bernie, 3
SANDF. *See* South African National Defence Force (SANDF)
SAP. *See* structural adjustment program (SAP)
Sarkozy, Nicolas, 96, 117, 120
Sarney, José, 378
Saudi Arabia, 619, 649
SAVAK, 614, 634
SCAP. *See* Supreme Commander for the Allied Powers (SCAP)
scheduled caste, **294**
Schengen Area, **193**
Schmidt, Helmut, 142
Schröder, Gerhard, 143
Schulz, Martin, 198
Schuman, Robert, 184
Schuman plan, 189
SCOPA. *See* Select Committee on Public Accounts (SCOPA)
Scotland, 42, 46, 59, 65, 66
Scotland Yard, 64
SDP. *See* Social Democratic Party (SDP)
SEA. *See* Single European Act (SEA)
Second Reich, 138–139
secularism, **89**
security policy, EU, 212–215
Select Committee on Public Accounts (SCOPA), 493
semi-presidential system, 106, 107, 578
semipublic agencies, France, 111
semipublic institutions, 63–64
  Brazil, 393–394
  Germany, 147–149
  Iran, 636–637
  Russian Federation, 580–581

Sen, Amartya, 16, 17, 22
Senate, U.S., 329–330, 352–354
separation of church and state, 89
separation of powers, **333**, 334, 345
Sepoy Rebellion, 282
September 11, 2001, 3, 4, 21
  Brazil after, 378–379
  France after, 95–96
  Germany after, 143–144
  India after, 287
  Iran after, 618–619
  Mexico after, 425
  U.S. after, 332, 350, 363
Serbia, 64
settlement
  of Britain, 43
  of Japan, 231
  of South Africa, 465, 467
settler state, **474**
7/7 bombings, 46, 79
sexenio, **438**, 444
Shagari, Shehu, 520
Shah of Iran, 613–615, 616–617, 628
shari'a, **529**, 533, 537–538, 543, 610, 614, **616**, 621, 634–635, 638
Shariati, Ali, 625–626
Sharpeville Massacre, 469–470
Shi'i Islam, 610, 618–619, 642–643, 648, 650–651
shogun, **232**
Shonekan, Ernest, 520
Sikhs, **279**
siloviki, **579**
Singh, Manmohan, 286, 301, 316
Single European Act (SEA), **186**, 192, 194
single-member districts (SMDs), 261, **262**
single member plurality (SMP) electoral sysetm, **334**
single nontransferable vote (SNTV), **261**
Sino-Japanese War, 236, 241
slavery, 330
small and medium size enterprises (SMEs), 243–244
small N analysis, 11
SMD. *See* single-member districts (SMDs)
SMEs. *See* small and medium size enterprises (SMEs)
SMP. *See* single member plurality (SMP) electoral sysetm
Smuts, Jan, 469
Snowden, Edward, 144
social capital, 360
social class, **20**
  Brazil, 381
  Britain, 75
  EU, 223–224
  France, 122
  India, 280, 292, 294
  Iran, 624–625
  Russian Federation, 594
Social Democratic Party (PSD), 375
Social Democratic Party (SDP)
  Britain, 71
  Germany, 138, 165, 166–167
  Japan, 259
  Nigeria, 540
social dumping, 192
socialism, **659**
social issues, 453
socialist, **99**
socialist democracy, 682, **683**
socialist market economy, **667**–668
Socialist Party, France, 94, 99–100, 117
social market economy, **147**
  Germany, 146–147, 148–149

social media, 14, 77, 174, 270, 361, 406–407, 454, 497, 501–502, 545–546, 597, 646, 691
social model, French, 128
social movements and protest, **19**
  Brazil, 370, 405–406
  Britain, 76–77
  China, 655–656, 661–662, 689–690
  EU, 218–221
  France, 97, 126
  Germany, 172–174
  India, 312–314
  Iran, 644–645
  Japan, 267–269
  Mexico, 452–453
  Nigeria, 544–545
  Russian Federation, 586, 594–596
  South Africa, 463–464, 500–501
  United States, 359–361
social policy
  Britain, 53–54
  EU, 210–211, 224–225
Social Progress Index (SPI), **17**, 18
social protection, 23
social sciences, 11
Social Security, **331**, 339, 363
social security, 54
social services, France, 101–102
social welfare programs
  Brazil, 385–386
  China, 670
  India, 292–294
  Iran, 624–626
  Japan, 244–245
  Mexico, 458
  Nigeria, 529
  Russian Federation, 570–572
  South Africa, 504
  United States, 331, 339, 340, 363
society and economy
  Brazil, 385–387
  Britain, 53–55
  China, 669–671
  France, 101–102
  Germany, 150–152
  India, 292–294
  Iran, 624–626
  Japan, 243–245
  Mexico, 435
  Nigeria, 527–529
  Russian Federation, 570–572
  South Africa, 478–480
  United States, 337–340
soft authoritarianism, **565**
software industry, 295
Sonoran Dynasty, 422–423
Sotomayor, Sonia, 349
South Africa, 462–508
  administrative structure, 464
  African resistance in, 469
  Anglo-Boer War, 468
  apartheid regime, 465, 468–471, 476–477
  black empowerment, 479–480
  BRICs and, 482–483
  cabinet, 485
  citizenship, 500
  collective identity in, 475, 500
  comparative politics, 475–476, 505–507
  constitution of, 483
  critical historical junctures in, 465–474
  democracy in, 475, 504, 506
  demographic trends, 505
  economic policy, 475, 477, 481
  economy of, 473–474, 475, 476–483, 504
  education system, 476–477
  education system in, 471, 472
  elections, 498–499

South Africa, (*Continued*)
  environmental issues, 480–481
  ethnic groups in, 466
  executive in, 464, 484–486
  facts and statistics, 31, 33, 35, 462, 466
  frontier, 467–468
  geographic setting, 465
  globalization and, 474, 481–482
  governance in, 483–492
  HIV/AIDS in, 479, 502–503
  inequality in, 478
  interest groups in, 500–501
  judiciary in, 464, 487–489
  languages in, 466
  legislature in, 464, 492–493
  making of modern, 463–476
  map of, 467, 490
  media in, 501–502
  military, 489
  party system in, 464, 493–498
  police, 487–489
  policy-making process in, 491–492
  political challenges and changing agendas in, 502–504
  political culture in, 500
  political development, 464–465
  political economy, 476–483
  political impact of technology in, 501–502
  political organization of, 464
  political parties in, 493–498
  politics in action, 463–464
  politics in transition, 502–507
  poverty in, 478, 504
  president of, 484–486
  regime history, 464
  religions in, 466
  representation and participation in, 492–502
  revolt and reform in, 472
  settlement of, 465, 467
  Sharpeville Massacre, 469–470
  social movements and protest in, 463–464
  social welfare programs in, 504
  society and economy in, 478–480
  state and economy in, 476–477
  state institutions, 487–491
  state organization, 483
  subnational government, 489–491
  unemployment, 505
  U.S. relations with, 486–487
  welfare state, 476–477
  youth in, 505
South African miracle, 472–474
South African National Defence Force (SANDF), 489
South China Sea, 4
South Korea, economy of, 15
sovereign democracy, **593**
Soviet Union, 558–559
  See also Russian Federation
  Cold War and, 185
  collapse of, 1, 15, 558, 563–565, 567, 599
  constitution of, 576
  de-Stalinization, 561
  Eastern Europe and, 141–142
  economic policy, 563
  founding of, 559–560
  perestroika and glasnost, 563
  reforms in, 2
  under Stalin, 560–561
  World War II and, 141, 560–561
Spain, 197
special relationship, **49**, 80
Sri Lanka, 21, 318
stagflation, 186, 191
Stalin, Josef, 2
Stalin, Joseph, 560–561

standards of living, 16, 435, 626
Standing Committee, **676**
state, 9–10, **10**
state and economy
  Brazil, 382–385
  Britain, 50–52
  China, 666–669
  France, 98–105
  Germany, 144, 146–149
  India, 290–291
  Iran, 622–624
  Japan, 241–243
  Mexico, 430–434
  Nigeria, 524–527
  Russian Federation, 568–570
  South Africa, 476–477
  United States, 334–337
state capitalism, **430**
state-controlled firms, Brazil, 393–394
state corporatism, **375**
state council, France, 112
State Council, **678**
state formation, **11**
state government. *See* subnational government
state institutions, 9, 10
  Brazil, 390, 393–396
  Britain, 64–65
  China, 679–681
  France, 111–114
  Germany, 154–155
  India, 299–302, 319–320
  Iran, 634–637
  Japan, 251–256
  Mexico, 441–443
  Nigeria, 536–538
  Russian Federation, 581–585
  South Africa, 487–491
  United States, 348–349
state-led economic development, **290, 376**
  Brazil, 393
  India, 290–291
state organization
  Brazil, 390
  Britain, 58–64
  China, 674
  France, 105–106
  Germany, 154–158
  India, 296–298
  Iran, 629
  Japan, 248–250
  Mexico, 438–441
  Nigeria, 532–533
  Russian Federation, 576–577
  South Africa, 483
  United States, 344–345
state-owned enterprises (SOEs), 525, 568, 667, 669
states, globalizing world of, 13–15
state technocrats, 382, **383**
statism, 97, 100, 130
statistical analysis, 11
Stop Trump Coalition, 77
strikes
  Britain, 51, 75
  China, 690
  France, 93
  Nigeria, 546
  South Africa, 471, 500–501
structural adjustment program (SAP), 524–525
student activism. *See* social movements and protest
student loans, 363
subnational government
  Brazil, 395
  Britain, 65–66
  China, 680

France, 112–113
Germany, 160–161
India, 302
Iran, 636
Japan, 255–256
Mexico, 443
Nigeria, 538
Russian Federation, 582–583
South Africa, 489–491
United States, 349–350
subsidiarity, 188, **203**
Sunni Islam, 610, 619, 643
Sun Yat-sen, 658
supranationality, 218
Supreme Commander for the Allied Powers (SCAP), **237**
Supreme Court
  Brazil, 394
  Britain, 65
  India, 294, 301
  Japan, 253–255
  Russian Federation, 582
  United States, 325, 348–349
Supreme Leader (Iran), **609**
Syria, 4, 14, 64, 95–96

T

Taisho democracy, 235–**236**
Taiwan, 659, 660
Taliban, 95, 618–619
Tamil Nadu, 318
tariffs
  Brazil, 389
  France, 91, 103
  India, 296
  South Africa, 475
  United States, 335
taxation
  Brazil, 384
  China, 670
  Japan, 271
  Nigeria, 538
  Russian Federation, 583
  United States, 331, 338
  value-added taxes, 191
Tea Party, 356
technocrats, **440**, 663
technologies, dual-use, 269–270
technology, political impact of
  in Brazil, 406–407
  in Britain, 77
  China, 690–691
  in EU, 221–222
  in France, 126
  in Germany, 174–175
  in India, 314–315
  Iran, 645–646
  in Japan, 269–270
  in Mexico, 453–454
  in Nigeria, 545–546
  Russian Federation, 596–597
  in South Africa, 501–502
  in United States, 361
Temer, Michel, 370
territorial disputes, Japan and, 260
terrorism
  9/11 attacks, 3, 4, 21
  Britain, 46, 76, 79
  cyberterrorism, 314
  EU and, 212
  fear of, 46
  France, 85–86, 96, 129–130
  India, 287, 301–302, 316
  Iran and, 618–619

Nigeria, 543–544
Pakistan, 287
Russia, 582, 584
United States and, 332, 350, 363
war on, 332, 379
Texas, 421
Thatcher, Margaret, 45, 51–52, 56, 60, 75, 78, 94, 100, 191
theocracies, 24, 608, **609**, 639, 647
Third Reich, 140–141, 145
Third Republic, France, 90–91
third way, 45–46, 53–54
Three Gorges Dam, 671–672
Tiananmen Square, 655–656, 661, 665
Tibet, ethnic conflict in, 11
Tokugawa Ieyasu, 232, 234
totalitarianism, **695**
tourism, France, 85–86
township, **469**
TPP. *See* Trans-Pacific Partnership (TPP)
trade agreements, 213, 243, 326
trade deficit, United States, 246–247, 336
trade unions. *See* labor unions
Transatlantic Trade and Investment Partnership (TTIP), 195, 213
transnational corporations, 13–14
Trans-Pacific Partnership (TPP), 243, 247
Treaty of Lisbon, 176
Treaty of Versailles, 139, 141
Truman Doctrine, 561
Trump, Donald J., 49, 79, 81, 96, 153, 187, 333, 336
   "America First" position of, 225, 229
   border wall and, 343
   election of, 3, 229, 325, 356
   elections, 354, 362
   environmental issues and, 341, 388
   EU and, 195, 213
   foreign policy of, 366
   immigration and, 364
   Iran and, 649, 650
   Mexico and, 416–418, 457–458
   profile of, 347
   Twitter use by, 361
TTIP. *See* Transatlantic Trade and Investment Partnership (TTIP)
Tudeh Party, 614, 641
Turkish migrants, 151
Twelve Imams, 610
Twenty-Sixth Amendment, 357
Twitter, 361, 502, 546
typology, **22**

U

Ukraine, 4, 565, 598, 599
Umkhonto-we-Sizwe, **471**
UN. *See* United Nations (UN)
unemployment
   Brazil, 385
   France, 101, 102
   Germany, 179
   India, 320
   Iran, 623, 645, 650
   Japan, 244
   Mexico, 428, 435
   Nigeria, 551
   Russian Federation, 596
   South Africa, 474, 478, 505
   youth, 179, 320, 505, 551, 650
UNFCCC. *See* UN Framework Convention on Climate Change (UNFCCC)
unfinished state, **513**
UN Framework Convention on Climate Change (UNFCCC), 194

Union Carbide, 313
Union of Soviet Socialist Republics (USSR). *See* Soviet Union
unitary state, **59**
United Democratic Front (UDF), 472
United Kingdom. *See* Britain
United Kingdom Independent Party (UKIP), 46–47, 71–72, 74
United Nations (UN), 7, 13, 239
United Russia Party, 588, 589, 593
United States, 324–368
   administrative structure, 329
   after 9/11, 332, 350, 363
   agriculture policy, 335
   Brazil and, 379
   British relationship with, 49, 80
   bureaucracy, 347–348
   cabinet of, 347–348
   China and, 247, 673
   citizenship, 330, 358–359
   Civil War, 330
   Cold War and, 185
   collective identities in, 333, 358–359, 364
   comparative politics, 365–366
   Constitution of, 325, 329, 334, 344–345
   critical historical junctures in, 326–332
   Cuba and, 366
   democracy in, 333
   demographic trends, 365
   divided government in, 331–332, 345
   economic competitiveness of, 209
   economic inequality in, 23
   economic policy, 333
   economy of, 333, 334–340
   elections in, 325, 329, 355–358
   environmental issues, 340–341
   ethnic groups in, 327
   ethnic minorities in, 362
   EU and, 213
   executive in, 329, 346–347
   facts and statistics, 31, 33, 35, 324, 327
   foreign policy, 332–333, 366
   France and, 96
   gender equality in, 337
   geographic setting, 326
   Germany and, 143–144
   globalization and, 332–333, 341–343, 366
   governance, 344–350
   Great Depression in, 330–331
   Great Recession in, 3
   immigration policy, 343
   immigration to, 333, 338–339, 364, 434, 457–458
   India and, 287
   inequality in, 337–338
   interest groups, 332, 351, 359–361
   Iran and, 614, 615, 619, 628, 649–650
   Japan and, 229, 241–242, 254, 269
   judiciary in, 329, 348–349
   labor unions in, 338
   languages in, 327
   legislature in, 325, 329–330, 351, 352–354
   making of modern, 325–334
   map of, 328
   media in, 361
   Mexico and, 416–418, 421, 427, 457–458
   military, 254, 269, 350
   national security agencies, 350
   New Deal era, 330–331
   Nigeria and, 531
   partisanship in, 331–332
   party system in, 329, 354–356
   policy-making process in, 350–351
   political challenges and changing agendas in, 362–364
   political culture of, 358–359

   political development of, 326–327
   political economy, 334–337
   political impact of technology in, 361
   political organization, 329
   political parties in, 354–356
   political system of, 329
   politics in action, 325
   politics in transition, 362–366
   populism in, 356
   postwar Europe and, 189
   presidential system, 62, 106
   president of, 299, 331, 346–347, 392
   public sector in, 336–337
   Reconstruction in, 330
   religions in, 327, 359
   representation and participation in, 352–361
   revolutionary era, 328–330
   social movements and protest in, 359–361
   social welfare programs, 331, 339, 340, 363
   society and economy in, 337–340
   South Africa and, 486–487
   state and economy in, 334–337
   state institutions, 348–349
   state organization, 344–345
   subnational government, 349–350
   taxation in, 338
   terrorism and, 363
   trade deficit, 246–247, 336
   World War II and, 331
   youth in, 365
universities, Germany, 171
University of Cape Town (UCT), 463
UN Security Council, 49, 64, 96, 239, 600
urban poverty, 432
U.S. dollar, 336
U.S.-Mexico border, 343, 427
U.S. military, 254, 269, 350
U.S. presidential election (2016), 11
   Russian interference in, 4
USSR. *See* Soviet Union

V

value-added taxes (VATs), 191
Van Duyn v. Home Office, 204
Van Gend en Loos v Nederlandse Administratie der Belastingen, 204
Van Rompuy, Herman, 198
Vargas, Getúlio Dornelles, 375, 391
VATs. *See* value-added taxes (VATs)
Vereniging Bond van Adverteerders v. the Netherlands State, 204
Vichy France, 91–93
Victoria (queen), 44, 80
Villa, Francisco (Pancho), 422
violence
   Mexico, 425, 427
   political, 316
vocational education system, Germany, 148
Volkswagen, 175
Voortrekkers, **467**
voter suppression, 357
voter turnout
   France, 119
   Germany, 169–170
   Japan, 263, 272
   South, 491
   United States, 357–358, 363
voting rights
   Britain, 44, 45
   United States, 330, 357
Voting Rights Act (1965), 330, 357

W

Wales, 42, 59, 65
Wall Street, 3
WannaCry, 77
war on drugs, 425
war on terrorism, 332, 379
warrant chiefs, **517**
Weimar Republic, **139**–140, 145
welfare state, **45**
   Brazil, 385–386
   Britain, 53
   France, 101–102, 128
   Japan, 244–245
   South Africa, 476–477
West Germany, 141–142
Westminster model, **50**, 484
Wilhelm II, 138
William of Normandy, 41
William the Conqueror, 88
women
   in Brazil, 381, 385, 405
   in China, 670–671
   in France, 102–103, 124–125
   in Germany, 151–152, 163–164, 172
   in government, 73–74
   in India, 304–305
   in Iran, 644
   in Japan, 244, 261, 267–268
   in labor force, 102, 151, 385
   in Mexico, 440
   in Nigeria, 529
   political representation of, 163–164, 261,
      304–305, 440
   in Russia, 594
   voting rights for, 357

women's movement
   in Brazil, 405
   in India, 313
   in Japan, 267–268
   in South Africa, 500
Workers' Party (PT), 400–401
workplace inequality, 210
works council, **148**
World Bank, 7, 13, 189, 239, 341–342
World Development Indicators (World Bank), 29
World Economic Forum, 49
World Factbook (CIA), 29
world trade, labor productivity and, 44
World Trade Organization (WTO), **13**, 76, 103,
   195, 291, 436, 475, 573, 600, 649
World War I, 44–45, 91, 138–139, 236
World War II, 2, 45, 91–92, 141, 171, 185, 283
   Japan and, 229, 236–237, 240
   Soviet Union and, 560–561
   U.S. and, 331
Worldwide Governance Indicators, 8
WTO. *See* World Trade Organization (WTO)

X

Xavier, Francis, 234
xenophobia, 79
Xi Jinping, 663, 676, 692

Y

Yanukovych, Victor, 565
Yar'Adua, Umaru Musa, 512, 521, 531,
   533, 534
Yavlinksy, Grigory, 591

Yeltsin, Boris, 563–564, 568, 577, 578, 579
youth
   Brazil, 410
   Britain, 80
   China, 694
   France, 102
   Germany, 178–179
   India, 320
   Iran, 650
   Japan, 272–273
   Mexico, 458–459
   Nigeria, 550–551
   Russian Federation, 602–603
   South Africa, 505
   United States, 365
Yugoslavia, 186, 214

Z

zaibatsu, **236**, 241
Zaire, 17
zamindars, **301**
Zapata, Emiliano, 422, 430
Zapatista Army of National Liberation
   (EZLN), 424
Zardari, Asaf Ali, 316
Zedillo, Ernesto, 425, 439, 443
Zille, Helen, 496, 497
zoku, **256**
Zulu kingdom, 467–468
Zuma, Jacob, 473–474, 482, 484,
   485–486, 492